Non-discrimination in Tax Treaty Law and World Trade Law

Series on International Taxation

VOLUME 72

Series Editors

Prof. Ruth Mason, University of Virginia School of Law
Prof. Dr Ekkehart Reimer, University of Heidelberg

Introduction & Contents

The Series on International Taxation deals with a wide variety of topics in the global tax arena. The authors include many of the field's leading experts as well as talented newcomers. Their expert views and incisive commentary have proven highly useful to practitioners and academics alike.

Objective

The volumes published in this series are aimed at offering high-quality analytical information and practical solutions to international tax practitioners.

Readership

Practitioners, academics and policy makers in international tax law.

Frequency of Publication

2-3 new volumes published each year.

The titles published in this series are listed at the end of this volume.

Non-discrimination in Tax Treaty Law and World Trade Law

The Impact of Formal, Substantive, and Subjective Approaches

Kasper Dziurdź

Wolters Kluwer

Published by:
Kluwer Law International B.V.
PO Box 316
2400 AH Alphen aan den Rijn
The Netherlands
E-mail: international-sales@wolterskluwer.com
Website: lrus.wolterskluwer.com

Sold and distributed in North, Central and South America by:
Wolters Kluwer Legal & Regulatory U.S.
7201 McKinney Circle
Frederick, MD 21704
United States of America
Email: customer.service@wolterskluwer.com

Sold and distributed in all other countries by:
Air Business Subscriptions
Rockwood House
Haywards Heath
West Sussex
RH16 3DH
United Kingdom
Email: international-customerservice@wolterskluwer.com

ISBN 978-94-035-0904-4

e-Book: ISBN 978-94-035-0912-9
web-PDF: ISBN 978-94-035-0920-4

To my parents

Table of Contents

Preface

My interest in equal treatment and non-discrimination provisions and why they can be understood so differently despite often similar wording laid the foundation for this work. I started to read about the concepts of equal treatment and non-discrimination in many areas of law including European law, human rights law, and constitutional law in order to get a feeling for how differently the non-discrimination clauses can be structured, applied, and interpreted. Against the insights I gained from this fundamental study, I decided to focus on economic non-discrimination provisions in two areas of international law: WTO law and tax treaty law. On the one hand, the general non-discrimination rules under WTO law cover both direct and indirect discriminations and require a rather sophisticated analysis of comparability. In addition, a violation may be justified under the general exceptions clauses. On the other hand, the concept of non-discrimination under tax treaty law extends only to cases of direct discrimination and allows for no justification. A simple test arguably solves all issues of comparability. Understanding the reasons for those vast differences motivated this study.

I would never have been able to write this habilitation thesis without the constant and invaluable support of Prof. Michael Lang, Prof. Josef Schuch, and Prof. Claus Staringer. More than ten years at the Institute for Austrian and International Tax Law, WU (Vienna University of Economics and Business) have greatly influenced my thinking and research skills and allowed me to become who I am today. Prof. Marjaana Helminen and Prof. Alexander Rust reviewed this study during my habilitation process, for which I owe a debt of gratitude. I had the opportunity to conduct research stays in Munich and Uppsala both of which allowed me to discuss, rethink, and shape my ideas. I owe many thanks to Prof. Wolfgang Schön and Prof. Bertil Wiman for their invitation and support. I especially want to thank Nathalie Bravo for supporting me in every way. Caroline Heber, Daniela Hohenwarter-Mayr, Christoph Marchgraber, Matthias Mayer, Karoline Spies, Viktoria Wöhrer, and Stephanie Zolles reviewed parts of this study, and I am grateful for their critical comments and suggestions. Also, the team of the Organisation for Economic Co-operation and Development (OECD) Archives provided me with important help during my research in Paris. Last but not least, I want to thank Jenny Hill for the language editing, the team of Newgen for the copy editing, and Kluwer Law International for accepting this study for publication.

This study was completed in August 2017, officially accepted as a habilitation thesis in September 2018, and updated thereafter. It was written during the tenure of an APART Fellowship of the Austrian Academy of Sciences at the Institute for Austrian and International Tax Law, WU (Vienna University of Economics and Business). Preliminary research was conducted as part of a project of the Austrian Science Fund (FWF). Heinrich Graf Hardegg'sche Stiftung also supported this study. I am very thankful for the support I received.

Vienna, January 2019

List of Abbreviations

AB	Appellate Body
ACT	Advanced Corporation Tax
Add.	Addendum
AOA	Authorized OECD Approach
Art.	Article
ATC	Agreement on Textiles and Clothing
BEPS	Base Erosion and Profit Shifting
BISD	Basic Instruments and Selected Documents
BIT	Bilateral Investment Treaty
CEN	Capital Export Neutrality
CIN	Capital Import Neutrality
CJEU	Court of Justice of the European Union
DOP	Dominican Peso
DSU	Dispute Settlement Understanding (Understanding on Rules and Procedures Governing the Settlement of Disputes)
EC	European Community/Communities
EEC	European Economic Community/Communities
e.g.	exempli gratia (for example)
et al.	et alii (and others)
et seq.	et sequens (and the following)
EU	European Union
fn.	Footnote
GATS	General Agreement on Trade in Services
GATT	General Agreement on Tariffs and Trade

GmbH	Gesellschaft mit beschränkter Haftung (limited liability company)
GST	Goods and services tax
i.e.	id est (that is)
Ibid.	ibidem (in the same place)
ILC	International Law Commission
incorp.	Incorporation
kl	Kilolitres
m.no(s).	Marginal Number(s)
MFN	Most-Favoured-Nation
NT	National Treatment
OECD	Organisation for Economic Co-operation and Development
OEEC	Organisation for European Economic Co-operation
OJ	Official Journal of the European Union
p(p).	Page(s)
para(s).	Paragraph(s)
PE	Permanent Establishment
POEM	Place of Effective Management
POM	Place of Management
PPM	Process and Production Method
PVA	Polyvinyl Alcohol
Rev.	Revision
SCM	Subsidies and Countervailing Measures
sec(s).	Section(s)
sent.	Sentence
SPS	Sanitary and Phytosanitary Measures
TBT	Technical Barriers to Trade
TFEU	Treaty on the Functioning of the European Union
TRIMs	Trade-Related Investment Measures
TRIPS	Trade-Related Aspects of Intellectual Property Rights
UK	United Kingdom of Great Britain and Northern Ireland
UN	United Nations
UNHCR	United Nations High Commissioner for Refugees
US	United States
USD	US Dollar
VAT	Value Added Tax
VCLT	Vienna Convention on the Law of Treaties
viz.	Namely

vs.	Versus
WTO	World Trade Organization
YBILC	Yearbook of the International Law Commission

List of Figures

List of Tables

CHAPTER 1

Introduction

This study will analyse two concepts of non-discrimination: non-discrimination under the law of the World Trade Organization (WTO) and non-discrimination under Article 24 of the Organisation for Economic Co-operation and Development (OECD) Model Tax Convention on Income and on Capital (OECD Model). The former concept includes the most-favoured-nation (MFN) and national treatment (NT) rules of the General Agreement on Tariffs and Trade (GATT) and the General Agreement on Trade in Services (GATS). The latter concept consists of non-discrimination rules that prohibit discrimination because of nationality or residence in certain precise circumstances.

On the one hand, the WTO Agreement constitutes a multilateral framework that promotes trade liberalization among 164 Members[1] for the purposes of which non-discrimination is of central importance. This framework meets acceptance throughout the world because of its multilateral nature and wide membership; the WTO is a quasi-universal organization.[2] Hence, the interpretation and scope of the MFN and NT rules of the GATT and GATS concern all Members from Afghanistan to Zimbabwe. Since the European Union (EU) is also a WTO Member, its own regulatory measures must also meet the non-discrimination requirements of WTO law.[3] On the other hand, double taxation conventions predominantly aim at avoiding international juridical double taxation and are usually concluded on a bilateral basis. It is safe to say that more than 3,000 double taxation conventions exist worldwide. They are largely based on the OECD Model, and their non-discrimination provisions thus resemble Article 24 of the OECD Model.

Both areas of international law address situations of discrimination in a different manner. The WTO Agreement does not require its direct effect in domestic legal orders, and all of the major trading members of the WTO deny it:[4] citizens and enterprises

1. A total of 164 countries are WTO Members since 29 July 2016 (reviewed on 6 January 2019).
2. DiMascio and Pauwelyn 2008, 53.
3. *See*, for instance, Búrca 2002, 185, 195.
4. *See*, for instance, Ruiz Fabri 2014.

cannot directly claim non-discriminatory treatment. Despite that, the WTO framework offers a forum for discussion, a dispute settlement mechanism for resolving conflicts, and means for imposing pressure so that Members make their domestic rules WTO-consistent. The non-discrimination provisions of double taxation conventions, by contrast, are directly enforceable in most cases: nationals and residents can generally claim non-discriminatory tax treatment in front of tax administrations and courts. Article 24 intends to prevail over contrary domestic law and thereby directly influence a taxpayer's position.[5]

The WTO Agreement and double taxation conventions have a different focus: open trade and double taxation, respectively. This explains why their non-discrimination rules are worded differently and have a different scope. However, this does not mean that there is no overlap. Article 24 of the OECD Model avoids discrimination precisely because certain differences in tax treatment are perceived to have a negative impact on cross-border business and trade. It even reaches beyond a convention's general scope by covering not only direct but also indirect taxes. WTO law also plays an important role in disciplining direct tax measures. Recently, for example, it has been discussed whether a destination-based taxation of corporate income is compatible with substantive WTO obligations.[6] In *Argentina – Financial Services* (2016), certain measures against harmful tax competition have been addressed with regard to their discriminatory effects; similar measures might be covered by Article 24 of the OECD Model as well.[7]

The concepts of non-discrimination under WTO law and Article 24 of the OECD Model are the subject of this study because of their nature and background. Both the non-discrimination clauses of the GATT and GATS and those of double taxation conventions are sources of international law and deal with economic matters and conditions of competition. They neither aim at deep integration between States nor focus on a particular region or group of countries. The scope of these non-discrimination clauses highlights the significant differences towards the EU fundamental freedoms that are of a regional nature and establish and foster the internal market within the EU. Bilateral investment treaties (BITs) also include MFN and NT clauses and are, just like double taxation conventions, concluded on a bilateral basis between different States. However, they are less suitable for a comparative analysis. There is no model for BITs in place that would be as universally accepted as the OECD Model for double taxation conventions. This makes it difficult to establish common principles of non-discrimination when different arbitral tribunals are confronted with different texts and render different decisions.[8] As far as the MFN and NT rules of the GATT and GATS

5. *See*, for instance, Rust 2015b m.no. 2. Although Article 24 *intends* to do so in order to succeed in its goal, this does not mean that tax treaty provisions must always prevail over contrary domestic law. Depending on a State's legal system, domestic law provisions giving effect to a treaty may not fully implement a non-discrimination rule, or domestic law provisions may later override a non-discrimination rule (treaty override).
6. *See*, for instance, Schön 2016.
7. *See*, for instance, Dziurdź 2016.
8. *See also* DiMascio and Pauwelyn 2008, 66; moreover, on the different approaches to 'likeness' and 'less favourable treatment' in international investment law, Mitchell, Heaton, and Henckels 2016, 64–88, 135–155.

are concerned, the Appellate Body is able to clarify and resolve conflicts between different panel reports and thereby ensures uniformity. Numerous disputes about MFN and NT obligations have been incited during the more than seventy years of GATT rules and more than twenty years since the creation of the WTO. This long-standing framework thus led to sufficient jurisprudence that allows identifying not only the principles of non-discrimination but also the history of how these principles have evolved over time. The work on the non-discrimination provisions of the OECD Model started in 1956 and has significantly developed since then. In 1977 and 2008, comprehensive updates to the OECD Commentary on Article 24 were made that try to ensure a certain level of common interpretation. Identically worded provisions that are based on the same version of the OECD Model should, in principle, be given a similar meaning even when interpreted by different domestic courts. Last, but not least, the wording of the analysed non-discrimination provisions is ambiguous and open to different meanings and concepts. Therefore, the interpretation must take special account of the broader context of the GATT and GATS and of double taxation conventions. All of this justifies taking a closer look at both areas of international non-discrimination law; establish to what extent formal, substantive, and subjective approaches are applied; determine the reasons for the approaches taken; and deduce conceptual implications for non-discrimination law.

This study will be structured in five parts:

> First, an analysis of the general MFN and NT rules of the GATT and GATS will be undertaken (Chapter 2). This analysis will focus on the meanings of 'likeness' and 'less favourable treatment' and on how the context of the non-discrimination provisions and the (non-)existence of general exceptions may influence these meanings and the burden of proof. Since the WTO framework must bring together objectives of trade liberalization with various regulatory purposes,[9] it will be demonstrated at which stages of analysis such regulatory purposes may play a role. In principle, general exceptions – that is, justifications[10] – acknowledge legitimate regulatory purposes such as protection of human, animal or plant life, or health. However, since general

9. In this study, terms such as 'regulatory purpose', 'policy objective', 'policy interest', and 'aim' will be used to describe various purposes such as environmental protection or avoidance of low or no taxation which have at least some alleged connection to an internal measure and can potentially be submitted as an argument against discrimination or a violation. Unless otherwise indicated, these terms are not indented to predetermine whether a particular purpose can be verified through subjective or objective evidence or turns out to be merely a pretext. *See*, by contrast, Mitchell, Heaton, and Henckels 2016, 15–20, who address possible meanings of 'regulatory purpose' and provide a distinct working definition that is based on objective evidence.

10. It is undisputed that, under WTO law, general exceptions clauses provide for a justification defence. *See*, instead of many, Van den Bossche and Zdouc 2013, 546: 'Article XX [of the GATT] is relevant, and will be invoked by a Member, *only* when a measure of that Member has been found to be inconsistent with another GATT provision [original emphasis]. In such a case, Article XX will be invoked to justify the GATT-inconsistent measure.' *See also* Article 36 of the TFEU, for which the general exception clause of Article XX of the GATT 1947 was the inspiration (Gaines and Olsen 2012, 205; Desmedt 2001, 462).

exceptions clauses are exhaustive, impose strict requirements for their application, or are sometimes missing, it has been suggested to consider regulatory purposes as a matter of 'likeness' or 'less favourable treatment'. An analysis of the general MFN and NT rules will outline how a justification defence can be integrated into any stage of a non-discrimination analysis.

Second, after determining what objectives the non-discrimination provisions of Article 24 of the OECD Model pursue, unresolved issues concerning comparability will be addressed (Chapter 3). A mechanical approach to comparability is usually applied to automatically resolve cases of potential discrimination. This approach basically requires all circumstances to be identical, allows focusing on only direct discrimination, and leaves no room for justifications. However, situations involving interlinked characteristics cannot be resolved in a consistent manner. Based on selected situations of potential discrimination, it will be demonstrated why contradictory results are sometimes reached and how arguments that are difficult to reconcile with a traditional test of comparability are nevertheless employed in order to argue in favour of or against discrimination. In some cases, it appears indispensable to go beyond a mechanical approach to comparability.

Third, an approach to non-discrimination will be suggested that openly considers all arguments that might speak for or against discrimination, regardless of whether such arguments are labelled as a justification (Chapter 4). This approach will supplement an adapted 'but for' test with a substantive analysis and thus suggest a two-step approach for determining whether circumstances are comparable. In a first step, all circumstances must be the same except for the protected characteristic and all attributes that are inevitably linked to this characteristic in a concrete case. This 'but for' test allows domestic tax measures to distinguish on any basis as long as they do not rely on a protected characteristic or an inevitably linked attribute. However, if a domestic tax measure refers directly or through an inevitably linked attribute to a protected characteristic in a concrete case, discrimination cannot yet be established; the measure is only prima facie discriminatory. In a second step, it has to be determined whether legitimate arguments for different treatment are reflected in an inevitably linked attribute, thereby preventing comparability, or whether all inevitably linked attributes must be ignored as a distinction on such a basis is unacceptable from a tax treaty perspective. This suggested two-step approach to comparability will then be applied to selected cases of potential discrimination and supplemented with additional considerations.

Fourth, as both the general MFN and NT rules of the GATT and GATS and the non-discrimination rules of Article 24 of the OECD Model face common conceptual challenges, these challenges will be identified and discussed (Chapter 5). It will be submitted that non-discrimination provisions necessarily establish a balance between competing policy interests, that regulatory purposes and policy arguments need not be a matter of a separate justification analysis, that it is often necessary to identify aims of a scrutinized measure in an objective manner even when dealing with comparability or treatment that is less favourable, and that formal approaches might be inconclusive or not provide for straightforward solutions which is the reason why substantive considerations appear indispensable. This chapter, therefore, aims to elaborate on what conceptual implications can be drawn from the concepts of non-discrimination under WTO law and Article 24 of the OECD Model.

Finally, a summary and conclusions will be offered (Chapter 6).

CHAPTER 2

General Non-discrimination Rules of the GATT and GATS

Non-discrimination is a central obligation under the multilateral trading system of the WTO. This chapter will begin with some preliminary remarks on the multilateral trading system of the WTO (section §2.01). Subsequently, an overview of the most important concepts of non-discrimination - MFN and NT - will be provided, and the difficulty of balancing trade and non-trade objectives will be addressed (section §2.02). In order to identify discrimination and a violation of substantive WTO obligations, it is necessary to perform an analysis that generally consists of 'likeness' (section §2.03), 'less favourable treatment' (section §2.04), and exceptions (section §2.05). It will be demonstrated how these steps of analysis are understood in different contexts and why all of the steps of analysis are, in principle, able to consider non-trade objectives in order to justify differences in treatment. Finally, the implications for the burden of proof will be discussed (section §2.06).

§2.01 PRELIMINARY REMARKS ON THE MULTILATERAL TRADING SYSTEM

Global trade has become an integral part of our daily lives, although the worldwide and interwoven chains of production often go unnoticed. In producing a computer mouse, not necessarily a complex product compared to mobile phones or other electronic devices, around 1,000 people in more than 100 enterprises and at least fifteen countries might be involved.[11] Therefore, it is a huge challenge to trace back the origins of all of the components and raw materials (aluminium, barium, copper, crude oil, gold, iron, nickel, palladium, ruthenium, silicon, silver, tin, titanium, etc.) that are needed for a computer mouse in order to ensure its fair production. An average vehicle may consist

11. *See* https://www.nager-it.de/maus/preisgestaltung and https://www.nager-it.de/static/pdf/lieferkette.pdf (visited on 6 January 2019).

of about 20,000 parts and depend on thousands of suppliers.[12] If an earthquake and tsunami in Japan leads to a shortage of a single component, the entire production of trucks at a United States (US) plant of one of the world's largest automobile manufacturers can stop.[13] Enterprises fundamentally rely on an unhindered flow of international trade in products and resources. In fact, many products, even local products, could hardly be manufactured without imports of materials, components, or equipment or without foreign services. They are now 'Made in the World'.[14]

Within the multilateral trading system of the WTO, 164 Members regulate their trade relations in the area of goods, services, and intellectual property. This open trading system is based on multilaterally agreed rules and grounded in the belief that all economies can benefit from open trade. Although the WTO began life as an international organization on 1 January 1995, its de facto predecessor,[15] the GATT 1947, greatly influenced trade liberalization and world trade in goods for nearly half a century.[16] With the Marrakesh Agreement Establishing the WTO of 1994 (the WTO Agreement), that is, the legal basis for the WTO trading system, the GATT remained in effect under the WTO framework, but it was updated and incorporated by reference as a legally distinct agreement (the GATT 1994). This means that, even though the GATT 1994 is legally distinct from the GATT 1947,[17] it consists of the original provisions in the GATT 1947.[18] Besides the GATT 1994, which is complemented by several other multilateral agreements on trade in goods, the GATS and the Agreement on Trade-Related Aspects of Intellectual Property Rights (TRIPS) became major pillars of the WTO.

The WTO Agreement serves as an umbrella agreement for the other WTO agreements that are annexed to it. They concern trade in goods (the GATT and other multilateral agreements on specific sectors or issues),[19] trade in services (the GATS, which also includes annexes on specific sectors)[20] as well as trade-related aspects of intellectual property rights (the TRIPS Agreement).[21] In addition, the WTO Agreement regulates the settlement of disputes in the Dispute Settlement Understanding (DSU)[22] and establishes a Trade Policy Review Mechanism.[23] Finally, the WTO Agreement includes plurilateral agreements[24] that are not binding on all WTO Members.[25] Unlike

12. Bunkley 2011.
13. Bunkley 2011.
14. Van den Bossche and Zdouc 2013, 13.
15. Van den Bossche and Zdouc 2013, 78.
16. Although the GATT 1947 was not an international organization but merely a multilateral agreement, it generated some fairly elaborate procedures for conducting its business. Therefore, the GATT 1947 is often referred to as a de facto organization.
17. Article II:4 of the WTO Agreement.
18. Paragraph 1(a) of the GATT 1994.
19. Annex 1A of the WTO Agreement.
20. Annex 1B of the WTO Agreement.
21. Annex 1C of the WTO Agreement.
22. Annex 2 of the WTO Agreement.
23. Annex 3 of the WTO Agreement.
24. Annex 4 of the WTO Agreement.
25. However, the agreements on dairy products and bovine meat were terminated in 1997; thus, only the agreements on trade in civil aircraft and government procurement are still in force.

the previous GATT 1947 system, the WTO Agreement is a single treaty instrument that was accepted by the WTO Members as a 'single undertaking'.[26] Since all of the trade agreements in the annex to the WTO Agreement are integral parts of it,[27] they represent an inseparable package of rights and disciplines.[28]

§2.02 NON-DISCRIMINATION AS A CENTRAL WTO OBLIGATION

[A] Benefits of Non-discrimination in World Trade

Within the WTO framework, all major agreements include non-discrimination provisions that require MFN and NT. They obligate the Members not to discriminate *between* their trading partners (MFN) or *against* their trading partners (NT). In fact, the principle of non-discrimination is a cornerstone of the WTO system. The preamble to the WTO Agreement already proclaims that the Members intend to contribute to the desired trade objectives 'by entering into reciprocal and mutually advantageous arrangements directed to the substantial reduction of tariffs and other barriers to trade and to the elimination of discriminatory treatment in international trade relations'.[29]

Generally speaking, discrimination distorts the market in favour of products that are more expensive and/or of lower quality[30] thereby disadvantaging superior products because of their origin. A discriminated trading partner may resort to countermeasures, and a continuous rise of trade barriers as well as a formation of trade cliques may lead to economic and political tensions.[31] As the WTO observes, '[h]istory is littered with examples of trade disputes turning into war'.[32] Therefore, prevention of discrimination is at the heart of the WTO.

If a WTO Member lowers a trade barrier or opens up its market, it has to do so for all of its trading partners. This means that all of the other WTO Members enjoy the benefits given to the most-favoured trading partner. Besides promoting liberalization by extending trade benefits to almost the whole world,[33] MFN treatment reduces complexity and transaction costs for Members as well as for importers and exporters.[34] Instead of granting many different trade benefits to different trading partners, the 'best' trade benefits are granted equally to all trading partners. MFN treatment further avoids a misallocation of resources and protects the value of trade concessions against future erosion.[35]

While foreign competition may lead to short-term disadvantages which usually concentrate on specific business sectors, it may also provide long-term benefits such as

26. AB Report, *Brazil – Desiccated Coconut*, 1997, p. 12.
27. Article II:2 and 3 of the WTO Agreement. Of course, the plurilateral trade agreements are only part of the WTO Agreement for those Members that have accepted them.
28. *See*, to this effect, AB Report, *Argentina – Footwear (EC)*, 2000, para. 81.
29. Third recital of the preamble to the WTO Agreement.
30. Van den Bossche and Zdouc 2013, 315.
31. Jackson 2000b, 61.
32. World Trade Organization 2008, 2.
33. Jackson 2000b, 60.
34. Jackson 2000b, 60–61.
35. Trebilcock and Howse 2005, 51–53.

lower prices, better quality, more innovation, and increased productivity that come step by step and spread over many people and enterprises.[36] Therefore, NT obligations together with specific rules against overly trade-restrictive measures prevent Members from protectionism. After a foreign product or service has entered the market, it must be treated as being equal to domestic products or services. This ensures that foreign and domestic products and services can compete on an equal footing, that is, without burdens placed for protectionist purposes other than tariffs. In addition, due to the NT obligations, trade concessions granted by a WTO Member cannot be undermined by adopting a substitute policy that discriminates against foreign products or services that benefited from these concessions.[37]

In the following, the general non-discrimination rules concerning MFN and NT will be outlined. First, the non-discrimination rules in the GATT and in other agreements related to trade in goods will be dealt with (section §2.02[B]). Subsequently, the corresponding MFN and NT rules in the GATS will be presented (section §2.02[C]), and the non-discrimination concept under the TRIPS Agreement will be introduced (section §2.02[D]). Finally, the issue of balancing trade and non-trade objectives (section §2.02[E]) will lead over to a detailed analysis of 'likeness', 'less favourable treatment', and general exceptions.

[B] GATT: Tariffs and Trade

[1] Article I: MFN

MFN treatment essentially means that concessions or advantages given to one trading partner must be extended to all trading partners. Accordingly, a WTO Member normally cannot discriminate between its trading partners: favour one, favour all.[38] This principle is so fundamental to trade in goods that it is enshrined at the very beginning of the GATT, in Article I:1:

> **Article I**
>
> *General Most-Favoured-Nation Treatment*
>
> 1. With respect to customs duties and charges of any kind imposed on or in connection with importation or exportation or imposed on the international transfer of payments for imports or exports, and with respect to the method of levying such duties and charges, and with respect to all rules and formalities in connection with importation and exportation, and with respect to all matters referred to in paragraphs 2 and 4 of Article III, any advantage, favour, privilege or immunity granted by any [Member] [[39]] to any product originating in or destined

36. Van den Bossche and Zdouc 2013, 23–24.
37. Trebilcock and Howse 2005, 83–84.
38. World Trade Organization 2015, 10, 34.
39. In the GATT 1947, the term 'contracting party' was used. Paragraph 2(a) of the GATT 1994 stipulates that '[t]he references to "contracting party" … shall be deemed to read "Member"'. Accordingly, in the context of the GATT 1994, the term 'Member' will be used even when quoting or referring to provisions that originated in the GATT 1947.

> for any other country shall be accorded immediately and unconditionally to the like product originating in or destined for the territories of all other [Members].

This MFN principle is central to the GATT because it prohibits discrimination among like products originating in or destined for different countries.[40] Products imported from another WTO Member cannot be treated less favourably than like products of any other trading partner, and products to be exported to another Member cannot be treated less favourably than like products destined for any other country, whether that country is a WTO Member or not. MFN treatment ensures that all Members have an equal opportunity to import from or export to other Members.[41]

Moreover, the prohibition of discrimination in Article I:1 of the GATT also serves as an incentive for concessions, negotiated reciprocally, to be extended to all other WTO Members on an MFN basis.[42] When a Member has an interest in exporting certain products to another Member, and vice versa, and when these Members, therefore, agree to reciprocally lower their tariffs on the products concerned, the tariff reductions must be extended to and benefit all of the other WTO Members as well. This means, however, that other Members may profit from the tariff reductions even if they did not grant any reduction in return ('free riders'). Consequently, the MFN treatment obligation complicates tariff negotiations, but these complications can be mitigated by abandoning negotiations on a product-by-product basis and turning to sectoral or formula approaches.[43]

Article I:1 of the GATT covers a broad range of measures. Basically, these measures can be divided into border measures and internal measures.[44] Border measures include customs duties, other charges imposed on or in connection with importation or exportation, and all rules and formalities in connection with importation and exportation. For example, import surcharges, export duties, customs fees, and quality inspection fees, as well as import and export prohibitions and quotas, tariff quotas, import licences, and customs formalities, constitute border measures that must meet the MFN treatment obligation.[45] Internal measures are not explicitly mentioned in Article I:1 of the GATT. Instead, Article I:1 refers to the provisions on NT in Article III:2 and 4 of the GATT. Therein, internal measures are defined as internal taxes or other internal charges of any kind, on the one hand (Article III:2) and as all laws, regulations, and requirements affecting the products' internal sale or use on the other hand (Article III:4). With respect to all these border and internal measures, any advantage, favour, privilege, or immunity, if granted by a WTO Member to any product originating in or destined for any other country, must be extended immediately and unconditionally to all like products regardless of their origin or destination.

40. AB Report, *Canada – Autos*, 2000, para. 84.
41. Van den Bossche and Zdouc 2013, 318, 346.
42. AB Report, *Canada – Autos*, 2000, para. 84. *See also*, however, McRae 2012, 4, who remarks that 'Article I:1 provides more than an incentive; it contains an obligation'.
43. Van den Bossche and Zdouc 2013, 430–431.
44. Van den Bossche and Zdouc 2013, 321.
45. Van den Bossche and Zdouc 2013, 321.

[2] Article III: NT

Article III of the GATT provides for NT. In its first paragraph, it establishes the general principle to non-discrimination that internal measures should not be applied so as to afford protection to domestic production. Thereafter, Article III stipulates specific non-discrimination obligations: in the second paragraph, obligations regarding internal taxation (fiscal measures) and, in the fourth paragraph, obligations regarding internal regulation (non-fiscal measures):

> **Article III**
>
> *National Treatment on Internal Taxation and Regulation*
>
> 1. The [Members] recognize that internal taxes and other internal charges, and laws, regulations and requirements affecting the internal sale, offering for sale, purchase, transportation, distribution or use of products, and internal quantitative regulations requiring the mixture, processing or use of products in specified amounts or proportions, should not be applied to imported or domestic products so as to afford protection to domestic production.
>
> 2. The products of the territory of any [Member] imported into the territory of any other [Member] shall not be subject, directly or indirectly, to internal taxes or other internal charges of any kind in excess of those applied, directly or indirectly, to like domestic products. Moreover, no [Member] shall otherwise apply internal taxes or other internal charges to imported or domestic products in a manner contrary to the principles set forth in paragraph 1.
>
> ...
>
> 4. The products of the territory of any [Member] imported into the territory of any other [Member] shall be accorded treatment no less favourable than that accorded to like products of national origin in respect of all laws, regulations and requirements affecting their internal sale, offering for sale, purchase, transportation, distribution or use.

It follows that Article III of the GATT prohibits discrimination because of foreign origin. A WTO Member normally cannot discriminate against its trading partners, which means that it cannot favour itself. Once a foreign product has been cleared through customs and has entered the market, it must be granted no less favourable treatment than like domestic products.

In practice, Members often discriminate against foreign products and often in a disguised manner. Measures that are formally neutral may have a negative impact on trade in foreign goods, thereby protecting domestic production from foreign competition. In this respect, Robert E. Hudec observes:[46]

> In any federal regime dedicated to maintaining open markets ... experience teaches that domestic regulations sometimes have a negative impact on trade. In some cases the negative trade effects are unintended, but on other occasions it has been clear that member governments are using domestic regulations to give local producers a competitive advantage. This tendency to misuse domestic regulatory measures for protectionist purposes is inevitable in a world where the commercial

46. Hudec 1998, 619.

interests of foreign states have little or no representation in the political life of the state enacting the measure.

Article III of the GATT aims at preventing such protectionism. As the Appellate Body stated in *Japan – Alcoholic Beverages II* (1996):[47]

> The broad and fundamental purpose of Article III is to avoid protectionism in the application of internal tax and regulatory measures. More specifically, the purpose of Article III 'is to ensure that internal measures "not be applied to imported or domestic products so as to afford protection to domestic production"'. Toward this end, Article III obliges Members of the WTO to provide equality of competitive conditions for imported products in relation to domestic products.

Article III of the GATT protects expectations of equal competitive relationships but not trade flows.[48] Thus, proof that a measure has actual trade effects is not necessary for establishing a violation. An additional purpose of Article III is to guarantee that internal measures of WTO Members do not undermine their commitments on tariffs under Article II of the GATT.[49] Members could be inclined to remove trade barriers by lowering and binding their tariffs on foreign products but, at the same time, enact internal measures, which would effectively create new trade barriers for such foreign products and thereby compensate for the tariff concessions.[50] Such a circumvention of tariff concessions is prevented by the obligation of treating foreign products no less favourably than like domestic products. However, the NT obligation is not limited to products that are the subject of tariff concessions. It is a general prohibition of discrimination that also extends to products not bound under Article II of the GATT.[51]

For the application of the NT obligation, it is important to determine whether a measure is a border measure or an internal measure.[52] Only internal measures fall within the scope of Article III of the GATT while border measures are dealt with by other provisions such as by Article II (tariff concessions), Article VII (valuation for customs purposes), and Article XI (general elimination of quantitative restrictions). In this respect, the Interpretative Note *Ad* Article III, the legal status of which is equivalent to that of other GATT provisions,[53] clarifies that whether a measure is applied at the time or point of importation is not decisive:

47. AB Report, *Japan – Alcoholic Beverages II*, 1996, p. 16 (footnotes omitted).
48. AB Report, *Japan – Alcoholic Beverages II*, 1996, p. 16 ('it is irrelevant that "the trade effects" ... are insignificant or even nonexistent; Article III protects expectations not of any particular trade volume but rather of the equal competitive relationship between imported and domestic products'). *See also*, for instance, AB Report, *Korea – Alcoholic Beverages*, 1999, paras 119–120; AB Report, *US – Tuna II (Mexico)*, 2012, para. 239. This has been confirmed for Article I:1 of the GATT as well. *See* AB Report, *EC – Seal Products*, 2014, paras 5.87–5.88.
49. Van den Bossche and Zdouc 2013, 353.
50. *See also* Cosbey and Mavroidis 2014, 288.
51. AB Report, *Japan – Alcoholic Beverages II*, 1996, pp. 16–17. *See also*, for instance, Hestermeyer 2011 m.no. 4; DiMascio and Pauwelyn 2008, 59–61; Jackson 1989, 209.
52. Van den Bossche and Zdouc 2013, 354.
53. *See*, for example, with respect to Article III:2, second sentence of the GATT, AB Report, *Japan – Alcoholic Beverages II*, 1996, p. 24.

> Any internal tax or other internal charge, or any law, regulation or requirement of the kind referred to in paragraph 1 which applies to an imported product and to the like domestic product and is collected or enforced in the case of the imported product at the time or point of importation, is nevertheless to be regarded as an internal tax or other internal charge, or a law, regulation or requirement of the kind referred to in paragraph 1, and is accordingly subject to the provisions of Article III.

What is important for an internal charge within the meaning Article III:2 'is that the *obligation* to pay a charge must accrue due to an internal event or factor, such as the distribution, sale, use or transportation of the imported product'.[54]

Under Article III of the GATT, it must be distinguished between fiscal and non-fiscal measures that are covered by Article III:2 and 4, respectively. Article III:2 applies to 'internal taxes or other internal charges of any kind', whereas Article III:4 concerns 'all laws, regulations and requirements affecting their internal sale, offering for sale, purchase, transportation, distribution or use'. Although following the same general purpose of avoiding protectionism, these non-discrimination rules set out different conditions for their application.

The first sentence of Article III:2 of the GATT provides that internal taxation on foreign products must not be levied 'in excess of' that on 'like domestic products'. The second sentence of Article III:2 of the GATT, by contrast, refers 'to the principles set forth in paragraph 1' and prohibits any internal taxation contrary to these principles. In this respect, the Interpretative Note *Ad* Article III:2 states:

> A tax conforming to the requirements of the first sentence of paragraph 2 would be considered to be inconsistent with the provisions of the second sentence only in cases where competition was involved between, on the one hand, the taxed product and, on the other hand, a directly competitive or substitutable product which was not similarly taxed.

While the first sentence of Article III:2 of the GATT thus uses the concept of 'like products', the second sentence refers to the broader concept of 'directly competitive or substitutable products', and while the first sentence prohibits taxation 'in excess of', the second sentence prohibits only taxation that is 'not similar'. Therefore, the second sentence covers certain products that are not 'like products',[55] but it balances this broader scope by permitting certain *de minimis* differences in taxation as determined on a case-by-case basis.[56] In addition, since the second sentence of Article III:2 specifically invokes the general principle enshrined in Article III:1 of the GATT, it must be separately determined whether a measure is 'applied ... so as to afford protection to domestic production'.[57] Accordingly, the first sentence involves two issues, 'like products' and taxation 'in excess of', whereas the second sentence involves three

54. AB Report, *China – Auto Parts*, 2009, para. 162 (original emphasis).
55. AB Report, *Japan – Alcoholic Beverages II*, 1996, pp. 19 and 25.
56. *Ibid.*, p. 23 with respect to Article III:2, first sentence of the GATT ('[e]ven the smallest amount of "excess" is too much') and p. 27 with respect to Article III:2, second sentence of the GATT ('this amount of differential taxation must be more than *de minimis* to be deemed "not similarly taxed" in any given case').
57. *Ibid.*, p. 24.

issues: 'directly competitive or substitutable products', 'not similarly taxed', and 'protective application'.

Article III:4 on internal regulation uses the concept of 'like products' and prohibits 'less favourable treatment'. It does not contain a provision similar or comparable to the second sentence of Article III:2 (*see also* Table 2.1). To what extent these differences in wording influence the meaning of 'like products' – a term employed by both the first sentence of Article III:2 and Article III:4 – will be discussed below (*see* section §2.03[E][2][a]).

Table 2.1 Structure of Article III:2 and 4 of the GATT

GATT Provision	*Products*	*Reference to Article III:1*	*Prohibition*
Article III:2, 1st sent.	like	no	in excess
Article III:2, 2nd sent.	directly competitive or substitutable	yes	not similar
Article III:4	like	no	less favourable

[3] Direct Taxation

It is often difficult to distinguish between fiscal and non-fiscal measures, that is between internal taxation (Article III:2) and internal regulation (Article III:4).[58] While value added taxes (VAT), sales taxes, and excise duties constitute fiscal measures within the meaning of Article III:2 of the GATT, it is disputed whether direct tax measures also belong to such fiscal measures or whether they are covered by Article III:4.[59] Arguably, direct taxes such as individual and corporate income taxes, capital gains taxes, and wealth taxes are not applied, directly or indirectly, to *products* and, therefore, do not meet the conditions of Article III:2.[60] At the same time, the MFN and NT provisions of the GATT (unlike those of the GATS) do not protect *producers*, as such; they merely protect products.

It can be replied, however, that the distinction between direct and indirect taxes is far from clear-cut, if not outdated.[61] Besides, even if a suitable distinction should be

58. *See also* Dziurdź 2016, 188–190.
59. For an in-depth analysis with further references, *see* Farrell 2013, especially at pp. 41 et seq.; moreover, Schön 2016, sec. 25.2.2.1.
60. *See*, for example, Van den Bossche and Zdouc 2013, 357, who state that '[i]ncome taxes are not covered by Article III:2, first sentence, since they are not internal taxes or other internal charges on *products*' (original emphasis). However, they also note that 'an income tax regulation can be considered to be an internal regulation and thus to fall within the scope of Article III:4 of the GATT'.
61. *See*, for example, Farrell 2013, 46–47; Schön 2004, 291.

agreed on,[62] direct taxes are not explicitly carved out from the GATT. On the contrary, direct tax measures may constitute a subsidy under Article XVI of the GATT even though this article refers to products and not to producers.[63] To the extent that direct taxes have a sufficient connection to products and thus may be regarded as being at least indirectly applicable to products, they can fall under the NT obligation of Article III:2 of the GATT.[64]

Moreover, Article III:4 of the GATT refers to 'all laws, regulations and requirements affecting their [the products'] internal sale, offering for sale, purchase, transportation, distribution or use'. Since the word 'affecting' is understood broadly as referring to measures that have an effect on imported goods,[65] also in direct tax matters special deductions (including accelerated depreciations), tax incentives, and tax quotas for products of domestic origin can constitute trade-related investment measures (TRIMs) that are inconsistent with Article III:4 of the GATT in so far as they encourage the use of domestic over imported products.[66] If direct taxes should not be regarded as fiscal measures within the meaning of Article III:2, they can still constitute

62. *See*, for example, footnote 58 to item (e) of the Annex I to the Agreement on Subsidies and Countervailing Measures (SCM Agreement) which defines, '[f]or the purpose of this Agreement', the term 'direct taxes' as 'taxes on wages, profits, interests, rents, royalties, and all other forms of income, and taxes on the ownership of real property' and the term 'indirect taxes' as 'sales, excise, turnover, value added, franchise, stamp, transfer, inventory and equipment taxes, border taxes and all taxes other than direct taxes and import charges [that is, especially tariffs and duties]'. For the definition of the term 'direct taxes' in the GATS, *see infra* n. 603.
63. *See*, for example, GATT, Report of the Working Party on Subsidies, L/1381, November 1960, which contains a non-exhaustive list of export subsidies in the sense of Article XVI:4 of the GATT 1947, including '[t]he remission, calculated in relation to exports, of *direct taxes* ... on industrial or commercial enterprises' (emphasis added). Moreover, according to Article 1.1(a)(1)(ii) of the SCM Agreement, a subsidy is deemed to exist if 'there is a financial contribution by a government or any public body within the territory of a Member', that is, not only when 'a government practice involves a direct transfer of funds' but also where 'government revenue that is otherwise due is foregone or not collected (e.g. fiscal incentives such as tax credits)'. Annex I to the SCM Agreement incorporates an illustrative list of export subsidies referring to '[t]he full or partial exemption remission, or deferral specifically related to exports, of *direct taxes* ... paid or payable by industrial or commercial enterprises' and '[t]he allowance of special deductions directly related to exports or export performance, over and above those granted in respect to production for domestic consumption, in the calculation of the base on which *direct* taxes are charged' (emphasis added; footnotes omitted). *See also* Farrell 2013, 50, 105 et seq.
64. *See also* AB Report, *Brazil – Taxation*, 2018, para. 5.15, which states that Article III:2, first sentence has a broad scope of application by disciplining not only internal taxes that directly affect products but also internal taxes that indirectly affect products and that it does not exclude measures from its scope that are directed at producers on their face.
65. World Trade Organization 2012 GATT 1994, paras 359 et seq.; AB Report, *Brazil – Taxation*, 2018, para. 5.16. *See also*, with respect to the GATS, AB Report, *EC – Bananas III*, 1997, para. 220.
66. *See also* the Agreement on Trade-Related Investment Measures (TRIMs) which deals with and further specifies which investment measures that relate to trade in goods are inconsistent with the obligation of NT provided for in Article III:4 of the GATT or with the obligation of general elimination of quantitative restrictions stipulated in Article XI:1 of the GATT. An illustrative list of such TRIMs is included in the Annex in para. 1 and also refers to local content requirements: 'TRIMs that are inconsistent with the obligation of national treatment ... include those ... compliance with which is necessary to obtain an advantage, and which require: (a) the purchase or use by an enterprise of products of domestic origin or from any domestic source, whether specified in terms of particular products, in terms of volume or value of products, or in terms of a proportion of volume or value of its local production ....'

'non-fiscal' measures under Article III:4. In both cases, by cross reference, they would be within the scope of Article I:1 of the GATT as well. Only measures not linked to products but, for example, exclusively linked to producers without direct or indirect repercussions on the related products would appear to be out of scope of the non-discrimination rules,[67] whereas qualifying income tax measures that have repercussions on the related products 'must ... be applied in such a way that they have the same effect on all imported products irrespective their origin and on imported as compared to domestic products'.[68]

[4] Other Provisions

Within the GATT, there is a number of other provisions that provide for MFN and NT obligations.[69] For example, Article V:5 obligates, with respect to all charges, regulations, and formalities in connection with transit that 'each [Member] shall accord to traffic in transit to or from the territory of any other [Member] treatment no less favourable than the treatment accorded to traffic in transit to or from any third country'. Article IX:1 requires with regard to marks of origin that 'each [Member] shall accord to the products of the territories of other [Members] treatment ... no less favourable than the treatment accorded to like products of any third country'. Article XIII:1, which deals with the non-discriminatory administration of quantitative restrictions, stipulates that 'no [import or export] prohibition or restriction shall be applied by any [Member] ... unless the importation of the like product of all third countries or the exportation of the like product to all third countries is similarly prohibited or restricted'. To a certain extent, these provisions are worded similarly as the general MFN and NT obligations, notably, by using the concepts of 'like products' and 'less favourable treatment'. Other provisions, however, provide for a very different wording. Article XVII:1, for instance, simply incorporates by reference 'the general principles of non-discriminatory treatment prescribed in this Agreement for governmental measures affecting imports or exports by private traders' which State trading enterprises must adhere to as well in their purchases or sales involving either imports or exports. Last, but not least, the general exceptions clause of Article XX contains a chapeau that requires that 'measures are not applied in a manner which would constitute a means of arbitrary or unjustifiable discrimination between countries where the same conditions prevail, or a disguised restriction on international trade' (*see* section §2.05[C]).

Besides the GATT, various other multilateral WTO agreements on trade in goods include specific MFN and NT provisions that reinforce or extend the general MFN and NT obligations. For example, Article 2.1 of the Agreement on Technical Barriers to Trade (TBT Agreement) combines MFN and NT obligations: 'in respect of technical regulations, products imported from the territory of any Member shall be accorded treatment no less favourable than that accorded to like products of national origin and

67. Davey and Pauwelyn 2000, 18, with respect to Article I:1 of the GATT.
68. Thiel 2005, 20–21, with respect to Articles I:1 and III:4 of the GATT.
69. For a detailed discussion, *see* Zedalis 1994.

to like products originating in any other country'. A similar MFN and NT provision is provided in Article 5.1.1 of the TBT Agreement with respect to conformity assessment procedures that is supplemented by an NT obligation in Article 5.2.1. Moreover, Article 2.3 of the Agreement on the Application of Sanitary and Phytosanitary Measures (SPS Agreement) requires Members to 'ensure that their sanitary and phytosanitary measures do not arbitrarily or unjustifiably discriminate between Members where identical or similar conditions prevail, including between their own territory and that of other Members'. Article 2.1 of the TRIMs Agreement specifies that 'no Member shall apply any TRIM that is inconsistent with the provisions of Article III' of the GATT, and the Agreement includes an illustrative list of such inconsistent TRIMs. Article 2.1 of the Agreement on Preshipment Inspection prescribes that '[u]ser Members shall ensure that preshipment inspection activities are carried out in a non-discriminatory manner, and that the procedures and criteria employed in the conduct of these activities are objective and are applied on an equal basis to all exporters affected by such activities', while Article 2.2 refers to the provisions of Article III:4 of GATT which must be respected to the extent that these are relevant.

All of the mentioned MFN and NT obligations are embedded in different contexts. These contexts may lead to different interpretations and understanding even when the respective provisions use the same or similar terms. In this study, the focus will lie on the general MFN and NT provisions enshrined in Articles I and III of the GATT and on the parallel provisions of the GATS. However, to the extent that other provisions and agreements relating to trade in goods shed light on the concept of non-discrimination under Articles I and III of the GATT, they will be dealt with as well. This especially concerns the TBT Agreement which shows that justifications may be a separate step of analysis or incorporated into 'less favourable treatment' depending on the specific context.

In essence, the WTO non-discrimination obligations regarding trade in goods prescribe that 'like products should be treated equally, irrespective of their origin'.[70] They aim at protecting equal conditions of competition by preventing discrimination between WTO Members (MFN) and against WTO Members (NT) because both kinds of discrimination equally distort the market and the allocation of resources thereby equally diminishing global wealth.[71]

[C] GATS: Trade in Services

[1] Article II: MFN

Under the GATS, the fundamental principles of non-discrimination are extended to trade in services. Article II:1 of the GATS provides for the MFN treatment obligation with respect to services and service suppliers:

70. AB Report, *EC – Bananas III*, 1997, para. 190.
71. Hudec 2000a, 108.

> **Article II**
>
> *Most-Favoured-Nation Treatment*
>
> 1. With respect to any measure covered by this Agreement, each Member shall accord immediately and unconditionally to services and service suppliers of any other Member treatment no less favourable than that it accords to like services and service suppliers of any other country.

This MFN principle prohibits discrimination among like services and service suppliers from different countries. If a WTO Member grants favourable treatment to certain services and service suppliers of another country, it must extend this treatment to all like services and service suppliers of any other Member. Put differently, a Member cannot treat foreign services and service suppliers less favourably than those of any other foreign country. As a consequence, the MFN treatment obligation ensures service suppliers from all WTO Members an equal opportunity to supply their like services abroad in another Member country.[72]

Besides the crucial elements of 'likeness' and 'less favourable treatment', a measure must be 'covered by this Agreement' in order to fall within the scope of Article II:1 of the GATS. According to Article I:1 of the GATS, the Agreement 'applies to measures by Members affecting trade in services'. For the purpose of the GATS, a 'measure' means any measure by a Member whether in the form of a law, regulation, rule, procedure, decision, administrative action, or any other form.[73] Moreover, 'services' includes any service in any sector except services supplied in the exercise of governmental authority.[74] Finally, trade in services is defined as the supply of a service in one of the four modes of supply:[75]

(1) mode 1: cross-border supply (the supply from the territory of one Member into the territory of any other Member);
(2) mode 2: consumption abroad (the supply in the territory of one Member to the service consumer of any other Member);
(3) mode 3: commercial presence (the supply by a service supplier of one Member, through commercial presence in the territory of any other Member);
(4) mode 4: presence of natural persons (the supply by a service supplier of one Member through the presence of natural persons of a Member in the territory of any other Member).

In the GATS, there is no definition of what a *supply* of a service is or when a measure *affects* trade in services. However, some examples are given: 'supply of a service' includes the production, distribution, marketing, sale, and delivery of a service,[76] and 'measures by Members affecting trade in services' include measures in respect of (i) the purchase, payment, or use of a service; (ii) the access to and use of

72. Van den Bossche and Zdouc 2013, 335, 346.
73. Article XXVIII(a) of the GATS. *See also* Article I:3(a) of the GATS.
74. Article I:3(b) of the GATS. *See also* Article I:3(c) of the GATS.
75. Article I:2(a)-(d) of the GATS.
76. Article XXVIII(b) of the GATS.

connected services that are required by those Members to be offered to the public generally; (iii) the presence, including commercial presence, of persons of a Member for the supply of a service in the territory of another Member.[77]

In *EC – Bananas III* (1997),[78] the Appellate Body clarified the meaning of the term 'affecting' by giving it a broad scope. In *US – FSC (Article 21.5 – EC)* (2002),[79] the Appellate Body transferred this reasoning to Article III:4 of the GATT. In particular, the Appellate Body did not require a measure to explicitly regulate or govern trade in services in order to affect, that is to have an effect on, trade in services. Moreover, measures can be found to fall within the scope of both the GATT and GATS, namely, if they involve a service relating to a particular good or a service supplied in conjunction with a particular good.[80]

[2] Article XVII: NT

While all measures by Members affecting trade in services automatically fall within the ambit of the MFN principle enshrined in Article II:1 of the GATS unless temporary exemptions have been listed,[81] the Members must commit themselves to market access and NT in specific sectors before the NT provision of Article XVII:1 of the GATS can be invoked:

> **Article XVII**
>
> *National Treatment*
>
> 1. In the sectors inscribed in its Schedule, and subject to any conditions and qualifications set out therein, each Member shall accord to services and service suppliers of any other Member, in respect of all measures affecting the supply of services, treatment no less favourable than that it accords to its own like services and service suppliers.[10]
>
> 2. A Member may meet the requirement of paragraph 1 by according to services and service suppliers of any other Member, either formally identical treatment or formally different treatment to that it accords to its own like services and service suppliers.
>
> 3. Formally identical or formally different treatment shall be considered to be less favourable if it modifies the conditions of competition in favour of services or service suppliers of the Member compared to like services or service suppliers of any other Member.
>
> [10] Specific commitments assumed under this Article shall not be construed to require any Member to compensate for any inherent competitive disadvantages which result from the foreign character of the relevant services or service suppliers.

77. Article XXVIII(c) of the GATS.
78. AB Report, *EC – Bananas III*, 1997, para. 220.
79. AB Report, *US – FSC (Article 21.5 – EC)*, 2002, paras 208–210.
80. AB Report, *EC – Bananas III*, 1997, para. 221.
81. *See* Article II:2 of the GATS. *See also* Annex on Article II Exemptions.

This means that there is an important difference when compared to trade in goods. While the NT obligation under the GATT is of general scope, under the GATS, it requires specific commitments that are listed in a Member's Schedule of Specific Commitments (Services Schedule). These commitments are entered into by each Member for specific services sectors with respect to certain modes of supply and often with additional limitations. Open trade in services, therefore, will require further rounds of negotiations with a view to achieving a progressively higher level of liberalization (progressive liberalization).[82]

It is noteworthy that, whereas the non-discrimination rules in the GATT protect only against a discriminatory treatment of *products*, the MFN and NT provisions in Articles II and XVII of the GATS refer to services and *service suppliers*. Article XXVIII(g) of the GATS defines the term 'service supplier' as 'any person that supplies a service'. Consequently, it cannot be argued that the GATS only applies to indirect taxes levied on services but not to direct taxes levied on service suppliers.[83] This potentially wide scope of the GATS had been recognized by the drafters. Article XIV(d) and (e) of the GATS contains general exceptions for direct taxes (*see* section §2.05[A]) which essentially relate to the aim of ensuring the equitable or effective imposition or collection of direct taxes (exception from NT) and the aim of avoiding international juridical double taxation (exception from MFN treatment).

[D] TRIPS: Intellectual Property Rights

Since the TRIPS Agreement protects against the unauthorized use of creations of the mind such as trademarks, patents, or literary and artistic works, it does not concern trade as such.[84] However, these days, the value of many goods and services is largely determined by intellectual property. Its unauthorized use is likely to affect the trade in these products or services.[85] Thus, the TRIPS Agreement contributes to international trade in goods and services by specifying minimum standards of protection of intellectual property rights and requiring effective enforcement of these rights.[86]

The TRIPS Agreement also contains general MFN and NT provisions. Article 3.1 of the TRIPS Agreement on NT provides:

> **Article 3**
>
> *National Treatment*
>
> 1. Each Member shall accord to the nationals of other Members treatment no less favourable than that it accords to its own nationals with regard to the protection[3] of intellectual property, subject to the exceptions already provided in, respectively, the Paris Convention (1967), the Berne Convention (1971), the Rome Convention or the Treaty on Intellectual Property in Respect of Integrated Circuits. ...

82. *See also* Article XIX of the GATS.
83. *See also* Beyer 2018, 352-353.
84. Van den Bossche and Zdouc 2013, 47.
85. Van den Bossche and Zdouc 2013, 47.
86. Van den Bossche and Zdouc 2013, 47.

> 3 For the purposes of Articles 3 and 4, 'protection' shall include matters affecting the availability, acquisition, scope, maintenance and enforcement of intellectual property rights as well as those matters affecting the use of intellectual property rights specifically addressed in this Agreement.

Moreover, Article 4 of the TRIPS Agreement enshrines the MFN principle:

> **Article 4**
>
> *Most-Favoured-Nation Treatment*
>
> With regard to the protection of intellectual property, any advantage, favour, privilege or immunity granted by a Member to the nationals of any other country shall be accorded immediately and unconditionally to the nationals of all other Members. ...

The MFN and NT obligations under the TRIPS Agreement have in common with the non-discrimination principles of the GATT and GATS that they require granting 'any advantage, favour, privilege or immunity ... immediately and unconditionally'[87] or 'treatment no less favourable'.[88] However, the obligations under the TRIPS Agreement also differ since they do not expressly require or define 'likeness' or comparability and do not refer to products or services and service suppliers. Instead, they refer to 'nationals of other Members' who are defined by the second sentence of Article 1.3 of the TRIPS Agreement: 'In respect of the relevant intellectual property right, the nationals of other Members shall be understood as those natural or legal persons that would meet the criteria for eligibility for protection provided for in the Paris Convention (1967), the Berne Convention (1971), the Rome Convention and the Treaty on Intellectual Property in Respect of Integrated Circuits, were all Members of the WTO members of those conventions'.[89] This reference to other international agreements in defining 'nationality' can be explained by the fact that the TRIPS Agreement, unlike the GATT and GATS which are instruments of negative integration,[90] prescribes certain minimum standards of protection and incorporates, by reference rights, obligations and exceptions from other conventions on intellectual property.

To date, relatively few panel reports have dealt with the general non-discrimination obligations of the TRIPS Agreement,[91] and the Appellate Body has rendered only one decision on this matter: *US – Section 211 Appropriations Act* (2002).[92] However, the Appellate Body stated in this decision that:[93]

> the national treatment obligation is a fundamental principle underlying the *TRIPS Agreement*, just as it has been in what is now the GATT 1994. The Panel was

87. Compare with Article I:1 of the GATT.
88. Compare with Article III:4 of the GATT and Article XVII:1 of the GATS.
89. *See also*, in detail, Lüers 2013 m.nos. 38–62.
90. *See*, for instance, Pauwelyn 2010, 421–422.
91. As far as can be seen: *Indonesia – Autos* (1998); *US – Section 211 Appropriations Act* (2002); *EC – Trademarks and Geographical Indications (US)* (2005); *EC – Trademarks and Geographical Indications (Australia)* (2005).
92. For a general overview and discussion of the intellectual property disputes at the WTO between 1995 and 2010, *see* Pauwelyn 2010.
93. AB Report, *US – Section 211 Appropriations Act*, 2002, para. 242.

> correct in concluding that, as the language of Article 3.1 of the *TRIPS Agreement*, in particular, is similar to that of Article III:4 of the GATT 1994, the jurisprudence on Article III:4 of the GATT 1994 may be useful in interpreting the national treatment obligation in the *TRIPS Agreement*.

To this effect, the Panel on *EC – Trademarks and Geographical Indications* (2005) decided, after referring to precedence under the GATT, that the NT obligation of Article 3.1 of the TRIPS Agreement also covers de facto discrimination and, notably, situations when conditions for registration of geographical indications differ when a geographical indication is located outside a WTO Member.[94] As a de facto matter, foreign applicants would almost exclusively seek to register geographical indications for products produced abroad.[95] Although the concepts developed under the GATT cannot be used in all cases or without caution under the TRIPS Agreement,[96] the GATT principles are relevant in interpreting the MFN and NT rules of the TRIPS Agreement.[97]

[E] Balancing Trade and Non-trade Objectives

Global trade is a means and not an end in itself.[98] This is recognized by the WTO Agreement in which all 164 Members observe not only that 'their relations in the field of trade and economic endeavour should be conducted with a view to ... expanding the production of and trade in goods and services' but also 'with a view to raising standards of living, ensuring full employment and a large and steadily growing volume of real income and effective demand, ... while allowing for the optimal use of the world's resources in accordance with the objective of sustainable development, seeking both to protect and preserve the environment and to enhance the means for doing so in a manner consistent with their respective needs and concerns at different levels of economic development'.[99] These objectives are pursued 'by entering into reciprocal

94. Panel Report, *EC – Trademarks and Geographical Indications (US)*, 2005, paras 7.131–7.213; Panel Report, *EC – Trademarks and Geographical Indications (Australia)*, 2005, paras 7.181–7.249.
95. Abbott, Cottier, and Gurry 2015, 74.
96. *See*, in particular, Kennedy 2015; moreover, Kamperman Sanders 2014, 293–297.
97. Kennedy 2015, 735, 739–740, 754 ('[GATT] jurisprudence can be applicable in TRIPS disputes ... [in] substantive issues surrounding basic GATT principles as adapted in Part I of TRIPS'; 'GATT principles are also relevant to substantive issues where they are present in the TRIPS text, notably the non-discrimination obligations, provided that the specific context within TRIPS and the object and purpose of that Agreement are taken into account').
98. *See also*, with respect to trade liberalization, Cottier and Schneller 2014, 4.
99. First recital of the preamble to the WTO Agreement. By contrast, the second recital of the preamble to the GATT 1947 mentions only the aims of 'raising standards of living, ensuring full employment and a large and steadily growing volume of real income and effective demand, developing the full [not optimal] use of the resources of the world and expanding the production and exchange of goods'. It mentions neither the objective of sustainable development nor the objective of protecting and preserving the environment. *See also* AB Report, *US – Shrimp*, 1998, paras 129, 131, 152–153, 155 where the Appellate Body referred to the qualifications of the objectives in the WTO Agreement and held that this preambular language 'must add colour, texture and shading' to the interpretation (para. 153). In addition, the GATT 1947 does not refer to the countries' different levels of economic development, whereas the second recital of the preamble to the WTO Agreement recognizes 'further that there is need for

and mutually advantageous arrangements directed to the substantial reduction of tariffs and other barriers to trade and to the elimination of discriminatory treatment in international trade relations'.[100]

Trade-restrictive measures may be necessary for pursuing interests that are outside the realm of trade liberalization. WTO law, therefore, provides for a set of rules to reconcile trade liberalization, market access, and non-discrimination rules with the need to protect and promote other societal values and interests.[101] A balance is sought between trade and non-trade objectives.[102] For example, while the MFN and NT rules of the GATT seek to eliminate discriminatory treatment in international trade relations, different treatment of goods may be necessary to protect and preserve the environment. Accordingly, it may be legitimate to restrict or disfavour trade in goods based on a product's negative environmental impact even if such a distinction has a disparate effect on products of certain foreign origin. MFN and NT obligations are designed to secure *fair* conditions of trade[103] and not to prohibit all distinctions on the basis of origin for whatever reason they are made. At the same time, there is an inherent risk that measures that seem to pursue legitimate policy interests amount to protectionism in disguise. It is thus necessary to strike a balance between illegitimate discrimination and legitimate distinctions even when both constitute an obstacle to trade by imposing trade barriers.

Trade liberalization under the WTO framework need not have a negative impact on non-trade objectives. On the contrary, an important aim of free trade is to stimulate competition and thereby allow superior products and services to succeed over those that are inferior (but subsidized or protected). From a consumer's perspective, a product or service may be superior if, for example, it involves no health risks, is environmentally sustainable, or has been produced under good working conditions. Moreover, WTO rules can break down trade barriers for important products that would not be available otherwise. As Peter Van den Bossche and Werner Zdouc point out, '[t]hrough trade, environmentally friendly products or life-saving medicines, that would not be available otherwise, become available to consumers and patients, respectively. At a more general level, trade generates the degree of economic activity and economic welfare that enables governments effectively to promote and protect the societal values and interests' that belong to their core tasks such as public health, consumer safety, the environment, employment, economic development, and national security.[104]

positive efforts designed to ensure that developing countries, and especially the least developed among them, secure a share in the growth in international trade commensurate with the needs of their economic development'.

100. Third recital of the preamble to the WTO Agreement.
101. Van den Bossche and Zdouc 2013, 544.
102. In the following, the term 'trade objectives' will be used for objectives that are specifically promoted by the multilateral trading system such as the protection of equal conditions of competitions whereas the term 'non-trade objectives' will be used for all other objectives and, notably, for those mentioned under general exceptions clauses or commonly regarded as core tasks of governments such as the protection of human, animal, or plant life or health.
103. World Trade Organization 2015, 12.
104. Van den Bossche and Zdouc 2013, 543–544.

Broadly generalized, the steps of a non-discrimination analysis under the general MFN and NT rules consist of a 'likeness' analysis, a 'less favourable treatment' analysis, and a justification defence in the form of general or specific exceptions. Thus, for establishing whether measures are inconsistent with the WTO non-discrimination rules, a 'likeness' analysis must first be conducted. 'Less favourable treatment' on the basis of foreign origin can constitute an unlawful trade barrier only if products or services and service suppliers are 'like', that is sufficiently similar or comparable. In a next step, however, regardless of whether a measure differentiates the 'like' directly (de jure) or indirectly (de facto) on the basis of origin, a justification defence is available. Article XX of GATT and Article XIV of the GATS enshrine general exceptions that may allow deviating from all substantive obligations thus including but not limited to the general MFN and NT obligations.[105] Besides that, the GATT and GATS also include security exceptions related to national security interests and the maintenance of international peace and security.[106] In addition, economic emergency exceptions,[107] regional trade exceptions,[108] and various rules providing for special and differential treatment of developing-country Members and least-developed-country Members[109] may permit a departure from the MFN and NT principles and other WTO obligations.

General exceptions may be invoked only when a measure of a Member has been found to be inconsistent with WTO obligations. As the Appellate Body observed in *Thailand – Cigarettes (Philippines)* (2011), 'an analysis of whether a measure infringes an obligation necessarily precedes, and is distinct from, the "further and separate" assessment of whether such measure is otherwise justified'.[110] Moreover, all listed exceptions are exhaustive and cannot be extended by other or 'unwritten' justification grounds.[111] General exceptions provide for a closed list of regulatory purposes that, under certain conditions, legitimize barriers to trade including deviations from the general MFN and NT obligations.

Many of the exceptions of the GATT and GATS reoccur in other WTO agreements. For example, the sixth recital of the preamble to the TBT Agreement mentions similar regulatory purposes to those stated in the general exceptions clause of Article XX of the GATT.[112] Article 2.2 of the TBT Agreement further refers to legitimate objectives including national security requirements, the prevention of deceptive practices, and

105. Article XIV of the GATS is to a certain extent different since its paras (d) and (e) relate only to the general NT and MFN obligations, respectively.
106. Article XXI of the GATT and Article XIV*bis* of the GATS.
107. Article XIX of the GATT and Agreement on Safeguards.
108. Article XXIV of the GATT and Article V of the GATS.
109. *See*, in particular, the 'Enabling Clause' (Decision on Differential and More Favourable Treatment, Reciprocity and Fuller Participation of Developing Countries, 28 November 1979, L/4903).
110. AB Report, *Thailand – Cigarettes (Philippines)*, 2011, para. 173.
111. *See*, for instance, Mavroidis 2000a, 129, 131.
112. The sixth recital of the preamble to the TBT Agreement and Article XX of the GATT both recognize the protection of human, animal, or plant life or health and the prevention of deceptive practice as legitimate objectives but subject measures that implement these regulatory purposes to the requirement that they 'are not applied in a manner which would constitute a means of arbitrary or unjustifiable discrimination between countries where the same conditions prevail[,] or a disguised restriction on international trade'.

the protection of human health or safety, animal or plant life or health, or the environment. Other agreements incorporate exceptions by cross reference such as Article 3 of the TRIMs Agreement by requiring, as appropriate, the application of all exceptions under the GATT.

Some agreements, however, do not contain a general exceptions clause nor do their non-discrimination provisions necessarily name or refer to such exceptions. For instance, Article 2.1 of the TBT Agreement contains a combined MFN and NT obligation in respect of technical regulations which is very similarly worded to the NT obligation of Article III:4 of the GATT[113] and overlaps in scope, but the TBT Agreement does not contain a general exceptions clause similar to Article XX of the GATT. Thus, the fact that no explicit exceptions are applicable to Article 2.1 of the TBT Agreement is relevant for interpreting this non-discrimination provision (*see* section §2.04[C][3]).

It follows that, in different WTO agreements, the delicate balance between the pursuit of trade liberalization and the Members' right to regulate is expressed in different ways.[114] When no general exceptions are available, general exceptions appear to be too limited, or their application is subject to strict requirements, the question arises whether non-trade objectives may be taken into account in another way. In the following, it will be demonstrated that, besides being a matter of justifications (section §2.05), legitimate policy interests can potentially influence 'likeness' (section §2.03) and 'less favourable treatment' (section §2.04).

§2.03 'LIKENESS' OF PRODUCTS OR SERVICES AND SERVICE SUPPLIERS

[A] Questions Regarding 'Likeness'

Whether products or services and service suppliers are alike is crucial for many non-discrimination rules under WTO law. This question, however, is difficult to answer. Is high alcohol beer like low alcohol beer?[115] Are cars selling for more than USD 30,000 just like cars selling for less?[116] Is vodka or whisky like shōchū (a Japanese distilled beverage)?[117] Are chrysotile asbestos fibres like polyvinyl alcohol (PVA), cellulose, and glass fibres?[118] Are soft drinks sweetened with fructose-glucose syrup like soft drinks sweetened with cane sugar?[119] Is tuna fished without dolphin protection like dolphin-safe tuna?[120] Are clove cigarettes like menthol cigarettes?[121] Are services and service suppliers from countries that do not cooperate in tax matters like services

113. Article 2.1 of the TBT Agreement and Article III:4 of the GATT both refer to imported products that 'shall be accorded treatment no less favourable than that accorded to like products of national origin'.
114. Du 2015, 67–68.
115. *See* GATT 1947 dispute DS23, 39S/206, *US – Malt Beverages*.
116. *See* GATT 1947 dispute DS31, *US – Auto Taxes*.
117. *See* WTO disputes DS8, DS10 and DS11, *Japan – Alcoholic Beverages II*.
118. *See* WTO dispute DS135, *EC – Asbestos*.
119. *See* WTO dispute DS308, *Mexico – Taxes on Soft Drinks*.
120. *See* WTO dispute DS381, *US – Tuna II (Mexico)*.
121. *See* WTO dispute DS406, *US – Clove Cigarettes*.

and service suppliers from cooperative countries?[122] What are the relevant criteria for establishing 'likeness' in all of these cases? Are these criteria the same for the purposes of the GATT and GATS, for the purposes of MFN and NT, for the purposes of all the rules and provisions which refer to 'likeness', or does the meaning of 'likeness' rather depend on the specific context and thus differ under each single agreement, rule, and provision?

To determine whether products are 'like', it is necessary to determine the appropriate standard of 'likeness' since products are always comparable or alike in some aspects but different in others. Thus, it is first necessary to specify the individual criteria by which 'likeness' is to be measured and then to determine – on the basis of the relevant criteria – the degree of 'likeness' required for establishing 'like products'.[123] In *EC – Asbestos* (2001), the Appellate Body observed to this effect that, when determining the meaning of 'like products' under Article III:4 of the GATT, three issues of interpretation must be resolved:[124]

(1) First, it must be established which characteristics or qualities are important in assessing the 'likeness' of products. For instance, most products will have many qualities and characteristics ranging from physical properties such as composition, size, shape, texture, and, possibly, taste and smell to the end-uses and applications of the product.
(2) Second, guidance is required in determining the degree or extent to which products must share qualities or characteristics in order to be 'like products'. Products may share only very few characteristics or qualities, or they may share many. Thus, in the abstract, the term 'like' can encompass a spectrum of differing degrees of 'likeness' or 'similarity'.
(3) Third, there must be an indication from whose perspective 'likeness' should be judged. For instance, ultimate consumers may have a view about the 'likeness' of two products that is very different from that of the inventors or producers of those products.

Although the question of 'likeness' is very much dependent on the specific provision and the context,[125] certain common criteria and considerations have been developed and further refined over time. In early disputes, an objective standard was applied (section §2.03[B]) which later, in 1970, was supplemented by a more economic approach known as the Border Tax Adjustments framework (section §2.03[C]). A few years before the establishment of the WTO, GATT panels developed a purpose-oriented standard of 'likeness' commonly referred to as the aim and effects test (section

122. *See* WTO dispute DS453, *Argentina – Financial Services*.
123. Hudec 2000a, 103. *See also* Regan 2006a, 192–193; Regan 2002, 445–446.
124. AB Report, *EC – Asbestos*, 2001, para. 92.
125. Already during discussions at the London session of the Preparatory Committee in 1946, it was stated that 'the expression ["like product"] had different meanings in different contexts of the Draft Charter'. *See* United Nations, Economic and Social Council, Preparatory Committee of the International Conference on Trade and Employment, Twelfth Meeting, held on 22 November 1946, EPCT/C.II/65, p. 2; World Trade Organization 1995, 1:35.

§2.03[D]). This test was rejected by the Appellate Body in one of its earliest decisions under the WTO framework. Instead, a competitive standard of 'likeness' has since then prevailed (section §2.03[E]).

[B] Objective Standard

[1] Physical Characteristics: A Proxy

Under the objective standard of 'likeness', the most important criterion for measuring 'likeness' is physical characteristics – the more products have the same physical characteristics, the more they can be said to be 'alike'.[126] Robert E. Hudec observes, in this respect, that 'it is usually difficult to understand why a difference in this or that physical characteristic, as such, should dictate that two products need not be treated the same',[127] notably, by failing to meet the condition of 'likeness' under an MFN or NT rule. In a policy sense, the objective standard of 'likeness' would appear to be a sterile concept:[128]

> [A] high degree of physical likeness can be a reliable proxy for many other criteria that do have policy content – criteria such as commercial interchangeability. The greater the physical identity of two products the more likely it is that they are interchangeable. ... As soon as any difference of physical characteristics is found, however, one has to resort to other criteria to determine whether the difference is relevant to the question of 'like' treatment.

If the physical characteristics of two products are identical, there likely exist good policy reasons to treat them equal whatever these reasons are.[129] Any potential reason against their equal treatment cannot be reflected in their physical characteristics. However, if two products are merely similar, that is, identical in some aspects but different in others, it is difficult to judge how they should be treated solely on the basis of their physical characteristics. Even small differences in physical characteristics, including differences in a single atom, may matter a great deal and distinguish, for instance, between a wonder drug and a useless chemical compound.[130] Therefore, it seems necessary to resort to the underlying policy objective for non-discriminatory

126. Hudec 2000a, 103.
127. Hudec 2000a, 103.
128. Hudec 2000a, 103.
129. *See also* Howse and Levy 2013, 336–337, who observe that '[i]n the case of truly similar products, there would not be economic justification for any different treatment of an imported product once it had crossed the border' and that 'there is a baseline economic presumption that identical products should receive identical regulatory and tax treatment' (but they also state that 'to really make ... products identical, they must have matching dimensions, materials, functionality, methods of production, and even spillovers from those methods of production'); moreover, Regan 2006a, 193, 202; Regan 2002, 446, 456, who observes that 'whatever the ultimate ground of "likeness", as objects become more alike in their physical properties, they tend to become more alike in whatever way we are ultimately concerned with', and 'if two objects are perfectly identical, then they must be alike in any other respects that interest us'; similarly, Howse and Regan 2000, 261.
130. Regan 2006a, 193; Regan 2002, 446.

treatment in light of the object and purpose of the treaty itself[131] such as the objective of protecting equal conditions of competition and avoiding protectionism.

A high degree of physical likeness need not be a reliable proxy for all criteria that do have policy content. Whether products are commercially interchangeable may be influenced by non-physical factors such as by environmental- or labour-friendly process and production methods (PPMs).[132] Such methods need not influence the physical characteristics of products but may nevertheless influence consumers' preferences. For example, a 'dolphin-safe' label for tuna may allow consumers to choose between tuna that was harvested in a way that endangered or saved the life of dolphins. If consumers strongly prefer 'dolphin-safe' tuna, this preference will not be reflected in the physical characteristics despite having an impact on interchangeability.[133] If commercial interchangeability is a policy criterion of interest for 'likeness', physical likeness might not constitute a reliable proxy. In fact, these days, many products are distinguished and perceived by consumers as different on the basis of intangible characteristics, including intellectual property. For this reason, the TRIPS Agreement protects against the unauthorized use of creations of the mind. If consumer perceptions are influenced by advertising and marketing, even physically identical products could be regarded as different just because they are branded with a different name or logo.[134]

It follows that similarity in physical characteristics is an important but inconclusive evidence that products are considered 'alike' in the marketplace and that they are commercially interchangeable.[135] As the Appellate Body observed in *Philippines – Distilled Spirits* (2012), 'products that have very similar physical characteristics may not be "like" ... if their competitiveness or substitutability is low, while products that present certain physical differences may still be considered "like" if such physical differences have a limited impact on the competitive relationship between and among the products'.[136] The products' physical characteristics are a relevant but imperfect proxy or only one of the relevant criteria for the nature and extent of the competitive relationship between and among the products.

131. *See also*, to this effect, Mitchell, Heaton, and Henckels 2016, 89, 95.
132. On PPMs, *see*, in detail, Conrad 2011; moreover, Charnovitz 2002; Howse and Regan 2000; Jackson 2000a; Hudec 2000b. On product-related and non-product-related PPMs, in particular, under the TBT Agreement, *see also* Marceau 2014, 325–328, with further references.
133. Such impact does not necessarily prevent different kinds of tuna from being considered 'like products'; label requirements, therefore, may lead to 'less favourable treatment'. *See* Panel Report, *US – Tuna II (Mexico)*, 2012, in particular paras 7.248–7.250; Partiti 2013, 80–81; Ankersmit and Lawrence 2012, 140–141; Nottage and Sánchez 2012, 61–62; moreover, AB Report, *US – Tuna II (Mexico)*, 2012 (commented by Crowley and Howse 2014); AB Report, *US – Tuna II (Mexico) (Article 21.5 – Mexico)*, 2015.
134. *See*, to this effect, H. Horn and Mavroidis 2004, 62–63.
135. *See also* Diebold 2011a, 137 ('purely qualitative and formal criteria such as physical characteristics and end-uses have no value in themselves but must be weighed and assessed through the lens of the actual consumer').
136. AB Report, *Philippines – Distilled Spirits*, 2012, para. 120.

[2] Early GATT 1947 Decisions

At the early beginning under the GATT 1947, the concept of 'like products' was understood to primarily rely on objective criteria, that is especially on physical properties and tariff classifications (which reflect physical properties), without paying much attention to competitive relationships.[137] Before the Working Party on Border Tax Adjustments suggested a more economic approach in 1970, however, only a few cases dealt with or were related to the MFN or NT 'like product' concept in the GATT 1947: *Brazil - Internal Taxes* (1949), *Australia - Ammonium Sulphate* (1950), and *Germany - Sardines* (1952).

In *Brazil — Internal Taxes* (1949),[138] the French delegation alleged that a higher tax imposed on French cognac compared to Brazilian *conhaque* would result in protection for the Brazilian cognac industry against competition from like foreign products which thereby violated Article III of the GATT 1947. However, the Brazilian delegation assured that a lower tax only applied to *conhaque de alcatrão, conhaque de mel* and *conhaque de gengibre* (tar, honey, and ginger *conhaque*), a type of beverage containing aromatic or medicinal substances which supposedly make it quite different from French cognac while Brazilian beverages similar to French cognac were subjected to a higher tax as well.[139] Since the members of the Working Party accepted this explanation[140] without any further analysis, no definite conclusions with respect to the 'like product' concept can be drawn.

In *Australia - Ammonium Sulphate* (1950),[141] the Working Party denied 'likeness' between two types of nitrogenous fertilizer, that is ammonium sulphate and sodium nitrate, due to their different tariff classifications. Although the Working Party did not try to give a definition of 'like products' and disregarded the question of whether the two fertilizers were directly competitive, it concluded 'that they were not to be considered as "like products" within the terms of Article I' of the GATT 1947.[142] The Working Party highlighted that the two products were listed as separate items and enjoyed different treatment in the Australian tariff and that, in the tariffs of other countries, the two products are also listed separately though, in certain cases, the rate is the same but, in others, the treatment is different. For the same reasons, the Working Party denied the existence of 'like products' under Article III:4 of the GATT 1947.[143] When subsequently examining whether tariff concessions on sodium nitrate granted by Australia to Chile had been nullified or impaired under Article XXIII of the GATT 1947, the Working Party emphasized, among other things, that the two types of

137. *See* Diebold 2011b, 836; Melloni 2005, 122.
138. *See also* Melloni 2005, 29-30.
139. GATT Working Party, *Brazil - Internal Taxes, Explanatory Note Submitted by the Brazilian Delegation*, GATT/CP.3/WP.7/2/Add.2, 26 May 1949.
140. GATT Working Party Report, *Brazil - Internal Taxes*, 1949, para. 7.
141. *See also* Melloni 2005, 68-70.
142. GATT Working Party Report, *Australia - Ammonium Sulphate*, 1950, para. 8.
143. *Ibid.*, para. 9.

fertilizer were 'closely related'[144] and recommended removing any competitive inequality between sodium nitrate and ammonium sulphate for use as fertilizers.[145]

As *Australia – Ammonium Sulphate* (1950) concerned a financial subsidy on ammonium sulphate, the Working Party's reference to the Australian tariff, that is to the practice of the same government in another unrelated area and to tariff classifications in other countries, might have been used to demonstrate that the product distinction was objectively justified and thus not discriminatory or protective in purpose.[146] The declared intention of the Australian government was not to give financial aid to producers of a certain type of fertilizer but to the producers of certain crops whose selling price was limited by price control and who preferred to use ammonium sulphate for technical reasons irrespective of price considerations.[147] Even though the Working Party relied on objective criteria and did not consider competitive aspects in its 'likeness' determination, it cannot be ruled out that it was influenced by policy considerations such as whether the distinction at issue aimed at protectionism.

Finally, in *Germany – Sardines* (1952),[148] preparations of European pilchards (sardines), European sprats, and Atlantic herrings, although closely related and considered by many as directly competitive, were surmised not to be 'like products' because the GATT Panel could not derive from the tariff negotiations and the customs tariff used in these negotiations (which classified the preparations under separate sub-items) that Germany and Norway had agreed expressly or tacitly to treat these preparations as if they were 'like products'.[149] Prior to and during the Torquay negotiations of 1951, the canned version of these products enjoyed the same customs treatment in Germany. Nevertheless, all three types of preparation of the same family were classified under separate sub-items in the customs tariff used in these negotiations, and the German delegation only agreed, upon request from Norway, to negotiate tariff reductions regarding European sprats and Atlantic herrings. As a result of the Torquay negotiations, customs duties on European sprats and Atlantic herrings were bound, and the duties on European pilchards (sardines) remained unbound. Later on, however, Germany reduced the customs duties on European pilchards which, as a result, fell below the level of the duties on European sprats and Atlantic herrings. Norway claimed, among other things, that the lower customs duties on preparations of European pilchards had to be extended to the other preparations on the basis of the MFN rule under Article I:1 of the GATT 1947.

Similar to *Australia – Ammonium Sulphate* (1950), the GATT Panel did not feel that it was called upon to give a definition of 'like products' or that it was necessary to decide whether the three types of preparation had to be generally treated as 'like products'. Instead, the Panel regarded it as sufficient to consider whether, in the conduct of the Torquay negotiations, Germany and Norway agreed expressly or tacitly to treat these preparations as if they were 'like products' for the purposes of the GATT

144. *Ibid.*, para. 12.
145. *Ibid.*, paras 15–17.
146. Hudec 2000a fn. 29 on p. 123.
147. GATT Working Party Report, *Australia – Ammonium Sulphate*, 1950, para. 15.
148. *See also* Zedalis 1994 fn. 135 on p. 79; Hudec 1990, 174–179.
149. GATT Panel Report, *Germany – Sardines*, 1952, paras 11 et seq.

1947.[150] Since during the Torquay Round the three types of preparations were consistently treated and in effect negotiated as if they were separate products, since apparently Norway relied on assurances obtained in the course of the negotiation rather than on the automatic operation of the MFN clause that equality of treatment in customs matters would be continued,[151] and since Germany did not unilaterally split up these preparations after it submitted its customs tariff at Torquay,[152] the GATT Panel saw no sufficient evidence that 'like products' had been agreed on and thus that the MFN obligation was violated.[153] However, when subsequently examining under Article XXIII of the GATT 1947 whether a benefit accruing to Norway directly or indirectly under the GATT had been nullified or impaired, the GATT Panel mentioned, among other things, that the products at hand 'are closely related and are considered by many interested parties as directly competitive'.[154] In the end, the Panel concluded that the competitive relationship between the various preparations had been upset by the more favourable treatment of European pilchards (sardines).[155]

According to Robert E. Hudec, *Germany – Sardines* (1952) must be understood against the backdrop of a common GATT tariff practice which treats such fine product distinctions as perfectly normal and legal tariff behaviour. This common practice would support a uniquely narrow concept of 'like product' under Article I:1 of the GATT for product distinctions made in tariffs but not for cases involving internal measures referred to in Article III:2 and 4 of the GATT and cross referenced by Article I:1 of the GATT (*see also* section §2.03[E][2][b]).[156] Although the GATT Panel did not want to definitely rule on the issue of 'likeness', it considered the context of the Torquay negotiations. Since Norway tacitly accepted and relied on a separate classification of the preparations during the negotiations of tariff concessions, the Panel denied Norway's subsequent claim of an MFN treatment violation in the context of tariffs even though preparations of European pilchards, European sprats, and Atlantic herring were in a competitive relationship.

[C] Border Tax Adjustments Criteria

[1] Some Suggested 'Likeness' Criteria

In 1970, the Working Party on Border Tax Adjustments released a report[157] that greatly influenced the approach for analysing 'likeness' under the GATT. This approach has mainly consisted of employing four general criteria:[158]

150. *Ibid.*, para. 12.
151. *Ibid.*, para. 13.
152. *Ibid.*, para. 14.
153. *Ibid.*, para. 15.
154. *Ibid.*, para. 16.
155. *Ibid.*, paras 16–17.
156. Hudec 2000a, 116–117; concurring Delimatsis et al. 2011, 260; Qin 2005, 241. *See also*, in detail, Davey and Pauwelyn 2000, 28–36; critically, Vranes 2009, 215–223.
157. GATT Working Party Report, *Border Tax Adjustments*, 1970, para. 18.
158. *See* AB Report, *EC – Asbestos*, 2001, para. 101.

(1) the properties, nature, and quality of the products;
(2) the end-uses of the products in a given market, that is the extent to which the products are capable of serving the same or similar end-uses;
(3) consumers' tastes and habits, that is the extent to which consumers perceive and treat the products as alternative means of performing particular functions in order to satisfy a particular want or demand; and
(4) the tariff classification of the products.[159]

In particular, the products' end-uses and consumers' tastes and habits allowed for a more nuanced perspective and added competitive elements to the analysis.[160] GATT panels used these criteria when deciding issues of 'likeness'[161] and later, under the WTO framework, the Appellate Body endorsed these criteria as well.[162] However, they were applied on a case-by-case basis, and, thus, the underlying policy considerations often remained unclear. In fact, the Border Tax Adjustments report did not really provide a comprehensive framework for analysing 'likeness'. After pointing out that the term '... like or similar products ...' occurs some sixteen times throughout the GATT 1947, the report merely stated:[163]

> The Working Party concluded that problems arising from the interpretation of the term should be examined on a case-by-case basis. This would allow a fair assessment in each case of the different elements that constitute a 'similar' product. Some criteria were suggested for determining, on a case-by-case basis, whether a product is 'similar': the product's end-uses in a given market; consumers' tastes and habits, which change from country to country; the product's properties, nature and quality. It was observed, however, that the term '... like or similar products ...' caused some uncertainty and that it would be desirable to improve on it; however, no improved term was arrived at.

For Robert E. Hudec, it is difficult to understand why so much respect is accorded to this passage of the report given that it is discussing the term 'like or similar' or 'similar' whereas the keywords of Articles I, III:2 and III:4 of the GATT are 'like product'.[164] Moreover, the criteria listed in the report were just 'suggestions', and these suggestions are merely *reported* by the Working Party but in no way officially recommended by it. Also, the criteria mentioned in the report are merely illustrative since only *some* criteria were suggested for determining, on a case-by-case basis, whether a product is 'similar'.[165] Read as a definition, the report of the Working Party calls for an analysis of both competitive factors and physical characteristics,[166] but it

159. With respect to the tariff classification, the Appellate Body noted that this criterion was not mentioned in the report on Border Tax Adjustments but was included by subsequent panels. *See* AB Report, *EC – Asbestos*, 2001, fn. 74 to para. 101.
160. *See also* Diebold 2011b, 836.
161. *See* AB Report, *Japan – Alcoholic Beverages II*, 1996, fn. 46 on p. 20, with further references.
162. *See*, for instance, AB Report, *Japan – Alcoholic Beverages II*, 1996, p. 20; AB Report, *EC – Asbestos*, 2001, paras 101–102.
163. GATT Working Party Report, *Border Tax Adjustments*, 1970, para. 18.
164. Hudec 2000a, 113.
165. Hudec 2000a, 113.
166. Hudec 2000a, 113.

does not take a position on how much weight should be given to each criterion and what the required degree of 'likeness' or 'similarity' is in a specific context. It only suggests that the examination should be conducted on a case-by-case basis.[167]

This case-by-case approach, as suggested in the report of the Working Party on Border Tax Adjustments, has been emphasized by panels and the Appellate Body ever since.[168] On the one hand, each individual case may involve different facts and circumstances (e.g., consumers' tastes and habits may differ in different markets; different WTO provisions may require different degrees of similarity) and thus 'likeness' must be approached on a case-by-case basis. On the other hand, a case-by-case approach is often called upon when it is unclear or difficult to explain *why* a certain decision is taken. The statement that 'like products' must be defined on a case-by-case basis 'suggests that the concept itself cannot be reduced to definable criteria, and thus that individual applications of the concept ... will differ for reasons cannot be explained'.[169]

[2] Later GATT 1947 Decisions

After the publication of the Border Tax Adjustments report in 1970, the suggested criteria began to influence the determination of 'likeness'. *EEC – Animal Feed Proteins* (1978)[170] dealt with a compulsory purchase programme for skimmed milk powder by the EEC that had the purpose to allow for increased utilization of denatured skimmed milk powder as a protein source for use in feedingstuffs for animals other than calves with a view of reducing the surplus stocks of skimmed milk powder held by governmental intervention agencies.[171] The issue arose whether all products used for the same purpose of adding protein to animal feeds, namely, vegetable proteins, skimmed milk powder as well as animal, marine, and synthetic proteins could be considered as 'like products' under Articles I and III of the GATT 1947.[172]

On the issue of 'likeness', the GATT Panel noted 'such factors as the number of products and tariff items carrying different duty rates and tariff bindings, the varying protein contents and the different vegetable, animal and synthetic origins of the protein products'. It concluded that these various protein products could not be considered as 'like products' within the meaning of Articles I and III.[173] It later repeated that animal, marine, and synthetic proteins could not be considered to be 'like' vegetable proteins,[174] but it also implied that the different kinds of vegetable proteins (soybeans and flour, soybean cakes and meals, other oilseeds and oilseed products, dehydrated forage

167. *See also* Regan 2006a, 210; Regan 2003, 756; Regan 2002, 465.
168. *See*, for instance, AB Report, *Argentina – Financial Services*, 2016, para. 6.26; AB Report, *EC – Asbestos*, 2001, paras 101–102; AB Report, *Japan – Alcoholic Beverages II*, 1996, pp. 20, 25.
169. Hudec 2000a, 101. *See also* Gupta 1997, 708, 709–710.
170. *See also* Melloni 2005, 71–73.
171. GATT Panel Report, *EEC – Animal Feed Proteins*, 1978, paras 1.1 and 2.3.
172. *Ibid.*, paras 3.2–3.4.
173. *Ibid.*, para. 4.2.
174. *Ibid.*, paras 4.11 and 4.20.

and feed preparations, and corn gluten feeds)[175] would constitute 'like products'.[176] Thus, the Panel focused on the properties and the tariff classification of the protein products and employed these criteria in order to deny 'likeness' between vegetable proteins, skimmed milk powder as well as animal, marine, and synthetic proteins. However, the Panel also turned to the question of 'directly competitive or substitutable products' within the meaning of Article III. It concluded that vegetable proteins and skimmed milk powder were technically substitutable in terms of their final use (as a protein source for use in feedingstuffs for animals other than calves) and that the effects of the EEC measures were to make skimmed milk powder competitive with these vegetable proteins (by fostering the use of otherwise less competitive skimmed milk powder).[177]

In *Spain – Unroasted Coffee* (1981),[178] Spain had introduced certain modifications in the tariff treatment applied to imports of unroasted coffee according to which imports into Spain of unroasted non-decaffeinated 'unwashed Arabica' and Robusta coffees were then subject to a tariff treatment that was less favourable than that accorded to 'mild' coffee.[179] As a main supplier of coffee to Spain and mainly exporting 'unwashed Arabica' but also Robusta coffee, Brazil claimed that the new tariff regime was in violation of the MFN treatment obligation stipulated by Article I:1 of the GATT 1947.[180] The Panel examined the question of 'like products' in some detail. It did not consider that organoleptic differences resulting from geographical factors, cultivation methods, the processing of the beans, and the genetic factor were sufficient reasons to allow for a different tariff treatment.[181] For the Panel, it was not unusual that, in the case of agricultural products, the taste and aroma of the end product would differ because of such factors.[182] Moreover, unroasted coffee was mainly, if not exclusively, sold in the form of blends that combined various types of coffee, and coffee in its end-use was universally regarded as a well-defined and single product intended for drinking.[183] Finally, since no other contracting party applied its tariff regime in respect of unroasted, non-decaffeinated coffee in such a way that different types of coffee were subject to different tariff rates,[184] the Panel concluded that all unroasted, non-decaffeinated coffee beans should be considered as 'like products' within the meaning of Article I:1,[185] leading to a violation of the MFN treatment obligation.[186]

It is notable about *Spain – Unroasted Coffee* (1981) that the GATT Panel not only considered the properties and tariff classification of the products in question but also the end-uses of the products. It can be argued, however, that consumers of unroasted

175. *Ibid.*, para. 2.11.
176. *Ibid.*, para. 4.20.
177. *Ibid.*, para. 4.3.
178. *See also* Hudec 1993, 140–141.
179. GATT Panel Report, *Spain – Unroasted Coffee*, 1981, para. 1.1.
180. *Ibid.*, para. 3.1.
181. *Ibid.*, para. 4.6.
182. *Ibid.*, para. 4.6.
183. *Ibid.*, para. 4.7.
184. *Ibid.*, para. 4.8.
185. *Ibid.*, para. 4.9.
186. *Ibid.*, para. 4.10.

coffee, that is roasters that produce coffee blends to be sold to final consumers, differentiate between various types of unroasted coffee for a good reason, for instance, in order to ensure consistent flavour or to create a specific flavour. Thus, for the relevant consumer, different types of unroasted coffee with different qualities and characteristics need not be capable of serving the same or similar end-uses, that is creating a coffee blend with the intended flavour. From this perspective, the Panel could have put more emphasis on the differences in properties of the various types of unroasted coffee, which might have led to significant differences in the end-use of unroasted coffee unlike the end-use of (usually) roasted coffee that is intended for drinking. Spain indeed argued that the existence of blends proved that the various types of unroasted coffee were not the same products.[187]

In *US – Superfund* (1987),[188] Canada, the EEC, and Mexico complained about US taxes on petroleum and certain imported substances. In particular, the US levied an excise tax on petroleum at higher rates for imported products.[189] When examining whether the tax was contrary to the NT requirement of the first sentence of Article III:2 of the GATT 1947, the Panel first determined whether domestic products subject to the tax (crude oil, crude oil condensates, and natural gasoline) were 'like' the imported products subject to the tax (crude oil, crude oil condensates, natural gasoline, refined and residual oil, and certain other liquid hydrocarbon products).[190] After referring to the suggestions in the Border Tax Adjustments framework, the Panel affirmed the existence of 'like products' within the meaning of the first sentence of Article III:2 by focusing only on the end-uses of the products.[191] According to the Panel, '[t]he imported and domestic products are ... either identical or, in the case of imported liquid hydrocarbon products, serve substantially identical end-uses'.[192] Of course, identical products serve identical end-uses, but since all the products subject to the tax on petroleum served substantially identical end-uses, they were all considered 'like products'. As a consequence, because the rate of tax applied to the imported products was higher than the rate applied to the 'like' domestic products, the Panel held that the tax on petroleum was inconsistent with the NT obligations.[193]

In the last case before the introduction of the aim and effects test, *Japan – Alcoholic Beverages I* (1987),[194] the EEC complained about various aspects of Japan's customs duties, taxes, and labelling practices on imported wines and alcoholic beverages. The GATT Panel comprehensively dealt with the question of whether different kinds of alcoholic beverages could be regarded as 'like products' or 'directly competitive or substitutable products' under the first and second sentences of Article III:2 of the GATT 1947, respectively. The Panel observed that past decisions on 'likeness' had been made on a case-by-case basis after examining a number of relevant

---

187. *Ibid.*, para. 3.8.
188. *See also* Melloni 2005, 31–33.
189. GATT Panel Report, *US – Superfund*, 1987, para. 2.2.
190. *Ibid.*, para. 5.1.1.
191. *Ibid.*, para. 5.1.1.
192. *Ibid.*, para. 5.1.1.
193. *Ibid.*, para. 5.1.1.
194. *See also* Melloni 2005, 33–35; Hudec 1993, 213–214.

facts, and it referred to the Border Tax Adjustments report and the criteria mentioned therein.[195] Then, the Panel decided to examine the issue of 'like products' on a product-by-product basis using the criteria of the Border Tax Adjustments framework as well as others recognized in previous GATT practice such as the classification of goods in customs tariffs.[196] In view of their similar properties, end-uses, and usually uniform classification in tariff nomenclatures, the Panel found that imported and domestic gin, vodka, whisky, grape brandy, fruit brandy, 'classic' liqueurs, unsweetened still wine, and sparkling wine should be considered as 'like products', respectively.[197] The Panel agreed that each category of alcoholic beverages constituted a well-defined and single product intended for drinking in its end-use and that minor differences in taste, colour, and other properties did not prevent products qualifying as 'like products'.[198]

Moreover, even though the Panel was of the view that the 'likeness' of products must be examined taking into account not only objective criteria (such as composition and manufacturing processes of products) but also the more subjective consumers' viewpoint (such as consumption and use by consumers), the Panel held that shōchū, a Japanese distilled beverage, and vodka could be considered as 'like products' because they were both white/clean spirits, made of similar raw materials, and their end-uses were virtually identical.[199] Although shōchū has certain traditional Japanese consumer habits such as being diluted with hot water before drinking it, the Panel found that the traditional Japanese consumer habits provided no reason for not considering vodka to be a 'like' product because consumer habits are variable in time and space, and differential taxes should not crystallize consumer preferences for traditional domestic products.[200]

Turning to the issue of 'directly competitive or substitutable products', the Panel stated that even if imported alcoholic beverages were not considered to be 'like' to Japanese alcoholic beverages, the flexibility in the use of alcoholic drinks and their common characteristics often offered an alternative choice for consumers leading to a competitive relationship.[201] Thus, the Panel concluded that imported and domestic distilled liquors (whisky, brandy, vodka, shōchū, etc.) among each other, liqueurs among each other, unsweetened and sweetened wines among each other, and sparkling wines among each other could be considered to be 'directly competitive or substitutable products'.[202]

The above-mentioned decisions demonstrate that the specific role of the physical characteristics, tariff classification, products' end-uses, and consumers' tastes and habits were not always articulated. It remains largely unclear what standards determined the relative relevance and weight of these factors in a particular case and how

195. GATT Panel Report, *Japan – Alcoholic Beverages I*, 1987, para. 5.6.
196. *Ibid.*, para. 5.6.
197. *Ibid.*, para. 5.6.
198. *Ibid.*, para. 5.6 with reference to *Spain – Unroasted Coffee* (1981).
199. *Ibid.*, para. 5.7.
200. *Ibid.*, para. 5.7.
201. *Ibid.*, para. 5.7.
202. *Ibid.*, para. 5.7.

the context of each non-discrimination rule as well as the measures under scrutiny influenced the decisions.[203] 'Rather than trying to build up a consistent set of decisions applying these factors, GATT tribunals have hastened to insist that such analysis must be done on a case-by-case basis; in effect, saying that they are not required to supply any general definitions that reconcile one decision with another.'[204]

[D] Purpose-Oriented Standard: Aim and Effects Test

[1] Introduction in US – Malt Beverages

In addition to using the Border Tax Adjustments criteria, GATT 1947 jurisprudence introduced a purpose-oriented or subjective standard of 'likeness' which became known as the aim and effects test. It was first developed in *US – Malt Beverages* (1992),[205] a case concerning various US measures relating to imported beer, wine, and cider. The state of Mississippi applied a lower tax rate to wines in which a certain variety of grape was used. Canada claimed that this lower tax rate violated the NT obligation of Article III:1 and 2 of the GATT 1947.[206]

First, the GATT Panel considered whether wine imported from Canada was 'like' the domestic wine in Mississippi made from the specified variety of grape. For the Panel, the 'like product' determination under the first sentence of Article III:2 of the GATT 1947 should not only examine the Border Tax Adjustments criteria but should also have regard to the basic purpose of Article III[207] as emphasized in Article III:1. After quoting Article III:1 which condemns a protective application of internal measures, the Panel stated that the purpose of Article III:[208]

> is thus not to prevent contracting parties from using their fiscal and regulatory powers for purposes other than to afford protection to domestic production. Specifically, the purpose of Article III is not to prevent contracting parties from differentiating between different product categories for policy purposes unrelated to the protection of domestic production.

The Panel then considered that the limited purpose of Article III of the GATT 1947 has to be taken into account in interpreting the term 'like products'.[209] Consequently, in determining whether two products subject to different treatment are 'like products', it is necessary to consider whether such product differentiation is being made 'so as to afford protection to domestic production'.[210]

203. *See also* Tsai 1999, 29–30, who observes that the Border Tax Adjustments criteria preceded virtually every attempt to interpret and apply the term 'like product' to a given Article III case but were regularly invoked 'without any subsequent discussion of their relevance or the manner of their application'.
204. Hudec 1998, 625.
205. *See also* Melloni 2005, 37–39, 81–84, 136–137; Westin 1997, 126–127.
206. GATT Panel Report, *US – Malt Beverages*, 1992, paras 5.23 et seq.
207. *Ibid.*, para. 5.24.
208. *Ibid.*, para. 5.25.
209. *Ibid.*, para. 5.25.
210. *Ibid.*, para. 5.25.

In applying those considerations to the Mississippi wine tax, the GATT Panel took into account the limited growing range of the specific variety of grape (only in the south-eastern US and the Mediterranean region) and the rather exceptional basis for a tax distinction.[211] This led the Panel to the view that the special tax treatment implied a geographical distinction that afforded protection to local production of wine to the disadvantage of wine produced where this type of grape could not be grown.[212] Since the US did not claim any public policy purpose other than to subsidize small local producers, the Panel concluded that the unsweetened still wine imported from Canada was 'like' the domestic still wine made from the specified variety of grape and that the particular distinction in favour of wine of a local variety afforded protection to Mississippi vintners. This is contrary to the first sentence of Article III:2 of the GATT 1947.[213]

Several US states also maintained restrictions on points of sale, distribution, and labelling based on certain alcohol content of beer, which means that the measures at issue differentiated between low alcohol beer and high alcohol beer to the disadvantage of the latter. Canada claimed that these restrictions discriminated against imported beer (a major portion of the low alcohol beer market was served by US manufacturers) and contravened Article III:1 and 4 of the GATT 1947.[214]

Again the GATT Panel started by examining whether low alcohol beer and high alcohol beer should be considered 'like products' under Article III:4 of the GATT 1947 and recalled its earlier statement on 'like product' determinations that such determinations should also be made in light of the purpose of Article III.[215] According to the Panel, the issue of 'like products' is significant: 'once products are designated as like products, a regulatory product differentiation, e.g. for standardization or environmental purposes, becomes inconsistent with Article III even if the regulation is not "applied ... so as afford protection to domestic production".'[216] Therefore, the Panel held that the 'like product' determination should be made in such a way that it does not unnecessarily infringe upon the regulatory authority and domestic policy options.[217]

After turning to the specific facts in *US – Malt Beverages* (1992), the Panel admitted that, on the basis of their physical characteristics, low alcohol beer and high alcohol beer are similar.[218] Since both Canadian and US beer manufacturers produced both high and low alcohol beer and since the regulations in question were origin neutral, as such, the burdens also did not fall more heavily on Canadian than on US

---

211. *Ibid.*, para. 5.26.
212. *Ibid.*, para. 5.26.
213. *Ibid.*, para. 5.26.
214. *Ibid.*, paras 5.70 et seq.
215. *Ibid.*, para. 5.71.
216. *Ibid.*, para. 5.72.
217. *Ibid.*, para. 5.72. *See*, critically, Vranes 2009, 204–205. Indeed, as the Appellate Body later held in *EC – Asbestos* (2001), a regulatory product differentiation between 'like products' does not automatically become inconsistent with Article III (*see* section §2.04[B][3]) – but it may become inconsistent.
218. *Ibid.*, para. 5.73.

producers.[219] Moreover, there was some evidence of a certain degree of market differentiation and specialization between high and low alcohol beer.[220]

All of this, however, did not suffice for the Panel to decide on the issue of 'like products'. Instead, the Panel acknowledged the policy goals and the legislative background of the laws regulating the alcohol content of beer, namely, to encourage the consumption of low alcohol beer over the beer with a higher alcohol content specifically for the purposes of protecting human life and health and upholding public morals or to raise additional tax revenue.[221] For the Panel, these regulatory purposes suggested 'that the alcohol content of beer has not been singled out as a means of favouring domestic producers over foreign producers'.[222] Since, in the end, there was no evidence 'that the choice of the particular [alcohol content] level has the *purpose or effect* of affording protection to domestic production' (emphasis added),[223] the Panel decided that low alcohol beer and high alcohol beer need not be considered as 'like products' in terms of Article III:4 of the GATT 1947.[224]

In short, the GATT Panel observed that the 'like product' determination under Article III:2 and 4 of the GATT 1947 should have regard to the purpose of Article III which is (as emphasized in Article III:1) to prevent protective measures but not to prevent differentiations for policy purposes unrelated to the protection of domestic production. Consequently, in determining whether two products that are subject to different treatment are 'like products', it is necessary to consider whether such product differentiation is being made 'so as to afford protection to domestic production'.[225] The regulatory purpose of a Member's measure that differentiates between products is relevant for the task of assessing the 'likeness' of products.

[2] Reapplication in US – Auto Taxes

Once more, the aim and effects test was applied in *US – Auto Taxes* (1994);[226] the decision was circulated only shortly before the creation of the WTO. It was not adopted and, therefore, remained without legal status due to the opposition of the complainant, the European Community (EC).[227] In this case, the EC complained against US regulations that distinguished between automobiles on the basis of their value (luxury tax) and fuel consumption (gas guzzler tax and fuel economy requirements). A luxury tax initially applied to certain luxury products including domestic and imported automobiles that sold for over USD 30,000. The EC claimed that the luxury tax violated the first sentence of Article III:2 of the GATT 1947 since a disproportionately large number of

219. *Ibid.*, para. 5.73.
220. *Ibid.*, para. 5.72.
221. *Ibid.*, para. 5.74.
222. *Ibid.*, para. 5.74.
223. *Ibid.*, para. 5.74.
224. *Ibid.*, para. 5.75.
225. *Ibid.*, paras 5.24–5.25 and 5.71–5.72.
226. *See also* Melloni 2005, 39–46, 85–86, 137–138; Westin 1997, 127–132; Snelson 1996; Haag 1995.
227. Charnovitz 1997, 199; Hudec 1998, 629.

automobiles that sold for more than USD 30,000 were European: European automobiles were, on average, larger and more expensive than US (or Japanese) automobiles. Accordingly, the EC argued that automobiles costing over USD 30,000 were 'like products' to automobiles costing less since they had the same end-use, basic physical characteristics, and tariff classification.[228]

Pursuant to the GATT Panel on *US – Auto Taxes* (1994),[229] however, automobiles selling for more than USD 30,000 could not, for the purposes of the luxury tax, be considered as 'like products' to automobiles selling for less.[230] In framing its reasoning, the Panel observed that the practical interpretative issue under Article III of the GATT 1947 was 'which differences between products may form the basis of regulatory distinctions by governments that accord less favourable treatment to imported products? Or, conversely, which similarities between products prevent regulatory distinctions by governments that accord less favourable treatment to imported products?'[231] After looking at the object and purpose of Article III, which is only to prohibit regulatory distinctions between products applied so as to afford protection to domestic production, and after referring to *US – Malt Beverages* (1992),[232] the Panel concluded that Article III of the GATT 1947 could not be interpreted as prohibiting government policy options that were not taken so as to afford protection to domestic production regardless of whether such policy options required distinctions based on the Border Tax Adjustments criteria or on other factors.[233] For the Panel, the step of determining 'likeness' would:[234]

> in all but the most straightforward cases, have to include an examination of the *aim and effect* of the particular tax measure. ... [I]ssues of likeness under Article III should be analyzed primarily in terms of whether less favourable treatment was based on a regulatory distinction taken so as to afford protection to domestic production.

For the GATT Panel, 'the phrase "so as to afford protection" called for an analysis of elements including the aim of the measure and the resulting effects'.[235] It explained its understanding of the relevant aim and effect as follows:[236]

> A measure could be said to have the *aim* of affording protection if an analysis of the circumstances in which it was adopted, in particular an analysis of the instruments available to the contracting party to achieve the declared domestic policy goal, demonstrated that a change in competitive opportunities in favour of domestic products was a desired outcome and not merely an incidental consequence of the pursuit of a legitimate policy goal. A measure could be said to have the *effect* of affording protection to domestic production if it accorded greater competitive opportunities to domestic products than to imported products. The [actual] effect

228. GATT Panel Report, *US – Auto Taxes*, 1994, unadopted, para. 5.2.
229. *Ibid.*, paras 5.5 et seq.
230. *Ibid.*, para. 5.15.
231. *Ibid.*, para. 5.6.
232. *Ibid.*, para. 5.7.
233. *Ibid.*, para. 5.8.
234. *Ibid.*, para. 5.9 (emphasis added).
235. *Ibid.*, para. 5.10.
236. *Ibid.*, para. 5.10 (original emphasis).

of a measure in terms of trade flows was not relevant ..., since a change in the volume or proportion of imports could be due to many factors other than government measures.

When examining whether the threshold distinction of USD 30,000 was drawn in order to afford protection to domestic production, the Panel appraised the US luxury tax as having the policy objective to raise revenue from sales of perceived 'luxury' products. This was consistent with setting a price threshold of USD 30,000, and setting it at a level at which only a small proportion of automobiles sold within the US market were taxed.[237] The fact that a large proportion of imports from the EC consisted of expensive automobiles and was affected by the measure did not demonstrate that the principal aim of the legislation was to closely target a distinct product category of imported automobile.[238] With respect to the effects of the luxury tax, the Panel did not find any conclusive evidence of a change in the conditions of competition favouring US automobiles.[239] On these grounds, because the threshold distinction of USD 30,000 in the luxury tax was not implemented in order to afford protection to domestic production, the Panel concluded that automobiles above and below that threshold value could not be considered as 'like products'.[240]

The GATT Panel applied basically the same approach to the gas guzzler tax.[241] It found, among other things, that the tax created an incentive to purchase automobiles that are more fuel-efficient and that this incentive would normally lead to increased conservation of fossil fuels.[242] Since the gas guzzler tax was not aimed at[243] and did not have the effect of[244] affording protection to domestic production, automobiles with a low fuel economy could not, for the purposes of the gas guzzler tax, be considered as 'like products' to automobiles with a high fuel economy.[245]

This 'likeness' approach focused not only on arguably objective criteria such as physical characteristics or on competitive relationships. It considered *why* a measure was taken by a Member and what effects it had, that is, whether the alleged regulatory purpose was bona fide and legitimate or whether it had a protective aim or protective effects,[246] although the concrete relationship between the 'aim' and the 'effects' when those factors point in different directions (e.g., when a product distinction has a bona fide regulatory purpose but also has protective market effects) remained unclear.[247]

237. *Ibid.*, para. 5.12. *See also*, however, Farber and Hudec 1996, 75, who observe that there was some evidence of protectionism; moreover, Snelson 1996, 477–478, 484–485, 490.
238. *Ibid.*, para. 5.12.
239. *Ibid.*, paras 5.13–5.14. *See*, critically, Ehring 2002, 967–968; Verhoosel 2002, 53; Mattoo and Subramanian 1998, 311–312; Snelson 1996, 492–493.
240. *Ibid.*, para. 5.15.
241. *Ibid.*, paras 5.21 et seq.
242. *Ibid.*, para. 5.24.
243. *Ibid.*, para. 5.24.
244. *Ibid.*, para. 5.25.
245. *Ibid.*, para. 5.26. *See*, critically, Haag 1995, 100–103.
246. *See also* Muller 2017, 159, who observes with regard to the aim and effects test that 'if the intent of a measure is not protectionist, i.e., it does not *aim* to afford protection, and does not have a protectionist *effect*, it is not considered discriminatory'.
247. Hudec 1998, 627–628.

[3] Pros and Cons of the Aim and Effects Test

Various advantages and disadvantages of the aim and effects test have been put forward and discussed.[248] Basically, the aim and effects test is based on the general principle of Article III:1 of the GATT which stipulates that measures 'should not be applied to imported or domestic products so as to afford protection to domestic production'. Whether a measure has protectionist aims and/or protectionist effects, therefore, should be relevant for establishing 'likeness'. However, the emergence of and support for[249] the aim and effects test can also be explained from a broader perspective. On the one hand, since virtually every regulatory measure has trade effects,[250] even measures that pursue non-protectionist aims such as social, cultural, or environmental interests could violate the NT provisions of Article III. Such discriminatory effects may be merely incidental, difficult to predict, or even change over time due to changes in trade flows and consumers' preferences. It thus seems questionable whether Article III intends to condemn all regulatory measures based only on their effects even when they distinguish between 'like products' on a facially neutral basis and for legitimate policy reasons. As already mentioned, Article III:1 is only concerned with measures that are 'applied ... so as to afford protection to domestic production'. On the other hand, the general exceptions clause of Article XX of the GATT might be seen as insufficient for saving all regulatory measures from violating substantive WTO obligations (*see* section §2.05[A]). Not all public policy purposes that are widely viewed as legitimate or important in liberal democratic societies are covered by the exceptions in Article XX of the GATT. For example, consumer protection (beyond life and health and prevention of deceptive practices) could remain outside of the scope of the exceptions clause.[251] When an exception is available, additional requirements for justifying a measure such as the least trade-restrictive test might be difficult to meet. As a consequence, regulatory measures that pursue non-protectionist aims could incidentally trigger a violation of substantive WTO obligations without being able to rely on appropriate justification. If basically every measure with adverse effects automatically leads to a violation, this could further suggest that the NT principle is an instrument of deregulation rather than non-discrimination.[252]

The aim and effects test considers non-protectionist purposes as an issue of 'likeness' in order to avoid situations when a measure with a disparate impact on imported products automatically violates non-discrimination obligations even without an intention of protectionism. By relying on the trade effects of a measure and on the bona fides of the alleged regulatory purpose behind it, already the question of a

248. For an overview of the main arguments for and against the aim and effects test, *see also* Diebold 2010, 78–80; H. Horn and Weiler 2004, 142–145; Horn and Weiler 2003, 28–32.
249. *See*, rather in favour of the aim and effects test, Reid 2010, 889–891; Roessler 2003; Regan 2003; Regan 2002 (also published in Regan 2006a); Tsai 1999; Hudec 1998; Roessler 1996, 28–31 (also published in Roessler 2000, 127–130).
250. H. Horn and Mavroidis 2004, 53; moreover, Serpin 2016, 224.
251. Howse and Regan 2000, 253; moreover, Ehring 2002, 955; Mavroidis 2000a, 129.
252. *See* Lydgate 2016, 440–442 with reference to Verhoosel 2002, 48; moreover, Cosbey and Mavroidis 2014, 291.

violation primarily depends on and is more precisely guided by the overarching purpose of the non-discrimination rules to separate bona fide regulation from trade protection.[253] In addition, the aim and effects test is able to open up the MFN and NT rules to additional policy considerations or emerging policy concerns that might not have been foreseen at the time when the closed list of general exceptions was codified thereby enhancing the regulatory autonomy of WTO Members.[254] As far as the enumerated list of social policies that can justify measures is regarded as being too narrow to cover all of the many kinds of policies that should be considered valid bases for regulatory actions,[255] the aim and effects test establishes a way of reaching a more reasonable balance between trade and non-trade objectives.

Some concerns about an inappropriate impact on the regulatory autonomy of WTO Members have been lessened only after the aim and effects test was applied in *US – Malt Beverages* (1992) and *US – Auto Taxes* (1994). It was sometimes assumed that basically every distinction between 'like products' could amount to de facto discrimination as soon as some 'like' domestic products are treated better than some 'like' imported products.[256] However, the Appellate Body later clarified in *EC – Asbestos* (2001) that this is not the case: 'less favourable treatment' requires a disproportionate impact on the whole group of 'like' imported products (*see* section §2.04[B][3]). In *Korea – Various Measures on Beef* (2001), moreover, the Appellate Body relaxed the least trade-restrictive test by weighing and balancing a series of factors, arguably giving more flexibility for recognizing legitimate policy interests (*see* section §2.05[B]). From this *ex post* perspective, the question of 'likeness' seems to be only a threshold question and not determinative for illegitimate discrimination.[257] Yet, even though a narrower interpretation of 'less favourable treatment' may exclude many incidental trade effects from being discriminatory and even though flexibility in applying the general exceptions clause may justify discriminatory treatment in a more balanced manner, situations may remain in which regulatory measures address 'like products' without a protectionist purpose but lead to a disparate impact and fail to be justified. Such a result may be seen as intended because discriminatory and unjustified effects necessarily imply protectionism or as ignoring the general principle of Article III:1 of the GATT because bona fide regulation should not be condemned.

It can even make a difference whether a regulatory purpose such as the protection of human life or health is considered and legitimatized at the 'likeness' level or only as a justification defence. Governments regard it as unacceptable to have their patently innocent and sensible regulations branded as a 'violation' of the WTO non-discrimination rules even if rescue under the general exceptions clause is possible.[258]

253. Hudec 1998, 628.
254. *See also* Choi 2002, 115–117; Roessler 2000, 129–130; Roessler 1996, 30–31; critically, Pillai 2002, 334–336.
255. Hudec 1998, 638.
256. *See*, for instance, GATT Panel Report, *US – Malt Beverages*, 1992, para. 5.72, which states that 'once products are designated as like products, a regulatory product differentiation ... becomes inconsistent with Article III'; moreover, Ehring 2002, 939–942.
257. *See*, to this effect, Pauwelyn 2008, 362.
258. *See* Regan 2003, 749, with reference to Hudec 1998, 639.

According to Henrik Horn and Joseph H. H. Weiler, in the realms of concept and symbol, '[i]t is wrong, it can be argued, to deal with the case of a State which adopts an origin neutral measure for a totally legitimate purpose, but which has the coincidental effect of giving an advantage to domestic production, as a violation of a non-discrimination provision requiring justification. Even if the result is the same, there is value in having cases dealt with in a correct normative context and in not diluting the notion of discrimination with activities which should not be so branded'.[259] It is further a question of constitutional identity, the way a society wants to understand its internal hierarchy of values, whether the default norm is liberalized trade and, for competing norms to prevail, they have to be justified, or whether the default value is autonomy of political and moral identity which requires justification only if purposefully abused.[260] Since the terms 'discrimination' and 'violation' have a negative connotation and since the rule-exception dichotomy may imply that trade liberalization, not human life or health, is the default or more important value, a justification defence in sensible matters is simply unacceptable to many people.[261] Robert Howse observes in respect of *EC – Asbestos* (2001) (*see* section §2.03[E][3]) that:[262]

> the normative messaging to outsider communities, such as asbestos victims and the public health community, of considering the products [asbestos and substitute products] 'like' and finding that distinguishing them [by imposing a ban on both domestic and imported asbestos] was discrimination was, to say the least, risky from the point of view of the WTO's legitimacy. This situation lent credence to the views of scholars, such as myself, who warned that there are dangers in impugning as 'discrimination' legitimate public policies simply based upon market disadvantage, which are blind to policy considerations, even if the policies could eventually be held to be justified under Article XX.

With the aim and effects test, it is possible to respect the genuine aim of protecting human life or health already at the 'likeness' level. As a consequence, the non-discrimination rules of the WTO framework do not need to interfere with such sensitive regulatory purposes to the extent those purposes are genuinely pursued.

Nevertheless, the aim and effects test can be criticized for valuing policy objectives at the 'incorrect' stage of analysis,[263] that is at the 'likeness' stage instead of the exception stage. Instead of providing for an exception to the MFN or NT obligations, legitimate policy objectives would become part of the criteria for defining the scope of the non-discrimination obligations. The aim and effects test could further lead to a non-exhaustive list of legitimate policy grounds without any further guidance on the conditions of application and without proportionality requirements. This might

259. H. Horn and Weiler 2004, 143; Horn and Weiler 2003, 30; similarly, Weiler 2009, 767–768.
260. H. Horn and Weiler 2004, 144; Horn and Weiler 2003, 31; similarly, Weiler 2009, 768–769. *See*, moreover, Ortino 2012, 28, 55 ('differentiating between ... [nationality discrimination and public policy justification] may be an indication of a ranking of interests that favours investment protection/liberalization over other legitimate policy interests').
261. Du 2016, 153; moreover, Du 2015, 72; Du 2011, 657, 664–665, 671.
262. Howse 2016, 47. *See*, moreover, Lydgate 2011, 169, 178.
263. *See also*, to this effect, Du 2016, 154–155, 163; Du 2015, 90, who favours a clear division of labour between Article III and Article XX of the GATT.

undermine the effectiveness of the WTO non-discrimination obligations to the detriment of free trade, impair predictability, lead to legal uncertainty,[264] and disrupt the delicate balance between the non-discrimination obligations and the general exceptions clause. In the words of Ming Du, '[l]ike it or not, WTO Members have agreed on a rule-exception structure'.[265] If Members wish to consider new policy interests for justifying measures, they should amend and extend the closed list of general exceptions instead of creating new exceptions to existing substantive obligations by introducing the aim and effects test.[266] If all of the asserted regulatory purposes are evaluated, and their legitimacy is determined at the 'likeness' stage, the role of the exceptions clauses with their explicit justification grounds and application requirements could even be rendered 'virtually redundant'.[267]

Nevertheless, the general exceptions in Article XX of the GATT and Article XIV of the GATS can justify all measures that breach substantive obligations, not only measures that are contrary to the general MFN or NT rules. Article XX of the GATT and Article XIV of the GATS, therefore, would retain a scope of application and would only partly, that is with respect to the non-discrimination provisions, play no independent role under the aim and effects test.[268] Moreover, even if no recourse would be taken to the general exceptions clauses when non-discrimination rules are applied, this would not diminish their importance. On the contrary, the list of exceptions would arguably provide, as part of the context, indispensable guidance about the legitimacy of policy purposes and thus would help to distinguish between legitimate and illegitimate aims at the 'likeness' level.

It is often difficult to objectively establish what the exact aim of a measure is, and there might be more than just one aim or underlying policy objective. Indeed, there might be a variety of different and possibly conflicting aims and policy goals.[269] Since it is necessary to establish the aims of the legislation under scrutiny with the aim and effects test and since it might be necessary to decide which aim of a multiplicity of aims should be determinative or what weight it should be given, the 'likeness' analysis may become vague instead of relying on clearly identifiable objectives or economic criteria.[270] However, it can be responded that similar difficulties arise when the legitimacy of a measure is evaluated under an exceptions clause. Also at this stage of analysis, it

264. *See*, to this effect, Zhou 2012a, 115; Vranes 2009, 204; Snelson 1996, 494.
265. Du 2016, 150; moreover, Du 2015, 90; Vranes 2009, 212.
266. *See*, to this effect, Mavroidis 2000a, 129–131.
267. Hudec 1998, 628–629. *See also*, for instance, Du 2011, 659 (but *see* p. 664); to this effect, Nielsen and Calle 2013, 57.
268. *See*, to this effect, Zhou 2012a, 86; Regan 2006a, 210; H. Horn and Weiler 2004, 142; Horn and Weiler 2003, 28–29; Regan 2002, 454–455; Howse and Regan 2000, 266.
269. *See also* Levy and Regan 2015, 363; moreover, AB Report, *US – Clove Cigarettes*, 2012, para. 115.
270. *See*, in particular, AB Report, *US – Clove Cigarettes*, 2012, para. 115, in which the Appellate Body voiced concerns that 'a panel … may not be able to reach a coherent result if, in determining likeness, it has to rely on various possible regulatory objectives of the measure. If a panel were to focus on one of the objectives of a measure to the exclusion of all others that are equally important, it may reach a somewhat arbitrary result in the determination of what are the like products at issue'.

is necessary to identify and verify what a measure's exact aims are[271] instead of relying on unproven claims.[272] This can be achieved through 'texts of statutes, legislative history, and pronouncements of government agencies or officials' as well as 'the structure and operation of the measure' and any other evidence.[273] By rejecting the aim and effects test, an objective assessment of a measure's aims is not avoided. In *US – Gasoline* (1996), the Appellate Body indicated with regard to Article XX(g) of the GATT that 'should it become clear that realistically, a specific measure cannot in any possible situation have any positive effect on conservation goals, it would very probably be because that measure was not designed as a conservation regulation to begin with'.[274] In *Korea – Various Measures on Beef* (2001), moreover, the Appellate Body was not convinced that Korea intended to establish a level of protection that *totally eliminated* fraud with respect to the origin of beef (domestic or foreign) sold by retailers.[275] This would have probably required a total ban on imports and not only certain restrictions on sales.[276] Apparently, because of this contradiction between the operation of the chosen instrument and the alleged intention of a total elimination of fraud, the Appellate Body assumed that, in effect, Korea intended to *considerably reduce* the number of cases of fraud[277] and continued to analyse Korea's justification defence under Article XX(d) of the GATT on this basis.[278] Also, in *EC – Seal Products* (2014),

271. *See* H. Horn and Mavroidis 2004, 52 ('intent is relevant in the context of Article XX'); Porges and Trachtman 2003, 786, 790, 797 ('aim and effects can also be considered in connection with GATT Article XX'); Fauchald 2003, 464 ('[b]oth the aim or purpose of the measure and the effects of the measure may possibly be relevant ... under the general exceptions').
272. *See also* Farber and Hudec 1996, 82, who observe that 'many claims of regulatory purpose are quite transparently bogus, having been dreamed up in the lawyers' offices only after the measure was challenged'.
273. AB Report, *US – Gambling*, 2005, para. 304. *See*, moreover, AB Report, *US – Tuna II (Mexico)*, para. 314; AB Report, *EC – Seal Products*, 2012, para. 5.144.
274. AB Report, *US – Gasoline*, 1996, pp. 21–22.
275. AB Report, *Korea – Various Measures on Beef*, 2001, para. 178.
276. *Ibid.*, para. 178.
277. *Ibid.*, para. 178.
278. *See also* Vranes 2009, 264–266 ('the Appellate Body did not accept the defendant's *stated* level of protection of its policy goal, but re-adjusted it by drawing an "inverse" inference from the measure adopted to the presumable level of protection'; original emphasis); Regan 2007, 359–360 ('Korea cannot assert a "desired level of protection" that is *higher* than the level achieved by the actual measure and then hold proposed alternatives to the standard Korea *asserts* as opposed to the standard its actual measure *achieves*'); critically, Du 2010, 1097–1098 ('[t]his explicit modification of Korea's regulatory objective is unacceptable as the AB has repeatedly reassured that a WTO Member has autonomy in pursuing legitimate regulatory policy and setting its own ALOP [appropriate level of protection]'). To be sure, the Appellate Body questioned the intended level of protection for the purposes of determining whether alternative measures were reasonably available; the application of Article XX(d) of the GATT as such was not appealed (para. 158). It should, in principle, be possible that a WTO Member intends to establish a high overall level of protection but implements a measure that only aims to achieve a lower level (notably, because this measure is part of a comprehensive policy comprising a multiplicity of interacting measures); this lower level of protection should arguably be relevant for assessing alternative measures in order to avoid a search for a *more*-effective alternative (*see* Bown and Trachtman 2009, 129). It seems that there is a thin line between questioning a Member's intention of a high level of protection if this level is not reflected in the measure under review and questioning the measure's aim to reach such a high level of protection.

multiple objectives were at stake. A ban on seal products combined with certain exceptions was held to have not only the principal objective to address EU public moral concerns regarding seal welfare but also the purpose to accommodate the interests of the Inuit and other indigenous communities traditionally engaged in the hunting of seals.[279] In order to take advantage of Article XX(a) of the GATT, it was not necessary to establish that the EU seal regime was *solely* motivated by public morals.[280]

Finally, if the aim and effects test is criticized for its 'subjectivity' and risk of result-oriented decisions,[281] it should be kept in mind that, as Tomer Broude and Philip I. Levy emphasize, even an economic analysis of 'likeness' which focuses primarily on competitive factors cannot be applied mechanically without a value judgment and subjective component.[282] It has already been observed that physical characteristics, as such, have no policy content (*see* section §2.03[B][1]).[283] Given that a Member should not be able to justify any protectionist action by pointing out even minor - perhaps absurd - physical differences between two products, it is necessary to attach a judgment as to whether those physical differences are significant.[284] If an economic analysis is adopted for determining whether there is a competitive relationship between two products, there is still no objective threshold beyond which these products should be considered 'like'.[285] Establishing a product's end-use is not an objective task, either.[286] On the one hand, menthol and clove cigarettes may be found to share a common end-use, that is, 'to be smoked'. On the other hand, their end-uses may be seen in 'satisfying an addiction to nicotine' and 'creating a pleasurable experience of cigarette taste'[287] - or in 'creating a pleasurable experience of clove taste' thereby implying that menthol cigarettes are different.[288] As there may be an overlap of different functions, a judgment as to whether these overlapping functions or end-uses speak in favour of 'likeness' is indispensable.[289] Thus, no approach to 'likeness' can completely avoid result-oriented decisions. Such risks can only be curtailed by taking

279. AB Report, *EC – Seal Products*, 2012, para. 5.167.
280. Conconi and Voon 2016, 221–224. *See also*, however, Mavroidis 2015, arguing that the EU introduced in one regulation two different measures aimed at two different objectives.
281. *See*, for instance, Davey and Pauwelyn 2000, 38.
282. *See*, in detail, Broude and Levy 2014, 372–378.
283. *See*, however, Appleton 2014, 123, who favours a greater emphasis on product characteristics with due deference to tariff classification and end-uses because product characteristics are readily ascertainable and, therefore, an objective criterion as is tariff classification and, to a lesser extent, end-uses. He further states that Coca-Cola and beer 'are certainly not like products based on product characteristics' and indicates that neither are clove cigarettes and tobacco cigarettes. He does not explain, however, why it is certain that these products have sufficiently different product characteristics to render them 'unlike' although both Coca-Cola and beer are composed mostly of water; have common end-uses of 'to be drunk', 'to quench thirst' (but beer also 'to provide pleasant intoxication'); and are available in many different flavours, such as Coca-Cola Cherry and Kriek Lambic (Belgian cherry lambic beer).
284. Broude and Levy 2014, 375; to this effect, Berrisch 2003 m.nos. 36, 41.
285. Broude and Levy 2014, 375–378; moreover, Mitchell, Heaton, and Henckels 2016, 94–95.
286. *See also* H. Horn and Mavroidis 2004, 63, who address the arbitrariness in the classification of various 'needs' that may be satisfied by products.
287. AB Report, *US – Clove Cigarettes*, 2012, paras 122–132.
288. Howse and Levy 2013, 340.
289. Broude and Levy 2014, 378–380. *See also*, however, H. Horn and Weiler 2004, 144; Horn and Weiler 2003, 31, who argue that a competition-based approach is 'objective' and does not

into account the object and purpose and the context of the non-discrimination provisions including the general exceptions and any other indications of legitimate and illegitimate policy interests.

[4] Rejection by the Appellate Body

With the aim and effects test, an approach had been suggested and applied that would allow considering regulatory purposes at the stage of the 'likeness' analysis thereby lessening the importance of a justification defence and preventing measures that genuinely pursue legitimate policy goals from being branded as a 'violation' or 'discrimination'. Under the WTO framework, however, the Appellate Body rejected, in *Japan – Alcoholic Beverages II* (1996) and *EC – Bananas III* (1997), the aim and effects test for the purposes of both the GATT and GATS.[290] It did so primarily by relying on the wording of the non-discrimination rules, notably, on the fact that the first sentence of Article III:2 as well as Article III:4 of the GATT do not refer specifically to the general principle enshrined in Article III:1 that internal measures 'should not be applied ... so as to afford protection to domestic production' even though this principle was used to substantiate the aim and effects test.[291] The second sentence of Article III:2 of the GATT contains such a textual reference but requires no 'likeness' of products. In the GATS, there is even no provision comparable to Article III:1 of the GATT. Therefore, according to the Appellate Body, the question of whether a measure has the purpose or effect of affording protection to domestic production or rather exclusively follows a legitimate regulatory purpose is not, as such, decisive for establishing or denying 'likeness'.[292]

Japan – Alcoholic Beverages II (1996) concerned internal taxes levied by Japan on certain alcoholic beverages.[293] Pursuant to the applicable tax law, various types of alcoholic beverages were classified into categories. Japanese's shōchū[294] constituted a separate category in addition to the categories of 'whisky/brandy', 'spirits' (including vodka), and 'liqueurs'. For each category, a specific amount of tax per litre of beverage was laid down based on a reference alcohol content. Overall, the tax per litre for Japanese 'shōchū' was considerably lower than those for 'whisky/brandy', 'spirits', and 'liqueurs'.

Both Japan and the US relied on the aim and effects test as a basis for their argumentation. Not surprisingly, the US argued that protective aims and effects existed

---

involve a value judgment in determining 'likeness'; moreover, Choi 2002, 112, who distinguishes between subjective *market-based* end-uses and more objective *general* end-uses (but without explaining how general end-uses should be determined).

290. AB Report, *Japan – Alcoholic Beverages II*, 1996, pp. 15 et seq.; AB Report, *EC – Bananas III*, 1997, paras 215–216, 241. *See also* Hudec 1998, 629–633.
291. GATT Panel Report, *US – Malt Beverages*, 1992, paras 5.25, 5.71–5.72.
292. *See also*, however, Cossy 2008, who argues for an improved aim and effects test under the GATS; moreover, Pauwelyn 2008, who instead focuses on 'less favourable treatment'.
293. *See also* Melloni 2005, 46–51; Charnovitz 1997, 198–203; Gupta 1997.
294. Although Japan contested that shochu was essentially a Japanese product, since a shochu-like product was produced in various countries outside Japan, a significant share of the Japanese shochu market was held by Japanese shochu producers. *See* Panel Report, *Japan – Alcoholic Beverages II*, 1996, para. 6.35.

whereas Japan denied such claims. By contrast, Canada and especially the EC seized the opportunity to criticize and defeat the aim and effects test, and both the Panel and the Appellate Body endorsed their approach.

Article III:2 of the GATT on fiscal measures contains two separate sentences, each imposing distinct,[295] although closely related,[296] NT obligations. While the first sentence employs the concept of 'like products', the second sentence uses the broader concept of 'directly competitive or substitutable products'. Furthermore, the first sentence does not refer specifically to the general principle set forth in Article III:1 of the GATT that measures 'should not be applied ... so as to afford protection to domestic production', while the second sentence contains such a textual reference. With this wording, context, and systematic relationship in mind, the Appellate Body stated in *Japan – Alcoholic Beverages II* (1996):[297]

> The terms of Article III must be given their ordinary meaning – in their context and in the light of the overall object and purpose of the *WTO Agreement*. Thus, the words actually used in the Article provide the basis for an interpretation that must give meaning and effect to all its terms. ... Article III:1 articulates a general principle that internal measures should not be applied so as to afford protection to domestic production. This general principle informs the rest of Article III. The purpose of Article III:1 is to establish this general principle as a guide to understanding and interpreting the specific obligations contained in Article III:2 and in the other paragraphs of Article III, while respecting, and not diminishing in any way, the meaning of the words actually used in the texts of those other paragraphs. In short, Article III:1 constitutes part of the context of Article III:2, in the same way that it constitutes part of the context of each of the other paragraphs in Article III. Any other reading of Article III would have the effect of rendering the words of Article III:1 meaningless, thereby violating the fundamental principle of effectiveness in treaty interpretation. Consistent with this principle of effectiveness, and with the textual differences in the two sentences, we believe that Article III:1 informs the first sentence and the second sentence of Article III:2 in different ways.

Even though the general principle enshrined in Article III:1 informs all of the other provisions of Article III, it informs them in different ways due to their textual differences.[298] Thus, the Appellate Body turned to the interpretation of the first sentence of Article III:2 of the GATT which uses the concept of 'like products' but does not refer specifically to the general principle set forth in Article III:1:[299]

> Article III:1 informs Article III:2, first sentence, by establishing that if imported products are taxed in excess of like domestic products, then that tax measure is inconsistent with Article III. Article III:2, first sentence does not refer specifically to Article III:1. There is no specific invocation in this first sentence of the general principle in Article III:1 that admonishes Members of the WTO not to apply measures 'so as to afford protection'. This omission must have some meaning. We believe the meaning is simply that the presence of a protective application need not

295. AB Report, *EC – Asbestos*, 2001, para. 94.
296. AB Report, *Canada – Periodicals*, 1997, p. 24.
297. AB Report, *Japan – Alcoholic Beverages II*, 1996, pp. 17-18 (footnotes omitted).
298. *See also* AB Report, *EC – Seal Products*, 2014, para. 5.114.
299. AB Report, *Japan – Alcoholic Beverages II*, 1996, pp. 18–20 (footnotes omitted).

> be established separately from the specific requirements that are included in the first sentence in order to show that a tax measure is inconsistent with the general principle set out in the first sentence. However, this does not mean that the general principle of Article III:1 does not apply to this sentence. To the contrary, we believe the first sentence of Article III:2 is, in effect, an application of this general principle. ... If the imported and domestic products are 'like products', and if the taxes applied to the imported products are 'in excess of' those applied to the like domestic products, then the measure is inconsistent with Article III:2, first sentence. ...
>
> Because the second sentence of Article III:2 provides for a separate and distinctive consideration of the protective aspect of a measure in examining its application to a broader category of products that are not 'like products' as contemplated by the first sentence, ... the first sentence of Article III:2 must be construed narrowly so as not to condemn measures that its strict terms are not meant to condemn. Consequently, ... the definition of 'like products' in Article III:2, first sentence, should be construed narrowly.

Since the first sentence of Article III:2 does not refer specifically to Article III:1, the Appellate Body concluded that there is no obligation of separately establishing the presence of a protective application. Under the aim and effects test, by contrast, the 'likeness' analysis also requires establishing that the Member's measure in question has the aim or effect of affording protection to domestic production. After having opposed the aim and effects test, the Appellate Body addressed the issue of how narrowly the first sentence of Article III:2 should be construed:[300]

> How narrowly is a matter that should be determined separately for each tax measure in each case. We agree with the practice under the GATT 1947 of determining whether imported and domestic products are 'like' on a case-by-case basis. The Report of the Working Party on Border Tax Adjustments ... set out the basic approach for interpreting 'like or similar products' generally in the various provisions of the GATT 1947 .... This approach was followed in almost all adopted panel reports after *Border Tax Adjustments*. This approach should be helpful in identifying on a case-by-case basis the range of 'like products' that fall within the narrow limits of Article III:2, first sentence in the GATT 1994. Yet this approach will be most helpful if decision makers keep ever in mind how narrow the range of 'like products' in Article III:2, first sentence is meant to be as opposed to the range of 'like' products contemplated in some other [WTO] provisions .... In applying the criteria cited in *Border Tax Adjustments* to the facts of any particular case, and in considering other criteria that may also be relevant in certain cases, panels can only apply their best judgement in determining whether in fact products are 'like'. This will always involve an unavoidable element of individual, discretionary judgement. We do not agree ... that distinguishing between 'like products' and 'directly competitive or substitutable products' under Article III:2 is 'an arbitrary decision'. Rather, we think it is a discretionary decision that must be made in considering the various characteristics of products in individual cases.

Thus, the Appellate Body did not provide much guidance for understanding the concept of 'likeness' except that the determination of 'like products' must be conducted on a case-by-case basis. Moreover, the context of the first sentence of Article III:2 as

300. AB Report, *Japan – Alcoholic Beverages II*, 1996, pp. 20–21 (footnotes omitted).

well as that of other WTO provisions must be considered. Regarding the context, however, the Appellate Body then emphasized – by evoking the well-known and often-cited image of an accordion – that 'likeness' is not an absolute but only a relative concept:[301]

> No one approach to exercising judgement will be appropriate for all cases. The criteria in *Border Tax Adjustments* should be examined, but there can be no one precise and absolute definition of what is 'like'. The concept of 'likeness' is a relative one that evokes the image of an accordion. The accordion of 'likeness' stretches and squeezes in different places as different provisions of the *WTO Agreement* are applied. The width of the accordion in any one of those places must be determined by the particular provision in which the term 'like' is encountered as well as by the context and the circumstances that prevail in any given case to which that provision may apply. We believe that, in Article III:2, first sentence of the GATT 1994, the accordion of 'likeness' is meant to be narrowly squeezed.

On the concrete facts, the Appellate Body affirmed the Panel's conclusion that shōchū and vodka are 'like products'.[302] This conclusion heavily relied on the fact that the only difference between them is the media used for filtration, which also means that both beverages share the most physical characteristics and have common end-uses.[303] For the Panel, the difference in the alcoholic strength did not preclude a finding of 'likeness' especially since alcoholic beverages are often consumed in a diluted form.[304] By contrast, the use of additives or ingredients or the appearance arising from manufacturing processes disqualified other alcoholic beverages such as gin, rum, whisky, and brandy from being 'like' to shōchū.[305] In this respect, the Appellate Body confirmed that distilled spirits and liqueurs other than vodka constitute only 'directly competitive or substitutable products'.[306]

Since *Japan – Alcoholic Beverages II* (1996) only dealt with fiscal measures and thus with Article III:2 of the GATT, the Appellate Body still had to decide on the aim and effects test with respect to Article III:4 of the GATT and to the GATS. Article III:4 on non-fiscal measures uses the concept of 'like products' but does not contain a two-sentence structure. It does not refer specifically to the general principle set forth in Article III:1. For this reason, the Appellate Body in *EC – Bananas III* (1997) rejected an enquiry into a 'protective application' for the purposes of determining discrimination.[307] Moreover, the Appellate Body rejected the aim and effects test for the purposes of the GATS as well, again based on the wording which lacks a provision similar to Article III:1 of the GATT and any references to such a provision:[308]

301. AB Report, *Japan – Alcoholic Beverages II*, 1996, p. 21. *See*, critically, Tsai 1999, 27–28, 39–40 ('a meaningless, but apt, metaphor'; 'a less than helpful and vague discussion').
302. *Ibid.*, p. 32.
303. Panel Report, *Japan – Alcoholic Beverages II*, 1996, para. 6.23.
304. *Ibid.*, para. 6.23.
305. *Ibid.*, para. 6.23.
306. AB Report, *Japan – Alcoholic Beverages II*, 1996, p. 32.
307. AB Report, *EC – Bananas III*, 1997, para. 216 (original emphasis).
308. *Ibid.*, para. 241.

> We see no specific authority either in Article II [MFN] or in Article XVII [NT] of the GATS for the proposition that the 'aims and effects' of a measure are in any way relevant in determining whether that measure is inconsistent with those provisions. In the GATT context, the 'aims and effects' theory had its origins in the principle of Article III:1 that internal taxes or charges or other regulations 'should not be applied to imported or domestic products so as to afford protection to domestic production'. There is no comparable provision in the GATS.

Although the aim and effects test did not survive long and was strongly rejected by the Appellate Body in *Japan – Alcoholic Beverages II* (1996) and *EC – Bananas III* (1997), the discussion about the aim and effects test did not cease. In fact, the main argument of the Appellate Body for rejecting the aim and effects test was the wording of the respective provisions. This literalism or unusually strict attachment to the exact words of the relevant provisions may be supported as wisely respecting the wording of the GATT and thereby saving the Appellate Body from political criticism.[309] Members may more likely be satisfied and accept WTO decisions when the Appellate Body adheres to what is explicitly written and agreed on by the Members. Nevertheless, the GATT is 'an old, and often badly drafted, instrument'.[310] Adhering strictly to the specific words of each provision without allowing for additional considerations based on their general policy unless expressly demanded suggests that the drafters possessed 'a rather uncommon degree of perfection in foresight and expression'.[311]

[5] Protective Application: An Objective Aim Test?

In *Japan – Alcoholic Beverages II* (1996), the Appellate Body ruled that the NT obligation under the second sentence requires something more than just an analysis of protective effects on competitive conditions.[312] It also requires an analysis of a protective application:[313]

> Unlike that of Article III:2, first sentence, the language of Article III:2, second sentence, specifically invokes Article III:1. The significance of this distinction lies in the fact that whereas Article III:1 acts implicitly in addressing the two issues that must be considered in applying the first sentence [i.e. 'like products' and taxation 'in excess of'], it acts explicitly as an entirely separate issue that must be addressed along with two other issues that are raised in applying the second sentence. Giving full meaning to the text and to its context, three separate issues must be addressed to determine whether an internal tax measure is inconsistent with Article III:2, second sentence. These three issues are whether:
> (1) the imported products and the domestic products are 'directly competitive or substitutable products' which are in competition with each other;
> (2) the directly competitive or substitutable imported and domestic products *are 'not similarly taxed'*; and

309. Hudec 1998, 633.
310. Hudec 1998, 633.
311. Hudec 1998, 641. *See also* Roessler 2003, 775-776.
312. Hudec 1998, 631.
313. AB Report, *Japan – Alcoholic Beverages II*, 1996, p. 24 (original emphasis).

(3) the dissimilar taxation of the directly competitive or substitutable imported domestic products *is 'applied ... so as to afford protection to domestic production'*.

Having concluded that the category of 'directly competitive or substitutable products' is broader than the concept of 'likeness' (how much broader has to be determined based on all of the relevant facts on a case-by-case basis)[314] and having decided that the phrase 'not similarly taxed' has a different meaning from the phrase 'in excess of', namely, that the tax burden must be more than *de minimis* (as determined on a case-by-case basis),[315] the Appellate Body turned to the question of when a measure is applied to afford protection to domestic production. Remember that this policy statement of Article III:1 is explicitly referred to in the second sentence of Article III:2 of the GATT and was used to substantiate the aim and effects test. According to the Appellate Body, determining whether directly competitive or substitutable products are not similarly taxed in a way that affords protection 'is not an issue of intent[,] ... [it] is an issue of how the measure in question is *applied*'.[316] Thus, pursuant to the second sentence of Article III:2 in connection with Article III:1 of the GATT, 'it does not matter that there may not have been any desire to engage in protectionism in the minds of the legislators or the regulators'.[317] Apparently, the Appellate Body feared that panels could start enquiring into the many subjective intentions that legislators or regulators may have.

Although the Appellate Body rejected any enquiry into subjective intentions, it essentially focused on the objectified intentions of a measure. Determining whether a measure is applied to afford protection to domestic production under the second sentence of Article III:2 of the GATT:[318]

> requires a comprehensive and objective analysis of the structure and application of the measure in question on domestic as compared to imported products. We believe it is possible to examine objectively the underlying criteria used in a particular tax measure, its structure, and its overall application to ascertain whether it is applied in a way that affords protection to domestic products.
>
> Although it is true that the aim of a measure may not be easily ascertained, nevertheless its protective application can most often be discerned from the design, the architecture, and the revealing structure of a measure. The very magnitude of the dissimilar taxation in a particular case may be evidence of such a protective application, ...

By using a concept of 'protective application', the Appellate Body applied an aim and effects test but for subjective elements, that is, an objective analysis of regulatory purpose.[319] Robert E. Hudec suggests that 'protective application' can be read as

314. *Ibid.*, p. 25.
315. *Ibid.*, pp. 26–27.
316. *Ibid.*, pp. 27–28 (original emphasis).
317. *Ibid.*, pp. 27–28.
318. *Ibid.*, p. 29.
319. Hudec 1998, 631.

'protective purpose'.[320] Although it is true that the aim of a measure may not be easily ascertained, its protective purpose can, nevertheless, most often be discerned from the design, the architecture, and the revealing structure of a measure.[321]

This view is supported by the Appellate Body's decision on *Chile – Alcoholic Beverages* (2000).[322] Therein, the Appellate Body differentiated between *subjective* intentions inhabiting the minds of individual legislators or regulators, on the one hand, and 'the statutory purposes or objectives – that is, the purpose or objectives of a Member's legislature and government as a whole – to the extent that they are given *objective* expression in the statute itself', on the other hand.[323] In this context, the Appellate Body referred to *Japan – Alcoholic Beverages II* (1996)[324] repeating that a measure's 'protective application can most often be discerned from the *design*, the *architecture*, and the revealing *structure* of a measure' (emphasis added by the Appellate Body).[325] Accordingly, it is possible to identify a measure's objectives or purposes as revealed or objectified in the measure itself[326] by finding that, even though distilled alcoholic beverages are taxed on a progressive basis depending on their alcohol content, in practice, this tax system operates largely as if there were only two tax brackets. The first (alcohol content of 35% or below) applies a certain fixed rate that ends at the point at which most domestic products are found, and the second (alcohol content in excess of 39%) applies a considerably higher rate that begins at the point at which most imports are found.[327] '[A] measure's purposes, objectively manifested in the design, architecture and structure of the measure, *are* intensely pertinent to the task of evaluating whether or not that measure is applied so as to afford protection to domestic production.'[328] While aims and effects are not pertinent to the question of whether products are substitutable or directly competitive, they are relevant to the issue of whether the measure in question is applied 'so as to afford protection' under the second sentence of Article III:2 of the GATT.[329]

320. Hudec 1998, 631; concurring Regan 2006a, 221; Regan 2002, 477; Howse and Regan 2000, 265; critically, Vranes 2009, 243–250.
321. *See also* Mitchell, Heaton, and Henckels 2016, 100–101 ('an "objective" aim'); Melloni 2005, 184–185 ('an *intent-based* test'; original emphasis); Qin 2005, 244 ('an approach that is not substantively different from the aim-and-effects approach'); H. Horn and Mavroidis 2004, 58 ('*[w]hat* is it that the structure reveals, if not that it is intended to protect?'; original emphasis); Porges and Trachtman 2003, 787 ('an analysis of objective, rather than subjective, intent'; 'a restructured, apparently more objective, aim and effects test'); Verhoosel 2002, 55–56 ('nothing but a painfully far-fetched attempt to define objective parameters which may be revealing of subjective intent'); differently, Zedalis 1997, 111 ('[t]he Appellate Body's opinion is clear in rejecting the aim component of the aim and effect test').
322. *See also* Melloni 2005, 189–190.
323. AB Report, *Chile – Alcoholic Beverages*, 2000, para. 62 (original emphasis).
324. AB Report, *Japan – Alcoholic Beverages II*, 1996, p. 29.
325. AB Report, *Chile – Alcoholic Beverages*, 2000, para. 71.
326. *Ibid.*, para. 71.
327. *Ibid.*, para. 66.
328. *Ibid.*, para. 71 (original emphasis).
329. Porges and Trachtman 2003, 793. *See also* Cottier and Oesch 2012, 161; Zhou 2012b, 1082–1083; Zhou 2012a, 105–106; Du 2011, 659–661; Pauwelyn 2008, 363–364; DiMascio and Pauwelyn 2008, 65, 83; Regan 2006a, 208–209; Qin 2005, 248; H. Horn and Mavroidis 2004, 58; Regan 2003, 739–740; Berrisch 2003 m.nos. 64–65; Regan 2002, 462–463; differently, Vranes 2009, 243–250, who argues that 'so as to afford protection' should not be regarded as a

[6] Objective Investigation into Aims

What the aims of a measure are and thus whether a measure follows a protective aim can be determined from the measure itself and its overall context. It is not necessary to rely on openly declared purposes in legislative materials or in other reports or statements[330] that may be missing or allege implausible aims if a measure is introduced for condemned reasons.[331] By examining the circumstances surrounding a measure's introduction, the criteria employed for a distinction and the actual, potential, and foreseeable effects on domestic and foreign products, conclusions about purposes can be drawn on an objective basis.[332] In addition, the very magnitude of the disadvantage in a particular case may be evidence of a protective application.[333] If a measure heavily disadvantages foreign products when compared to domestic products, it seems to be more difficult to argue that its enactment had no protective intentions and that all negative consequences for foreign products are mere coincidence. Conversely, if a measure has neither actual negative effects nor potential negative effects on foreign products in a significant amount and thus if a measure lacks protective effects, it is unlikely that protectionist purposes would lie behind such a measure.[334] In addition, the Appellate Body stated in *Chile – Alcoholic Beverages* (2000) that trying 'to relate the observable structural features of the measure with its declared purposes ... is [a task that is] unavoidable in appraising the application of the measure as protective or not of domestic production'.[335] This suggests that a well-founded and innocent explanation of the measure's design, architecture, and structure may speak against protectionist intentions even if the measure has a disparate impact on foreign products whereas an inconsistency between declared purposes and observable structural features may reinforce protectionist intentions.

Already in *US – Auto Taxes* (1994), the GATT Panel relied on an objective assessment of the aim. Thus, the proposed aim and effects test was not about subjective intentions or aims.[336] In explaining what it understood as the aim of a

---

self-standing criterion but as an interpretative guideline that – in the sense of a flexible system – levels the two-sentence structure of Article III:2: in the case of 'directly competitive or substitutable products' that are close competitors, a test similar to that of Article III:2, first sentence ('in excess of') will apply, whereas, in the case of such products that are more remote competitors, a finding of 'not similarly taxed' will normally require a greater degree of disparate impact and/or a greater extent of differential taxation.

330. *See also* Regan 2006a, 206; Regan 2002, 460.
331. But *see* Regan 2001, 1890, who observes that protectionist purposes are often explicitly stated, which is perhaps not so surprising when considering that politicians want credit for their efforts on behalf of constituents or contributors.
332. *See also* Regan 2006a, 206; Regan 2002, 460, who regards the text, structure, and foreseeable effects of a measure as objective evidence; moreover, Regan 2001, 1886.
333. AB Report, *Japan – Alcoholic Beverages II*, 1996, p. 29; AB Report, *Chile – Alcoholic Beverages*, 2000, para. 66.
334. *See also* H. Horn and Mavroidis 2004, 56.
335. AB Report, *Chile – Alcoholic Beverages*, 2000, para. 72. *See also* Regan 2006a, 208–209; Regan 2002, 462–463.
336. *See also* Hudec 1998, 631–632 ('[u]nder at least some understandings of the "aim and effects" approach ... it could be argued that the analysis of "aim" was never meant to go beyond an objective analysis of purpose in the first place').

measure, the GATT Panel referred to the circumstances in which the measure was adopted and in particular to the instruments available to achieve the declared domestic policy goal.[337] Moreover, when determining whether a change in competitive opportunities in favour of domestic products was a desired outcome and not merely an incidental consequence of the pursuit of a legitimate policy goal, the Panel rejected an enquiry solely into statements by legislators:[338]

> [A]n assessment of the aim of the legislation could not be based solely on such statements or on other preparatory work. The aim of the legislation had also to be determined through the interpretation of the wording of the legislation as a whole.

It is, of course, impossible to read the minds of the people who prepared or enacted legislation or regulation. Undocumented intentions are consequently irrelevant under Article III of the GATT. However, this does not mean that evidence about a measure's purposes should be ignored if it is available. In *Canada – Periodicals* (1997),[339] the Appellate Body referred, among other things, to legislative documents and several statements of the Government about Canada's explicit policy objectives in introducing the measure at issue (e.g., 'we must protect ourselves against split-runs coming from foreign countries and, in particular, from the United States') before concluding that, for this reason and others, 'the design and structure' of the measure in question was 'clearly to afford protection to the production of Canadian periodicals'.[340] Several subjective statements about the aim of the Canadian measure contributed to the conclusion that the *objective* aim or the 'application' of this measure was protective and thus violated the second sentence of Article III:2 of the GATT. According to Amelia Porges and Joel P. Trachtman, *Canada – Periodicals* (1997) illustrates that 'in real life litigation, undisputed damaging factual evidence of intent will have an impact on the outcome of a case'.[341] Similarly, Emily Lydgate observes that the rejection of 'aim' in favour of 'objective' structure in *Japan – Alcoholic Beverages II* (1996) 'likely shifted the emphasis away from certain types of "subjective" evidence, such as reviewing preparatory materials of the legislation, and suggests that any statements regarding the purpose of the regulation, even within the regulation, are not a valid source of evidence', but in *Canada – Periodicals* (1997), the Appellate Body has nevertheless made reference to just such evidence.[342] Robert Howse and Donald Regan further conclude that 'in its discussion of "affording protection", the Appellate Body ... may or may not have rejected "the aims and effects test", but it clearly did not reject consideration of aims and effects'.[343] It is perfectly possible to determine a measure's

337. GATT Panel Report, *US – Auto Taxes*, 1994, unadopted, para. 5.10.
338. *Ibid.*, para. 5.12.
339. *See also* Melloni 2005, 51–54.
340. AB Report, *Canada – Periodicals*, 1997, pp. 30–32.
341. Porges and Trachtman 2003, 791.
342. Lydgate 2016, 439. *See*, moreover, Mitchell, Heaton, and Henckels 2016, 103–104; Neven and Trachtman 2013, 309–310; Regan 2006b, 985–986; Regan 2006a, 206; Melloni 2005, 187; Regan 2002, 460; in general Diebold 2011b, 849 ('[e]ven though the Appellate Body emphasized that the test ... is about protective *application*, not about protective *intent*, indications of protectionist intent regularly flow into the legal analysis'; original emphasis).
343. Howse and Regan 2000, 266.

purpose 'on the basis of its structure, its effects, the intuitive compellingness of the distinctions it draws, whether the claimed regulatory goal is shared with other legal systems or multilateral regimes, the measure's timing, and so on, without any reference to explicit statements of [subjective] purpose',[344] but all evidence must be carefully evaluated, including evidence of subjective intent, when such evidence exists.[345]

In a different context, when determining 'necessity' under the general exceptions clauses of the GATT and GATS, the Appellate Body also noted that an independent and objective assessment of a measure's objective and of the effectiveness of a regulatory approach may be 'evidenced, for example, by texts of statutes, legislative history, and pronouncements of government agencies or officials' as well as by 'the structure and operation of the measure' and by other evidence in the record.[346] Moreover, the Appellate Body considered the broader context of a measure, namely the existence of a comprehensive strategy designed and implemented to deal with certain policy issues.[347] Such a comprehensive strategy may indicate that the aims and purposes of a measure are authentic.

It is further worth mentioning that some rules on trade in goods explicitly call for an objectified aim and effects test by integrating justifications into the analysis of a trade restriction.[348] According to Article 2.2 of the TBT Agreement:

> Members shall ensure that technical regulations are not prepared, adopted or applied *with a view to or with the effect of* creating unnecessary obstacles to international trade [emphasis added]. For this purpose, technical regulations shall not be more trade-restrictive than necessary to fulfil a legitimate objective, taking account of the risks non-fulfilment would create. Such legitimate objectives are, *inter alia*: national security requirements; the prevention of deceptive practices; protection of human health or safety, animal or plant life or health, or the environment. In assessing such risks, relevant elements of consideration are, *inter alia*: available scientific and technical information, related processing technology or intended end-uses of products.

In this context, the TBT Agreement requires balancing the trade-restrictive effects with certain legitimate policy objectives that are listed but non exhaustive. Article 2.2 of the TBT Agreement thus integrates a justification defence into its analysis of a violation because the TBT Agreement contains no general exceptions clause. It is necessary, among other things, to '[independently and objectively] assess what a Member seeks to achieve by means of a technical regulation' in particular by taking

344. Howse and Regan 2000, 265.
345. Howse and Regan 2000, 264–266; to this effect, Regan 2006b, 985–986.
346. AB Report, *US – Gambling*, 2005, para. 304. *See also* AB Report, *EC – Seal Products*, 2014, para. 5.144, with reference to *US – Tuna II (Mexico)*, 2012, para. 314, where the Appellate Body stated that, in seeking to identify the objective of a measure, all evidence in the record must be taken into account including the texts of statutes, legislative history, and other evidence regarding the structure and operation of the measure at issue.
347. AB Report, *Brazil – Retreaded Tyres*, 2007, paras 154–155.
348. *See also* Hudec 1998, 642–644.

into account 'the texts of statutes, legislative history, and other evidence regarding the structure and operation of the measure'.[349]

The second sentence of Article III:2 of the GATT calls for an objectified aim and effects test by requiring proof of dissimilar taxation (effects) and a protective application (objectified aim). This requirement of protective application does not call for an enquiry into subjective intentions but rather for an objective assessment of a measure's purposes, something which is also known from the general exceptions clauses and Article 2.2 of the TBT Agreement. While all available evidence must be considered, the measure's aim may be identified through its design, architecture, and structure without necessarily relying on 'subjective' evidence.

[E] Competitive Standard

[1] Competitive Relationship in the Marketplace

Comparisons under the WTO framework are not conducted in a vacuum. Rather, they serve certain policy purposes as embodied in the WTO agreements and the particular provisions. Since the WTO is about trade and commerce, 'it seems reasonable to start with the assumption that "likeness" is (or should be) a commercial concept, meant to describe one or more market phenomena'.[350]

Under the GATT 1994, a standard that primarily focuses on the competitive relationship has been explicitly recognized and continuously applied. After referring to the general principle in Article III:1, which is to ensure equality of competitive conditions by avoiding protectionism,[351] the Appellate Body concluded in *EC – Asbestos* (2001) that 'the word "like" in Article III:4 is to be interpreted to apply to products that are in ... a competitive relationship [in the marketplace]. Thus, a determination of "likeness" under Article III:4 is, fundamentally, a determination about the nature and extent of a competitive relationship between and among products'.[352] Indeed, '[i]f there is – or could be – *no* competitive relationship between

349. AB Report, *US – Tuna II (Mexico)*, 2012, para. 314, with reference to AB Report, *US – Gambling*, 2005, para. 304. *See also* AB Report, *US – COOL*, 2012, para. 371; moreover, Marceau 2013, 14–15; Meltzer and Porges 2013, 718–719. In addition, besides determining whether a particular objective is legitimate, an assessment of whether a technical regulation is 'more trade-restrictive than necessary' involves an evaluation of a number of factors including '(i) the degree of contribution made by the measure to the legitimate objective at issue; (ii) the trade-restrictiveness of the measure; and (iii) the nature of the risks at issue and the gravity of consequences that would arise from non-fulfilment of the objective(s) pursued by the Member through the measure. In most cases, a comparison of the challenged measure and possible alternative measures should be undertaken. In particular, it may be relevant for the purpose of this comparison to consider whether the proposed alternative is less trade restrictive, whether it would make an equivalent contribution to the relevant legitimate objective, taking account of the risks non-fulfilment would create, and whether it is reasonably available'. *See* AB Report, *US – Tuna II (Mexico)*, 2012, para. 322 (footnote omitted); AB Report, *US – COOL*, 2012, para. 378.
350. Hudec 2000a, 104.
351. AB Report, *EC – Asbestos*, 2001, paras 97–98.
352. *Ibid.*, para. 99.

products, a Member cannot intervene, through internal taxation or regulation, to protect domestic production'.[353]

Additionally, the Appellate Body confirmed that the Border Tax Adjustments criteria are 'neither a treaty-mandated nor a closed list of criteria'. Rather they are 'simply tools to assist in the task of sorting and examining the relevant evidence' which do 'not dissolve the duty or the need to examine, in each case, *all* of the pertinent evidence'.[354] This means that there is no closed list of criteria for 'likeness'. All of the potentially relevant criteria must be examined on a case-by-case basis.[355] Moreover, the Appellate Body clarified that 'although each criterion addresses, in principle, a different aspect of the products involved, which should be examined separately, the different criteria are interrelated'.[356] For instance, physical properties shape and limit the end-uses to which products can be devoted, and consumer perceptions may similarly influence traditional uses of products.[357] When assessing 'likeness' based on the four criteria set forth in the Border Tax Adjustments report, all of the evidence relating to each of those four criteria should be examined and weighed along with any other relevant evidence in order to make an overall determination of whether the products at issue can be characterized as 'like'.[358]

Later, in *Philippines – Distilled Spirits* (2012), the Appellate Body also held with respect to the first sentence of Article III:2 of the GATT that 'the determination of "likeness" ... is, fundamentally, a determination about the nature and extent of a competitive relationship between and among imported and domestic products'.[359] Such a determination is carried out by considering the Border Tax Adjustments criteria and what impact they have on the competitive relationship.[360]

Supposedly objective criteria such as physical properties and tariff classification continue to influence the 'likeness' analysis. In this sense, the Appellate Body stated in *EC – Asbestos* (2001) that, although physical properties are not decisive for the 'likeness' of products, 'the extent to which products share common physical properties may be a useful indicator of "likeness"', and the physical properties 'may also influence how the product can be used, consumer attitudes about the product, and tariff classification'.[361] However, whereas a high degree of physical likeness can be a reliable proxy for many other criteria such as commercial interchangeability (*see* section §2.03[B][1]), the relevance and weight of physical differences should be determined on the basis of the extent they change or leave unchanged the competitive

353. *Ibid.*, para. 117 (original emphasis).
354. *Ibid.*, para. 102 (original emphasis). *See also* AB Report, *Philippines – Distilled Spirits*, 2012, para. 131.
355. *See*, critically on this 'case-by-case approach' and on other layers of additional discretion, Hudec 1998, 625, 634.
356. AB Report, *EC – Asbestos*, 2001, para. 102.
357. *Ibid.*, para. 102.
358. *Ibid.*, para. 109.
359. AB Report, *Philippines – Distilled Spirits*, 2012, para. 170. *See also* Neven and Trachtman 2013.
360. *See* Bronckers and McNelis 2000, 347; Bronckers and McNelis 1999, 75, who observe that the emphasis on 'competition in the marketplace ... ties together the different and disparate elements of the "like-product" determination ..., and allows them to be given their proper weight in a coherent analysis'.
361. AB Report, *EC – Asbestos*, 2001, para. 111.

relationship.[362] For instance, products with quite different physical properties may be capable of performing similar or identical end-uses[363] and, therefore, such products may nevertheless be in a competitive relationship in the marketplace.

[2] Accordion of 'Likeness' Stretches and Squeezes

[a] GATT: NT

Yet '[t]he accordion of "likeness" stretches and squeezes in different places as different provisions of the *WTO Agreement* are applied'.[364] As the term 'like products' appears in many different provisions and in numerous agreements, '[i]n each of the provisions ..., the term must be interpreted in light of the context, and of the object and purpose, of the provision at issue, and of the object and purpose of the covered agreement in which the provision appears'.[365] Accordingly, the meanings of 'like products' in the first sentence of Article III:2 as well as Article III:4 of the GATT need not be identical.[366]

Despite the fact that both the first sentence of Article III:2 of the GATT (fiscal measures) and Article III:4 of the GATT (non-fiscal measures) use the concept of 'likeness' and even though, under both provisions, the determination of 'likeness' is, fundamentally, a determination about the nature and extent of a competitive relationship, the required degree of 'likeness' differs. Article III:2 contains two separate sentences with the first sentence using the concept of 'like products' and the second sentence the broader concept of 'directly competitive or substitutable products'. Against this background, the Appellate Body decided in *Japan – Alcoholic Beverages II* (1996) that, in the first sentence of Article III:2, 'the accordion of "likeness" is meant to be narrowly squeezed'.[367] By contrast, since Article III:4 does not contain a two-sentence structure but instead a single obligation that applies solely to 'like products',[368] the Appellate Body decided in *EC – Asbestos* (2001) that 'the "accordion" of "likeness" stretches in a different way in Article III:4'.[369]

In order to apply the general principle in Article III:1 consistently, Members should not be able to use non-fiscal in lieu of fiscal measures to protect domestic production.[370] '[T]here is no sharp distinction between fiscal regulation, covered by Article III:2, and non-fiscal regulation, covered by Article III:4. Both forms of regulation

362. *See also* AB Report, *EC – Asbestos*, 2001, para. 114, where the Appellate Body stated that the examination of physical properties of products must take into consideration those physical properties 'that are likely to influence the competitive relationship between products in the marketplace'.
363. *Ibid.*, para. 112.
364. AB Report, *Japan – Alcoholic Beverages II*, 1996, p. 21.
365. AB Report, *EC – Asbestos*, 2001, para. 88.
366. *Ibid.*, para. 89.
367. AB Report, *Japan – Alcoholic Beverages II*, 1996, p. 21. *See also* pp. 18 et seq.; AB Report, *Canada – Periodicals*, 1997, p. 22.
368. AB Report, *EC – Asbestos*, 2001, paras 94–96.
369. *Ibid.*, para. 96.
370. *Ibid.*, para. 99.

can often be used to achieve the same ends.'[371] Confronted, on the one hand, with the different language of Article III:2 and Article III:4 but recognizing, on the other hand, that these rules pursue the same general purpose and, therefore, that the scope of the NT obligation should not significantly differ between fiscal and non-fiscal measures, the Appellate Body sought for a solution that would bring these diverging arguments together. As a result, the Appellate Body vaguely stated that 'the scope of "like" in Article III:4 is broader than the scope of "like" in Article III:2, first sentence', but it 'is certainly *not* broader than the *combined* product scope of the *two* sentences of Article III:2 of the GATT 1994'.[372]

This jurisprudence demonstrates that, depending on the specific context, the term 'like products' may have partly different scopes even when it is used by the same non-discrimination article and fosters the same general principle of preventing protective measures. While certain general or traditional 'likeness' criteria have become well established and their weight and relevance are now assessed from a competitive perspective, it is not possible to independently define or determine the exact meaning of 'like' without considering each specific provision. Even when using a competitive standard to determine whether products are 'like' based on the Border Tax Adjustments criteria and other factors, several possible degrees of competitiveness and thus of 'likeness' exist. Therefore, it must be determined which degree of competitiveness is meant to be required under the respective provision and why.[373] To describe one 'likeness' definition as broader than the other while leaving all further considerations to a case-by-case analysis does not provide clear guidance of the appropriate standard of 'likeness' in a particular case.[374]

[b] GATT: MFN

Article I:1 of the GATT contains a single MFN treatment obligation that applies not only to border measures but also 'to all matters referred to in paragraphs 2 and 4 of Article III', that is, to internal taxes and internal regulatory measures. Article I:1 thus uses the term 'like product' only once with respect to all of these different types of measures. This implies that the standard of 'likeness' under Article I:1 may vary depending on the measure in question.

Under the first sentence of Article III:2 of the GATT, a narrow standard of 'likeness' applies because the second sentence establishes the broader concept of 'directly competitive or substitutable products'. Article I:1, however, refers to Article III:2 in general and uses only the concept of 'like products' without containing a two-sentence structure. Therefore, it can be argued that, when examining an internal fiscal measure from an MFN perspective, a broader concept of 'like products' applies in

371. *Ibid.*, para. 99.
372. *Ibid.*, para. 99 (original emphasis). *See*, critically, Qin 2005, 250.
373. *See*, to this effect, Hudec 1998, 626.
374. *See also*, critically, Appleton 2014, 105–106 ('undermines predictability and therefore WTO legitimacy'; 'the Appellate Body cannot define what is a like product, but knows like products when it sees them'); moreover, Mitchell, Heaton, and Henckels 2016, 45–46, 57.

order to compensate, at least to some extent, for the missing concept of 'directly competitive or substitutable products'.[375] When examining this internal fiscal measure from an NT perspective, however, a narrower concept of 'likeness' applies because different treatment of 'unlike' products (first sentence) may still lead to discrimination if these products are 'directly competitive or substitutable products' (second sentence). The scope of 'likeness' under Article I:1 for the purposes of both fiscal and non-fiscal measures could thus be similar to the one under Article III:4 for the purposes of non-fiscal measures: both provisions engage only in the concept of 'likeness' and do not contain a two-sentence structure similar to Article III:2.

Identifiable differences with respect to the scope and meaning of 'likeness' may also exist within Article I:1 of the GATT between border measures and internal measures since these measures are embedded in different policy contexts.[376] Particularly tariffs have always made rather fine product distinctions, for example, on the basis of differences in materials of construction, method of manufacture, plant or animal species, value ('value brackets'), shape, size or dimension, or quality.[377] Arguably, this common practice has been accepted by the WTO Members as being appropriate regardless of the competitive significance or purpose of such product characteristics.[378] While, with regard to internal measures, the policy of the MFN and NT obligations is to eliminate market distortions, the policy of the GATT with regard to tariffs is to allow market distortions.[379] Tariffs - by definition, an obstacle to international trade - are allowed, although within certain limits. The MFN treatment obligation sets limits with regard to tariffs as well, but the different policy context of tariffs might influence the scope of the MFN treatment rule itself and especially the concept of 'like products' in this particular context.

A policy of tariff protection requires 'to draw lines between products in order to confine protection to those imports which do in fact threaten domestic producers, and also to confine tariff liberalization to those products for which the removal will be found acceptable to domestic interests'.[380] In addition, the GATT policy is to reciprocally lower tariffs by negotiation. However, if some Members are not willing to grant equivalent concessions for the benefit of a tariff reduction in return, discrimination against these 'free riders' by making fine product distinctions in tariffs appears to be, tacitly, an accepted practice.[381] As a consequence, the MFN obligation of Article I:1 prevents discrimination in the context of tariffs when a country is almost explicitly referred to, that is, when a tariff differentiation is so unique that it cannot have any

---

375. *See* Davey and Pauwelyn 2000, 35–36.
376. *See* Davey and Pauwelyn 2000, 27–28.
377. Hudec 2000a, 110.
378. Hudec 2000a, 110. *See also* Davey and Pauwelyn 2000, 29, 31, who state that '[t]he practice of allowing Members to establish fine distinctions in tariff schedules seems supported by GATT practice generally' and conclude that 'for purposes of interpreting tariff schedules, WTO/GATT case law accords considerable discretion to Members in subdividing products into different tariff categories for purposes of Article II without fear of violating Article I:1'.
379. Hudec 2000a, 108.
380. Hudec 2000a, 108–109.
381. Hudec 2000a, 109.

conceivable taxonomic function.[382] For example, the 1904 German tariff concession to Switzerland lowered the tariff on female cattle older than one and a half year that were reared at a spot at least 300 metres above sea level and having at least one month's grazing each year at a spot at least 800 metres above sea level.[383] All other fine tariff distinctions that are based on an objective characteristic, even if they aim at limiting concessions to products that will not threaten domestic producers or at discriminating against 'free riders', arguably remain unaffected by the MFN obligation.[384] This could speak for a quite narrow concept of 'likeness' under Article I:1 as far as tariff measures are concerned (any objective difference between products would justify a separate tariff classification) but for a broader and competitive concept of 'likeness' under Article I:1 with regard to internal measures referred to in Article III:2 and 4 of the GATT.[385]

[c] GATS

Under the GATS, the term 'like services and service suppliers' must also partly rely on different criteria than the 'like product' concept under the GATT.[386] Especially *physical* properties and *tariff* classifications cannot lead to meaningful results with intangible services. Other intrinsic characteristics and classifications can be employed and relied on instead. Under both the GATT and GATS, the establishment of 'likeness' thus constitutes a flexible concept that adapts to each specific provision and each particular context.

In *Argentina – Financial Services* (2016), the Appellate Body confirmed that the concept of 'likeness' under Articles II:1 and XVII:1 of the GATS is based on whether services and service suppliers are in a competitive relationship. At the same time, certain deviations from the concept of 'likeness' under the GATT are indispensable. In the context of both trade in goods and trade in services, 'likeness' refers to something that is similar.[387] Based on the context in which the word 'like' appears in the provisions of Articles II:1 and XVII:1 of the GATS, it can be concluded that the concept of 'likeness' of services and service suppliers is concerned with the competitive relationship of services and service suppliers.[388] Since it is difficult, if not impossible,

382. Hudec 2000a, 111.
383. *See Zusatzvertrag zum Handels- und Zollvertrage zwischen dem Deutschen Reiche und der Schweiz vom 10. Dezember 1891*, Fassung vom 12. November 1904, Deutsches Reichsgesetzblatt vom 24. Mai 1905, Nummer 21, Seiten 330-355, Anlage A. *See also*, for instance, Charnovitz 2002, 68; Hudec 2000a, 109; Jackson 2000b, 59; Curzon 1965 fn. 1 on p. 60.
384. Hudec 2000a, 110–112.
385. Hudec 2000a, 112; critically and differently, Vranes 2009, 215–223.
386. *See also*, in detail on the concept of 'likeness' under the GATS, Diebold 2010; moreover, Delimatsis et al. 2011, 258–260, who argue that the broad market-based standard of 'directly competitive or substitutable' under the second sentence of Article III:2 of the GATT is directly transferable to national treatment in services under Article XVII of the GATS; similarly, Mattoo 1997, 127.
387. AB Report, *Argentina – Financial Services*, 2016, para. 6.21.
388. *Ibid.*, paras 6.22–6.25.

in the abstract to indicate precisely where on a spectrum of degrees of 'competitiveness' or 'substitutability' the word 'like' falls, the likeness of services and service suppliers can only be determined on a case-by-case basis, taking into account the specific circumstances of the particular case.[389]

What is being compared for 'likeness' is different in the context of trade in goods and trade in services.[390] Articles II:1 and XVII:1 of the GATS refer to 'like services and service suppliers'. By contrast, the MFN and NT rules of the GATT refer to 'like products', but they do not include a reference to 'like producers':[391]

> [T]he reference to 'services and service suppliers' indicates that considerations relating to both the service and the service supplier are relevant for determining 'likeness' under Articles II:1 and XVII:1 of the GATS. The assessment of likeness of services should not be undertaken in isolation from considerations relating to the service suppliers, and, conversely, the assessment of likeness of service suppliers should not be undertaken in isolation from considerations relating to the likeness of the services they provide. We see the phrase 'like services *and* service suppliers' as an integrated element for the likeness analysis under Articles II:1 and XVII:1, respectively. Accordingly, separate findings with respect to the 'likeness' of services, on the one hand, and the 'likeness' of service suppliers, on the other hand, are not required. Because the 'likeness' analysis serves to assess the competitive relationship of the 'services *and* service suppliers' at issue, the particular features of that competitive relationship, in the circumstances of any specific case, will determine the relative weight to be accorded in the analysis of 'likeness' to considerations relating to the service and the service supplier, respectively. In any event, in a holistic analysis of 'likeness', considerations relating to both the service and the service supplier will be relevant, albeit to varying degrees, depending on the circumstances of each case.

After referring to the Border Tax Adjustments criteria and summarizing their relevance,[392] the Appellate Body recalled that the analysis of 'likeness' serves the same purpose in the context of both trade in goods and trade in services, namely, to determine whether the products or services and service suppliers, respectively, are in a competitive relationship with each other.[393] Thus, the traditional criteria for assessing 'likeness' in the context of trade in goods, to the extent they are relevant, may be employed also in assessing 'likeness' in the context of trade in services provided that they are adapted as appropriate to account for the specific characteristics of trade in

389. *Ibid.*, para. 6.26.
390. *Ibid.*, para. 6.27.
391. *Ibid.*, para. 6.29 (original emphasis; footnotes omitted). *See also* Muller 2016, 829–831, who concludes that 'the Appellate Body appears to favour the cumulative approach [both the likeness of services and the likeness of service suppliers must be demonstrated] with nevertheless some nuance: consideration of the likeness of both terms is necessary, albeit to varying degrees depending on the circumstances of each case'. Arguably, this nuanced approach corresponds to the merged test suggested by Diebold 2010, 217–219 (*see also* Delimatsis et al. 2011, 261–263) according to which both supplier-related and services-based factors are considered in order to determine the competitive relationship as a whole. On this issue, *see*, moreover, Connolly 2015, 69–71; Krajewski and Engelke 2008 m.nos. 35–38.
392. *Ibid.*, para. 6.30.
393. *Ibid.*, para. 6.31.

services.[394] For example, the characteristics of services and service suppliers or consumers' preferences in respect of services and service suppliers may constitute relevant 'likeness' criteria.[395] Furthermore, the classification and description of services under, for instance, the United Nations (UN) Central Product Classification could constitute a relevant adaptation of the original criterion of tariff classification.[396] However, there is neither a treaty-mandated nor a closed list of criteria for the purposes of establishing 'likeness' under the GATS,[397] and the different modes of supply as defined in Article I:2 may require additional considerations that would be unique to the GATS.[398]

[3] Importance of Health Risks in **EC – Asbestos**

Although the Appellate Body rejected the aim and effects test and endorsed a competitive standard of 'likeness', policy reasons for a regulatory distinction may be reflected by the traditional Border Tax Adjustments criteria and the nature and extent of a competitive relationship between and among products. France introduced prohibitions of asbestos fibres and products containing these fibres for the purpose of protecting the lives and health of workers and consumers coupled with certain limited and temporary exceptions concerning chrysotile asbestos fibres. Canada complained, among other things, that those prohibitions were inconsistent with the NT obligation under Article III:4 of the GATT. In *EC – Asbestos* (2001),[399] therefore, the issue arose whether chrysotile asbestos fibres are 'like' PVA, cellulose, and glass fibres and whether cement-based products containing the former fibres are 'like' cement-based products containing the latter fibres. It was particularly disputed whether considerations of the health risk factors relating to asbestos could be relevant in determining whether 'like products' existed under Article III:4 of the GATT.

Protection of human life and health is the main, if not the only, regulatory aim pursued by a measure banning asbestos fibres. This policy interest of 'protect[ing] human ... life or health' is explicitly mentioned as a general exception in Article XX(b) of the GATT. Although a justification defence is available, this did not prevent the Appellate Body from concluding that the toxicity of chrysotile asbestos fibres and the non-toxicity of other fibres may be considered as part of a determination of 'likeness' under the Border Tax Adjustments framework, notably, as a highly significant physical difference and as influencing the consumers' tastes and habits.[400] According to the Appellate Body, consideration of this evidence relating to health risks does not nullify the effect of the justification defence of Article XX(b) because 'Article III:4 and Article XX(b) are distinct and independent provisions ... each to be interpreted on its own' and

394. *Ibid.*, para. 6.31.
395. *Ibid.*, para. 6.32.
396. *Ibid.*, para. 6.32.
397. *Ibid.*, para. 6.32.
398. *Ibid.*, para. 6.33.
399. *See also*, for instance, Melloni 2005, 102–109; Footer and Zia-Zarifi 2002, 136–140; McConnell 2002, 157–162, 174–177; Breining-Kaufmann 2001, 1172–1173, 1176–1177.
400. AB Report, *EC – Asbestos*, 2001, paras 104 et seq.

because 'a less frequent recourse to Article XX(b) does not deprive the exception in Article XX(b) of *effet utile*'.[401]

The Appellate Body held that evidence relating to the health risks associated with a product may be pertinent in an examination of 'likeness', not as a separate criterion but under the existing criteria of physical properties and consumers' tastes and habits.[402] When determining the relevance of physical properties, it is necessary to examine those properties 'that are likely to influence the competitive relationship between products in the marketplace'.[403] Since the microscopic particles and filaments of chrysotile asbestos fibres are carcinogenic in humans, this carcinogenicity constitutes a defining aspect of the physical properties and results in a highly significant physical difference to PVA, cellulose, and glass fibres.[404] It follows that evidence relating to health risks may be relevant in assessing the competitive relationship in the marketplace between allegedly 'like' products.[405] To the extent that non-trade policy concerns are reflected by the Border Tax Adjustments criteria (such as concerns about health risk may be reflected by physical characteristics), they can already be considered when assessing the 'likeness' of products. In such cases, there may be no need to rely on explicit justification grounds and their requirements for application.

Even though the toxicity of chrysotile asbestos fibres made it clear for the Appellate Body that the products at issue were physically very different,[406] this was not the end of the analysis. The other Border Tax Adjustments criteria had to be considered as well because they can overcome the indication that products are not 'like'. Since Article III of the GATT is concerned with competitive relationships in the marketplace and since it is impossible to protect the domestic production of products by taxing or regulating other products that are not and cannot be in a competitive relationship, evidence about the extent to which products can serve the same or similar functions (end-uses) and the extent to which consumers are - or would be - willing to choose one product instead of another to perform those functions (consumers' tastes and habits) is highly relevant evidence in assessing 'likeness'.[407] In this respect, however, the Appellate Body placed a very heavy burden on Canada 'to establish that, despite the pronounced physical differences, there is a competitive relationship between the products such that[,] *all* of the evidence, taken together, demonstrates that the products are "like"'.[408]

The Panel's analysis of the end-uses and consumers' tastes and habits did not satisfy the Appellate Body, especially because the Panel evaluated only similar end-uses but not different end-uses[409] and because it refrained from examining consumers' tastes and habits altogether.[410] Therefore, the Appellate Body itself tried to

401. *Ibid.*, para. 115.
402. *Ibid.*, para. 113. *See also* AB Report, *US – Clove Cigarettes*, 2012, paras 117–120.
403. *Ibid.*, para. 114.
404. *Ibid.*, paras 114 and 135–136 (and *see also* paras 128 and 142 on cement-based products).
405. *Ibid.*, para. 115.
406. *Ibid.*, para. 118.
407. *Ibid.*, para. 117.
408. *Ibid.*, paras 118 and 136 (original emphasis).
409. *Ibid.*, paras 119 and 137–138.
410. *Ibid.*, para. 120.

establish to what extent the health risks associated with chrysotile asbestos fibres influence consumers' tastes and habits.[411] Although the Appellate Body did not wish to speculate on what the evidence regarding the consumers (in this case, the manufacturers who incorporate the fibres into another product) would have indicated, it wished to highlight 'that consumers' tastes and habits regarding *fibres* ... are very likely to be shaped by the health risks associated with a product which is known to be highly carcinogenic'.[412] Of course, as the Appellate Body recognized, some dangerous products, such as tobacco, are widely used despite the known health risks,[413] but the Appellate Body in this particular case was persuaded that ultimate consumers' decision not to buy products with sufficiently great risks, and other factors such as a potential civil liability relating to health risks or additional costs associated with safety procedures were sufficient to conclude that the health risks of chrysotile asbestos fibres likely influence consumers' behaviour with respect to the different fibres.[414]

It can be critically remarked that, if the health risks of chrysotile asbestos fibres indeed influenced consumers' tastes and habits to a greater extent, there would have been no need for France to introduce prohibitions of asbestos fibres and products containing these fibres. Since France introduced these prohibitions, apparently, consumers did not sufficiently take account of the health risks to meet the intended level of health protection. It can thus be argued that, in *EC – Asbestos* (2001), from a competitive perspective, the toxicity or non-toxicity of the different fibres was not a significant physical difference and did not sufficiently influence consumers' tastes and habits. The legislator saw a need to regulate and prohibit the use of toxic asbestos fibres because consumers apparently regarded toxic and non-toxic fibres as similar or equivalent products and did not adequately take account of the health risks imposed by chrysotile asbestos fibres.[415]

Robert Howse comments on *EC – Asbestos* (2001) that '[t]he Appellate Body pulled a rabbit out of a hat, as it were' and improvised brilliantly.[416] It 'could say health was relevant, not for public policy considerations but, rather, for consumer behaviour considerations',[417] thereby responding to a legitimacy challenge posed in this case if a

411. *Ibid.*, para. 122.
412. *Ibid.*, para. 122 (original emphasis).
413. *Ibid.*, fn. 103 to para. 122.
414. *Ibid.*, para. 122 (and *see also* paras 130 and 145 on cement-based products). *See*, moreover, Meltzer and Porges 2013, 709 ('the Appellate Body incorporated [in the like product analysis] a reference to regulatory aims, but only to the extent that these reflect consumer preferences').
415. *See* Davis 2017, 37, who states that '[t]he presence of asbestos in a product is largely inconsequential in these regards [physical characteristics, consumers' tastes and habits, the product's end-uses in a given market and tariff classification], despite the obvious health risks that it poses' and that the Panel on *EC – Asbestos* (2001) thus found that health is not a determinant of product likeness; moreover, Cosbey and Mavroidis 2014, 293–294, who generally observe that, typically, the reason why there is a need to treat products differently is that buyers do *not* make the desirable distinction – that is, market likeness is often part of the reason why products are *not* policy like; similarly, Marceau and Trachtman 2014, 361; Meltzer and Porges 2013, 713; Englisch 2008, 485–486; H. Horn and Weiler 2004, 149–150; Regan 2006a, 211–212; Horn and Weiler 2003, 37–38; H. Horn and Mavroidis 2004, 60; Porges and Trachtman 2003 fn. 56 on p. 795; Regan 2002, 465–466.
416. Howse 2016, 48.
417. Howse 2016, 48.

ban of toxic and, in fact, life-threatening products would have been branded as discrimination but maintaining a competitive standard of 'likeness'.[418] Thus, regulatory interests were taken into account by adopting the perspective of consumer behaviour in an idealized marketplace where consumers have full information and negative externalities have already been internalized to some extent and not the perspective of the regulator, as such.[419] Emily Lydgate further observes that the Appellate Body asserted that consumers would not prefer asbestos, but this conclusion was not based on evidence, and its reasoning represented a departure from an objective analysis of consumer preferences by introducing an extra-market dimension, although the Appellate Body disingenuously presented it as objective.[420]

Because the Appellate Body still tried to adhere to a competitive standard of 'likeness', it did not completely exclude the possibility of 'likeness' between chrysotile asbestos fibres and PVA, cellulose, and glass fibres. It placed a high burden on Canada to prove that, despite the significant physical differences relating to public health risk, these products were 'like' due to their end-uses, consumers' tastes and habits, and their tariff classification. Canada did not satisfy its burden.[421] This means that, in principle, it would have been possible for Canada to prove that the fibres in question were in a competitive relationship that was sufficient to establish 'like products' when considering and weighing conclusive evidence on all the Border Tax Adjustments criteria.

One of the three Members of the Appellate Body – in a concurring statement – submitted that chrysotile asbestos fibres should have been definitely characterized as not 'like' PVA, cellulose, and glass fibres just because of their serious health risks, that is, even without considering end-uses and consumers' tastes and habits and without prioritizing the role of competitive relationships:[422]

> It is difficult for me to imagine what evidence relating to economic competitive relationships as reflected in end-uses and consumers' tastes and habits could outweigh and set at naught the undisputed deadly nature of chrysotile asbestos fibres, compared with PCG fibres [PVA, cellulose, and glass fibres], when inhaled by humans, and thereby compel a characterization of 'likeness' of chrysotile asbestos and PCG fibres. ...
>
> [T]he necessity or appropriateness of adopting a 'fundamentally' economic interpretation of the 'likeness' of products under Article III:4 of the GATT 1994 does not appear to me to be free from substantial doubt.

---

418. Howse 2016, 47–48. *See also* Howse and Türk 2006, 96–97; Howse and Türk 2001, 304–305.
419. Howse and Türk 2006, 93–94; Howse and Türk 2001, 301–302. *See*, moreover, Regan 2006a, 211–212; Regan 2002, 466, who argues that how fully informed and rational consumers would behave is not an empirically observable economic fact – 'rational' is a normative concept – and that, therefore, the Appellate Body relied on its own regulatory purpose, that is, its own views about how consumers should behave.
420. Lydgate 2011, 168–170, 177–180, 184–187. *See*, moreover, Mitchell, Heaton, and Henckels 2016, 48–52; Englisch 2008, 388, 485–486; Horn and Mavroidis 2008, 1119–1120; Regan 2006a, 210–213; H. Horn and Weiler 2004, 150–151; Horn and Weiler 2003, 38–39; Porges and Trachtman 2003, 795; Regan 2002, 465–468.
421. *See*, in particular, AB Report, *EC – Asbestos*, 2001, para. 141 (and also para. 147).
422. AB Report, *EC – Asbestos*, 2001, paras 152, 154.

EC – Asbestos (2001) illustrates that regulatory purposes and the underlying policy interests may influence consumers' tastes and habits and the traditional criteria of 'likeness' under a competitive standard. Also, such policy interests may reflect highly significant physical differences. To a certain extent, therefore, regulatory purposes and traditional justifications such as the protection of human life and health or the preservation of the environment may already prevent 'likeness' of products.[423] Moreover, *EC – Asbestos* (2001) evidences conflicting views about the relevance of competitive relationships and whether serious health risks should definitely prevent 'likeness' regardless of end-uses and consumers' tastes and habits. Later, however, the Appellate Body stressed in *US – Clove Cigarettes* (2012) that the regulatory concerns underlying a measure such as the health risks associated with a given product may be relevant to an analysis of the 'likeness' criteria but only to the extent they have an impact on the competitive relationship between and among the products concerned, that is, to the extent they are reflected in the products' competitive relationship.[424]

[4] Continuous Relevance of Policy Considerations

Even though the aim and effects test was rejected by the Appellate Body, policy considerations continue to influence the non-discrimination analysis outside of the justification stage. Most prominently, Robert E. Hudec argues that it appears impossible to assess discrimination under WTO law and differentiate between bona fide regulation and a disguised trade restriction without being aware of and at least unconsciously influenced by the aims and effects of a measure.[425] In *Japan – Alcoholic Beverages II* (1996), the Appellate Body utilized the image of an accordion to illustrate the importance of the context for the interpretation and application of the 'like product' concept (*see* section §2.03[E][2]). By this, however, the Appellate Body also added several layers of additional discretion.[426] Not only is the determination made whether imported and domestic products are 'like' on a case-by-case basis,[427] but the accordion of 'likeness' can be made larger or smaller depending upon the particular legal and factual context in which an issue is being decided,[428] and the application of the Border Tax Adjustments criteria 'will always involve an unavoidable element of individual, discretionary judgement'.[429] Such discretion can be used to arrive at any decision:[430]

423. *See also*, to this effect, Búrca 2002, 193.
424. AB Report, *US – Clove Cigarettes*, 2012, paras 119–120.
425. Hudec 1998, 634–635; concurring Neven and Trachtman 2013, 302. *See also*, for example, Regan 2006a; Regan 2002, and Regan 2003, who presents many arguments as to why it is indispensable to consider the regulatory purpose in determining 'like products'. *See*, however, Davey and Pauwelyn 2000, 38, who argue against the aim and effects test by stating that the 'likeness' analysis should be limited to the most objective differences between products, namely, those linked to the physical characteristics of the product itself, in order to avoid result-oriented decisions on 'likeness' which do not take into account the legitimate criteria for distinguishing between products referred to in Article XX of the GATT.
426. Hudec 1998, 634.
427. AB Report, *Japan – Alcoholic Beverages II*, 1996, p. 20.
428. *Ibid.*, p. 21.
429. *Ibid.*, pp. 20–21.

> Tribunals usually call for such discretion when they are being asked to resolve important issues under legal criteria that make little or no policy sense. ... Once the tribunal comes to a conclusion about who should win, it fashions an analysis, in terms of the meaningless criteria it has been asked to apply, that makes the case come out that way. Given the likelihood that decisions written in this manner will have a high degree of inconsistency, the tribunals naturally seek to give such decisions as much armor-plating as possible by claiming the widest possible range of discretion. ... So long as the tribunal gets it right most of the time – that is, decides its cases according to the larger community's perception of right and wrong behavior – the decisions tend to be accepted, and in an opaque sort of way they even succeed in guiding conduct toward the proper goals.

It is likely that WTO tribunals will rely on the aim and effects test when using their discretion and framing their decisions based on the flexible accordion of 'likeness'. According to Robert E. Hudec, 'panel members will instinctively want to know whether the measure has a bona fide regulatory purpose and to what extent its market effects are protective'.[431] Thus, the aim and effects test was an attempt to bring this covert analysis into the open where, supposedly, the quality of decision is improved because the real criteria of decision can be addressed openly.[432] By refusing to apply the aim and effects test, these criteria and considerations for differentiating between bona fide regulation and a disguised trade restriction remain underground instead of being transparently discussed at the 'likeness' level.[433]

Indeed, although in *Japan – Alcoholic Beverages II* (1996), the Appellate Body distinguished between protective aims and a measure's protective application, there seems to be little difference between these two concepts (*see* section §2.03[D][5]). In *EC – Asbestos* (2001), moreover, the Appellate Body arguably considered regulatory purposes to deny 'likeness' but without admitting it (*see* section §2.03[E][3]). At least some considerations of regulatory purposes and their legitimacy and importance remained hidden behind supposedly objective criteria of physical properties and consumers' tastes and habits.[434]

It seems that, regardless of which approach to 'likeness' is followed, value judgments need to be made at some point. It is necessary to determine whether differences in physical characteristics matter, how to establish a product's relevant end-uses and deal with overlaps, or at which point products become 'unlike' because of their insufficient competitive relationship in actual or ideal circumstances. Such judgments may involve some discretion, but they should be guided by the context and

430. Hudec 1998, 634.
431. Hudec 1998, 634–645. *See also* Lydgate 2016, who observes that, in some disputes, compelling policy objectives shape the outcome of a supposedly market-based analysis; and Iacovides 2014, 345, who suspects that, in *US – Clove Cigarettes* (2012), the Appellate Body clothed a suspicion of protectionism with the seeming objectivity of economics and found 'likeness' on evidence that was inconclusive and based on an application of the methodology of relevant market definition that was flawed.
432. Hudec 1998, 635.
433. Hudec 1998, 635.
434. *See also* Mitchell, Heaton, and Henckels 2016, 156, who conclude from an in-depth analysis of WTO jurisprudence that '[t]he Appellate Body repeatedly rejected "aim" or "object" inquiries, only to engage in them either openly or, more commonly, under guises such as "protective application", physical properties, consumer preferences or causation'.

purpose of a particular non-discrimination provision. By discussing the aims and effects of a measure, all facts and circumstances that might inevitably influence the relative importance and weight of the Border Tax Adjustments criteria and any other criteria of 'likeness' can be laid open. In order to increase transparency, any decision on 'likeness' should explain why these aims and effects were relevant or not and why they have or have not influenced each of the relevant factors in a concrete case.

§2.04 'LESS FAVOURABLE TREATMENT': DE JURE AND DE FACTO

[A] De Jure and De Facto Discrimination

[1] Discrimination Through Origin-Neutral Treatment

After 'like' products or services and service suppliers have been identified, it is necessary to determine whether certain products or services and service suppliers are treated identically or differently and whether such treatment results in 'less favourable treatment' by reason of foreign origin or destination.[435] If foreign products or services and service suppliers are treated less favourably compared to other foreign (MFN) or domestic (NT) 'like' products or services and service suppliers, a violation of an MFN or NT rule, respectively, can be established.

Not all MFN and NT rules use the concept of 'less favourable treatment'. Whereas the general MFN and NT rules in the GATS, that is, Article II:1 (MFN) and Article XVII:1 (NT), both use the phrase 'treatment no less favourable', in the GATT, only the general NT rule regarding non-fiscal measures, Article III:4 of the GATT, employs this phrase. Article III:2 of the GATT on fiscal measures instead uses the expressions '[taxed] in excess of' (first sentence) and 'not similarly taxed' (second sentence) while Article I:1 of the GATT on MFN treatment requires that 'any advantage, favour, privilege or immunity ... shall be accorded immediately and unconditionally to the like product'. Thus, different non-discrimination provisions oppose different levels of different treatment. There is no single threshold that must be reached before disadvantages become discriminatory.[436] Nevertheless, certain general questions arise regardless of the specific terms employed such as why do the MFN and NT rules cover both de jure and de facto discrimination, against what standard a certain impact on foreign origin should be measured, and whether regulatory purposes may play a role.

When a measure directly refers to origin and thereby disadvantages a certain foreign origin, this can be a case of de jure discrimination. Peter Van den Bossche and Werner Zdouc hold that '[a] measure may be said to discriminate in law (or *de jure*) in a case in which it is clear from reading the text of the law, regulation or policy that it treats the product from one WTO Member less favourably than the like product from

435. Article I:1 of the GATT applies not only to importation but also to exportation. Accordingly, any advantage, etc., granted by any Member to any product destined for any other country must be accorded to the 'like product' destined for the territories of all other Members.

436. *See supra* n. 56.

another WTO Member or country'.[437] By contrast, measures that are more sophisticated and do not directly refer to origin may nevertheless in practice, that is, in fact, lead to treatment that is less favourable by reason of foreign origin.[438] Such measures can be a case of de facto discrimination. Similarly, Lothar Ehring defines de jure discrimination as cases in which the disadvantage imposed on foreign products is already discernible from the legislation in question while de facto discrimination can occur when the conclusion that foreign products are disadvantaged is possible 'only after additionally taking into account the *factual* circumstances at issue' either because no distinction is drawn or because a distinction is drawn on the basis of a criterion other than origin.[439]

Generally, therefore, three different types of measures may be distinguished:

(1) measures that differentiate between 'like products' by expressly referring to origin (de jure discrimination);[440]
(2) measures that differentiate between 'like products' by referring to a facially neutral characteristic which, for factual reasons, predominantly affects products with foreign origin (de facto discrimination); and
(3) measures that do *not* differentiate between 'like products' and instead provide for equal treatment, but this treatment has a negative or more burdensome impact on products with foreign origin (de facto discrimination).[441]

437. Van den Bossche and Zdouc 2013, 319.
438. *See also* Hudec 1998, 620, 623, who describes de facto discrimination as involving regulatory measures that do not explicitly distinguish between foreign and domestic products (called 'origin-neutral') but which have a disproportionate impact or impose a burden on foreign products that is, for some reason, viewed as wrong or illegitimate.
439. Ehring 2014, 36 (original emphasis).
440. This also includes measures that treat foreign products in the same manner as most but not all 'like' domestic products, for instance, by favouring only certain local or regional goods or even only a single domestic producer or supplier. *See* Ehring 2002, 923.
441. In *Dominican Republic – Import and Sale of Cigarettes* (2005), for example, a tax stamp requirement for cigarette packets constituted treatment that was less favourable of imported cigarettes even though it applied to both domestic and imported cigarettes. Tax stamps could be affixed on packets of domestic cigarettes as part of the production process, while, in the case of imported cigarettes, an additional process had to be undertaken. This additional process entailed added costs and led to imported cigarettes being presented to final consumers in a less appealing manner. *See* Panel Report, *Dominican Republic – Import and Sale of Cigarettes*, 2005, paras 7.180 et seq. (this finding of an NT violation had not been appealed; *see* AB Report, *Dominican Republic – Import and Sale of Cigarettes*, 2005, paras 57–58). *See also*, however, Englisch 2008, 397, who suggests that *Dominican Republic – Import and Sale of Cigarettes* (2005) could be seen as a case of de jure discrimination against imported cigarettes because only domestic producers were provided with tax stamps in advance that could then be affixed as part of the production process. However, it should be noted that this distinction between domestic and foreign producers and products might have only been the logical consequence of the tax stamp requirement, that is the requirement that a tax stamp must be affixed on cigarette packets *in the territory of the Dominican Republic*, which applied to both domestic and imported cigarettes and was, as such, a formally identical requirement (para. 7.180).

WTO non-discrimination obligations cover both de jure and de facto discrimination. This is not necessarily apparent from the wording.[442] Under the GATT, the MFN obligation in Article I and the NT obligation in Article III do not explicitly state that facially neutral criteria or criteria other than foreign origin can constitute discrimination or that formally identical treatment may be considered less favourable. Nevertheless, it is undisputed that such forms of discrimination are covered. In *Korea – Various Measures on Beef* (2001), for instance, the Appellate Body highlighted that '[a] formal difference in treatment between imported and like domestic products is ... neither necessary, nor sufficient, to show a violation of Article III:4'.[443] With respect to the MFN obligation in Article I, the Appellate Body further stated in *Canada – Autos* (2000) that:[444]

> the words of Article I:1 do not restrict its scope only to cases in which the failure to accord an 'advantage' to like products of all other Members appears *on the face* of the measure, or can be demonstrated on the basis of the words of the measure. Neither the words '*de jure*' nor '*de facto*' appear in Article I:1. Nevertheless, we observe that Article I:1 does not cover only 'in law', or *de jure*, discrimination. ... Article I:1 covers also 'in fact', or *de facto*, discrimination.

Under the GATS, the MFN treatment provision in Article II also does not explicitly recognize the concept of de facto discrimination. It merely refers to 'treatment no less favourable' of like services and service suppliers. Article XVII:2 and 3 of the GATS on NT, by contrast, refers to the concept of de facto discrimination by stating that a Member may meet the NT requirement 'by according to services and service suppliers of any other Member, either formally identical treatment or formally different treatment to that it accords to its own like services and service suppliers' and that '[f]ormally identical or formally different treatment shall be considered to be less favourable if it modifies the conditions of competition in favour of services or service suppliers of the Member compared to like services or service suppliers of any other Member'.[445] This means that:

442. *See also* Ehring 2014, 35, who observes that all NT obligations in the WTO Agreement do not feature this terminology of de jure and de facto discrimination.
443. AB Report, *Korea – Various Measures on Beef*, 2001, para. 137. *See*, moreover, para. 136, quoting from the GATT Panel Report, *US – Section 337 Tariff Act*, 1989, para. 5.11: 'it also has to be recognised that there may be cases where the application of formally *identical* legal provisions would in practice accord less favourable treatment to imported products and a contracting party might thus have to apply different legal provisions to imported products to ensure that the treatment accorded them is in fact no less favourable' (emphasis added by the Appellate Body). *See also*, however, Englisch 2008, 396, 420–424, who believes that no discrimination can be established without some distinction between 'like products' or 'like services and service suppliers'; differently, for instance, Berrisch 2003 m.no. 76; Verhoosel 2002, 21–22 ('an obligation not simply to accord identical treatment ... but to differentiate--adapt–domestic regulation if such differentiation is necessary to provide no less favourable treatment'); Roessler 2000, 124; Roessler 1996, 26 ('an obligation to accord formally different treatment').
444. AB Report, *Canada – Autos*, 2000, para. 78 (original emphasis; footnotes omitted).
445. *See* Muller 2017, 152, 155–156; Muller 2016, 835, who links the rule's coverage of 'formally identical treatment or formally different treatment' to de jure and de facto discrimination; moreover, WTO, *Guidelines for the Scheduling of Specific Commitments under the General*

- formally different treatment of like services and service suppliers may constitute no discrimination;[446]
- formally identical treatment of like services and service suppliers may constitute no discrimination;
- formally different treatment of like services and service suppliers may constitute discrimination; and
- formally identical treatment of like services and service suppliers may constitute discrimination.[447]

It follows that a Member's measure need not explicitly refer to origin in order to conflict with the non-discrimination obligations. Origin-neutral measures that do not distinguish between like services and service suppliers may be discriminatory as well. What matters pursuant to Article XVII:3 is that the treatment 'modifies the conditions of competition in favour of [domestic] services or service suppliers ... compared to like services or service suppliers of any other Member'.

Since there is a difference in the wording between the MFN rule and the NT rule under the GATS, and since only the latter considers formally identical treatment as potentially discriminatory, it could be argued *a contrario* that formally identical treatment cannot lead to discrimination under the MFN provision and that such a form of de facto discrimination is not covered by Article II. However, the Appellate Body rejected such a conclusion in *EC – Bananas III* (1997):[448]

> The GATS negotiators chose to use different language in Article II and Article XVII of the GATS in expressing the obligation to provide 'treatment no less favourable'. The question naturally arises: if the GATS negotiators intended that 'treatment no less favourable' should have exactly the same meaning in Articles II and XVII of the GATS, why did they not repeat paragraphs 2 and 3 of Article XVII in Article II? But that is not the question here. The question here is the meaning of 'treatment no less favourable' with respect to the MFN obligation in Article II of the GATS. There is more than one way of writing a *de facto* non-discrimination provision. ... The obligation imposed by Article II is unqualified. The ordinary meaning of this provision does not exclude *de facto* discrimination. Moreover, if Article II was not applicable to *de facto* discrimination, it would not be difficult – and, indeed, it would be a good deal easier in the case of trade in services, than in the case of trade in goods – to devise discriminatory measures aimed at circumventing the basic purpose of that Article.

Agreement on Trade in Services (GATS), S/L/92, 28 March 2001, para. 13; Li 2010, 89; Hudec 1998, 639; critically, Flett 2014, 74–76.

446. In such a case, it could also be argued that these services and service suppliers are not in fact 'like' and, therefore, their formally different treatment does not constitute discrimination – but this is not the approach taken by Article XVII:2 of the GATS.

447. In such a case, it could also be argued that these services and service suppliers are not in fact 'like' and, therefore, their formally identical treatment constitutes discrimination – but this is not the approach taken by Article XVII:3 of the GATS. *See*, however, Englisch 2008, 421, who argues that Article XVII:2 and 3 of the GATS refers only to whether an express reference to origin is made and that, also for this reason, some formal distinction is required for discrimination.

448. AB Report, *EC – Bananas III*, 1997, paras 233–234.

> For these reasons, we conclude that 'treatment no less favourable' in Article II:1 of the GATS should be interpreted to include *de facto,* as well as *de jure,* discrimination.

Articles I and III of the GATT as well as Article II of the GATS do not expressly mandate a concept of de facto discrimination (only Article XVII of the GATS does so), but they also do not exclude such a concept. Therefore, despite various differences in wording, the basic purpose of these non-discrimination provisions indicates that formally identical and formally different treatment can be considered to be less favourable and that facially neutral measures are covered as well.

[2] De Jure Distinctions Illegitimate Per Se?

When a non-discrimination rule covers both de jure and de facto discrimination, differences in assessing discrimination may arise. Origin-based measures are regarded as being discriminatory by definition.[449] For instance, Lothar Ehring states that '[i]t is obvious that any internal regulation openly distinguishing between ... ["like"] national and foreign goods to the detriment of the latter violates' the NT obligation of Article III:4 of the GATT.[450] Similarly, for William J. Davey and Joost Pauwelyn, if regulatory distinctions 'are made exclusively on the basis of the origin of the product ... no doubt Article I:1 would be violated. ... A simple "but for" test can reveal this kind of violation: "but for" the country of origin, would the products be treated alike?',[451] or in the words of Robert E. Hudec, 'the explicitly different treatment is viewed as evidence that discrimination against foreign goods is a deliberate policy'[452] and, thus, such distinctions based on origin are a priori illegitimate.[453] Because of its deliberate character, de jure discrimination is likely to cause a greater-than-normal degree of opposition.[454]

By contrast, measures that do not directly refer to origin require a more sophisticated non-discrimination analysis and 'scrutiny becomes more complicated'.[455] It is argued that only with such facially neutral measures it is necessary to conduct an in-depth analysis of 'likeness' and 'less favourable treatment', whereas 'likeness' and 'less favourable treatment' may generally be taken for granted when measures explicitly differentiate by reason of origin.[456] Thus, measures that openly provide for treatment that is less favourable by reason of foreign origin appear to be illegitimate per se, whereas origin-neutral measures demand additional proof that they de facto provide for treatment that is less favourable by reason of foreign origin.[457]

449. Van den Bossche and Zdouc 2013, 319.
450. Ehring 2002, 923.
451. Davey and Pauwelyn 2000, 25.
452. Hudec 1998, 621.
453. Hudec 1998, 623.
454. Hudec 1998, 621.
455. Ehring 2002, 923.
456. *See also* Regan 2001 fn. 4 on p. 1856, p. 1887, who suggests that it may be presumed that explicit discrimination has a protectionist purpose unless some strong justification is positively demonstrated; moreover, Regan 2006b, 985.
457. *See also,* for instance, Regan 2006a, 202; Regan 2002, 455–456.

Nevertheless, just as facially neutral measures can de facto refer to foreign origin, origin-based measures can de facto refer to some other potentially legitimate factor.[458] An express reference to certain origin, therefore, may not be solely based on origin, as the dispute *Argentina – Financial Services* (2016) illustrates.[459] In *Argentina – Financial Services* (2016), Panama raised concerns with respect to various rules that targeted tax havens and low-tax regimes.[460] Argentina provided for a different tax treatment based on a list of 'countries with low or no taxes' that included Panama. For instance, with regard to credits, loans, and placement of funds, Argentina presumed a higher creditor's net profit if the creditor was a banking or financial institution based in a listed country and, therefore, levied a higher withholding tax. Panama claimed that this measure was contrary to the MFN obligation of Article II:1 of the GATS.[461] Argentina also established different criteria concerning the possibility of deducting expenses incurred in transactions with foreign parties. While such deductions were generally governed by the accrual rule, that is the expenses were deductible at the time at which the underlying obligation was contracted, the time of actual payment was relevant if the counterparty was from a listed country. Even though, in both cases, the expenses were ultimately deductible, Panama claimed that this difference in treatment was inconsistent with both Article II:1 (MFN) and Article XVII (NT) of the GATS.[462]

Argentina subsequently amended its legislation to the effect that the negative list of 'countries with low or no taxes' became a positive list of countries considered to be cooperative for the purposes of tax transparency. Consequently, there was then a difference in treatment between cooperative and non-cooperative countries.[463] Despite that, in Panama's view, the amendment 'simply provided for cosmetic changes to the rules at issue and did not substantially modify the measure that had given rise to this dispute'.[464] In order to resolve this dispute, the Panel on *Argentina – Financial Services* (2016) delivered its report in September 2015[465] which was followed by a report of the Appellate Body in April 2016.[466]

It is interesting to note that, in *Argentina – Financial Services* (2016), uncertainty prevailed about whether the difference in treatment by reference to the list of cooperative countries was exclusively based on the supplier's origin[467] and whether,

458. *See also* Regan 2006a, 202–203; Regan 2002, 456–457, who admits that an origin-specific measure may be necessary to achieve an 'origin-neutral' (i.e., non-protectionist) purpose; to this effect, Regan 2006b, 985.
459. *See also* Dziurdź 2016, 192–193, 200–203.
460. *Argentina – Financial Services*, Request for Consultations by Panama, WT/DS453/1, G/L/1019, S/L/396 (19 December 2012); *Argentina – Financial Services*, Request for the Establishment of a Panel by Panama, WT/DS453/4 (14 May 2013).
461. *Ibid.*, WT/DS453/1, pp. 1–2, and WT/DS453/4, pp. 1–2.
462. *Ibid.*, WT/DS453/1, p. 6, and WT/DS453/4, pp. 4–5.
463. *See*, in detail, Rybnik 2014.
464. Dispute Settlement Body, Minutes of Meeting, Held in the Centre William Rappard on 24 June 2013, WT/DSB/M/333, pp. 15–17, at p. 16 (30 August 2013).
465. For a discussion, *see* Hahn et al. 2016, 345–352.
466. For a case summary, *see* Carlson 2016.
467. *See* Panel Report, *Argentina – Financial Services*, 2016, paras 7.118 et seq.; Third Party Written Submission by the European Union, Ares(2014)1824204, pp. 13–14, paras 48–50 (4 June 2014); Responses of the United States to the Panel's Questions for the Third Parties Following the First Panel Meeting, pp. 3–4 (13 October 2014).

therefore, 'likeness' could be deemed to exist. Without paying attention to the background of the list, an exclusive reference to origin can be assumed. Thus, the list is merely a list of origins. If, however, it is taken into account that the list was compiled on the basis of the countries' cooperativeness (transparency, exchange of information, etc.), it can be argued that origin is not the actual reason for different treatment. Rather, the countries' cooperativeness is the direct reason for differentiation or the countries' (un)cooperativeness itself may be regarded as a substitute for concerns regarding the imposition or collection of taxes in respect of services and service suppliers from the respective jurisdictions. Depending on which information and factual circumstances are taken into account for the purposes of the legal analysis, measures may be regarded as operating either exclusively because of origin or other grounds.

On appeal, the Appellate Body dealt with the question of whether a presumption approach is appropriate under the GATS, that is whether 'likeness' may be established without analysing the relevant 'likeness' criteria by demonstrating that the measure at issue makes a distinction between services and service suppliers based exclusively on origin.[468] In principle, the Appellate Body approved this approach under both the GATT and the GATS[469] (but it raised some concerns regarding trade in services).[470] Nevertheless, even though the Panel presumed 'likeness', the Appellate Body reversed the Panel's findings. Under the presumption approach, the services and service suppliers may be considered 'like' when a measure provides for different treatment *exclusively* on the basis of origin. The Panel only made a finding that the difference in treatment between cooperative and non-cooperative countries was 'due to origin' and not that it was based *exclusively* on origin.[471] On the contrary, the Panel stated that the distinction at issue was based not on origin per se but on the regulatory framework inextricably linked to such origin.[472] Also, the Panel considered that the possibility for Argentina to have access to tax information could be taken into account in the 'likeness' analysis provided that this 'other factor' affects the competitive relationship.[473] In the absence of a finding that the measures at issue provided for a distinction

468. AB Report, *Argentina – Financial Services*, 2016, para. 6.35.
469. *See also* Muller 2016, 832, who states that in *Argentina – Financial Services* (2016), 'the Appellate Body specified that there is a presumption of "likeness" where a measure provides for a distinction based exclusively on origin'.
470. According to the Appellate Body in *Argentina – Financial Services* (2016), measures allowing the application of a presumption of 'likeness' under the GATT will typically be measures involving a de jure distinction between products of different origin (para. 6.36). Also, when a measure provides for a distinction based exclusively on origin, there will or can be services and service suppliers that are the same in all respects except for origin and, accordingly, 'likeness' can be presumed without resorting to the relevant 'likeness' criteria. However, compared to trade in goods, the scope for such a presumption under the GATS would be more limited, and establishing 'likeness' based on the presumption may often involve greater complexity (para. 6.38). The determination of 'likeness' under the GATS involves consideration of both the service and the service supplier which may render the analysis of whether or not a distinction is based exclusively on origin more complex (para. 6.39). In addition, determining origin may be a complex matter in the context of trade in services, and different modes of supply add an additional layer of complexity (para. 6.40).
471. *Ibid.*, paras 6.54–6.61.
472. *Ibid.*, para. 6.56.
473. *Ibid.*, para. 6.57.

based *exclusively* on origin and by failing to conduct an in-depth analysis of 'likeness', the Panel erred in finding 'likeness' 'by reason of origin'.[474]

At the same time, the Appellate Body emphasized that it had taken no view on whether the services and service suppliers of cooperative countries were 'like' the services and service suppliers of non-cooperative countries or 'like' Argentine services and service suppliers.[475] Thus, whether a distinction between cooperative and non-cooperative countries is based *exclusively* on origin even when certain policy rationales (such as the aim of having access to tax information) underlie this origin-based distinction[476] was not answered. It is clear, however, that an express reference to foreign origin does not automatically imply that this distinction is based *exclusively* on origin and that 'likeness', therefore, may be presumed.

In *Korea – Various Measures on Beef* (2001),[477] the Appellate Body further decided that an origin-based distinction does not allow for a presumption of 'less favourable treatment'. Korea introduced a dual retail system that, as Korea argued, assured perfect regulatory symmetry between imported and domestic beef. It obligated retailers to decide whether they wanted to sell either exclusively domestic or exclusively imported beef (larger retailers, however, could sell both imported and domestic beefs but only in separate sales areas). Korea submitted that it was neutral with respect to foreign origin as retailers could choose freely to sell only domestic beef or only imported beef.[478] While the Panel believed that '[a]ny regulatory distinction that is based exclusively on criteria relating to the nationality or the origin of the products is incompatible with Article III',[479] which implied that Korea's dual retail system for beef accorded treatment less favourable to imported beef than to like Korean beef, the Appellate Body rejected this interpretation.[480] Although the Korean measure formally separated the selling of imported beef and domestic beef and thereby potentially limited 'side-by-side' comparison and encouraged consumer perceptions of 'differences',[481] that formal separation, *in and of itself*, did not necessarily compel 'less favourable treatment'.[482]

This means that formally different treatment by reason of origin does not necessarily imply 'less favourable treatment'.[483] It is neither justified to assume that a measure that distinguishes between products on the basis of their origin necessarily distinguishes between 'like products' nor that it provides for 'less favourable treatment' to products of foreign origin. Instead, it must be determined, based on a

474. *Ibid.*, para. 6.61.
475. *Ibid.*, para. 6.80.
476. *Ibid.*, paras 6.62–6.63.
477. *See also* Colares and Canterberry 2017, 115–117; Melloni 2005, 97–101.
478. AB Report, *Korea – Various Measures on Beef*, 2001, paras 17, 131.
479. Panel Report, *Korea – Various Measures on Beef*, 2001, para. 627.
480. AB Report, *Korea – Various Measures on Beef*, 2001, paras 135–138.
481. *Ibid.*, para. 141.
482. *Ibid.*, para. 144.
483. *See also* Du 2016, 142; Du 2015, 74, who observes that, in *Korea – Various Measures on Beef* (2001), the Appellate Body 'made it clear that a formal difference in treatment between imported products and like domestic products, even if based exclusively on the origin of the products, is neither necessary, nor sufficient, to show a violation of Article III:4'.

competitive standard, whether such formally different treatment amounts to 'less favourable treatment' by modifying the conditions of competition. All of this makes it doubtful whether measures that explicitly refer to origin can be viewed as illegitimate per se instead of merely indicating potential discrimination.[484]

[B] Competitive Standard

[1] Detrimental Impact on Competitive Relationship

Since the purpose of the general non-discrimination rules is to provide equality of competitive conditions,[485] and since the determination of 'likeness' is, fundamentally, a determination about the nature and extent of a competitive relationship between and among products (*see* section §2.03[E][1]), the determination of 'less favourable treatment' is, fundamentally, a determination about a measure's detrimental impact on this competitive relationship. Already in *US – Section 337 Tariff Act* (1989), the Panel found that the 'no less favourable treatment' requirement under the GATT is an expression of the underlying principle of equality of treatment of imported products compared to the treatment given either to other foreign products under the MFN standard or to domestic products under the NT standard of Article III.[486] The words 'treatment no less favourable' in Article III:4 call for effective equality of opportunities for imported products.[487]

This understanding of the 'treatment no less favourable' obligation as ensuring effective equality of competitive opportunities has been consistently applied in later GATT and WTO decisions.[488] An internal measure is discriminatory and contrary to Article III:4 of the GATT only if it modifies the conditions of competition in the relevant market to the detriment of imported products when compared to competing (and, therefore, arguably 'like') domestic products.[489] In other words, a measure accords 'less favourable treatment' to imported products if it provides domestic 'like' products with a competitive advantage in the market over imported 'like' products.[490]

As already mentioned, the Appellate Body confirmed in *Korea – Various Measures on Beef* (2001) that regulatory distinctions based on origin need not be inconsistent with Article III:4 of the GATT.[491] On the one hand, such formally different treatment may be more favourable to imported products. On the other hand, it may be equal in substance if it does not modify the conditions of competition. In addition,

484. *See also* AB Report, *Thailand – Cigarettes (Philippines)*, 2011, para. 130, where the Appellate Body held that an explicit reference to origin may be a significant indication but not conclusive evidence of 'less favourable treatment'.
485. *See*, with respect to Article III, AB Report, *Japan – Alcoholic Beverages II*, 1996, p. 18.
486. GATT Panel Report, *US – Section 337 Tariff Act*, 1989, para. 5.11.
487. *Ibid.*, para. 5.11.
488. Van den Bossche and Zdouc 2013, 395.
489. AB Report, *Korea – Various Measures on Beef*, 2001, para. 137; AB Report, *Dominican Republic – Import and Sale of Cigarettes*, 2005, para. 93; AB Report, *Thailand – Cigarettes (Philippines)*, 2011, para. 128; AB Report, *EC – Seal Products*, 2014, paras 5.108–5.110.
490. AB Report, *Dominican Republic – Import and Sale of Cigarettes*, 2005, para. 93.
491. AB Report, *Korea – Various Measures on Beef*, 2001, paras 135–137.

facially neutral measures that do not formally distinguish based on origin may nevertheless violate the NT obligation. What really matters is not formalism but the impact on the conditions of competition.

With respect to the Korean dual retail system for beef, the Appellate Body concluded that, even though individual retailers could freely choose to sell only domestic beef or only imported beef, a vast majority chose to sell domestic beef when the system was introduced. This legal necessity of making a choice virtually excluded imported beef from the retail distribution channels and thus suddenly and drastically reduced the commercial opportunity for imported beef.[492] Due to the lack of equality of competitive conditions entailed by the dual retail system, 'less favourable treatment' was accorded to imported beef.[493]

Turning from the GATT to the GATS, it is noteworthy that a very similar, if not the same, competitive standard of 'less favourable treatment' applies. Article XVII:3 of the GATS expressly provides for a competitive meaning of 'less favourable treatment' with respect to the NT obligation by stating that any treatment 'shall be considered to be less favourable if it *modifies the conditions of competition* in favour of services or service suppliers of the Member compared to like services or service suppliers of any other Member' (emphasis added). However, footnote 10 to Article XVII states that the NT obligation 'shall not be construed to require any Member to compensate for any inherent competitive disadvantages which result from the foreign character of the relevant services or service suppliers'. In many cases, services and service suppliers of foreign origin have competitive disadvantages that are inherent to their foreign character. For example, the mere existence of cross-border regulatory diversity represents a burden for service suppliers,[494] or foreign service suppliers may need to overcome longer physical distances to customers when compared to domestic competitors.[495] Article XVII of the GATS does not require Members to introduce measures that compensate for such inherent disadvantages. However, the Members are not allowed to introduce measures that further reinforce or create disadvantages so that, in effect, competitive disadvantages result from or are caused by such measures.[496]

492. *Ibid.*, paras 145–147.
493. *Ibid.*, para. 148. *See*, critically, H. Horn and Mavroidis 2009a, 127–128, who submit that '[t]he number of outlets was most likely, the direct outcome of the quota in place: the imported beef could satisfy only a *small* fraction of the demand; most traders would be interested in carrying the more expensive domestic beef' (original emphasis).
494. Muller 2017, 156.
495. *See also* Muller 2016, 836, who refers to restrictions such as the need to work in the local language and adapt to local traditions or commercial practice; moreover, Krajewski and Engelke 2008 m.no. 45.
496. *See*, in particular, AB Report, *Argentina – Financial Services*, 2016, para. 6.104, where the Appellate Body clarified that the 'inherent competitive disadvantages' result from the 'foreign character' of the relevant services or service suppliers rather than from the contested measure adopted by the importing Member and, therefore, the 'inherent competitive disadvantages' must be distinguished from the measure's impact on the conditions of competition in the marketplace. The NT obligation is not about the relative competitive advantages or disadvantages of the services and service suppliers that are *not* caused by the contested measure. Rather, the standard of 'treatment no less favourable' must be based on the impact on the conditions of competition that *results from* the contested measure.

[2] *Different Approaches to 'Less Favourable Treatment'*

Under both the GATT and GATS, the general non-discrimination provisions rely on a competitive standard when comparing the treatment of imported products (or foreign services and service suppliers) to the treatment given either to domestic products (NT) or other foreign products (MFN). Treatment is 'less favourable' if it affects the conditions of competition to the detriment of foreign origin.

Since the concept of 'likeness' does not demand complete identity in every respect, products that share important characteristics can differ in other aspects without losing their 'likeness'. A measure may consequently favour some 'like products' and disfavour others, potentially both among imports and domestic (NT) or other foreign (MFN) products.[497] For example, if all types of beer are regarded as 'like products' from the perspective of their competitive relationship, it is possible to establish subgroups of 'like products' other than on the basis of origin, such as the subgroups of low and high alcohol beer. Origin-neutral regulation[498] may differentiate between these subgroups by treating high alcohol beer differently than low alcohol beer. This raises the question of whether it is sufficient to find some imported beer (with a high alcohol content) that is treated less favourably than some domestic beer (with a low alcohol content), whether only high alcohol beer or only low alcohol beer can be compared to each other, or whether a different approach to establishing 'less favourable treatment' has to be applied.

It should be remembered that, even if a measure does not distinguish between 'like products' at all neither on the basis of origin nor on the basis of any other characteristic, it may treat imported products less favourably (*see* section §2.04[A][1]). In such a case, the measure at issue may also divide 'like products' into four subgroups when the more intense burden falls not on all foreign products, and some 'like' domestic products are burdened more intensively as well: more and less burdened 'like products' both of domestic and foreign origin.[499]

In all cases in which subgroups of domestic and foreign 'like products' can be established on the basis of product-related characteristics, the question is whether origin-neutral measures violate a non-discrimination rule only if they impose a greater overall disadvantage on the aggregate group of imports than on the aggregate group of comparable domestic (NT) or other foreign (MFN) products or whether it suffices that

497. Ehring 2002, 924.
498. On de jure discrimination, *see* Ehring 2014, 53–54, who submits that one single imported product being treated less favourably de jure than one 'like' domestic product suffices for a breach of Article III:4 of the GATT; treatment that is more favourable of other imported products cannot be balanced against such less favourable treatment. *See also*, to this effect, Howse and Türk 2006 fn. 55 on p. 90; Ortino 2008 fn. 24 on p. 182; Ortino 2004, 260; Ehring 2002, 946–947; Howse and Türk 2001 fn. 55 on pp. 297–298; differently, Englisch 2008, 427, who critically remarks that it is not clear why a different standard should be applied in such cases; but *see also* pp. 445–447 where he argues that origin-based distinctions that disadvantage a whole (sub)group of 'like' imported products when compared to a corresponding (sub)group of 'like' domestic products always lead to treatment that is less favourable under Article III:4.
499. Ehring 2002 fn. 10 at p. 925.

they disfavour some imports compared to some 'like' domestic (NT) or other foreign (MFN) products.[500] If it is possible to compare the treatment accorded to any foreign product with the more favourable treatment accorded to any 'like' domestic product, imported high alcohol beer can be compared with domestic low alcohol beer in order to establish 'less favourable treatment'. Accordingly, a Member could violate an NT obligation if it introduced an origin-neutral measure which would burden high alcohol beer unless that measure would be justified. Such a violation would persist even if the burden falls similarly on domestic and foreign beer (*see* Figure 2.1 and Table 2.2) and even if domestic beer suffers a disproportionately higher burden (*see* Figure 2.2 and Table 2.3). What matters is that there is some imported beer that is treated less favourably than some 'like' domestic beer. As Lothar Ehring describes, '[t]his means that it is always possible to find a violation ..., as long as the disfavoured type is (potentially) imported and the favoured type exists domestically. Even when imported products overwhelmingly receive the better treatment and most domestic goods fall in the less advantageous category, there is still a violation'.[501] Under this approach, the best treatment accorded to any 'like' domestic product would have to be accorded to *all* 'like' imported products to meet the non-discrimination obligations.[502]

Figure 2.1 Comparability: Different Treatment of Subgroups (1)

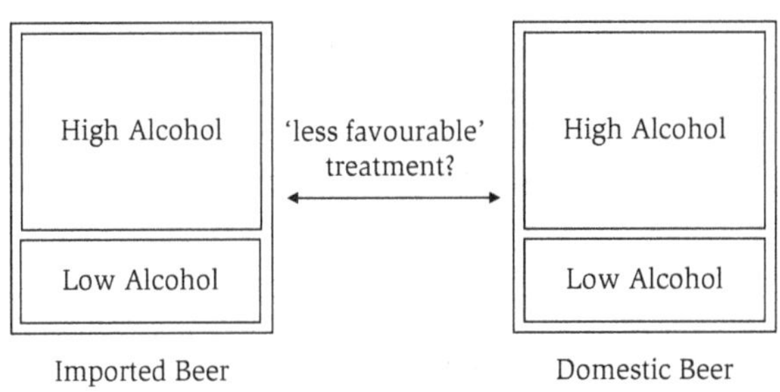

Table 2.2 Subgroups of 'Like Products': Equivalent Burdens

Alcohol Content	*Imported Beer*	*Domestic Beer*	*Treatment*
high	80%	80%	burdensome
low	20%	20%	favourable
	100%	100%	

500. Ehring 2002, 922.
501. Ehring 2002, 924.
502. Diebold 2011b, 844. To be precise, however, it would also be possible to grant the same treatment to all 'like' domestic and imported products, and this treatment could be the best treatment or the worst treatment previously available. *See also* Ehring 2002, 955–957.

Figure 2.2 Comparability: Different Treatment of Subgroups (2)

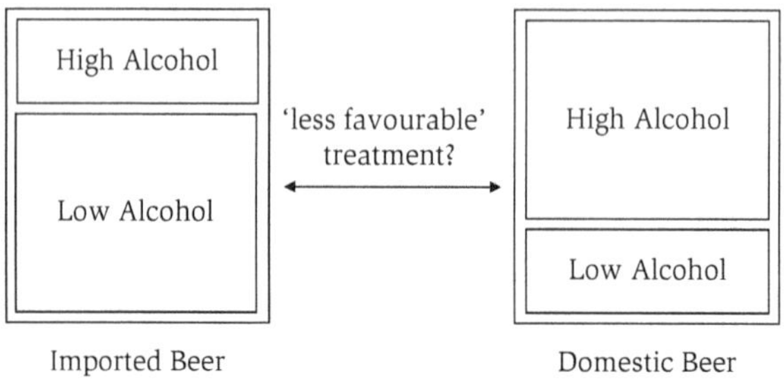

Table 2.3 Subgroups of 'Like Products': Lower Burden on Imports

Alcohol Content	*Imported Beer*	*Domestic Beer*	*Treatment*
high	20%	80%	burdensome
low	80%	20%	favourable
	100%	100%	

By contrast, when looking at the aggregated groups of imports and 'like' domestic (NT) or other foreign (MFN) products, the whole group of imported beer comprising the subgroups of low and high alcohol beer must be compared to the whole group of domestic beer. Discrimination due to 'less favourable treatment' can only exist if imported beer suffers a disproportionate or asymmetric disadvantage compared to domestic beer. Accordingly, a Member would not violate an NT obligation if it introduced an origin-neutral measure that would burden high alcohol beer as long as this differentiation between high and low alcohol beer does not have a disproportionate impact on imported beer (*see* again Figures 2.1 and 2.2 and Tables 2.2 and 2.3). For this equivalence to exist, 'it is necessary that, as a whole and relatively, the entire groups of imports and domestic products bear the burden in an equivalent proportion'.[503] In this case, 'the disadvantage arising from the measure for parts of both domestic and imported like products is not even indirectly related to origin. It is only related to the origin-neutral (e.g. physical) characteristics on which it depends'.[504] If, however, the overall burden is comparatively heavier for imported beer than for domestic beer, that is if 'most imports fall into the disfavoured regulatory category and/or most domestic products fall into the favoured group',[505] discrimination exists (*see* Figure 2.3 and Table 2.4).[506] Due to the composition of imports and domestic goods most, but not all, imported beer is treated less favourably and most, but not all, 'like' domestic beer is granted favourable treatment. Thus, even though favourable treatment is granted to some products of foreign origin as well and certain products of domestic origin are also

503. Ehring 2002, 925.
504. Ehring 2002, 925.
505. Ehring 2002, 925.
506. Obviously, also in this case, a comparison of some imported products with some domestic 'like' products would lead to discrimination.

treated less favourably, de facto discrimination is at hand because overall, imported beer is treated less favourably than 'like' domestic beer.

Figure 2.3 Comparability: Different Treatment of Subgroups (3)

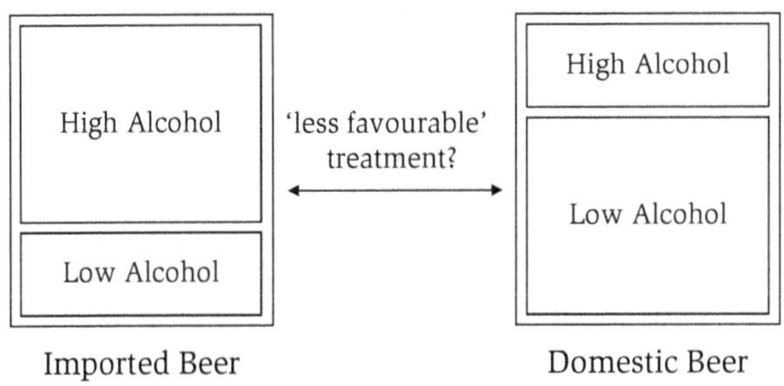

Table 2.4 Subgroups of 'Like Products': Higher Burden on Imports

Alcohol Content	*Imported Beer*	*Domestic Beer*	*Treatment*
high	80%	20%	burdensome
low	20%	80%	favourable
	100%	100%	

For the purpose of establishing 'less favourable treatment', it would theoretically be possible to compare only those imported and domestic (NT) or other foreign (MFN) products that fall under a particular subgroup of 'like products'. If a measure distinguishes between low and high alcohol beer, the comparisons could take place between imported and domestic low alcohol beer only and between imported and domestic high alcohol beer only. Since there is no difference in treatment within each of these subgroups neither on the basis of origin nor on the basis of any other product characteristic, de facto discrimination could never occur unless the equal treatment of beer within a subgroup would result in a qualitatively higher burden on imported high alcohol beer than on domestic high alcohol beer or on imported low alcohol beer than on domestic low alcohol beer.[507] 'By definition, origin-neutral rules then would not be able to give rise to less favourable treatment, unless the imposed burden is qualitatively heavier for imported goods.'[508]

Such an approach to 'less favourable treatment' would achieve a similar result as a very narrow interpretation of 'likeness'.[509] If any regulatory distinction based on product characteristics, except for origin, prevented 'likeness', the concept of de facto

507. Ehring 2002, 927–928, 959. On a similar argument submitted in *EC – Seal Products* (2014), *see* Nielsen and Calle 2013, 53–54.
508. Ehring 2002, 959.
509. Ehring 2002, 928: 'If the interpretation of "likeness" is sufficiently narrow, it may prevent the differently treated goods from entering the same product category (like products). If the differently treated goods are not "like" there can, as a consequence, be no violation ... However, it is clear that the regulatory distinction itself cannot, as a general rule, be sufficient for the conclusion that goods are no longer "like" one another. Such an approach would ...

discrimination would become largely meaningless. Only a direct reference to origin could establish discrimination within such a very narrow category of 'like products'. If any regulatory distinction based on product characteristics, except for origin, created separate subgroups of 'like products' and thereby restricted the issue of 'less favourable treatment' to the domain of each separate subgroup, hardly any cases of de facto discrimination would remain except for cases in which equal treatment within a subgroup would have a disparate impact on foreign origin.

[3] Comparison of Whole Groups of 'Like Products'

There are three fundamentally different approaches to 'less favourable treatment' (and to 'in excess of' as well as to 'not similarly taxed'):

(1) one that compares some imported products to some 'like' domestic (NT) or other foreign (MFN) products and effectively prohibits all distinctions between 'like products' thereby severely limiting the regulatory autonomy of WTO Members;
(2) one that compares the whole group of imported products to the whole group of 'like' domestic or other foreign products and requires a disparate impact on the whole group of imports thereby leaving more scope for regulatory distinctions;[510] and
(3) one that compares only within each separate subgroup of 'like products' and effectively accepts any regulatory distinction based on a product characteristic thereby hardly leaving cases of de facto discrimination.[511]

With respect to 'not similarly taxed' under the second sentence of Article III:2 of the GATT, the Appellate Body rejected the third approach in *Chile – Alcoholic Beverages* (2000). With respect to 'treatment no less favourable' under Article III:4 of the GATT, the Appellate Body relied on the second approach in *EC – Asbestos* (2001) thereby rejecting the first approach. As a consequence, under the GATT, one has to compare the whole group of imported products to the whole group of 'like' domestic (NT) or other foreign (MFN) products.

In *Chile – Alcoholic Beverages* (2000), Chile argued that all distilled alcoholic beverages with a specific alcohol content were subject to identical ad valorem tax rates irrespective of their origin and thus invited the Appellate Body 'to focus exclusively on a comparison of the relative tax burden on domestic and imported products *within each fiscal category*'.[512] Even though all distilled alcoholic beverages of a specific alcohol content were taxed similarly, the Appellate Body pointed out that 'the group of directly competitive or substitutable products in this case is broader than simply the products

render the concept of *de facto* discrimination meaningless and permit an easy circumvention of many non-discrimination disciplines.'

510. *See also*, for instance, Ehring 2002, 925, 962, 973.
511. *See also*, to this effect, Vranes 2009, 232; Regan 2006a, 214; Regan 2002, 469.
512. AB Report, *Chile – Alcoholic Beverages*, 2000, para. 51 (original emphasis).

within each fiscal category'.[513] The objective of Article III is to provide equality of competitive conditions 'for *all* directly competitive or substitutable imported products in relation to domestic products, and not simply for *some* of these imported products'.[514] As a consequence, the Appellate Body took into account *all* of the distilled alcoholic beverages in *each and every* fiscal category, that is *all* of the directly competitive or substitutable domestic and imported products, and compared the tax burden on all imported products with the tax burden on all domestic products.[515]

In an obiter dictum in *EC – Asbestos* (2001), the Appellate Body further held with respect to Article III:4 of the GATT that, in order to violate the NT obligation, a measure must accord to the group of 'like' *imported* products 'less favourable treatment' than it accords to the group of 'like' *domestic* products:[516]

> [E]ven if two products are 'like', that does not mean that a measure is inconsistent with Article III:4. A complaining Member must still establish that the measure accords to the group of 'like' *imported* products 'less favourable treatment' than it accords to the group of 'like' *domestic* products. The term 'less favourable treatment' expresses the general principle, in Article III:1, that internal regulations 'should not be applied ... so as to afford protection to domestic production'. If there is 'less favourable treatment' of the group of 'like' imported products, there is, conversely, 'protection' of the group of 'like' domestic products. However, a Member may draw distinctions between products which have been found to be 'like', without, for this reason alone, according to the group of 'like' *imported* products 'less favourable treatment' than that accorded to the group of 'like' *domestic* products.

Under Article III:4 of the GATT, in order to claim 'less favourable treatment', it does not suffice to find some 'like' domestic products that enjoy better treatment than some 'like' imported products. Such an approach would automatically condemn all regulatory distinctions between products that have been found to be 'like' for whatever reason these distinctions are made. Thus, even origin-neutral measures that predominantly favour imports over 'like' domestic products could violate Article III:4.[517] As later confirmed in *US – Clove Cigarettes* (2012),[518] *EC – Asbestos* (2001) speaks in favour of a different approach.[519] A disproportionate or asymmetric overall impact to

513. *Ibid.*, para. 52 (original emphasis).
514. *Ibid.*, para. 52 (original emphasis).
515. *Ibid.*, paras 52–53.
516. AB Report, *EC – Asbestos*, 2001, para. 100 (original emphasis). *See also* Ehring 2014, 36–37; Ehring 2002, 942–946; Wiers and Mathis 2001, 222–224. For an in-depth analysis of preceding jurisprudence, *see*, moreover, Ehring 2002, 931–942.
517. Ehring 2002, 924, 953, 959; similarly, Vranes 2009, 234.
518. AB Report, *US – Clove Cigarettes*, 2012, para. 193.
519. *See also* Ehring 2014, 36–37, 42–44; in detail, Ehring 2002, 943–946; moreover, Du 2016, 143–144; Du 2015, 74; Marceau and Trachtman 2014, 362–363; Meltzer and Porges 2013, 709–710; Ortino 2012, 26–27; Diebold 2011b, 843; Vranes 2009, 238–239; Pauwelyn 2008, 364–365; Englisch 2008, 394–395, 428–436; Ortino 2008, 181–182; Ortino 2004, 257–260. According to Howse and Türk 2006, 90–91, 97; Howse 2002, 515; Howse and Türk 2001, 297–299, 305 and Porges and Trachtman 2003, 796; the Appellate Body seemed to suggest in *EC – Asbestos* (2001) that an analysis similar to that concerning 'so as to afford protection to domestic production' under the second sentence of Article III:2 – an objective assessment of a measure's purpose (*see* section §2.03[D][6]) – would be required under Article III:4 as well.

the detriment of imports must be assessed by comparing the whole group of favoured and disfavoured 'like' imported products with the whole group of favoured and disfavoured 'like' domestic products. As a consequence, the fact alone that some 'like' domestic products are granted treatment that is more favourable is not sufficient to trigger discrimination under Article III:4. Also, the fact that some 'like' domestic products are treated less favourably is not sufficient to disprove discrimination[520] and neither is the fact that some 'like' imported products are also treated more favourably. The impact on the conditions of competition between the two aggregated *groups* of 'like products' - imported and domestic products - must be analysed. This conversely means that regulatory distinctions between 'like products' on the basis of their characteristics are permitted as long as these distinctions do not detrimentally affect the conditions of competition between the groups of imported and domestic products.

Moreover, and as can be concluded from *Chile – Alcoholic Beverages* (2000), it is irrelevant for the purposes of NT whether the burdened or favoured subcategory of 'like products' is predominantly of foreign or domestic origin.[521] What matters is whether the proportion of burdened and favoured 'like' imported products is higher than the proportion of burdened and favoured 'like' domestic products.[522] For instance, based on kilolitres, if the market for high alcohol beer is dominated by domestic products with a market share of over 99%[523] and thus less than 1%[524] of high alcohol beer constitutes imported beer, there still may be 'less favourable treatment' when imports predominantly consist of high alcohol beer and domestic products of low alcohol beer (*see* Table 2.5). If the overall volume of imported beer is small, the volume of imported high alcohol beer is small as well. Nevertheless, the whole group of imports, when compared to the whole group of 'like' domestic products, remains detrimentally affected by a measure disfavouring high alcohol beer when the relative number of imported high alcohol beer in the group of imports (80%) is higher than the relative number of domestic high alcohol beer in the group of 'like' domestic products (20%).

See, critically, Ehring 2002, 945–946; moreover, Zhou 2012a, 109–111; Vranes 2009, 239–240. This view, however, has been rejected by the Appellate Body in *EC – Seal Products* (*see* section §2.04[C][3]).

520. Ehring 2002, 964.
521. AB Report, *Chile – Alcoholic Beverages*, 2000, para. 67. *See also*, in detail, Ehring 2002, 964–965; critically, H. Horn and Mavroidis 2004, 59.
522. *See also* Ehring 2002, 964: 'A factual asymmetry will exist if imports are underrepresented in the favoured sub-category or if domestic goods are underrepresented in the disfavoured sub-category. Underrepresented means that the quantitative ratio between favoured and disfavoured goods is lower than within the group of like products of the other origin'.
523. 20,000 kl ÷ (20,000 kl + 80 kl) = 99.6%.
524. 80 kl ÷ (20,000 kl + 80 kl) = 0.4%.

Table 2.5 Subgroups of 'Like Products': Higher Burden on Low-Quantity Imports

Alcohol Content	*Domestic Beer*	*Imported Beer*	*Treatment*
high	20,000 kl (20%)	80 kl (80%)	burdensome
low	80,000 kl (80%)	20 kl (20%)	favourable
	100,000 kl (100%)	100 kl (100%)	

Until now, the subgroups of 'like products' only suffered a burden or not, and the issue was whether the proportions of burdened imports and of 'like' domestic products were equivalent or disparate. A burden could be a ban of or a sale restriction on certain products such as a ban of high alcohol beer or an obligation to sell high alcohol beer in special stores. However, many measures, including tax measures, provide for varying burdens, for instance, by imposing a progressive tax rate which increases with certain thresholds of alcohol content (tax brackets). In such cases, many different burdens are imposed on 'like products' and thus many different subgroups are created. It is then necessary to qualify and quantify the relevant burdens and their intensity for the purposes of 'less favourable treatment' in order to determine whether the whole group of imported products suffers a disparate impact compared to the whole group of 'like' domestic (NT) or other foreign (MFN) products.[525] No solution will fit all cases.[526] In *Chile – Alcoholic Beverages* (2000), for instance, since the measure in question operated largely as if there were only two tax brackets, the Appellate Body simplified matters by only looking at the lowest and highest tax brackets that covered most imported and 'like' domestic products, respectively.[527] Thereby, the Appellate Body diminished the relevant subgroups to highly burdened and least burdened 'like products', leaving aside the tax brackets in between that appeared of minor practical importance.

When a measure detrimentally affects the competitive relationship of imported products compared to 'like' domestic products, these actual effects may be considered as evidence that 'less favourable treatment' of imported products exists.[528] However, the examination of whether a measure involves 'less favourable treatment' need not be based on the actual effects[529] since Article III also protects the expectations of equal competitive relationships.[530] It is sufficient that a measure may have a potential effect of treating imported products less favourably and that it may prevent future imports of products that do not yet compete in the marketplace. Yet, as held in *Thailand –*

525. *See also* Ehring 2002, 965, who proposes to calculate the weighted average of the tax imposed on imports and 'like' domestic or other foreign products, respectively, in order to take account of both the degree of the asymmetric distribution and the extent of the differentiation, that is the amount of the difference between the various tax rates.
526. In particular, it is often difficult to quantify burdens imposed by non-fiscal measures. Actually, even a simple ban can be of different intensity because the economic burden associated with compliance may vary significantly. *See* Ehring 2002, 966.
527. AB Report, *Chile – Alcoholic Beverages*, 2000, para. 53.
528. AB Report, *Thailand – Cigarettes (Philippines)*, 2011, para. 134.
529. AB Report, *Japan – Alcoholic Beverages II*, 1996, p. 16; AB Report, *Canada – Periodicals*, 1997, p. 18; AB Report, *US – FSC (Article 21.5 – EC)*, 2002, para. 215; AB Report, *Thailand – Cigarettes (Philippines)*, 2011, para. 134.
530. *See supra* n. 48.

Cigarettes (Philippines) (2011), the question of potential effects is not a question of probability:[531]

> [A]n analysis of less favourable treatment should not be anchored in an assessment of the degree of likelihood that an adverse impact on competitive conditions will materialize. Rather, an analysis under Article III:4 must begin with careful scrutiny of the measure, including consideration of the design, structure, and expected operation of the measure at issue. Such scrutiny may well involve - but does not require - an assessment of the contested measure in the light of evidence regarding the actual effects of that measure in the market. In any event, there must be in every case a genuine relationship between the measure at issue and its adverse impact on competitive opportunities for imported versus like domestic products to support a finding that imported products are treated less favourably.

[C] Purpose-Oriented Standard

[1] Arguments in Favour of Policy Considerations

A competitive standard of 'less favourable treatment' looks only at the actual and potential effects of a measure on the competitive relationships between and among 'like products'. It does not matter whether, for instance, a ban on asbestos fibres was introduced in order to protect human life and health, tax brackets were set at specific levels to take into account the dangers and long-term costs of alcoholic beverages, or 'like products' are treated differently in order to protect domestic production.[532] There must only be an asymmetry in the composition of (potential) imports and 'like' domestic products that is responsible for the rule's disparate impact on imports to the advantage of domestic products.[533]

It is anything but surprising that, in the realm of de facto discrimination, facts matter and not only the explicit language of the laws at issue.[534] However, when the facts decide about discrimination, this may lead to unexpected results. The composition in the market, that is the allocation of the subgroups between imports and 'like' domestic products, depends on a large number of market forces including production decisions, capacities and technologies, trade patterns, sales and marketing activities, and consumers' preferences. A measure's impact and whether it will predominantly disfavour foreign or domestic goods may be difficult to predict and change constantly. In fact, every regulatory measure likely has some impact on trade and may incidentally disfavour products of certain foreign origin more than other products at one point in time. Since it is 'undisputed that WTO Members have the right to determine the level

531. AB Report, *Thailand – Cigarettes (Philippines)*, 2011, para. 134.
532. However, such an analysis can matter under the second sentence of Article III:2 of the GATT for determining, after it is established that directly competitive or substitutable products are not similarly taxed, whether a measure is applied so as to afford protection to domestic production (*see* section §2.03[D][5]).
533. Ehring 2002, 925.
534. Ehring 2002, 961; *see also* pp. 967, 696, 973.

of protection of health that they consider appropriate in a given situation',[535] it would appear superficial, for instance, to blame a Member for discrimination and require justification solely because a measure distinguishes between 'like products' based on their health risks and happens to have a detrimental impact on imported products without bad faith. Robert E. Hudec states that:[536]

> a one-dimensional analysis of competitive impact has obvious shortcomings as a normative basis for prohibiting national regulations. Given that all regulatory measures impose some burden on the regulated businesses, and that such burdens are often distributed according to fortuitous market circumstances that are not even known (or at least not investigated) at the time the regulation is promulgated, the fact that in some cases a measure causes a disproportionate burden on foreign interests may be nothing more than a matter of random distribution of unintended effects. These effects could just as easily, and often do, turn out to be disproportionately burdensome to domestic interests. To say that such unintended and essentially random market effects justify invalidating the regulation is a normative proposition that would not find much acceptance in most WTO capitals. To the contrary, one would expect most governments to demand at least some evidence of bad faith, or at least gross negligence, before assenting to that conclusion.

It is consequently argued that a disparate impact should not be automatic grounds for a violation of Article III of the GATT; it is essential to consider the reason.[537] Initially, it was suggested to consider the regulatory purpose as an issue of 'likeness' by applying the aim and effects test (*see* section §2.03[D]). After the Appellate Body rejected this test for the purposes of both the GATT and GATS, however, the focus shifted to the meaning of 'less favourable treatment'.[538]

Under a purpose-oriented standard of 'less favourable treatment', whether a measure provides for 'less favourable treatment' is also determined on the basis of whether it genuinely pursues a legitimate policy objective or rather has a protective purpose. It does not suffice for 'less favourable treatment' that a measure detrimentally affects the competitive relationship of imported products compared to 'like' domestic products. A measure's detrimental impact must not be the result of a legitimate policy objective. Under this approach, the objectively assessed purposes of a measure can be a question of 'less favourable treatment'.[539] The measure can provide for such treatment and violate a non-discrimination obligation only if it does not pursue a legitimate policy objective. This allows excluding situations from being discriminatory when the disparate impact is attributable to the pursuit of legitimate policy interests.

535. AB Report, *EC – Asbestos*, 2001, para. 168.
536. Hudec 1998, 639.
537. Lydgate 2016, 425-426, with reference to Hudec 1998; Regan 2002 (also published in Regan 2006a); Regan 2003; Reid 2010.
538. *See*, in particular, Pauwelyn 2008; Ehring 2002; moreover, Du 2016, 141; Du 2015, 74; Diebold 2011b, 834.
539. *See also* Porges and Trachtman 2003, especially at pp. 786, 789-790; moreover, Flett 2014; Flett 2013; Pauwelyn 2008, 360-367 (commenting on Cossy 2008); but *see* Ehring 2002, 946, who argues with regard to 'less favourable treatment' under Article III:4 of the GATT that 'it ... seems impossible to consider, in addition to the design and the effect of the measure, whether its aim is legitimate enough to offset a discriminatory effect'.

[2] *Genuine Relationship to an Adverse Impact*

In *Dominican Republic – Import and Sale of Cigarettes* (2005), the Appellate Body stated that 'the existence of a detrimental effect on a given imported product resulting from a measure does not necessarily imply that this measure accords less favourable treatment to imports if the detrimental effect is explained by factors or circumstances unrelated to the foreign origin of the product'.[540] This has been understood as an implication of a purpose-oriented standard of 'less favourable treatment' according to which adverse effects on the conditions of competition may be regarded as 'no less favourable' if there is a non-protectionist explanation.[541] Subsequently, however, the Appellate Body clarified that this statement was not meant to suggest that an additional enquiry is necessary as to whether such detrimental impact is related to the foreign origin of the products or explained by other factors or circumstances.[542] It must rather be ascertained that a disparate impact on imported products is attributable to the specific measure at issue. As stated in *Thailand – Cigarettes (Philippines)* (2011), 'there must be in every case a genuine relationship between the measure at issue and its adverse impact on competitive opportunities for imported versus like domestic products to support a finding that imported products are treated less favourably'.[543] This is a test of 'causation' that determines whether any alleged disparate impact is caused by the specific measure at issue or by some other factors or which causal factor is a closer cause for the disparate impact.[544]

How can such a genuine relationship between the measure at issue and its adverse impact on competitive opportunities for imported versus like domestic products be identified? All origin-neutral measures may have a disparate impact on imports. Even measures that impose an identical burden on both importers and domestic producers (for instance, the same flat rate fee for obtaining a licence, the same minimum corporate tax in a low-profit situation) may lead to a higher pro rata burden on imports as soon as market shares differ. In *Dominican Republic – Import and Sale of Cigarettes* (2005), the same bond requirement fixed at USD 5 million for both importers and producers to ensure payment of taxes (the measure)[545] and a smaller market share

540. AB Report, *Dominican Republic – Import and Sale of Cigarettes*, 2005, para. 96.
541. *See*, for instance, Du 2016, 146–147; Du 2015, 76–77. *See*, moreover, Cossy 2008, 345–346; Pauwelyn 2008, 365–366; DiMascio and Pauwelyn 2008, 83. In fact, the Appellate Body noted in *US – Clove Cigarettes* (2012) that this statement 'when read in isolation, could be viewed as suggesting that further inquiry into the rationale for the detrimental impact is necessary'. *See* AB Report, *US – Clove Cigarettes*, 2012, fn. 372 to para. 179.
542. AB Report, *US – Clove Cigarettes*, 2012, fn. 372 to para. 179; moreover, AB Report, *EC – Seal Products*, 2014, paras 5.104–5.105. *See also*, in detail, Du 2016, 146–148; Du 2015, 76–78; Ehring 2014, 48–53.
543. AB Report, *Thailand – Cigarettes (Philippines)*, 2011, para. 134.
544. Du 2016, 147–148, 156–157; Du 2015, 78; moreover, Conconi and Voon 2016, 219–220. *See also* Zhou 2012b, 1087–1088, 1091, 1114–1115, who discusses this understanding but also argues that 'the Appellate Body has continued to leave open the question of whether an assessment of origin-unrelated factors or means-ends relationship is merely a "causation" test, which concerns effects only, or such an assessment should also involve a consideration of non-protectionist policy objectives when necessary'; moreover, Mitchell, Heaton, and Henckels 2016, 108–112.
545. AB Report, *Dominican Republic – Import and Sale of Cigarettes*, 2005, para. 93.

of one importer compared to two domestic producers of cigarettes (the factual circumstances)[546] resulted in higher pro rata costs entailed by the bond requirement for imported cigarettes. As Lothar Ehring observes, 'a *de facto* discriminatory impact is never attributable in full to the measure, and is always a function also of facts'.[547] Therefore, the different market shares, as such, cannot automatically prevent the existence of de facto discrimination.

A 'but for' test - but for the existence of the disputed measure, would the adverse impact have occurred? - is not sufficient to show a genuine relationship. Ming Du points out that when applying a 'but for' test to *Dominican Republic – Import and Sale of Cigarettes* (2005), the uniform bond requirement was surely a causal factor because, without the bond requirement, the disparate impact would not have arisen.[548] Despite that, the Appellate Body attributed the detrimental impact to the market shares and not to the bond requirement:[549]

> [I]mported products are treated less favourably than like products if a measure modifies the conditions of competition in the relevant market *to the detriment of imported products*. However, the existence of a detrimental effect on a given imported product resulting from a measure does not necessarily imply that this measure accords less favourable treatment to imports if the detrimental effect is explained by factors or circumstances unrelated to the foreign origin of the product, such as the market share of the importer in this case. In this specific case, the mere demonstration that the per-unit cost of the bond requirement for imported cigarettes was higher than for some domestic cigarettes during a particular period is not, in our view, *sufficient* to establish 'less favourable treatment' under Article III:4 of the GATT 1994. Indeed, the difference between the per-unit costs of the bond requirement ... is explained by the fact that the importer of ... cigarettes has a smaller market share than two domestic producers (the per-unit cost of the bond requirement being the result of dividing the cost of the bond by the number of cigarettes sold on the Dominican Republic market). In this case, the difference between the per-unit costs of the bond requirement ... does not depend on the foreign origin of the imported cigarettes.

The difference between the per-unit costs of the bond requirement did not directly depend on the foreign origin of the imported cigarettes. However, the concept of de facto discrimination also covers origin-neutral measures that do not differentiate between 'like products' at all but nevertheless lead to a disproportionate burden on foreign origin (*see* section §2.04[A][1]). This can be the case when it is, in practice, more difficult for imports to meet certain requirements or obligations that are imposed equally on all 'like products'. *Any* adverse impact on competitive opportunities for imported products vis-à-vis 'like' domestic products that is caused by a particular measure may potentially be relevant for the purpose of establishing 'less favourable

546. *Ibid.*, para. 96.
547. Ehring 2014, 52–53.
548. Du 2016, 156.
549. AB Report, *Dominican Republic – Import and Sale of Cigarettes*, 2005, para. 96 (original emphasis; footnotes omitted).

treatment' and de facto discrimination.[550] In some circumstances, formally different treatment may thus be required if identical treatment causes an adverse impact on competitive opportunities for imported products.

Even in *Dominican Republic – Import and Sale of Cigarettes* (2005), the Appellate Body recognized that 'a measure that applies equally to importers and domestic producers might, in some circumstances, nevertheless be inconsistent with Article III:4'.[551] In this case, the bond requirement was imposed equally on both importers and domestic producers, but it led to a disproportionate burden on imports. To what extent the measure should have considered the concrete market shares, that is the volumes of production or sales, in order to avoid 'less favourable treatment' was exactly the question.[552] Yet, in *Dominican Republic – Import and Sale of Cigarettes* (2005), the Appellate Body gave priority to the market shares as an explanation for the disparate impact. Therefore, it deemed the nexus between the measure establishing the bond requirement and the trade impact as insufficient for 'less favourable treatment'.[553] As a result, there was no obligation to consider market shares even though this would have been possible by varying the amount of the bond requirement based on the market shares and even though this would have even better ensured the equality of competitive conditions. Ming Du thus considers the denial of the causal relationship between the disputed measure and the detrimental impact in *Dominican Republic – Import and Sale of Cigarettes* (2005) as not entirely convincing.[554] Arguably, 'the Appellate Body recognized that to ensure absolute equality of treatment in all circumstances is too costly and that it would make the design and implementation of a *bona fide* regulation unnecessarily complicated'; the uniform bond requirement had only an incidental and unintended disparate impact on imported cigarettes.[555]

[3] Special Context (only) under the TBT Agreement

After the Appellate Body clarified that its decision in *Dominican Republic – Import and Sale of Cigarettes* (2005) was not meant to imply that 'less favourable treatment' under

550. *See*, to this effect, AB Report, *US – Tuna II (Mexico)*, 2012, para. 225; moreover, Crowley and Howse 2014, 328–329.
551. AB Report, *Dominican Republic – Import and Sale of Cigarettes*, 2005, para. 94.
552. *See also* Ehring 2014, 53, who observes that the flat-fee nature of the measure at issue inherently gave rise to the possibility of discrimination through equal treatment (of unequal situations); moreover, Davey and Maskus 2013, 178, who state that 'one can speculate that the Appellate Body would have upheld a Panel conclusion that the bond requirement modified the conditions of competition to the detriment of importers if the Panel had found that importers are typically smaller firms than domestic suppliers, and that, accordingly, a bond requirement would impose heavier costs on them on a per-item basis'.
553. *See also* AB Report, *EC – Seal Products*, 2014, para. 5.336, where the Appellate Body implied that if a disparate market impact could be attributed *entirely* to private choice, there would be no 'genuine relationship' between this disparate impact and the measure at issue; critically, Du 2016, 156, who observes that '[i]n reality, a disparate market impact can hardly be caused *entirely* by private choice and the measure at issue does not play any role in causing such an adverse impact' (original emphasis).
554. Du 2016, 157.
555. Du 2016, 157. *See also* Ortino 2008, 183–184, 186, who derives from *Dominican Republic – Import and Sale of Cigarettes* (2005) that an adverse impact has to be more than *de minimis*.

Article III:4 of the GATT is concerned with regulatory purposes,[556] it also decided that regulatory purposes may influence 'less favourable treatment' under the TBT Agreement. Such treatment cannot be established if a disproportionate burden on foreign products stems exclusively from legitimate regulatory distinctions. This raises the question of whether a similar approach should be followed under the non-discrimination provisions of the GATT and GATS.

Article 2 of the TBT Agreement establishes obligations on the preparation, adoption, and application of technical regulations by central government bodies. It contains a combined MFN and NT obligation in Article 2.1 and prescribes that technical regulations must not have the 'aim or effect' of creating unnecessary obstacles to international trade in Article 2.2 (*see also* section §2.03[D][6]):

> **Article 2**
>
> *Preparation, Adoption and Application of Technical Regulations by Central Government Bodies*
>
> With respect to their central government bodies:
>
> 2.1 Members shall ensure that in respect of technical regulations, products imported from the territory of any Member shall be accorded treatment no less favourable than that accorded to like products of national origin and to like products originating in any other country.
>
> 2.2 Members shall ensure that technical regulations are not prepared, adopted or applied with a view to or with the effect of creating unnecessary obstacles to international trade. For this purpose, technical regulations shall not be more trade-restrictive than necessary to fulfil a legitimate objective, taking account of the risks non-fulfilment would create. Such legitimate objectives are, *inter alia*: national security requirements; the prevention of deceptive practices; protection of human health or safety, animal or plant life or health, or the environment.

In contrast to Article 2.2 of the TBT Agreement, Article 2.1 does not incorporate an explicit justification test. It merely requires that 'treatment no less favourable' must be accorded to 'like products' of certain foreign origin. In addition, the TBT Agreement does not contain a general exceptions clause comparable to Article XX of the GATT. Thus, in *US – Clove Cigarettes* (2012), the issue arose whether regulatory purposes and legitimate policy objectives may be considered under Article 2.1 of the TBT Agreement at all and, if yes, whether they are part of the 'likeness' or 'less favourable treatment' analysis.

Initially, the Panel on *US – Clove Cigarettes* (2012)[557] regarded the regulatory context as being relevant for the 'likeness' analysis under Article 2.1 of the TBT Agreement.[558] On appeal, the Appellate Body rejected this 'likeness' test to the extent that the underlying regulatory concerns are not reflected in the products' competitive

556. AB Report, *US – Clove Cigarettes*, 2012, fn. 372 to para. 179.
557. Panel Report, *US – Clove Cigarettes*, 2012, especially at para. 7.119.
558. This approach has also been favoured by Mavroidis 2013, who submits that 'likeness' in the TBT context should be understood as policy likeness and not as market likeness; moreover, Mitchell and Voon 2011, 417; differently, Broude and Levy 2014, who find it impossible to ignore regulatory purpose in discrimination cases but also argue that, while there is not much economic difference in analysing regulatory purpose separately from more observable market

relationship.[559] Instead, it considered the regulatory context for the purposes of 'less favourable treatment'. According to this approach,[560] 'less favourable treatment' under Article 2.1 of the TBT Agreement exists only if the differentiating measure is not based exclusively on legitimate regulatory distinctions such as the protection of human life or health by reducing the attractiveness and palatability of cigarettes for young and potential smokers:[561]

> [T]he object and purpose of the *TBT Agreement* is to strike a balance between, on the one hand, the objective of trade liberalization and, on the other hand, Members' right to regulate. This object and purpose therefore suggests that Article 2.1 should not be interpreted as prohibiting any detrimental impact on competitive opportunities for imports in cases where such detrimental impact on imports stems exclusively from legitimate regulatory distinctions.
>
> Accordingly, the context and object and purpose of the *TBT Agreement* weigh in favour of reading the 'treatment no less favourable' requirement of Article 2.1 as prohibiting both *de jure* and *de facto* discrimination against imported products, while at the same time permitting detrimental impact on competitive opportunities for imports that stems exclusively from legitimate regulatory distinctions. ...
>
> In making this determination [whether a detrimental impact on imports stems exclusively from a legitimate regulatory distinction rather than reflecting discrimination against the group of imported products], a panel must carefully scrutinize the particular circumstances of the case, that is, the design, architecture, revealing structure, operation, and application of the technical regulation at issue, and, in particular, whether that technical regulation is even-handed, in order to determine whether it discriminates against the group of imported products.

---

considerations, this sequencing (competition-oriented analysis of 'likeness', consideration of regulatory purpose as a factor in 'less favourable treatment') does add political logic, analytical focus, and formal transparency.

559. AB Report, *US – Clove Cigarettes*, 2012, paras 112 et seq.

560. This approach has also been favoured by Flett 2014 (for Article XVII of the GATS); Flett 2013; Zhou 2012b, 1110–1122; Zhou 2012a, 106–112; (for Article III:4 of the GATT); and Zhou 2012a, 112–117 (for Article III:2, first sentence of the GATT if interpreted to cover de facto discrimination). *See*, moreover, Pauwelyn 2008, 362–367, who has suggested that a number of elements including evidence of protectionist or non-protectionist purposes should play a role in establishing de facto discrimination (less favourable treatment) under both the GATT and GATS.

561. *Ibid.*, at paras 174–175, 182. *See also* paras 169 et seq., 215; AB Report, *US – Tuna II (Mexico)*, 2012, paras 211 et seq.; AB Report, *US – COOL*, 2012, paras 268 et seq. (but critically with regard to the Appellate Body's analysis Colares and Canterberry 2017; Mitchell, Heaton, and Henckels 2016, 125–128; Mavroidis and Saggi 2014; Mavroidis 2013, 520–522); AB Report, *US – Tuna II (Mexico) (Article 21.5 – Mexico)*, 2015, paras 7.26, 7.30 et seq.; Flett 2014, 58–62, who submits that 'the aim and effects of the measure are relevant [under Article 2.1 of the TBT Agreement], not at the stage of the product analysis but rather at the stage of the less favourable treatment analysis'; Flett 2013, 60–63, 88 ('*a more elaborate aim and effects test*, not in the framework of a product or *like product* analysis, but rather in the framework of an analysis of *less favourable treatment*'; original emphasis); similarly, Cosbey and Mavroidis 2014, 296 ('obvious parallels with the now-rejected aims and effect test'); Zhou 2012b, 1100–1105, 1111 ('an assessment of both the *effect* and the *aim* of the measure'; original emphasis); moreover, Broude and Levy 2014; Appleton 2014, 107–117; Marceau 2013, 6–12; Norpoth 2013, 585–590; Voon 2012; McGrady 2012.

It should be noted that the analysis of whether the detrimental impact on imports stems exclusively from a legitimate regulatory distinction is only available when a technical regulation does not de jure discriminate against imports.[562] Apparently, it is presumed that a technical regulation cannot exclusively pursue a legitimate objective if it expressly refers to origin.[563] This contrasts with the general exceptions that are available under Article XX of the GATT that legitimize very similar regulatory purposes as those that are presumably legitimate under Article 2.1 of the TBT Agreement but without distinguishing between de jure and de facto discrimination.[564] Moreover, under what conditions a detrimental impact on competitive opportunities stems *exclusively* from legitimate regulatory distinctions and how to establish whether a technical regulation is *even-handed* based on its design, architecture, revealing structure, operation, and application are the subjects of considerable debate. Although the Appellate Body provided some guidance,[565] it is not exactly clear how to establish even-handedness and whether the exceptions of Article XX of the GATT together with the chapeau are fully integrated into the analysis of 'less favourable treatment' or what, if any, substantial differences remain.[566]

Article 2.1 of the TBT Agreement and Article III:4 of the GATT both refer to imported products which 'shall be accorded treatment no less favourable than that accorded to like products of national origin'. Accordingly, Article 2.1 of the TBT Agreement is very similarly worded to the NT obligation of Article III:4 of the GATT,

562. AB Report, *US – Clove Cigarettes*, 2012, para. 182; AB Report, *US – COOL*, 2012, para. 271; AB Report, *US – Tuna II (Mexico) (Article 21.5 – Mexico)*, 2015, para. 7.32.
563. *See also* Valinaki 2016, 71–72, who finds a possible explanation in the overall nature of the TBT Agreement and its role in promoting harmonization, mutual recognition, transparency, and recognition of equivalence; apart from the fact that origin is not a 'technical' feature, distinguishing products based upon their origin would seriously impair the attainment of these goals and hamper international trade and production efficiency.
564. *See*, for instance, Hudec 1998, 622. *See also* Alcover and Garcés 2016, 366–367, who criticize that, unlike under Article III:4 of the GATT, there seems to be a double legal standard of 'treatment no less favourably' under Article 2.1 of the TBT Agreement which might prove problematic because a de jure discriminatory technical regulation, in principle, would always be in violation of Article 2.1 of the TBT Agreement – with no possibility of justification – whereas a de jure violation of Article III:4 of the GATT could arguably be justified under Article XX of the GATT.
565. AB Report, *US – Tuna II (Mexico)*, 2012, paras 282 et seq.; AB Report, *US – COOL*, 2012, paras 340 et seq.; AB Report, *US – Tuna II (Mexico) (Article 21.5 – Mexico)*, 2015, paras 7.87 et seq. *See also* Zell 2016, 10–11; Hahn et al. 2016, 334–339.
566. *See* AB Report, *EC – Seal Products*, 2014, paras 5.127–5.128, where the Appellate Body stated with reference to AB Report, *US – Clove Cigarettes*, 2012, para. 96 that, under the TBT Agreement, the balance between the desire to avoid creating unnecessary obstacles to international trade and the recognition of Members' right to regulate is not, in principle, different from the balance set out in the GATT 1994 and dismissed concerns about divergent outcomes because the European Union had not pointed to any concrete examples of a legitimate objective that could factor into an analysis under Article 2.1 of the TBT Agreement (open list of objectives) but would not fall within the scope of Article XX of the GATT 1994 (closed list of objectives). *See*, critically, Mitchell, Heaton, and Henckels 2016, 132–134. *See also*, however, AB Report, *EC – Seal Products*, 2014, paras. 5.310–5.312, where the Appellate Body stressed that while 'there are important parallels', 'there are [also] significant differences between the analyses under Article 2.1 of the TBT Agreement and the chapeau of Article XX of the GATT 1994'. *See*, not least, Valinaki 2016, 73–86; Houston-McMillan 2016, 553–559; Zell 2016, 10–14; Alcover and Garcés 2016, 367; Levy and Regan 2015, 365–370.

their scopes of application in respect of technical regulations overlap,[567] and both require 'treatment no less favourable'. Moreover, the sixth recital of the preamble to the TBT Agreement mentions similar regulatory purposes to those stated in the general exceptions clause of Article XX of the GATT. Both recognize the protection of human, animal, or plant life or health and the prevention of deceptive practice as legitimate objectives but subject measures that implement these regulatory purposes to the requirement that they 'are not applied in a manner which would constitute a means of arbitrary or unjustifiable discrimination between countries where the same conditions prevail[,] or a disguised restriction on international trade'.[568]

Despite these similarities, the Appellate Body rejected, in *EC – Seal Products* (2014),[569] an equal legal standard for the non-discrimination obligations under Article III:4 of the GATT and Article 2.1 of the TBT Agreement on the basis of contextual and systematic considerations.[570] Thus, not only the accordion of 'likeness' but also the accordion of 'less favourable treatment' stretches and squeezes in different places as different provisions are applied:[571]

> [T]he TBT Agreement does not contain a general exceptions clause similar to Article XX of the GATT 1994. This does not mean, however, that Members do not have a right to regulate under the TBT Agreement. Instead, the sixth recital of the preamble of the TBT Agreement suggests that a Member's right to regulate should not be constrained if the measures taken are necessary to fulfil certain legitimate policy objectives, and provided that they are not applied in a manner that would constitute a means of arbitrary or unjustifiable discrimination or a disguised restriction on international trade, and are otherwise in accordance with the provisions of the Agreement. ... [I]t is the specific context of Article 2.1 of the TBT Agreement ... that supports a reading that Article 2.1 does not operate to prohibit *a priori* any restriction on international trade [in cases where the detrimental impact stems exclusively from legitimate regulatory distinctions].

567. *See* AB Report, *US – Clove Cigarettes*, 2012, para. 91; Du 2016, 149; Du 2015, 89.
568. Sixth recital of the preamble to the TBT Agreement.
569. AB Report, *EC – Seal Products*, 2014, paras 5.97 et seq. *See also* paras 5.78 et seq.; Du 2016, 148–155; Du 2015, 88–92; Connolly 2015, 77–82; Flores Elizondo 2014, 317–318. A different result has been suggested by Flett 2013; Zhou 2012b, 1110–1122; Zhou 2012a, 106–112; and not excluded by Neven and Trachtman 2013, 313, 325 ('[t]here appears to be room ... in "less favourable treatment" under Article III:4, to include the question of nonprotectionist regulatory rationales for differential treatment') whereas Nielsen and Calle 2013, 56 have stated that '[i]t is ... a very logical conclusion to draw that given the existence of Article XX in the GATT, there is no basis to import the concepts of "legitimate regulatory distinction" and "evenhandedness" into Articles I or III'. *See*, moreover, Mitchell, Heaton, and Henckels 2016, 131–135, who nevertheless suggest including a 'stems exclusively from a legitimate regulatory distinction' analysis for the purposes of determining 'less favourable treatment' under Article III:4 of the GATT (and, for that matter, under Articles I:1 and III:2) if a measure does not fall within the scope of any of the paragraphs of Article XX of the GATT.
570. *See also*, however, AB Report, *EC – Seal Products*, 2014, paras 5.115–5.117, where the Appellate Body considered that, 'just as the omission of a textual reference to Article III:1, in Article III:2, first sentence, must be given meaning, so too must the absence of a reference to Article III:1 in Article III:4' and that 'for the purposes of an analysis under Article III:4, a panel is [therefore not] required to examine whether the detrimental impact of a measure on competitive opportunities for like imported products stems exclusively from a legitimate regulatory distinction'.
571. AB Report, *EC – Seal Products*, 2014, paras 5.124–5.125 (footnotes omitted).

> By contrast, ... the obligations assumed by Members to respect the non-discrimination disciplines under Articles I:1 and III:4 of the GATT 1994 are balanced by a Member's right to regulate in a manner consistent with the requirements of the separate general exceptions clause of Article XX and its chapeau. In our view, the fact that, under the GATT 1994, a Member's right to regulate is accommodated under Article XX, weighs heavily against an interpretation of Articles I:1 and III:4 that requires an examination of whether the detrimental impact of a measure on competitive opportunities for like imported products stems exclusively from a legitimate regulatory distinction.

While certain regulatory purposes justify discriminatory treatment based on a closed list of general exceptions under the GATT, they influence, as part of the context, the existence of 'less favourable treatment' under the TBT Agreement. As a result, very similar considerations are relevant in analysing whether illegitimate and unjustifiable discrimination exists although the regulatory purposes are resorted to and the different underlying aims are balanced at different stages of analysis (*see also* Figure 2.4).

Figure 2.4 GATT and TBT Agreement: Market-Based and Policy-Based Tests

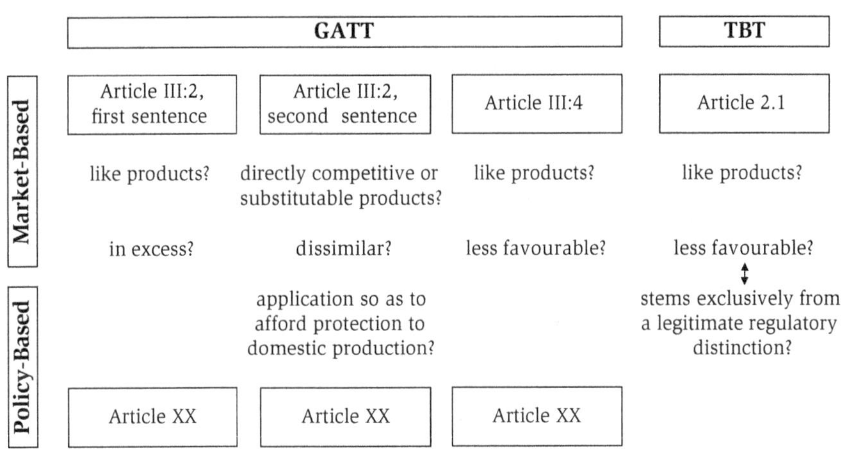

[4] *Rejection Also for Purposes of the GATS*

In *Argentina – Financial Services* (2016),[572] the Appellate Body held that the 'less favourable treatment' standard under both the MFN and NT provisions of the GATS is focused on a measure's modification of the conditions of competition and does not contemplate a separate and additional enquiry into regulatory objectives.[573] Neither the fact that the MFN and NT provisions of the GATS have a potentially broad scope of application (this is not unique to the GATS)[574] nor the fact that these provisions also

572. *See also* Muller 2017, 162–166; Mitchell, Heaton, and Henckels 2016, 119–120; Dziurdź 2016, 205.
573. AB Report, *Argentina – Financial Services*, 2016, para. 6.106.
574. *Ibid.*, para. 6.109.

refer to 'service suppliers' indicates a different legal standard of 'treatment no less favourable'.[575] Under the structure of the GATS, Members can rather utilize certain flexibilities that are available to them uniquely under the GATS when undertaking their GATS commitments, and their obligations are qualified by exceptions or other derogations (*see* especially Article XX of the GATS on schedules of specific market access commitments and NT obligations).[576] Furthermore, the GATS sets out general exceptions and security exceptions from obligations under that Agreement in the same manner as does the GATT.[577] The Appellate Body held that, through these flexibilities and exceptions, the GATS seeks to strike a balance between a Member's obligations assumed under the Agreement and that Member's right to pursue national policy objectives.[578] This balance also reinforces the established legal standard for 'treatment no less favourable' under the non-discrimination provisions of the GATS.[579] 'Where a measure is inconsistent with the non-discrimination provisions, regulatory aspects or concerns that could potentially justify such a measure are more appropriately addressed in the context of the relevant exceptions. Addressing them in the context of the non-discrimination provisions would upset the existing balance under the GATS.'[580]

Also, the Appellate Body did not endorse concerns regarding the limited scope of the general exceptions contained in Article XIV of the GATS (*see* section §2.05[A]) or that the non-discrimination provisions of the GATS could unduly restrict national policy objectives.[581] As long as Members comply with their GATS obligations and commitments, they are free to pursue national policy objectives that they consider appropriate.[582] Members, on a daily basis, regulate services sectors and pursue a wide range of national policy objectives without violating their obligations under the GATS.[583] Therefore, an interpretation of the term 'treatment no less favourable' that is based on a measure's detrimental impact on the conditions of competition does *not* prevent a Member from pursuing a wide range of national policy objectives beyond those identified in the exceptions.[584]

The Appellate Body noted that its interpretation of the non-discrimination obligations of the GATS chimes with that of the MFN and NT obligations in the context of the GATT.[585] Although the Appellate Body had adopted a different approach to the relevance of regulatory concerns in determining 'treatment no less favourable' under Article 2.1 of the TBT Agreement,[586] this approach cannot be transposed to the

575. *Ibid.*, para. 6.111.
576. *Ibid.*, para. 6.112.
577. *Ibid.*, para. 6.113.
578. *Ibid.*, para. 6.114.
579. *Ibid.*, para. 6.115.
580. *Ibid.*, para. 6.115.
581. *See* third and fourth recitals of the preamble to the GATS which states that the WTO Members desire 'giving due respect to national policy objectives' and recognize 'the right of Members to regulate, and to introduce new regulations, on the supply of services within their territories in order to meet national policy objectives'.
582. AB Report, *Argentina – Financial Services*, 2016, para. 6.117.
583. *Ibid.*, para. 6.117.
584. *Ibid.*, para. 6.118.
585. *Ibid.*, para. 6.119.
586. *Ibid.*, para. 6.120.

non-discrimination provisions of the GATS.[587] While the TBT Agreement does not contain a general exceptions clause, the GATS provides not only various exceptions but also flexibilities unique to the GATS that establish a balance between a Member's non-discrimination obligations and that Member's right to regulate.[588] Neither the text and context of the MFN and NT provisions of the GATS nor the object and purpose of the GATS provide a basis for a legal standard whereby certain regulatory aspects can convert 'less favourable treatment' into 'treatment no less favourable'.[589] However, this does not suggest that any evidence relating to the regulatory aspects, notably the regulatory aspects of having access to tax information, must a priori be excluded.[590] To the extent that such evidence has a bearing on the conditions of competition, it might be taken into account to determine whether the measure at issue modifies the conditions of competition.[591]

In *Argentina – Financial Services* (2016), the Appellate Body criticized the Panel's view that a measure that neutralizes an unintended competitive advantage is not inconsistent with the NT obligation of the GATS. The Panel held that Argentina's defensive measures, rather than giving Argentine services and service suppliers an advantage, neutralized an 'unintended competitive advantage' enjoyed by non-cooperative jurisdictions owing to the lack of exchange of tax information with Argentina on their suppliers.[592] According to the Appellate Body, however, 'ensuring equal competitive conditions, which is required by the legal standard of "treatment no less favourable", is *not* the same as guaranteeing that one group of services or products does not have any competitive advantage over another group'.[593] It means to guarantee equality of *opportunities* to compete in the marketplace rather than to guarantee that all like services and service suppliers are equally *competitive*.[594] Article XVII of the GATS provides no basis for permitting discriminatory measures to neutralize a competitive advantage that results from the regulatory framework in the country of origin of certain foreign service suppliers.[595]

§2.05 GENERAL EXCEPTIONS CLAUSES (JUSTIFICATIONS)

[A] Closed and Perhaps Too Limited List of Exceptions

If a measure violates an MFN or NT rule, it might still be possible for a Member to maintain it. Under the GATT and GATS, there are a number of exceptions that allow

587. A different result has been suggested by Flett 2014.
588. *Ibid.*, para. 6.121.
589. *Ibid.*, para. 6.126.
590. *Ibid.*, para. 6.127.
591. *Ibid.*, para. 6.127.
592. Panel Report, *Argentina – Financial Services*, 2016, para. 7.515. *See also*, similarly, Cottier, Delimatsis, and Diebold 2008 m.no. 46.
593. AB Report, *Argentina – Financial Services*, 2016, para. 6.144 (original emphasis).
594. *Ibid.*, para. 6.144.
595. *Ibid.*, para. 6.145.

justifying WTO-inconsistent measures. In particular, Article XX of the GATT contains a closed list of general exceptions:[596]

> **Article XX**
>
> *General Exceptions*
>
> Subject to the requirement that such measures are not applied in a manner which would constitute a means of arbitrary or unjustifiable discrimination between countries where the same conditions prevail, or a disguised restriction on international trade, nothing in this Agreement shall be construed to prevent the adoption or enforcement by any [Member] of measures:
>
> (a) necessary to protect public morals;
> (b) necessary to protect human, animal or plant life or health;
> (c) relating to the importations or exportations of gold or silver;
> (d) necessary to secure compliance with laws or regulations which are not inconsistent with the provisions of this Agreement, including those relating to customs enforcement, the enforcement of [State] monopolies ..., the protection of patents, trade marks and copyrights, and the prevention of deceptive practices;
> (e) relating to the products of prison labour;
> (f) imposed for the protection of national treasures of artistic, historic or archaeological value;
> (g) relating to the conservation of exhaustible natural resources if such measures are made effective in conjunction with restrictions on domestic production or consumption;
> (h) undertaken in pursuance of obligations under any intergovernmental commodity agreement ...,
> (i) involving restrictions on exports of domestic materials necessary to ensure essential quantities of such materials to a domestic processing industry ...,
> (j) essential to the acquisition or distribution of products in general or local short supply ....

This general exceptions clause requires a two-tier test for determining whether a restriction on trade is justified.[597] First, it must be determined whether a regulatory purpose of a Member's measure falls under at least one of the exceptions listed under Article XX of the GATT. For that purpose, a certain nexus between the pursued regulatory purpose and the policy objective permitted by Article XX must be established (for instance, the measure at issue must be *necessary* to protect public morals). Thereafter, the introductory sentence of Article XX, commonly referred to as the chapeau, sets forth requirements for the application of the provisionally justified measure. The first step is to analyse the measure itself and whether it pursues a legitimate aim as stipulated by Article XX. The second step is to analyse the application of the – in principle – legitimate measure that cannot constitute a means of arbitrary or

596. For a comparison with Article 36 of the TFEU, *see* Gaines and Olsen 2012.

597. *See*, for example, AB Report, *US – Gasoline*, 1996, p. 22; AB Report, *US – Shrimp*, 1998, paras 118 and 147; AB Report, *US – Gambling*, 2005, para. 292; AB Report, *Dominican Republic – Import and Sale of Cigarettes*, 2005, para. 64; AB Report, *Brazil – Retreaded Tyres*, 2007, para. 139; AB Report, *EC – Seal Products*, 2014, para. 5.169.

unjustifiable discrimination between Members where the same conditions prevail or a disguised restriction on international trade.

Due to the similar structure, these steps of analysis are also essential when evaluating the closed list of general exceptions under Article XIV of the GATS:[598]

Article XIV

General Exceptions

Subject to the requirement that such measures are not applied in a manner which would constitute a means of arbitrary or unjustifiable discrimination between countries where like conditions prevail, or a disguised restriction on trade in services, nothing in this Agreement shall be construed to prevent the adoption or enforcement by any Member of measures:

(a) necessary to protect public morals or to maintain public order;[5]
(b) necessary to protect human, animal or plant life or health;
(c) necessary to secure compliance with laws or regulations which are not inconsistent with the provisions of this Agreement including those relating to:
  (i) the prevention of deceptive and fraudulent practices or to deal with the effects of a default on services contracts;
  (ii) the protection of the privacy of individuals in relation to the processing and dissemination of personal data and the protection of confidentiality of individual records and accounts;
  (iii) safety;
(d) inconsistent with Article XVII [NT], provided that the difference in treatment is aimed at ensuring the equitable or effective[6] imposition or collection of direct taxes in respect of services or service suppliers of other Members;
(e) inconsistent with Article II [MFN], provided that the difference in treatment is the result of an agreement on the avoidance of double taxation or provisions on the avoidance of double taxation in any other international agreement or arrangement by which the Member is bound.

5 The public order exception may be invoked only where a genuine and sufficiently serious threat is posed to one of the fundamental interests of society.

6 Measures that are aimed at ensuring the equitable or effective imposition or collection of direct taxes include measures taken by a Member under its taxation system which:

(i) apply to non-resident service suppliers in recognition of the fact that the tax obligation of non-residents is determined with respect to taxable items sourced or located in the Member's territory; or
(ii) apply to non-residents in order to ensure the imposition or collection of taxes in the Member's territory; or

598. *See* AB Report, *US – Gambling*, 2005, paras 291–292, where the Appellate Body concluded that, due to the fact that both Article XX of the GATT and Article XIV of the GATS set out general exceptions from substantive obligations and use similar language (notably the term 'necessary' and the requirements set out in their respective chapeau), the previous decisions under Article XX of the GATT are also relevant under Article XIV of the GATS. Accordingly, Article XIV of the GATS contemplates a two-tier analysis which requires first to determine whether the challenged measure falls within the scope of a general exception by addressing a particular interest as well as by entailing a sufficient nexus or 'degree of connection' to that interest and, second, to consider the requirements of the chapeau.

(iii) apply to non-residents or residents in order to prevent the avoidance or evasion of taxes, including compliance measures; or
(iv) apply to consumers of services supplied in or from the territory of another Member in order to ensure the imposition or collection of taxes on such consumers derived from sources in the Member's territory; or
(v) distinguish service suppliers subject to tax on worldwide taxable items from other service suppliers, in recognition of the difference in the nature of the tax base between them; or
(vi) determine, allocate or apportion income, profit, gain, loss, deduction or credit of resident persons or branches, or between related persons or branches of the same person, in order to safeguard the Member's tax base.

Tax terms or concepts in paragraph (d) of Article XIV and in this footnote are determined according to tax definitions and concepts, or equivalent or similar definitions and concepts, under the domestic law of the Member taking the measure.

Article XIV of the GATS resembles certain exceptions that can be found in Article XX of the GATT. It covers measures necessary to protect human, animal, or plant life or health[599] as well as measures necessary to secure compliance with laws or regulations that are not inconsistent with the provisions of the GATS (although it gives different examples).[600] It further mentions measures that are necessary to protect public morals and supplements this exception with measures necessary to maintain public order.[601] However, it also lacks some exceptions that are more closely related to trade in goods.[602] Furthermore, Article XIV of the GATS adds specific exceptions related to direct taxes[603] because the general MFN and NT rules of the GATS protect not only services but also service suppliers.[604]

Various policy objectives might not have been anticipated when the agreements were drafted. In fact, the policy justifications under the general exceptions clause of Article XX of the GATT 'are quite limited, reserved to what might be called the most compelling sort of regulatory interests'.[605] It is further believed that the general

599. Article XIV(b) of the GATS; compare with Article XX(b) of the GATT.
600. Article XIV(c) of the GATS; compare with Article XX(d) of the GATT.
601. Article XIV(a) of the GATS; compare with Article XX(a) of the GATT.
602. Article XX(c) and (e) to (j) of the GATT.
603. Article XXVIII(o) of the GATS defines '[f]or the purpose of this Agreement' the term 'direct taxes' as 'all taxes on total income, on total capital or on elements of income or of capital, including taxes on gains from the alienation of property, taxes on estates, inheritances and gifts, and taxes on the total amounts of wages or salaries paid by enterprises, as well as taxes on capital appreciation'.
604. Article XIV(d) and (e) of the GATS.
605. Hudec 1998, 622. *See also* Roessler 2003, 777, who emphasizes that, from the exhaustive list of policy purposes in Article XX, only three objectives are relevant in practice for internal measures inconsistent with Article III of the GATT: the protection of public morals; the protection of human, animal, or plant life or health; and the conservation of natural resources; moreover, Du 2016, 152 ('[i]t is questionable whether this closed list [of Article XX] written 60 years ago is adequate to rescue various legitimate government regulations in the twenty-first century'); Du 2015, 72; Du 2011, 665; Porges and Trachtman 2003, 786, 797; Roessler 2000, 129; Tsai 1999, 54; Mattoo and Subramanian 1998, 307–308, 313–314; Roessler 1996, 30; differently, Weiler 2009, 767; H. Horn and Weiler 2004, 142–143; Horn and Weiler 2003, 29 ('Article XX GATT is broad and sufficiently open-textured to cater for most exigencies').

exceptions clause of Article XIV of the GATS has a narrow scope as 'the list of policy purposes that justify derogation to trade liberalization is exhaustive and does not reflect the reality of the regulation in the service sector'.[606] This perceived limitation is one reason why so much emphasis is put on 'likeness' and 'less favourable treatment'. Without discrimination, there is no need to take recourse to explicit and arguably too limited justifications. While it is not possible to deal with all regulatory purposes that might be important to a WTO Member in this study, some examples and potential solutions regarding environmental concerns, redistributive taxes, and rules countering low or no taxation will illustrate why the general exceptions clauses are sometimes regarded as being insufficient.

The aim of protecting and preserving the environment is recognized under the WTO Agreement as a goal of national and international policy.[607] Yet, environmental protection, as such, is not a general exception under the GATT and GATS. Any environmental interests of a WTO Member must be within the scope of other exceptions in order to justify measures that violate substantive WTO obligations. For this purpose, the exceptions concerning human, animal, or plant life or health under Article XX(b) of the GATT and Article XIV(b) of the GATS as well as those relating to the conservation of exhaustible natural resources under Article XX(g) of the GATT play a major role.[608] According to WTO jurisprudence, these general exceptions have a potentially wide scope. For instance, clean air (although a rather abstract and relative notion)[609] as well as sea turtles (which are capable of reproduction and, in that sense, 'renewable')[610] constitute natural resources that may be facing the danger of exhaustion. The term 'natural resources' is not 'static' in its content or reference but rather 'by definition, evolutionary'.[611] Also, public moral concerns such as moral concerns regarding seal welfare can be relevant under Article XX(a) of the GATT and Article XIV(a) of the GATS.[612]

It had been argued that unilateral trade measures that address environmental challenges arising from conduct outside of a Member's territory would not be eligible for an exception because of their extra-jurisdictional application.[613] This very controversial view was overturned in *US – Shrimp* (1998) in which the Appellate Body held

606. Muller 2017, 156; similarly, Muller 2016, 841.
607. First recital of the preamble to the WTO Agreement.
608. *See also* Charnovitz 1991, who reviews the history of Article XX of the GATT and concludes that the general exceptions clause was designed to encompass environmental measures; just about everything except perhaps the preservation of scenic vistas 'relates squarely either to the life or health of living organisms or to the conservation of truly exhaustible resources like clean air, fossil fuels, and stratospheric ozone' (p. 55).
609. Panel Report, *US – Gasoline*, 1996, para. 6.37 (this aspect was not appealed; *see* AB Report, *US – Gasoline*, 1996, pp. 11–12).
610. AB Report, *US – Shrimp*, 1998, paras 127–134.
611. *Ibid.*, para. 130. *See also* Howse 2002, 502–503; Mavroidis 2000b, 85–86; Bree 1998, 106–109.
612. AB Report, *EC – Seal Products*, 2014, paras 5.194 et seq. *See also*, for instance, Serpin 2016; Howse, Langille, and Sykes 2015; for a preceding analysis of Article XX(a) of the GATT, moreover, Charnovitz 1998.
613. GATT Panel Report, *US – Tuna I (Mexico)*, 1991, unadopted, paras 5.22 et seq. *See also* Roessler 2000, 131–135; Roessler 1996, 32–35; Hudec 1996, 117–199; in favour of a territorial limitation, for instance, McDorman 1991, 520–523; critically, Howse and Regan 2000, 272–279; Charnovitz 1994, 339–341; McDonald 1993, 430–433, 442–443.

that 'conditioning access to a Member's domestic market on whether exporting Members comply with, or adopt, a policy or policies unilaterally prescribed by the importing Member may, to some degree, be a common aspect of measures falling within the scope of one or another of the exceptions (a) to (j) of Article XX'.[614] It is thus possible to justify measures that address global environmental concerns even on a unilateral basis although some doubts exist with regard to 'non-living resources' under the GATS. Since the GATS does not contain an exception similar to Article XX(g) of the GATT, it is not precisely clear whether Article XIV(b) of the GATS can be interpreted extensively to cover conservation of all 'non-living resources' as protection of human, animal, or plant life or health.[615] When a measure that aims at protecting and preserving the environment falls under a general exception of the GATT or GATS, it is still subject to additional requirements ('necessary' or 'relating to', chapeau) in order to be justified. By this, a balance between trade and non-trade objectives is pursued.

While the general exceptions of the GATT and GATS generally offer a defence for trade-restrictive but environmental-friendly measures, this does not mean that an exception is available for every supposedly legitimate regulatory purpose. If a Member introduces a tax on automobiles above USD 30,000, such as in *US – Auto Taxes* (1994), if automobiles below and above USD 30,000 are, in principle, 'like products', and if the tax on automobiles hits imports more than domestic production, arguably, the first sentence of Article III:2 of the GATT 1994 is violated. Therefore, it would be necessary to justify this type of discrimination, or otherwise, the tax would illegitimately violate substantive WTO obligations. A luxury tax may pursue the aim of taxing those consumers on a progressive basis who can afford the most expensive automobiles. It is at least questionable whether such a social policy objective would be covered by Article XX of the GATT.[616] As far as can be seen, Article XX(a) of the GATT could be the only relevant justification. It concerns measures that are necessary to protect public morals. A very liberal interpretation of 'public morals' would be required to cover a redistribution policy that is achieved by a progressive tax on specific high-value goods.[617]

Article XIV(d) and (e) of the GATS largely excludes direct taxes from the scope of the MFN and NT rules.[618] However, these exceptions might not encompass all

614. AB Report, *US – Shrimp*, 1998, para. 121. *See*, moreover, Cosbey and Mavroidis 2014, 292, 294–295; Howse 2012, 445–447; Howse and Neven 2003, 53–54, 64–65; Howse 2002, 500–501; Mavroidis 2000b, 74–76; Chang 2000, 34–39; Bree 1998, 110–112; but also Jackson 2000a, 306, who observes that this is a very nuanced sentence (note the word 'may') that leaves open whether a unilateral measure can be justified under Article XX of the GATT. In *US – Shrimp (Article 21.5 – Malaysia)* (2001), however, the Appellate Body stated that '[t]his statement expresses a principle that was central to our ruling in *United States – Shrimp*' (para. 138). Yet, this does not necessarily mean that there need not be a nexus between the environmental challenge and the Member imposing the measure. *See*, in detail, Young 2014; moreover, Horn and Mavroidis 2008.

615. *See*, for instance, Cottier, Delimatsis, and Diebold 2008 m.nos. 34–36.

616. *See also* Ehring 2002, 955, who states that, in the realm of 'socio-economic policies in general (e.g. luxury tax), Article XX is not available'; moreover, Conconi and Voon 2016, 223; Roessler 2000, 129; Mattoo and Subramanian 1998, 308; Roessler 1996, 30.

617. *See also* H. Horn and Mavroidis 2004 fn. 43 on p. 55.

618. But *see* Beyer 2018, 369–372, who proposes a restrictive interpretation of Article XIV(e) under which only those provisions of a tax treaty directly related to the avoidance of double taxation are covered by Article XIV(e), whereas measures that, in fact, grant an unrelated advantage are

measures against harmful tax competition and Base Erosion and Profit Shifting (BEPS).[619] This is especially true for targeted interest limitation rules that limit deductions of arm's-length interest when the income is subject to no or low taxation, particularly in the event that the recipient is a resident of a tax haven, is subject to a low statutory tax rate, or receives a favourable tax exemption or reduction.[620] From the perspective of the MFN and NT obligations under the GATT and GATS, targeted interest limitation rules could raise concerns[621] and, therefore, call for a justification defence.

Article XIV(c) of the GATS justifies 'measures ... necessary to secure compliance with laws or regulations which are not inconsistent with the provisions of this Agreement including those relating to ... the prevention of deceptive and fraudulent practices'. When laws or regulations provide for tax liability without being inconsistent with the provisions of the GATS, defensive measures may be taken to secure compliance with these laws or regulations and thereby secure the collection of tax. However, if measures against low-tax jurisdictions are taken despite the fact that these jurisdictions cooperate in tax matters (tax transparency, exchange of information, etc.) and thus all taxes legally due in a country can be secured and collected from both residents and non-residents, a justification under Article XIV(c) of the GATS becomes doubtful. A compensatory measure for another Member's sovereign decision to establish a favourable tax regime appears not to be covered by this general exception even if some service suppliers might relocate their business to take advantage of such benefits.

Article XIV(d) of the GATS requires that measures inconsistent with Article XVII on NT must be 'aimed at ensuring the equitable or effective imposition or collection of direct taxes in respect of services or service suppliers of other Members' in order to be justified. Although various examples of measures that are aimed at ensuring the equitable or effective imposition or collection of direct taxes are given in the GATS,[622] they predominantly deal with measures taken by a Member that distinguish between service suppliers in recognition of the fact that non-residents are taxed on a territorial basis and residents on a worldwide basis,[623] apply to non-resident service suppliers in order to ensure the imposition or collection of taxes in the Member's territory[624] or safeguard the Member's tax base, for instance, by applying the arm's-length principle in attributing income to permanent establishments (PEs) or related persons.[625] Moreover, they include measures that apply to consumers of services supplied in or from the territory of another Member in order to ensure the imposition on or collection of taxes

out of scope; the mere fact that an agreement carries the words 'avoidance of double taxation' in its title is insufficient for the application of Article XIV(e).

619. *See* in this context, OECD, Final Report on BEPS Action 5.

620. *See*, in detail, Dziurdź 2016, sec. 6.3.2.

621. *See* Thiel 2005, 22, 40–42, 45–47, who reports concerns regarding domestic anti-avoidance legislation aimed specifically at tax havens and low-tax jurisdictions. *See also* Hofbauer 2004b; Gross 2003; Orava 2002; Grynberg and Chilala 2001 (also published in Grynberg and Chilala 2002); Scott 2001. *See*, moreover, Dziurdź 2016, sec. 6.3.

622. *See* footnote 6 to Article XIV(d) of the GATS.

623. *Ibid.*, items (i) and (v).

624. *Ibid.*, item (ii).

625. *Ibid.*, item (vi).

from such consumers derived from sources in the Member's territory.[626] These examples of measures justified under Article XIV(d) of the GATS thus relate to the principles of worldwide and territorial taxation, to the right of a Member to protect its tax base, and to the various implications of these fundamental tax principles. They do not appear to concern harmful tax competition or measures that compensate for another Member's decision to tax income with a low tax rate or to not tax at all.

Article XIV(d) of the GATS also includes an example of measures applying to non-residents or residents in order to prevent the avoidance or evasion of taxes including compliance measures.[627] This purpose, however, might not be appropriate for justifying non-deductibility rules countering low-tax regimes. Even though the fact that another Member is a tax haven or provides for a low level of taxation may be exploited by taxpayers for avoidance or evasion purposes, a service supplier that is established in such a country need not necessarily be involved in exploitation practices. In particular, if a Member decides to grant a competitive advantage to its service suppliers in the form of tax incentives or a reduced tax rate, this does not call into question that its service suppliers may be well established, follow a business purpose, and possess economic substance. A low level of taxation in a particular country may trigger or contribute to but cannot be equated with avoidance or evasion practices. Non-deductibility measures that apply to low-taxed payments and counter low-tax regimes, therefore, might not be sufficiently aimed at ensuring an equitable or effective imposition or collection of direct taxes under Article XIV(d) of the GATS, especially if they primarily aim at preventing low taxation, as such, and not only or primarily low taxation in cases of tax avoidance or evasion.[628]

While a Member may rely on Article XIV(c) of the GATS in order to secure compliance with its GATS-consistent laws or regulations or on Article XIV(d) of the GATS in order to ensure the equitable or effective imposition or collection of direct taxes, it might be difficult to justify measures that broadly penalize service suppliers from tax havens or low-tax jurisdictions regardless of whether an exchange of tax information is possible. Such measures would not appear to merely secure a Member's own tax base or to be targeted against tax avoidance or evasion schemes but rather aim to discourage or to compensate for the use of certain other tax jurisdictions. An unjustified violation of substantive WTO obligations might be an intended result under the GATS. However, when Members are concerned with harmful tax competition and BEPS just as with climate change or extinction of sea turtles, they will try to rescue their measures, notably, by arguing that low-taxed services and service suppliers are not

626. *Ibid.*, item (iv).
627. *Ibid.*, item (iii).
628. On the concepts of 'tax evasion' and 'tax avoidance', *see* Panel Report, *China – Auto Parts*, 2009, para. 7.335. *See also* footnote 6 to Article XIV(d) of the GATS, which states that '[t]ax terms or concepts in paragraph (d) of Article XIV and in this footnote are determined according to tax definitions and concepts, or equivalent or similar definitions and concepts, under the domestic law of the Member taking the measure'.

'like' high-taxed services and service suppliers[629] or that different treatment does not lead to 'less favourable treatment'.[630]

Article XX of the GATT as well as Article XIV of the GATS essentially comprise measures that are recognized as exceptions to substantive WTO obligations because the domestic policies embodied in such measures have been recognized as important and legitimate in character.[631] This also implies that a Member may unilaterally decide whether it wants to pursue these policies. If it does so, other Members can either comply with these policies as well or must face trade restrictions which, as such, would be contrary to substantive WTO obligations. Yet, there is a danger that Members could use and misuse these legitimate policies for trade-protectionist purposes. Therefore, the WTO provisions set out certain requirements that must be fulfilled in order to justify a violation of WTO obligations. In particular, there must be a certain nexus between a Member's measure and a legitimate policy objective, and a measure cannot be applied in a certain discriminatory or restrictive way.

[B] Nexus Requirements Involving a Holistic Process

Article XX of the GATT uses different terms for the required nexus between a Member's measure and a legitimate policy objective: 'necessary' - in paragraphs (a), (b), and (d); 'essential' - in paragraph (j); 'relating to' - in paragraphs (c), (e), and (g); 'for the protection of' - in paragraph (f); 'in pursuance of' - in paragraph (h); and 'involving' - in paragraph (i). Consequently, the Appellate Body concluded in *US – Gasoline* (1996) that '[i]t does not seem reasonable to suppose that the WTO Members intended to require, in respect of each and every category, the same kind or degree of connection or relationship'.[632] Article XIV(a) to (c) of the GATS, by contrast, relies on the term 'necessary' for the purposes of all the general exceptions. Only the somewhat more specific exceptions from MFN and NT obligations for direct taxes employ different terms: 'aimed at' - in paragraph (d); and 'the result of' - in paragraph (e).

A societal objective that is often relied on is the protection of human, animal, or plant life or health under Article XX(b) of the GATT and Article XIV(b) of the GATS. In order to be provisionally justified, a measure must be 'necessary' to fulfil this policy objective. It is not clear, however, why a generally WTO-inconsistent measure must be 'necessary' to protect human, animal, or plant life or health, whereas, under Article XX(g) of the GATT, it must only be 'relating to' the conservation of exhaustible natural resources.[633] This raises the question of whether measures that are designed to protect

629. *See*, in detail, Dziurdź 2016, sec. 6.3.3.
630. *See*, in detail, Dziurdź 2016, sec. 6.3.4.
631. AB Report, *US – Shrimp*, 1998, para. 121.
632. AB Report, *US – Gasoline*, 1996, pp. 17–18.
633. *See also* Vranes 2009, 282 ('relating to ... appears to establish a lower threshold of justification ... than ... necessary'); Kapterian 2010, 105; Schoenbaum 1997, 276.

human life or health are subjected to stricter scrutiny than measures that aim at the conservation of exhaustible natural resources.[634]

Korea – Various Measures on Beef (2001) introduced the current approach to the interpretation and application of the 'necessity' requirement.[635] Before that, the term 'necessary' was generally understood as requiring domestic regulation to be the least trade-restrictive method of achieving the desired goal without weighing and balancing various characteristics of the chosen measure.[636] This basically meant that the measure had to be indispensable to be 'necessary',[637] which often represented an insurmountable hurdle for justifying discrimination. Robert Howse remarks that '[i]t was possible to defeat a defence under Article XX just by dreaming up a theoretical less trade restrictive alternative policy that could serve the GATT member state's objective, regardless of its costs, its feasibility and the degree of certainty or uncertainty as to whether, in real world conditions, the policy would actually attain the GATT member state's objective'.[638]

Starting from *Korea – Various Measures on Beef* (2001), a more sophisticated and fine-tuned test has been developed that arguably strikes a better balance between trade liberalization and national regulatory autonomy.[639] A necessity analysis involves a holistic process of 'weighing and balancing' a series of factors including the importance of the objective furthered by the challenged measure, the contribution of the measure to that objective and the trade restrictiveness of the measure, and then a comparison between the challenged measure and possible alternatives with all of this being done while taking into account the interests or values at stake.[640] With this holistic approach, which was later applied by the Appellate Body to other exceptions as well,[641] namely, to Article XX(a)[642] and (b)[643] of the GATT and

---

634. To be precise, Article XX(g) of the GATT additionally requires that the measures concerned must be 'made effective in conjunction with restrictions on domestic production or consumption'. According to the Appellate Body, this means that the measures must be 'promulgated or brought into effect together with restrictions on domestic production or consumption of natural resources. ... The clause is a requirement of *even-handedness* in the imposition of restrictions, in the name of conservation, upon the production or consumption of exhaustible natural resources'. *See* AB Report, *US – Gasoline*, 1996, pp. 20–21 (original emphasis). Nevertheless, Article XX(c) and (e) of the GATT also uses the term 'relating to' but does not contain such an additional clause.
635. Van den Bossche and Zdouc 2013, 556, 563; in detail, Mitchell and Henckels 2013, 126–135.
636. Marceau and Trachtman 2014, 368–375, 406–408; Du 2010, 1090–1092. *See also*, for instance, GATT Panel Report, *US – Section 337 Tariff Act*, 1989, para. 5.26; moreover, Montini 1997, 122–123.
637. Howse 2016, 49.
638. Howse 2016, 48. *See also*, critically, Kapterian 2010, 101–106; Schoenbaum 1997, 276–277; differently, Farber and Hudec 1996, 81, who state that although 'it is always possible to imagine *some* less restrictive alternative to any given regulation ..., GATT tribunals have exercised good judgment and common sense in this exercise'.
639. Du 2011, 665–668; critically, Kapterian 2010.
640. *See*, for example, AB Report, *EC – Seal Products*, 2014, paras 5.169, 5.214.
641. Moreover, in *Dominican Republic – Import and Sale of Cigarettes* (2005), the Appellate Body applied the concept of weighing and balancing again to Article XX(d) of the GATT. *See* AB Report, *Dominican Republic – Import and Sale of Cigarettes*, 2005, paras 65 et seq.
642. AB Report, *EC – Seal Products*, 2014, paras 5.169, 5.214.
643. AB Report, *EC – Asbestos*, 2001, paras 171–172; AB Report, *Brazil – Retreaded Tyres*, 2007, paras 142–143, 156, 178 and 210.

Article XIV(a)[644] and (c)[645] of the GATS, justifications are subject to a flexible necessity test. This test amounts to a proportionality analysis in practical terms.[646] However, it does not include a test of 'proportionality *stricto sensu*', that is, a cost-benefit balancing.[647] Only the measure at issue and not the desired public policy goal and the chosen level of protection can be scrutinized.[648]

With respect to Article XX(d) of the GATT ('necessary to secure compliance with [GATT-consistent] laws or regulations'), the Appellate Body first reasoned in *Korea – Various Measures on Beef* (2001) that, as Robert Howse remarks,[649] 'necessity' does not necessarily mean necessary:[650]

> We believe that, as used in the context of Article XX(d), the reach of the word 'necessary' is not limited to that which is 'indispensable' or 'of absolute necessity' or 'inevitable'. ... As used in Article XX(d), the term 'necessary' refers, in our view, to a range of degrees of necessity. At one end of this continuum lies 'necessary' understood as 'indispensable'; at the other end, is 'necessary' taken to mean as 'making a contribution to.' We consider that a 'necessary' measure is, in this continuum, located significantly closer to the pole of 'indispensable' than to the opposite pole of simply 'making a contribution to'.

In this context, the Appellate Body recalled its interpretation of Article XX(g) of the GATT which requires a measure 'relating to' the conservation of exhaustible

644. AB Report, *US – Gambling*, 2005, paras 305–307.
645. AB Report, *Argentina – Financial Services*, 2016, paras 6.204, 6.227 et seq.
646. *See*, for instance, Cottier and Oesch 2012, 158, 164, 173; Gaines and Olsen 2012, 209, 210–212, 229; for a broader analysis of proportionality and balancing in WTO law, moreover, Andenas and Zleptnig 2008.
647. *See* Ortino 2009, 142–146; Ortino 2008, 187–190, 193, who discusses whether 'necessity' is really about balancing different societal values such as protection of public health against trade (cost-benefit balancing) – in EU law terminology, the test of 'proportionality *stricto sensu*' – or is merely a mechanism to determine whether no less trade-restrictive alternatives are reasonably available to achieve a Member's desired public policy goal without calling the public policy goal and the chosen level of protection into question (cost-effectiveness test). He suggests that the Appellate Body should clarify in favour of the latter approach. *See*, moreover, Vranes 2009, 283, who concludes that 'the Appellate Body has not balanced the importance of the legitimate policy goal pursued and a measure's trade effects against each other so as to determine whether even the least trade restrictive means has disproportionate effects on trade ...: rather, the Appellate Body merely referred to these criteria in order to lay open the factors influencing the *degree of scrutiny* applicable under the test of necessity', and similar considerations apply to the Appellate Body jurisprudence under the chapeau (original emphasis); to this effect, Van den Bossche 2008 (although pointing out that the Appellate Body in *Brazil – Retreaded Tyres* (2007) might have introduced a new requirement of 'material contribution'; but *see* AB Report, *EC – Seal Products*, 2014, paras 5.209–5.216, where the Appellate Body rejected a standard of 'materiality' as a generally applicable predetermined threshold of contribution); Neumann and Türk 2003a, 208–214, 227–231; Neumann and Türk 2003b, 115–122, 137–142 (concluding that proportionality *stricto sensu* is not a category of written WTO law nor did the Appellate Body introduce it in its jurisprudence); Desmedt 2001, 476; not least, Regan 2007 (demonstrating in detail that the Appellate Body has never engaged in cost-benefit balancing); differently, for instance, Sykes 2003.
648. *See*, for instance, Berrisch 2003 m.no. 235. *See also*, however, AB Report, *Korea – Various Measures on Beef*, 2001, para. 178; and *supra* n. 278.
649. Howse 2016, 49.
650. AB Report, *Korea – Various Measures on Beef*, 2001, para. 161 (footnote omitted).

natural resources.[651] This requirement is more flexible textually than the 'necessity' requirement found in Article XX(d). However, the Appellate Body also noted that, under the more flexible 'relating to' standard of Article XX(g), it accepted, in *US – Gasoline* (1996),[652] a measure because it presented a '*substantial* relationship', that is *a close and genuine* relationship of ends and means, with the conservation of clean air,[653] and it accepted, in *US – Shrimp* (1998),[654] a measure because it was '*reasonably related*' to the protection and conservation of sea turtles.[655] This observation that the word 'necessary' includes but does not necessarily mean 'indispensable' and that the term 'relating to' does not include every possible relationship[656] indicates some convergence of these standards. Although they may involve a different kind or degree of connection or relationship, measures that are not indispensable may be 'necessary' to protect human, animal, or plant life or health,[657] and measures somehow aimed at the conservation of exhaustible natural resources need not be 'relating to' this legitimate interest.

In *Korea – Various Measures on Beef* (2001), the Appellate Body subsequently explained that, when assessing whether a measure is necessary to secure compliance of a WTO-consistent law or regulation under Article XX(d) of the GATT, three aspects may be taken into account:

(1) In appropriate cases, the relative importance of the common interests or values that the law or regulation to be enforced is intended to protect. The more vital or important those common interests or values are, the easier it

651. *Ibid.*, fn. 104 to para. 161.
652. AB Report, *US – Gasoline*, 1996, p. 19.
653. *See also* AB Report, *US – Shrimp*, 1998, para. 136, where the Appellate Body stated that the substantial relationship in *US – Gasoline* between the measure at stake (the means) and the legitimate policy goals (the ends) was 'close and genuine'.
654. AB Report, *US – Shrimp*, 1998, para. 141.
655. *See also* AB Report, *China – Raw Materials*, 2012, para. 355, with reference to AB Report, *US – Shrimp*, 1998, para. 136. In *US – Shrimp* (1998), the Appellate Body noted that the measure at issue, based on its general structure and design, was 'fairly narrowly focused' also because exceptions from the import ban existed which related 'clearly and directly to the policy goal' (para. 138). Accordingly, the measure was 'not a simple, blanket prohibition' and 'not disproportionately wide in its scope and reach in relation to the policy objective'. On those grounds, the Appellate Body inferred that the means were, in principle, 'reasonably related to the ends' and that the means and ends relationship was 'observably a close and real one' and 'substantial' (para. 141).
656. *See also* Appleton 1997, 132–133, who observes that, in *US – Gasoline* (1996), the Appellate Body opted for a narrower interpretation of the phrase 'relating to' than that suggested by its ordinary meaning.
657. In *Brazil – Retreaded Tyres* (2007), the Appellate Body further noted that an import ban might be regarded as 'necessary' under Article XX(b) of the GATT 'on the basis of a demonstration that the import ban at issue is *apt to produce a material contribution* to the achievement of its objective' (para. 151; emphasis added). *See*, moreover, Bown and Trachtman 2009, 125–126, who critically observe that the Appellate Body relied on an unknown but presumed positive and 'material' contribution to health and that 'simply making a [material] contribution to' the goal was enough.

would be to accept as 'necessary' a measure designed as an enforcement instrument.[658]

(2) The extent to which the measure contributes to the realization of the end pursued, the securing of compliance with the law or regulation at issue. The greater the contribution, the more easily a measure might be considered to be 'necessary'.[659]

(3) The extent to which the compliance measure produces restrictive effects on international commerce, that is in respect of a measure inconsistent with Article III:4, restrictive effects *on imported goods*. A measure with a relatively slight impact on imported products might more easily be considered as 'necessary' than a measure with intense or broader restrictive effects.[660]

This holistic approach to 'necessary' was then summarized as follows:[661]

> In sum, determination of whether a measure, which is not 'indispensable', may nevertheless be 'necessary' within the contemplation of Article XX(d), involves in every case a process of weighing and balancing a series of factors which prominently include the contribution made by the compliance measure to the enforcement of the law or regulation at issue, the importance of the common interests or values protected by that law or regulation, and the accompanying impact of the law or regulation on imports or exports.

In addition, the process of weighing and balancing is comprehended in the determination of whether a WTO-consistent alternative measure that the Member concerned could 'reasonably be expected to employ' is available or whether a less WTO-inconsistent measure is 'reasonably available'.[662] A preliminary conclusion that the challenged measure is 'necessary' must be confirmed by comparing it with its possible alternatives.[663] The result of such a comparison should be considered in the light of the importance of the interests or values at stake.[664] On the basis of this analysis, it is established whether the challenged measure is 'necessary' or, alternatively, whether another, less WTO-inconsistent measure is 'reasonably available'.[665] An alternative measure is 'reasonably available' when it is less trade restrictive while providing an equivalent contribution to the achievement of the objective that is

658. AB Report, *Korea – Various Measures on Beef*, 2001, para. 162. On the assessment of the importance by WTO tribunals, *see* Mitchell and Henckels 2013, 128–130; moreover, Du 2010, 1096–1101; Regan 2007, 352–353.
659. *Ibid.*, para. 163.
660. *Ibid.*, para. 163. *See also* AB Report, *China – Publications and Audiovisual Products*, 2010, para. 310.
661. *Ibid.*, para. 164.
662. *Ibid.*, para. 166.
663. AB Report, *US – Gambling*, 2005, para. 307. *See also* AB Report, *Brazil – Retreaded Tyres*, 2007, paras 156, 178; moreover, AB Report, *EC – Seal Products*, 2014, para. 5.215 (and, in particular, fn. 1299 where the Appellate Body clarified that a preliminary determination of necessity is not required before proceeding to compare the challenged measure with possible alternatives; only *if* a panel reaches a preliminary conclusion that a measure is necessary, then this result must be confirmed by comparing the measure with possible alternatives).
664. AB Report, *US – Gambling*, 2005, para. 307.
665. *Ibid.*, para. 307.

pursued.[666] An alternative measure may be found not to be 'reasonably available' when it is impossible to implement[667] or is merely theoretical in nature because, for instance, it imposes an undue burden on the Member, such as prohibitive costs or substantial technical difficulties.[668] Moreover, when considering an alternative measure, the risks arising out of the implementation of the possible alternative must also be taken into account.[669] An alternative measure is only reasonably available if it allows the Member to achieve its desired level of protection with respect to the objective that is pursued.[670] It is a fundamental principle that WTO Members have the right to determine the level of protection that they consider appropriate in a given situation.[671]

Overall, the weighing and balancing of the different factors 'is a holistic operation that involves putting all the variables of the equation together and evaluating them in relation to each other after having examined them individually, in order to reach an overall judgement'.[672] Based on the chosen level of protection that a Member considers appropriate in a given context, the contribution of the measure at issue to the achievement of the objective pursued by it has to be weighed against the measure's trade restrictiveness, taking into account the importance of the interests or the values underlying the objective and whether less trade restrictive but equally effective alternatives are reasonably available.[673]

[C] Chapeau Requirements Establishing a Final Balance

[1] Requirement of Reasonableness

When a Member's measure violates a substantive GATT or GATS obligation but meets the specific requirements of a general exception under Article XX of the GATT or Article XIV of the GATS, it is only provisionally justified. The measure's application must still meet the requirements of the chapeau. Article XX of the GATT and Article XIV of the GATS open their list of exceptions with a quite similar introductory sentence, that is the chapeau. Measures that pursue a legitimate policy goal can be regarded as GATT compliant '[s]ubject to the requirement that such measures are not applied in a manner which would constitute a means of arbitrary or unjustifiable discrimination between countries where the same conditions prevail, or a disguised restriction on international trade', or as GATS compliant '[s]ubject to the requirement that such measures are not

666. AB Report, *Brazil – Retreaded Tyres*, 2007, para. 156.
667. AB Report, *EC – Asbestos*, 2001, para. 169.
668. AB Report, *US – Gambling*, 2005, para. 308. *See also* AB Report, *Brazil – Retreaded Tyres*, 2007, para. 171.
669. AB Report, *Brazil – Retreaded Tyres*, 2007, para. 174.
670. AB Report, *US – Gambling*, 2005, para. 308, with reference to AB Report, *EC – Asbestos*, 2001, paras 172–174 and AB Report, *Korea – Various Measures on Beef*, 2001, para. 180. *See also* AB Report, *Brazil – Retreaded Tyres*, 2007, paras 156, 170, 210; AB Report, *China – Publications and Audiovisual Products*, 2010, para. 319; moreover, Mitchell and Henckels 2013, 134–135.
671. AB Report, *EC – Asbestos*, 2001, para. 168; AB Report, *Brazil – Retreaded Tyres*, 2007, paras 140 and 210. *See*, however, Du 2010; moreover, Vranes 2009, 264–266.
672. AB Report, *Brazil – Retreaded Tyres*, 2007, para. 182. *See*, critically, Du 2010, 1095–1096.
673. *Ibid.*, para. 210.

applied in a manner which would constitute a means of arbitrary or unjustifiable discrimination between countries where like conditions prevail, or a disguised restriction on trade in services'. Even when discriminatory measures violate an MFN or NT obligation but fall under a general exception and are provisionally justified, they are still subject to the conditions of non-discrimination and non-restriction.[674]

As the Appellate Body stated in *US – Gasoline* (1996), '[t]he chapeau by its express terms addresses, not so much the questioned measure or its specific contents as such, but rather the manner in which that measure is applied'.[675] When determining whether the requirements of the chapeau are met, the measure has already been judged as pursuing a legitimate policy objective and as being without appropriate alternatives; the remaining question is about the *application* of the provisionally justified measure.[676]

The object and purpose of the chapeau is generally the prevention of abuse or misuse of the exceptions from substantial obligations.[677] In essence, however, this means that the chapeau is about refining proportionality, seeking a balance between the legitimate policy objectives pursued by a Member's measure and the other Members' rights under the GATT or GATS. In *US – Gasoline* (1996), the Appellate Body explained that 'the measures falling within the particular exceptions must be applied reasonably, with due regard both to the legal duties of the party claiming the exception and the legal rights of the other parties concerned'.[678] Later, the Appellate Body reinforced this statement in *US – Shrimp* (1998):[679]

> [The chapeau of Article XX] embodies the recognition on the part of WTO Members of the need to maintain a balance of rights and obligations between the right of a Member to invoke one or another of the exceptions of Article XX ..., on the one hand, and the substantive rights of the other Members under the GATT 1994, on the other hand. Exercise by one Member of its right to invoke an exception ..., if abused or misused, will, to that extent, erode or render naught the substantive treaty rights ... of other Members. Similarly, because the GATT 1994 itself makes available the exceptions of Article XX, in recognition of the legitimate nature of the policies and interests there embodied, the right to invoke one of those exceptions is not to be rendered illusory. The same concept may be expressed from a slightly different angle of vision, thus, a balance must be struck between the *right* of a Member to invoke an exception under Article XX and the *duty* of that same Member to respect the treaty rights of the other Members. To permit one Member to abuse or misuse its right to invoke an exception would be effectively to allow

674. In *US – Shrimp* (1998), the Appellate Body explicitly confirmed that *first* the specific exceptions must be examined, and only then the requirements of the chapeau must be assessed and not the other way round. *See* AB Report, *US – Shrimp*, 1998, paras 117–122.
675. AB Report, *US – Gasoline*, 1996, p. 22.
676. *See also* AB Report, *US – Shrimp*, 1998, para. 115; AB Report, *US – Gambling*, 2005, para. 339; AB Report, *Brazil – Retreaded Tyres*, 2007, para. 215; critically, Bartels 2015, 98–101; moreover, Vranes 2009, 278; Desmedt 2001, 473–475.
677. AB Report, *US – Gasoline*, 1996, p. 22. *See also* AB Report, *US – Shrimp*, 1998, para. 151; AB Report, *Brazil – Retreaded Tyres*, 2007, paras 224, 227.
678. AB Report, *US – Gasoline*, 1996, p. 22.
679. AB Report, *US – Shrimp*, 1998, para. 156 (original emphasis). *See also*, however, Charnovitz 2007, 703, who is critical of the notion that WTO Members have a legal 'right' in WTO law to have their exports accepted by other WTO Members.

> that Member to degrade its own treaty obligations as well as to devalue the treaty rights of other Members. If the abuse or misuse is sufficiently grave or extensive, the Member, in effect, reduces its treaty obligation to a merely facultative one and dissolves its juridical character, and, in so doing, negates altogether the treaty rights of other Members. The chapeau was installed ... to prevent such far-reaching consequences.

Article XX of the GATT as well as Article XIV of the GATS set forth limited and conditional exceptions from the obligations of the substantive provisions. Any measure, to finally qualify for an exception, must also satisfy the requirements of the chapeau.[680] Furthermore, according to the Appellate Body, the chapeau is an expression of the principle of good faith.[681] It serves to ensure that Members' rights to avail themselves of exceptions are exercised reasonably so as not to frustrate the rights accorded to other Members by the substantive rules[682] and exercised in good faith to protect legitimate interests but not as a means to circumvent one Member's obligations towards other WTO Members.[683] Interpreting and applying the chapeau is essentially the delicate task of 'locating and marking out a line of equilibrium between the right of a Member to invoke an exception ... and the rights of the other Members under varying substantive provisions ..., so that neither of the competing rights will cancel out the other and thereby distort and nullify or impair the balance of rights and obligations'.[684] Where this line of equilibrium is located is not exactly spelled out by the Appellate Body. It is 'not fixed and unchanging'.[685] Resembling the case-by-case approach of the 'likeness' analysis, 'the line [of equilibrium] moves as the kind and the shape of the measures at stake vary and as the facts making up specific cases differ'.[686]

The chapeau establishes a balance between, on the one hand, the right of Members to adopt and maintain trade-restrictive measures that pursue legitimate policy interests and, on the other hand, the right of other Members to trade.[687] This balance is accomplished by dismissing an application of measures that lead to arbitrary or unjustifiable discrimination between countries when the same or like conditions prevail or lead to a disguised restriction on trade. Although 'arbitrary discrimination', 'unjustifiable discrimination', and 'disguised restriction' are mentioned separately and constitute separable standards,[688] they may be read side by side; they impart meaning to one another.[689] Since the object and purpose is to avoid abuse or illegitimate use of the exceptions, 'the kinds of considerations pertinent in deciding whether the application of a particular measure amounts to "arbitrary or unjustifiable discrimination",

680. *Ibid.*, para. 157.
681. *Ibid.*, para. 158.
682. AB Report, *US – Gambling*, 2005, para. 339.
683. AB Report, *Brazil – Retreaded Tyres*, 2007, para. 215.
684. AB Report, *US – Shrimp*, 1998, para. 159.
685. *Ibid.*, para. 159.
686. *Ibid.*, para. 159.
687. Van den Bossche and Zdouc 2013, 574.
688. *See*, for example, AB Report, *US – Gasoline*, 1996, pp. 23–25; and AB Report, *US – Shrimp*, 1998, paras 120, 150, where these standards are listed separately.
689. AB Report, *US – Gasoline*, 1996, p. 25.

may also be taken into account in determining the presence of a "disguised restriction" on international trade'.[690]

It is notable that, when a measure that violates an MFN or NT rule is provisionally justified, the chapeau requires another non-discrimination test. However, the nature and quality of this discrimination under the chapeau is different from the discrimination in the treatment that was already found to be inconsistent with an MFN or NT obligation.[691] As the Appellate Body acknowledged in *US – Gasoline* (1996), '[t]he provisions of the chapeau cannot logically refer to the same standard(s) by which a violation of a substantive rule has been determined to have occurred'.[692] A discriminatory but provisionally justified measure, therefore, is not automatically discriminatory in its application for the purposes of the chapeau. According to Andrew D. Mitchell and Caroline Henckels, 'the chapeau effectively acts as a second check to determine whether the measure is really being applied in good faith in circumstances where it is necessary to achieve a legitimate objective'.[693]

[2] Application in **US – Shrimp**

US – Shrimp (1998) is a leading case not only because it allowed addressing environmental challenges arising from conduct outside of a Member's territory but also because, after a first detailed analysis in *US – Gasoline* (1996),[694] it comprehensively dealt with the requirements of the chapeau.[695] The US imposed an import ban on shrimp and shrimp products from countries that had not used certain devices for the protection of sea turtles in catching shrimp, namely essentially the same devices that all US shrimp trawl vessels were required to use. This measure, therefore, aimed at influencing other countries to adopt the same standards of protection, and it was not consistent with Article XI:1 of the GATT (general elimination of quantitative restrictions). Recognizing that sea turtles constitute 'exhaustible natural resources'[696] and that the measure was 'relating to' the conservation of exhaustible natural resources[697] and 'made effective in conjunction with restrictions on domestic production or consumption',[698] the Appellate Body confirmed the applicability of Article XX(g) of the GATT. However, the US failed to meet the requirements of the chapeau as the application of the measure constituted a means of arbitrary and unjustifiable discrimination between countries where the same conditions prevailed. Although the US pursued a legitimate policy goal, the application of the measure led to a violation of GATT obligations.

690. *Ibid.*, p. 25.
691. AB Report, *US – Shrimp*, 1998, para. 150, with reference to AB Report, *US – Gasoline*, 1996, p. 23.
692. AB Report, *US – Gasoline*, 1996, p. 23.
693. Mitchell and Henckels 2013, 136.
694. *See*, for instance, Appleton 1997, 133–136.
695. *See also* Howse 2002, 504–511; Gaines 2001, 770–842; Mavroidis 2000b, 78–83; Chang 2000, 39–43; Bree 1998, 116–129.
696. AB Report, *US – Shrimp*, 1998, paras 127–134.
697. *Ibid.*, paras 135–142.
698. *Ibid.*, paras 143–145.

Unjustifiable discrimination existed because the US required other WTO Members, if they wished to exercise their GATT rights, to adopt a regulatory programme for the protection of sea turtles that was not merely comparable but, rather, essentially the same as that applied in the US.[699] As the Appellate Body stated, 'it is not acceptable, in international trade relations, for one WTO Member to use an economic embargo to *require* other Members to adopt essentially the same comprehensive regulatory program, to achieve a certain policy goal, as that in force within that Member's territory, *without* taking into consideration different conditions which may occur in the territories of those other Members'.[700] Accordingly, unjustifiable discrimination 'results not only when countries in which the same conditions prevail are differently treated, but also when the application of the measure at issue does not allow for any inquiry into the appropriateness of the regulatory program for the conditions prevailing in those ... countries'.[701] Furthermore, the US measure relied on a certification process and, as a result, shrimp caught using methods identical to those employed in the US had been excluded from the US market solely because they had been caught in waters of countries that had not been certified by the US. The resulting situation was difficult to reconcile with the declared policy objective of protecting and conserving sea turtles.[702] For similar reasons, that is because the US imposed a single, rigid, and unbending requirement to adopt essentially the same comprehensive regulatory programme as in the US, without enquiring into the appropriateness, the Appellate Body found that not only unjustifiable discrimination but also arbitrary discrimination existed in this particular case.[703]

In *US – Shrimp* (1998), the Appellate Body moreover condemned that the US failed to engage certain Members exporting shrimp to the US in serious, across-the-board negotiations with the objective of concluding bilateral or multilateral agreements for the protection and conservation of sea turtles before enforcing the import prohibition against the shrimp exports of those other Members.[704] An import prohibition, the Appellate Body observed, 'is, ordinarily, the heaviest "weapon" in a Member's armoury of trade measures'.[705] Unjustifiable discrimination thus arose because the US negotiated seriously with some but not with other Members exporting shrimp to the US and nevertheless imposed an import ban of unilateral character on the shrimp exports

699. *Ibid.*, para. 163.
700. *Ibid.*, para. 164 (original emphasis).
701. *Ibid.*, para. 165.
702. *Ibid.*, para. 165. *See also* Howse 2002, 506.
703. *Ibid.*, para. 177. In addition, the Appellate Body condemned that the certification process for the confirmation of such a comprehensive regulatory programme was not transparent and predictable (no formal opportunity to be heard and to respond, no formal written, reasoned decision, and no formal legal procedure for review or appeal) and thus led to arbitrary discrimination (*see* paras 178 et seq.).
704. *Ibid.*, paras 166 et seq. *See also* Howse 2002, 507–509, who demonstrates that 'the AB never held that the requirements of the chapeau, in and of themselves, impose a *sui generis* duty to negotiate'; to this effect, Chang 2000, 41–43; differently, McRae 2000, 234, for whom 'it appears unlikely that unilateral measures ... will meet the requirements of the *chapeau*'; ('[a]t the minimum there will have to be some indication that negotiations were attempted').
705. *Ibid.*, para. 171.

of those other Members.[706] Lastly, the application of the measure in question resulted in differential treatment among various countries desiring certification due to differences in the length of the 'phase-in' periods that were granted.[707] All of those differences in treatment in their cumulative effect constituted 'unjustifiable discrimination' under the chapeau.[708]

In this sense, an equilibrium between the Members' rights and obligations is often better achieved by negotiating bilateral or multilateral agreements or by finding flexible solutions that consider the particular conditions prevailing in other countries. However, the chapeau does not presuppose bilateral or multilateral agreements nor accommodation of every possible difference in conditions.[709] In *US – Shrimp (Article 21.5 – Malaysia)* (2001), the Appellate Body later held that, under the chapeau, a measure should be sufficiently flexible to take into account the specific conditions prevailing in *any* exporting Member. Yet, this does not mean that there must be specific provisions in the measure aimed at specifically addressing the particular conditions in *every individual* exporting Member, notably, by anticipating and providing explicitly for the specific conditions prevailing and evolving in *every individual* Member.[710] In addition, the Appellate Body clarified that there is no requirement to conclude a multilateral agreement in order to successfully invoke the general exceptions clause. As much as possible, a multilateral approach is strongly preferred, and all Members must be given similar opportunities to negotiate an international agreement. Yet, it is one thing to *prefer* a multilateral approach in the application of a measure that is provisionally justified; it is another to require the conclusion of a multilateral agreement as a condition of avoiding 'arbitrary or unjustifiable discrimination' under the chapeau of Article XX of the GATT.[711]

Requiring formally different treatment, that is condemning formally identical treatment as discrimination, does not necessarily imply that the non-discrimination rule itself determines the treatment that is required. Pursuant to the decisions in *US – Shrimp* (1998) and *US – Shrimp (Article 21.5 – Malaysia)* (2001), a measure should be sufficiently flexible to take into account relevant differences. Otherwise, it may violate the non-discrimination requirements of the chapeau. At the same time, the chapeau does not prescribe any specific procedure or the exact criteria that need to be taken into account. In adopting and enforcing a measure that pursues legitimate policy goals, the chapeau gives Members a certain margin of appreciation. A wide range of possible solutions exists, and these solutions may all be sufficiently flexible to meet the requirements of the chapeau.

In *Brazil – Retreaded Tyres* (2007), the Appellate Body generalized the ideas expressed in *US – Gasoline* (1996), *US – Shrimp* (1998), and *US – Shrimp (Article 21.5*

706. *Ibid.*, para. 172.
707. *Ibid.*, paras 173–175.
708. *Ibid.*, para. 176.
709. *See also* Howse 2002, 509–511.
710. AB Report, *US – Shrimp (Article 21.5 – Malaysia)*, 2001, para. 149.
711. *Ibid.*, para. 124. *See also* Howse and Neven 2003, 52–53, 64, who regard this as the Appellate Body's most significant holding in *US – Shrimp (Article 21.5 – Malaysia)* (2001); critically, Gaines 2001, 804–820.

– *Malaysia)* (2001) about when discrimination is arbitrary or unjustifiable. The primary issue is the cause or the rationale of the discrimination and whether that cause or rationale is satisfactory or legitimate in the light of the policy objective being pursued.[712] It follows that 'the analysis of whether the application of a measure results in arbitrary or unjustifiable discrimination should focus on the cause of the discrimination, or the rationale put forward to explain its existence'.[713] General exceptions are abused or misused by a Member and, thus, arbitrary or unjustifiable discrimination exists under the chapeau when a measure is applied in a discriminatory manner between countries where the same conditions prevail, 'and when the reasons given for this discrimination bear no rational connection to the objective ..., or would go against that objective'.[714] The effects of the discrimination, that is the quantitative impact on the achievement of the objective and to what extent that achievement is undermined, are not relevant, as such.[715] In certain cases, however, they 'may be a relevant factor, among others, for determining whether the cause or rationale of discrimination is acceptable or defensible and, ultimately, whether the discrimination is justifiable'.[716]

The chapeau constitutes the final step of balancing competing policy objectives. While the non-discrimination analysis focuses on the WTO Members' substantive rights to open trade without discrimination by relying on a competitive standard of 'likeness' and 'less favourable treatment', the justification defence allows a Member to defend its discriminatory measure based on certain legitimate policy interests. A balance between these rights is sought not only by limiting the legitimate policy interests through a closed list of exceptions (although interpreted in a liberal and evolutionary manner) but also by requiring a certain close, yet flexible, nexus between the measure at issue and the policy goal that is pursued. Finally, the chapeau ensures that the Member respects other Members' rights in applying its provisionally justified measure while being able to reach its desired level of protection.

In 1997, Arthur E. Appleton observed that it was 'much easier to invoke Article XX(g) to protect exhaustible natural resources, such as petroleum and fish stocks, than to invoke Article XX(b) to protect human life' and asked whether 'perhaps like fish, mankind falls under both provisions'.[717] By putting more emphasis on the chapeau and thereby allowing for more scrutiny in *US – Gasoline* (1996) and *US – Shrimp* (1998)[718] while later relaxing the 'necessity' requirement through a flexible weighing and balancing test in *Korea – Various Measures on Beef* (2001), the Appellate Body was able to adopt a more sensible approach to the application of the general exceptions. As the preservation of human life and health is 'both vital and important in the highest degree',[719] this policy interest cannot be taken lightly or prevail over trade interests

712. AB Report, *Brazil – Retreaded Tyres*, 2007, para. 225.
713. *Ibid.*, para. 226.
714. *Ibid.*, para. 227. *See also* Davies 2009, 518-521.
715. *Ibid.*, para. 229. *See also* Davies 2009, 512-518.
716. *Ibid.*, para. 230.
717. Appleton 1997, 136.
718. *See also* McRae 2000, 227 ('new life has been breathed into the *chapeau*').
719. AB Report, *EC – Asbestos*, 2001, para. 172.

only if its pursuit is indispensable even though the wording of the general exceptions could indicate otherwise.[720]

§2.06 PROCEDURAL ASPECTS: THE BURDEN OF PROOF

[A] What and on Whom Is the 'Burden of Proof'?

Under the general MFN and NT rules of the GATT and GATS, it is possible to differentiate between certain steps of analysis, notably, between 'likeness', 'less favourable treatment', and general exceptions (justifications). In this context, the question of the burden of proof arises. What must a Member prove in order to succeed with its claim of illegitimate discrimination or to rebut such a claim?

US – Wool Shirts and Blouses (1997) addressed whether India or the US had the burden of demonstrating that there has or has not been an infringement of the obligations assumed under Article 6 of the Agreement on Textiles and Clothing (ATC).[721] Although this dispute was not related to non-discrimination obligations, the Appellate Body made important statements about the burden of proof under the WTO dispute settlement system. It essentially adhered to the view that:[722]

> the burden of proof rests upon the party, whether complaining or defending, who asserts the affirmative of a particular claim or defence. If that party adduces evidence sufficient to raise a presumption that what is claimed is true, the burden then shifts to the other party, who will fail unless it adduces sufficient evidence to rebut the presumption.
>
> In the context of the GATT 1994 and the *WTO Agreement*, precisely how much and precisely what kind of evidence will be required to establish such a presumption will necessarily vary from measure to measure, provision to provision, and case to case.

In addition, the Appellate Body distinguished between 'positive rules establishing obligations in themselves' and other provisions such as Article XX of the GATT which are 'limited exceptions from obligations' and 'in the nature of affirmative defences'.[723] For the Appellate Body, '[i]t is only reasonable that the burden of establishing such a defence should rest on the party asserting it'.[724] After the Appellate Body held that Article 6 of the ATC constitutes 'a fundamental part of the rights and obligations of WTO Members' and not a limited exception from obligations or an affirmative defence, it concluded that the party claiming a violation (in this case, India) must assert and prove its claim,[725] that is present evidence and argument sufficient to

720. *See also* Vranes 2009, 282.
721. The ACT terminated on 1 January 2005.
722. AB Report, *US – Wool Shirts and Blouses*, 1997, p. 14 (footnote omitted).
723. *Ibid.*, p. 16.
724. *Ibid.*, p. 16 (footnote omitted).
725. *Ibid.*, p. 16.

establish a presumption or prima facie case[726] of violation.[727] Only thereafter does the onus shift to the respondent (in this case, the US) to bring forward evidence and argument to disprove the claim,[728] that is to rebut the presumption or prima facie case.[729] Differently than in other international courts and tribunals, a prima facie case rule has become a central and established feature of judicial decision-making and is used in all WTO cases and not merely in cases when evidence is difficult to obtain.[730]

It is not precisely clear what 'burden of proof' means under the WTO dispute settlement system, what the standards of proof for establishing a prima facie case are, and why the burden of proof 'shifts'[731] or 'moves'[732] after establishing such a prima facie case.[733] In this respect, the concepts and terminology used by the Appellate Body are asserted as being 'disturbingly ambiguous and potentially misleading'.[734] Some confusion may also stem from different understandings of 'burden of proof' in common and civil law. While common law distinguishes between the burden of production and the burden of persuasion,[735] in civil law, the burden of persuasion is the key component of burden of proof.[736]

In common law practice, evidence is presented sequentially.[737] Therefore, the complainant must present evidence at the outset to support its version of all of the disputed facts and all of the mixed questions of law and fact[738] in order to convince the court that there is, in fact, a case to be tried (burden of production).[739] If the complainant meets its burden of production, this does not mean, however, that it has met its burden of persuasion.[740] The complainant still bears the risk that, after evaluating all of the evidence and arguments presented by both sides, the court will be in equipoise and will thus have to dismiss the complainant's claim (burden of persuasion or risk of non-persuasion).[741] In this situation of uncertainty, the benefit of the doubt goes to the respondent.[742] While the burden of production may shift back and forth between the complainant and respondent (initial claim, rebuttal, further rebuttal, etc.), the burden of persuasion generally stays with the complainant and does not

726. Apparently, the Appellate Body equates a complainant presenting a prima facie case with raising a rebuttable presumption in the complainant's favour. *See* Barceló III 2009, 26, 35, with reference to AB Report, *US – Wool Shirts and Blouses*, 1997, p. 14, and AB Report, *EC – Hormones*, 1998, para. 98.
727. AB Report, *US – Wool Shirts and Blouses*, 1997, p. 13.
728. *Ibid.*, pp. 16–17.
729. *Ibid.*, p. 13.
730. Foster 2010, 52.
731. AB Report, *US – Wool Shirts and Blouses*, 1997, p. 14.
732. AB Report, *EC – Hormones*, 1998, para. 98.
733. *See*, for instance, Pauwelyn 1998; Unterhalter 2008; Taniguchi 2008; Pfitzer and Sabune 2008; Barceló III 2009; Pfitzer and Sabune 2009; Grando 2009.
734. Barceló III 2009, 23.
735. *See* Pauwelyn 1998, 229; Taniguchi 2008, 555–559; Barceló III 2009, 27; Pfitzer and Sabune 2009, 10.
736. *See* Taniguchi 2008, 560–561; Barceló III 2009, 33; moreover, Grando 2009, 70–83.
737. Barceló III 2009, 28.
738. Barceló III 2009, 278.
739. Pfitzer and Sabune 2009, 8.
740. Barceló III 2009, 28.
741. Barceló III 2009, 27.
742. Barceló III 2009, 27. *See also* Pauwelyn 1998, 229; Pfitzer and Sabune 2009, 8.

shift.[743] In civil law practice, by contrast, evidence is normally submitted simultaneously.[744] Therefore, the concept of a burden of production has a very limited meaning;[745] the burden of persuasion captures the real meaning of burden of proof.[746] This burden of proof generally rests on the complainant during the proceedings and may only be discharged or not.[747]

Arguably, therefore, the burden of proof understood as the duty to persuade in order to ultimately succeed with a claim or defence always stays with the same party throughout the proceedings and never shifts to the other party;[748] it may only be on different parties as far as different claims or defences are concerned. After all of the evidence and arguments have been submitted by both the complainant and the respondent, either the complainant has to ultimately convince the adjudicating body that the respondent has violated a provision (otherwise, the benefit of the doubt will be given to the respondent, and the complainant will lose its claim of a violation) or the respondent has to ultimately convince that body that it has not violated a provision (otherwise, the benefit of the doubt will be given to the complainant, and the complainant will win its claim of a violation). Correspondingly, either the complainant has to ultimately convince the adjudicating body that the respondent cannot rely on a justification (otherwise, the benefit of the doubt will be given to the respondent, and the respondent will win its defence of justifiability) or the respondent has to ultimately convince that body that it can rely on a justification (otherwise, the benefit of the doubt will be given to the complainant, and the respondent will lose its defence of justifiability).

Nevertheless, the Appellate Body established that, under the WTO framework, 'the burden [of proof] ... shifts to the other party' once a prima facie case has been made.[749] Such a shifting would make perfect sense from a procedural point of view (burden of production), but, under the WTO dispute settlement system, all evidence is submitted and evaluated before any interim findings of fact, applicable law, or WTO

743. Barceló III 2009, 29. *See also* Taniguchi 2008, 558–559; Pfitzer and Sabune 2009, 9.
744. Barceló III 2009, 33.
745. Barceló III 2009, 33.
746. Barceló III 2009, 34. *See also* Pauwelyn 1998, 229; Taniguchi 2008, 560–561; Pfitzer and Sabune 2009, 9.
747. Pauwelyn 1998, 230; Taniguchi 2008, 561 ('[t]he burden always rests with the same party and it is only tentatively treated as having been fulfilled unless the other party succeeds in producing evidence sufficient to bring the proof back to a state of uncertainty'); Pfitzer and Sabune 2009, 9–10. Yasuhei Taniguchi also notes, however, in practice, it can amount to a shifting of the burden of proof when a prima facie proof (*Anscheinsbeweis*) can be made easily by showing a clear and simple fact. *See* Taniguchi 2008, 561–562. On whether presumptions may affect the burden of proof, *see*, for instance, Unterhalter 2008, 545–547; Grando 2009, 85, 93–96; Barceló III 2009, 34–36; Foster 2010, 58–59.
748. *See*, for instance, Pauwelyn 1998, 230, 232 ('[t]he burden of proof (in its real sense), as a fundamental substantive obligation, does not shift'; '[t]his does, of course, not mean that the burden of proof will always rest on the same party'); Unterhalter 2008, 544, 549–550; Taniguchi 2008, 558–559; Pfitzer and Sabune 2009, 10; moreover, Hariharan 2012, 808, who, therefore, regards the phrases 'the burden of proof shifts' and 'the burden of proof moves' as a 'mere game of words or not a matter of interpretation and not to be intended to have their literal meaning'.
749. AB Report, *US – Wool Shirts and Blouses*, 1997, p. 14. *See also* AB Report, *EC – Hormones*, 1998, paras 98, 109. Moreover, the Appellate Body explained in *EC – Hormones* (1998) that 'a *prima*

violations are made by a panel.[750] The procedural WTO framework does not allow for a separate consideration of a rebuttal only after a prima facie case has been made.[751] Both sides generally submit evidence and arguments simultaneously and not in ordered sequence.[752] Since there is no strict temporal sequence to present evidence,[753] the concept of a burden of production in a WTO proceeding is relatively meaningless.[754] The statements of the Appellate Body about a 'shifting' of the burden of proof appear ambiguous.

[B] Possible Implications of a 'Prima Facie Case'

As early as 1998, Joost Pauwelyn raised concerns about the GATT 1947 and emerging WTO jurisprudence on the burden of proof.[755] He considers the major source of confusion as lying in the terminology used to express the rules on the burden of proof and in the often overlooked distinction between the *determination* of who bears the burden of proof and the process of presenting or evaluating the evidence necessary to decide whether or not the burden of proof has been *discharged*.[756] In order to discharge the burden of proof, presumptions may be invoked, for example, by creating or relying on prima facie (but inconclusive) evidence.[757] This presumption technique, however, is only a tool that can be used by a tribunal in the *evaluation* of evidence once the *determination* of who bears the burden of proof has been made; a tool only used in the event the evidence submitted is inconclusive.[758] A presumption of truth that is not rebutted will be enough to accept a fact as a matter of law.[759] It does not affect the *determination* of which party bears the burden of proof for a specific allegation[760] because a presumption technique can only be used *after* a decision on who bears the burden of proof has been made, and this is in order to decide whether the burden of proof has been discharged.[761]

Joost Pauwelyn submits that the Appellate Body has embraced the presumption technique but tends to characterize it as the basic rule on who bears the burden of proof in a WTO dispute settlement.[762] It thus seemingly confused the determination of who bears the burden of proof with the process of evaluating evidence in order to check

facie case is one which, in the absence of effective refutation by the defending party, requires a panel, as a matter of law, to rule in favour of the complaining party presenting the *prima facie* case' (para. 104).

750. Pfitzer and Sabune 2009, 5.
751. AB Report, *Korea – Dairy*, 2000, para. 145; moreover, H. Horn and Mavroidis 2009a, 115; Mavroidis 2004, 167–168.
752. Taniguchi 2008, 566, 568; Barceló III 2009, 38.
753. Taniguchi 2008, 565; Pfitzer and Sabune 2009, 11.
754. Barceló III 2009, 36.
755. Pauwelyn 1998.
756. Pauwelyn 1998, 228, 233.
757. Pauwelyn 1998, 234, 246, 256–257.
758. Pauwelyn 1998, 234–235, 252, 256–257.
759. Pauwelyn 1998, 235, 246, 256–257.
760. Pauwelyn 1998, 235, 252.
761. Pauwelyn 1998, 253.
762. Pauwelyn 1998, 235, 252, 258.

whether the burden of proof (burden of persuasion) has been discharged.[763] Moreover, it seems that the GATT/WTO case law did not adopt the requirement of providing a prima facie case in order to proceed (burden of production) known in common law.[764] Instead of stating that 'the burden of proof moves'[765] or 'shifts'[766] after a prima facie case has been made, it is better to formulate this 'shift' as a shift in the burden to come forward with evidence or simply as an obligation to rebut a presumption.[767]

John J. Barceló III argues with reference to *Canada – Aircraft* (1999)[768] that the Appellate Body is apparently using 'prima facie case' to simply mean a plausible case for the complainant.[769] In this context, 'burden-shifting' seems to be best understood as a way of saying that, if the complainant makes a plausible case, the respondent will lose (or will probably lose) unless it rebuts that case.[770] It is only at the panel's final ruling, however, that we learn whether the complainant's case, in light of any rebuttal evidence from the respondent, was nevertheless convincing enough to win.[771] Given that the panel never performs a separate test to determine whether the complainant has established a prima facie case, the burden of production is effectively merged into the burden of persuasion, and it is the latter concept that dominates the panel's decision-making process.[772] Put differently, the overriding issue arguably is the non-shifting burden of persuasion.[773] If, after the parties have presented all of their evidence and arguments, the panel is unpersuaded or in equipoise, the party with the burden of persuasion loses.[774]

James Headen Pfitzer and Sheila Sabune suggest that the Appellate Body might have created a novel concept related to the application of the burden of proof by blending the concept of the prima facie standard as related to the burden of production with the concept of the burden of persuasion.[775] Under the prima facie standard employed by the Appellate Body, it seems that the complainant has to present a prima

763. Pauwelyn 1998, 235.
764. Pauwelyn 1998, 242.
765. AB Report, *EC – Hormones*, 1998, para. 98.
766. AB Report, *US – Wool Shirts and Blouses*, 1997, p. 14.
767. Pauwelyn 1998, 254.
768. AB Report, *Canada – Aircraft*, 1999, para. 192: the Appellate Body stated that a panel may need information from the respondent before or after a complaining Member has established its complaint on a prima facie basis and also in order to evaluate evidence already before it in the course of determining whether the complainant has established a prima facie case.
769. Barceló III 2009, 41.
770. Barceló III 2009, 41. *See also*, however, Unterhalter 2009, 549 (similarly, Pfitzer and Sabune 2009, 22): '[I]f a prima facie case is simply evidence which if believed would place the opposing party at some risk of losing the case, then the concept of a prima facie case is contingent and does not elucidate the primary issue concerning the burden of proof: namely, upon whom does the ultimate burden rest to satisfy the decision-maker at the end of the case that proof has been furnished to the required standard. The burden of proof in its true sense does not shift, it rests upon a party throughout the case, and that party must at the end of the case satisfy the burden of proof, upon a consideration of all the evidence adduced in the case.'
771. Barceló III 2009, 41.
772. Barceló III 2009, 41.
773. Barceló III 2009, 24, 39, 42–43.
774. Barceló III 2009, 39.
775. Pfitzer and Sabune 2009, 25.

facie case in order to move the case forward (burden of production) and also in order to emerge victorious with the case (burden of persuasion).[776]

As can be seen, the terminology used by the Appellate Body leaves room for different understandings and has led to an intense discussion about the concept of the burden of proof under the WTO dispute settlement system.[777] Although the precise meaning and consequences of a burden-shifting and a prima facie case remain controversial, it is important to note that the Appellate Body places the initial burden of proof on different parties depending on whether violations (positive rights) or defences (exceptions) are at stake. At the outset, positive rights require the complainant to establish a prima facie case that its claim of a violation is legitimate before, in the words of the Appellate Body, the burden of proof 'shifts' to the respondent, whereas exceptions require the respondent to establish a prima facie case that its defence of an exception is legitimate before the burden of proof 'shifts' to the complainant.

[C] Alternating Burdens under the MFN and NT Rules

Since the MFN and NT obligations under the GATT and GATS constitute substantive obligations, it is for the Member that claims a violation of a non-discrimination obligation (the complainant) to provide sufficient evidence and argument[778] in order to establish a prima facie case of a violation. Only then does the burden of proof shift to the accused Member (the respondent) to rebut the claim of a violation. This means that the complainant must provide legal arguments and evidence for 'likeness' and for 'less favourable treatment'. Unless a prima facie case of inconsistency is made, the respondent's measure will be treated as WTO consistent. When the complainant has established a prima facie case of a WTO violation, it is then for the respondent to rebut this presumption by providing legal arguments and evidence that the products or services and service suppliers in question are not 'like' or that no 'less favourable treatment' is at hand.

Conversely, after discrimination under a general MFN or NT clause has been established, it is the burden of the respondent to provide sufficient evidence that a general exception is applicable because general exceptions constitute limited exceptions from positive obligations and, therefore, affirmative defences. As a general rule, the burden of proof for an 'exception' falls on the respondent, that is on the party

776. Pfitzer and Sabune 2009, 25.

777. *See also* Kim 2007; Unterhalter 2008; Taniguchi 2008; H. Horn and Mavroidis 2009b; Grando 2009; H. Horn and Mavroidis 2009a; Foster 2010.

778. Even though a tribunal or court is expected to know the law (*iura novit curia*; *see also* AB Report, *EC – Tariff Preferences*, 2004, para. 105), the Appellate Body clarified in *US – Gambling* (2005) that '[a] *prima facie* case must be based on "evidence *and* legal argument" put forward by the complaining party in relation to *each* of the elements of the claim'. Moreover, '[t]he evidence and arguments underlying a *prima facie* case ... must be sufficient to identify the challenged measure and its basic import, identify the relevant WTO provision and obligation contained therein and explain the basis for the claimed inconsistency of the measure with that provision'. *See* AB Report, *US – Gambling*, 2005, paras 140–141 (original emphasis; footnote omitted).

asserting the affirmative of a particular defence.[779] After the respondent has established a prima facie case of a justification under a general exceptions clause, again the burden shifts to the complainant to bring forward evidence and argumentation to rebut the presumption of a justified measure. However, even though it is well established that the respondent invoking an affirmative defence bears the burden of demonstrating that its measure, found to be WTO-inconsistent, satisfies the requirements of the invoked defence such as the requirement that a measure is 'necessary' to achieve legitimate policy objectives, the Appellate Body held in *US – Gambling* (2005) that the respondent need not show 'that there are *no* reasonably available alternatives to achieve its objectives'.[780] In particular, the respondent 'need not identify the universe of less trade-restrictive alternative measures and then show that none of those measures achieves the desired objective. The WTO agreements do not contemplate such an impracticable and, indeed, often impossible burden'.[781] Instead of the respondent being required to prove that alternatives are not reasonably available, the complainant has to raise WTO-consistent alternative measures when rebutting a prima facie case of a 'necessary' measure.[782]

Therefore, the respondent must make a prima facie case that its measure is, for instance, 'necessary' by putting forward sufficient evidence and arguments.[783] The respondent may, but need not, point out why alternative measures are not reasonably available.[784] If, based on that evidence, a panel concludes that the respondent has made a prima facie case that the challenged measure is 'necessary', it, as a matter of law, is required to rule in favour of the respondent presenting the prima facie case in the absence of effective refutation by the complainant.[785] However, the complainant has the opportunity to produce sufficient evidence to rebut the prima facie case. The complainant may do so by raising a WTO-consistent alternative measure that, in its view, the respondent should have taken.[786] Then the respondent will be required to demonstrate why its challenged measure remains 'necessary' in the light of that alternative[787] or, otherwise, it will lose its defence.[788]

When analysing whether a measure provides a sufficient nexus to a legitimate policy interest by being 'necessary', three steps of alternating burden can be distinguished. The first step is a weighing and balancing process in which the burden of establishing a prima facie case falls to the respondent. The second step is the question of reasonably available yet less restrictive alternatives whereby the burden falls to the

779. AB Report, *EC – Tariff Preferences*, 2004, para. 104, in particular with reference to AB Report, *US – Wool Shirts and Blouses*, 1997, p. 14.
780. AB Report, *US – Gambling*, 2005, para. 309 (original emphasis).
781. *Ibid.*, para. 309.
782. *Ibid.*, para. 311.
783. *Ibid.*, para. 310.
784. *Ibid.*, para. 310.
785. *Ibid.*, para. 310.
786. *Ibid.*, para. 311.
787. *Ibid.*, para. 311.
788. *See also* AB Report, *Brazil – Retreaded Tyres*, 2007, para. 156; AB Report, *China – Publications and Audiovisual Products*, 2010, para. 319; AB Report, *EC – Seal Products*, 2014, paras 5.169, 5.261.

complainant.[789] The third step is to disprove such alternatives where the burden again falls to the respondent.[790] Finally, after it is established by the respondent that its measure violating a non-discrimination obligation is provisionally justified under a general exception, the respondent has to show that the application of its measure does not constitute abuse of such an exception under the chapeau. According to the Appellate Body, that is necessarily a heavier task than that involved in showing that an exception under Article XX of the GATT or Article XIV of the GATS encompasses the measure at issue.[791] This means that the burden of proof under the chapeau will be more difficult to discharge than that under any of the individual paragraphs of the general exceptions.[792]

The burden to provide further evidence in order to succeed with a claim or defence repeatedly shifts during the analysis of justifications. Yet, it has to be remembered that a panel does not separately decide during the course of the proceedings whether a prima facie case has been successfully made or rebutted. All of the evidence is evaluated together before a decision is taken by a panel. With regard to justifications, therefore, it can be argued that the burden of persuasion always rests on the respondent - it never shifts[793] - and only comes into play if all of the evidence is inconclusive or in equipoise. In such a case, the respondent will not have discharged its burden of persuasion and will not be able to justify its measure. Nevertheless, a prima facie case of a justification, unrebutted by the complainant, suffices as proof for justifying a measure[794] even if the evidence submitted by the respondent is not irrefutable and thus even if a higher degree of evidence than simply establishing a prima facie case would be required to fully discharge the respondent's burden of persuasion.[795] A prima facie case describes not only a threshold of proof or evidence to be passed[796] but also a certain standard of proof. This standard of proof remains vague. '[P]recisely how much and precisely what kind of evidence will be required to establish such a presumption [*prima facie* case] will necessarily vary from measure to measure, provision to provision, and case to case',[797] and 'similarly, this reasoning applies with regard to the quantity and nature of evidence required to *rebut* a *prima facie* case of inconsistency'.[798]

789. *See*, however, Mitchell and Henckels 2013, 133, who submit that 'this should not be taken to mean that the burden of proof then switches to the complainant to show that a reasonable alternative exists'.
790. Kruse 2013, 391-392.
791. AB Report, *US – Gasoline*, 1996, pp. 22-23. *See also* AB Report, *EC – Seal Products*, 2014, para. 5.297.
792. Pauwelyn 1998 fn. 38 at pp. 239-240.
793. *See*, for instance, Condon 2014, 343.
794. *See*, to this effect, AB Report, *EC – Hormones*, 1998, para. 104.
795. Pauwelyn 1998, 254.
796. On the problems with this understanding of a prima facie case as a threshold requirement, *see*, however, Grando 2009, 111-114.
797. AB Report, *US – Wool Shirts and Blouses*, 1997, p. 14.
798. AB Report, *US – Clove Cigarettes*, 2012, para. 281. *See also* Foster 2010, 52, 54 ('[a]t present, [in international adjudication] there seems only a fine distinction between the potentially undisciplined use of *prima facie* case approaches and the exercise of discretion in the weighing of evidence'; 'it seems, in practice the *prima facie* case approach also operates through the exercise of judicial discretion in the WTO'; '[t]he standard involved in establishing a *prima*

[D] Difference Between Exceptions and Exclusions?

Under the WTO dispute settlement proceedings, the burden of proof is used to describe different aspects regarding the submission and evaluation of evidence. The initial burden of proof rests on the complainant with respect to claims and on the respondent with respect to defences. While it is presumed that the respondent has not violated a non-discrimination obligation because the complainant bears the burden of proving such a violation, as soon as a violation has been established, it is presumed that the respondent has illegitimately violated a non-discrimination obligation because the burden of proving a justification is on the respondent.[799] Therefore, the question arises, what is the difference between claims and defences or between substantive obligations and exceptions from such obligations?

In *EC – Hormones* (1998), the Appellate Body dealt with the burden of proof under the SPS Agreement.[800] It rejected the Panel's approach of characterizing Article 3.3 of the SPS Agreement ('Members may introduce or maintain sanitary or phytosanitary measures which result in a higher level of sanitary or phytosanitary protection than would be achieved by measures based on the relevant international standards, guidelines or recommendations, if ...') as an exception to the general obligation contained in Article 3.1 ('Members shall base their sanitary or phytosanitary measures on international standards, guidelines or recommendations, where they exist, except as otherwise provided for in this Agreement, and in particular in paragraph 3'). Instead of a 'general rule–exception' relationship such as that between the MFN and NT obligations of Articles I and III and the exceptions of Article XX of the GATT, the Appellate Body conceived the relationship between Articles 3.1 and 3.3 of the SPS Agreement as qualitatively different:[801]

> Article 3.1 of the *SPS Agreement* simply excludes from its scope of application the kinds of situations covered by Article 3.3 of that Agreement, that is, where a Member has projected for itself a higher level of sanitary protection than would be achieved by a measure based on an international standard. Article 3.3 recognizes the autonomous right of a Member to establish such higher level of protection, provided that that Member complies with certain requirements in promulgating SPS measures to achieve that level. The general rule in a dispute settlement

facie remains unarticulated and susceptible to variation'); Unterhalter 2008, 551–552 ('[i]t is not altogether clear what such a variable standard entails, nor how it may be determined on a casuistic basis'); critically, Pauwelyn 1998, 258 ('[t]he risk is that panels and/or the Appellate Body may use this, in practice, very open rule [on burden of proof] as a tool to support result-oriented findings'); Grando 2009, 126–127. Yet, in *US – Clove Cigarettes* (2012), the Appellate Body dealt extensively with the question of how to establish a prima facie case and how to rebut such a case under Article 2.12 of the TBT Agreement (paras 276–297). It stated, among other things, that 'the burden of proof in respect of a particular provision of the covered agreements *cannot* be understood in isolation from the overarching logic of that provision, and the function which it is designed to serve. On the contrary, it is by having regard for the function and rationale of a particular provision that an adjudicator can, adequately, assess the manner in which the burden of proof should be allocated under that provision'. *See* AB Report, *US – Clove Cigarettes*, 2012, para. 286 (original emphasis).

799. *See also* Foster 2010, 62–63.

800. AB Report, *EC – Hormones*, 1998, paras 97 et seq.

801. *Ibid.*, para. 104 (original emphasis).

> proceeding requiring a complaining party to establish a *prima facie* case of inconsistency with a provision of the *SPS Agreement* before the burden of showing consistency with that provision is taken on by the defending party, is *not* avoided by simply describing that same provision as an 'exception'. In much the same way, merely characterizing a treaty provision as an 'exception' does not by itself justify a 'stricter' or 'narrower' interpretation of that provision than would be warranted by examination of the ordinary meaning of the actual treaty words, viewed in context and in the light of the treaty's object and purpose, or, in other words, by applying the normal rules of treaty interpretation.

Even though Article 3.1 of the SPS Agreement uses the expression '*except* as otherwise provided for in this Agreement, and in particular in [Article 3] paragraph 3' (emphasis added), the Appellate Body rejected the idea that Article 3.3 constitutes an exception to Article 3.1. Instead, Article 3.3 constitutes, in substance, a mere 'exclusion' of Article 3.1 or an 'autonomous right' regardless of whether it is described as an 'exception' or not. Accordingly, Article 3.3 does not constitute an affirmative defence. Unlike under Article XX of the GATT,[802] the burden of proof does not shift to the respondent but remains with the complainant. It follows that the burden is on the complainant to prove and to initially establish a prima facie case that there is an international standard, that the measure in dispute is not based on this standard under Article 3.1 of the SPS Agreement and, additionally, that the measure is not justified under Article 3.3 of the SPS Agreement as the respondent has not complied with the requirements of this 'exclusion'.

While the burden of proof with respect to an 'exception' is on the respondent, in the case of an 'exclusion', the burden of proof is on the complainant.[803] The difference between an 'exception' (i.e., a provision that establishes an exception to another provision) and an 'exclusion' (i.e., a provision that excludes the application of another provision) is subject to controversy.[804] It is not easily identifiable,[805] and its determination may involve a tacit but potentially significant normative judgment.[806] Even the Appellate Body admitted that 'this distinction [between an exclusion and an exception, or defence] may not always be evident or readily applicable'.[807] Moreover, the WTO jurisprudence is criticized for lacking a coherent approach to the allocation of the

802. In *US – FSC (Article 21.5 – EC)* (2002), the Appellate Body stated with reference to its findings in *EC – Hormones* (1998) that '[i]n the case of the GATT 1994 provisions, ... Article XX does not establish any "positive obligations" relevant to determining the proper scope of the obligations imposed under Articles I and III. Instead, Article XX sets out circumstances in which Members are entitled to "adopt or maintain" measures that are inconsistent with the obligations imposed under other provisions of the GATT 1994, such as Articles I and III'. *See* AB Report, *US – FSC (Article 21.5 – EC)*, 2002, para. 127. Therefore, it is necessary to establish whether a provision determines, in part, the proper scope of obligations or whether it provides an exception to obligations. In this respect, Article XX of the GATT constitutes an exception to obligations. Accordingly, the burden of proving that the conditions of Article XX are fulfilled rests on the respondent.
803. Grando 2006, 619; Grando 2009, 154.
804. Grando 2006; Broude 2007; Unterhalter 2009; Grando 2009, 151–224.
805. *See*, for instance, Kim 2007, 250.
806. *See*, to this effect, Foster 2010, 85.
807. AB Report, *EC – Tariff Preferences*, 2004, para. 88.

burden of proof and for relying on arbitrary criteria.[808] According to Michelle T. Grando, the confusing ways in which panels and the Appellate Body have described this distinction between an 'exception' and an 'exclusion' suggests that the distinction is artificial.[809]

Michelle T. Grando raises the critique that while an 'exception' and the rule it is providing an exception from are understood to be in conflict (but the exception prevails as *lex specialis*),[810] an 'exclusion' and the rule that it excludes are apparently not in conflict because they have different scopes of application; that is they do not overlap.[811] Caroline E. Foster also explains to this effect that '[o]n the Appellate Body's approach a provision that applies instead of another provision, rather than simultaneously, will not be an exception'.[812] However, Michelle T. Grando argues that there is no conflict or overlap in both cases.[813] The drafters of the agreements explicitly dealt with any possible conflict that could arise when they included words and phrases such as 'except' in Article 3.1 of the SPS Agreement or 'nothing in this Agreement shall be construed to prevent' in Article XX of the GATT.[814] Both expressions explicitly allow for deviations from other rules.[815] 'Therefore, it is clear that ... [owing] to the action of the drafters there is no conflict or overlap between Articles I and XX of the GATT just as there is no conflict or overlap between Articles 3.1 and 3.3 of the SPS Agreement.'[816] Due to legislative action, it is clear which provision applies to a certain situation.[817] Consequently, no conflict of norms analysis is required.[818] Instead of relying on alleged differences between 'exceptions' and 'exclusions', the allocation of the burden of proof 'should be based on considerations specific to the question of proof [and] the efficient functioning of the legal process'.[819]

Neither the language nor the importance of a provision appears to be decisive when determining whether it constitutes an 'exception' or 'exclusion'. For instance, even though the Appellate Body considered in *US – Wool Shirts and Blouses* (1997) – before deciding that Article 6 of the ATC is not an 'exception' – that this provision reflects a 'carefully drawn balance of rights and obligations of Members' and that it is 'a fundamental part of the rights and obligations of WTO Members',[820] the Appellate Body also stated in *EC – Tariff Preferences* (2004) that 'characterizing the Enabling Clause as an exception ... does not undermine the importance of the Enabling Clause within the overall framework of the covered agreements'.[821] A 'stricter' or 'narrower'

808. *See*, for instance, Pauwelyn 1998, 252; Grando 2006, 615, 617, 619, 629, 631, 655; Grando 2009, 151, 168, 179, 182, 223. For an overview, *see*, moreover, Condon 2014, 337–340.
809. *See*, with further references, Grando 2006, 619; Grando 2009, 154.
810. *See* Charnovitz et al. 2004, 257.
811. Grando 2006, 630; Grando 2009, 181–182.
812. Foster 2010, 69.
813. Grando 2006, 630; Grando 2009, 182.
814. Grando 2006, 630–631; Grando 2009, 182.
815. Grando 2006, 631; Grando 2009, 182.
816. Grando 2006, 631; Grando 2009, 182.
817. Grando 2006, 631; Grando 2009, 182.
818. Grando 2006, 631; Grando 2009, 182.
819. Grando 2006, 631; Grando 2009, 182.
820. AB Report, *US – Wool Shirts and Blouses*, 1997, p. 16.
821. AB Report, *EC – Tariff Preferences*, 2004, para. 95.

interpretation of exceptions was expressly rejected in *EC – Hormones* (1998) as well.[822] Indeed, exceptions may pursue important policy objectives and, therefore, are not necessarily considered subordinate to substantive WTO provisions.[823] It also did not matter for the Appellate Body that Article 3.3 of the SPS Agreement is described as an 'exception' by using the word 'except' in Article 3.1; it still constitutes an 'exclusion'.[824] Even the structure and purpose of 'exceptions' and 'exclusions' may be considered the same and, yet, the burden of proof is different.[825] It is thus doubtful whether the precise wording of a provision matters.[826] It is not clear why the burden of proof should be allocated differently when a provision that establishes an exception is at issue.[827] What is so special about an 'exception' that it would imply a different allocation of the burden of proof?[828] Does not an exception merely define the scope of a rule?[829] Michelle T. Grando suggests that the drafters may have preferred to create a separate paragraph or article with 'exceptions' merely for reasons of convenience, that is in order to avoid having to incorporate 'exceptions' into several or all paragraphs or articles although it is often possible to draft provisions in a way that the 'exception' is contained in the rule.[830] It is questionable whether the style of drafting represents a considered judgment as to the allocation of the burden of proof.[831]

David Unterhalter argues, however, that positive rules (exclusions) and affirmative defences (exceptions) should be distinguished from each other by reference to the regulatory purpose underlying the rules.[832] If a measure breaches the MFN obligation of Article I:1 of the GATT, the invocation of a general exception under Article XX of the GATT does not diminish that breach; rather, the exception condones the breach in the face of proof that the measure is required for another purpose that the agreement allows.[833] By contrast, a measure taken under Article 3.3 of the SPS Agreement (measures may, under certain conditions, pursue a higher level of protection than international standards) is not justified by recourse to an independent principle that

822. AB Report, *EC – Hormones*, 1998, para. 104.
823. AB Report, *EC – Tariff Preferences*, 2004, para. 95. *See also* Kruse 2013, 392.
824. AB Report, *EC – Hormones*, 1998, para. 104.
825. *See* Grando 2006, 632 ('the distinction created between Articles 3.1 and 3.3 of the SPS Agreement, and Article XX of the GATT is not based on the substance or the purpose of those Articles'); Grando 2009, 184; Unterhalter 2009, 215–216 ('[t]he structure of … [Article 3.3 of the SPS Agreement and Article XX of the GATT] is much the same, yet their characterization under the typology of the Appellate Body is different').
826. *See also* Broude 2007, 229 ('[t]he textual structuring of provisions tells us little about either their substantive relationship or their burden-of-proof classification; the same normative results can be achieved through different textual formulations'); Unterhalter 2009, 218, 220 ('[i]t is not possible to determine whether a provision is a positive rule or an affirmative defence simply by analyzing the text of the provision in question').
827. Grando 2006, 634; Grando 2009, 186.
828. Grando 2006, 635; Grando 2009, 187.
829. Grando 2006, 635; Grando 2009, 187.
830. Grando 2006, 635–636; Grando 2009, 188.
831. Grando 2006, 636; Grando 2009, 188.
832. Unterhalter 2009, 218.
833. Unterhalter 2009, 219.

conflicts with the purposes underlying Article 3.1 (measures should follow international standards) or any other provision of the SPS Agreement.[834] Article 3.3 simply sets out an alternative regime of obligations by framing positive rules that may be followed as an alternative to the positive rules set out in Article 3.1.[835] In the view of David Unterhalter, it follows that the distinction between 'exclusions' and 'exceptions' is intended to capture the distinction between a rule that allows a party to justify its failure to observe an obligation of general application and a rule that permits a party to engage in conduct that is regulated under an alternative scheme of regulation.[836] To this effect, Tomer Broude concludes from *EC – Hormones* (1998) that Articles 3.1 and 3.3 of the SPS Agreement 'act as separate, alternative rules governing different situations: the former applies to SPS measures "based on" international standards, the latter applies to measures resulting "in a higher level" of protection'.[837] In substance, the Appellate Body found that Articles 3.1 and 3.3 of the SPS Agreement are independent positive rules (obligations), 'the scope of whose application is mutually exclusive' and 'each of which may be violated under its own terms (and cannot be violated contemporaneously by the same measure)'.[838]

This discussion on the burden of proof demonstrates that there is no predetermined or readily identifiable difference between substantive rights, the scope of which is limited by 'exclusions', and separate 'exceptions' to substantive rights including justifications. A provision may be regarded as defining the scope of a right or obligation by limiting it or as an exception to an unlimited substantive right and, therefore, as a defence which leads to a shift of the burden of proof from the complainant to the respondent. However, it is important for the burden of proof whether the scope of a non-discrimination clause is limited by an excluding provision (for instance, by excluding certain measures from coverage or by limiting the scope of 'likeness' or 'less favourable treatment') or whether a separate exception or justification to a non-discrimination clause is established. In the former case, the complainant has to prove that the scope of the non-discrimination clause is not limited by the excluding provision. In the latter case, the respondent has to prove that even though the non-discrimination clause is applicable, discrimination is justified by an exception. In spite of those procedural differences between an 'exclusion' and an 'exception', the effects of both types of provisions can be the same: no illegitimate violation of substantive WTO obligations.

[E] Repercussions on the Aim and Effects Test?

Under the aim and effects test, 'likeness' and thus the scope of an MFN or NT clause depends on whether a measure has protectionist aims and/or protectionist effects (*see* section §2.03[D]). An additional argument against this test relates to the concern that

834. Unterhalter 2009, 219.
835. Unterhalter 2009, 219.
836. Unterhalter 2009, 221.
837. Broude 2007, 223.
838. Broude 2007, 223.

the burden of proof, which lies with the respondent under the general exceptions, would be subtly but effectively shifted to the complainant.[839] If the complainant were to prove that the measure in question pursues a protective purpose, this could create an additional burden for the complainant. In order to succeed with its discrimination claim, the complainant would have to prove that the legitimate purpose mentioned by the respondent was not the real purpose but protectionism[840] or, if the respondent did not submit any legitimate purpose, that the measure aims at protectionism rather than at any legitimate purpose. Thus, when applying the aim and effects test, the complainant would have the burden of showing the aims of a particular measure 'which sometimes can be indiscernible'.[841] It could be up to the complainant to produce a prima facie case that the measure has both the aim and effect of affording protection to domestic production. Once the complainant has demonstrated that this is the case, only then would the respondent have to present evidence to rebut the claim of 'likeness'.[842]

However, the aim and effects test need not involve an additional burden for the complainant. It could be argued that the question is only about legitimate policy purposes and not about protective purposes since protective purposes may be presumed. Under this approach, the complainant would have to make a prima facie case of 'likeness' on the basis of the Border Tax Adjustments criteria without enquiring into aims and purposes. After establishing such a prima facie case, the burden would shift to the respondent who then could prove on the basis of legitimate policy purposes and their necessity that the products or services and service suppliers are not 'like'.[843] It could thus be the obligation of the respondent to bring forward a legitimate policy objective and prove that the measure in question genuinely pursues this purpose. If the measure is prima facie necessary to pursue a legitimate policy goal, as evidenced by the respondent, no 'likeness' could be established. If, by contrast, the aim of the measure is *not* to pursue a legitimate policy goal because the respondent was not able to provide sufficient evidence for such a goal or if the measure is *not* necessary because a less WTO-inconsistent measure is reasonably available, 'likeness' could exist regardless of whether the complainant has proven a protectionist purpose. Since the burden of proof under the general exceptions also need not be exceedingly onerous for the respondent, Rudi Kruse concludes that the debate about whether or not regulatory purposes (notably, those related to PPMs) should be relevant at the level of 'likeness' is 'truly

839. *See* Panel Report, *Japan – Alcoholic Beverages II*, 1996, paras 4.13, 4.41, 4.44, where the European Community raised this concern and which the Panel followed in paras 6.16–6.17; moreover, Du 2015, 73 ('the complainant would bear the burden of showing not only discriminatory effects, but also that the aim of the measure is to afford protection to domestic production'); Piérola 2012, 348; Du 2011, 659; Hestermeyer 2011 m.no. 34; Choi 2002, 118; to this effect, Nielsen and Calle 2013, 57 ('if the entire Article XX is imported into the tests in Articles I and III, ... the burden of proof for Article XX would have shifted to the complaining party'); Pillai 2002, 336; Van Calster 2001, 117, 119; but *see also* H. Horn and Mavroidis 2004, 55, who believe that recourse to Article XX of the GATT brings serious problems for the complainant; similarly, Porges and Trachtman 2003, 786, 797.

840. Panel Report, *Japan – Alcoholic Beverages II*, 1996, para. 4.44.

841. *Ibid.*, para. 6.16.

842. *Ibid.*, paras 4.32, 6.17.

843. *See also*, to this effect, Weiler 2009, 766; H. Horn and Weiler 2004, 142; Horn and Weiler 2003, 29; Mattoo 1997, 131–133.

academic – of theoretical interest, but little practical relevance' when considering the allocation of the burden of proof.[844]

In fact, the GATT Panel noted in *US – Malt Beverages* (1992), with respect to a lower tax rate to wines applied by the US state of Mississippi, that 'the United States [the respondent] did not claim any public policy purpose for this Mississippi tax provision other than to subsidize small local producers'.[845] This led the Panel to conclude that 'unsweetened still wines are like products and that the particular distinction in the Mississippi law in favour of still wine of a local variety *must be presumed*, on the basis of the evidence submitted to the Panel, to afford protection to Mississippi vintners' (emphasis added).[846] With the aim and effects test, the burden to provide evidence for non-protectionist purposes was with the respondent. Because the respondent did not provide sufficient evidence for a legitimate policy purpose, the products in question were deemed 'like' based on the traditional 'likeness' criteria. Therefore, the Border Tax Adjustments criteria defined the prima facie position in *US – Malt Beverages* (1992) even when the *decisive* criterion was a non-protectionist purpose.[847] 'This suggests that even if regulatory purpose is to be the *decisive* criterion to determine whether products are "like", it is not necessarily the case that the complainant will have the burden of establishing that fact'.[848]

It is also noteworthy that with respect to 'less favourable treatment' under Article 2.1 of the TBT Agreement which does not exist if the detrimental impact on imported products stems exclusively from legitimate regulatory distinctions (*see* section §2.04[C][3]), the Appellate Body did not require the complainant to prove without any doubt that the detrimental impact does not stem exclusively from legitimate regulatory distinctions.[849] To make a prima facie case of 'less favourable treatment', which would suggest that the challenged measure is inconsistent with Article 2.1 of the TBT Agreement, it is sufficient for the complainant to show detrimental impact and, for example, adduce evidence and arguments showing that the measure is not even-handed. If, however, the respondent shows that the detrimental impact on imported products stems exclusively from a legitimate regulatory distinction, it follows that the challenged measure is not inconsistent with Article 2.1 of the TBT Agreement. Moreover, the Appellate Body added in *US – Tuna II (Mexico) (Article 21.5 – Mexico)* (2015) that 'having promulgated the technical regulation containing the regulatory distinctions that result in the detrimental impact, the responding Member will be best situated to adduce the arguments and evidence needed to explain why, contrary to the complainant's assertions, the technical regulation *is* even-handed and thus why the

844. Kruse 2013, 393 (original emphasis); similarly, Regan 2006a fn. 23 on pp. 195–196; Regan 2002 fn. 23 on p. 449 ('it will often not make much difference whether we consider regulatory purpose under Article III or Article XX').
845. GATT Panel Report, *US – Malt Beverages*, 1992, para. 5.26.
846. *Ibid.*, para. 5.26.
847. Kruse 2013, 385.
848. Kruse 2013, 387 (original emphasis).
849. AB Report, *US – Tuna II (Mexico)*, 2012, para. 216; AB Report, *US – COOL*, 2012, para. 272; AB Report, *US – Tuna II (Mexico) (Article 21.5 – Mexico)*, 2015, paras 7.32–7.33.

detrimental impact on imports stems exclusively from a legitimate regulatory distinction'.[850] Although the burden of proof is on the complainant, a prima facie case of inconsistency including a lack of even-handedness pushes the respondent into a defensive position with regard to the regulatory purpose of the measure at issue.[851]

Apart from these considerations, the NT obligation in the second sentence of Article III:2 of the GATT actually requires that the complainant prove that a measure is applied so as to afford protection to domestic production in order to succeed with a claim of discrimination.[852] In *Chile – Alcoholic Beverages* (2000), the Appellate Body held that 'a measure's purposes, objectively manifested in the design, architecture and structure of the measure, *are* intensely pertinent to the task of evaluating whether or not that measure is applied so as to afford protection to domestic production' under the second sentence of Article III:2 of the GATT.[853] Accordingly, the complainant has to prove whether a measure has an objectively manifested purpose of affording protection (*see* section §2.03[D][5]). From the perspective of the burden of proof, therefore, it remains doubtful why a measure's regulatory purposes should not influence the question of 'likeness' as envisaged by the aim and effects test even though an arguably similar analysis is required when claiming a violation of the second sentence of Article III:2 of the GATT. In both cases, the ultimate burden of proof is on the complainant. Despite that, a prima facie case of a protective purpose can be established by the complainant on the basis of the objective structure and effect of the measure in question. Thereafter, the burden to rebut the prima facie case of a protective purpose would be on the respondent.[854] For an effective rebuttal, a mere statement of objectives pursued by the responding Member would not suffice.[855] This suggests that, even if the burden of proof falls on the complainant, in many cases, the burden of providing further evidence (especially to rebut a prima facie case) will nevertheless fall on the respondent.[856] Whether regulatory purposes are considered as a justification defence only after discrimination has been established or whether they influence 'likeness', 'so as to afford protection to domestic production', or 'less favourable treatment' need not have a substantial or practical impact on the burden of proof under WTO law.

---

850. AB Report, *US – Tuna II (Mexico) (Article 21.5 – Mexico)*, 2015, para. 7.33 (original emphasis).
851. *See also* Valinaki 2016, 75–76, who submits that the Appellate Body allocates the same burden of proof to both the complainant and the respondent and that the respondent is required under both the GATT and the TBT Agreement to 'justify' its measure; moreover, Alcover and Garcés 2016, 363, 367–368, who comment that the complainant's burden of proof, although Article 2.1 of the TBT Agreement is not an exception, might not be as heavy as it seems; Zell 2016, 7, who describes the 'stems exclusively from a legitimate regulatory distinction' test as being an affirmative defence; and Condon 2014, 344–345, who criticizes the approach of the Appellate Body for creating confusion but suggests that perhaps the correct characterization is that 'proof of less favorable treatment may raise a presumption that the treatment is based on nationality, which the respondent can rebut by proving that the discrepant treatment is the by-product of a legitimate government goal not based on national origin'.
852. Kruse 2013, 386.
853. AB Report, *Chile – Alcoholic Beverages*, 2000, para. 71 (original emphasis).
854. Regan 2006a fn. 23 on pp. 195–196; Regan 2003, 752; Regan 2002 fn. 23 on p. 449.
855. AB Report, *Chile – Alcoholic Beverages*, 2000, para. 71.
856. Kruse 2013, 386.

CHAPTER 3

Article 24 of the OECD Model: Tensions and Unresolved Issues

This chapter on the current concept of non-discrimination under Article 24 of the OECD Model will deal with the question of comparability and with the difference between direct and indirect discrimination. After some preliminary remarks (section §3.01), the non-discrimination rules of Article 24 will be outlined (section §3.02). Although they are criticized for being incoherent and incomplete, they pursue important policy objectives that deserve an in-depth analysis (section §3.03). This analysis will be followed by a discussion of the various comparability requirements that pursue a single concept of comparability but, nevertheless, raise specific issues (section §3.04). Afterwards, the current approach to non-discrimination under Article 24 will be presented: a strict comparability test regards basically all differences in circumstances as relevant, rejects a concept of indirect discrimination, and allows for no justifications (section §3.05). Selected cases of potential discrimination will illustrate, however, that this understanding of comparability cannot convincingly identify the grounds for different tax treatment when protected and unprotected characteristics overlap, at least not without implicit policy judgments (section §3.06).

§3.01 PRELIMINARY REMARKS ON THE OECD MODEL AND COMMENTARY

As soon as a person is active or has property in more than one State, more than one State may want to impose a tax on that person's income or capital. International juridical double taxation, therefore, may arise when comparable taxes are imposed in two (or more) States on the same taxpayer in respect of the same subject matter and for identical periods.[857] In order to provide relief from such double taxation, States conclude bilateral double taxation conventions, also referred to as tax treaties. These

857. Introduction to the 1992–2017 OECD Model, para. 1 (similarly 1977: para. 3).

conventions determine in which State certain income or capital is taxable and how relief from double taxation has to be granted. In order to eliminate negative effects of discrimination and to promote international commerce, a majority also contains non-discrimination provisions that protect foreign persons and enterprises from discriminatory tax treatment.

Most double taxation conventions follow the OECD Model to a large extent. In 1963, the OECD released the first OECD Model with the title 'Draft Double Taxation Convention on Income and Capital'; the expression 'Draft Convention' indicated that it was a draft to be used in drafting double taxation conventions and not that it was an unfinished model. In 1977, a major revision of the OECD Model was published with the title 'Model Double Taxation Convention on Income and on Capital'. Since 1992, the 'Model Tax Convention on Income and on Capital' is continually updated. Changes to the OECD Model have been made in 1992, 1994, 1995, 1997, 2000, 2002,[858] 2005, 2008, 2010, 2014,[859] and 2017.

Article 24 of the OECD Model contains provisions dealing with the elimination of tax discrimination.[860] It provides certain specific grounds that a State may not use to discriminate for the purposes of taxation. In relation to nationals of the treaty partner State, Article 24 prohibits discrimination by reason of nationality (paragraph 1) and contains similar protection for stateless persons (paragraph 2). In relation to residents of the treaty partner State, Article 24 prohibits discrimination in cases of PEs belonging to treaty partner residents (paragraph 3), deductions of certain payments and debts to treaty partner residents (paragraph 4), and enterprises owned or controlled by treaty partner residents (paragraph 5).[861]

Article 24 of the UN Model[862] will not be explicitly dealt with in this study as there are generally no differences in wording when compared to the corresponding versions of the OECD Model.[863] Similarly, even though the OECD Estate, Inheritance and Gift Model[864] contains non-discrimination rules in Article 10 that prohibit discrimination

858. Note that the report entitled 'The 2002 Update to the Model Tax Convention' was adopted by the OECD Council on 28 January 2003; therefore, it is sometimes referred to as the 2003 Update.

859. As the 2012 Update to Article 26 (Exchange of Information) of the OECD Model and its Commentary is not considered as a separate update to the OECD Model, the changes were again included in the 2014 Update.

860. This is, in particular, indicated by the title of Article 24: 'Non-Discrimination'.

861. Avery Jones, Depret, et al. 1991b, 311.

862. United Nations, Model Double Taxation Convention between Developed and Developing Countries (2017); previous versions were released in 1980, 2001, and 2011.

863. This means that, except for a reference to a different paragraph of Article 12 where the restriction concerning non-arm's-length royalty payments is located and (since 2017) an additional reference to Article 12A on fees for technical services, the non-discrimination clauses of the 2017 UN Model are identical to the ones of the 2017 OECD Model; the same holds true for the 2011 UN Model (2010 OECD Model), 2001 UN Model (2000 OECD Model), and the 1980 UN Model (1977 OECD Model). However, the UN Commentary contains additional comments. *See* 2017 UN Commentary on Article 24, after paras 60, 75, 80. *See also* Bammens and Vanistendael 2016, sec. 3.

864. OECD, Model Double Taxation Convention on Estates and Inheritances and on Gifts (1982); a previous version was released in 1966 with the title 'Draft Convention for the Avoidance of Double Taxation on Estates and Inheritances' and contained non-discrimination provisions that resembled Article 24(1), (2), (3), (5), and (6).

because of nationality, these provisions merely resemble Article 24(1), (2), and (6) of the OECD Model and will not be specifically analysed.

Although this study is devoted to the meaning of the non-discrimination provisions of the OECD Model, it is important to keep in mind that the OECD Model cannot provide protection against discrimination to a taxpayer. Only a specific tax treaty can do so. The relevant means of interpretation, or at least their perceived weight, may be different depending on whether the Contracting States relied on an older or newer version of the OECD Model, agreed on deviations or additions to it, understood a tax treaty as a 'living instrument',[865] or concluded it at a specific point in time in which certain statements have not yet been included or deleted from the OECD Commentary. Thus, the result of interpretation may be different as well. For instance, Article 24(1) of the US Model[866] provides that 'for the purposes of United States taxation, United States nationals who are subject to tax on a worldwide basis are not in the same circumstances as nationals of [the other Contracting State] who are not residents of the United States'. Such a provision is not included in the OECD Model. Yet, as long as it is unclear what meaning Article 24 has without such deviations and additions, it is also unclear whether that provision merely confirms a particular interpretation that could be derived from the OECD Model anyway (clarification) or rather changes the meaning and scope (modification). A deviation from the OECD Model in one specific tax treaty can further point to an *argumentum e contrario* with regard to all other conventions or merely confirm a long-standing interpretation of all conventions.[867] Therefore, as deviations do not contribute to an understanding of non-discrimination provisions in conventions that adhere to the OECD Model, they will not be addressed.

Besides focusing on the wording, context, and object and purpose of the non-discrimination provisions, this study will take account of the historical development of the OECD Model and the statements in the OECD Commentary. According to Article 31 of the Vienna Convention on the Law of Treaties (VCLT), '[a] treaty shall be interpreted in good faith in accordance with the ordinary meaning to be given to the terms of the treaty in their context and in the light of its object and purpose', whereas the OECD Model and the OECD Commentary are covered by Article 32 of the VCLT as a supplementary means of interpretation.[868] Recourse may (not shall) be had to supplementary means of interpretation in order to confirm the meaning resulting from the application of Article 31 of the VCLT or to determine the meaning when the interpretation according to Article 31 of the VCLT '[l]eaves the meaning ambiguous or obscure' or '[l]eads to a result which is manifestly absurd or unreasonable'.

865. *See* Nieminen 2015b, 784–795.
866. 2016 United States Model Income Tax Convention.
867. *See* Lang 2007a, 199–202, who criticizes a decision of the Austrian Supreme Administrative Court (Verwaltungsgerichtshof), 19 December 2006, 2005/15/0158, according to which the 1995 amendment to Article 3(2) of the OECD Model that was intended to clarify a 'dynamic' reference to domestic meanings of undefined terms constituted an argument for a 'static' reference under a previously concluded tax treaty that contained no such amendment.
868. *See*, in detail, Nieminen 2015a, 638–645; Dziurdź 2013c, sec. 2.2.

Nevertheless, under the VCLT, interpretation is a single combined operation[869] rather than a straight-lined process.[870] If the meaning is clear but supplementary means of interpretation do not confirm this clear meaning, it is possible to reconsider whether everything is really as clear as initially assumed.[871] Thus, as Martti Nieminen observes,[872] Articles 31 and 32 of the VCLT allow that the question of clarity is reconsidered if recourse to supplementary means, including the OECD Commentary, does not confirm the prima facie clear meaning but contradicts it. In that case, the task of the interpreter is to re-evaluate whether the treaty term in its context and in the light of the treaty's object and purpose may, after all, have more than one possible meaning. If the answer after the second round of thinking is that there indeed are alternative meanings, supplementary means can be used to determine which one is correct. Instead, if the interpreter remains convinced that the authentic means allow only one possible interpretation, that interpretation prevails notwithstanding what is provided in the supplementary means. This way, the interpreter is able to make full use of the supplementary means without 'destroying the hierarchy between Articles 31 and 32 of the VCLT'.

As the general rule of interpretation often leaves the meaning of a treaty and its provisions ambiguous, supplementary means of interpretation are important in practice;[873] the term 'supplementary' corresponds with the French term '*complémentaire*'

869. ILC Report 1966, YBILC 1966 II, pp. 219–220 (m.no. 8).
870. *See also* Gardiner 2015, 32 ('interpretation may require going round the circle more than once if a factor presents itself under an element of the rules later in the list and which appears to outweigh one already taken up'); Torres Bernárdez 1998, 726 ('interpretation … is a legal operation which should combine the various permitted elements and means of interpretation as they may be present in the case, while keeping *open* the interpretation until the very conclusion of the interpretative process'; original emphasis).
871. *See*, in particular, Gardiner 2015, 351, 355 ('[n]on-confirming preparatory work could … lead to exploration of a hitherto unnoticed ambiguity in the text and reopen evaluation of the meaning'; '"confirm" offers the option of not confirming and the possibility of transforming the exercise into one where the preparatory work leads to revisiting the application of the general rule to find a permissible interpretation which is then confirmed'; '[a]nother possibility is that the investigation may lead to a conclusion that there is a hitherto unperceived ambiguity … such that the exploration of the preparatory work is transformed from a potential confirming role to one of determining the meaning').
872. Nieminen 2015a, 647–648.
873. *See*, for example, Gardiner 2015, 25, 348 ('[t]he classification of such material [preparatory work] … as "supplementary means of interpretation" has not in practical terms diminished its importance'; '[t]he prerequisites for using supplementary means to "determine" the meaning are ambiguity, obscurity, absurdity, or unreasonableness … [but] these clear lines of approach (particularly confirmation) were not intended to be applied too rigidly, nor are they in practice'); Dörr 2012 m.nos. 27, 32, 34 ('Art 32 allows reference to supplementary means of interpretation … in a much more liberal manner than it is usually perceived'; 'the confirmative mode of using supplementary means of interpretation possesses … *de facto* a relevance similar to that of the general rule of interpretation'; 'the elastic concept of ambiguity … clearly outweighs the – alleged – supplementary character of the interpretative means identified in Art 32'); Villiger 2009 Article 32, m.no. 11 ('it is difficult to imagine situations where the means of Article 32 may not be employed'; 'Article 32 permits use of these means in most situations and does not restrict the manner in which they may be employed'); but more cautiously Sinclair 1984, 141–142 ('recourse is permissible in carefully controlled circumstances'; '[r]ecourse … must always be undertaken with caution and prudence').

rather than implying 'subsidiary' means.[874] Article 32 of the VCLT only prohibits interpreting a tax treaty solely on the basis of the OECD Commentary and other supplementary means of interpretation, that is independently of the wording, context, and object and purpose.[875]

It is sometimes argued that explanations in the OECD Commentary may lead to a special meaning under Article 31(4) of the VCLT that the Contracting States intended to give to a term by following the OECD Model.[876] Nevertheless, it is important to verify this intention. Unlike with definitions that are part of the text of a treaty, whether the Contracting States adhered to or deviated from the OECD Model and the origins of the terms used (OECD Model, UN Model, domestic law, a preceding treaty, etc.) are not the ordinary meaning, context, or object and purpose of a tax treaty. An intention to give a term a special meaning, therefore, is derived on the basis of supplementary means of interpretation - but this does not render the OECD Commentary less relevant. It remains a sometimes more, sometimes less important means of interpretation, the weight of which depends on how its explanations interact with all other available means of interpretation. In other words, 'the relative value ... is not fixed but varies from case to case'.[877]

The provisions of the OECD Model generally refer to 'a resident of a Contracting State' and to 'the other Contracting State'. For the purposes of this study, a Contracting State will be termed as 'the source State' as soon as the taxpayer in question is not a resident of that State regardless of what and where the source of income or capital is believed to be; 'the source State' is thus equivalent to 'the non-residence State'.[878] However, since different persons may be involved in a case and these persons may be residents of different Contracting States, the term 'allegedly discriminating State' (State A) will be used as well; this State supposedly discriminates due to some connection to the other Contracting State (State B). Finally, a State that is not a Contracting State to the tax treaty of primary interest will be referred to as 'the third State' (State C). If, for example, a taxpayer is a resident of State A, maintains a PE in State B, and receives income from State C that is taxable in all three States, the non-discrimination provisions of the tax treaty between State A and State B are particularly relevant. It

874. Villiger 2009 Article 32, m.no. 7. *See also* Gardiner 2015, 358 ('supplementary means can[not] be characterized as always *subordinate* to the general rule'; original emphasis); Sinclair 1984, 115–116 ('the *travaux préparatoires* of a treaty ... are [not] relegated to a subordinate, and wholly ineffective, role'; 'no rigid temporal prohibition on resort to the *travaux préparatoires* of a treaty was intended'; '[t]he distinction ... intended rather to ensure that the supplementary means do not constitute an alternative, autonomous method of interpretation divorced from the general rule').

875. *See*, to this effect, Nieminen 2015a, 658 ('the subtle but theoretically important distinction on the interpretative weight between the authentic means of Article 31 VCLT and the supplementary means of Article 32 VCLT is that if there is no way of reconciling the interpretation suggested by supplementary means with the wording, context and purpose of the treaty, the interpretation arising from the primary means must prevail notwithstanding how convincing the evidence from the supplementary means, including the OECD Commentaries'). *See*, moreover, Dziurdź 2013c, sec. 2.1.

876. *See*, to this effect, Ault 1993, 65; similarly, Lang and Brugger 2008, 99–100; Lang 1994a, 18–23; moreover, Lang 2011b, 285.

877. Nieminen 2015a, 636.

878. *See* Vogel 2005.

follows that State A is the residence State, State B is the source State (the non-residence State), and State C is the third State. When applying the non-discrimination provisions of the tax treaty between the residence State and the source State, a tax treaty between the residence State and the third State or between the source State and the third State may exist as well.

§3.02 OVERVIEW OF THE NON-DISCRIMINATION RULES OF ARTICLE 24

[A] Non-discrimination Based on Nationality

[1] Article 24(1): Nationality

In May 1956 when the work on the OECD Model basically started, the Organisation for European Economic Co-operation (OEEC)[879] Fiscal Committee set up Working Party No. 4 to study discrimination in taxation on the grounds of nationality or on similar grounds.[880] After circulating a questionnaire and receiving replies, the Working Party delivered its first report in January 1957.[881] Therein it suggested a nationality non-discrimination provision because such a type of discrimination seldom occurred: a person's nationality is not relevant for tax liability as fiscal domicile determines whether a person is subject to full or limited tax liability.[882] In addition, the Working Party believed that the OEEC Member countries were opposed to such a type of discrimination. It identified various initiatives against discrimination based on nationality which included Article 21 of the European Convention on Establishment of December 1955 as well as provisions in various bilateral conventions, notably, commercial conventions, conventions on employment, conventions on establishment, conventions of friendship, and conventions for the avoidance of double taxation.[883] Since the Working Party felt that 'it can conclude that the Member countries of the O.E.E.C. are not in favour of discriminatory taxation on grounds of the taxpayer's nationality' and that they 'acknowledge in general the importance of eliminating the few cases of discrimination that still exist between them',[884] the principle of non-discrimination on the grounds of nationality was given formal recognition.

Article 24(1) of the OECD Model, therefore, prohibits discrimination because of nationality. It is worded in the 2017 version of the OECD Model as follows:[885]

879. Organisation for European Economic Co-operation (OEEC); superseded by the Organisation for Economic Co-operation and Development (OECD) in September 1961.
880. OEEC, FC/M(56)1, p. 4; OEEC, TFD/FC/2. For a historical analysis of Article 24, *see also* Bammens 2012, 33–62; Rodríguez Nepote 2011; Avery Jones 2009, 28–49; Lang 2007b; Lang 2006.
881. OEEC, FC/WP4(57)1.
882. *Ibid.*, pp. 1–2.
883. *Ibid.*, p. 3.
884. *Ibid.*, p. 3.
885. In the following, all quotations will refer to the 2017 OECD Model unless otherwise stated.

Article 24

Non-Discrimination

1. Nationals of a Contracting State shall not be subjected in the other Contracting State to any taxation or any requirement connected therewith, which is other or more burdensome than the taxation and connected requirements to which nationals of that other State in the same circumstances, in particular with respect to residence, are or may be subjected. This provision shall, notwithstanding the provisions of Article 1, also apply to persons who are not residents of one or both of the Contracting States.

With regard to the personal scope of the non-discrimination provision, the 1963 OECD Model lacked the second sentence of Article 24(1). This sentence was added in 1977 to ensure that nationals of a Contracting State who are residents of a third State are not discriminated against because of nationality as well.[886] The application of the nationality non-discrimination rule to nationals who are residents of a third State had been a point of disagreement when the 1977 OECD Model was prepared.[887] Several Delegations believed that a conflict between Article 1 and Article 24 existed[888] and that this conflict would not necessarily be solved in favour of a wider scope of Article 24 as arguably intended by the drafters of the 1963 OECD Model. Thus, the majority of the Fiscal Committee agreed to make clear that the principle of non-discrimination for nationals should also apply to nationals who are residents of a third State[889] and to make clear in the Commentary that the 1977 amendment to Article 24(1) was for the purposes of clarification so that the *a contrario* argument could not be applied to

886. *See also* 2008–2017 OECD Commentary on Article 24, para. 6 (1977–2005: para. 2).

887. *See* OECD, TFD/FC/173, p. 2 (the Japanese Delegation believed that Article 24(1) does not apply to a national of a Contracting State being resident in neither of the Contracting States as Article 1 restricts the application of Article 24); OECD, FC/WP25(66)1, pp. 4–5 (Working Party No. 25 argued against this interpretation with regard to nationals but not necessarily with regard to stateless persons); OECD, FC/M(66)2, pp. 4–5 (the Fiscal Committee discussed this issue but, for the time being, left aside whether the text of Article 24 should be amended, although the general view was that Article 24 should apply to all nationals of the Contracting States irrespective of their residence); OECD, FC/WP28(68)2, pp. 3–4 (Working Party No. 28 regarded a conflict between Article 1 and Article 24 as a valid interpretation, noted that several Delegations considered that a wider interpretation was intended by the Fiscal Committee when Article 24 was formulated, and suggested amendments in order to remove this conflict if such a wider interpretation meets with general acceptance); OECD, DAF/FC/69.17, p. 8 (some Delegates expressed themselves in agreement with Working Party No. 28 that Article 24 should be liberated from the restrictive effect of Article 1).

888. OECD, FC/WP28(68)2, p. 4.

889. OECD, DAF/FC/70.5, p. 1. *See also* OECD, DAF/FC/71.6, p. 1, where the Fiscal Committee again adopted the amendment proposed by Working Party No. 4 (OECD, FC/WP4(71)1, pp. 3–4) to include the expression 'whether or not resident in one of the Contracting States'. It is not precisely clear when and why this expression was redrafted into its current form of a separate sentence; it was still included in OECD, CFA/WP1(71)1, p. 2; OECD, CFA/WP1(73)6, p. 2; and, after a revision by the Steering Group (OECD, DAF/CFA/WP1(73)13, p. 1), in OECD, CFA/WP1(73)10, p. 55; and OECD, CFA(73)15, p. 59. However, already in 1968, Working Party No. 28 suggested adding a second sentence to Article 24 stating that '[t]he provisions of this Article shall not be limited by the provisions of Article 1'. *See* OECD, FC/WP28(68)2, p. 4; OECD, FC/WP28(68)2 Corrigendum.

conventions based on the 1963 OECD Model.[890] This intention of a clarification later became blurred.[891]

It follows that the benefits of Article 24(1) do not depend on Article 1 and whether the taxpayer is a resident of a Contracting State. If the taxpayer is a national of a Contracting State but a resident of a third State, that person can claim non-discriminatory tax treatment in the other Contracting State. Conversely, a national of a third State has no rights under Article 24(1) even if that person is a resident of a Contracting State. Only nationals of a Contracting State are protected. This means that, under a tax treaty between State A and State B, the following simplified[892] situations are covered by the non-discrimination clause:[893]

- Nationals of State B who are residents of State B can claim a tax treatment from State A that is no more burdensome than that applied to nationals of State A who are residents of State B.
- Nationals of State B who are residents of State A can claim a tax treatment from State A that is no more burdensome than that applied to nationals of State A who are residents of State A.
- Nationals of State B who are residents of State C, a third State, can claim a tax treatment from State A that is no more burdensome than that applied to nationals of State A who are residents of State C.

The expression 'in particular with respect to residence' was added to the OECD Model in 1992 in order to substantiate the requirement of 'in the same circumstances'.[894] This addition was preceded by decisions of French courts ruling that when nationality and residence are linked to each other, distinctions based on residence may amount to prohibited discrimination because of nationality.[895]

Article 24(1) not only concerns situations of taxation that is more burdensome. It also prohibits a Contracting State from subjecting nationals of the other Contracting State to other taxation than its own nationals, that is taxation on the basis of different legal rules.[896] It is not necessary to prove that a different treatment actually resulted in taxation that is more burdensome; 'the mere possibility that a different treatment ...

890. OECD, DAF/FC/70.5, p. 1.
891. *See* OECD, FC/WP4(71)1, pp. 3–4 (Working Party No. 4 proposed a new paragraph to be included in the OECD Commentary in order to clarify that Article 24(1), because of its historical origin and its original justification and scope, should be regarded as an autonomous provision for which application is not restricted by Article 1); OECD, DAF/FC/71.6, p. 1 (the Fiscal Committee adopted this proposal); OECD, CFA/WP1(71)1, p. 3; OECD, DAF/CFA/WP1/71.10, p. 3 (some improvements in drafting); OECD, DAF/CFA/WP1/72/3, p. 4 (adoption); OECD, CFA/WP1(73)6, p. 3; OECD, CFA/WP1(73)10, p. 57; OECD, CFA(73)15, p. 61; and OECD, DAF/CFA/WP1/76.19, p. 112 (an autonomous character is no longer mentioned). *See*, moreover, 2008–2017 OECD Commentary on Article 24, para. 6 (1977–2005: para. 2).
892. It is assumed that the respective national is a resident of only one State and, therefore, cases of dual residence are ignored for the moment.
893. Raad 1986, 84.
894. *See*, for instance, Raad 1992, 674–675.
895. *See* Bammens 2012, 99–108; Moldenhauer 1995a; Moldenhauer 1995b; Lazarski 1989.
896. *See*, for instance, Wassermeyer and Schwenke 2016 m.no. 20; Rust 2015b m.no. 30; Rust 2015c m.no. 42; Rust 2010, 630; Vogel 1997 Article 24, m.no. 35.

might lead to more burdensome taxation is sufficient to invoke Article 24(1).'[897] By that, any requirement connected with taxation is also addressed.

Although Article 24(1) prohibits 'other taxation' and thus different tax treatment, it is argued in the literature[898] and in the OECD Commentary[899] that Article 24(1) does not prohibit preferential treatment of foreigners. According to the OECD Commentary, since Article 24(1) 'has been deliberately framed in a negative form'[900] and 'since the principal object of this clause is to forbid discrimination in one State against the nationals of the other, there is nothing to prevent the first State from granting to persons of foreign nationality, for special reasons of its own, ... [[901]] certain concessions or facilities which are not available to its own nationals'.[902] A prohibition of preferential treatment of foreigners would lead to the creation of a tax liability. Just because tax treaties aim at avoiding double taxation and, therefore, normally do not create taxing rights does not necessarily mean that they are prohibited from doing so (although constitutional laws or laws incorporating a tax treaty might provide otherwise). Nevertheless, the creation of taxing rights is generally not the purpose of a tax

897. Rust 2015b m.no. 30; likewise, Rust 2015c m.no. 30; Vogel 1997 Article 24, m.no. 35.
898. *See*, for instance, Loukota and Jirousek 2016 m.no. 5; Wassermeyer and Schwenke 2016 m.nos. 2c, 20; Rust 2015b m.nos. 3 and 32; Rust 2015c m.nos. 3, 44; Munhoz Ribeiro 2015, 337–338; Pannwitz 2012 m.no. 15; Dommes and Metzler 2006, 129–130; Arnold 1991, 37; Vogel 1997 Article 24, m.no. 35b; Debatin 1970, 131; Schuch and Stieglitz 2006, 416 (who therefrom conclude that 'other or more burdensome taxation' under Article 24(1) equals 'taxation ... less favourably levied' under Article 24(3); disadvantageous tax treatment is covered by both non-discrimination clauses regardless of whether there is a higher tax burden in terms of money); Moritz 2003, 226; differently, Burgstaller and Obermair 2006, 192. John F. Avery Jones, Henri-Robert Depret, et al. acknowledge that the words '*other or* more burdensome' might suggest that discrimination in favour of foreigners is prohibited under Article 24(1) as well. However, the authors argue that, since 'other taxation' refers to a tax different from that to which nationals are subject and 'more burdensome taxation' to a different quantum of tax, these two together mean that, while there is nothing to prevent the taxing State from charging nationals of the other State less of the same tax, it cannot charge a different tax or the same tax on a different occasion even if it is less burdensome, although normally, the taxpayer is unlikely to complain if it did. *See* Avery Jones, Depret, et al. 1991b, 325–326. Accordingly, it seems that the authors believe that Article 24(1) prohibits discrimination in favour of foreigners but only when such favourable treatment is reached through a different tax. Kees van Raad similarly submits that an interpretation of 'other taxation' as prohibiting taxation of foreigners on a different legal basis (*see* Vogel 1997 Article 24, m.no. 35), regardless of the actual tax burden, would produce many challenges of taxation procedures developed for practical reasons. He rather favours the hypothesis of Willem Dirksen that, historically, 'other' might refer to other taxes (in the past, foreigners were often subjected to special levies) and 'more burdensome' to the same type of taxes but levied in a more burdensome way. *See* Raad 1986, 93; differently, Silva 2016b, 76–77 ('[other taxation derives from the fact that a person] may not benefit from certain tax rules ... irrespectively of whether the non-application of such rules leads to a higher tax burden or to being subject to different taxes'); Toifl 1996, 155; Moldenhauer 1995a, 82–83.
899. 2008–2017 OECD Commentary on Article 24, para. 14 (1963: para. 8; 1977–2005: para. 9).
900. *See*, critically, Bammens 2012, 129–130.
901. In 1977, the following (omitted) expression was added to the OECD Commentary: 'or in order to comply with a special stipulation in a double taxation convention, such as, notably, the requirement that profits of permanent establishments are to be taxed on the basis of separate accounts [since 2010: in accordance with Article 7]'. *See* OECD, FC/WP4(69)1, pp. 14–15; OECD, DAF/FC/70.5, p. 4; OECD, FC/WP4(71)1, p. 5; OECD, DAF/FC/71.6, pp. 1–2; OECD, CFA/WP1(71)1, p. 5.
902. 2008–2017 OECD Commentary on Article 24, para. 14 (1963: para. 8; 1977–2005: para. 9).

treaty, which speaks against an interpretation of Article 24(1) that would require taxation of foreigners by prohibiting preferential treatment.[903]

From a historical perspective,[904] the words 'other or more burdensome' in Article 24(1) may be understood as a single concept which does not object to preferential taxation of foreigners but aims at preventing lengthy discussions about whether different taxation is 'more burdensome' or not. When Working Party No. 4 of the OEEC Fiscal Committee drafted the nationality non-discrimination clause, it initially used the expression 'other, higher or more burdensome' (French original: '*différente, plus élevée ou plus lourde*').[905] The Belgian Delegation proposed to the Working Party to simplify the nationality non-discrimination clause by replacing the mentioned expression with 'more burdensome'.[906] Although the Working Party was not opposed to the text being simplified, it considered that the amendment 'would leave room for conflicting judgments on the question whether any given taxation is more burdensome or not than some other taxation'.[907] It believed that it probably would be better to merely prohibit 'other taxation' which would also rule out heavier taxation.[908] At the same time, the Working Party explicitly held that '[i]n its negative form, moreover, and due regard being had to the considerations on which it is founded, an equivalent treatment clause drafted in this way should not, in the Working Party's view, prevent a State from granting, for special reasons of its own, certain concessions or facilities to foreign nationals which would not be available to its own nationals'.[909]

After this exchange of views, the Fiscal Committee agreed on the current wording 'other or more burdensome' (French original: '*autre ou plus lourde*').[910] It then asked Working Party No. 4 to submit a new draft Article with a Commentary taking account of the discussions.[911] In this new Commentary, the Working Party explained that the words 'other or more burdensome' mean that 'tax may not be in another form (no different tax, no different mode of computing the taxable amount, no different rate, etc.) and that the formalities connected with the taxation (returns, payment, prescribed times, etc.) may not be more onerous'.[912] As the OECD Commentary still states today, 'when a tax is imposed on nationals and foreigners in the same circumstances, it must be in the same form as regards both the basis of charge and the method of assessment,

903. *See also* Rust 2015b m.no. 3; Rust 2015c m.no. 3.
904. *See also* Lang 2006, 44–46; Avery Jones 2009, 33–34.
905. OEEC, FC/WP4(57)1, p. 4.
906. OEEC, FC/WP4(57)2, p. 2.
907. *Ibid.*, p. 2.
908. *Ibid.*, p. 2.
909. *Ibid.*, p. 2. Already in its report of January 1957 on tax discrimination on grounds of nationality or similar grounds, Working Party No. 4 recognized that a Member country's legislation may lay down 'more favourable taxation treatment for nationals of a foreign country … than for its own nationals' but decided to omit this category of discrimination from its study 'because the Member country is able to decide of its own accord to end the discrimination against its own nationals'. *See* OEEC, FC/WP4(57)1, pp. 1–2.
910. OEEC, FC/M(57)2, p. 3. Initially, Working Party No. 4 used the French wording '*différente, plus élevée ou plus lourde*' in its report of January 1957 but suggested the wording '*autre, plus élevée ou plus lourde*' in its supplementary report of May 1957; both had been translated as 'other, higher or more burdensome'. *See* OEEC, FC/WP4(57)1, p. 4; OEEC, FC/WP4(57)2, p. 10.
911. OEEC, FC/M(57)2, p. 4.
912. OEEC, FC/WP4(57)3, pp. 5 and 7.

its rate must be the same and, finally, the formalities connected with the taxation (returns, payment, prescribed times, etc.) must not be more onerous for foreigners than for nationals'.[913]

While the term 'other taxation' in Article 24(1) covers not only different taxes but also different tax bases and rates, the nationality non-discrimination clause does not prohibit preferential taxation of foreigners even though, from a formal perspective, such treatment vis-à-vis nationals also constitutes 'other taxation'. Conversely, whether or not taxation is indeed 'more burdensome' should not raise points for discussion as long as the foreigner in question is taxed differently than a comparable national and claims to be discriminated against due to nationality. In such a case, no proof of 'more burdensome taxation' should be required.[914]

Since Article 24(1) protects against discrimination because of nationality, it is important to define 'nationality'. Article 24(2) initially contained a definition of the term 'national'. This definition moved to Article 3(1)(f) in 1992[915] and Article 3(1)(g) in 2000.[916] It underwent minor changes in 2003:[917]

913. 2008–2017 OECD Commentary on Article 24, para. 15 (1963: para. 9; 1977–2005: para. 10). Niels Bammens comments similarly as Raad 1986, 93, and Avery Jones, Depret, et al. 1991b, 325–326 that, from a historical perspective, 'other taxation' refers to the situation in which a foreigner is subject to a different tax entirely, whereas 'more burdensome taxation' refers to the situation when a foreigner is subject to the same tax as a national but this tax is levied in a more burdensome manner (*see also* Bammens and Vanistendael 2016, sec. 2.1.4.2). Nevertheless, on the basis of the quoted statements of the OECD Commentary, he concludes that apparently discrimination in favour of foreigners is possible but limited to the requirements (formalities) connected with the taxation. *See* Bammens 2012, 124–132. If this view is followed, discrimination in favour of foreigners would apparently be prohibited under Article 24(1) as far as the taxation (the basis of charge, the method of assessment, the rate of tax, etc.) is concerned. *See also*, however, Haslehner 2009, 66–67, 258, who submits a contrary interpretation. According to Werner Haslehner, the term 'other' in Article 24(1) only refers to the requirements connected with the taxation while the taxation must be proven to be 'more burdensome' in order to find a violation of Article 24(1). With regard to the (procedural) requirements connected with the taxation, it is often difficult to prove whether other requirements are indeed more burdensome. Conversely, if the same requirements are applied, a comparison of the tax burdens can easily be made; more burdensome tax treatment of foreigners is prohibited; preferential tax treatment of foreigners is allowed.

914. *See also*, to this effect, Lang 2006, 44–45, who concludes from a historical analysis that the expression 'other or more burdensome taxation' intends to cover all forms of higher taxation even if such taxation is not 'more burdensome' without doubt; moreover, Kubaile 2013 m.nos. 23, 80, who notes that 'other or more burdensome taxation' spares the sometimes difficult proof of a greater tax burden; similarly, Rust 2015b m.no. 30; Rust 2015c m.no. 42; Pannwitz 2012 m.no. 15; differently, Dommes and Metzler 2006, 130, who regard 'other ... taxation' (but not 'other ... connected requirements') as meaningless and believe that proof of 'more burdensome taxation' is always required.

915. *See* already OECD, FC/WP4(69)1, p. 9 and Corrigendum, p. 1, in which the United Kingdom Delegation reportedly pointed out that the term 'national' is employed not only in Article 24 but also in Article 4(2)(d) and felt that it would be more logical to transfer the definition of 'national' to Article 3; this suggestion had also been made by the Turkish Delegation. *See*, moreover, OECD, DAF/CFA/WP1/73.2, p. 2, where the Steering Group recommended shifting this definition to Article 3; and OECD, DAF/CFA/WP1/73.5, p. 1, where Working Party No. 1 agreed to the conclusions of the Steering Group.

916. In that year, Article 14 on independent personal services was deleted, which led to additional definitions of the terms 'enterprise' and 'business' in Article 3(1)(c) and (h), respectively.

917. Some redrafting took place by adding the words 'in relation to a Contracting State', and Article 3(1)(g)(i) now uses 'nationality or citizenship' instead of 'nationality'.

Article 3

General Definitions

1. For the purposes of this Convention, unless the context otherwise requires: ...

(g) the term 'national', in relation to a Contracting State, means:
  (i) any individual possessing the nationality or citizenship of that Contracting State; and
  (ii) any legal person, partnership or association deriving its status as such from the laws in force in that Contracting State;

It is beyond the scope of this study to comprehensively deal with the definition of nationality. However, it is important to mention that nationality may coincide with residence, notably, when the nationality of individuals or the place of incorporation of legal persons is used as a criterion for establishing worldwide tax liability. This raises questions regarding the concept of non-discrimination under Article 24(1), which will be extensively analysed below (*see* section §3.06[C]).

[2] Article 24(2): Statelessness

It is estimated that there are at least ten million stateless people in dozens of countries around the world.[918] These people are also protected from tax discrimination due to their statelessness. Article 24(2)[919] resembles the non-discrimination obligation of Article 24(1) and, since 1997, it substantiates the condition of 'in the same circumstances' by adding the phrase 'in particular with respect to residence':[920]

> 2. Stateless persons who are residents of a Contracting State shall not be subjected in either Contracting State to any taxation or any requirement connected therewith, which is other or more burdensome than the taxation and connected requirements to which nationals of the State concerned in the same circumstances, in particular with respect to residence, are or may be subjected.

Article 24(2) enables NT to be accorded to stateless persons, that is individuals who are not considered as a national by any State under the operation of its law.[921] A very similar rule can be found in the Convention relating to the Status of Stateless Persons of 1954 (the 1954 Convention). This diminishes the need for corresponding tax treaty provisions. According to Article 29(1) of the 1954 Convention, '[t]he Contracting States shall not impose upon stateless persons duties, charges or taxes, of any description whatsoever, other or higher than those which are or may be levied on their

918. *See* http://www.unhcr.org/pages/49c3646c155.html (visited on 6 January 2019).
919. Prior to 1992, the non-discrimination clause was contained in Article 24(3). It was redesignated as Article 24(2) when the definition of nationality moved to Article 3(1).
920. Reportedly, it was intended to add this phrase already in 1992 but, for some reason, it was not. *See* OECD, DAFFE/CFA/WP1(94)9, p. 43 (Issue 126); OECD, DAFFE/CFA/WP1/MR(95)2, p. 16 (paras 47–50); OECD, DAFFE/CFA/WP1(95)5, p. 6 (paras 21–24), OECD, DAFFE/CFA/WP1(95)5REV1, p. 4 (paras 15–18); OECD, DAFFE/CFA/WP1(95)5/REV2, pp. 4–5 (paras 17–20); OECD, DAFFE/CFA/WP1(95)5/REV3, p. 17 (para. 75).
921. 2008–2017 OECD Commentary on Article 24, para. 32 (1977: para. 20; 1992–2005: para. 18). *See*, moreover, OECD, FC/WP4(71)1, pp. 9–10.

nationals in similar situations'. Currently, there are ninety-one States parties to the 1954 Convention.[922] In those States, stateless persons are accorded national tax treatment by the 1954 Convention while the respective non-discrimination provisions in tax treaties only extend NT to persons who are excluded from the 1954 Convention's application[923] (namely, persons presently receiving protection or assistance from an organ or agency of the UN other than the United Nations High Commissioner for Refugees (UNHCR), those enjoying the rights and obligations of nationality in their State of residence, war criminals, serious non-political criminals, and similar persons).[924] In other States in which no protection is given by the 1954 Convention, non-discrimination provisions based on Article 24(2) of the OECD Model gain importance.[925]

Instead of relying on the criterion of nationality of the other Contracting State, Article 24(2) requires stateless persons to be residents of a Contracting State. This has been ensured in the 1977 OECD Model by adding an explicit requirement of residence.[926] Thus, arguably, the additional expression '[stateless persons] who are residents of a Contracting State' in Article 24(2)[927] clarified that Article 1 restricts the scope of the non-discrimination clause regarding stateless persons,[928] whereas the second sentence of Article 24(1) changed the scope of the nationality non-discrimination clause by adding that it 'shall, notwithstanding the provisions of Article 1, also apply to persons who are not residents of one or both of the Contracting States'.[929] It may also be argued, however, that both Article 24(1) and Article 24(2) always applied independently of Article 1 which means that the second sentence of Article 24(1) merely clarified this wider scope (*see* section §3.02[A][1]). Conversely, the addition to Article 24(2) limited the application of this non-discrimination clause to stateless persons who are residents of a Contracting State.[930] This view is confirmed by

922. *See* https://treaties.un.org/pages/ViewDetailsII.aspx?src = TREATY&mtdsg_no = V-3&chapter = 5&lang = en (visited on 1 November 2018).
923. 2008-2017 OECD Commentary on Article 24, para. 27 (1977: para. 15; 1992-2005: para. 13). *See*, moreover, OECD, FC/WP4(71)1, pp. 9-10.
924. Article 1(2) of the 1954 Convention.
925. *See also* Dziurdź 2010b, 247-248.
926. Nevertheless, the OECD Commentary contains an alternative provision without a residence requirement so that, in all cases, stateless persons enjoy the most favourable treatment accorded to nationals of the State concerned. *See* 2008-2017 OECD Commentary on Article 24, para. 30 (1977: para. 18; 1992-2005: para. 16).
927. To be precise, the non-discrimination provision on stateless persons was contained in Article 24(3) of the 1977 OECD Model. In order to avoid confusion, only the current numbering of the non-discrimination rules will be used in this study.
928. Rust 2015b m.no. 47; Rust 2015c m.no. 82; Bruns 2013 m.no. 80; differently, Wassermeyer and Schwenke 2016 m.no. 7.
929. Rust 2015b m.no. 28; Rust 2015c m.no. 40; Bruns 2013 m.no. 52; differently, Wassermeyer and Schwenke 2016 m.no. 15; Hageböke 2005 m.no. 35; Kubaile 2013 m.nos. 2.2, 17.
930. On this issue, *see also* Bammens 2012, 180-181; Dommes and Metzler 2006, 96-97; Raad 1986, 84, 86-87. *See*, moreover, OECD, DAF/FC/70.5, p. 5, where the Rapporteur of Working Party No. 4 was inclined to amend the text of Article 24(2) to make it clear that it applied only to stateless persons who were residents of one of the Contracting States. The Delegations for Belgium, Germany, and Luxembourg supported this view. Moreover, *see* OECD, FC/WP4(71)1, pp. 9-10, where this decision is explained as avoiding that stateless persons resident in a third State are placed in a more favourable situation than non-resident nationals of the Contracting

the fact that, after it had been decided to amend the non-discrimination provision concerning stateless persons by including a requirement of residence, Working Party No. 1 of the Committee on Fiscal Affairs asked to mention in the OECD Commentary 'that it was left open to the Contracting States to give the provisions ... either a wider scope (*in accordance with the present provisions of the [1963] Model Convention*) or a narrower scope' (emphasis added).[931] Indeed, if nationals of a Contracting State who are residents of a third State were not covered by Article 24(1), they could never claim non-discriminatory tax treatment. They would be neither a resident of a Contracting State nor a national of a third State thereby not being able to rely on protection against discrimination for the reason of nationality at all. Since nationality, unlike residence, is generally not relevant for taxation purposes, it is not clear why Article 24(1) should erode protection of nationals in such situations by requiring an additional nexus of residence.[932] If stateless persons who are residents of a third State are not covered by Article 24(2), in contrast, they may still rely on such non-discrimination provisions of their residence State's tax treaty network as that State's nationality is obviously no condition for non-discrimination due to statelessness.

Article 24(2) has a wider scope than any other non-discrimination provision in Article 24.[933] It protects a person in both Contracting States, in the residence State, and in the source State.[934] Hence, stateless persons who are residents of a Contracting State can claim national tax treatment in that State.[935] It does not matter whether or not they have a connection to the other Contracting State or any other State in the world; purely

States, although this explanation appears unclear given that nationals resident in a third State are also protected against discrimination under Article 24(1). *See*, similarly, 2008–2017 OECD Commentary on Article 24, paras 28–29 (1977: para. 16–17; 1992–2005: para. 14–15), which states that, by excluding stateless persons who are residents of neither Contracting State from the scope of Article 24(2), 'such a clause prevents their being privileged in one State as compared with nationals of the other State'. It is interesting to note that, when the OECD Fiscal Committee adopted the amendment to the non-discrimination clause on stateless persons, it also asked to substitute 'residents' with 'resident nationals' in the following explanation of the requirement of residence: 'the scope of a clause extending national treatment to stateless persons should, in order to avoid placing stateless persons in a more favourable position than residents [afterwards: resident nationals] of third States, be limited to stateless persons who are residents of the Contracting States.' *See* OECD, FC/WP4(71)1, p. 10; OECD, DAF/FC/71.6, p. 2. This indicates that stateless persons who are resident in a third State should not be treated more favourably than nationals of that third State who are also resident therein. However, Working Party No. 4 apparently missed substituting 'residents' with 'resident nationals'. *See* OECD, CFA/WP1(71)1, p. 6. Later on, this explanation was redrafted to its current (unfortunately ambiguous) wording without any apparent intention to modify its (lost) content. *See* OECD, DAF/CFA/WP1/71.10, p. 4; moreover, OECD, DAF/CFA/WP1/72/3, p. 4 (adoption).

931. OECD, DAF/CFA/WP1/71.3, p. 1. *See also* OECD, DAF/CFA/WP1/71.10, p. 4; moreover, OECD, DAF/CFA/WP1/72/3, p. 4 (adoption).
932. *See also* Debatin 1970, 133.
933. Raad 1986, 85.
934. Article 24(2) states that '[s]tateless persons who are residents of a Contracting State shall not be subjected *in either Contracting State* to any taxation or any requirement connected therewith, which is other or more burdensome' (emphasis added).
935. However, the OECD Commentary contains an alternative provision that restricts the scope of the non-discrimination clause to the treatment in the source State. Accordingly, no national treatment is required in the residence State of the stateless person (unless Article 29(1) of the 1954 Convention applies). *See* 2008–2017 OECD Commentary on Article 24, para. 31 (1977: para. 19; 1992–2005: para. 17).

domestic situations are covered as well. Protection is granted to all stateless persons who are residents of a State as soon as Article 24(2) is included in a single tax treaty.[936]

Article 29(1) of the 1954 Convention protects stateless persons regardless of their residence. Article 24(2) of the OECD Model, in contrast, requires stateless persons to be residents of a Contracting State. According to Niels Bammens[937] and Alexander Rust,[938] if the Contracting States of a tax treaty that includes Article 24(2) of the OECD Model have also signed and ratified the 1954 Convention, a conflict arises concerning the scope of protection for stateless persons who are residents of neither Contracting State. Whereas Article 24(2) of the OECD Model restricts NT to residents, Article 29(1) of the 1954 Convention does not contain such a restriction and applies regardless of residence.[939]

It is true that Article 24(2) of the OECD Model does not obligate a State to grant non-discriminatory treatment to stateless persons who are residents of neither Contracting State. However, Article 24(2) does not object to such treatment being granted. There is also no indication that the Contracting States to a bilateral tax treaty intend to modify and thereby limit the scope of their obligations under the multilateral 1954 Convention. Therefore, it is possible to achieve a harmonious reading of the non-discrimination provisions. As both provisions require non-discrimination in certain cases without prohibiting non-discrimination in other cases, they can be applied simultaneously without raising conflicts or being opposed to each other. Article 29(1) of the 1954 Convention provides for non-discriminatory treatment to non-resident persons who are not covered by Article 24(2) of the OECD Model while Article 24(2) of the OECD Model does not object to such treatment being granted under Article 29(1) of the 1954 Convention. Just because the non-discrimination rules have a partly different scope of application (Article 24(2) of the OECD Model additionally protects persons presently receiving protection or assistance from an organ or agency of the UN other than the UNHCR and also covers requirements connected with taxation; Article 29(1) of the 1954 Convention additionally protects stateless persons who are residents of a third State), this does not trigger issues in their concurrent application.

Despite the fact that there is no conflict with the 1954 Convention, the phrase 'who are residents of a Contracting State' in Article 24(2) has a practical relevant meaning and scope of application. If a stateless person is excluded from the Convention's application pursuant to Article 1(2) of the 1954 Convention, that individual can rely on Article 24(2) of the OECD Model but only if that person is a resident of a Contracting State. This restriction to residents of a Contracting State 'prevails' as the 1954 Convention does not apply. In all other cases, however, a stateless person can rely on both Article 24(2) of the OECD Model and Article 29(1) of the 1954 Convention if the

936. *See also* Dziurdź 2010b, 247–248.
937. Bammens 2012, 181–184.
938. Rust 2015b m.no. 48.
939. A similar line of reasoning, although in a different context, is followed by Adolfo J. Martín Jiménez. He argues that, since Article 10 of the OECD Estate, Inheritance and Gift Model is narrower in scope than Article 24 of the OECD Model (on Income and on Capital), an estate, inheritance, and gift tax treaty may limit the effect and objective scope of the non-discrimination clause in an income and capital tax treaty. *See* Martín Jiménez 2005, 439.

individual is a resident of a Contracting State or only on Article 29(1) of the 1954 Convention if a resident of neither Contracting State.[940]

Article 24(2) extends the effects of Article 24(1) to stateless persons. Therefore, 'other or more burdensome ... taxation' and 'connected requirements' are covered. A Contracting State cannot treat stateless persons differently and thereby presumably more burdensome than nationals who are 'in the same circumstances, in particular with respect to residence'. At this point, it should be mentioned that the following analysis of the concept of non-discrimination will often refer to tax distinctions between nationals and foreigners and to Article 24(1) only. This will be done for the sake of clarity, not to imply substantial differences between Article 24(1) and Article 24(2). All of the conclusions reached on Article 24(1) will be conceptually valid for both non-discrimination obligations.

[B] Non-discrimination Based on Residence

[1] Article 24(3): Permanent Establishments

In income and capital tax legislation, nationality is rarely used as a criterion for the treatment of taxpayers. Rather, different rules are provided for residents and non-residents, that is for persons who are subject to full (worldwide) and limited (source-based) tax liability, respectively. For instance, residents may be taxed on a net basis and by applying a progressive scale of rates whereas non-residents may be taxed on a gross basis and subject to other tax rates. Advantages concerning the deduction of expenses, the depreciation of assets, or the carry-forward of losses may be restricted to residents. While such differences in treatment are generally accepted in international tax law, an exception exists in Article 24(3):[941]

> 3. The taxation on a permanent establishment which an enterprise of a Contracting State has in the other Contracting State shall not be less favourably levied in that other State than the taxation levied on enterprises of that other State carrying on the same activities. This provision shall not be construed as obliging a Contracting State to grant to residents of the other Contracting State any personal allowances, reliefs and reductions for taxation purposes on account of civil status or family responsibilities which it grants to its own residents.

In March 1957, Working Party No. 4 of the OEEC Fiscal Committee concluded that the replies to its questionnaire had 'shown beyond doubt that the form of discrimination in question here occurs but very rarely'.[942] It mentioned earlier, however, that differences in treatment existed in a number of OEEC Member countries concerning expenditure incurred abroad, relief for losses, and (notional) methods of profit computation.[943] The PE non-discrimination clause suggested by Working Party

940. *See*, to this effect, Raad 1986, 87–88.
941. Prior to 1992, the non-discrimination clause was contained in Article 24(4). It was redesignated as Article 24(3) when the definition of nationality moved to Article 3(1).
942. OEEC, FC/WP4(57)2, p. 6. *See also* Lang 2011d, 12–13.
943. OEEC, FC/WP4(57)1, p. 6.

No. 4 initially referred to a less favourable computation of a PE's profits,[944] but the only real difference was seen in whether it would apply to capital taxes as well.[945] Today, the PE non-discrimination clause is the most relevant non-discrimination provision in practice.[946]

The main purpose of the PE non-discrimination clause lies in a contribution to equal conditions of competition between resident and non-resident enterprises (*see* section §3.03[D][1]). If a non-resident enterprise expands its business to the source State through a PE, the competitive opportunities should not be negatively influenced by the source State. Article 7(2) determines the profits that are taxable in the source State by treating the PE as a separate and independent enterprise;[947] the source State is principally not allowed to tax other profits than those attributable to the PE. Article 24(3) extends this hypothetical independence by ensuring that the attributable profits are not taxed more heavily in the source State than the profits of a comparable resident enterprise. Both provisions together contribute to equal conditions of competition. The second sentence of Article 24(3), however, permits the source State to deny any personal allowances, reliefs, and reductions for taxation purposes on account of civil status or family responsibilities. Only the residence State should be responsible for such benefits in order to avoid double benefits in cross-border situations (*see* section §3.03[D][2]).

Article 24(3) covers 'a permanent establishment which an enterprise of a Contracting State [the residence State] has in the other Contracting State [the source State]'. Therefore, it requires 'an enterprise' and 'a permanent establishment'. According to Article 3(1)(d), the term 'enterprise of a Contracting State' means an enterprise carried on by a resident of a Contracting State. Since the 2000 deletion of Article 14 on independent personal services, Article 3(1)(c) defines that the term 'enterprise' applies to the carrying on of any business. Article 3(1)(h) provides that the term 'business' includes the performance of professional services and of other activities of an independent character. Thus, as the OECD Model contains a definition of the term 'enterprise', Article 3(2) on undefined terms cannot apply.[948] An autonomous tax treaty meaning of 'enterprise' prevails over an automatic recourse to a domestic tax law meaning.[949]

Article 5 defines the term 'permanent establishment'. Article 7(1) further provides that the business profits that are attributable to a PE in the source State may be taxed in that State. To determine such profits, Article 7(2) deems a PE to be a separate and independent enterprise. Whether this is a wise approach for attributing profits to a PE or whether the concept of a PE is a suitable concept for modern-day business cannot be questioned under Article 24(3). With the expression '[t]he taxation on a

944. *Ibid.*, p. 7.
945. OEEC, FC/WP4(57)2, pp. 6–7; OEEC, FC/M(57)2, p. 4.
946. *See*, for instance, Rust 2015b m.no. 55; Rust 2010, 638; Debatin 1970, 131.
947. How far this concept goes has been the subject of considerable debate and therefore led to changes to Article 7 of the OECD Model in 2010. *See* OECD, Attribution of Profits Report 2010. However, already Article 7(2) of the 1963 OECD Model referred to 'a distinct and separate enterprise', and Article 7(4) required for a method of apportionment to lead to results that are in accordance with the principles laid down in Article 7.
948. Lang 2011d, 16–17.
949. On the meaning of 'enterprise', *see* Lang 2011d, 9–20.

permanent establishment', Article 24(3) refers in particular to the business profits that are attributable to a PE in the source State. It only scrutinizes how the source State exercises its tax sovereignty with respect to these business profits and does not question the legitimacy of allocation decisions.[950] Income or capital (or functions, assets, and risks) must be allocated to a PE before Article 24(3) can be applied.

Profits that are attributable to a PE situated in the source State under Article 7(2) and that are, therefore, taxable in the source State under Article 7(1) are protected by the PE non-discrimination clause. It is unclear, however, whether the same is true with respect to business profits that are not governed by Article 7(1) but by a more specific allocation rule. According to the prevailing opinion in the literature,[951] Article 24(3) also applies with respect to profits derived by an enterprise that are governed by Article 6 (income from immovable property), Article 8 (shipping, inland waterways transport, and air transport), and Article 17 (entertainers and sportspersons).[952] In situations when an allocation rule does not rely on a PE for the purpose of allocating taxing rights among the Contracting States, tax discrimination may also be prohibited. Of course, a precondition is that, pursuant to Article 5, a PE actually exists in the source State and

950. *See also* Bammens and Vanistendael 2016, secs. 2.3.1.1, 2.3.3.1.2.1, 6.1.1, according to whom the framework within which Article 24(3) applies is determined by Article 7 or, in other words, the scope of application of Article 24(3) is limited to the taxation of profits attributed to a PE under Article 7. It should be noted, however, that Article 24(3) also applies to taxes on capital that are not governed by Article 7 but by Article 22(2).

951. Haslehner 2016a m.no. 19; Loukota and Jirousek 2016 m.no. 27; Rust 2015b m.no. 59 (but differently, Rust 2015c m.no. 98); Reimer 2015 m.nos. 43a, 204; Munhoz Ribeiro 2015, 340–341; Lang 2011d, 13–15; Haslehner 2009, 175–176, 228; Tumpel and Stangl 2006, 72–73; H. Loukota 2005, 58–59; Saccardo 2003, 275–277; Toifl 2003, 267–268; Avery Jones, Depret, et al. 1991b, 330; Raad 1986, 135–136. Moreover, in the Article 5 Discussion Draft 2011 (m.nos. 5–9) and the Article 5 Revised Discussion Draft 2012 (m.nos. 5–9), a Working Group composed of Delegates to Working Party No. 1 of the OECD Committee on Fiscal Affairs suggested that the following be added to the OECD Commentary on Article 5: '[t]he determination of whether or not an enterprise of a Contracting State has a permanent establishment in the other Contracting State must be made independently from the determination of which provisions of the Convention apply to the profits derived by that enterprise.' *See also* Hoor 2012, 208; Bendlinger 2011, 532; now, moreover, 2017 OECD Commentary on Article 5, para. 9. In 1969, Working Party No. 4 of the OECD Fiscal Committee reported that the Delegations were divided over whether the term 'profits of an enterprise' to which Article 24(3) refers extends to agricultural profits. *See* OECD, FC/WP4(69)1, p. 8–9. *See also*, against an application of Article 24(3) to PEs of agricultural or forestry enterprises (or even to all immovable property attributable to a PE), Bammens and Vanistendael 2016, secs. 2.3.1.1, 2.3.3.1.2.2, 6.1.1; Bammens 2012, 185–187, 188–189, 229–231; Vogel 1997 Article 24, m.no. 121; implicitly also Dürrschmidt 2015 m.no. 41a.

952. It should be noted that the German Federal Fiscal Court (Bundesfinanzhof), in its decision of 27 October 2011, I R 26/11, denied the existence of an enterprise under Article 6 and, consequently, rejected a concept of a PE with respect to income from agriculture or forestry. *See*, critically, Engel and Hilbert 2012. Also, the Austrian Constitutional Court (Verfassungsgerichtshof) assumed in its decision of 15 March 1990, B 758/88, B 759/88, that the non-discrimination clause of Article 24(3) does not apply to income from agriculture or forestry covered by Article 6. *See*, critically, Staringer and Jettmar 2006, 403–405. Nevertheless, it appears undisputed that, at least under Article 8, an enterprise exists (Article 8 actually uses the term 'enterprise') and thus the PE non-discrimination provision may apply. *See*, for instance, the decision of the German Federal Fiscal Court (Bundesfinanzhof) of 22 April 1998, I R 54/96, in which the Court granted protection under Article 24(3) in the context of Article 8. *See also*, for example, Lang 2014, 60; W. Loukota 2005, 332; Lang and Loukota 2003, 70.

that the profits (even though they are taxable in the source State regardless of a PE) are connected to that PE within the meaning of Article 7(2) – they would be attributable if Article 7 was applied.

Article 24(1) prohibits other or more burdensome taxation or any requirement connected therewith. Article 24(3) prohibits taxation that is less favourable. Arguably, 'less favourable' under Article 24(3) is used as a synonym to 'more burdensome' under Article 24(1) but not to 'other' taxation.[953] This difference in wording thus indicates that, under the PE non-discrimination clause, 'it does not constitute discrimination to tax non-resident persons differently, for practical reasons, from resident persons, as long as this does not result in more burdensome taxation for the former than for the latter'.[954] Since it is the result alone that counts[955] and since connected requirements are not covered by Article 24(3),[956] it appears permissible to assess the profits of a PE and to collect the tax differently, that is 'to adapt the mode of taxation to the particular circumstances in which the taxation is levied',[957] as long as the PE is not taxed more heavily than a resident enterprise.[958]

As outlined above (*see* section §3.02[A][1]), the phrase 'other or more burdensome' in Article 24(1) is not meant to prohibit favourable tax treatment of foreigners; taxation may differ between foreigners and nationals as long as it favours foreigners. In situations of uncertainty about whether certain tax treatment that is claimed to be more burdensome is indeed just that, the word 'other' tips the balance in favour of more

953. *See*, for instance, Rust 2015b m.no. 66; Avery Jones, Depret, et al. 1991b, 331; differently, Oesterhelt 2015 m.no. 103; Schuch and Stieglitz 2006, 415–417.
954. 2008–2017 OECD Commentary on Article 24, para. 34 (1977: para. 22; 1992–2005: para. 20; similarly, 1963: para. 16). *See also*, for instance, Wassermeyer and Schwenke 2016 m.no. 49; Hohenwarter 2010, 173–174; Hohenwarter and Weninger 2006, 248; W. Loukota 2005, 339–340; Raad 1986, 141. As far as can be seen, to John F. Avery Jones, Henri-Robert Depret, et al., this difference in wording merely indicates that the charging of a *different tax* on a PE is permitted by Article 24(3) as long as the quantum of tax is not greater than that payable by a resident. *See* Avery Jones, Depret, et al. 1991b, 331. Accordingly, different modes of taxation within the *same tax* are not covered by 'other taxation' under Article 24(1) and are thus permitted under both Article 24(1) and Article 24(3) as long as they do not lead to more burdensome taxation (para. 1) or less favourable taxation (para. 3), that is, a greater quantum of tax. If it is assumed, however, that 'other taxation' under Article 24(1) refers to different modes of taxation within the same tax as well, the difference between 'other or more burdensome' (para. 1) and 'less favourably levied' (para. 3) supports a result-oriented interpretation of discrimination under Article 24(3).
955. 2008–2017 OECD Commentary on Article 24, para. 34 (1963: para. 16; 1977: para. 22; 1992–2005: para. 20).
956. *See*, however, Schuch and Stieglitz 2006, 414–415.
957. 2008–2017 OECD Commentary on Article 24, para. 34 (1977: para. 22; 1992–2005: para. 20; similarly, 1963: para. 16).
958. *See*, for instance, Rust 2015b m.no. 66; Rust 2015c m.no. 104; Kubaile 2013 m.no. 37; Hageböke 2004 m.no. 71; Goldberg and Glicklich 1992, 91–92; Avery Jones, Depret, et al. 1991b, 331; Engelschalk 1988, 102; Raad 1986, 141; Debatin 1970, 135; differently, Loukota and Jirousek 2016 m.nos. 37–42, who argue that a different tax collection procedure such as a withholding tax may also constitute less favourable taxation on a PE; moreover, Schuch and Stieglitz 2006, 415–417. *See also* OEEC, FC/WP4(57)2, p. 6 ('[t]he provision envisaged leaves a country completely free to devise special rules for computing the profits of a permanent establishment of a foreign enterprise, so long as such profits are not thereby less favourably computed than the profits of national enterprises'); OEEC, FC/M(57)2, p. 4; OEEC, FC/WP4(57)3, pp. 6 and 12.

burdensome taxation and thereby helps to establish prohibited tax discrimination. It follows that, under Article 24(1), a proof of different taxation together with a claim of more burdensome taxation or discrimination should suffice for the application of the non-discrimination rule. Under Article 24(3), in contrast, taxation must actually be less favourably levied or levied differently but for no practical reason[959] in order to constitute prohibited tax discrimination.[960] In any case, other or more burdensome requirements connected with taxation are not covered by Article 24(3).[961]

Article 24(3) protects the non-resident enterprise that conducts business in the source State through a PE and deals only with the taxation on the PE. When establishing less favourable taxation, only the tax burden on the PE has to be compared with that of a domestic enterprise.[962] Accordingly, when a higher tax is levied on another person, such as on the shareholder of the non-resident enterprise, this fact cannot be taken into account for the comparison of the tax burdens.[963]

[2] Article 24(4): Deductibility

Article 24(4) of the OECD Model provides for the non-discrimination principle in respect of certain payments and debts to non-resident persons. While the first sentence deals with income taxation and the deductibility of disbursements, the second sentence of Article 24(4) contains a very similar rule for capital taxation:

> 4. Except where the provisions of paragraph 1 of Article 9, paragraph 6 of Article 11, or paragraph 4 of Article 12, apply, interest, royalties and other disbursements paid by an enterprise of a Contracting State to a resident of the other Contracting

959. *See* 2008–2017 OECD Commentary on Article 24, para. 34 (1963: para. 16; 1977: para. 22; 1992–2005: para. 20). In this context, the question arises of which practical reasons should allow for 'different taxation' and how differently 'different taxation' can legitimately be. *See also* Haslehner 2009, 252, 258–260. It is worth mentioning that Working Party No. 4 of the OEEC Fiscal Committee believed that the words 'shall not be less favourably assessed' give the right to apply different taxation so long as this does not result in taxation that is more burdensome. However, it also mentioned that 'the States should limit their claims in this respect, by endeavouring not to resort to different taxation unless it is in keeping, not only with their own conceptions, but also with generally accepted standards'. *See* OEEC, FC/WP4(57)3, p. 12; moreover, Avery Jones 2009, 39–40.
960. Werner Haslehner argues that not only a higher nominal tax burden but also liquidity costs and cash-flow disadvantages may lead to taxation of a PE that is less favourable (for instance, when the same amount of tax is levied by way of a withholding tax at an earlier point in time and without compensation for this time difference). *See* Haslehner 2009, 258–261, 377–378; similarly, Oesterhelt 2015 m.no. 104; Tumpel and Stangl 2006, 80, 90; to this effect, also Schuch and Stieglitz 2006, 423. In fact, such liquidity costs and cash-flow disadvantages could be covered as taxation levied differently but for no practical reasons. This approach would render liquidity costs and cash-flow disadvantages not discriminatory per se but would require additional proof of why it is incomprehensible to tax a PE differently than resident enterprises in a particular case. To a certain extent, this approach would involve a justification analysis at the level of 'less favourable treatment'. *See also* Hohenwarter 2010, 626.
961. *See* Avery Jones, Depret, et al. 1991b, 331 ('[c]onnected requirements are not mentioned in this provision, no doubt because a permanent establishment may well need to be taxed in a different way from a resident'); differently, Schuch and Stieglitz 2006, 414–415.
962. Rust 2015b m.no. 66.
963. Rust 2015b m.no. 66; Rust 2015c m.no. 104. *See*, moreover, Rust 2004, 392–393.

> State shall, for the purpose of determining the taxable profits of such enterprise, be deductible under the same conditions as if they had been paid to a resident of the first-mentioned State. Similarly, any debts of an enterprise of a Contracting State to a resident of the other Contracting State shall, for the purpose of determining the taxable capital of such enterprise, be deductible under the same conditions as if they had been contracted to a resident of the first-mentioned State.

Article 24(4) was added to the OECD Model in 1977[964] because certain States disallowed the deduction of interest and royalty payments unless the recipient also resided in that State or was taxable in that State.[965] It was considered desirable that the deduction should be allowed in these cases regardless of residence. Article 24(4) thus protects resident enterprises (the payor or debtor) against discrimination based on the residence of another person (the recipient or creditor).

Article 24(4) is motivated by concerns that the Contracting States might substitute juridical with economic double taxation in order to compensate for a loss of tax revenue caused by a tax treaty (*see* section §3.03[E][1]). When a resident of a Contracting State pays interest or royalties to a resident of the other Contracting State, Articles 11 and 12 apply to the recipient and limit the taxing rights of the first-mentioned State. At the same time, such payments usually constitute deductible expenses for the payor and, therefore, lower the taxable base in the State of the payor. This State, therefore, is confronted with a double burden; it loses taxing rights for interest or royalties under Articles 11 and 12, respectively, and it deducts interest or royalties from the taxable base, which lowers its tax revenue.

While it is widely (but perhaps wrongly) believed that such a double loss of tax revenue is a reason why Article 15(2)(b) and (c), the 183-day rule on income from employment, grants taxing rights to the source State where the remuneration for employment is deductible,[966] a double loss of tax revenue is no reason for the State of the payor to compensate by denying a deduction of interest and royalties that are paid to a non-resident recipient. A prohibition of a deduction could save the State of the payor from its double burden, but it could also create economic double taxation through non-deductible payments at the level of the payor and taxable income at the level of the recipient. Article 24(4) thus explicitly prohibits different treatment based on whether the recipient is subject to tax or not, that is based on whether the recipient is a resident or non-resident. The deduction should not be forbidden by reason of the fact that the tax payable by the recipient of such interest or royalties is reduced or not levied in the State of source in the application of Articles 11 and 12, respectively. 'Any other method of procedure might cancel out the beneficial effects of the measures taken to avoid double taxation.'[967]

---

964. Prior to 1992, the non-discrimination clause was contained in Article 24(5). It was redesignated as Article 24(4) when the definition of nationality moved to Article 3(1).
965. *See* 1963 OECD Commentary on Article 11, para. 17; and on Article 12, para. 9. *See also* Rust 2015b m.no. 91; Rust 2015c m.no. 137.
966. *See*, in detail, Dziurdź and Pötgens 2014, 404–406; Dziurdź 2013a, 123–124; Dziurdź 2013c, sec. 3.2, with further references.
967. 1963 OECD Commentary on Article 11, para. 17; and on Article 12, para. 9.

Article 24(4) does not include any express comparability requirements (*see* section §3.04[B][3]). It merely states that payments and debts must be 'deductible under the same conditions' as in a domestic context. All requirements for the deduction, including the amount and the timing of the deduction, must not be less favourable.[968] Despite that, the OECD Commentary believes that Article 24(4) 'does not prohibit additional information requirements with respect to payments made to non-residents since these requirements are intended to ensure similar levels of compliance and verification in the case of payments to residents and non-residents'.[969]

It should be mentioned further that Article 24(4) contains an exception or carve-out for non-arm's-length payments and debts; discrimination because of the recipient's or creditor's residence is prohibited '[e]xcept where the provisions of paragraph 1 of Article 9, paragraph 6 of Article 11, or paragraph 4 of Article 12, apply'. What role this statement plays (*see* Chapter 4, section §4.04[A][4]) and whether it is a prerequisite for excluding non-arm's-length transactions from non-discrimination obligations will be analysed in connection with Article 24(5), which does not provide for such a carve-out (*see* Chapter 4, section §4.04[A][5]).

[3] Article 24(5): Ownership and Control

Article 24(5)[970] protects resident enterprises against discrimination based on the residence of their shareholders. It is worded similarly to Article 24(1) and (2):

> 5. Enterprises of a Contracting State, the capital of which is wholly or partly owned or controlled, directly or indirectly, by one or more residents of the other Contracting State, shall not be subjected in the first-mentioned State to any taxation or any requirement connected therewith which is other or more burdensome than the taxation and connected requirements to which other similar enterprises of the first-mentioned State are or may be subjected.

Article 24(5) complements the other non-discrimination provisions.[971] If a company of a Contracting State conducts business in the other Contracting State, it is protected by Article 24(1) against discrimination based on nationality, that is its incorporation in the first-mentioned State. If that company conducts business in the other Contracting State through a PE, the income and capital that is attributable to this PE are protected by Article 24(3) against discrimination based on residence. Finally, when that company conducts business in the other Contracting State through a subsidiary, this subsidiary, as a resident of the other Contracting State, is protected by Article 24(5) against discrimination based on the residence of its shareholder, that is the parent company. Article 24(5) consequently allows an investor to conduct business

968. Rust 2015b m.no. 99.
969. 2008–2017 OECD Commentary on Article 24, para. 75.
970. In 1977, when the deductibility non-discrimination clause was added to the OECD Model, the non-discrimination clause on ownership and control moved from Article 24(5) to Article 24(6). In 1992, it became Article 24(5) when the definition of nationality moved to Article 3(1).
971. *See also* Haslehner 2016a m.no. 32.

in the other Contracting State through a company (the subsidiary)[972] resident therein without this company being discriminated against on the basis of the investor's residence. This view is supported by the Thin Capitalisation Report, according to which Article 24(5) is aimed broadly at preventing 'tax protectionism', that is the deterrence by tax measures of investment from outside the country.[973]

It is also argued that Article 24(5) indirectly protects or benefits not only the non-resident investor[974] but also the investor's residence State; this State may only be willing to provide relief from economic double taxation at the investor's level if the State of the subsidiary does not tax this company higher than other comparable enterprises.[975] In addition, Article 24(5) might not only be concerned with the investor or the investor's State. It might also secure a particular allocation of taxing rights as stipulated by the tax treaty. Since non-resident shareholders in a resident company imply a loss of taxing rights under the tax treaty with regard to dividends and capital gains, a Contracting State should not respond by creating economic double taxation, that is, by discriminating against resident enterprises on the basis of their shareholders' residence (*see* section §3.03[E][2]).

Article 24(5) prohibits other or more burdensome taxation or connected requirements. All taxation rules should be applied without regard to the shareholder's residence, or they may otherwise lead to prohibited tax discrimination. Moreover, Article 24(5) protects '[e]nterprises of a Contracting State' as defined in Article 3(1)(c), (d), and (h). Such enterprises can be carried on by individuals or by other persons, notably, corporations. Nevertheless, since the non-discrimination clause also requires direct or indirect ownership or control of the capital of the protected enterprise and since it is impossible to own or control the capital of individuals, only enterprises carried on by corporations or other entities are addressed by Article 24(5). If a partnership is subject to a particular tax as a resident person, discrimination based on where its partners reside is prohibited as well.[976]

It is important to strictly distinguish between the taxation of the enterprise that is carried on by a resident person and the taxation of the shareholder or partner who wholly or partly owns or controls, directly or indirectly, the capital of that enterprise. Article 24(5) scrutinizes only the tax treatment of the resident enterprise, not the tax treatment of the non-resident shareholder or partner.[977] Therefore, it is prohibited to

972. Although 'the subsidiary' implies that the investor is 'the parent company', it should be noted that an investor under Article 24(5) may also be an individual.
973. OECD, Thin Capitalisation Report, para. 66(b) on p. 27.
974. *See* Munhoz Ribeiro 2015, 342–343; Allevato Neto 2015, 554; Bruns 2013 m.no. 148; Rust 2010, 641; Bronselaer and Heyvaert 2009 m.no. 23.83; Burgstaller and Obermair 2006, 189.
975. Bennett 2006, 463–464; moreover, Rust 2015b m.no. 105; Rust 2015c m.no. 160; Bruns 2013 m.no. 148; Rust 2010, 641, 656.
976. *See*, to this effect, Freeden, Häck, and Schaumburg 2017 m.no. 4.64; Rust 2015b m.no. 107; Rust 2015c m.no. 163; Hageböke 2005 m.no. 103; Fischer-Zernin 1997 m.no. 53; Raupach 1966, 89; somewhat differently, Burgstaller and Obermair 2006, 175–177, who apparently require an opaque treatment of a partnership for income tax purposes and, therefore, would not apply Article 24(5) to other taxes if a fiscally transparent partnership is involved; similarly, Wassermeyer and Schwenke 2016 m.no. 89; Haslehner 2016a m.no. 33; Haslehner 2009, 81–82.
977. *See* Vanistendael 2016, 251; Wassermeyer and Schwenke 2016 m.no. 86; Silva 2016b, 74–75, 109–111; Bammens and Vanistendael 2016, sec. 2.5.1.2.1; Loukota and Jirousek 2016 m.no.

tax a resident enterprise other or more burdensome when its shareholder is a non-resident instead of a resident, but it is permissible to tax this shareholder other or more burdensome than a resident shareholder. In the words of the OECD Commentary, the provision of Article 24(5) 'and the discrimination which it puts an end to, relates to the taxation only of enterprises and not of the persons owning or controlling their capital'.[978]

[C] Taxes of Every Kind and Description

Article 24(6)[979] defines the substantive scope of the non-discrimination clauses:

> 6. The provisions of this Article shall, notwithstanding the provisions of Article 2, apply to taxes of every kind and description.

The origins of this paragraph and the expression 'taxes of every kind and description' can be traced back to the work of Working Party No. 4.[980] The nationality non-discrimination provision in the Working Party's report of January 1957 on tax discrimination on the grounds of nationality or similar grounds covered only taxes on income and capital, and on estates, inheritances and gifts.[981] Thereupon, the Swiss Delegation suggested not maintaining this limitation but to cover taxes and contributions in general. By including an additional clause and, in particular, using the expression 'of every kind and description', the aim was 'to prevent discriminatory treatment in relation to all taxes whatever'.[982] It seems that this wide scope of Article

---

120; Allevato Neto 2015, 557–558; Rust 2015c m.no. 164; Bruns 2013 m.nos. 148, 165; Kubaile 2013 m.no. 74; Raad 2012, 163; Bammens 2012, 380; Bronselaer and Heyvaert 2009 m.no. 23.83; De Broe 2008, 552–553; Helminen 2007, 107; Hageböke and Käbisch 2006, 851; Baker 2006 m.no. 24B.07; Burgstaller and Obermair 2006, 187; Rust 2005, 28; Baker 2004, 210; Hageböke 2005 m.no. 102; Rust 2003b, 659; Moritz 2003, 236; Toifl 2003, 268; Brendt 2003, 902; Fischer-Zernin 1997 m.no. 56; Lang 1994b, 152; Hughes 1996, 390; Hinnekens 1995, 225; Hosson and Michielse 1989, 474; Raad 1986, 186; Debatin 1981 III m.nos. 332, 334; Rädler and Raupach 1966, 394.

978. 2008–2017 OECD Commentary on Article 24, para. 76 (1963: para. 18; 1977–2005: para. 57). *See also* OEEC, FC/WP4(57)3, p. 13, where Working Party No. 4 of the OEEC Fiscal Committee already clarified with the quoted statement that it is the taxation of the companies and not of their shareholders that is in question. *See* Lang 2006, 40–41; Lang 2007b, 107; Avery Jones, Baker, et al. 2011b, 185–186; Avery Jones, Baker, et al. 2011a, 542–543.
979. In 1977, when the deductibility non-discrimination clause was added to the OECD Model, the clause on the relevant taxes moved from Article 24(6) to Article 24(7). In 1992, it became Article 24(6) when the definition of nationality moved to Article 3(1).
980. *See also* Brandstetter 2011, 138–141; Dziurdź 2010b, 239–240.
981. OEEC, FC/WP4(57)1, pp. 1 et seq. (and in particular p. 4).
982. OEEC, FC/WP4(57)2, pp. 1–2. *See also* OEEC, FC/M(57)2, pp. 3–4. It is worth mentioning that the Fiscal Committee initially defined the term 'taxation' (French original: '*imposition*') in accordance with the proposal of the Swiss Delegation as 'contributions of every kind and description' (French original: '*les contributions de toute nature ou dénomination*'). This definition was later translated into English as 'taxes of every kind and description'. *See* OEEC, FC/WP4(57)4, p. 5. As far as can be seen, the French definition then changed from '*les contributions de toute nature ou dénomination*' (draft report by the Fiscal Committee of February 1958) to '*les impôts de toute nature ou dénomination*' (revised draft report by the Fiscal Committee of April 1958) without any explanation. *See* OEEC, FC(58)2, p. 21; FC(58)2(Rev.1) Part I, pp. 24 (English) and 22 (French). In the 1963 OECD Commentary on

24 was driven by the view that all discrimination is undesirable as an impediment to international trade. John F. Avery Jones, Philip Baker, et al. find some evidence that the concern was that, if not so extended, States could get around the intent of Article 24 by subjecting the relevant taxpayer to a discriminatory tax not within the covered range (e.g., a tax on turnover with the rate set in such a way that it operated much like a tax on income).[983]

Article 24(6) of the 1963 OECD Model stated that '[i]n this Article the term "taxation" means taxes of every kind and description'. Therefore, while the meaning of 'taxation' was broad, it was still possible to argue that the scope of Article 24 was restricted by Article 2, or at least that it was not precisely clear what taxes were covered.[984] Thus, in 1977, the wording changed by referring to an application of the non-discrimination provisions 'notwithstanding the provisions of Article 2'. This change meant to clarify the meaning of Article 24(6), namely, that the non-discrimination rules of Article 24 also apply to taxes not within the scope of the Convention.[985] Consequently, they apply to all taxes levied by, or on behalf of, a State, its political subdivisions, or local authorities[986] such as, income taxes, capital taxes, estate, inheritance and gift taxes, VAT or goods and services taxes (GST),[987] sales taxes, turnover taxes, excise taxes, capital duties,[988] and local property taxes.[989]

It is worth mentioning that Working Party No. 4 of the OECD Fiscal Committee suggested in 1971 to include in the Commentary that:[990]

> the term [taxation] covers taxes of every kind or description payable compulsorily, finally, and without counterpart, in order to meet the expenditure of the State, its political sub-divisions or its local authorities. It follows that the provisions of Article 24 do not apply to three categories of levies which do not have the character of a tax, namely:
>
> - dues payable in consideration of services rendered;

Article 24, para. 19, the French words '*les contributions de toute nature ou dénomination*' remained. *See also* OEEC, FC(58)2(Rev.1) Part II, pp. 28 (English) and 29 (French).

983. Avery Jones, Baker, et al. 2011b, 190–191; Avery Jones, Baker, et al. 2011a, 547–548. *See also* Rust 2015b m.no. 123; Rust 2015c m.no. 180; Brandstetter 2011, 135.
984. *See* OECD, FC/WP4(69)1, p. 12; OECD, DAF/FC/70.5, p. 5.
985. *See*, for instance, Wassermeyer and Schwenke 2016 m.no. 11; Rust 2015b m.no. 122; Rust 2015c m.no. 180; Oesterhelt 2015 m.no. 149; Bruns 2013 m.no. 24; Vogel 1997 Article 24, m.no. 175; Raad 1986, 201; to this effect, also Kumpf 1982, 175; Bellstedt 1973, 115–116; Debatin 1970, 132; Rädler and Raupach 1966, 251, 367; Raupach 1966, 86–87; Heining and Timbart 1961 m.no. 143.
986. 2008-2017 OECD Commentary on Article 24, para. 81 (1963: para. 19; 1977: para. 58; 1992–2005: para. 60). On the meaning of 'taxes of every kind and description', *see also* Díaz Prado 2015, 578–586; Brandstetter 2011, sec. 3.1.2.3.1; Dommes and Metzler 2006, 99–102; Martín Jiménez 2005, 438–439.
987. Rust 2015b m.no. 124; Lang 2011a, 331–334; Maisto 2011a, 53–57 (although concluding that the application of Article 24 to VAT cases is almost theoretical); Bourgeois and Römer 2009, 1233–1247; Raad 1986, 202. *See*, however, on Article 24(3), Zalasiński 2007, 467; critically Bourgeois and Römer 2009, 1244–1245; Maisto 2011a, 54.
988. *See*, for instance, Valkenburg 1995; Debatin 1981 III m.no. 311; Bellstedt 1973, 115–121.
989. Avery Jones, Depret, et al. 1991b, 345; Raad 1986, 202. On social security contributions, *see also* Díaz Prado 2015, 585–586; in detail, moreover, Brandstetter 2011, sec. 3.1.1.8.
990. OECD, FC/WP4(71)1, p. 21.

- parafiscal levies payable for the benefit of certain public or private co-operations;
- contributions paid to social security institutions.

Furthermore, it should be understood that [c]ustoms duties, although presenting the character of a tax, do not, in view of their non-recurrent character and special regulation, fall within the scope of Article 24.

However, the Fiscal Committee decided (unfortunately without any reported reasoning) to keep the text of the OECD Commentary[991] which basically repeats the wording of Article 24(6) without giving any additional guidance.[992]

Although the non-discrimination provisions of Article 24 apply to taxes of every kind and description,[993] the application of these provisions to taxes other than on income and capital is not always straightforward.[994] In particular, the PE non-discrimination rule imposes conditions for its application which might be difficult to meet with some taxes that are not levied on persons.[995] Article 24(3) concerns '[t]he taxation on a permanent establishment [as defined in Article 5][996] which an enterprise of a Contracting State has in the other Contracting State'. Article 3(1)(d) defines the term 'enterprise of a Contracting State' as 'an enterprise carried on by a resident of a Contracting State'. Article 4(1) requires for residence in a Contracting State liability to tax by reason of domicile, residence, place of management, or any other criterion of a similar nature, and this requirement usually corresponds to a comprehensive liability to tax - full tax liability - based on the taxpayer's personal attachment to the State concerned.[997] It could thus be argued that impersonal taxes that are levied on objects, sales, or transactions and not on persons are not within the ambit of Article 24(3).

Article 24(3) indeed presupposes a resident person, and residence might be difficult to establish with impersonal taxes. On the one hand, it is not convincing to refer to residence under an income or capital tax system when dealing with other taxes.[998] A person might be subject to full tax liability in both Contracting States in regard to income. In such a case, the tiebreaker rules of Article 4(2) and (3) decide about the residence State for tax treaty purposes. However, this residence State can be the source State concerning capital, especially if a capital tax is only levied in the other Contracting State. To rephrase, there might be two different residence States under Article 4, that is one for income tax purposes and one for capital tax purposes.[999] When the non-discrimination provisions are applied to a tax other than on income and

991. OECD, DAF/FC/71.6, p. 4.
992. 1963 OECD Commentary on Article 24, para. 19 (similarly 1977: para. 58; 1992–2005: para. 60; 2008–2017: para. 81).
993. However, Article 24(4) only refers to 'taxable profits' and 'taxable capital', which indicates a more limited scope. *See also* Haslehner 2016a m.nos. 28, 40.
994. *See also*, for instance, Díaz Prado 2015, 594–595.
995. *See also* Dziurdź 2010c, 266–271.
996. Maisto 2011a, 54–56; Dziurdź 2010c, 268; Bourgeois and Römer 2009, 1246.
997. 1963–2017 OECD Commentary on Article 4, para. 3.
998. Dziurdź 2010c, 268–269.
999. *See*, however, Ismer and Riemer 2015 m.no. 21, who deal with a situation where a person is only liable to one specific tax and argue that although each tax has to be assessed individually, liability to one tax can be sufficient for residence and thus for treaty entitlement with respect to all taxes; similarly, Lüdicke 2015 m.no. 20.

capital, no preference for income tax residence or capital tax residence is apparent.[1000] Moreover, a person (for instance, a transparent partnership) may not be a resident for income and capital tax purposes but subject to other taxes.[1001] All of these issues question the relevance of such residence concepts.[1002] On the other hand, impersonal taxes on objects, sales, or transactions do not heavily use a criterion of residence, if at all. When Article 4 is applied to value added taxes, for instance, no distinction between full and limited tax liability of a person can be relied on; only supplies are taxed in a particular State. On initial consideration, without full (value added) tax liability, a person cannot be a resident under Article 4 and without a resident of a Contracting State, Article 24(3) cannot be applied.

Nevertheless, when objects, sales, or transactions are taxed or even when the ultimate burden is expected to fall on consumers, enterprises may, in effect, be taxed differently depending on their residence. For example, a VAT exemption for small and medium-sized enterprises may allow an enterprise to supply goods and services for a lower price than its competitors or to achieve higher profits.[1003] If this exemption is restricted to resident enterprises, non-resident enterprises may suffer from less favourable tax treatment.[1004] It is not precisely clear why, in such a case, the legal technique of a tax should prevent the non-discrimination provisions of Article 24 from applying.[1005] Moreover, even without full tax liability, tax treaty residence under Article 4 can be established.[1006] Some income tax systems are designed on a territorial basis. They subject to tax only income sourced in the State concerned without distinguishing between residents and non-residents or between full and limited tax liability. The second sentence of Article 4(1) states that 'the term "resident of a Contracting State" ... does not include any person who is liable to tax in that State in respect only of income from sources in that State'.[1007] Yet, the OECD Commentary puts this sentence into perspective: the second sentence of Article 4(1) 'has to be interpreted in the light of its object and purpose ... because it might otherwise exclude from the scope of the Convention all residents of countries adopting a territorial principle in their taxation, a result which is clearly not intended'.[1008]

1000. Dziurdź 2010c, 268–269.

1001. Dziurdź 2010c, 269. Michael Lang conversely argues that, since partnerships can qualify as residents for VAT purposes when applying the PE non-discrimination clause, they should also qualify as residents for income tax purposes even if they are not subject to income tax in the (residence) State to which they have a close personal connection. *See* Lang 2011a, 334–337.

1002. *See also*, to this effect, Rust 2015b m.no. 107; likewise, Rust 2015c m.no. 163, who states that the application of Article 24(5) 'to partnerships can, therefore [since Article 24(5) applies to all taxes and not only in respect of those on income and capital], not depend on whether or not the partnership is subject to income and/or capital tax in its State of organization. It has to be asked whether the partnership is subject to the particular (discriminatory) tax itself'.

1003. Dziurdź 2010c, 267.

1004. Dziurdź 2010c, 267.

1005. Dziurdź 2010c, 267–268.

1006. Dziurdź 2010c, 269.

1007. *See also* Lang 2011a, 333, who notes that the second sentence of Article 4(1) only refers to income and capital and, therefore, cannot limit the concept of residence for the purposes of VAT.

1008. 2008–2017 OECD Commentary on Article 4, para. 8.3 (similarly 1992–2005: para. 8).

States that have a territorial tax system and, consequently, do not tax residents on a worldwide basis may, nevertheless, distinguish between taxpayers on the basis of residence, notably when granting personal tax deductions. Such concepts of residence can be utilized for the purposes of determining whether a person has a personal attachment to the State concerned and, therefore, whether that person is a resident of that State under Article 4.[1009] When dealing with taxes on objects, sales, or transactions, it should be possible to establish residence under Article 4 in a similar way.[1010] Although a concept of residence may not be an essential part of a tax system, it may be employed for specific tax distinctions and thereby raise concerns about tax discrimination. This 'less fundamental' concept of residence may then be relevant for applying the non-discrimination provisions of Article 24.

§3.03 AIMS AND OBJECTIVES OF THE NON-DISCRIMINATION CLAUSES

[A] Criticisms of a Too Limited Scope of Article 24

Article 24 prohibits tax discrimination because of nationality (paragraphs 1 and 2) and residence (paragraphs 3, 4, and 5) 'in certain precise circumstances'.[1011] It is not a general prohibition of tax discrimination or a general equal treatment clause.[1012] Article 24(3), for instance, protects PEs of non-resident enterprises from discriminatory taxation based on residence. It does not address non-business income and capital such as income from employment. Article 24(4) and (5) protects resident enterprises with regard to their relationship to certain non-residents who have provided them with products, services, or capital. If non-residents, as such, face negative tax consequences due to this relationship, they are not protected. In addition, the non-discrimination provisions of Article 24 focus on the treatment of foreign persons making inbound investments, not on domestic persons making outbound investments thereby falling short of providing full protection from discrimination against cross-border trade and investment.[1013]

1009. Dziurdź 2010c, 269.
1010. Dziurdź 2010c, 270; critically Haslehner 2016a m.no. 18, who distinguishes between the substantive scope that is extended to taxes of every kind and description under Article 24(6), and the personal scope that remains limited to taxes on income and on capital under Article 4. Only the partners of a transparent partnership are tax treaty residents and, therefore, able to claim non-discriminatory VAT treatment under Article 24(3) with regard to their PE, that is the partnership even if it is a taxable person for VAT purposes. This view could create problems, however, if the partnership is treated as transparent for income tax purposes but as opaque for capital tax purposes.
1011. 2008–2017 OECD Commentary on Article 24, para. 1.
1012. *See*, for instance, Haslehner 2016c, 1; Hoyos Jiménez 2016, 27–28, 38; Silva 2016b, 71; Schwarz 2015, sec. 24.050 (p. 396); Avery Jones, Baker, et al. 2011b, 194; Avery Jones, Baker, et al. 2011a, 552; Bruns 2007, 580; Staringer and Jettmar 2006, 402; Toifl 2003, 266.
1013. Bennett 2006, 465–466. *See*, generally, Brown and Mintz 2010 ('[Article 24] fails to achieve fully international tax neutrality or capital export neutrality and improves capital import neutrality only in much defined circumstances'); Mason 2010; Warren 2001; Graetz 2001; Green 1994; moreover, Graetz 2003, 436–486.

Article 24 employs different wording to achieve its goals. Certain differences between the non-discrimination clauses intentionally establish a different level of protection;[1014] others rather cause confusion. Article 24(1) and (2) uses the expression 'in the same circumstances', Article 24(3) relies on 'the same activities', Article 24(4) contains no explicit comparability requirements, and Article 24(5) compares to 'other similar enterprises', all not necessarily contributing to a clear concept of comparability. Above all, it is basically undisputed that the non-discrimination rules of Article 24 only prohibit direct discrimination (*see* section §3.05[B]). Article 24 consequently focuses on certain, rather narrow, types of discrimination without extending to economically similar tax distinctions.

For such reasons, Article 24 is viewed as an 'odd collection of paragraphs, which ... reveals no overarching theory',[1015] 'an incoherent collection of fairly narrow clauses'[1016] without 'any apparent structure and philosophy',[1017] a clause that 'lacks a coherent guiding principle'[1018] and a non-discrimination obligation that adheres to an 'incoherent, incomplete, uncertain, ineffective and outdated conceptual framework'.[1019] Article 24 is 'an amalgam of isolated obligations'[1020] and 'characterized by the lack of an organizing principle: there is no unifying policy that binds the different provisions together'.[1021] It has also been observed that Article 24 'bears no obvious relationship with the rest of the treaty'[1022] and has a different regulatory aim; it governs the 'how' rather than the 'if' of taxation.[1023] Indeed, the allocation rules of Articles 6 to 22 and the methods for elimination of double taxation of Articles 23A and 23B decide whether the residence State or the source State has a right to tax income or capital and to what extent, whereas Article 24 governs the way in which either State may exercise such taxing rights.[1024] The OEEC Fiscal Committee, therefore, already noted in its draft report on its activities of February 1958 that the question of discrimination 'has no connection with problems of double taxation'.[1025]

1014. Article 24(1), (2), and (5) prohibits other or more burdensome taxation and connected requirements, whereas Article 24(3) prohibits less favourable taxation. As already mentioned, this difference in wording is understood to imply that, under Article 24(3), it does not constitute discrimination to tax non-resident persons differently, for practical reasons, from resident persons as long as this does not result in taxation that is more burdensome for the former than for the latter. *See* 2008–2017 OECD Commentary on Article 24, para. 34 (1977: para. 22; 1992–2005: para. 20; similarly, 1963: para. 16).
1015. Bennett 2006, 439.
1016. Raad 1988b, 347; similarly, Raad and Bosman 2016, 67.
1017. Raad 1986, 255.
1018. Mason 2010, 138; similarly, Brauner 2014, 347; Baker 2006 m.no. 24B.05; Jeffery 1999, 72–73.
1019. L. Hinnekens and Hinnekens 2008, 52. *See also* Hinnekens 2008, 248.
1020. Bammens and Vanistendael 2016, sec. 1.1.2.4.
1021. Bammens and Vanistendael 2016, sec. 1.1.1.1; similarly, Vanistendael 2016, 240.
1022. Bennett 2006, 439. *See also* Friedlander 2002, 81; Raad 1986, 202.
1023. Haslehner 2016c, 2, 11; Haslehner 2016a m.no. 2; Haslehner 2009, 50–51. *See also* Rust 2015b m.no. 10; Rust 2015c m.no. 8; Rust 2010, 632; Lehner 2001, 332; Lehner 2000, 466.
1024. Alexander Rust, for instance, distinguishes between Article 24(3) and Article 7(2). Unlike Article 7(2), the non-discrimination provision is silent about how much income can be attributed to a PE. It only deals with the question of how the income attributable to the PE can be taxed. *See* Rust 2015b m.no. 68; Rust 2015c m.no. 108.
1025. OEEC, FC(58)2, p. 12. *See also* OEEC, FC(58)2(Rev.1) Part I, p. 12; OEEC, C(58)118 Part I, p. 13; moreover, Debatin 1963a, 293.

It may be criticized that Article 24 offers no overarching and comprehensive concept of non-discrimination but rather deals with selected cases of discrimination through differently worded provisions with a rather limited scope of application. It does not cover many distinctions between residents and non-residents or between cross-border and domestic investments which may have a negative impact on international trade.[1026] Various gaps, therefore, question a sound and coherent policy of the non-discrimination clauses. Nevertheless, Article 24 is related to other parts of a tax treaty in terms of policy. Both double taxation and discriminatory taxation constitute an impediment to international trade. Just as the elimination of double taxation is not an objective in itself but is based on the assumption that double taxation constitutes an obstacle to trade; non-discrimination is also not an objective in itself but is based on the assumption that discriminatory treatment creates market distortions.[1027] By establishing equal conditions of competition with regard to taxation,[1028] Article 24 contributes to the promotion of cross-border investment[1029] and the development of bilateral economic relations.[1030] Article 24 'forms a key element of double taxation conventions that complements the core provisions concerning the allocation and limitation of taxing rights'.[1031] Similarly, not only the elimination of double taxation and non-discrimination but also the exchange of information[1032] and assistance in tax collection[1033] contribute to an international tax system that not only prevents overtaxation but also secures taxation in international relations by targeting tax evasion and fraud.

[B] Residence as a Fundamental Tax Treaty Principle

Article 24(1) and (2) prohibits discrimination because of nationality but not because of residence.[1034] It holds that, for the purposes of establishing nationality discrimination, a foreigner and a national must be 'in the same circumstances, in particular with respect to residence'. Article 24(3), (4), and (5), by contrast, prohibits discrimination because of residence and not for other reasons. Before analysing what different aims

1026. *See also* Raad 1988b, 347, who observes that '[t]he existing non-discrimination clauses ... do not take a broad neutrality approach in respect of either taxable persons (non-residents vs. residents) or taxable income (foreign income vs. domestic income) nor do they effectively deal with the entire catalogue of foreign-unfriendly practices of many countries'. For a discussion of how Article 24 could be improved, *see* Matthews 1993.
1027. Bammens 2016, 110–111; Bammens 2012, 1028. *See also* Haslehner 2016c, 3–4; Haslehner 2016a m.no. 2; Jeffery 1999, 72; moreover, Silva 2016a, 227, who mentions that avoidance of double taxation and prevention of non-discrimination constitute the means to achieve the (higher) goal of promoting international trade and foreign direct investments as well as providing legal (tax) certainty.
1028. *See also* Vanistendael 2016, 252.
1029. Bammens and Vanistendael 2016, sec. 1.1.2.1.
1030. H. Loukota 2005, 56. *See also* Introduction to the 2017 OECD Model, para. 15.5; moreover, Raad 2005, 137, who points out that Article 24 serves a wider goal of tax treaties, that is to promote the free movement of persons, business, and capital; similarly, Raad and Bosman 2016, 75; Haslinger and Petritz 2006, 357.
1031. Haslehner 2016c, 2.
1032. Article 26 of the OECD Model.
1033. Article 27 of the OECD Model.
1034. *See,* instead of many, Arnold 2011, 370.

these non-discrimination clauses specifically pursue and what role 'residence' plays in these contexts, it appears necessary to begin with a broader discussion of the concept of residence. This is especially since three different meanings can be distinguished: residence under domestic tax law which usually corresponds to full tax liability, residence under Article 4(1) which refers to residence under domestic tax law, and tax treaty residence under the entire Article 4, including the tiebreaker rules of Article 4(2) and (3) for cases of dual residence.

States usually distinguish between different scopes of tax liability, notably, between full and limited tax liability, for various policy reasons. First of all, full tax liability or worldwide taxation often goes hand in hand with a consideration of a taxpayer's overall ability to pay tax. Individuals (and, less commonly, legal persons) are taxed on a progressive basis which means that the tax rate increases as the worldwide income or capital increases. Various personal allowances and deductions that cannot be attributed to specific sources of income or capital[1035] or to a specific State are provided, such as deductions for medical expenses and family allowances. If a State subjects a taxpayer to full tax liability, this may also mean that losses from sources located outside that State can be deducted immediately from all taxable profits.[1036] In addition, full tax liability in a State ensures that if other States do not tax particular items of income or capital on a territorial basis, these items remain taxable in at least one State. Unless a tax exemption in particular under Article 23 A is applicable, this allows preventing non-taxation of income and capital. Last, but not least, practical considerations motivate States to subject persons without a close personal attachment to their territory to limited tax liability on a territorial basis, that is only on income from sources in that State or capital situated therein. If a taxpayer is out of reach because that individual resides outside of a State's territory and has no other personal connection or nexus, it may prove difficult to assess and verify that taxpayer's worldwide income and capital. Thus, if a State taxed a taxpayer on a worldwide basis as soon as some income is derived from sources in that State (for instance, due to a short-term presence) or some capital is located therein, administrative burdens would arise that could be regarded as excessive. Special withholding procedures and gross taxation commonly ensure taxation on a territorial basis in situations of limited tax liability without requiring having to deal with a taxpayer's overall ability to pay tax.

Since most States distinguish between full and limited tax liability, the OECD Model is influenced by these distinctions. Article 1 determines the personal scope of application. A tax treaty applies to 'persons who are residents of one or both of the Contracting States'. Article 4(1) defines the term 'resident of a Contracting State' as 'any person who, under the laws of that State, is liable to tax therein by reason of his domicile, residence, place of management or any other criterion of a similar nature'. It does not include 'any person who is liable to tax in that State in respect only of income

1035. *See*, for instance, Raad 2010, 154 ('[d]eductions for personal circumstances are mostly related to overall income').

1036. However, such a loss deduction need not be granted in particular if foreign profits are tax exempt. *See* 1977–2017 OECD Commentary on Articles ,23 A and 23 B, para. 44.

from sources in that State or capital situated therein'.[1037] This definition of 'residence' thus refers to a comprehensive liability to tax (full tax liability) based on a taxpayer's personal attachment to the State concerned,[1038] that is to the concept of residence adopted in the domestic laws of the Contracting States.[1039] In addition, conventions do not lay down standards that the provisions of the domestic laws on 'residence' have to fulfil in order that claims for full tax liability can be accepted between the Contracting States. In this respect, the States take their stand entirely on the domestic laws.[1040]

Article 4(1) contains some common criteria of personal attachment that may lead to full tax liability under domestic law ('domicile, residence, place of management'), whereas the OECD Commentary mentions some other criteria of a similar nature that cause residence under Article 4(1) if used as a basis for full tax liability: continuous stay, stay for a certain period, performance of services on board a ship that has a certain home harbour,[1041] and work as a diplomat or as another person in government service.[1042] It is sometimes argued that 'any other criterion of a similar nature' which also leads to residence under Article 4(1) cannot be of a purely legal nature but must be locality related, as indicated by 'domicile, residence [and] place of management'.[1043] This arguably excludes full tax liability because of nationality.[1044] However, it remains unclear why, in such cases, a tax treaty should not avoid international juridical double taxation.[1045] It further appears to be difficult to draw a distinction to recognized criteria that are mentioned in the OECD Commentary, notably, to deemed (and, therefore, merely legal) residence of diplomats in government service.[1046] It follows that persons who are subject to full tax liability in a State due to a 'residence fiction' are a resident of that State under Article 4(1) even if they have no physical connection to that State: no presence, no abode, no home, no domicile, etc.[1047] In addition, even an individual who performs services on board a ship that has its home harbour in a State may be a resident of that State,[1048] supposedly even if the individual has never been in that State.

1037. This second sentence was added to Article 4(1) of the OECD Model in 1977. Prior to that, only the 1963 OECD Commentary on Article 4, para. 10, stated that '[a]n individual ... is not to be considered a "resident of a Contracting State" in the sense of the Convention if, although not domiciled in that State, he is considered as a resident according to the national law and is only subject to a limited taxation on the income arising in that State'. *See also* 2008–2017 OECD Commentary on Article 4, para. 8.1 (1977–2005: para. 8).

1038. 1963–2017 OECD Commentary on Article 4, para. 3.

1039. 1977–2017 OECD Commentary on Article 4, para. 8 (1963: para. 10).

1040. 1963–2017 OECD Commentary on Article 4, para. 4.

1041. 1963–2017 OECD Commentary on Article 4, para. 3.

1042. 1977–2017 OECD Commentary on Article 4, para. 8.

1043. *See*, for example, Lüdicke 2015 m.no. 29; Ismer and Riemer 2015 m.no. 57; Wassermeyer and Kaeser 2013 m.no. 39; Staringer 2008, 74–75; Vogel 1997 Article 4, m.no. 24.

1044. *See* Ismer and Riemer 2015 m.nos. 3, 61; Wassermeyer and Kaeser 2013 m.no. 40; Staringer 2008, 75; Vogel 1997 Article 4, m.no. 30. *See*, moreover, Raad 1986, 130–131, who discusses the question of whether nationality, if employed as a circumstance producing full tax liability, can lead to residence under Article 4(1) and states that although there is evidence that the term 'residence' encompasses 'nationality', no firm conclusions can be drawn.

1045. *See also* Raad 1986, 131.

1046. *See* 1977–2017 OECD Commentary on Article 4, para. 8.

1047. This is also admitted by Ismer and Riemer 2015 m.no. 58 ('[t]he connection stems from a legal relationship').

1048. *See*, to this effect, 1977–2017 OECD Commentary on Article 4, para. 3.

Therefore, it is submitted that nationality may be grounds for full tax liability under domestic law and thus for residence under Article 4(1).

Situations when both Contracting States subject a taxpayer to limited tax liability are not covered by a tax treaty. If a taxpayer is not a resident of either Contracting State because the person is taxed in neither State on a comprehensive basis, the conditions of Article 1 are not fulfilled. This is confirmed by the OECD Commentary according to which only two typical cases of conflict are intended to be solved by a tax treaty: conflicts between two residences and between residence and source or situs.[1049] A tax treaty consequently supposes that the Contracting States subject at least some persons to tax on a comprehensive basis, that is to full tax liability. As sometimes both Contracting States may subject a person to full tax liability, a solution for conflicts of dual residence is provided. Article 4(2) and (3) contains various criteria to establish the residence State for tax treaty purposes in cases where a taxpayer is a resident of both States under Article 4(1).

After the residence State and the source State have been determined under the entire Article 4, the allocation rules of Articles 6 to 22 and the methods for elimination of double taxation of Articles 23 A and 23 B limit the taxing rights of both Contracting States. Depending on the meaning of 'source', it can be argued that both the residence State and the source State potentially have a right to tax items of income and capital that have their source or are located abroad. For instance, if an enterprise of the residence State receives dividends from a third State, these dividends may be attributable to a PE in the source State and, therefore, taxable in that State under Article 7.[1050] Since 2008, however, the OECD Commentary has followed a different meaning of 'source' as far as the second sentence of Article 4(1) is concerned ('liable to tax … in respect only of income from sources in [a Contracting State]'). It claims that the effects of a tax treaty may transform full tax liability under domestic law into 'limited tax liability' for tax treaty purposes. This sentence also excludes 'persons who are not subject to comprehensive liability to tax in a Contracting State because these persons, whilst being residents of that State under that State's tax law, are considered to be residents of another State pursuant to a treaty between these two States' from the definition of a resident.[1051] A resident of a Contracting State, that is a person subject to full tax liability under domestic law, therefore, may become a non-resident for the purposes of another tax treaty if that State loses the tiebreaker under Article 4(2) or (3). A tax treaty consequently limits the source State's taxing rights based on criteria of source or situs to the effect of limited tax liability.

1049. 1963-2017 OECD Commentary on Article 4, para. 2.

1050. *See*, for instance, Langoth 2004, 33.

1051. 2008-2017 OECD Commentary on Article 4, para. 8.2. *See also* Ismer and Riemer 2015 m.nos. 43-44; Arnold 2009b, 178-179; Zhai 2009, 1122; Russo 2008, 465; Sasseville 2006, 42-44; critically Fett 2014, 471-484, who concludes that there are two equally defensible interpretations of the second sentence of Article 4(1); moreover, Lehner 2015 m.nos. 120-121a; Lüdicke 2015 m.no. 36; Eilers 2015 m.no. 5; Raad 2009; Vann 2009, 252-254; Avery Jones 2006, 137-138.

Although this view remains controversial,[1052] it will not be questioned in this study.[1053] It will thus be taken for granted that the source State is allowed to tax only income from sources in that State and capital situated therein, whereas the residence State is allowed to tax all of the remaining income and capital. However, even if this view is rejected and it is argued that a tax treaty does not by itself create situations of a taxpayer being effectively taxed on a territorial basis or that the second sentence of Article 4(1) does not refer to such situations, what matters for the purposes of this study is the fact that residence influences the allocation of taxing rights. In general, the source State has more limited taxing rights than the residence State.

From all of this, it can be concluded that a tax treaty recognizes and is based on differences between full and limited tax liability. Moreover, the Contracting States are not only allowed to tax on a worldwide or territorial basis but also allowed to distinguish between different taxpayers by taxing some taxpayers (residents) on a worldwide and other taxpayers (non-residents) on a territorial basis. Accordingly, the Contracting States are not expected to subject all persons falling within their tax jurisdiction to one single type of tax liability (although they may do so and, indeed, some States tax both residents and non-residents on a territorial basis).[1054] They are free to choose the criteria of personal attachment that lead to full tax liability and thereby to residence under Article 4(1). On this basis, after the residence State and the source State have been determined under the entire Article 4, taxing rights are allocated among the Contracting States, and this allocation may be more or less favourable to a Contracting State depending on whether it is the residence State or the source State.

1052. Before the OECD Commentary dealt with this issue, the prevailing opinion in the literature assumed that it would be possible to be a resident of both Contracting States for the purposes of Article 4(1) of any other tax treaty and that a dual resident may thus invoke the tax treaty network of both Contracting States. *See*, for instance, Lehner 2008 m.nos. 20, 23–25; Burgstaller and Obermair 2006, 183; Burgstaller 2005, 238–242; W. Loukota and Stefaner 2005, 262–264; Gusmeroli 2005, 12; Langoth 2004, 33; Dommes and Herdin 2004; Gerdes 2004, 205–211; Kolb et al. 2002, 479–480 (but already mentioning that this position is being reviewed); Lüdicke 1999, 738–742; Avery Jones and Bobbett 1999, 16, 19; Staringer 1999, 149–152; Vogel 1997 Article 4, m.no. 31a; Huemer 1996, 109; Großmann 1995, 86–92; García Prats 1994, 482–484; Raad 1993, 301; Gennep 1991 (but also commenting that there is no common opinion in the Dutch tax literature); Raad 1988c, 6–8; Raad 1988d, 243; Raad 1988a; Raad 1986, 130. *See also*, however, Betten 1989; Gennep 1991, 141, who reports on a different view of the Dutch Under-Minister of Finance (critically Raad 1990); and Fett 2014, 476–477; Smit 2002; Vogel 2002a, 2; Damen 2001; Kort 2001, who reports on a decision of the Supreme Court of the Netherlands (Hoge Raad) in case No. 35557 of 28 February 2001, BNB 2001/295c.

1053. *See*, instead, Dziurdź 2013c, sec. 6.2.2; moreover, Raad 2009; Schlager 2008.

1054. 2008–2017 OECD Commentary on Article 4, para. 8.3 (1992–2005: para. 8).

[C] Article 24(1): Prohibiting Arbitrary Treatment of Foreigners

[1] Nationality, as Distinct from Residence

[a] Context and Systematics

When approaching the question of why Article 24(1) prohibits discrimination because of nationality, inevitably, the issue arises whether Article 24(1) also prohibits tax distinctions by reason of residence (for instance, different tax rates, different deductible amounts, etc.) if certain items of income or capital are within a State's tax jurisdiction both with residents and non-residents. As a matter of fact, nationals of a State are usually residents of that State and foreigners are predominantly non-residents. A tax measure of a Contracting State (State A) that favours residents or disadvantages non-residents may consequently lead to a disproportionate tax burden on nationals of the other Contracting State (State B) if State A nationals are more likely to be residents whereas State B nationals are more likely to be non-residents. Therefore, it seems legitimate to ask whether a tax distinction on the basis of residence can be equated with a prohibited tax distinction on the basis of nationality even when differences in nationality are not inevitably linked to differences in residence.

Just because the OECD Model fundamentally relies on residence (*see* section §3.03[B]) does not necessarily mean that tax distinctions between residents and non-residents should always be permitted or viewed as legitimate; the non-discrimination provisions of Article 24(3), (4), and (5) demonstrate this. Article 24(1), therefore, could prohibit certain tax distinctions between residents and non-residents and thereby complement the other non-discrimination provisions that explicitly deal with residence. If a State, for instance, imposes a higher tax rate on income of non-resident employees or grants personal tax deductions to only resident taxpayers, this could arguably lead to prohibited tax discrimination because of nationality.

An argument against an extension of Article 24(1) to distinctions because of residence lies in systematic considerations. The first sentence of Article 24(3) contains a non-discrimination provision that prohibits distinctions between resident and non-resident enterprises as far as PEs are concerned. The second sentence of Article 24(3) excludes certain personal tax benefits from this non-discrimination obligation. If Article 24(1) protected PEs of non-resident enterprises against such discrimination as well, the role of Article 24(3) would be diminished to mere interpretative guidance or to a superfluous provision that regulates a situation of discrimination that is already covered by Article 24(1).[1055] Instead of assuming that Article 24(3) is of such minor importance, it seems more convincing to argue that the PE non-discrimination clause protects against forms of discrimination that are not covered by the nationality non-discrimination clause. Accordingly, tax distinctions on the basis of residence are arguably not covered by Article 24(1).

1055. *See*, to this effect, Rust 2015b m.nos. 16 and 36; Rust 2015c m.nos. 18, 49; Haslehner 2009, 64; Loukota 2006, 273; Raupach 1966, 88; critically Toifl 2003, 306.

However, Article 24(1) could also be seen as a supplementary non-discrimination provision. If certain tax distinctions on the basis of residence do not lead to discrimination under Article 24(3), they could still do so under Article 24(1). This would not render Article 24(3) meaningless but would rather provide enhanced protection in situations that are not covered by other non-discrimination provisions. Comparability under Article 24(1) between residents and non-residents could be denied if relevant differences in tax liability exist or if personal tax circumstances have already been considered once and thus should not be considered twice. Comparability could be confirmed if personal tax circumstances have not yet been considered or if taxable non-business income is at stake. Article 24(1) could even incorporate a threshold that would have to be surpassed before other or more burdensome treatment of non-residents would have a sufficiently negative effect on foreigners in order to constitute discrimination, whereas Article 24(3) would continue to prohibit even minor differences in tax burdens that disadvantage PEs of non-resident enterprises.

[b] Historical Implications

A systematic analysis of the relationship between Article 24(1) and Article 24(3) does not necessarily explain why tax distinctions on the basis of residence should be entirely excluded from the scope of the nationality non-discrimination clause. Nevertheless, the historical background indicates a rather narrow scope of Article 24(1). As the OECD Commentary mentions, the nationality non-discrimination provision was inspired by the same type of provisions in other conventions:[1056]

> [T]he principle of non-discrimination, under various descriptions and with a more or less wide scope, was applied in international fiscal relations well before the appearance, at the end of the 19th Century, of the classic type of double taxation conventions. Thus, in a great many agreements of different kinds (consular or establishment conventions, treaties of friendship or commerce, etc.) concluded by States, especially in the 19th Century, in order to extend and strengthen the diplomatic protection of their nationals wherever resident, there are clauses under which each of the two Contracting States undertakes to accord nationals of the other State equality of treatment with its own nationals. The fact that such clauses subsequently found their way into double taxation conventions has in no way affected their original justification and scope.

According to Michael Lang and Walter Loukota, this favours a rather narrow scope of Article 24(1) when compared to the concept of non-discrimination within the EU.[1057] In addition, almost no State (the US being a notable exception)[1058] uses

1056. 2008–2017 OECD Commentary on Article 24, para. 6 (1977–2005: para. 2). *See also* OEEC, FC/WP4(57)1, p. 3; OEEC, FC(58)2, p. 12; and OEEC, FC(58)2(Rev.1) Part I, p. 13, where Working Party No. 4 and the OEEC Fiscal Committee referred to various other conventions that already prohibited discrimination based on nationality. *See*, moreover, Oberascher 2006.
1057. *See* Lang and Loukota 2003, 69; critically Toifl 2003, 306–307.
1058. *See*, for instance, Rienstra 2017, sec. 1.1.4.1.: 'US citizens are treated as residents of the United States for US federal income tax purposes regardless of where they physically reside, i.e. whether they physically reside within or without the United States'.

nationality as a basis for full tax liability, at least when individuals are concerned. For such a reason, as early as 1957, Working Party No. 4 of the OEEC Fiscal Committee, which drafted the nationality non-discrimination provision, had the impression that Article 24(1) would only be of limited practical relevance[1059] (although a similar statement was later made with regard to the PE non-discrimination clause).[1060] It mentioned that 'in none of the Member countries of the O.E.E.C. does tax legislation make liability to tax dependent on a person's nationality'[1061] and that the replies to its questionnaire indicated that discrimination because of nationality:[1062]

> occurs only exceptionally. The main reason for this is that tax legislations generally place on the same footing all taxpayers having their fiscal domicile in the Member country's territory, just as they treat alike all taxpayers having their fiscal domicile outside its territory. What exceptions there are consist for the most part in giving larger personal reliefs for family circumstances, etc., to the nationals of the Member country concerned than to nationals of other countries ....

Moreover, after observing various developments with regard to the elimination of nationality discrimination, Working Party No. 4 concluded that:[1063]

> the Member countries of the O.E.E.C. acknowledge in general the importance of eliminating the few cases of discrimination that still exist between them and of giving formal recognition, through the medium of Conventions, to the principle of non-discrimination on grounds of nationality.

When discussing the PE non-discrimination provision, Working Party No. 4 of the OEEC Fiscal Committee clearly separated its statements on nationality discrimination from its statements on residence discrimination. In fact, the programme of work of the OEEC Fiscal Committee already distinguished between considerations of nationality and other considerations such as residence.[1064] According to Working Party No. 4, its statements on nationality discrimination would not take into consideration:[1065]

> inequalities of treatment resulting from differences in domicile. If State A, for one reason or another, thinks fit to tax persons not domiciled in its territory differently from persons who are, the result will be that its own and foreign nationals will be treated differently, depending on whether they are domiciled in its territory or not. According to present usages, some other State B will not as a general rule have grounds for complaint by reason that persons domiciled in its territory will be taxed by State A differently from a person domiciled in the territory of State A. Neither will it be justified in complaining of the fact that a person domiciled in its own territory and at the same time possessing its nationality will be taxed by State A differently from a national of State A who at the same time is domiciled in the territory of State A, provided that State A does not tax a national of State B,

1059. OEEC, FC/WP4(57)1, pp. 1-3. *See also* Lang 2006, 35-36; Lang 2007b, 105; moreover, Sasseville 2013, 348, who argues that Article 24(1) was always intended to have a very limited scope and, therefore, should not be applicable to distinctions based on tax residence.
1060. *See* OEEC, FC/WP4(57)2, p. 6; moreover, Lang 2006, 38-39; Lang 2007b, 106.
1061. OEEC, FC/WP4(57)1, p. 1.
1062. *Ibid.*, p. 2.
1063. *Ibid.*, p. 3.
1064. OEEC, FC/M(56)1, p. 3.
1065. OEEC, FC/WP4(57)1, pp. 5-6.

domiciled in State B, differently from one of its own nationals not domiciled in its territory.

The Working Party further commented that '[t]he purpose of this [nationality non-discrimination] provision is to end the discrimination whereby a State, when dealing with two persons *who are in absolutely like circumstances [French original: se trouvant tout à fait dans la même situation] but are of different nationalities* taxes one more favourably than the other for the sole reason that the first is a national while the other is not. In other words, the provision does away with the difference in taxation treatment that is based *solely* on difference in nationality'.[1066] In two follow-up examples presented by the Working Party, a national of State A who is domiciled in State A was compared to a national of State B who is likewise domiciled in State A. Also, a national of State A who is domiciled in State B was compared to a national of State B who is likewise domiciled in State B.[1067]

Some Delegates also mentioned that 'the same circumstances' under Article 24(1) can only exist when residence does not differ.[1068] In a reply to the Council of Europe on matters concerning non-discriminatory fiscal treatment in the European Convention on Establishment of Companies, the Fiscal Committee explained that its proposed provision drafted along the lines of Article 24(1) is solely designed to give the same treatment in the same situation, notably, from the point of view of residence as defined by the place of effective management (POEM).[1069] This view is still reflected in the OECD Commentary: '[I]f a Contracting State … distinguishes between its own nationals according to whether they reside in its territory or not, that State cannot be obliged to give nationals of the other State who do not reside in its territory the same treatment as it gives its resident nationals but it undertakes to extend to them the same treatment as is available to its nationals who reside in the other State.'[1070]

By contrast, Working Party No. 4 held that '[n]ationality plays no part in this type of discrimination' with respect to the PE and the ownership non-discrimination clauses.[1071] Also, the Working Party believed that tax distinctions between residents and non-residents are rather viewed as legitimate while tax distinctions between nationals and non-nationals may more likely justify complaints. It desired to eliminate

1066. OEEC, FC/WP4(57)3, p. 6 (original emphasis). Subsequently, the English translation of '*se trouvant dans la même situation*' changed from 'in the like circumstances' to 'in the same circumstances'. *See infra* n. 1217.

1067. *Ibid.*, pp. 6–7.

1068. *See* OEEC, FC/M(57)3, p. 6. The Delegate for Germany considered that, under Article 24(1), persons taxed on the whole and persons taxed on only part of their income were not 'in the like circumstances' and could be treated differently with regard to tax reliefs or different rates of tax. The Delegate for France considered that the expression 'in the like circumstances' implied, among other things, the like circumstances from the point of view of residence, which means that resident foreigners should receive the same treatment as resident nationals and, likewise, non-resident foreigners the same treatment as non-resident nationals.

1069. OEEC, TFD/FC/134, pp. 3–4 (para. 10).

1070. 2008–2017 OECD Commentary on Article 24, para. 8 (1994–2005: para. 4; similarly, 1963: para. 3; 1977–1992: para. 4).

1071. OEEC, FC/WP4(57)3, pp. 11 and 13. *See also* OEEC, FC/WP4(57)4, p. 2.

differences in treatment between domiciled and non-domiciled persons in selected cases only, notably, in regard to the computation of profits realized through a PE.[1072]

It follows that the PE non-discrimination clause was not envisaged to constitute a specification of the nationality non-discrimination clause. It rather deals with a different type of discrimination, that is with discrimination based on situs, domicile, or residence as being distinct from discrimination based on nationality.[1073] Article 24(1), on the other hand, protects only against discrimination based on nationality and not against discrimination based on residence, a view that can also be traced back to early writings on the OECD Model.[1074]

[c] Reference to Residence

Since 1992, the same circumstances, 'in particular with respect to residence', must exist in order to establish comparability under Article 24(1). This added expression supports the view that residence cannot be equated with nationality and thus that tax distinctions based on residence are, in principle, legitimate from a tax treaty perspective. It was, however, a response to developments in France that suggested otherwise, notably, that distinctions based on residence could be prohibited when nationality and residence formally overlap.[1075] In 1991, the Delegate for France presented a note on a recent decision of the French Court of Cassation (Cour de Cassation)[1076] to Working Party No. 1 of the OECD Committee on Fiscal Affairs. It seemed to suggest that Article 24(1) could be applied to prevent discrimination based on residence, a suggestion that was also put forward in a decision of the EC Court of Justice.[1077,1078] While the Working Party agreed that this was not the right interpretation to be given to Article 24(1), it was generally felt that there was no need to amend the provisions of the OECD Model as the decision appeared to be based, to a large extent, on specific provisions of French domestic law.[1079] However, it was also agreed that the OECD Commentary could be clarified in this respect.[1080]

Despite this agreement, the Delegation for France proposed that the wording of Article 24(1) be amended in order to apply it only to individuals and to clarify that individuals must be in the same circumstances, 'notably with respect to residence'

1072. OEEC, FC/WP4(57)1, pp. 6–7.
1073. As the OECD Commentary still states today, Article 24(3) is concerned with 'discrimination based not on nationality but on the actual situs of an enterprise'. *See* 2008–2017 OECD Commentary on Article 24, para. 33 (1963: para. 14; 1977: para. 21; 1992–2005: para. 19); critically about the term 'actual situs' Raad 1986, 128.
1074. *See*, for instance, Debatin 1963b, 21–22: 'Das Verbot der steuerlichen Diskriminierung untersagt aber *nicht* Besteuerungsunterschiede, die an andere Merkmale [als die Staatsangehörigkeit] anknüpfen [original emphasis]. Das gilt vor allem für die Unterscheidung zwischen unbeschränkter und beschränkter Steuerpflicht ...'.
1075. *See supra* n. 895.
1076. Cour de Cassation, 21 December 1990, No. 88-15744.
1077. CJEU, 8 May 1990, C-175/88, *Biehl*.
1078. OECD, DAFFE/CFA/WP1/M(91)1, sec. VIII. *See also* OECD, DAFFE/CFA/WP1(91)1.
1079. OECD, DAFFE/CFA/WP1/M(91)1, sec. VIII.
1080. *Ibid.*, sec. VIII.

(French original: '*notamment au regard de la résidence*').[1081] Although the OECD Commentary confirmed a clear distinction between nationality and residence, this fundamental distinction was not recognized by certain courts.[1082] This is why France had found it preferable to amend Article 24(1) rather than to modify the OECD Commentary, which could be clarified on certain aspects but the legal value of which was still uncertain.[1083]

Subsequently, Working Party No. 1 decided to establish a special Working Group and to send out a short questionnaire[1084] that offered a choice between maintaining the status quo, restricting the scope of Article 24(1) to individuals who are in the same situation regarding residence, adding only 'notably with respect to residence', or amending only the OECD Commentary.[1085] On the basis of the replies,[1086] the Steering Group on the Revision of the Model recommended amending Article 24(1) by adding 'notably with respect to residence' and to modify the OECD Commentary that this added expression was only a clarification.[1087] The main question subsequently discussed by Working Party No. 1 was whether a change was required to both the Article and the Commentary or only to the Commentary, but the Steering Group's recommendation was followed as it provided useful clarification with respect to a principle with which all Delegates agreed.[1088]

From a historical perspective, therefore, nationality and residence must be distinguished from each other when analysing potential cases of discrimination under Article 24(1). This is now confirmed with the express requirement of 'the same circumstances, in particular with respect to residence'. Article 24(1) is strictly limited to discrimination because of nationality. It does not extend to the much more common tax distinctions because of residence. Its aims and objectives thus appear unimportant from a tax point of view, at least in practice.

Nevertheless, the fact that tax distinctions on the basis of nationality are rather rare does not render non-discrimination because of nationality undesirable. On the contrary, when the nationality non-discrimination provision was drafted, tax distinctions because of nationality were seldom which indicates that such distinctions were generally not an integral part of domestic tax systems. Most income and capital tax systems do not aim at subjecting nationals to tax but instead focus on residents and non-residents, on a taxpayer's ability to pay tax, on personal circumstances, on specific sources of income or capital, on promotion of research and development, etc. Most policy objectives that a domestic tax system pursues, therefore, constitute no suitable explanation and justification for tax distinctions by reason of nationality. Their explanation may more likely be found in the political calculation that is unrelated to taxation such as in favouring or not disadvantaging nationals because of their stronger

1081. OECD, DAFFE/CFA/WP1(91)5.
1082. *Ibid.*
1083. *Ibid.*
1084. OECD, DAFFE/CFA/WP1/M(91)2, sec. VII.
1085. OECD, DAFFE/CFA/WP1(92)4, Annex I.
1086. OECD, DAFFE/CFA/WP1(92)4, Annex II; OECD, DAFFE/CFA/WP1(92)17.
1087. OECD, DAFFE/CFA/WP1(92)4.
1088. OECD, DAFFE/CFA/WP1/M(92)1, sec. V.

participation in politics in particular by voting and standing for elections. In political reality, foreigners often have less voice than nationals and generally no right to vote which diminishes their chances to successfully protest against burdensome tax treatment. They provide an obvious target for States that wish to maximize their tax revenues at the lowest political cost,[1089] and, therefore, they are a target that must remain protected under Article 24(1) against both current and future discriminations,[1090] arguably unless a connection to a legitimate policy goal can be made. Frans Vanistendael emphasizes this arbitrariness of distinctions based on nationality in matters of taxation:[1091]

> It is precisely because nationality is to a large extent not relevant in determining the tax jurisdiction, that it cannot reasonably be used as a criterion to make a distinction in tax treatment. Making a distinction on the basis of nationality would be almost as arbitrary as making a distinction based on gender, race or religion.

Finally, according to Michael J. Graetz, the fundamental idea that everyone, including foreigners, is entitled to equal treatment before the law is grounded in concern for fairness and mutual respect.[1092]

[2] Nationality, Grounds for Residence

Article 24(1) aims to ensure that all residents and all non-residents benefit from the same tax measures regardless of their nationality. In contrast to Article 24(3), (4), and (5), it does not limit a State's freedom to distinguish on the basis of residence. Brian J. Arnold describes this as perhaps the most important feature of Article 24(1).[1093] Tension might arise, however, when a Contracting State employs nationality as a basis for full tax liability and residence. Article 24(1) prohibits discrimination because of nationality. Therefore, it is not clear whether it also prohibits a State to tax nationals on a worldwide basis because of their nationality.

Since 'residence' under Article 4(1) can be understood to refer to all criteria of personal attachment that can lead to full tax liability under domestic law, including nationality (*see* section §3.03[B]), it is questionable why Article 24(1) should subsequently prohibit such explicit references to nationality that are necessary to establish

1089. *See*, to this effect, Arnold 1991, 10; moreover, Rust 2013b, 71–72.
1090. *See also*, however, Pinto Nogueira 2017, 395, who comments that '[i]t is rather odd to conventionally prohibit "nationality non-discrimination" in tax systems that already do not entail any distinction based on nationality'. Similarly, *see* Arnold 1991, 45, 261, who regards Article 24(1) as largely unnecessary and of little practical significance since most States have never discriminated widely against foreigners but also submits that it is, nevertheless, valuable for this principle to be reiterated in double taxation conventions; moreover, Böckli 1979, 4, who views Article 24(1) as relying on a criterion coming from an ivory tower and, therefore, without practical relevance.
1091. Vanistendael 2010, 177. *See also* Van Brussel 2015, 354.
1092. Graetz 2001, 300.
1093. Arnold 1991, 33.

full tax liability and corresponding differences in tax treatment.[1094] It can rather be assumed that the Contracting States should remain free to tax nationals on a worldwide basis and foreigners in otherwise identical circumstances on a territorial basis without being required by Article 24(1) to extend all of the benefits of full tax liability to foreigners or to tax foreigners on a worldwide basis as well (but *see also* section §3.06[C][2] for a different view).

It must be further acknowledged that the OECD Model itself distinguishes between nationals and foreigners.[1095] When an individual is a resident of both Contracting States under Article 4(1), first of all, Article 4(2)(a) provides that a permanent home should determine the residence State. If this does not lead to a conclusive result because a permanent home is available in both Contracting States, the criterion of closer personal and economic relations (centre of vital interests) is used as a tiebreaker. If a centre of vital interest cannot be determined or if no permanent home is available in either Contracting State, Article 4(2)(b) relies on a habitual abode. If this tiebreaker fails again, Article 4(2)(c) looks at nationality. It provides that an individual 'shall be deemed to be a resident only of the State of which he is a national'. This means that, under a tax treaty between State A and State B (and disregarding cases of no or dual nationality for which Article 4(2)(d) refers to mutual agreement), a national of State A may be a tax treaty resident of State A and a national of State B in otherwise identical circumstances may be a tax treaty resident of State B.

Certain allocation rules of the OECD Model assign taxing rights only to the residence State. Items of income not sourced in a Contracting State but connected to a third State,[1096] royalties under Article 12 that are not effectively connected to a PE, gains from the alienation of property dealt with by Article 13(5), pensions under Article 18, items of income dealt with by Article 21, and elements of capital addressed by Article 22(4) are taxable only in the residence State. If this residence State is determined through nationality, differences in nationality may have important implications for the allocation of taxing rights. Items of income and capital may be taxable only in State A if a State A national is involved and only in State B if a State B national is involved.

Overall, this means that the allocation rules allow a Contracting State to tax its own nationals on a broader basis than foreigners. Conversely, they prohibit a State to tax foreigners on certain items of income and capital because of their foreign nationality. As State A may tax its own nationals on a broader basis than State B nationals, this initially does not appear to be problematic under Article 24(1). When nationality determines tax treaty residence under Article 4(2)(c), protected foreigners (i.e.,

1094. *See also* Haslehner 2009 fn. 178 on pp. 59–60, who states that the Contracting States have autonomy to choose between nationality and residence as a basis for tax liability and that Article 24 does not intend to restrict this autonomy.

1095. This is also highlighted by Bronselaer and Heyvaert 2009 m.no. 23.16 ('[o]ccasionally, the Treaty explicitly allows discrimination based on nationality').

1096. For instance, Article 15(1) provides that 'salaries, wages and other similar remuneration derived by a resident of a Contracting State in respect of an employment shall be taxable only in that State unless the employment is exercised in the other Contracting State'. This means that remuneration derived in respect of an employment exercised in a third State is taxable only in the residence State. A change in residence leads to a change in taxing rights.

non-residents for treaty purposes) are taxed on fewer items of income and capital than nationals and are thereby favoured.

Article 19 deals with government service and partly relies on nationality for the purposes of allocating tax rights to either the residence State or the source State. From a Contracting State's perspective, certain items of income may either be taxable in that State or not, depending on nationality. As a general rule, Article 19(1)(a) provides that '[s]alaries, wages and other similar remuneration paid by a Contracting State ... to an individual in respect of services rendered to that State ... shall be taxable only in that State'. If an individual, therefore, renders such services to the source State (the State of which the person is not a resident), the remuneration is taxable only in the source State. Article 19(1)(b), however, provides an exception to this rule that is based on nationality: 'such ... remuneration shall be taxable only in the other Contracting State [the residence State] if the services are rendered in that State and the individual is a resident of that State who: (i) is a national of that State; or (ii) did not become a resident of that State solely for the purpose of rendering the services'. In certain circumstances, nationality may thus determine whether the remuneration for government service is taxable only in the residence State or the source State. Article 19(2)(b) provides a similar rule with respect to pensions. If, for example, an individual provides services to the source State in the residence State and did not become a resident of the residence State solely for the purpose of rendering the services to the source State, that person is taxable only in the residence State if a national of that State or in the source State if not such a national.

As with Article 4(2)(c), initially, there appears to be no problem of tax discrimination: the residence State taxes only its own nationals and exempts nationals of the source State as well as nationals of third States; the source State taxes only its own nationals as well as nationals of third States and exempts nationals of the residence State. A tax exemption, as such, does not appear problematic under Article 24(1). However, States may provide for different tax benefits depending on how much income or capital remains taxable within their territory under a tax treaty. If more income or capital remains taxable, more or additional tax benefits may be granted. For instance, a taxpayer subject to tax in State A with a higher proportion of income or capital might receive higher personal and family allowances and other deductions, in particular if State A apportions these tax-free amounts.[1097] In cases when the tiebreaker rule of Article 4(2)(c) decides about the residence State for tax treaty purposes or when the allocation rules of Article 19(1)(b) or (2)(b) apply, the effective scope of tax liability in State A as well as the amount of tax benefits granted by State A may thus depend on nationality. Although the domestic tax law is facially neutral with respect to nationality, differences in taxing rights that are caused by differences in nationality might lead to differences in treatment between nationals and foreigners under domestic tax law.

In all cases for which no problems of dual residence arise; those in which problems of dual residence are solved by relying on a criterion of permanent home, centre of vital interest, habitual abode or mutual agreement; and all of those in which

1097. *See* 1977–2017 OECD Commentary on Articles 23 A and 23 B, para. 42.

Article 19(1)(b) and (2)(b) does not apply or does not need to refer to nationality, a State is free, under Article 24(1), to connect tax benefits to certain tax liability and, accordingly, to grant treatment that is more beneficial if a higher amount of income or capital is taxable in that State under a tax treaty. In all of these cases, apparently no violation of Article 24(1) can arise because no connection to nationality exists. In addition, the OECD Commentary acknowledges that the residence State may apportion personal allowances and deductions based on the income and capital that remains taxable in that State under a tax treaty.[1098] It would be surprising if, in certain situations that involve a subordinate tiebreaker rule or income for government service, Article 24(1) would blame a State for discriminating against foreigners by connecting tax benefits to certain amounts of taxable income or capital solely because these amounts happen to be influenced by tax treaty rules that rely on nationality.

Assuming, for these reasons, that a Contracting State is allowed under Article 24(1) to connect different tax benefits to different scopes of tax liability even though, in some cases, nationality may have an influence on these benefits after applying a tax treaty, there are some grounds to believe that a State is also allowed to use nationality as a basis for different tax liability under domestic tax law, notably, to distinguish between full and limited tax liability. Since a tax treaty itself uses nationality in order to provide for a different allocation of taxing rights in certain situations, a State cannot be blamed for relying on nationality to provide for a similar tax distinction, a distinction between full and limited tax liability, or between worldwide and territorial taxation.

[D] Article 24(3): Contributing to Equal Conditions of Competition

[1] Equal Treatment of Economically Similar Situations

Although residence is crucial for the purposes of allocating taxing rights under a tax treaty, this does not mean that all tax distinctions because of residence are sacrosanct. They may be scrutinized under Article 24(3) when a non-resident enterprise is taxable in a Contracting State due to a PE.

A policy background of Article 24(3) lies in the concept of capital import neutrality (CIN). Such neutrality is said to prevail if similar investments in a given State are subject to the same effective tax rate whether they are made by domestic investors or by foreign investors.[1099] Under the exemption method of Article 23 A, the residence State of an enterprise exempts the income or capital that is attributable to a PE in the source State. As a consequence, the activities carried on through the PE are taxable only in the source State. The effective tax rate is not influenced by the level of taxation in the residence State. This allows the enterprise of the residence State to compete in the source State on an equal tax footing with enterprises of the source State. By applying the exemption method, the residence State facilitates equal conditions of

1098. *Ibid.*, para. 42.

1099. *See* Green 1994, 116; moreover, Musgrave 2005b, 50–51: capital import neutrality describes '[a] condition in which the same effective tax rate applies to all capital income earned within a given country, regardless of the investor's country of residence'.

competition between its own enterprises and enterprises of the source State as far as the activities carried on in the source State are concerned.[1100] For example, if the source State offers tax incentives for research and development, the lower tax in the source State is not offset by a higher tax in the residence State.

Article 24(3) contributes to this neutrality in the source State. It prohibits the source State from levying less favourable taxation on a PE with regard to attributable income or capital. Such less favourable taxation would modify the conditions of competition for the benefit of resident enterprises and, conversely, to the disadvantage of non-resident enterprises.[1101] This would impede the concept of CIN and, therefore, is prohibited under the PE non-discrimination clause.[1102] Referring back to the previous example, the source State is not allowed to influence the conditions of competition in favour of its own enterprises and thereby influence the effective tax rate with regard to the activities carried on in the source State by granting tax incentives to resident enterprises but not to non-resident enterprises.

Article 24(3) is less closely related to the concept of capital export neutrality (CEN).[1103] Such neutrality is said to prevail if the tax system does not distort an investor's decision regarding whether to invest at home or abroad.[1104] Under the credit method of Article 23 B, the residence State of an enterprise taxes the income or capital that is attributable to a PE but grants a credit for the tax paid in the source State. The effective tax rate with regard to the activities carried on through the PE amounts to at least the tax rate in the residence State. If the tax rate in the residence State is higher than in the source State, an enterprise of the residence State bears a higher tax burden than enterprises of the source State. However, it bears the same tax burden as other enterprises of the residence State that have not invested abroad. By applying the credit method, the residence State maintains neutrality between its own resident enterprises regardless of whether they invest at home or abroad.

In these cases, Article 24(3) ensures that the source State does not levy less favourable taxation on PEs at the expense of the residence State. Without the non-discrimination clause, the source State could be inclined to levy a higher tax on non-resident enterprises, for instance, by denying tax incentives. This would increase the amount of tax that is paid in the source State and creditable in the residence State thereby lowering the tax revenue of the residence State to the advantage of the source State. While this would not necessarily affect the taxpayer's tax burden and, therefore, not deter investment in the source State (due to the effects of the credit method, the higher tax in the source State may be offset by a lower tax in the residence State), discriminatory taxation could lead to an unintended shift of tax revenue from the

1100. Rust 2015b m.no. 56; Rust 2015c m.no. 94a; Rust 2013b, 77; Rust 2010, 640, 647.

1101. *See also*, for instance, Rust 2010, 640, 647; Rust 2004, 395; Adonnino 1993, 53; Zöchling 1994, 18; Raad 1986, 127; Debatin 1981 III m.no. 309; Debatin 1970, 131, 134.

1102. *See* Green 1994, 124, 134–136, 163; Green 1998 fn. 42 on pp. 88–89; moreover, Warren 2001, 163–164; Ault and Sasseville 2010, 102.

1103. *See* Green 1994, 124–129, 162.

1104. *See* Green 1994, 116; moreover, Musgrave 2005a, 45–46: capital export neutrality describes 'a situation in which the overall burden of taxation on capital owned by resident entities of a given country is the same whether that capital is invested abroad or at home'.

residence State to the source State. Article 24(3) avoids such consequences. Arguably, the non-discrimination clause protects the residence State against excessive credit obligations and thereby restrains the residence State from repealing or restricting its foreign tax credit system.[1105] Lastly, in cases when discriminatory taxation in the source State leads to a tax burden that exceeds the creditable amount of tax in the residence State, Article 24(3) contributes to equal conditions of competition between resident and non-resident enterprises with regard to the activities carried on in the source State even under the credit method.

Robert A. Green puts forward another view on the policy background of Article 24(3) and (5). He argues that ownership neutrality, meaning that tax rules should not interfere with market forces that result in assets being owned by the firms that can use them most productively, is a more appropriate goal for the taxation of foreign direct investment than CEN or CIN.[1106] Since Article 24 prohibits a Contracting State from imposing discriminatory taxes on enterprises that are carried on (paragraph 3), owned, or controlled (paragraph 5) by non-residents, it promotes ownership neutrality and, therefore, is desirable from the standpoint of global economic efficiency.[1107]

In addition, Michael J. Graetz criticizes the strong reliance on the traditional concepts of CEN, CIN, and on the corresponding goal of advancing worldwide economic efficiency when discussing international tax policy.[1108] In his view, multiple principles may explain measures that deal with the taxation of cross-border investments and even claims on behalf of adopting policies of both CEN and CIN seem to be grounded not only in concerns for economic efficiency. 'While potential economic inefficiencies are the primary concern of advocates of CEN and CIN, issues of fairness are implicated in this criterion as well.'[1109]

It should be noted that, from a historical perspective,[1110] Working Party No. 4 of the OEEC Fiscal Committee did not extensively deal with the advantages of a PE non-discrimination clause. It merely highlighted that 'for the purpose of *imposition of tax*, the permanent establishment is to be treated as an independent enterprise. Consequently, the permanent establishment becomes, so to speak, an independent enterprise carried on in the State in which it is installed'.[1111] The Working Party felt that the profits of such a PE should not be computed differently solely on the grounds that the operator has fiscal domicile out of that State.[1112] In support of this opinion, the

1105. Haslehner 2016c, 3–4; Rust 2015b m.no. 56; Rust 2015c m.no. 94a; Rust 2013b, 77–78; Rust 2010, 640, 646–647; Warren 2001, 160; Green 1998 fn. 42 on pp. 88–89 with reference to Ault 1992, 574–576; critically Green 1994, 128–129; Friedlander 2002, 76–77. *See also* Mason 2010, 134, who mentions that the residence State may be reluctant – for revenue reasons – to credit discriminatory taxes levied by the source State; moreover, Avery Jones, Baker, et al. 2011b, 191–194; Avery Jones, Baker, et al. 2011a, 548–552.

1106. Green 1994, 116, 138–144. *See also* Desai and Hines 2003, 487–497, 499; Kane 2006; moreover, Mason and Knoll 2012, 1021, 1051–1055, 1115–1116.

1107. Green 1994, 116, 144–152, 162–164.

1108. Graetz 2001, 261–336. *See also* Mason 2010, 134, who acknowledges that other values may be at work besides locational (CEN) and competitive (CIN) neutrality.

1109. Graetz 2001, 305.

1110. *See also* Lang 2006, 38–39; Lang 2007b, 105–106.

1111. OEEC, FC/WP4(57)1, p. 7 (original emphasis).

1112. *Ibid.*, p. 7.

Working Party invoked a PE non-discrimination provision that was incorporated in a number of double taxation conventions concluded by the OEEC Member countries whereby an enterprise carried on by a non-resident is not to be subjected, in respect of the profits (and of the capital) of a PE, to tax that is other or more burdensome than that to which enterprises carried on by residents are subjected.[1113] Later, the Working Party recalled that '[t]here is a close connection between this provision [the provision suggested by the Working Party] and the clause to be found in most Conventions for the avoidance of double taxation, namely, that the profits of a permanent establishment of a foreign enterprise are to be computed in principle as if the permanent establishment constituted an independent enterprise'.[1114] It also stated that the non-discrimination principle regarding PEs 'is of great importance for the development of commercial and industrial activity across the frontiers',[1115] and its purpose is to do away with differences in treatment 'in situations which are entirely similar from the economic point of view'.[1116] Moreover, the OEEC Fiscal Committee reported that Article 24(3) 'will give firms greater security in expanding their international business'.[1117]

It is thus somewhat unclear to what extent considerations related to CIN, CEN, ownership neutrality, or fairness had been a reason for introducing the PE non-discrimination clause into the OECD Model. Nevertheless, this does not prevent Article 24(3) from at least partly facilitating these concepts and from making non-discrimination desirable. Also, since Article 7 attributes business profits to a PE in the source State based on the concept of an independent enterprise, it is difficult to see a major reason for subsequently taxing these attributed profits higher than those of an independent enterprise. If the situations of resident and non-resident enterprises in the source State are entirely similar from the economic point of view and from the point of view of Article 7, taxes should not work against this similarity by discriminating between enterprises because of their residence. Whether non-discriminatory tax treatment in the source State actually allows non-resident enterprises to compete in the source State on an equal tax footing or whether tax benefits from such non-discrimination are offset in the residence State through a lower tax credit or unprotected discrimination of outbound investments depends on the facts and circumstances of each individual case. Despite these uncertainties about the actual impact of Article 24(3), the policy purposes for taxing PEs no less favourably than resident enterprises remain strong and important. Article 24(3) ensures that economically similar situations in the source State are treated equally by that State and thereby potentially contributes to equal conditions of competition and promotes international commerce.

1113. *Ibid.*, p. 7.
1114. OEEC, FC/WP4(57)2, pp. 5–6. *See also* OEEC, FC/WP4(57)3, p. 11 ('computed as if it constituted a separate enterprise').
1115. OEEC, FC/WP4(57)2, p. 6.
1116. OEEC, FC/WP4(57)3, p. 11.
1117. OEEC, FC(58)2, p. 13; OEEC, FC(58)2(Rev.1) Part I, p. 13; OEEC, C(58)118 Part I, p. 14.

[2] Exception for Personal and Family Circumstances

Article 24(3) on PEs contains a second sentence that permits less favourable treatment of non-residents vis-à-vis residents:

> This provision shall not be construed as obliging a Contracting State to grant to residents of the other Contracting State any personal allowances, reliefs and reductions for taxation purposes on account of civil status or family responsibilities which it grants to its own residents.

This sentence can be traced back to an observation of the Delegate for Germany that Article 24(3) 'should relate to the taxation of the permanent establishment, independently of its owner'.[1118] He suggested specifying in the text of Article 24(3) that nothing should be construed as obliging a country to grant non-residents the same reliefs or the same treatment regarding the rates of tax as its own residents enjoyed.[1119] While the Delegate for the United Kingdom (UK) agreed, the Delegate for Belgium voiced concerns because the suggested amendment would deprive Article 24(3) of a great deal of its value.[1120] Following this discussion, the OEEC Fiscal Committee decided that Working Party No. 4 would present a draft stating that the provisions of Article 24(3) were not to be construed as obliging a Contracting State to grant non-residents the same tax reliefs as to its own residents (without mentioning, however, the question of rates of tax).[1121] This led Working Party No. 4 to present the second sentence of Article 24(3)[1122] which was then adopted by the Fiscal Committee.[1123]

Whether this second sentence contains an exhaustive list of personal allowances, reliefs, and reductions – 'on account of civil status or family responsibilities' – or whether all types of personal allowances, reliefs, and reductions are excluded from the scope of the non-discrimination clause is subject to debate.[1124] According to the OECD

1118. OEEC, FC/M(57)3, p. 6. *See also* Lang 2006, 39–40.
1119. *Ibid.*, p. 6.
1120. *Ibid.*, p. 6.
1121. *Ibid.*, p. 7.
1122. OEEC, FC/WP4(57)4, pp. 1 and 3–4.
1123. OEEC, FC/M(58)1, p. 7.
1124. Based on the wording of the second sentence of Article 24(3), it is not clear whether this reference to civil status or family responsibilities is just an example for relevant personal circumstances. The OECD Commentary also does not deal with this issue; it only refers to individuals in this context. *See* 2008–2017 OECD Commentary on Article 24, para. 36 (1977: para. 24; 1992–2005: para. 22; similarly, 1963: para. 15). However, the OECD Commentary has mentioned since 2008 with regard to dividend distributions made by non-resident enterprises that '[p]aragraph 3 is restricted to the taxation of the profits from the activities of the permanent establishment itself and does not extend to the taxation of the enterprise as a whole. This is confirmed by the second sentence of the paragraph, which confirms that tax aspects related to the taxpayer that owns the permanent establishment, such as personal allowances and deductions, are outside the scope of the paragraph'. *See* 2008–2017 OECD Commentary on Article 24, para. 59. While the OECD Commentary does not explicitly state that the second sentence of Article 24(3) applies to corporation or that it covers all personal circumstances such as, arguably, dividend distributions (corporations have no civil status or family responsibilities), this sentence is meant to confirm that dividend distributions made by a non-resident enterprise are not covered by Article 24(3). In the literature, the views are

Commentary, the second sentence of Article 24(3) 'is designed mainly to ensure that such persons [individuals who are residents of a Contracting State and have a permanent establishment in the other State] do not obtain greater advantages than residents, through entitlement to personal allowances and reliefs for family responsibilities, both in the State of which they are residents, by the application of its domestic laws, and in the other State by virtue of the principle of equal treatment'.[1125] As this sentence limits the scope of the non-discrimination clause, the taxpayer is prevented from obtaining personal allowances and benefits twice: once in the residence State and once in the source State.[1126] It can even be argued that double benefits would distort equal conditions of competition between resident and non-resident enterprises in the source State, so this sentence enhances the object and purpose of the non-discrimination clause as a whole.

Although the OECD Commentary fears that double benefits could be obtained without the second sentence of Article 24(3), this limitation to the PE non-discrimination clause may also lead to a complete loss of such benefits. If the residence State exempts the income or capital that is attributable to a PE in the source State under Article 23 A and if no substantial income or capital remains taxable in the residence State, personal allowances and benefits may have no effect in the residence State if they presuppose a sufficiently high tax base or tax liability. At the same time, the source State in which the income or capital is taxable is not obligated to grant personal allowances and benefits. Therefore, a taxpayer with all or a major part of that person's income or capital being taxed in the source State may not benefit from personal allowances, reliefs, and reductions at all, neither in the residence State nor in the source State.[1127]

A solution could lie in a proportional consideration of personal allowances and reliefs in both the residence State and the source State. To the extent that the income or capital is taxable in a Contracting State, the respective State could be responsible for granting personal allowances and reliefs. Indeed, the OECD Commentary mentions this option: the second sentence of Article 24(3) 'leaves it open to the State in which the permanent establishment is situated whether or not to give personal allowances and

divided. Many authors interpret the second sentence of Article 24(3) as comprising all personal allowances, reliefs, and reductions but only as far as individuals are concerned (*see*, for instance, Wassermeyer and Schwenke 2016 m.no. 59; Rust 2015b m.nos. 70, 79; Rust 2015c m.nos. 109, 120; Kubaile 2013 m.no. 57; Pannwitz 2012 m.no. 26; Tumpel and Stangl 2006, 85, 87; W. Loukota 2005, 342; Hageböke 2004 m.nos. 82–83; Fischer-Zernin 1997 m.no. 37), whereas other authors argue that personal (or general) circumstances of corporations are excluded from the non-discrimination obligations as well; these authors do not only rely on the second sentence of Article 24(3) but rather interpret both sentences of Article 24(3) as a single coherent concept (*see*, in particular, Debatin 1970, 134–136; Sass 1966, 107–110; differently, for instance, Rust 2015b m.no. 70; Rust 2015c m.no. 109; Kubaile 2013 m.nos. 59–61; Pannwitz 2012 m.no. 26; Haslehner 2009, 268–269, 377; Rust 2004, 393; Fischer-Zernin 1997 m.nos. 37–38; Storck 1980, 87–89; Hintzen 1976, 2227).

1125. 2008–2017 OECD Commentary on Article 24, para. 36 (1977: para. 24; 1992–2005: para. 22). *See also* OECD, FC/WP4(71)1, p. 19; OECD, DAF/FC/71.6, p. 3; OECD, CFA/WP1(71)1, pp. 8–9.

1126. Rust 2015b m.nos. 55, 80.

1127. *See also* CJEU, 14 February 1995, C-279/93, *Schumacker*.

reliefs to the persons concerned in the proportion which the amount of the permanent establishment's profits bears to the world income taxable in the other State'.[1128] If both Contracting States pursue this approach, double benefits can be prevented while single benefits are ensured. The problem is that Article 24(3) does not prevent the residence State from fully considering a taxpayer's personal circumstances, and it does not obligate the source State to at least proportionally consider such circumstances.

An additional reason for this sentence could lie in the fact that the residence State is arguably in a better position than any other State to consider the personal circumstances of a taxpayer. A taxpayer generally has a closer personal connection to the residence State than to the source State[1129] which makes it easier for the residence State to take account of personal factors. In addition, the residence State usually subjects its residents to full tax liability which allows it to consider the overall ability to pay tax when calculating the deductible amounts and personal reliefs. By contrast, the source State subjects non-residents to limited tax liability. It might further face practical difficulties in gathering and verifying information about a taxpayer's worldwide circumstances.[1130] That might also be a reason why the non-discrimination clause of Article 24(3) does not obligate the source State to grant personal allowances, reliefs, and reductions.

In the context of pensions, the OECD Commentary on Article 18 emphasizes the special role of the residence State regarding personal circumstances:[1131]

> According to this Article [18], pensions paid in respect of private employment are taxable only in the State of residence of the recipient. Various policy and administrative considerations support the principle that the taxing right with respect to this type of pension, and other similar remuneration, should be left to the State of residence. For instance, the State of residence of the recipient of a pension is in a better position than any other State to take into account the recipient's overall ability to pay tax, which mostly depends on worldwide income and personal circumstances such as family responsibilities. This solution also avoids imposing on the recipient of this type of pension the administrative burden of having to comply with tax obligations in States other than that recipient's State of residence.

In addition, the OECD Commentary on Article 18 states that 'the State of residence is in a better position to provide for adequate taxation of pension payments as it is easier for that State to take into account the worldwide income, and therefore the overall ability to pay tax, of the recipient so as to apply appropriate rates and personal

1128. 2008–2017 OECD Commentary on Article 24, para. 36 (1977: para. 24; 1992–2005: para. 22). *See also* OECD, FC/WP4(71)1, p. 19; OECD, DAF/FC/71.6, p. 3; OECD, CFA/WP1(71)1, p. 9.

1129. This is evidenced by the personal factors that lead to tax treaty residence under Article 4.

1130. *See also* Wattel 2000, 215, who observes that '[s]ource States often feel that they are not able to take into account personal circumstances of non-residents pro rata for lack of information on those personal circumstances. Neither do they usually have information on the worldwide income of non-residents: they only know of the source income that has been earned within their territory'. In addition, '[t]ax returns of non-residents [which in principle could report worldwide income and provide information on personal circumstance] are difficult to check, and if only relatively small amounts of source income are involved, it is scarcely worth the effort'.

1131. 2005–2017 OECD Commentary on Article 18, para. 1.

allowances'.[1132] However, the residence State need not consider all personal circumstances:[1133]

> It may be the intention of a State [which uses the exemption method under Article 23 A] that its residents always enjoy the full benefit of their personal and family allowances and other deductions. In other States these tax free amounts are apportioned. In many States personal or family allowances form part of the progressive scale, are granted as a deduction from tax, or are even unknown, the family status being taken into account by separate tax scales.

The second sentence of Article 24(3) thus reveals special policy considerations regarding personal circumstances. The PE non-discrimination rule does not require the source State to extend certain personal allowances and deductions to non-residents because the residence State is already expected to grant them. They should not be granted twice, that is, in both Contracting States. This sentence also reinforces the idea that there are principal differences between full and limited tax liability. Since Article 24(3) is concerned only with income and capital attributable to a PE, the source State should not be required by the non-discrimination rule to grant deductions and expenses that are not related to specific sources of income or capital. Conversely, the OECD Model expects (but does not obligate) the residence State to consider such personal circumstances because the residence State, by taxing the worldwide income and capital, is in a better position to do so.

A connection, therefore, exists between certain personal allowances and deductions, on the one hand, and the different connections to a State that lead to different scopes of tax liability, on the other hand. A Contracting State that taxes on a worldwide basis (full tax liability) due to a personal connection to its territory presumably considers the personal circumstances of the taxpayer in question. A Contracting State that taxes on a territorial basis (limited tax liability) presumably ignores the personal circumstances. The second sentence of Article 24(3) is based on this presumption. Although a proportional consideration of personal expenses and deductions in each Contracting State would be a viable and perhaps an even better solution than leaving the responsibility for taking care of personal circumstances solely to the residence State,[1134] the OECD Model does not require the Contracting States to proportionally consider the overall ability of the taxpayer in question to pay tax.

1132. *Ibid.*, para. 17.

1133. 1977–2017 OECD Commentary on Articles 23 A and 23 B, para. 42.

1134. *See* Raad and Bosman 2016, 80: 'In that approach [fractional taxation] not only the residence country but also the source country (-ies) should compute the taxpayer's worldwide income and the resulting tax, and restrict the tax they effectively impose to the fraction thereof that corresponds with the fraction that the source country income is of the worldwide income. As a consequence of this approach, the taxpayer is entitled in each of the source countries from which he derives income, to effectively enjoy on a pro rata-parte basis the same benefits that are available to residents of that source country'. *See also* Raad 2010; Raad 2001; Wattel 2000.

[E] Article 24(4) & (5): Safeguarding Allocation of Taxing Rights

[1] No Compensation for Non-taxation of Recipients

[a] Context and Systematics

Article 24(4) prohibits different conditions for the deduction of interest, royalties, and other disbursements that are paid by a resident of a Contracting State to a resident of the other Contracting State, and it provides a similar provision for debts. Accordingly, the taxpayer in question is a resident of the allegedly discriminating State (the residence State) and subject to full tax liability in that State. Under Article 24(4), the residence State may not distinguish between payments and debts based on whether the recipient or creditor is a resident or a non-resident. If the recipient or creditor is not a tax treaty resident of or subject to full tax liability in the residence State, that State must deduct payments or debts under the same conditions as if they were paid or owed to a resident.

Article 24(4) thus involves two different persons: a resident taxpayer who claims a tax deduction for payments or debts and a non-resident recipient or creditor. It addresses the resident payer or debtor and protects that person against different conditions for deduction that are based on whether the recipient or creditor is a resident or non-resident. Although it may be said that the non-resident recipient or creditor is indirectly protected against discrimination as well, only the tax treatment of the resident payer or debtor is subject to the non-discrimination obligations. Thus, as long as the non-resident recipient or creditor does not maintain a PE in the allegedly discriminating State (in which case, the PE non-discrimination clause would apply), that person cannot complain about less favourable tax treatment by reason of residence. Only the resident payer or debtor may complain about discrimination for such a reason.

The reason for this scope of Article 24(4) lies in the fact that the non-resident recipient or creditor, instead of being protected against discrimination, is already protected against taxation in the allegedly discriminating State. In particular, Article 11 on interest, Article 12 on royalties, and Article 21(4) on capital grant taxing rights to the State of which the recipient or creditor is a resident if no PE or immovable property is involved. The allocation rules, therefore, leave the allegedly discriminating State with no or only limited taxing rights. With no or limited taxation, less need for protection against discrimination at the level of the non-resident recipient or creditor arises.[1135]

However, the resident payer or debtor is within the full tax jurisdiction of the allegedly discriminating State and, therefore, concerns about discrimination remain. With regard to the object and purpose of Article 24(4), the current version of the OECD Commentary does not provide any insights but merely restates the scope of the non-discrimination clause:[1136]

1135. *See also* Rust 2004, 392; Rust 2010, 646.
1136. 2008–2017 OECD Commentary on Article 24, para. 73 (1977: para. 56; 1992–2005: para. 55).

> This paragraph is designed to end a particular form of discrimination resulting from the fact that in certain countries the deduction of interest, royalties and other disbursements allowed without restriction when the recipient is resident, is restricted or even prohibited when he is a non-resident. The same situation may also be found in the sphere of capital taxation, as regards debts contracted to a non-resident.

Niels Bammens and Frans Vanistendael argue that the underlying idea of Article 24(4) is that States may wish to disallow the deduction of payments because they believe that their domestic tax base could be eroded if residents are able to shift income abroad through payments to a (related) non-resident; Article 24(4) seeks to ensure that such measures would not discriminate.[1137] Werner Haslehner further explains that the discriminatory measures that are targeted by Article 24(4) usually pursue the idea of compensating for a deduction and reduction in tax at the level of the payer or debtor by levying tax at the level of the recipient or creditor, respectively. This is (at least partly) not possible due to the allocation rules of a tax treaty if the recipient or creditor is resident abroad.[1138] Indeed, since the allocation rules rely on residence, tax treaty residence may influence the allocation of taxing rights. Under Article 11, interest arising in one Contracting State and paid to a recipient who is a resident of the other Contracting State may be taxed in that other State, that is the residence State of the recipient, while the first-mentioned State is left with only limited taxing rights. Under Article 12, royalties arising in one Contracting State and beneficially owned by a recipient who is a resident of the other Contracting State may be taxed only in that other State. If the recipient was a resident of the first-mentioned State, by contrast, this State would principally have full taxing rights under Article 7(1) as business profits or under Article 21(1) as private income.[1139] Tax treaty residence thus determines which Contracting State has a right to tax such items of income (but certain exceptions apply when a PE is involved).[1140] Last, but not least, Article 21(4) grants the residence State of the creditor the exclusive taxing right for capital (but with important exceptions concerning immovable property and PEs).[1141] Although residence is not the sole criterion for the allocation of taxing rights, as the allocation rules usually rely on various other factors as well, a change in residence may cause a substantial change in taxing rights.

It could be argued that what a State loses with payments made by its own residents to non-residents (deduction but no taxation) it gains with payments made by non-residents to its own residents (no deduction but taxation). Yet, although the tax treaty rules apply reciprocally, the actual effects of a particular allocation rule need not be the same in both Contracting States, particularly if the trade relationships are unbalanced. In order to maintain or gain more tax revenue, a Contracting State could

1137. *See* Bammens and Vanistendael 2016, sec. 2.4.1; likewise, Bammens 2012, 335. This view has already been put forward by Raad 1986, 174.
1138. Haslehner 2009, 72–73.
1139. Article 12 would not apply as the royalties would still arise in the first-mentioned State and thus not in the other Contracting State.
1140. Articles 11(4) and 12(3) of the OECD Model.
1141. Article 21(1) to (3) of the OECD Model.

be inclined to take measures that provide compensation for its loss of taxing rights, notably, by denying or disadvantaging deductions of payments made or debts owed to non-residents. Instead of fully taxing the non-resident recipient or creditor on payments or receivables as envisaged under the domestic tax law but prohibited under the tax treaty, the allegedly discriminating State could tax the resident payer or debtor by disallowing a deduction of these payments or debts. This measure would effectively turn juridical into economic double taxation. If the allegedly discriminating State denies a deduction at the level of the resident payer or debtor in order to compensate for its loss of taxing rights under the tax treaty, both Contracting States economically tax the same items of income or capital but at the level of different taxpayers, that is once at the level of the recipient or creditor (inclusion) and once at the level of the payer or debtor (no deduction).

Article 24(4) prohibits discrimination for the reason of residence. More specifically, it prohibits tax distinctions at the level of the resident payer or debtor that are based on the recipient's or creditor's residence. If the allegedly discriminating State imposes domestic tax measures that disallow or disadvantage deductions to non-residents but not to residents because non-residents generally indicate a loss of taxing rights under the tax treaty, payments or debts to non-residents are not deductible under the same conditions as if they had been paid or contracted to residents. As a consequence, the non-discrimination obligations of Article 24(4) are violated. This article, in effect, ensures that a particular allocation of taxing rights that is based on residence cannot be undone by a Contracting State through domestic tax measures that disadvantage deductions of payments or debts to non-resident recipients or creditors.

[b] Historical Implications

The purpose of Article 24(4) is confirmed by the OECD Commentary and the historical background of the non-discrimination clause. A non-discrimination rule regarding payments and debts was only added to the 1977 OECD Model. Already before this addition, however, the 1963 OECD Commentary condemned discrimination of payments:[1142]

> Certain countries do not allow interest [Article 12: royalties] paid to be deducted for the purposes of the payer's tax unless the recipient also resides in the same State or is taxable in that State. Otherwise they forbid the deduction. The Fiscal Committee considers it desirable that the deduction in question should also be allowed in cases where the interest is [Article 12: where the royalties are] paid by a resident of a Contracting State to a resident of the other State, the case of fraud being, of course, reserved; it considers that the deduction should not be forbidden simply because the tax payable by the recipient of such interest is reduced [Article 12: of such royalties is not levied] in the State of source in application of the proposed Article. Any other method of procedure might cancel out the beneficial effects of the measures taken to avoid double taxation.

1142. 1963 OECD Commentary on Article 11, para. 17; and on Article 12, para. 9.

The first two sentences of this statement were unchanged after Article 24(4) was included in the OECD Model. They are still part of the OECD Commentary and refer to the fact that certain countries forbid a deduction of payments unless the recipient also resides in the same State or is taxable in that State.[1143] The other sentences of this comment were replaced with a reference to Article 24(4). 'The question whether the deduction should also be allowed in cases where the interest is [Article 12: where the royalties are] paid by a resident of a Contracting State to a resident of the other State, is dealt with in paragraph 4 of Article 24.'[1144]

Although the current version of the OECD Commentary does not refer to the fact that domestic tax rules that deny a deduction to non-resident recipients might cancel out the beneficial effects of the tax treaty measures taken to avoid double taxation, the mention of this fact in the 1963 OECD Commentary nevertheless indicates the reason why the Fiscal Committee initially recommended non-discrimination with regard to deductions of certain payments and later decided to introduce a deductibility non-discrimination rule in Article 24(4).

When digging deeper into the historical development of Article 24(4), two interesting facts can be derived. First, the Swiss Delegation pressed the OEEC Fiscal Committee to introduce a deductibility non-discrimination provision and also proposed the introduction of Article 24(5) on ownership and control. Second, the Commentary's implication that the purpose of Article 24(4) is to safeguard a particular allocation of taxing rights is confirmed.

In its supplementary memorandum to the second report on the direct taxation of patent royalties and similar payments of November 1958, Working Party No. 8 of the OEEC Fiscal Committee mentioned that the Swiss Delegation asked it to consider whether it would be proper to insert a provision in the draft Article on royalties that royalties would be deductible for the purposes of the payer's tax.[1145] The Working Party did not welcome this suggestion:[1146]

> The Working Party knows of no current tax Convention containing such a clause. It would appear that the sole object of the tax Conventions is to avoid double taxation on one taxpayer only. The Swiss proposal tends therefore to widen the concept of double taxation as embodied in the Conventions. The Working Party does not consider it expedient to depart in regard to royalties from the practices hitherto followed, particularly as the question might also arise in connection with other categories of income, e.g. interest.

Despite this rejecting answer of the Working Party, the Swiss Delegation remained persistent. At the 10th Session of the Fiscal Committee held later in November 1958, the Delegate for Switzerland pointed out that it was necessary to settle the question of the deductibility of royalties for the purposes of the payer's tax.[1147] For

1143. 1977-2017 OECD Commentary on Article 11, para. 4; and on Article 12, para. 2.
1144. *Ibid.*
1145. OEEC, FC/WP8(58)3, p. 3.
1146. *Ibid.*, p. 3.
1147. OEEC, FC/M(58)5, p. 9.

quite some time, this question remained open for discussion.[1148] Only at the 20th Session of the Fiscal Committee held in September 1960 did the Delegate for Switzerland raise this issue again (he had also suggested a general provision on this question in June 1960) but, yet again, 'Working Party No. 8 had been unable to accept this provision which would be a new departure for there was no juridical double taxation as far as the individual, or the company, was concerned, although there was economic double taxation'.[1149] After various statements:[1150]

> [t]he Delegate for Switzerland felt that his Delegation's note had not been thoroughly enough examined by Working Party No. 8. He was not asking for the interest and royalties to be automatically deducted from the payer's income, but that when this deduction was granted by a country to its own residents it should not be precluded solely on account of the fact that the tax payable by the recipient was reduced in accordance with the provisions of the Article under discussion. It was not therefore a question of discriminating in favour of non-residents, but of avoiding discrimination between non-residents and residents.

After the 20th Session of the Fiscal Committee, the Swiss note was circulated to all of the members of the Committee.[1151] In this note, the Swiss Delegation explained its intention behind the non-discrimination provision in further detail:[1152]

> Under most taxation laws, interest and royalties paid by a taxpayer to a third party are expenses which may be deducted from the gross income in order to arrive at the taxable income. There are exceptions to this rule, however.
>
> (a) Under certain countries' laws the payer may not deduct interest and royalties from his income; but he is allowed or required to deduct the tax payable from the interest or royalties he pays to his creditor. Thus the taxation of the creditor is secured.
> (b) Other tax laws allow the deduction of interest and royalties in principle, but disallow it if the creditor is not resident in the same State or if he is not taxable in the same State. By this means too, interest and royalties can be taxed by the State of the payer's residence. ...
>
> When the domestic law generally disallows the deduction of interest and royalties for the purposes of the payer's tax, it is the gross income that is taxed. In such a case, no provision in a Convention which provides relief from the taxes levied on interest and royalties can be invoked to justify the deduction of such interest and royalties from the payer's taxable income.
>
> The position is different if the deduction is allowed as a general rule but disallowed in certain particular cases. In such case the tax is charged on the net income, and if the deduction is disallowed of interest and royalties paid, for example, to a non-resident creditor, the debtor is taxed in place of the creditor. This frustrates the provision in the Convention providing relief from tax on interest and royalties, for no tax is borne by the creditor. Of course, such a possibility must be precluded. ...

1148. OEEC, FC/WP8(58)4, p. 2; OEEC, FC/M(60)2, p. 15; OEEC, FC/WP8(60)1, p. 3; OEEC, TFD/FC/98, p. 3.
1149. OEEC, FC/M(60)5, p. 9.
1150. *Ibid.*, p. 10.
1151. *Ibid.*, p. 10; OEEC, TFD/FC/102.
1152. OEEC, TFD/FC/102, pp. 3-5.

> In view of the importance of the question, the Swiss Delegation proposes a general provision which might be formulated as follows:
>
> 'Interest (royalties) paid by a resident of a Contracting State to a resident of the other Contracting State may be deducted from the gross income of the first-mentioned under the same conditions as and to the extent that such deduction is permitted where the recipient is a resident of the same State as the payer. Such deduction shall not be precluded by reason merely that the tax payable by the recipient on such interest (royalties) is reduced in accordance with this Article ....'

At the 22nd Session of the Fiscal Committee held in January 1961, the Delegate for Switzerland agreed to the question of deductibility being mentioned solely in the Commentary on the draft Articles concerning interest and royalties.[1153] Therefore, a draft Commentary on this question was prepared. Working Party No. 8 (royalties) phrased the question of deductibility as follows:[1154]

> The Article [on the taxation of royalties] does not settle the question of the deductibility of the royalties for the purpose of the payer's tax. In principle, this matter comes under the laws of the State of the payer's residence.
>
> If, however, after the signature of a Convention, a State, with the object of indirectly countering the effect of its relinquishment of the tax at the source, were to introduce into its law a rule prohibiting the deduction for the purposes of the payer's tax of royalties paid to a non-resident, then, in the Fiscal Committee's view, such a measure would be incompatible with the objects of paragraph 1 of the Article.

Working Party No. 11 (interest) expressed this issue in somewhat different terms,[1155] and its explanation was later adopted by the Fiscal Committee:[1156]

> Certain countries do not allow interest paid to be deducted for the purposes of the payer's tax unless the recipient also resides in the same State or is taxable in that State. In any other case they forbid the deduction. The Committee considers it desirable that the deduction in question should also be allowed in cases where the interest is paid by a resident of a Contracting State to a resident of the other State, with of course provision to prevent fraud; it considers that the deduction should not be forbidden simply because the tax payable by the recipient of such interest is reduced in the State of source in application of the proposed Article [on the taxation of interest]. Any other method of procedure might cancel out the beneficial effects of the measures taken to avoid double taxation.

The current wording of the OECD Commentary[1157] still resembles this quoted explanation of Working Party No. 11. Therefore, it seems evident that the intention behind Article 24(4) was to protect the allocation of taxing rights agreed by the Contracting States in the tax treaty. Nevertheless, this object and purpose was not mentioned again when Article 24(4) was added to the 1977 OECD Model. As Working Party No. 4 reported in 1969, the Belgian Delegation proposed a new paragraph to be

1153. OEEC, FC/M(61)1, p. 15.
1154. OEEC, FC/WP8(61)1, p. 9. *See also* OEEC, FC/WP8(61)2, p. 8.
1155. OEEC, FC/WP11(61)1, p. 8. *See also* OEEC, FC/WP11(61)2, p. 8.
1156. OEEC, FC/M(61)3, p. 3.
1157. 1977–2017 OECD Commentary on Article 11, para. 4; and on Article 12, para. 2.

inserted into Article 24 which, except for some minor drafting changes, corresponded to the current wording of Article 24(4):[1158]

> Except where Articles 9, 11, paragraph 6, and 12, paragraph 4, apply, interest, royalties and other disbursements paid by an enterprise of a Contracting State to a resident of the other Contracting State shall, for the purpose of determining the taxable profits of such enterprise, be deductible [under the same conditions][1159] as if they had been paid to a resident of the first-mentioned State.
>
> Similarly, any debts of an enterprise of a Contracting State to a resident of the other Contracting State shall, for the purposes of determining the taxable capital of such enterprise, be deductible [under the same conditions][1160] as if they had been contracted to a resident of the first-mentioned State.

According to the Belgian Delegation, such provisions would end the discrimination resulting from the fact that, in certain countries, the deduction of interest, royalties, and other disbursements that is allowed without restriction when these are paid to a resident is restricted or even prohibited when they are paid to a non-resident.[1161] The Belgian Delegation's proposal for a new non-discrimination clause was then agreed upon by the Fiscal Committee without any reported discussion.[1162] As the OECD Commentary on Articles 11 and 12 was adapted to reflect these changes to Article 24,[1163] there is a good reason to believe that the deductibility non-discrimination clause continued to reflect the policy concerns that were already raised in preparation of the 1963 OECD Model. Article 24(4) thus addresses domestic tax measures that impede the agreed allocation of taxing rights by turning prevented juridical double taxation into unrelieved economic double taxation, that is, by taxing the payer or debtor in place of the recipient or creditor, respectively.

[c] Taxing Rights as a Substitute

Article 24(4) appears to have two different kinds of discriminatory domestic tax measures in mind:

1158. OECD, FC/WP4(69)1, p. 10.

1159. This expression was not included in the English version until OECD, CFA(73)15, p. 59 (i.e., not in OECD, FC/WP4(69)1, p. 10; OECD, FC/WP4(71)1, p. 20; OECD, CFA/WP1(73)6, p. 2; and OECD, CFA/WP1(73)10, p. 55), although the French original contained the expression '*dans les mêmes conditions*' from the very beginning.

1160. For the same reasons as mentioned in the previous footnote, this expression was not included in the English version until OECD, CFA(76)7 Part II, p. 52.

1161. OECD, FC/WP4(69)1, p. 10. *See also* OECD, FC/WP4(71)1, p. 20, where Working Party No. 4 suggested including this statement in the Commentary; moreover, OECD, CFA/WP1(71)1, p. 9; 2008–2017 OECD Commentary on Article 24, para. 73 (1977: para. 56; 1992–2005: para. 55).

1162. OECD, DAF/FC/70.5, p. 3. *See also* OECD, FC/WP4(71)1, p. 20; OECD, DAF/FC/71.6, p. 4; OECD, CFA/WP1(71)1, p. 2.

1163. Compare the 1963 OECD Commentary on Article 11, para. 17, and on Article 12, para. 9, with the 1977–2017 OECD Commentary on Article 11, para. 4, and on Article 12, para. 2.

(1) tax measures that are simply based on residence – no deduction 'unless the recipient also resides' in the allegedly discriminating State;[1164] and
(2) tax measures that distinguish based on taxing rights – no deduction 'unless the recipient ... is taxable in that State'.[1165]

In the first scenario, the domestic tax law of the allegedly discriminating State grants no deduction unless the recipient also resides in that State. Article 24(4) prohibits discrimination because of the recipient's or creditor's residence. A Contracting State consequently cannot deny a deduction of payments or debts or impose different conditions for the deduction based on the fact that the recipient or creditor is not a resident of that State for domestic or tax treaty purposes but, rather, a resident of the other Contracting State.

In the second scenario, the domestic tax law of the allegedly discriminating State grants no deduction unless the recipient is within that State's tax jurisdiction for tax treaty purposes or unless the recipient is actually subject to tax in that State. Thus, the decisive criterion is not residence but taxing rights. A deduction is allowed even if a non-resident recipient is at stake provided that this recipient remains taxable in the allegedly discriminating State.

Article 24(4) obligates the Contracting States to impose the same conditions for deduction with regard to residents and non-residents. With its wording, it condemns measures that distinguish based on the recipient's or creditor's residence and not based on whether the recipient or creditor is taxable. Yet, the OECD Commentary appears to suggest that both distinctions should be covered.[1166]

In some cases, the tax treaty may grant the allegedly discriminating State taxing rights for payments or receivables even if a non-resident recipient or creditor is at stake. For instance, if the non-resident recipient or creditor maintains a PE in the allegedly discriminating State, Articles 11(4), 12(3), and 22(2) grant this State in which the PE is situated taxing rights with respect to the attributable income or capital. This means that the allegedly discriminating State may tax the non-resident recipient or creditor on the payments received or on the capital represented by the receivables, respectively. As it has tax jurisdiction over these items of income or capital, its domestic tax law might distinguish not on the basis of residence but, more accurately, on the basis of taxing rights. In cases when no differences in taxing rights between residents and non-residents exist, it will stipulate the same conditions for deduction at the level of the payer or creditor, and no concerns will arise under Article 24(4).

In other cases, especially Articles 11(1) and (2), 12(1), and 22(4) may limit the taxing rights of the allegedly discriminating State, notably, when no PE and no other source of income or capital is located in that State. Being displeased with its loss of taxing rights, the allegedly discriminating State might disadvantage corresponding deductions to the recipient or creditor. If certain payments or receivables are not taxable within its tax jurisdiction at the level of the non-resident recipient or creditor

1164. 1977–2017 OECD Commentary on Article 11, para. 4; and on Article 12, para. 2.
1165. *Ibid.*
1166. *Ibid.*

(because they are taxable in the other Contracting State), the allegedly discriminating State might deny a deduction at the level of the resident payer or debtor. This saves it from fiscal disadvantages (deduction and no taxation) but also cancels out the beneficial effects of the tax treaty measures that are taken to avoid juridical double taxation. In effect, the allegedly discriminating State replaces juridical double taxation that is avoided by the tax treaty with unrelieved economic double taxation, although it does not refer to residence but to taxing rights. It does not discriminate in all cases when non-resident recipients or creditors are involved but only in specific cases when the tax treaty limits its taxing rights in particular due to non-residence.

Article 24(4) could easily be circumvented if it would only cover measures that directly refer to residence. A domestic tax measure that accounts for a loss of taxing rights due to non-residence under the tax treaty could easily avoid the threat of discrimination under Article 24(4) if it was allowed to refer to a particular allocation of taxing rights. For instance, instead of prohibiting a deduction of payments when the recipient is a non-resident (discrimination because of residence), the domestic tax measure of a State could prohibit a deduction of payments when they are not taxable within that State's tax jurisdiction due to the tax treaty, that is, when a particular tax treaty provision limits the State's taxing rights. In such a case, the domestic tax measure would, from a formal perspective, not take account of whether the recipient is a resident or a non-resident. If the taxing rights with respect to these payments are allocated under the tax treaty only on the basis of residence or if residents are regarded as always being taxable under the tax treaty in particular when the credit method under Article 23 B is applied, the omission of a direct reference to residence does not necessarily lead to changes in the scope of the scrutinized measure; the criterion of taxing rights might address non-residents only.

Based on the object and purpose of Article 24(4), it should not matter whether the domestic tax measure under scrutiny directly refers to the residence of the recipient or creditor or whether it reaches a very similar result through a reference to taxation or taxing rights as determined by the allocation rules of the tax treaty. Since the allocation rules are fundamentally based on residence and since Article 24(4) pursues the aim of safeguarding the allocation decisions that have been agreed in the tax treaty by the Contracting States, a reference to a particular allocation of taxing rights might be seen as a substitute for residence. All domestic tax measures of a State that lead to economic double taxation for the reason that the tax treaty, when applied to the recipient or creditor, restricts that State's taxing rights because a non-resident is involved should consequently violate Article 24(4) regardless of the legal technique. If a State thus prohibits a deduction or imposes different conditions of deductibility when the recipient or creditor is not taxable in that State, the object and purpose of Article 24(4) speaks for covering such situations as prohibited tax discrimination as well (*see also* Chapter 4 section §4.03[B][2][d]).[1167]

1167. *See*, to this effect, Pöllath and Rädler 1980, 21–22. Kees van Raad, however, emphasizes that the OECD Commentary distinguishes between residence of the recipient and taxing rights of the recipient: 'Certain countries do not allow interest [Article 12: royalties] paid to be deducted for the purposes of the payer's tax unless the recipient also resides in the same State

[2] No Compensation for Non-taxation of Owners?

[a] Context and Systematics

Article 24(5) on ownership and control prohibits other or more burdensome tax treatment of resident enterprises if their capital is owned or controlled by a resident of the other Contracting State. Accordingly, the taxpayer in question is a resident of the allegedly discriminating State (the residence State) and subject to full tax liability in that State. Pursuant to Article 24(5), the residence State may not distinguish based on ownership or control as far as residence is concerned. Even if the residence State has no tax jurisdiction over the person owning or controlling the capital of the resident enterprise, it must treat the resident enterprise the same as if its capital was owned or controlled by a resident. The fact that the capital of a resident enterprise (subsidiary) is owned or controlled by a resident of the other Contracting State (parent company, investor, or shareholder) should not lead to tax disadvantages.

As outlined above (*see* section §3.02[B][3]), Article 24(5) is aimed at preventing tax protectionism, that is the deterrence by tax measures of investment from outside the country. Furthermore, Article 24(5) indirectly protects not only the investor but also the investor's residence State; this State may only be willing to provide relief from economic double taxation at the investor's level if the State of the subsidiary does not tax this company higher than other comparable enterprises. It may also be argued, however, that Article 24(5) is aimed at safeguarding the agreed allocation of taxing rights. Just as with deductible payments and debts under Article 24(4), dividend distributions and ownership of shareholdings indicate a loss of taxing rights under the tax treaty if non-resident shareholders are involved.

How taxing rights are divided among the Contracting States is partly determined by residence. If no PE is involved, dividends are taxable under Article 10(1) primarily in the Contracting State of which the beneficial owner (the shareholder) is a resident while, under Article 10(2), the other State is left with only limited taxing rights. Additionally, capital gains from the alienation of shares, the value of which is not predominantly represented by immovable property, are taxable under Article 13(5) only in the Contracting State of which the alienator (the shareholder) is a resident. Last, but not least, the capital represented by shares is taxable under Article 22(4) only in the residence State of the capital owner (the shareholder). To the extent that these allocation rules rely on residence for the purpose of allocating taxing rights to the Contracting States, differences in residence may lead to substantial differences in

or is taxable in that State. Otherwise they forbid the deduction. The question whether the deduction should also be allowed in cases where the interest is [Article 12: where the royalties are] paid by a resident of a Contracting State to a resident of the other State, is dealt with in paragraph 4 of Article 24.' *See* 1977–2017 OECD Commentary on Article 11, para. 4; and on Article 12, para. 2. While the first sentence mentions both residence and taxing rights, the last sentence refers to Article 24(4) for the case when the disallowance of the deduction is based on residence. This comment could, therefore, also be interpreted as indicating that a disallowance based on taxing rights is *not* covered by Article 24(4). *See* Raad 1986 fn. 8 on p. 176.

taxation. Since the Contracting States have agreed on such tax consequences, they expect each other not to enact domestic tax measures that could render this agreement or those rules ineffective. This context of Article 24(5) supports the argument that the goal behind the ownership non-discrimination provision is to protect the allocation of taxing rights as agreed by the Contracting States in the tax treaty and to prevent the Contracting States from turning juridical into economic double taxation. Thus, the fact that some items of income or capital that belong to the shareholder are not taxable in the allegedly discriminating State (because the shareholder is a non-resident) should not lead to other or more burdensome taxation of the resident enterprise, the capital of which is owned or controlled by that shareholder.

Without the non-discrimination clause of Article 24(5), by contrast, a Contracting State could prevent juridical double taxation by surrendering taxing rights in favour of the other Contracting State but afterwards turn this initiative into economic double taxation by disadvantaging foreign-owned enterprises. For instance, in the case of dividends, if the shareholder is a resident of the other Contracting State, the allegedly discriminating State might partly have no taxing rights under Article 10(1) and (2), whereas it would be allowed to fully tax a resident shareholder (while facing crediting obligations for foreign tax under Article 23 A or 23 B). Being displeased with such a loss of tax revenue due to non-residency, the allegedly discriminating State might provide for other or more burdensome tax treatment of the resident enterprise, the capital of which is owned or controlled by the non-resident shareholder. What the allegedly discriminating State has lost under the tax treaty at the level of the shareholder could be regained by taxing the underlying of the shareholding, that is the resident enterprise.[1168] Article 24(5), however, prohibits such discriminatory treatment.

[b] Historical Implications

From a historical perspective,[1169] there exists little evidence of the objectives of Article 24(5), especially when compared to Article 24(4). In its first report of January 1957 on tax discrimination, Working Party No. 4 of the OEEC Fiscal Committee did not suggest an ownership non-discrimination provision.[1170] Rather, the Swiss Delegation sent written comments on the Working Party's report and proposed, among others, a provision 'which is designed to prevent discrimination on the ground that an enterprise of one country is controlled by persons domiciled in another country'.[1171] This provision, which replicated the language in the tax treaty between the UK and Switzerland of 1954,[1172] was worded as follows:[1173]

1168. *See*, however, Avery Jones 2009, 44–45, who regards Article 24(5) more like an extension of Article 24(1) to prevent discrimination purely on account of foreign ownership when this did not give rise to different nationality, as defined to mean governing law.
1169. *See also* Lang 2006, 40–41; Lang 2007b, 106–107; Avery Jones 2009, 40–48; Avery Jones, Baker, et al. 2011b, 181–191; Avery Jones, Baker, et al. 2011a, 538–549.
1170. OEEC, FC/WP4(57)1.
1171. OEEC, FC/WP4(57)2, p. 7.
1172. Avery Jones, Baker, et al. 2011b, 182; Avery Jones, Baker, et al. 2011a, 538–539; Avery Jones 2009, 42–43.
1173. OEEC, FC/WP4(57)2, p. 8.

> The income, profits and capital of an enterprise of one of the States, the capital of which is wholly or partly owned or controlled, directly or indirectly, by one or more persons domiciled in the other State, shall not be subjected in the first-mentioned State to any taxation which is other, higher or more burdensome than the taxation to which other similar enterprises of that first-mentioned State in the like circumstances are or may be subjected in respect of the like income, profits and capital.

The Swiss Delegation suggested both an ownership non-discrimination provision and a deductibility non-discrimination provision. Although the Swiss Delegation only explained the intended objectives behind the last-mentioned provision (*see* section §3.03[E][1][b]), an argument can be made that both provisions pursue similar aims. Apparently, the Swiss Delegation was aware of the problem that Contracting States might turn juridical into economic double taxation after concluding a tax treaty in order to regain tax revenue. While not providing sufficient evidence to reach conclusive results, the fact that the Swiss Delegation suggested including both an ownership non-discrimination provision and a deductibility non-discrimination provision could indicate a potential link between these provisions.[1174] In fact, both non-discrimination provisions as enshrined in Article 24(4) and (5) are conceptually very similar. They protect a resident taxpayer against discrimination based on the residence of another person, and this other person, the recipient, creditor, or shareholder is subject in the allegedly discriminating State only to source taxation due to the allocation rules of the tax treaty. Just as a State might be dissatisfied with losing taxing rights with regard to payments and debts when a non-resident recipient or creditor is at stake, a State might be dissatisfied with losing taxing rights with regard to dividends and capital gains when a non-resident shareholder is at stake.

It could also be argued that discriminatory tax treatment of a subsidiary is prohibited under Article 24(5) because, otherwise, the subsidiary's State could increase its tax revenue at the expense of the parent company's State without affecting the overall tax burden. This would be the case if the latter State, in the case of a dividend distribution from the subsidiary to the parent company, provides the parent company with an indirect tax credit for the underlying corporate tax paid by the subsidiary in order to avoid economic double taxation.[1175] Similarly, if the parent company's State avoids economic double taxation through a dividend or participation exemption, it might expect the subsidiary's State to not undo its efforts by discriminating against the subsidiary. Nevertheless, since the OECD Model contains neither a dividend or participation exemption nor an indirect tax credit for underlying corporate tax, it seems reasonable to place greater emphasis on a connection to the allocation rules and on concerns about turning juridical into economic double taxation through discrimination against resident enterprises because of their relationship to a non-resident shareholder.

1174. It should also be mentioned, however, that the origins of the provision on ownership and control can be traced back to the UK's tax treaty practice. *See* Avery Jones, Baker, et al. 2011b, 181–182; Avery Jones, Baker, et al. 2011a, 538; Avery Jones 2009, 40–41.

1175. *See* Avery Jones, Baker, et al. 2011b, 193–194; Avery Jones, Baker, et al. 2011a, 551–552.

It is interesting to note that Working Party No. 4 approved (subject to slight modifications)[1176] the suggestion of the Swiss Delegation even though it saw little practical relevance of such a non-discrimination provision.[1177] For the Working Party '[i]t would appear that the discrimination in question arises only very rarely' in the OEEC Member countries.[1178] Indeed, the Working Party stated that 'it is not easy to see how the Swiss Delegation's proposal can have any real significance' and 'it is inconceivable that ... [a company of State A] could be subjected to discriminatory treatment ... on the ground that it is controlled by persons domiciled in State B'.[1179] Nevertheless, such a non-discrimination provision 'will be of the fullest importance in relations with [non-OEEC Member] countries which see no objection in applying such discrimination'.[1180]

This view on the practical relevance of the non-discrimination provisions should be treated with caution. The Working Party saw a connection of Article 24(5) to the company's nationality which 'is sometimes determined by reference to the country of origin of the capital invested in it and of the individuals controlling it'.[1181] Since the Working Party's proposal of a nationality non-discrimination provision similar to Article 24(1) already had 'the effect ... that in determining a company's nationality one must look to the law governing companies',[1182] the non-discrimination provision on ownership and control was seen as being of little practical relevance. In addition, the Working Party expressed the opinion that even the PE non-discrimination rule would be of little practical relevance in the OEEC Member countries. According to the Working Party, the replies to its questionnaire 'have shown beyond doubt that the form of discrimination in question here occurs but very rarely in the Member countries of the O.E.E.C. It feels, however, that the value of the [PE non-discrimination] provision, as indeed of the Article as a whole, is this, that the Member countries of the O.E.E.C., by their formal adherence to the principle of non-discrimination, will help to propagate this principle which is so vital for the development of international economic relations'.[1183] By denying any practical consequences, the Working Party tried to meet the main concerns of most Delegates about an impact on their country's tax law and to convince them to adopt the suggested non-discrimination provisions.[1184] As the OEEC Member countries supposedly did not discriminate anyway, they did not have to fear any consequences. Still, a non-discrimination standard in tax matters would encourage third countries to adhere to the principle of non-discrimination as well.[1185]

1176. Working Party No. 4 only replaced 'an enterprise of one of the States' with 'an enterprise established in a Member country of the O.E.E.C' as well as 'in the other State' with 'in some other Member country' and made some other corresponding amendments. *See* OEEC, FC/WP4(57)2, p. 10.
1177. *See also* Avery Jones, Baker, et al. 2011b, 182–184; Avery Jones, Baker, et al. 2011a, 539–541; Avery Jones 2009, 41–42; Lang 2006, 40; Lang 2007b, 106–107.
1178. OEEC, FC/WP4(57)2, p. 8.
1179. *Ibid.*, p. 8.
1180. *Ibid.*, p. 8.
1181. *Ibid.*, p. 8.
1182. *Ibid.*, p. 8.
1183. *Ibid.*, p. 6.
1184. *See also* Lang 2007b, 108.
1185. *See also* Lang 2011d, 13.

[F] Implications for Dual Residents (Tiebreaker)

As outlined above (*see* section §3.03[B]), 'residence' may have different meanings in different tax treaty contexts. It is thus unclear whether 'residence' under Article 24(3), (4), and (5) refers to full tax liability under domestic law and to all underlying criteria that lead to full tax liability and residence under Article 4(1) or to tax treaty residence under the entire Article 4, including the tiebreaker rules of Article 4(2) and (3) in cases of dual residence. A Contracting State may not only discriminate against non-residents who are tax treaty residents of the other Contracting State but also against its own tax treaty residents if they remain subject to full tax liability in the other Contracting State and thus if they remain residents of the other Contracting State under Article 4(1) but not under Article 4(2) or (3). As the first-mentioned State is actually discriminating against its own tax treaty residents, it could be argued that no discrimination under Article 24(3), (4), and (5) can be at hand. However, whether these non-discrimination provisions cover situations when a State discriminates against its own tax treaty residents[1186] has to be answered against the backdrop of their objectives.[1187]

Article 24(3) pursues the objective of contributing to equal conditions of competition between resident and non-resident enterprises (*see* section §3.03[D][1]). In principle, this means that, as far as PEs are concerned, all tax benefits that relate to attributable income or capital must be granted equally even if the taxpayer in question has no personal connection to the State concerned. If the taxpayer is subjected to limited tax liability and, therefore, treated as a non-resident under Article 4(1) and the entire Article 4, the PE non-discrimination clause grants protection. If the taxpayer establishes a personal connection to the State concerned that triggers full tax liability and residence under Article 4(1) but not under the entire Article 4, again Article 24(3) prohibits discrimination because of residence. As the taxpayer is a non-resident under the entire Article 4, a PE may exist under Article 7, and thus protection under Article 24(3) is not questioned. Finally, if the taxpayer is a resident of the State concerned under Article 4(1) and the entire Article 4 without being a dual resident, there can be no discrimination. Rather, the tax treatment of the taxpayer – a resident of the State concerned who has no personal connection to the other Contracting State – determines how comparable non-resident enterprises should be treated under Article 24(3). In all of those cases, the State concerned is allowed to tax income or capital that is attributable to the PE regardless of how closely the taxpayer in question is integrated into that State's economy, and all of those cases are treated equally either because a resident is involved or because Article 24(3) prohibits less favourable treatment of non-residents.

Given that Article 24(3) contributes to equal conditions of competition by requiring equal treatment of all of those cases, it is not clear why the State concerned should be allowed to discriminate in rather exceptional circumstances, namely, if it

1186. Or to be precise with regard to Article 24(4) and (5): it discriminates against resident enterprises that pay disbursements or owe debts to its own tax treaty residents (para. 4) or that are owned or controlled by its own tax treaty residents (para. 5).

1187. *See also*, to this effect, Lang 2008, 227–228.

does not lose but wins the tiebreaker rules of Article 4(2) and (3). It can even be argued that, with more integration, not less but more protection against discrimination should be granted.[1188] Four situations based on the personal connection to the allegedly discriminating State can be distinguished:

(1) no personal connection to that State;[1189]
(2) weak personal connection to that State;[1190]
(3) strong personal connection to that State;[1191] and
(4) sole personal connection to that State.[1192]

It would remain dubious why cases (1) and (2) should be treated no less favourably than case (4), whereas case (3) should not be protected at all even though, in all of these cases, income or capital is attributable to a PE and taxable in that State, arguably asking for equal conditions of competition. From this perspective, it should not matter whether the allegedly discriminating State has taxing rights as the source State or as the residence State as long as the involvement of the other Contracting State as a tax jurisdiction causes tax disadvantages for taxable income or capital. Even in a situation of dual residence when the allegedly discriminating State wins the tiebreaker under Article 4(2) or (3) and becomes the residence State for tax treaty purposes, less favourable tax treatment because of full tax liability and residence under Article 4(1) in the other Contracting State should be prohibited to the extent a PE exists in the residence State within the meaning of Article 5.[1193]

It could be argued that, if the allegedly discriminating State is the residence State for tax treaty purposes, no PE exists in that State under Article 7. Without a PE, Article 24(3) cannot apply. However, while it is true that Article 7 does not address a PE in the residence State but only a PE in the source State, this does not mean that it prohibits such a concept under Article 24(3). Article 5 defines the term 'permanent establishment' in a neutral manner regardless of the Contracting State in which a PE is located and regardless of which allocation rule is applied; it defines the term '[f]or the purposes of this Convention'. Consequently, a PE and, notably, a fixed place of business may exist not only in situations where an allocation rule other than Article 7 applies[1194] but also in the residence State. It follows that Article 24(3) protects against all forms of discrimination because of residence as soon as a PE within the meaning of Article 5 is at hand.

Similar to that under Article 24(3), the concept of residence under the deductibility non-discrimination clause should not only refer to tax treaty residence under the entire Article 4 but should also cover full tax liability and residence under Article 4(1).

1188. *See*, to this effect, Rust 2003b, 660.
1189. A resident of only the other Contracting State.
1190. A resident of both Contracting States; tiebreaker is lost.
1191. A resident of both Contracting States; tiebreaker is won.
1192. A resident of only the allegedly discriminating State.
1193. *See*, however, Haslehner 2009, 181, who states that the tiebreaker rules of Article 4(2) and (3) apply for the purpose of determining residence under Article 24(3).
1194. *See*, in particular, Article 15(2)(c) of the OECD Model.

Alexander Rust notes that the application of the tiebreaker rules would lead to strange results:[1195] A Contracting State would be prohibited from discriminating against the resident payer or debtor when that State may not tax the recipient or creditor because it has lost the tiebreaker (the recipient or creditor would be a resident of the other Contracting State). A Contracting State, however, would be allowed to discriminate against the resident payer or debtor even if that State is entitled to tax the recipient or creditor because it has won the tiebreaker (the recipient or creditor would not be a resident of the other Contracting State). For this reason, Article 24(4) protects against distinctions based on differences in tax liability and residence under Article 4(1) and the entire Article 4. It does not matter whether the allegedly discriminating State requires residence in that State for a tax benefit or whether it refuses a tax benefit if residence exists in the other Contracting State.[1196]

Since Article 24(4) aims at avoiding that a Contracting State disadvantages resident payers or debtors when it has lost taxing rights with regard to non-resident recipients or creditors (*see* section §3.03[E][1]), it could be questioned why a Contracting State should be prohibited from differentiating based on residence when it has won the tiebreaker and not lost any taxing rights. It could further be questioned why a Contracting State should be prohibited from differentiating based on residence if it has not lost any taxing rights for other reasons, for instance, because the recipient or creditor maintains a PE in that State under Article 7 or Article 22(2). This issue is not necessarily related to situations of dual residence. A tax distinction based on residence is indeed broader than necessary to compensate for a loss of taxing rights. Conversely, a tax distinction based on taxing rights is more precise but should still be regarded as discrimination when taxing rights are effectively a substitute for residence. Thus, a tax distinction based on taxing rights may conflict with Article 24(4) when taxing rights are influenced by residence, but this does not necessarily prevent Article 24(4) from condemning all tax distinction based on residence if there is no other explanation than to compensate for a loss in taxing rights in as many situations as possible. After all, such a distinction simply discriminates against more persons than necessary, but it still discriminates on the basis of residence for illegitimate reasons and should be prohibited in all cases.

Similar considerations can also be made with regard to the ownership non-discrimination clause. There is no apparent reason why, at some time during the transition between not being personally connected to the allegedly discriminating State at all and being a single-resident shareholder of that State, protection under Article 24(5) should stop. Article 24(5) should rather protect against discrimination even in situations when the shareholder is a tax treaty resident of the allegedly discriminating State but continues to be subject to full tax liability in the other Contracting State; the

1195. Rust 2015b m.no. 97; Rust 2015c m.no. 145.

1196. *See*, moreover, Freeden, Häck, and Schaumburg 2017 fn. 8 to m.no. 4.62; Wassermeyer and Schwenke 2016 m.no. 73; Kubaile 2013 m.no. 67; Wunderlich 2009 m.no. 35; Haslehner 2009, 75; Hofstätter and Ressler 2006, 211–213; Rust 2003b fn. 21 on p. 660.

tiebreaker rules of Article 4(2) and (3) are not relevant for determining the shareholder's residence with respect to Article 24(5).[1197]

Under Article 24(3), (4), and (5), the scope of protection, therefore, is not restricted by an overly narrow meaning of residence. If, for instance, in both State A and State B, incorporation *or* the POEM of a company leads to full tax liability under domestic law and residence under Article 4(1), a domestic tax measure of State A that requires incorporation *and* the POEM in that State for granting a tax benefit is initially discriminating because of residence against: (1) a dual-resident company that is incorporated in State A but has its POEM in State B; (2) a dual-resident company that has its POEM in State A but is incorporated in State B; and (3) a non-resident company that is incorporated and has its POEM in State B – regardless of whether the tiebreaker rule of Article 4(3) relies on incorporation or the POEM.[1198]

§3.04 IDENTITY OF ALL RELEVANT ASPECTS AS A CONCEPT OF COMPARABILITY

[A] Same Concept Despite Differences in Wording?

Article 24 contains several non-discrimination provisions that pursue different aims. Article 24(1) prohibits different tax treatment between nationals and foreigners because nationality generally plays no role in taxation. Article 24(3) prohibits different tax treatment between residents and non-residents as far as a PE is concerned in order to contribute to equal conditions of competition in economically similar situations. Article 24(4) and, arguably, also Article 24(5) prohibit different tax treatment based on the recipient's, creditor's, or shareholder's residence in order to avoid that a Contracting State compensates for its loss of taxing rights. Based solely on the wording of Article 24, moreover, each non-discrimination provision appears to pursue a different concept of comparability. Article 24(1) on nationality requires that the persons who are compared must be 'in the same circumstances, in particular with respect to residence'.[1199] Article 24(3) stipulates that a PE of a non-resident enterprise must be compared to a resident enterprise 'carrying on the same activities'. Article 24(4) on the deduction of payments and debts lays down no explicit comparability requirements; it only demands 'the same conditions' for deductibility to apply. Article 24(5) on foreign ownership and control refers to 'similar enterprises'.

Although the wording of Article 24 imposes different comparability requirements under each of its provisions, the OECD Commentary argues that the different non-discrimination clauses pursue a common concept of comparability:[1200]

1197. Rust 2015b m.no. 106; Rust 2015c m.no. 162; Haslehner 2009, 83–84; Burgstaller and Obermair 2006, 186; Rust 2003b, 660; differently, Toifl 2003, 276.

1198. *See also*, to this effect, Ribbrock 2005, 402–403; Rust 2005, 28; Rust 2003b, 659; concurring Wunderlich 2009 m.no. 51.

1199. In the following, Article 24(2) will not be separately mentioned to the extent that there are no substantial differences when compared to Article 24(1). Hence, conclusions reached with regard to Article 24(1) can be applied *mutatis mutandis* under Article 24(2).

1200. 2008–2017 OECD Commentary on Article 24, para. 3. *See also* Haslehner 2016c, 9–10.

> The various provisions of Article 24 prevent differences in tax treatment that are solely based on certain specific grounds (*e.g.* nationality, in the case of paragraph 1). Thus, for these paragraphs to apply, other relevant aspects must be the same. The various provisions of Article 24 use different wording to achieve that result (*e.g.* 'in the same circumstances' in paragraphs 1 and 2; 'carrying on the same activities' in paragraph 3; 'similar enterprises' in paragraph 5).

Thus, the OECD Commentary first emphasizes what the non-discrimination provisions of Article 24 have in common: they prevent differences in tax treatment that are solely based on certain specific grounds. For this reason, the OECD Commentary concludes that the underlying concept of comparability can be described in common terms; all relevant aspects, except for the specific grounds that are protected by a non-discrimination clause, must be the same.

It is worth highlighting that the OECD Commentary refers to all *relevant* aspects thereby implying that irrelevant differences in circumstances do not prevent comparability.[1201] Moreover, the OECD Commentary does not specifically mention Article 24(4).[1202] This could lead to arguments about whether this non-discrimination provision pursues a different concept of comparability. At the same time, however, the OECD Commentary refers to '[t]he various provisions of Article 24', arguably including Article 24(4), and it describes the explicit comparability requirements of Article 24(1), (2), (3), and (5) as only examples ('e.g.') for the different wording used to achieve the same result. Article 24(4) also prevents differences in tax treatment that are solely based on certain specific grounds, namely the residence of the recipient or creditor. Arguably, the Commentary does not mention Article 24(4) because no explicit comparability requirements can be found in this non-discrimination clause and not because a completely different concept of comparability should be pursued.

This basic understanding that the non-discrimination rules of Article 24 involve a common concept of comparability is supported by Kees van Raad. He submits that a 'same circumstances' requirement may be considered redundant.[1203] Identity of relevant circumstances is implied in the very concepts of non-discrimination and equal treatment.[1204] It is clear, Kees van Raad argues, that when a State extends a favour that it normally restricts to persons who have a certain characteristic (e.g., the nationality of that State) to persons who do not have such a characteristic, this gesture does not

1201. *See also* 2008–2017 OECD Commentary on Article 24, paras 7, 17–18; critically Haslehner 2016c, 9–10, 15 ('[the OECD Commentary] only requires the same [circumstances] with respect to "all relevant aspects", prompting the question which aspects might be ignored'; '[this intended simplification] is more likely to unnecessarily complicate matters, by stirring debates about what is and what is not *relevant*'; original emphasis).

1202. *See also* Bammens 2012, 344.

1203. Raad 1986, 88–89; similarly, Raad 1992, 675; differently, Santiago 2009, 255. As will be illustrated below, Kees van Raad submits that a 'same circumstances' requirement may be considered redundant not only to emphasize that comparability is required under Article 24 and that comparability may be phrased in abstract terms under all of its non-discrimination provisions. He also believes that the question of relevance should play no role because all circumstances, except for the protected characteristic, should be identical or otherwise lead to incomparability. Therefore, he also proposes a concrete and rather strict comparability standard.

1204. Raad 1986, 88.

release these latter persons from any further requirements upon which the original granting of the favour may depend.[1205] A 'same circumstances' requirement is thus redundant in non-discrimination rules that term a specific circumstance non-discriminatory, as is done in Article 24 that gives circumstances such as nationality, residence, and foreign ownership a non-discriminatory status.[1206] This means that even if such a rule does not expressly refer to 'same circumstances', such circumstances are required for its application. Accordingly, the 'same circumstances' requirement is redundant under Article 24(1).[1207] Also, the express 'same activities' test under Article 24(3)[1208] and the 'similar enterprises' requirement under Article 24(5)[1209] should be applied as supplemented by an implied 'same circumstances' requirement. Last, but not least, identity of circumstances and conditions is also inherent in Article 24(4).[1210]

It should be noted in favour of Kees van Raad's view that Working Party No. 4 assumed an implied comparability test as well.[1211] In its report on tax discrimination on the grounds of nationality or similar grounds of January 1957, the Working Party proposed a nationality non-discrimination provision that did not contain a 'same circumstances' requirement.[1212] According to Working Party No. 4, 'it is not necessary to lay down separately the condition essential to the provision in question, namely, that similar circumstances [French original: une situation analogue] must exist; rather ... such a condition is already implied' in the proposed provision.[1213] In response to the Working Party's proposal, the Belgian and Swiss Delegations proposed including an 'in identical/similar circumstances' (French original: '*une situation identique/semblable*') requirement.[1214] Although Working Party No. 4 was 'still of opinion that such an addition is unnecessary, and that it is obvious that the text suggested could not imply the extension to foreign nationals of the treatment appropriate to the country's own nationals whose tax circumstances were different',[1215] it had no objection to the proposed addition being adopted, with the following wording: 'in the like circumstances' (French original: '*se trouvant dans la même situation*').[1216] This wording was later translated into English as 'in the same circumstances'.[1217]

1205. Raad 1986, 88-89.
1206. Raad 1986, 89.
1207. Raad 1986, 89.
1208. Raad 1986, 140.
1209. Raad 1986, 189.
1210. Raad 1986, 176.
1211. *See also* Avery Jones 2009, 32-33.
1212. OEEC, FC/WP4(57)1, p. 4: 'The nationals of a Member country of the O.E.E.C. shall not be subjected in the territory of any other Member country to any taxation or any requirement connected therewith, ... which is other, higher or more burdensome than the taxation and connected requirements to which the nationals of the latter country are or may be subjected'.
1213. *Ibid.*, p. 4.
1214. OEEC, FC/WP4(57)2, p. 2.
1215. *Ibid.*, p. 2.
1216. *Ibid.*, pp. 2 and 10.
1217. As far as can be seen, the term '*se trouvant dans la même situation*' was translated as 'in the like circumstances' in the following documents: OEEC, FC/WP4(57)2, p. 2; OEEC, FC/M(57)2, p. 3; OEEC, FC/WP4(57)3, pp. 3, 5 and 6; OEEC, FC/M(57)3, p. 6. This term was,

There are some grounds to believe that the explicit comparability requirements of Article 24(1), (2), (3), and (5) can be subsumed under a common concept of comparability that requires the identity of all of the relevant aspects or circumstances. It is not precisely clear, however, what role these comparability requirements then play or why they are worded differently if they merely point to a single concept of comparability. They might have been drafted without too much thought about their exact meaning, or they might carry specific implications about comparability. In the following, some specific implications will be discussed that are relevant only for each individual non-discrimination clause and cannot be generalized. This analysis will then be followed by a broader discussion of the concept of comparability under Article 24 and how to determine the relevant aspects or circumstances.

[B] Specific Questions Regarding Comparability

[1] Article 24(1): Same or Similar Circumstances

In regard to Article 24(1), the OECD Commentary explains the condition of 'the same circumstances, in particular with respect to residence' in further detail:[1218]

> The expression 'in the same circumstances' refers to taxpayers (individuals, legal persons, partnerships and associations) placed, from the point of view of the application of the ordinary taxation laws and regulations, in substantially similar circumstances both in law and in fact. The expression 'in particular with respect to residence' makes clear that the residence of the taxpayer is one of the factors that are relevant in determining whether taxpayers are placed in similar circumstances.

Distinguished authors criticize that the OECD Commentary does not adhere to a sufficiently strict and exact comparability standard.[1219] By relying on substantially *similar* circumstances, arguably, the Commentary deviates from the wording of Article 24(1) that imposes a precise condition of 'in the *same* circumstances'. In referring to similar, rather than identical, circumstances, no doubt the Commentary intended to prevent arguments about minor differences in circumstances, but it has had the opposite effect at least as far as differences of fact are concerned.[1220] John F. Avery Jones, Henri-Robert Depret, et al. report that some supposed differences in factual circumstances were inappropriately used to place nationals and foreigners in different situations under Article 24(1).[1221] It was suggested that expatriated nationals abroad have generally preserved close personal and economic connections to their country of origin, and the majority of these persons will take up residence in their country of origin

for the first time, translated as 'in the same circumstances' in the third supplementary report of Working Party No. 4: OEEC, FC/WP4(57)4, p. 4.

1218. 2008-2017 OECD Commentary on Article 24, para. 7 (1992-2005: para. 3; similarly, 1963: para. 2; 1977: para. 3).

1219. *See* Bammens 2012, 86; Raad 1992, 675 ('[the Commentary's] explanation ... upsets the very notion of non-discrimination'); Avery Jones, Depret, et al. 1991b, 312-313.

1220. Avery Jones, Depret, et al. 1991b, 312.

1221. Avery Jones, Depret, et al. 1991b, 312.

again while foreigners do not have such close personal and economic connections.[1222] According to John F. Avery Jones, Henri-Robert Depret, et al., rather than looking at hypothetical nationals in general (and assuming differences with respect to the preservation of personal and economic relations), the comparison should be made with a hypothetical national who was factually identical to the foreign national in all relevant matters except nationality.[1223] It would have been better if the OECD Commentary had not referred to *similar* factual circumstances so that one was required to compare the real taxpayer with a hypothetical taxpayer in identical factual circumstances except, of course, for their nationality.[1224]

However, the expression 'substantially similar' (instead of 'identical' or 'the same') could merely point to the fact that all *relevant* aspects except for the protected characteristic must be the same in order to establish comparability.[1225] Prohibited discrimination because of nationality should not be denied under Article 24(1) solely because 'the same circumstances' do not literally exist. In this sense, substantially similar circumstances exist when all of the differences in circumstances are irrelevant. Niels Bammens similarly submits that minor differences in circumstances can also be relevant to taxation.[1226] The decisive question, therefore, should be whether the circumstances that are relevant are identical.[1227] Factors that are irrelevant to the tax measure at issue, such as the possibility that non-resident nationals have closer personal and economic ties to their State of nationality than non-resident foreigners have to that State, should not be taken into account.[1228] This obviously raises the question of how the relevant and irrelevant differences in circumstances can be determined (*see* section §3.05[A]).

A major discussion concerning the nationality non-discrimination clause relates to the issue of whether differences in residence always prevent comparability between foreigners and nationals. At first glance, they do so. Since 1992, the wording of Article 24(1) expressly requires 'the same circumstances, in particular with respect to residence' to exist, and the OECD Commentary regards this statement as a clarification.[1229] Problems arise, however, if nationality leads to full tax liability and thereby to residence for tax treaty purposes. Whether differences in legal circumstances between foreigners (limited tax liability) and nationals (full tax liability) prevent discrimination is the subject of debate (*see* section §3.06[C]). Those persons are not in identical circumstances both in law and in fact but, arguably, they might be 'in substantially

1222. Avery Jones, Depret, et al. 1991b, 312.
1223. Avery Jones, Depret, et al. 1991b, 312–313.
1224. Avery Jones, Depret, et al. 1991b, 313.
1225. 2008–2017 OECD Commentary on Article 24, paras 3, 7, 17–18 ('relevant aspects'; 'relevant factors'; 'no relevance whatsoever').
1226. Bammens 2012, 86.
1227. Bammens 2012, 86–87.
1228. Bammens 2012, 84.
1229. 2008–2017 OECD Commentary on Article 24, para. 7 (1992–2005: para. 3). *See also*, for instance, Rust 2015b m.no. 36; Rust 2015c m.no. 49; Oesterhelt 2015 m.no. 19; Bruns 2013 m.no. 15; Kubaile 2013 m.no. 2.2; Avery Jones 1996, 46; Lehner 1995, 30; to this effect, moreover, Debatin 1963b, 21–22; differently, Raad and Bosman 2016, 70; Raad 2012, 163–164; Schilcher and Stefaner 2006, 162–163; Raad 2005, 130–131; Toifl 2004, 331; Toifl 2003, 291–292, 303–304, 313.

similar circumstances' if differences in residence are not relevant in a concrete case and, thus, if all of the relevant circumstances are 'the same'.

[2] Article 24(3): Same (Sector of) Activities

Article 24(3) requires 'the same activities' for the purposes of comparability. During the drafting of the PE non-discrimination clause, Working Party No. 4 did not pay much attention to this phrase.[1230] The first draft of the provision compared the computation of a PE's profits to 'similar profits' of a resident operator.[1231] The Swiss Delegation suggested that the non-discrimination clause should not be restricted to the computing of profits but should also apply to taxes on capital. The text proposed by the Swiss Delegation contained the expressions 'an enterprise ... conducted in the like manner' and 'in respect of the like income, profits or capital'.[1232] The Working Party proposed a different wording that used the expression 'engaged in the like business' (French original: '*exerçant la mĕme activité*').[1233] In the English translation, this expression was later replaced by 'carrying on the same activities', though it remained as '*exerçant la mĕme activité*' in the original French version.[1234]

Nevertheless, Article 24(3) arguably relies on 'the same activities' for a reason. A PE belonging to a non-resident enterprise cannot be in exactly the same circumstances as a resident enterprise.[1235] In the words of Niels Bammens and Frans Vanistendael, 'a PE is, by definition, never in "the same circumstances" as a resident' and 'there will always be significant (factual and legal) differences between a PE and a resident'.[1236]

A PE is not a legally separate and independent enterprise. It is only a legal concept or fiction[1237] that merely exists for tax treaty purposes. This part of an enterprise cannot, in general,[1238] conclude legally binding contracts, own assets, or bear risks except hypothetically when applying Article 7(2) in order to attribute profits under the

1230. *See also* Dziurdź 2010b, 249–250.
1231. OEEC, FC/WP4(57)1, p. 7; OEEC, FC/WP4(57)2, p. 10.
1232. OEEC, FC/WP4(57)2, pp. 6–7.
1233. *Ibid.*, p. 7. *See also* OEEC, FC/M(57)2, p. 4; OEEC, FC/WP4(57)3, p. 3.
1234. OEEC, FC/WP4(57)4, p. 4. *See also* OEEC, FC/WP4(58)1, p. 3. It is further worth mentioning that, in preparation of the 1977 OECD Model, the Portuguese Delegation proposed that the words 'in the same circumstances' be added at the end of the first sentence of Article 24(3). *See* OECD, FC/WP4(69)1, p. 10. However, without any reported discussion, the OECD Fiscal Committee agreed not to make this amendment. *See* OECD, DAF/FC/70.5, p. 2.
1235. *See*, to this effect, Avery Jones, Depret, et al. 1991b, 331; Arnold 1991, 37; O'Brien 1978, 568–569; Patrick 1978, 706. *See*, moreover, Bronselaer and Heyvaert 2009 m.no. 23.56, who comment that, in Belgium, a PE and a resident company are, as a matter of principle, not in the same circumstances because they are subject to a different tax regime (non-resident income tax versus corporate income tax).
1236. Bammens and Vanistendael 2016, sec. 2.3.2.1.1; likewise, Bammens 2012, 193–194.
1237. However, the word 'fiction' may be misleading because a PE under Article 5 presupposes a certain presence for its legal existence, for example a place of business or physical presence. *See* Dziurdź 2014, 135–136.
1238. Agreements between different parts of an enterprise can sometimes be legally binding. If a partnership having legal capacity or even a company under a 'check-the-box' regulation is treated as transparent for tax purposes, it may be regarded as constituting a PE for its partners or shareholders, respectively. In such cases, it is possible that a single part of the enterprise

authorized OECD approach (AOA).[1239] It also cannot be a resident for tax treaty purposes under Article 4 (but *see* Chapter 4 section §4.04[D][1]). According to the OECD Commentary, difficulties thus arise because of:[1240]

> the actual nature of the permanent establishment, which is not a separate legal entity but only a part of an enterprise that has its head office in another State. The situation of the permanent establishment is different from that of a domestic enterprise, which constitutes a single entity all of whose activities, with their fiscal implications, can be fully brought within the purview of the State where it has its head office.

If 'the same circumstances' were required, there would be a risk that inherent factual and legal differences between a PE of a non-resident enterprise and a legally separate and independent enterprise would automatically prevent comparability. By only requiring 'the same activities', Article 24(3) allows ignoring these inherent differences and is thus able to successfully prevent tax discrimination. Nevertheless, to what extent certain characteristics are inherent to a PE is often unclear. For instance, a PE does not, as such, distribute dividends; only the non-resident enterprise to which the PE belongs is able to declare and pay out dividends to its shareholders. Whether this fact suffices for denying relief from economic double taxation is disputed (*see* Chapter 4 sections §4.04[E][2][d] and §4.04[E][4]).

Although the explicit comparability requirement of 'the same activities' appears to ensure that PEs can be compared to resident enterprises, Article 24(3) can also be criticized for using a too relaxed comparability standard by merely focusing on 'activities'.[1241] This comparability requirement appears to limit itself to certain operations, processes, or functions or to something being done.[1242] The OECD Commentary even notes that Article 24(3) has the purpose 'to end all discrimination in the treatment of permanent establishments as compared with resident enterprises belonging to the same *sector of* activities' (emphasis added).[1243] This seems to involve a more relaxed comparability standard than 'the same activities'. Therefore, it could be argued that this condition for comparability does not extend to legal circumstances. For example, a PE may belong to an enterprise of an individual or of a corporation. If it was assumed that 'the same activities' do not comprise legal circumstances, a PE belonging to an enterprise of a non-resident individual would be comparable to and could not be taxed less favourably than an enterprise of a resident corporation as long as both carry on the same activities or belong to the same sector of activities. Taken literally, 'the same activities' would not account for differences in legal and factual circumstances that exist between individuals and corporations. A State, therefore, would be prohibited from applying different rates of tax or different tax systems to these persons as soon as

(the partnership/company as the PE or a partner/shareholder as the head office) legally owns assets, assumes risks, or possesses capital or contracts with separate enterprises. *See* Dziurdź 2014, 145.

1239. *See*, with further references, Dziurdź 2014, 138–141.
1240. 2008–2017 OECD Commentary on Article 24, para. 39 (1977–2005: para. 23).
1241. Bammens and Vanistendael 2016, sec. 2.3.2.1.1.
1242. *See also* Raad 1986, 140.
1243. 2008–2017 OECD Commentary on Article 24, para. 35 (1977: para. 23; 1992–2005: para. 21).

a PE is involved. Most differences between personal and corporate income tax systems could potentially be incompatible with Article 24(3).

Such an intrusive impact on a State's domestic tax policy is not intended by Article 24(3) and is unanimously rejected.[1244] The OECD Commentary states that the tax treatment of a PE 'should be compared to that of [a resident] enterprise ... that has a legal structure that is similar to that of the [non-resident] enterprise to which the permanent establishment belongs. Thus, for example, paragraph 3 does not require a State to apply to the profits of the permanent establishment of an enterprise carried on by a non-resident individual the same rate of tax as is applicable to an enterprise of that State that is carried on by a resident company'.[1245] Although the legal structure need not be linked to the activities performed by an enterprise, it is captured by 'the same activities' or at least by an implied 'same circumstances' requirement.[1246]

At the same time, the assumption that the legal structure must be identical for the purposes of comparability under Article 24(3) could impose impossible or too strict requirements. In cases when incorporation leads to residence (*see* section §3.06[C]), a non-resident company has, by definition, a different legal structure than a resident company because these persons derive their status, as such, from the laws in force in different States, that is their States of incorporation. If the PE non-discrimination clause is not to be rendered meaningless in such cases, a substantially similar legal structure must suffice.[1247] While a non-resident enterprise carried on by an individual should not be comparable to a resident enterprise carried on by a company, a non-resident enterprise carried on by a German limited liability company (GmbH) should remain comparable to a resident enterprise carried on by an Austrian limited liability company (GmbH) and vice versa.[1248] This means that 'the same activities' or an implied 'same circumstances' requirement covers more than only the activities of the enterprises (it covers the legal structures as well). At the same time, it does not require the legal structures to be identical (similarity of the legal structures suffices). This again raises the question of how the relevant and irrelevant differences in circumstances can be determined (*see* section §3.05[A]).

1244. *See*, for instance, Bammens and Vanistendael 2016, sec. 2.3.2.1.1 ('other considerations (such as legal structure) may be taken into account as well'; 'identical in all relevant respects'); Bammens 2012, 194; Rust 2004, 393; Zorman 2003, 286–287; Raad 1986, 140.

1245. 2008–2017 OECD Commentary on Article 24, para. 37. *See also*, to this effect, Rust 2015b m.no. 62; Rust 2015c m.no. 103; Rädler and Raupach 1966, 393.

1246. *See*, moreover, Debatin 1970, 135, who emphasizes the fact that a PE is a dependent part of a non-resident enterprise but must be compared to a separate and independent resident enterprise. This requires the assumption of legal personality according to the circumstances of the non-resident enterprise.

1247. It could be argued that if, after applying Article 24(3), differences in legal structure prevent equal treatment, these differences amount to prohibited discrimination because of nationality under Article 24(1). However, if Article 24(1) is not included in a particular tax treaty or if its scope is limited to individuals, Article 24(3) could become largely meaningless as far as differences in residence coincide with differences in incorporation and legal structure.

1248. *See also* Haslehner 2016a m.no. 21; Haslehner 2009, 60, 226–227; Tumpel and Stangl 2006, 76; Raad 1986, 135, 137; as regards Article 24(1), moreover, Schilcher and Stefaner 2006, 152–154; Hageböke 2004 m.no. 40.

A somewhat related issue concerns the activities of a non-resident enterprise that are not carried on through the PE and whether these activities may be relevant for comparability purposes under Article 24(3) or, rather, must be ignored. In some cases, such other activities may not influence the taxation on the PE if, for instance, the domestic tax law of the source State taxes both residents and non-residents on a territorial basis or if all of the activities of the non-resident enterprise are carried on through the PE in the source State, which means that no other activities and places of business exist[1249] (*see* Figure 3.1).[1250]

Figure 3.1 Comparability Involving Only One PE

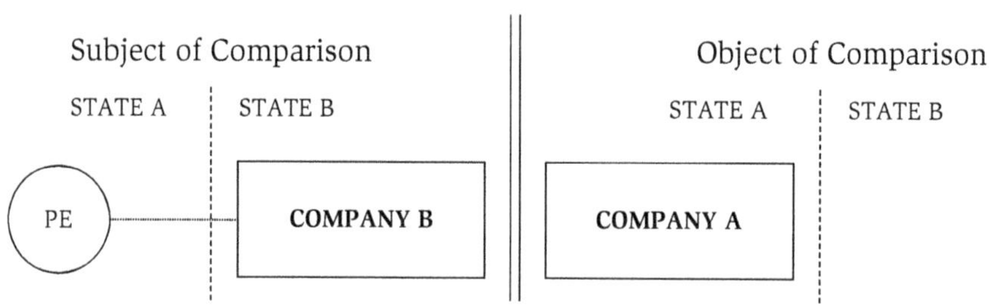

In other cases, however, if the non-resident enterprise carries on other activities as well, these other activities may potentially influence the taxation on the PE. It is often stated that it is not the PE that is protected against discrimination under Article 24(3) but the non-resident enterprise with regard to the income or capital that is attributable to the PE.[1251] This could imply that the other activities of the enterprise (and the income therefrom and the capital associated therewith) cannot be ignored. If, for instance, the head office in the residence State constitutes a fixed place of business within the meaning of Article 5, the PE of the non-resident enterprise in the source State must be compared to a resident enterprise that maintains such a fixed place of business abroad. Comparison must be made to a resident enterprise that conducts the same activities as

1249. It is thinkable, for instance, that a company is a resident of a Contracting State due to its incorporation but without carrying on business through a fixed place of business in that State. If the tiebreaker rule of Article 4(3) deviates from the OECD Model by relying on incorporation, a company may maintain a PE (place of management) in the source State but not in the residence State. Similar situations arise if an individual is a resident of a Contracting State but carries on the enterprise entirely in the other Contracting State. *See also* Rust 2015b m.no. 60; Rust 2015c m.no. 99.

1250. In this figure, the comparable resident enterprise of State A (the object of comparison) carries on the same activities as the PE of the non-resident enterprise of State B (the subject of comparison). As a consequence, the fixed place of business in State A, deemed to belong to the comparable resident enterprise of State A, is not specifically indicated.

1251. *See*, for instance, Wassermeyer and Schwenke 2016 m.no. 46; Rust 2015b m.no. 57; Rust 2015c m.no. 95; Bruns 2013 m.no. 85; Rust 2010, 638; Haslehner 2009, 223–224; Wunderlich 2009 m.no. 22; Schön 2006, 27; Tumpel and Stangl 2006, 76; Hageböke 2004 m.nos. 64–65; Raad 1986, 133; Vogel 1970, 354.

the whole non-resident enterprise to which the PE belongs.[1252] For an appropriate comparison to a resident enterprise, the PE in the source State (PE 1) must become the head office of a resident enterprise, and the head office in the residence State (PE 2) must become a PE (*see* Figure 3.2), even though only the taxation on the first-mentioned PE can be scrutinized.

Figure 3.2 Comparability Considering the Whole Non-resident Enterprise

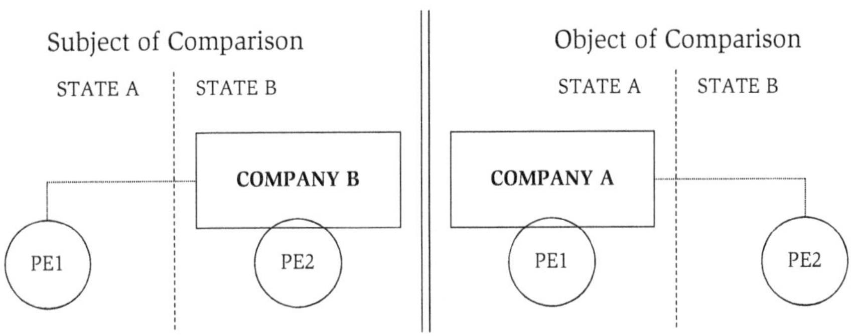

The fact that Article 24(3) is merely concerned with '[t]he taxation on a permanent establishment' could also mean that both the taxation of the other activities of the enterprise (tax advantages in the residence State, therefore, cannot compensate for tax disadvantages in the source State) and the existence of the other activities, as such, should be ignored. Comparison can only be made to a resident enterprise that carries on 'the same activities' as the PE in the source State and no other activities (*see* Figure 3.3).[1253]

1252. *See also* Vogel 1997 Article 24, m.no. 122, who comments on New York Court of Appeals, 12 October 1993, *Reuters Ltd. v. Tax Appeals Tribunal* et al. that 'the comparison with a domestic enterprise which has the same structure worldwide as that of the enterprise operating the permanent establishment ... will only be necessary in exceptional situations, viz. when this structure is actually of importance of the taxation of the enterprise concerned', thereby in principle approving such a comparison; moreover, Rust 2015c m.no. 100; differently, for instance, Haslehner 2009, 225; critically also Kaplan 1992.

1253. *See*, for instance, Bhuta 2015, 385–387, 394–397; Wandl 2015, 438–439; Haslehner 2009, 225; Tumpel and Stangl 2006, 76–77; Schneeweiss 2006, 317; Zöchling 1990, 51.

Figure 3.3 Comparability Limited to the PE

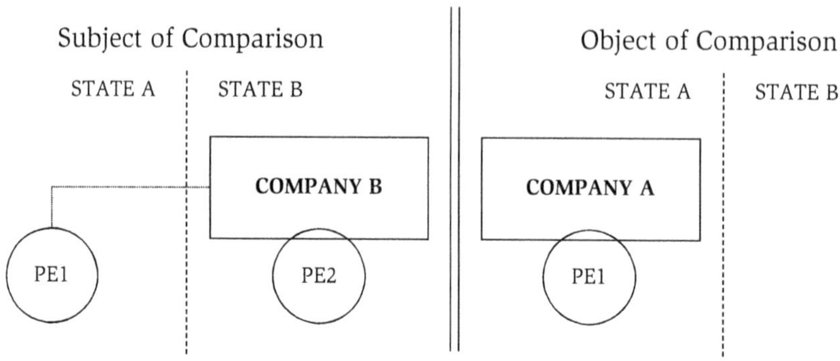

Lastly, it is sometimes suggested that comparison should be made to a subsidiary in the source State of a non-resident parent company (*see* Figure 3.4).[1254] It remains unclear, however, why comparison should not be made to a parent company in the source State that holds shares in a non-resident subsidiary[1255] and how to proceed with enterprises carried on by individuals.[1256]

Figure 3.4 Comparability Assuming a Parent–Subsidiary Relationship

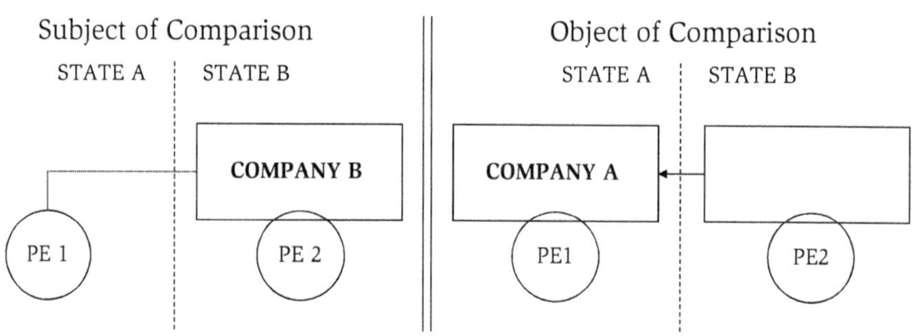

William C. Gifford already observed in 1978 that the truncated language of Article 24(3) unfortunately gives rise to an elliptical comparison – 'the same activities' as what, the

1254. *See*, to this effect, Raad 2008, 164–171; similarly, Silva 2016b, 121; Pitkänen 2015, 476–479, 482–487; Ismer 2012, 824; critically Hohenwarter 2010, 624; moreover, Haslehner 2016a m.no. 21; Oliver 1977, 151–152.
1255. In fact, if the tiebreaker rule of Article 4(3) deviates from the OECD Model by relying on incorporation, the POEM of the whole enterprise may be located at the PE in the source State. It could consequently be argued that if the PE is deemed to be a separate company under Article 24(3), the head office in the residence State becomes a subsidiary of the parent company in the source State.
1256. *See also* Oesterhelt 2015 m.no. 96.

PE or the enterprise of which the PE is a part?[1257] This issue had also been considered by Working Party No. 1 of the OECD Committee on Fiscal Affairs,[1258] but no relevant statements have been included in the OECD Commentary. When discussing progressive scales of tax rates, it will be submitted that better arguments speak in favour of considering the activities of the whole non-resident enterprise. Accordingly, the worldwide income or capital may influence the non-discriminatory tax rate (*see* Chapter 4 section §4.04[B]). Under Article 24(3), when residence is deemed to be different, the activities of the whole non-resident enterprise, regardless of where they are carried on or whether they are attributable to the PE, may be relevant if they influence the taxation on the PE.

[3] Article 24(4): Same Conditions for Deductibility

Article 24(4) includes no explicit comparability requirements. It merely requires that payments and debts are deductible 'under the same conditions'. This omission might be understood in two different ways: either it does not change anything about the comparability requirements because a 'same circumstances' test is inherent in all non-discrimination provisions,[1259] or there are no specific comparability requirements, implying a broader scope of comparability.[1260] According to the latter view, payments made to non-residents would always be comparable to payments made to residents, regardless of any remaining differences in circumstances. Whether the recipient is a taxable or tax-exempt individual or corporation or whether the recipient is carrying on charitable or gainful undertakings would not matter for the purposes of comparability. This view, therefore, could lead to a conceptual deviation from the other non-discrimination clauses that rely on sameness or similarity of circumstances, activities, or enterprises. If more differences in circumstances are regarded as irrelevant, comparability can be more easily established.

Niels Bammens submits an example of a domestic thin capitalization rule that denies deduction of payments made by residents to tax-exempt persons, including non-residents that are not subject to taxation in that State but also residents that are tax

1257. Gifford 1978, 60–61, 66–67, further argues that the term 'activities' should be read to refer only to the business operations that a PE conducts in the State in which it is situated.

1258. *See* OECD, DAFFE/CFA/WP1/MR(95)2, p. 24 (paras 69–71), where Philip T. Kaplan raised the issue that it is unclear whether a PE is to be compared with a resident enterprise having the same dimensions as the PE or having the same dimensions as the worldwide enterprise of which the PE forms a part. *See*, moreover, Kaplan 1992. It is further reported that the Steering Group on the Revision of the Model Tax Convention discussed proposed amendments to the OECD Commentary put forward in OECD, DAFFE/CFA/WP1/MR(95)2/REV6 (a document that, unfortunately, was not available for the purposes of this research) and agreed to present proposals to Working Party No. 1. *See* OECD, DAFFE/CFA/WP1/MR/M(97)1, p. 4.

1259. Raad 1986, 176–177; critically Bammens 2012, 344, who submits that, under the current wording of Article 24, interpreting Article 24(4) as including an implicit 'same circumstances' test would be subject to debate, if not incorrect.

1260. Bammens 2012, 339–343, 345–346. *See also* Bammens and Vanistendael 2016, sec. 2.4.2, who additionally mention, however, that this omission has not given rise to significant issues in practice, so it seems that Article 24(4) is interpreted as containing an implicit 'same circumstances' requirement.

exempt for specific reasons such as charitable organizations.[1261] Without any comparability requirements, payments made to non-residents (no deduction) would be comparable to both payments made to tax-exempt residents (no deduction) and payments made to taxable residents (deduction).[1262] Phrased differently, the question of whether comparable payments made to residents are deductible has to be answered with both yes (in some cases) and no (in other cases).[1263]

If payments made to non-residents (no deduction) are regarded as comparable to both payments made to tax-exempt residents (no deduction) and payments made to taxable residents (deduction), this need not raise conceptual problems. It could be argued that Article 24(4) should grant the best treatment of residents (deduction) to all payments made to non-residents, that Article 24(4) should only be violated if the domestic tax measure affects non-residents disproportionally heavier than residents (which would be the case unless a significant number of residents is tax exempt), or that no discrimination should arise as long as not literally all payments to residents are favoured over all payments to non-residents. A policy defence could even be incorporated into 'under the same conditions' if it is concluded that such conditions exist in substance as long as formally identical or formally different conditions are imposed for legitimate policy reasons. Finally, as Niels Bammens apparently suggests, all conditions for deductibility could be seen as legitimate or 'the same' unless they explicitly refer to or are a perfect substitute for residence.[1264] For example, if all payments to tax-exempt persons are non-deductible regardless of their residence, they are arguably deductible 'under the same conditions'.[1265]

It should be mentioned that the interpretation of 'under the same conditions' suggested by Niels Bammens is, as for the result, difficult to distinguish from a 'same circumstances' requirement that regards all or most differences in circumstances as relevant.[1266] As the law applies equally to all to whom it applies,[1267] the law also prescribes equal conditions for its application to all whom it concerns. Even a blatant discriminatory condition for deductibility of paying to a resident recipient is, so to speak, the same condition with respect to all payments made to residents and non-residents. This understanding of 'under the same conditions' would render Article 24(4) meaningless. If this requirement, therefore, is understood as a mere prohibition of explicit references to residence, a deduction is granted 'under the same conditions' as soon as a reference is made to any other characteristic. In terms of comparability, it could be said that differences with regard to this other characteristic render situations between residents and non-residents incomparable. Article 24(4) is not violated because a distinction is made on the basis of a characteristic other than residence (the

1261. Bammens 2012, 339.
1262. Bammens 2012, 339–340, 343, 1020–1021.
1263. Bammens 2012, 440.
1264. Bammens 2012, 345–347.
1265. Bammens 2012, 345.
1266. In fact, Niels Bammens speaks of 'a comparability requirement of sorts', the difference being that it does not incorporate a test of relevance. *See* Bammens 2012, 345–347.
1267. Tussman and tenBroek 1949, 345.

deduction is granted 'under the same conditions') or because residents and non-residents are treated differently as they differ with regard to this other characteristic, arguably rendering situations incomparable (residents and non-residents are not 'in the same circumstances'). Overall, the omission of explicit comparability requirements under Article 24(4) may leave open how comparability should be determined, but it does not avoid a decision on how broad or narrow the scope of Article 24(4) should be.

[4] Article 24(5): Similar (Foreign?) Enterprises

Article 24(5) prescribes a comparison of resident enterprises, the capital of which is owned or controlled by residents of the other Contracting State, with 'other similar enterprises'. Unlike Article 24(3) and (4), Article 24(5) does not specifically require a comparison involving a resident. Rather, it leaves open whether the term 'similar' requires domestic or foreign ownership and control, that is whether a resident enterprise that has non-resident shareholders who are residents of the other Contracting State should be compared to a resident enterprise that also has non-resident shareholders but who are residents of a third State or whether comparison should be made with a domestically owned or controlled enterprise. Nothing in the present language prohibits comparing to enterprises controlled by residents of a third State.[1268] Today, it is almost undisputed, however, that a cross-border shareholding must be compared to a domestic shareholding, that is to a resident company that is owned or controlled by resident shareholders.[1269] When Article 24(5) was adopted in February 1958, the OEEC Fiscal Committee indeed 'agreed that the expression "other similar enterprises established in the territory of that first-mentioned Contracting Party" referred to enterprises not under foreign control'.[1270]

The statement that comparison should be made to 'enterprises not under foreign control'[1271] allows claiming that comparison should always be made to resident

1268. Raad 1986, 188. *See*, moreover, Bagci 2019, 27; Oliver 1993, 436–437; Hosson and Michielse 1989, 484.
1269. *See* Silva 2016b, 78–81; Bammens and Vanistendael 2016, sec. 2.5.2.1; Haslehner 2016a m.no. 35; Rust 2015b m.no. 114; Rust 2015c m.no. 167; Allevato Neto 2015, 555–556; Elliffe 2013b, 29–30; Elliffe 2013a, 630–631; Silva 2013, 110; Bruns 2013 m.no. 157; Bammens 2012, 403–405; Avery Jones, Baker, et al. 2011a, 563; Avery Jones, Baker, et al. 2011b, 204; Hohenwarter 2010 fn. 2645 on p. 606; Rust 2010, 641–642; Haslehner 2009, 84; Bronselaer and Heyvaert 2009 m.no. 23.85; De Broe 2008, 554–556, 558–559; Burgstaller and Obermair 2006, 196–197; Hohenwarter and Weninger 2006, 252; Scapa Passalacqua and Henie 2005, 39; Rust 2005, 28; Danon 2004, 338; Burgstaller 2004, 289–290, 292; Oliver 2004, 80–83; Toifl 2003, 311; Papotti 2003, 320–321; Lang 2003a, 258; Rust 2003b, 659; Gouthière 2002, 162; Michielse 1997, 571–572; Fischer-Zernin 1997 m.no. 59; Hughes 1996, 390; Doernberg 1995, 100; Lang 1994b, 153; Avery Jones, Depret, et al. 1991b, 339; Avery Jones, Depret, et al. 1991a, 438–439; Doernberg and Raad 1990, 204; Oliver 1989; Raad 1988b, 351; Raad 1986, 188–189; Pott 1982, 228; Debatin 1981 III m.no. 332; Meilicke 1980, 106. *See also* OECD, Article 24 Discussion Draft 2007, para. 88; moreover, Bruns 2008, 488, who states that this has now been clarified in the 2008–2017 OECD Commentary on Article 24, paras 77–79. *See*, however, Bagci 2019.
1270. OEEC, FC/M(58)2, p. 5. *See also* Silva 2016b, 79; Avery Jones, Baker, et al. 2011b, 204; Avery Jones, Baker, et al. 2011a, 563; Avery Jones 2009, 46–47.
1271. *Ibid.*

enterprises that are directly or indirectly owned by resident shareholders only.[1272] If, in a concrete case, all direct and indirect non-resident shareholders are protected against discrimination – or to be precise, if the resident enterprise is protected against discrimination with regard to all of its direct and indirect non-resident shareholders (protected shareholders) – because all shareholders are residents of the other Contracting State, comparison has to be made to a resident enterprise that is solely owned by resident shareholders (*see* Figure 3.5).

Figure 3.5 Deeming Protected Shareholders to Be Residents (Bilateral)

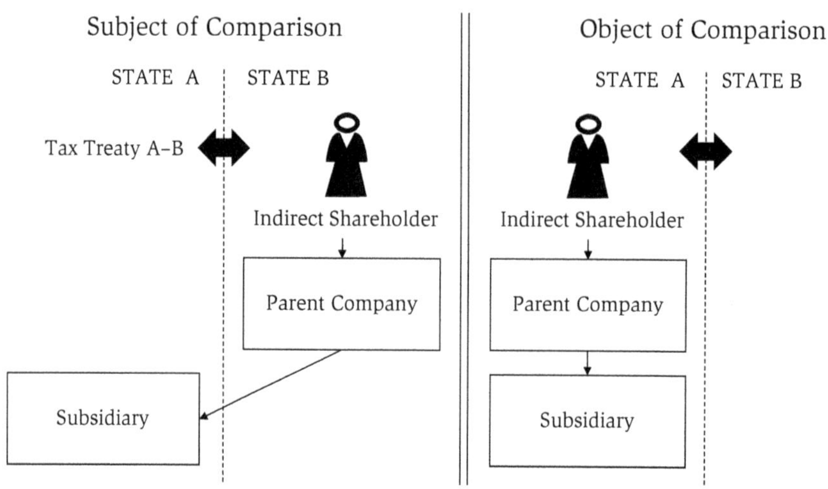

In triangular situations, however, the comparison becomes more complex. Assume that a resident enterprise of a Contracting State (State A) is directly owned by a shareholder from a third State (State C) with which no tax treaty exists. As soon as this enterprise is indirectly owned by a protected shareholder of the other Contracting State (State B), comparison to a better-treated enterprise owned exclusively by resident shareholders would arguably be possible if a comparison must always be made to an enterprise not under foreign control (*see* Figure 3.6). This would also be true if the residence of the protected indirect shareholder has no effect on the tax treatment under scrutiny and thus if the disadvantage at issue arises due to the ownership by the direct shareholder from the third State. In such a case, a change in the residence of all of the protected and unprotected non-resident shareholders would accord a tax advantage, arguably leading to prohibited tax discrimination under Article 24(5) even though a

1272. *See*, for instance, Hintsanen and Viitanen 2004; and Penttilä 2008, 264, who report on such a ruling of the Finish Supreme Administrative Court (korkein hallinto-oikeus), 22 June 2004, KHO:2004:65 (English translation in Simpson 2005); moreover, Bronselaer and Heyvaert 2009 m.nos. 23.91–23.92; basically concurring Bammens 2012, 378–379, although arguing that it is also necessary to determine whether a non-resident intermediary company constitutes a relevant characteristic for the domestic tax measure at issue; critically Silva 2016b, 127–131; De Broe 2008, 559–560.

change in the residence of the protected shareholder alone would not lead to a change in tax treatment.

Figure 3.6 Deeming All Shareholders to Be Residents (Triangular)

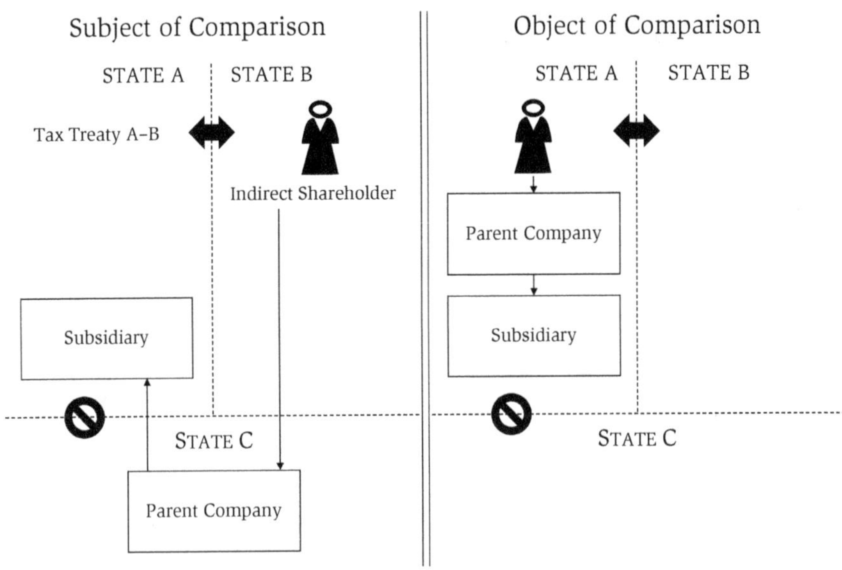

This basically means that a single direct or indirect minority shareholder would allow a resident enterprise to claim non-discriminatory treatment with regard to all of its direct and indirect shareholders including shareholders from third States with which no tax treaty exists. There is no indication that Article 24(5) intends to have such a broad scope. Therefore, it is submitted that it is possible to compare to a resident enterprise without any non-resident shareholders, that is to an enterprise not under foreign control only if all direct and indirect non-resident shareholders are protected by Article 24(5). If not all shareholders are protected, by contrast, comparison has to be made to a resident enterprise that is owned by both resident shareholders and unprotected non-resident shareholders. For example, if a resident enterprise of State A is indirectly owned by a protected shareholder of State B and directly owned by an unprotected shareholder of State C, comparison has to be made to a resident enterprise of State A that is indirectly owned by a shareholder of State A but still directly owned by a shareholder of State C (*see* Figure 3.7).

Figure 3.7 Deeming Protected Shareholders to Be Residents (Triangular)

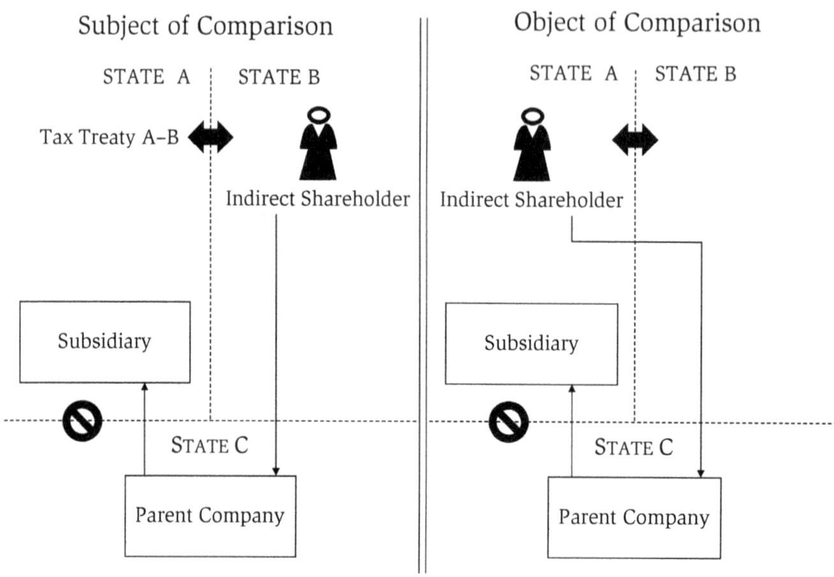

Moreover, it is worth mentioning that the non-discrimination rule of Article 24(5) also initially used the words 'in the same circumstances' (French original: '*se trouvant dans la même situation*'), which qualified similar enterprises.[1273] These words had been deleted because, pursuant to Working Party No. 4 of the OEEC Fiscal Committee, 'they might lead to misunderstanding' and 'add nothing to the meaning of the provision'.[1274] If the expression 'in the same circumstances' would have added nothing to the meaning, this supports the view that implicit comparability requirements are provided and that a 'same circumstances' test may be applied under Article 24(5).[1275] Also, according to Niels Bammens, it seems that 'similar' does not add anything substantial to the interpretation.[1276] All relevant elements, apart from foreign ownership of relevant shareholders, must be identical.[1277] This means that circumstances at the level

1273. *See* OEEC, FC/WP4(57)2, p. 10; OEEC, FC/WP4(57)3, p. 3; OEEC, FC/WP4(57)4, p. 5. Note that the original expression '*se trouvant dans la même situation*' was translated into English as 'in the like circumstances' in OEEC, FC/WP4(57)2 and OEEC, FC/WP4(57)3, while the ultimate translation of this expression which is still used in Article 24(1) and (2) was introduced in OEEC, FC/WP4(57)4. *See also supra* n. 1217.

1274. OEEC, FC/WP4(58)1, p. 4. *See also* Avery Jones, Baker, et al. 2011b, 187–188; Avery Jones, Baker, et al. 2011a, 544–545; Avery Jones 2009, 46.

1275. Raad 1986, 189.

1276. Bammens 2012, 408.

1277. Bammens 2012, 392–393, 408. *See also* Haslehner 2016a m.no. 35; Hohenwarter 2010, 603; Haslehner 2009, 85. *See*, however, Avery Jones, Depret, et al. 1991b, 340, who call into question whether the OECD Commentary's definition of 'same circumstances' (substantially similar circumstances both in law and in fact) applies under Article 24(5); similarly, Cleave 2008, 94–95; Cleave 2007, 606, who argues that, since Article 24(5) does not contain a 'same circumstances' requirement, 'it seems that the paragraph should apply if the enterprise

of relevant shareholders may be relevant,[1278] of course, except for the protected characteristic of the shareholders' residence in order not to render Article 24(5) superfluous.[1279]

[C] Comment on the Concept of Comparability

In order to establish prohibited tax discrimination under Article 24, tax treatments must be compared. Although in other areas of law it is possible to establish discrimination without comparison,[1280] Article 24 is framed around comparability, imposes explicit comparability requirements,[1281] and, therefore, requires comparison. There is also nothing wrong in assuming that Article 24 entails a single concept of comparability that applies to all non-discrimination provisions. All relevant aspects, apart from the protected characteristic (nationality or residence), must be the same. It should not be overlooked, however, that this concept of comparability is very abstract or, to put it in exaggerated terms, empty of content.[1282] It is of little help without a comparability standard that specifies the relevant aspects of a particular case.[1283] It further reminds of the principle that equals should be treated equally and unequals unequally. Without defining which characteristics should lead to equality or inequality of persons or situations, this equal treatment principle is difficult to apply as a legal rule or leaves room for different judgments as all persons and situations are comparable in some aspects but different in others.[1284] Therefore, it is necessary to establish a comparability standard that determines which aspects are relevant and may render situations (in)comparable and which aspects are irrelevant and thus do not influence comparability.[1285]

If a 'same circumstances' requirement is regarded as redundant and implicit to all non-discrimination provisions of Article 24, this does not answer the decisive question of how the relevant circumstances should be determined and whether different aspects may be relevant depending on the facts and circumstances of a particular case. While

---

controlled by non-residents is subjected to taxation or a requirement connected therewith that is other or more burdensome, regardless of whether there might be other reasons for that treatment than the question of control'.

1278. *See also*, to this effect, Bammens 2013a, 168; differently, Knobbe-Keuk 1993, 63.
1279. *See*, for instance, Lang 1994b, 153.
1280. *See infra* n. 2274 and accompanying text.
1281. Article 24(4) is an exception but, nevertheless, calls for comparability as it demands same conditions for deductibility with regard to resident and non-resident recipients.
1282. *See* Westen 1982b. Peter Westen's thesis that the principle of equality is empty of content led to many critical comments and an extensive discussion: Burton 1982; Westen 1982a; Chemerinsky 1983; D'Amato 1983; Westen 1983a; Greenawalt 1983; Westen 1983b; Karst 1983; Simons 1985; Rosenfeld 1988; Westen 1990; Waldron 1991; Peters 1997; Greenawalt 1997; Sarnoff 1999a; Peters 1999; Sarnoff 1999b; Simons 2000; Peters 2000.
1283. *See also* Dziurdź and Marchgraber 2015, 15–16.
1284. *See*, for instance, Dziurdź and Marchgraber 2015, 15–16; Cordewener 2002, 178–179; Peters and Snellaars 2001, 13; Westen 1982b, 544.
1285. *See also* Santiago 2009, 254, who argues that similarity of situations should only be required in connection with what are considered to be relevant factors, but this does not solve the problem of comparability as it is still necessary to determine what factors should be considered to be relevant in a given situation and those which are not.

'the same circumstances' speaks for the identity of circumstances, this requirement does not specify which circumstances must be identical and thus whether all or only certain specific circumstances must be 'the same'. For 'the same circumstances' to be present, it could suffice that all relevant circumstances are identical; irrelevant differences in circumstances could be ignored. In different cases and in different legal contexts, different characteristics could be relevant for the purposes of comparability.

In fact, each non-discrimination provision is embedded in a different legal context, pursues different aims, and covers different forms of discrimination. Even though a common concept of comparability may be worded in abstract terms and applied to all non-discrimination provisions of Article 24, the actual result of a comparability analysis may be very different depending on which provision is applied and which specific attribute is protected. Since Article 24(1) protects against discrimination because of nationality, differences in nationality do not prevent comparability, but differences in residence may do so. Since Article 24(3), (4), and (5) protects against discrimination because of residence, differences in residence do not prevent comparability, but differences in nationality might, in principle, do so (see, however, Chapter 4 section §4.04[C][5][a]). In different contexts, different characteristics may become relevant and lead to incomparability of persons or situations.

It is thus necessary to distinguish between rather abstract concepts of comparability – all relevant aspects must be the same, the circumstances must be the same, etc. – and a concrete comparability standard that defines the relevant aspects or circumstances in a concrete case or at least provides an approach for their determination. The statement of the OECD Commentary that 'other relevant aspects [except for the protected grounds] must be the same' under Article 24[1286] and the view voiced by Working Party No. 4 that tax benefits should not be extended in different tax circumstances[1287] offer little guidance as to the aspects that should be regarded as relevant.

The explicit comparability requirements of Article 24 constitute a more important indication of a particular comparability standard for each non-discrimination provision, although they often remain inconclusive. Article 24(3) is a good example in this respect. A PE is a legally dependent part of a non-resident enterprise. It might never be in circumstances that are identical to those of a separate and independent enterprise. Article 24(3), therefore, should not be rendered meaningless by an overly strict 'same circumstances' test. The relaxed requirement of 'the same activities' is designed to ensure that inherent differences between PEs and resident enterprises do not prevent comparability. Nevertheless, it does not cover various important differences in legal and factual circumstances that are unrelated to the activities of an enterprise (*see* section §3.04[B][2]). This illustrates that the explicit comparability requirements provide guidance but cannot answer the question of comparability on a stand-alone basis. Additional guidance from the context of the non-discrimination rules is needed to determine which differences in circumstances are relevant in a concrete case.

1286. 2008–2017 OECD Commentary on Article 24, para. 3.
1287. OEEC, FC/WP4(57)2, p. 2. *See also* OEEC, FC/WP4(57)1, p. 4.

§3.05 CURRENT APPROACH TO NON-DISCRIMINATION UNDER ARTICLE 24

[A] Determining Relevant Differences in Circumstances

Comparability is about distinguishing between relevant and irrelevant differences in circumstances, that is, between differences that prevent comparability and those that may be ignored. It has a great impact on the scope of Article 24 because all characteristics that render situations incomparable allow for differences in treatment. Without comparability, there is no discrimination. Without discrimination, distinctions can be maintained. By defining which differences in circumstances prevent comparability, the scope of Article 24 may be limited or enlarged.

If too many differences in circumstances are ignored due to their supposed irrelevance, Article 24 could end up with an unduly broad scope of application. For instance, foreigners could be comparable to nationals under Article 24(1) even if their residence differs, raising the question of whether tax distinctions based on residence lead to discrimination because of nationality. If too many differences are taken into account due to their supposed relevance, Article 24 could become ineffective or easy to circumvent. For example, foreigners could be incomparable to nationals under Article 24(1) if their arguably relevant entitlement to a passport of a particular State differs. Which circumstances are relevant is probably the most important but also the most challenging issue under Article 24.[1288]

Two slightly different ways of determining comparability can be discerned, that is one that effectively regards all differences in circumstances as relevant and one that judges on their relevance from the perspective of the domestic tax law:

(1) Under the first approach, all circumstances except for the protected attribute must be the same, which means that all differences in circumstances are relevant and prevent comparability. This approach is based on ideas of Helmut Debatin,[1289] comes closest to the view of Kees van Raad,[1290] and is not different from the view of Alexander Rust in substance.[1291]

(2) Under the second approach, the relevance of circumstances must be determined from the perspective of the domestic tax law, which means that certain

1288. *See also* Bammens 2012, 14, who acknowledges that, in assessing whether different treatment is discriminatory, the issue of comparability is, by far, the most complex one because it is often excruciatingly difficult to determine which aspects are relevant and which are not.

1289. Already in 1970, Helmut Debatin dealt with the non-discrimination provisions of Article 24 in some great detail. He argued that discrimination must be determined by comparing the tax treatment in question with the tax treatment without the protected characteristic (foreign nationality or non-residence), that is the tax treatment in otherwise the same circumstances. Differences in tax treatment that disappear are a manifestation of discrimination and, therefore, prohibited. Differences in tax treatment that remain are triggered by other reasons and no case of discrimination under Article 24. *See* Debatin 1970, 132.

1290. Raad 1986.

1291. Rust 2015b.

> differences in circumstances may be ignored. This approach accords to the view of Niels Bammens[1292] and is supported by the OECD Commentary.[1293]

Since it would not be useful to try to list all of the circumstances (besides residence) that may be relevant for tax purposes in a nationality non-discrimination clause, Kees van Raad suggests simply avoiding the issue of relevance: 'The question as to which circumstances are tax-relevant and which are not can simply be avoided by requiring for purposes of comparison that all circumstances, except the one indicated by the nondiscrimination clause, be the same.'[1294] Even circumstances such as skin colour, therefore, must be assumed to be the same in the comparison of the tax treatments although, of course, most of the circumstances will turn out to have no importance for tax treatment that is received.[1295]

This first approach does not require verifying whether a particular aspect is indeed relevant. All differences in circumstances, regardless of their relevance or of what 'relevance' actually means, prevent comparability. It follows that, under Article 24, there automatically is no comparability if there is any difference in circumstances; differences in circumstances cannot be ignored. All differences, however small or unsubstantial, can be seen as being relevant for the purposes of comparability. This also means that the implied 'same circumstances' requirement under Article 24 includes a concrete comparability standard; everything, apart from nationality or residence, must be identical and all differences are, in effect, relevant.

By contrast, Niels Bammens does not refer to all aspects (except for the protected attribute) but to all *relevant* aspects which must be the same thereby distinguishing between relevant and irrelevant differences in circumstances: '[I]t must be ascertained whether the characteristics that are *relevant* to the measure at issue are identical.'[1296] Since situations are never comparable in the abstract, the aspects that are relevant must be determined in light of the measure at issue.[1297] Comparability depends on determining which characteristics are relevant.[1298] It is not necessary that all differences in circumstances prevent comparability:[1299]

> [A] non-discrimination rule that prohibits only discrimination on the basis of nationality will be violated only if *all characteristics other than nationality* are identical among subject and object of comparison. Clearly, such an interpretation would render the non-discrimination rule entirely ineffective, as any difference,

1292. Bammens 2012 (*see*, for instance, p. 1013, where he states that Article 24 entails a standard according to which situations are considered to be comparable if the relevant characteristics are identical, the relevance of characteristics is always determined by the measure under scrutiny, and characteristics that are inherently linked to the protected characteristic are disregarded). *See*, moreover, Bammens and Vanistendael 2016, secs. 1.1.2.1, 2.1.3.2.1, 2.3.2.1.1; moreover, to this effect, O'Brien 1978, 557.

1293. 2008–2017 OECD Commentary on Article 24, paras 3, 7 and 17–18. *See also* Bammens 2012, 78.

1294. Raad 1986, 90, with reference to Debatin 1970, 132.

1295. Raad 1986, 90.

1296. Bammens 2012, 17 (original emphasis).

1297. Bammens 2012, 14.

1298. Bammens 2012, 26.

1299. Bammens 2012, 120 (original emphasis).

however irrelevant, would mean that there is no discrimination. For this reason, the comparability test ... is inherently concerned with characteristics that are *relevant* for the issue under scrutiny.

Situations are comparable if the characteristics that are relevant from the perspective of the domestic measure are identical.[1300] It follows that, in order to apply Article 24(1), a comparison must be made between the subject of comparison and the object of comparison which must be 'in the same circumstances, in particular with respect to residence'.[1301] As a result, all relevant factual circumstances (apart from nationality) must be the same.[1302] Factors that are irrelevant to the tax measure at issue (e.g., the possibility that non-resident nationals have closer personal and economic ties to their State of nationality than non-resident foreigners have to that State) should not be taken into account.[1303] For this reason, it cannot be said a priori that nationals are rendered incomparable by their difference in residence.[1304] They are incomparable only if that difference in residence is relevant from the perspective of the measure at issue.[1305]

Niels Bammens does not discuss in detail how the relevance should be determined from the perspective of the domestic tax law, but he offers some examples. If a taxpayer's ability to pay in a given State is reflected by that person's scope of tax liability in that State, 'then that scope of tax liability is certainly relevant from the perspective of domestic measures that grant benefits in order to take account of taxpayers' personal ability to pay tax'.[1306] By contrast, when a domestic tax measure is solely intended to prevent double taxation of dividends, the taxpayer's scope of tax liability is irrelevant from the perspective of such a measure.[1307] Moreover, Niels Bammens argues that, clearly, being listed on a State's stock exchange is irrelevant for the purposes of that State's measure concerning the deductibility of a liquidated subsidiary's losses.[1308] Accordingly, that characteristic should not prevent comparability between non-listed foreign corporations and listed national corporations that are in otherwise identical circumstances even if the benefits at issue are granted only to listed national corporations.[1309] This might indicate that all foreign corporations could claim the benefits at issue although these benefits would not be available to non-listed national corporations.[1310]

1300. Bammens 2012, 78.
1301. Bammens 2012, 83.
1302. Bammens 2012, 84.
1303. Bammens 2012, 84.
1304. Bammens 2012, 78, 92.
1305. Bammens 2012, 78, 92, 1016.
1306. Bammens 2012, 92.
1307. Bammens 2012, 92.
1308. Bammens 2012, 122.
1309. Bammens 2012, 122.
1310. *See*, moreover, Bammens 2012, 438 ('it is unclear ... why being listed [on a stock exchange in the allegedly discriminating State where only residents can be so listed] is a relevant characteristic in light of the possibility to carry forward losses'). If beneficial tax treatment depends on a stock exchange requirement, no explicit reference to residence is made. Nevertheless, if only resident companies can be listed on a stock exchange in the allegedly discriminating State and, consequently, only resident companies can benefit from a tax

Alexander Rust also distinguishes between relevant and irrelevant differences in circumstances. He emphasizes that, under Article 24(1), differences other than nationality allow discrimination only if these other differences are relevant for the distinction.[1311] To determine whether a difference is relevant or, to say it in other words, whether the distinction is based on this other criterion and not on nationality, one has to ask the question whether the same taxpayer would have obtained the benefit had that person possessed the nationality of the other Contracting State.[1312] If you deem the taxpayer to be a national of the other Contracting State and leave all other circumstances the same, then the discrimination is based on nationality if the taxpayer is now entitled to the tax benefit.[1313] With the help of the test, it is easy to determine which circumstances are and are not relevant.[1314] By contrast, discrimination is based on other criteria, and Article 24(1) is not violated if the taxpayer is still not entitled to the tax benefit after deeming that person to be a national of the other Contracting State.[1315]

It is worth noting that Alexander Rust uses a specific test to evaluate the relevance of differences in circumstances. In order to establish whether a difference is relevant, only the protected characteristic is deemed to be different. If discrimination does not cease to exist, it is not based on the protected characteristic but on another criterion that is relevant for the distinction at issue. Thus, if a measure refers to a criterion that is not nationality or residence, this criterion automatically establishes relevant differences in circumstances. All circumstances are relevant except for nationality or residence as soon as they are employed as grounds for different tax

---

measure, non-resident companies are generally excluded from tax advantages that are granted to some specific resident companies. This interesting example raises various issues: is the fact that a company is listed on a stock exchange in the allegedly discriminating State a relevant comparability factor or can all non-resident (non-listed) companies be compared to all resident (listed and non-listed) companies? In the latter case, can non-resident non-listed companies really be compared to resident non-listed companies (same treatment) and, at the same time, to resident listed companies (different treatment), or should this comparison rather depend on whether the non-resident company at stake is listed on a stock exchange in the other Contracting State or anywhere else in the world? If comparability between non-resident and resident companies can only be established as long as they are listed on any stock exchange, why should the fact of being listed anywhere on a stock exchange be a relevant comparability factor? What is actually the reason for this stock exchange requirement, and why is a particular stock exchange required? Is the allegedly discriminating State aiming at strengthening its own capital market, which is not as such prohibited by Article 24, or does it assume that listed companies are subject to extensive reporting obligations and less likely to participate in aggressive tax planning or loss-trading transactions and should, therefore, receive a particular tax advantage? *See also* Arnold 2009a, 271, who comments that it is not readily apparent that listing on a foreign stock exchange is the equivalent of listing on a domestic stock exchange, and, as a result, it is not clear that a resident subsidiary of a publicly listed non-resident company is in the same circumstances as a resident subsidiary of a publicly listed resident company.

1311. Rust 2015b m.no. 35.
1312. Rust 2015b m.no. 35.
1313. Rust 2015b m.no. 35. *See also* Rust 2015c m.no. 48; Rust 2010, 631; Rust 2004, 393.
1314. Rust 2010, 631.
1315. Rust 2015b m.no. 35.

treatment.[1316] This is, in substance, a very different concept of 'relevance' than that pursued by Niels Bammens. Alexander Rust argues that, if a measure distinguishes on the basis of a criterion that is not the protected attribute, this criterion automatically establishes relevant differences in circumstances. As for the result, this approach corresponds to that of Kees van Raad.[1317] Niels Bammens, by contrast, also takes account of the aims and intentions of the domestic tax measure under scrutiny such as the aim of taking account of taxpayers' personal ability to pay tax.[1318] Even if a measure explicitly refers to a facially neutral characteristic such as to a stock exchange criterion, this criterion may be irrelevant for the purposes of comparability.[1319]

It is essential to establish which differences in circumstances are relevant and, therefore, prevent comparability. In this respect, it is possible to divide the current approach to non-discrimination under Article 24 into two categories: either all differences in circumstances except for the protected characteristic prevent comparability (all differences, therefore, are treated as relevant for the purposes of rejecting discrimination) or their relevance must be determined from the perspective of the domestic tax law. Both ways for determining the relevant differences in circumstances have one important thing in common: they tend to confirm comparability only if a protected characteristic is directly employed as grounds for different tax treatment, which conversely means that they regard most differences in circumstances as relevant. All or almost all differences in circumstances except for the protected attribute suffice to reject tax discrimination. As will be seen, a reason for this strictness lies in the intention to limit the scope of Article 24 to cases of direct discrimination.

[B] Verifying Direct and Rejecting Indirect Discrimination

It is basically undisputed that Article 24 does not entail a concept of covert or indirect discrimination.[1320] It only prevents overt or direct discrimination. Indirect forms,

1316. *See*, to this effect, Rust 2015b m.nos. 35, 62, 115 ('[t]he legal form, structure and activities performed are only of relevance if the domestic tax law distinguishes on the basis of these criteria'); similarly, Munhoz Ribeiro 2015, 346.
1317. *See also* Rust 2015b m.nos. 61–62.
1318. Bammens 2012, 92.
1319. Bammens 2012, 122, 438.
1320. *See*, for instance, Lüdicke 2017, 293; Wassermeyer and Schwenke 2016 m.no. 2e; Haslehner 2016a m.no. 3; Bammens and Vanistendael 2016, secs. 1.1.2.2, 2.1.1.1; Rust 2015b m.no. 5; Rust 2015c m.no. 5; Oesterhelt 2015 m.no. 2; Bruns 2013 m.nos. 5, 60, 142, 165; Elliffe 2013b, 38; Rust 2013b, 76; Bammens 2012, 58, 63–64, 1014; Pannwitz 2012 m.nos. 3, 16; Rust 2010, 634; Hageböke 2005 m.no. 6; H. Loukota 2005, 57; Lüdicke 2005, 485; Jeffery 1999, 72; Thömmes 1997, 804–805; differently, Toifl 2003, 307–308, 313, who argues for a concept of indirect discrimination and for justifications under Article 24(1) in its version before 1992. In addition, Alexander Rust submits that, when the EU fundamental freedoms oblige EU Member States to grant non-discriminatory tax treatment, such results should be reached through a more extensive interpretation of Article 24 rather than by assuming that domestic tax law violates EU law obligations and that EU law, therefore, takes precedence. *See* Rust 2015b m.nos. 17, 38, 81, 116; Rust 2015c m.nos. 19, 62, 121, 150, 169; concurring Hageböke 2004 m.no. 27; similarly, Lehner 2001, 333, 335, 337; differently, Haslehner 2016a m.no. 9; Bammens 2016, 123–135; Bammens 2013b, 182–186; Bammens 2012, 1057–1064; Garrido 2009, 175.

therefore, are not within its scope even if the domestic tax measure under scrutiny, in most instances, burdens protected persons by ostensibly differentiating on the basis of a neutral criterion.[1321] Under Article 24(1) and (2), only measures that directly refer to nationality lead to illegitimate discrimination. Under Article 24(3), (4), and (5), only distinctions that are directly based on residence are prohibited. The non-discrimination provisions would seem to elevate form over substance by refusing to acknowledge a potentially discriminatory impact of provisions that do not happen to be drafted in such a way as to target perfectly and exclusively protected persons (i.e., foreigners or non-residents).[1322]

A strict comparability standard contributes to this distinction between direct and indirect discrimination.[1323] Since all relevant circumstances except for the protected characteristic must be the same in order to establish comparability under Article 24, there remain no other relevant grounds that could lead to illegitimate discrimination against protected taxpayers, that is to discrimination through indirect means.[1324] For instance, if the expression 'in the same circumstances' requires residence to be the same under Article 24(1), differences in residence may be used as grounds for different tax treatment without leading to indirect discrimination by reason of nationality. Such differences in residence prevent comparability from the outset. Only direct references to nationality remain prohibited by the nationality non-discrimination clause.

When comparing the subject of comparison (i.e., the situation or category that is protected by the non-discrimination rule) with the object of comparison (i.e., the situation or category that is used as the benchmark in assessing whether discrimination has occurred), it is essential to determine the characteristics that are relevant to the comparison.[1325] If a non-discrimination rule is concerned only with direct discrimination, the subject and the object of comparison must be identical in all relevant aspects other than the common characteristic that characterizes the protected group[1326] (the protected attribute).[1327] For example, if a non-discrimination rule intends to protect

1321. It should be noted that, sometimes, the distinction between direct and indirect discrimination is understood in a different way: direct discrimination occurs when a person's circumstances (foreign or no nationality or non-residence) result in discrimination against this person (paras 1, 2, and 3), while indirect discrimination occurs when a person's circumstances (non-residence) result in discrimination not against this person but against another (resident) person (paras 4 and 5). *See*, for instance, Raad and Bosman 2016, 68; Silva 2016b, 75; L. Hinnekens and Hinnekens 2008, 21–22; De Broe 2008, 544–545, 552; Bennett 2006, 443; Raad 2005, 129–130; Hosson and Michielse 1989, 483; Raad 1986, 173. Although it is important under Article 24 to distinguish between these two types of discrimination, they will not be referred to as cases of direct or indirect discrimination.

1322. Bennett 2006, 469.

1323. *See also* Haslehner 2016c, 5 ('whether article 24 covers hidden or "indirect" discrimination cannot be disentangled from the appropriate understanding of "comparability"').

1324. *See also* Bruns 2007, 580, who observes that this comparability test generally precludes a concept of indirect discrimination.

1325. Bammens 2012, 10.

1326. Bammens 2012, 10.

1327. Niels Bammens actually uses the concept of 'the comparative attribute', which is also called the *tertium comparationis*. This concept apparently refers to a quality which the subject and the object of comparison have in common and which is the point of comparison. It might, for instance, refer to nationality or residence. Then the comparative attribute 'nationality' would include both nationals and non-nationals of a particular State, while the comparative attribute

non-residents (the subject of comparison), the object of comparison consists of residents who are identical to the subject of comparison in all relevant aspects other than their non-residence.[1328] Similarly, if a non-discrimination rule intends to protect non-nationals (the subject of comparison), the object of comparison consists of nationals who are identical in all relevant respects apart from nationality.[1329] Niels Bammens mentions that, in order for a non-discrimination rule to cover only direct discrimination, the comparability test must be interpreted as strictly as possible.[1330] That is to say, the comparability test must require all relevant elements other than the protected attribute to be the same.[1331] Although he relies on relevance and does not believe that all differences in circumstances should automatically be relevant, he still adheres to a strict comparability standard. In general, all circumstances must be identical in order to limit the scope of Article 24 to direct discrimination as apparently intended by the Contracting States.[1332]

[C] Avoiding Policy Considerations and Value Judgments

It is widely believed that comparability under Article 24 can be established without policy considerations and value judgments. Comparability is a rather mechanical exercise regardless of whether all differences in circumstances are, in effect, relevant or whether their relevance is determined from the perspective of the domestic tax law. An enquiry into policy issues is not necessary. This point turns comparability into a mechanical assessment and into an arguably simple task.[1333] It turns a strict comparability test into a mechanical comparability test.

Therefore, when discussing the concept of non-discrimination under Article 24, comparability is contrasted with justifications. Article 24 does not entail a concept of

---

'residence' would include both residents and non-residents of a particular State. Accordingly, when assessing whether direct discrimination occurs, all relevant aspects must be identical except for nationality or residence (the comparative attribute), respectively.

1328. Bammens 2012, 11.
1329. Bammens 2012, 12.
1330. Bammens 2012, 12.
1331. Bammens 2012, 12.
1332. Alexander Rust, however, applies a strict comparability standard to conclude that Article 24 does not extend to indirect discrimination. Article 24(1) is not violated if a taxpayer, after deeming the person to be a national and leaving all other circumstances the same, is still not entitled to a tax benefit. According to Alexander Rust, this test shows that indirect discrimination (discrimination that is based on another criterion than nationality but which typically discriminates against foreigners) is not prohibited by Article 24(1). *See* Rust 2015b m.no. 35. It may thus appear unclear whether a strict comparability standard should be preferred and applied in order to cover direct discrimination only or, rather, whether the fact that the explicit or implicit comparability requirements ('the same circumstances', etc.) require a strict comparability standard contributes to a narrow scope of Article 24.
1333. *See* Bammens 2016, 99 ('[article 24] is applied in a strictly mechanical way'); Bammens 2012, 26, 174, 1014–1015 ('[article 24] may be applied as a strictly mechanical tool, without any margin for flexibility'; 'the discrimination test ... should ... be a mechanical analysis into comparability and equal treatment'); Rust 2010, 632 ('[the suggested] test is very easy to handle'; 'it is clear whether or not the particular non-discrimination provision is violated'); similarly, Raad and Bosman 2016, 73; Raad 2005, 134; Rust 2004, 393.

justifications.[1334] The non-discrimination provisions of this article have an absolute character; the Contracting States may not derogate therefrom.[1335] A distinction on the basis of a protected characteristic is prohibited and automatically violates it.[1336] Moreover, such different treatment cannot be justified by legitimate reasons.[1337] There is no room for arguing contrary to the ordinary meaning of the terms of Article 24 that different treatment is justified.[1338] The article merely lists a number of circumstances requiring at least equal treatment, regardless of whether the grounds are justified (or perfectly reasonable from a tax policy perspective) or not.[1339] Since no justifications are available, it is not possible to balance a Contracting State's policy interests against the aim of preventing discrimination because of nationality or residence.[1340] Article 24 may be applied as a strictly mechanical tool without any margin for flexibility.[1341]

Justifications could give leeway for policy considerations, balancing decisions, value judgments, and discretion. As many different courts from different countries decide on tax treaty issues, this could lead to international disagreement over the relevance of specific unwritten justifications. In order to avoid such problems and to ensure legal certainty, many voices in the literature argue that it is better to reject justifications under Article 24 and to keep with a mechanical comparability test.[1342] Alexander Rust, for instance, states that a concept of justification should not be introduced under Article 24 'as long as no world tax court exists to resolve potential disputes'.[1343] Justifications would require courts to balance the objective achieved by

1334. *See*, for instance, Freeden, Häck, and Schaumburg 2017 m.no. 4.49; Lüdicke 2017, 293, 298; Wassermeyer and Schwenke 2016 m.no. 2e; Haslehner 2016a m.no. 4; Bammens 2016, 99, 108–110 (although concluding that the traditional view that Article 24 does not offer any room for justification grounds is not entirely correct, but it is not far from the truth either); Rust 2015b m.nos. 4 and 132; Rust 2015c m.no. 4; Oesterhelt 2015 m.no. 4; Schänzle 2015 m.no. 9; Munhoz Ribeiro 2015, 338; Bruns 2013 m.nos. 10, 56; Bammens 2013b, 179; Rust 2013b, 76; Bammens 2012, 59, 169, 171, 1014–1015, 1030–1033; Haslehner 2012, 596; Pannwitz 2012 m.no. 18; Rust 2010, 635, 648; Haslehner 2009, 274–295, 377; Hageböke and Käbisch 2006, 855; Baker 2006 m.no. 24B.27; Raad 2005, 134–135; Hageböke 2005 m.no. 6; Lüdicke 2005, 485; Rust 2004, 394; Rust 2003b, 661; Avery Jones, Depret, et al. 1991b, 345–347; Debatin 1981 III m.no. 300; to this effect, although not excluding that justifications are part of a comparability assessment, Schön 2006, 17. *See also*, however, Hohenwarter and Weninger 2006, 254–264, who do not categorically exclude justifications under Article 24 even if such justifications are only considered as a limitation of a provision's scope and, in particular, as a reason to deny comparability; moreover, Toifl 2003, 307–308, 313, who argues for a concept of indirect discrimination and for justifications under Article 24(1) in its version before 1992; similarly, Gosch 2007, 1560.
1335. Rust 2015b m.nos. 4, 132.
1336. Rust 2015b m.nos. 4, 132.
1337. Rust 2015b m.nos. 4, 132.
1338. Avery Jones, Depret, et al. 1991b, 345–346.
1339. Avery Jones, Depret, et al. 1991b, 346.
1340. *See* Haslehner 2009, 275–277, 377.
1341. Bammens 2012, 26.
1342. *See* Vanistendael 2016, 246–247, 253; Rust 2015b m.nos. 4, 131–132; Bammens 2012, 174, 1033–1034; Rust 2010, 648–649; Haslehner 2009, 294–295, 377. *See also* Raad 1988b, 350, who holds that, if exceptions must be permitted in a specific non-discrimination clause, it is preferable that the exceptions be enumerated; only then can a non-discrimination clause serve the purpose for which it was designated, that is to offer security to protected persons, and in respect of objects and relations.
1343. Rust 2015b m.no. 4.

the discrimination (which arguably corresponds to the policy objective pursued by the domestic tax law under scrutiny) against the disadvantages suffered by the taxpayer therefrom.[1344] For Alexander Rust, such balancing decisions require a value judgment.[1345] Different courts would, almost inevitably, come to different conclusions about the legitimacy of such justifications.[1346] Therefore, the chances of reaching a common interpretation of Article 24 would be made far more difficult.[1347] The current situation covering only cases of direct discrimination but leading automatically to a violation facilitates the application of Article 24 and ensures legal certainty.[1348]

Similarly, Niels Bammens holds that it would not be advisable to incorporate justification grounds in Article 24.[1349] 'Justification is a matter of policy, while the discrimination test should be strictly neutral and free from interference from policy objectives.'[1350] If different courts have different conceptions of the appropriate balance between a State's interest in exercising its tax sovereignty and a taxpayer's interest in not being discriminated against, the result would be a fragmented application of Article 24.[1351] As there is no single judicial body ensuring a uniform policy on the appropriate degree of tax integration as implied by a particular justification grounds, the use of an open standard under Article 24 allowing for any public policy reason to be invoked is impossible and could lead to a considerable degree of uncertainty.[1352] Justification is a matter of policy, while the discrimination test under Article 24 should be strictly neutral and free from interference from policy objectives.[1353] It follows that policy considerations 'should not affect the discrimination test, which should instead be a mechanical analysis into comparability and equal treatment'.[1354]

Under Article 24, all relevant circumstances must be identical; only then can comparability of persons or situations be confirmed. This comparability test is applied more or less automatically or mechanically because every difference in circumstances is, in effect, relevant or because the relevance of differences can be determined quite easily from the perspective of the domestic tax law. Under the first approach, even the smallest differences in circumstances prevent comparability and, thus, no complicated questions about relevance, including questions about policy, arise. Under the second approach, differences in circumstances do not automatically prevent comparability if they are irrelevant, but the question of relevance can be answered from the perspective of the domestic tax law without a need for value judgments. Although the aspect of relevance could theoretically be used to open up comparability to policy considerations

1344. Rust 2015b m.nos. 4, 132; Rust 2010, 648; similarly, Bammens 2016, 111 ('the justification analysis comes down to balancing a state's interest in exercising its tax sovereignty against a taxpayer's interest in not being discriminated against').
1345. Rust 2015b m.nos. 4, 131–132; Rust 2010, 648; similarly, Bammens 2016, 111; Bammens 2012, 1033.
1346. Rust 2015b m.nos. 4, 132; Rust 2010, 648.
1347. Rust 2015b m.nos. 4, 132; Rust 2010, 648.
1348. Rust 2015b m.no. 131.
1349. Bammens 2016, 111; Bammens 2012, 174, 1033–1034.
1350. Bammens 2012, 174.
1351. Bammens 2016, 111; Bammens 2012, 1033–1034.
1352. Bammens 2016, 111; Bammens 2012, 1033–1034.
1353. Bammens 2012, 174.
1354. Bammens 2012, 174.

(depending on which differences in circumstances are regarded as 'relevant' from a policy perspective, different results under Article 24 could be reached), this is arguably prevented by linking the question of relevance to domestic tax law. According to Niels Bammens, 'the relevance requirement is a factual (objective) test, which leaves little room for discretion, whereas justification requires an appraisal to be made, a comparative (and subjective) assessment between different conflicting interests'.[1355]

Justifications are not available under Article 24 in order to avoid policy questions and value judgments. Since discrimination cannot be justified, a narrow scope of application should be preferred, that is no indirect discrimination.[1356] The aim of reaching a limited scope of the non-discrimination provisions can be reached through a strict comparability standard. The aim of avoiding policy questions and value judgments can be reached through a mechanical application of this standard. Comparability under Article 24 arguably combines everything that justifications are not able to provide: a limited scope of application without a need for balancing decisions.

§3.06 COMPARABILITY TEST: CONCEPTUAL ISSUES WITH LINKED ATTRIBUTES

[A] Overlap of Protected and Unprotected Attributes

Conceptual issues arise when protected and unprotected attributes overlap. In order to assess discrimination under Article 24, tax treatments of persons must be compared. A strict and mechanical comparability standard limits the scope of the non-discrimination provisions to cases of direct discrimination and is arguably free of policy considerations and value judgments. Since all relevant legal and factual circumstances except for the protected characteristic must be the same, the appropriate object of comparison can differ from the subject of comparison only with regard to the protected characteristic and irrelevant attributes. However, the protected characteristic of nationality or residence may be directly linked to or overlap with an unprotected attribute and thereby trigger unprotected differences in circumstances. For instance, nationals of a State may be entitled to a passport of that State and taxed on a worldwide basis due to their nationality. This means that differences in nationality may be connected or automatically lead to differences in passport entitlement and tax liability. If the taxpayer in question is deemed to have a different nationality, that individual may necessarily be entitled to a different passport and subject to different tax liability. If differences in passport entitlement and tax liability are ignored as being irrelevant, they do not hinder comparability under Article 24(1). If differences in passport entitlement and tax liability are taken into account as being relevant, they prevent comparability and discrimination. It is not clear whether it is possible to regard certain differences in

1355. Bammens 2012, 174.
1356. Rust 2015b m.no. 16; Rust 2015c m.nos. 5, 18; Rust 2010, 649. *See also* Haslehner 2012, 596, according to whom it is not surprising that comparability is construed narrowly under Article 24 since the determination of comparability and a relevant different treatment are the only crucial elements of the non-discrimination analysis; there is no room for justification.

circumstances (tax liability) as relevant and others (passport entitlement) as irrelevant despite a similar link to nationality. A comparability standard must provide definite answers about this issue, that is how to deal with unprotected differences in circumstances that are linked to protected differences in nationality or residence.

Referring back to the previously mentioned approaches for determining which attributes are relevant (*see* section §3.05[A]), there are, in principle, two solutions:

(1) First, literally all differences in circumstances can be regarded as relevant for comparability purposes which means that comparability and discrimination would have to be denied. Arguably, differences in passport entitlement prevent comparability under Article 24(1) just like differences in tax liability.
(2) Second, differences in circumstances can be regarded as relevant for comparability purposes only if they are relevant to the domestic tax measure under scrutiny. This might allow distinguishing between passport entitlement and tax liability even when both attributes are similarly linked to nationality.

Under the first approach, tension with the objective of preventing tax discrimination could arise. As soon as the protected attribute (nationality) triggers some unprotected differences in circumstances (passport entitlement or tax liability), discrimination would have to be denied. Since this would render Article 24 largely meaningless,[1357] there appears to be agreement that at least certain differences in circumstances that are directly or too closely linked to the protected attribute should not prevent comparability and should thus be ignored.[1358] Nevertheless, there is disagreement as to which differences in circumstances should be ignored in which situations. As far as Article 24(1) is concerned, no one has questioned that differences in passport entitlement should be ignored (*see* section §3.06[B]), but different views with regard to tax liability exist (*see* section §3.06[C]).

Under the second approach, the requirement of 'relevance' could constitute a suitable means to establish a distinction between cases in which an unprotected attribute should not prevent comparability (irrelevant differences in circumstances)

1357. If it is argued that everything except for nationality must be the same, passports must arguably be the same as well: a national of State B who is entitled to a passport of State B but not of State A can only be compared to a national of State A who is entitled to a passport of State B but not of State A. Such conditions for comparability would render an appropriate comparison almost impossible. However, it can be argued that especially as long as the domestic tax measure under scrutiny does not explicitly refer to passport entitlement, differences in passport entitlement are irrelevant and can be ignored (this approach does not succeed if the measure in question explicitly refers to passport entitlement) or that just as differences in nationality cannot prevent comparability, differences in directly connected or inextricably linked factors, even if relevant, cannot prevent comparability either.

1358. *See*, for instance, 2008–2017 OECD Commentary on Article 24, para. 1, which states that Article 24(1) 'would prevent a different treatment that is really a disguised form of discrimination based on nationality such as a different treatment of individuals based on whether or not they hold, or are entitled to, a passport issued by the State'. This conversely means that a different treatment of individuals based on whether or not they are a national of the State constitutes discrimination despite potential differences in passport entitlement. In fact, even Kees van Raad regards residence and full tax liability as interchangeable notions under Article 24(3), (4), and (5). *See* Raad 1986, 141, 176, 189.

and cases in which an unprotected attribute should render persons or situations incomparable (relevant differences in circumstances). Nevertheless, if 'relevance' is determined solely from the perspective of the domestic tax measure under scrutiny, that is without considering which differences should be regarded as relevant from the perspective of the non-discrimination provisions, there again is a risk that this determination could lead to results that contravene the principal objective of avoiding tax discrimination. Given that a State will always be able to justify discrimination by some policy argument because it is unlikely to introduce arbitrary discrimination in its law,[1359] a domestic tax measure that refers to nationality, passport entitlement, tax liability, or listing on a stock exchange (in order to strengthen that State's capital market) must regard this criterion as relevant for achieving its policy goal. If a measure refers to passport entitlement, this criterion might be just as relevant as a criterion of nationality, and if a measure refers to nationality, it probably does so for a reason even if this reason is not of a fiscal nature and might not be acceptable under Article 24. It would indeed appear strange to argue that a measure that aims at discriminating because of nationality and, therefore, employs a criterion of nationality refers to an irrelevant criterion from the perspective of that measure. Nothing else can be true if a measure refers to passport entitlement or any other facially neutral but linked attribute.

Therefore, it appears to be necessary to go beyond a domestic perspective and to find some other reason why certain 'relevant' differences in circumstances (passport entitlement) should be ignored but other linked differences in circumstances (tax liability) should not or under which conditions linked differences in circumstances should be ignored under Article 24. As will be illustrated in greater detail below, such situations in which a protected characteristic coincides with an unprotected attribute raise issues that are the most controversial. The fact that different approaches and solutions are suggested in the literature indicates that even a strict comparability standard cannot solve cases of discrimination in a mechanical way.

[B] Nationality or Differences in Passport?

Based on a traditional understanding of direct discrimination, a measure must explicitly refer to nationality under Article 24(1) and (2) or to residence under Article 24(3), (4), and (5) to conflict with the respective non-discrimination clause.[1360] When a measure, by its practical effects but not its explicit terms, discriminates against a protected person, no discrimination under Article 24 can arise.[1361] To be precise, whether a measure favours nationals or residents or burdens foreigners or non-residents has no effect on the existence of discrimination,[1362] but, as soon as some other criterion is employed, no discrimination can arguably exist under Article 24.

1359. Avery Jones, Depret, et al. 1991b, 347.
1360. *See*, for instance, Wassermeyer and Schwenke 2016 m.no. 2e; Bennett 2006, 466-467; Staringer and Jettmar 2006, 390.
1361. *See* Bennett 2006, 466-467.
1362. *See*, to this effect, Rust 2003b, 660; Avery Jones, Depret, et al. 1991b, 323. Thus, if an individual is a national of both Contracting States, State A and State B, it is possible for

Such a narrow understanding of direct discrimination would allow Contracting States to circumvent the non-discrimination obligations of Article 24 quite easily. Instead of linking tax disadvantages directly to nationality or residence, a State could differentiate on the basis of an equivalent characteristic. For instance, in order to avoid an explicit reference to nationality, a State could link disadvantages to an entitlement to a certain passport. Circumventing the obligations of Article 24 would largely be a matter of legal technique.[1363]

Presumably, for this reason, the OECD Commentary rejects an overly narrow approach to direct discrimination under Article 24(1):[1364]

> Article [24] should not be unduly extended to cover so-called 'indirect' discrimination. For example, whilst paragraph 1, which deals with discrimination on the basis of nationality, would prevent a different treatment that is really a disguised form of discrimination based on nationality such as a different treatment of individuals based on whether or not they hold, or are entitled to, a passport issued by the State, it could not be argued that non-residents of a given State include primarily persons who are not nationals of that State to conclude that a different treatment based on residence is indirectly a discrimination based on nationality for purposes of that paragraph.

According to the OECD Commentary, a passport requirement is really a disguised form of discrimination based on nationality.[1365] An entitlement to a passport is too closely connected to nationality and, therefore, cannot convert direct into indirect discrimination for the purposes of Article 24(1). Since nationality entitles an individual to a passport, a hypothetical change in nationality must also trigger a hypothetical change in passport entitlement when comparing a foreigner to a hypothetical national in otherwise identical circumstances. As a result, since a reference to passport entitlement is, in substance, equivalent to a direct and prohibited reference to nationality, discrimination may exist under Article 24(1) even if the domestic tax measure under scrutiny does not expressly refer to the prohibited grounds for different tax treatment.

Similarly, Niels Bammens submits that a criterion that is inextricably linked to a protected attribute should be disregarded for comparability purposes. 'Inextricably linked' means that the presence or absence of the relevant characteristic depends

discrimination to take place under Article 24(1) if there is a provision of State A's law directed against State B nationals (or foreign nationals generally) regardless of whether or not they are also nationals of State A. In such a situation, a national of State A is actually treated other or more burdensome than other nationals of State A because of dual nationality. In order to establish comparability under Article 24(1), therefore, the individual must be deemed to be a national of State A only. On a similar issue regarding dual residents, *see also* Chapter 3 section §3.03[F].

1363. *See*, to this effect, Lang and Loukota 2003, 69; Lang 1999, 159; moreover, Dommes and Metzler 2006, 120; Schilcher and Stefaner 2006, 162–163; Toifl 2003, 303.

1364. 2008–2017 OECD Commentary on Article 24, para. 1.

1365. *See also* Bammens 2012, 58–59, 112, who distinguishes between indirect discrimination and 'disguised' discrimination and additionally argues that holding a passport issued by a State is a characteristic that is inextricably linked with nationality; likewise, Bammens and Vanistendael 2016, sec. 1.1.2.2; moreover, Schänzle 2015 m.no. 10; Bruns 2013 m.no. 5.

entirely on the value of the protected attribute.[1366] For instance, with respect to a nationality non-discrimination rule, *all* non-nationals and *no* nationals must share that characteristic, or vice versa.[1367] Thus, if a relevant characteristic is found to be different between the subject and the object of comparison, it is still necessary to verify whether that characteristic is inextricably linked to the protected attribute.[1368] If it is not, it renders the situations incomparable, which means that there is no discrimination.[1369] If it is, it should be disregarded.[1370]

Given the identity of the protected attribute and the inextricably linked characteristic and since the subject and the object of comparison are, by definition, different in regard to the protected attribute, the inextricably linked characteristic would automatically render the situations incomparable if it was taken into account for comparability purposes.[1371] Then a State could easily evade direct discrimination by replacing a distinction on the basis of the protected attribute with a distinction on the basis of the inextricably linked characteristic even though both distinctions would lead to identical results. This would render any non-discrimination rule entirely ineffective.[1372] For this reason, when conducting a comparability test, a rule that prohibits direct discrimination should disregard characteristics that are inextricably linked to the protected attribute.[1373] According to Niels Bammens, such characteristics could only reappear in a justification analysis and justify discrimination,[1374] but no justifications are available under Article 24.

At the same time, the fact that a State may not discriminate under Article 24 by employing an inextricably linked characteristic does not imply that the non-discrimination provisions are being interpreted as also precluding indirect discrimination.[1375] Indirect discrimination must be distinguished from 'disguised' discrimination.[1376] In the latter case, the measure at issue is aimed at the protected persons, but a seemingly innocent distinguishing criterion is used in order to disguise the discrimination.[1377] That is to say, instead of distinguishing on the basis of the prohibited criterion, the distinction is made on the basis of a criterion that is inextricably linked to the prohibited criterion.[1378] Entitlement to a passport could constitute such an attribute that is inextricably linked to nationality provided that all nationals of a given State are entitled to a passport of that State, and all foreigners are never entitled to such a

1366. Bammens 2012, 18.
1367. Bammens 2012, 18.
1368. Bammens 2012, 17.
1369. Bammens 2012, 17.
1370. Bammens 2012, 17.
1371. Bammens 2012, 17.
1372. Bammens 2012, 17.
1373. Bammens 2012, 18.
1374. *See*, to this effect, Bammens 2012, 993.
1375. Bammens 2012, 17.
1376. Bammens 2012, 58.
1377. Bammens 2012, 58.
1378. Bammens 2012, 58.

passport.[1379] Niels Bammens regards the criterion of holding a passport as being inextricably linked to nationality.[1380]

Contrary to what may be intuitively assumed, the criterion of holding or being entitled to a passport is not necessarily a perfect substitute for or completely interchangeable with the protected characteristic of nationality.[1381] First of all, nationals are usually not required to hold a passport and, thus, not all nationals need to have one. In addition, some nationals may not be entitled to a passport for national security or health reasons, notably, in order to ensure legal prosecution or prevent a cross-border spread of incurable diseases.[1382] If a rule of a State provides treatment that is more burdensome to all who hold or are entitled to a foreign passport, it would then miss those foreigners who are not entitled to one (and it might include nationals who possess a dual citizenship).[1383] Instead, if a rule of a State provides treatment that is more favourable to all who hold or are entitled to a passport issued by this State, some nationals who are not entitled to one might be disfavoured together with all foreigners (or at least those who do not possess a dual citizenship). Therefore, it cannot be said a priori that an entitlement to a passport of a State is inextricably linked to nationality of that State; not all nationals may have a right to obtain a passport. To complicate matters, an 'alien's passport', that is, a travel document for foreign nationals or stateless persons, might exist as well.[1384] A passport requirement is only an indirect and imperfect reference to nationality but, according to the OECD Commentary, it may still lead to direct discrimination on the basis of nationality.[1385]

This approach of the Commentary is viewed critically by Werner Haslehner.[1386] In principle, the approach should be praised for its attempt to make a clear distinction between, on the one hand, prohibited discrimination that is based directly on the criterion that is protected under Article 24 and, on the other hand, disadvantages that are based on related or similar but different criteria and thus fall outside the narrow scope of any of the non-discrimination provisions.[1387] In order to avoid a formalistic approach that would yet again allow Contracting States an escape that would be all too easy to fabricate, Article 24 also covers such disadvantages that are merely disguised as 'indirect' by replacing a protected criterion with a requirement that is equivalent to it in all but name.[1388] Whereas a rejection of a concept of indirect discrimination under

1379. Bammens 2012, 18.
1380. Bammens 2012, 122.
1381. *See also* Dziurdź 2016, 218.
1382. *See*, for instance, § 14 of the Austrian Passport Act (Passgesetz).
1383. Kees van Raad mentions that if a person happens to be a national of both Contracting States, his privileged status in both States makes application of Article 24(1) unnecessary. *See* Raad 1986, 80; similarly, Zalasiński 2007, 463. However, if a Contracting State discriminates against foreigners instead of favouring its own nationals, Article 24(1) might still be necessary to prevent discrimination (unless that State discriminates against foreigners with the additional condition that they are not nationals at the same time). *See also*, to this effect, Van Brussel 2015, 358; Bammens 2012 fn. 127 on p. 67.
1384. *See*, for instance, §§ 88 et seq. of the Austrian Aliens' Police Act (Fremdenpolizeigesetz).
1385. 2008-2017 OECD Commentary on Article 24, para. 1.
1386. Haslehner 2016c, 6-7; moreover, Haslehner 2016a m.no. 3.
1387. Haslehner 2016c, 6.
1388. Haslehner 2016c, 7.

Article 24 prevents an unworkable open discrimination clause, an acceptance of a disguised form of direct discrimination prevents Article 24 from being so narrow that it becomes wholly ineffective.[1389] However, the Commentary does not clarify how close the relationship between the protected criterion and its 'equivalent' needs to be and thereby raises many questions.[1390] If a Contracting State favours all persons who hold a domestic passport, does it matter that there are domestic nationals who may not hold such passport if it is clear that no foreign national could possibly have one?[1391]

In certain situations, all nationals may be residents and all foreigners may be non-residents (*see* section §3.06[C]). According to the OECD Commentary, a reference to residence still does not need to lead to direct discrimination under Article 24(1);[1392] residence may remain a relevant comparability factor even if a change in nationality necessarily triggers a corresponding change in residence, and vice versa (*see also* Chapter 4 section §4.03[A]). Thus, when residence is completely interchangeable with nationality and appears to constitute a better proxy for nationality than entitlement to a passport, it may, nevertheless (but not always),[1393] establish relevant differences in circumstances.

A formal differentiation between direct and indirect discrimination could regard a distinction based on passports as an unprotected matter of indirect discrimination and a distinction based on residence as a protected situation of direct discrimination because of nationality. There need to be good reasons why a distinction based on residence (full or limited tax liability), unlike a distinction based on passports, should not violate Article 24(1) even if nationality is completely interchangeable with both passports and residence. How close the relationship between nationality and a substitute must be in order to assume direct discrimination; why, in certain cases, a perfect substitute or a criterion directly linked to nationality does not suffice for establishing direct discrimination under Article 24(1); and why, in other cases, the same criterion may nevertheless lead to prohibited discrimination are the decisive questions. When differentiating between direct and indirect discrimination under Article 24, a formal approach that merely looks at express references to a protected characteristic is doomed to fail.

[C] Nationality or Differences in Residence?

[1] Nationality May Coincide with Residence

Residence is central to most modern income and capital tax systems because distinctions between full and limited tax liability are normally based on residence.[1394]

1389. Haslehner 2016c, 7.
1390. Haslehner 2016c, 7.
1391. Haslehner 2016c, 7.
1392. 2008-2017 OECD Commentary on Article 24, paras 21, 24–25 (Examples 2 and 5).
1393. *Ibid.*, para. 23 (Example 4).
1394. *See*, instead of many, Kuleshova 2005, 454. In this context, 'residence' stands for various criteria that lead to full tax liability under domestic law including domicile and place of abode but excluding nationality.

Nationality, by contrast, is seldom used to define a State's tax jurisdiction, although the US tax system is a notable exception.[1395] This is true, at least, with respect to individuals. When dealing with persons other than individuals, incorporation may sometimes lead to nationality, full tax liability, and residence. Therefore, it may be difficult to distinguish between nationality and residence if both concepts are formally identical, that is if both rely on incorporation. Article 24(1), however, only prohibits discrimination for reason of nationality; tax distinctions for reason of residence are not prohibited. This raises the question of whether it is possible to differentiate between nationality and residence despite their overlap.

Nationality is a rather straightforward concept as far as individuals are concerned. In most cases, it can be clearly distinguished from residence. Article 3(1)(g)(i) defines the term 'national' as any individual possessing the nationality or citizenship of a Contracting State and thereby refers to each State's particular rules on the acquisition or loss of nationality or citizenship.[1396] Article 4(1) defines the term 'resident of a Contracting State' as 'any person who, under the laws of that State, is liable to tax therein by reason of his domicile, residence, place of management or any other criterion of a similar nature', and 'who is [not] liable to tax in that State in respect only of income from sources in that State or capital situated therein'. Although nationality is not explicitly mentioned as a relevant criterion for tax treaty residence, it arguably constitutes a 'criterion of a similar nature' (*see* section §3.03[B]). Nationality can establish a sufficient personal attachment to a Contracting State and thereby lead to residence in that State for tax treaty purposes if it triggers comprehensive taxation (full tax liability) under domestic law. Nevertheless, as already indicated, the nationality of individuals is seldom used as a criterion for full tax liability; both nationals and foreigners may be residents or non-residents. As a consequence, the nationality non-discrimination provision is only of little practical importance where individuals are concerned.[1397]

It is quite common, by contrast, that legal persons are nationals of a particular State and, at the same time, residents of that State, whereas foreign persons are considered to be non-residents.[1398] In principle, there would be a broad range of criteria available for determining the nationality of corporations. Kees van Raad mentions incorporation (subdivided between the jurisdiction under which the entity was originally created and the jurisdiction under which it is presently organized); nationality or residence of the shareholders; nationality or residence of the management; location of the effective management (which involves a spectrum of choices from rather formal aspects of management location to a highly composite control test); and principal place

1395. *See*, for instance, Vanistendael 2010, 176–177.
1396. 1992–2017 OECD Commentary on Article 3, para. 8; 1977 OECD Commentary on Article 24, para. 11 (1963: para. 10).
1397. *See*, for instance, Rust 2015b m.no. 26; Rust 2015c m.no. 36; Van Brussel 2015, 354; Adonnino 1993, 42.
1398. *See*, for instance, Raad 2005, 130; Arnold 2011, 370; Vanistendael 2010, 177–178; Wunderlich 2009 m.no. 18.

of business.[1399] For tax treaty purposes, however, Article 3(1)(g)(ii) defines the term 'national' as any legal person, partnership, or association deriving its status as such from the laws in force in a Contracting State. Accordingly, the place of incorporation of a legal person generally determines the nationality.[1400] At the same time, the place of incorporation is often used by domestic law to establish residence and full tax liability. It further constitutes a 'criterion of a similar nature' under Article 4(1) which may lead to residence for tax treaty purposes.[1401] As a result, unlike with individuals in which nationality and residence generally remain separate and distinguishable concepts, incorporation may lead to both nationality under Article 3(1)(g)(ii) and residence under Article 4(1).[1402] In these cases, nationality and residence of legal persons[1403] coincide; nationals are automatically residents (which means that they are subject to full tax liability), and foreign persons generally remain non-residents.

Up to now, when stating that nationality and residence may coincide, reference was made to full tax liability under domestic law and residence under Article 4(1).[1404]

1399. Raad 1986, 81–82. *See also* 1992–2017 OECD Commentary on Article 3, para. 9; 1977 OECD Commentary on Article 24, para. 12 (1963: para. 11), which states that '[i]n defining the nationality of companies, certain States have regard less to the law that governs the company than to the origin of the capital with which the company was formed or the nationality of the individuals or legal persons controlling it'.

1400. It should be mentioned that there might be a difference between the place at which a corporation was originally created and the place at which it is at present organized. Article 3(1)(g)(ii) refers to the Contracting State the laws of which define the status of a corporation at the time when the tax treaty is applied. If the laws in force use criteria other than incorporation to determine the status of a corporation (real seat, central administration, registered office, place of central management, and control), these other criteria become relevant under Article 3(1)(g)(ii) for the purpose of determining nationality. In the following, however, for the sake of simplicity, no distinction between incorporation and such other criteria or between different understandings of 'incorporation' will be made. It will be assumed that 'incorporation' covers all possible criteria that allow a legal person, partnership, or association to derive its status as such from the laws in force in a Contracting State within the meaning of Article 3(1)(g)(ii).

1401. *See* 2008–2017 OECD Commentary on Article 24, para. 17.

1402. *See*, for example, Haslehner 2016c, 12 ('residence and nationality are not only frequently overlapping as a practical matter, but are often inextricably linked as a legal matter so as to make both criteria seem exchangeable'); Van Brussel 2015, 361; Haslehner 2009, 61.

1403. After defining the nationality of individuals, Article 3(1)(g)(ii) deals with the nationality of 'any legal person, partnership or association', a concept which should coincide with 'a person other than an individual' under Article 4(3). At the same time, Article 3(1)(a) and (b) defines the term 'person' as 'an individual, a company and any other body of persons' and the term 'company' as 'any body corporate or any entity that is treated as a body corporate for tax purposes'. For the purposes of this study, the persons of interest are individuals and other persons that are subject to income or capital tax. Thus, for instance, transparent or hybrid partnerships will not be dealt with. In the following, the terms 'legal person', 'corporation', and 'company' will be used interchangeably for a person other than an individual that is subject as such to income or capital tax and that is, therefore, a 'company' within the meaning of Article 3(1)(b).

1404. John F. Avery Jones, Henri-Robert Depret, et al. point out that, in some countries, nationals are taxed on the basis of their worldwide income without describing them as residents. *See* Avery Jones, Depret, et al. 1991b, 312. For the purposes of this study, no distinction between a State taxing its nationals and residents in the same way and a State deeming its nationals to be residents will be made. It will be taken for granted that full tax liability due to nationality, even if nationals are not deemed 'residents', is sufficient for residence under Article 4(1). Accordingly, full tax liability and residence under Article 4(1) will be used interchangeably.

The same criterion that determines nationality pursuant to Article 3(1)(g) also triggers full tax liability under domestic law and thereby leads to residence under Article 4(1). From a domestic perspective, incorporation leads to full tax liability. From a treaty perspective, incorporation leads to nationality under Article 3(1)(g) and to residence under Article 4(1).[1405] In many States, however, not only incorporation but also other criteria are employed as reasons for full tax liability, notably, a place of management. Often incorporation *or* a place of management in a State establishes full tax liability and thereby residence in that State under Article 4(1). This has two implications. First, a foreign company, that is a company not incorporated in a State, may nevertheless be a resident of that State if it has its place of management therein. Although it is not subject to full tax liability due to its incorporation (a foreign company is, by definition, incorporated abroad), it may be subject to full tax liability by reason of its place of management. Second, it is normally impossible for a national company incorporated in a State to be a non-resident, that is subject to limited tax liability in that State, even if its place of management is located abroad. A national company is, by definition, incorporated in that State and incorporation suffices for full tax liability. Accordingly, a national company cannot be a non-resident company under Article 4(1).[1406]

This raises the question of whether an appropriate comparator exists for a foreign non-resident company. When incorporation (nationality) triggers full tax liability and residence, a national non-resident company cannot legally exist. For example, from State A's perspective, a foreign company incorporated in State B having its place of management in State A can be compared to a national company incorporated in State A having its place of management in State A; both are subject to full tax liability in and residents of State A (*see* Figure 3.8 and Table 3.1). It is unclear, however, whether a foreign company incorporated in State B and having its place of management in State B can be compared to a national company incorporated in State A and having its place of management in State B; the foreign company is subject as a non-resident to limited tax liability in State A, whereas the national company is subject as a resident to full tax liability by reason of its incorporation (*see* Figure 3.9 and Table 3.1). If comparability is confirmed especially because legal differences in tax liability are directly connected to protected differences in nationality, a measure that distinguishes between persons

1405. For reasons of simplicity, it is often said that nationality leads to residence. This is indeed true when individuals are at stake; the definition of nationality in Article 3(1)(g)(i) simply refers to the domestic concept of nationality or citizenship. With respect to legal persons, however, a more autonomous concept of nationality has been chosen in Article 3(1)(g)(ii). Therefore, it is better said that incorporation determines both nationality and residence and not that nationality leads to residence. In other words, nationality and residence are linked through the criterion of incorporation or, to be precise, through the laws in force in a Contracting State from which a legal person derives its status as such. *See also* Bammens 2012, 74.

1406. There are two exceptions, however. First, according to the 2008–2017 OECD Commentary on Article 4, para. 8.2, if the tiebreaker rules of a tax treaty with a third State deem a national company to be a resident of that third State (notably, because of the POEM located therein), incorporation does not lead to tax treaty residence under Article 4(1). Second, a State's domestic law can stipulate that a national company should not be subject to full tax liability if it becomes a tax treaty resident of another State (*see*, for instance, Sasseville 2006, 45–48; Avery Jones 2006, 138–140; Avery Jones and Bobbett 1999, 20), which leads to similar results as the view advocated by the OECD Commentary.

subject to full and limited tax liability would at least partly conflict with the nationality non-discrimination clause. If comparability is denied because legal differences in tax liability establish relevant differences in circumstances despite their connection to nationality, a measure that distinguishes between persons subject to full and limited tax liability would fulfil the non-discrimination obligations of Article 24(1).

Figure 3.8 No Differences in Tax Liability in State A

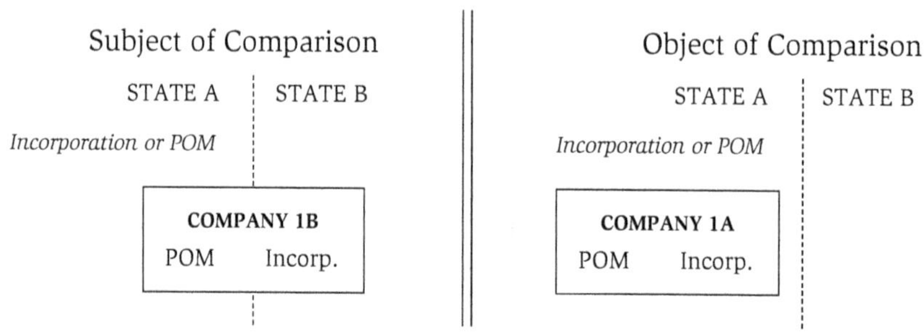

Figure 3.9 Inevitable Differences in Tax Liability in State A

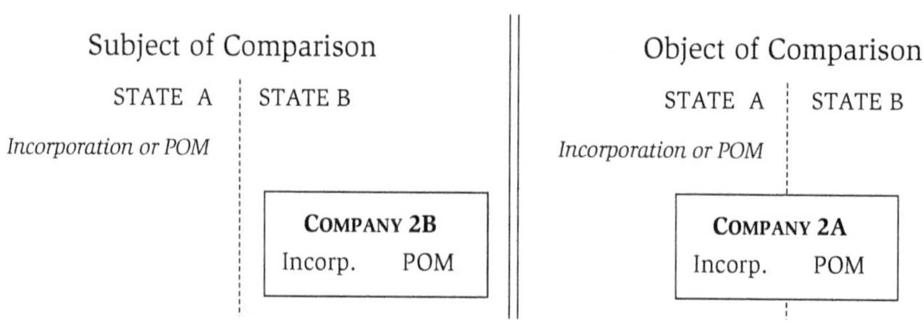

Table 3.1 Missing Comparator: State A National Subject to Limited Tax Liability

	State A	*State B*	*Nationality*	*Tax in State A*
Company 1B	POM	incorp.	State B	full liability
Company 1A	POM & incorp.	–	State A	full liability
Company 2B	–	incorp. & POM	State B	limited liability
Company 2A	incorp.	POM	State A	full liability

[2] Linked Attributes Do Not Prevent Comparability

When nationality leads to full tax liability and, consequently, when differences in nationality trigger differences in residence under Article 4(1), it can be argued that foreigners and nationals should be treated equally despite the remaining differences in tax liability and residence. All attributes that are legally linked to nationality should not prevent comparability under Article 24(1). Klaus Vogel explains that, in situations when the criteria for nationality and residence of corporations are described in different terms but are identical in substance, a Contracting State should not be able to circumvent the non-discrimination obligations of Article 24(1) by referring to the criteria for residence thereby rendering the nationality non-discrimination clause practically meaningless.[1407] When a dividend or participation exemption or a split-rate company tax system is restricted to resident (national) corporations, Article 24(1) may thus extend these benefits to non-resident (foreign) corporations.[1408]

Kees van Raad also submits that when a State employs nationality as a basis for its tax jurisdiction by subjecting its nationals to full tax liability and foreigners to limited tax liability, it cannot apply nationality as grounds for non-discrimination at the same time because its jurisdictional basis would always violate the nationality non-discrimination clause.[1409] If local incorporation triggers full tax liability under the tax law of a State and that State nevertheless concludes a tax treaty with a nationality non-discrimination clause that follows Article 24(1) of the OECD Model, it must extend all benefits attached to such full liability to foreign corporations[1410] even though, unlike national corporations, they are only subject to limited tax liability.[1411] Countries that employ nationality (or an underlying criterion such as incorporation) as a basis for full tax liability, therefore, should be very careful about concluding a tax treaty that fully incorporates Article 24(1). With such an unrestricted non-discrimination clause, they promise non-residents (foreigners) a treatment similar to that of its residents (nationals) in respect to all attributes of full tax liability (e.g., group consolidation regime, participation exemption), and this may lead to undesirable effects.[1412]

Kees van Raad brings the example of the US which does not consider an alien who is not subject to worldwide US tax liability and a US citizen who is subject to be in same circumstances because the difference in the scope of tax liability is a relevant difference in circumstances under Article 24(1).[1413] However, as US nationality automatically means worldwide tax liability in the US, it does not make sense to suggest, on the one hand, that foreign nationals should be treated in the same way as US nationals but, on the other, to maintain that foreign nationals who are not subject to US worldwide tax liability are not in the same circumstances as US nationals who, by their very nationality, are so subject.[1414] For Kees van Raad, it is clearly unreasonable to refer to a difference in a direct consequence of this nationality as a non-neutral circumstance when nationality is agreed upon as a tax-neutral circumstance.[1415] Any

1407. Vogel 1970, 352, 356.
1408. Vogel 1970, 352–353.
1409. Raad 1986, 75.
1410. Raad 1986, 75.
1411. *See also* Raad 1988b, 349–350; Raad 1982, 183–187.
1412. Raad 1988b, 349.
1413. Raad 1986, 91.
1414. Raad 1986, 91.
1415. Raad 1982, 187. To be precise, as in the US, both nationals and residents of the US are subject to full tax liability (*see also* Raad 1986, 102, 108), full tax liability is a legal consequence of US

other conclusion would be tantamount to an attempt to justify discriminatory treatment.[1416] Thus, the 'same circumstances' requirement is met in situations when a foreign-managed domestically incorporated corporation is subject to full tax liability and a foreign-managed foreign-incorporated corporation is not subject to full tax liability.[1417]

If the law provides a type of differential treatment based on nationality (for instance, nationals may not be extradited whereas foreigners may), the result is impossibility of 'similar circumstances in law'; then, a foreigner is *not* in a similar legal position as a national.[1418] Kees van Raad, therefore, believes that the OECD Commentary's explanation of the 'same circumstances' requirement, namely, that taxpayers must be placed 'in substantially similar circumstances both in law and in fact'[1419] is conceptually incorrect.[1420] With regard to 'similar circumstances in fact', all facts must be identical except for the very aspect protected under the non-discrimination clause.[1421] As the requirement of similarity in factual circumstances flows from the very concept of specific non-discrimination, it is superfluous.[1422] By contrast, the requirement of 'similar circumstances in law' is of a different nature.[1423] Only if a given basis for non-discrimination (e.g., nationality) has no legal consequences whatsoever will persons differing from each other in this respect (e.g., foreigners and nationals) be in identical 'circumstances in law'. However, if the law does make a distinction in respect of specific grounds for non-discrimination, such as nationality, then a foreigner is *not* in a similar legal position to a national.[1424] To forbid foreigners to invoke a nationality non-discrimination rule because the law provides a type of differential treatment based on nationality (resulting in impossibility of 'similar circumstances in law') would not make sense;[1425] then, virtually any existing instance of discrimination would escape from constituting a violation of Article 24(1).[1426] Thus, the requirement of 'similar circumstances in law' must be dismissed.[1427] As the difference in nationality is eliminated as possible grounds for differential treatment by Article 24(1), all of the consequences that flow from the difference in nationality must also be covered by this

nationality, but limited tax liability is a legal consequence of foreign nationality only if a foreigner is not a resident of the US.

1416. Raad 1986, 91–92; Raad 1982, 187.
1417. Raad 1988b, 349–350.
1418. Raad 1988b, 350.
1419. 2008–2017 OECD Commentary on Article 24, para. 7 (1963: para. 2; 1977–2005: para. 3).
1420. Raad 1988b, 350; concurring Santiago 2009, 255–256, who adds, however, that distinctions between law and fact are always artificial due to an intimate connection that prevents real separation.
1421. Raad 1988b, 350.
1422. Raad 1988b, 350.
1423. Raad 1988b, 350.
1424. Raad 1988b, 350.
1425. Raad 1988b, 350.
1426. Raad 1992, 675.
1427. Raad 1988b, 350. *See also*, to this effect, Goldberg and Glicklich 1992, 86–87, who state that '[t]he phrase "in the same circumstances" would appear to mean the same *factual* circumstances, since the question being addressed is whether the situations are treated the same under the law ..., yet some questions that seem factual, such as residence, may really be mixed questions of fact and law' (original emphasis).

provision.[1428] Therefore, a difference in the scope of tax liability, such as residence or non-residence, flowing directly from the difference in nationality should be treated in a non-discriminatory manner as well.[1429]

Instead of foisting a 'benefit' upon foreigners (no full tax liability, that is an exemption from tax on foreign income and capital) and then proceeding to tax them more heavily as a consequence,[1430] a State could also subject both nationals and foreigners to tax on their worldwide income and capital. It could grant them equally all of the advantages and disadvantages of a worldwide tax system.[1431] Article 24(1), however, is not necessarily giving foreigners an option to be subject to worldwide taxation if all nationals are so subject.[1432] It only requires extending all benefits to foreigners that are granted to nationals. As a consequence, Article 24(1) arguably requires extending all benefits that are connected to full tax liability even if these foreigners remain subject to limited tax liability and, therefore, retain other benefits.

Since 1992, discrimination under Article 24(1) may only arise if foreigners and nationals are 'in the same circumstances, in particular with respect to residence'. Kees van Raad interprets this adjustment as a change in the scope of the nationality non-discrimination provision; the scope has become narrower than before.[1433] Article 24(1) now protects against other or more burdensome treatment based on pure foreign nationality (and no longer of other or more burdensome treatment stemming from – in many States – the related effect of foreign nationality, that is not being taxed on a worldwide basis).[1434] With this change, tax distinctions between residents and non-residents can no longer be scrutinized under Article 24(1) even if they directly relate to differences in nationality. This is only true, however, when a tax treaty adheres to the new wording of Article 24(1)[1435] and arguably only with regard to distinctions between residents and non-residents and not with regard to other distinctions that might also be directly connected to protected differences in nationality.[1436]

1428. Raad 1982, 183–188 (and in particular p. 187).
1429. Avery Jones, Depret, et al. 1991b, 313 (view of Kees van Raad). *See*, moreover, Avery Jones 2009, 33, who holds that the reference to similar circumstances in *law* is strange; clearly the discriminatory legal provision must be excluded from the circumstances in law.
1430. O'Brien 1978, 551, 558–559.
1431. *See also* O'Brien 1978, 551 ('cannot the nonresident alien respond by requesting that ... [a Contracting State that subjects nonresident nationals to tax on their worldwide income] not exempt his foreign source income in the first place, and thereafter not deny him the benefits of the nondiscrimination article?'); moreover, Goldberg and Glicklich 1992, 66 ('any existing discrimination could have been solved by allowing the taxpayer to elect to include his worldwide income and be taxed as a resident').
1432. *See*, differently, Rust 2015c m.no. 59; Bruns 2013 m.no. 58.
1433. Raad and Bosman 2016, 70; Raad 2012, 163–164; Raad 2005, 130–131. *See also*, to this effect, Schilcher and Stefaner 2006, 162–163; Toifl 2004, 331; Toifl 2003, 291–292, 303–304, 313.
1434. Raad and Bosman 2016, 70; Raad 2005, 131.
1435. *See*, however, 2008-2017 OECD Commentary on Article 24, para. 7 (1992–2005: para. 3) which holds that the expression 'in particular with respect to residence' was regarded by the OECD Committee on Fiscal Affairs only as a useful clarification thereby implying that the former and the current version of Article 24(1) should not be interpreted differently.
1436. *See*, however, Schilcher and Stefaner 2006, 163–165, who believe that, under restrictive conditions, 'the same circumstances, in particular with respect to residence' may be present between foreign and national corporations even if these corporations are subject to different scopes of tax liability due to their nationality.

[3] *Linked Attributes Might Prevent Comparability*

John F. Avery Jones, Henri-Robert Depret, et al., with the exception of Kees van Raad, suggest, by contrast, that comparison should not be attempted when nationality triggers residence (full tax liability) and, therefore, when no non-resident national can exist.[1437] In cases when both a foreigner and a hypothetical national would not be taxed under a State's domestic tax law as either residents (full tax liability) or non-residents (limited tax liability), they cannot be compared to each other.[1438] When comparison is impossible, no discrimination under Article 24(1) can be established.[1439] In such cases, the circumstances that must be 'the same' under Article 24(1) are legally very different.[1440] From the point of view of the application of the ordinary taxation laws and regulations, the taxpayers are not even in substantially similar circumstances legally.[1441]

As a result, a State may subject its nationals to full tax liability and foreigners to limited tax liability.[1442] All advantages that are granted to nationals due to their full tax liability but not to foreigners due to their limited tax liability need not be extended. Such different treatment does not constitute discrimination under Article 24(1) due to a lack of comparability. Even though the State itself decided to tax nationals as residents on the basis of their worldwide income and, thus, even though the State itself created legal differences between nationals and foreigners, those legal differences prevent comparability under Article 24(1).[1443]

John F. Avery Jones, Henri-Robert Depret, et al. recognize that this view may be difficult to reconcile with the view that Article 24(1) permits positive discrimination. Although Article 24(1) prohibits '*other* or more burdensome' taxation, it does not prohibit more favourable taxation of foreigners (*see* section §3.02[A][1]). Therefore, it could be argued that, by taxing nationals but not foreigners on their worldwide income, a State is merely exercising a permitted positive discrimination in favour of foreigners.[1444] It would follow that making a comparison between foreigners and nationals is

1437. Avery Jones, Depret, et al. 1991b, 314, 327.
1438. Avery Jones, Depret, et al. 1991b, 314.
1439. Avery Jones, Depret, et al. 1991b, 314, 321. *See also* Avery Jones 2009, 32–33, who states that nobody can hypothetically be in identical circumstances as a non-resident national if nationality is the test for residence as is common for corporations, in which case the comparison cannot be made and there can be no discrimination.
1440. Avery Jones, Depret, et al. 1991b, 314.
1441. Avery Jones, Depret, et al. 1991b, 314.
1442. Of course, foreigners can also be subjected to full tax liability on the basis of a criterion other than nationality such as domicile, residence, or place of management.
1443. *See also*, to this effect, Bennett 2006, 446, who states that a corporation that is not a US 'national' is, virtually by definition, not 'in the same circumstances' as a corporation that is a US national because the dividing line between full and limited tax liability is the same as the nationality criterion, namely, whether the corporation is incorporated under US laws; similarly, L. Hinnekens and Hinnekens 2008, 24; moreover, Arnold 2011, 371, who takes the view that, even if residence and nationality are synonymous under a State's domestic law (i.e., the test of corporate residence is based exclusively on the place of incorporation as it is in the US), there is no discrimination.
1444. Avery Jones, Depret, et al. 1991b, 326. *See also* O'Brien 1978, 551, 558–559, who refers to a benefit of an exemption from tax by being subject only to limited tax liability.

possible, and all of the benefits given to nationals should also be given to foreigners.[1445] Positive discrimination by not taxing foreigners on a worldwide basis would not prevent comparability with respect to advantages granted only to nationals even when nationality is the sole criterion for full tax liability. However, John F. Avery Jones, Henri-Robert Depret, et al. doubt if this is intended.[1446]

It should be critically remarked that denying comparability between foreigners and nationals under Article 24(1) because of legal differences in their tax liability that are directly related to their nationality may not be fully convincing when viewed from the perspective of an individual foreigner whose entire income is derived from sources located in the allegedly discriminating State.[1447] As the foreigner is, in fact (and despite the individual's legal status of limited tax liability), being subjected to tax in that State on that person's worldwide income,[1448] no relevant differences in tax liability appear to exist when compared to a national who is also, in fact, being subjected to tax in that State on the worldwide income.[1449] Nevertheless, at least when a foreigner earns income from sources located outside of the allegedly discriminating State, actual differences in the tax liability exist between nationals (full tax liability) and foreigners (limited tax liability), and these legal differences might prevent comparability under Article 24(1).

[4] Tiebreaker Residence: A Way Out?

[a] Place of Effective Management

As illustrated above, two fundamentally different approaches can be identified with regard to Article 24(1) in cases when nationality triggers full tax liability and residence under Article 4(1):[1450]

(1) Under the first view most prominently argued by Kees van Raad (*see* section §3.06[C][2]), all consequences flowing from nationality, including full tax liability and residence, must be ignored when a foreigner is compared to a hypothetical national. Just as a different nationality obviously cannot prevent comparability, legal differences connected to or caused by nationality cannot prevent comparability. As a result, a foreigner subject to limited tax liability as a non-resident can be compared to a national subject to full tax liability as a resident if nationality leads to residence.

1445. Avery Jones, Depret, et al. 1991b, 326.
1446. Avery Jones, Depret, et al. 1991b, 326.
1447. O'Brien 1978, 557.
1448. O'Brien 1978, 557–558.
1449. *See also* Lehner 2001, 333, who argues that the expression 'in particular with respect to residence' need not be opposed to an assumption of 'the same circumstances' in certain exceptional situations even if differences in residence exist.
1450. *See also* Bammens and Vanistendael 2016, sec. 2.1.3.2.2.

(2) Under the second view most prominently supported by John F. Avery Jones, Henri-Robert Depret, et al. (*see* section §3.06[C][3]), legal differences between full tax liability and limited tax liability, and thus between residence and non-residence, generally prevent comparability. Accordingly, a foreigner subject to limited tax liability as a non-resident cannot be compared to a national subject to full tax liability as a resident if nationality leads to residence. An appropriate comparison is impossible because no non-resident national can exist.

John F. Avery Jones, Henri-Robert Depret, et al. qualify this concept of comparability by considering the tiebreaker rules of Article 4(2) and (3).[1451] In certain cases, a non-resident foreigner can be compared to a resident national, namely, if that resident national becomes a non-resident under Article 4(2) or (3) by reason of a criterion other than nationality. When a hypothetical State A national would, if the circumstances were the same as those of a State B national, be taxed for treaty purposes as a resident of State B, that person is treated by State A in the same way as a State B national who is resident in State B.[1452] To state it differently, consider that a State B national resident in State B is compared to a hypothetical State A national resident in State B. When nationality leads to full tax liability under State A's internal law, the tiebreaker rules should hypothetically be applied in order to determine whether the hypothetical dual-resident taxpayer (the object of comparison) is resident for tax treaty purposes under the entire Article 4 in the same State as the single-resident taxpayer (the subject of comparison).[1453] If they are resident for tax treaty purposes in the same State, namely, in State B, their circumstances may become comparable even if differences in tax liability remain under State A's internal law. In so far as residence must be considered as one of the circumstances embraced by the words 'in the same circumstances', then it should be judged by the definitions in the tax treaty and not by reference to internal law.[1454]

When incorporation leads to both nationality under Article 3(1)(g) and residence under Article 4(1), the tiebreaker in Article 4(3) can be relied on. States that use incorporation and a place of management as a sufficient personal nexus for full tax liability often include a tiebreaker rule in their conventions that follows Article 4(3) of the OECD Model. Prior to 2017, this provision relied on the POEM, a criterion that is still relied on in most double taxation conventions.[1455] In cases of dual residence under Article 4(1), that is when a company is a resident of both Contracting States, the POEM is often the deciding factor about residence for tax treaty purposes. As a consequence, there is only one residence State when applying the treaty provisions; the decisive criterion for residence is not incorporation (nationality) but, generally, the POEM. A

1451. Avery Jones, Depret, et al. 1991b, 314, 321–322, 327.
1452. Avery Jones, Depret, et al. 1991b, 314.
1453. Avery Jones, Depret, et al. 1991b, 321.
1454. Avery Jones, Depret, et al. 1991b, 322.
1455. Pursuant to Article 4 of the Multilateral Convention to Implement Tax Treaty Related Measures to Prevent BEPS (2016), however, this tiebreaker can be changed to mutual agreement. Article 4(3) of the 2017 OECD Model switched to mutual agreement as well.

foreign company that is a non-resident of a State, therefore, can be compared to a national company that is a resident of that State under Article 4(1) if this national company becomes a non-resident under Article 4(3). In such situations, nationality and tax treaty residence can be clearly distinguished from each other.

For example, from State A's perspective, a foreign company incorporated in State B and having its POEM in State A can be compared to a national company incorporated in State A and having its POEM in State A. Both are tax treaty residents under the entire Article 4 in State A (*see also* Table 3.2 and compare Company 1B with Company 1A).[1456] In addition, a foreign company incorporated in State B and having its POEM in State B can be compared to a national company incorporated in State A and having its POEM in State B. Both are tax treaty residents under the entire Article 4 in State B (*see also* Table 3.2 and compare Company 2B with Company 2A). The fact that the foreign company is subject to limited tax liability in State A whereas the national company is subject to full tax liability because of its incorporation does not matter for the purposes of comparability when the tiebreaker rule of Article 4(3) is relied on. A domestic tax measure of State A that provides for favourable treatment only to companies incorporated or subject to full tax liability in State A consequently violates the non-discrimination obligations.

Table 3.2 Comparators with Tiebreaker (POEM)

	State A	*State B*	*Nationality*	*Residence*
Company 1B	POEM	incorp.	State B	State A
Company 1A	POEM & incorp.	–	State A	State A
Company 2B	–	incorp. & POEM	State B	State B
Company 2A	incorp.	POEM	State A	State B

[b] Reasons for Ignoring Remaining Differences

Article 24(1) uses the expression 'in the same circumstances, in particular with respect to residence'. It is not precisely clear why 'in particular with respect to residence' should refer to the tax treaty residence under the entire Article 4, including the tiebreaker rules of Article 4(2) and (3), without considering remaining differences in residence under Article 4(1) and domestic tax law. Indeed, Kees van Raad suggests that the reference to 'residence' in Article 24(1) is imprecise and should rather be understood as a reference to worldwide tax liability under domestic tax law.[1457] Why should

1456. *See*, moreover, Bennett 2006, 446, who emphasizes that '[f]or other countries ... [than the US] the coverage of corporations under Article 24(1) could well have more practical effect, because many countries use not only place of incorporation but also ... place of effective management as their criterion for imposing worldwide taxation. Accordingly, if such a country has an income tax provision that distinguishes between two corporations based on their place of incorporation, that provision could run afoul of Article 24(1) if both corporations are effectively managed in that country ...'.

1457. Raad and Bosman 2016, 69; Raad 2005, 130–131.

a foreigner who is subject to limited tax liability be compared to a hypothetical national subject to full tax liability as soon as tax treaty residence is equal? Although the national may become a non-resident for tax treaty purposes under Article 4(2) or (3),[1458] full tax liability under domestic law and residence under Article 4(1) remain unaffected. In principle, these remaining differences in circumstances could prevent comparability and thereby permit different tax treatment on the basis of incorporation or tax liability to be maintained.

Probably the main reason why the tiebreaker rules of Article 4(2) and (3) are considered as being able to overrule remaining differences in tax liability under domestic law is the fact that they potentially affect the effective scope of tax liability. If, for instance, a foreign company incorporated in State B that has its POEM in State B is compared to a hypothetical national company incorporated in State A that has its POEM in State B, their scopes of tax liability initially differ. While the foreign company is subject to full tax liability only in State B, the national company is a dual resident and subject to full tax liability in both State A (incorporation) and State B (POEM).[1459] Consequently, the tiebreaker rules should be hypothetically applied.[1460] This deems the national company to be a tax treaty resident of State B where its POEM is located. As a result:

- the subject of comparison is a foreign company incorporated in State B that is subject to full tax liability only in State B and a tax treaty resident of State B; and
- the object of comparison is a national company incorporated in State A that is subject to full tax liability in both State A and State B but a tax treaty resident of State B.

This does not yet prevent legal differences in the scopes of tax liability. A national company of State A is subject to full tax liability in State A, whereas a foreign company of State B is not subject to full tax liability in State A. However, in cases when these taxpayers have their POEM in State B, the tiebreaker in Article 4(3) assimilates their circumstances. Since State A loses the tiebreaker with respect to a national company that has its POEM in State B, the applicable tax treaty between State A and State B deems State B to be the residence State of the company and State A to be the source State. According to the OECD Commentary, the source State has taxing rights only in respect of income from sources in that State and capital situated therein[1461] which means that the application of the tax treaty to the dual-resident national company puts this company in a position that is substantially similar to that of the foreign company incorporated in State B. Both are subject to tax only in relation to sources in State A, and both are subject to 'limited tax liability' in State A within the meaning of the second sentence of Article 4(1). Situations of full tax liability when a tax treaty leads to source

1458. Or, to be precise: a resident of the other Contracting State.
1459. Of course, the foreign company could still be a resident of State A if it had a place of management but not its place of *effective* management in State A.
1460. Avery Jones, Depret, et al. 1991b, 321.
1461. 2008–2017 OECD Commentary on Article 4, para. 8.2.

taxation due to a lost tiebreaker and situations of limited tax liability under domestic law are regarded as being equivalent for the purposes of Article 24(1). Certain inherent legal differences that continue to exist are apparently not able to prevent comparability under Article 24(1); they are, from a tax treaty perspective, legally irrelevant.[1462]

As previously discussed, the approach of Kees van Raad is that all attributes that are legally linked to nationality should be ignored (*see* section §3.06[C][2]). It could be argued that, while differences in tax liability under domestic law and in residence under Article 4(1) are a direct consequence of differences in nationality, this is not the case with differences in the POEM and with corresponding differences in tax treaty residence under the entire Article 4. As a consequence, the former differences must automatically be ignored for comparability purposes, whereas the POEM must be located in the same State in order to establish comparability under Article 24(1).

John F. Avery Jones, Henri-Robert Depret, et al., by contrast, argue precisely that differences in circumstances that are a direct consequence of differences in nationality should not be automatically ignored but might rather prevent comparability (*see* section §3.06[C][3]). This could mean that they always prevent comparability regardless of where the POEM is located. As outlined above, however, John F. Avery Jones, Henri-Robert Depret, et al. disregard these differences in certain situations, namely, when the POEM is located in the same State and the tiebreaker rule of Article 4(3) relies on the POEM. They apparently consider the broader context of the nationality non-discrimination clause, notably the fact that a lost tiebreaker may render a resident (national) subject to tax liability like a non-resident (foreigner); that a tiebreaker rule may rely on the POEM, that is an unprotected characteristic; and that remaining differences directly stemming from nationality should not prevent 'the same circumstances' under Article 24(1) as they appear irrelevant from a tax treaty perspective.

As long as the tiebreaker rule of Article 4(3) relies on the POEM, both approaches to comparability lead to identical results, although for different reasons. Under the first approach, the remaining differences in tax liability under domestic law and in residence under Article 4(1) are ignored because they are legally linked to the protected characteristic. Under the second approach, these remaining differences are ignored

1462. In cases when the POEM of a foreign company of State B is located in State A, however, that State could argue that it is willing to give advantages only to a national company incorporated in State A because a foreign company incorporated in State B is already receiving these benefits in State B due to full tax liability under domestic law regardless of tax treaty residence. Indeed, even though a tax treaty may limit State B's taxing rights to an extent equivalent with limited tax liability, a tax treaty need not prevent State B from granting tax benefits to State B nationals that are subject to full tax liability under domestic law. Therefore, State A could argue that, even though both the subject and the object of comparison are residents of State A for tax treaty purposes, the remaining legal differences between a State B national and a State A national – full and limited tax liability in State B – are relevant and render their situations incomparable. State A would submit that it is not discriminating the foreign company incorporated abroad because of its incorporation but because of the fact that the foreign company is subject to full tax liability abroad and, therefore, already receives (or should receive) the benefits in State B that State A confines to its own nationals. Whether the domestic tax law of State A indeed pursues this aim and whether this aim is acceptable from the perspective of Article 24(1) appears to be an issue that cannot be solved with a mechanical comparability test.

because they appear, in many cases,[1463] irrelevant against the backdrop of the same residence under the entire Article 4.

[c] Incorporation (Alternative Tiebreaker)

Cases remain in which nationality and residence are formally indistinguishable from each other even when the tiebreaker rules are applied. This is especially true when the tiebreaker in Article 4(3) deviates from the OECD Model by not relying on the POEM but on the place of incorporation. Consider, for instance, a situation when incorporation leads to full tax liability under both State A's and State B's domestic tax law. Incorporation triggers both nationality under Article 3(1)(g)(ii) and residence under Article 4(1). Assume, moreover, that the tiebreaker in Article 4(3) deviates from the OECD Model by using the place of incorporation as the decisive criterion for tax treaty residence. All companies incorporated in State A are nationals and tax treaty residents of State A, whereas all companies incorporated in State B are nationals and tax treaty residents of State B regardless of their POEM (*see also* Table 3.3). Assume, finally, that a measure of State A favours companies incorporated or subject to full tax liability in State A. As this distinction favours only companies of State A, it might constitute discrimination by reason of nationality under Article 24(1).

Table 3.3 Comparators with Alternative Tiebreaker (Incorporation)

	State A	*State B*	*Nationality*	*Residence*
Company 1B	POEM	incorp.	State B	State B
Company 1A	POEM & incorp.	–	State A	State A
Company 2B	–	incorp. & POEM	State B	State B
Company 2A	incorp.	POEM	State A	State A

John F. Avery Jones, Henri-Robert Depret, et al. imply that, if nationality decides the tax treaty residence under the tiebreaker rules, no comparability can exist between a non-resident foreigner and a hypothetical resident national; the legal differences in circumstances with regard to tax treaty residence under the entire Article 4 prevent

1463. Avery Jones, Depret, et al. 1991b, 321, state that tax treaty residence in the same State, that is in State B, will not lead to same circumstances in all cases under Article 24(1). If a State B national resident in State B is compared to a hypothetical State A national resident in State B who is, due to that person's nationality, also resident in State A, and when both taxpayers are, for tax treaty purposes, resident in State B, the tax regime applicable to the dual-resident State A national may be so different from that of the State B national that comparison remains impossible. In particular, if a State A national receives a benefit in State A because of internal law residence, and if the tax treaty residence in State B cannot take away this benefit (although the treaty assigns the corresponding income to State B), treaty residence in State B may not lead to comparable circumstances between this hypothetical taxpayer and a State B national resident in State B. One is still comparing an internal law resident of State A with a non-resident even though, for tax treaty purposes, they are both residents of State B, and such a comparison is impossible under Article 24(1).

comparability when applying the nationality non-discrimination clause.[1464] Therefore, they ignore differences in tax liability that are directly connected to nationality as long as tax treaty residence is identical and independent of nationality. As soon as differences in tax treaty residence are directly connected to nationality, however, these differences can no longer be ignored; comparability and discrimination because of nationality must be dismissed.

Above, it was implicitly assumed that incorporation *or* a place of management in a State establishes full tax liability and thereby residence in that State for tax treaty purposes under Article 4(1). This may be a common situation but need not always be the case. In some States, incorporation may be the sole criterion for full tax liability and residence.[1465] This simplifies matters as all national companies are residents and all foreign companies are non-residents under both domestic tax law and Article 4(1) regardless of where the place of management is actually located. It is not necessary to specifically deal with situations when a foreign company has its place of management in the allegedly discriminating State and is subject to full tax liability as a resident despite its foreign nationality, whereas a national company in otherwise identical circumstances would also be subject to full tax liability. Moreover, if both Contracting States rely only on incorporation, even tax treaty residence under the entire Article 4 cannot be formally distinguished from nationality regardless of whether the tiebreaker in Article 4(3) follows the OECD Model (POEM) or employs other criteria. Since nationality is the sole criterion for full tax liability in both Contracting States, cases of dual residence cannot arise from the outset. Taken together, nationality and residence may be formally indistinguishable from each other if incorporation decides on cases of dual residence under Article 4(3) or when incorporation is the sole basis for full tax liability in both Contracting States.

In cases when a distinction on the basis of incorporation, tax liability, domestic residence, or tax treaty residence is, from a formal perspective, necessarily a distinction on the basis of nationality, the approaches of John F. Avery Jones, Henri-Robert Depret, et al. and Kees van Raad fundamentally differ. Non-resident foreigners cannot be compared to resident nationals, or non-resident foreigners can be compared to resident nationals, respectively. Although both approaches lead to definite results about discrimination, they lead to contradictory results.

While the solution proposed by Kees van Raad leads to results that might be difficult to understand from a policy perspective (the nationality non-discrimination clause could require an extension to non-residents of all of the benefits granted to residents),[1466] the solution proposed by John F. Avery Jones, Henri-Robert Depret, et

1464. Avery Jones, Depret, et al. 1991b, 321.

1465. *See*, to this effect, OECD, DAFFE/CFA/WP1(91)1, p. 2 ('the French Cour de Cassation ... has ruled that, under French law, the two concepts of companies' nationality and residence concur'); Moldenhauer 1995a, 78–79; moreover, Bennett 2006, 446.

1466. *See*, for instance, Raad 2005, 130, who admits that it is doubtful whether the States concerned indeed intend to grant to foreign (non-resident) corporations that they tax on a territorial basis the right to be taxed not other or more burdensome than domestic corporations that they subject to worldwide taxation due to their domestic incorporation; similarly, Raad and Bosman 2016, 69.

al. principally preserves the fundamental distinction between residence and non-residence even when residence is connected to nationality. While the former solution automatically condemns distinctions based on passport entitlement as discrimination because of nationality, the latter solution requires further considerations. It requires disregarding differences in circumstances that are directly connected to differences in nationality but have no effect on the actual scope of tax liability from a tax treaty perspective (notably, differences in passport entitlement and tax liability under domestic law if a State loses the tiebreaker). By contrast, tax treaty residence under the entire Article 4 is a relevant factor that prevents comparability even if, in a particular case, this factor is directly connected to differences in nationality. The latter solution, therefore, implicitly introduces a distinction between relevant and irrelevant differences in circumstances which is a distinction that cannot be made automatically.

[5] Distinction Based on an 'Inextricable Link'

Niels Bammens submits the idea that only inextricably linked characteristics should be ignored when they are relevant to a domestic tax measure. An example of a characteristic that is inextricably linked to a protected attribute could be worldwide tax liability if all residents of a given State are subject to it while non-residents are never subject to it.[1467] In this case, worldwide tax liability would be inextricably linked to residence and, therefore, should be disregarded under a residence non-discrimination rule.[1468] Differences with respect to worldwide tax liability, even when relevant for the measure at issue, would consequently not render the situations incomparable.[1469]

Accordingly, even if differences in residence or full tax liability are relevant to a domestic tax measure, they should be ignored for the purposes of comparability under Article 24(1) if they are inextricably linked to differences in nationality. It follows that, when nationality (incorporation) and residence (full tax liability and tax treaty residence) are inextricably linked to each other, it does not matter whether residence is a relevant comparability factor. If it is irrelevant, it must be ignored and does not prevent comparability. If it is relevant but inextricably linked to nationality, it must still be disregarded and does not prevent comparability. In such a case, a tax distinction based on nationality or residence amounts to prohibited tax discrimination because of nationality under Article 24(1).

Niels Bammens extensively deals with cases in which nationality and residence overlap. For example, when a non-resident US national is subject to worldwide taxation because of US nationality, the decisive question is whether that person is in the same legal circumstances as a non-resident foreigner who is only subject to limited tax liability. The difference in the scope of tax liability is, at a first glance, a relevant difference in circumstances.[1470] According to Niels Bammens, however, the different

1467. Bammens 2012, 18.
1468. Bammens 2012, 18.
1469. Bammens 2012, 20.
1470. Bammens 2012, 87. *See also* Bammens and Vanistendael 2016, sec. 2.1.3.2.1.

legal circumstances (limited or full tax liability) are inextricably linked to the differences in nationality.[1471] As nationality is exactly the basis of the differentiation that is prohibited under Article 24(1) and, consequently, must be ignored in order to assess whether the circumstances are the same, all of the differences caused by nationality must also be ignored.[1472] It would indeed be contradictory to refer to differences between the subject and the object of comparison that are direct consequences of the difference in nationality in order to argue that the situations are incomparable.[1473] If a legislature is prohibited from attaching burdensome tax consequences to non-nationality, it should also be prohibited from attaching burdensome tax consequences to a factor that was introduced by the legislature itself in order to substitute nationality.[1474] Even though it has been argued that all relevant legal circumstances, including full or limited tax liability, must be the same in order to make the comparison, this argument can be countered by holding that nationality must be ignored when making the comparison.[1475] Therefore, all consequences flowing from nationality must be ignored as well.[1476] This would mean that the difference in scope of tax liability, being a direct consequence of nationality, cannot be invoked as a difference in legal circumstances that would render the comparison impossible.[1477] Niels Bammens, therefore, is rather critical of the view that legal differences flowing from differences in nationality should, as relevant differences, automatically prevent 'same circumstances' under Article 24(1). From a conceptual perspective, it is difficult to accept that characteristics that are inherent in the protected attribute can render the situations incomparable.[1478]

It is not exactly clear why, according to Niels Bammens,[1479] full or limited tax liability in the US is inextricably linked to US nationality. Niels Bammens defines 'inextricably linked' as meaning that the presence or absence of a characteristic (full tax liability) depends entirely on the value of the protected attribute (nationality).[1480] All of the situations in which a non-national is involved must share that characteristic while none of the situations in which a national is involved must have that characteristic.[1481] No US national can share the characteristic of limited tax liability when US nationality always leads to worldwide taxation. However, to the extent that foreigners are subjected to full tax liability in the US for reasons unrelated to their nationality (e.g., due to their domicile in the US), not all non-US nationals share the characteristic of limited tax liability. Some foreigners may be subject to full tax liability which should exclude nationality and full tax liability from being inextricably linked to each other. It consequently remains unclear why differences in tax liability should be disregarded for

1471. Bammens 2012, 88. *See also* Bammens and Vanistendael 2016, sec. 2.1.3.2.1.
1472. Bammens 2012 fn. 192 on p. 88.
1473. Bammens 2012 fn. 192 on p. 88.
1474. Bammens 2012, 90.
1475. Bammens 2012, 90.
1476. Bammens 2012, 90.
1477. Bammens 2012, 90–91.
1478. Bammens 2012, 92.
1479. Bammens 2012, 88.
1480. Bammens 2012, 18.
1481. Bammens 2012, 18.

the purposes of comparability given that only inextricably linked or irrelevant criteria may be ignored under a non-discrimination rule that concerns direct but not indirect discrimination.

Of course, all US nationals are subject to full tax liability *on the basis of their nationality* (if not already due to other criteria), and no foreigner is subject to full tax liability *on such a basis*; the characteristic 'subject to full tax liability on the basis of US nationality' is inextricably linked to nationality. At the same time, however, it is questionable whether this narrow characteristic can be relevant to the domestic tax measure under scrutiny. If that measure distinguishes on the broader basis of full or limited tax liability regardless of the reasons for such a liability (nationality, domicile, residence, etc.), it can be argued that only the scope of tax liability as such is relevant to the measure at issue. Therefore, even if the inextricably linked characteristic 'subject to full tax liability on the basis of US nationality' is disregarded, the characteristic 'subject to full tax liability' is not inextricably linked to nationality, cannot be disregarded, and prevents comparability.

In a highly interesting case in which French nationals were deemed to be residents of France,[1482] not all French nationals were deemed to be such residents but only those who had transferred their residence to Monaco (and not even all of them since exceptions applied).[1483] Therefore, it can be argued that deemed residence and nationality were not inextricably linked to each other. French nationality did not lead to deemed residence in all situations involving the protected attribute (nationality). In many situations, French nationals remained non-residents.[1484] Nevertheless, pursuant to Niels Bammens, the *deemed* residence of French nationals was inextricably linked to their nationality.[1485] Characteristics that are inextricably linked to the protected attribute should be disregarded.[1486] Accordingly, differences in deemed residence should be disregarded for comparability purposes, which would render a comparison between nationals (deemed residents) and non-nationals (not deemed residents) possible. Niels Bammens does not discuss why the characteristic 'deemed residence' and not only the broader characteristic 'residence' was relevant to the domestic tax measure under scrutiny. As far as can be seen, this measure simply taxed all non-residents potentially more burdensome than all residents regardless of the reasons for full or limited tax liability.

Niels Bammens approves an approach according to which no appropriate object of comparison (a non-resident national company) can be hypothesized in situations when incorporation leads to both nationality and residence.[1487] In other words, a non-resident foreign company is not in the same circumstances with respect to residence as a national company if nationality equals residence. Consequently, it

1482. Bammens 2012, 109–110.
1483. Bammens 2012 fn. 246 on p. 109.
1484. *See* Bammens 2012, 18.
1485. Bammens 2012, 111–112.
1486. Bammens 2012, 111–112.
1487. Bammens 2012, 96.

cannot be said that there is discrimination contrary to the nationality non-discrimination clause.[1488] Even in situations when the criteria for determining nationality and residence overlap, '[i]t clearly follows from the wording of [Article 24] that nationality discrimination is prohibited only in cases where the taxpayer is in the same circumstances with respect to residence as a hypothetical national taxpayer'.[1489] On another case, Niels Bammens comments that residence as a relevant characteristic is not inherently linked with nationality if it is possible for non-national corporations to be resident (because of their management and control) and, conversely, for national corporations to be non-resident (because of a lost tiebreaker rule).[1490] A non-resident non-national cannot be considered comparable to a resident national under Article 24(1).[1491]

It follows that, according to Niels Bammens, residence is not inextricably linked to nationality even if nationality leads to residence because there might also be other reasons for residence (such as a corporation's management and control), and some nationals may be non-residents. If this reasoning is applied to the previous examples concerning US and French individuals, this should arguably mean that residence is not inextricably linked with US nationality if it is possible for foreigners to be resident in the US (for instance, because of their domicile) or that residence is not inextricably linked with French nationality if it is possible for French nationals (who reside neither in Monaco nor in France) to be non-resident in France – but, for Niels Bammens, these cases involve an 'inextricable link'.

Niels Bammens' concept of an 'inextricable link' is problematic because it relies on undisclosed assumptions about the relevant perspective. A protected attribute may, or may not, be inextricably linked to an unprotected attribute depending on which protected persons are taken into account. For instance, Article 24(1) protects both individuals and corporations against discrimination because of nationality. If all protected persons, that is individuals and corporations, are taken as a reference point, different tax treatment based on whether or not a person holds or is entitled to a passport is not inextricably linked to differences in nationality. Corporations may be nationals within the meaning of Article 3(1)(g) without being able to obtain a passport, not to mention that even some national individuals may not hold, or be entitled to, a passport (*see* section §3.06[B]). Similarly, even if incorporation (nationality) fully coincides with residence of corporations under both domestic and tax treaty law, nationality is still not inextricably linked to residence if individuals can be both residents and non-residents regardless of their nationality.[1492] However, if protected and unprotected characteristics partly overlap or are partly linked to each other, it is

1488. Bammens 2012, 96.
1489. Bammens 2012, 96.
1490. Bammens 2012, 116–117, 121.
1491. Bammens 2012, 117.
1492. *See*, to this effect, Bammens 2012, 429, who argues with regard to Article 24(5) that the shareholder's liability to advanced corporation tax (ACT) is not inextricably linked to the shareholder's residence in particular because resident individuals are not liable to advanced corporation tax (ACT). With this argument, however, a group taxation regime that does not apply to resident individuals could also succeed in being non-discriminatory under Article 24(5).

only necessary to sufficiently narrow down the relevant perspective in order to establish an inextricable link.[1493] If basically all differences in circumstances except for nationality or residence are regarded as relevant, an inextricable link may exist in some cases even if there is no such link in other cases. If only individuals who had transferred their residence to Monaco are taken into account and all other individuals and corporations are ignored, an inextricable link between nationality and (deemed) residence may be assumed, although individuals who had transferred their residence to any other State are non-residents, and those who had not transferred their residence are residents regardless of their nationality. To bring another example, Niels Bammens implies that, when non-resident corporations are, by definition, not subject to corporate tax in a State, a criterion of being subject to corporate tax in that State is inextricably linked to residence; this holds true even if domestic tax-exempt corporations are also not subject to corporate tax despite their residence.[1494] Such an inextricable link indeed exists if all tax-exempt corporations and all individuals are disregarded. If tax-exempt corporations are taken into account, however, it cannot be said that only residents and not non-residents, or vice versa, are addressed by this criterion. Which protected persons are taken into account is decisive for confirming or denying an inextricable link. A decision on that matter is likely based on arguments that remain hidden behind a supposedly simple concept of an 'inextricable link'.

[6] Special Role of Linked Differences in Residence

Werner Haslehner, after analysing the OECD Commentary's statements on comparability,[1495] deals in detail with situations in which the hypothesizing of nationality carries certain automatic consequences under a country's law.[1496] To establish the cause of a disadvantage, a comparison must be made. In doing so, two possible approaches exist on how to deal with legal differences that are directly attached to the protected criterion.[1497] When hypothesizing the object of comparison:

- nationality needs to be added to the taxpayer with all attendant consequences that follow from nationality, or
- everything but nationality must be held the same.

Under the first approach (*see also* section §3.06[C][2]), a tax system that uses nationality as a criterion for distinguishing between full and limited tax liability would often appear to violate Article 24(1).[1498] Under the second approach (*see also* section §3.06[C][3]), in cases in which legal differences other than the discrimination in

1493. *See also* Bammens 2012, 432, who then admits that if the question of whether the shareholder is an individual or a company is a relevant characteristic for the purposes of the measure under scrutiny and thereby narrows down the appropriate comparison, the shareholder's liability to advanced corporation tax (ACT) might become inextricably linked with residence.
1494. Bammens 2012, 406–407.
1495. Haslehner 2016c, 9–10, 14–18.
1496. Haslehner 2016c, 18–29. *See also* Haslehner 2009, 59–64.
1497. Haslehner 2016c, 18.
1498. Haslehner 2016c, 18.

question are directly attached to nationality, the comparison is impossible and thus no discrimination arises.[1499] When, for instance, full tax liability is attached directly to nationality, it is impossible to hypothesize a national who is subject to only limited tax liability in the way a foreigner is.[1500]

Werner Haslehner proposes a middle way between the two approaches that could satisfy the need for a more logical comparability analysis and minimize the instances when a comparison is simply 'not possible'.[1501] This middle way would draw a distinction between a company's residence as an attendant consequence to nationality and any other such legal consequences.[1502] In so doing, this approach would also serve to reconcile the suggested prohibition of 'disguised discrimination' - different treatment of individuals based on whether or not they hold or are entitled to a passport violates Article 24(1)[1503] - with the more restrictive reading of Article 24(1) that distinctions based on residence do not constitute 'disguised discrimination' even in cases when nationality and residence coincide, notably, when incorporation leads to both nationality and residence.[1504]

First, according to this proposal, it is necessary to test whether the factor on which a disadvantage is based is a complete substitute for the protected factor.[1505] If this is the case, any different treatment based on the substitute should be prima facie prohibited as 'disguised discrimination' under Article 24(1).[1506] However, a complete substitute requires that all nationals necessarily possess the quality of that substitute and all non-nationals are automatically excluded from it[1507] (*see also* section §3.06[C][5]). According to Werner Haslehner, such would be the case for the entitlement to a passport of a State instead of nationality.[1508]

This test would only very rarely identify the condition of corporate residence as such a complete substitute for nationality, namely, only when all of the companies that are incorporated are automatically considered resident and no foreign-incorporated company could be considered as such.[1509] Yet, even in those exceptional cases in which residence is indeed a complete substitute of nationality, the comparison may still be denied.[1510] Werner Haslehner emphasizes that, since 1992, Article 24(1) explicitly requires equal circumstances with respect to residence.[1511] Moreover, even without such a requirement, a non-resident should not be considered comparable to a resident.[1512] First, the OECD Model is construed around this distinction which, in itself, creates a strong argument to interpret the nationality non-discrimination rule in such a

1499. Haslehner 2016c, 18.
1500. Haslehner 2016c, 18.
1501. Haslehner 2016c, 19.
1502. Haslehner 2016c, 19.
1503. *See* 2008-2017 OECD Commentary on Article 24, para. 1.
1504. Haslehner 2016c, 19.
1505. Haslehner 2016c, 19.
1506. Haslehner 2016c, 19.
1507. Haslehner 2016c, 19.
1508. Haslehner 2016c, 19.
1509. Haslehner 2016c, 19.
1510. Haslehner 2016c, 20.
1511. Haslehner 2016c, 20.
1512. Haslehner 2016c, 20.

way as to conform to the structural basis of the treaty as a whole.[1513] Second, Article 24(3) and (5) contains explicit provisions that protect non-residents directly and indirectly from being treated less favourably than residents.[1514] If Article 24(1) was interpreted to also cover that distinction, little room would remain for the application of those provisions, in particular Article 24(3) with its additional conditions and narrower scope of protection.[1515]

As a result of this systematic interpretation, a comparison between residents and non-residents should fail even for those cases when nationality and residence are complete substitutes.[1516] One should never hypothesize a change in residence to that of the actual taxpayer when defining the comparator even if nationality and residence overlap in all cases.[1517] If the otherwise correct comparator would have a different State of residence, the comparison must fail.[1518] By contrast, any other factor that comes directly and necessarily attached to a change of nationality should be so hypothesized and thus also be considered an inappropriate basis for a distinction in taxation in light of Article 24(1).[1519]

In brief, Werner Haslehner distinguishes between residence and other factors even if all of these factors are a complete substitute of nationality; residence must always remain in the same State, but all other such factors must change with differences in nationality. He argues based on the context of Article 24(1): differences in residence are either explicitly acknowledged (the OECD Model is based on this notion) or explicitly dealt with (namely, in the other non-discrimination provisions). All inextricably linked attributes should be ignored except for residence.

[7] Comment on the Proposed Solutions

On the one hand, if a facially neutral criterion is employed for a tax distinction, it may coincide with nationality. On the other hand, if nationality is used for a tax distinction, it may coincide with residence. While Article 24(1) prohibits discrimination because of nationality, it does not prohibit discrimination because of other grounds. Thus, the issue arises whether discrimination exists in cases when it is difficult, if not impossible, to formally distinguish between nationality and residence. When a protected characteristic (nationality) overlaps with an unprotected characteristic (residence), it can be argued that a distinction based on either characteristic automatically (*see* section §3.06[C][2]) or never (*see* section §3.06[C][3]) leads to tax discrimination, that the tiebreaker rules must be considered in order to determine tax treaty residence (*see* section §3.06[C][4]), that residence may only be ignored if it is irrelevant or inextricably linked to nationality (*see* section §3.06[C][5]), or that residence plays a special role

1513. Haslehner 2016c, 20.
1514. Haslehner 2016c, 20.
1515. Haslehner 2016c, 20.
1516. Haslehner 2016c, 20.
1517. Haslehner 2016c, 20.
1518. Haslehner 2016c, 20.
1519. Haslehner 2016c, 20.

and, unlike other interchangeable characteristics, is always relevant for comparability purposes (*see* section §3.06[C][6]).

Only the first two approaches amount to a pure mechanical comparability test that can be applied without further considerations. If a protected characteristic triggers additional differences in circumstances, these differences can either always be ignored or always be treated as preventing comparability. As soon as the tiebreaker rules are taken into account, a concept of 'inextricably linked' is introduced or residence is distinguished from other interchangeable characteristics, there is more to consider with the non-discrimination analysis. It has to be determined why tax treaty residence can be treated differently from residence under domestic tax law, that is why certain linked differences in tax liability under domestic law can be ignored as long as tax treaty residence remains identical. A concept of 'inextricably linked' may be understood rather strictly – all protected persons and no unprotected persons must have a characteristic, or vice versa (a definition that even passport entitlement as a substitute for nationality would not meet) – or a more 'flexible' meaning may be preferred. Either way, this meaning depends on preceding decisions about which cases should be taken into account for the purposes of defining 'all' and 'no persons' and which should be ignored. If a contextual analysis indicates that tax treaty residence should be treated differently than other linked characteristics, the question arises of whether exceptions may apply. If tax treaty residence is always regarded to be a relevant attribute, States could circumvent the non-discrimination provisions by linking disadvantages to tax treaty residence instead of nationality. If, in a particular case, nationality, full tax liability, and tax treaty residence are formally indistinguishable from each other, a Contracting State could refer to arguably relevant differences in tax treaty residence in order to discriminate, for instance, in the area of VAT without violating Article 24(1) and (6). Finally, if tax treaty residence is a relevant difference in circumstances regardless of its link to nationality, the question arises why other characteristics should not be similarly relevant. Just as an analysis of the context of Article 24(1) confirms that tax treaty residence has to be a relevant attribute, it might also regard some other linked attribute as similarly relevant.

There indeed exist good reasons why differences in tax treaty residence should be considered as being relevant and preventing comparability under Article 24(1) even if they are linked to differences in nationality. Article 24(1) has not only required 'the same circumstances, in particular with respect to residence' since 1992, but the entire OECD Model is based on a fundamental distinction between residence and non-residence (*see* section §3.03[B]). Historically, the nationality non-discrimination clause did not intend to interfere with this fundamental distinction nor with the States' freedom to employ nationality as grounds for full tax liability (*see* section §3.03[C]). By contrast, differences in residence under domestic tax law (full or limited tax liability) need not prevent comparability if they leave tax treaty residence and taxing rights unaffected. This approach to non-discrimination under Article 24(1) comes close to the solutions proposed by John F. Avery Jones, Henri-Robert Depret, et al., and Werner Haslehner as it values differences in circumstances based on the context of Article 24(1) including the other non-discrimination rules and the tax treaty as a whole. It is necessary to derive from the context why certain factors that are directly linked to nationality (for instance, tax treaty residence) prevent comparability, although other factors that are similarly linked to nationality (for instance, passports or domestic residence) do not necessarily do so.

Under a comparability test that requires all relevant aspects except for nationality to be the same, different results may be reached for cases in which nationality and residence coincide depending on which differences in circumstances are considered relevant. It is possible to regard all differences linked to nationality as relevant or irrelevant, allowing for an automatic assessment of discrimination. In order to reach results that better correspond to the objectives of the non-discrimination provisions, however, it appears preferable to enquire into the legal context of the domestic tax law and the tax treaty. This is at least partly done by treating linked differences in tax treaty residence differently than linked differences in other attributes. As far as inevitably linked characteristics are concerned, the contradictory approaches to comparability under Article 24(1) demonstrate that it is not always easy to determine the relevant differences in circumstances and, therefore, whether discrimination exists. As will be discussed in greater detail below (*see* Chapter 4 section §4.03[A][2]), it is necessary to supplement a strict comparability test with a substantive analysis that determines whether differences in circumstances that are inevitably linked to differences in nationality in a concrete case are relevant or must be ignored.

[D] Residence or Differences in Low or No Taxation?

[1] Issues with Hybrid Mismatch Arrangements

In order to address undesirable situations of low or no taxation, States introduce measures that deny a deduction of payments at the level of the payer if these payments are not sufficiently taxed at the level of the recipient. Such measures also include rules that address hybrid mismatch situations; the payer's State treats the payments as deductible interest, but the recipient's State treats the payments as exempt dividends.[1520]

Article 24(4) could condemn non-deductibility rules that counter hybrid mismatch arrangements[1521] as far as interest within the meaning of Article 11(3) is concerned.[1522] This non-discrimination provision essentially requires that 'interest,

1520. On a comparative policy analysis of equity and debt, *see* Schön et al. 2014.

1521. *See*, for instance, Zanutto Velasques 2015, 488–489. Some thoughts on non-deductibility rules countering hybrid mismatch arrangements were also published in Dziurdź 2016, sec. 6.4. This study represents the views of the author more accurately.

1522. Article 24(4) uses the term 'interest', while Article 11(3) defines the term 'interest' as 'income from debt-claims of every kind, whether or not secured by mortgage and whether or not carrying a right to participate in the debtor's profits ...'. However, Article 11(3) only defines '[t]he term "interest" as used in this Article [11]'. This could imply that the meaning stipulated in Article 11(3) cannot be used for the purposes of Article 24(4). If this view is followed, Article 24(4) would use the insofar undefined term 'interest' which, according to Article 3(2), has a domestic law meaning 'unless the context otherwise requires'. It then could be argued that, indeed, the context otherwise requires, namely, an autonomous meaning of 'interest'. Although Article 11(3) would not define the term 'interest' for the purposes of Article 24(4),

royalties and other disbursements paid by an enterprise of a Contracting State to a resident of the other Contracting State shall, for the purpose of determining the taxable profits of such enterprise, be deductible under the same conditions as if they had been paid to a resident of the first-mentioned State'. A comparability test that deems the recipient's residence to be different could imply discrimination. With a change in residence, a hybrid mismatch may disappear which allows for a deduction. Certain payments to non-residents are treated differently than payments to residents. In addition, as a non-deductibility rule that specifically targets hybrid mismatch arrangements may only apply in cross-border situations, that is when payments that qualify as interest under domestic tax law are treated as exempt dividends by the other Contracting State, the non-deductibility rule as such could be regarded as an additional condition for the purposes of the interest deduction. This means that, contrary to Article 24(4), the interest would not be deductible under the same conditions as if it had been paid to a resident. On the other hand, it could be replied that the same conditions apply to all domestic and cross-border interest deductions. In fact, all interest, regardless of the recipient's residence, is being tested for the existence of a hybrid mismatch. From this perspective, it would not matter whether the underlying hybrid mismatch criterion predominantly or only concerns non-residents or cross-border cases as indirect discrimination is not covered by Article 24(4).

Alexander Rust specifically addresses the question of whether a non-deductibility rule that targets hybrid mismatch arrangements may violate the non-discrimination clause of Article 24(4).[1523] He submits that Article 24(4) only prohibits discrimination based on the residence of the recipient.[1524] A distinction based on criteria other than residence is still permitted.[1525] In cases when a rule counters hybrid mismatch arrangements, 'the denial of the deduction is not based on residence of the enterprise receiving the payments. The reason for the non-deductibility is that the payments are tax exempt at the level of the recipient company'.[1526]

---

it would constitute a relevant context under Article 3(2) and would influence the meaning of 'interest' for the purposes of the non-discrimination rule. Moreover, in cases when no interest within the meaning of Article 11(3) is at hand, it can be discussed whether such payments, notably, dividends, constitute 'other disbursements' under Article 24(4). It is beyond the scope of this study to analyse this issue in detail and, therefore, it is assumed that hybrid payments either constitute 'interest' or 'other disbursements' under Article 24(4). *See* Bammens and Vanistendael 2016, sec. 2.4.4.2; Haslehner 2016a m.no. 29; Tomazela 2015; Bammens 2013a, 150–153; Bammens 2012, 352–356; Haslehner 2009, 76–77; De Broe 2008, 545–549; Hofstätter and Ressler 2006, 217; Lang 1994b, 150; Lang 1991, 69; Sommerhalder 1996, 93; Hosson and Michielse 1989, 483; Raad 1986, 178. *See also* Raad 1986, 175, who argues that, since the wording of Article 24(4) contains no indication that the 'other disbursements' must be *similar* to interest and royalties, it appears reasonable to challenge, for example, a denial of a dividend paid deduction in respect of dividends distributed to non-residents; differently, Fischer-Zernin 1997 m.no. 43; moreover, Zanutto Velasques 2015, 497–501, who believes that a dividend is not a payment covered by the non-discrimination rule of Article 24(4) and that exploring the definition of 'other disbursements' is irrelevant in the context of hybrid financial instruments.

1523. Rust 2015d, 311–312; Rust 2015e, 93.
1524. Rust 2015d, 312.
1525. Rust 2015d, 312.
1526. Rust 2015d, 312.

Alexander Rust considers the argument that residence of the recipient and tax exemption of the payments constitute criteria that are linked to each other and, therefore, a different tax treatment based on whether or not these payments are exempt from tax must necessarily result in a discriminatory distinction based on the residence of the recipient. 'One could argue that residence in the other Contracting State and tax exemption of the payments are linked: in general, if the recipient is a company resident in the other Contracting State the payments will be regarded as dividends and are, therefore, tax exempt.'[1527]

For Alexander Rust, however, two arguments can be put forward against this view. First, payments to a company resident in the allegedly discriminating State may also be non-deductible. Second, payments to a company resident in the other Contracting State need not always be non-deductible. It follows that residence and tax exemption are not identical criteria because 'residence in the other Contracting State is neither a necessary nor a sufficient condition'[1528] for a tax exemption.

First, 'if the payment is made to another resident enterprise which has a permanent establishment in the other Contracting State and the payments are attributable to the permanent establishment the payments will not be deductible either as they are tax exempt at the level of the permanent establishment'.[1529] Therefore, if burdensome treatment of non-residents is extended to certain residents (in this case, to resident enterprises that have a PE in the other Contracting State), no discrimination under Article 24(4) arises.[1530]

Second, 'if the recipient is a company resident in the other Contracting State which has a permanent establishment in the first Contracting State and the payments are attributable to the permanent establishment then the payments will be deductible although received by a non-resident enterprise'.[1531] This apparently means that, if burdensome treatment is not extended to all non-residents (in this case, not to non-resident enterprises that have a PE in the allegedly discriminating State), no discrimination under Article 24(4) arises.[1532]

1527. Rust 2015d, 312.
1528. Rust 2015d, 312.
1529. Rust 2015d, 312.
1530. *See also* Haslehner 2016a m.no. 71.
1531. Rust 2015d, 312.
1532. *See also* Haslehner 2016a m.no. 71; Wunderlich 2009 m.no. 36. It is argued to this effect that, if not all foreign-owned enterprises but only enterprises owned by non-resident shareholders who do not maintain a PE in the allegedly discriminating State are disadvantaged by a group taxation regime, there is no discrimination by reason of residence under Article 24(5); the reason for different tax treatment is the existence of a PE. *See*, for instance, Frotscher 2011, 699, 701; similarly, Schwenke 2013, 46; moreover, French Supreme Administrative Court (Conseil d'État), 15 December 2004, *Société de promotion écologique*, No. 257337; critically Bammens 2012, 118–119, 389–391, fn. 910 on p. 393, and p. 473 (but *see also* pp. 474–475); Lazarski 2005.

[2] Traditional Approach to Comparability

Before turning to the issue of whether burdensome taxation of residents or favourable taxation of non-residents may avoid discrimination, it is necessary to consider that, under the current approach to non-discrimination under Article 24, the starting point of a comparison is the taxpayer in question. In order to establish discrimination, a payment to a non-resident recipient for which the taxpayer in question claims a deduction must be compared with a payment to a resident recipient. Although Article 24(4) does not contain any explicit comparability requirements, all relevant aspects, except for the recipient's residence, must be the same (*see* section §3.04[A]). Thus, the persons being compared must be in substantially similar circumstances both in law and in fact.[1533] If tax treatments differ, prohibited tax discrimination is occurring. Alexander Rust also suggests that, in order to find out whether the discrimination is based exclusively on the criterion of residence, it is necessary to deem the taxpayer (or, in this case, the recipient) to be a resident of the allegedly discriminating State and leave all other facts unchanged. If the taxpayer will then be entitled to the benefit, it is proven that the discrimination is based on residence.[1534]

It should be remembered that two slightly different views with regard to the determination of the relevant comparability factors exist (*see* section §3.05[A]):

(1) Under the first approach, all circumstances except for the protected attribute must be the same, which means that all differences in circumstances are relevant and prevent comparability.
(2) Under the second approach, the relevance of circumstances must be determined from the perspective of the domestic tax law, which means that certain differences in circumstances may be ignored.

As far as anti-hybrid mismatch rules are concerned, these approaches should lead to identical results. Under Article 24(4), the protected attribute is the recipient's residence. If all circumstances except for the recipient's residence must be the same in order to establish comparability, differences in the existence of a hybrid mismatch are relevant as they are not protected. If, by contrast, it must be determined whether differences in the existence of a hybrid mismatch are relevant from the perspective of the domestic tax law (because irrelevant differences in circumstances may be ignored), it appears difficult to argue that those differences are irrelevant to a measure that specifically targets hybrid mismatch arrangements. Thus, relevant differences in the existence of a hybrid mismatch should render circumstances incomparable under Article 24(4), which arguably means that a tax distinction on the basis of such a facially neutral characteristic can never amount to prohibited tax discrimination.

If this was the end of the non-discrimination analysis, it would not be necessary to consider whether a non-deductibility rule that specifically targets hybrid mismatch

1533. *See*, to this effect, 2008–2017 OECD Commentary on Article 24, paras 3, 7.
1534. *See*, with regard to Article 24(4), Rust 2015c m.no. 145; moreover, with regard to Article 24(3) and (5), Rust 2015b m.nos. 61, 109; Rust 2015c m.no. 165.

arrangements also disadvantages payments to resident recipients. Since the existence of a hybrid mismatch is not the protected attribute, it must remain identical or else it prevents comparability. As long as only hybrid mismatch situations can be compared to each other, a hybrid mismatch criterion does not lead to relevant differences in tax treatment between resident and non-resident recipients. All situations with a mismatch are treated identically regardless of residence, and all situations without a mismatch are treated identically regardless of residence. Alternatively, no suitable comparator – a resident recipient involved in a hybrid mismatch in otherwise identical circumstances – is available. Without a suitable comparator, assessment of comparability is impossible. As a consequence, if the criterion that a measure employs as the basis for a tax distinction (the existence of a hybrid mismatch) renders situations incomparable, this measure is sacrosanct.

[3] Inevitably Linked Differences in Circumstances

Tension arises because facially neutral characteristics may also lead to prohibited tax discrimination under Article 24 if they are sufficiently linked to a protected characteristic. This is most evident in cases when a measure refers to passport entitlement (*see* section §3.06[B]) but also discussed in cases in which nationality leads to, or appears indistinguishable from, residence (*see* section §3.06[C]). If a Contracting State uses a passport requirement instead of a nationality criterion, differences in passport entitlement do not render the legal and factual circumstances of foreigners and nationals incomparable under Article 24(1). If a foreigner is thus deemed to be a national under Article 24(1), not only nationality but also passports can be considered to be different without preventing comparability in order to determine whether this change in nationality leads to a discriminatory change in tax treatment. Similarly, the question arises whether the existence of a hybrid mismatch is sufficiently linked to the recipient's residence in order to be regarded as being interchangeable with residence for the purposes of Article 24(4). If a non-resident recipient is deemed to be a resident recipient, it is unclear whether a hybrid mismatch can also be considered to be different without preventing comparability.

With regard to Article 24(5), the ownership non-discrimination provision, Alexander Rust discusses situations in which protected and unprotected characteristics coincide.[1535] In order to find out whether the discrimination is based exclusively on the criterion of residence of the shareholders, the following test must be conducted: deem the shareholders to be a resident of the Contracting State in which the enterprise at issue is a resident and leave all other facts unchanged.[1536] If the resident enterprise will then be entitled to the benefits, it is proven that the discrimination is based on the residence of its shareholders.[1537] If, however, the discrimination is based on a criterion that is linked to the residence of the shareholders, Article 24(5) is also violated if the shareholders who are deemed to be a resident would fulfil the other requirement as

1535. Rust 2015b m.no. 109; likewise, Rust 2015c m.no. 165.
1536. Rust 2015b m.no. 109.
1537. Rust 2015b m.no. 109.

well.[1538] Article 24(5) 'prohibits not only discrimination based on residence but also on all criteria that trigger residence and all criteria that automatically follow from the status of being a resident, such as unlimited tax liability'.[1539] For example, the criterion 'subject to a tax assessment' is closely linked to the criterion 'residence' but is not identical to it if only resident taxpayers who are not tax exempt are subject to a tax assessment.[1540] In cases when the measure in question distinguishes on the basis of whether shareholders are subject to a tax assessment, the comparability test should be applied as well:[1541] deem the shareholders to be a resident and leave all other facts unchanged. If the resident enterprise will then be entitled to the benefits (because resident shareholders will be subject to a tax assessment), it is proven that the discrimination is based on the residence of its shareholders. However, in the case of a tax-exempt entity as a shareholder, the test would not be passed.[1542] Even if the tax-exempt entity is deemed to be a resident, the resident enterprise would still not be entitled to the benefits as the tax-exempt entity is not subject to a tax assessment.[1543]

When taking this view for granted, a view that Alexander Rust also submits with regard to Article 24(4),[1544] a hybrid mismatch criterion would be similarly linked in certain situations to the recipient's residence and, therefore, should lead to prohibited tax discrimination. A change in the recipient's residence may sometimes lead to full and unrestricted tax liability in the allegedly discriminating State and thereby avoid a hybrid mismatch situation in particular if no PE is involved.

Therefore, it is important to distinguish between cases that involve a PE and cases that do not. A non-resident company that receives hybrid payments may be a resident of the other Contracting State based on its incorporation or POEM but need not maintain a fixed place of business in that other State.[1545] Moreover, even if the non-resident company maintains a fixed place of business in the other Contracting State, this does not necessarily mean that the hybrid payments must be attributable to that PE under Article 11(4) in conjunction with Article 7(2).[1546] As a fallback rule, the

1538. Rust 2015b m.no. 109.
1539. Rust 2015b m.no. 106. *See also* Rust 2005, 28; Rust 2003b, 659; concurring Hageböke 2005 m.no. 7; Wunderlich 2009 m.no. 51.
1540. Rust 2015b m.no. 109.
1541. Rust 2015b m.no. 109.
1542. Rust 2015b m.no. 109.
1543. Rust 2015b m.no. 109.
1544. Rust 2015c m.no. 145.
1545. Although such situations may be seldom, they are not impossible. Article 5(1) defines the term 'permanent establishment' as 'a fixed place of business through which the business of an enterprise is wholly or partly carried on'; pursuant to Article 5(2)(a), the term 'permanent establishment' includes especially a place of management. However, it is thinkable that a company has no PE in the State from which it is managed since the examples in Article 5(2) are to be seen against the background of the general definition given in Article 5(1) and, therefore, the requirements of Article 5(1) must be met. *See* 2017 OECD Commentary on Article 5, para. 45 (similarly 1977: para. 11; 1992–2014: para. 12). When there is no *fixed* place of business from which the company is managed, the place of management does not constitute a PE within the meaning of Article 5.
1546. Alternatively, Article 7(2) applies without recourse to Article 11(4) if the hybrid payments do not constitute 'interest' within the meaning of Article 11(3) but are, nevertheless, covered by Article 24(4) as 'other disbursements'. *See also supra* n. 1522.

payments remain taxable under Article 11(1) in the residence State of the recipient, while Article 11(2) grants the allegedly discriminating State a limited right to tax.[1547] Such situations that do not involve a PE are of particular interest because the recipient's residence determines the relevant tax jurisdiction for the hybrid payments. Since the residence State of the recipient in principle has a full right to tax,[1548] a change in residence necessarily leads to a change in tax jurisdiction. If the allegedly discriminating State becomes the residence State of the recipient, it obtains full tax jurisdiction over the deductible interest payments[1549] and, by taxing these payments, it prevents a hybrid mismatch situation of a deduction and no inclusion.

A non-resident tax-exempt entity must be compared to a resident tax-exempt entity when the facially neutral criterion 'subject to a tax assessment' is used even though this criterion is not identical to the criterion 'residence'.[1550] Similarly, a non-resident recipient without a PE must be compared to a resident recipient without a PE when the facially neutral criterion 'hybrid mismatch' is employed as grounds for different tax treatment. When considering only those situations that do not involve a PE, the question of whether interest is taxed or exempt at the level of the recipient is linked to the recipient's residence. In the allegedly discriminating State, hybrid payments made to non-resident recipients that do not maintain a fixed place of business in the other Contracting State (and do not maintain a PE in any other State) are treated less favourably than hybrid payments made to resident recipients that also do not maintain a fixed place of business in that other State. Similarly, if payments cannot be attributed to a PE of a non-resident recipient even though a PE exists, the treatment of these payments must be compared to the payments made to a resident recipient when these payments are also not attributable to a PE. Since residence (full tax liability) in the allegedly discriminating State precludes a tax-exempt hybrid mismatch situation as long as no PE is involved, non-resident recipients remain involved in a hybrid mismatch solely by reason of their foreign residence.

It follows that, by looking only at individual cases that do not involve a PE, the existence of a hybrid mismatch and the recipient's residence become interchangeable criteria. The recipient at issue, a company resident in State B that does not maintain a PE in State B, would not be involved in a hybrid mismatch if it was resident in the allegedly discriminating State, that is State A (*see* Figure 3.10 and Table 3.4). Consequently, it can be argued that, in these situations, non-deductibility rules based on the existence of a hybrid mismatch lead to discrimination by reason of residence thereby violating Article 24(4). Even though, in other cases, non-resident recipients may not cause disadvantages if they have a PE in the allegedly discriminating State (*see* Figure

1547. Alternatively, they are taxable under Article 7(1) only in the residence State of the recipient if the hybrid payments do not constitute 'interest' within the meaning of Article 11(3) but are, nevertheless, covered by Article 24(4) as 'other disbursements'.

1548. However, the residence State of the recipient is obligated to grant a credit under Article 23 A(2) or 23 B(1) for the tax paid in the allegedly discriminating State pursuant to Article 11(2).

1549. Since the interest is then paid by a resident of the allegedly discriminating State to another resident of that State, Article 11 is not applicable. Article 7(1) consequently provides a full right to tax to the allegedly discriminating State since no PE is involved.

1550. Rust 2015b m.no. 109; Rust 2015c m.nos. 145, 165.

3.11 and Table 3.4) or resident recipients may cause disadvantages as well if they have a PE in the other Contracting State and the allegedly discriminating State exempts the hybrid payments that are attributable to the PE (*see* Figure 3.12 and Table 3.4), this does not justify a different outcome in cases that do not concern a PE.

Figure 3.10 Hybrid Mismatch Situation Involving No PE

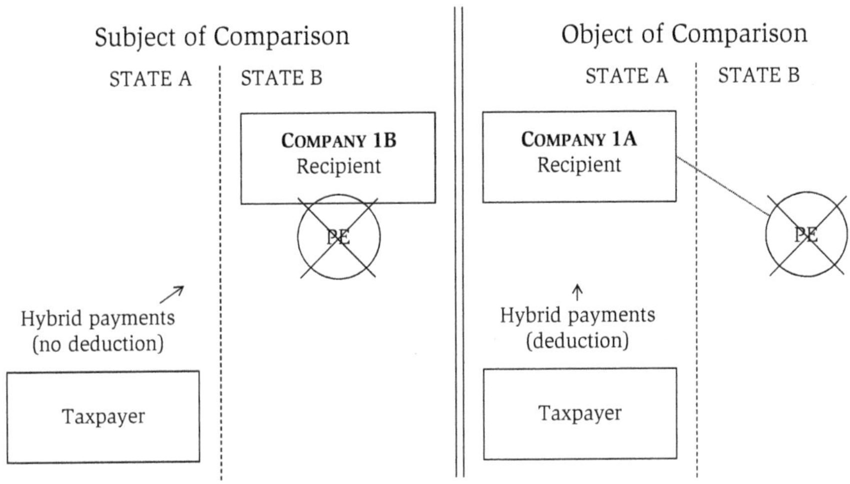

Figure 3.11 No Hybrid Mismatch Situation Due to a Taxable PE

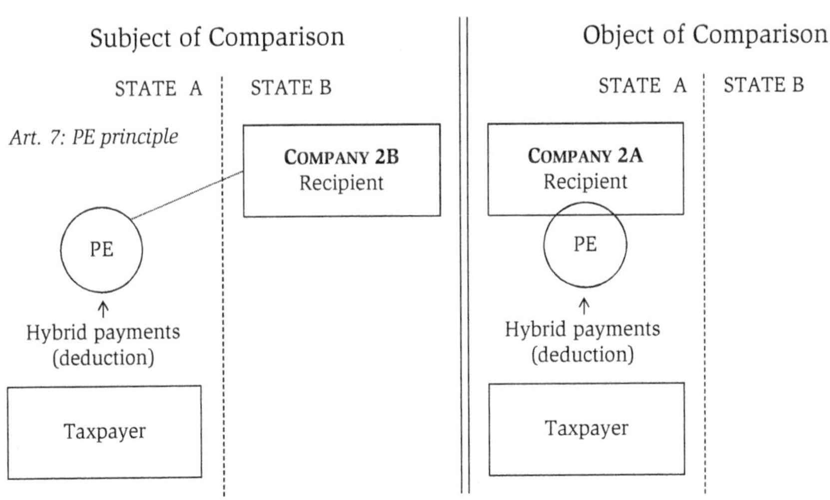

Figure 3.12 Hybrid Mismatch Situation Involving an Exempt PE

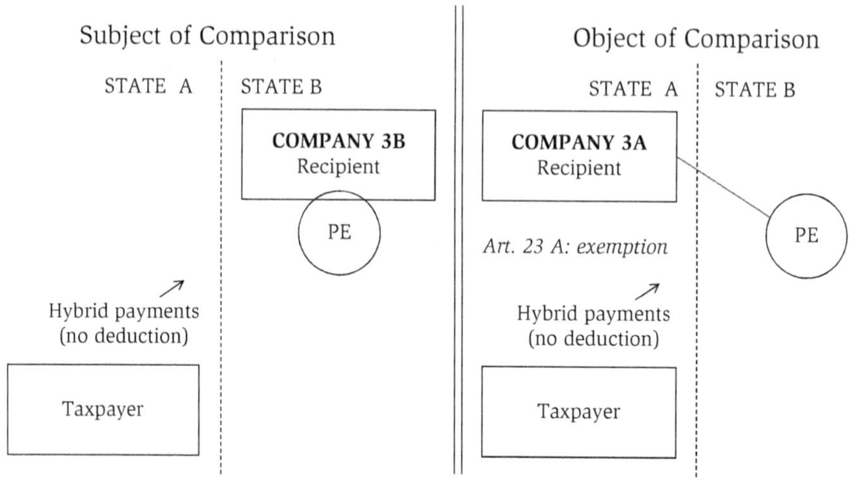

Table 3.4 When Are Hybrid Payments Deductible in State A?

	Residence	*Attribution to PE*	*Mismatch/ Exemption*	*Deduction*
Company 1B	State B	–	yes	no
Company 1A	State A	–	no	yes
Company 2B	State B	State A	no	yes*
Company 2A	State A	State A	no	yes
Company 3B	State B	State B	yes	no
Company 3A	State A	State B	yes**	no

* However, a deduction could be denied if the non-deductibility rule of State A only looks at whether a mismatch can potentially arise and not at whether the payments are actually exempt, that is if the existence of a PE in State A is ignored.

** A mismatch situation arises if State A uses the exemption method under Article 23 A; it need not arise if State A applies the credit method under Article 23 B.

If all circumstances except for the recipient's residence and linked attributes must be the same under Article 24(4), situations with and without a PE are not comparable to each other. A non-resident recipient of hybrid payments that does not maintain a PE in a State cannot be compared to a resident recipient of hybrid payments that has a PE in that State as the legal and factual circumstances differ. Even if the non-deductibility rule treats both hybrid mismatch situations identically by denying a deduction, discrimination under Article 24(4) is not avoided. Incomparable hybrid mismatch situations, that is situations with and without a PE are treated identically, but equal treatment of incomparable situations does not save different treatment of comparable situations from being discriminatory.

[4] Existence of a PE Irrelevant?

In order to argue against prohibited tax discrimination under Article 24(4), comparability could be assessed not only from the perspective of an individual case that does not involve a PE but also from a broader perspective. All hybrid mismatch cases, irrespective of whether they involve a PE, could be regarded as comparable to each other under Article 24(4). If the domestic tax measure under scrutiny does not differentiate on the basis of whether a PE exists but employs a hybrid mismatch criterion, the existence of a PE arguably is an irrelevant comparability factor[1551] or it at least becomes doubtful whether the existence of a PE is relevant to that measure.[1552] Payments made to a non-resident recipient that is involved in a hybrid mismatch (without a PE) can, consequently, be compared to payments made to a resident recipient that is also involved in a hybrid mismatch (because of a PE). If both hybrid mismatch situations are targeted by a non-deductibility rule, there arguably is no discrimination because of the recipient's residence. This comparison, therefore, ignores certain facts and circumstances of an individual case, notably, the existence of a PE, and compares the recipient at issue to a hypothetical recipient that is in somewhat different circumstances.[1553]

Ignoring differences in circumstances with respect to the existence of a PE initially means, however, that non-deductible payments made to non-resident recipients can be compared to both:

- non-deductible payments made to resident recipients – they are non-deductible because these residents maintain a PE in the other Contracting State; and
- deductible payments made to resident recipients – they are deductible because these residents do not maintain a PE in the other Contracting State.

Without further assumptions about comparability, such non-deductible payments, therefore, are comparable to deductible and non-deductible payments at the same time. Although this broader comparison need not necessarily raise conceptual problems (*see* section §3.04[B][3]), it could at least support a claim of discrimination.

Thus, everything is based on the question of whether differences in the existence of a hybrid mismatch are relevant for comparability purposes. If the existence of a hybrid mismatch is a relevant comparability factor, cases that involve a hybrid mismatch cannot be compared to cases that lack one. A comparison of payments made

1551. *See*, to this effect, Rust 2015b m.no. 35.
1552. *See*, to this effect, Bammens 2013b, 178, who argues that under a thin capitalization rule in which interest is not deductible if paid to a non-resident shareholder or to a tax-exempt resident shareholder, the corporate status of the shareholder is not a relevant characteristic for the purpose of the thin capitalization rule. As a result, a resident company with a non-resident corporate shareholder can validly be compared to a resident company with a resident non-corporate shareholder (e.g., a tax-exempt entity).
1553. Goldberg and Glicklich 1992, 65, describe this approach to comparability as a generic comparison that ignores the specific facts involved and looks instead to a hypothetical taxpayer and the *potentially* applicable facts and circumstances.

to a non-resident recipient that is not taxed on these payments due to a hybrid mismatch (no deduction) with payments made to a resident recipient that is fully taxed on these payments (deduction) remains unsuccessful because legal differences in the existence of a hybrid mismatch render the circumstances incomparable. As a result, a deduction granted for taxable payments made to resident recipients need not be extended to exempt payments made to non-resident recipients. Only situations in which a hybrid mismatch arises can be compared to each other. As long as payments made to such an appropriate comparator, a resident recipient in a hybrid mismatch situation (*see* Figure 3.13), are non-deductible as well, there is no discrimination of payments made to non-resident recipients.

Figure 3.13 Hybrid Mismatch Situation with Residents (Exemption Method)

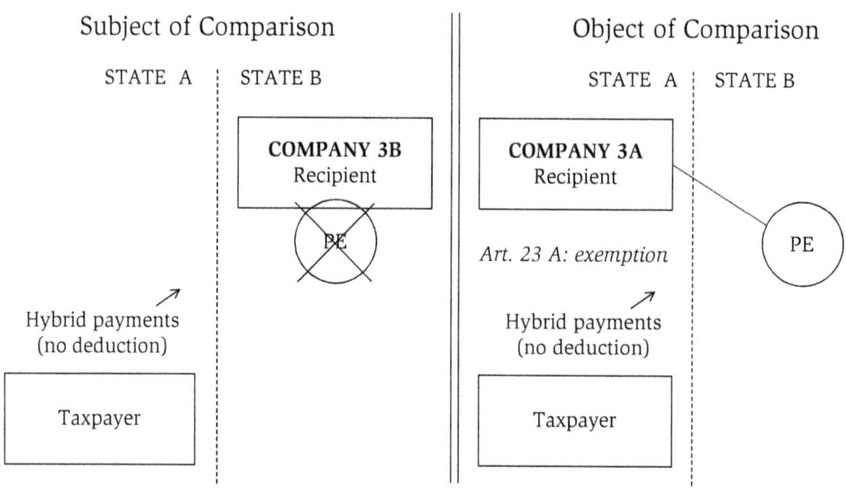

Ignoring differences in legal and factual circumstances as far as a PE is concerned makes a comparison to an equally treated resident recipient possible (while abandoning a strict comparability test that takes account of all of the facts and circumstances of an individual case). However, the decisive point that leads to a denial of discrimination under Article 24(4) is the conclusion that the existence of a hybrid mismatch is a relevant comparability factor. Only for this reason is a case of non-deductible hybrid payments involving a non-resident recipient not to be compared to a case of deductible non-hybrid payments involving a resident recipient.[1554] It still remains unclear on what basis it can be concluded that differences in the existence of a hybrid mismatch prevent comparability. Since facially neutral tax distinctions such as a passport requirement

1554. *See also*, to this effect, Krabbe 1984, 129, who argues that 'similar enterprises' under Article 24(5) must take account of whether or not the shareholder is fully subject to tax in the allegedly discriminating State and, therefore, concludes that all foreign-owned enterprises (the shareholder is not fully subject to tax because of non-residence) are treated the same as all similar domestic-owned enterprises (the shareholder is not fully subject to tax because of a tax exemption). The same is true with regard to Article 24(4).

may also lead to tax discrimination under Article 24, the fact that the recipient's residence is not explicitly referred to by the rule under scrutiny cannot be decisive.

In addition, as long as the existence of a hybrid mismatch is a relevant comparability factor despite being linked to the recipient's residence, it actually does not matter whether comparison is made to an equally treated hybrid mismatch situation involving a resident recipient (as differences in the existence of a PE are ignored) or a non-resident recipient without a PE is considered to be in a unique situation (as resident recipients cannot be involved in a hybrid mismatch without a PE). In both cases, discrimination has to be denied because Article 24(4) requires comparability, and hybrid mismatch situations are not comparable to situations without it. This is true even if, in a concrete case, a change in residence would avoid a hybrid mismatch and lead to favourable tax treatment.

[5] Argument: Discrimination Also in Domestic Cases

[a] No Domestic Situation: Credit Method

Perhaps the most compelling argument against discrimination under Article 24 is the fact that, sometimes, States disadvantage some of their own nationals or residents as well. In such situations, it is generally assumed that nationality or residence, respectively, is not the actual reason for different tax treatment. Instead, there must be some other explanation or grounds for different tax treatment that is not sufficiently linked to the protected characteristic. With regard to non-deductibility rules countering hybrid mismatch arrangements, if payments to resident recipients that maintain a PE in the other Contracting State are non-deductible as well,[1555] residence as such cannot be decisive for non-deductibility.

The problem with this argument is that if less favourable treatment of some unprotected persons would automatically avoid tax treaty discrimination in all cases, a State might be able to circumvent the non-discrimination obligations by replacing a protected characteristic with an almost equivalent but imperfect substitute, notably, by arbitrarily disadvantaging some payments to resident recipients as well. Completely different results would be reached under Article 24 depending on whether just a single unprotected person is also affected. For instance, if certain nationals are not entitled to a passport for national security or health reasons (*see* section §3.06[B]), their disadvantageous tax treatment could theoretically prevent discrimination under Article 24(1) since some nationals would be treated less favourably as well. Michael Lang and Walter Loukota observe to this effect that such an overly formal understanding of the

1555. Notably, if the PE receives payments that are treated as exempt dividends by the other Contracting State while the allegedly discriminating State, although it regards these payments as taxable interest of a resident taxpayer, exempts these payments under Article 23 A as business profits that are attributable to the PE in the other Contracting State. In such a case, the payments are exempt in both the allegedly discriminating State and the other Contracting State.

non-discrimination rules could render them meaningless.[1556] Besides that, it is not precisely clear which unprotected persons need to be disadvantaged in order to avoid discrimination under Article 24. If a benefit is limited to certain nationals, for instance to national corporations that are residents of the allegedly discriminating State, all national individuals and some national corporations also do not qualify for the benefit. Nevertheless, as Niels Bammens remarks, the fact that *some* nationals of the allegedly discriminating State are not entitled to the benefit does not detract from the conclusion that excluding all non-nationals may give rise to nationality discrimination.[1557]

The further problem with this argument is that discrimination would have to be confirmed as soon as no payments to resident recipients are disadvantaged[1558] even if the domestic tax measure under scrutiny pursues an objective that does not appear to conflict with the aims of the non-discrimination provisions. In effect, the domestic objective of targeting hybrid mismatch arrangements would fail or succeed, and the tax treaty objective of avoiding tax discrimination in certain precise circumstances would arguably be impaired or not affected depending on whether some disadvantaged payments to resident recipients happen to exist.

If the allegedly discriminating State taxes its residents on a worldwide basis and employs the credit method pursuant to Article 23 B, payments to resident recipients might never be disadvantaged. A resident of the allegedly discriminating State might never be involved in a hybrid mismatch even if hybrid payments are attributable to a PE in the other Contracting State. Despite maintaining such a PE and receiving payments that the other Contracting State treats as exempt dividends, the allegedly discriminating State taxes its residents on such payments and is only prepared to grant a tax credit. It thereby prevents all negative consequences of a hybrid mismatch situation, that is a deduction and no inclusion. A non-deductibility rule that focuses on whether payments are tax exempt due to a hybrid mismatch, therefore, might never apply to situations involving resident recipients (*see* Figure 3.14).

1556. *See* Lang and Loukota 2003, 69; Lang 1999, 159; moreover, Toifl 2003, 303.
1557. Bammens 2012, 120–121.
1558. *See also*, to this effect, Haslehner 2016a m.no. 71, who would confirm discrimination under Article 24(4) if a rule countering low or no taxation disadvantages no resident recipients (because the allegedly discriminating State applies the credit method) and all non-resident recipients (because the other Contracting State provides for a low general tax rate); he would reach a different results, however, if not all non-resident recipients are disadvantaged (because the other Contracting State favours only specific recipients).

Figure 3.14 No Hybrid Mismatch Situation with Residents (Credit Method)

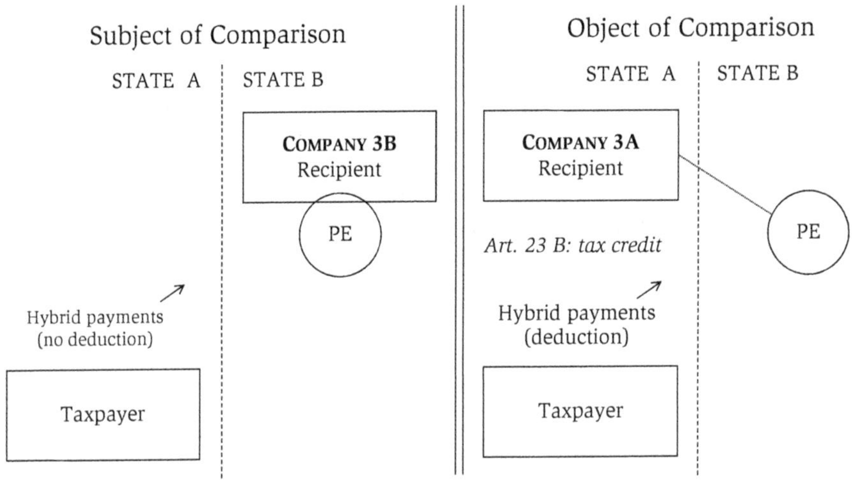

If the criterion of a hybrid mismatch disadvantages only payments to non-resident recipients because resident recipients cannot be involved in a hybrid mismatch, there appears little room for arguing that differences in the existence of a hybrid mismatch should not be equated with the protected characteristic of the recipient's residence. In all cases, regardless of whether a PE is involved, a change in residence inevitably leads to a change in tax liability, avoids a hybrid mismatch, and allows for a deduction. This could lead to the conclusion that the criterion of a hybrid mismatch is too closely linked to the recipient's residence and that all corresponding differences in circumstances should be ignored. If a non-resident recipient is deemed to be a resident in order to determine whether this change in residence triggers a discriminatory change in deductibility, a hybrid mismatch should also be deemed to be different without preventing comparability. A non-resident recipient that is involved in a hybrid mismatch becomes comparable to a resident recipient that is not involved in one. Arguably, there is prohibited tax discrimination because of the recipient's residence.

It is also not precisely clear under which conditions no payments to resident recipients are disadvantaged. As Article 24(4) is part of a bilateral tax treaty, it could be argued that, if the allegedly discriminating State employs the credit method under this tax treaty and, therefore, prevents hybrid mismatch situations in which resident recipients are active in the other Contracting State, no disadvantages arise with regard to resident recipients. This view would ignore the fact that the allegedly discriminating State might employ the exemption method under a tax treaty with a third State and that certain payments to resident recipients, notably those that maintain a PE in that third State, might lead to a hybrid mismatch and be targeted by an anti-hybrid mismatch rule. If the result of the non-discrimination analysis depends solely on whether payments to resident recipients are disadvantaged as well, a decision has to be made whether all payments, even if connected to a PE in a third State, or only payments involving the Contracting States should be taken into account.

Despite that, the allegedly discriminating State might rely on the credit method throughout its tax treaty network, which leaves the problem that hybrid payments to resident recipients might never be disadvantaged regardless of whether these recipients maintain a PE in any other State. On the one hand, it can be argued that a non-deductibility rule specifically targeting hybrid mismatch arrangements would violate the non-discrimination obligations of Article 24(4) only in such rather exceptional situations. On the other hand, it can be questioned whether the relevance of the existence of a hybrid mismatch and the result of the non-discrimination analysis should depend solely on whether some hybrid payments to resident recipients are disadvantaged as well.

Overall, the fact that a State extends burdensome tax treatment to situations involving resident recipients does not appear to constitute an ultimate argument against discrimination. In an individual case but also in all situations when the allegedly discriminating State uses the credit method under Article 23 B, a hybrid mismatch may be inevitably linked to residence. Only payments to non-resident recipients might be subject to burdensome tax treatment even if the domestic tax measure under scrutiny formally applies to all hybrid mismatch situations regardless of residence. Given that certain differences in circumstances may be ignored for comparability purposes provided that they are sufficiently linked to the protected characteristic, differences in the existence of a hybrid mismatch might also be ignored. This would arguably lead to comparability between hybrid mismatch situations and differently treated situations without a hybrid mismatch.

[b] *Targeting Low or No Taxation in General*

In order to avoid tax discrimination under Article 24(4), a State could be inclined to extend treatment that is less favourable to domestic situations more broadly. Instead of specifically tackling hybrid mismatch arrangements and risking that no payments to resident recipients are disadvantaged, a State could deny deductions in all domestic and cross-border cases of low or no taxation. In a domestic context, low or no taxation may arise, for example, when tax-exempt non-profit organizations are involved. If payments are not sufficiently taxed at the level of the recipient, a deduction would be denied at the level of the payer regardless of the recipient's residence.[1559]

1559. *See*, for instance, Tomazela 2015, who holds that differences in tax liability do not constitute valid grounds for restricting a deduction of hybrid expenses under Article 24(4) unless a payment made to a resident without full tax liability (e.g., a tax-exempt entity) is also non-deductible. Moreover, with regard to Article 24(5), Bammens 2016, 115; Bammens 2013b, 178, states that if a domestic tax measure mainly affects non-residents but also some residents (e.g., tax-exempt residents), this is a case of indirect discrimination on the basis of residence, which goes beyond the scope of Article 24 as it has traditionally been interpreted. *See also*, however, Schnitger and Oskamp 2014, 392–393, who report on an in effect different view of the German Federal Fiscal Court (Bundesfinanzhof) in the decisions of 8 September 2010, I R 6/09, and 16 January 2014, I R 30/12.

It not clear why the correct comparator for a hybrid mismatch case should be a tax-exempt entity such as a non-profit organization. It would be necessary to ignore differences in legal and factual circumstances regarding the reason for the interest not being taxed, that is, on the one hand, the different understanding of equity and debt and, on the other hand, the non-profit activities. As a result, enterprises that conduct their business for profit would be compared to non-profit organizations which usually have different aims and perform different activities[1560] or have nothing in common except for the fact that they are also disadvantaged.[1561] By contrast, if all relevant circumstances except for the recipient's residence and linked attributes are required to be identical, a comparison of a non-resident recipient involved in a hybrid mismatch to a resident non-profit organization is impossible as conducting business for profit does not equal conducting business for non-profit purposes, and those factors are not linked to the recipient's residence.[1562]

An argument for applying a broader comparability test could be that the relevance of the comparability factors must be judged from the perspective of the domestic tax measure under scrutiny that aims at preventing low or no taxation. This means that whether or not the payments are tax exempt at the level of the recipient becomes a relevant comparability factor, whereas all other differences in circumstances between recipients, including the reason for such a tax treatment of the payments, must be ignored. A non-resident recipient of tax-exempt payments (exemption due to a hybrid mismatch or non-profit activities) is comparable to a resident recipient of tax-exempt payments (exemption due to non-profit activities). As long as both situations are treated identically by the non-deductibility rule, there arguably is no discrimination because of the recipient's residence.

1560. *See*, for instance, Zanutto Velasques 2015, 503–506, who discusses a comparison of a non-resident payee to a resident tax-exempt entity but is sceptical about this comparison; moreover, Doernberg and Raad 1990, 203–204, who describe the question of whether only residence should be changed or whether comparison should be made to a tax-exempt entity as '[t]he heart of the non-discrimination issue' and further observe that there is a fundamental difference between domestic tax-exempt and foreign tax-exempt recipients of interest: a domestic tax-exempt recipient is tax exempt because of *what* the recipient does, whereas a foreign recipient may be tax exempt because of *where* it does whatever it does; similarly, Doernberg 1995, 97–99.

1561. *See* Pott 1982, 226, who observes that, in such a case, the persons compared have nothing in common except for the legal consequences they bear due to the fact that they are both not subject to full tax liability although for different reasons.

1562. As a consequence, it is argued that the fact that interest deductions are denied not only for payments to related foreign persons but also for payments to related domestic tax-exempt entities is a sham since the proper comparison is between the non-resident business entity and a comparable resident business entity. *See*, for instance, Bennett 2006, 453, 467, with reference to Ault and Tillinghast 1992, 258–259 ('it is not appropriate to compare domestic tax-exempt organizations with foreign business organizations'); moreover, to this effect, Lüdicke 2005, 486–487; Papotti 2003, 322; Brendt 2003, 902; Doernberg 1995, 97–99; Doernberg and Raad 1990, 203–204; Pott 1982, 226; Meilicke 1981, 28–29; Meilicke 1980, 106; Pöllath and Rädler 1980, 22, 23. *See*, however, Glicklich and Goldberg 1993, 730, who report that '[s]ince [in the US] consolidated returns are denied to commonly owned domestic corporations if the shareholder (domestic *or* foreign) is not a corporation, it is not clear that there is any discrimination' under Article 24(5) when such benefit is allowed to two domestic corporations wholly owned by a domestic corporation but not to two domestic corporations wholly owned by a foreign corporation.

However, as long as the existence of a tax exemption is a relevant comparability factor, resident recipients that are covered by the non-deductibility rule need not actually exist in order to avoid tax discrimination under Article 24(4). Based on the assumption that only tax-exempt or low-taxed payments can be compared to each other (as differences in taxation render circumstances incomparable), the only appropriate comparator for a non-resident recipient of tax-exempt payments is a resident recipient of tax-exempt payments. If no such resident recipient can legally exist because the allegedly discriminating State does not provide for any tax exemptions to its residents, no appropriate comparator is available. Accordingly, the unique case of a non-resident recipient of tax-exempt payments cannot be compared to any other case and thus can be treated arbitrarily without violating Article 24(4).

This situation is conceptually no different from the situation in which differences in the existence of a PE are ignored in order to allow comparison of a non-resident recipient to an equally treated resident recipient (*see* section §3.06[D][4]). If a non-deductibility rule employs the criterion of a hybrid mismatch, the issue is whether differences in its existence are relevant. If a non-deductibility rule employs the criterion of low or no taxation, the issue is whether differences in taxation are relevant regardless of any remaining differences in the existence of a PE or in the reason for a tax exemption. As a consequence, the decisive issue appears to be whether *some* cases of disadvantaged resident recipients are indispensable in order to regard differences in the existence of a hybrid mismatch or in taxation to be relevant in *all* cases[1563] or whether their relevance can also be established without requiring resident recipients to be disadvantaged.

[6] Argument: Discrimination Not in All Foreign Cases

Another argument against discrimination concerns the fact that States also sometimes favour certain foreigners or non-residents. With regard to non-deductibility rules countering hybrid mismatch arrangements, if payments to non-residents that maintain a PE in the allegedly discriminating State are deductible as well,[1564] residence as such cannot be decisive for non-deductibility.

It is not precisely clear why it should be possible to avoid tax treaty discrimination because of residence under Article 24(4) by simply limiting burdensome tax treatment to selected non-residents, such as to non-residents who do not maintain a PE[1565]

1563. This includes cases when a change in the recipient's residence inevitably leads to a change in tax treatment.

1564. Notably, if the PE receives payments that are treated as exempt dividends by the other Contracting State, but the allegedly discriminating State regards these payments as taxable interest of a non-resident taxpayer and taxes these payments under Article 11(4) in conjunction with Article 7(1) and (2) as business profits that are attributable to the PE in the allegedly discriminating State.

1565. *See* Bammens 2012, 389–391, fn. 910 on p. 393, and p. 473, who discusses a domestic tax measure that grants benefits to all domestic-owned enterprises and to foreign-owned enterprises provided that the shares in the latter are held by a PE; even though the distinction is also based on the fact that the non-resident owner does not have a PE to which the shares would be attributable, discrimination under Article 24(5) is not necessarily avoided. *See also*,

or to female non-residents.[1566] Combinations of a protected characteristic with other qualifying characteristics are actually quite common. Seldom is residence the sole condition for certain tax treatment. For instance, often a fundamental distinction between individuals and corporations is made. If a supposedly discriminatory tax measure provides an advantage to resident corporations, the condition of residence is qualified with the personal characteristic of being a corporation. Similarly, the fact that a non-deductibility rule specifically addressing hybrid mismatch arrangements does not apply to all cases involving protected non-residents can be seen as a qualifying condition for (non-)deductibility. The domestic tax measure under scrutiny does not apply to all non-residents but only to those that are not individuals and do not maintain a PE in the allegedly discriminating State.

Both the conditions of being a corporation and of not maintaining a PE in the allegedly discriminating State may further be an implicit condition to a non-deductibility rule. If a rule employs a hybrid mismatch criterion in order to provide for different tax treatment and if such a hybrid mismatch cannot legally arise with individuals, the condition of a hybrid mismatch implicitly includes the condition of being a corporation. If a rule employs a hybrid mismatch criterion and if such a hybrid mismatch cannot legally arise with corporations that maintain a PE in the allegedly discriminating State, the condition of a hybrid mismatch implicitly includes the condition of not maintaining a taxable PE. From a formal point of view, there is no difference between these conditions.

It thus remains open why tax measures that disadvantage only non-residents that do not maintain a taxable PE in the allegedly discriminating State should be viewed differently from tax measures that disadvantage only non-resident corporations but not non-resident individuals. Arguing that a non-deductibility rule specifically targeting hybrid mismatch arrangements is compliant with Article 24(4) because it does not apply to non-resident corporations that have a PE in the allegedly discriminating State seems like arguing that this non-deductibility rule is not discriminatory because it does not apply to non-resident individuals. In both cases of non-application, the payments are taxed at the level of the recipient, for some reason, and actually regardless of residence. This is either because the recipient maintains a taxable PE in the allegedly discriminating State to which the payments at issue are attributable as taxable interest or because the recipient is an individual and cannot enjoy a dividend exemption. It would be surprising if a State could automatically escape discrimination under Article 24(4) by simply limiting its non-deductibility rules to corporations or by submitting

---

however, Bammens 2012, 474–475, where he argues that, if PEs of non-resident enterprises are subject to a State's tax like resident enterprises, this characteristic 'subject to tax at the normal rate', when used as grounds for different tax treatment, may be relevant for comparability purposes and prevent discrimination under Article 24(5) as it is not inextricably linked to residence. In effect, if a domestic tax measure grants benefits to all domestic-owned enterprises and to certain foreign-owned enterprises by employing a facially neutral characteristic ('subject to tax at the normal rate'), discrimination may arguably be avoided if this characteristic is relevant from a domestic perspective – but not if it is irrelevant.

1566. *See* again Bammens 2012, 390, who provides an example of a measure that discriminates specifically against female foreigners.

that, since payments to non-resident individuals are deductible, residence as such cannot be decisive for non-deductibility. When seen from a different angle, the non-deductibility rule imposes certain conditions for being able to claim a tax deduction. If favourable tax treatment of non-resident individuals does not prevent discrimination under Article 24(4), favourable tax treatment of non-resident recipients that maintain a taxable PE in the allegedly discriminating State should also be of no concern.

Even if it is accepted that granting favourable tax treatment to non-resident recipients that maintain a taxable PE suffices for denying discrimination under Article 24(4), certain non-deductibility rules countering hybrid mismatch arrangements might still remain suspect to discrimination. Both the payer's State and the recipient's State may target hybrid mismatch arrangements. If the recipient's State counters these arrangements by subjecting exempt dividends to tax, this does not necessarily mean that a non-deductibility rule in the payer's State becomes inapplicable. On the contrary, both anti-hybrid mismatch rules might apply, raising problems of circularly linked rules and potentially leading to economic double taxation.[1567] Non-deductibility rules, therefore, need not take account of whether the interest is actually taxed in the other Contracting State or at the level of a PE in any other State. They might only look at whether different definitions of equity and debt are at stake by referring to the general tax treatment in the other Contracting State. Such non-deductibility rules could conflict with Article 24(4) because they would deny a deduction of all payments to non-residents that are or could potentially be involved in a hybrid mismatch regardless of actual taxation or exemption. They would, therefore, also target payments to non-resident recipients that maintain a taxable PE in the allegedly discriminating State.

[7] *Comment on the Discussed Arguments*

A strict comparability test that deems residence to be different could, in some cases, imply that non-deductibility rules specifically targeting hybrid mismatch arrangements or low or no taxation lead to prohibited tax discrimination under Article 24(4). When no PE is involved or no non-profit organization is at stake, a change in residence leads to a change in tax jurisdiction and taxation and, therefore, may turn non-taxation into taxation and allow for a deduction. Just as a requirement of holding a passport may be closely linked to nationality under Article 24(1), a requirement of not being involved in a hybrid mismatch may be closely linked to residence under Article 24(4). Some nationals may not hold a passport, and some residents may also be involved in a hybrid mismatch, but such cases do not necessarily avoid an inevitable link in a concrete case.

As soon as it is argued that a distinction on the basis of a hybrid mismatch cannot be equated with a distinction on the basis of residence despite an inevitable link in a concrete case, a strict comparability test is supplemented with additional arguments. For some undisclosed reason, the facially neutral criterion 'subject to a tax assessment' may lead to discrimination because of residence, although the facially neutral criterion

1567. *See* Dziurdź 2013b.

'not involved in a hybrid mismatch' should not lead to discrimination because of residence even though both criteria are closely linked to residence. Depending on which protected and unprotected persons are taken into account – individuals and corporations, only corporations, only corporations receiving hybrid payments, only corporations receiving hybrid payments that are not attributable to a PE, etc. – the connection between these facially neutral criteria and residence may further be regarded as being closer or more remote. Again, choosing the 'right' perspective appears to involve some additional assumptions that are not related to a strict comparability test.

The attempt to dissect a link between a hybrid mismatch and residence in a concrete case by pointing to other cases in which certain payments to non-resident recipients are not disadvantaged might appear like arguing that a corporate tax measure cannot be discriminatory because it does not disadvantage non-resident individuals. Nevertheless, the fact that not 'all' non-resident recipients of payments are addressed by a non-deductibility rule and that this rule, therefore, has a rather precise scope is not irrelevant. It might support the view that there is a reason for different tax treatment that need not be residence, at least from a domestic perspective. After all, an anti-hybrid mismatch rule addresses not all non-resident recipients, not all non-resident corporations, not all payments but only deductible interest payments, not all such payments but only payments that are treated as exempt dividends by the other Contracting State, and usually not even all such hybrid payments but only payments that are not taxable in the allegedly discriminating State due to a PE. In such rather unique cross-border situations, a hybrid mismatch and residence may be formally indistinguishable from each other, but this does not necessarily mean that the domestic tax measure under scrutiny aims at disadvantaging payments to non-resident recipients solely because of foreign residence.

Another argument against discrimination is the fact that some hybrid or low-taxed payments to resident recipients may also be addressed by a facially neutral non-deductibility rule. On the one hand, the Contracting States could thereby circumvent the non-discrimination obligations by arbitrarily disadvantaging just a single unprotected person. Also, there may be no disadvantaged payments to resident recipients if the allegedly discriminating State employs the credit method pursuant to Article 23 B or grants no tax exemptions to its residents. Such non-deductibility rules could, therefore, violate or be consistent with the non-discrimination obligations of Article 24(4) depending on the chosen legal technique and on how double taxation is avoided, that is through exemption or tax credit. On the other hand, the search for domestic situations that are disadvantaged as well tries to dissect the link between the protected characteristic and the criterion for different tax treatment. It tries to make differences in the existence of a hybrid mismatch relevant in all cases, including cases in which a change in the recipient's residence leads to a change in tax treatment because, in certain cases, a change in the recipient's residence has no influence on non-deductibility. Since resident recipients may also be disadvantaged, notably, when they maintain a PE that is involved in a hybrid mismatch, the existence of a hybrid mismatch should not be equated with the recipient's residence, at least from a domestic perspective.

Situations involving hybrid mismatch arrangements illustrate that a strict comparability test may regard anti-hybrid mismatch rules as discriminatory under Article 24(4) due to an inevitable link between a hybrid mismatch and residence in a concrete case. Probably because such rules and their aims do not appear to be condemned by Article 24(4) if the object and purpose of this non-discrimination clause is taken into account, additional arguments are introduced that try to dissect this link in a concrete case by considering how other cases are treated. As will be discussed in greater detail below (*see* Chapter 4 section §4.03[B][2]), the fact that certain resident recipients are also disadvantaged or not all non-resident recipients are disadvantaged is neither a necessary nor a sufficient argument against discrimination under Article 24(4). It is, however, an important part of a substantive analysis that tries to demonstrate that the domestic tax measure under scrutiny genuinely pursues a distinct objective – targeting hybrid mismatch arrangements or low or no taxation – and that this objective should not be equated with the protected characteristic of residence from a tax treaty perspective.

CHAPTER 4

Article 24 of the OECD Model: Suggested Comparability Test

This chapter will attempt to refine the current approach to comparability under Article 24 and propose solutions for linked attributes. Article 24 is concerned with unjustified differences in tax treatment, which means that it incorporates a balance between competing policy interests, considers justifications as issues of comparability, and also mentions some specific justifications (section §4.01). The goal of the non-discrimination analysis under Article 24 is to identify the actual reason for different tax treatment and whether this reason is a protected characteristic. A two-step approach will be suggested (section §4.02):

(1) First, as it should not matter whether a domestic tax measure expressly refers to a protected characteristic or employs a substitute, it is necessary to deem the protected characteristic and all attributes that are inevitably linked to that characteristic to be different while leaving all other circumstances the same. If this 'but for' test leads to a change in tax treatment, there is prima facie discrimination; otherwise, the claim of discrimination can be denied.
(2) Second, if there is prima facie discrimination, it has to be determined with a substantive analysis whether the protected characteristic (discrimination) or an inevitably linked attribute (no discrimination) constitutes the actual reason for different tax treatment. At this stage, other cases and their treatment may be taken into account in order to assess the reasons for the distinction from a domestic perspective, but these reasons must also be balanced against the objectives of the non-discrimination obligations.

This two-step approach will then be applied to the discussed cases concerning nationality and residence as well as hybrid mismatch arrangements when protected and unprotected characteristics overlap (section §4.03). Finally, various practical cases of potential discrimination will be presented and solved on the basis of the suggested approach to non-discrimination under Article 24 (section §4.04).

§4.01 DISCRIMINATION IS ABOUT UNJUSTIFIED DIFFERENCES IN TREATMENT

[A] Balance Between Competing Policy Interests

Article 24 addresses 'tax discrimination in certain precise circumstances'[1568] instead of constituting a broad and general equal treatment clause.[1569] It imposes numerous requirements for non-discrimination as to which situations should be covered, how comparability should be established,[1570] when differences in taxation should be regarded as less favourable or more burdensome, and whether exceptions for certain personal circumstances or non-arm's-length payments should apply.

Despite those precise requirements, Article 24 does not operate in a policy vacuum. Given that every domestic and international non-discrimination rule pursues or contributes to some broader or narrower policy objective instead of eliminating discrimination for no particular reason, the non-discrimination provisions of Article 24 must also reflect objectives that have been valued as desirable from a policy perspective. Article 24 eliminates tax discrimination in order to protect persons against certain arbitrary, unjustified, or unreasonable tax distinctions; contributes to equal conditions of competition between resident and non-resident enterprises; and strengthens the economic relations of the Contracting States (*see* Chapter 3 section §3.03) – but many different and legitimate domestic policy interests should not be branded as discrimination. Moreover, every tax treaty that is based on the OECD Model pursues certain policy goals (facilitation of the exchange of goods and services and movements of capital, technology, and persons by avoiding international juridical double taxation, prevention of tax evasion by strengthening the cooperation in tax matters between the Contracting States, etc.), generally respects certain policy decisions taken under domestic tax law (distinction between full and limited tax liability, consideration of certain personal circumstances only in the residence State, etc.), and is silent about many issues and questions, particularly those unrelated to international juridical double taxation such as environmental protection, prevention of unemployment, and consumer protection.

Article 24 also establishes a balance between potentially competing policy interests: the policy aims of the domestic tax system and the measure under scrutiny as well as those of the tax treaty and the non-discrimination provisions. Certain tax distinctions that pursue legitimate objectives from a domestic perspective may contravene the objectives of the non-discrimination provisions, and vice versa. In this respect, the OECD Commentary on Article 24 observes that '[a]ll tax systems incorporate *legitimate* distinctions based, for example, on differences in liability to tax or

1568. 2008–2017 OECD Commentary on Article 24, para. 1.
1569. *See supra* n. 1012.
1570. *See* Haslehner 2009, 279–280; Hohenwarter and Weninger 2006, 253.

ability to pay' and that the non-discrimination provisions of Article 24 'seek to *balance* the need to prevent *unjustified* discrimination with the need to take account of these *legitimate* distinctions' (emphasis added).[1571] Article 24 consequently incorporates decisions about justified and unjustified differences in tax treatment that have been made by the drafters of the OECD Model and the Contracting States who have agreed to include the non-discrimination provisions of Article 24 in a tax treaty with a specific wording and scope.

Since the non-discrimination provisions of Article 24 lay down precise requirements for their application, they may not allow for an open-ended assessment of domestic policy interests or for flexibility and discretion in balancing these interests against the principal purpose of preventing tax discrimination. Since strict comparability requirements regard most differences in circumstances as relevant, discrimination can only exist in certain precise circumstances that involve a too close or direct reference to a protected characteristic. A separate consideration of justifications is thereby rendered largely superfluous. It might, therefore, be argued that the non-discrimination provisions of Article 24, in predefining an appropriate balance, are clear in every respect and must be applied without taking account of domestic policy interests or rendering further balancing decisions. However, even in that case, Article 24 still has important consequences and policy implications. A denial of comparability and discrimination allows domestic policy aims (e.g., economic or social motives) to succeed whereas an existence of comparability and discrimination impedes such policy aims.

Put another way, whether a domestic tax measure is allowed to pursue its policy aims depends on whether discrimination exists. If there are indeed very good reasons to distinguish between nationals and foreigners because, for example, only nationals are subject to full tax liability, Article 24 frustrates such reasons if discrimination is confirmed (apparently these reasons are not good enough from a tax treaty perspective), but it does not touch upon them if discrimination is denied. This means that, even if the non-discrimination analysis under Article 24 requires ignoring all domestic motives for a particular tax distinction as they cannot compensate for discriminatory effects,[1572] it does decide on whether a domestic tax measure can pursue a particular policy aim in a chosen manner.

On the one hand, the non-discrimination provisions of Article 24 pursue objectives that have a policy background by prohibiting tax discrimination in certain precise circumstances. On the other hand, the result of the non-discrimination analysis under Article 24 necessarily has an impact on whether domestic tax measures may succeed in

---

1571. 2008–2017 OECD Commentary on Article 24, para. 1.

1572. *See* Raad 1986, 77, who comments on Article 24(1) that more burdensome tax treatment 'need not be intended to discriminate against foreign nationals. It is only the effect that counts. Domestic economic and social motives cannot compensate for such effect'. *See also*, similarly, Vogel 1997 Article 24, m.no. 37a ('[t]he purpose of the discriminatory tax treatment is irrelevant'); Vogel 1970, 350; Debatin 1970, 132; moreover, Bammens 2012, 140, who also states, however, that '[i]t is possible that this aim [of a provision] could be important when assessing whether certain characteristics are relevant in the comparability analysis'.

their policy goals although, in many cases, it leaves domestic policy interests unaffected. Article 24 lays down specific comparability requirements, focuses on selected situations involving foreigners or non-residents, and prescribes a closed list of exceptions with regard to personal circumstances and non-arm's-length payments. Arguably, it thereby solves all issues of comparability without taking account of domestic policy interests and without leaving room for different judgments depending on what objectives a scrutinized measure pursues. In that way, Article 24 itself establishes a definite, appropriate, and clear balance between competing policy interests and ensures a uniform interpretation by different interpreters, decision-makers, or courts.

However, previous parts of this study have demonstrated that Article 24 is not always easy to apply; the wording of the non-discrimination provisions does not always provide clear and straightforward solutions. This raises the question of whether policy considerations should play a more prominent role in the non-discrimination analysis. Instead of assuming that the non-discrimination provisions of Article 24 distinguish between justified and unjustified differences in tax treatment by providing unambiguous comparability requirements and by requiring that comparability be assessed in a mechanical way, this distinction could be sought through a substantive analysis, namely, by openly considering potential reasons for different tax treatment from a domestic perspective and by judging on their legitimacy from a tax treaty perspective. This does not mean that an interpreter, decision-maker, or court would be allowed to decide completely freely on cases of discrimination under Article 24 or be able to introduce personal value judgments. On the contrary, precisely what distinctions should be viewed as legitimate or lead to prohibited tax discrimination would remain a matter of interpretation guided by all relevant means of interpretation. If the wording of Article 24 is not perfectly clear and leaves open whether discrimination exists in a particular case, it appears indispensable to enquire into the policy background of the non-discrimination provisions and the tax treaty as a whole, that is deeper into the intended balance between legitimate distinctions and unjustified discrimination, instead of rendering decisions solely on the basis of a supposedly simple comparability test. Thus, this intended balance is not necessarily between the objective achieved by the discrimination and the disadvantages suffered by the taxpayer therefrom;[1573] it is between the objective pursued by the domestic tax measure under scrutiny and the objective pursued by the particular non-discrimination provision. It is a balance that the allegedly discriminating State is legally obligated to achieve and that cannot always be reached in a formal manner or without policy considerations.

[B] Reasons for No Separate Justification Analysis

Questions of comparability may overlap with questions of treatment that is less favourable and with questions of justification. As no predetermined or universally

1573. *See* Rust 2015b m.nos. 4, 132; Rust 2010, 648; similarly, Bammens 2016, 111.

accepted delineation exists between a comparability analysis, a less favourable treatment analysis, and a justification analysis, policy arguments can potentially be evaluated and balanced against each other at all of these stages of examination.[1574] Whether they succeed in justifying different treatment by influencing comparability or less favourable treatment or by constituting separate grounds of justification depends on each individual non-discrimination provision. Reaching an appropriate balance between legitimate distinctions and unjustified discrimination, therefore, is not solely a matter of justifications as it may be a matter of comparability as well.

Initially, Article 24 could be open to complex balancing decisions and an open-ended outcome regardless of whether the non-discrimination analysis is limited to comparability and less favourable treatment or allows for justifications. Without taking a closer look at the wording, context, and purpose of each non-discrimination provision, comparability could be interpreted broadly and denied only if legitimate domestic policy purposes render situations incomparable, thereby justifying different tax treatment at the level of comparability, or a separate justification analysis could be introduced. If comparability is to be understood more strictly or if justifications are to be rejected, there must be an explanation for this.

There is no reason to believe that if non-discrimination clauses explicitly list all protected characteristics that should be treated neutrally without mentioning any justifications, they offer no room for discussion about unwritten justifications or that they must necessarily involve a strict comparability standard.[1575] Article 24 of the

---

1574. *See also* Bammens 2012, 990–991, who admits that justification grounds can generally also be phrased in terms of comparability and that both comparability and justification arguments may relate to the purpose of the domestic measure at issue; Hohenwarter 2010, 181–182, who emphasizes that the reasons for a denial of comparability or for a limitation of the scope of Article 24 are predominantly considered as a matter of justification under EU law; Staringer and Schneeweiss 2007, 238; moreover, with regard to EU law, Vanistendael 2016, 230; Wattel 2016 ('the Court ... routinely mixes up objective (non)comparability and justification grounds'; '[t]he same grounds ... is thus sometimes labelled as "incomparability" and sometimes as "justification"'); Wattel 2015; Hohenwarter and Weninger 2006, 243, 256, 264; Lang 2005a, 369 ('die auf der Vergleichbarkeits- und auf der Rechtfertigungsebene zu prüfenden Aspekte [sind] weitgehend austauschbar'); Cordewener 2002, 163–166, 483, 673 ('Vergleichbarkeits- und Rechtfertigungstest ... [sind] die zwei perspektivisch entgegengesetzten Ausgangspunkte ein und derselben rechtlichen Prüfung'; '[sind] untrennbar miteinander verbunden ... und [gehen] fließend ineinander über'; 'für den Ausgang der Diskriminierungsprüfung letztlich irrelevant'); Lang 1996, 37; similarly but critically, Toifl 2003, 174–175. *See also*, however, Haslehner 2009, 275, who argues that, even though a denial of comparability and an approval of a justification may lead to same results, a difference between these steps of analysis lies in the fact that justifications demand considerations of proportionality, notably, by weighing and balancing competing policy interests; differently, Wattel 2016, 274, 281–282; Wattel 2015, 550, 553.

1575. *See*, differently, Raad 1995, 192, who argues that the non-discrimination rules of Article 24 generally prohibit differential treatment on the basis of a protected attribute and are thus simple and absolute; when the conditions laid down in these rules are met, States should apply them without restriction. *See*, moreover, Raad 1986, 7–15: 'Discrimination' nowadays implies less favourable treatment, the grounds for which are unreasonable, arbitrary, or irrelevant (p. 8). Whether a distinction is unreasonable, arbitrary, or irrelevant is a matter of subjective judgment (pp. 8–9). An 'open' approach to non-discrimination which, for instance, plainly forbids 'discrimination' without listing forbidden grounds for differential treatment requires courts to determine whether the use of a given fact or circumstance as the basis for differential treatment amounts to discrimination (pp. 9, 14). By contrast, when forbidden

OECD Model is often compared to the general non-discrimination clause of Article 18 of the Treaty on the Functioning of the European Union (TFEU) ('any discrimination on grounds of nationality shall be prohibited') as well as to the EU fundamental freedoms that substantiate the general non-discrimination clause.[1576] In particular, both Article 24(1) of the OECD Model and Article 18 of the TFEU explicitly prohibit discrimination on grounds of nationality, but Article 18 of the TFEU has a much broader scope. It also covers different treatment of residents and non-residents as indirect discrimination on the basis of nationality,[1577] whereas Article 24(1) is restricted to cases of direct discrimination. At the same time, justifications play a vital role under Article 18 of the TFEU,[1578] whereas the tax treaty non-discrimination clauses of Article 24 are absolute and do not allow for any implicit or unwritten justifications. A strict comparability standard and a rejection of justifications cannot be solely based on the fact that Article 24(1) of the OECD Model specifically refers to the protected characteristic of nationality without providing for any exceptions.[1579]

It is fair to say, however, that these non-discrimination provisions are embedded in two very different legal contexts and that important differences in the purposes of the OECD Model and the EU framework warrant independent interpretation and different scopes.[1580] A bilateral tax treaty aims at a very different level of integration when compared to the EU framework. Accordingly, the different functions of the non-discrimination provisions must be considered.[1581] Non-discrimination is a cornerstone of the EU's internal market concept to guarantee the free movement of people, goods, services, and capital. This justifies a broad interpretation of the EU non-discrimination rules.[1582] By contrast, Article 24 of the OECD Model contains special rules that are not necessary for achieving the primary treaty objectives of eliminating double taxation and preventing tax evasion and do not aim to contribute to the creation of a highly integrated market. This argues, together with other means of interpretation (*see* Chapter 3 section §3.03), in favour of a more narrow interpretation of Article 24 and in particular of the nationality non-discrimination clause.[1583]

---

grounds for differential treatment are specifically (and exhaustively) spelled out in the law, personal judgment is eliminated (pp. 9–10). Differential treatment based on the forbidden grounds that are specifically mentioned constitutes discrimination per se, or, conversely, differential treatment is permitted unless it is based on a designated 'forbidden ground' (p. 10). Since non-discrimination clauses drafted according to Article 24 of the OECD Model never blankly prescribe non-discrimination but always list the circumstances which, for tax purposes, should be treated neutrally, they offer no room for discussion of whether a given type of differential treatment violates any – unwritten – legal (or moral) principle (p. 15).

1576. *See*, for example, Bammens and Vanistendael 2017, sec. 5; Vanistendael 2016; Bammens 2016; Bammens 2012, 1013–1034; Garrido 2009; Staringer and Schneeweiss 2007; Raad 2005.

1577. *See*, for instance, CJEU, 8 May 1990, C-175/88, *Biehl*.

1578. *Ibid*. For a detailed analysis of indirect discrimination under EU law, *see also* Tobler 2005.

1579. *See also*, to this effect, Hohenwarter 2010, 180–181; Hohenwarter and Weninger 2006, 254–255; Schilcher and Stefaner 2006, 161; Toifl 2003, 279.

1580. *See also*, to this effect, Mason 2010, 136–137; moreover, Vanistendael 2010, 190; Garrido 2009, 169, 174; Hahn 2005, 526.

1581. Rust 2015b m.no. 16; Rust 2015c m.no. 18.

1582. Rust 2015b m.no. 16; Rust 2015c m.no. 18; Lang and Loukota 2003, 69.

1583. Vanistendael 2016, 241, 253–254; Rust 2015b m.no. 16; Rust 2015c m.no. 18; Vogel 1997 Article 24, m.no. 5e; similarly, Haslehner 2016a m.no. 9; Lang and Loukota 2003, 69; critically

If a narrow scope of Article 24 is intended, justifications could narrow down the scope of Article 24 even further. In particular, discrimination could be justified for reasons that cannot be pinned down to relevant differences in legal or factual circumstances.[1584] Although justifications are often introduced as a second step in the field of constitutional and EU law after broadening the scope of fundamental rights in order to limit the applicability of those rights,[1585] in the field of tax treaty law, justifications could also be introduced in addition to a strict comparability standard. Thus, it is not clear why justifications should necessarily imply or presuppose a more lenient or relaxed comparability standard.[1586]

Justifications may be regarded as implying value judgments. If a value judgment is understood as a judgment about the rightness or wrongness of certain treatment by balancing different policy purposes or interests, it requires a particular set of values on which to rely. Nevertheless, value judgments are not arbitrary decisions that should be avoided whenever possible. They can also be made on the basis of values that are inherent in a legal system.[1587] When looking at the wording, the object and purpose as well as the context of all of the relevant laws and regulations including but not limited to the allegedly discriminatory measure and the non-discrimination provisions, it can be determined which aims these laws and regulations pursue, which values they involve, and which policy interests they bring or represent. In order to decide on whether discrimination is justified, it might be necessary to weigh different and possibly conflicting policy interests against each other. This may be a difficult task that

Toifl 2003, 305. Niels Bammens notes, however, that the non-discrimination clauses of Article 24 also pursue similar goals as the EU fundamental freedoms, namely, to remove discriminatory obstacles to trade in order to ensure equal conditions of competition and advance economic development. It is incorrect to assume that a tax treaty is merely intended to remove double taxation. *See* Bammens 2016, 110–111, 125; Bammens 2012, 6, 1013, 1028. While it is true that the non-discrimination clauses of Article 24 and the EU fundamental freedoms have certain goals in common and that a tax treaty is not merely intended to remove double taxation, there still exist many differences in particular with regard to the level of integration which arguably imply different approaches to non-discrimination.

1584. *See also* Rust 2015b m.no. 132, who mentions that a strict interpretation of Article 24 according to which a distinction on the basis of the prohibited criterion automatically leads to a violation of the non-discrimination provision may certainly deprive courts of the necessary flexibility as there may be good reasons to discriminate in some situations; similarly, Avery Jones, Depret, et al. 1991b, 345, who observe that Article 24 may be felt to be too inflexible in not recognizing so-called valid reasons for what would appear to be discriminatory tax provisions that are designed to preserve the integrity of the tax system.

1585. Rust 2015b m.no. 131. *See also* Schön 2006, 17 ('mit einer Ausweitung des Normbereichs der [EU-]Diskriminierungsverbote [geht] stets auch eine Ausweitung der Rechtfertigungsmöglichkeiten für Ungleichbehandlungen einher').

1586. However, *see also* Haslehner 2009, 293, who mentions that the scope of the non-discrimination provisions of Article 24 is very narrow and limited to specific cases of different treatment, which appears to speak against a further limitation through justifications and that the introduction of unwritten justifications under Article 24 would virtually require a broad scope of protection of the non-discrimination provisions; moreover, Haslehner 2016c, 6–7 ('[a]s a flipside to this narrow scope, article 24 allows no escapes ... via "reasonable justifications"').

1587. *See*, to this effect, Pöschl 2008, 186–189, 310; Korinek and Holoubek 1999, 44–45; ('the criteria for objective justification ... must be derived from the legal system itself which has codified the relevant values'); Korinek and Holoubek 1991, 84–85; Antoniolli 1956, 647.

requires complex decisions and may leave room for discretion and different results, but it does not make value judgments extraordinary, arbitrary, or an intuitive feeling of an interpreter, decision-maker, or court. Value judgments may allow for flexibility and discretion when reaching decisions about an appropriate balance between competing interests and purposes, but such a balance within a legal framework is not a purely subjective matter or a matter of personal opinion. If certain arguments or policy interests are particularly strong and tip the balance in favour of or against discrimination, they should be able to do so regardless of which court has to render a decision in a particular case.

Therefore, there is no reason to be overly worried about disagreement between different courts, at least not more than with regard to other tax treaty provisions. It is true that no world tax court exists that could be responsible for interpreting all bilateral tax treaty provisions and thereby ensure a common interpretation of Article 24.[1588] It is true that balancing decisions between competing policy interests often involve flexibility and discretion and need not be predetermined or automatically established. Nevertheless, interpreting non-discrimination provisions and reaching balanced results about discrimination need not be a different task than interpreting allocation rules or any other rules of a tax treaty. A single provision in itself may entail various policy considerations that have led to its particular but not always clear wording. Deciding on a meaning of a tax treaty provision may, therefore, involve a balancing decision between various arguments and means of interpretation. Articles 31 to 33 of the VCLT provide rules of interpretation, but these rules do not prescribe which arguments or means of interpretation should prevail over others and, therefore, leave some room for different judgments. It may be said that an interpreter, decision-maker, or court renders a value judgment when interpreting the law. Indeed, the same terms of a tax treaty have sometimes been interpreted differently by different courts despite the fact that, in principle, they should have been interpreted the same.[1589] Also, in situations when the wording is open to more than one meaning, the OECD Commentary as it is worded when a tax treaty is concluded may disclose a common intention of the Contracting States or tip the balance, particularly if its reasoning does not contradict other means of

1588. *See* Rust 2015b m.no. 4.

1589. For instance, the meaning of the term 'beneficial owner' has been subject to controversy and was understood differently by different courts. *See*, in detail, Lang et al. 2013. This disagreement arguably has its roots in policy questions: to what extent should tax treaty benefits be granted in situations which might be regarded as tax avoidance, to what extent should an interposed taxpayer be able to rely on tax treaty benefits, to what extent should domestic decisions on the allocation of income to a particular person govern the meaning of 'beneficial owner', etc. Apparently, the questions of what constitutes tax avoidance for the purposes of a tax treaty, to what extent the term 'beneficial owner' is intended to cover such situations, and to what extent a mere reference to an allocation of income under domestic tax law is made with the term 'beneficial owner' involves complex legal questions which cannot be answered out of the box. Various views may be taken in this respect and, accordingly, different understandings of 'beneficial owner' have emerged. Moreover, different means of interpretation may point in different directions and support one or another meaning. Interpretation is not an automatism and as subjective (or objective) as justifications can be.

interpretation. Which justifications could be accepted under Article 24 remains somewhat ambiguous, but the OECD Commentary could provide guidance just as it provides guidance on comparability.[1590]

A complete denial of justifications under Article 24, therefore, is not necessarily convincing. If a narrow scope of Article 24 is intended, this speaks rather for and not against justifications. Although justifications may require complex balancing decisions between competing policy interests, these decisions are far from being arbitrary. In addition, there are various ways of securing a common understanding of Article 24 even if justifications were accepted. Justifications need not pose problems that are unknown to other treaty provisions and conventions. Giving tax treaty terms a concrete meaning often requires balancing decisions between different and potentially competing arguments that, in practice, lead to different results being reached by different interpreters, decision-makers, or courts. Finally, comparability issues may also involve difficult balancing decisions and interpretation problems. Value judgments, therefore, are not avoided with a rejection of justifications.

Nevertheless, concerns about conflicting value judgments, disagreement, and uncertainty might have influenced the drafting of Article 24 and contributed to precise comparability requirements. An in-depth analysis of the specific aims of the non-discrimination provisions as well as of their wording and context reveals that a narrow scope of Article 24 and in particular of the nationality non-discrimination provision was indeed intended (*see* Chapter 3 section §3.03) and, therefore, speaks for a rather strict comparability standard. Article 24 contains precisely drafted non-discrimination clauses that deliberately cover a limited number of discriminatory situations. A strict comparability standard regards most differences in circumstances as relevant and provides broad policy space for domestic tax measures as long as domestic policy interests are pursued without too closely or directly relying on a protected attribute. It thereby contributes to a narrow scope of Article 24.

[C] Potential Justifications Prevent Comparability

Since the scope of Article 24 is so narrowly defined, the need for safety valves (i.e., justification grounds) is not quite as pressing.[1591] Potential justifications are considered as an issue of comparability and succeed in preventing discrimination as long as they are reflected in relevant differences in legal or factual circumstances. Put another way,

1590. *See*, to this effect, Avery Jones, Depret, et al. 1991b, 347 (but the authors also consider that if a list of exceptions to the wording of the OECD Model would be included in the OECD Commentary to deal with the more obvious points, this would only be a limited solution); moreover, Bammens 2012, 1029, who puts the difference between the tax treaty non-discrimination provisions and the EU fundamental freedoms (which are uniformly interpreted by the CJEU) into perspective by pointing out that the OECD aspires to ensure that tax treaties worldwide follow the template of the OECD Model, resulting in a network of identical treaties that are all interpreted in accordance with the OECD Commentary.

1591. Bammens 2016, 99; Bammens 2012, 1015; similarly, Bruns 2013 m.no. 10.

differences in circumstances that could amount to a separate justification[1592] or to an indirect reference to a protected characteristic prevent comparability. If, for instance, differences in residence prevent comparability under Article 24(1), distinctions based on residence do not lead to discrimination because of nationality. No separate justifications are needed for such tax distinctions.[1593] There is no need to consider under Article 24(1) that the residence State might be in a better position to take into account personal and family circumstances of its residents or that the source State might encounter problems when enforcing its taxing rights and, therefore, might have good reasons for levying withholding tax only on non-residents; differences in residence as well as connected differences in a State's position to take into account personal and family circumstances[1594] and to enforce its tax claims[1595] prevent comparability. A potential justification cannot be accepted under Article 24 only if it bears no relationship to differences in circumstances. It is consequently not possible to freely balance a Contracting State's policy interests against the aim of preventing tax discrimination. Article 24 has already predetermined an appropriate balance by imposing strict comparability requirements.

Comparability takes the role of a separate justification analysis.[1596] Whether certain circumstances in law or in fact are relevant for comparability purposes is a question of whether differences in these circumstances justify different treatment from a tax treaty perspective. Werner Haslehner admits that the choice of the appropriate comparator generally presupposes a value judgment but counters that this judgment is instructed and guided by the explicit requirements of the wording of the non-discrimination provisions.[1597] Indeed, the wording of the non-discrimination provisions of Article 24 provides important guidance and imposes specific comparability requirements. No room for other value judgments remains. Nevertheless, the wording is not in all cases clear. For example, in cases when protected and unprotected characteristics overlap, it may be ambiguous which value judgments Article 24 incorporates with its comparability requirements, where the equilibrium between legitimate and unjustified tax distinctions lies and which distinctions, therefore, should be viewed as legitimate.

1592. *See also* Peters and Snellaars 2001, 13, who hold that, in general, a justification for different treatment can be found either in a difference in factual circumstances or in the legitimate aim of the rule under scrutiny.
1593. *See*, to this effect, Bruns 2013 m.no. 10.
1594. In C-279/93, *Schumacker*, the CJEU employed similar arguments to argue that residents and non-residents are not, as a rule, in a comparable situation. *See* CJEU, 14 February 1995, C-279/93, *Schumacker*, paras 31–34. The second sentence of Article 24(3) that provides an exception from non-discrimination obligations is based on such arguments. Arguably, non-residents and residents are in a comparable situation as far as a PE is concerned, but less favourable treatment is justified (*see* section §4.01[D]).
1595. In C-290/04, *Scorpio*, the CJEU decided that a withholding tax only for non-residents is justified by the need to ensure the effective collection of tax. *See* CJEU, 3 October 2006, C-290/04, *Scorpio*, paras 35–36. *See also*, however, CJEU, 22 December 2008, C-282/07, *Truck Center*, in which the CJEU considered similar arguments as an issue of comparability; critically De Broe and Bammens 2009.
1596. *See also* Schön 2006, 17.
1597. Haslehner 2009, 294–295. *See also* Dommes and Metzler 2006, 126.

In such cases, different arguments for and against a particular result must be evaluated and balanced against each other at the level of comparability. Questions of comparability, therefore, may involve complex legal questions that cannot be answered in a mechanical way but, instead, require value judgments.[1598] It must be decided whether certain differences in circumstances that are linked to a protected characteristic are relevant and render persons or situations incomparable and thus whether these differences justify different tax treatment. If a separate analysis of justifications is denied under Article 24, this does not always allow establishing discrimination by merely looking at the 'clear' wording of the provisions at issue or by relying on an automated non-discrimination test. Also and perhaps most important, arguments should not be disregarded just because they are considered to be 'justifications' for some undisclosed reason.[1599] Almost every argument that is labelled as a 'justification' can just as well influence comparability by establishing relevant differences in legal or factual circumstances, and vice versa. Therefore, while arguments are sometimes wrongly rejected under Article 24 because of their supposed classification as 'justifications', it is conversely argued that, under EU law, many justifications in tax matters are, in fact, an issue of comparability and establish relevant differences in circumstances.[1600] Finally, while Article 24 is subject to an autonomous interpretation based on Articles 31 to 33 of the VCLT without being influenced by domestic concepts of non-discrimination, this does not prevent a so defined concept of non-discrimination to take account of domestic objectives and to consider whether these objectives, if reflected in differences in circumstances, may be brought into balance with the principal aim of preventing tax discrimination because of nationality or residence.[1601] A main reason for rejecting justifications and focusing on comparability, a 'fear' of value judgments, does not leave Article 24 with a value-free analysis.

[D] Wording Provides for Specific Justifications

A strict comparability standard under Article 24 does not completely eliminate a need for further guidance as to which differences in tax treatment should be regarded as legitimate. Some non-discrimination clauses explicitly authorize distinctions that are directly based on a protected characteristic thereby allowing the Contracting States to

1598. *See also*, for instance, Fredman 2011, 168 ('the choice of comparator itself requires a value judgment as to which aspects of the comparator are relevant and which irrelevant'); Toifl 1996, 152, 179–180; moreover, regarding the Austrian equal treatment principle, Korinek and Holoubek 1999, 44 ('even the identification of comparable issues requires value judgments'); Korinek and Holoubek 1991, 83; Gassner 1970, 4–5.

1599. *See*, differently, Haslehner 2016a m.no. 62; Bammens 2012, 253–254 ('[this] constitutes a justification argument'; '[a]rguments of this kind have no place under article 24'); Tumpel and Stangl 2006, 87.

1600. *See*, for instance, Lyal 2003, 74 ('in each case where the Court ... has then gone on to examine the possibility of objective justification under a rule of reason, the discussion returns to what is in reality an examination of the comparability of situations'; '[t]hose [rule of reason] justifications amount in practice to grounds for the conclusion that there is an objective, relevant difference between the domestic and the trans-frontier situation'); moreover, in detail, Wattel 2016; Wattel 2015.

1601. *See*, differently, Haslehner 2009, 277.

pursue specific policy aims and ensuring an appropriate balance between legitimate and unjustified tax distinctions. It is actually even argued that, since Article 24 explicitly permits certain otherwise discriminatory tax distinctions, no other implicit or unwritten justifications should be allowed.[1602]

The second sentence of Article 24(3) expressly permits discrimination against non-residents for specific policy reasons (*see* Chapter 3 section §3.03[D][2]):

> This provision shall not be construed as obliging a Contracting State to grant to residents of the other Contracting State any personal allowances, reliefs and reductions for taxation purposes on account of civil status or family responsibilities which it grants to its own residents.

It is not clear, however, whether this sentence is merely declaratory in nature or rather constitutes an exception to the non-discrimination obligations:

- On the one hand, the first sentence of Article 24(3) can be understood as being strictly focused on PEs. Therefore, it does not extend to personal allowances, reliefs, and reductions on account of civil status or family responsibilities. Such benefits arguably have no sufficient connection to the activities carried on through a PE in the source State. Because of this limited scope, it cannot be said that PEs of non-resident enterprises are comparable to resident enterprises with regard to personal circumstances. The second sentence of Article 24(3) merely confirms this interpretation which can already be derived from the first sentence. It constitutes a clarification that removes any doubt.[1603]
- On the other hand, while personal tax benefits might be viewed as bearing a closer connection to a taxpayer's overall ability to pay tax or to certain personal circumstances (childcare, sickness, exceptional burdens, etc.) than to a particular State or source of income or capital,[1604] they are nevertheless intended to be deducted from or calculated on the basis of the tax payable or the income or capital subject to tax in a State. This relationship between personal circumstances and taxation could suffice for establishing comparability between resident and non-resident enterprises under the first sentence of Article 24(3) as far as PEs are concerned. A PE non-discrimination clause could, therefore, require at least a partial extension of personal tax benefits.[1605] In that case, the second sentence of Article 24(3) can be seen as offering the source State a defence to uphold its different and, in principle, discriminatory tax treatment based on residence. It thus limits the scope of the first sentence

1602. *See*, to this effect, Rust 2004, 396; moreover, Haslehner 2009, 278, 293.
1603. *See*, for instance, Bammens and Vanistendael 2016, sec. 2.3.4, who believe that 'this reservation [Article 24(3), second sentence] seems redundant, as only enterprises are entitled to protection under the provision, and as it applies only to the taxation of the PE itself'; critically Haslehner 2009, 268–269.
1604. *See*, for instance, Wattel 2000, 214.
1605. *See*, to this effect, Haslehner 2016a m.no. 27; Haslehner 2009, 268–269. By contrast, the CJEU decided in C-279/93, *Schumacker* that the source State is not obligated to consider a non-resident's personal circumstances because residents and non-residents are not in a comparable situation, but exceptions apply if that taxpayer's personal circumstances cannot be considered in the residence State; critically, for instance, Lang 2005c; Avery Jones 1996.

> which would cover all kinds of discrimination. Without this express limitation, the source State would arguably discriminate against non-resident enterprises if it did not consider personal circumstances like with resident enterprises.[1606]

Taking an obligation to tax PEs of non-resident enterprises no less favourably than comparable resident enterprises as a reference point, a State is not bound by this obligation if an exception exists or if a violation of this obligation is justified. The second sentence of Article 24(3), therefore, can be viewed as such an exception or justification.[1607] It allows for a deviation from the general non-discrimination obligations of the first sentence of Article 24(3) regarding PEs. Yet, the policy aims pursued by the second sentence can just as well be considered as an issue of comparability. Arguably, relevant differences in circumstances between resident and non-resident enterprises exist insofar as personal tax benefits are concerned. For various reasons that are reflected in legal and factual circumstances, the residence State is in a better position than any other State to consider the personal circumstances of its taxpayers[1608] and thus residents and non-residents are never comparable in this respect. In addition, a PE of a non-resident enterprise would not be comparable to a resident enterprise if, unlike that resident enterprise in a purely domestic situation, it is able to obtain personal allowances and benefits twice.[1609] Comparability could thus be denied to the extent that the residence State of the non-resident enterprise already grants such benefits in relation to the profits that are attributable to the PE in the source State. With this approach to comparability, the first sentence of Article 24(3) would achieve the intended results.

If the first sentence of Article 24(3) contained a 'perfect' comparability test, there would be no need for the second sentence. Apparently, however, the first sentence could also be understood as an obligation to proportionately consider personal circumstances in the source State through personal allowances, reliefs, and reductions on account of civil status or family responsibilities irrespective of whether these benefits are thereby granted twice. The second sentence of Article 24(3) prevents this result. It thereby confirms that comparability is not always straightforward, that not all questions of comparability can be solved with simple comparability requirements, and that sometimes express statements are needed to establish without a doubt what distinctions are justified from a tax treaty perspective. Whether this second sentence is an express clarification, limitation, exclusion, exception, or justification, it remains a provision that allows distinguishing between resident and non-resident enterprises in

1606. *See*, to this effect, Vogel 1970, 350, who describes the permission of the second sentence as a derogation from the rule of the first sentence; Haslehner 2016a m.no. 27; Haslehner 2009, 267–269, 274, 281–282, 293, sees the effect of the second sentence as a limitation of the scope of protection which has a constitutive effect; Vanistendael 2016, 232, comments that Article 24(3) approaches the taxation of income of resident and non-resident individuals as being comparable, although it makes an exception for certain personal tax benefits.

1607. *See also* Hohenwarter and Weninger 2006, 256, who comments that the second sentence of Article 24(3) contains a de facto justification; similarly, Moritz 2003, 239.

1608. 2005–2017 OECD Commentary on Article 18, para. 1.

1609. 2008–2017 OECD Commentary on Article 24, para. 36 (1977: para. 24; 1992–2005: para. 22).

order to reach specific policy goals. Such tax distinctions are justified from a tax treaty perspective.

Other provisions of Article 24 also contain limitations. The first sentence of Article 24(4) explicitly excludes non-arm's-length payments from its non-discrimination obligations regarding deduction of payments. 'Except where the provisions of paragraph 1 of Article 9, paragraph 6 of Article 11, or paragraph 4 of Article 12, apply', disbursements paid by an enterprise of a resident to a non-resident must be deductible under the same conditions as if they had been paid to a resident. It can be said that Article 24(4) does not cover such non-arm's-length payments or that discriminatory treatment of these payments is excluded from the non-discrimination obligations and thereby justified.[1610] In the end, non-arm's-length payments can be treated differently, and the Contracting States are thus permitted to apply their complex transfer pricing or similar profit adjustment rules only in cross-border situations[1611] (*see also* section §4.04[A][4]). Instead of relying on the argument that non-arm's-length payments made to non-residents are not comparable to such payments made to residents due to the different legal circumstances that they trigger in cross-border situations (*see* section §4.04[A][5]), Article 24(4) explicitly settles this issue.

Article 24 excludes certain areas of taxation from the scope of its non-discrimination provisions for specific policy reasons. Whether these exceptions are included in a separate sentence, paragraph, or article and are titled as 'exceptions' or 'justifications' appear to be matters of legal technique. Whether these exceptions are viewed as limiting the substantive scope of non-discrimination obligations or as justifying discriminatory treatment or whether they merely clarify and provide guidance as to which differences in circumstances should be relevant is a different way of expressing the same result: the non-discrimination obligations do not prevent a State from treating certain protected persons differently. In that way, a balance between the objective of eliminating tax discrimination between residents and non-residents and the objective of providing personal tax benefits only to residents or allowing special treatment of non-arm's-length payments is established. It is sometimes justified to treat residents and non-residents differently.

[E] OECD Commentary Mentions Justifications

Not only does the wording of Article 24 provide for certain exceptions that could be an issue of comparability. The OECD Commentary also deals with borderline cases of discrimination and phrases questions of comparability in terms of justifications.[1612] In cases when comparability is difficult to establish, the OECD Commentary discusses

1610. *See also* Bammens 2016, 103, 110; Bammens 2012, 1021, 1033, who regards the arm's-length standard as one of the few examples of actual justification grounds under Article 24; moreover, L. Hinnekens and Hinnekens 2008, 33, 40, who state that Article 24(4) provides for a justification for discriminatory measures.

1611. Rust 2015b m.no. 92; Rust 2015c m.no. 138.

1612. *See also* Hohenwarter and Weninger 2006, 254–264.

various arguments for and against discrimination which could just as well be considered as separate justifications.

Under Article 24(1), a non-resident foreigner need not be comparable to a non-resident national. According to the OECD Commentary, Article 24(1) 'does not apply where a national of a Contracting State (State [B]) who is also a resident of State [B] is taxed less favourably in the other Contracting State (State [A]) than a national of State [A] residing in a third State (for instance, as a result of the application of provisions aimed at discouraging the use of tax havens) as the two persons are not in the same circumstances with respect to their residence'.[1613] Thus, from the perspective of State A which is allegedly discriminating against State B nationals, a State B national need not be comparable to a State A national even when both are subject to limited tax liability in State A, that is even when both are non-residents. State A may make distinctions not only between residents and non-residents but also between different non-residents.

At a first glance, it is not clear why a non-resident foreigner should not always be comparable to a non-resident national or why they should not necessarily be in the same circumstances, in particular with respect to residence. Both are non-residents from the perspective of the allegedly discriminating State and, arguably, this is the only thing that counts.[1614] However, the OECD Commentary implies that there might be good reasons to distinguish between non-residents, such as the aim of discouraging the use of tax havens.[1615] From the perspective of this specific objective, not only differences between residents and non-residents with respect to their full or limited tax liability but also differences between non-residents with respect to their tax jurisdiction are relevant for the purposes of the non-discrimination analysis. In other cases, however, when no objective of combating tax havens is involved, the OECD Commentary claims that even residence as such and, therefore – contrary to the wording[1616] – differences with respect to residence may be irrelevant under Article 24(1); resident nationals and non-resident foreigners may be in substantially similar circumstances both in law and in fact.[1617] It thus cannot be easily assumed that every difference in circumstances always or automatically prevents comparability nor that a difference in circumstances can always or automatically be disregarded if it is linked to a protected

1613. 2018–2017 OECD Commentary on Article 24, para. 8 (1994–2005: para. 4).

1614. *See* Bammens and Vanistendael 2016, secs. 2.1.3.1.1–2.1.3.1.2; Bammens 2012, 65–66.

1615. This is also admitted by Bammens and Vanistendael 2016, sec. 2.1.3.1.2; Bammens 2012, 65–66 ('it is possible that there are particular reasons to distinguish between different types of non-residents').

1616. Since 1992, Article 24(1) explicitly requires that the nationals of each Contracting State must be 'in the same circumstances, *in particular with respect to residence*' (emphasis added).

1617. 2008–2017 OECD Commentary on Article 24, para. 23, with an example of a payroll tax in which the fact that a national company will not have the same residence for tax treaty purposes as a foreign company 'has no relevance at all with respect to the different tax treatment under the payroll tax' (this example will be discussed in detail in section §4.03[A][2][e]). *See also* 2008–2017 OECD Commentary on Article 24, para. 18: 'Whilst residents and non-residents are usually not in the same circumstances for the purposes of paragraph 1, it is clear, however, that this is not the case where residence has no relevance whatsoever with respect to the different treatment under consideration.' *See* Haslehner 2016c, 10, who also remarks that, according to the OECD Commentary, even residence may

characteristic. Depending on the underlying objective of the domestic tax law, legal and factual differences relating to residence appear in a different light and have different legal relevance.

Also in the context of public bodies and services as well as in the context of private institutions not for profit that perform activities for the purposes of public benefit (non-profit organizations), the OECD Commentary frames its comparability analysis in terms of a justification. '[I]f a State accords immunity from taxation to its own public bodies and services, this is *justified* because such bodies and services are integral parts of the State and at no time can their circumstances be comparable to those of the public bodies and services of the other State' (emphasis added).[1618] Admittedly, the wording of the OECD Commentary indicates that, since there is no comparability, the distinctions in question are justified. It is more reasonable to assume, however, that comparability is denied since such distinctions are justified.[1619] Indeed, not all taxation privileges granted to public bodies and services are justified and prevent comparability. In the case of State corporations carrying on gainful undertakings 'to the extent that these can be regarded as being on the same footing as private business undertakings, the provisions of paragraph 1 will apply to them'[1620] and, therefore, comparability is at least partly possible.

In addition, the OECD Commentary states that 'if a State accords taxation privileges to certain private institutions not for profit, this is clearly *justified* by the very nature of these institutions' activities and by the benefit which that State and its nationals will derive from those activities' (emphasis added).[1621] Justifications are clearly spelled out, but the Commentary is silent about comparability. A private

potentially be an irrelevant factor in determining comparability under Article 24(1); moreover, Wiman 2013, 334–335, who observes that 'in the same circumstances, in particular with respect to residence' is not the same as saying that the compared persons must be residents of the same State.

1618. 2008–2017 OECD Commentary on Article 24, para. 12 (1977–2005: para. 7; 1963: para. 6). *See also* OEEC, FC/WP4(59)3, pp. 9–10, in which Working Party No. 4 of the OEEC Fiscal Committee commented that a State's own '[public] bodies and services can never be in comparable circumstances to those of the public bodies and services of another State: their position in relation to the State to which they belong is a unique one'; moreover, Lang 2006, 36–37; Avery Jones 2009, 34–36.

1619. *See* Wassermeyer and Schwenke 2016 m.no. 22, who remark that the OECD Commentary gives the false impression that justifications may remove discrimination although this is a question of meeting the conditions laid down in Article 24(1), a question which admittedly shows features of a justification analysis; Hohenwarter and Weninger 2006, 256–257, who, in principle, accept the OECD Commentary's arguments as a matter of comparability but emphasize that these arguments could just as well be considered as justifications; differently, Tumpel and Stangl 2006, 75, who regard the Commentary's arguments as an issue of justification and, therefore, suggest rejecting these arguments in the context of Article 24(3); but also Haslehner 2009, 282–283, who is critical about putting too much emphasis on the term 'justified' in this context.

1620. 2008–2017 OECD Commentary on Article 24, para. 12 (2000–2005: para. 7; similarly, 1977–1997: para. 7; 1963: para. 6).

1621. 2008–2017 OECD Commentary on Article 24, para. 13 (1977–2005: para. 8; 1963: para. 7). *See also* OEEC, FC/WP4(59)3, p. 10, in which Working Party No. 4 of the OEEC Fiscal Committee stated that private institutions not for profit 'have a unique position in relation to the State to which they belong, since the taxation privileges are accorded them ... because their activities are performed for purposes of public benefit which are specific to that State'.

institution not for profit is not comparable to a private institution for profit only by implication, and a private institution not for profit that conducts activities for the benefit of the State in question is not comparable to a private institution not for profit that conducts activities for the benefit of another State.[1622]

On the issue of whether Article 24(3) obligates the source State to extend special treatment of dividends received in respect of holdings owned by PEs (*see also* section §4.04[E][2]), the OECD Commentary states that opinions differ and brings forward several policy arguments for and against an extension[1623] all of which can be traced back to conflicting views about the scope of Article 24(3) that arose when the 1977 OECD Model was drafted.[1624] States that consider that assimilating PEs to their own enterprises does not entail any obligation to accord such special treatment to PEs

1622. *See* Bammens 2012, 1032, who states that this seems to be justification grounds but, in reality, it is an aspect of the comparability test; and Bammens 2012, 169–174, wherein he criticizes the OECD Commentary for mentioning grounds for a justification and confusing the important steps of comparability and justification. *See*, moreover, Bammens 2016, 108–109 ('it seems that the lack of information as regards non-residents ... may constitute a justification ground'); Hohenwarter and Weninger 2006, 257–258.

1623. 2008–2017 OECD Commentary on Article 24, paras 48–54 (1992–2005: paras 29–35; 1977: paras 31–37).

1624. *See* OECD, FC/WP4(71)1, pp. 17–19 (the Rapporteur of Working Party No. 4 addressed this issue and was rather inclined to think that benefits should be granted to PEs); OECD, DAF/FC/71.6, p. 3 (the Delegate for the United Kingdom desired a new provision to be added to Article 24(3) so that dividends paid by a resident subsidiary to a non-resident parent company could not escape taxation in the subsidiary's State; the Delegates for Luxembourg and the Netherlands basically shared the view of the Rapporteur); OECD, CFA/WP1(71)1, p. 3 (Working Group No. 4, which succeeded Working Party No. 4, included the proposal of the Delegate for the United Kingdom in Article 24 and omitted dealing with relief from economic double taxation in the Commentary); OECD, DAF/CFA/WP1/71.3, p. 2 (the Delegate for Belgium pointed to this omission and considered that any alleviations for dividends should be equally applied to a PE; the Delegates for France, the Netherlands, Norway, Switzerland, and the United States shared this point of view; the Delegates for Austria, Finland, Germany, and Turkey considered this interpretation to be incorrect; the Delegate for the United Kingdom explained the objective of its proposal); OECD, DAF/CFA/WP1/71.10, pp. 4–6 (Working Group No. 4, as instructed by Working Party No. 1, proposed a Commentary arguing in favour of relief from economic double taxation unless States 'clarify' otherwise in their bilateral conventions); OECD, CFA/WP1(71)8, p. 1 (the Australian Delegation objected to an extension of tax relief on inter-corporate dividends under Article 24(3) as, in this way, dividend withholding tax on repatriated profits could be avoided if no compensatory tax liability, such as a 'branch profits tax', is applied); OECD, DAF/CFA/WP1/71.10(Add.1), pp. 1–2 (Working Group No. 4 additionally addressed risks of abuse by transferring holdings and Article 24's autonomous character and general scope in relation to other tax treaty provisions, notably, Article 10); OECD, DAF/CFA/WP1/72/3, p. 4 (as it was still impossible to reconcile the conflicting views, Working Party No. 1 asked Working Group No. 4 to prepare new texts taking account of certain considerations); OECD, CFA/WP1(72)8, pp. 7–9 (Working Group No. 4 proposed revised comments); OECD, DAF/CFA/WP1/73.2, p. 2 (the Delegation for the United Kingdom proposed to withdraw its suggestion for a new provision); OECD, DAF/CFA/2584, pp. 3–5 (the Rapporteur of Working Group No. 4 made various amendments following a meeting of the Steering Group); OECD, CFA/WP1(73)6, pp. 9–11 (Working Group No. 4 submitted its final report); OECD, DAF/CFA/WP1(73)8, pp. 4–5 (Working Party No. 1 adopted the new Commentary subject to an expansion of arguments in favour of relief from economic double taxation); OECD, DAF/CFA/WP1/73.11, pp. 1–2 (the Delegate for the Netherlands and the Rapporteur prepared expanded arguments in favour of relief); OECD, DAF/CFA/WP1/73.12, p. 1 and OECD, DAF/CFA/WP1(73)13, p. 4 (Working Party No. 1 adopted this amendment).

'*justify* their position on various grounds' (emphasis added).[1625] It is necessary to decide whether a PE is comparable to domestic enterprises with respect to dividends that are received. This should be an easy and value-free task under a mechanical comparability test. Despite that, all arguments put forward in the OECD Commentary for and against comparability are policy arguments that relate to potential aims of the domestic tax measure under scrutiny:[1626] the aim of fully avoiding economic double taxation[1627] and the different interests in this aim;[1628] the aim of ensuring substance and single taxation;[1629] the aim of receiving compensation for a loss of tax revenue by taxing redistributed dividends;[1630] the aim of avoiding treatment that is more favourable for non-resident enterprises so that they do not receive benefits without fulfilling all required conditions;[1631] and the aim of not contributing to tax avoidance structures.[1632]

Lastly, Article 24(4) requires deductions to be made 'under the same conditions', but the OECD Commentary states that Article 24(4) 'does not prohibit additional information requirements with respect to payments made to non-residents'.[1633] When looking only at the wording, additional information requirements for a deduction do not constitute 'the same conditions'. Nevertheless, the OECD Commentary interprets 'the same conditions' more narrowly than the wording initially suggests and does so for a reason: 'since these requirements are intended to ensure similar levels of compliance and verification in the case of payments to residents and non-residents'.[1634] Similarly, the OECD Commentary states with regard to Article 24(5) that '[i]n the case of transfer pricing enquiries, ... additional information requirements which would be more stringent than the normal requirements, or even a reversal of the burden of proof, would not constitute discrimination within the meaning of the Article',[1635] even if such additional information requirements would only apply in cases involving non-resident shareholders.[1636]

1625. 2008–2017 OECD Commentary on Article 24, para. 50 (1992–2005: para. 31; 1977: para. 33).
1626. Tumpel and Stangl 2006, 87, therefore, reject these arguments as they arguably constitute justifications which, according to the prevailing opinion, are not available under Article 24.
1627. 2008–2017 OECD Commentary on Article 24, para. 49 (1992–2005: para. 30; 1977: para. 32).
1628. *Ibid.*, paras 50, 31 and 33, respectively.
1629. *Ibid.*, paras 49, 30 and 32, respectively.
1630. *Ibid.*, paras 50, 31 and 33, respectively.
1631. *Ibid.*, paras 50, 31 and 33, respectively.
1632. *Ibid.*, paras 50–41, 31–32 and 33–34, respectively.
1633. 2008–2017 OECD Commentary on Article 24, para. 75; differently, for instance, Haslehner 2009, 79; Arnold 1991, 39.
1634. *Ibid.*, para. 75. *See*, critically, Bammens 2013a, 159; Bammens 2012, 348–349, 359–360, 364, 1030–1032, who submits that this position is difficult to reconcile with the clear wording of Article 24(4), although he admits that differences in available information could be seen as an aspect of comparability which, in turn, raises the question of whether such differences arise only with non-residents and never with residents, that is whether they are inextricably linked to residence and, therefore, constitute justification grounds.
1635. 2008–2017 OECD Commentary on Article 24, para. 80 (1992–2005: para. 59).
1636. *See*, critically, Bammens 2012, 451–451; moreover, Burgstaller and Obermair 2006, 201, who suggest two explanations for this result: either there is no comparability or differences in treatment are justified; this illustrates that comparability and justification are largely interchangeable; to this effect, also Hohenwarter and Weninger 2006, 263. *See*, however, Haslehner 2016a m.no. 37, who argues that such additional information requirements usually apply

Since non-residents are located outside of the source State's territory and since it may, therefore, be more difficult or even impossible to obtain or verify information from non-residents, additional information requirements may aim at compensating for these difficulties that arguably do not arise with residents. According to the OECD Commentary, Article 24(4) and (5) takes account of these differences in legal and factual circumstances between residents and non-residents because these differences relate to justifiable intentions. It apparently does not matter that these differences in circumstances could be linked to residence and that distinctions based on residence are, in principle, prohibited under Article 24(4) and (5). Issues and concerns about the availability of information may lead to relevant differences in circumstances and may thus justify a denial of comparability even in cases when a distinction is directly based on a protected characteristic.

Overall, the OECD Commentary's statements demonstrate that it is, in principle, possible to solve issues of discrimination through comparability alone thereby rejecting a separate analysis of justifications. Under such an approach, however, arguments that some may label as 'justifications' continue to be relevant, notably, by influencing comparability. Although a strict comparability standard narrows down the scope of Article 24 and renders justifications largely superfluous, the non-discrimination analysis still determines which domestic policy aims may be pursued and which have to be abandoned due to their discriminatory effect. Article 24 thereby establishes a balance between legitimate and illegitimate or justified and unjustified tax distinctions. Although this balance is largely predetermined through the conditions of the non-discrimination provisions, the wording is far from being clear-cut. Article 24 apparently requires explicit clarifications, exceptions, or justifications with regard to specific policy purposes concerning personal tax benefits and non-arm's-length payments. Last, but not least, various differences in circumstances may be connected to nationality or residence and raise the question of whether they should be ignored. Therefore, it is no surprise that arguments that could just as well serve as separate justification grounds are discussed by the OECD Commentary as an issue of comparability.

§4.02 SUBSTANTIVE ANALYSIS OF DISCRIMINATION UNDER ARTICLE 24

This part will suggest a solution for many issues that arise under Article 24. It will first summarize the conceptual limitations of the traditional approach to non-discrimination under this article, an approach which basically consists in the application of a 'but for' test (section §4.02[A]). Such shortcomings are not necessarily a reason to abandon a 'but for' test, but they are a reason to seek refinements. It will be argued that a domestic legal technique should be irrelevant; whether a measure directly refers to a protected attribute or uses a substitute should not lead to different

in other cases involving associated enterprises as well and, therefore, the reason for different treatment is not the shareholder's residence but the potential profit shifting.

results (section §4.02[B]). Rather, a two-step approach may be applied to identify the reason for different tax treatment from a tax treaty perspective:

(1) First, a 'but for' test determines whether a change in the protected attribute leads to a change in tax treatment in a concrete case (section §4.02[C]). Prima facie discrimination exists if the domestic tax measure under scrutiny either refers to the protected characteristic or to a facially neutral attribute that is linked to the protected characteristic. At this stage, it does not matter how other cases are treated or whether there is a link between the facially neutral attribute and the protected characteristic in other cases as well.
(2) Second, a substantive analysis determines whether the reason for different tax treatment lies in the protected characteristic or in an inevitably linked but relevant attribute (section §4.02[D]). This analysis requires taking account of the reasons for different tax treatment from a domestic perspective, objectively identified by considering the design, scope, and effects of the domestic tax measure under scrutiny and by judging these purposes from a tax treaty perspective, that is by determining whether they are legitimate or unjustified in view of the objectives of the non-discrimination provisions.

[A] Conceptual Limitations of a 'But For' Test

Article 24 only prohibits discrimination on the basis of a protected characteristic. In the words of the OECD Commentary, this article prevents 'differences in tax treatment that are solely based on certain specific grounds'.[1637] Also, according to Alexander Rust, 'one has to analyse the reason for the discrimination'.[1638] Article 24 is only violated 'if the "foreignness" is the reason for the discrimination' whereas '[d]istinctions on the basis of other criteria are still possible'.[1639] As a consequence, the question of whether discrimination exists under Article 24 can be seen as an enquiry into the reason for different tax treatment.[1640]

1637. 2008–2017 OECD Commentary on Article 24, para. 3. In this context, the term 'solely' should not be understood to mean that different tax treatment must depend only on nationality or residence. The requirement of being a national or resident may be qualified by many other conditions, such as by being an individual or corporation, conducting a certain type of business, or investing in certain property. Thus, if a special depreciation rate is granted only to resident individuals who invest in machinery, differences in tax treatment between such residents and non-resident individuals who also invest in machinery may be solely based on residence for the purposes of Article 24. *See also* section §4.02[C][3].
1638. Rust 2015b m.no. 111.
1639. Rust 2010, 631.
1640. *See also*, for instance, Silva 2016b, 74; Silva 2013, 108 ('the reason for discrimination'); Kostohryz 2015, 534, 546, 550 ('the real reason for the different treatment'); Elliffe 2013b, 34; Elliffe 2013a, 613 ('the *cause* of the discrimination'; original emphasis); Avery Jones, Baker, et al. 2011a, 553–554; Avery Jones, Baker, et al. 2011b, 197; ('the reason (or ultimate cause)'; 'the real ground').

A strict comparability test is applied to identify the reason for different tax treatment. This test demands that the appropriate comparator is in the same circumstances, except for nationality or residence, as the taxpayer in question.[1641] Therefore, it eliminates all relevant differences in circumstances and, as a consequence, all relevant reasons for different tax treatment except for nationality or residence. The relevant person must be deemed to be a national or resident and all other facts must be left unchanged. If the disadvantage disappears, the reason for different treatment lies in the protected attribute. If the disadvantage remains, the reason for different treatment is not caused by the protected attribute. As pointed out by Werner Haslehner, 'where everything else is equal, the only remaining difference between two taxpayers can safely be identified as the cause for any different treatment'.[1642]

Such a comparability test, however, has conceptual limitations. If it requires all relevant circumstances to be identical and does not regard all circumstances as relevant, it provides no answers as to which factors are relevant and which may be ignored for the purposes of comparability. An exact determination of all relevant and irrelevant comparability factors is rather a precondition for its application. Therefore, it merely resembles an abstract concept of comparability that leaves the decisive question about the relevant circumstances open. If this test instead requires literally all circumstances to be identical (and, therefore, regards all circumstances as relevant or at least all circumstances that are explicitly referred to by a tax measure), it amounts to a 'but for' test - but for the protected characteristic, would the tax treatment be different? - that suffers from important shortcomings when a protected characteristic coincides with an unprotected attribute.[1643]

When a protected characteristic is deemed to be different, an unprotected attribute may also become different if the taxpayer in question possesses both characteristics. It is then unclear whether the grounds for different tax treatment lies in the protected or unprotected characteristic. For instance, nationality may lead to residence (*see* Chapter 3 section §3.06[C]) or residence may prevent a hybrid mismatch (*see* Chapter 3 section §3.06[D]). If nationality is deemed to be different under Article 24(1), residence may also be different. If residence is deemed to be different under Article 24(4), a hybrid mismatch may also disappear. It is thus unclear whether the reason for different tax treatment lies in the protected characteristic or, rather, in the connected but unprotected attribute. This distinction is important, however, given that Article 24(1) does not prohibit tax distinctions based on residence, and Article 24(4) is not concerned with anti-hybrid mismatch rules. Similarly, Article 24(5) protects against discrimination because of the shareholder's residence and not because of the recipient's residence. If a non-resident shareholder receives payments, deeming the shareholder to be a resident may lead to differences in tax treatment. It remains unclear

1641. *See*, instead of many, Hohenwarter and Weninger 2006, 253.
1642. Haslehner 2012, 597.
1643. *See also* Haslehner 2016a m.no. 3, who admits that finding an appropriate comparator is difficult if a change in a protected characteristic inevitably leads to a change in other circumstances.

whether the reason for these differences lies in the shareholder's residence, in the recipient's residence, or in both or in a yet unknown characteristic.

A protected characteristic can always overlap with or be inherently linked to some unknown unprotected attributes. Deeming a protected characteristic to be different while leaving other factors unchanged thus cannot provide definite answers about the reason for different tax treatment unless it is ensured that the protected attribute is completely independent from other facts and circumstances. Only if it could be ensured that nationality is not linked to differences in passports, voting rights, tax liability, etc., or that residence is not linked to differences in nationality, tax cooperation, hybrid mismatches, tax exemptions, tax collection mechanisms, etc., could a 'but for' test prove that the reason for different tax treatment lies solely in nationality or residence, respectively. Otherwise, if a link to other facts and circumstances cannot be excluded, a change in nationality or residence might necessarily lead to a change in all of these other characteristics that might constitute the actual grounds for different tax treatment. For instance, if a change in nationality leads to a change from limited to full tax liability, and this change in tax liability avoids a hybrid mismatch, a 'but for' test could imply that a targeted anti-hybrid mismatch rule disadvantages solely because of nationality. It would give the misleading impression that it is a value-free standard that can find a single and unequivocal cause for different tax treatment (in this case: nationality), although there may be other reasons as well; 'but for' the hybrid mismatch or 'but for' the limited tax liability, there would also be no disadvantage.[1644]

It is always possible to find some reasons why, for example, differences in tax liability but not differences in passports should prevent comparability of foreigners and nationals even if, in a concrete case, a change in nationality automatically leads to a change in both tax liability and passports. However, such reasons cannot be rooted in a 'but for' test or in a mechanical application of a strict comparability standard;[1645] they require a substantive analysis. Therefore, it is no surprise that often facts and circumstances that are not relevant to a 'but for' test are considered for the purposes of comparability under Article 24. If deeming a protected characteristic to be different does not provide satisfactory solutions, that is if a 'but for' test would allow States to circumvent the non-discrimination obligations of Article 24 or would prohibit crucial tax distinctions that do not seem to be in opposition to the non-discrimination provisions, additional arguments about discrimination are brought forward. A concept of 'inextricably linked' attributes is introduced or it is argued that partly linked attributes should always, sometimes, or never be ignored. There is an attempt to distinguish not only between direct and indirect discrimination but between direct, disguised, and indirect discrimination. It is further submitted that, in some other cases, nationals or residents of the allegedly discriminating State are treated less favourably as well or that only very specific foreigners or non-residents are disadvantaged due to

1644. *See*, to this effect, Fredman 2011, 208–209.

1645. *See also* Haslehner 2016c, 16–17, who remarks that it is not clear why in cases in which a change in nationality (incorporation) leads to a change in tax liability, tax treaty residence, and tax treatment should not be regarded as really a disguised form of discrimination based on nationality such as using a taxpayer's right to a passport instead of nationality directly.

their unique characteristics. Lastly, the objectives of the domestic tax measure under scrutiny are implicitly taken into account and their legitimacy is evaluated from a tax treaty perspective.

[B] Domestic Legal Technique Initially Irrelevant

All of these problems concerning linked characteristics could be avoided, and non-discrimination could be assessed in a mechanical way if Article 24 prohibited only formal references to a protected characteristic without any exceptions. An explicit reference to nationality or residence would always lead to prohibited tax discrimination provided that all other conditions of application (taxation that is other or more burdensome, or connected requirements; taxation that is less favourable on a PE; certain payments or debts; certain ownership or control; etc.) would be fulfilled as well. This concept would be straightforward to apply, it would leave no room for discretion or different judgments, and it would make it very easy for States to circumvent the non-discrimination obligations.

On the one hand, the Contracting States could avoid the application of Article 24 by distinguishing on the basis of a facially neutral attribute.[1646] After all, a reference to a facially neutral attribute does not constitute a formal or explicit reference to a protected characteristic. It may only lead to very similar results. Being entitled to or holding a passport is such a facially neutral characteristic even though it might address most or all nationals or foreigners. On the other hand, the Contracting States could create unintended situations of discrimination by formally relying on a protected characteristic. If incorporation (i.e., nationality) is used as a basis for full tax liability and tax treaty residence, the Contracting States would be allowed to refer to them but prohibited from referring to incorporation under Article 24(1) even though both references lead to identical results.[1647] Alternatively, the Contracting States could be prohibited from employing incorporation as a basis for full tax liability and tax treaty residence because, in doing so, they would refer to nationality. Finally, it could be argued that a reference to a criterion that leads to full tax liability (domicile, residence, place of management, etc.) or even to full tax liability as such does not constitute a direct reference to residence under Article 4(1) and, therefore, is perfectly in line with the non-discrimination obligations of Article 24(3), (4), and (5).

1646. *See also* Van Brussel 2015, 365, who is concerned about undesired situations that could arise if residence was always taken into account as a relevant circumstance under Article 24(1) even though nationality and residence may be intertwined: 'States could impose legislation which discriminates based on nationality while it is formulated in such a way so it appears to discriminate on the basis of residence.'

1647. *See also*, to this effect, Raupach 1966, 87, who argues that a distinction based on a company's seat is not a distinction based on incorporation for the purposes of a capital duty as a distinction between a person's domicile (seat) and nationality is also made for the purposes of an income tax; critically Bellstedt 1973, 117–119.

Such an overly formal approach to non-discrimination under Article 24 is widely rejected.[1648] In particular with regard to passports, no one has questioned that the Contracting States should be prohibited from circumventing the nationality non-discrimination clause in such a simple way. While this intended result seems undisputed, all of the arguments that are submitted in this respect do not appear to be fully convincing. Although a State might treat individuals differently 'based on whether or not they hold, or are entitled to, a passport issued by the State',[1649] a State might also grant tax benefits only to individuals who actually hold a passport issued by the State.[1650] Unlike with passport entitlement, it is not possible to argue that there is an inevitable legal connection between the facially neutral characteristic and the protected characteristic. A national must apply for a passport in order to hold one and must, in fact, hold a passport in order to receive a tax benefit. In addition, there is no 'inextricable link' between these characteristics. Some nationals might not hold a passport of the State and, therefore, might be disadvantaged as well. Nevertheless, the fact remains that foreigners (unless they possess dual nationality) have no possibility to hold a passport while nationals may apply for such a passport if they want to receive a tax benefit. Also, a category of 'disguised discrimination' does not explain why such facially neutral distinctions should be branded as discrimination. The expression 'direct discrimination' is not used by Article 24 and merely describes a particular result of interpretation. The idea that this article is limited to cases of direct discrimination is not self-evident. An abstract or perceived meaning of 'direct discrimination' should consequently have no influence on the scope of it. The interpretation of Article 24 in accordance with the rules of interpretation of Articles 31 to 33 of the VCLT should rather determine the actual scope of the non-discrimination provisions regardless of what 'direct', 'disguised', or 'indirect discrimination' is believed to mean.

1648. Alexander Rust, for instance, submits that Article 24(5) 'prohibits not only discrimination based on residence but also on all [facially neutral] criteria that trigger residence and all [facially neutral] criteria that automatically follow from the status of being a resident, such as unlimited tax liability'. *See* Rust 2015b m.no. 106; moreover, Rust 2005, 28; Rust 2003b, 659; concurring Hageböke 2005 m.no. 7; Wunderlich 2009 m.no. 51; similarly, Meilicke 1981, 28 ('[o]bviously the prohibition of discrimination ... cannot be circumvented through reference to another legal category which, in turn, refers to foreign residents'); Meilicke 1980, 106. Niels Bammens employs a concept of 'inextricably linked' and observes, among other things, that '[i]f a legislature is prohibited from attaching burdensome tax consequences to non-nationality, it should also be prohibited from attaching burdensome tax consequences to a factor which was introduced by the legislature itself in order to substitute nationality'. *See*, for example, Bammens 2012, 90. Kees van Raad argues that under Article 24(3), the implicitly required 'same circumstances' do not include full tax liability because such liability is a sequel to residence, and if a PE cannot reasonably be asked to meet a certain requirement or if it is utterly unable to meet it because of its lack of independent legal status, then such a requirement should not apply. In addition, under Article 24(4), it also appears reasonable to exclude from 'the same conditions' those that are narrowly related to the residence status of the comparable recipient, such as full tax liability, and under Article 24(5) to treat residence and full tax liability as interchangeable notions. *See* Raad 1986, 141, 147, 176, 189; concurring De Broe 2008, 550–551. *See also* 2008–2017 OECD Commentary on Article 24, para. 1, which refers to disguised forms of discrimination.

1649. 2008–2017 OECD Commentary on Article 24, para. 1.

1650. *See also* Haslehner 2016c, 7.

On the one hand, the Contracting States should not be able to circumvent the non-discrimination obligations by employing facially neutral criteria such as passports. On the other hand, legitimate tax distinctions should not be prohibited by the non-discrimination provisions merely because they happen to coincide with a protected characteristic. A mechanical approach to comparability fails to appropriately balance those objectives. A better starting point of the non-discrimination analysis under Article 24, therefore, is the principle that the domestic legal technique as such should not matter. It should not matter whether a domestic tax measure refers to nationality or passports, nationality or residence, incorporation or nationality, full tax liability or tax treaty residence, residence or taxation, a hybrid mismatch or residence, etc. Regardless of whether a domestic tax measure distinguishes on the basis of a facially neutral characteristic or a protected attribute, it can or cannot lead to prohibited tax discrimination under Article 24.

This starting point leaves open how close the connection between grounds for different tax treatment and a protected attribute must be in order to establish discrimination in a particular case, but it has an important implication: discrimination should not be confirmed or denied for only formal reasons. If the domestic tax measure under scrutiny explicitly distinguishes on the basis of a protected characteristic, this might render the measure suspicious but does not suffice for discrimination under Article 24. It is possible that the protected characteristic is not the reason for different tax treatment but merely used as a substitute for a linked and unprotected attribute. If the domestic tax measure distinguishes on the basis of a facially neutral attribute, this does not suffice for denying discrimination. It is possible that this attribute is merely used as a substitute for a linked and protected characteristic. While it is not yet clear when such a link should be assumed and how the reason for different treatment should be determined, it is clear that the formal design of a measure should not be the end of the analysis.

[C] 1st Step: Formal Application of a 'But For' Test

[1] Requirement of only One Single Comparator

At the beginning of the non-discrimination analysis, a foreigner or non-resident is treated less favourably than a national or resident, respectively. This may raise suspicion of discrimination and open an in-depth enquiry. At the same time, however, differences in tax treatment between protected and unprotected persons are not the exception but the rule. A foreigner may earn more income than a national and, therefore, may be treated less favourably by being required to pay a proportionately higher tax under a progressive tax system. A national may have children and, consequently, be treated more favourably than a foreigner without children by receiving a childcare allowance. Such effects cannot be scrutinized under Article 24 as they do not amount to discrimination because of nationality or residence. This might seem too obvious, but it requires proof that the criterion employed for different tax treatment has no sufficient link to a protected characteristic, which conversely means that nationality or residence has no effect on taxation.

Tax distinctions cannot be scrutinized under Article 24 if they do not show a sufficiently close connection to a protected characteristic. Hence, the question arises of how close the relationship must be between a criterion employed as grounds for different tax treatment and a protected characteristic. Since it should not matter which legal technique a domestic tax measure employs and, thus, whether or not it explicitly refers to a protected characteristic, every measure can, in principle, lead to prohibited tax discrimination under Article 24 provided that its facially neutral criterion disadvantages only or predominantly protected persons or perhaps just one single protected person. Therefore, it is unclear under what conditions discrimination can exist if a facially neutral criterion affects certain foreigners or non-residents and what impact a domestic tax measure must have on these persons.

If the Contracting States intended to give especially Article 24(1) a rather narrow scope, they must have regarded many characteristics and factors as being relevant for the purposes of comparability. If, for instance, a domestic tax measure distinguishes on the basis of residence, it distinguishes on the basis of a relevant characteristic, and thus it can never lead to prohibited tax discrimination under Article 24(1) due to a lack of comparability. There is indeed overwhelming evidence that residence constitutes a relevant comparability factor for the purposes of Article 24(1) and that distinctions on such a basis are generally permitted (*see* Chapter 3 section §3.03[C]). However, since the States have an unlimited number of facially neutral characteristics at their disposal to distinguish between different taxpayers, it is unlikely that evidence on the relevance of each facially neutral characteristic will be available. It is unclear, for example, whether differences in language skills should render situations incomparable under Article 24(1) or whether they should be equated with differences in passports that lead to 'disguised' discrimination because of nationality.

Whether a taxpayer is discriminated against depends on whether a domestic tax measure is discriminatory, and vice versa. If a domestic tax measure is not discriminatory at all, it also cannot discriminate against a taxpayer in a concrete case. If it discriminates against a taxpayer, it is at least partly discriminatory. With a 'but for' test, the starting point of the non-discrimination analysis is the taxpayer in question. However, this is not the only possible approach to non-discrimination. Under a group or class approach, the starting point is a group of protected persons to which the taxpayer in question belongs and a group of comparable persons. This approach would require determining of which persons each group should be composed of and what effects a domestic tax measure should have in order to condemn a distinction based on a facially neutral characteristic (passports, language skills, distance to work, etc.) as discrimination. If a passport requirement has a strong disparate impact on the group of protected persons (foreign individuals) when compared to the group of unprotected persons (national individuals), it could constitute discrimination even if some protected persons (who possess a dual citizenship) are not disadvantaged or some unprotected persons (who are not entitled to a passport for national security or health reasons) are disadvantaged as well. If a distinction based on language skills has a much weaker impact on the group of protected persons (foreign individuals) when compared to the group of unprotected persons (national individuals), discrimination could be denied in all cases even if some protected persons (without sufficient language skills) suffer disadvantages compared to some unprotected persons (with sufficient language skills). Under such an approach, a domestic tax measure could only be discriminatory or not as a whole, that is in all cases or in no cases, and a taxpayer could claim discrimination in a concrete case only on such a basis.

The question of what characteristics are relevant for the purposes of comparability influences and is influenced by the question of whether a group of persons (certain foreigners or non-residents) should be compared to another group of persons (comparable nationals or residents, respectively) or, rather, whether a single person (the taxpayer in question) should be compared to another single person (a hypothetical taxpayer), rendering all other persons incomparable due to some relevant characteristics. By regarding most differences in circumstances as relevant and thereby narrowing down the possible comparators, one hypothetical taxpayer with otherwise identical characteristics may remain which allows a comparison to a single person instead of to a group of persons. By ignoring differences in circumstances, by contrast, persons in somewhat different circumstances become comparable to each other and form groups of protected and unprotected persons.

In this respect, the wording of Article 24 is not clear and might even suggest different approaches: Article 24(1) protects 'nationals' and compares them to other 'nationals'. Article 24(2) addresses 'stateless persons' and compares them to 'nationals'. Article 24(3) deals with the taxation on 'a permanent establishment' of 'an enterprise' and compares that taxation to the taxation on other 'enterprises'. Article 24(4) refers to 'an enterprise' paying to 'a [non-]resident' and compares this situation to a situation in which such an enterprise pays to 'a resident'. Article 24(5) concerns 'enterprises' owned or controlled by 'residents' and compares them to other 'enterprises'. Based on the wording, it could be argued that a group of persons should be compared to another group of persons (paragraphs 1, 2, and 5), a single person should be compared to a group of persons (paragraph 3), and a single person should be compared to another single person (paragraph 4).

There are some grounds to believe, however, that under all of these non-discrimination provisions, the taxpayer in question[1651] should be compared to one single person.[1652] Within a broader group of persons, some persons might have

1651. *See* OECD, Article 24 Discussion Draft 2007, paras 19–20: 'The test for discrimination can theoretically be applied at the level of the individual taxpayer who is adversely affected, or at the level of his class of taxpayers as a whole. In other words, is it possible to consider that a tax measure does not violate a non-discrimination provision if one particular taxpayer is treated less favourably but other taxpayers in the same group enjoy advantages from that measure? The Working Group agreed that the correct interpretation of the provisions of Article 24 is that the comparison should be at the level of the individual taxpayer and not at the level of the class of taxpayers to whom the taxpayer belongs. It did not consider, however, that changes to the Commentary were needed to clarify that this was the correct interpretation of the provisions of the Article.' *See*, moreover, Bammens 2012, 57.

1652. *See also*, with regard to Article 24(1), Bruns 2013 m.no. 53 ('Betrachtung der individuellen Besteuerung'; 'keine Gruppenbetrachtung'); with regard to Article 24(3), Gifford 1978, 65, 67–68 ('[t]he permanent establishment clause should be interpreted to protect every … permanent establishment of a treaty partner enterprise who is subject to heavier taxation

different characteristics (some non-resident nationals might have retained close personal and economic relations; other non-resident nationals might not have done so) or may even be treated differently by a domestic tax measure (some payments to residents may be deductible, other payments to residents not). If a protected group of persons (foreigners or non-residents) was compared to a group of comparable persons (nationals or residents) and if, within both groups, some persons would be treated differently than others, it would be necessary to qualify when a measure has a sufficiently negative impact on the protected group. Thus, for example, if it is assumed that residence generally does not prevent comparability under Article 24(1), some persons within the protected group of foreigners could receive worse treatment (because they are non-residents) and others could receive better treatment (because they are residents), and the same would hold true for the group of comparable nationals (*see* Figure 4.1). It would be necessary to define whether favourable tax treatment of a single person within the group of comparable persons suffices for extending that treatment to all protected persons – that is, the best treatment enjoyed by (resident) nationals would have to be extended to all (resident and non-resident) foreigners – how disproportionately a measure must treat these groups in order to trigger relevant effects or whether a single unfavourably treated (non-resident) national within the group of comparable persons suffices for denying discrimination with regard to all (resident and non-resident) foreigners. Above all, it would be necessary to define how narrow or broad a particular group of persons should be and whether, for instance, individuals and corporations or non-profit organizations and other corporations should be part of the same group. Such issues also arise if a single person is compared to a group of comparable persons who are treated differently (*see* Figure 4.2) and if residence is replaced with language skills, distance to work, or any other facially neutral criterion.

Figure 4.1 Comparability (Persons/Persons): Other Taxation?

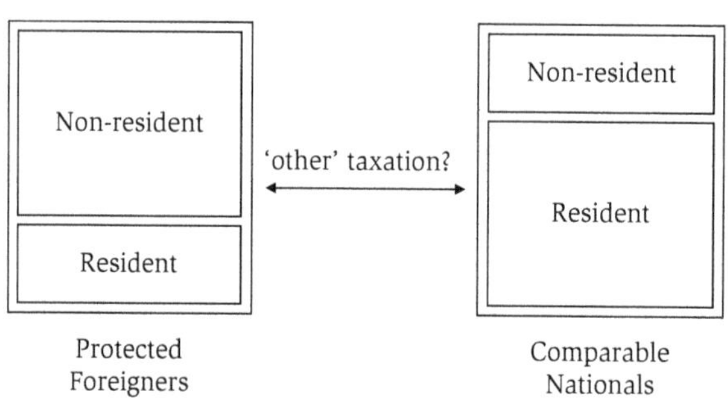

because of its particular circumstances, even though permanent establishments as a class receive equal treatment'); differently, Krabbe 1984, 129, who argues that, since Article 24(4) and (5) does not distinguish between individuals and corporations, discrimination can be confirmed or denied only for all of them.

Figure 4.2 Comparability (Person/Persons): Other Taxation?

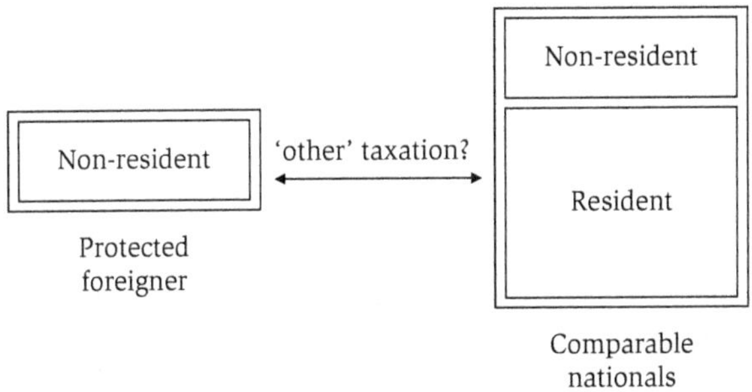

By contrast, by regarding all or almost all of the differences in circumstances as being relevant and thereby narrowing down the possible comparators, only two comparable persons may remain: the subject of comparison, that is, the person who is protected by the non-discrimination rule, and the object of comparison, that is, the person who is employed as the benchmark in assessing whether discrimination has occurred. Thus, for example, if the protected foreigner in question receives worse treatment and the comparable national in otherwise identical circumstances receives better treatment, this difference in treatment is suspect to discrimination regardless of how other protected or unprotected persons are treated (*see* Figure 4.3). Since it is generally known how the domestic tax law treats any particular taxpayer, the appropriate object of comparison need not actually exist but may be a hypothetical taxpayer for whom the protected attribute is deemed to be different. What matters is that a single comparable taxpayer remains for whom the tax treatment is known and does not depend on any further assumptions.

Figure 4.3 Comparability (Person/Person): Other Taxation

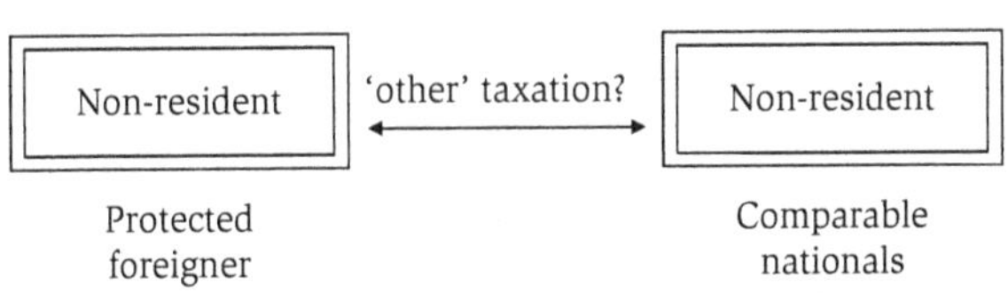

If differences in circumstances are treated as irrelevant for comparability purposes, this enlarges the group of comparable persons who may then be treated differently depending on the domestic tax law. By contrast, if the group of comparable persons is narrowed down to one single hypothetical taxpayer, this allows for a simple comparison as to whether the tax treatment is different or the same. This relationship allows drawing some conclusions with regard to the intended scope of the non-discrimination provisions:[1653] Article 24(1), (2), and (5) prohibits 'other or more burdensome' taxation and connected requirements. If certain persons are treated differently than others within a group of comparable nationals or residents, it is difficult to determine whether this group of persons is treated '*other* or more burdensome' than a group of protected persons. As a whole, there might always be some differences in treatment between these groups even if some, many, or perhaps most protected persons are not taxed differently than comparable persons. As already mentioned, it would be necessary to establish how many persons within a group of comparable nationals or residents must be treated differently than foreigners or non-residents, respectively, in order to conclude that a group of protected persons is taxed differently within the meaning of Article 24(1), (2), or (5): all persons, proportionately more persons, a single person, etc. Although such an approach can be reconciled with the expressions 'more burdensome' and 'less favourable' taxation, the term 'other' indicates that comparability should be construed narrowly in order to compare the taxpayer in question to one single hypothetical taxpayer who is treated and taxed in only one - other or the same - way.

In addition, if certain differences in circumstances between protected and unprotected persons would automatically be treated as irrelevant for comparability purposes as soon as they are not a basis for a distinction under domestic tax law, it could be argued that taxation and requirements connected therewith may be more burdensome for protected persons even when they are not formally different. For instance, if a foreigner who speaks only a foreign language would be regarded as comparable to a national who speaks a national language, an obligation for both to submit a tax declaration in a national language could have in fact a more burdensome effect on that foreigner (*see* Figure 4.4). Comparing a broader group of foreigners to a broader group of comparable nationals could also show a disparate impact on foreigners despite formally equal treatment (*see* Figure 4.5).

Figure 4.4 Comparability (Person/Person): More Burdensome Requirements?

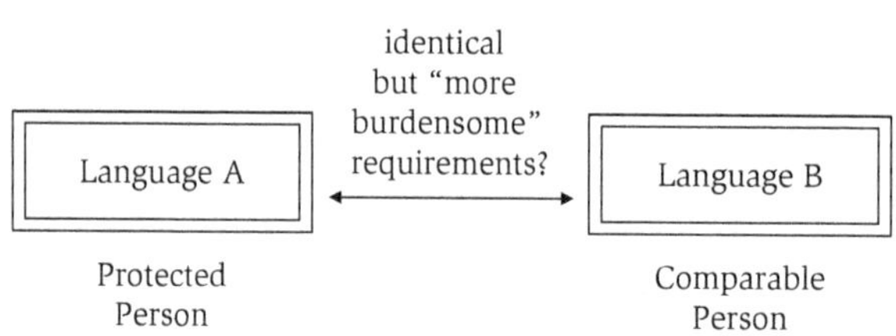

1653. *See also* Arnold 1991, 36, who observes that it is unclear under Article 24(1) whether the relative tax burdens on foreigners and nationals are to be compared on a class or an individual basis and also remarks that the '"more burdensome taxation"' requirement is closely related to the '"same circumstances"' requirement, since it is essential to know whose tax burdens are being compared.

Figure 4.5 Comparability (Persons/Persons): More Burdensome Requirements?

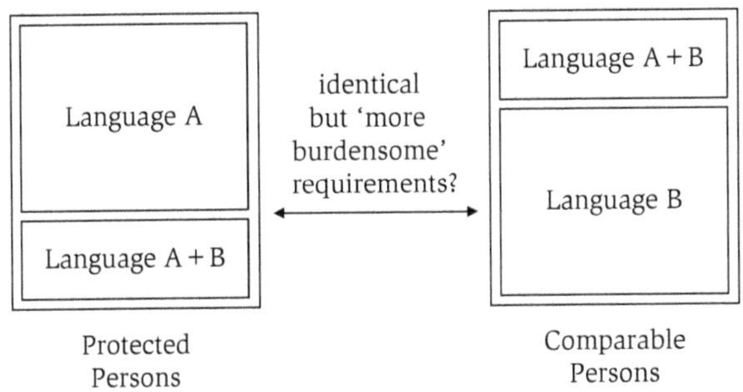

Yet again, the prohibition of 'other' taxation and connected requirements indicates that identical treatment should not lead to discrimination under Article 24. Rather, other treatment is required for discrimination under Article 24, just as the expressions '[taxation] less favourably levied' and 'more burdensome [taxation]' are understood to presuppose differences in tax burdens[1654] and thus differences in tax treatment (although the OECD Commentary might imply a different approach with regard to connected requirements).[1655] By assuming, for these reasons, that language skills and all other attributes are relevant comparability factors even if not used as grounds for different tax treatment, comparability may only be established between persons speaking the same languages, etc. As a consequence, all questions about a disparate impact due to formally equal treatment are avoided.

As far as can be seen, this idea of finding one single appropriate comparator is an important basis of the current approach to non-discrimination under Article 24 (*see* Chapter 3 section §3.05[A]). If all or almost all differences in circumstances (or all that are expressly used by a measure)[1656] prevent comparability, it can be ensured that one single taxpayer remains. This taxpayer can be used as the benchmark for comparison without dealing with questions of disparate impact or 'indirect discrimination'. As William C. Gifford observes, 'this approach offers a relatively simple objective standard

1654. This is particularly true with regard to Article 24(3). *See* 2008–2017 OECD Commentary on Article 24, para. 34 (1977: para. 22; 1992–2005: para. 20; similarly, 1963: para. 16).

1655. According to the OECD Commentary, Article 24(1) requires that 'a tax … must be in the same form as regards both the basis of charge and the method of assessment, its rate must be the same and, finally, the formalities connected with the taxation (returns, payment, prescribed times, etc.) must not be more onerous for foreigners than for nationals'. *See* 2008–2017 OECD Commentary on Article 24, para. 15 (1963: para. 9; 1977–2005: para. 10). While 'the same' tax treatment suffices for not leading to 'other or more burdensome taxation', the Commentary apparently is not satisfied with 'the same' formalities. It might thereby imply that even 'the same' formalities could be more onerous for foreigners than for nationals, leading to prohibited tax discrimination under Article 24(1). This approach would inevitably require comparison between protected and unprotected persons in somewhat different circumstances so that equal requirements could have different impact in practice.

1656. However, as already mentioned, if only grounds for different tax treatment that are expressly employed by a domestic tax measure prevent comparability, the question could arise whether equal treatment leads to discrimination under Article 24 by effectively causing more burdensome or less favourable taxation due to certain remaining differences in circumstances.

of discrimination and does not involve the evidentiary tangles and subjective analysis which the "class" approach would entail'[1657] (but it is submitted that the former standard also becomes 'subjective' when protected and unprotected characteristics overlap, and the latter standard is 'objective' if a well-defined benchmark for determining groups of comparable persons and assessing disparate impact exists). This approach is also supported by the fact that a tax treaty is not about invalidating or condemning tax measures as a whole if they lead to juridical double taxation or discrimination. It rather grants individual rights to taxpayers who are residents of one or both of the Contracting States, including a right not to be discriminated against. Thus, the focus is on how a taxpayer is treated and taxed in a concrete case, whether this taxation leads to juridical double taxation or to prohibited tax discrimination, and whether that taxpayer should be able to object to taxation in a Contracting State, notably, by claiming an exemption, tax credit, or non-discriminatory treatment.[1658]

[2] Ignoring All Linked Attributes (For Now)

If it is taken for granted that, under Article 24, comparison must be made to one single hypothetical taxpayer and not to a larger group of comparable and perhaps differently treated persons, it makes sense to begin the non-discrimination analysis with a 'but for' test that requires everything to be the same except for nationality or residence. This test excludes all situations of tax treatment that could otherwise account for a group of differently treated but comparable persons: a foreigner who claims discrimination is not comparable to both individuals and corporations, a foreigner who has children but does not receive a childcare allowance is not comparable to nationals both with and without children, a PE of a non-resident enterprise is not comparable to resident enterprises earning different amounts of income or carrying on different activities, etc. All of these differences in circumstances are relevant for the purposes of comparability under Article 24 in order to remain with one single appropriate comparator that is treated and taxed in only one way and subject to only one specific tax burden.

By implication, this comparability test also suffices for denying discrimination in all situations when the grounds for different tax treatment has evidently no connection to a protected characteristic. If nationality or residence is deemed to be different but this causes no change in taxation, it can rightly be concluded that there is no tax treaty discrimination in the case at issue. Thus, if a foreigner is deemed to be a national or if a non-resident is deemed to be a resident while all other facts and circumstances remain identical, the fact that the tax treatment remains unaffected proves that there is no discrimination under Article 24.

However, this test cannot require that literally all circumstances remain identical. If this was the case, the non-discrimination provisions of Article 24 could be easily circumvented and would be rendered ineffective. For example, deeming nationality to

1657. Gifford 1978, 68.

1658. On a similar argument, *see* DiMascio and Pauwelyn 2008, 77–78, 82 ('[b]ecause their [the investment agreements'] goal is to protect individual investors from injury, ... no group analysis comparing the entire "domestic pool" to the entire "imported pool" is called for').

be different while requiring everything else to be identical would mean that certain circumstances both in law (entitlement to a passport, voting rights, etc.) and in fact (holding a passport, etc.) would have to remain identical. It could then be argued that such an appropriate comparator cannot exist and thus, without an appropriate comparator, comparability and discrimination have to be denied. Alternatively, it would have to be assumed that this impossible comparator would, in reality, actually exist. In both cases, a facially neutral tax measure that distinguishes because of passports would not be discriminatory under Article 24(1), either because an appropriate comparator with a different nationality but the same passports (or rights to passports) cannot really exist or because passports would, despite better knowledge, remain identical and would consequently cause no differences in tax treatment; both the subject and the object of comparison would be treated in the same way as they would possess the same passports.

As a consequence, it is necessary to limit the requirement of identity of circumstances. Starting with the taxpayer in question and searching for one single hypothetical taxpayer in order to compare tax treatments, all circumstances must remain identical except for the following characteristics:

- the protected characteristic, that is nationality or residence;[1659] and
- all circumstances both in law and in fact that are inevitably linked to the protected characteristic in the situation at issue.

This 'inevitable link' is only about a link in a concrete case. It is not a question of whether the presence or absence of a characteristic depends entirely on the value of the protected attribute in all cases that are considered to be relevant (*see* Chapter 3 section §3.06[C][5]). Therefore, it is not a question of whether an inevitable link also exists in other cases. If deeming nationality to be different inevitably means that an entitlement to a passport becomes different, there is a sufficient link between these characteristics even when some other foreigners, if there were nationals, would not be entitled to a passport for national security or health reasons. If deeming nationality to be different inevitably means that tax liability becomes different by changing from limited to full tax liability, there is a sufficient link between these characteristics even when other foreigners, if they were nationals, would remain subject to limited tax liability. If deeming residence to be different inevitably means that tax liability becomes different by changing from limited to full tax liability and, as a consequence, a hybrid mismatch disappears, there is a sufficient link between these characteristics even when a hybrid mismatch would remain due to an exempt PE in other cases. If deeming residence to be different allows for deductibility of payments because these payments become taxable, there is a sufficient link to residence even when no such link would exist in other cases,

1659. Since Article 24(3), (4), and (5) also protects against discrimination because of full tax liability and residence under Article 4(1) even if the relevant person is a tax treaty resident of the allegedly discriminating State under the entire Article 4 (*see* Chapter 3 section §3.03[F]), deeming residence to be different does not only mean that full tax liability under Article 4(1) and residence under the entire Article 4 must be deemed to exist in the allegedly discriminating State (if not already existing), but it must also be assumed that the relevant person does not remain subject to full tax liability under Article 4(1) in the other Contracting State.

notably, when a non-resident non-profit organization is at stake that is exempt from tax regardless of residence. In a concrete case, all of these linked characteristics must be deemed to be different together with nationality or residence. Accordingly, even if a tax measure is facially neutral by referring to passport entitlement or tax liability instead of nationality or to a hybrid mismatch or tax exemption instead of residence, nationality or residence may have an effect on taxation in a concrete case which suffices for prima facie discrimination under Article 24.

Such an inevitable link between a protected characteristic and other circumstances is of a legal nature in many cases: nationality and a passport entitlement, nationality and voting rights, nationality and tax liability or residence, residence and a hybrid mismatch or tax exemption, etc. Nevertheless, an inevitable link may also exist if a protected person as such has certain characteristics that can be relevant for taxation. If a non-resident individual who owns certain shareholdings and receives certain payments is deemed to be a resident individual, this person has a different residence not only in the function of a shareholder but also in the function of a recipient of payments. Of course, it would be possible to assume that this person sells its shares to another non-resident person or that another non-resident person receives the payments instead, but the fact remains that there is a factual link between the recipient's and the shareholder's residence in the form of a single person in this concrete case. Under Article 24(4) and (5), if that person's residence is deemed to be different, both the shareholder's and the recipient's residence must inevitably be different. If this test leads to differences in tax treatment, there is prima facie discrimination under both non-discrimination provisions regardless of which results a 'but for' test would show in other cases in which the recipient and the shareholder are in fact different persons.

Admittedly, since deeming a protected characteristic to be different requires an assumption of something that is not real, it might not always be clear whether an inevitable link between two characteristics exists in a concrete case. A change in a protected characteristic, for instance, might require further action in order to qualify for a tax benefit. While a change in nationality usually leads to a change in passport entitlement, benefits might be granted only to persons who actually hold a passport of a State. Therefore, it is not clear whether a foreigner who is deemed to be a national has applied for a different passport as well and under which conditions the facially neutral characteristic of actually holding a passport can be inevitably linked to nationality in a concrete case. While this issue should not be taken lightly, it does not appear to be specific to the suggested approach to non-discrimination under Article 24. It is rather unclear whether certain additional requirements for a tax benefit, such as an actual application for a passport, are merely formal in nature and, therefore, should be disregarded or assumed to be met for the purposes of Article 24.

All relevant circumstances except for the protected attribute must be the same. Given that it does not matter under Article 24 whether a domestic tax measure expressly refers to a protected characteristic or uses a substitute and given that the non-discrimination provisions are seeking for one single hypothetical comparator, it is necessary to regard all circumstances as relevant provided that they are not inevitably linked to the protected characteristic in a concrete case. Comparability thereby sorts out all unsuspicious tax distinctions that raise no concerns about discrimination. Conversely, a 'but for' test is able to demonstrate that the protected attribute has an effect on taxation in a concrete case either because it is explicitly relied on or because an inevitable legal or factual link exists in this case to other grounds for different tax treatment. It regards all tax distinctions as prima facie discriminatory when a change in the protected attribute has an inevitable effect on taxation.

[3] Treatment of Other Cases Irrelevant

As has been argued above, it does not matter for the purposes of a 'but for' test how other cases are treated and whether same or similar disadvantages may also arise in other cases involving protected or unprotected persons. Besides the fact that a 'but for' test takes a concrete case as its basis and deems the protected characteristic to be different in this concrete case, there is also another reason why it initially should not matter how other cases are treated. It would be almost always possible to find some other cases in which unprotected persons or not all protected persons are disadvantaged. Indeed, domestic tax measures seldom grant benefits to all nationals or residents or deny benefits to all foreigners or non-residents even if they expressly refer to a protected characteristic. They usually combine a protected characteristic with unprotected attributes.[1660]

As soon as a protected characteristic, that is foreign nationality or foreign residence, comes into play, this characteristic may have two types of relationships to other attributes, although combinations are also possible:

(1) having the protected characteristic *or* an unprotected characteristic may lead to a tax disadvantage;[1661] or
(2) having the protected characteristic *and* an unprotected characteristic may lead to a tax disadvantage.[1662]

First, there may be measures pursuant to which a protected characteristic *or* an unprotected characteristic leads to a tax disadvantage. For example, if a childcare allowance is only granted to nationals who have children, the protected characteristic of foreign nationality or the unprotected characteristic of having no children (or of being a corporation) suffices for a denial of this tax benefit. In a situation of a foreigner who has no children or a foreign corporation, deeming nationality to be different and leaving all other circumstances the same ('but for' test) does not result in any difference in tax treatment. As a consequence, in these cases, the protected characteristic of

1660. *See also* Bammens 2012, 117–118, 120–121, 389–392, 473, who mentions certain combinations of nationality and residence, of domestic or foreign ownership and attribution to a PE or ownership by a corporation, and of nationality and gender; such combinations do not necessarily prevent discrimination under Article 24.
1661. Or, instead, *not* having the protected characteristic *and* an unprotected characteristic may lead to a tax advantage.
1662. Or, instead, *not* having the protected characteristic *or* an unprotected characteristic may lead to a tax advantage.

foreign nationality can be excluded as the reason for different tax treatment. In a situation when a foreigner with children is involved, deeming nationality to be different and leaving all other circumstances the same ('but for' test) prevents the tax disadvantage at issue. In this concrete case, the protected characteristic of foreign nationality has a relevant and prima facie discriminatory effect on taxation, although some nationals (namely, nationals without children and national corporations) are treated less favourably as well.

Second, there may be measures pursuant to which a protected characteristic *and* an unprotected characteristic lead together to a tax disadvantage. This conversely means that some foreigners or non-residents receive tax benefits as well. If a childcare allowance is granted to nationals who have children and to foreigners who have more than two children, the protected characteristic of foreign nationality and the unprotected characteristic of having children, but not more than two children, lead together to a tax disadvantage (and the unprotected characteristic of having no children or of being a corporation can still be seen as alternative grounds for that tax disadvantage). In a situation when a foreigner with children, but not more than two children, is involved, deeming nationality to be different and leaving all other circumstances the same ('but for' test) prevents the tax disadvantage at issue. In this concrete case, the protected characteristic of foreign nationality has a relevant and prima facie discriminatory effect on taxation. All other cases are of no particular concern to Article 24 as the tax benefit is granted (individuals with more than two children) or denied (individuals without children, corporations) regardless of nationality.

If a 'but for' test thus establishes a relevant effect on taxation, neither the fact that some nationals or residents are also disadvantaged in other cases nor the fact that some foreigners or non-residents are not disadvantaged can initially constitute a suitable argument against discrimination under Article 24.[1663] The fact that individuals who have no children do not receive a childcare allowance or that foreigners who have more than two children receive a childcare allowance does not render a situation of a foreigner who has children, but not more than two children, less discriminatory when a 'but for' test demonstrates that differences in nationality have a relevant effect on taxation in this particular case. As the non-discrimination analysis is concerned with one single taxpayer by comparing that taxpayer to another taxpayer and not to a group of comparable persons, a tax distinction constitutes prima facie discrimination if a 'but for' test shows a relevant effect on taxation in a concrete case regardless of what happens in other cases and how other persons, that is incomparable persons, are treated.

1663. *See also*, to this effect, Pott 1982, 226 ('Gleichheit liegt ... nicht schon dann vor, wenn eine Gruppe von Ansässigen nachgewiesen wird, deren Vergütungen ebenfalls dem Abzugsverbot unterliegen'); Meilicke 1981, 28 ('the mere fact that the ... legislation does not exclusively disadvantage foreign shareholders does not alter the fact that in a particular instance the resulting increased tax liability incurred by foreign-controlled corporations is precisely a consequence of the foreign residence of their shareholders'); Meilicke 1980, 106.

[D] 2nd Step: Substantive Analysis of Linked Attributes

[1] Establishing Linked but Relevant Attributes

A 'but for' test deems the protected characteristic and all inevitably linked attributes to be different but requires all other circumstances to remain identical. It demonstrates, in a concrete case, that the protected characteristic has an inevitable effect on taxation by causing taxation to be different. Nevertheless, an appropriate balance between the objectives of the domestic tax measure under scrutiny and the objectives of the non-discrimination clauses has not yet been found. A 'but for' test ignores all attributes that are linked to the protected characteristic thereby not being able to appreciate their relevance. Yet, under Article 24, an inevitably linked but unprotected characteristic can prevail as actual grounds for different tax treatment thereby justifying the tax distinction at issue. Since inevitably linked but unprotected characteristics are neither always relevant nor can they always be disregarded, a substantive analysis must determine their relevance. By regarding an unprotected characteristic as being relevant despite its inevitable link to nationality or residence, it is possible to deny discrimination in a concrete case even when a 'but for' test indicates a different result.

This approach to comparability under Article 24 allows distinguishing between cases in which a domestic tax measure violates the non-discrimination obligations by relying too closely but not necessarily formally on a protected characteristic without providing for a legitimate explanation from a tax treaty perspective and cases in which an initially suspicious tax distinction genuinely pursues objectives that are fully in line with the non-discrimination obligations even if, in both cases, a 'but for' test establishes prima facie discrimination. If a 'but for' test, as a first step, demonstrates a sufficiently close connection between a tax disadvantage and a protected attribute in a concrete case, it is necessary to conduct a substantive analysis into the reason for different tax treatment as a second step. This substantive analysis will focus not only on the taxpayer in question but will also consider the scope and design of the domestic tax measure under scrutiny, that is to which other protected or unprotected persons it may or may not apply and *why* it might or might not do so.

This second step is not a mechanical exercise:

(1) It is necessary to determine what objectives the domestic tax measure under scrutiny pursues in particular by taking account of how that measure treats other cases and situations involving somewhat different facts and circumstances.[1664] Given that the domestic law usually does not treat taxpayers differently for no reason,[1665] this analysis allows objectively establishing the reason for different tax treatment from a domestic perspective or, if a Contracting State claims a reason for different tax treatment other than

1664. *See also* Hohenwarter 2010, 607, 626 ('das Erfordernis der Vergleichbarkeit der Situationen [ist] ... auch unter Berücksichtigung des Normzwecks und der Systematik der potentiell diskriminierenden Regelung des nationalen Steuerrechts [zu prüfen]').
1665. *See* Avery Jones, Depret, et al. 1991b, 347.

nationality or residence, to verify that this reason is indeed genuinely pursued. Thus, by verifying to what extent a particular objective manifests itself in the wording, scope, design, architecture, and structure of a domestic tax measure in each individual case, an alleged reason for different tax treatment can be turned into an objective that is genuinely pursued by that measure.

(2) It is also necessary to consider what objectives the non-discrimination provisions of Article 24 pursue (*see* already Chapter 3 section §3.03). This allows determining which reasons for a tax distinction should be branded as discrimination and which reasons appear perfectly legitimate or do not cause any particular concerns from a tax treaty perspective. For example, proof that residence plays a fundamental role for tax treaty purposes might allow making a distinction between residence and passports even when these characteristics are similarly linked to nationality. In addition, Article 24 protects rather than impedes an agreed allocation of taxing rights. This renders tax distinctions that aim at compensating for a loss of taxing rights at least suspicious.

(3) As the non-discrimination provisions of Article 24 cannot be viewed in isolation from the rest of the treaty, they raise some issues about their relationship to other tax treaty provisions. It is unclear, for instance, in which cases tax treaty rules expressly authorize discriminatory tax treatment and whether concerns about reciprocity influence the scope of Article 24. In interpreting Article 24 and determining the precise scope of the non-discrimination provisions, therefore, it is necessary to take account of the broader tax treaty context and of conceptual issues that may arise therefrom.

(4) Finally, in an overall assessment, it has to be established whether the reason for different tax treatment from the perspective of the domestic tax law is, in substance, able to justify a prima facie discriminatory tax distinction from the perspective of the non-discrimination provisions thereby rendering linked differences in circumstances relevant for comparability purposes:

  (a) There is discrimination, that is the actual reason for different tax treatment is the protected characteristic, if the domestic tax measure relies directly or indirectly on the protected characteristic so that a change in the protected characteristic leads to a change in the tax treatment in a concrete case ('but for' test) and, in addition, if: (i) no particular reason for this tax distinction can be found; (ii) the objectively determined reason for different tax treatment from a domestic perspective is legitimate but not reflected in linked attributes in the case at issue (by implication, this reason may only justify tax distinctions in other cases); or (iii) the objectively determined reason for different tax treatment contravenes the objectives of the non-discrimination provisions and, therefore, must be equated with a prohibited tax distinction.

  (b) There is no discrimination, that is the actual reason for different tax treatment is not the protected characteristic, if the domestic tax measure provides for a tax distinction that has no relevant relationship to the protected characteristic in a concrete case ('but for' test) or, alternatively, if: (i) it formally relies on the protected characteristic, but this characteristic succeeds as a suitable proxy for a tax distinction that is in line with the objectives of the non-discrimination provisions of Article 24 and reflected in linked attributes in the case at issue; or (ii) it employs a facially neutral criterion that is linked to the protected characteristic but the reason for this tax distinction does not contravene the objectives of the non-discrimination provisions.

[2] Implications of a Substantive Analysis

This approach to non-discrimination can be brought in line with an abstract concept of comparability which requires all relevant aspects except for the protected characteristic to be the same. If the actual reason for different tax treatment is, in substance, a protected characteristic, differences in the protected characteristic and in legal and factual circumstances that are linked to it must be viewed as irrelevant and can be ignored. Although these aspects might be highly relevant to the domestic tax measure under scrutiny, they are irrelevant for the purposes of the non-discrimination provisions. If the actual reason for different tax treatment is not, in substance, a protected characteristic, all differences in legal and factual circumstances that reflect the actual reason for different tax treatment are relevant despite their link to the protected characteristic. As a consequence, the legitimate reason or unprotected grounds for different tax treatment renders situations incomparable as it is based on relevant differences in circumstances. When a 'but for' test demonstrates an inevitable link between the protected characteristic and differences in circumstances that reflect, for instance, social or economic motives, it is necessary to judge on these motives and on whether they interfere with the principal aim of preventing tax discrimination instead of mechanically confirming or denying discrimination.

Although a State will always be able to justify discrimination by some policy argument because it is unlikely to introduce arbitrary discrimination in its law,[1666] this does not mean that every allegedly good reason for different tax treatment prevents comparability. It is necessary to distinguish between permitted and condemned reasons from a tax treaty perspective.[1667] Just as not every policy argument in favour of discrimination necessarily constitutes a legitimate justification, not every policy argument that relates to differences in legal or factual circumstances automatically prevents comparability. Only if a policy argument is genuinely reflected in linked differences in

1666. Avery Jones, Depret, et al. 1991b, 347.
1667. John F. Avery Jones, Henri-Robert Depret, et al. believe, by contrast, that 'a state will always be able to justify discrimination by some policy argument because it is unlikely to introduce arbitrary discrimination in its law' and that 'there is no international norm against which such policy arguments could be measured'. *See* again Avery Jones, Depret, et al. 1991b, 347. It is submitted, however, that the provisions of Article 24 and of the tax treaty as a whole constitute the relevant international norm and, therefore, not every policy argument in favour of discrimination is acceptable from a tax treaty perspective.

legal or factual circumstances and these linked differences are judged as relevant under Article 24, can comparability be denied. It is thus not possible to deny comparability by concluding that a characteristic is relevant from only a domestic perspective. It also has to be relevant from a tax treaty perspective. If, for instance, a tax measure of a State has the purpose of avoiding erosion of the domestic tax base due to profits being shifted abroad and consequently denies certain deductions of non-taxable payments based on the characteristic 'subject to tax in this State', this characteristic is apparently relevant from a domestic perspective. Nevertheless, it might still be illegitimate under Article 24(4) or (5) given that residence may influence tax liability and taxing rights in a concrete case and that the Contracting States should not compensate for a loss of taxing rights by denying arm's-length deductions and creating economic double taxation.[1668]

At the same time, it appears indispensable to take account of domestic objectives. Article 24 distinguishes between legitimate and unjustified tax distinctions in order to leave the former unaffected but condemn the latter as prohibited tax discrimination. A comparability standard that disregards the reason for different tax treatment from a domestic perspective would have to treat nationals and foreigners, or residents and non-residents, either as comparable or as incomparable to each other in a particular situation regardless of which domestic tax measure is applied and what objectives this measure pursues. Article 24 would have to decide on comparability in the abstract and disconnected from any particular domestic tax measure.[1669] If, for example, a foreigner is subject to limited tax liability although, as a national, would be subject to full tax liability, comparability between that foreigner and a hypothetical national would have to be confirmed or denied regardless of whether a domestic tax measure distinguishes on the basis of nationality in order to take account of a taxpayer's personal circumstances in situations of worldwide taxation or in order to levy an additional head tax on foreigners for populist reasons. Similarly, if all tax-exempt payments would always be comparable to each other but not to taxable payments under Article 24(4), a non-deductibility rule targeting low or no taxation would likely pass the non-discrimination test. However, since a comparison of non-deductible hybrid payments made to non-resident recipients and tax-exempt (non-hybrid) payments made to resident recipients (such as deductible donations to non-profit organizations) would also appear permissible, a non-deductibility rule specifically targeting hybrid mismatch arrangements could turn out to be discriminatory. If a comparability standard, therefore, does not consider the reason for different tax treatment from a domestic perspective, it might lead to results that appear to be over- or under-inclusive based on the objectives of the non-discrimination clauses (*see* Chapter 3 section §3.03).

1668. *See*, differently, Bammens 2013a, 169; Bammens 2012, 474–475, who in effect argues that such a characteristic is not inextricably linked to residence (non-residents may also be subject to tax in particular if they maintain a PE) and, therefore, there is no discrimination because of residence under Article 24(5) if this characteristic is relevant from a domestic perspective (it is relevant from the perspective of the purpose to avoid erosion of the domestic tax base due to profits being shifted abroad).

1669. For a similar suggestion with respect to WTO and international investment law, *see* Mitchell, Heaton, and Henckels 2016, 88–90.

Instead of accepting such shortcomings, a more convincing solution lies in openly taking account of a domestic measure's objectives and establishing to what extent these objectives contravene the objectives of Article 24 or represent legitimate grounds for different tax treatment. To this effect, the OECD Commentary states that '[t]he expression "in the same circumstances" refers to taxpayers ... placed, *from the point of view of the application of the ordinary taxation laws and regulations*, in substantially similar circumstances both in law and in fact' (emphasis added).[1670] Although this statement is somewhat ambiguous (it could imply that comparability has to be determined solely from the point of view of the application of the ordinary taxation laws and regulations without taking account of the objectives of the non-discrimination provisions), it correctly emphasizes the domestic perspective on a particular tax distinction for the purposes of establishing prohibited tax discrimination under Article 24. Arguably, in all cases when the actual reason for different tax treatment lies not in nationality but in residence (*see* Chapter 3 section §3.06[C]) or not in residence but in an interlinked hybrid mismatch (*see* Chapter 3 section §3.06[D]), the reason for such treatment is evaluated from a domestic perspective as well.

[3] Scope and Design of a Domestic Tax Measure

[a] Genuinely Pursued Objectives

It is necessary to verify that an alleged reason for different tax treatment is genuinely pursued by a domestic tax measure. Inevitably linked attributes should not become relevant for comparability purposes under Article 24 by merely claiming that there is a good reason for a tax distinction that is somehow reflected in inevitably linked attributes. A reason for different treatment claimed by a State must be reflected in the scope and design of the domestic tax measure before it can be accepted as a legitimate reason for different tax treatment from a tax treaty perspective.

This is not an enquiry into subjective intentions of people drafting a particular measure but can rather be compared to an enquiry into the object and purpose within the meaning of Article 31(1) of the VCLT. It is an objective analysis that attempts to identify a measure's purposes as revealed and objectified in the measure itself, that is as manifested in its wording, scope, design, architecture, and structure. If a domestic tax measure genuinely pursues certain aims and distinguishes for a reason instead of arbitrarily taxing different persons differently, its scope and design likely reflect these objectives by relying on corresponding differences in circumstances. This conversely means that conclusions about its actual and foreseeable effects and its envisaged objectives can be drawn from its scope and design.

Arguments against discrimination under Article 24 that refer to some purely domestic situations that are also treated less favourably or to other cross-border situations that are not disadvantaged try to emphasize that the genuine objective of the domestic tax measure under scrutiny is not to discriminate against protected persons

1670. 2008–2017 OECD Commentary on Article 24, para. 7 (1963: para. 2; 1977–2005: para. 3).

but to distinguish on the basis of some other legitimate grounds. Such arguments refer to other cases in which the domestic tax measure under scrutiny does or does not apply and thus to the measure's scope and design. Although it is almost inevitable that a prima facie discriminatory tax measure disadvantages some unprotected persons or not all protected persons (*see* section §4.02[C][3]), the persons addressed by a particular tax measure provide important insights about the measure's objectives. While the effect that counts with a 'but for' test is limited to the facts and circumstances of a concrete case, the effects in other cases may confirm or call into question a particular objective for different tax treatment that the domestic tax measure allegedly pursues.

An illustrative example of how the reason for different tax treatment is determined on the basis of a measure's scope and design concerns the relationship between Article 24(4) and Article 24(5).[1671] If a non-deductibility rule denies a deduction of all payments to non-residents, it also covers payments to non-resident shareholders although it is facially neutral with regard to this characteristic. Such payments received by a non-resident shareholder would be deductible if that shareholder/recipient was a resident. A 'but for' test, therefore, renders this non-deductibility rule prima facie discriminatory under Article 24(4) and (5). In this concrete case, the criterion of being a recipient coincides with the criterion of being a shareholder; both criteria have the same effect.

Article 24(5) only covers distinctions based on the shareholder's residence. Article 24(4) only covers distinctions based on the recipient's residence. According to Alexander Rust, therefore, a conflict with Article 24(5) has to be denied.[1672] Arguably, the reason for discrimination is not the shareholder's but the recipient's residence.[1673] John F. Avery Jones, Philip Baker, et al. hold to this effect that:[1674]

> The ownership provision requires not only that both factors (ownership and non-residence) are present, but also that the denial of the relief under the domestic grouping provision must be *by reason of* ownership by a non-resident, reflecting a *causal relationship* .... If the ground for the difference in treatment is non-residence but not ownership, although ownership happens to be present (and vice versa), that is not sufficient, at least where only the application of the ownership provision is in question; and it is not enough that both non-residence and

1671. For an overview, *see also* Silva 2016b, 117–118.

1672. Rust 2015b m.no. 111; Rust 2015c m.no. 165a.

1673. *See also* Lüdicke 2011b, 648, who submits that, since the German thin capitalization rule was also applicable if the shareholder was a resident as long as the recipient was an associated or qualified non-resident, it is doubtful whether the discrimination was actually based on foreign ownership.

1674. Avery Jones, Baker, et al. 2011a, 536; Avery Jones, Baker, et al. 2011b, 180 (original emphasis). *See*, moreover, Avery Jones, Baker, et al. 2011a, 555–561, 585; Avery Jones, Baker, et al. 2011b, 197–202, 224; also referring to US Tax Court, 27 March 2002, *Square D Co. v. Commissioner*, 118 T.C. 299 (2002); affirmed by US Court of Appeals, Seventh Circuit, 13 February 2006, No. 04-4302, 438 F.3d 739 (2006); commented by Bammens 2012, 442–444; Vogel 2002b, 286; now similarly 2008–2017 OECD Commentary on Article 24, para. 79. Silva 2016b, 118, comments that the application of either Article 24(4) or Article 24(5) thus 'depends on identifying the proper *grounds for the discriminatory treatment*' (original emphasis), that is debtor–creditor relationship or company–shareholder relationship.

ownership are present without their combination being the cause of the difference in treatment.

This reason for discrimination can only be established by taking the entire scope of the domestic tax measure into account or by using hypothetical facts.[1675] It is not sufficient to consider only the facts of the case at issue or to deem the taxpayer in question to be a resident and leave all other circumstances the same. While all payments to non-resident shareholders are disadvantaged and would not be disadvantaged if these shareholders were residents, no tax benefit is granted with regard to non-resident recipients even if resident shareholders are at stake (discrimination also in cases involving resident shareholders), but a tax benefit is granted with regard to resident recipients even if non-resident shareholders are at stake (no discrimination in cases involving non-resident shareholders). As can be seen in this and many other examples,[1676] the overall scope of the measure provides a crucial implication about the actual reason for different tax treatment.[1677]

In terms of comparability, it could be argued that, under Article 24(5), a foreign-owned resident that makes a payment to a non-resident recipient (no deduction) should be compared to a domestic-owned resident that makes a payment to a non-resident recipient (no deduction).[1678] In following this argument, the non-resident recipient and shareholder is split into two different spheres, that is that of being a

1675. *See* Avery Jones, Baker, et al. 2011a, 558; Avery Jones, Baker, et al. 2011b, 199, who imply that, if it is not possible to consider other facts in the case at issue when the payment was not made to the shareholder, '[t]he same approach can be applied using hypothetical facts which demonstrate that the ground for ... [different tax treatment], resulting in more burdensome taxation, is the residence of the recipient, and not ownership'.

1676. *See*, for instance, Kostohryz 2015, 546–548, who considers the fact that all payments to non-resident associated enterprises (parent companies, sister companies, other related parties) and not only payments to non-resident shareholders are covered by a non-deductibility rule countering low or no taxation to be 'the most important argument to support the idea that the foreign ownership is not the reason for different treatment'; moreover, Haslehner 2016a m.no. 37, who argues that additional information requirements usually apply not only to foreign-owned resident enterprises but also in other cases involving associated enterprises and, therefore, the reason for different tax treatment under Article 24(5) is not the shareholder's residence but the potential profit shifting. *See also* UK First-tier Tribunal (Tax Chamber), *FCE Bank plc v. HMRC*, 24 March 2010, [2010] UKFTT 136 (TC), para. 10: 'Suppose ... the Appellant was claiming to be able to accept a surrender of losses from its US parent company. It might be said that there was factually more burdensome taxation of the Appellant than would have occurred if the parent company had been UK (as opposed to US) resident (since in that situation the Appellant would have been entitled to group relief for the UK parent's losses). But the ground for the difference would not be US ownership. Group relief would also have been denied if the US surrendering company had been a subsidiary, or a sister company, of the claimant company (with a common UK resident parent). In other words although there happens in this example to be US ownership, the real ground for the denial of relief is that the surrendering company is US resident whether or not it is the owner'.

1677. This result could also be framed in a rather formal manner, namely, that the identity of the taxpayer in question must overlap explicitly and exclusively with the non-discrimination provision's description of the protected person. *See* Bennett 2006, 467–468. However, this exclusive overlap can only be identified by establishing whether recipients of payments other than non-resident shareholders may be covered as well and thus by considering the overall scope of the domestic tax measure under scrutiny.

1678. Bammens and Vanistendael 2016, sec. 2.5.2.2; Bammens 2013a fn. 55 on p. 165; Bammens 2012, 444; similarly, Haslehner 2012 fn. 42 on p. 609.

recipient and a shareholder.[1679] For the purposes of hypothesizing the appropriate comparator, the same person becomes a resident shareholder but remains a non-resident recipient in order to reach the 'appropriate' result: no discrimination because of the shareholder's residence under Article 24(5). Although the recipient and the shareholder are one and the same person and thus the recipient's residence cannot be separated from the shareholder's residence in this particular case, a factually impossible comparator is deemed to exist.

According to the suggested approach to non-discrimination under Article 24, by contrast, the non-resident recipient and shareholder must be deemed to be a resident recipient and shareholder ('but for' test), which allows for a deduction. Since the shareholder's residence and the recipient's residence are inevitably linked to each other in this concrete case, it is necessary to conduct a substantive analysis in order to establish whether differences in the shareholder's residence are relevant and prevent comparability under Article 24(4) or whether the differences in the recipient's residence are relevant and prevent comparability under Article 24(5). For this purpose, it is indispensable to consider the scope and design of the domestic tax measure in order to determine the reason for different tax treatment from a domestic perspective. The fact that other payments to non-resident recipients are disadvantaged despite domestic ownership and that other payments to resident recipients are not disadvantaged despite foreign ownership verifies that the reason for different tax treatment is the recipient's and not the shareholder's residence. Although the recipient's residence is linked to the shareholder's residence in this concrete case, it is a relevant comparability factor for the purposes of the ownership non-discrimination clause and thereby prevents comparability and discrimination because of the shareholder's residence.

[b] Effects and Other Means

Depending on the criterion a domestic tax measure employs as grounds for different tax treatment, the measure may have very different effects in different cases. This is most evident in situations in which a domestic tax measure employs a facially neutral criterion for different tax treatment. Unlike with an explicit reference to nationality or residence, it is likely that a facially neutral characteristic will advantage or disadvantage nationals and foreigners as well as residents and non-residents. If, for example, a facially neutral measure prohibits a deduction of hybrid payments, it has different effects than a measure that prohibits a deduction of all payments to non-residents. If a Contracting State claims to distinguish not by reason of residence but by reason of low or no taxation in a hybrid mismatch situation, the scope and design of the domestic tax measure is more likely to support this alleged purpose if it employs a hybrid mismatch criterion rather than if all payments to non-residents are treated as non-deductible.

Conversely, if the domestic tax measure denies a deduction to all non-residents, it is more difficult to argue that this measure does so solely for the purpose of

1679. Rust 2015b m.no. 111 ('[e]ven if the recipient of the payments is at the same time the shareholder of the company making the payments both characteristics have to be distinguished'); Rust 2015c m.no. 165a; Rust 2010, 643–644; moreover, Isakova 2015, 519.

preventing low or no taxation in a hybrid mismatch situation. Although it will effectively tackle all cases of low or no taxation involving non-residents, it is both over- and under-inclusive. It covers too many cases that raise no policy concerns at all and might not cover some cases when residents are involved in a hybrid mismatch. Therefore, if a 'but for' test demonstrates in a particular case that both types of measures are inevitably linked to residence and have the same effects because a change in residence avoids a hybrid mismatch, the question of how other cases that involve different facts and circumstances are treated may support or question the argument that even though, in this particular case, no distinction between a criterion of residence and a hybrid mismatch criterion can formally be drawn (both criteria deny a deduction), a distinction between these linked characteristics must be drawn in substance.

It is not possible to give a formula for how a domestic tax measure should be designed or which actual and foreseeable effects on protected and unprotected persons it should have in order to support any particular objective. Such measures are usually embedded in, or connected to, other measures, form part of an often complex domestic tax system, and may rely on different legal techniques while leading to the same or similar results. In addition, it seems clear that a non-deductibility rule that specifically targets hybrid mismatch arrangements has and will always have very different effects than a measure that denies a deduction of all payments to non-residents. Therefore, conclusions about these measures' objectives can be drawn. In other situations, however, certain effects may not be foreseeable, may change over time, or may turn out to be different than foreseen. Hence, a case-by-case analysis should take account of the scope and design of a domestic tax measure and its corresponding effects, and it should individually consider how much weight should be given to such evidence.

Moreover, while the focus of a non-discrimination analysis under Article 24 often lies on the scope and design of the domestic tax measure under scrutiny, other arguments for or against any particular purpose should not be ignored. If a systematic or historical analysis provides evidence about a particular objective that the measure pursues with its reliance on a protected or facially neutral characteristic, this evidence should also be taken into account. Article 24 demands an objective assessment of the reasons for a particular distinction under domestic tax law before analysing whether these reasons conform to, or violate, a non-discrimination obligation. It does not exclude certain forms of evidence from consideration. It also does not offer rules for weighing relevant evidence. To this effect, '[a]ll the various elements, as they were present in any given case, would be thrown into the crucible, and their interaction would give the legally relevant interpretation'.[1680]

After objectively determining the reason for different tax treatment from a domestic perspective, it must still be determined whether this reason is legitimate from a tax treaty perspective. It does not suffice to disadvantage some nationals or residents in order to escape prohibited tax discrimination under Article 24.[1681] Although there

1680. ILC Report 1966, YBILC 1966 II, pp. 219–220 (m.no. 8).

1681. *See also* Arnold 2011, 371 ('the taxpayer's argument might be that just because there are some obscure circumstances in which a [national] corporation ... would not be a ... [resident] corporation should not excuse a provision that otherwise discriminates on grounds of

might be good reasons from a domestic perspective why, for instance, not only all non-residents but also resident tax-exempt non-profit organizations and resident individuals are denied a tax benefit (resident individuals are not corporations and should not benefit from corporate tax measures; non-profit organizations already benefit from a tax exemption; and non-resident corporation are tax exempt under a tax treaty), it must still be assessed whether such reasons are valid from a tax treaty perspective.

Thus, not only the fact that certain residents (individuals, tax-exempt non-profit organizations, etc.) are disadvantaged together with non-residents constitutes a convincing argument against discrimination under Article 24. It is also the fact that the domestic tax measure under scrutiny pursues a particular aim, that this aim is genuinely reflected in that measure's scope and design and, most importantly, that the aim does not contravene the aims of the non-discrimination provisions of Article 24. Conversely, it does not suffice for the purposes of establishing prohibited tax discrimination to demonstrate that only foreigners or non-residents are disadvantaged. If no nationals or residents suffer from a particular tax burden, there may still be a reason for this tax distinction that is legitimate and acceptable from a tax treaty perspective despite being linked to a protected characteristic.[1682]

[c] Multilateral Perspective

Indications about a measure's objectives may also be derived by analysing its actual and foreseeable effects not only from a bilateral perspective that is limited to nationals or residents of the Contracting States but also from a multilateral perspective that includes nationals or residents of third States. Article 24 is not about MFN treatment; this is beyond doubt. Nevertheless, since Article 24 aims at preventing discrimination because of nationality or residence and not for other reasons, it is important to understand the purposes for which a domestic tax measure has been enacted and whether it, in substance, disadvantages taxpayers because of their nationality or residence. Since domestic tax measures very seldom disadvantage persons from only one specific State,[1683] they potentially apply to nationals or residents from third States as well. An enquiry into the grounds for different treatment from a domestic perspective, therefore, should not be limited to a bilateral perspective.

nationality'); Lang and Loukota 2003, 69; Toifl 2003, 303; Lang 1999, 159; moreover, Rosenbloom 1991, 90–91, who mentions (less favourable) taxation of non-foreign exempt organizations as one of several 'jerry-rigged and disingenuous solutions' for avoiding discrimination under Article 24; similarly, Isakova 2015, 517 ('an artificial means'); Mattern 2014, 560 ('ein Feigenblatt ohne einen signifikanten praktischen Anwendungsbereich').

1682. *See*, differently, Krabbe 1984, 129, who states that, under Article 24(5), discrimination can only be denied if foreign-owned enterprises are comparable to domestic-owned enterprises that are also disadvantaged.

1683. *See*, for instance, Meilicke 1980, 106 ('eine speziell ... [gegen einen Staat] gerichtete Diskriminierung ... [kommt] praktisch nur bei seltenen völkerrechtlichen Auseinandersetzungen (vgl. die Iran-Krise) vor'); Arnold 1991, 10 ('no developed country unilaterally discriminates against non-residents depending on their country of residence').

When a State enacts a domestic tax measure, not only nationals or residents of one particular State need to be addressed. For instance, State A might grant tax advantages to its own nationals or residents and thereby burden all foreigners or non-residents. When applying the non-discrimination provisions of the tax treaty between State A and State B, only the treatment of nationals or residents of State B matters. Therefore, it is clear that these provisions do not protect nationals or residents of third States. However, in order to determine whether nationals or residents of State B are discriminated against, it is necessary to assess the reason for different tax treatment from a domestic perspective before deciding on its legitimacy. Since the domestic tax measure under scrutiny is unlikely to address only nationals or residents of State B, it seems necessary to evaluate that measure's complete scope.

In fact, the basic idea behind a multilateral perspective is the same as with less favourable treatment of a State's own nationals or residents. If a State genuinely pursues an objective that is distinguishable from blatant discrimination because of nationality or residence, it is rather unlikely that adequate grounds for different tax treatment will not disadvantage any of that State's own nationals or residents. For instance, if a State is concerned with income or capital that is not subject to taxation in any State, it is unlikely that only non-residents will be negatively affected by a criterion of 'low or no taxation' given that, in many States, tax exemptions are granted to residents as well. Similarly, even if a State's own residents are not disadvantaged at all, it is unlikely that a facially neutral criterion will disadvantage residents of all other States in a similar manner. A multilateral perspective assumes that the domestic tax measure pursues an objective that is potentially distinguishable from discrimination because of nationality or residence if it does not disadvantage all foreigners or non-residents in an identical way but only specific foreigners or non-residents from specific States.

If it is concluded from the scope and design of a domestic tax measure, from that measure's actual and foreseeable effects, and from other means of interpretation that, from a domestic perspective, this allegedly discriminatory measure indeed genuinely pursues a particular objective, this may mean that, 'from the point of view of the application of the ordinary taxation laws and regulations',[1684] relevant differences in circumstances exist between the subject and the object of comparison in a concrete case. Nevertheless, as already mentioned, it is still necessary to determine whether this objective is compatible with the aims of the non-discrimination provisions. If it is, no discrimination under Article 24 can exist even if, in a bilateral context, only non-residents suffer disadvantages. In that case, inevitably linked differences in circumstances that reflect a legitimate objective are relevant for comparability purposes and prevent comparability. If, by contrast, the reason for different tax treatment from a domestic perspective cannot be brought in line with the aims of the non-discrimination provisions, it must be equated with a prohibited tax distinction. In that case, inevitably linked differences in circumstances are irrelevant for comparability purposes and must be ignored irrespective of how relevant they might be from a domestic perspective.

1684. 2008–2017 OECD Commentary on Article 24, para. 7 (1963: para. 2; 1977–2005: para. 3).

[E] Main Characteristics of the Suggested Approach

In conclusion, the suggested approach to non-discrimination under Article 24 depends neither on any particular legal technique nor on subtle differences in the scope and design of a domestic tax measure. A State can neither avoid discrimination by replacing protected grounds for different tax treatment with a facially neutral but, in substance, equal characteristic nor by 'arbitrarily' disadvantaging some of its own nationals or residents as well. Finding one single national or resident who is treated less favourably does not suffice for denying claims of discrimination of foreigners or non-residents just as concluding that no nationals or residents are treated less favourably does not suffice for establishing discrimination. A two-step approach is suggested in order to: (1) exclude all persons from comparison who differ in circumstances that are not inevitably linked to nationality or residence; and (2) substantively address the issue whether inevitably linked differences in circumstances constitute legitimate grounds for different tax treatment despite their connection to nationality or residence in a concrete case.

(1) First, a 'but for' test hypothesizes an appropriate comparator by deeming the protected characteristic, nationality or residence, and all necessarily connected attributes to be different while requiring all other facts and circumstances to remain the same. With this test, one single comparator can be identified, which is either treated differently than or the same as the taxpayer in question. Whereas same tax treatment allows denying claims of discrimination, different tax treatment does not allow confirming discrimination because inevitably linked attributes have not yet been addressed – the domestic tax measure under scrutiny is only prima facie discriminatory.
(2) Second, a substantive analysis determines whether inevitably linked attributes that have been deemed to be different together with nationality or residence can be seen as actual grounds for different tax treatment from a tax treaty perspective. This analysis allows distinguishing between:
    (a) inevitably linked attributes that are relevant for comparability purposes under domestic tax law and under Article 24 and which, therefore, prevent comparability and justify different tax treatment; and
    (b) inevitably linked attributes that are irrelevant under domestic tax law or under Article 24 and which, therefore, do not prevent comparability but allow establishing prohibited tax discrimination in a concrete case.

In this respect, the scope and design of the domestic tax measure under scrutiny may have important implications about that measure's objectives, purposes, and aims. Whether the measure disadvantages unprotected persons or favours protected persons in other cases can support particular grounds for different tax treatment.

A tax distinction that a 'but for' test regards as prima facie discriminatory in a concrete case can only be upheld if the domestic tax measure under scrutiny genuinely pursues a legitimate objective that is reflected in inevitably linked differences in circumstances in a concrete case. In order to be regarded as legitimate, this objective must be manifested in that measure's scope and design and cannot contravene the aims of the non-discrimination provisions. Thus, the suggested approach to non-discrimination has the following main characteristics that distinguish it from a mechanical approach to non-discrimination:

- Discrimination cannot be confirmed just because a change in the protected attribute leads to a change in tax treatment or because a State's own nationals or residents are never disadvantaged – inevitably linked but relevant differences in circumstances in a concrete case may prevent comparability.
- Discrimination cannot be denied just because some nationals or residents are disadvantaged as well or because not all foreigners or non-residents are disadvantaged – a change in the protected attribute may lead to a change in tax treatment and no inevitably linked but relevant differences in circumstances may exist in a concrete case.
- Policy arguments in favour or against discrimination cannot be ignored just because of their supposed classification as 'justifications' – if they are reflected in inevitably linked differences in circumstances in a concrete case, they may be relevant from a tax treaty perspective.
- It initially does not matter whether a domestic tax measure explicitly refers to nationality or residence or employs a facially neutral but linked characteristic – but different effects in other cases may have important implications about that measure's objectives, which then have to be evaluated and judged upon from a tax treaty perspective.
- A measure need not be discriminatory as a whole, it may also be discriminatory in some cases but not in others – if a domestic tax measure explicitly refers to nationality or residence or to some other criterion in order to pursue a legitimate objective, this objective may be reflected in inevitably linked but relevant differences in circumstances in some cases but not in others.
- Last, but not least, relevant differences in circumstances can neither be determined in the abstract, that is, without considering the purposes of the domestic tax measure, nor only from a domestic perspective – since '[t]he non-discrimination provisions of the Article seek to balance the need to prevent unjustified discrimination with the need to take account of these legitimate distinctions',[1685] these provisions can establish an appropriate balance only by taking both domestic and tax treaty objectives into account.

1685. 2008–2017 OECD Commentary on Article 24, para. 1.

§4.03 COMPARABILITY TEST: PROPOSED SOLUTION FOR LINKED ATTRIBUTES

[A] Overlap of Nationality and Residence Revisited

[1] 1st Step: Application of a 'But For' Test

If a State does not employ nationality as grounds for full tax liability at all, a 'but for' test is able to demonstrate that no discrimination exists under Article 24(1) with regard to all tax distinctions that relate to full or limited tax liability. A change in nationality does not trigger any differences in tax liability and, thus, in tax treatment. Accordingly, there is an insufficient connection to nationality.

As soon as nationality influences tax liability in some cases, a 'but for' test may regard facially neutral tax distinctions based on full or limited tax liability as prima facie discriminatory. It does so regardless of whether nationality and residence fully or only partly overlap. It further does not matter whether some nationals are disadvantaged as well (arguably for other reasons) or whether not all foreigners are disadvantaged. Therefore, if a State deems nationals who move to another State to remain subject to full tax liability for a certain period of time, deems national diplomats and government workers to be subject to full tax liability when they reside abroad, or subjects all nationals to full tax liability regardless of where they reside, tax benefits that are only granted in situations of full tax liability may be prima facie discriminatory in some cases, notably, if a foreigner moves to another State, a foreign diplomat or government worker resides abroad, or a foreigner is not subject to full tax liability, respectively. As tax liability is inevitably linked to nationality in those situations, both nationality and tax liability must be deemed to be different, thereby leading to prima facie discrimination with a 'but for' test.

However, a definite answer as to whether discrimination under Article 24(1) exists cannot yet be provided. It is neither convincing to argue that, in such cases, the nationality non-discrimination clause is always violated (as full tax liability is based on the protected characteristic) nor that Article 24(1) is never violated (as full tax liability establishes relevant differences in circumstances). It is a matter of a substantive analysis to assess whether nationality is the actual reason for different tax treatment or whether a legitimate reference to differences between full and limited tax liability is made.

In the cases of particular interest (*see* Chapter 3 section §3.06[C]), incorporation of a company determines both its nationality under Article 3(1)(g)(ii) and its residence under Article 4(1). Thus, a national company is subject to full tax liability as a resident, and a foreign company is subject to limited tax liability as a non-resident. Often, however, not only incorporation but incorporation *or* the place of management leads to full tax liability under domestic law. With regard to facially neutral distinctions based on tax liability, this means that not all foreign corporations are treated less favourably. If a tax benefit is granted to all corporations that are subject to full tax liability in the allegedly discriminating State, all national corporations regardless of their place of management and foreign corporations that have their place of management in that

State receive a tax benefit. With regard to those foreign corporations a 'but for' test is not able to demonstrate any differences in tax treatment; the place of management suffices for a tax benefit. Conversely, foreign corporations that have their place of management abroad are prima facie discriminated against as, in this case, a change in nationality inevitably leads to a change in tax liability and, therefore, to a change in tax treatment. If a domestic tax measure employs a facially neutral criterion of tax liability that is only partly linked to nationality, a 'but for' test establishes prima facie discrimination in some cases but rejects a sufficient connection to nationality in others.

Different results may also arise with explicit references to incorporation. If a tax benefit is granted only to corporations that are incorporated *and* have their place of management in the allegedly discriminating State even though either criterion suffices for full tax liability, a 'but for' test is not able to demonstrate any differences in tax treatment with regard to foreign corporations that have their place of management abroad. Their place of management leads to a tax disadvantage regardless of their nationality or tax liability; national corporations also suffer from less favourable treatment if they have their place of management abroad. Conversely, all foreign corporations that have their place of management in the allegedly discriminating State are prima facie discriminated against as a change in nationality inevitably leads to a change in tax treatment. A 'but for' test is consequently able to demonstrate, in some cases, that no discrimination is occurring while it establishes a sufficient connection to nationality in other cases and leaves them to a substantive analysis for further consideration.

Before turning to a substantive analysis, it is important to identify all of the differences in circumstances that are inevitably linked to nationality in a concrete case since those differences may subsequently prevent comparability. First of all, foreign corporations that have their place of management abroad are subject to limited tax liability in the allegedly discriminating State. Deeming their nationality to be different leads to full tax liability in that State. Thus, the characteristic of full or limited tax liability in that State is inevitably linked to nationality in this particular case. In addition, a change in incorporation can lead to a change in tax liability in the other Contracting State if that State uses incorporation as the sole grounds for full tax liability or if the place of management is not located therein. Accordingly, the characteristic of full or limited tax liability in the other Contracting State can also be inevitably linked to nationality. If the tiebreaker in Article 4(3) deviates from the OECD Model by relying on incorporation, a change in incorporation (nationality) inevitably leads to a change in tax treaty residence. Finally, there may be various other characteristics that are inevitably linked to nationality. As Article 3(1)(g)(ii) defines the term 'national' as 'any legal person, partnership or association deriving its status as such from the laws in force in that Contracting State', a change in nationality may also lead to a change in the relevant rules for capital maintenance, liquidation, or other rules related to company law. All of these differences in circumstances can potentially be relevant for comparability purposes, however, not with a 'but for' test but with a substantive analysis.

[2] 2nd Step: Relevance of Linked Attributes

[a] General Remarks

If a 'but for' test establishes prima facie discrimination under Article 24(1), there remain no differences in circumstances without an inevitable connection to differences in nationality. This conversely means that only foreign nationality or an inevitably linked characteristic can be the reason for different tax treatment under Article 24(1). Whether such an inevitably linked characteristic is relevant for comparability purposes and thereby prevents discrimination or whether foreign nationality prevails as the actual reason for different tax treatment still has to be determined. It is necessary to objectively verify what purposes the domestic tax measure under scrutiny pursues and whether they can be judged as legitimate from a tax treaty perspective or rather amount to a prohibited tax distinction because of nationality.

At this point, it is worth dealing with the solution proposed by the OECD Commentary. Since 2008, it addresses situations in which nationality leads to full tax liability and, thus, to residence under Article 4(1). Pursuant to the OECD Commentary, a State may grant more beneficial treatment to nationals who are subject to full tax liability due to their nationality. Accordingly, a State does not violate Article 24(1) if it provides other or more burdensome treatment to foreigners who are not subject to full tax liability:[1686]

> The expression 'in the same circumstances' can in some cases refer to a person's tax situation. This would be the case, for example, where a country would subject its nationals, or some of them, to a more comprehensive tax liability than non-nationals (this, for example, is a feature of the United States tax system). As long as such treatment is not itself a violation of paragraph 1, it could not be argued that persons who are not nationals of that State are in the same circumstances as its nationals for the purposes of the application of the other provisions of the domestic tax law of that State with respect to which the comprehensive or limited liability to tax of a taxpayer would be relevant (*e.g.* the granting of personal allowances).

Initially, the OECD Commentary leaves open whether a country may subject its nationals to a more comprehensive tax liability than non-nationals without violating the nationality non-discrimination clause ('*[a]s long as* such treatment is not itself a violation').[1687] However, from the context and the subsequent examples of the OECD Commentary, it can be concluded that nationality (incorporation) may lead to full tax liability under a State's domestic law without violating Article 24(1) with respect to persons other than individuals;[1688] the same should hold true concerning individuals. When a State, such as the US, subjects individuals who are nationals of that State to taxation on a worldwide basis (full tax liability), foreigners who are not so subject cannot claim tax benefits that are only granted to persons who are subject to full tax

1686. 2008–2017 OECD Commentary on Article 24, para. 9.
1687. *See also*, critically, Bammens 2012, 91–92.
1688. 2008–2017 OECD Commentary on Article 24, paras 17 et seq.

liability. It does not matter that these foreigners, if they were nationals, would be subject to full tax liability and would, therefore, receive all of the benefits with a 'but for' test. It also does not matter that the State itself decided to employ nationality as a criterion for full tax liability and thereby introduced legal differences in the scope of tax liability that directly relate to nationality. Since a State may tax its nationals on a worldwide basis and thereby differently than foreigners (*see also* Chapter 3 section §3.03[C][2]), it may also tax its nationals differently than foreigners 'for the purposes of the application of the ... provisions of the domestic tax law ... with respect to which the comprehensive or limited liability to tax of a taxpayer would be relevant'.[1689]

Under the domestic law of many countries, the incorporation or registration of companies, which usually determines nationality under Article 3(1)(g)(ii), also 'constitutes the criterion, or one of the criteria, to determine the residence of companies for the purposes of Article 4'.[1690] Although incorporation may thus lead to both nationality and residence, the OECD Commentary strictly distinguishes between these two characteristics:[1691]

> Since paragraph 1 of Article 24 prevents different treatment based on nationality but only with respect to persons or entities 'in the same circumstances, in particular with respect to residence', it is therefore important to distinguish, for purposes of that paragraph, a different treatment that is solely based on nationality from a different treatment that relates to other circumstances and, in particular, residence. As explained ... above, paragraph 1 only prohibits discrimination based on a different nationality and requires that all other relevant factors, including the residence of the entity, be the same. The different treatment of residents and non-residents is a crucial feature of domestic tax systems and of tax treaties; when Article 24 is read in the context of the other Articles of the Convention, most of which provide for a different treatment of residents and non-residents, it is clear that two companies that are not residents of the same State for purposes of the Convention (under the rules of Article 4) are usually not in the same circumstances for purposes of paragraph 1.

This means that, according to the OECD Commentary, it is possible to discern 'a different treatment that is solely based on nationality from a different treatment that relates to ... residence'[1692] even when nationality triggers residence and a 'but for' test establishes prima facie discrimination. Also, the Commentary mentions two arguments in favour of this conclusion. It refers to the crucial feature of domestic tax systems that distinguish between residents and non-residents and thereby assumes that this crucial feature will be rather accepted than prohibited by the nationality non-discrimination clause. Moreover, tax treaties also distinguish between residents and non-residents by presupposing full tax liability for tax treaty residence under Article 4(1), ultimately establishing only one residence State for treaty purposes under Article 4(2) and (3) in cases of dual residence, and relying on 'a resident of a Contracting State' in most of the

1689. 2008–2017 OECD Commentary on Article 24, para. 9.
1690. *Ibid.*, para. 17.
1691. *Ibid.*, para. 17.
1692. *Ibid.*, para. 17.

tax treaty provisions. From this context, the Commentary concludes 'that two companies that are not residents of the same State for purposes of the Convention … are usually not in the same circumstances for purposes of paragraph 1'.[1693]

At this point, it could be assumed that, according to the OECD Commentary, differences in residence should always be relevant and, therefore, should always prevent comparability even if they are inevitably linked to differences in nationality. However, as explicitly stated in the OECD Commentary, residents and non-residents are only *usually* not in the same circumstances under Article 24(1). 'Whilst residents and non-residents are usually not in the same circumstances for the purposes of paragraph 1, it is clear, however, that this is not the case where residence has no relevance whatsoever with respect to the different treatment under consideration.'[1694]

Since the OECD Commentary admits that differences in circumstances and, in particular, differences in residence may be irrelevant under Article 24(1), the question arises as to when residence is irrelevant. In the OECD Commentary, five examples try to answer this question by taking the objectives of both the domestic tax law and the tax treaty provisions into account.[1695] As will be illustrated below, when a change in nationality leads to a change in residence with a 'but for' test, sometimes inevitably linked differences in residence are relevant[1696] and sometimes not.[1697] In this context, the criterion of relevance allows distinguishing between cases in which no or only a discriminatory reason for different tax treatment can be objectively identified and cases when the allegedly discriminating State, although formally relying on a protected or inevitably linked characteristic, pursues objectives that in no way contravene the aims of Article 24(1).[1698]

Accordingly, the OECD Commentary does not only apply a 'but for' test – a change in nationality leads to a change in tax treatment – but also conducts a substantive analysis. It implicitly asks for the reasons why differences in circumstances lead to differences in tax treatment under domestic tax law and whether these reasons can be equated with a prohibited tax distinction from a tax treaty perspective. If these reasons constitute legitimate grounds for different treatment from the perspective of Article 24(1) and the tax treaty as a whole, corresponding differences in circumstances prevent comparability and discrimination. If, however, differences in tax treatment cannot be justified with a legitimate purpose but rather amount to a prohibited tax distinction because of nationality, the OECD Commentary ignores all corresponding differences in circumstances that are inevitably linked to nationality, including inevitably linked differences in residence. Thus, the examples of the OECD Commentary can be brought fully in line with the suggested approach to non-discrimination under Article 24.

1693. *Ibid.*, para. 17.
1694. *Ibid.*, para. 18 (*see also* para. 17).
1695. *Ibid.*, paras 19–25.
1696. *Ibid.*, paras 21, 24–25 (Examples 2 and 5).
1697. *Ibid.*, para. 23 (Example 4).
1698. *See also* Van Brussel 2015, 365, 372, 375, who comments that 'the relevance of residence can be seen as a sort of safeguard against domestic tax measures that artificially introduce a different treatment based on residence in order to avoid the application of Article 24(1)'.

[b] *Example 1: Dividend Exemption (Part 1)*

Example 1 concerns a case in which a tax exemption that refers to incorporation violates Article 24(1). Although differences in incorporation may lead to differences in tax liability and residence under Article 4(1), incorporation need not be the sole nexus that establishes full tax liability in a State: the place of (effective) management may also trigger residence. According to the OECD Commentary, a company incorporated in a State and a company incorporated abroad may be in the same circumstances under Article 24(1) if they are both subject to full tax liability in that State and, in addition, if that State is the residence State for tax treaty purposes under the entire Article 4 including the tiebreaker rule of Article 4(3):[1699]

> Under the domestic income tax law of State A, companies incorporated in that State or having their place of effective management in that State are residents thereof. [2017 addition: Under the domestic income tax law of State B, only companies that have their place of effective management in that State are residents thereof.] The State A – State B tax convention is identical to this Model Tax Convention. The domestic tax law of State A provides that dividends paid to a company incorporated in that country by another company incorporated in that country are exempt from tax. Since a company incorporated in State B that would have its place of effective management in State A would be a resident of State A for purposes of the State A – State B Convention, the fact that dividends paid to such a company by a company incorporated in State A would not be eligible for this exemption, even though the recipient company is in the same circumstances as a company incorporated in State A with respect to its residence, would constitute a breach of paragraph 1 absent other relevant different circumstances.

In State A, incorporation or the POEM leads to full tax liability and residence under Article 4(1). A national company incorporated in State A, therefore, is a resident of State A under Article 4(1). A foreign company incorporated in State B is also a resident of State A under Article 4(1) if it has its POEM in State A. Accordingly, both a national and a foreign company may be subject to full tax liability in State A. That is the case in Example 1 as the POEM is located in State A. Nevertheless, the exemption from tax in State A distinguishes on the basis of incorporation and, thus, on the basis of nationality. It does not distinguish on the basis of full or limited tax liability or on the basis of tax treaty residence. Since there are no relevant differences in circumstances with respect to residence, Article 24(1) is breached (*see* Figure 4.6).

1699. 2008–2017 OECD Commentary on Article 24, para. 20 (Example 1).

Figure 4.6 Discriminatory Dividend Exemption (Example 1)

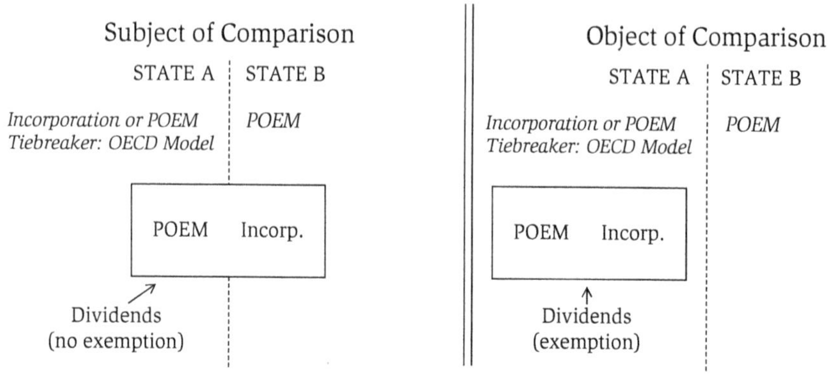

When approaching this example with a 'but for' test, nationality (incorporation) must be deemed to be different together with all inevitably linked attributes. Since the domestic tax measure under scrutiny explicitly relies on incorporation while all other conditions for the exemption (dividends, a receiving company, a paying company incorporated in State A) are fulfilled, differences in nationality lead to differences in tax treatment in this concrete case. The fact that some nationals are treated less favourably as well (notably, individuals who receive dividends), that some nationals benefit from the exemption despite being a non-resident of State A for tax treaty purposes (notably, national companies that have their POEM in State B), or that all foreigners are disadvantaged speaks neither for nor against prima facie discrimination. A 'but for' test establishes prima facie discrimination in this concrete case regardless of how other cases are treated.

As a next step, it is necessary to consider whether differences in circumstances that are inevitably linked to nationality may nevertheless justify differences in tax treatment by being relevant and preventing comparability. Tax liability under the domestic tax law of State A and tax treaty residence under the entire Article 4 cannot constitute such relevant differences in circumstances as they do not differ. Since the foreign company incorporated in State B has its POEM in State A, it is subject to full tax liability in State A, a resident of State A within the meaning of Article 4(1) and a tax treaty resident of State A under the entire Article 4. All of these characteristics cannot justify differences in tax treatment as they are not inevitably linked to nationality and do not differ after applying a 'but for' test.

Other inevitably linked differences in circumstances may still exist and could potentially be relevant under Article 24(1). If the foreign company of State B would be subject to full tax liability in State B due to its incorporation in that State whereas a national company of State A that is incorporated and has its POEM in State A would be subject only to limited tax liability in State B, a change in nationality would inevitably lead to a change in tax liability in State B. In order to succeed in making such a difference in circumstances relevant for comparability purposes under Article 24(1), it would be necessary to prove that it is relevant to the domestic tax measure under scrutiny and that it constitutes legitimate grounds for different tax treatment from a tax treaty perspective. It could, for instance, be argued that the dividend exemption is granted to national companies and denied to foreign companies because the latter might already receive a similar dividend exemption in their State of incorporation where they are subject to full tax liability: differences in tax liability in State B, therefore, arguably matter and should be distinguished from differences in nationality. Since 2017, however, the OECD Commentary states that '[u]nder the domestic income tax law of State B, only companies that have their POEM in that State are residents thereof'. There are no differences in tax liability in State B as long as the POEM is located in State A.

In addition, when taking a closer look at the measure's scope and design, such an alleged purpose of the tax distinction at issue would become questionable. If a national company of State A has its POEM in State B or in a third State, it might be subject to full tax liability in and a tax treaty resident of that other State. Despite that, it would still be eligible for the dividend exemption in State A. Thus, even though such a nationality company of State A might also receive a similar dividend exemption in another State where it is subject to full tax liability as well, this would not be taken into account by the domestic tax measure under scrutiny. It consequently remains doubtful whether State A would be able to make a case that differences in tax liability in State B or other inevitably linked differences related to rules on capital maintenance or liquidation, etc., matter despite full tax liability and tax treaty residence in State A.

[c] *Example 2: Dividend Exemption (Part 2)*

[i] Differences in Residence

Example 2 again concerns a case involving a tax exemption, but the legal context is different. Under the domestic tax law of State A, only incorporation leads to full tax liability and not the POEM. Furthermore, the tax treaty between State A and State B deviates from the OECD Model. In cases of dual residence, the tiebreaker in Article 4(3) uses incorporation as the decisive criterion for tax treaty residence:[1700]

> Under the domestic income tax law of State A, companies incorporated in that State are residents thereof and companies incorporated abroad are non-residents. The State A – State B tax convention is identical to this Model Tax Convention except that paragraph 3 of Article 4 provides that if a legal person is a resident of both States under paragraph 1 of that Article, that legal person shall be deemed to be a resident of the State in which it has been incorporated. The domestic tax law of State A provides that dividends paid to a company incorporated in that country by another company incorporated in that country are exempt from tax. Paragraph 1 does not extend that treatment to dividends paid to a company incorporated in State B. Even if a company incorporated in State A and a company incorporated in State B that receive such dividends are treated differently, these companies are not in the same circumstances with regards to their residence and residence is a

1700. *Ibid.*, para. 21 (Example 2). For a very similar example, *see* Avery Jones and Bobbett 2008, 50–51 (Case 1).

relevant factor in this case (as can be concluded, for example, from paragraph 5 of Article 10, which would prevent the subsequent taxation of dividends paid by a non-resident company but not those paid by a resident company).

In this case, no facts about the POEM are given. It is hence unclear whether the POEM of the company incorporated in State B is located in State A, State B, or a third State. It is also unclear whether, under the domestic tax law of State B, only incorporation (like in State A) or only the POEM leads to full tax liability or whether both criteria are alternative grounds for full tax liability and residence under Article 4(1). Since the OECD Commentary does not deal with these issues, they apparently would not affect the conclusion that there is no breach of the non-discrimination obligations. However, it is clear from the facts that, under the domestic tax law of State A, only incorporation leads to full tax liability and that the POEM is of no importance. A company incorporated in another State cannot be a resident of State A under Article 4(1) even if it has its POEM therein; it remains a non-resident (*see* Figure 4.7).

Figure 4.7 Legitimate Dividend Exemption (Example 2)

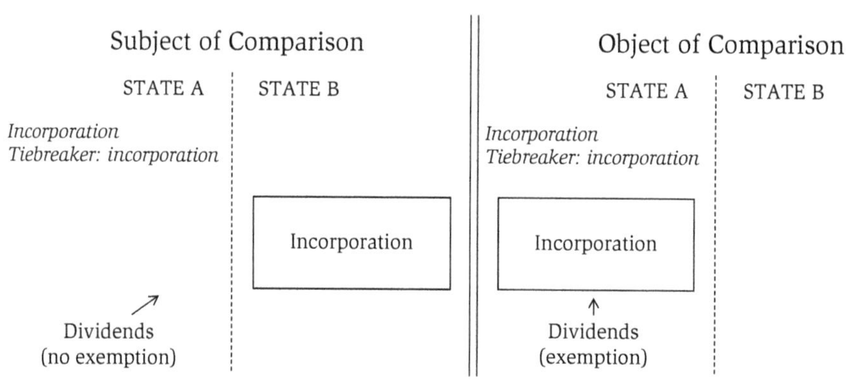

When approaching this example with a 'but for' test, nationality (incorporation) must be deemed to be different together with all inevitably linked attributes. Since the domestic tax measure under scrutiny explicitly relies on incorporation while all other conditions for the exemption (dividends, a receiving company, a paying company incorporated in State A) are fulfilled, differences in nationality lead to differences in tax treatment in this concrete case. A 'but for' test, therefore, establishes prima facie discrimination.

As a next step, it is necessary to consider whether differences in circumstances that are inevitably linked to nationality may nevertheless justify differences in tax treatment by being relevant and preventing comparability. For this purpose, it is first necessary to consider why the OECD Commentary emphasizes that the tiebreaker in Article 4(3) of the tax treaty between State A and State B deviates from the OECD Model by using incorporation as the decisive factor for tax treaty residence and not the POEM. As already mentioned, Example 2 does not specify the role of the POEM. However, the tiebreaker in Article 4(3) may only play a role in this bilateral context if, under the domestic tax law of State B, a criterion other than incorporation also leads to full tax liability. Otherwise, if companies incorporated in State B were residents thereof and companies incorporated abroad were non-residents (i.e., if only incorporation would lead to full tax liability under the domestic laws of both State A and State B), a company of State A or State B could never be a dual resident given that it can be incorporated or registered in only one State at the same time; Article 4(3) would never apply. It is thus possible to assume that the company in question, which is supposedly discriminated against by State A due to its incorporation in State B, has its POEM in State B and that both criteria are an alternative reason for full tax liability and residence under Article 4(1) in that State. This assumption renders Article 4(3) relevant when comparing to a national company of State A that has its POEM in State B and that is, therefore, a dual resident.

If it is taken for granted that the POEM is grounds for full tax liability in State B, both the company incorporated in State B (the subject of comparison) and the company incorporated in State A (the object of comparison) are subject to full tax liability in State B due to their POEM therein. With respect to the subject of comparison, that is the company of State B, no problems of dual residence arise. By contrast, the object of comparison, that is the company of State A, is a dual resident. Its incorporation in State A leads to full tax liability and residence under Article 4(1) in State A, and its POEM in State B leads to full tax liability and residence under Article 4(1) in State B. Article 4(3) has to break the tie.

Two potentially relevant differences in circumstances that are inevitably linked to differences in incorporation (nationality), therefore, can be identified:

(1) First, only incorporation in State A leads to full tax liability therein. The foreign company of State B is subject to limited tax liability in State A, whereas the national company of State A is subject to full tax liability.
(2) Second, as the national company remains subject to full tax liability in State B due to its POEM therein, the tiebreaker rule solves this case of dual residence in favour of State A by relying on incorporation. The foreign company of State B is a tax treaty resident of State B, whereas the national company is a tax treaty resident of State A.

Both characteristics, that is full tax liability in State A and tax treaty residence in State A, are inevitably linked to nationality in this concrete case as they explicitly rely on incorporation. In order to succeed in making these differences in circumstances relevant for comparability purposes, it is necessary to prove that they are relevant to the domestic tax measure under scrutiny and that they constitute legitimate grounds for different treatment from a tax treaty perspective.

[ii] Subsequent Taxation

Just because inevitably linked differences in circumstances exist between the subject and the object of comparison with respect to their tax liability in State A and their residence under the entire Article 4, this does not necessarily mean that these differences prevent comparability under Article 24(1). Indeed, the OECD Commentary implies several times that these differences must also constitute relevant differences in circumstances.[1701] Consequently, the Commentary explains why these differences are relevant in Example 2. It states that residence is a relevant factor in this concrete case because, for example, Article 10(5) 'would prevent the subsequent taxation of dividends paid by a non-resident company but not those paid by a resident company'.[1702]

The domestic tax law of State A provides that dividends paid to an intermediate company incorporated in that country by another company incorporated in that country are exempt from tax.[1703] Therewith, the domestic tax law apparently aims at preventing economic double taxation when a company already taxed on its profits in State A pays dividends to another company that is also taxable in State A. Under such a system, corporation tax is first levied to the company generating profits (first level), then all of the dividends out of these profits remain exempt if they are received by an intermediate company and, finally, the dividends are taxed in the hands of individuals (second level). State A, therefore, may have an interest in taxing such dividends at least once, either in the hands of individuals who ultimately receive the dividends or, if this should prove to be impossible, in the hands of any other taxpayer. Accordingly, besides preventing economic double taxation at inter-company level, the dividend exemption may also entail the objective that dividends paid out of taxable profits should be taxed once in State A, if not at the level of individuals as the ultimate recipients then at the level of any other taxpayer including an intermediate company.

This qualified aim of preventing economic double taxation might explain why dividends paid to a non-resident intermediate company are not exempt in State A. If a resident company pays dividends to another resident company, State A keeps the right to tax these dividends at a later time in the hands of another taxpayer, namely, when these dividends are redistributed by the latter company. Under Article 10(2), the latter company as a resident intermediate company has a sufficient nexus to State A which allows State A to levy withholding tax up to 15% of the gross amount of the dividends (but the tax is reduced to 5% of the gross amount of the dividends if the beneficial owner is a company that directly holds a participation of at least 25%). Knowing that its tax revenue is only postponed, State A may be prepared to exempt dividends in the hands of the resident intermediate company. This exemption of dividends that are received is compensated by taxation of redistributed dividends at a later time. By contrast, if a resident company pays dividends to a non-resident company, State A's right to tax these dividends at a later time in the hands of another taxpayer is limited. Under Article 10(2), the latter company as a non-resident intermediate company does not establish a sufficient nexus to State A.[1704] Article 10(5) generally prohibits State A

1701. 2008–2017 OECD Commentary on Article 24, paras 3, 7, 17–18.
1702. *Ibid.*, para. 21 (Example 2).
1703. *Ibid.*, para. 21 (Example 2).
1704. *See also* Avery Jones and Bobbett 2008, 51, who point to the policy of the OECD Model to allow source taxation (at a reduced rate) of dividends paid to non-resident shareholders; 'it would be unfortunate if a withholding tax on such dividends were found to be in violation of Article 24(1)'.

from subsequently taxing a person on dividends received from a non-resident intermediate company even when these dividends are paid out of profits originating in State A. Consequently, State A might not be prepared to exempt dividends in the hands of a non-resident intermediate company (*see* Figure 4.8).

Figure 4.8 Legitimate Dividend Exemption (Example 2): Redistribution (1)

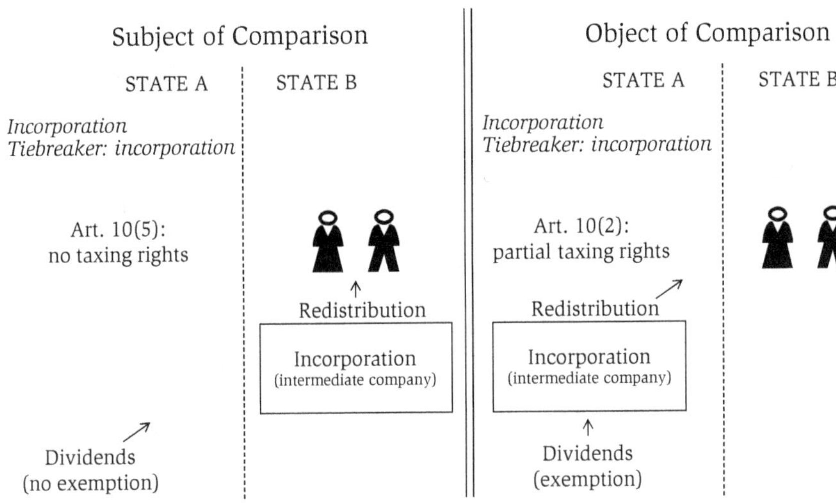

From the perspective of State A, a dividend exemption would be contrary to the aim of exercising taxing rights at least once with respect to dividends paid out of profits arising in State A. This corresponding decision not to exempt dividends in cases when it is impossible to tax those dividends subsequently is, according to the OECD Commentary, respected by Article 24(1) even when the measure in question overtly distinguishes on the basis of incorporation, that is nationality. In Example 2, even though incorporation (nationality) and residence coincide, differences in residence are relevant and prevent comparability under Article 24(1) because Article 10(5) 'would prevent the subsequent taxation of dividends paid by a non-resident company but not those paid by a resident company'.[1705]

Although the Commentary's analysis is rather brief, it indicates a reason for relying on incorporation under domestic tax law ('the subsequent taxation of dividends') and accepts this reason as being legitimate from a tax treaty perspective ('residence is a relevant factor in this case').[1706] The dividend exemption of State A relies on incorporation because incorporation is the sole grounds for full tax liability under the domestic law of State A, and this scope of tax liability is not substantially limited by the tax treaty between State A and State B, either because State A is the sole residence State under Article 4(1) or because the tiebreaker in Article 4(3) solves cases

1705. 2008–2017 OECD Commentary on Article 24, para. 21 (Example 2).
1706. *Ibid.*, para. 21 (Example 2).

of dual residence in favour of State A, again by relying on incorporation. Differences in incorporation (nationality) inevitably lead to differences in tax liability and tax treaty residence, and the latter differences in turn influence the subsequent taxation of dividends. According to the OECD Commentary, these differences in circumstances are, in substance, relevant for comparability purposes even though they are inevitably linked to incorporation (nationality).

[iii] Additional Considerations

Some objections can be raised against the conclusion of the OECD Commentary. It should not suffice for avoiding discrimination under Article 24(1) to merely allege that the subsequent taxation of dividends is State A's main concern and the reason why the dividend exemption relies on incorporation. It should rather be verified whether State A genuinely pursues this objective. Incorporation, full tax liability, and tax treaty residence in State A are formally indistinguishable from each other under the tax treaty between State A and State B. Yet, this need not be the case with other double taxation conventions. If, for instance, the tiebreaker in the tax treaty between State A and State C relies on the POEM, a national company of State A can be a non-resident for tax treaty purposes if it has its POEM in State C. Accordingly, Article 10(5) of the tax treaty between State A and State C prevents the subsequent taxation of dividends paid by such a national company of State A just as it prevents the subsequent taxation of dividends paid by a foreign company of State C in otherwise identical circumstances. Despite that, the domestic tax law of State A grants the dividend exemption to the national company but denies it to the foreign company. This should not only lead to prohibited tax discrimination under Article 24(1) of the tax treaty between State A and State C. This should also put the objective of ensuring the subsequent taxation of dividends into question. Even without differences in the subsequent taxation of dividends, the domestic tax law of State A apparently continues to discriminate. If it discriminates regardless of whether Article 10(5) provides for different tax consequences, it is not clear why differences in the subsequent taxation of dividends should suddenly become relevant for the purposes of Article 24(1) of the tax treaty between State A and State B just because Article 10(5) is applicable in a concrete case.

In addition, the relevance of differences in the subsequent taxation of dividends could also depend on whether redistributed dividends are actually not taxable in State A thereby requiring an in-depth analysis of whether Article 10(5) indeed restricts State A's taxing rights in a particular case. Article 10(5) prohibits State A from taxing any subsequent dividends paid by a non-resident intermediate company that is incorporated and resident in State B even if such dividends consist of profits or income arising in State A, but it contains exceptions.[1707] If dividends paid by a non-resident company

1707. Article 10(5) states that '[w]here a company which is a resident of a Contracting State [State B] derives profits or income from the other Contracting State [State A], that other State [State A] may not impose any tax on the dividends paid by the company, *except insofar as such dividends are paid to a resident of that other State [State A] or insofar as the holding in respect of which the dividends are paid is effectively connected with a permanent establishment*

are received by a resident of State A or attributable to a PE situated in State A, State A has the right to tax these dividends under Articles 7, 10, or 21. Article 10(5) does not impede State A's right to tax and, consequently, offers no justification for different tax treatment.

Arguably, to the extent that State A has the right to tax subsequent dividends paid by the intermediate company incorporated and resident in State B, there exists no justification for State A to refuse the exemption for dividends that the intermediate company receives from a resident company. In such a case, differences in incorporation and thereby differences in residence should not matter to the domestic tax measure under scrutiny that aims at preventing economic double taxation. Both the profits generated in State A and the dividends paid out of these profits remain, in the end, taxable in State A even if the exemption for dividends is extended to the intermediate company from State B. To the extent that differences in incorporation (nationality) do not influence the taxing rights of State A, they should not be used to reject a claim of discrimination because of nationality under Article 24(1).[1708]

It can be replied to this argument that even if the intermediate company that is incorporated and resident in State B subsequently pays out dividends to a resident of State A, State A cannot fully regain its taxing rights. It is true that Article 10(5) does not restrict State A from taxing in such a case. Nevertheless, while Article 10(1) allows State A to tax the dividends, Article 10(2) provides limited taxing rights to State B of which the intermediate company is a resident. State A, therefore, is obligated to grant a tax credit under Article 23 A(2) or 23 B(1) which lowers State A's tax revenue. By contrast, if the intermediate company is a resident of State A, State A generally has full taxing rights with respect to all of the persons involved. It is able to fully tax both the profits generated in State A and the dividends paid out of these profits. This arguably renders linked differences in taxing rights relevant for comparability purposes (*see* Figure 4.9).

---

situated in that other State [State A], ... even if the dividends paid ... consist wholly or partly of profits or income arising in such other State [State A]' (emphasis added).

1708. In this context, timing issues arise: it might be unknown who will receive the subsequent dividends paid at a later time by the intermediate company from State B. Consequently, it might be unclear whether State A will have the right to tax the subsequent dividends or whether Article 10(5) will prevent such taxation. It still remains questionable, however, whether these timing issues might justify a complete denial of benefits under Article 24(1).

Figure 4.9 Legitimate Dividend Exemption (Example 2): Redistribution (2)

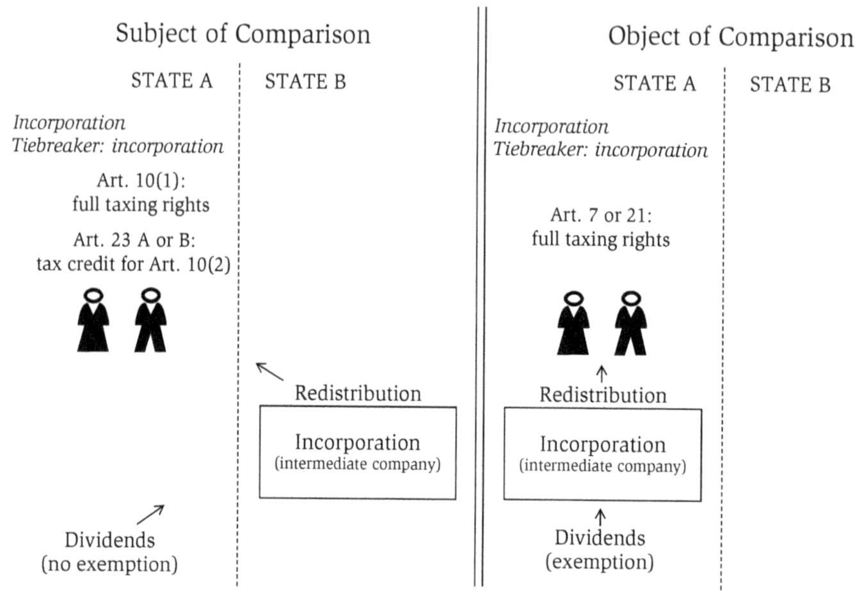

If dividends are paid to a non-resident intermediate company, taxing rights might be restricted under Article 10(5) or Article 10(2) in conjunction with Article 23 A(2) or 23 B(1) when these dividends are subsequently paid out by this intermediate company. This might justify a general denial of the exemption for dividends paid to such non-residents. However, cases remain in which differences in residence have no impact on State A's taxing rights. When an intermediate company pays out dividends to a PE located in State A (*see* Figure 4.10) or to a PE located outside of State A (*see* Figure 4.11), the dividends may remain fully taxable or not taxable in State A, respectively, regardless of whether the intermediate company is a resident or non-resident of State A. In such cases, differences in residence that are inevitably linked to differences in nationality do not appear relevant under the nationality non-discrimination clause.

Figure 4.10 Legitimate Dividend Exemption (Example 2): Redistribution (3)

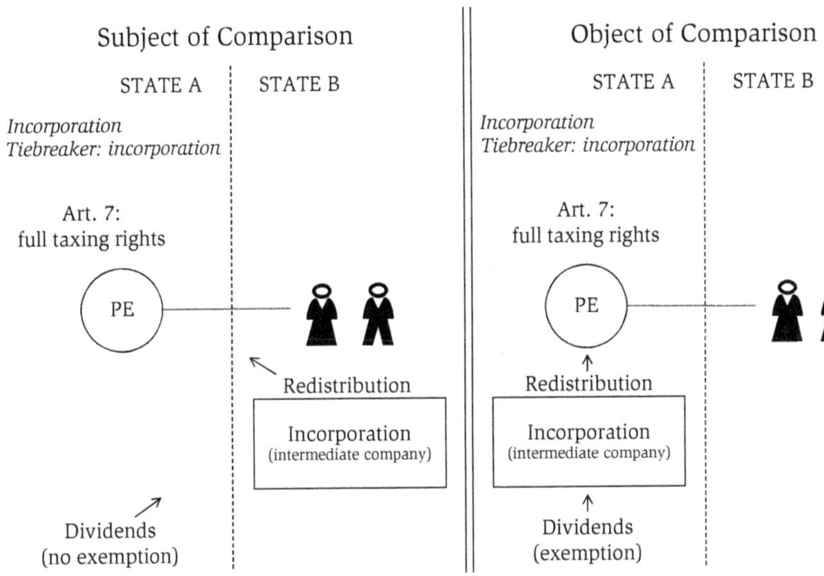

Figure 4.11 Legitimate Dividend Exemption (Example 2): Redistribution (4)

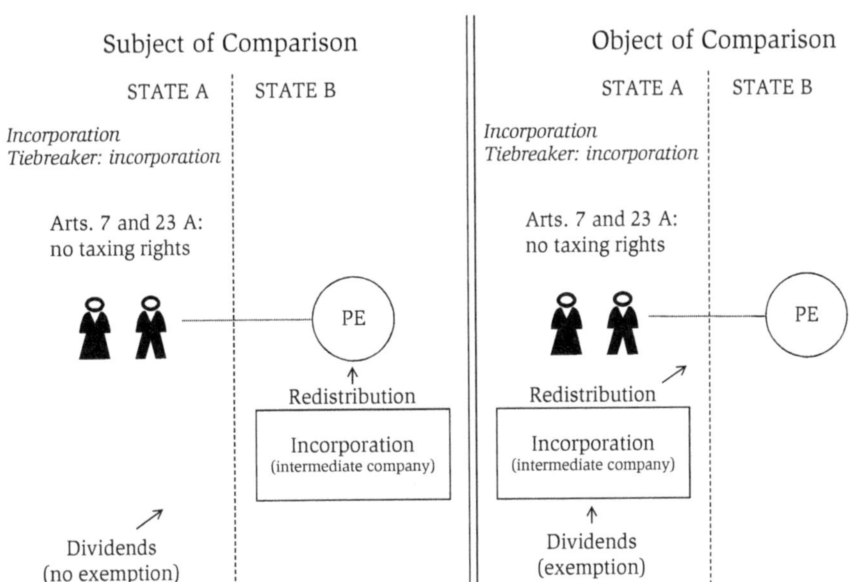

All in all, Example 2 deals with a case in which differences in tax liability and tax treaty residence are inevitably linked to differences in nationality in a concrete case. A 'but for' test deems all of these characteristics to be different, regardless of which characteristic is formally relied on, and establishes prima facie discrimination. Nevertheless, the OECD Commentary identifies a legitimate reason for the tax distinction at issue, namely the subsequent taxation of dividends. It can be doubted whether this reason is indeed genuinely pursued by the domestic tax measure under scrutiny. It can be further discussed why this reason should always be able to establish relevant differences in circumstances even if the relevant tax treaty rules, despite their reliance on inevitably linked differences in tax treaty residence, do not influence the subsequent taxation of dividends in a concrete case. However, an analysis of Article 24(1) confirms that differences in tax liability and corresponding tax distinctions are not a concern to the nationality non-discrimination clause (*see* Chapter 3 section §3.03[C]). Since differences in tax treaty residence might potentially influence State A's taxing rights with regard to redistributed dividends, residence might be regarded as a relevant comparability factor even if it is inevitably linked to nationality in a concrete case. Therefore, it might permit a denial of the dividend exemption without violating the non-discrimination obligations of Article 24(1).

[d] Example 3: Exchange of Information

[i] Ambiguous Description

Example 3 is probably the most interesting but also the most complex and ambiguous example. It deals with a triangular case in which residence is arguably relevant for the purposes of Article 24(1):[1709]

> Under the domestic income tax law of State A, companies that are incorporated in that State are residents thereof. Under the domestic tax law of State B, companies that have their place of effective management in that State are residents thereof. The State A – State B tax convention is identical to this Model Tax Convention. The domestic tax law of State A provides that a non-resident company that is a resident of a State with which State A does not have a tax treaty that allows for the exchange of tax information is subject to an annual tax equal to 3 per cent of the value of its immovable property instead of a tax on the net income derived from that property. A company incorporated in State B but which is a resident of a State with which State A does not have a tax treaty that allows for the exchange of tax information cannot claim that paragraph 1 prevents the application of the 3 per cent tax levied by State A because it is treated differently from a company incorporated in State A. In that case, such a company would not be in the same circumstances, with respect to its residence, as a company incorporated in State A and the residence of the company would be relevant (*e.g.* for purposes of accessing the information necessary to verify the net income from immovable property derived by a non-resident taxpayer).

1709. 2008–2017 OECD Commentary on Article 24, para. 22 (Example 3). This example is most probably inspired by decisions of French courts regarding a 3 % tax on the value of French real property held by certain foreign real property holding companies. *See supra* n. 895.

In this example, State A uses incorporation as a triggering event for full tax liability and residence under Article 4(1). State B, by contrast, relies on the POEM. This apparently means that only a company incorporated in State A is a resident of State A and only a company having its POEM in State B is a resident of State B. Conversely, a company having its POEM in State A but incorporated abroad is not subject to full tax liability in State A, and a company incorporated in State B but having its POEM abroad is not subject to full tax liability in State B.[1710] In such cases, a company is a resident of neither Contracting State, the conditions of Article 1 in connection with Article 4(1) are not fulfilled, and the tax treaty between State A and State B does not apply.[1711]

The foreign company (the subject of comparison) that must be compared to a national company of State A under Article 24(1) is '[a] company incorporated in State B but which is a resident of a State with which State A does not have a tax treaty that allows for the exchange of tax information'.[1712] Hereafter, this third State will also be referred to as State C. It is not exactly clear what the term 'a resident of a [third] State' means in this context, but most probably it refers to the POEM in that State. Clearly, the company in question is incorporated in and a national of State B. It cannot be incorporated in State C as well.[1713] Moreover, the POEM constitutes the decisive tiebreaker under Article 4(3) of the tax treaty between State A and State B if based on the pre-2017 OECD Model. For these reasons it may be assumed that the foreign company in question is incorporated in State B but has its POEM in a third State, that is State C. This company is not subject to full tax liability in State A because it is not incorporated in State A. It is also not subject to full tax liability in State B because it does not have its POEM in State B. It is not a resident of either State A or State B. It follows that under Article 1, the conditions for the application of the tax treaty between State

1710. *See* especially Examples 1 and 5 which explicitly state that, under the domestic income tax law of State A, companies incorporated in that State *or having their place of effective management in that State* are residents thereof. By contrast, Example 3 only provides that '[u]nder the domestic income tax law of State A, companies that are incorporated in that State are residents thereof' and that '[u]nder the domestic tax law of State B, companies that have their place of effective management in that State are residents thereof'. Interestingly, however, Examples 2 and 4 explicitly mention that, under the domestic income tax law of State A, companies incorporated in that State are residents of State A *and companies incorporated abroad are non-residents*, implying that the POEM in State A will not lead to residence. Therefore, it is unclear whether the only criteria that lead to full tax liability and residence are incorporation under the domestic tax law of State A and the POEM under the domestic tax law of State B. Put differently, it is unclear whether a company not incorporated in State A is always a non-resident even if it has its POEM in State A and whether a company without its POEM in State B is always a non-resident even if it is incorporated therein. Nevertheless, from the context, it can be concluded that the expressly mentioned criteria in Example 3 (incorporation in State A and the POEM in State B) are the only relevant criteria for residence. If both incorporation and the POEM could lead to residence in State A, arguably, both the POEM and incorporation could lead to residence in State B as well, and vice versa. It would then remain unclear why the OECD Commentary only mentions incorporation with respect to State A and the POEM with respect to State B instead of stating that, under the domestic income tax laws of both Contracting States, incorporation or the POEM leads to residence.

1711. Such cases may also lead to dual non-residence and to non-taxation if a company is incorporated in State B and has its POEM in State A.

1712. 2008–2017 OECD Commentary on Article 24, para. 22 (Example 3).

1713. At least not if the criteria for incorporation do not differ between the States involved, which is assumed in this case. *See also supra* n. 1400.

A and State B are not fulfilled. Article 24(1), however, applies 'notwithstanding the provisions of Article 1, also ... to persons who are not residents of one or both of the Contracting States'. Consequently, State A is prohibited from discriminating because of nationality against the foreign company incorporated in State B even though this company is subject to limited tax liability as a non-resident in both State A and State B.

Under the domestic tax law of State A, 'a non-resident company that is a resident of a State with which State A does not have a tax treaty that allows for the exchange of tax information is subject to an annual tax equal to 3 per cent of the value of its immovable property instead of a tax on the net income derived from that property'.[1714] The expressions 'a non-resident company' and 'a resident of a State' that are used to specify the scope of the special tax rule on immovable property are ambiguous. It is unclear whether they refer to incorporation or to the POEM. It could be argued that, since the domestic tax law of State A stipulates that incorporation is the relevant criterion for full tax liability and residence, the domestic tax law regulating the taxation of income from immovable property must also distinguish on the basis of incorporation. This would mean, however, that a company incorporated in State B would be granted the same tax treatment as a company incorporated in State A. Since the tax treaty between State A and State B is identical to the OECD Model and, therefore, includes Article 26 on the exchange of tax information, a company incorporated in State B ('a non-resident company') would be incorporated in a State ('a resident of a State') with which exchange of information is possible, State B.

In order to account for Example 3 as a potential case of discrimination, it could be assumed instead that the domestic tax law of State A distinguishes on the basis of the POEM. A company that has its POEM abroad ('a non-resident company') and in a State ('a resident of a State') with which State A does not have a tax treaty that allows for the exchange of tax information would be subject to different tax treatment. However, this understanding would again lead to strange results. A company incorporated in State B would be granted the same treatment as a company incorporated in State A if both have their POEM in State C. Since there is no tax treaty with an exchange of tax information clause in force between State A and State C, all companies having their POEM in State C would be treated the same regardless of their incorporation (nationality).[1715] This result, however, would be inconsistent with the explanation of the OECD Commentary that, in Example 3, '[a] company incorporated in State B but which is a resident of a State with which State A does not have a tax treaty that allows for the exchange of tax information ... *is treated differently* from a company incorporated in State A' (emphasis added). Apparently, different tax treatment is present in State A and must somehow be related to incorporation.

All of these considerations and issues can be brought together if the domestic tax law of State A (according to which 'a non-resident company that is a resident of a State

1714. *Ibid.*, para. 22 (Example 3).

1715. This conclusion is reached by Van Brussel 2015, 369–371: '[W]hen applying the domestic law in this example, "*residence*" is understood as referring to the place of effective management. In this case Article 24(1) is not violated, since a company incorporated in State A but a resident of State C and a company incorporated in State B but also a resident of State C will both be subjected to the same less favourable treatment'.

with which State A does not have a tax treaty that allows for the exchange of tax information is subject to [different treatment]')[1716] actually refers to both incorporation and the POEM: 'a non-resident company' refers to a company not incorporated in State A and 'a resident of a [third] State' refers to a company that has its POEM in that State (or which is a tax treaty resident of that State). Accordingly, the domestic tax law of State A provides that a company not incorporated in State A that has its POEM in a third State, State C, with which State A does not have a tax treaty that allows for the exchange of tax information is treated differently and potentially more burdensome than a company incorporated in State A.

It follows that a company incorporated in State A is not 'a non-resident company'. For this reason, the special tax rule on immovable property does not apply irrespective of the POEM. With this understanding, different treatment based on incorporation becomes possible under the domestic tax law of State A even when, for comparability purposes under Article 24(1), the POEM remains in State C. With a 'but for' test, a company incorporated in State B with its POEM in State C (the subject of comparison) is treated differently compared to a company incorporated in State A with its POEM in State C (the object of comparison) because incorporation in State A renders the special tax rule on immovable property inapplicable. A change in nationality leads to a change in tax treatment.

In sum, Example 3 concerns a company incorporated in State B which has its POEM in State C that is treated differently by State A than a company incorporated in State A which has its POEM in State C (*see* Figure 4.12). Although a 'but for' test confirms differences in tax treatment connected to nationality in this concrete case, the question remains whether this prima facie discriminatory treatment amounts to discrimination based on nationality or whether, in a next step, a substantive analysis is able to identify inevitably linked but relevant differences in circumstances.

Figure 4.12 Legitimate Information Requirements (Example 3)

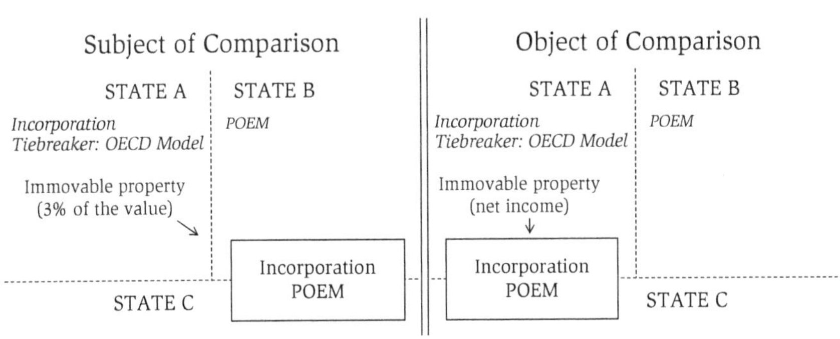

1716. 2008–2017 OECD Commentary on Article 24, para. 22 (Example 3).

[ii] Differences in Residence

According to the OECD Commentary, there is no discrimination under Article 24(1) in Example 3. 'In that case, such a company [incorporated in State B] would not be in the same circumstances, with respect to its residence, as a company incorporated in State A and the residence of the company would be relevant (*e.g.* for purposes of accessing the information necessary to verify the net income from immovable property derived by a non-resident taxpayer).'[1717] In this statement, the expression 'not ... in the same circumstances, with respect to its residence'[1718] cannot refer to the POEM even though the tiebreaker in Article 4(3) of the tax treaty between State A and State B relies on this criterion if it is based on the pre-2017 OECD Model. If a foreign company incorporated in State B (the subject of comparison) is compared to a national company incorporated in State A (the object of comparison), the POEM is not inevitably linked to nationality and, therefore, remains in the same State, State C. By contrast, as only incorporation leads to full tax liability under the domestic law of State A, a foreign company incorporated in State B is not subject to full tax liability in State A (and it never can be as long as it remains incorporated in State B), whereas a national company incorporated in State A is subject to full tax liability therein. There is an inevitable link between nationality and tax liability in State A. Consequently, the Commentary's statement that the subject of comparison is 'not ... in the same circumstances, with respect to its residence'[1719] as the object of comparison may refer to differences in residence from the perspective of the domestic tax law of State A which uses incorporation as the sole criterion for full tax liability and residence. Since a company incorporated in State B is a non-resident company under the domestic tax law of State A, it arguably cannot be compared to a company incorporated and, therefore, resident in State A.

Werner Haslehner criticizes the OECD Commentary for being somewhat inconsistent in Example 3.[1720] Previously, the Commentary refers to residence 'for purposes of the Convention (under the rules of Article 4)'[1721] and, in Example 2, rejects comparability on the basis of tax treaty residence and not only on the basis of residence under the domestic tax law of State A.[1722] Nevertheless, in Example 3, the Commentary appears to limit itself to residence from the perspective of the domestic tax law of State A. Taking into account the standard tiebreaker rule of Article 4(3), both the subject and the object of comparison are exclusively residents of a third State, State C.[1723] If the OECD Commentary relied on residence 'for purposes of the Convention (under the rules of Article 4)',[1724] it would have to confirm comparability and discrimination because of nationality because both the subject and the object of comparison have their POEM in State C. Since the OECD Commentary denies the same circumstances in

1717. *Ibid.*, para. 22 (Example 3).
1718. *Ibid.*, para. 22 (Example 3).
1719. *Ibid.*, para. 22 (Example 3).
1720. Haslehner 2016c, 17.
1721. 2008-2017 OECD Commentary on Article 24, para. 17.
1722. *Ibid*, para. 21 (Example 2).
1723. Haslehner 2016c, 17.
1724. 2008-2017 OECD Commentary on Article 24, para. 17.

Example 3, however, it can only be reasoned that the Commentary does not rely on tax treaty residence, which is contrary to its other explanations and examples.

Yet, the OECD Commentary's approach is perfectly in line with the suggested approach to non-discrimination under Article 24. The question is not which single meaning of 'residence' should be relevant for the purposes of Article 24(1) and whether the POEM, as it is used as the tiebreaker in Article 4(3) of the relevant tax treaty between State A and State B if based on the pre-2017 OECD Model, should suffice for comparability. The question is whether differences in circumstances exist that are inevitably linked to nationality but can nevertheless be regarded as relevant for comparability purposes. In Example 2, differences in domestic tax liability in State A, in residence under Article 4(1) and in tax treaty residence under the entire Article 4, are inevitably linked to differences in nationality in particular because the tiebreaker in Article 4(3) relies on incorporation. Due to a substantive analysis, differences in tax treaty residence can be regarded as relevant. In Example 3, the POEM as the tiebreaker in Article 4(3) is not linked to nationality and, therefore, does not differ between the subject and the object of comparison with a 'but for' test. However, other differences in circumstances and other meanings of 'residence' are inevitably linked to nationality; the OECD Commentary considers them as relevant.

Although the OECD Commentary can be criticized for not being precise by using the general term 'residence' for different characteristics in different examples, it cannot be criticized for the fact that it regards different characteristics as being relevant in different cases in which different characteristics are inevitably linked to nationality. In Example 3, it has to be determined why differences in tax liability under the domestic tax law of State A (and potentially also differences in residence under the entire Article 4 if they do not depend on the POEM) should prevent comparability for the purposes of the nationality non-discrimination clause even though these differences are inevitably linked to differences in nationality.

When taking a closer look at tax treaty residence, Example 3 is a complex case. As already outlined above, the subject of comparison, that is the foreign company incorporated in State B that has its POEM in State C, is not a resident under the tax treaty between State A and State B. It has no personal connection to State A, incorporation in State B does not lead to full tax liability and residence in State B, and the POEM in a third State, State C, is generally irrelevant from the perspective of the tax treaty between State A and State B. At the same time, it is not known from the facts of the case whether a tax treaty exists between State A and State C or between State B and State C. Although the OECD Commentary mentions that 'State A does not have a tax treaty [with State C] that allows for the exchange of tax information',[1725] it arguably does not matter in this context whether State A has not concluded a tax treaty at all or whether it has concluded a tax treaty but without an exchange of tax information clause. In both cases, the special tax rule on immovable property should apply as no tax information can be exchanged.

1725. 2008-2017 OECD Commentary on Article 24, para. 22 (Example 3).

If it is assumed that neither State A nor State B has concluded a tax treaty with State C, no tax treaty residence can be established in Example 3. If it is assumed instead that a tax treaty is in force with State C, it still remains unclear whether the tiebreaker in Article 4(3) of that treaty follows the OECD Model (POEM or, since 2017, mutual agreement) or relies on some other criterion (incorporation). In Example 3, references to tax treaty residence initially appear problematic because the subject of comparison is not a tax treaty resident under the tax treaty between State A and State B and might not be a tax treaty resident under any other tax treaty as well. At the same time, relying on the POEM just because Article 4(3) of the tax treaty between State A and State B envisages this criterion as a tiebreaker for cases of dual residence if based on the pre-2017 OECD Model does not appear convincing. Why should the POEM suffice for comparability if, in this particular case (no case of dual residence), it is legally irrelevant both under the domestic tax law of State A and under the tax treaty itself?

Although the POEM is not at all connected to nationality, inevitably linked differences in tax treaty residence can exist when the object of comparison is considered as well, that is the national company incorporated in State A having its POEM in State C. Under the domestic tax law of State A, companies that are incorporated in that State are residents thereof. It follows that the hypothetical object of comparison is a resident of State A under Article 4(1) of the tax treaty between State A and State B. Unlike the subject of comparison that is a tax treaty resident of neither State A nor State B, the object of comparison is a tax treaty resident of State A. While both the foreign and the national company have their POEM in State C and insofar no differences in circumstances exist, it still can be argued that they are 'not ... in the same circumstances, with respect to ... residence'[1726] because the foreign company that is incorporated in State B (the subject of comparison) is a tax treaty resident of neither Contracting State, but the national company incorporated in State A (the object of comparison) is not only subject to full tax liability as a resident under the domestic tax law of State A but also a tax treaty resident of State A under the entire Article 4.

This conclusion about differences in tax treaty residence presupposes that there is no tax treaty in force between State A and State C or that a tax treaty between these States deviates from the OECD Model by using incorporation as the tiebreaker under Article 4(3). Otherwise, if the POEM was the tiebreaker under a tax treaty between State A and State C, State C would be the residence State for tax treaty purposes and State A would be the source State. As a consequence, at least according to the OECD Commentary,[1727] the object of comparison, that is the hypothetical national company incorporated in State A having its POEM in State C, would not be a resident of State A under Article 4(1) of the tax treaty between State A and State B. It would be liable in State A only for the income from sources in that State or capital situated therein. In such a case, both the subject and the object of comparison would not be a tax treaty resident of either Contracting State.

Nevertheless, regardless of whether the foreign company of State B and the national company of State A are both considered to be non-residents for tax treaty

1726. *Ibid.*, para. 22 (Example 3).
1727. 2008–2017 OECD Commentary on Article 4, para. 8.2.

purposes or whether incorporation in State A necessarily leads to differences in tax treaty residence, certain other inevitably linked differences in circumstances remain: the foreign company of State B is not subject to full tax liability under the domestic law of State A, whereas the national company of State A is subject to full tax liability because of its incorporation in State A. In Example 3, the decisive question thus remains unanswered: why should differences in residence under the domestic tax law of State A or, if appropriate, corresponding differences in tax treaty residence be relevant in this particular case? State A taxes a foreign company incorporated in State B as a taxpayer subject to limited tax liability. Accordingly, only income from sources in State A is subject to tax therein. By contrast, a national company incorporated in State A is taxed on a worldwide basis. It is unclear why this difference in the scope of tax liability should be relevant for the domestic tax measure under scrutiny, that is for taxing the income from immovable property located in State A. After all, the measure that potentially violates Article 24(1) is only concerned with the taxation of income from immovable property located in State A. It only applies to non-residents that are taxed on a territorial basis in State A and only deals with income that always remains taxable in State A regardless of residence.[1728]

Income from immovable property located in State A always remains taxable in State A regardless of whether the taxpayer is a resident or non-resident under the domestic tax law of State A or the tax treaty. Regarding the subject of comparison, the allocation rules of the treaty between State A and State B are not applicable because the foreign company in question is not a resident of either Contracting State. In addition, Article 6 of any tax treaty (for instance, between State A and State C) would grant State A, as the source State, the taxing rights with respect to income from immovable property located in State A. Concerning the object of comparison, the allocation rules of the treaty between State A and State B would also grant State A the taxing rights for income from immovable property located in State A. Since the hypothetical national company would be incorporated in State A, it would be a resident of State A under the domestic tax law and under Article 4 of the tax treaty between State A and State B (unless State A loses the tiebreaker rules of another tax treaty). Although Article 6 would not be applicable because the immovable property would not be located in the other Contracting State, that is State B, Article 7 or 21 would grant the taxing rights to State A which, in this case, is the residence State. All in all, State A always has the right to tax the income from immovable property located in State A. Therefore, as no differences in taxing rights with regard to the immovable property located in State A are apparent, it is doubtful why inevitably linked differences in tax liability or tax treaty residence should matter in Example 3. These differences could rather constitute a pretext for discrimination because of nationality which means that they should be

1728. To be precise, State A could also tax, on a territorial basis, income from immovable property located outside its territory if that property has some other close connection to its territory (for instance, if immovable property located outside of State A is functionally, not physically, attributable to a PE located in State A), but usually the location or situs of immovable property is used by States to determine the scope of limited tax liability.

regarded as irrelevant and allow establishing comparability and tax discrimination under Article 24(1).

[iii] Exchange of Information

The OECD Commentary mentions a policy explanation for why certain differences in circumstances that are inevitably linked to incorporation matter in Example 3. A company incorporated in State B 'would not be in the same circumstances, with respect to its residence, as a company incorporated in State A and the residence of the company would be relevant (*e.g.* for purposes of accessing the information necessary to verify the net income from immovable property derived by a non-resident taxpayer)'.[1729] Although the OECD Commentary equates incorporation with residence and thereby implies that differences in the scope of tax liability matter, it is at least questionable whether such a case for tax liability can be made.[1730] State A appears to have concerns regarding information that is necessary to assess the net income derived from immovable property in cases when a company has no personal connection to its territory. Conversely, as incorporation constitutes a sufficient personal connection for full tax liability and residence in State A, it may allow State A to access and verify information for the purposes of taxing immovable property located in State A.

Nevertheless, the POEM in State A, even though it does not lead to full tax liability and residence, appears to suffice for accessing and verifying such information as well. Given that '[t]he domestic tax law of State A provides that a non-resident company [a company not incorporated in State A] that is a resident of a State [has its place of effective management in a State] with which State A does not have a tax treaty that allows for the exchange of tax information is subject to [different treatment]',[1731] a company may be incorporated or have its POEM in State A in order to avoid the application of the special tax rule on immovable property. If a foreign company incorporated abroad has its POEM in State A, it arguably cannot be 'a resident of a State with which State A does not have a tax treaty that allows for the exchange of tax information'.[1732] It follows that a company incorporated in State B but having its POEM in State A is not subject to potentially more burdensome taxation.

From a policy perspective, such an understanding of the domestic tax law of State A provides meaningful results. A sufficiently close personal connection to State A for the purposes of gathering or verifying information need not depend on full tax liability in State A. State A seeks to rely on exchange of tax information clauses in order to assess and verify the net income derived from immovable property located in State A only if a company has no nexus to State A because it is incorporated and has its POEM abroad. Without an exchange of tax information clause, a different tax assessment substitutes information requests and thereby considers the value of the immovable property instead of the net income derived from that property. Not all foreign

1729. 2008–2017 OECD Commentary on Article 24, para. 22 (Example 3).
1730. *See also* Loukota and Jirousek 2016 m.no. 17.
1731. *Ibid.*, para. 22 (Example 3).
1732. *Ibid.*, para. 22 (Example 3).

companies are disadvantaged as certain foreign companies may have a sufficient personal nexus to State A or may be located in a State with which exchange of tax information is possible. Consequently, as it appears from the facts of the case, the POEM in State A suffices as a personal nexus for gathering information about net income from immovable property located in State A even though this nexus does not lead to full tax liability in State A.

It can be further assumed that incorporation in State A also suffices as a personal nexus to State A even if, in certain cases, this nexus does not lead to full tax liability in State A within the meaning of the second sentence of Article 4(1). If State A has concluded a tax treaty with State C that follows the pre-2017 OECD Model, except that it contains no exchange of tax information clause, State A loses the tiebreaker under Article 4(3) in cases when a national company incorporated in State A has its POEM in State C. State C would be the residence State for tax treaty purposes, and State A would be the source State. As a consequence, the company in question would be liable to tax in State A only for income from sources in State A or capital situated therein. Arguably, the company would not be a resident of State A under any other tax treaty concluded by State A including the tax treaty between State A and State B.[1733] Nevertheless, incorporation in State A would still appear to constitute a sufficient personal connection for obtaining information about the net income from immovable property located in State A. Since the special tax rule presupposes 'a non-resident company',[1734] that is a company not incorporated in State A, it could never apply to a company incorporated in State A even if that company is taxed in State A on a territorial basis. This illustrates that even without full tax liability in State A within the meaning of the second sentence of Article 4(1), there might be a sufficient nexus. State A is able to obtain and verify all information and to tax the income from immovable property on a net basis if a company is incorporated in or has its POEM in that State.

Since this substantive analysis of the scope and design of the domestic tax measure under scrutiny indicates that the issue of full or limited tax liability is not at all relevant for the purposes of taxing the income from immovable property located in State A on a net basis, 'residence' either cannot be a relevant difference in circumstances under Article 24(1) or cannot mean 'differences in tax liability'. In fact, the factors of incorporation, the POEM, and the existence of a tax treaty with an exchange of tax information clause all appear to constitute a proxy for concern regarding the availability and validity of information that is required for taxing the net income from immovable property.[1735] In Example 3, the POEM is neither located in State A nor in a State with which State A has concluded a tax treaty that allows for the exchange of tax information. In this concrete case, therefore (but not necessarily in other cases) differences in incorporation trigger differences in tax treatment. Although full tax liability and tax treaty residence are inevitably linked to nationality – the foreign company of State B is not subject to full tax liability in State A and not a tax treaty resident; the national company of State A is subject to full tax liability in State A and a

1733. 2008–2017 OECD Commentary on Article 4, para. 8.2.
1734. 2008–2017 OECD Commentary on Article 24, para. 22 (Example 3).
1735. *See also*, to this effect, Van Brussel 2015, 370.

tax treaty resident of that State – these inevitably linked differences in circumstances do not appear relevant for the domestic tax measure under scrutiny and, therefore, cannot be accepted as relevant differences under Article 24(1). However, differences in the accessibility and verification of information are also inevitably linked to differences in nationality in this concrete case (but not necessarily in other cases). It can further be concluded that these differences are relevant from a domestic perspective.

Nevertheless, it has to be determined whether the reason for different tax treatment under the domestic tax law of State A is acceptable from a tax treaty perspective or whether it should amount to prohibited tax discrimination because of nationality. In Example 3, the OECD Commentary regards policy concern about the accessibility and verifiability of information as justified under Article 24(1). When taking a look at the broader context of the non-discrimination provisions, Article 26 on the exchange of tax information indicates that State A and State B have concerns about tax information in cross-border situations and, therefore, seek to enhance their exchange of tax information. It is at least reasonable to conclude that differences with regard to tax information may be considered relevant for the purposes of Article 24(1) even if they are inevitably linked to differences in nationality in a concrete case. Article 24(1), it can be argued, only prevents discrimination because of nationality but not discrimination because of potential problems regarding the access to and verification of tax information. For the purposes of taxing the income from immovable property in Example 3, incorporation is genuinely used together with other criteria as a proxy for concerns about the accessibility and verifiability of information. Thus, the fact that the measure under scrutiny uses a proxy for such policy concerns that coincides with nationality in a concrete case should not automatically mean that discrimination is at hand.

Even though the OECD Commentary has reached a reasonable result, this result cannot be explained by differences in residence. Instead, differences in potentially available and verifiable information render circumstances different in spite of an inevitable link to nationality. Why such information is relevant from a domestic perspective, whether such information requirements are in line with the objective of Article 24(1) to prevent discrimination because of nationality, and whether the factors used as a proxy for (in)sufficient information such as incorporation are justified and, thus, relevant for comparability purposes are the decisive questions. They can hardly be answered with a 'but for' test as they additionally require a substantive analysis that openly addresses all of the differences in circumstances that are inevitably linked to differences in nationality in a concrete case.

In this context, it can be asked why a tax treaty that allows for the exchange of tax information is not sufficient for information purposes when it is concluded with the State in which the company is incorporated (State B). Why does the domestic tax measure under scrutiny demand such a tax treaty to be in force with the State in which the company has its POEM (State C) even though incorporation in the allegedly discriminating State (State A) prevents potentially more burdensome treatment?[1736] If

1736. *See also* Van Brussel 2015, 370, who points out that the tax treaty 'between State A and State B provides for the exchange of information. Thus, the company incorporated in State B is

it concluded in a concrete case that there are no inevitably linked differences in circumstances with regard to the access of the information necessary to verify the net income from immovable property, a substantive analysis cannot save a prima facie discriminatory measure from violating the non-discrimination obligations of Article 24(1).

[e] Example 4: Payroll Tax Rate

In Example 4, the OECD Commentary regards differences in tax liability under domestic tax law, in residence under Article 4(1), and in tax treaty residence under the entire Article 4 as irrelevant even though all of these differences are inevitably linked to differences in nationality in a concrete case. A comparison of this example with Example 2 demonstrates that distinctions formally based on the same protected characteristic may either be in line with or violate the nationality non-discrimination clause of Article 24(1) depending on whether a substantive analysis is able to render linked differences in circumstances to be relevant for comparability purposes:[1737]

> Under the domestic income tax law of State A, companies incorporated in that State are residents of State A and companies incorporated abroad are non-residents. The State A – State B tax convention is identical to this Model Tax Convention except that paragraph 3 of Article 4 provides that if a legal person is a resident of both States under paragraph 1 of that Article, that legal person shall be deemed to be a resident of the State in which it has been incorporated. Under State A's payroll tax law, all companies that employ resident employees are subject to a payroll tax that does not make any distinction based on the residence of the employer but that provides that only companies incorporated in State A shall benefit from a lower rate of payroll tax. In that case, the fact that a company incorporated in State B will not have the same residence as a company incorporated in State A for the purposes of the A–B convention has no relevance at all with respect to the different tax treatment under the payroll tax and that different treatment would therefore be in violation of paragraph 1 absent other relevant different circumstances.

The first two sentences of this example provide identical information as the first two sentences of Example 2. State A uses only incorporation as a triggering event for full tax liability and residence, and the tiebreaker in Article 4(3) of the tax treaty between State A and State B deviates from the OECD Model by using incorporation as well. No information is given about the POEM. Therefore, it is unclear what role the POEM plays under the domestic tax law of State B (*see* Figure 4.13).

---

subjected to a different treatment even though the information could be exchanged and, as a consequence, should be available'.

1737. 2008–2017 OECD Commentary on Article 24, para. 23 (Example 4).

Figure 4.13 Discriminatory Payroll Tax Rate (Example 4)

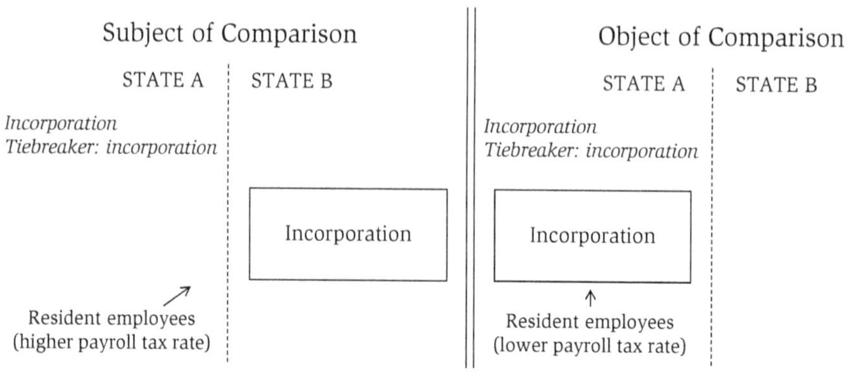

As explained with regard to Example 2, the most interesting case involves a foreign company incorporated in State B that has its POEM in State B while incorporation or the POEM leads to full tax liability and residence in State B; in that case, the tiebreaker in Article 4(3) may become relevant for the purposes of the non-discrimination analysis. With a 'but for' test, such a company (the subject of comparison) must be compared to a dual-resident company incorporated in State A that has its POEM in State B (the object of comparison). In other words, the POEM remains in State B while nationality (incorporation) changes together with all inevitably linked attributes. This test leads to differences in tax treatment because only companies incorporated in State A benefit from a lower rate of payroll tax. Accordingly, this tax distinction is prima facie discriminatory.

Nevertheless, a substantive analysis may still identify differences in circumstances that are inevitably linked to nationality but should be regarded as relevant for comparability purposes under Article 24(1). A company incorporated and having its POEM in State B is a tax treaty resident of State B, but a dual-resident company incorporated in State A having its POEM in State B is a tax treaty resident of State A since the tiebreaker in Article 4(3) solves this case in favour of State A. It follows that the subject of comparison, the foreign company of State B, necessarily is a tax treaty resident of State B, whereas the object of comparison, the national company of State A, necessarily is a tax treaty resident of State A; differences in incorporation inevitably lead to differences in tax treaty residence. In addition, only the national company of State A is subject to full tax liability under the domestic tax law of State A, whereas the foreign company of State B is not subject to full tax liability.

Although these inevitably linked differences in circumstances and, in particular, differences with regard to tax treaty residence are present in both Example 2 and Example 4, the OECD Commentary reaches different conclusions. In Example 2, Article 24(1) is not violated because differences in residence are relevant despite their link to nationality (*see* section §4.03[A][2][c]). In Example 4, by contrast, the OECD Commentary concludes that 'the fact that a company incorporated in State B will not have the same residence as a company incorporated in State A for the purposes of the A–B convention has no relevance at all with respect to the different tax treatment ... and that different treatment would therefore be in violation of paragraph 1 absent other relevant different circumstances'.[1738] Apparently, either differences in residence merely constitute a pretext for discrimination from a domestic perspective or an arguably good reason for different tax treatment must nevertheless be equated with prohibited tax discrimination because of nationality.

In Example 4, 'all companies that employ resident employees are subject to a payroll tax that does not make any distinction based on the residence of the employer but that provides that only companies incorporated in State A shall benefit from a lower rate of payroll tax'.[1739] With this statement, the OECD Commentary appears to emphasize that, for the purposes of payroll tax, incorporation of the employer that coincides with residence under the domestic tax law of State A and with tax treaty residence under the entire Article 4 is completely irrelevant except for the purposes of the tax rate. State A's payroll tax does not make any distinction based on the residence of the employer, but it makes a distinction based on the incorporation of the employer as far as the tax rate is concerned.

In fact, what objectives a particular tax system pursues, how that tax system is designed, and how the domestic tax measure under scrutiny fits into that tax system may have important implications for whether inevitably linked differences in circumstances can be regarded as relevant. If neither tax treaty residence nor nationality of a particular person (employer) plays a role for any other tax provision within a particular tax system (payroll tax), it is more difficult to argue that differences in residence are relevant and should prevent comparability even though they correspond to protected differences in nationality. By contrast, if residence is a fundamental condition for all personal tax benefits within a tax system (personal income tax), there is some contextual underpinning that differences in residence remain fundamental to the domestic tax measure at issue regardless of any link to nationality as long as that measure deals with personal tax benefits. Tax systems that differentiate between residents and non-residents usually do so with respect to various advantages and disadvantages from the scope of tax liability (worldwide or territorial taxation) to special family deductions and tax-free allowances. Thus, if a tax system such as a payroll tax distinguishes between residents (nationals) and non-residents (non-nationals) only for the purposes of prescribing a higher or lower rate of tax, a systematic reason for different tax treatment becomes, at the least, doubtful.

It is also necessary to consider that the payroll tax is, in fact, a territorial tax system. 'Under State A's payroll tax law, all [resident and non-resident, national and foreign] companies that employ resident employees are subject to a payroll tax.'[1740] Thus, resident *employees* establish a relevant territorial connection to State A just as, in other cases, resident persons distributing dividends or paying interest may establish a relevant connection for source taxation. From this perspective, since both resident and non-resident employers are subject to the same tax and to the same tax base regardless

1738. 2008–2017 OECD Commentary on Article 24, para. 23 (Example 4).
1739. *Ibid.*, para. 23 (Example 4).
1740. *Ibid.*, para. 23 (Example 4).

of their incorporation, a distinction between resident and non-resident employers at the level of the tax rate appears dubious. The OECD Commentary thus rightly concludes that 'different treatment would ... be in violation of paragraph 1 absent other relevant different circumstances'.[1741] While, in principle, there could be valid and justified reasons for such a distinction that would prevent comparability under Article 24(1) despite a link to nationality, such reasons and corresponding differences in circumstances are not apparent from the facts of the case.

Overall, Example 4 is a great illustration that tax distinctions based on exactly the same protected characteristic and concerning the same inevitably linked differences in circumstances may lead to different results under Article 24(1) depending on what purpose the measure in question pursues and whether this purpose is legitimate from a tax treaty perspective. If no genuine purpose is apparent, such as in Example 4 concerning a payroll tax, discrimination under Article 24(1) has to be confirmed. A 'but for' test renders a tax distinction on the basis of nationality as being suspect of constituting prohibited tax discrimination and a substantive analysis is not able to establish an inevitably linked characteristic that could be regarded as the actual grounds for different tax treatment and be distinguished from nationality. If, however, a genuine purpose can be identified, such as in Example 2, and if this purpose is in line with the objectives of the non-discrimination provisions, differences in circumstances prevent comparability and discrimination under Article 24(1) despite being inevitably linked to differences in nationality in a concrete case.

[f] Example 5: Group Consolidation

Example 5 is the last example of the OECD Commentary. It denies an extension of group consolidation regimes to foreign companies that are non-residents due to their incorporation abroad:[1742]

> Under the domestic income tax law of State A, companies incorporated in that State or which have their place of effective management in that State are residents of the State and companies that do not meet one of these two conditions are non-residents. Under the domestic income tax law of State B, companies incorporated in that State are residents of that State. The State A – State B tax convention is identical to this Model Tax Convention except that paragraph 3 of Article 4 provides that if a legal person is a resident of both States under paragraph 1 of that Article, that legal person shall be deemed to be a resident only of the State in which it has been incorporated. The domestic tax law of State A further provides that companies that have been incorporated and that have their place of effective management in that State are entitled to consolidate their income for tax purposes if they are part of a group of companies that have common shareholders. Company X, which was incorporated in State B, belongs to the same group as two companies incorporated in State A and all these companies are effectively managed in State A. Since it was not incorporated in State A, company X is not allowed to consolidate its income with that of the two other companies.

1741. *Ibid.*, para. 23 (Example 4).
1742. 2008–2017 OECD Commentary on Article 24, paras 24–25 (Example 5).

> In that case, even if company X is a resident of State A under the domestic law of that State, it is not a resident of State A for purposes of the Convention by virtue of paragraph 3 of Article 4. It will therefore not be in the same circumstances as the other companies of the group as regards residence and paragraph 1 will not allow it to obtain the benefits of consolidation even if the different treatment results from the fact that company X has not been incorporated in State A. The residence of company X is clearly relevant with respect to the benefits of consolidation since certain provisions of the Convention, such as Articles 7 and 10, would prevent State A from taxing certain types of income derived by company X.

When approaching this example with a 'but for' test, nationality (incorporation) must be deemed to be different together with all inevitably linked attributes. Since the domestic tax measure under scrutiny explicitly relies on incorporation while all other conditions for group consolidation (a group of companies that have common shareholders, POEM in State A) are fulfilled, differences in nationality lead to differences in tax treatment in this concrete case. The fact that some nationals are treated less favourably as well (notably, individuals, companies that are not part of a group, companies that are part of a group but which have their POEM abroad and cannot rely on the PE non-discrimination clause) or that all foreigners are disadvantaged speaks neither for nor against prima facie discrimination. A 'but for' test establishes prima facie discrimination in this concrete case regardless of how other cases are treated.

As a next step, it is necessary to consider whether differences in circumstances that are inevitably linked to nationality may nevertheless justify differences in tax treatment by being relevant and preventing comparability. Unlike in Examples 2, 3, and 4 in which the domestic income tax law of State A relies only on incorporation but, in accordance with Example 1, companies incorporated in State A or having their POEM in State A are residents thereof. Accordingly, both a foreign company incorporated in State B that has its POEM in State A (the subject of comparison) and a national company incorporated in State A that has its POEM in State A (the object of comparison) are subject to full tax liability in State A because the POEM suffices for residence in State A (*see* Figure 4.14). As tax liability and residence under Article 4(1) in State A do not differ, it is not possible to justify different tax treatment on this basis.

Figure 4.14 Legitimate Group Consolidation Regime (Example 5)

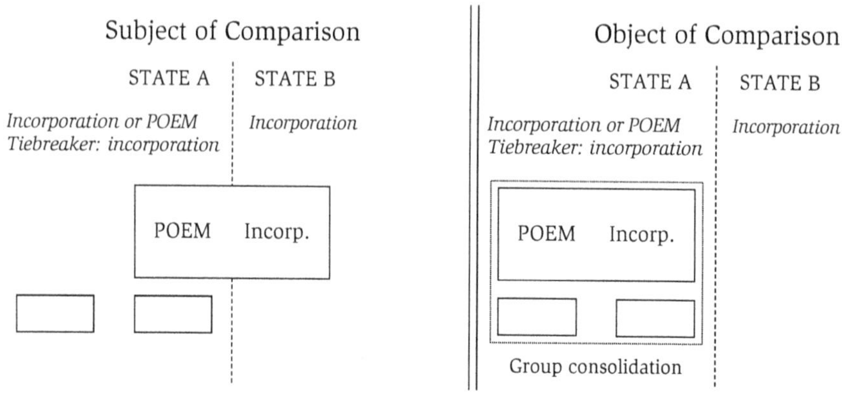

However, according to the OECD Commentary, tax treaty residence must be considered as well.[1743] In Example 5, State B relies only on incorporation as a triggering event for full tax liability and residence. Moreover, it negotiated a tax treaty with State A that deviates from the OECD Model. In cases of dual residence, the tiebreaker in Article 4(3) provides that incorporation determines the residence State for tax treaty purposes. It follows that a company incorporated in State B is always a resident of State B for tax treaty purposes even if it has its POEM in State A. State A, due to the application of the tax treaty, is able to tax that company only for income from sources in State A or capital situated therein.[1744] By contrast, a company incorporated in State A is a resident of State A for tax treaty purposes and, therefore, subject to broader tax liability in State A, although State A is obligated to prevent double taxation of income from sources in State B or capital situated therein. In Example 5, differences in nationality thus lead to differences in tax treaty residence because incorporation is the decisive tiebreaker in cases of dual residence.

Although differences in incorporation inevitably trigger differences in tax treaty residence, it must be determined whether such differences play a role from a domestic perspective and whether they can be accepted as being relevant under Article 24(1). For the OECD Commentary, no discrimination exists because differences in incorporation lead to differences in tax treaty residence due to Article 4(3). In addition, 'residence … is clearly relevant with respect to the benefits of consolidation since certain provisions of the Convention, such as Articles 7 and 10, would prevent State A from taxing certain types of income'[1745] derived by a company incorporated in State B even if this company has its POEM in State A.

The OECD Commentary might implicitly assume that the group consolidation regime aims at consolidating only those profits and losses that are taxable in State A.

1743. *See*, for instance, 2008–2017 OECD Commentary on Article 24, para. 17.
1744. 2008–2017 OECD Commentary on Article 4, para. 8.2.
1745. *Ibid.*, para. 25 (Example 5).

Due to consolidation, profits of one company are not taxed because they are offset by losses of another company. At the same time, the losses of that other company are utilized and, therefore, any future profits will not be offset by these losses. This means that the group consolidation regime primarily provides liquidity or cash-flow advantages (*see also* section §4.04[C][1]). Since losses can be offset immediately, profits are taxed only later. This also means that a State may only be prepared to consider losses if it is also able to tax corresponding profits later on.

If a non-resident company, that is a company incorporated abroad, would participate in a group consolidation regime in State A, there could be a risk that losses of that company are used and offset against taxable profits in State A, but corresponding profits are not taxed in that State later on. In the case that the non-resident company suffers losses, it could claim group consolidation benefits on the basis of Article 24(1) for all of its losses, but, in the case that the non-resident company makes profits, it simply could not rely on Article 24(1) and, therefore, would be taxed only on its profits that have their source in State A. This could mean that the losses would be considered in State A due to Article 24(1), but the corresponding profits would not be taxed since the taxing rights would remain with the residence State of that company, that is State B. As the OECD Commentary highlights, '[c]ertain provisions of the Convention, such as Articles 7 and 10, would prevent State A from taxing certain types of income derived by a company incorporated in State B even if this company has its place of effective management in State A'.[1746] From a domestic perspective, therefore, it makes sense to prohibit group consolidation with companies that are treated as non-residents for tax treaty purposes even if they are subject to full tax liability under domestic law. Otherwise, certain benefits would have to be extended under Article 24(1) without being able to ensure later taxation (but *see also* section §4.04[C][2][d]).

Some support for this view can also be found in the scope and design of the domestic tax measure under scrutiny when considered from a multilateral perspective. Pursuant to the domestic tax law of State A, 'companies that have been incorporated *and* that have their place of effective management in that State are entitled to consolidate their income for tax purposes if they are part of a group of companies that have common shareholders', whereas 'companies incorporated in that State *or* which have their place of effective management in that State are residents of the State' (emphasis added).[1747] A national company of State A is not able to participate in group consolidation if it has its POEM abroad even though it is subject to full tax liability. State A might thereby ensure that only tax treaty residents are eligible for group consolidation. If some of State A's tax treaties, in contrast to the tax treaty between State A and State B, rely on the POEM as a tiebreaker in Article 4(3), a national company of State A that has its POEM abroad might not be a tax treaty resident of State A; group consolidation would then be denied as well. Thus, the fact that State A requires both incorporation and the POEM to be in State A in order to qualify for group consolidation might support the alleged purpose that only tax treaty residents of State A should benefit from group consolidation.

1746. *Ibid.*, para. 25 (Example 5).
1747. *Ibid.*, para. 24 (Example 5).

At the same time, the fact that State A refers to both incorporation and the POEM instead of directly relying on tax treaty residence makes the domestic tax measure under scrutiny too limited in its scope. When a tax treaty relies on the POEM in Article 4(3), both a foreign company that has its POEM in State A and a national company that has its POEM in State A are tax treaty residents of State A despite their differences in incorporation. Accordingly, the domestic tax measure under scrutiny might violate the non-discrimination obligations of Article 24(1) of such a treaty. A 'but for' test would indicate prima facie discrimination. Since tax treaty residence would not differ, it would not be available as an inevitably linked but relevant characteristic that could justify differences in tax treatment. Even though the condition of incorporation was intended to be used for an arguably legitimate reason, this legitimate reason cannot succeed if it is not reflected in inevitably linked differences in circumstances in a concrete case.[1748]

If it is concluded that the cumulative criteria of incorporation and the POEM, in spite of being an imperfect proxy for tax treaty residence, genuinely aim at preventing group consolidation of companies that are non-residents for tax treaty purposes, differences in tax treaty residence could be regarded as relevant. Nevertheless, in Example 5, it could be questioned whether a substantive analysis should always render inevitably linked differences in tax treaty residence as being relevant. While it is true that Articles 7 and 10 on business profits and dividends would prevent State A from taxing certain types of income derived by a company resident in State B, State A may still have taxing rights for other types of income. If a company incorporated and resident in State B has a PE in State A, State A has the taxing rights for the business profits that are attributable to that PE under Article 7 and for all of the dividends received by that PE under Article 10(4) in conjunction with Article 7. From this perspective, the Commentary's reference to Articles 7 and 10 as an explanation for why differences in tax treaty residence should be relevant holds true only for those types or parts of income that are not taxable in State A.

Incorporation is a suitable proxy for differences in residence but not a suitable proxy for differences in taxing rights. Given that group consolidation is about consolidating taxable profits and losses, differences in residence could only partly prevent comparability. It could be argued that differences in residence and corresponding differences in taxing rights should be relevant under Article 24(1) only to the extent that income is not taxable in State A due to the application of the tax treaty between State A and State B. To the extent that income remains taxable in State A when a PE exists in that State, differences in residence become irrelevant under Article 24(1) as they have no impact on the taxing rights of State A. As a consequence, a foreign company that is resident in State B could be regarded as comparable to a national company that is resident in State A insofar as they are both taxable in State A and, thus,

1748. This example further highlights that the same domestic tax measure might overall pursue a legitimate purpose but, depending on the facts and circumstances of a particular case, still lead to prohibited tax discrimination if that purpose is not reflected in differences in circumstances that are inevitably linked to differences in nationality, notably, if the tiebreaker in Article 4(3) does not rely on incorporation but on the POEM.

no inevitably linked differences in taxing rights exist. A general prohibition of consolidation due to foreign incorporation and tax treaty residence would at least partly constitute discrimination because of nationality under Article 24(1).

It could be responded that even if a company incorporated in State B maintains a PE in State A, certain relevant differences between this company and a company incorporated in State A remain. If a company incorporated in State A pays dividends out of the profits that have been taxable (and possibly consolidated) in State A, the recipient is subject to tax on those dividends in State A. Even if the recipient of the dividends is a non-resident, Article 10(2) generally permits State A to tax those dividends up to a certain amount. By contrast, if a non-resident company pays dividends out of the profits derived by a PE in State A, the recipient is generally not subject to tax on those dividends in State A unless the recipient itself is resident in State A or has a PE therein.[1749] Profits derived by a PE in State A may usually be transferred to the head office of a company that is incorporated and resident in State B without any tax consequences while profits derived by a company incorporated in State A will likely trigger tax on dividends if those dividends are paid to a company incorporated and resident in State B. All of these differences in circumstances are also inevitably linked to differences in nationality when incorporation determines tax treaty residence.

Instead of regarding differences in residence as irrelevant and looking at whether inevitably linked differences in taxing rights or other relevant differences in circumstances exist, the OECD Commentary takes a different approach. Since differences in residence may potentially have an impact on State A's taxing rights, since State A is apparently concerned with its taxing rights, and since such broader concerns also appear legitimate from the perspective of the non-discrimination provisions, there is no discrimination at all. State A can prohibit group consolidation for all of the companies incorporated in State B with respect to all types of income without violating the non-discrimination obligations of Article 24(1). Indeed, Article 24(3) is a better-targeted non-discrimination rule that addresses the question of whether differences in tax treatment based on tax treaty residence should be permitted or branded as discrimination if a State has taxing rights with regard to a PE (*see* section §4.04[C][2]).

[B] Overlap of Residence and Low or No Taxation Revisited

[1] 1st Step: Application of a 'But For' Test

The OECD Commentary does not discuss whether non-deductibility rules specifically countering hybrid mismatch arrangements or low or no taxation are suspect to discrimination under Article 24(4). Only in the Final Report on BEPS Action 2 is it argued that anti-hybrid mismatch rules under domestic tax law do not appear to raise concerns about a possible conflict with Article 24(4) and (5):[1750]

1749. *See also* Article 10(5) of the OECD Model.
1750. OECD, Final Report on BEPS Action 2, para. 448. *See also* Schnitger and Oskamp 2014, 392–393.

> Some of the domestic law recommendations to neutralise the effects of hybrid mismatch arrangements ... may impact payments to non-residents more than they will impact payments to residents. This, however, is not relevant for the purposes of Article 24 as long as the distinction is based on the treatment of the payments in the hands of the payers and recipients. The fact that a mismatch in the tax treatment of an entity or payment is less likely in a purely domestic context (i.e. one would expect a country to be consistent in the way it characterises domestic payments and entities) cannot be interpreted as meaning that rules that are strictly based on the existence of such a mismatch are treating payments to non-residents, or to non-resident owned enterprises, differently from the way payments to residents, or resident-owned enterprises, are treated under domestic law.

Hybrid mismatch arrangements can be effectively addressed by different kinds of non-deductibility rules. For the purposes of Article 24(4), it is worth distinguishing between three types of tax measures that may be used against non-taxation:

(1) First, a non-deductibility rule of a State may specifically target hybrid mismatch arrangements. Therefore, it may employ a facially neutral criterion 'hybrid mismatch' that denies a deduction of a payment if a different classification of a financial instrument as equity or debt leads to a conflict in tax treatment and to a situation of a deduction and no inclusion.
(2) Second, a non-deductibility rule of a State may not only target hybrid mismatch arrangements but all cases of insufficient taxation. Therefore, it may employ a facially neutral criterion 'low or no taxation' that denies a deduction if a payment is not or insufficiently taxed in any State. Conversely, high taxation in any State, or in all States taken together, suffices for a deduction regardless of which State is actually able to tax.
(3) Third, a non-deductibility rule of a State may target all cases of no taxation in that State. Therefore, it may employ a facially neutral criterion 'not subject to tax in this State' that denies a deduction if a payment is not taxed in that State for whatever reason (tax exemption, no full or limited tax liability, no taxing rights under a tax treaty, etc.) irrespective of whether that payment is subject to tax in another State.

With regard to non-deductibility rules that specifically target hybrid mismatch arrangements, in some cases, a change in residence may lead to full and unrestricted tax liability in the allegedly discriminating State and, therefore, avoid a hybrid mismatch. This is in particular true if no PE is involved or if the income of a PE abroad would be taxed and a tax credit would be granted under Article 23 B. With a 'but for' test, a change in residence may consequently lead to a change in tax treatment and thereby establish a sufficient link between the criterion for different tax treatment and the protected characteristic of the recipient's residence. It does not matter that, in other cases involving somewhat different facts and circumstances, payments to resident recipients may be disadvantaged as well in particular if a PE is located abroad of which the income is exempt under Article 23 A. It also does not matter that not all payments to non-resident recipients are disadvantaged as non-resident individuals and corporations that are not part of a hybrid mismatch arrangement allow for a deduction. For the purposes of determining whether the protected characteristic has relevant effects on taxation and whether the tax distinction is prima facie discriminatory in a concrete case, a 'but for' test focuses only on the taxpayer in question and on the facts and circumstances of that individual case.

With regard to non-deductibility rules that target all cases of insufficient taxation and, therefore, employ a facially neutral criterion 'low or no taxation', there is prima facie discrimination in some additional situations. If a non-resident recipient without a PE benefits from a favourable tax regime in the other Contracting State, a change in residence may lead to a change in tax treatment, notably, if a resident recipient in otherwise identical circumstances would be subject to tax in the allegedly discriminating State without benefiting from a favourable tax regime. This allows establishing prima facie discrimination with a 'but for' test in a concrete case even though the results in other cases may be different. It does not matter that, in certain situations, both Contracting States may provide for a favourable tax regime, for instance, to non-profit organizations and, therefore, a change in residence may not lead to a change in tax treatment if non-profit organizations are involved.[1751] In all cases when the State of the recipient, unlike the State of the payer, grants tax benefits that lead to low or no taxation, a non-deductibility rule that targets such situations leads to prima facie discrimination with a 'but for' test.

Finally, with regard to non-deductibility rules of a State that target cases of no taxation in that State and, therefore, employ a facially neutral criterion 'not subject to tax in this State', even more situations are prima facie discriminatory. If a non-resident recipient without a PE is taxed in the other Contracting State, a change in residence may lead to a change in tax treatment, notably, if the non-resident recipient carries on activities that would not qualify for a tax exemption in the allegedly discriminating State. Although (or rather because) this recipient is taxed in the other Contracting State, a deduction of the payments is denied. As a consequence, a change in residence allows establishing prima facie discrimination with a 'but for' test in this concrete case.

As far as non-deductibility rules countering hybrid mismatch arrangements, situations of low or no taxation, or situations of not being subject to tax in a State are concerned, it is always possible to find some cases in which a 'but for' test leads to prima facie discrimination. It is not convincing to argue that a State can avoid discrimination under Article 24(4) in all of those cases simply by disadvantaging payments to tax-exempt resident recipients together with all payments to non-resident recipients. With a 'but for' test, only corporations carrying on gainful undertakings can be compared to each other thereby disregarding individuals and tax-exempt non-profit organizations due to their fundamentally dissimilar situation.[1752] Which activities a person performs and whether this person is an individual or a corporation is not a

1751. *See also* Raad 1986, 177: 'The required same circumstances and conditions permit the disallowance of payments to persons who are nonresident (or are in a position closely related thereto) only if payments to resident persons in the same circumstances can be deducted. Accordingly, if, e.g., resident nonprofit institutions are exempt from taxation and for that reason payments to them are not deductible, the disallowance of a payment to a similar nonresident institution is permitted under the clause'.

1752. *See also supra* n. 1562.

matter that would be inevitably linked to the protected characteristic. Deeming the recipient's residence to be different does not render non-resident corporations carrying on gainful undertakings comparable to resident individuals or tax-exempt non-profit organizations. Nevertheless, the scope and design of the domestic tax measure under scrutiny may be considered with a substantive analysis.

[2] 2nd Step: Relevance of Linked Attributes

[a] General Remarks

If a 'but for' test establishes prima facie discrimination under Article 24(4), there remain no differences in circumstances without an inevitable connection to differences in residence. This conversely means that only the recipient's residence or an inevitably linked characteristic can be the reason for different tax treatment under Article 24(4). Whether such an inevitably linked characteristic is relevant for comparability purposes and thereby prevents discrimination or whether the recipient's residence prevails as the actual reason for different tax treatment still has to be determined. It is necessary to objectively verify what purposes the domestic tax measure under scrutiny pursues and whether these purposes can be judged as legitimate from a tax treaty perspective or rather amount to a prohibited tax distinction because of residence.

In the cases discussed here, the domestic tax measure under scrutiny relies on a facially neutral characteristic. When deeming the recipient's residence to be different, a 'but for' test, therefore, is able to demonstrate relevant differences in tax treatment only if this facially neutral characteristic inevitably changes as well. As a consequence, in all cases that have remained suspect to discrimination with a 'but for' test, there remains at least one difference in circumstances that could be regarded as relevant for comparability purposes despite its inevitable link to the recipient's residence: a difference in the existence of a hybrid mismatch, a difference in whether the payments are subject to low or no taxation, or a difference in whether the payments are subject to tax in the allegedly discriminating State. As will be seen below, not all of these differences in circumstances reflect justified reasons for different tax treatment. Not all inevitably linked characteristics, therefore, can be accepted as establishing relevant differences for comparability purposes.

[b] Example 1: Hybrid Mismatches

If a State enacts a non-deductibility rule that specifically targets hybrid mismatch arrangements, in certain cases, a change in the recipient's residence and in all inevitably linked attributes leads to a change in tax treatment. In these cases, as a second step, it has to be determined on a substantive basis whether differences in the existence of a hybrid mismatch, despite being inevitably linked to protected differences in the recipient's residence, are relevant. For this purpose, it is necessary to analyse what objectives the domestic tax measure under scrutiny pursues and whether these objectives are in line with or contradict the objectives of the non-discrimination clause of Article 24(4).

It might seem clear that a non-deductibility rule that employs a facially neutral criterion of a hybrid mismatch genuinely aims at countering hybrid mismatch arrangements and not at disadvantaging non-resident recipients because of their foreign residence. This might seem less clear if this rule disadvantages only payments to non-resident recipients and never applies in purely domestic situations. Nevertheless, the fact that no unprotected persons are disadvantaged is no reason to confirm discrimination under Article 24 just as the fact that some unprotected persons are also disadvantaged is no reason to deny discrimination. If a rule disadvantages only foreigners or non-residents, it may still pursue a goal that is, in substance, different from nationality or residence. A non-deductibility rule that relies on a criterion of a hybrid mismatch may thus pursue a higher goal from a domestic perspective even if it never affects payments to resident recipients. Proof for such a genuine objective can consist in the context and historical development of that anti-hybrid mismatch measure (previous rules addressing such situations, relationship to other rules targeting unintended situations of low or no taxation, parliamentary materials identifying the reasons for that measure's introduction, etc.), but it must also be manifested in that measure's scope and design.

Not all payments to non-resident recipients are disadvantaged by a non-deductibility rule countering hybrid mismatch arrangements; only very specific payments are disadvantaged. This fact may objectively support grounds for different tax treatment that is different from residence. Apparently, the allegedly discriminating State decided not to deny a deduction of all payments to non-resident corporations but only specific payments (interest payments) that enjoy certain tax treatment that stems from a different classification of a financial instrument as equity or debt in cross-border situations provided that such payments are not taxed in any State (no taxable PE). A measure that is precisely drafted and facially neutral and disadvantages only specific persons in specific situations may point to a genuine objective of avoiding non-taxation even if that measure happens to disadvantage only protected persons. If certain situations can arise only in a cross-border context, this does not automatically mean that foreign residence is the only explanation for measures that apply to such situations.

In addition, if the rule under scrutiny addresses hybrid mismatch situations involving resident recipients that have a PE in the other Contracting State or in a third State, this reinforces the objective of countering hybrid mismatch arrangements. It does not necessarily matter whether, between the Contracting States, only non-resident recipients can be involved in a hybrid mismatch (notably, if the credit method is applied by the allegedly discriminating State). In a different bilateral context, resident recipients may still be involved in a hybrid mismatch (notably, if the exemption method is applied by the allegedly discriminating State) and trigger tax disadvantages. This is a logical consequence if that rule's genuine aim is to counter hybrid mismatch arrangements. Payments to resident recipients that are or may potentially be disadvantaged as well, therefore, constitute a strong argument against a simple equation of the facially neutral criterion for different tax treatment with the protected characteris tic. This does not mean that non-resident recipients without a PE should be compared to resident recipients with a PE if both are involved in a hybrid mismatch. A 'but for' test requires the (non-)existence of a PE to remain identical. Rather, the fact that certain resident recipients with a PE cause disadvantages in some cases dissects the link between the criterion of a hybrid mismatch and the protected attribute of the recipient's residence in all cases even if, in a concrete case, a change in residence inevitably leads to a change in tax treatment with a 'but for' test.

If it is objectively verified that a non-deductibility rule genuinely pursues a purpose that is different from discrimination by reason of the recipient's residence from a domestic perspective, it is still necessary to determine whether this purpose is in line with or contradicts the aims of the non-discrimination clause. Article 24(4) aims to ensure that the Contracting States do not frustrate the allocation of taxing rights and the avoidance of juridical double taxation under the tax treaty. A Contracting State should not be able to undo the beneficial effects of especially Articles 11, 12, and 22 by denying a deduction of payments or debts and thereby turning juridical into economic double taxation (*see* Chapter 3 section §3.03[E][1]). Thus, the question arises whether a Contracting State may deny a deduction for other reasons without violating Article 24(4), notably because of a hybrid mismatch, or whether such a reason should be equated with a condemned tax distinction.

Situations that can be regarded as discrimination because of residence under Article 24(4) include cases when a Contracting State disadvantages or denies a deduction due to the fact that certain items of income or capital are not taxable within its jurisdiction but in the other Contracting State. Initially, for the purposes of establishing such discrimination under Article 24(4), it does not matter whether the other Contracting State actually exercises its taxing rights. As the allocation rules of the tax treaty do not force a Contracting State to tax, discriminatory conditions for a deduction may also exist if the other Contracting State is allowed to tax under the tax treaty but does not exercise its taxing rights, for instance, due to a tax exemption under its domestic tax law. This is true as long as the reason for different tax treatment lies in the fact that the allegedly discriminating State relinquished its taxing rights under the tax treaty in favour of the other Contracting State and is now dissatisfied with the result. If the tax treaty assigns taxing rights to the other Contracting State, the prohibited criterion of no taxing rights in the allegedly discriminating State – no deduction 'unless the recipient … is taxable in that [allegedly discriminating] State'[1753] (*see also* Chapter 3 section §3.03[E][1][c]) – includes situations when the other Contracting State is allowed to tax under the tax treaty and indeed levies a tax as well as situations when the other Contracting State is allowed to tax under the tax treaty but does not exercise its taxing rights.

A hybrid mismatch criterion does not solely rely on the fact that the allegedly discriminating State has lost taxing rights under the tax treaty. It also relies on the fact that the payments are not taxed at all in the allegedly discriminating State, in the other Contracting State, or in a third State. By specifically targeting hybrid mismatch

1753. 1977–2017 OECD Commentary on Article 11, para. 4; and on Article 12, para. 2.

arrangements, a Contracting State thus prohibits a deduction not because it is prevented by the tax treaty from taxing payments received by non-residents but because such payments are not taxable at all due to a different classification of a financial instrument as equity or debt. On the one hand, the payments are not taxed in the allegedly discriminating State either because the recipient has an insufficient connection for full or limited tax liability or because the allocation rules of the tax treaty prohibit it from taxing (or at least limit its taxing rights).[1754] On the other hand, the payments are not taxed in the other Contracting State because that State qualifies them as dividends and stipulates a corresponding tax exemption under its domestic tax law and thereby contributes to a hybrid mismatch situation. Tax distinctions that aim at preventing situations of no taxation due to a different classification of a financial instrument as equity or debt, therefore, appear to be of no concern to the deductibility non-discrimination clause. A Contracting State does not try to compensate for its loss of taxing rights under the tax treaty by relying on a criterion of a hybrid mismatch. Article 24(4), on the other hand, does not appear to aim at preventing the Contracting States from specifically targeting situations of no taxation due to a hybrid mismatch arrangement even if, in some or all cases, a hybrid mismatch may be inevitably linked to residence.

It follows that differences in the existence of a hybrid mismatch are relevant for comparability purposes even if they are inevitably linked to differences in the recipient's residence. A substantive analysis allows concluding that, by employing the facially neutral criterion 'hybrid mismatch', the genuine aim of targeting situations of no taxation due to a hybrid mismatch cannot be equated with a condemned compensation for a loss of taxing rights from a tax treaty perspective. A non-deductibility rule specifically targeting hybrid mismatch arrangements may be maintained under Article 24(4) as a non-discriminatory tax measure. It relies on inevitably linked but relevant differences in circumstances regarding the existence of a hybrid mismatch. This is true even if no payments to resident recipients are disadvantaged in a bilateral context, that is even if a change in the recipient's residence always leads to a change in tax treatment.

[c] Example 2: Low or No Taxation

Instead of specifically targeting hybrid mismatch arrangements, States may also introduce measures that counter low or no taxation in general, notably, when deductible interest is not taxed at a specific minimum rate. Such measures may thus prohibit a deduction if payments are not taxed at all or taxed at a low rate and allow a deduction if payments are sufficiently taxed regardless of which State exercises taxing

1754. Article 11(2) grants limited taxing rights to the allegedly discriminating State and 'full' taxing rights to the other Contracting State but with a crediting obligation under Article 23 A(2) or 23 B(1). Accordingly, the allegedly discriminating State may only partly lose taxing rights and the other Contracting State may only partly be allowed to tax. Also, such an allocation of taxing rights is no reason for the allegedly discriminating State to provide for different conditions of deductibility under Article 24(4).

rights. In some cases of low or no taxation, a change in the recipient's residence may lead to a change in the level of taxation and thereby allow for a deduction if the allegedly discriminating State taxes its residents on a worldwide basis and provides for a sufficiently high tax rate and for no exemptions. Since the deductibility of the payments is inevitably linked to the recipient's residence with a 'but for' test in such cases, there is prima facie discrimination. However, a substantive analysis may still render differences in the level of taxation as being relevant and thereby prevent comparability despite an inevitable link to the recipient's residence in a concrete case.

In order to succeed in avoiding comparability and discrimination under Article 24(4), it is necessary to verify that the domestic tax measure under scrutiny pursues an aim that can be distinguished from discrimination because of the recipient's residence and that this aim is legitimate from a tax treaty perspective. This substantive analysis is conceptually similar to the analysis concerning non-deductibility rules specifically targeting hybrid mismatch arrangements (*see* section §4.03[B][2][b]) although the focus lies on differences in the overall level of taxation and not on differences in the existence of a hybrid mismatch.

A non-deductibility rule countering low or no taxation might never apply to resident recipients if the allegedly discriminating State taxes its residents on a worldwide basis, provides for a sufficiently high tax rate and for no exemptions, and uses the credit method under Article 23 B. Accordingly, in a bilateral context, such a non-deductibility rule may only apply to non-resident recipients of the other Contracting State. Therefore, it may be difficult to establish on a formal basis whether the allegedly discriminating State pursues an objective of preventing low or no taxation or whether it rather discriminates by reason of the recipient's residence even though it employs a facially neutral characteristic. Legitimate grounds for different treatment (overall level of taxation not specifically motivated by a loss of taxing rights) may be difficult to distinguish from illegitimate grounds for different treatment (limited or no taxation in the allegedly discriminating State due to the tax treaty concluded with the other Contracting State).

If the other Contracting State is a low-tax jurisdiction, a majority of non-resident recipients of that other State may be negatively affected by a criterion of low or no taxation. Nevertheless, a closer look may reveal that this criterion does not disadvantage non-resident recipients of that other State without distinction. A low-tax jurisdiction may provide for a high individual income tax rate and, therefore, may favour only corporations in order to attract capital and investment. It follows that payments to non-resident recipients of the other Contracting State may not be disadvantaged when individuals are at stake. In addition, if non-resident recipients of the other Contracting State maintain a PE or are subject to tax for some other reason in a high-tax jurisdiction, including the allegedly discriminating State, the payments may be subject to a sufficiently high tax rate thereby allowing for a deduction. As only specific non-residents of the other Contracting State are targeted, this may indicate a purpose that, from a domestic perspective, need not be equated with the recipient's residence.

In addition, even if a non-deductibility rule applies to all non-resident recipients of the other Contracting State because residence in that other State always suffices for non-deductibility, a multilateral perspective may nevertheless support a substantive distinction between the criterion of low or no taxation and the recipient's residence. In one bilateral context, the statutory tax rate of the other Contracting State may be sufficiently high so that the rule countering low or no taxation will have no scope of application. In another bilateral context, the statutory tax rate of the other Contracting State may be too low so that tax disadvantages will always be triggered. Thus, a non-deductibility rule countering low or no taxation may apply to non-residents from some States more extensively than to non-residents from other States. Although Article 24 is not about MFN treatment and does not object to different treatment between non-residents of different States, these different effects may still have important implications. Apparently, the allegedly discriminating State is not bluntly treating payments to non-resident recipients less favourably than payments to its own residents. It has chosen certain characteristics for different tax treatment that may negatively affect all non-residents from one State, some non-residents from another State, and no non-residents from yet another State – and for a reason. Such different effects in different contexts may confirm that the reason for different tax treatment from a domestic perspective is not the recipient's residence even if, in a particular bilateral context, all deductions of payments to non-resident recipients are denied by a non-deductibility rule.

Furthermore, if the allegedly discriminating State provides for a tax exemption or favourable tax regime to some of its own residents, the fact that a non-deductibility rule also denies a deduction of payments to such resident recipients further supports the conclusion that the recipient's residence is not, as such, decisive from a domestic perspective. If, in a concrete case, a non-resident recipient is subject to low or no taxation but would not qualify for a tax exemption or favourable tax regime as a resident of the allegedly discriminating State, a 'but for' test leads to prima facie discrimination because the recipient's residence and all inevitably linked differences in circumstances, including the level of taxation, are deemed to be different. Nevertheless, the fact that other resident recipients in somewhat different situations would qualify for a tax exemption or favourable tax regime in the allegedly discriminating State and would, therefore, also be targeted by the domestic tax measure under scrutiny dissects the link between the criterion of low or no taxation and the protected attribute of the recipient's residence.

At this point, it should be emphasized that, similar to anti-hybrid mismatch rules, the aim of avoiding situations of low or no taxation appears to be a legitimate tax distinction under Article 24(4) as long as high taxation in any State suffices for favourable tax treatment. A criterion of low or no taxation does not solely rely on the fact that the allegedly discriminating State has lost taxing rights under the tax treaty. It also relies on the fact that the payments are not sufficiently taxed at all in the allegedly discriminating State, in the other Contracting State, in a third State, or in all States taken together. Situations of low or no taxation, therefore, can be distinguished from situations involving a loss of taxing rights. A Contracting State does not try to compensate for a loss of taxing rights under the tax treaty by relying on a criterion of low or no taxation. Article 24(4), on the other hand, does not appear to aim at preventing the Contracting States from countering situations of low or no taxation even if, in some or all cases, residence may have influence on the overall amount of tax.

It follows that differences in the level of taxation are relevant for comparability purposes even if they are inevitably linked to differences in the recipient's residence. A substantive analysis allows concluding that, by employing the facially neutral criterion 'low or no taxation', the genuine aim of targeting situations of low or no taxation cannot be equated with a condemned compensation for a loss of taxing rights from a tax treaty perspective. A non-deductibility rule addressing situations of low or no taxation may be maintained under Article 24(4) as a non-discriminatory tax measure. It relies on linked but relevant differences in circumstances regarding the level of taxation. This is true even if no payments to resident recipients are disadvantaged in a bilateral context, that is, even if a change in the recipient's residence always leads to a change in tax treatment.

It is worth noting that a measure may also explicitly refer to residence in specific States that are known as low-tax jurisdictions by employing a list of tax havens instead of referring to a certain level of taxation and thereby using a facially neutral criterion. This explicit reference to residence does not automatically lead to prohibited tax discrimination under Article 24(4). Such a measure may disadvantage no payments to resident recipients and only selected payments to non-resident recipients. In one bilateral context, all non-resident recipients may be disadvantaged if the other Contracting State is a low-tax jurisdiction. In another bilateral context, no non-resident recipients may be disadvantaged if the other Contracting State is not regarded as a tax haven. From a multilateral perspective, not all non-resident recipients are disadvantaged but only those from specific States. Such a distinction between different non-resident recipients should trigger an enquiry into why specific States have been chosen and thereby whether the measure under scrutiny genuinely pursues an objective that is different from the recipient's residence and from a compensation for a loss of taxing rights.

The criterion of being a resident of a listed tax jurisdiction may not be perfectly targeted if it only refers to residence in a low-tax jurisdiction without taking account of whether the payments at issue are actually subject to low or no taxation; non-resident recipients that are resident in a tax haven may be subject to sufficiently high taxation in another State, and resident recipients that are resident in the allegedly discriminating State may be subject to low or no taxation if specific tax exemptions are granted by that State or if they maintain a tax-exempt PE abroad. This fact that the domestic tax measure under scrutiny is not as precisely targeted as it could be does not necessarily call into question its genuine objective of countering low or no taxation. This fact rather allows establishing discrimination in all cases when the objective of countering low or no taxation is not reflected in inevitably linked differences in circumstances.

For example, if a non-resident recipient is resident in a low-tax jurisdiction and, therefore, treated less favourably than a resident recipient even though the payments are attributable to a taxable PE in a high-tax jurisdiction, a change in residence and all inevitably linked characteristics leads to a prima facie discriminatory change in tax treatment. Subsequently, however, as the taxation at the level of the PE is not inevitably linked to the recipient's residence, there are no differences in the level of taxation that could justify that tax distinction. Even though the domestic tax measure under scrutiny may genuinely pursue the objective of countering situations of low or no taxation and even though this objective is, in principle, legitimate from a tax treaty perspective, there are no actual differences in the level of taxation that could be relevant for denying comparability in this concrete case. Similarly, if the non-resident recipient is subject to low or no taxation and a change in the recipient's residence leads to a change in tax treatment but not in the level of taxation (notably, because the allegedly discriminating State also grants a tax exemption), again, the level of taxation does not constitute an inevitably linked but relevant characteristic that could render circumstances incomparable. When a measure is not precisely targeted but only refers to residence in a low-tax jurisdiction, it can be discriminatory under Article 24(4) even if it pursues a legitimate objective because this objective might not be reflected in inevitably linked differences in circumstances in a concrete case. In effect, there is no tax discrimination only when that measure is actually effective in countering situations of low or no taxation.

[d] Example 3: Lost Taxing Rights

Perhaps the most interesting example concerns non-deductibility rules that employ a facially neutral criterion 'not subject to tax in this State'. This criterion is not meant to refer to no taxation in general but to no taxation in the allegedly discriminating State. It denies a deduction even if the payments at issue are taxed in the other Contracting State or in a third State because they are not subject to tax in the allegedly discriminating State. Such a non-deductibility rule predominantly affects non-resident recipients either because these recipients are not subject to full or limited tax liability in the allegedly discriminating State or because the tax treaty prohibits the allegedly discriminating State from taxing. It does not negatively affect all non-resident recipients because some may be taxed in the allegedly discriminating State due to a PE. Additionally, it may affect some resident recipients if their income is exempt under Article 23 A when they maintain a PE in another State or if they receive a tax exemption for other reasons such as for being a non-profit organization.

If a non-resident recipient would qualify as a resident for a tax exemption in the allegedly discriminating State and a deduction, therefore, would be denied as well, a change in residence does not lead to differences in tax treatment with a 'but for' test. This means that discrimination can be denied without a substantive analysis. However, this does not lessen concerns about tax discrimination in other cases when the recipient's residence has an inevitable effect on the tax treatment of the payments. The question arises whether differences in the fact that the non-resident recipient is not subject to tax in the allegedly discriminating State whereas a resident recipient would be so subjected constitutes a relevant characteristic for comparability purposes despite an inevitable link to the recipient's residence.

From a domestic perspective, it can be argued that the non-deductibility rule under scrutiny aims at disadvantaging all payments to recipients that are not subject to tax in the allegedly discriminating State regardless of the reason for non-taxation and regardless of the recipient's residence. Indeed, this objective could be seen as genuine and verified on the basis of the scope and design of the domestic tax measure notably because payments to resident recipients are also disadvantaged if they are not subject to tax in the allegedly discriminating State due to a tax exemption under domestic tax law. Nevertheless, in order to render differences in circumstances relevant for comparability purposes, it is necessary to consider the objectives of the non-discrimination clause of Article 24(4). It has to be decided from a tax treaty perspective whether the genuine aim of allowing deductions of payments in a State only when these payments are subject to tax in this State is legitimate and whether corresponding differences in circumstances, therefore, prevent comparability under Article 24(4) even if they are inevitably linked to the recipient's residence in a concrete case.[1755]

International juridical double taxation that is prevented by the tax treaty should not be turned into a legally different but economically comparable form of double taxation. Article 24(4) consequently objects to non-deductibility rules and different conditions for deduction that are driven by the aim of compensating for a loss of taxing rights (*see* Chapter 3 section §3.03[E][1]). Even if the domestic tax measure under scrutiny does not discriminate against all payments involving non-resident recipients and even if it does not explicitly refer to residence but, rather, to whether the payments are subject to tax in the allegedly discriminating State at the level of the recipient – no deduction 'unless the recipient ... is taxable in that State'[1756] – discrimination because of the recipient's residence may be established.

A domestic tax measure may formally rely on a single facially neutral criterion 'not subject to tax in this State' but nevertheless disadvantage payments to residents and non-residents for very different reasons. Some persons are affected by this criterion because, as residents or non-residents, they qualify or would qualify for a tax exemption for specific reasons such as for being a non-profit organization. A 'but for' test sorts out these cases as unsuspicious. In other cases, however, a change in residence leads to a change in tax treatment because residence means full tax liability in the allegedly discriminating State together with broader taxing rights under the tax treaty. It follows that differences in tax liability as well as differences in taxing rights are inevitably linked to protected differences in the recipient's residence. No other differences in circumstances are apparent. In particular, there is generally no difference in the overall level of taxation that could matter from a domestic perspective. If a non-resident recipient pays no tax in the allegedly discriminating State, it is not true that it is 'exempt' from tax in the same way that a non-profit organization, for example, is exempt from tax; the tax is merely paid elsewhere.[1757] By not taking this factor into account and by not appreciating whether the payments are subject to no, low, or high taxation in any other tax jurisdiction and what the overall level of taxation is, the

1755. *See*, in effect differently, Bammens 2012, 339–340, who believes that if a domestic thin capitalization rule of a State disadvantages payments to non-residents that are not subject to taxation in that State and also payments to residents that are tax exempt for specific reasons such as charitable organizations, the fact that the recipient is not subject to tax in the allegedly discriminating State is a relevant characteristic from the perspective of that State's thin capitalization rule; a same circumstances requirement under Article 24(4), therefore, would require comparison of a non-resident recipient to a tax-exempt resident recipient and consequently deny discrimination: both recipients are treated equally (i.e., no deduction).

1756. 1977–2017 OECD Commentary on Article 11, para. 4; and on Article 12, para. 2.

1757. Ault and Tillinghast 1992, 259.

domestic tax measure under scrutiny is only concerned with whether the tax is paid in the allegedly discriminating State. Such a reason for different tax treatment is in direct opposition to the aims of the non-discrimination clause of Article 24(4), namely, to prevent a Contracting State from turning juridical into economic double taxation when certain payments are not taxed within its tax jurisdiction but in the other Contracting State.

States pursue such objectionable aims. Richard L. Doernberg and Kees van Raad, for instance, suspect that 'the real purpose of the [U.S.] earnings-stripping provision is to take away any reduced rate of U.S. taxation on interest paid by U.S. corporate borrowers to treaty-based foreign lenders. What the United States has negotiated in treaty provisions corresponding to Article 11 of the U.S. Model, Congress has unilaterally renegotiated ...'.[1758] Thus, the enactment of the earnings stripping provision 'was a back-door effort to undermine tax treaty provisions that the United States already had negotiated but now disavowed'.[1759] Article 24(4) protects against discrimination in order to prevent States from enacting such rules. When a change in the recipient's residence leads to a change in tax treatment and when no inevitably linked differences in circumstances remain except for differences in tax liability and taxing rights, this tax distinction cannot be justified from a tax treaty perspective. All of these inevitably linked differences in circumstances are irrelevant based on a substantive analysis. Therefore, it is possible to establish comparability and prohibited tax discrimination because of the recipient's residence.

Under Article 24(4), a Contracting State is free to deny a deduction of payments if these payments are subject to a tax exemption for specific reasons such as for being a non-profit organization or if they are subject to low or no taxation regardless of which State has taxing rights in a concrete case. Conversely, a State is prohibited from treating payments differently depending on whether it has retained or lost taxing rights. A two-step analysis is able to distinguish between these legitimate and illegitimate grounds for different tax treatment. In a first step, a 'but for' test denies discrimination in all situations when the protected characteristic of the recipient's residence has no unavoidable effect on the tax treatment under scrutiny, and it establishes prima facie discrimination in all other cases regardless of whether the domestic tax measure expressly refers to the recipient's residence or uses a facially neutral characteristic. In a second step, a substantive analysis must openly approach all inevitably linked differences in circumstances that have not yet been considered. Depending on what objectives a domestic tax measure genuinely pursues and whether these objectives are acceptable from a tax treaty perspective, certain inevitably linked differences in circumstances must either be regarded as relevant or ignored. Thus, differences in the existence of a hybrid mismatch or in the overall level of taxation are relevant under Article 24(4) as they do not contravene the aim of preventing the Contracting States from turning juridical into economic double taxation. Therefore, they prevent comparability and discrimination. By contrast, differences in tax liability and taxing rights cannot be accepted as legitimate under Article 24(4) even if they are relevant from a

1758. Doernberg and Raad 1990, 205; similarly, Doernberg 1995, 101.
1759. Doernberg 1995, 104.

domestic perspective. Such differences in circumstances must be ignored despite an inevitable link to the recipient's residence in a concrete case.

§4.04 ANALYSIS OF SELECTED CASES OF POTENTIAL DISCRIMINATION

A 'but for' test supplemented with a substantive analysis allows denying discrimination in all cases when a protected characteristic has no influence on taxation. It further allows to comprehensively address interlinked characteristics by taking domestic and tax treaty objectives into account. This suggested approach to non-discrimination may raise challenges because discrimination cannot be established in a mechanical manner. Nevertheless, solutions for such challenges can be found by thoroughly analysing the domestic and tax treaty provisions at issue and by taking account of all available means of interpretation in a particular case.

Since it is not always easy to determine what objectives tax treaty provisions pursue or how certain provisions interact with Article 24, this part will deal with selected cases of potential discrimination in order to discuss various issues that are important for identifying linked but relevant characteristics. First, it has to be considered whether tax treaty provisions implicitly or expressly authorize discriminatory tax treatment (section §4.04[A]). If a 'but for' test leads to prima facie discrimination under Article 24, other tax treaty provisions may indicate inevitably linked but relevant differences in legal circumstances or, to the same result, permit otherwise discriminatory tax distinctions. Another question specifically related to the PE non-discrimination clause is whether certain facts and circumstances must be ignored for comparability purposes due to the comparability requirements of this clause. This will be discussed in connection to the issue of whether a progressive scale of rates can be applied to a PE of a non-resident enterprise by taking the enterprise's worldwide activities into account (section §4.04[B]). Article 24 further raises the issue of whether group taxation regimes must be extended to PEs and foreign-owned enterprises or, rather, whether inevitably linked differences in circumstances regarding a potential loss of taxing rights or a double deduction of losses prevent comparability (section §4.04[C]). Finally, complex questions arise with regard to domestic tax measures that avoid juridical (section §4.04[D]) and economic (section §4.04[E]) double taxation.

[A] Authorization of Tax Discrimination

[1] Allocation Rules Do Not Discriminate as Such

Articles 6 to 22 allocate taxing rights between the Contracting States. Together with Articles 23 A and 23 B, they allow taxation, exempt income or capital, limit taxation up to a certain gross amount, or grant a credit for foreign tax, but they do not require taxation. In exercising their taxing rights, the Contracting States are free to exempt certain items of income or capital or to grant special tax deductions or other benefits under their domestic tax laws. If they do so in a discriminatory manner, the non-discrimination provisions of Article 24 may require an extension of such benefits to foreigners or non-residents. Conversely, without taxing rights or without their exercise, no discrimination can arise.[1760] It follows that, if a tax treaty rule only allows but does not require a Contracting State to tax income or capital, there can be no conflict between this rule and the non-discrimination provisions.

Niels Bammens provides an example in which the tax treaty between State A and State B expressly provides, in deviation from the OECD Model, that State A may levy withholding taxes up to 15% regarding dividends paid to State A nationals residing in State B, while State A may levy withholding taxes up to 25% regarding dividends paid to State B nationals residing in State B. He concludes that such a rule, which allocates taxing powers in respect of dividend payments, clearly discriminates on the basis of nationality.[1761]

However, under the tax treaty between State A and State B, State A may, but is not required to, levy a higher tax in regard to dividends paid to State B nationals when compared to State A nationals. If State A's domestic tax law levies a withholding tax of 15% or lower, regardless of nationality, State B nationals will remain subject to the same tax treatment as State A nationals irrespective of a 'discriminatory' allocation of taxing powers in the tax treaty. Thus, the allocation rule does not, as such, violate the non-discrimination clause of Article 24(1). State B nationals will be subject to other or more burdensome taxation under Article 24(1) only if State A's domestic tax law makes full use of that State's taxing powers and levies a higher tax on State B nationals. The question then is whether the Contracting States had the intention to legitimize such nationality discrimination under their domestic tax laws by providing for a 'discriminatory' allocation of taxing powers in the tax treaty and thereby aiming at limiting the scope of Article 24(1) in these circumstances. This might but need not be the case.

To this effect, Alexander Rust comments on a decision[1762] that there is no conflict between Article 24(3) and an allocation rule on shipping and air transport that allows the source State to levy a tax on non-resident enterprises up to a certain gross amount even if, in a particular case, no tax would be levied on resident enterprises due to a loss situation. As the allocation rule does not require the source State to levy a tax but only restricts taxation up to a certain amount, by not levying a tax, the source State fulfils the requirements of the non-discrimination clause without violating the allocation rule.[1763] To use another example, although Article 11(2) permits the source State to tax non-residents with up to 10% of the gross amount of the interest, this does not mean that the source State is automatically permitted to treat residents and non-residents differently, for instance, by exempting residents only or by taxing non-residents on a gross basis and residents on a net basis.[1764] If the source State exempts residents from

1760. *See* Rust 2004, 392; Rust 2010, 646.
1761. Bammens 2012, 144.
1762. German Federal Fiscal Court (Bundesfinanzhof) of 22 April 1998, I R 54/96. *See also* Bammens 2012, 210–211.
1763. Rust 2015b fn. 23 to m.no. 10; Rust 2015c m.no. 8; Rust 2010, 632–633.
1764. *See*, differently, Rust 2010, 645. It should be noted that Article 24(3) prohibits discrimination because of residence only if a non-resident enterprise maintains a PE in the source State. In

tax, it could rather be obliged to exempt non-residents as well thereby being prevented from making use of its taxing rights.[1765]

A somewhat similar issue arises under Article 7. It could be argued that the rules on the attribution of profits to a PE of Article 7 interfere with the PE non-discrimination clause of Article 24(3). If a PE can be seen as a separate and independent enterprise for the purposes of Article 24(3), a deviation from the separate entity approach under Article 7(2) could pose problems.[1766] Before the 2010 update to the OECD Model, Article 7(4) permitted the application of an indirect method of profit attribution (pro rata apportionment). If such an indirect method leads to an attribution of profits to a PE in the source State even though no or less profits would be attributable directly on an arm's-length basis, Article 24(3) might be violated.[1767] If, by contrast, a PE is regarded as a dependent part of a non-resident enterprise, a full adherence to the separate entity approach under Article 7(2) could raise concerns about discrimination.[1768]

Again, Article 7 only allows the source State to tax the attributed profits (and not more than that); it does not obligate the source State to tax. Therefore, it cannot be made responsible for discrimination without domestic tax measures that make use of taxing rights. Under its domestic tax law, the source State is always free to tax less than it is allowed to tax under Article 7 in order to meet the non-discrimination obligations of Article 24(3).[1769] In addition, Article 24(3) refers to a specific type of income or capital that is taxable in the source State ('[t]he taxation on a permanent establishment'). It might take the attribution of profits under Article 7 or the determination of the business property under Article 22 for granted without showing a preference for any particular method of attribution.[1770] Also, with a 'but for' test, a change in residence does not lead to a change in the activities carried on in the source State nor

that case, Article 11(2) does not apply because Article 11(4) refers back to Article 7. Article 24, therefore, does not contain any provision that could require equal treatment of residents and non-residents in situations when Article 11 is applicable.

1765. *See*, by contrast, Raad 1986, 177, who states that, to the extent Articles 11 and 12 permit the source State to tax payments to non-resident recipients, nothing in these provisions requires the source State to subject similar payments to resident recipients to at least equal taxation; Article 24(4) cannot be construed as overriding these other treaty provisions even if such taxation at the level of the recipient is viewed as wholly or partly offsetting a deduction and thereby leading to non-deductibility at the level of the payer. Kees van Raad apparently assumes that, if an allocation rule permits the source State to tax a non-resident, the source State can levy a tax on that non-resident but not on comparable residents without violating a non-discrimination clause that prohibits discrimination because of residence. Otherwise, the source State would have to levy tax on both residents and non-residents in order to make use of its taxing rights. This result is arguably intended neither by the allocation rule nor by the non-discrimination clause. *See also* Baker 2004, 210, who submits that, if Article 24(5) prohibited a State to impose a withholding tax on dividends paid to a non-resident shareholder only, there would be a conflict between Article 10 and Article 24(5).

1766. *See* Bammens 2012 fn. 428 on p. 195; moreover, Shalav and Faber 2005, who discuss whether the limitations on the separate entity approach and in particular the non-deductibility of certain deemed payments may constitute a breach of Article 24(3), although they also emphasize that the issue stems primarily from the domestic law of the State concerned.

1767. *See* Ault and Kaplan 1980, 82–84; differently, Rust 2015b m.no. 67; Rust 2015c m.no. 106; Ault and Tillinghast 1992, 268–269; Raad 1986, 139–140.

1768. *See* Haslehner 2009, 233–234.

1769. *See* Haslehner 2009, 234.

1770. *See* Haslehner 2009, 236.

in the allocation of taxing rights with regard to these activities. A PE in the source State must consequently be compared to a resident enterprise that achieves the same amount of profits or losses for tax treaty purposes.

Article 7(2) attributes profits not only for the purposes of limiting the taxing rights of the source State but also for the purposes of providing relief from double taxation in the residence State under Article 23 A or 23 B. This was made explicit in 2010 by adding to Article 7(2) that the attribution of profits is made '[f]or the purposes of this Article and Article [23 A] [23 B]'.[1771] Transactions between a PE of a non-resident enterprise and other parts of that enterprise are, in effect, valued at arm's length in both Contracting States. It follows that, if residence changes and the source State becomes the residence State and vice versa, Article 7(2) should lead to the same attribution of profits to the different parts of an enterprise. Although residual profits and especially profits that have their source solely in a third State might be attributed differently, there is no change in the attribution of profits with regard to the protected activities carried on in the source State.[1772] Therefore, one cannot complain that the tax treaty prescribes a particular method of attribution. Article 7 provides for a maximum amount of taxable profits and, together with Article 23 A or 23 B, for a corresponding exemption or tax credit, but it does not raise any issues of discrimination under Article 24(3) regardless of which method of attribution it employs.

[2] Article 7 and Domestic Attribution of Income

Whether the domestic tax law provides for different methods of attribution based on residence and potentially infringes Article 24(3) is a different question. Article 24(3) scrutinizes whether the source State's domestic tax measures impose a different tax burden with regard to certain activities based on whether a resident or non-resident enterprise is involved. After Article 7 attributed a particular amount of profits or losses to a PE in the source State and thereby limited the taxing rights of that State, the PE must be compared to a resident enterprise that achieves the same amount of profits or losses for tax treaty purposes. Even if the amount of attributed profits under domestic tax law is not higher than the amount of attributed profits under Article 7, it might be higher than the amount of profits that would be attributable to a resident enterprise in otherwise identical circumstances. A 'but for' test can consequently lead to prima facie discrimination if differences in residence lead to differences in treatment. Although discrimination cannot arise from the method of attribution under Article 7, it can arise from the method of attribution under domestic tax law.

1771. *See also* Russo 2004, 481, who remarks on earlier versions of Article 7(2) that '[t]he residence state must also determine the profits attributable to the PE considering it as a separate entity ... for purposes of granting double taxation relief'.

1772. If profits are attributable to a PE in the source State under Article 7(2) and, therefore, taxable in that State, they are apparently not attributable to any other part of the enterprise based on the functions performed, assets used, and risks assumed. If any other part of the enterprise, therefore, becomes a PE due to a change in residence, the (non-)attribution of these profits should remain unaffected.

If the domestic tax law does not apply transfer pricing rules to domestic transactions within a resident enterprise but only to cross-border transactions, this does not constitute a problem under Article 24(3) as long as domestic transactions within a PE of a non-resident enterprise are not subject to such rules as well. Conversely, if the domestic tax law subjects cross-border transactions between a PE of a non-resident enterprise and other parts of that enterprise to transfer pricing rules, this also does not constitute a problem as long as such rules are applied to cross-border transactions between a resident enterprise and other parts of that enterprise as well.

In this respect, it does not matter whether the expression 'the same activities' in Article 24(3) is understood to focus only on the activities carried on through the PE or on all of the activities carried on by the non-resident enterprise (*see* Chapter 3 section §3.04[B][2]). On the one hand, if comparability is limited to the activities carried on in the source State through the PE thereby ignoring all other activities, transactions between different parts of a resident enterprise must also be ignored for the purposes of Article 24(3). Their treatment and valuation cannot establish discrimination. It would seem inconsistent to require a comparable resident enterprise to exercise the same activities as the PE but then to complain that transactions between one part of that resident enterprise carrying on the same activities as the PE and another part of that enterprise carrying on different activities do not lead to tax consequences in a purely domestic context.[1773]

On the other hand, if it is taken into account that a PE is only a dependent part of a non-resident enterprise and that transactions between different parts of an enterprise may influence the domestic profits derived from the activities carried on in the source State through the PE, Article 24(3) can only prohibit an application of different methods for the valuation of such transactions. Thus, the non-discrimination clause obligates the source State to value cross-border transactions no differently in cases when a local PE is interacting with the remaining foreign parts of the non-resident enterprise than in cases when a local part of a resident enterprise is interacting with the remaining foreign (not local!)[1774] parts of that enterprise. As long as these situations lead to the same domestic profits that stem from the activities carried on in the source State, the

1773. But *see* Haslehner 2009, 236–239, 375–376, who in the end suggests comparing a PE of a non-resident enterprise to a resident subsidiary of a non-resident enterprise. As far as can be seen, Werner Haslehner is concerned with the fact that, within a resident enterprise and unlike in a cross-border context, transactions between one part of the enterprise carrying on the same activities as the PE and another part of the enterprise carrying on other activities do not lead to deemed profits; the arm's-length principle is not applicable in a purely domestic context. Therefore, he initially assumes that all activities take place in the source State and within the same resident enterprise in order to illustrate concerns about discrimination. As a solution, he suggests making a comparison to a resident enterprise of the source State (a subsidiary) carrying on the same activities as the PE while the other activities are carried on by a different enterprise (a non-resident associated enterprise) outside of the source State, leading to an application of the arm's-length principle. If, however, the other activities were not assumed to take place in the source State in the first place, no concerns about discrimination would arise.

1774. *See*, differently, Baker and Collier 2006, 57–58, who compare a cross-border situation involving a foreign head office and a local PE to a purely domestic situation involving a local head office and a local PE; moreover, W. Loukota 2005, 337.

domestic tax law meets the obligations of Article 24(3). In fact, even when employing an indirect method of attribution, the source State may exercise the allocated taxing rights under its domestic tax law without necessarily calculating the domestic profits differently than with resident enterprises.[1775]

Problems of discrimination only arise if the domestic profits of a PE are determined differently than the domestic profits of a head office, that is if the domestic profits that are attributable to certain activities carried on in the source State differ depending on whether a resident or non-resident enterprise is at stake. Although the source State may apply the same method of attribution as stipulated by Article 7 in order to determine the domestic profits that are attributable to the activities carried on through a PE, it may apply a more favourable method of attribution or a different definition of domestic profits as far as resident enterprises are concerned.[1776] For example, the domestic tax law could fully apply the separate entity approach of Article 7(2) when determining the taxable profits of a local PE but not recognize any internal dealings between a resident enterprise and foreign parts of that enterprise when determining the taxable profits of a local head office. This difference in treatment, in principle, constitutes prohibited discrimination under Article 24(3). A change in residence leads to a change in tax treatment with a 'but for' test and linked but relevant differences in circumstances are not apparent.

[3] Treatment Authorized by Other Treaty Rules

The question arises whether the fact that the domestic tax law adheres to the method of attribution that is stipulated by the tax treaty itself legitimizes different tax treatment. In such a case, a 'but for' test leads to prima facie discrimination, and there appear to be no linked differences in circumstances that could be regarded as relevant except for the different domestic methods of profit attribution that are scrutinized under Article 24(3). Nevertheless, the Contracting States could have implicitly or expressly intended in Article 7(2) to authorize such differences in tax treatment between PEs and resident enterprises.

Instead of being in conflict with Article 24, tax treaty provisions may expressly permit the domestic tax law to discriminate. For instance, the text of a tax treaty may provide that the non-discrimination provisions of Article 24 do not apply to certain domestic tax measures such as to thin capitalization rules.[1777] Whether this wording limits the scope of Article 24 or whether a conflict between thin capitalization rules and the non-discrimination provisions should be solved in favour of thin capitalization

1775. *See also*, to this effect, Raad 1986, 139, who argues that, if the domestic profit of a resident enterprise (which is part of a larger unit producing the same overall profit as the whole enterprise to which the PE belongs) is determined by the indirect method, the same profit and no discrimination would result.

1776. *See also* Reyes 2011, 302.

1777. *See*, in particular, the reservation on Article 24(4) in the 2008–2017 OECD Commentary on Article 24, para. 91 (similarly 1977: para. 66; 1992–2005: para. 70), where France wishes to reserve the possibility of applying the provisions in its domestic laws relative to the limitation to the deduction of interest paid by a French company to an associated or related company.

rules is less important than the fact that the Contracting States voiced a certain intention. They intended not to apply Article 24 to thin capitalization rules. In that sense, the OECD Commentary is right in stating that 'the provisions of the Article [24] must be read in the context of the other Articles of the Convention so that measures that are mandated or expressly authorised[[1778]] by the provisions of these Articles cannot be considered to violate the provisions of the Article [24]'.[1779] In the words of Niels Bammens, 'where the treaty partners expressly preserve domestic measures that discriminate in the treaty', their common intention to do so cannot be ignored. '[I]f it was the intention of the treaty partners to uphold such discriminatory treatment, the non-discrimination provision cannot remedy this discrimination.'[1780]

When a tax treaty provision expressly authorizes discriminatory tax treatment, it provides for a deviation from the non-discrimination obligations of Article 24. Nevertheless, there may also be borderline cases in which no express authorization of discrimination can be found but where the allocation rules could implicitly authorize discriminatory tax treatment. Niels Bammens notes that the Contracting States are free to bilaterally agree on deviations from Article 24. If they choose to do so, whether implicitly or expressly, whether in Article 24 or elsewhere, then the scope of application of Article 24 is restricted accordingly.[1781]

If an allocation rule grants a particular Contracting State a right to tax or limits that State's taxing powers, it does so for a reason and usually not without justification. Therefore, it might be difficult to argue that domestic tax measures that draw sound consequences from a particular allocation of taxing rights or that adhere to what a tax treaty allows should be condemned under Article 24. For instance, if Article 10 deviates from the OECD Model, avoids economic double taxation by exempting dividends at the level of resident enterprises and, therefore, not at the level of PEs carried on by non-resident enterprises, this could be understood as an implicit authorization to treat non-residents and residents differently thereby making the non-discrimination obligations of Article 24(3) inapplicable to such situations. Moreover, the acceptance of the arm's-length principle in various provisions of the OECD Model could implicitly allow for a distinction between arm's-length and non-arm's-length payments even if only non-residents are negatively affected by such a distinction. Article 7(4) of the pre-2010 OECD Model could indicate an intention of the Contracting States to permit an indirect calculation of profits of a PE not only for tax treaty purposes but also for domestic tax purposes regardless of whether this method is applied to resident enterprises as well. Lastly, Article 7(2) could be seen as an authorization to apply any method for the attribution of profits under domestic tax law as long as PEs of non-resident enterprises are not taxed above what Article 7(2) prescribes by applying the arm's-length standard.

1778. Although the OECD Commentary refers only to measures that are mandated or expressly authorized, it is not clear why it should make a difference whether an authorization is express or implicit. *See* Haslehner 2016c, 11.
1779. 2008–2017 OECD Commentary on Article 24, para. 4.
1780. Bammens 2012, 144; similarly, Bammens and Vanistendael 2016, sec. 6.2.1.
1781. Bammens 2012, 197. *See also* Bammens and Vanistendael 2016, sec. 6.1.1; Haslehner 2016c, 11.

Indeed, there are some arguments for the view that the method of attribution prescribed by Article 7 should not lead to discrimination under Article 24(3) even if it is applied only to non-resident enterprises. Article 7(4) of the pre-2010 OECD Model refers to an apportionment that may be customary in a Contracting State, apparently referring to an apportionment under domestic tax law which, if in accordance with the principles contained in Article 7, can be applied for tax treaty purposes as well. If this customary method of attribution under domestic tax law is adopted for tax treaty purposes, it arguably should not be condemned as discrimination under Article 24(3) just because it applies only to non-resident enterprises. Or, in general terms, the Contracting States agreed in Article 7 on a particular method of attribution in order to determine the maximum amount of profits that may be taxed in the source State, and they presumably agreed on this particular method for a reason. If the source State makes use of these taxing rights by employing the same method of attribution under domestic tax law (or if, conversely, Article 7(4) of the pre-2010 OECD Model acknowledges a domestic method of attribution), it is difficult to see why unintended distortions should arise from the perspective of the non-discrimination clause.[1782] Niels Bammens argues to this effect that, if Article 7 implicitly or expressly mandates the domestic method of attribution, then the intention of the Contracting States to mandate a difference in treatment between PEs and resident enterprises should be respected, which means that Article 24(3) has not been infringed.[1783]

At the same time, there is a risk that the source State could circumvent the obligations of Article 24(3) by applying different methods of attribution based on residence under domestic tax law. It could employ a treaty-acknowledged method of attribution in order to determine the domestic profits of a PE but a very different method to resident enterprises carrying on the same activities. For instance, all profits from the same activities could be deemed to arise outside of the source State, or all earnings could be deemed to be offset by equal expenses, leading to a domestic tax base of zero. While profits that are attributable to a PE would be taxed in the source State based on the same method of attribution as envisaged under Article 7, resident

1782. *See* 2008–2017 OECD Commentary on Article 24, para. 42: '[I]t is clear that the application of transfer pricing rules based on the arm's length standard in the case of transfers from a permanent establishment to its head office (or vice versa) cannot be considered to be a violation of paragraph 3 even if such rules do not apply to transfers within an enterprise of the Contracting State where the permanent establishment is located. Indeed, the application of the arm's length standard to the determination of the profits attributable to a permanent establishment is mandated by paragraph 2 of Article 7 and that paragraph forms part of the context in which paragraph 3 of Article 24 must be read; also, since Article 9 would authorise the application of the arm's length standard to a transfer between a domestic enterprise and a foreign related enterprise, one cannot consider that its application in the case of a permanent establishment results in less favourable taxation than that levied on an enterprise of the Contracting State where the permanent establishment is located.' *See also*, to this effect, Raad 1986, 139–140, according to whom the fact that an indirect method is explicitly provided for in Article 7(4) of the pre-2010 OECD Model renders unlikely that this provision could be interpreted as conflicting with another provision such as Article 24(3); similarly, Rust 2015b m.no. 67; Rust 2015c m.no. 106; Ault and Tillinghast 1992, 268–269 ('the non-discrimination clause should not be construed to override the express rule which is adopted [that is, either a direct or an indirect method of attribution of expenses to a permanent establishment]').

1783. Bammens 2012, 196, 202–203, 310–311. *See also* Bammens and Vanistendael 2016, sec. 6.1.1.

enterprises of the source State could carry on the same activities without any or with less taxable profits. Arguably, the source State would only make use of its taxing rights with regard to non-resident enterprises as expressly authorized under Article 7 and without violating the non-discrimination obligations of Article 24(3).

It thus appears more convincing to require the source State to apply the same method of attribution to both resident and non-resident enterprises. This means that the domestic profits of a non-resident enterprise (i.e., the profits that stem from the activities carried on through the PE) should be determined in the same manner as the domestic profits of a resident enterprise (i.e., the profits that stem from the same activities and are not subject to a tax treaty exemption or not taken into account when calculating the maximum credit for foreign tax). Transactions between a local PE and a foreign head office of a non-resident enterprise should be valued or apportioned no differently than transactions between a local head office and foreign parts of a resident enterprise in order to result in the same amount of domestic profits. Transactions within a local PE must remain immaterial if transactions within a local head office also remain immaterial.

As a result, two independent limitations with regard to PEs in the source State exist. First, the domestic profits cannot exceed the amount that is determined by the method of attribution under Article 7. Second, the domestic profits cannot be calculated less favourably than domestic profits of a comparable resident enterprise under Article 24(3). Article 7 does not mandate or authorize a particular domestic method of attribution. It provides for an autonomous method of attribution that prescribes the maximum amount of profits that may be taxed in the source State, while the source State still has to observe the non-discrimination obligations when applying its domestic methods of attribution for determining the relevant amount of profits and the tax base.

[4] Carve-Out for Non-arm's-length Payments

Article 24(4) prescribes that discrimination because of the recipient's residence is prohibited '[e]xcept where the provisions of paragraph 1 of Article 9, paragraph 6 of Article 11, or paragraph 4 of Article 12, apply'. It is not precisely clear why Article 24(4) contains such a carve-out; the OECD Commentary does not give any explanation. Therefore, it is necessary to take a closer look on how non-arm's-length payments are addressed by those tax treaty provisions.

Article 9(1) allows a Contracting State to include in the profits of an associated enterprise any profits which, by reason of special conditions (i.e., the participation directly or indirectly in the management, control, or capital of an enterprise), have not accrued. Article 9(1) thereby incorporates the arm's-length principle: non-arm's-length conditions may be adjusted to arm's-length conditions in cross-border situations. A declared income of 80 from an intra-group transaction may be adjusted to an arm's-length income of 100. In addition, since Article 9(1) has the purpose of protecting associated enterprises against arbitrary transfer pricing adjustments[1784] and avoiding

1784. *See* 1997–2017 OECD Commentary on Article 9, para. 2 (1977–1995: para. 1; similarly, 1963).

economic double taxation by requiring corresponding adjustments under Article 9(2), it also prohibits a State from taxing profits above an arm's-length amount.[1785] A declared income of 80 from an intra-group transaction cannot be adjusted to a non-arm's-length income of 120. Otherwise, if an adjustment under Article 9(1) could be based on any amount, a corresponding adjustment under Article 9(2) would have to be based on this amount as well – this seems unacceptable without a common standard for adjustments – or unrelieved economic double taxation would remain.[1786]

As a consequence, Article 9(1) allows a Contracting State to adjust non-arm's-length to arm's-length conditions under its domestic tax law but also prohibits subjecting associated enterprises to a higher tax by pricing or classifying transactions in deviation from the arm's-length standard. Article 9(1) thus imposes limitations that are similar to those of allocation rules. It limits taxing rights by prohibiting taxing more than an arm's-length amount without requiring a State to levy tax. Rather, a domestic legal basis is needed for transfer pricing adjustments.[1787] If a Contracting State taxes a lower amount of profits than it would be allowed to tax under Article 9(1) because it has not implemented domestic provisions addressing non-arm's-length transactions, Article 9(1) does not obligate that State to tax at arm's length nor does it constitute a legal basis for arm's-length adjustments.

Article 11(6) limits the benefits of Article 11 to the arm's-length amount of interest payments and thereby allows the Contracting States to tax the excess part of the payments according to their domestic laws, 'due regard being had to the other provisions of this Convention'. Similarly, Article 12(4) limits the benefits of Article 12 to the arm's-length amount of royalty payments. Both provisions only address the taxation at the level of the recipient and cover various kinds of special relationships that may be a reason for non-arm's-length amounts, including a relationship by blood or marriage.[1788] In addition, the OECD Commentary on Article 11 notes that Article 11(6) permits only the adjustment of the rate at which interest is charged and not – unlike Article 9(1)[1789] –

1785. *See*, for instance, Marres 2016b, 2–3; Marres 2016a, 39–41; Kofler 2015 m.nos. 6, 12–15, 34; Eigelshoven 2015 m.nos. 3, 20; Bammens 2013a, 150; Bammens 2012, 351; Wittendorff 2010, 196–199; Lang 1994b, 131–133, 136; Lang 1991, 64–65; Lüthi 1991, 451; Knobbe-Keuk 1993, 64; Pott 1982, 224–225; Pöllath and Rädler 1982a; Pöllath and Rädler 1982b; Pöllath and Rädler 1980, 20; Debatin 1980, 3; differently, for instance, Krabbe 1984, 127–128.

1786. *See also* Lüthi 1991, 451, who observes that there is no obligation under Article 9(2) to grant a correlative adjustment for adjusted profits not in conformity with the arm's-length principle; similarly, Lang 1994b, 136, who therefrom concludes that Article 9(1) also requires adhering to the arm's-length principle in order to avoid economic double taxation; moreover, 1992–2017 OECD Commentary on Article 9, para. 6 (similarly 1977: para. 3).

1787. *See*, for instance, Kofler 2015 m.nos. 6, 10–11; Eigelshoven 2015 m.nos. 3, 18–19; Mitra 2007, 5; Lang 1994b, 131; Knobbe-Keuk 1992, 407; Lang 1991, 63–64; Lüthi 1991, 451. *See also*, however, Vinnitskiy 2016, 164–165, who reports on an apparently different conclusion of Russian courts but also comments that this conclusion is 'more than questionable' and that an adjustment permitted by Article 9(1) should be prescribed in domestic legislation.

1788. 1992–2017 OECD Commentary on Article 11, para. 34, and on Article 12, para. 24 (1963: paras 35 and 22; 1977: paras 32 and 19, respectively).

1789. *See*, for instance, De Broe 2008, 504–506; Lang 1994b, 133–134; Lüthi 1991, 451; moreover, 1997–2017 OECD Commentary on Article 9, para. 3 (1992–1995: para. 2); OECD, Transfer Pricing Guidelines 2010, para. 1.65. *See also*, however, Wittendorff 2010, 163 ('Article 9(1) requires the form of the transaction to be recognized'); Michielse 1997, 568, 572 ('[t]he term "condition" has a rather limited meaning'; 'only the (excessive) remuneration can be changed

the reclassification of the loan in such a way as to give it the character of a contribution to equity capital.[1790]

When a Contracting State makes transfer pricing adjustments only in cross-border situations in order to meet the arm's-length standard, this is perfectly in line with Articles 9(1), 11(6), and 12(4). Such transfer pricing adjustments could, however, result in a lower amount of deductible payments than in purely domestic situations thereby leading to different conditions of deduction. As the recipient is a non-resident, only an arm's-length amount can be deducted at the level of the resident payer. If the recipient was a resident, no arm's-length adjustments would be made under domestic tax law and thus a higher amount of payments would be deductible. Article 24(4) could consequently require a deduction of a non-arm's-length amount in cross-border situations. Such equal treatment would be unproblematic under Article 9(1) given that this provision does not prohibit a deduction of more than an arm's-length amount.[1791]

With its carve-out, Article 24(4) makes clear that the Contracting States are entitled to disallow deductions to associated non-residents for excessive or non-arm's-length interest and royalty payments even if a deduction of such payments would be granted to associated residents. It is not discriminatory to apply profit adjustment rules with regard to non-arm's-length payments exclusively to cross-border transactions.[1792] As far as payments are not made at arm's length and trigger differences in tax treatment for this reason, they are outside of the scope of the non-discrimination clause. This is also true if the provisions of Articles 9(1), 11(6), and 12(4), as such, do not lead to an arm's-length adjustment at the level of the payer in a concrete case either because they are irrelevant to the payer or because they prohibit neither a deduction above arm's length nor a denial of a deduction for reasons unrelated to association. They apply only at the level of the recipient or only permit, not require, arm's-length adjustments, but they still apply for the purposes of Article 24(4) and thereby exclude discrimination.[1793]

---

by applying Article 9(1)'); moreover, Baranger 2004, 289, who reports that the French Supreme Administrative Court (Conseil d'État), 30 December 2003, *SA Andritz*, No. 233894, followed the view that Article 9(1) only relates to transfer pricing matters and not to issues related to thin capitalization thereby implying that it is possible to compare the conditions of a loan with 'normal conditions' but not to examine the opportunity to use debt financing over equity financing; similarly, Baker 2004, 211–212 ('the judgement of the *Conseil d'État* implies that ... the equivalent of Art. 9 of the OECD Model do[es] not permit the tax administration to adjust the debt/equity ratio'). For an overview, *see also* Kofler 2015 m.nos. 99, 103–104, with further references.

1790. 1992–2017 OECD Commentary on Article 11, para. 35. *See also* OECD, Thin Capitalisation Report, para. 61 on p. 25.

1791. Of course, if less than an arm's-length deduction is granted under domestic tax law although independent enterprises (and resident associated enterprises) would receive such a deduction, this leads to higher non-arm's-length profits, a result to which Article 9(1) is opposed. In that case, it does not seem to matter whether Article 24(4) also requires an arm's-length deduction or whether Article 24(4) gives priority to Article 9(1) and does not apply; Article 9(1) already requires taxation of no more than arm's-length profits and, if necessary, Article 9(2) requires a corresponding adjustment. *See also*, to this effect, Marres 2016b, 9; Marres 2016a, 55–56; Bammens 2013a, 150, 155–157; Bammens 2012, 351–352.

1792. Bammens and Vanistendael 2016, sec. 2.4.4.1. *See also*, to this effect, Rust 2015b m.no. 92; Rust 2015c m.no. 138; Rust 2010, 640; Mitra 2007, 3.

1793. *See also*, to this effect, Marres 2016b, 8–9; Marres 2016a, 54–57 ('the function of the reference to articles 11(6) and 12(4) is that any arm's length adjustment is exempt from the application

[5] *Thin Capitalization Rules and Arm's Length*

Article 24(5), the ownership non-discrimination clause, contains no exception for non-arm's-length interest payments. This could mean that if a thin capitalization rule addresses non-arm's-length interest payments to non-resident shareholders either by reclassifying them into dividends for domestic purposes or by denying a deduction, its application might constitute discrimination under Article 24(5). Article 9(1) protects against transfer pricing adjustments that do not adhere to the arm's-length standard whereas other adjustments that meet the arm's-length principle are allowed but not required. Article 9(1), therefore, does not require transfer pricing adjustments of a non-arm's-length deduction to a lower arm's-length deduction. In addition, Article 11(6) concerns the taxation at the level of the recipient and not the deduction at the level of the payer.[1794] Without being in conflict with Articles 9(1) and 11(6), Article 24(5) could consequently prohibit an adjustment of payments from a non-arm's-length amount to a lower arm's-length amount if this adjustment is based on the shareholder's residence.

This view that Article 24(5) obligates a Contracting State to grant a non-arm's-length deduction of payments to a non-resident shareholder if such a deduction is granted for payments to a resident shareholder appears to be compatible with Articles 9(1) and 11(6) just as with any other allocation rule. Werner Haslehner emphasizes that allocation rules only grant taxing rights but prescribe no obligation to tax and that Article 24 would be rendered meaningless if every taxing right provided for by an allocation rule was non-discriminatory per se:[1795]

> The distributive rules of article 6 to article 21 [and the relief provisions] certainly do not *mandate* any particular tax measure. They merely limit a contracting state's right to exercise its domestic tax laws. As such, they only *mandate* the reduction of taxes ... and thus seem incapable of interfering with the demands of article 24. ... If it were sufficient for any other provision in a double taxation convention permitting taxation to trump it, article 24 would not merely be severely limited in its role, but rendered completely superfluous. For any tax measure to be applied it must be permitted by all provisions of a double tax convention, so the non-discrimination provision would not add anything to the protection of taxpayers under this interpretation.

---

of article 24(4)'; 'the carve-out [in article 24(4)] pertains to all measures that are in conformity with the arm's length *standard* embedded in article 9(1) and/or article 11(6), irrespective of whether these provisions, in fact, apply'; original emphasis).

1794. *See also,* for instance, Rust 2015b m.no. 112; Rust 2015c m.no. 165a, according to whom Article 11(6) 'does clearly not restrict the scope of Article 24(5) ... as this provision only deals with tax treatment at the level of the recipient of the payments and not with the deductibility of the payments at the level of the payor', and who believes that Article 9 'should not be given priority over Article 24(5) ... either'; similarly with regard to Article 9, Wassermeyer and Schwenke 2016 m.no. 102.

1795. Haslehner 2016c, 10–11 (original emphasis). *See also* Haslehner 2009 fn. 959 on p. 229; moreover, Haslehner 2012, 609, where he points out that compliance with the allocation rules of a tax treaty can only be a minimum requirement for lawful taxation and cannot automatically shield from discrimination claims.

Article 24 provides an additional layer of obligations. It limits the exercise of taxing rights rather than applying only when allocation rules do not prescribe any tax consequences.[1796] Thus, without an implicit or explicit exception for non-arm's-length payments, Article 24(5) appears to encompass all payments to non-resident shareholders regardless of Articles 9(1) and 11(6) and other allocation rules.[1797]

Since 2008, however, the OECD Commentary deals with the relationship of Article 24 to other tax treaty rules. It holds that Article 24 cannot be interpreted as prohibiting tax measures that are permitted by the provisions of other Articles[1798] and illustrates this with an example on thin capitalization rules:[1799]

> [I]f under a State's domestic thin capitalisation rules, a resident enterprise is not allowed to deduct interest paid to a non-resident associated enterprise, that rule ... could be in violation of paragraph 4 to the extent that different conditions would apply for the deduction of interest paid to residents and non-residents and it will therefore be important to determine, for purposes of that paragraph, whether the application of the rule is compatible with the provisions of paragraph 1 of Article 9 or paragraph 6 of Article 11 ... [[1800]]. This would also be important for purposes of paragraph 5 in the case of thin capitalisation rules that would apply only to enterprises of a Contracting State the capital of which is wholly or partly owned or controlled, directly or indirectly, by non-residents. Indeed, since the provisions of paragraph 1 of Article 9 or paragraph 6 of Article 11 form part of the context in which paragraph 5 must be read (as required by Article 31 of the *Vienna Convention on the Law of Treaties*), adjustments which are compatible with these provisions could not be considered to violate the provisions of paragraph 5. [[1801]]

1796. *See* Haslehner 2016c, 11 ('a second layer of protection'); Haslehner 2016a m.no. 7; Haslehner 2012, 609 ('[Article 24's] role is precisely to provide a limit to the exercise of taxing power'); Rust 2010, 632 ('a double layer of obligations'); Haslehner 2009 fn. 959 on p. 229 and pp. 333, 374.

1797. *See also*, to this effect, Rust 2015b m.no. 112; Rust 2015c m.no. 165a, who states that, as Article 24(5) does not contain a caveat, its scope is not restricted by Article 9; differently, Avery Jones, Depret, et al. 1991b, 344, who agree that Article 24(5) should not be construed as conflicting with Article 9.

1798. 2008–2017 OECD Commentary on Article 24, para. 4.

1799. *Ibid.*, para. 79.

1800. Reference is made to the following statements in the 2008–2017 OECD Commentary on Article 24, para. 74: 'Paragraph 4 does not prohibit the country of the borrower from applying its domestic rules on thin capitalisation insofar as these are compatible with paragraph 1 of Article 9 or paragraph 6 of Article 11. However, if such treatment results from rules which are not compatible with the said Articles and which only apply to non-resident creditors (to the exclusion of resident creditors), then such treatment is prohibited by paragraph 4.' *See also*, critically, Marres 2016b, 8–9; Marres 2016a, 55–56.

1801. Before 2008, the OECD Commentary stated that '[p]aragraph 5, though relevant in principle to thin capitalisation, is worded in such general terms that it must take second place to more specific provisions in the Convention. Thus paragraph 4 (referring to paragraph 1 of Article 9 and paragraph 6 of Article 11) takes precedence over this paragraph in relation to the deduction of interest'. *See* 1992–2005 OECD Commentary on Article 24, para. 58; moreover, OECD, Thin Capitalisation Report, para. 66(b) on p. 27. This view, however, is widely rejected in the literature; Article 24(4) and Article 24(5) can be applied simultaneously. *See*, for instance, Wassermeyer and Schwenke 2016 m.nos. 2b, 102; Marres 2016b, 10; Marres 2016a, 58; Rust 2015b m.no. 111; Rust 2015c m.nos. 6, 165a (but differently, Rust 2003a m.nos. 6, 160); Böhmer 2014, 165; Staringer and Schneeweiss 2007, 231; Burgstaller and Obermair 2006, 188; Hofstätter and Ressler 2006, 224–226; Toifl 2003, 269; Nitikman 2000, 35; Piltz 1996, 134; Toifl 1996, 143; Lang 1994b, 154–155; Lang 1991, 70; Hosson and Michielse 1989,

Indeed, it may be derived from the context of Article 24(5) that concerns regarding non-arm's-length payments are generally legitimate from a tax treaty perspective as numerous rules address non-arm's-length transactions. Article 9 is probably the most important rule in this respect, but also Articles 7(2), 11(6), and 12(4) incorporate such concerns about non-arm's-length payments. In the same vein, Article 24(4) contains an exclusion of non-arm's-length payments. This background constitutes an important argument for distinguishing between non-arm's-length and residence. Article 24(5) prohibits discrimination because of the shareholder's residence, not because of the failure to meet the arm's-length standard. As concerns about BEPS through non-arm's-length transactions mostly arise in a cross-border context, it may make sense to apply the arm's-length principle to certain transactions only in cross-border situations.[1802] Consequently, the decisive question appears to be whether thin capitalization rules that do not comprehensively target all non-arm's-length payments to associated enterprises but only interest payments to non-resident shareholders are solely pursuing the aim of distinguishing between arm's-length and non-arm's-length payments. If a non-resident shareholder receives non-arm's-length payments, a change in residence leads to a change in tax treatment with a 'but for' test thereby establishing prima facie discrimination. Yet, with a substantive analysis, inevitably linked but relevant differences in circumstances may exist.

Since non-arm's-length interest payments to shareholders arguably imply that, from a domestic perspective, there is or should be a dividend distribution, a deduction is denied. For treaty purposes, this may have the following implications:[1803]

- On the one hand, if these payments constitute dividends within the meaning of Article 10(3) because they originate from corporate rights, Article 11(6) is not applicable. Nevertheless, Article 9(1) likely permits the domestic tax law to reclassify the loan in such a way as to give it the character of a contribution to equity capital or at least to treat the excess amount of (domestic) interest as non-deductible if no reclassification is made or allowed.
- On the other hand, if these payments constitute interest within the meaning of Article 11(3) because they originate from debt claims, Article 11(6) permits the adjustment of the rate at which interest is charged so that the excess amount of interest is governed by other provisions. Although this has no immediate

483; to this effect, also Avery Jones, Depret, et al. 1991b, 343–344, who note that both Article 24(4) and Article 24(5) might be seen as 'more specific'; similarly, Bammens 2013a, 165; Bammens 2012, 466–467; De Broe 2008, 562; differently, for instance, Helminen 2007, 108; Hageböke 2005 m.no. 4; Hageböke and Käbisch 2006, 850; Vogel 1997 Article 24, m.no. 160; moreover, Moritz 2003, 226–227, with further references. *See also*, not least, Haslehner 2009, 89–90; Friedlander 2002, 87.

1802. *See*, for instance, Ault and Sasseville 2010, 111; Marres 2016b, 8; Marres 2016a, 54.

1803. In this context, it is assumed that special conditions exist under both Article 9(1) and Article 11(6) although Article 9(1) does not cover, for instance, relationship by blood or marriage and that the definitions of 'dividends' and 'interest' in Articles 10(3) and 11(3) are at least largely autonomous and, therefore, do not depend on how payments are classified under thin capitalization rules or other provisions of domestic tax law.

implications for the deductibility of these payments,[1804] Article 9(1) likely permits the domestic tax law to treat the excess amount of interest as non-deductible.[1805]

Articles 9(1) and 11(6) only apply in cross-border situations when a resident and a non-resident transact with each other on a non-arm's-length basis thereby distinguishing on the basis of residence in cases that could potentially be covered by Article 24(5). Moreover, in all cases when non-arm's-length payments are treated as non-deductible, no protection is granted under Article 24(4) due to the exclusion of non-arm's-length payments. Against this background, it is doubtful why thin capitalization rules that deny a deduction of non-arm's-length payments to non-resident shareholders should pursue objectives that are illegitimate from a tax treaty perspective or contravene the aims of the non-discrimination clause of Article 24(5).[1806] Although differences in the shareholder's residence are not inevitably linked to whether payments are at arm's length – if a non-resident shareholder receives

1804. *See*, however, 1992–2017 OECD Commentary on Article 11, para. 35, which states that 'this paragraph [6] can affect not only the recipient but also the payer of excessive interest and if the law of the State of source permits, the excess amount can be disallowed as a deduction, due regard being had to other applicable provisions of the Convention'. This conclusion is only acceptable if it is considered that Article 24(4) refers to Article 11(6) so that the latter may affect the former with regard to whether different conditions for deduction of excessive interest are acceptable or constitute prohibited tax discrimination. *See also*, critically, Marres 2016b, 7, 8; Marres 2016a, 52, 54–55.

1805. This is particularly true if Article 9(1) does not rely on the definitions of 'dividends' and 'interest' pursuant to Articles 10(3) and 11(3), respectively. *See*, for instance, Lang 1994b, 134. In this case, non-arm's-length interest payments within the meaning of Article 11(3) could be partly treated as non-deductible dividends under domestic tax law without necessarily conflicting with Article 9(1). A follow-up issue is how these non-arm's-length interest payments should be treated for tax treaty purposes. Article 11(6) excludes the excess amount from the scope of Article 11 but without changing its classification as 'interest'; Article 11(6) even refers to 'the [excess] amount of the interest, having regard to the debt-claim for which it is paid'. Article 7 or 21 could be applicable instead, although this would normally mean that the State of the payer would lose taxing rights over the excess amount. Therefore, it seems plausible to consider Article 10 as well. Although the interest payments continue to be 'interest' within the meaning of Article 11(3), that is income from debt claims, the excess amount could be treated like a hidden dividend distribution and, thus, as if it was income from corporate rights within the meaning of Article 10(3).

1806. *See also*, to this effect, Ault and Sasseville 2010, 117 ('since Art. 9(1) specifically authorizes the application of domestic law rules that have the effect of adjusting the profits of associated enterprises according to the arm's length principle, it seems reasonable, when reading Art. 24(5) in the context of the whole OECD Model, to conclude that a similar exception applies to the non-discrimination rule of that paragraph'); Bammens 2013a, 157, 164, 171; Bruns 2013 m.nos. 172, 175; De Broe 2008, 562; Hofstätter and Ressler 2006, 223; Elliffe 2013b, 37–38; Elliffe 2013a, 609–611 (at least in respect of tax treaties negotiated from 1986 onwards); Bammens 2012, 465–466, 472, 477; Avery Jones, Depret, et al. 1991b, 344; differently, Marres 2016b, 10; Marres 2016a, 58–59 ('[i]f article 24(4) ... is part of the context of article 24(5), this may be an argument for a similar interpretation of a similar term, but not an argument in favour of an exception that is explicitly provided for in one but not in the other provision'); Haslehner 2016a m.no. 38; Rust 2015b m.no. 112; Rust 2015c m.no. 165a; Mitra 2007, 5–7; Piltz 1996, 134; Lang 1994b, 154, 156. *See*, moreover, German Federal Fiscal Court (Bundesfinanzhof), 8 September 2010, I R 6/09 (comments by Lüdicke 2011b); and 16 January 2014, I R 30/12, rejecting an implicit carve-out under Article 24(5); concurring Wassermeyer and Schwenke 2016 m.no. 102.

non-arm's-length payments, a change in residence does not change the amount of these payments - Articles 9(1), 11(6), 12(4), and 24(4) indicate that:

- the Contracting States aim at applying tax treaty rules other than Articles 11 and 12 to non-arm's-length interest and royalty payments;
- the Contracting States should be allowed to make transfer pricing adjustments under domestic tax law even if these adjustments increase taxable profits as long as the arm's-length standard is adhered to; and
- the Contracting States should not be prohibited from denying a deduction in such cases, notably, if they legitimately reclassify equity into debt or interest into dividends for domestic purposes.

This means that, while other tax treaty rules do not authorize discriminatory tax treatment under Article 24(5), they authorize the Contracting States in certain situations to apply different rules to non-arm's-length payments as far as non-resident recipients are concerned. They thereby indicate differences in legal circumstances between residents and non-residents because of arguably different profit shifting opportunities. Such differences could be regarded as relevant under Article 24(5) even when they are inevitably linked to residence in a concrete case. In fact, a similar approach is taken in cases in which nationality and residence coincide under Article 24(1): Article 4(3) may create relevant differences in legal circumstances between national and foreign corporations when incorporation leads to full tax liability but not to tax treaty residence (*see* Chapter 3 section §3.06[C][4]).

A counter-argument could be that there does not appear to be a rationale for a carve-out for transfer pricing adjustments under Article 24(5). Whereas the rationale is evident in respect of Article 24(4), 'it does not make sense to accept different transfer pricing regimes for domestic-owned and foreign-owned enterprises'.[1807] If the domestic tax measure under scrutiny would really aim at preventing profit shifting opportunities, it would have to employ the recipient's residence and not the shareholder's residence as the appropriate grounds for different tax treatment. To such tax distinctions, Article 24(5) would not apply anyway because the reason for different tax treatment would then lie in the recipient's residence. However, since the domestic tax measure under scrutiny addresses only non-arm's-length interest payments that are made to direct or indirect shareholders, profit shifting opportunities with other associated enterprises remain and put that measure's aims into question. When a change in the shareholder's residence leads to change in tax treatment in a concrete case, a substantive analysis could, therefore, imply that the reason for different tax treatment cannot be explained with profit shifting opportunities and thus lies in the shareholder's residence.

While with a substantive analysis it is indeed necessary to determine whether the allegedly discriminating State genuinely pursues an objective that is different from the shareholder's residence, it cannot be said that a thin capitalization rule that addresses

1807. Marres 2016b, 10; Marres 2016a, 58–59. *See also*, similarly, Rust 2015b m.no. 112; Rust 2015c m.no. 165a; Isakova 2015, 522.

only non-arm's-length interest payments to non-resident shareholders is not countering BEPS. This thin capitalization rule, for instance, may be only one of many defensive tax measures addressing non-arm's-length transactions. Therefore, it may make sense from a State's perspective to apply, on the one hand, different transfer pricing regimes for domestic-owned and foreign-owned enterprises under specialized thin capitalization rules and, on the other hand, to complement such rules by other measures that apply different transfer pricing regimes for resident and non-resident recipients, excluding shareholders. All in all, there are some reasons to believe that, if a thin capitalization rule addresses only foreign-owned enterprises by denying a deduction of non-arm's-length interest payments to non-resident shareholders, it relies on inevitably linked but relevant differences in legal circumstances indicated by Articles 9(1), 11(6), 12(4), and 24(4). Such differences prevent comparability for the purposes of the ownership non-discrimination clause and thereby justify differences in tax treatment.

[B] Progressive Tax Rate and Foreign Income

[1] Progressivity and Overall Ability to Pay Tax

Article 24(3) is relevant for enterprises that conduct business in the source State through a PE regardless of whether such enterprises are carried on by corporations or individuals.[1808] Since individuals are often subject to a progressive tax (this is now less common with legal persons), the issue arises whether the source State may calculate the tax rate on the basis of the income and capital of the whole enterprise including profits, losses, and property sourced or located outside of the source State or only on the basis of the income and capital that is attributable to a PE in the source State.

A progressive tax is designed to increase the tax rate as the taxable amount increases. If the taxpayer earns more income or possesses more property, that person pays a proportionately higher tax on all taxable income or capital. Conversely, if the taxpayer earns less income or possesses less property, that person pays a proportionately lower tax so that, put differently, a certain minimum amount of income or capital remains at least largely untaxed. By applying a progressive scale of rates, the average tax rate increases with a higher and decreases with a lower tax base. From a policy perspective, a progressive tax aims at subjecting persons with a higher ability to pay to a proportionately higher tax than persons with a lower ability to pay. What 'ability to pay' means and to what tax treatment a particular ability to pay should lead are controversial issues that cannot be answered in the abstract, that is without a benchmark derived from, for instance, a constitutional framework or a specific tax system.[1809] Yet, if it can be determined that a certain higher amount of income or capital leads to a higher ability to pay tax, a progressive scale of rates constitutes a means for levying a proportionately higher tax.

1808. *See*, for instance, Rust 2015b m.no. 60; Rust 2015c m.no. 99; Zhai 2009, 1108; Tumpel and Stangl 2006, 72; Adonnino 1993, 55; Raad 1986, 133.

1809. *See*, critically, Gassner and Lang 2000b; Gassner and Lang 2000a; but *see also* Hey 2015, sec. 3 m.no. 41.

States may limit their attention to their territory by taxing both residents and non-residents on a territorial basis and thereby ignoring foreign income and capital.[1810] Similarly, States may calculate their progressive tax rate by taking only income and capital sourced or situated within their territory into account. A progressive scale of rates does not necessarily imply a particular basis for progression. It rather leaves open what income and capital, that is all items of income and capital or only certain items as identified by their nexus or classification, should lead to an assumption of a higher ability to pay tax and to a higher average tax rate. Initially, from the point of view of a progressive tax system, ability to pay may be determined on a worldwide or territorial basis.

However, many States tax residents on a worldwide basis and non-residents on a territorial basis. In this way, States subject residents to full tax liability in order to consider, among other things, their overall or worldwide ability to pay tax, whereas they subject non-residents to limited tax liability and thereby distinguish based on whether income or capital is sourced or located domestically or abroad. States manifest their intention to consider a resident's ability to pay tax on a worldwide basis by taxing residents on such a basis and applying a progressive scale of rates accordingly, that is on a worldwide basis as well.

This intention could be disrupted by tax treaty exemptions for both the residence State and the source State. A tax treaty may, in effect, turn worldwide taxation into territorial taxation. This is particularly visible when a Contracting State subjects a person to full tax liability under its domestic tax law but becomes the source State for tax treaty purposes under the tiebreaker rules of Article 4(2) or (3). According to the OECD Commentary, such a person is not subject to comprehensive liability to tax in the source State for the purposes of any other tax treaty even though that individual remains a resident of that State under domestic tax law.[1811] Also, if the residence State of a taxpayer provides an exemption under Article 23 A for income or capital that is allocated to and taxable in the other Contracting State, the amount of income or capital that remains taxable in the residence State is reduced. If no income or capital is sourced or located in a third State, the residence State is actually taxing only income from sources in that State or capital situated therein. By granting an exemption in order to avoid juridical double taxation, one of the Contracting States must lower its tax base. When the residence State does so by exempting income or capital, it forfeits its right to tax on a worldwide basis even though it may still aim at considering the taxpayer's overall ability to pay tax.

If a tax treaty exemption would require the residence State to calculate a progressive tax rate not on a worldwide basis but on a territorial basis, that is without taking into account the exempt income or capital, taxpayers could escape higher progressivity in a cross-border situation.[1812] A distribution of income or capital among

1810. *See*, in particular, 2008-2017 OECD Commentary on Article 24, para. 8.3 (1992-2005: para. 8), which argues that residents of States adopting a territorial principle in their taxation are not excluded from the scope of a tax treaty under the second sentence of Article 4(1).
1811. 2008-2017 OECD Commentary on Article 4, para. 8.2.
1812. *See*, for instance, Raad 2005, 139-140; Lüdicke 1999, 744.

several States leads to a lower amount of income or capital that remains taxable in each State. If each State, including the residence State, applies a progressive tax by calculating the relevant tax rate only on the basis of the taxable income or capital, the average tax rate in each State is reduced. As a consequence, the accumulated tax burden of the taxpayer is lower than in a purely domestic situation and the taxpayer can take advantage of splitting income or capital between different States. Conversely, if the same overall amount of income or capital would be earned or located in only one State, that State would assume a higher ability to pay tax and would apply a higher average tax rate.

In order to prevent such advantages in a cross-border context and to consider a taxpayer's overall ability to pay tax even if that taxpayer is active in several States, many States calculate the applicable tax rate not on a territorial basis but on a worldwide basis regardless of whether they grant exemptions. This means that even when a State does not, in fact, tax on a worldwide basis because certain income or capital is exempt under a tax treaty, it calculates the progressive tax rate as if it would be allowed to tax on a worldwide basis. Articles 23 A(3) and 23 B(2) explicitly allow the residence State to do so. Which level of progression is reached thus depends on the worldwide income or capital. On this basis, the average tax rate is determined[1813] and applied to the income or capital that is actually subject to tax.

Not only the residence State but also the source State may have an interest in calculating a progressive tax rate on a worldwide basis. In principle, therefore, the source State may also wish to take a taxpayer's overall ability to pay tax into account even when it does not tax all income or capital of a taxpayer. For example, the source State might subject a non-resident taxpayer to limited tax liability but nevertheless aim at applying the same average tax rate to the taxable income and capital of that taxpayer as it would apply to a resident taxpayer with the same worldwide income or capital.[1814] Additionally, if a taxpayer is a resident of both Contracting States under domestic tax law, the worldwide income or capital might automatically be considered for the purposes of calculating the tax rate both in the residence State and in the source State.[1815] Accordingly, the source State in which a PE is located might also have an interest in taxing the income or capital that is attributable to the PE on the basis of the worldwide tax circumstances with respect to the applicable tax rate. It would thereby contribute to taxation based on the taxpayer's ability to pay tax as determined from a worldwide perspective. If each State taxes income or capital on a territorial basis but calculates its progressive tax rate that is applied to that income or capital on a worldwide basis, the overall ability to pay tax is taken into account in each State. Regarding the tax base, the consideration of the worldwide income or capital in more

1813. This is done by first computing the tax liability as it would arise without the tax treaty exemptions, that is by applying the progressive tax rate to the overall amount of income or capital and then by dividing this tax liability by the overall amount of income or capital. *See also* Rust 2015a m.no. 84.

1814. *See*, to this effect, Djanani and Hartmann 2000, 322. However, in practice, taxation of non-residents is often based on objective criteria disregarding all elements of ability to pay (zero bracket, personal expenses, progressive tax rates, etc.). *See* Rust 2015a m.no. 87.

1815. *See also* Rust 2015a m.no. 87.

than one State leads to international juridical double taxation, a consequence which a tax treaty aims to avoid. Regarding the tax rate, by contrast, it is only logical to consider the worldwide income or capital in more than one State if each State aims to take account of a taxpayer's overall ability to pay tax.

[2] Solution Proposed by the OECD Commentary

Article 24(3) requires non-discriminatory taxation on a PE. Therefore, it could prohibit the source State from considering the worldwide income or capital for the purposes of calculating the applicable tax rate. To apply a progressive scale of rates on a worldwide basis, the source State must take into account the income or capital that is not attributable to the PE even though the taxation on the PE cannot be more burdensome than the taxation levied on resident enterprises carrying on the same activities. It is thus unclear whether the tax burden on the income or capital that is attributable to the PE can be calculated on the basis of the activities of the whole non-resident enterprise as far as the tax rate is concerned or only on the basis of the activities carried on through the PE.

According to the OECD Commentary, Article 24(3) permits the source State to consider the worldwide income or capital of a non-resident enterprise for tax rate purposes when taxing a PE of this enterprise:[1816]

> When the taxation of profits made by companies which are residents of a given State is calculated according to a progressive scale of rates, such a scale should, in principle, be applied to permanent establishments situated in that State. If in applying the progressive scale, the permanent establishment's State takes into account the profits of the whole company to which such a permanent establishment belongs, such a rule would not appear to conflict with the equal treatment rule, since resident companies are in fact treated in the same way .... States that tax their own companies in this way could therefore define in their bilateral conventions the treatment applicable to permanent establishments.
>
> When a system of taxation based on a progressive scale of rates includes a rule that a minimum rate is applicable to permanent establishments, it cannot be claimed *a priori* that such a rule is incompatible with the equal treatment principle. The profits of the whole enterprise to which the permanent establishment belongs should be taken into account in determining the rate applicable according to the progressive scale. The provisions of the first sentence of paragraph 3 are not observed only if the minimum rate is higher.

At first, the OECD Commentary takes the view that the worldwide tax circumstances may be considered for the purposes of calculating the tax rate that is applicable to a PE.[1817] Articles 23 A(3) and 23 B(2) safeguard the principle of progression for the residence State. In calculating the amount of tax on the income or capital of a resident

1816. 2008–2017 OECD Commentary on Article 24, paras 56–57 (1977: paras 39–40; 1992–2005: paras 37–38).
1817. It is noteworthy that the OECD Commentary is rather cautious in this context by using the expression 'would not appear to conflict' and suggesting that the Contracting States could bilaterally define the envisaged treatment. *See* Oesterhelt 2015 m.no. 85.

enterprise, the residence State may take into account the income or capital that is exempt in the residence State under a tax treaty. Thus, in calculating the amount of the non-discriminatory tax under Article 24(3), the source State may also take into account the income or capital that is not taxable in the source State. This further implies that the income or capital that is not attributable to a particular PE but nevertheless taxable in the source State (for instance, because private immovable property or another PE is situated in the source State) may also influence the progressive tax rate without violating Article 24(3).

As soon as a progressive tax rate calculated on a worldwide basis leads to lower taxation on a PE than a progressive tax rate calculated on a territorial basis, the OECD Commentary changes its position. If the worldwide income or capital of the non-resident enterprise is lower than that of the PE, Article 24(3) arguably does not prevent the source State from considering only the income or capital of the PE:[1818]

> However, even if the profits of the whole enterprise to which the permanent establishment belongs are taken into account when applying either a progressive scale of rates or a minimum rate, this should not conflict with the principle of the separate and independent [before 2010: distinct and separate] enterprise, according to which the profits of the permanent establishment must be determined under paragraph 2 of Article 7. The minimum amount of the tax levied in the State where the permanent establishment is situated is, therefore, the amount which would be due if it were a separate and independent [before 2010: distinct and separate] enterprise, without reference to the profits of the whole enterprise to which it belongs. The State where the permanent establishment is situated is, therefore, justified in applying the progressive scale applicable to resident enterprises solely to the profits of the permanent establishment, leaving aside the profits of the whole enterprise when the latter are less than those of the permanent establishment. This State may likewise tax the profits of the permanent establishment at a minimum rate, provided that the same rate applies also to resident enterprises, even if taking into account the profits of the whole enterprise to which it belongs would result in a lower amount of tax, or no tax at all.

It appears that the OECD Commentary takes a contradictory approach:[1819] the worldwide income or capital of a non-resident enterprise may increase the taxation on a PE without violating the non-discrimination obligations but losses suffered by or debts attributable to other parts of the enterprise, if they lead to a lower worldwide income or capital than that of the PE, need not lower the taxation on the PE and may thereby even lead to competitive disadvantages.[1820] In order to justify this view, the OECD Commentary relies on Article 7(2). For the purposes of determining the profits that are attributable to a PE, Article 7(2) hypothesizes the PE to be a separate and independent enterprise. According to the OECD Commentary, Article 24(3) 'should not conflict with the principle of the separate and independent enterprise'[1821] by requiring to take into account the income and capital of the whole enterprise when this would result in a lower amount or no tax at all due to a progressive scale of rates.

1818. 2008-2017 OECD Commentary on Article 24, para. 58 (1977: para. 41; 1992-2005: para. 39).
1819. *See* Haslehner 2016a m.no. 24; Bhuta 2015, 382-385; Haslehner 2009, 307-308.
1820. *See* Bhuta 2015, 384.
1821. 2008-2017 OECD Commentary on Article 24, para. 58 (1977: para. 41; 1992-2005: para. 39).

Article 7(2) is part of the context of Article 24 and may thus be relevant for the interpretation of Article 24(3).[1822] Despite that, its principle of separateness and independence could only favour a separation of the PE from other parts of the enterprise regardless of whether these other parts incur profits or losses and whether the applicable tax rate thereby increases or decreases. Article 7(2) could favour taxation based on a progressive tax rate that solely considers the PE's functions and activities when the PE is in a profit situation even if the whole enterprise suffers losses (or earns less profits); the PE would be taxed as a separate and independent enterprise. Then Article 7(2) would also have to favour taxation based on a progressive tax rate that solely considers the PE's functions and activities if the whole enterprise earns higher profits than the PE; the progressive tax rate should only take the PE's profits into account. There is no indication that the PE should be more or less separate and independent under Article 7(2) or for the purposes of the non-discrimination clause depending on how the other parts of the non-resident enterprise succeed in their business.

Besides that, it is doubtful whether Article 7(2) may indeed lead to such a complete separation of a PE for the purposes of non-discrimination. Article 7(2) is concerned with the allocation of taxing rights, not with tax rates. It determines the profits or losses that are attributable to a PE in the source State. It does not address how these profits or losses should be taxed under the source State's domestic tax law, including the applicable tax rate. Whether the source State imposes a tax on attributable income that is less favourable than a corresponding tax on income of resident enterprises is an issue to be solved under Article 24(3). Income as identified by Article 7 must first be attributed to a PE in the source State before Article 24(3) can scrutinize whether the source State calculates the tax base differently or subjects the tax base to a different tax rate which leads to taxation that is less favourable for the PE when compared to resident enterprises. In addition, Article 7(2) does not deal with taxes other than on income although, for instance, taxes on capital as well as taxes on estates, inheritances, and on gifts are also covered by Article 24(3) and may be calculated on the basis of a progressive scale of rates. Finally, as the OECD Commentary on Article 7 mentions, '[t]he separate and independent enterprise fiction that is mandated by paragraph 2 is restricted to the determination of the profits that are attributable to a PE. It does not extend to create notional income for the enterprise which a Contracting State could tax as such under its domestic law by arguing that such income is covered by another Article of the Convention ...'.[1823] If the fiction of Article 7(2) does not extend to other allocation rules that deal with specific types of business income such as with interest, it is not clear why the fiction should nevertheless extend to the PE non-discrimination clause. 'Indeed, the fiction mandated by paragraph 2 ... merely applies to determine the profits attributable to the permanent establishment for the purposes of Articles 7, 23 A and 23 B',[1824] arguably without touching upon the issue

1822. *See*, to this effect, Hohenwarter 2010, 180.
1823. 2010–2017 OECD Commentary on Article 7, para. 28.
1824. *Ibid.*, para. 28.

of whether the attributed profits are taxed in a discriminatory manner by disregarding foreign losses for the purposes of calculating the tax rate that is applicable to the profits.

Contrary to the view of the OECD Commentary, no conflict between Article 24(3) and Article 7(2) can arise. Article 24(3) deals with the same business profits that are attributable to a PE in the source State under Article 7(2) without influencing this attribution. Article 7(2) attributes the same business profits to a PE regardless of what tax rate the source State applies with or without the non-discrimination obligations. The approach of the OECD Commentary can only succeed if it is understood that Article 7(2), in addition to setting a maximum amount of tax that may be levied in the source State, permits the source State to tax this amount under its domestic tax law as if no other parts of the non-resident enterprise existed. In fact, the OECD Commentary speaks of '[t]he *minimum* amount of the tax levied in the State where the permanent establishment is situated' (emphasis added) and refers to 'the amount which would be due if it were a separate and independent [before 2010: distinct and separate] enterprise'.[1825] Article 7(2) arguably permits the source State to tax a certain amount in isolation from all other sources of income, including income that is not attributable to the PE at issue but taxable in the source State. Given that Article 24(3) considers the activities of the whole non-resident enterprise as the benchmark for the purposes of progressivity and, therefore, allows applying a higher progressive tax rate on a worldwide basis, this means that Article 7(2) implicitly authorizes discriminatory tax treatment between resident and non-resident enterprises when Article 24(3) would otherwise require applying a lower progressive tax rate on a worldwide basis.[1826] It is at least doubtful whether Article 7(2) can be interpreted in this way.

When taking a look at the historical development of the Commentary's statements, Article 7 was initially used to argue against a tax rate that takes account of the worldwide income or capital unless the proviso safeguarding progression is extended for the benefit of the source State. It is reported that, in 1971, the Delegates for France, Belgium, Switzerland, and the US believed that, in principle, the same rates should be applied to a resident company as to a PE whereas the Delegates for Austria, Germany, and Turkey were not prepared to accept such a solution and considered that a differential treatment was justified by the fact that a PE was taxed only on the profits that it realized.[1827] In response, Working Group No. 4 prepared comments that rejected the view put forward in particular by the Austrian Delegation that States are justified in applying to non-residents a 'minimum rate' that is higher than the rate normally applicable to residents with the same level of income as the former.[1828] Such a 'minimum rate' would not only disregard the clear terms of Article 24(3), but, according to the Working Group, it would likely be incompatible 'with the "distinct and separate enterprise" principle laid down in Article 7 which, while it primarily concerns the determination of the permanent establishment's profits, nevertheless contains the

1825. 2008–2017 OECD Commentary on Article 24, para. 58 (1977: para. 41; 1992–2005: para. 39).
1826. *See* 2008–2017 OECD Commentary on Article 24, para. 4 ('measures that are mandated or expressly authorised by the provisions of these Articles [the other Articles of the Convention] cannot be considered to violate the provisions of the Article [24]').
1827. OECD, DAF/CFA/WP1/71.3, pp. 2–3.
1828. OECD, DAF/CFA/WP1/71.10(Add.1), pp. 2–3.

idea that the permanent establishment must be assimilated to a resident enterprise for taxation purposes'.[1829] In addition, the Working Group drew a connection between the justification of such a 'minimum rate', that is compensation for the fact that the tax liability of non-residents is limited to income arising in the State concerned and the 'reservation of the progression' made by Article 23 A in favour of the residence State.[1830] It was conceivable for the Working Group that this 'reservation of the progression' might be extended in bilateral conventions to the source State so as to meet the points made by the Austrian Delegation.[1831] Thus, the Working Group believed that a tax rate calculated on a worldwide basis or a corresponding 'minimum rate' could only be applied to a PE if the progression is also reserved in favour of the source State since, otherwise, Article 24(3) in the context of Article 7 required assimilating a PE to a resident enterprise.

It seems that the Austrian Delegation was not satisfied with this as Working Party No. 1 took note of the need to revise the exposition of the Austrian Delegation's position[1832] and Working Group No. 4 prepared new comments:[1833]

> When the taxation of profits made by companies resident in a given State is calculated according to a proportional rate, or a scale of progressive rates regardless of what is done with such profits, such rate or scale should, in principle, be applied to permanent establishments situated in that State, on the same footing as though they constituted distinct and separate enterprises. However, States which employ a scale of progressive rates for taxing companies are left free in their bilateral conventions, insofar of course as they use the exemption method ... (in favour solely of the State of residence), to stipulate that for the purpose of taxing profits of permanent establishments the 'reservation of the progression' clause contained in ... Article [23 A] shall be extended for the benefit of the States where such permanent establishments are situated. On the other hand, the retention of a minimum rate for permanent establishments that is higher than the ordinary rate appears incompatible with the principle of equal treatment ....

After the Steering Group discussed the proposals of the Working Group,[1834] the view that Article 24(3) in the context of Article 7 requires ignoring other income that is not attributable to a PE for the purposes of the tax rate was effectively reversed by holding that it does not appear to conflict with Article 24(3) to take into account the global income in applying a progressive tax scale.[1835] At first, these statements were not adopted by Working Party No. 1 as the Rapporteur was asked to submit a new text in order to avoid any contradiction with the comments on the second sentence of Article

1829. *Ibid.*, p. 3.
1830. *Ibid.*, p. 3.
1831. *Ibid.*, p. 3.
1832. OECD, DAF/CFA/WP1/72/3, p. 4.
1833. OECD, CFA/WP1(72)8, p. 9.
1834. OECD, DAF/CFA/WP1/73.1, p. 2; OECD, DAF/CFA/WP1/73.2, p. 2 (unfortunately, DAF/CFA/2516 of 4 January 1973 containing revised texts of Article 24 and the Commentary as well as DAF/CFA/2517 of 5 January 1973 containing observations by the German Delegate concerning the Commentary on Article 24 were not available for the purposes of this research, and no conclusions of the second meeting of the Steering Group have been found).
1835. OECD, DAF/CFA/2584, pp. 5–6; OECD, CFA/WP1(73)6, p. 11. *See also* 2008–2017 OECD Commentary on Article 24, paras 56–57 (1977: paras 39–40; 1992–2005: paras 37–38).

24(3) and to take into account the comments on the proviso safeguarding progression.[1836] A new text was not submitted, however. Instead, the Rapporteur of Working Group No. 4 prepared an amendment to the Commentary that included a new paragraph dealing with the minimum amount of the tax that may be levied in the source State in order to avoid a contradiction with the principle of the distinct and separate enterprise.[1837]

[3] Comparability: Ignoring All Other Activities?

[a] Requirement of 'The Same Activities'

If the source State applies a progressive tax rate on a worldwide basis even though it only taxes income or capital that is attributable to a PE, it aims at different treatment when compared to a resident enterprise that carries on the same activities as the PE. At the same time, it aims at identical treatment when compared to a resident enterprise that carries on the same activities as the non-resident enterprise to which the PE belongs. In terms of comparability, the decisive issue appears to be whether the PE must be compared to: (i) a resident enterprise that exercises only 'the same activities' as the PE; or (ii) a resident enterprise that exercises 'the same activities' as the non-resident enterprise, even though only '[t]he taxation on a permanent establishment' can be scrutinized and thus the taxation of the activities other than those carried on through the PE is not protected (*see also* Chapter 3 section §3.04[B][2]). As Harshal Bhuta puts it, the decisive question appears to be whether the PE or the non-resident enterprise to which the PE belongs really is the subject of comparison under Article 24(3), which arguably determines the appropriate object of comparison and the relevant activities.[1838]

It can be argued that Article 24(3) requires completely eliminating all activities from the comparability analysis other than those of the PE. Articles 7 and 22(2) limit the taxing rights of the source State to income or capital that is attributable to a PE. Article 24(3) is only concerned with '[t]he taxation on a permanent establishment'. Arguably, a comparable resident enterprise 'carrying on the same activities' cannot obtain or possess more income and capital than a PE as a hypothetically separate and independent enterprise obtains or possesses under Articles 7 and 22(2). This means that everything regarding the PE must be the same, but everything else must be ignored: profits, losses, and capital sourced or located outside of the source State or not attributable to the PE (even if taxable in the source State) play no role and cannot affect the tax rate. As a result, an effectively higher tax rate on the PE calculated by reference to the profits of the whole enterprise violates the non-discrimination obligations, but an

1836. OECD, DAF/CFA/WP1(73)8, pp. 4–5.
1837. OECD, DAF/CFA/WP1/73.11, p. 2; moreover, OECD, DAF/CFA/WP1/73.12, p. 1; OECD, DAF/CFA/WP1(73)13, p. 4 (adoption). *See also* 2008–2017 OECD Commentary on Article 24, para. 58 (1977: para. 41; 1992–2005: para. 39).
1838. Bhuta 2015, 385.

effectively lower tax rate on the PE need not be applied even if the whole enterprise suffers losses.

It can be replied, however, that Article 24(3) imposes no such limitations for the purposes of comparability. Although the non-discrimination rule is only concerned with '[t]he taxation on a permanent establishment' and, therefore, allows ignoring the taxation on other parts of the enterprise, it does not prohibit from taking other activities into account when dealing with the taxation on a PE. On the contrary, even though the expression 'carrying on the same activities' refers to the activities of a PE and thereby limits the focus of attention to the taxation of the activities carried on through a PE of a non-resident enterprise, certain other legal and factual circumstances must be taken into account for the purposes of determining whether resident and non-resident enterprises are comparable to each other, including the enterprises' legal structure (*see also* Chapter 3 section §3.04[B][2]). As a consequence, an effectively higher tax rate on the PE calculated by reference to the profits of the whole enterprise is perfectly in line with the non-discrimination obligations, but an effectively lower tax rate on the PE must be granted when the whole enterprise suffers losses.

Alexander Rust submits a similar line of reasoning. Since the non-resident enterprise (the taxpayer) and not the PE is protected against discrimination with respect to the income attributable to the PE,[1839] it is not correct to deem the legal personality of the PE for the purposes of applying the non-discrimination clause.[1840] If the PE is thus not regarded as a separate entity but as a dependent part of the whole enterprise, it is logical that, for calculating the tax rate applicable to the income of the PE, it does not violate Article 24(3) to take the entire income of the enterprise into account provided that the tax rate of resident enterprises is also calculated on the basis of the worldwide income.[1841]

With a 'but for' test, all circumstances both in law and in fact, except for the protected characteristic and inevitably linked attributes, must be same in order to identify whether a difference in tax treatment constitutes prima facie discrimination. All such circumstances, therefore, deny comparability if they differ in a concrete case. As the activities carried on in a Contracting State or a third State are not inevitably linked to the protected attribute of residence, they must remain identical when comparing a PE to a resident enterprise. Nevertheless, the issue remains whether the PE non-discrimination clause limits the meaning of 'all circumstances' to the protected activities thereby requiring ignoring all other activities or the consequences therefrom. In this respect, Article 24(3) contains ambiguous wording. It addresses '[t]he taxation on a permanent establishment' of a non-resident enterprise and requires a comparable resident enterprise to carry on 'the same activities'. This might imply that only the activities of the PE can be taken into account for the purposes of comparability and treatment that is less favourable. In its second sentence, however, Article 24(3) refers to the non-resident enterprise to which the PE belongs.[1842] Therefore, it is not clear

1839. *See also supra* n. 1251.
1840. Rust 2015b m.no. 57; Rust 2015c m.no. 95.
1841. Rust 2015b m.no. 67; Rust 2015c m.no. 105.
1842. *See also* Rust 2015b m.no. 57; Rust 2015c m.no. 95; critically Bhuta 2015, 386.

whether Article 24(3) requires ignoring certain circumstances (the activities other than those of the PE) even though they are not inevitably linked to the protected characteristic or whether all activities of the whole non-resident enterprise must be taken into account with a 'but for' test, which means that they could potentially influence the taxation on a PE and the taxation of a comparable resident enterprise.

[b] Safeguarding Progression under Article 23

Although the wording of Article 24(3) is ambiguous and the explanations in the OECD Commentary are contradictory, some useful insights may be derived from the context of Article 24(3) and, notably, from Articles 23 A(3) and 23 B(2). In general, a tax treaty is not concerned with tax bases and tax rates. Its rules allocate taxing rights by defining certain categories of income and capital (for instance, business profits) and by permitting one Contracting State to exercise its tax jurisdiction while requiring the other State to prevent juridical double taxation through exemption or tax credit. Whether a Contracting State taxes on a gross or net basis and what tax rate it applies is of no concern to a tax treaty.[1843] Thus, the Contracting States enjoy much leeway in defining their domestic tax bases and rates as long as they do not violate the non-discrimination obligations of Article 24.

In addition, Articles 23 A(3) and 23 B(2) safeguard the resident State's application of a progressive scale of rates on a worldwide basis: 'Where in accordance with any provision of the Convention income derived or capital owned by a resident of a Contracting State is exempt from tax in that State, such State may nevertheless, in calculating the amount of tax on the remaining income or capital of such resident, take into account the exempted income or capital.' It follows that the residence State may take into account income or capital that is exempt under the tax treaty when calculating the tax rate on the remaining income or capital.[1844] A tax treaty exemption only restricts the tax base for the calculation of the amount of income or capital that is taxable in the residence State but not the tax base for the calculation of the applicable tax rate.[1845] This allows the residence State to tax at a rate that corresponds to the taxpayer's overall ability to pay tax.[1846]

It is subject to debate whether Articles 23 A(3) and 23 B(2) merely clarify that a tax treaty exemption limits a Contracting State's taxing rights solely with regard to the tax base and, therefore, has no impact on the applicable tax rate.[1847] This question is of

1843. Although Articles 10 and 11 specify a maximum percentage of the gross amount of dividends and interest, the source State may still tax this income on a net basis by applying any tax rate as long as the tax does not exceed the prescribed amount. Therefore, it can be said that, under Articles 10 and 11, dividends and interest are only partly exempt in the source State.

1844. Rust 2015a m.no. 80.

1845. Rust 2015a m.no. 80.

1846. Rust 2015a m.no. 81.

1847. For an overview, *see* Rust 2015a m.nos. 88–89; in favour of a clarification Smit 2016, 306–309 ('a tax base exemption is only concerned with the allocation of taxation powers in relation to items of income and not with … the taxpayer's ability to pay tax'); Müller 2015 m.no. 8; Djanani and Hartmann 2000, 323, 325; Widhalm 1995, 165–166; Firlinger 1995, 313; Lechner 1982, 92–93; moreover, Lang 2011c, 387–389, who stresses that it is not unusual in a legal

particular importance to the source State which might also have an interest in applying a progressive tax rate on a worldwide basis. If the allocation rules would exempt income or capital not only from the tax base but also for the purposes of calculating the tax rate that is applicable to taxable income or capital, the source State would be forbidden to apply a progressive tax rate that takes account of the taxpayer's overall ability to pay tax. Articles 23 A(3) and 23 B(2) safeguard the application of such a progressive tax rate only with respect to the residence State. However, the OECD Commentary believes that the source State is free to apply its progressive tax rate regardless of whether the tax treaty explicitly addresses this issue.[1848] It follows that, while Article 23 A(3) explicitly allows the residence State to consider exempt income or capital for tax rate purposes, according to the OECD Commentary[1849] and voices in the literature,[1850] no *argumentum a contrario* can be drawn with regard to the source State. Neither tax treaty exemptions nor Articles 23 A(3) and 23 B(2) prevent the source State from calculating a progressive tax rate on a worldwide basis and from taking exempt income or capital for that purpose into account.

This result was not always that clear. In its preliminary report on methods for avoidance of double taxation of income of 1959, Working Party No. 15 of the OEEC Fiscal Committee concluded for reasons of simplicity that 'the full exemption system [that is, exemption without progression] is the most suitable for adoption in the State of source where that State gives up its right to tax a certain income'.[1851] It suggested a proviso safeguarding progression which, as with Articles 23 A(3) and 23 B(2), gave permission to the residence State without mentioning the source State.[1852] In response,

system that rules are introduced that are just explanatory and not really necessary; similarly, but also arguing for an *argumentum a contrario* if there is an express proviso safeguarding progression, Vogel 2008 m.nos. 40–41, 213–214; Vogel 1997 Article 23, m.nos. 69–69a, 208–209; differently, Dorn 1926, 102 ('[es wird] nicht nur Doppelbesteuerung vermieden, sondern Progression erspart'); Riemenschneider 1995, 187–190.

1848. 1977–2017 OECD Commentary on Articles 23 A and 23 B, para. 56 (similarly 1963: paras 35–36).

1849. *Ibid. See also* Grotherr 2016 m.no. 136; Rust 2015a m.no. 90 (the 1963 OECD Commentary 'already made clear that the non-residence State may apply a proviso safeguarding progression'); Haslehner 2016b, 49; Smit 2016, 308; Müller 2015 m.no. 9; Djanani and Hartmann 2000, 323; Lüdicke 1997, 657–658; Widhalm 1995, 168; Graf zu Ortenburg 1975, 485.

1850. Rust 2015a m.no. 90; Ismer 2015 m.no. 210; Smit 2016, 306–309; Müller 2015 m.no. 9; Djanani and Hartmann 2000; Widhalm 1995, 168–169; Firlinger 1995, 313; Widmer 1993a m.nos. 43.2, 73.1; Widmer 1993b m.nos. 43.2, 73.1; Graf zu Ortenburg 1975, 485; Debatin 1972, 1944; differently, Bammens 2012, 242–243; Vogel 2008 m.nos. 40–41, 213–214; Vogel 1997 Article 23, m.nos. 69–69a, 208–209; Riemenschneider 1995, 187–190; Flick and Wassermeyer 1974, 575; Hellwig 1973, 19.

1851. OEEC, FC/WP15(59)1 Part I, pp. 8, 13.

1852. *Ibid.*, p. 18. *See also* the revised draft in OEEC, FC/WP15(59)2, p. 2, which was later extensively discussed by the members of the Fiscal Committee: 'Where a resident of one of the Contracting States derives income from sources in the other Contracting State and that income, in accordance with this Convention, may be taxed in that other Contracting State, the Contracting State in which the person is resident shall ... exempt such income from tax but may, in calculating its tax, apply the rate of tax which would have been applicable if such income had not been so exempted.' Compare to Article 23 A(1) of the 1963 OECD Model: 'Where a resident of a Contracting State derives income or owns capital which, in accordance with the provisions of this Convention, may be taxed in the other Contracting State, the first-mentioned State shall ... exempt such income or capital from tax but may, in calculating

the Delegate for Switzerland thought that the tax rate could also be graduated by the source State as it was by the residence State and asked for an alteration,[1853] the Delegate for France favoured exemption without progression for the source State but exemption with progression for the residence State,[1854] and the Italian Delegation submitted a proposal[1855] that gave both the residence State and the source State the possibility of applying exemption with progression.[1856]

At the 16th Session of the Fiscal Committee in February 1960, the application of exemption with progression by the source State was extensively discussed.[1857] As Working Party No. 15 was composed of Denmark and Ireland, the Delegate for Denmark explained that it was the opinion of the Working Party that the source State cannot apply exemption with progression and that this resulted *a contrario* from the text of the suggested provision.[1858] The Delegate for France believed that the source State ought not to take the total income of the taxpayer into account.[1859] The Delegate for Switzerland did not consider that the suggested provision prevented the source State from applying exemption with progression.[1860] It would rather be fair for the source State to be allowed to consider a taxpayer's ability to pay in that way.[1861] The Delegate for Sweden thought that the suggested provision could restrict the right of the source State to apply exemption with progression but, for practical reasons, the source State ought to be free to apply exemption with progression if it so desired.[1862] The Delegate for the Netherlands agreed with this view provided that the system chosen was applied not only when it was to the source State's advantage but also when it was to its disadvantage and believed that it was not necessary to make a specific reference to the source State in the proviso safeguarding progression.[1863] The Delegate for Portugal shared this view and suggested dealing with this issue in the Commentary.[1864] The Delegate for Belgium and the Delegate for Germany were not in favour of the application of exemption with progression by the source State.[1865] The Delegate for Italy pointed to and further explained the proposal of the Italian Delegation.[1866] After general consultation among the members of the Fiscal Committee, it was found that:[1867]

tax on the remaining income or capital of that person, apply the rate of tax which would have been applicable if the exempted income or capital had not been so exempted.'

1853. OEEC, FC/M(59)2, p. 7.
1854. OEEC, FC/M(59)5, p. 5.
1855. OEEC, TFD/FC/81.
1856. OEEC, FC/M(59)5, p. 9.
1857. OEEC, FC/M(60)1, pp. 9-11.
1858. *Ibid.*, p. 9.
1859. *Ibid.*, p. 10.
1860. *Ibid.*, p. 10.
1861. *Ibid.*, p. 10.
1862. *Ibid.*, p. 10.
1863. *Ibid.*, p. 10.
1864. *Ibid.*, p. 10.
1865. *Ibid.*, p. 10.
1866. *Ibid.*, p. 10.
1867. *Ibid.*, p. 10.

> no Delegate objected to the application of exemption with progression by the country of residence; with the exception of the Delegate for Sweden, all Delegates were of the opinion that it would be necessary to provide for its application in Article B [later Article 23 A]. With the exception of the Delegate for Ireland, none of the Delegates objected to the application of exemption with progression by the country of source.

Disagreement followed with regard to whether the source State would be allowed to apply the exemption with progression only to income that was taxable in accordance with the terms of the Convention, to all income in the source State, or to total income.[1868] With a few exceptions, the Delegates were of the opinion that it would not be necessary to settle this question in an Article and that it would suffice if it were covered in the Commentary.[1869] Thus, the Working Party made it clear in the Commentary 'that Article B [later Article 23 A] in no way prejudices the application by the country of source of the provisions of its national legislation concerning this matter, and that any limitations on the right of the country of source would have to be made the subject of bilateral negotiations',[1870] a statement which can still be found in the OECD Commentary today.[1871] Interestingly, therefore, even though agreement was reached that both the residence State and the source State should be allowed to apply exemption with progression on the basis of their domestic tax laws without any restrictions imposed by a tax treaty, almost all Delegates saw a need for an express proviso safeguarding progression with regard to the residence State but no need with regard to the source State.

In preparation of the 1977 OECD Model, the issue of safeguarding progression came up again[1872] and was dealt with by the re-established Working Group No. 15. A number of Delegates feared that the proviso safeguarding progression, if it continued to be part of the exemption in Article 23 A(1) of the 1963 OECD Model,[1873] would not apply to Articles 8 and 19 that grant an exclusive right to tax and do not require an exemption under Article 23 A(1); not all Delegates shared this view.[1874] In addition, Working Group No. 15 observed that, unless there is an express limitation of the rate

1868. *Ibid.*, p. 11.
1869. *Ibid.*, p. 11.
1870. *Ibid.*, p. 11. *See also* OEEC, FC/WP15(60)1, p. 9: 'The application in the State of source of a system of exemption with progression is not affected by what is stated in the Article [later Article 23 A].' *See*, moreover, OEEC, FC/WP15(60)2, p. 15 (para. 36); 1963 OECD Commentary on Articles 23 A and 23 B, para. 36 (first sentence also 1977–2017: para. 56): 'The form of the Article [23 A] does not prejudice the application by the State of source of the provisions of its national legislation concerning the progression. If two Contracting States wish to clarify whether, or to what extent, the State of source shall have the right to use a progression they are left free to do so in bilateral negotiations.'
1871. 1977–2017 OECD Commentary on Articles 23 A and 23 B, para. 56 (similarly 1963: para. 36).
1872. OECD, DAF/CFA/WP1/73.5, pp. 3–4.
1873. Article 23 A(1) of the 1963 OECD Model: 'Where a resident of a Contracting State derives income or owns capital which, in accordance with the provisions of this Convention, may be taxed in the other Contracting State, the first-mentioned State shall ... exempt such income or capital from tax but may, in calculating tax on the remaining income or capital of that person, apply the rate of tax which would have been applicable if the exempted income or capital had not been so exempted.'
1874. OECD, CFA/WP1(74)2, pp. 9–10, 11 (paras 30–32, 36).

of tax, the source State is free to apply the provisions of its national legislation concerning the progression.[1875] At the level of Working Party No. 1 of the OECD Committee on Fiscal Affairs, while the Delegate for Austria and the Delegate for the Netherlands considered that the Contracting States should insert a special provision in the Convention if they wished to reach this result (for the latter Delegate, the fact that the proviso safeguarding progression only addressed the residence State led logically to the conclusion that the source State could not take into consideration income exempted for the purposes of determining a progressive rate of tax), the Delegate for Germany and the majority of the Working Party 'considered that the State of source was free to apply its legislation in the absence of provisions in the Convention to the contrary and that it was unnecessary to insert special provisions to that effect'.[1876] Due to this discussion, Working Party No. 1 decided to have a clear provision that would adopt an 'overall rate' as a general rule for both Contracting States.[1877]

Working Group No. 15 suggested the following provision which did not specifically refer to the residence State and, therefore, allowed the source State to consider exempted income or capital for the purposes of the tax rate as well:[1878]

> Where in accordance with the provisions of the Convention income derived or capital owned by a person is exempt from tax in a Contracting State, such Contracting State may nevertheless, in calculating tax on the remaining income or capital of such person, apply the rate of tax which would have been applicable if the exempted income or capital had not been so exempted.

This suggestion was then rejected by Working Party No. 1 for reasons which remain unknown: 'After a long discussion on this matter, the Working Party agreed to mention in the Article the right of the State of residence to apply progressive rates, and to mention in the Commentary that the State of source could do likewise by bilateral Convention, but only in the case of income arising in that State.'[1879] Apparently, Working Party No. 1 was now against a consideration of the 'global' or world income for the purposes of the tax rate in the source State. It decided that, in contrast to the previously agreed suggestion of Working Group No. 15, the proviso safeguarding progression 'would limit the use of exemption with progression to the country of residence' and 'unless otherwise agreed by Convention, only the State of residence could use the method of exemption with progression'.[1880]

For again unknown reasons, however, the proviso safeguarding progression ultimately continued to relate only to the residence State,[1881] and the OECD Commentary was not adapted to reflect the views of Working Party No. 1. It continued to state that '[t]he form of the Article does not prejudice the application by the State of source of the provisions of its national legislation concerning progression'.[1882] Only the

1875. *Ibid.*, p. 5 (para. 16).
1876. OECD, DAF/CFA/WP1/75.8, pp. 2, 4.
1877. *Ibid.*, pp. 2, 4. *See also* OECD, CFA/WP1(75)5, p. 5 (paras 11–14).
1878. OECD, CFA/WP1(75)5, p. 9 (*see also* pp. 25–26, 30).
1879. OECD, DAF/CFA/WP1/75.14, p. 2.
1880. *Ibid.*, pp. 3, 7.
1881. OECD, CFA/WP1(76)1, pp. 2–3; OECD, CFA/WP1(76)4, pp. 1–2.
1882. OECD, CFA/WP1(76)1, p. 18; OECD, CFA/WP1(76)4, p. 18.

statements on the different ways of calculating the progression in the source State (including on a worldwide basis)[1883] and on possible clarifications through bilateral negotiations[1884] were slightly modified[1885] and later deleted, arguably without changing the meaning of the tax treaty provisions with regard to the possibility of applying progressive tax rates on a worldwide basis.

[c] Implications for PEs

Given that, under a tax treaty, both the residence State and the source State may, in principle, calculate their progressive tax rate by including income or capital that is not taxable in the respective State, there is an argument for reaching the same result under Article 24(3). From the perspective of the source State, especially in situations of dual residence, the situation of a PE may be very similar to any other situation in which income or capital is taxable within its tax jurisdiction; taxable income or capital is subjected to a progressive tax rate under domestic tax law, and this tax rate is calculated on a worldwide basis if not prohibited by Article 24(3). Although it could be argued that Article 24(3) simply condemns certain treatment that other tax treaty provisions do not specifically address, it would still be difficult to understand why Article 24(3) should prohibit progressive taxation on a worldwide basis as soon as a PE is involved even though Articles 23 A(3) and 23 B(2) do not prohibit the source State from doing so in all other cases and would even expressly permit the source State, if it was the residence State, to continue doing so. If there exists no apparent reason for prohibiting the source State from taking the taxpayer's overall ability to pay tax into account, Article 24(3) should arguably not prevent the source State from taking the taxpayer's overall ability to pay tax into account either.

1883. OECD, CFA/WP1(76)1, p. 18 (modifying); OECD, DAF/CFA/WP1/75.14, p. 3 (deleting); OECD, CFA/WP1(76)4, p. 18. *See also* 1963 OECD Commentary on Articles 23 A and 23 B, para. 35: 'A question arises, however, when a State of source which applies a progressive tax scale gives up the right to tax and the non-resident taxpayer derives other income from that State. Different principles may be applied by a State of source in determining its progression. Its internal tax law may provide for the calculation of the progression on the global income of the taxpayer or only on the total income arising to the taxpayer in the State of source.'

1884. OECD, CFA(76)7 Part III, p. 122 (unfortunately, DAF/CFA/WP1/76.19(Add.) of 12 November 1976, which likely contains an interim version of section II and section III of the OECD Commentary on Articles 23 A and 23 B, was not available for the purposes of this research). *See also* 1963 OECD Commentary on Articles 23 A and 23 B, para. 36: 'If two Contracting States wish to clarify whether, or to what extent, the State of source shall have the right to use a progression they are left free to do so in bilateral negotiations.'

1885. As Working Party No. 1 advised taking the 1963 OECD Commentary on Articles 23 A and 23 B, paras 35–36 as a basis but to exclude all references to 'global' or world income in para. 35 (*see* OECD, DAF/CFA/WP1/75.14, p. 2), Working Group No. 15 merely mentioned in the revised Commentary that the domestic tax law of the source State may calculate a progressive scale of rates by taking into account all income arising in the source State thereby omitting the fact that all income, regardless of where it is arising, could be taken into account as well. *See* OECD, CFA/WP1(76)1, p. 18.

This argument is particularly supported by the fact that no unintended distortions arise if the source State considers exempt income or capital for tax rate purposes.[1886] Since a progressive tax rate, even when calculated on a worldwide basis, is only applied to taxable income or capital, it proportionately considers the taxpayer's overall ability to pay without a danger of a double dip. Although both States take into account the taxpayer's overall ability to pay for tax rate purposes, corresponding advantages or disadvantages (lower or higher tax rate) only affect the taxable income or capital. This means that the same tax treaty rules that determine how the taxing rights are allocated between the Contracting States also determine to what extent the Contracting States may consider a taxpayer's overall ability to pay by applying a progressive tax rate. From a policy perspective, a progressive tax rate calculated on a worldwide basis, therefore, leads to meaningful results. All considerations that might have played a role in designing the progressive scale of rates (tax-free amount, ability to pay tax, etc.) are considered in each Contracting State in proportion to the amount of the income or capital that is taxable in the respective State. Only the personal tax circumstances that are mentioned in the second sentence of Article 24(3)[1887] are excluded from the scope of the non-discrimination provision and are thus envisaged to be taken into account only in the residence State, not in the source State.

Based on a contextual analysis, it can been argued that the aim of calculating a progressive tax rate on a worldwide basis constitutes a valid and legitimate objective from a tax treaty perspective, as evidenced by Articles 23 A(3) and 23 B(2). Therefore, if a Contracting State applies a progressive tax rate that takes the entire income or capital of a resident enterprise into account, this tax rate should constitute the relevant benchmark for treating PEs on an equal footing under Article 24(3). As far as the tax rate is concerned, the activities of the whole enterprise must be taken into account in determining the non-discriminatory taxation on a PE. This is only possible, however, if the activities of the whole enterprise are not ignored. A 'but for' test thus requires the activities of the whole enterprise to remain identical as long as they are not inevitably linked to the protected attribute of residence. A comparable resident enterprise carries on the same activities as the whole non-resident enterprise even though only the taxation on the PE can be scrutinized (*see* Figure 4.15). While the taxation of the income from the activities other than those of the PE has no impact on whether the

1886. *See*, to this effect, Smit 2016, 308 ('the progressivity rule ... seeks to ensure no unfavourable or preferential tax treatment of non-resident taxpayers as concerns their ability to pay tax'); Raad 2005, 139–140, 141–142. *See also*, however, Djanani and Hartmann 2000, 324, 325, who oppose a calculation of a progressive tax rate on a worldwide basis in cases when a taxpayer is subject to limited tax liability under domestic tax law and personal tax circumstances, therefore, are not taken into account; critically, moreover, Bhuta 2015, 381–382; Bammens 2012, 242–243.

1887. *See* Rust 2015b m.nos. 67 and 79; Rust 2015c m.no. 105, who argues that there is no obligation to grant the benefits of the zero bracket to non-resident individuals because the second sentence of Article 24(3) applies to a progressive tax rate to the extent that the source State has integrated the zero bracket into its tax rate structure; likewise, Kubaile 2013 m.no. 51; Haslehner 2009, 270–271, 339–340; Tumpel and Stangl 2006, 85; differently, Bammens 2012, 244–245; OECD, Article 24 Discussion Draft 2007, para. 71, which argues that 'the tax-free threshold is related to the amount of income and not to the civil status or family responsibilities of the taxpayer'; but *see also* Haslehner 2009, 271–272, who criticizes this conclusion.

taxation on the PE is less favourably levied – tax advantages granted by the residence State or the source State that are related to such other activities cannot compensate for taxation that is less favourable on the PE[1888] – these other activities may influence the taxation on the PE as far as the application of a progressive scale of rates is concerned.

Figure 4.15 Comparability Considering the Whole Non-resident Enterprise

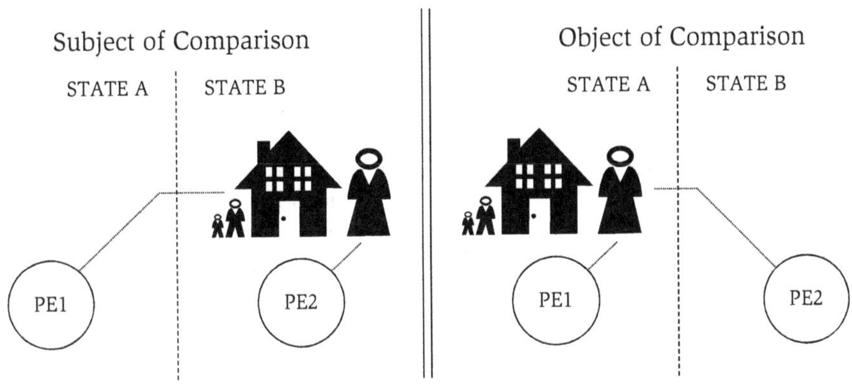

If the source State taxes resident enterprises by calculating a progressive tax rate on a worldwide basis, that is by including exempt profits and losses, it cannot tax PEs differently. If the progressive tax rate is increased through a consideration of a taxpayer's overall ability to pay tax, the source State is not violating the non-discrimination obligations of Article 24(3) as long as the taxation on the PE is based on this tax rate or not higher than that.[1889] If the progressive tax rate is thereby decreased, in particular if other parts of the enterprise suffer losses, however, Article 24(3) obligates the source State to apply this lower tax rate to the PE.[1890] Although Article 24(3) does not prohibit from applying an effectively higher tax rate that is calculated by reference to the profits of the whole enterprise, it requires applying an effectively lower tax rate when the whole enterprise suffers losses. As long as other tax treaty provisions do not authorize different tax treatment, the non-discrimination clause compares the taxation on a PE to the taxation on a resident enterprise that carries on the same activities as the non-resident enterprise to which the PE belongs.

1888. *See*, for instance, Haslehner 2016a m.no. 22; Rust 2015b m.no. 64 ('[a] disadvantageous treatment in the PE State cannot be compensated by tax advantages granted in the residence State'); Rust 2015c m.no. 100; Rust 2004, 392; Avery Jones, Depret, et al. 1991b, 336; Gifford 1978, 68.
1889. *See also*, to this effect, Rust 2015b m.no. 67 ('for calculating the tax rate applicable to the PE income it does not violate Article 24(3) OECD and UN MC to take the entire income of the enterprise into account'); Rust 2015c m.no. 105; Sass 1966, 108; differently, Bhuta 2015, 385-387, 394-400; Bammens 2012, 245.
1890. *See*, differently, Bhuta 2015, 385-387, 394-400.

[4] *Deduction of Foreign Losses and Carry Forward*

[a] *Deemed Taxation on a Worldwide Basis?*

A 'but for' test takes account of the activities of the whole non-resident enterprise for the purposes of determining the non-discriminatory taxation on a PE. This allows the source State to apply a progressive scale of rates on a worldwide basis. It could also be argued, however, that foreign losses suffered abroad should be offset against domestic profits in order to ensure non-discriminatory taxation.[1891] If the PE was a resident enterprise, it could deduct such foreign losses from its domestic profits, at least in some States.[1892] Thus, but for foreign residence and all inevitably linked attributes, a deduction of the foreign losses from the domestic profits would be possible in the source State. This is not an issue of whether the foreign losses can be carried forward in the source State even though they are not attributable to the PE and, therefore, exempt.[1893] It is an issue of how to determine the tax burden with regard to the activities carried on through the PE and whether the non-discriminatory tax burden under Article 24(3) is zero if the whole enterprise suffers losses. What is true with regard to the tax rate – the activities of the whole enterprise are relevant if they influence the taxation on the PE – could also be true with regard to the tax base.[1894] Put another way, if a comparable resident enterprise would not be taxed at all since the foreign losses would be deducted from the domestic profits, can it still be argued that there is tax levied on the domestic profits and that the PE, therefore, may be taxed on these profits without discrimination under Article 24(3)?

Conversely, if the PE suffers losses in the source State whereas the whole non-resident enterprise achieves profits, the PE as a resident enterprise would be subject to full tax liability, the credit method under Article 23 A(2) or 23 B(1) could apply and thus, after offsetting the PE's domestic losses against the foreign profits, no

1891. *See also* Kaplan 1992, 287, who critically observes that '[i]n the case of a company conducting its business in more than one jurisdiction, this comparison [of the worldwide operations] requires that income, expenses, etc. of non-United States branches of the company be taken into account in testing for discrimination …. … If the … company maintaining a United States branch has profits in the United States but losses abroad, the effect of the … comparison would be to import those losses into the United States. This is so because a United States company with the same United States and foreign branches would be entitled to deduct foreign losses against its United States profits'.

1892. *See* 1977–2017 OECD Commentary on Articles 23 A and 23 B, para. 44.

1893. There is, therefore, no contradiction with the statements of the 2008–2017 OECD Commentary on Article 24, para. 40 (1977: para. 26; 1992–2005: para. 24) that '[i]t is hardly necessary to specify that in the case of permanent establishments it is the loss on their own business activities [before 2010: as shown in the separate accounts for these activities] which will qualify for such carry-forward'. *See*, however, Lang 1990, 37.

1894. *See also* Bammens 2012, 240, who states that 'either the PE is considered as a separate entity – in which case it is not appropriate to take account of the non-resident's worldwide profits [for the purpose of determining the rate applicable for the taxation on a PE] – or it is not considered as a separate entity – in which case article 24(3) would require that other facilities concerning worldwide profits be applied to the PE as they are applied to residents (e.g. the taking into account of foreign losses)'; similarly, Oesterhelt 2015 m.no. 77, who regards this issue as being closely related to comparability.

loss carry-forward would be available. Arguably, no loss carry-forward must be granted to the loss-making PE if the whole enterprise achieves profits.[1895] This is not an issue of whether the domestic losses are already considered in the residence State, whether such a tax advantage in the residence State can compensate for a tax disadvantage in the source State in order to avoid a double deduction of losses, or whether the tax treatment in the residence State should matter under Article 24(3).[1896] It is an issue of how resident enterprises are treated under the source State's domestic tax law and whether a cross-border offsetting of profits and losses would be possible with resident enterprises. Just as personal tax circumstances relate to the whole enterprise but influence the taxation on the PE and, therefore, are addressed by the second sentence of Article 24(3) (*see* section §4.01[D]), a cross-border offsetting of profits and losses arguably determines the tax burden of the whole enterprise and thereby the non-discriminatory tax burden with regard to the activities carried on through the PE regardless of the treatment in the residence State.

Under the AOA (separate entity approach),[1897] a profitable PE in the source State may be taxed in that State even if the enterprise as a whole suffers losses, and a loss-making PE in the source State may not be taxed in that State even if the enterprise as a whole achieves profits.[1898] This does not mean, however, that Article 7(2) mandates different treatment between PEs and resident enterprises or requires taxing residents on a worldwide basis and non-residents (PEs) on a territorial basis. If a profitable PE in the source State was a resident enterprise, it could be taxed in that State regardless of how the other parts of the enterprise succeed in their business. A tax treaty does not require worldwide taxation of resident enterprises nor a deduction of losses suffered abroad. Therefore, it is not true that resident enterprises pay tax in their residence State only when the entire enterprise achieves a profit whereas, under the

1895. *See*, to this effect, H. Loukota 1989b, 29; similarly, H. Loukota 1990b, 62–64, although implying that in certain situations Article 24(3) might provide differently; critically Zöchling 1990, 51; Wundsam and Zöchling 1990, 101–102; thereafter H. Loukota 1990a, 163, recognizing that Article 24(3) may indeed require a loss carry-forward even if the whole enterprise achieves profits provided that the losses at issue are not deducted twice; moreover, H. Loukota 2005, 60–64; critically with regard to this condition for a loss carry-forward Lang 1990, 36–38, concluding that Article 24(3) always requires a loss carry-forward because the profits and losses that are not taxable in the source State are irrelevant for the purposes of the PE non-discrimination clause, actually regardless of whether the appropriate comparator is a resident enterprise carrying on the same activities as the PE or a resident enterprise carrying on the same activities as the whole non-resident enterprise. On this issue from an Austrian perspective, *see also* Austrian Supreme Administrative Court (Verwaltungsgerichtshof), 16 February 2006, 2005/14/0036 and 28 November 2007, 2007/14/0048; moreover, Boekhorst 1991; Beiser 1991; Zöchling 1993, 309–310; Hruschka and Bendlinger 2003; Faller 2003, 49–55; Schneeweiss 2006; Kempinger 2007; Kofler 2009; Haslehner 2009, 325–331; Bammens 2012, 214–219; Schuch and Fürnsinn 2015 m.nos. 4–6, 10–13; Haslehner 2016a m.nos. 62–64; Loukota and Jirousek 2016 m.nos. 51–70.

1896. *Confer* Rust 2015b m.no. 64; Rust 2015c m.no. 100; Tumpel and Stangl 2006, 76–77.

1897. *See*, in particular, OECD, Attribution of Profits Report 2010.

1898. 2008 OECD Commentary on Article 7, para. 11 ('the directive of paragraph 2 may result in profits being attributed to a permanent establishment even though the enterprise as a whole has never made profits; conversely, that directive may result in no profits being attributed to a permanent establishment even though the enterprise as a whole has made profits'); similarly, 2010–2017 OECD Commentary on Article 7, para. 17.

AOA, PEs may pay tax even if the entire enterprise suffers a loss.[1899] Rather, a Contracting State may adopt a territorial principle in its taxation even with regard to its residents.[1900] In doing so, that State may disregard both foreign profits and losses, which means that it may tax its residents on domestic profits even if foreign losses lead to an overall loss. In addition, the OECD Commentary on Articles 23 A and 23 B mentions that several States, in applying Article 23 A, treat foreign losses in the same manner as they treat foreign profits: as the residence State, they do not allow deduction of a loss incurred from a PE situated in the source State.[1901] Even if foreign losses lead to an overall loss, the residence State may subject domestic profits to tax. States, therefore, can tax both residents and non-residents on a territorial basis or exempt both foreign profits and losses thereby ensuring equal treatment of residents and non-residents.

Despite that, States sometimes allow a deduction of foreign losses when resident enterprises are at stake even when foreign profits are exempt under a tax treaty.[1902] By contrast, States often prohibit a deduction of foreign losses when non-resident enterprises are at stake. This difference in treatment is not imposed by Article 7(2) and the AOA (separate entity approach) but rather related to the domestic concepts of full and limited tax liability. It can raise concerns about discrimination under Article 24(3) as soon as the activities of the whole non-resident enterprise are taken into account for determining the non-discriminatory taxation on a PE. Just as foreign profits or losses may influence the progressive tax rate that is applicable to a PE, they may influence the tax base that is applicable to a PE.

Probably for this reason it is argued that, with regard to the tax base, the PE must be compared to a resident enterprise that performs no other activities and achieves no other profits or losses than those of the PE.[1903] It is consequently argued that the fact that foreign losses cannot be offset against domestic profits of a PE even though this would be possible with resident enterprises that carry on the same (and other)

1899. *See*, differently, Haslehner 2009, 233.
1900. 2008–2017 OECD Commentary on Article 4, para. 8.3 (1992–2005: para. 8).
1901. 1977–2017 OECD Commentary on Articles 23 A and 23 B, para. 44. It is not precisely clear whether a tax treaty with its terms 'income', 'profits', 'remuneration', etc. exempts both profits and losses, which means that a deduction of foreign losses must be specifically provided for under domestic tax law as an additional tax benefit or in deviation from a tax treaty or whether a tax treaty addresses only positive income thereby preserving a deduction of foreign losses in all situations of full tax liability unless otherwise provided under domestic tax law. *See*, for instance, Rust 2015a m.nos. 23–25, with further references; moreover, Vogel 1997 Article 23, m.nos. 71–75; Vogel 1996, 4–5 ('[h]eute wird diese Auffassung, daß das *Abkommen* die Verrechnung freigestellter Verluste verbiete, nirgendwo mehr ernstlich vertreten'; original emphasis); Krabbe 1985, 80–81; Vogel 1982, 66–68; differently, that is, rather in favour of a tax treaty exemption of both profits and losses, Schuch 1998b, 168–179; to this effect, also H. Loukota 1989a m.no. 669; Philipp 1971, 140–142; Debatin 1965, 49; Debatin 1963b, 44; critically Lechner 1996, 87–91; Lechner 1995, 144–150. *See*, moreover, Hohenwarter 2004, 224–227, who thereafter also deals with a decision of the Austrian Supreme Administrative Court (Verwaltungsgerichtshof), 25 September 2001, 99/14/0217, which allowed a deduction of foreign losses despite exempt profits; and Hohenwarter 2010, 249–254.
1902. *See* again 1977–2017 OECD Commentary on Articles 23 A and 23 B, para. 44.
1903. *See* Haslehner 2009, 225, 236, 306, 328.

activities cannot be considered as discrimination.[1904] Conversely, if domestic losses of a PE cannot be carried forward in situations when foreign profits have been accrued, this may lead to discrimination under Article 24(3).[1905]

If indeed the expression 'carrying on the same activities' does not refer to the whole non-resident enterprise but only to the PE,[1906] and if only the profits of the PE may be allocated to a comparable resident enterprise under Article 24(3),[1907] the same should hold true with regard to the tax rate.[1908] It is not necessarily logical why, for the purposes of the tax base but not for the purposes of the tax rate, all activities other than those of the PE should be ignored. In addition, if only the activities carried on through the PE are relevant under Article 24(3), all other sources of income and capital, even if taxable in the source State, have to be ignored as well, including all profits or losses that are attributable to another PE in the source State.[1909]

[b] Solution Based on Linked Characteristics

If it is accepted that, under Article 24(3), the activities of the whole enterprise must be considered for the purposes of calculating a tax on the basis of a progressive scale of rates, it is not possible to simply ignore those activities with a 'but for' test when dealing with other tax measures, including those which focus on the tax base. It is only possible to ignore characteristics that are inevitably linked to the protected attribute of residence and to leave their relevance to a substantive analysis. On a substantive basis, therefore, it could be argued that inevitably linked differences in legal or factual circumstances are relevant and prevent comparability as far as the tax base, but not the tax rate, is concerned. Since a tax treaty basically inherits a fundamental distinction between residents and non-residents (*see* Chapter 3 section §3.03[B]) and on this basis allocates the taxing rights between the Contracting States, notably, by limiting the tax base (exemptions and limited taxing rights on a gross basis) but not the tax rate (proviso safeguarding progression), a distinction between the tax base and the tax rate could also be made under Article 24(3).[1910]

It appears that after applying a 'but for' test, not many differences in circumstances other than protected differences in tax liability and residence remain. This

1904. *See*, to this effect, Haslehner 2009, 236 ('aus der Kalkulation der Betriebsstättengewinne unabhängig vom Gesamtgewinn ... [kann sich] keine Diskriminierung ... ergeben').
1905. *See* Haslehner 2009, 236, 303, 326-327.
1906. *See* Haslehner 2009, 225; Toifl 1996, 156; Tumpel 1992, 656; Zöchling 1990, 51.
1907. *See*, for example, Haslehner 2016a m.nos. 21, 64; Haslehner 2009, 236, 306, 328; Tumpel and Stangl 2006, 76-77; Toifl 1996, 157; Zöchling 1994, 18-19; Tumpel 1994, 381.
1908. *See*, to this effect, Bhuta 2015, 385-387, 394-400.
1909. *See also* Loukota and Jirousek 2016 m.nos. 71-72, 75; Bhuta 2015, 400-401; H. Loukota 2005, 62; Hruschka and Bendlinger 2003, 276-277.
1910. *See also* Haslehner 2009, 306, who observes that even though under Article 24(3) the comparable resident enterprise is assumed to make the same profits as those that are attributable to the PE, this need not be the case for the purposes of the tax rate. This assumption is made under Article 24(3) only because other profits are usually not taxable in the source State under Article 7 and, therefore, not relevant. However, Article 7 is not concerned with the tax rate in the source State that can, therefore, be influenced by Article 24(3).

seems to suggest that the only reason why foreign profits or losses cannot be taken into account for the purposes of determining the tax on the income of a PE is the fact that the taxpayer in question is subject to limited tax liability. In addition, some arguments speak against a distinction between the tax base and the tax rate. Whether a tax advantage is granted through a lower tax base or through a lower tax rate need not lead to different results. It might not matter, for instance, whether the tax base is subjected to the half of the normal tax rate or whether the half of the tax base is subjected to the normal tax rate. If the foreign losses are high enough to lower both the tax base of the PE and the progressive tax rate to zero, it might also not matter whether the foreign losses are considered through the tax base or the tax rate.[1911]

If the source State exempts foreign profits of its resident enterprises under the tax treaty but deducts and later reintegrates foreign losses, Article 24(3) also might require doing so with regard to PEs; the foreign losses should lower the tax base with respect to the profits that are attributable to the PE as this influences the taxation on the PE. From a tax treaty perspective, it is not necessarily clear why PEs and resident enterprises should be treated differently if no differences in taxing rights with regard to the activities exist. As the source State grants a liquidity or cash-flow advantage only to resident enterprises, it puts PEs of non-resident enterprises in a less favourable tax situation. A resident enterprise is allowed to pay no tax on its domestic profits if it suffers losses abroad whereas a non-resident enterprise is taxed on its domestic profits that are attributable to a PE. This result contravenes the principal objective of Article 24(3) to contribute to equal conditions of competition between resident and non-resident enterprises. A loss-making enterprise is, as a whole, losing money if it is taxed on 'isolated' profits that are attributable to a PE, which consequently diminishes its competitive position (negative impact on cash-flows, lower reserves or need for new capital through equity or debt, corresponding costs of capital, etc.) when compared to loss-making enterprises that does not pay taxes. Ekkehart Reimer, therefore, is right in stating that, under Article 24(3), losses incurred in the residence State (State R) shall be taken into account by the source State (State P) where the PE is located 'if, and only if, State P would allow a set-off of losses incurred by a PE which a taxpayer who is a resident of State P maintains in State R'.[1912] Helmut Loukota and Heinz Jirousek further mention the example of a transparent partnership that belongs to one resident and one non-resident partner and constitutes a PE for the latter. If the resident partner is able to claim a foreign loss deduction under domestic tax law for a share in the partnership's income, the non-resident partner should be able to claim such treatment as well.[1913]

Conversely, if profits that are exempt under the tax treaty do not lower a loss carry-forward of the source State's resident enterprises, profits that are not attributable to a PE or to other taxable sources of income and, therefore, exempt under the tax treaty

1911. *See*, to this effect, for instance, Widhalm 1995, 158; Mössner 1985, 156; Lechner 1982, 93; Vogel 1982, 67–68; critically Lechner 1996, 88–89, who demonstrates that, if foreign losses are considered through the tax rate, they can be fully considered only if the amount of the foreign losses equals the amount of the taxable profits which is almost impossible in practice; moreover, Vogel 1996, 5–9.

1912. Reimer 2014 m.no. 256.

1913. Loukota and Jirousek 2016 m.nos. 88–89.

also should not lower a loss carry-forward of non-resident enterprises.[1914] If a resident enterprise is allowed to carry forward its losses even though it achieves profits abroad, whereas a non-resident enterprise is not allowed to carry forward its losses (it is, therefore, taxed on its domestic profits that are attributable to a PE in following years), these enterprises are treated differently despite the fact that the source State is allowed to tax the same sources of income for the purposes of Article 24(3). Thus, there are some grounds to believe that it constitutes discrimination under Article 24(3) to principally deny a loss carry-forward to a PE when the whole enterprise achieves profits if resident enterprises could carry forward their losses in such situations involving a tax treaty exemption of these profits.

However, it can be argued that there is a risk of a permanent double deduction of losses if foreign losses are offset against domestic profits or if a loss carry-forward is granted by disregarding exempt profits. Inevitably linked but relevant differences in circumstances arguably exist if resident enterprises that carry on the same cross-border activities as the whole non-resident enterprise would receive a permanent loss deduction in one State and a liquidity or cash-flow advantage in another State, whereas an extension of tax benefits under Article 24(3) would lead to a permanent loss deduction in both Contracting States. If the domestic tax measure under scrutiny aims at preventing such situations and, therefore, treats PEs differently, this can constitute a legitimate objective from the perspective of Article 24(3). Otherwise, Article 24(3) would contribute to unequal conditions of competition by effectively favouring non-residents and would thereby run counter its own objectives.[1915] This argument would further require a consideration of the tax treatment in the residence State, something that Article 24(3) neither authorizes nor prohibits with its wording. If such inevitably linked differences in circumstances can be identified, therefore, if there is a risk of a double deduction of losses and recapturing mechanisms are not able to turn a loss deduction into a liquidity or cash-flow advantage, prohibited tax discrimination might be denied. In all other cases, however, liquidity or cash-flow advantages due to an overall loss situation that are granted to resident enterprises should be granted to PEs as well.

A double deduction of losses, as such, need not necessarily raise policy concerns, in particular if recapturing mechanisms are in place or if the other side of the coin is double taxation of profits. Nevertheless, interpreting Article 24(3) as requiring a temporary loss deduction like with resident enterprises might create problems in triangular situations.[1916] Assume that a resident of State B suffers losses of 100 in State B but achieves profits of 100 in State A and 100 in a third State, State C, all through PEs (*see* Figure 4.16). If a resident enterprise of State A is allowed to deduct foreign losses (losses arising in State B) even though corresponding foreign profits (profits arising in State B) are tax exempt, regardless of whether exempt profits are made in other States (per-country approach), it is reasonable to conclude that the PE in State B should also

1914. *See also*, to this effect, Beiser 1991, 17.
1915. *See* Hohenwarter 2010, 182–183.
1916. On a somewhat similar issue involving a third-State PE of a dual-resident company, *see* Hohenwarter 2004, 254–260.

be allowed to deduct such foreign losses under Article 24(3) of the tax treaty between State A and State B even though corresponding foreign profits are not attributable to the PE and, therefore, exempt in State A. As a consequence, tax is levied neither in State A nor in State B. Indeed, the overall income in these two States is zero. However, what is true under the tax treaty between State A and State B should also hold true under the tax treaty between State B and State C. If State C, therefore, is required to deduct foreign losses (losses arising in State B) in order to meet its non-discrimination obligations, tax is levied neither in State B nor in State C. All in all, this means that a temporary loss deduction of 100 is granted in both State A and State C. Although the worldwide income of the taxpayer in question is 100, no tax is levied in any State due to Article 24(3), a result which could not be reached in a purely domestic situation.

Figure 4.16 Double Loss Deduction in a Triangular Situation

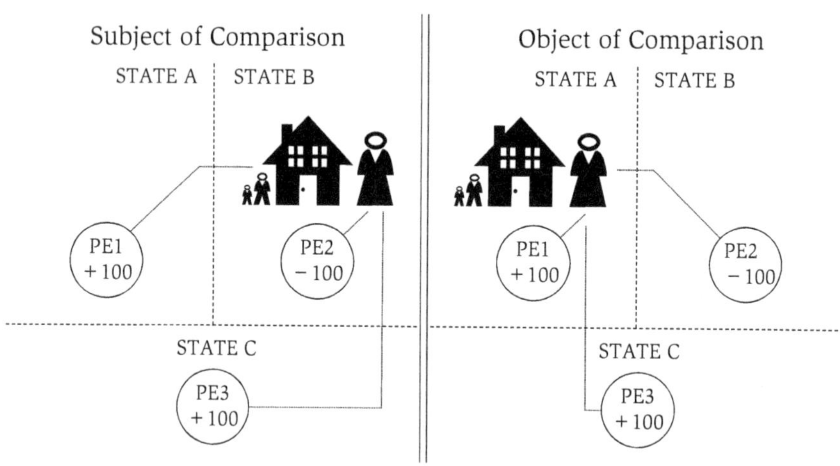

It is debatable whether the reason for this result lies not so much in the non-discrimination obligations but in the fact that the domestic tax laws of both State A and State C allow deducting foreign losses on a per-country basis even though foreign profits exist. Also, it could be argued that Article 24(3) is part of a bilateral tax treaty and, therefore, unable to take account of such 'unintended' situations; discrimination should be avoided in any case. It can be responded that, in such situations, inevitably linked differences in circumstances between resident and non-resident enterprises might be regarded as relevant under Article 24(3) thereby preventing comparability in regard to a deduction of foreign losses. Tax systems that allow resident enterprises to deduct foreign losses are generally based on the idea that such a loss deduction with a recapturing mechanism will only be possible in one State, that is the residence State. A multiple application of such a system through Article 24(3) in more than one State could lead to results that would be in direct opposition to that system's objective. This could speak in favour of regarding inevitably linked differences in a potential double deduction of losses in triangular situations as relevant for comparability purposes under Article 24(3) but only for the purposes of the tax base since such concerns do not arise with regard to the tax rate. It remains open whether this should always hold true as far as a deduction of foreign losses from a PE's tax base is concerned or only if there indeed exist similar non-discrimination obligations in triangular situations and when a risk of such a double deduction of losses is, therefore, not merely theoretical.

[c] OECD Discussions about Foreign Losses

Until today, the OECD Commentary does not explicitly deal with the issue of whether a PE may be taxed on its domestic profits if a resident enterprise would not be taxed on such profits because it would be able to lower these profits through a temporary deduction of foreign losses. Only by implication does the OECD Commentary deny an obligation to grant a temporary loss deduction under Article 24(3). If it is assumed that, for the purposes of applying a progressive scale of rates, Article 7(2) implies that '[t]he minimum amount of the tax levied in the State where the PE is situated is ... the amount which would be due if it were a separate and independent [before 2010: distinct and separate] enterprise, without reference to the profits of the whole enterprise to which it belongs',[1917] the same should hold true with regard to the tax base. It is worth noting, however, that this issue has been discussed as early as in 1963, and the views had been divided.

In May 1963, the US Delegation raised several unresolved issues which, in its opinion, required further study.[1918] Among other things, it criticized the concept of 'other or more burdensome' as too vague and posed the following question:[1919]

> Consider an enterprise which operates at a loss in its world-wide activities but is nevertheless subjected to tax by a country in which it has a permanent establishment because the permanent establishment itself has a profit. Since a company subject to full tax liability would not pay taxes if it operated at a loss, is the imposition of tax on the permanent establishment in such a case discriminatory?

This question was subsequently addressed by Working Party No. 4 of the OECD Fiscal Committee[1920] consisting of Delegates of France, Japan, and Spain[1921] in its report of July 1966. It denied discrimination under Article 24(1) because the distinction at issue depends not on the enterprise's nationality but on the enterprise's residence.[1922] According to the Working Party, 'it has always been recognised ... that States remain free, despite the provisions of paragraph 1 of that Article [24], to apply different regulations to non-residents than those applied to residents on condition that the regulations apply respectively to all non-residents and to all residents without distinction as to nationality'.[1923]

1917. 2008–2017 OECD Commentary on Article 24, para. 58 (1977: para. 41; 1992–2005: para. 39).
1918. OECD, TFD/FC/158.
1919. *Ibid.*, p. 5.
1920. OECD, FC/WP4(66)1, pp. 4–8.
1921. *See also* OECD, FC/M(64)4, p. 5.
1922. OECD, FC/WP4(66)1, p. 5.
1923. *Ibid.*, p. 5.

With regard to Article 24(3), the Working Party noted that mere consideration of the provisions of that clause will not resolve the question of discrimination; the question is, in fact, also connected to the application of the provisions of Article 7(2).[1924] Article 7(2) lays down that the profits of a PE must be determined by the difference between its income and its expenditure, independently of the overall results of the enterprise.[1925] This supports the idea that 'there is discrimination only in the case in which a State applies, in determining the profits earned from the activities of a permanent establishment, rules less favourable than those applied to domestic enterprises'.[1926]

Nevertheless, for Working Party No. 4, this was not the end of the analysis. 'The question may clearly still be raised whether the principle of taxation ... as laid down in Article 7 must be abandoned when the enterprise as a whole has made losses.'[1927] Although the Working Party believed they had no competence to answer this question as a whole, it gave an argument in favour of abandoning this principle, basically implying that such taxation could have negative effects on the competitive position of non-resident enterprises in the source State:[1928]

> [I]f an enterprise which has made losses as a whole but is nonetheless taxed in a country in which it has a permanent establishment on the grounds that such establishment, taken in isolation, has made a profit, such taxation may be levied only on the capital or reserves of the enterprise, which will increase its losses and may, if repeated for several years in succession, cause it to abandon all or part of its activities. This cannot fail to do harm not only to the country in which the enterprise has its head office but also to the country in which it has its permanent establishment.

At the same time, the Working Party pointed out that the application of Article 24(3) would give rise to serious practical difficulties in establishing that the loss is genuine and that it would have the effect of giving the PEs of foreign companies treatment that is more favourable than that given to subsidiaries set up by the same or other foreign companies although the tax system must remain as impartial as possible towards different social structures.[1929]

This issue was then discussed in late 1966 at the 26th session of the OECD Fiscal Committee.[1930] The Delegate for Switzerland basically considered that such differences in treatment regarding foreign losses would appear to constitute discrimination under Article 24(3).[1931] The Delegate for Austria thought that no discrimination arose if a PE was always treated as a separate entity, that is both in a profit and loss situation.[1932] The Delegate for the US agreed that a PE should be treated as an entity, and no

1924. *Ibid.*, p. 6.
1925. *Ibid.*, p. 6.
1926. *Ibid.*, p. 7.
1927. *Ibid.*, p. 7.
1928. *Ibid.*, p. 7.
1929. *Ibid.*, pp. 7-8.
1930. OECD, TFD/FC/211, pp. 2-3. *See also* OECD, FC/M(67)1, p. 3.
1931. *Ibid.*, p. 2.
1932. *Ibid.*, p. 2.

deduction of foreign losses should be possible.[1933] The Delegate for the UK agreed with this view and pointed out that, under Article 7, it was always assumed that a PE should be taxed as a separate entity.[1934] The Delegate for the US then basically suggested a comparison to a subsidiary of a foreign company, whereas the Delegate for Switzerland could not agree with this view.[1935] The Chairman thought that these problems would be resolved if Article 7 was more precise and contained a provision that a PE must be treated in the same way as a resident enterprise not only in regard to the method of calculation of profits (which Article 7 already provided for) but - in contrast to other allocation rules such as Articles 10 to 12 which provided only for allocation of taxing rights - also on other matters such as rates, administrative obligations, etc.[1936] The Delegate for the Netherlands emphasized that Article 7(2) and Article 24(3) had different purposes, that Article 7 was essentially a rule on allocation of profits, while Article 24 was concerned with national legislation.[1937] The Delegate for Luxembourg also emphasized that, no matter how precisely Article 7 were drafted, it would still be necessary for Article 24 to prevent discrimination.[1938]

Although the Delegates did not agree on whether PEs should be allowed to deduct foreign losses under Article 24(3), in the end, they focused on the meaning and relevance of Article 7 rather than on the wording and the comparability requirements of Article 24(3). At least some Delegates also recognized that the idea of treating a PE as a separate and independent enterprise was not directly enshrined in Article 24(3) but rather derived from Article 7. In addition, Article 7 would have to be interpreted as being more than a traditional allocation rule in order to influence the application of the PE non-discrimination clause.

After receiving answers to a questionnaire,[1939] Working Party No. 4 observed that practically all of the OEEC Member countries who answered the questionnaire refused, in determining the taxable profits of PEs of non-resident legal persons, to take into account any losses incurred in respect of the overall business of such enterprises.[1940] Their view is that this position is the logical consequence of the principle that the PE of a non-resident legal person must be regarded as an independent enterprise and treated as such. In this context, the Working Party referred to the 1963 OECD Commentary which explained the principal objective of Article 24(3) as follows:[1941]

> Strictly speaking, the type of discrimination which this paragraph is designed to end is discrimination based not on nationality, but on the actual situs of an enterprise. It therefore affects without distinction, and irrespective of their nationality, all residents of a Contracting State who have permanent establishments in the other Contracting State. In this connection, while it is true that most Conventions for the avoidance of double taxation lay down the principle that, for the

1933. *Ibid.*, p. 2.
1934. *Ibid.*, p. 2.
1935. *Ibid.*, p. 2.
1936. *Ibid.*, p. 2.
1937. *Ibid.*, pp. 2–3.
1938. *Ibid.*, p. 3.
1939. OECD, FC/WP4(68)1, p. 2.
1940. OECD, FC/WP4(69)1, pp. 4, 13.
1941. 1963 OECD Commentary on Article 24, para. 13.

> purpose of charging tax, a permanent establishment of an enterprise of a Contracting State in the other Contracting State must be regarded as an independent enterprise and treated as such, nevertheless the other State does not always extend to the permanent establishment the full benefit of the treatment it applies to its own enterprises. Thus, the permanent establishment may not be allowed the same depreciation facilities, or a proportion of the principal enterprise's overheads is not always allowed to be attributed to the permanent establishment, or any losses incurred by the permanent establishment are not allowed to be set off. The purpose of paragraph [3] is to put an end to these differences in treatment ....

In a certain way, a reason why Article 24(3) was introduced in the first place – PEs are taxed less favourably than resident enterprises under domestic law even though they are treated as independent enterprises under Article 7 – was used by Working Party No. 4 to deny discrimination. Since PEs are treated as independent enterprises under Article 7, no less favourable taxation can arise under Article 24(3) if losses that are not attributable to a PE of a non-resident enterprise are ignored for the purposes of the tax base even though they would not be ignored with resident enterprises carrying on the same activities as the whole non-resident enterprise.

This supposed influence of Article 7 on Article 24(3) was again emphasized by Working Party No. 4 in a later report.[1942] Article 7 deals with methods of computing the profits that are attributable to the PE in respect of given activities; if it specifies that the PE must be regarded as a 'distinct and separate enterprise', this is only in regard to such activities and only for the purpose of determining the profits arising therefrom.[1943] Article 24(3) contemplates equality of treatment with resident enterprises only from the same standpoint of the activities carried on by the PE.[1944] According to the Working Party, the final reference to 'enterprises of that other State carrying on the same activities' admits of no doubt on this point.[1945] In addition, the Working Party saw this observation as being consistent with the view that a distinction should be drawn between the actual fact of the carrying on of activities in a State by a non-resident enterprise and the overall situation of the enterprise,[1946] notably, by denying discrimination when a difference in treatment reflects the inherent difference that exists between the concept of the PE and that of the resident company.[1947]

As far as can be seen, this issue was not discussed thereafter, which might imply that the OECD Fiscal Committee, the work of which was continued by Working Party No. 1 when the Committee on Fiscal Affairs was established in 1971, was satisfied with this answer. It is worth noting, however, that the issue of progressivity was subsequently dealt with and thus the idea of connecting Article 24(3) to the principle of separateness and independence under Article 7(2) found its way into the OECD Commentary not in regard to the tax base but concerning the tax rate (*see* section §4.04[B][2]). This means that, while Article 24(3) scrutinizes only the taxation on a PE, it generally considers the activities of the whole non-resident enterprise in order to

1942. OECD, FC/WP4(71)1, pp. 14–15.
1943. *Ibid.*, p. 14.
1944. *Ibid.*, p. 14.
1945. *Ibid.*, p. 14.
1946. *Ibid.*, p. 14.
1947. OECD, FC/WP4(69)1, p. 11.

apply a (higher) non-discriminatory tax rate on a worldwide basis or to take account of the legal structure. Any different result, such as a minimum amount of tax that may be levied on a PE without discrimination or a distinction between the tax base and the tax rate as far as foreign losses are concerned, must be derived from the context of Article 24(3), including the provisions of Articles 7, 23 A, and 23 B.

[C] Group Taxation and Consolidation Regimes

[1] Purposes Behind Group Taxation Regimes

Income tax law, in general, treats a company as a separate taxable unit from its shareholders.[1948] This prevents deferral of tax or an attribution of profits of a widely held company to individual shareholders.[1949] In today's modern world, however, a corporate group often operates in substance as a single enterprise.[1950] In many States, provisions take account of this development by stipulating special tax treatment for group members that are associated with each other through their participation, ownership, or common control. Such rules treat corporate groups similar to single enterprises by allowing for consolidation, pooling, or transfer of profits or losses or for an intra-group transfer of assets on a tax-free basis.[1951]

In the following, the focus will lie on the first-mentioned type of provisions, that is provisions that deal with an intra-group offsetting of profits and losses. Such provisions will be referred to as group taxation regimes irrespective of their specific design. There is a wide variety of rules on group taxation and their design varies greatly.[1952] Group taxation regimes in different States are described as heterogeneous, diverse,[1953] and often differing substantially.[1954] On the one hand, group members may be allowed to transfer their losses but not profits (group relief), their profits but not losses (group contribution), or both their profits and losses while remaining a separate taxpayer. On the other hand, group members may be allowed to consolidate their entire income even by being treated as part of their parent company and ceasing to exist for income tax purposes (fiscal transparency). Some group taxation regimes may be rather flexible by allowing to freely choose the participating group members and the direction of a profit or loss transfer, whereas others may require all group members to participate and transfer their income vertically to their parent company. In addition, some regimes may be irrevocable as long as a sufficiently integrated corporate group exists, whereas

1948. Ting 2013, 3, 5.
1949. Ting 2013, 14–15.
1950. Ting 2013, 3, 5.
1951. *See*, for a comparative analysis, Ting 2013; Ault and Arnold 2010, 397–402; Princen and Gérard 2008; Vanistendael 2008, sec. 3.4; Masui 2004; Lüdicke and Rödel 2004; moreover, on various issues in designing a group taxation system, Wiman 2000.
1952. *See*, for instance, Pitkänen 2015, 465–466; Avery Jones, Baker, et al. 2011a, 537; Avery Jones, Baker, et al. 2011b, 180–181; Ault and Arnold 2010, 397.
1953. Princen and Gérard 2008, 174–175, 185.
1954. Ting 2013, 39.

others may allow group members to leave quite easily or only impose a minimum time period for their participation.[1955]

Despite many differences in their design, group taxation regimes generally aim at treating legally separate persons as a single taxpayer or economic unit. Their introduction may be justified primarily with policy objectives related to neutrality and competitiveness (because simplicity is difficult to achieve in practice).[1956] As soon as a sufficient connection between group members exists, group taxation regimes may allow pooling, consolidating, or transferring profits or losses and thereby provide liquidity or cash-flow advantages.[1957] If a group member suffers losses, instead of carrying forward these losses and utilizing them in future years, it may be allowed to offset them against profits of another group member. While these profits are no longer taxed, a loss carry-forward is no longer available and, thus, future profits are taxed instead. By applying a group taxation regime to a corporate group, losses are offset earlier and profits are taxed at a later point in time.

Although group taxation regimes principally lead to temporary tax advantages, definite advantages may also arise. They may even be intended if they would be available to a single enterprise as well. For instance, a loss carry-forward might be subject to a time limitation. Against this risk of not being able to offset losses against future profits if an enterprise remains in a loss position for a longer period of time, a group taxation regime may lead to a definite advantage, that is to an earlier offsetting of losses and thereby to a utilization.[1958] A group taxation regime may also provide no advantages in a particular year. If all group members make profits, consolidation of their income need not lower their overall tax burden. Whether a group taxation regime is favourable to a corporate group depends on the tax position of each member and on how that regime is designed, what benefits it offers, and what measures would otherwise be in place.

In a cross-border context, concerns about tax advantages that would be unavailable in a purely domestic situation may explain why non-resident enterprises are generally not eligible to join group taxation. States are worried about their taxing rights

1955. This very generic description is based on information derived from Ting 2013; Ault and Arnold 2010, 397–402; Princen and Gérard 2008; Vanistendael 2008, sec. 3.4; Masui 2004.

1956. Ting 2013, 19–26, 62–73, 97–98. *See also* Princen and Gérard 2008, 175 ('[i]n principle, ... tax neutrality [between a single company and a corporate group] stimulates tax legislators to introduce group taxation regimes'); critically Masui 2004, 34–37. Yoshihiro Masui is critical about tax neutrality and submits that broader policy decisions and developments regarding economic concentration and business combinations often influence a particular tax policy for corporate groups, although it is still possible to argue why group taxation regimes may be necessary in a more specific context (for instance, immediate offset of losses incurred in initial stages of new operations carried on through a subsidiary, reduction, or elimination of a need for transfer pricing scrutiny, etc.). It is also worth mentioning that Yoshihiro Masui does not endorse simplicity as an argument for group taxation regimes but rather holds that '[a]dministrative complexity is inevitable'. *See* Masui 2004, 36; differently, Boulogne 2011, 171 ('reduced administrative burden'), with reference to an argument that group taxation may allow to make a single tax return and to treat intra-group transactions as neutral for tax purposes, which renders documentation of transfer prices unnecessary.

1957. *See*, for instance, Allevato Neto 2015, 559; moreover, Boulogne 2011, 171, with reference to CJEU, 13 December 2005, C-446/03, *Marks & Spencer*, para. 32.

1958. *See also*, to this effect, Allevato Neto 2015, 559.

and about a definite deduction of foreign losses of non-resident enterprises from taxable profits of resident group members since they may not be able to tax foreign profits of non-resident enterprises.[1959] Antony Ting states that the primary reasons for the exclusion of non-resident companies are revenue concerns and administrative costs, concerns about avoidance and abuse, and the fact that extending residence taxing rights to non-resident companies is generally unacceptable.[1960]

However, EU Member States are required by the fundamental freedoms to extend their scope of group taxation regimes to cover taxable PEs of non-resident companies.[1961] They are also not allowed to deny benefits to resident companies because of their connection through an intermediary non-resident EU company[1962] or ownership by a common non-resident EU parent company.[1963] In all of these cases, only taxable profits and losses are at stake. This suggests that it is possible to adapt group taxation regimes to cover such cross-border situations without raising unsolvable problems of avoidance or abuse and without losing taxing rights. Still, the question remains whether the non-discrimination provisions of Article 24(3) and (5) also require an extension of group taxation regimes to PEs and foreign-owned resident enterprises.

[2] Grouping with a PE

[a] Group Structure and Relationship

A group taxation regime may allow resident enterprises to pool, consolidate, or transfer their profits or losses, while non-resident enterprises may be excluded from these benefits even when they maintain a PE. Therefore, if a PE of a non-resident enterprise generates profits, it cannot offset the profits against losses of resident group members. If, by contrast, this PE was a resident enterprise, it could become part of a tax group and would consequently pay no or less tax. Since participation in a tax group explicitly depends on residence, a change in residence leads to a change in tax treatment. Unless it is argued that, from a multi-year perspective, a group taxation regime provides only for liquidity or cash-flow advantages and, thus, its non-application does not result in a higher overall amount of tax (different but no less favourable taxation on a PE),[1964] a 'but for' test establishes prima facie discrimination under the PE non-discrimination clause of Article 24(3).

It is then necessary to consider on a substantive basis whether differences in circumstances between resident and non-resident enterprises exist that are inevitably linked to differences in residence but nevertheless prevent comparability. Although resident enterprises are subject to full tax liability and non-resident enterprises to

1959. *See also* Raad 2008, 157–158, who emphasizes, however, that it would be possible to only deduct foreign losses of non-resident enterprises and to implement a 'clawback' mechanism.
1960. Ting 2013, 102–103, 274. *See also*, for instance, Masui 2004, 55 ('revenue concerns and administrative costs'); Adda 2008, 239 ('potential abuses').
1961. CJEU, 6 September 2012, C-18/11, *Philips Electronics*.
1962. CJEU, 27 November 2008, C-418/07, *Papillon*.
1963. CJEU, 12 June 2014, C-39/13 to C-41/13, *SCA Group Holding*.
1964. *See*, critically, Hohenwarter 2010, 625–626.

limited tax liability, such differences in circumstances cannot be considered relevant. They amount to protected differences in tax liability and residence. Honouring them without any particular reason or justification would render Article 24(3) meaningless.[1965] In addition, differences in taxing rights with regard to the business carried on in the source State do not exist. A non-resident enterprise is taxable in the source State under Article 7(1) because the business is carried on in that State through a PE. Conversely, a resident enterprise would also be taxable in that State under Article 7(1) because the business in question would not be carried on in any other State. As differences in residence do not lead to differences in taxing rights as far as the activities carried on through the PE are concerned, at least these taxing rights cannot qualify as inevitably linked but relevant characteristics in a concrete case.

Nevertheless, the OECD Commentary rejects an application of Article 24(3):[1966]

> [T]he equal treatment principle of paragraph 3 only applies to the taxation of the permanent establishment's own activities. That principle, therefore, is restricted to a comparison between the rules governing the taxation of the permanent establishment's own activities and those applicable to similar business activities carried on by an independent resident enterprise. It does not extend to rules that take account of the relationship between an enterprise and other enterprises (*e.g.* rules that allow consolidation, transfer of losses or tax-free transfers of property between companies under common ownership) since the latter rules do not focus on the taxation of an enterprise's own business activities similar to those of the permanent establishment but, instead, on the taxation of a resident enterprise as part of a group of associated enterprises. Such rules will often operate to ensure or facilitate tax compliance and administration within a domestic group. It therefore follows that the equal treatment principle has no application.

As the OECD Commentary rightly observes, only '[t]he taxation on a permanent establishment' is a concern to the PE non-discrimination clause. However, this taxation may also depend on other parts of the non-resident enterprise. As the examples of a progressive tax rate (*see* section §4.04[B]) and a split-rate company tax system that avoids economic double taxation (*see* section §4.04[E][4]) demonstrate, the activities or dividend distributions of the entire non-resident enterprise may influence the tax treatment of the PE.[1967] For the OECD Commentary, it is also 'clear that … the tax treatment in one Contracting State of the permanent establishment of an enterprise of the other Contracting State should be compared to that of an enterprise of the

1965. *See* Papotti 2003, 328 ('[s]hould liability to tax on worldwide income be a relevant factor …, a permanent establishment would under no circumstances be regarded as being comparable to a resident enterprise'; 'Art. 24(3) [would be] completely meaningless'). *See also*, however, Ting 2013, 262; Sparagna 2004, 726; Goldberg and Glicklich 1992, 99, who report on a different view in the US; moreover, Ault and Tillinghast 1992, 271–272 ('[t]he consolidation privilege seems clearly premised on the idea that all of the includible corporations will be fully subject to US taxation on their world-wide income'; 'it would be impossible to assure that the permanent establishment would in fact resemble a fully taxable domestic entity'); critically Gifford 1978, 62–63, 66–67 ('such an analysis in effect nullifies the permanent establishment clause's protection of permanent establishments').

1966. 2008–2017 OECD Commentary on Article 24, para. 41. *See also* Loukota and Jirousek 2016 m.no. 29; Sasseville 2008, 135; Holmes and Löser 2004, 536 (opinion reportedly voiced by Jacques Sasseville); critically, for instance, Pitkänen 2015, 474–476.

1967. *See also* Pitkänen 2015, 475.

first-mentioned State that has a legal structure that is similar to that of the enterprise to which the permanent establishment belongs'.[1968] Apparently, the legal structure of the entire non-resident enterprise is taken into account for determining the appropriate comparator. The PE, as such, does not have any particular legal structure[1969] just as it does not have any particular owners or shareholders.

For the purposes of determining whether a PE is being discriminated against, Article 24(3) should thus consider that the entire non-resident enterprise belongs to a group of associated enterprises. In order to hypothesize an appropriate comparator with a 'but for' test, it should be assumed not only that the PE as a resident enterprise would have the same legal structure and would carry on the same activities as the whole non-resident enterprise to which it belongs but also that it would have the same owners or shareholders.[1970] Therefore, it would be part of a corporate group and could benefit from group taxation with regard to the activities carried on in the source State. If a group taxation regime addresses the taxation of a resident enterprise as part of a group of associated enterprises, this does not prevent Article 24(3) from scrutinizing the taxation on a PE as long as this taxation depends on factors related to the enterprise's ownership or control.[1971]

It follows that, if a group taxation regime requires a particular shareholder relationship or association between resident enterprises, a PE should be able to establish such a connection with resident enterprises as well. On the one hand, if the non-resident enterprise to which the PE belongs is owned or controlled by a resident enterprise, the PE as a resident enterprise would also be owned or controlled by that resident enterprise (*see* Figure 4.17), and if the non-resident enterprise is owned or controlled by another non-resident enterprise, the PE would also be owned or controlled by that other non-resident enterprise (*see* Figure 4.18).[1972] On the other hand, if the non-resident enterprise to which the PE belongs owns or controls a resident enterprise, the PE as a resident enterprise would also own or control that resident enterprise.

1968. 2008–2017 OECD Commentary on Article 24, para. 37.
1969. *See also*, for instance, Pitkänen 2015, 476; Rust 2015b m.no. 57; Rust 2015c m.nos. 95, 103.
1970. *See*, to this effect, Hohenwarter 2010, 624–625; Papotti 2003, 325–326; Lang 2003a, 255.
1971. *See also* L. Hinnekens and Hinnekens 2008, 30, who argue that the participation of a PE in a group consolidation regime relates to the profits (or losses) of the PE itself and that, based on Article 24(3), a PE should be entitled to the same tax incentives and relief mechanisms as a resident company exercising the same activities, including group relief; moreover, Pitkänen 2015, 480.
1972. In such a situation, a concurrent application of Article 24(5) could prohibit different tax treatment between foreign-owned and domestic-owned enterprises. *See also* section §4.04[C][5][a].

Figure 4.17 PE of a Domestic-Owned Subsidiary

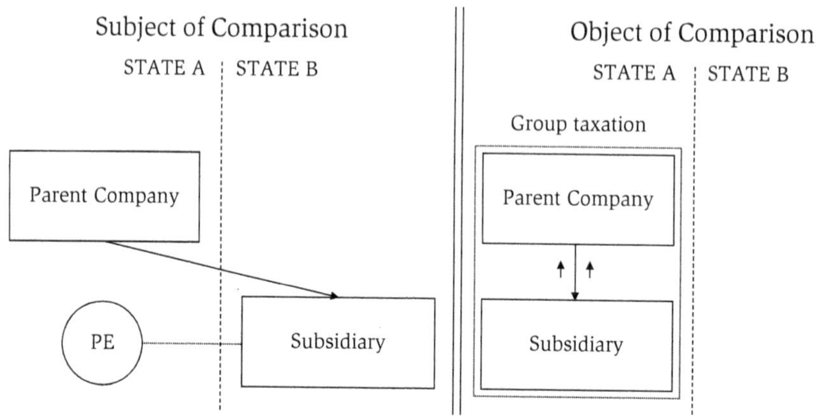

Figure 4.18 PE of a Foreign-Owned Sub-subsidiary

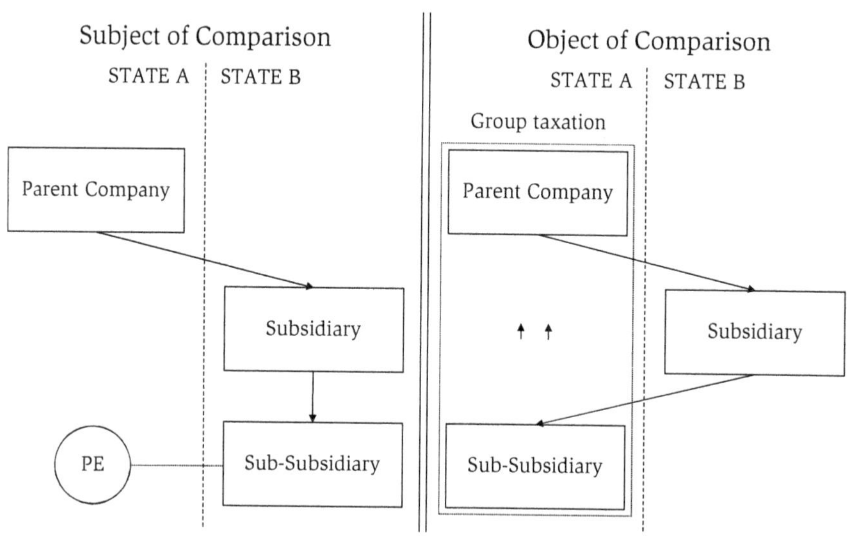

To be precise, whether the shareholding in a resident enterprise is attributable to the protected permanent establishment (PE 1) (*see* Figure 4.19) or to another part of the enterprise (PE 2) (*see* Figure 4.20) has no influence on the ownership chain. Even if, under Article 7(2), the shareholding is not economically owned by the protected PE, the ownership chain is not broken.[1973] Therefore, an extension of group taxation might be possible under Article 24(3)[1974] provided that a resident enterprise would qualify for

1973. *See*, differently, Papotti 2003, 327.
1974. In addition, Article 24(5) could apply at the level of the foreign-owned resident enterprise.

group taxation as a participating group member even if it economically holds the shareholding through another part of the enterprise located abroad and not through its head office. It can only be asked whether the fact that the shareholding is not attributable to the protected PE could prevent taxation of resident group members[1975] and, therefore, justify differences in tax treatment on the basis of inevitably linked but relevant differences in circumstances (*see* section §4.04[C][2][d]).

Figure 4.19 Shareholding Attributable to the PE

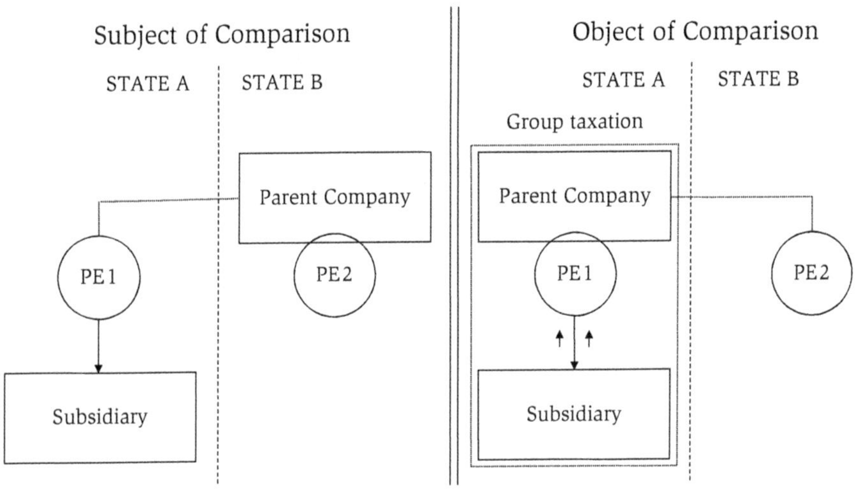

1975. On this issue, *see* Hohenwarter 2010, 639–642.

Figure 4.20 Shareholding Not Attributable to the PE

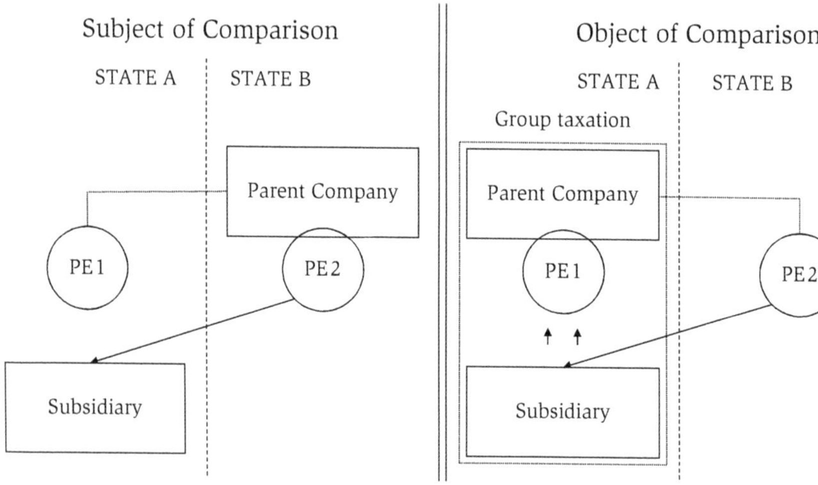

[b] *Discrimination in a Loss Situation?*

Group taxation regimes address a corporate group as a whole in order to bring its tax treatment closer to that of a single enterprise. They may stipulate a bundle of tax consequences (transfer of profits, transfer of losses, tax neutrality within a group with regard to shareholdings, etc.) to achieve their objective of providing an overall liquidity or cash-flow advantage to a corporate group. When considering each individual group member in isolation, however, a group taxation regime may have very different tax consequences. It may either lead to advantages (profits are allocated to or relieved by losses of another group member and, therefore, not taxed) or disadvantages (losses are allocated to or offset against contributed profits of another group member and, therefore, not available).[1976] If such tax consequences are scrutinized in isolation under Article 24(3), certain benefits could be extended to PEs without extending corresponding disadvantages. Although a non-application of a group taxation regime may lead to tax treatment that is less favourable for a corporate group as a whole if a transfer of losses from a PE to another group member would lower that corporate group's overall tax burden in a particular year, it need not result in less favourable tax treatment for that loss-making PE itself.

Assume that a non-resident company of State B maintains a PE in State A through which it substantially participates in a resident company. If the PE was a resident enterprise of State A, it could benefit from group taxation. All profits and losses of its subsidiary would be allocated to it. However, since the PE is only part of a non-resident enterprise, each company is taxed separately (*see* Figure 4.21). This raises the question

1976. Papotti 2003, 326, does not regard such a situation as a disadvantage to a loss-making PE but rather as equal treatment of non-resident and resident enterprises because, with and without group taxation, no profits of that enterprise are taxed: the tax burden is always zero.

of whether discrimination because of residence under Article 24(3) is at hand if the PE makes profits or losses.

Figure 4.21 PE of a Parent Company

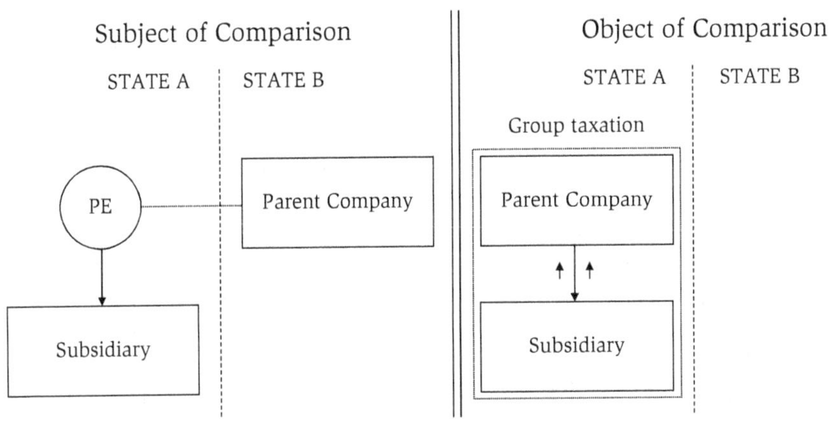

When looking at the PE in isolation, the group taxation regime could either lead to favourable or unfavourable tax treatment. This is not an issue of comparability but of whether taxation on a PE is 'less favourably levied'. If the PE makes profits whereas the subsidiary suffer losses, the group taxation regime would allow offsetting the losses of the subsidiary against the profits of the PE and would thus prevent or reduce taxation on the PE. Article 24(3) should, therefore, extend group taxation to the PE in order to prevent tax treatment that is less favourable compared to that of resident enterprises.[1977] If the PE suffers losses whereas the subsidiary makes profits, the group taxation regime could be seen as a tax disadvantage to the PE. Instead of being able to carry forward its losses, the PE would effectively lose the losses as they would be offset against the profits of the subsidiary. The PE would further suffer from higher taxation in future years as no loss carry-forward would be available to offset its profits. Article 24(3) should consequently not extend the group taxation regime to the PE. It arguably does not constitute less favourable taxation to pay no taxes and to maintain a loss carry-forward.[1978]

If a group taxation regime is designed in a way that only profits may be contributed to a group member, the result is very similar. A profitable PE could rely on Article 24(3) in order to get relief from taxation.[1979] By contrast, resident group members would not be able to contribute their profits to a loss-making PE since they,

1977. *See*, to this effect, Avery Jones, Depret, et al. 1991b, 332 ('possible discrimination exists where the [resident] corporation [whose shares are attributable to the permanent establishment] has losses which would reduce the tax on the permanent establishment if it were a resident corporation'); moreover, Lang 2003a, 254–255, 258.

1978. *See also* Pitkänen 2015, 480; Hohenwarter 2010, 626–627.

1979. *See* Scapa Passalacqua and Henie 2005, 37, 40, 44.

not the PE, would be taxed less favourably by reason of someone else's residence.[1980] As long as the PE is part of a tax group, it could avoid taxation of its profits under Article 24(3) if group members suffer losses, but it would accumulate loss carry-forwards even if group members make profits.[1981]

If a group taxation regime is designed in a way that only losses may be transferred to a group member, it could not apply to PEs at all. A loss-making PE would not be treated less favourably by being prevented from transferring its losses and losing its loss carry-forward. Although resident group members could potentially rely on Article 24(5) in order to transfer their losses to a profitable PE, namely, by claiming discrimination because of their shareholder's residence, Article 24(5) would fail to apply if the non-resident enterprise to which the PE belongs is a subsidiary of a resident group member (*see* again Figure 4.17).

A one-sided application of Article 24(3) could lead to tax consequences that would not be in line with principal objectives of a group taxation regime.[1982] While some regimes may be rather flexible by allowing to individually choose each transfer of profits or losses, others may be stricter by stipulating obligatory consequences for both profits and losses, for instance, by requiring to allocate income to a specific company. In addition, a group taxation regime may envisage a minimum time period or even require all sufficiently connected enterprises to participate in a tax group without being able to revoke after opting in. Such strict conditions for group taxation highlight that, while a group taxation system may have different effects on individual group members and in different years, it constitutes a complete package that should lead to an overall benefit regardless of individual tax positions. If Article 24(3) required extending certain benefits to a PE of a non-resident enterprise (notably, offsetting profits of a PE against losses of other group members) without requiring a corresponding extension of other group benefits (notably, forfeiting losses of a PE and offsetting them against profits of other group members), it would disturb this envisaged package. By dissecting a group taxation regime into its different parts and extending only some parts to PEs, Article 24(3) could lead to tax consequences that would not only contravene the regime's principal objective of treating all group members as a single taxpayer but would also be different within a tax group than in purely domestic situations.

Therefore, it can be argued in line with the OECD Commentary[1983] that resident and non-resident enterprises are not comparable to each other under Article 24(3) as far as group taxation regimes are concerned. This argument would not rely on the assumption that group taxation regimes do not address the taxation of the PE's own activities. It would rather focus on the principal objective of treating a corporate group as a single economic unit. This objective could be frustrated by a one-sided and somewhat arbitrary application of Article 24(3) to profitable but not loss-making PEs. When a group taxation regime is aimed at also affecting losses of resident enterprises in order to offset them against profits of other resident enterprises, Article 24(3) should

1980. *See* Scapa Passalacqua and Henie 2005, 38, 40.
1981. *See also* Pitkänen 2015, 481.
1982. *See*, to this effect, Pitkänen 2015, 481.
1983. 2008–2017 OECD Commentary on Article 24, para. 41.

not interfere with this aim by requiring group taxation only when a profitable PE is at stake. As a consequence, the inability of Article 24(3) to address both profits and losses would arguably allow this domestic objective to prevail thereby establishing inevitably linked but relevant differences in legal circumstances between PEs and resident group members. While a resident group member would face tax consequences with regard to both its profits and losses, a non-resident group member could face no such tax consequences, neither under domestic tax law nor under Article 24(3).

Although the source State by itself created those differences in legal circumstances, namely, by excluding non-resident enterprises from group taxation or not using a technique that focuses only on a transfer of profits, it is not required to adapt its group taxation system. Under Article 24(1), if a State taxes only its nationals on a worldwide basis, it created differences in circumstances by itself with regard to the scope of tax liability, which may prevent comparability as far as specific tax benefits (notably, personal allowances, reliefs, and reductions) are concerned, despite an inevitable link to nationality (*see* section §4.03[A]). Under Article 24(3), if a State applies a group taxation regime only to resident enterprises, it created differences in circumstances by itself with regard to the treatment of a group as a single economic unit, which may prevent comparability as far as specific tax benefits (notably, transfers of profits) are concerned, despite an inevitable link to residence. In the former case, tax treaty discrimination can be denied because Article 24(1) does not obligate a State to tax foreigners on a worldwide basis while only such taxation would maintain a system's coherence of connecting both advantages and disadvantages to full tax liability. Thus, nationals and foreigners are situated differently if they are subject to a different scope of tax liability. In the latter case, tax treaty discrimination can be denied because Article 24(3) does not obligate a State to transfer or consolidate losses of PEs while only such taxation would maintain a system's coherence of addressing both profits and losses within a tax group. Thus, residents and non-residents are situated differently if they are subject to a different taxation regime, that is, group or no group taxation. If Article 24(3) objects to taxation that is less favourable only when a profitable PE is not able to participate in group taxation whereas it does not object to taxation when a loss-making PE is not allowed to forfeit its losses to the benefit of other group members and the entire corporate group, there are some arguments against an application of Article 24(3) to group taxation regimes.

[c] *Group Taxation as a Single Tax Advantage*

In order to succeed with those arguments against an application of Article 24(3), the taxation on a PE must be less favourably levied in some situations but not in others although a group taxation regime would aim at applying in all of these situations and would indeed apply if a resident enterprise was at stake. Thus, the meaning of 'taxation … less favourably levied' is important. Under Article 24(3), different taxation is not automatically prohibited, 'it is the result alone which counts'.[1984] By merely looking at the tax burden or total amount of tax, it can be argued that a loss-making PE is not taxed less favourably by being excluded from group taxation. Rather, under a group taxation regime, it would lose its losses and its loss carry-forward while its tax burden would remain zero, or it would become taxable on additional profits and suffer from higher taxation if profits of other group members were allocated to it.

Raul-Angelo Papotti suggests an alternative interpretation of 'taxation ... less favourably levied'.[1985] In contrast to Article 24(1), (2), and (5), the PE non-discrimination clause does not prohibit 'other or more burdensome' taxation (*see also* Chapter 3 section §3.02[B][1]). This does not necessarily mean, however, that a mere comparison of tax burdens suffices under Article 24(3). As a PE is only a dependent part of a non-resident enterprise, some inherent differences in legal circumstances compared to resident enterprises always persist. Such differences should not automatically prevent comparability under Article 24(3) but may be relied on by a State in order to 'tax non-resident persons differently, for practical reasons, from resident persons, as long as this does not result in more burdensome taxation'.[1986] This conversely means that other taxation may be prohibited under Article 24(3) not only if it results in taxation that is more burdensome but also if it is not hinged upon differences in nature between PEs and separate enterprises.[1987] As long as the PE claims to be discriminated against by being treated differently than resident enterprises, that is by not being able to participate in a tax group, and as long as the PE's actual nature does not call for any differential treatment, the tax burden in a particular year and constellation should not be decisive for confirming or rejecting taxation that is less favourable under Article 24(3).[1988] A certain tax treatment may ultimately be unfavourable in terms of both the results (what must be paid in terms of money) and accorded preferences.[1989] Article 24(3) might be interpreted as generally pointing to any tax preference or opportunity that may have an impact upon taxation rather than (solely) what should be due in terms of tax liability.[1990]

To this effect, Sami Pitkänen suggests considering 'the whole group consolidation regime a single tax benefit being comprised of many rules', which means that 'disallowing this benefit from the PE when it incurs a loss would be less favourably levied taxation on the PE'.[1991] Kees van Raad also states that the term 'taxation' can be understood in the same way as under Article 24(1) and that it also covers rules on loss

1984. 2008–2017 OECD Commentary on Article 24, para. 34 (1963: para. 16; 1977: para. 22; 1992–2005: para. 20). *See also*, for instance, Rust 2015b m.nos. 30 and 66; Rust 2015c m.nos. 42, 104, who holds that Article 24(3) 'is exclusively based on a comparison of tax burdens', that is what must be paid in terms of money; similarly, Avery Jones, Depret, et al. 1991b, 331 ('quantum of tax'); differently, Schuch and Stieglitz 2006, 415–417.
1985. Papotti 2003, 326–328.
1986. 2008–2017 OECD Commentary on Article 24, para. 34 (1977: para. 22; 1992–2005: para. 20; similarly, 1963: para. 16).
1987. Papotti 2003, 326.
1988. Papotti 2003, 326.
1989. Papotti 2003, 326.
1990. Papotti 2003, 327.
1991. Pitkänen 2015, 481–482.

compensation, elections, and special regimes.[1992] Josef Schuch and Alexander Stieglitz argue that 'other or more burdensome taxation' under Article 24(1), as it does not prohibit taxation that is more favourable for foreigners, equals 'taxation ... less favourably levied' under Article 24(3) and, therefore, disadvantageous tax treatment is covered by both clauses regardless of whether there is a higher tax burden in terms of money.[1993] Last, but not least, Niels Bammens and Frans Vanistendael submit that, if a PE is not entitled to engage in a loss transfer with a subsidiary, 'it is obvious that the PE itself is less favourably treated than a resident company. Clearly, by not being able to transfer the losses, the PE suffers a disadvantage' that is condemned by Article 24(3).[1994]

Indeed, it is questionable whether a mere comparison of tax burdens would do justice to Article 24(3) especially when a group taxation regime is at stake. Such a regime may have a very different impact on individual group members even if, from a group perspective, it ultimately benefits all enterprises, including their PEs, by providing liquidity or cash-flow advantages. When taking this background into account, it should not matter under Article 24(3) whether a PE is in a profit or loss situation in a particular year and whether profits or losses are transferred from or to a PE. Similarly, it should not matter whether a group taxation regime actually leads to a liquidity or cash-flow advantage for a corporate group in a particular year or overall. Instead, a group taxation regime in its entirety should be considered as a tax measure, preference, option, or opportunity that leads to taxation that is less favourable if it is refused to a PE based on residence.

If it is neither necessary to consider each individual tax effect of a group taxation regime in isolation[1995] nor to compare individual, overall, or group-wide tax burdens in order to establish tax treatment that is less favourable under Article 24(3), it is possible to address both profits and losses of a PE and to consolidate income in accordance with a group taxation regime's objective irrespective of residence. When viewing a group taxation regime as a bundle of rights and obligations which, as such, may lead to taxation that is less favourable for a PE, a State is required to allow PEs full participation in a tax group. No relevant differences in legal circumstances with regard to the interrelated treatment of both profits and losses can then exist.

To sum up, if the expression 'taxation ... less favourably levied' in Article 24(3) is understood in a way that only profitable PEs may suffer from discriminatory tax treatment with regard to a group taxation regime, legitimate policy concerns about a one-sided extension of such regimes arise. This, in turn, could justify a tax distinction between resident and non-resident enterprises and thereby prevent comparability

1992. Raad 1986, 142.
1993. Schuch and Stieglitz 2006, 415–417.
1994. Bammens and Vanistendael 2016, sec. 2.3.3.1.1.
1995. *See*, however, Silva 2016b, 102–108; Silva 2013, 114–116, who discusses whether one should make a separate discrimination test concerning each of the benefits associated with group taxation regimes – per element – or whether an overall approach is more appropriate. It is submitted in this study that, if certain benefits are claimed in isolation, inevitably linked differences in circumstances regarding other connected benefits or disadvantages might prevent comparability if they are regarded as relevant with a substantive analysis.

under Article 24(3) due to inevitably linked but relevant differences in legal circumstances. However, better arguments speak in favour of regarding a denial of participation in a tax group as taxation that is less favourable regardless of whether a PE makes profits or losses. Following this view and in order to comply with the non-discrimination obligations, a PE must be allowed to fully join a tax group.[1996]

[d] No Modification of Taxing Rights

Nonetheless, a State could respond that it excludes non-resident enterprises from group taxation not because of their non-residence but because of its insufficient tax jurisdiction and a consequent fear about losing taxing rights over income of resident group members. Depending on how a group taxation regime is specifically designed and how a corporate group is structured, allowing a PE to participate in a tax group could mean that the taxable profits of resident group members would be allocated to a non-resident enterprise under domestic tax law. Given that a tax treaty does not determine to whom income should be allocated but rather refers to such a domestic allocation decision,[1997] profits of resident group members, therefore, would become income of a non-resident enterprise for tax treaty purposes.

Although a PE of a non-resident enterprise provides a sufficient nexus for taxation under Article 7(1), it is taxable only with respect to the profits that are attributable to the PE based on the functions it performs, the assets it uses, the risks it assumes, and the capital it requires for its activities.[1998] Arguably, the profits of a resident group member that would be allocated to the non-resident enterprise under a group taxation regime in order to meet the non-discrimination obligations of Article 24(3) do not relate to the functions performed by the PE. This is even the case if the PE economically owns the shareholding in the resident group member. It performs the significant functions relevant to the economic ownership of the shareholding but not the activities carried on by the resident group member that lead to the profits at issue. On the other hand, the resident group member cannot automatically be treated as a PE of the non-resident enterprise because, pursuant to Article 5(7), the fact that a company controls or is controlled by another company 'shall not of itself constitute either company a permanent establishment of the other'.[1999]

For tax treaty purposes, the profits of the resident group member, therefore, would not be attributable to the PE. As residual profits, they would belong to the head

1996. *See also*, to this effect, Brugger 2008, 198, who regards the fact that a non-resident enterprise operating a PE may not opt for group taxation as treatment that is less favourable under Article 24(3); moreover, Oberascher and Staringer 2007, 40; Dommes and Schuch 2007 fn. 24 on p. 354; Wiesner and Mayr 2005, 569; Trenkwalder 2005, 417; Holmes and Löser 2004, 536 (opinion reportedly voiced by Theo J. Keijzer). On a different decision of the Spanish Supreme Court (Tribunal Supremo) – most probably the decision of 15 July 2002, *Solvay et Cie*, 4517/1997, but *see also* the decision of 12 February 2003, *Solvay et Cie*, 8720/1998 –, *see*, critically, Vogel 2003, 39.
1997. *See*, in general, Lang 1992, 101–102.
1998. This is at least true if the AOA (separate entity approach) is applied. *See* OECD, Attribution of Profits Report 2010; moreover, Article 7(2) of the 2010–2017 OECD Model.
1999. *See also*, for instance, Rust 2003b, 661.

office of the non-resident enterprise. Consequently, while Article 24(3) would obligate the source State to apply its group taxation regime in a non-discriminatory manner by permitting the PE to participate in group taxation, Article 7(1) would prohibit the taxation of the profits that are thereupon allocated to the non-resident enterprise under the group taxation regime.

While the source State is principally allowed to tax all profits of a resident enterprise under Article 7, including all residual profits that are allocated to that enterprise for domestic tax purposes under a group taxation regime, a non-resident enterprise is subject to tax only with regard to its own activities carried on in the source State through a PE. If profits of resident group members cannot be attributed to a PE of a non-resident enterprise and potentially remain untaxed, differences in legal circumstances between resident and non-resident enterprises arise from a domestic and tax treaty perspective. Only with resident enterprises is it legally ensured that income of other resident group members could be taxed under a group taxation regime, whereas non-resident enterprises imply that income of resident group members cannot be taxed and that legitimate taxing rights are potentially lost.

This fear about losing taxing rights is largely unfounded, however:[2000]

- When a group taxation regime allows group members to consolidate or transfer profits or losses without disregarding their identity for taxation purposes, it can be argued that each group member continues to be individually entitled to tax treaty benefits.[2001] This means that, if a PE of a non-resident enterprise participates in a tax group, all resident group members remain taxable under domestic tax law and for tax treaty purposes. It does not matter that their profits or losses are pooled at the level of the PE or that the tax is technically paid by the non-resident enterprise. The source State, that is the State of the PE, is allowed to tax its resident group members and does not lose any taxing rights by extending group taxation under Article 24(3).
- When a group taxation regime completely disregards the identity of resident group members and treats them as fiscally transparent by allocating their profits and losses to the non-resident enterprise, the principles of the OECD Partnership Report,[2002] potentially implemented through Articles 3 and 11 of the Multilateral Convention,[2003] can be relied on.[2004] Such income conveys no tax treaty benefits as long as the other Contracting State, that is the residence State of the non-resident enterprise, does not allocate it to that enterprise as

2000. *See also* Lüdicke 2011a; Schnitger and Berliner 2011; Demschner and Stefaner 2009, 17.
2001. *See*, to this effect, Lüdicke 2011a, 743–746; Schnitger and Berliner 2011, 754–757; Demschner and Stefaner 2009, 17; Brugger 2008, 189–190; Dommes and Schuch 2007, 359–362; Staringer 1999, 354–355, 361; Schuch 1998a, 178–181; differently, Lang 2003b, 216–218; Lang 2001, 597.
2002. *See*, critically, Lang 2001; Lang 2000d; Lang 2000c; Lang 2000b; Lang 2000a.
2003. Multilateral Convention to Implement Tax Treaty Related Measures to Prevent BEPS (2016). *See also* Article 1(2) and (3) of the 2017 OECD Model.
2004. *See also*, for instance, Schnitger and Berliner 2011, 757–579 and Link 2008, who discuss the principles of the OECD Partnership Report in the context of group consolidation regimes.

well.[2005] The source State remains free to tax the non-resident enterprise on all profits that were originally obtained by or can be traced back to its resident group members because a negative conflict of allocation arises with regard to these profits. Article 7 does not prevent the source State from taxing the non-resident enterprise even without a PE because the enterprise cannot claim tax treaty benefits for the income that is allocated to it in the source State but not in the residence State.

- Finally, if the other Contracting State also treats group members as fiscally transparent and thereby avoids a negative conflict of allocation, or if the principles of the OECD Partnership Report are rejected, and the domestic income allocation of the source State is taken as a basis for tax treaty entitlement, the income-generating activities of these group members effectively become the activities of the non-resident enterprise to which the PE belongs.[2006] Since these activities – not the group members, as such – likely establish a PE in the source State pursuant to Article 5(1) if they are carried on through a fixed place of business, all profits initially derived by the group members can be attributed to a PE in the source State.[2007] This may even be true if the profits are sourced in a third State provided that a functional relationship with the activities carried on in the source State exists.[2008] Article 5(7) is not relevant just as it is not relevant with a partnership or 'check-the-box company' that is treated as fiscally transparent by both Contracting States.

The source State keeps its tax jurisdiction with regard to both the PE and its resident group members even if it extends group taxation under Article 24(3). Only when both Contracting States apply their group taxation regime cross-border and both States treat group members as fiscally transparent, residual profits that were originally obtained by resident group members but are functionally unrelated to the activities carried on in the source State might change their tax jurisdiction for tax treaty purposes.[2009] In such cases, it can be argued that a PE of a non-resident enterprise is not similarly situated as a resident enterprise for the purposes of extending group taxation

2005. *See also* 2000–2014 OECD Commentary on Article 1, para. 6.2: 'Where, for instance, the State of source treats a domestic partnership [the resident group members] as fiscally transparent and therefore taxes the partners [the non-resident enterprise] on their share of the income of the partnership [the resident group members], a partner [the non-resident enterprise] that is resident of a State that taxes partnerships [the resident group members] as companies would not be able to claim the benefits of the Convention between the two States with respect to the share of the partnership's [the resident group members'] income that the State of source taxes in his [the non-resident enterprise's] hands since that income, though allocated to the person claiming the benefits of the Convention under the laws of the State of source, is not similarly allocated for purposes of determining the liability to tax on that item of income in the State of residence of that person'.
2006. *See*, to this effect, Lüdicke 2011c, 846; moreover, 2017 OECD Commentary on Article 5, para. 56 (2000–2014: para. 19.1), basically submitting that the activities of a fiscally transparent partnership may establish a PE for each partner.
2007. *See*, to this effect, Demschner and Stefaner 2009, 17; Brugger 2008, 193–195; Aigner 2004, 129–130; differently, Schnitger and Berliner 2011, 760; Lang 2003b, 220–221.
2008. *See*, to this effect, Fett 2014, 5.
2009. *See also* Hohenwarter 2010, 639–642.

under Article 24(3) as evidenced by the fact that an inclusion of that PE in a tax group could affect the allocation of taxing rights under the tax treaty (*see also* section §4.04[C][3]). In other cases, however, a limitation of a group taxation regime to resident enterprises cannot be justified.

At this point, other justifications for different tax treatment could be brought forward: a PE of a non-resident enterprise is not comparable to a resident enterprise because it belongs to an enterprise that is subject to full or limited tax liability in more than one State which might lead to a temporary or permanent loss deduction in more than one State,[2010] or because only resident enterprises can be entrusted with obligations that ensure or facilitate tax compliance and administration. Whether such differences in circumstances, if they are inevitably linked to differences in residence in a concrete case, are indeed relevant to a group taxation regime requires further analysis. It is not clear, however, whether such reasons would be able to outweigh the objective of Article 24(3) of putting PEs of non-resident enterprises on an equal footing with resident enterprises. In particular, an abstract possibility of using losses twice in cross-border situations unlikely suffices for concluding that inevitably linked differences in legal or factual circumstances are relevant in a concrete case. Overall, since the strongest argument against discrimination – a loss of taxing rights by transferring profits of resident group members to a PE of a non-resident enterprise – seems largely unfounded and since a denial of group taxation benefits may lead to taxation that is less favourable regardless of whether profits or losses are transferred, stronger arguments speak in favour of extending group taxation benefits to PEs under Article 24(3).

[3] Grouping with a Non-resident Enterprise

Group taxation regimes may prohibit a resident enterprise from consolidating with a non-resident enterprise and, therefore, may provide for different tax treatment based on residence. While it was analysed above whether such tax distinctions between resident and non-resident enterprises constitute prohibited tax discrimination under Article 24(3) if a non-resident enterprise maintains a PE in the allegedly discriminating State, this section will now address a different situation from the perspective of the ownership non-discrimination clause of Article 24(5). When a resident enterprise is owned or controlled by a non-resident enterprise (but not vice versa!), the question arises whether group taxation between these two enterprises may be denied when no PE is involved.

Assume that a resident company of State A is owned by a non-resident company of State B. If the resident subsidiary was owned by a resident enterprise of State A, it could benefit from group taxation. All profits and losses would be allocated to its parent company. However, since the parent company is a non-resident enterprise, each company is taxed separately (*see* Figure 4.22). This raises the question of whether discrimination because of the shareholder's residence is at hand under Article 24(5) if the resident subsidiary makes profits or losses.

2010. *See*, for instance, Pitkänen 2015, 480–481; Lüdicke et al. 2014, 380.

Figure 4.22 Resident Enterprise and a Non-resident Parent Company

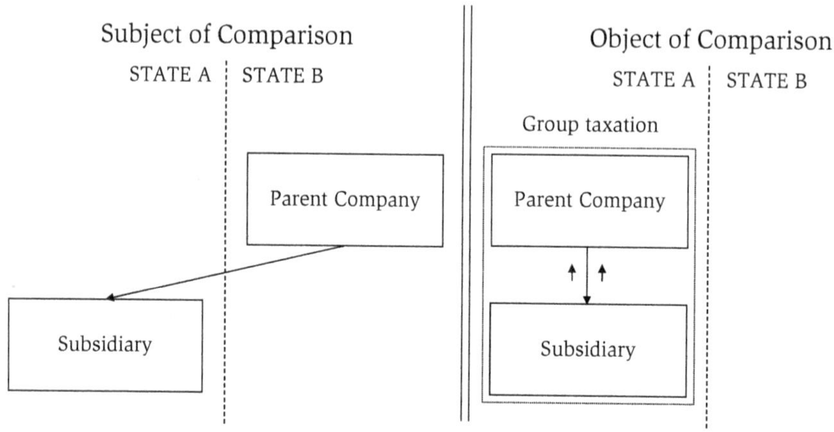

It is worth noting that the OECD Commentary rejects an application of the non-discrimination clause of Article 24(5) to group taxation regimes:[2011]

> Since the paragraph relates only to the taxation of resident enterprises and not to that of the persons owning or controlling their capital, it follows that it cannot be interpreted to extend the benefits of rules that take account of the relationship between a resident enterprise and other resident enterprises (*e.g.* rules that allow consolidation, transfer of losses or tax-free transfer of property between companies under common ownership). For example, if the domestic tax law of one State allows a resident company to consolidate its income with that of a resident parent company, paragraph 5 cannot have the effect to force the State to allow such consolidation between a resident company and a non-resident parent company. This would require comparing the combined treatment of a resident enterprise and the non-resident that owns its capital with that of a resident enterprise of the same State and the resident that owns its capital, something that clearly goes beyond the taxation of the resident enterprise alone.

Group taxation regimes combine the tax treatment of several enterprises. According to the OECD Commentary, such combined treatment is not within the scope of Article 24(5) as the non-discrimination clause deals only with the tax treatment of resident enterprises. Indeed, if a resident enterprise suffers losses, it could be questioned whether a group taxation regime favours that enterprise by transferring these losses to another enterprise thereby refusing a loss carry-forward (*see also* section §4.04[C][2][b]). From a group perspective, only liquidity or cash-flow advantages may be intended that cannot be assessed in isolation by focusing only on an individual group member. Similarly as under Article 24(3), it can be replied, however, that a group taxation regime can be seen as a single tax advantage consisting of an integrated set of rules, the non-application of which may lead to 'other or more burdensome ...

2011. 2008–2017 OECD Commentary on Article 24, para. 77; concurring Bruns 2013 m.no. 167.

taxation' under Article 24(5).[2012] This prevents an assessment of the combined treatment of several enterprises when determining whether a group taxation regime influences the tax burden of a resident group member in a particular year. It is not necessary to look at whether this group member makes profits or losses and how other group members succeed in their business. In fact, the expression '*other* or more burdensome ... taxation' under Article 24(1) and (5) intends to prevent discussions about whether a particular tax measure actually leads to a tax disadvantage in a particular situation when a tax distinction is based on the protected characteristic (*see* Chapter 3 section §3.02[A][1]).

Therefore, it is possible to disregard the concrete effects of a group taxation regime on the entire group (no 'combined treatment')[2013] and leave open whether the regime leads to a tax disadvantage at the level of the resident enterprise in question.[2014] If the resident enterprise claims to be discriminated against due to different treatment with regard to a group taxation regime, this should suffice for concluding that other or more burdensome taxation is at hand. Bruno da Silva further observes[2015] that the OECD Commentary discusses whether a group consolidation regime may lead to other or more burdensome taxation for a company and thereby violate the nationality non-discrimination rule of Article 24(1) if it requires certain nationality or residence[2016] (*see also* section §4.03[A][2][f]). It does not question discrimination on the basis of a 'combined treatment' argument but rather focuses on comparability and the reason for different tax treatment.

In order to confirm discrimination under Article 24(5), it must be established whether other or more burdensome taxation is due to the shareholder's residence. Other reasons for different tax treatment do not lead to discrimination. '[I]f the domestic tax law of one State allows a resident company to consolidate its income with that of a resident parent company', the question arises whether Article 24(5) can 'have the effect to force the State to allow such consolidation between a resident company and a non-resident parent company'.[2017] As the domestic tax measure under scrutiny directly refers to residence (it allows only resident enterprises to consolidate), a change in the shareholder's residence may lead to a change in tax treatment with a 'but for' test and thereby establish prima facie discrimination. If the non-resident parent company was a resident of the allegedly discriminating State, it could participate in a tax group

2012. *See also*, to this effect, Silva 2016b, 96; Silva 2013, 110–111; Gosch 2012b, 702; Hohenwarter 2010, 606; Papotti 2003, 324; moreover, Boulogne 2011, 173–174, 176, who interprets 'other taxation' as covering different tax treatment in a loss situation; and Ståhl 2000, 198, who reports that the Swedish Supreme Administrative Court (Regeringsrätten) in its decision of 26 November 1993, RÅ 1993 ref. 91 I, regarded a denial of a group contribution that would lead to an additional tax burden on a foreign-owned group company (and to a lower tax burden on another group company together with a subsequent tax equalization) as 'other' taxation and therefore confirmed discrimination against that company; critically Bammens 2012, 462–463.
2013. *See also*, to this effect, Silva 2016b, 89.
2014. *See*, however, Wunderlich 2009 m.no. 50, who doubts whether a loss-making subsidiary is disadvantaged under Article 24(5) by not being able to participate in a group with its non-resident parent company; only the parent company is disadvantaged.
2015. Silva 2016b, 89; Silva 2013, 109–110.
2016. 2008–2017 OECD Commentary on Article 24, para. 24–25 (Example 5).
2017. *Ibid.*, para. 77.

together with its resident subsidiary. At a first glance, its non-residence is the reason for different tax treatment.

In a second step, it is necessary to consider on a substantive basis whether differences in circumstances that are inevitably linked to differences in residence can be regarded as relevant. Therefore, it is necessary to determine for what reason the domestic tax measure under scrutiny refers to residence and whether this reason is in opposition to the non-discrimination clause or rather constitutes legitimate grounds for different tax treatment. As far as group taxation regimes are concerned, a reason for a limitation to resident enterprises could lie in concerns about losing taxing rights over income of resident group members. Inevitably linked differences in circumstances between domestic-owned and foreign-owned group members regarding their taxation in situations of domestic and cross-border group taxation, respectively, could consequently prevent comparability under Article 24(5).

If the income of a resident enterprise would be consolidated with the income of a non-resident enterprise, the allocation of taxing rights could be affected. For instance, by applying Article 24(5) and extending a group taxation regime cross-border to non-resident enterprises, the profits of a resident enterprise could be allocated to and consolidated with the losses of a non-resident enterprise. Since the allegedly discriminating State would not tax the profits of the resident enterprise immediately, it would expect to tax them (or other profits in return) at a later point in time. John F. Avery Jones, Philip Baker, et al. describe this taxation as the quid pro quo that the resident enterprise is expected to deliver in return for participating in group taxation but might be unable to deliver if it is owned by a non-resident enterprise that must be involved in group taxation.[2018] Since the non-resident enterprise is not within the State's tax jurisdiction and is generally protected under the tax treaty from taxation in that State unless it maintains a PE therein,[2019] the State concerned might not be able to tax the profits of the resident enterprise at all, neither at the level of the resident enterprise (the profits are allocated to the non-resident enterprise and offset against that enterprise's losses)[2020] nor at the level of the non-resident enterprise (the non-resident enterprise is not taxable under Article 7 on its profits without a PE).[2021]

It can be responded that a negative conflict of allocation arises if the allegedly discriminating State but not the other Contracting States allocates the profits of the resident enterprise to the non-resident enterprise under a group taxation regime. Thus, the allegedly discriminating State is allowed to tax the non-resident enterprise. Whether a PE exists or to which enterprise it might belong is not an issue (*see* already section §4.04[C][2][d]). Yet, although this is true from a tax treaty perspective, there might be no basis for taxation of the non-resident enterprise under domestic tax law.[2022] Cross-border group taxation, therefore, could prevent the allegedly discriminating State from taxing the profits that were initially derived by the resident enterprise

2018. Avery Jones, Baker, et al. 2011a, 566; Avery Jones, Baker, et al. 2011b, 207.
2019. *See also* Raad 1986, 193; moreover, Silva 2016b, 84; Silva 2013, 109; Rust 2003b, 661.
2020. *See* Rödder and Schönfeld 2011, 887 ('hat zwar eine Betriebsstätte, aber keine Einkünfte').
2021. *See* Rödder and Schönfeld 2011, 887 ('hat die Einkünfte, aber keine Betriebsstätte').
2022. *See*, for instance, Rödder and Schönfeld 2011, 888.

even though the tax treaty would allow taxing these profits at the level of the non-resident enterprise.[2023]

A group taxation regime could accommodate for such unintended tax consequences by providing for a recapturing mechanism.[2024] If taxable profits of a resident enterprise are offset against losses of a non-resident enterprise, these profits could be recaptured at the level of the resident enterprise as soon as the non-resident enterprise earns profits. This would not only ensure that taxable profits are indeed taxed and that no double non-taxation arises[2025] but also that they are taxed in the State of the resident enterprise, that is in the allegedly discriminating State. Alternatively, in the case of a negative conflict of allocation, if the other Contracting State does not take the transferred profits into account,[2026] the allegedly discriminating State could subject the non-resident enterprise to tax under its domestic tax law without any treaty limitation.

Nevertheless, Article 24(5) cannot substitute for such a recapturing mechanism or basis for taxation. As long as the allegedly discriminating State does not introduce a recapturing mechanism or a basis for taxation of non-resident enterprises that have no PE but participate in a tax group, it can argue that inevitably linked but relevant differences in legal circumstances between resident and non-resident enterprises exist in a concrete case. If a resident enterprise transfers its profits to a resident enterprise, these profits remain taxable at the level of a different taxpayer or are offset against losses and economically taxed at a later point in time (notably, when a lower loss carry-forward leads to taxation of future profits). If a resident enterprise transfers profits to a non-resident enterprise, by contrast, these profits may remain untaxed and permanent tax advantages might arise that are not available in purely domestic situations.[2027]

2023. John F. Avery Jones, Philip Baker, et al. argue that Article 24(5) cannot require a Contracting State to permit a transfer of the tax position of its subsidiary to a non-resident parent company because Articles 7 and 21 would not permit that Contracting State to tax such income when it is not income attributable to a PE of the parent company – in brief, the treaty cannot require under Article 24(5) what it does not permit under Articles 7 and 21. *See* Avery Jones, Baker, et al. 2011a fn. 123 on p. 566; Avery Jones, Baker, et al. 2011b fn. 191 on p. 207. It is worth mentioning, however, that Articles 7 and 21 permit non-taxation of resident and non-resident enterprises. This means that Article 24(5) would be fully in line with Articles 7 and 21 if it required a Contracting State to apply a group taxation regime to its subsidiary and a non-resident parent company even if that State would no longer be allowed to tax that subsidiary's income. Articles 7 and 21, therefore, only support a particular domestic objective (safeguarding the exercise of taxing rights with regard to a resident subsidiary) which must still be brought into balance with the objectives of Article 24(5).

2024. *See also* Raad 2008, 157–158, who states that a State will not have tax jurisdiction over non-resident enterprises and, therefore, it is understandable not to permit cross-border group taxation but who also emphasizes that it would be possible to only deduct foreign losses of non-resident enterprises and to implement a 'clawback' mechanism.

2025. On these concerns, *see* Hohenwarter 2010, 609.

2026. *See*, for instance, Rust 2015b m.no. 113 ('the profit transfer from one State to another State would lead to a loss of tax revenue in the first State and the second State would generally not take the transferred profit into account'); Rust 2015c m.no. 166; Gosch 2012b, 702; Gosch 2012a, 18; Hohenwarter 2010, 609; Rust 2003b, 661.

2027. *See* Rust 2015b m.no. 113; Rust 2015c m.no. 166; Hohenwarter 2010, 609; moreover, Silva 2016b, 84; Silva 2013, 109; Rust 2010, 642; Rust 2003b, 660–661.

While, under Article 24(5), the non-residence of the shareholder cannot be used as grounds for different tax treatment of the resident taxpayer in question, a certain allocation of taxing rights at the level of the resident taxpayer may lead to different tax treatment without violating Article 24(5). Article 24 does not aim at modifying the allocation of taxing rights that has been agreed on by the Contracting States.[2028] On the contrary, Article 24(3) explicitly relies on a particular allocation of taxing rights as it presupposes an attribution of profits or property to a PE. Article 24(4) was even designed to protect the allocation of taxing rights by preventing States from turning juridical into economic double taxation (*see* Chapter 3 section §3.03[E][1]). Article 24(5) might also aim at ensuring that a Contracting State does not tax resident enterprises less favourably when their shareholders are non-residents and when that State, therefore, has lost taxing rights with regard to these shareholders (*see* Chapter 3 section §3.03[E][2]). Since the non-discrimination provisions do not touch upon the allocation of taxing rights but rather aim at preserving the allocation, they should not be interpreted as requiring the allegedly discriminating State to disregard its taxing rights in favour of the other Contracting State, notably, by effectively forfeiting taxing rights over income of resident enterprises only in cross-border situations.

If a State withholds tax benefits of a group taxation regime to a resident enterprise because this enterprise's shareholder is a non-resident, this may constitute prima facie discrimination with a 'but for' test. If a State withholds tax benefits of a group taxation regime to a resident enterprise because it is afraid of not being able to exercise its taxing rights over income of this resident enterprise, the grounds for different tax treatment are not, as such, in opposition to Article 24(5) even if there is an inevitable link to the shareholder's residence. In such a case, the State wants to make use of its legitimate taxing rights and uses the shareholder's residence as a reasonable proxy. Article 24(5) should not contravene this intention by forcing the State to allocate income to another non-resident taxpayer under a group taxation regime if this taxpayer is not within that State's full tax jurisdiction.[2029]

2028. *See also*, to this effect, Silva 2016b, 84; Silva 2013, 109 ('the interpretation and application of tax treaty non-discrimination should not affect the allocation of taxing rights').

2029. *See also*, to this effect, Silva 2016b, 83–89; Rust 2015b m.no. 113; Rust 2015c m.nos. 166–166a; Allevato Neto 2015, 562–564; Silva 2013, 109; Bammens 2012, 456–457; Lüdicke 2011c, 846–847; Avery Jones, Baker, et al. 2011a, 535, 537; Avery Jones, Baker, et al. 2011b, 179, 180; Boulogne 2011, 176; Raad 2008, 160–161; Avery Jones and Bobbett 2008, 53; Rust 2003b, 660–661; Goldberg and Glicklich 1992, 99; Ault and Tillinghast 1992, 277; Raad 1986, 192–193. Bammens and Vanistendael 2016, sec. 2.5.1.2.2 also mention that a reason why Article 24(5) would not apply in a specific case involving a group treatment regime may be the fact that the allocation rules of the treaty preclude the allegedly discriminating State, that is the State of the subsidiary, from taking account of the non-resident parent's taxable results, but that should be assessed on a case-by-case basis. *See*, however, Scapa Passalacqua and Henie 2005, 39, 44 ('[t]here are also arguments in favour of allowing a ... [resident] subsidiary of a foreign parent company to be allowed to grant a group contribution to its foreign parent company'); Lang 2003a, 258–259; and German Federal Fiscal Court (Bundesfinanzhof), 9 February 2011, I R 54, 55/10 (commented by Rust 2013a; Lüdicke 2011c), which decided that a loss of taxing rights does not justify different tax treatment as justifications are not available under Article 24(5) and, therefore, is willing to accept that cross-border consolidation will lead to double non-taxation; concurring Freeden, Häck, and Schaumburg 2017 m.no. 4.65; Wassermeyer and Schwenke 2016 m.no. 101; Gosch 2012b, 701–705; Gosch 2012a, 17–22;

It is difficult to formally distinguish between cases in which a State is displeased with losing taxing rights with regard to non-resident shareholders and, therefore, taxes foreign-owned enterprises more heavily than domestic-owned enterprises and cases in which a State is afraid of losing taxing rights with regard to resident enterprises and, therefore, taxes foreign-owned enterprises more heavily than domestic-owned enterprises (i.e., no group taxation between resident and non-resident enterprises). Nevertheless, a substantive distinction must be made. In both situations, the State might initially be unable to tax a resident enterprise if it extends the group taxation benefits under Article 24(5) and transfers the profits of that resident enterprise to a non-resident enterprise in order to offset them against foreign losses. If the group taxation regime aims only at providing temporary benefits, such temporary benefits should not be denied under Article 24(5) even if a non-resident shareholder is involved. However, if the State would be unable to tax those transferred profits on a definite basis, no discrimination should be established. Thus, if an extension of its group consolidation regime to non-resident enterprises would not only grant tax benefits that are possible in purely domestic situations (in particular, liquidity or cash-flow advantages) but would lead to definite benefits that are contrary to both the purpose of the group taxation regime (only temporary benefits: the profits should be taxed later in time) and the allocation of taxing rights under the tax treaty (the allegedly discriminating State is allowed to tax the profits of its resident enterprises), a denial of group taxation benefits does not constitute discrimination because of the shareholder's residence. Inevitably linked but relevant differences in legal circumstances with regard to the taxing rights over income of resident group members prevent comparability.

This domestic purpose of not losing taxing rights over income of resident group members could be reinforced by the fact that the group taxation regime allows PEs of non-resident enterprises to consolidate with resident enterprises. Although Article 24(3) already requires group taxation (*see* section §4.04[C][2]), such a scope and design would support the objective of granting benefits only in situations when the taxing rights are not endangered and denying benefits in other cases when a loss of taxing rights could be triggered. This purpose could further be substantiated by the fact that the domestic tax law generally prohibits resident enterprises from consolidating with non-resident enterprises regardless of whether that non-resident enterprise is a shareholder. Such a scope and design of the group taxation regime would emphasize that the State's concerns and considerations in drafting the measure under scrutiny did not contravene the objectives of Article 24(5) but were rather driven by the objective of consolidating taxable profits and losses without creating permanent tax advantages. Although the group taxation regime would still distinguish based on residence, it would not discriminate because of the shareholder's residence. It would not discriminate against all non-resident shareholders (those maintaining a PE would be allowed to

critically, for instance, Kusch and Schöneborn 2012; Mössner 2011, 349–350 (but concurring so far as Article 24(5) is concerned); Mitschke 2011; Frotscher 2011; Rödder and Schönfeld 2011; Dötsch 2011; Behrens 2011; on a preceding decision (29 January 2003, I R 6/99, '*Delaware*'), moreover, Rust 2003b.

participate with their taxable income) and would discriminate against other non-resident enterprises as well (for instance, against non-resident subsidiaries and sister companies unless they maintain a PE). In terms of comparability, the fact that a group taxation regime would affect the allocation of taxing rights and thus the taxation of resident group members beyond liquidity or cash-flow advantages would render these non-resident enterprises incomparable to resident enterprises for the purposes of Article 24(5) even if, in a concrete case, a change in the shareholder's residence leads to a change in tax treatment.

[4] Grouping Between Resident Enterprises

It appears to be justified to prohibit cross-border consolidation in order to avoid double non-taxation of resident enterprises. If two resident enterprises have a common non-resident parent company, however, they may want to consolidate their profits and losses without necessarily including their parent company in the tax group. If a group taxation regime presupposes a resident parent company for establishing a tax group, consolidation is denied unless Article 24(5) can be relied on.

Assume that two resident sister companies of State A are both owned by a non-resident company of State B. If the two sister companies were both owned by a resident enterprise of State A, they could benefit from group taxation. All profits and losses of the two sister companies would be consolidated. However, since the parent company is a non-resident enterprise, each company is taxed separately (*see* Figure 4.23). This raises the question of whether discrimination because of residence under Article 24(5) is at hand if, in a purely domestic situation, a tax group could be established without including the common parent company.

Figure 4.23 Resident Enterprises and a Non-resident Parent Company (a)

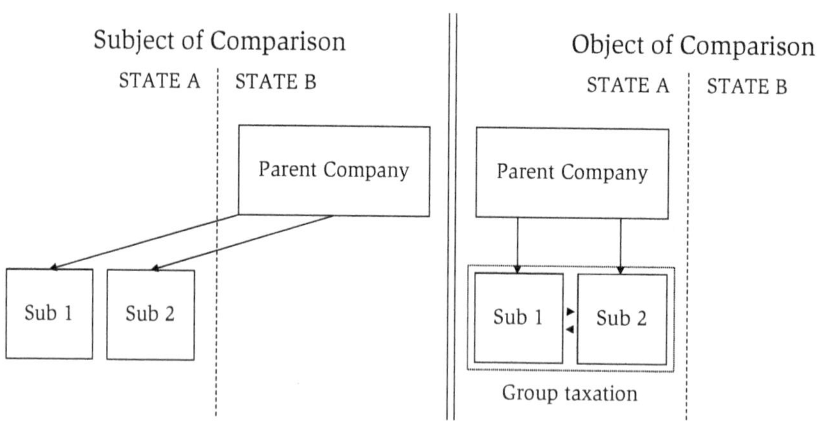

If group taxation between two resident sister companies is denied because of their shareholder's residence, a 'but for' test establishes prima facie discrimination. A change in the shareholder's residence leads to a change in tax treatment. On a substantive level, a potential loss of taxing rights cannot be brought forward as a justification. A change in the parent company's residence may, of course, lead to a change in taxing rights as far as the income and capital of the parent company is concerned. Such differences in circumstances, however, amount to protected differences in tax liability and residence under Article 24(5).[2030] Also, there are no linked differences in circumstances with regard to the income and capital of the resident sister companies. Their profits remain taxable in the allegedly discriminating State even if they are consolidated under a group taxation regime regardless of whether there is a resident or non-resident shareholder.[2031]

The fact that certain residents, notably, resident individuals and tax-exempt corporations such as non-profit organizations, cannot act as a common shareholder in order to establish a sufficient link between two resident sister companies does not avoid discrimination.[2032] A change in residence with a 'but for' test does not inevitably transform a company into an individual or a business organization into a non-profit organization. Accordingly, there exist no inevitably linked differences in circumstances that could prevent comparability on such a basis. A group taxation regime that distinguishes between foreign-owned and domestic-owned enterprises, therefore, discriminates because of the shareholder's residence without providing for any legitimate explanation that would be based on inevitably linked attributes. Consequently, under Article 24(5), the two resident sister companies should be allowed to establish a tax group and to consolidate their profits and losses.[2033]

According to John F. Avery Jones, Philip Baker, et al., this is only true as long as it is possible to consolidate profits and losses of two resident sister companies without including their common parent company in a purely domestic situation (or when the taxation of their parent company is not affected by the substance of the grouping process even if the parent company is involved in the computation or making returns of the combined profits and losses).[2034] A group taxation regime may require including

2030. *See*, for example, Papotti 2003, 321–322.

2031. *See also* Brugger 2008, 198, who mentions that Austria, as the allegedly discriminating State, has a right to tax the profits of resident subsidiaries irrespective of whether the participation of the non-resident holding company in these resident subsidiaries can be attributed to a PE in that State; the intention to safeguard the right to tax the profits, therefore, does not serve as a justification under Article 24(5).

2032. *See*, for example, Papotti 2003, 322.

2033. *See also*, to this effect, Silva 2016b, 89–90, 97–98; Vanistendael 2016, 251; Allevato Neto 2015, 560–562; Silva 2013, 109, 113–114; Ismer 2012, 824; Raad 2008, 161–162; Staringer 2005, 498–499.

2034. Avery Jones, Baker, et al. 2011a, 566–567, 571–575; Avery Jones, Baker, et al. 2011b, 206–208, 212–215. *See also* Rust 2015b m.no. 113; Rust 2015c m.no. 166. In contrast to these views, the Article 24 Discussion Draft 2007 states that, as Article 24(5) is limited to the taxation of the resident enterprise itself and generally excludes issues related to the taxation of the group to which the enterprise belongs, no consolidation of two subsidiaries of a foreign parent would be required under Article 24(5). *See* OECD, Article 24 Discussion Draft 2007, para. 14. However, the OECD Commentary does not explicitly deal with this situation of two resident subsidiaries. *See* 2008–2017 OECD Commentary on Article 24, para. 77 ('paragraph 5 cannot have the effect to force the State to allow such consolidation between a resident company and a *non-resident parent* company'; emphasis added). *See*, moreover, Raad 1986,

the parent company, in particular if all income is allocated vertically to the parent company or if subsidiaries are treated as fiscally transparent and cease to exist for tax purposes (*see* Figure 4.24). In a purely domestic situation, sister companies, therefore, might be unable to consolidate their income without the inclusion of their common parent company. Conversely, the parent company's involvement might be indispensable as only the parent company may remain effectively subjected to taxation.[2035]

Figure 4.24 Resident Enterprises and a Non-resident Parent Company (b)

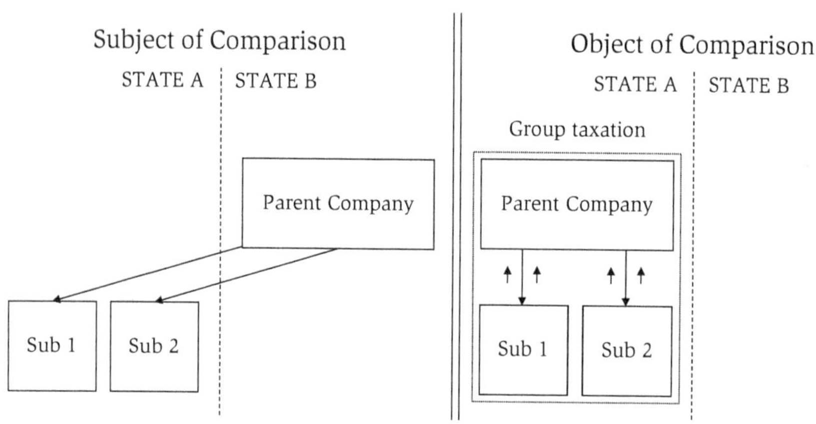

Arguably, cross-border situations should not be treated more favourably than domestic situations by allowing group taxation without a parent company. If a group taxation regime of a State requires participation of a resident parent company, Article 24(5) can neither obligate that State to include a non-resident parent company (*see* section §4.04[C][3]) nor to modify its group taxation system so that certain group structures are allowed in cross-border situations only. The true cause of the different tax treatment and the dissimilarity between foreign-owned and domestic-owned enterprises is the difference in the parent company's tax position and not, as such, non-resident ownership.[2036] A change in the parent company's residence inevitably leads to a change in its tax position with regard to its participation in a tax group. It follows that foreign-owned enterprises are not comparable to domestic-owned enterprises that benefit from group taxation because the former cannot include their common parent company in a tax group even though domestic tax law requires doing so whereas the latter can include their common parent company in a tax group and thereby fulfil all requirements for group taxation. If such differences in legal circumstances are treated as relevant under Article 24(5) even though they depend on

192, who is sceptical about consolidation between two resident sister companies under Article 24(5) if the domestic tax law does not allow consolidation without inclusion of the common parent company; to this effect, also Ault and Tillinghast 1992, 277–278.

2035. Avery Jones, Baker, et al. 2011a, 574–575; Avery Jones, Baker, et al. 2011b, 214.

2036. Avery Jones, Baker, et al. 2011a, 574–575; Avery Jones, Baker, et al. 2011b, 214.

residence, comparability can only be established with domestic-owned enterprises that do not participate in group taxation. In that case, no less favourable tax treatment arises.[2037]

Prohibited grounds for different tax treatment, that is the residence of the parent company, may be inherently connected to potentially legitimate grounds for different tax treatment, that is the non-participation of the parent company in a tax group that prevents group taxation in a purely domestic situation. Whether the common parent company can be part of a tax group depends on its residence. If the common parent company is a non-resident enterprise, it cannot participate in group taxation, and its subsidiaries do not benefit either. If the common parent company is a resident enterprise, it can participate in group taxation and its subsidiaries benefit as well. While the non-participation of a non-resident parent company in a tax group does not violate the ownership non-discrimination clause (*see* again section §4.04[C][3]), this does not necessarily explain why it should be permissible to prohibit group taxation in all cases and in particular between two resident sister companies. In order to regard the fact that only a resident parent company can participate in a tax group as a relevant difference in circumstances, it is necessary to establish on a substantive basis why participation of the parent company is required and whether this reason is legitimate from a tax treaty perspective.

Various techniques are available for the purposes of treating a corporate group as a single economic unit: treating separate enterprises as fiscally transparent, transferring profits and/or losses vertically to a parent company, transferring profits and/or losses vertically to a subsidiary, transferring profits and/or losses vertically or horizontally to any group member, etc. All of these techniques may lead to identical results. Thus, a State should not be able to circumvent the non-discrimination obligations of Article 24(5) by slightly modifying its group taxation system. If a resident holding company does not earn any income but only holds substantial shareholdings in two resident sister companies, it initially does not matter whether a group taxation regime allows consolidation or transfer of income between these two sister companies alone or requires allocating their income to the resident holding company and thereby integrating taxation of all three companies to a fundamental degree. In a cross-border situation involving a non-resident holding company, however, the first system would violate the non-discrimination obligations of Article 24(5) if it prohibited group taxation between the two resident sister companies, whereas the second system could arguably be maintained because tax treatment that is more favourable of cross-border situations is not required.[2038]

Instead of relying on formal differences between group taxation regimes, it should be considered why a domestic group taxation regime requires a parent company to participate in group taxation. This requirement may create inevitably linked but

2037. *See also* Raad 1986, 192, who argues that the implied 'same circumstances' requirement appears to prohibit consolidation under Article 24(5) as the object of comparison (two resident subsidiaries with a resident parent company) cannot consolidate without inclusion of the parent company.

2038. *See also* Trenkwalder 2005, 417.

relevant differences in legal circumstances and thereby outweigh the aims of the non-discrimination clause of Article 24(5) only if it pursues a genuine reason and is not merely a matter of legal technique or administrative obligations.

The fact that the domestic tax law does not stipulate any particular technique for consolidating two sister companies should not suffice for denying comparability and discrimination.[2039] It could just as well be argued that, if it is not possible for foreign-owned enterprises to include their common parent company in a tax group even though domestic tax law requires doing so, this is only a legal consequence of their foreign ownership and, thus, a result of discrimination. In other words, as the group taxation regime discriminates against foreign-owned enterprises under Article 24(5), it is only logical that it provides for no technique that would allow non-discriminatory taxation. This alone should be no reason for denying comparability or justifying different tax treatment under Article 24(5) regarding consolidation of foreign-owned enterprises without their common parent company.[2040] John F. Avery Jones, Philip Baker, et al. also argue that, if the parent company is only involved in group taxation as a matter of computation and making returns, and foreign-owned enterprises remain effectively subjected to taxation in the same manner as domestic-owned enterprises, Article 24(5) may potentially apply.[2041] Otherwise, States could easily circumvent the non-discrimination obligations by making the parent company responsible for some purely technical matters of consolidation, arguably in both domestic and cross-border situations, and subsequently requiring the parent company's residence for group taxation.[2042]

The situation might be different, however, if group taxation benefits regarding profits and losses of sister companies are linked to tax consequences or concessions that can only be applied at the level of or by including their parent company. It has been argued that a group of corporations can consolidate only when there is a common parent company because only when dividends received by that parent company are free of tax can transactions between sister companies in the group be allowed to proceed on a tax-deferred basis without concern that these might involve shifts of value amounting in substance to constructive dividends (hidden profit distributions) to the shareholder(s).[2043] It could also be argued that consolidation of profits and losses of resident sister companies should only be possible if shareholdings in them are tax neutral at the level of a common parent company in order to avoid inappropriate instances of double taxation or deduction.[2044] Yet, the force of these arguments is

2039. *See*, however, Hohenwarter 2010, 654, who believes that such a consolidation would jeopardize the integrity of the Austrian vertical system for allocating group income.

2040. *See also*, to this effect, Silva 2016b, 100–101; Allevato Neto 2015, 566–572; Silva 2013, 113–114; Boulogne 2011, 176; Papotti 2003 fn. 17 on p. 322; moreover, Bagci 2019.

2041. Avery Jones, Baker, et al. 2011a, 567, 571; Avery Jones, Baker, et al. 2011b, 208, 212. *See also*, with regard to an intermediate group company from an Austrian perspective, Hohenwarter 2010, 609–613.

2042. *See also* Allevato Neto 2015, 569.

2043. Ault and Tillinghast 1992, 277–278.

2044. *See* Masui 2004, 40–42 ('[a] more general solution [for inappropriate instances of double taxation or deduction] is to grant a parent company a full participation exemption for both dividends and capital gains/losses').

subject to scrutiny and must be weighed against the objective of preventing discrimination under Article 24(5). It might be doubtful, for instance, whether tax neutrality of shareholdings in resident sister companies is indeed needed if the common parent company is not included in the tax group and two separate layers of tax (subsidiary – parent company) are fully maintained. Double taxation or deduction of profits or losses first directly at the level of the sister companies and then indirectly at the level of the parent company in the form of capital gains or losses would be nothing more than a result of treating the parent company as a separate taxable entity without being inconsistent with a combination of the taxation on the resident sister companies.[2045]

Therefore, it is necessary to evaluate why a domestic group taxation regime does not allow group taxation without a shareholder or parent company, whether these reasons are reflected in inevitably linked differences in circumstances in a concrete case, and whether these reasons are legitimate from the perspective of Article 24(5). This allows answering whether the non-participation of a non-resident parent company in a tax group leads to relevant differences in circumstances with regard to resident enterprises that claim group taxation or whether these differences in circumstances are irrelevant and may be ignored. In the latter case, Article 24(5) would allow a comparison of foreign-owned enterprises (when the parent company does not participate in group taxation) to domestic-owned enterprises that participate in group taxation (because the parent company participates in group taxation as well) thereby establishing discrimination.

It should once again be emphasized that an obligatory technique of vertically allocating income to a parent company instead of allowing to choose the direction of a transfer of profits or losses does not, as such, suffice for inevitably linked but relevant differences in legal circumstances. While Article 24(5) does not require consolidation of taxable income of resident enterprises with non-taxable income of a non-resident parent company (*see* section §4.04[C][3]), it could require consolidation of taxable income of resident enterprises technically by allocating that income to a non-resident parent company and carving out that parent company's non-taxable income from consolidation. Raul-Angelo Papotti similarly argues that Article 24(5) should require an extension of full consolidation to a non-resident parent company even if that extension would be inconsistent with some basic principles of domestic taxation (i.e., only postponement and no infinite deferral of taxation on profits from intra-group transactions under a group consolidation regime).[2046] In addition, he suggests carving out the parent company's profits by relying on Article 7, which means that the parent company's income would be excluded from the consolidated amount (unless it is attributable to a PE).[2047] This apparently means that Article 24(5) should be applied

2045. On a similar argument, *see* Hohenwarter 2010, 612. *See also*, however, Hohenwarter 2010, 654.
2046. Papotti 2003, 322.
2047. Papotti 2003, 322.

without caring about taxability of income[2048] and only thereafter should all limitations imposed by Article 7 be considered.[2049]

An allocation without consolidation of taxable income to a non-resident parent company for group taxation purposes does not necessarily affect a State's taxing rights under a tax treaty.[2050] This allocation can be seen as a question of calculation, tax liability, or technicality that has no impact on a resident group member's tax treaty entitlement. Alternatively, if group members are effectively treated as fiscally transparent, a negative conflict of allocation may arise. In such a case, either no tax treaty benefits are available if the principles of the OECD Partnership Report, potentially implemented through Articles 3 and 11 of the Multilateral Convention, are followed,[2051] or group members become PEs of the non-resident parent company if the principles of the OECD Partnership Report are not applied. Such PEs also exist and permit taxation when both Contracting States adhere to fiscal transparency and, in that way, avoid a negative conflict of allocation. All solutions safeguard taxing rights (*see* already section §4.04[C][2][d]) and, therefore, allow extending group taxation to foreign-owned resident enterprises without leading to unintended tax consequences.

The allegedly discriminating State may submit that, after allocating income of a resident group member to a non-resident parent company, it would not be able to tax that income under its domestic tax law for technical reasons even though it retained taxing rights and would be allowed to tax under the tax treaty.[2052] It is then effectively arguing that, since it discriminates against foreign-owned resident enterprises and has not yet found a satisfactory solution for non-discriminatory tax treatment that would allow it to fully exercise its taxing rights, its distinction should be justified by rendering circumstances incomparable.

It is not clear whether this argument can succeed under Article 24(5). In order to avoid unintended tax consequences, the allegedly discriminating State can itself accommodate non-resident ownership and adapt its domestic tax law accordingly.[2053] On the other hand, many if not all differences in legal circumstances between protected and unprotected persons could be eliminated by a State through changes in its domestic or tax treaty law, including differences in taxing rights. Therefore, it is doubtful whether such differences should be regarded as irrelevant for comparability purposes for this reason alone. If a group taxation regime is designed in a way that Article 24(5) would prohibit the allegedly discriminating State from taxing its resident

2048. Papotti 2003, 322.
2049. This solution, however, could raise conceptual problems if it is assumed that Article 7 carves out profits but not losses, that is if it does not prohibit the allegedly discriminating State from deducting foreign losses even when Article 7 exempts or carves out foreign profits.
2050. *See also* Schnitger 2014, 588; Lüdicke 2011c, 846; Lüdicke 2011a; Schnitger and Berliner 2011; concurring Behrens 2012, 489; differently, for instance, Schwenke 2013, 45; Gosch 2012b, 704–705; Gosch 2012a, 22; Boulogne 2011, 176 ('the inclusion of a non-resident enterprise in a tax group would conflict with the allocation [of taxing rights]'); German Federal Fiscal Court (Bundesfinanzhof), 9 February 2011, I R 54, 55/10.
2051. *See also*, to this effect, Pinetz and Spies 2014b, 513–514.
2052. *See*, for instance, Pinetz and Spies 2014b, 512; moreover, Schnitger and Berliner 2011, 760–761, who conclude from a German perspective that there may be no domestic legal basis for making full use of taxing rights and, therefore, favour legislative amendments.
2053. *See also* Pinetz and Spies 2014a, 475.

group members even though only their income would be consolidated at the level of a common non-resident parent company, or if such a consolidation is inherently connected to certain tax consequences that require participation of a common parent company in a tax group, this could justify differences in tax treatment due to inevitably linked but relevant differences in legal circumstances in a concrete case. Just as it appears doubtful whether Article 24(3) requires a domestic group taxation system concerning both profits and losses to accommodate to a non-discriminatory transfer of profits but not losses (*see* section §4.04[C][2][b]), it appears doubtful whether Article 24(5) requires establishing a legal basis for group taxation of non-resident enterprises in order to exercise taxing rights over income of resident enterprises.

To sum up, regardless of how a group taxation regime is specifically designed and whether it allows offsetting profits and losses in a domestic context without a parent company, group taxation must be extended to resident enterprises with a common non-resident parent company if all of these enterprises would be eligible for group taxation in a purely domestic situation. Article 24(5) can even require including a non-resident parent company in a tax group for technical purposes of consolidation, calculation, and tax liability without including that company's income thereby allowing foreign-owned resident enterprises to consolidate their income without touching foreign profits or losses of a non-resident parent company. However, if reasons beyond mere technicalities and design decisions can explain why a parent company must actively participate in a tax group, relevant differences in legal circumstances may arise. Such differences, despite their inevitable link to residence, would then justify differences in tax treatment and would lead to incomparability between foreign-owned and domestic-owned enterprises with regard to a group taxation regime.

[5] Concurrent Application of Non-discrimination Rules

[a] Application to One Taxpayer

Article 24 contains several non-discrimination rules that may overlap.[2054] An overlap does not imply a conflict. All non-discrimination provisions of Article 24 aim at preventing disadvantageous tax treatment. Although they may be broader, narrower, or simply different in their scope, it is hardly possible that one non-discrimination provision requires something that another non-discrimination provision prohibits. Accordingly, no priority between the non-discrimination rules needs to be established, including Article 24(4) and (5).[2055] If a domestic tax measure refers to more than one protected characteristic for providing disadvantageous tax treatment, however, some conceptual problems with respect to comparability may arise with a 'but for' test.

2054. *See*, with regard to Article 24(1) and (3), Vogel 1970, 351; in detail, Bammens and Vanistendael 2016, sec. 6.1.4; Haslehner 2012; Bammens 2012, 485–492.
2055. Before 2008, the OECD Commentary argued that, in certain cases, Article 24(4) might be seen as a more specific provision and, therefore, should take precedence over Article 24(5). This view, however, is widely rejected in the literature; Article 24(4) and Article 24(5) can be applied simultaneously. *See supra* n. 1801.

A domestic tax measure may simultaneously discriminate because of nationality and because of residence. It may disadvantage all foreigners and all non-residents, including non-resident foreigners, by granting tax benefits only to resident nationals. If a national is a non-resident, that individual suffers a disadvantage; if a resident is a foreigner, that person suffers a disadvantage; and, if a person is both a non-resident and a foreigner, the individual suffers a disadvantage as well. Article 24(1) prohibits discrimination because of nationality but not because of residence. Article 24(3) prohibits discrimination because of residence as far as a PE is concerned but not because of nationality. It could thus be argued that a domestic tax measure that simultaneously disadvantages non-residents and foreigners does not violate Article 24(1) and (3) when a non-resident foreigner is at stake.[2056] If everything except for nationality and inevitably linked attributes must be identical for comparability under Article 24(1), no different tax treatment between a non-resident foreigner and a non-resident national can be established as both incur a disadvantage. If everything except for residence and inevitably linked attributes must be identical for comparability under Article 24(3), no different tax treatment between a non-resident foreigner maintaining a PE and a resident foreigner can be established as both incur a disadvantage. Similarly, if a non-resident foreigner is deemed to be a national under Article 24(1), that person remains discriminated against because of residence. If that person is deemed to be a resident under Article 24(3), the discrimination remains because of nationality. A change in the protected characteristic does not influence the tax treatment, which should arguably imply that the protected characteristic is not the cause for the tax disadvantage at issue.

Since Article 24(1) protects foreigners and, since Article 24(3) protects non-residents, Article 24(1) and (3) taken together must protect non-resident foreigners as well.[2057] In order to reach this apparently meaningful result, the comparability test could be relaxed by comparing a non-resident foreigner to a resident national under both Article 24(1) and (3) even when nationality and residence are not inevitably linked to each other in a concrete case. Since Article 24(3) condemns certain tax distinctions based on residence, this is an indication that such tax distinctions should not render Article 24(1) ineffective. Corresponding differences in circumstances, therefore, should be ignored under Article 24(1) when a non-resident foreigner is at stake. A non-resident foreigner may consequently be compared to a resident national. As a resident national receives tax treatment that is more favourable, Article 24(1) read in the context of Article 24(3) requires an extension of such favourable treatment to a

2056. *See also* Haslehner 2016c, 21; Haslehner 2016a m.no. 8; Haslehner 2012, 597; Haslehner 2009, 90; Bammens 2012, 485–486; to this effect, Avery Jones, Baker, et al. 2011b, 220; Avery Jones, Baker, et al. 2011a, 580.

2057. *See*, to this effect, Bammens and Vanistendael 2016, sec. 6.1.4.2; Haslehner 2016c, 21–23; Haslehner 2016a m.no. 8; Silva 2016b, 119–220; Rust 2015b m.no. 55; Haslehner 2012; Haslehner 2009, 90–91; Bammens 2012, 485–486, 491–492. *See*, moreover, Avery Jones, Baker, et al. 2011b, 217; Avery Jones, Baker, et al. 2011a, 577, who state that the approach of considering Article 24 in the context of the rest of the treaty might suggest that, if a State has made a commitment against two different types of discrimination, they should be capable of being combined at least so long as it is possible to do so.

non-resident foreigner. Conversely, since Article 24(1) condemns certain tax distinctions based on nationality, this is an indication that such tax distinctions should not render Article 24(3) ineffective. Corresponding differences in circumstances (or the condition that favourable tax treatment is only granted to nationals),[2058] therefore, should be ignored under Article 24(3). Again, a non-resident foreigner may be compared to a resident national. This means that, with a 'but for' test, not only inevitably linked attributes but also all protected attributes, that is, all attributes that cannot constitute grounds for different tax treatment due to other non-discrimination rules leave comparability unaffected.[2059]

An alternative approach suggested by Werner Haslehner makes tax-treaty-compliant taxation the relevant baseline for non-discriminatory treatment. It applies the non-discrimination rules of Article 24 to hypothetical comparators in order to determine the appropriate tax treatment under a particular non-discrimination clause.[2060] A non-resident foreigner can only be compared to a non-resident national under Article 24(1) and to a resident foreigner under Article 24(3). If a domestic tax measure grants favourable tax treatment to resident nationals only, both hypothetical comparators initially suffer disadvantages, at least under domestic law. However, the lawful tax treatment of each hypothetical comparator should be determined and then compared to the actual tax treatment of the taxpayer in question. All measures in force in the allegedly discriminating State including tax treaty measures and other non-discrimination rules should be considered.

Under this approach, the appropriate comparator under Article 24(1), a non-resident national, could claim non-discriminatory tax treatment under Article 24(3) if that person maintains a PE. Thus, the tax treatment of the non-resident foreigner should be compared to that of a non-resident national who is taxed in accordance with the non-discrimination obligations of Article 24(3), that is no less favourable taxation on a PE than on resident enterprises carrying on the same activities. The appropriate comparator under Article 24(3), a resident foreigner, could claim non-discriminatory tax treatment under Article 24(1). Thus, the tax treatment of the non-resident foreigner should be compared to that of a resident foreigner who is taxed in accordance with the non-discrimination obligations of Article 24(1), that is no other or more burdensome

2058. *See*, to this effect, Avery Jones, Baker, et al. 2011b, 220; Avery Jones, Baker, et al. 2011a, 580, who mention the argument that foreign nationality could not be held against a person who is protected against residence discrimination because that would violate the nationality non-discrimination provision and thus, in applying a residence non-discrimination provision, one must posit either that this person should be treated as a national (this alternative approach also suggested by Werner Haslehner will be discussed below) or that this condition of being a national should be ignored such that the only reason left causing disadvantageous tax treatment is non-residence which, in turn, violates the residence non-discrimination provision.

2059. If such other non-discrimination provisions offer a lower level of protection than, for instance, Article 24(1) because they only prohibit taxation that is less favourable (para. 3) instead of other or more burdensome taxation or connected requirements (para. 1), protected differences in circumstances could only be disregarded for the purposes of claims that do not exceed this lower level of protection; differences in residence, therefore, would prevent comparability under Article 24(1) as far as connected requirements are concerned.

2060. Haslehner 2012, 598–602; Haslehner 2016c, 21–23; Haslehner 2016a m.no. 8.

taxation on a resident foreigner than on resident nationals situated in the same circumstances. In this way, both non-discrimination clauses may be applied simultaneously and assimilate the treatment of a non-resident foreigner to that of a resident national.[2061]

[b] Application to Two Taxpayers

While this alternative approach suggested by Werner Haslehner is very appealing, it also entails certain limitations that could allow States to circumvent the non-discrimination obligations of Article 24. A group taxation regime may allow transferring profits or losses between a contributing resident company and a receiving resident company only if these persons have a common resident shareholder. Group taxation is thus denied if a non-resident parent company is involved (*see* Figure 4.25). When applying Article 24(5) at the level of the contributing company, the non-resident parent company is deemed to be a resident. Nevertheless, group taxation can still be denied because the receiving company continues to have a non-resident parent company and, therefore, cannot participate in group taxation (*see* Figure 4.26).

Figure 4.25 Resident Enterprises and a Non-resident Parent Company (c)

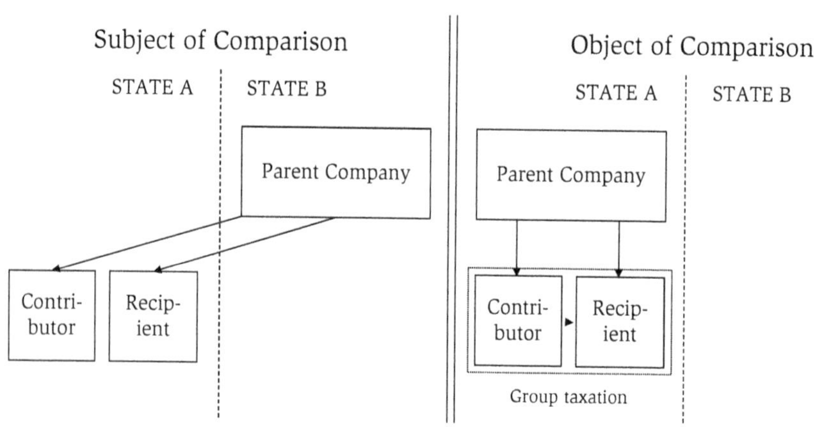

2061. *See also*, on combining Article 24(1), (3), and (5), Haslehner 2012, 605–607, and on combining non-discrimination rules in different tax treaties, Haslehner 2012, 610–616; moreover, Silva 2016b, 122–131.

Figure 4.26 Resident Enterprises and a Non-resident Parent Company (d)

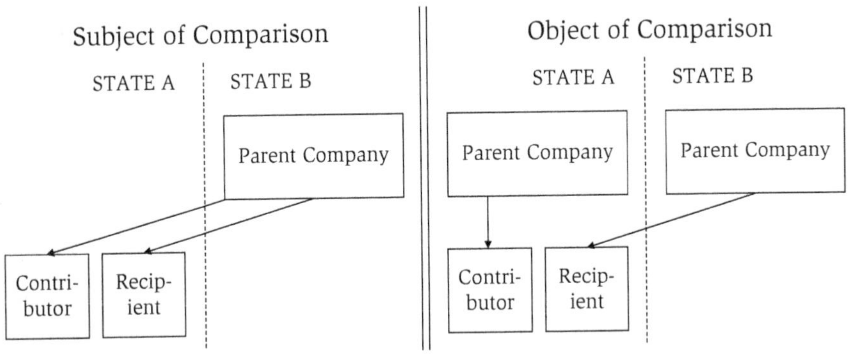

Article 24(5) protects the contributing company against discrimination because of its shareholder's residence, not against discrimination because of the fact that another person has a non-resident shareholder. Although that other person, the receiving company, is also protected against discrimination because of its shareholder's residence, this does not necessarily have impact on the lawful tax treatment of the contributing company. Thus, denying group taxation constitutes the lawful tax treatment of the contributing company because that company can rely on Article 24(5) only with regard to its own shareholder and not with regard to the receiving company's shareholder. As a consequence, the receiving company keeps its non-resident parent company. Its legal and factual position cannot be deemed to be different when Article 24(5) is applied at the level of the contributing company.

Although the contributing and the receiving company's shareholder is one and the same person, it is not necessarily clear why assumptions made for the purposes of establishing comparability under Article 24(5) at the level of the receiving company (the non-resident parent company is deemed to be a resident) should also be valid at the level of the contributing company. Given that Article 24(5) is applied independently at the level of different taxpayers, all assumptions should also be made independently without influencing each other. It is actually submitted with regard to Article 24(5) that a person may be deemed a resident for one purpose but remain a non-resident for another purpose even when only one taxpayer is potentially discriminated against. If a deduction of a payment to a non-resident shareholder is denied to a resident company, the 'recipient' of that payment is deemed to be a resident, but the 'shareholder' of that company remains a non-resident even though the recipient and the shareholder are one and the same person.[2062] If it is possible to deem a non-resident person a resident for one purpose (shareholder) but a non-resident for another purpose (recipient) when applying Article 24(5) at the level of one single taxpayer, it should be possible to deem a non-resident parent company a resident at the level of the contributing company but a non-resident at the level of the receiving company. Article 24(5) applied at the level

2062. *See*, Rust 2010, 643–644; moreover, Isakova 2015, 519.

of the contributing company does not require group taxation because a domestic-owned contributing company would also not be allowed to participate as long as the receiving company has a non-resident parent company. Conversely, Article 24(5) applied at the level of the receiving company does not require group taxation because a domestic-owned receiving company would also not be allowed to participate as long as the contributing company has a non-resident parent company.

If it is argued, by contrast, that the common non-resident parent company must be deemed to be a resident for both the contributing company and the receiving company as soon as Article 24(5) is applied to any of them[2063] because there is an inevitable link between the function of being the contributing company's parent company and that of being the receiving company's parent company not in law but in fact (*see* section §4.02[C][2]), situations remain in which Article 24(5) offers no relief from burdensome tax treatment. Assume that the contributing company and the receiving company are indirectly held by the same ultimate resident shareholder but each is directly owned by a different non-resident company. Group taxation is denied because each company is directly owned by a non-resident enterprise. If both were directly owned by a resident enterprise, group taxation would be possible (*see* Figure 4.27). Article 24(5) applied at the level of the contributing company deems that company's direct shareholder to be a resident, but group taxation is still denied because the receiving company is owned by a non-resident shareholder (*see* Figure 4.28). Article 24(5) applied at the level of the receiving company deems that company's direct shareholder to be a resident, but group taxation is still denied because the contributing company is owned by a non-resident shareholder.

2063. *See* Haslehner 2012, 613.

Figure 4.27 Resident Enterprises with Different Non-resident Shareholders (a)

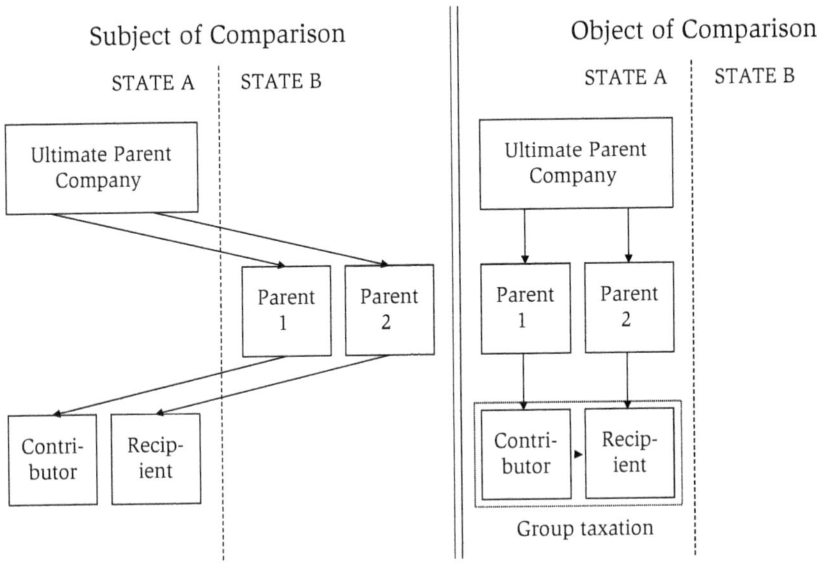

Figure 4.28 Resident Enterprises with Different Non-resident Shareholders (b)

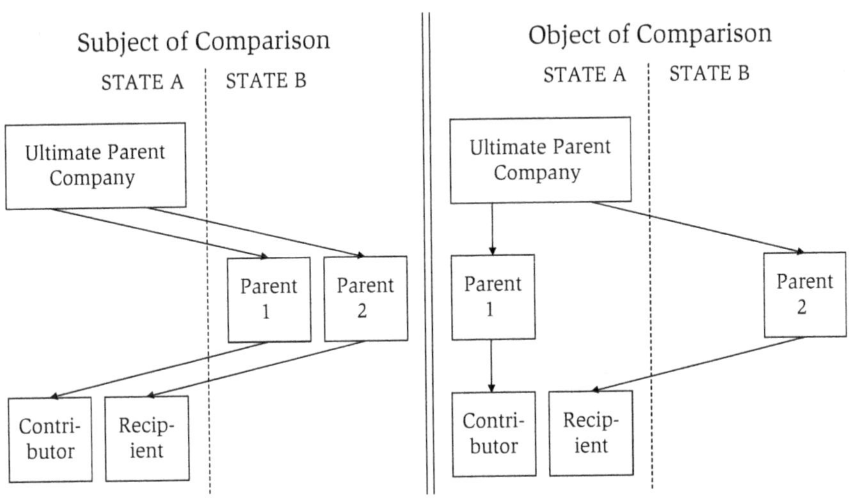

Whether the contributing company is allowed to transfer its profits or losses depends on the tax position of the receiving company, and vice versa. It could be argued that such complex discrimination cannot be relieved by Article 24(5) because a combined application of Article 24(5) at the level of different taxpayers fails due to the too narrow scope of the non-discrimination clause. Article 24(5) does not allow a company to claim discrimination based on the fact that another company is owned by a non-resident shareholder.[2064] Indeed, Article 24 only addresses specific persons and only protects against specific kinds of discrimination. It does not protect other persons against discrimination even if tax disadvantages arise for the same or similar reasons. For instance, Article 24(1) protects nationals against discrimination because of their nationality, but this nationality may be used as grounds for different tax treatment of other persons.[2065] With a 'but for' test, all characteristics of these other persons must remain identical even if they are also protected by a non-discrimination rule.

Nevertheless, if a joint assessment of spouses is only allowed when both spouses are nationals, it seems odd to deny their protection just because of the fact that they demand a *joint* assessment and that, consequently, each nationality matters for both of them. If the domestic tax measure under scrutiny prescribes legal consequences for both taxpayers, the protection against discrimination of both taxpayers should be considered in determining the non-discriminatory scope of application. In a group context, it is also difficult to see why the allegedly discriminating State should be able to avoid discrimination by interconnecting the requirements for group taxation of different taxpayers even though certain requirements are, in substance, rendered obsolete by the non-discrimination provisions. If the contributing company is treated differently because of the receiving company's shareholder without affecting the tax position of the receiving company, this treatment does not lead to discrimination under Article 24(5). However, if both the contributing company and the receiving company are treated differently because of the receiving company's shareholder as their tax treatment is connected or combined, it only makes sense to disregard the fact that the receiving company has a non-resident shareholder (or the condition that the receiving company must have a resident shareholder) when applying Article 24(5) at the level of the contributing company. After all, if the contributing company does not participate in group taxation, the receiving company cannot participate either, and vice versa. This approach allows the contributing company to participate in group taxation which in turn allows the receiving company to make use of Article 24(5) and to successfully claim non-discriminatory tax treatment as well.[2066]

Similar issues can also arise under Article 24(3) when at least two different enterprises must rely on non-discrimination provisions in order to successfully consolidate or transfer their profits or losses. For instance, if a non-resident enterprise claims group taxation between its PE and a foreign-owned resident enterprise, it is not clear whether it can succeed (*see* Figure 4.29). Group taxation could be denied not

2064. *See*, to this effect, Haslehner 2012, 613–614; differently (although not explicitly considering formal problems of a simultaneous application) Saccardo 2003, 279.

2065. *See* Raad 1986, 77, who gives the example of a child allowance made dependent on the nationality of the child as not contrary to Article 24(1); similarly, Rust 2015c m.no. 52; Kubaile 2013 m.no. 18; Moritz 2003, 232.

2066. *See also* Silva 2016b, 126–127 with reference to Haslehner 2012, 614, who describes this approach as 'an *integrated view* according to which a group member may claim the protection of any non-discrimination clauses even those that protect formally other group members, but which are materially relevant as they affect the tax position of the whole group' (original emphasis).

because of its non-residence, which is prohibited under Article 24(3),[2067] but because of the fact that it envisages group taxation with a foreign-owned resident enterprise although it cannot rely on Article 24(5). Similarly, that foreign-owned resident enterprise could be denied group taxation not because of its non-resident shareholder, which would be prohibited under Article 24(5), but because it claims group taxation with a PE of a non-resident enterprise although it cannot rely on Article 24(3).[2068]

Figure 4.29 PE and a Foreign-Owned Group Subsidiary

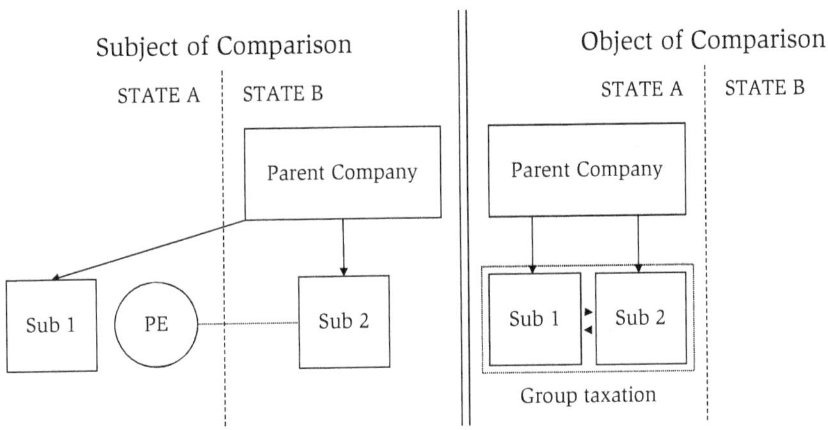

Issues may also arise when PEs of two non-resident enterprises want to form a tax group. If the PEs were resident enterprises, they would be eligible for group benefits. Since the PEs are only part of non-resident enterprises and since non-resident enterprises cannot participate in group taxation, each PE is taxed separately (*see* Figure 4.30). This again raises the question of whether discrimination because of residence is at hand. A State could argue that it is not discriminating against a PE of a non-resident enterprise because of its residence but because of the other enterprise's residence.

2067. In addition, if the PE of the non-resident enterprise (Sub 2) is deemed to be a resident enterprise under Article 24(3), it would have a non-resident shareholder (Parent Company), but it could claim non-discriminatory treatment under Article 24(5), that is the same tax treatment as if its shareholder (Parent Company) was a resident enterprise.

2068. *See also*, to this effect, Silva 2016b, 121, although he believes that applying the two-step approach (making tax-treaty-compliant taxation the relevant baseline for non-discriminatory treatment) would lead to a different result.

Figure 4.30 PEs of Non-resident Group Members

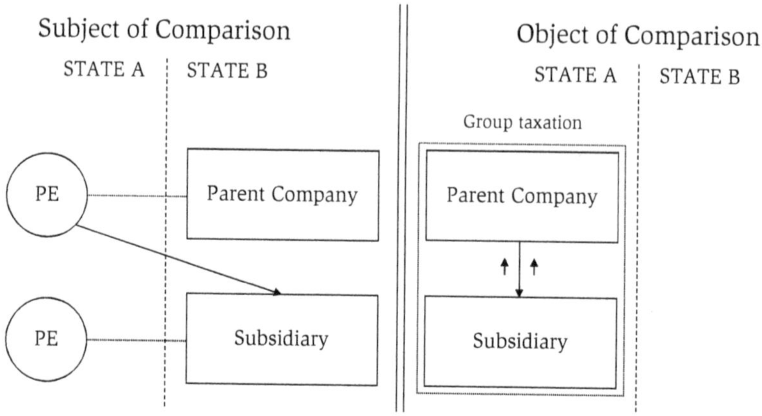

Again, if a person is protected against discrimination for certain reasons by a non-discrimination clause and if such reasons are used as grounds for different treatment of another taxpayer, this treatment does not, as such, create problems under Article 24. If a person is protected against discrimination for certain reasons by a non-discrimination clause, if such reasons are used as grounds for different treatment of another taxpayer and, in addition, if this different treatment of that other taxpayer influences the tax treatment of the protected person, discrimination under Article 24 should be affirmed with regard to both taxpayers. A PE of a non-resident enterprise should not be denied consolidation with a PE of another non-resident enterprise because of its enterprise's non-residence nor because of the other enterprise's non-residence. This means that both differences in residence must be disregarded with a 'but for' test as they are both protected under a non-discrimination rule of Article 24 and both influence the tax treatment of the taxpayer in question.

[D] Relief from Juridical Double Taxation

[1] Article 24(3) and Tax Treaty Entitlement

It is disputed whether, under Article 24(3), the source State is obligated to grant relief from international juridical double taxation to PEs when it does so with regard to its resident enterprises. According to the Introduction to the OECD Model, '[i]nternational juridical double taxation can be generally defined as the imposition of comparable taxes in two (or more) States on the same taxpayer in respect of the same subject matter and for identical periods. Its harmful effects on the exchange of goods and services and movements of capital, technology and persons are so well known that it is scarcely necessary [1992–1994: hardly needed] to stress the importance of removing the obstacles that double taxation presents to the development of economic relations between countries'.[2069] As tax treaties aim at avoiding juridical double taxation, the question of whether Article 24(3) obligates the source State to avoid such double taxation is often equated with the question of whether the non-discrimination clause obligates the source State to apply its tax treaty network to PEs.[2070]

PEs, as such, are not eligible for tax treaty benefits. Article 1 does not refer to PEs but to 'persons who are residents of one or both of the Contracting States' and the tax treaty concept of residence is legally distinct from the tax treaty concept of a PE. Article 4(1) uses certain criteria (person, personal attachment, full tax liability, no source taxation, etc.) in order to define the tax treaty concept of residence. Article 5 uses other criteria (fixed place of business, period of presence, dependent agent, etc.) in order to define the tax treaty concept of a PE. These definitions thus introduce separate and independent tax treaty concepts.

Nevertheless, those concepts may sometimes rely on very similar facts and circumstances. Article 5(1) defines the term 'PE' as a fixed place of business through which the business of an enterprise is wholly or partly carried on without referring to any particular Contracting State. This means that a PE may, in principle, exist in either Contracting State. For instance, a corporation may have a place of management within the meaning of Article 5(2)(a) in one or both of the Contracting States. At the same time, such a place of management in a State may lead to residence under Article 4(1) if this connection to that State establishes full tax liability under domestic law. If this is true for both Contracting States, the place of *effective* management determines the residence State for tax treaty purposes under the tiebreaker rules of Article 4(3) if based on the pre-2017 OECD Model. What constitutes a PE in one State under Article 5, therefore, may be hard to distinguish from residence in that State under Article 4; the same circumstances that establish a PE under Article 5 may lead to residence under Article 4, and vice versa.

It is often argued that a PE is not a person within the meaning of Article 3(1)(a) - a term used in a very wide sense[2071] including an individual, a company, and any other body of persons - and, therefore, fails to meet the requirements for residence under Article 4(1).[2072] However, a 'check-the-box company' may be treated as fiscally transparent for income tax purposes. Its place of management may establish a PE for another person to which all income of that corporation is allocated. This company or a similar investment vehicle might further not be treated as fiscally transparent for capital tax purposes and consequently remain a person within the meaning of Article 3(1)(a). If it is accepted that fiscally transparent persons cannot be a resident of a Contracting State under Article 4(1) with regard to items of income that are allocated to

2069. Introduction to the 1992–2017 OECD Model, para. 1 (similarly 1977: para. 3).

2070. *See also* Raad 1986, 152, who mentions that often the question about relief from juridical double taxation would be phrased as whether the PE can invoke that treaty; however, this is legally incorrect as the entrepreneur, not the PE, is the taxpayer.

2071. 1963–2017 OECD Commentary on Article 3, para. 2.

2072. *See*, for instance, Ismer and Riemer 2015 m.no. 15; Fett 2014, 5, 24; Wassermeyer and Kaeser 2013 m.no. 1; García Prats 1994, 477; moreover, 2008–2017 OECD Commentary on Article 24, para. 68; differently, Langoth 2004, 30–32.

another person by that State,[2073] it seems that a person could constitute a PE for income tax purposes and a PE could arguably be a person.

Yet, while there may be an overlap in the requirements for residence and a PE, these concepts are legally independent, relied on for different purposes, and mutually exclusive with regard to specific tax treaty benefits. Even if a 'check-the-box company' is treated as fiscally transparent for income tax purposes but not for capital tax purposes, maintains a fixed place of business within the meaning of Article 5, and meets the requirements of Article 4 with regard to residence for capital tax purposes due to that fixed place of business, for each tax treaty benefit, it can either be a resident itself or a PE of another resident but not a resident PE of another resident. Article 7 also strictly distinguishes between 'an enterprise of a Contracting State' (i.e., an enterprise carried on by a resident of a Contracting State)[2074] and 'a permanent establishment'. Thus, a PE belonging to a resident of a Contracting State is not eligible for tax treaty benefits just as immovable property belonging to a resident of a Contracting State is not eligible for tax treaty benefits. Again, these are very different tax treaty concepts even though their criteria may overlap, for instance, when a person's domicile leads to residence under Article 4(1) and constitutes immovable property within the meaning of Article 6(2).

Article 24(3) scrutinizes the taxation on a PE in the source State. What constitutes a PE (for instance, a place of management of a corporation) can, in principle, lead to residence under a tax treaty concluded by the source State with a third State. After all, the first sentence of Article 4(1) mentions various factors that can lead to residence, including a 'place of management or any other criterion of a similar nature'. A fixed place of business can consequently constitute a PE under one tax treaty and, as it belongs to a person, lead to residence under another tax treaty. Even if a PE is not considered to be a person, the person to which the PE belongs may be a resident of the State in which the PE is located due to the facts and circumstances that establish the PE. Such cases may also be referred to as cases of dual residence. What constitutes a PE within the meaning of Article 5 of one tax treaty leads to full tax liability of a person under the source State's domestic tax law and, therefore, to residence under the first sentence of Article 4(1) of another tax treaty.[2075]

However, according to the OECD Commentary, since the source State may tax in respect only of income from sources in that State or capital situated therein under the former tax treaty, residence under the latter tax treaty cannot be established due to the second sentence of Article 4(1).[2076] When a fixed place of business leads to full tax liability of a person under the source State's domestic law, the tax treaty network of the

2073. *See*, for instance, 2000–2014 OECD Commentary on Article 1, para. 4.

2074. Article 3(1)(d) of the OECD Model.

2075. *See also* Fett 2014, 12, who mentions that a 'dual resident triangular case' may effectively be a 'PE triangular case', with the exception that a tax treaty between the source State and a third State may potentially apply; similarly, Zhai 2009, 1106, 1121–1122; García Prats 1994 fn. 61 on p. 482.

2076. 2008–2017 OECD Commentary on Article 4, para. 8.2. *See also* Zhai 2009, 1122; differently, Langoth 2004, 33, who argues that a PE in the source State is not only taxed with income sourced in that State but also taxable on the worldwide income attributable to the PE. *See also supra* n. 1051 and n. 1052 and accompanying text.

source State is not available to the enterprise to which the fixed place of business belongs. Being limited in its taxing rights, the source State cannot become the residence State for the purposes of any other tax treaty.

When a personal connection within the meaning of Article 4(1) or any other connection to the source State meets the requirements for a PE under the tax treaty between the residence State and the source State, the question arises whether Article 24(3) requires an extension of tax treaty benefits granted to resident enterprises of the source State under the tax treaty between the source State and a third State. This question only concerns a unilateral or one-sided extension in the source State of benefits deriving from that treaty. The third State cannot be bound by the non-discrimination provisions contained in the tax treaty between the residence State and the source State,[2077] only the source State might be obligated to extend to PEs (or, more specifically, to enterprises of the residence State which maintain a PE in the source State) the tax treaty benefits that are available to its residents.

[2] Distinction Between Domestic and Treaty Relief?

[a] Guidance of the OECD Commentary

In a triangular situation when three (or more) States are involved, Article 24(3) may require an extension of exemptions or tax credits that are envisaged in another tax treaty. While juridical double taxation with regard to PEs is generally avoided between the two Contracting States, juridical double taxation may continue to exist if the two Contracting States and a third State subject certain items of income or capital to tax. Under the tax treaty between the residence State and the source State, primary taxing rights are granted to the source State in which the PE is located. When the third State levies tax on profits that are attributable to that PE because these profits have a sufficient connection to the third State as well, the source State and the third State both contribute to a situation of juridical double taxation that the residence State might not be able to avoid: it either exempts the profits of the PE (Article 23 A) or it may not levy sufficient tax to grant a credit for the tax paid in both the source State and the third State (Article 23 B).[2078] For this reason, non-discriminatory tax treatment under Article 24(3) could avoid juridical double taxation by extending to PEs the benefits of the tax treaty that the source State has concluded with the third State.

When a State avoids juridical double taxation with residents but not with non-residents, it apparently aims at providing for different treatment because of

2077. Rust 2015b m.no. 74, referring to Article 34 of the VCLT: 'A treaty does not create either obligations or rights for a third State without its consent.' *See also* Rust 2015c m.no. 115; Loukota and Jirousek 2016 m.no. 78; Fett 2014, 121; Kubaile 2013 m.no. 56; Raad 2012, 166–167; Rust 2010, 639; Zhai 2009, 1106; Lang, Lüdicke, and Riedweg 2006, 77; Langoth 2004, 26; Friedhelm 2002, 616; Helde 2000, 99–100; Raad 1995, 197; García Prats 1994, 480–481; Raad 1993, 299; Avery Jones, Depret, et al. 1991b, 337.

2078. *See*, for instance, Fett 2014, 107; Haslehner 2009, 353–354; Langoth 2004, 23–24; García Prats 1994, 475–477.

residence. Such an explicit reference to residence may establish prima facie discrimination with a 'but for' test. If the PE of a non-resident enterprise was a resident enterprise, the source State would subject that enterprise to full tax liability under domestic law, and the tax treaty between the residence State and the source State would not limit the application of the tax treaty between the source State and a third State. As Article 1 of that tax treaty determines that most tax treaty benefits[2079] are only granted to residents of either State, a prima facie discriminatory tax distinction is at stake. Nevertheless, it must also be determined on a substantive basis whether this distinction, which is formally based on residence, pursues an objective that is reflected in inevitably linked but relevant differences in circumstances in a concrete case.

With regard to domestic tax measures that avoid international juridical double taxation, the OECD Commentary on Article 24 has a clear opinion:[2080]

> [W]hen foreign income is included in the profits attributable to a permanent establishment, it is right ... to grant to the permanent establishment credit for foreign tax borne by such income when such credit is granted to resident enterprises under domestic laws.

In addition, the OECD Commentary on Articles 23 A and 23 B confirms that, under Article 24(3), 'any relief provided for in the domestic laws of [the source State] (double taxation conventions excluded) for residents of [the source State] is also to be granted to a permanent establishment in [the source State] of an enterprise of [the residence State]'.[2081] Accordingly, when a domestic tax measure of the source State grants credit for foreign tax to resident enterprises, it is right to apply Article 24(3) and to grant PEs credit for foreign tax as well. The OECD Commentary mentions no arguments against such an approach.[2082]

By contrast, the OECD Commentary on Article 24 takes no definite position on whether such credits for foreign tax should be extended to PEs under Article 24(3) if they are granted under a tax treaty between the source State and a third State. As outlined above, this treaty does not apply to persons who are neither a resident of the source State nor a resident of the third State but maintain a PE in the source State that is protected by Article 24(3) of the tax treaty between the residence State and the source State. In the context of Articles 23 A and 23 B, the OECD Commentary implies that

2079. Article 24(1) states that '[t]his provision shall, notwithstanding the provisions of Article 1, also apply to persons who are not residents of one or both of the Contracting States'.

2080. 2008–2017 OECD Commentary on Article 24, para. 67 (similarly 1977: para. 51; 1992–2005: para. 49).

2081. 1977–2017 OECD Commentary on Articles 23 A and 23 B, para. 10, with reference to the 2008–2017 OECD Commentary on Article 24, paras 67–72 (1977: paras 51–55; 1992–2005: paras 49–54).

2082. *See also* Bammens and Vanistendael 2016, sec. 2.3.3.3.3, who argue that if relief from juridical double taxation is granted to residents of the source State in the domestic law of that State, 'then it would clearly be incompatible with that [PE non-discrimination] clause to deny relief to the PE'; moreover, Raad 1986, 151–152, according to whom it appears that under Article 24(3) the source State is required to extend any unilateral relief rules that are applicable to residents, and Raad 1988b, 348; similarly, Haslehner 2009, 331–333, who concludes that relief from juridical double taxation under domestic tax law must be extended to PEs of non-resident enterprises; to this effect, Fett 2014, 114; Ault and Tillinghast 1992, 269–271.

Article 24(3) does not require an extension of tax treaty benefits but only 'any relief provided for in the domestic laws of [the source State] (double taxation conventions excluded)'.[2083] In the context of Article 24, however, the OECD Commentary includes the following statements that indicate disagreement between the OECD member countries not with regard to the objective of avoiding juridical double taxation but with regard to the scope of the non-discrimination clause:[2084]

> When the permanent establishment in a Contracting State of a resident enterprise of another Contracting State receives dividends or interest from a third State, then the question arises as to whether and to what extent the Contracting State in which the permanent establishment is situated should credit the tax that cannot be recovered from the third State.
>
> There is agreement that double taxation arises in these situations and that some method of relief should be found. The majority of member countries are able to grant credit in these cases on the basis of their domestic law or under paragraph 3. States that cannot give credit in such a way or that wish to clarify the situation may wish to supplement the provision in their convention with the Contracting State in which the enterprise is resident by wording that allows the State in which the permanent establishment is situated to credit the tax liability in the State in which the income originates to an amount that does not exceed the amount that resident enterprises in the Contracting State in which the permanent establishment is situated can claim on the basis of the Contracting State's convention with the third State. If the tax that cannot be recovered under the convention between the third State and the State of residence of the enterprise which has a permanent establishment in the other Contracting State is lower than that under the convention between the third State and the Contracting State in which the permanent establishment is situated, then only the lower tax collected in the third State shall be credited. ...

There is thus agreement that international juridical double taxation may arise in triangular situations and that some method of relief should be found. However, the OECD Commentary does not explicitly recognize that Article 24(3) extends tax treaty benefits granted under a tax treaty between the source State and a third State to PEs located in the source State. It only mentions that the majority of the OECD member countries are able to grant credit in these cases on the basis of their domestic law *or* under Article 24(3), but some OECD member countries are not able to do so without an explicit provision in their tax treaty. Apparently, the OECD member countries have divergent views on whether Article 24(3) may extend benefits of another tax treaty.[2085] Nevertheless, they agree that, from a policy perspective, international juridical double taxation should be avoided even in these triangular situations.

In the situations at issue, a tax treaty measure is under scrutiny. Since, pursuant to Article 1, '[t]his Convention shall apply to persons who are residents of one or both of the Contracting States', a tax treaty between the source State (A) and a third State (C) does not apply to a resident of the residence State (B) even when that person maintains a PE in the source State (*see* Figure 4.31). According to the OECD Commentary, this is

2083. 1977–2017 OECD Commentary on Articles 23 A and 23 B, para. 10.
2084. 2008–2017 OECD Commentary on Article 24, paras 69–70 (similarly 1992–2005: paras 51–52).
2085. *See also* Rust 2015b fn. 159 to m.no. 73.

even true when that person is a resident and subject to full tax liability under the domestic tax law of the source State.[2086] This different tax treatment between residents and non-residents in the source State is a direct consequence of the requirements of Article 1 in connection with Article 4 and of other tax treaty rules. Article 1, without doubt, discriminates based on residence. Thus, the tax treaty measure under scrutiny aims at discriminating because of residence as it restricts benefits to residents of a Contracting State, in this case, to residents of the source State or the third State.

Figure 4.31 Tax Treaty Benefits in a Triangular Situation

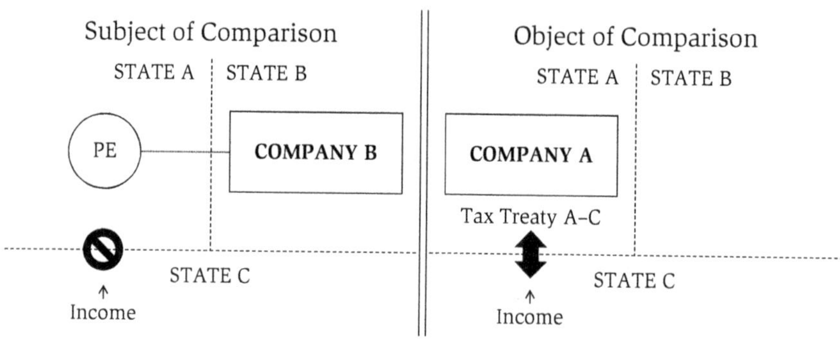

Under the tax treaty between the residence State and the source State, however, the question remains of whether this apparent purpose of restricting tax treaty benefits to residents of the source State or the third State can be brought into balance with the non-discrimination obligations of Article 24(3). In terms of comparability, two solutions are possible. On the one hand, a PE in the source State to which the tax treaty between the source State and the third State does not apply may be viewed as comparable to a resident enterprise of the source State to which the tax treaty applies given that the scope of the tax treaty is directly linked to the protected characteristic of residence for no apparent or legitimate policy purpose. A change in residence leads to a change in tax treatment and thereby establishes prima facie discrimination. An objection on a substantive basis remains unsuccessful. On the other hand, inevitably linked differences in legal circumstances with regard to the applicability of the tax treaty between the source State and the third State and, notably, differences in reciprocity may arguably render a PE in the source State incomparable to a resident enterprise of the source State. Although the OECD Commentary suggests adding a provision which would definitely provide some relief from juridical double taxation,[2087] this proposal has no bearing on the interpretation of Article 24(3) if such a provision is not contained in a tax treaty. It might merely restate what can already be

2086. 2008–2017 OECD Commentary on Article 4, para. 8.2.
2087. 2008–2017 OECD Commentary on Article 24, para. 70 (1992–2005: para. 52) suggests adding the following words after the first sentence of Article 24(3): 'When a permanent establishment in a Contracting State of an enterprise of the other Contracting State receives dividends or interest from a third State and the holding or debt-claim in respect of which the dividends or

derived from the non-discrimination principle concerning PEs, expand the non-discrimination obligations of Article 24(3), or even limit them by requiring tax credits but not dealing with and, therefore, arguably not requiring exemptions.[2088]

[b] *Reciprocal Nature of Tax Conventions*

[i] No MFN Treatment

An important argument against Article 24 covering tax distinctions in double taxation conventions is based not on the legal nature of such conventions but on their reciprocity. According to Niels Bammens, reciprocity refers to the fact that the rights and obligations of one Contracting State are directly linked to those of the other Contracting State.[2089] A bilateral tax treaty thus expresses a mutual but conditional exchange of legal rights and obligations.[2090] For instance, the reason why one Contracting State agrees to accord subjects of the other Contracting State non-discriminatory treatment is the desire for reciprocity, that is, that the other State will treat the first State's subjects in a non-discriminatory manner.[2091]

This principle of reciprocity is also addressed by the OECD Commentary on Article 24 in the context of MFN treatment:[2092]

---

interest are paid is effectively connected with that permanent establishment, the first-mentioned State shall grant a tax credit in respect of the tax paid in the third State on the dividends or interest, as the case may be, by applying the rate of tax provided in the convention with respect to taxes on income and capital between the State of which the enterprise is a resident and the third State. However, the amount of the credit shall not exceed the amount that an enterprise that is a resident of the first-mentioned State can claim under that State's convention on income and capital with the third State.' Before the 1997 update, however, it was only held that '[the State of the permanent establishment] shall grant a tax credit in respect of the tax paid in the third State ..., but the amount of such credit shall not exceed the amount calculated by applying the appropriate rate provided for under the convention with respect to taxes on income and on capital between the Contracting State of which the enterprise is a resident and the third State'. This was a drafting error that was brought to the attention of Working Party No. 1 by John F. Avery Jones and corrected thereafter. *See* OECD, DAFFE/CFA/WP1/MR(95)2, p. 18 (paras 54–55); OECD, DAFFE/CFA/WP1(95)5, p. 8 (paras 30–32); OECD, DAFFE/CFA/WP1(95)5REV1, pp. 5–6 (paras 22–24); OECD, DAFFE/CFA/WP1(95)5/REV2, pp. 6–8 (paras 26–29); OECD, DAFFE/CFA/WP1(95)5/REV3, pp. 13–15 (paras 62–66); OECD, DAFFE/CFA/WP1(96)17, pp. 13–15 (paras 38–43); OECD, DAFFE/CFA/WP1/M(97)1, p. 6 (adoption).

2088. *See also*, critically on the OECD Commentary's suggestion of an additional wording, Helde 2000, 159–169; Staringer 1994, 78–81.
2089. Bammens 2012, 151.
2090. Bammens 2012, 151.
2091. Bammens 2012, 152–153.
2092. 2008–2017 OECD Commentary on Article 24, para. 2. *See also*, critically, Haslehner 2016c, 7–8. In addition, the OECD Commentary states that 'paragraph [1] establishes the principle that for purposes of taxation discrimination on the grounds of nationality is forbidden, and that, subject to reciprocity, the nationals of a Contracting State may not be less favourably treated in the other Contracting State than nationals of the latter State in the same circumstances'. *See* 2008–2017 OECD Commentary on Article 24, para. 5 (1963–2005: para. 1); moreover, Bammens 2012, 151–154, 163–168.

> [T]he provisions of the Article cannot be interpreted as to require most-favoured-nation treatment. Where a State [State A] has concluded a bilateral or multilateral agreement which affords tax benefits to nationals or residents of the other Contracting State(s) party to that agreement [State B], nationals or residents of a third State [State C] that is not a Contracting State of the treaty may not claim these benefits by reason of a similar non-discrimination provision in the double taxation convention between the third State [State C] and the first-mentioned State [State A]. As tax conventions are based on the principle of reciprocity, a tax treatment that is granted by one Contracting State [State A] under a bilateral or multilateral agreement to a resident or national of another Contracting State party to that agreement [State B] by reason of the specific economic relationship between those Contracting States may not be extended to a resident or national of a third State [State C] under the non-discrimination provision of the tax convention between the first State [State A] and the third State [State C].

In this situation, State A affords various tax benefits (no taxation or exemption, tax credit, non-discriminatory treatment, etc.) to foreigners or non-residents, notably, to nationals or residents of State B. For instance, State A may be prohibited by Article 7(1) of the tax treaty between State A and State B from taxing a resident of State B when a building site in State A lasts for not more than twelve months under Article 5(3). According to the OECD Commentary, the non-discrimination provisions of the tax treaty between State A and State C do not require State A to extend the tax benefits granted under the tax treaty between State A and State B to other foreigners or non-residents, notably, to nationals or residents of State C. This means that State A is not required to grant an exemption for business profits of a resident of State C when a building site in State A that lasts for not more than twelve months establishes a PE under the tax treaty between State A and State C because of a shorter time period in Article 5(3). Even if the definition of a PE in the tax treaty between State A and State C is less favourable than the definition in the tax treaty between State A and State B (taxation versus no taxation in State A), a resident of State C cannot claim in State A the same tax treatment as a resident of State B.

This conclusion is not controversial.[2093] As it is already clear from the wording of the non-discrimination provisions (perhaps with the exception of Article 24(5) which merely prompts a comparison to 'similar enterprises'), Article 24 is not concerned with MFN treatment,[2094] that is with the tax treatment in State A either of State C nationals compared to State B nationals or of State C residents compared to State B residents. State A may treat State B nationals or residents better than State C nationals or residents irrespective of whether tax benefits are granted under the tax treaty between State A and State B or unilaterally under the domestic tax law of State A.

Nevertheless, the OECD Commentary points to the principle of reciprocity on which double taxation conventions are based.[2095] State A and State B have a particular economic relationship. Because of this relationship, they have concluded a bilateral

2093. *See also*, to this effect, Haslehner 2016c, 7–8.
2094. This does not mean, however, that MFN treatment is unknown to non-discrimination provisions in tax treaty practice. *See* Hofbauer 2006, 296–299; Hofbauer 2005a, 166–180; Hofbauer 2004a, 670–672; moreover, Hofbauer 2005b.
2095. 2008–2017 OECD Commentary on Article 24, para. 2.

double taxation convention that provides for tax benefits and thereby establishes certain tax distinctions. Since State B is prepared to give up taxing rights, State A is prepared to give up equivalent taxing rights, and vice versa. With this balanced agreement, both States aim at mutually benefiting from economic growth by fostering international commerce and exchange of labour. State A and State C, by contrast, might have a very different economic relationship. State A, therefore, might not be prepared to give up the same taxing rights vis-à-vis State C as it was prepared to give up vis-à-vis State B. Such important differences in bilateral relationships were already recognized by Working Party No. 4 of the OEEC Fiscal Committee in 1957:[2096]

> [I]t may happen that a Member country [A], under the terms of a Convention, treats nationals of Member country [B] more favourably than the nationals of other Member countries [C], but puts the latter on the same footing as its own nationals. Although ... there is some departure from the principle of equality of treatment between taxpayers who – leaving aside their different nationalities – are placed in exactly the same circumstances, ... 'such tax discrimination on grounds of nationality' – which can be eliminated merely by incorporation of the most favoured nation clause – is based on very special economic, financial or political relations and interests between the two contracting parties [A and B] which are not to be found vis-à-vis other Member countries [C] or, if they are, are not of the same degree.

It does not appear justified to extend tax treaty benefits that State A grants to nationals or residents of State B also to nationals or residents of State C. With its emphasis on the principle of reciprocity,[2097] the OECD Commentary gives an explanation for why Article 24 does not contain an MFN clause. Clearly, State A is not obligated to extend the tax treaty benefits that it grants to nationals or residents of *State B* to nationals or residents of State C, and it is not obligated to extend the tax treaty benefits that it grants to nationals or residents of *State C* to nationals or residents of State B. However, the decisive question remains whether State A is obligated to extend the tax treaty benefits that it grants to its own nationals or residents of *State A*, including all benefits that are contained in double taxation conventions concluded with other States, to nationals or residents of State C when the tax treaty between State A and State C contains provisions that prohibit discrimination of nationals or residents of State C or to nationals or residents of State B when the tax treaty between State A and State B contains such provisions drafted in accordance with Article 24 of the OECD Model.

[ii] Conflict of Treaty Rules?

Niels Bammens argues that the principle of reciprocity and the resulting relative effect of tax treaties speak against an extension of benefits provided for by a tax treaty.[2098]

2096. OEEC, FC/WP4(57)1, pp. 1–2.
2097. 2008–2017 OECD Commentary on Article 24, para. 2.
2098. Bammens 2012, 61–62, 98, 112–114, 133, 146–147, 148–149, 258–259, fn. 610 on p. 263, fn. 705 on p. 298, pp. 306–308.

Such benefits are reciprocal by their very nature.[2099] They are restricted (on a reciprocal basis) to residents or nationals of either Contracting State.[2100] This reciprocity and the balance of the tax treaty that results therefrom would be undermined if residents or nationals of third States could claim the same benefits on the basis of a non-discrimination provision in another treaty.[2101] As a result of this reciprocal nature, the benefit cannot be extended to residents or nationals of a third State.[2102] In other words, benefits granted under a tax treaty to residents or nationals of the Contracting States cannot be extended to residents or nationals of third States on the basis of a non-discrimination provision in another tax treaty because these benefits are granted on a reciprocal basis and, therefore, are limited to residents or nationals of the Contracting States.[2103] They are not among the benefits in respect of which Article 24 seeks to ensure non-discriminatory treatment.[2104]

Niels Bammens thus believes that Article 24 of the tax treaty between the residence State and the source State respects the reciprocal nature of double taxation conventions concluded with third States and, therefore, is limited in its scope to non-reciprocal benefits. He does not argue – although this argument would have some force – that such a tax treaty to which the residence State is not a party forbids the source State to unilaterally or one-sidedly extend tax treaty benefits to non-residents because of its reciprocal nature (Article 1),[2105] whereas Article 24 of the tax treaty between the residence State and the source State demands doing so thereby creating a conflict of treaty provisions.[2106] By contrast, Francisco Alfredo García Prats submits that pursuant to Article 30(4)(b) in connection with Articles 26 and 59 of the VCLT, the source State should not be able to invoke the limited effect of the tax treaty between the source State and the third State to limit the scope of the tax treaty between the residence State and the source State,[2107] which supposedly speaks for an extension of tax treaty benefits under Article 24.

As the source State is a party to both the tax treaty with the residence State and that with the third State, it is obligated to follow both conventions. Such situations are actually quite common in triangular cases in which two different conventions apply to a resident taxpayer. Although the residence State derives no rights and obligations from

2099. Bammens 2012, 146, 149.
2100. Bammens 2012, 146, 308.
2101. Bammens 2012, 149, 308.
2102. Bammens 2012, 146.
2103. Bammens 2012, 146.
2104. Bammens 2012, 307.
2105. Thus, while it is clear that Article 1 does not grant tax treaty benefits to persons who are not residents of one or both of the Contracting States, it would have to be argued that Article 1, stating that '[t]his Convention shall apply to persons who are residents of one or both of the Contracting States' implicitly forbids the Contracting States to extend the benefits to any other person through any other means in particular because this would upset the treaty's balance. *See also* Debatin 1981 III m.no. 329: 'Der den DBA zugrunde liegende Gesichtspunkt der Gegenseitigkeit verbietet, einen Vertragstaat aus seinem Abk. mit dem *einen* Partnerstaat zur Anwendung seines Abk. mit einem *anderen* Staat zu zwingen, wenn dieses Abk. einer solchen Erstreckung entgegensteht' (original emphasis).
2106. *See*, in particular Bammens 2012, 308 ('there is no conflict').
2107. García Prats 1994, 479–480. *See*, moreover, Martín Jiménez, García Prats, and Calderón Carrero 2001, 245; Helde 2000, 96.

the tax treaty between the source State and the third State, the source State might be obligated, on the one hand, to provide non-discriminatory tax treatment to PEs under the tax treaty with the residence State and, on the other hand, not to extend tax treaty benefits to non-residents and their PEs under the tax treaty with the third State (assuming that Article 1 indeed forbids or objects to this extension of benefits). A conflict of treaty provisions arises, as it is impossible to both grant and not grant tax treaty benefits to PEs. This conflict has to be solved through the *lex posterior* principle pursuant to Article 30 of the VCLT or on the basis of some other grounds such as the object and purpose of Article 24 and that of Article 1.[2108] It may be solved by not granting tax treaty benefits to non-residents which then makes the source State responsible under international law for the conclusion and application of a treaty (the tax treaty with the third State) the provisions of which are incompatible with its obligations towards another State under another treaty (the tax treaty with the residence State), or it may be solved by granting tax treaty benefits to non-residents, which again makes the source State responsible under international law for the conclusion and application of a treaty (the treaty with the residence State) the provisions of which are incompatible with its obligations towards another State under another treaty (the tax treaty with the third State). Pursuant to Jan Klabbers, such situations are unlikely to cause major concerns in practice:[2109]

> A [the source State] has a taxation agreement with B [the residence State]; A concludes a conflicting one with C [the third State]: what to do? Often enough, the terms of the two treaties, in this sort of case, can be easily reconciled, and if not, neither B nor C will lose a lot of sleep over being confronted with a Janus-faced A. For one thing, the treaty with either B or C can usually be renegotiated without much further ado. These cases then end up being less than spectacular – and less than problematic.

[iii] Impact of Reciprocity

As already mentioned, Niels Bammens argues that the non-discrimination provisions of Article 24 do not require a State to extend benefits stipulated by other tax treaties even if the State's own nationals or residents benefit. On the one hand, the tax treaty between State A and State B does not require State A to extend tax treaty benefits granted to *State C* nationals or residents because it does not contain an MFN clause. On the other hand, the tax treaty between State A and State B does not require State A to extend tax treaty benefits granted to *State A* nationals or residents because it honours the fact that the tax treaty between State A and State C was concluded on a reciprocal basis and, therefore, should not apply with respect to State B nationals or residents. This idea that the tax treaty between State A and State C should not apply with respect to State B nationals or residents must be derived from the principle of reciprocity that is embodied in the tax treaty between State A and State C. Yet, the non-discrimination

2108. On conflicts of treaty provisions, *see also* Bravo 2016, 282–291, with further references.
2109. Klabbers 2009, 33.

provisions of the tax treaty between State A and State B are at stake. Although the tax treaty between State A and State B requires – on a reciprocal basis[2110] – non-discrimination, it arguably honours the reciprocal and thereby limited scope of the tax treaty between State A and State C. To this extent, it limits its own scope as well. Article 24 does not apply because it does not intend to interfere with the envisaged reciprocity of other legal instruments.[2111] Inevitably linked differences in circumstances between residents and non-residents, that is differences in the reciprocal application of the tax treaty between State A and State C, arguably prevent comparability under Article 24(3) of the tax treaty between State A and State B. While residents of State A contribute to the reciprocal application of the tax treaty between State A and State C, non-residents of State A who are resident in State B would inevitably disturb the reciprocal application if the tax treaty benefits were extended to them through a non-discrimination provision of another tax treaty, that is of the tax treaty between State A and State B.

There are certain problems with this view, however.[2112] Domestic tax measures that grant a tax benefit to resident enterprises but deny such a benefit to PEs of non-resident enterprises may also rely on reciprocity. For instance, they may grant a credit for foreign tax to resident enterprises in order to avoid juridical double taxation but may only do so subject to reciprocity, that is if the other State knows a similar provision that also provides relief from juridical double taxation in reverse situations. Although, in such a case, the States have not agreed on reciprocal rights and concessions by concluding a tax treaty, their intentions are clear: either both States reciprocally provide for relief from juridical double taxation in their bilateral relations as far as residents and only residents are concerned or neither State provides for relief. If reciprocity played a role for the purposes of applying Article 24(3), the non-discrimination clause would arguably not obligate extending domestic relief from juridical double taxation to PEs if this relief is meant to be granted only to residents on a reciprocal basis.

Apart from this, reciprocity with regard to the operation of treaty norms is an ambiguous concept. It may consist of the bestowing of either identical or equivalent rights and obligations on each other.[2113] Thus, reciprocity may exist when the Contracting States have different obligations provided that these obligations are considered to be equal in value, notably, because they are interdependent or linked to each other. While it is generally assumed that a tax treaty is based on the principle of reciprocity and that thereby a 'balanced' or 'equal' allocation of taxing rights is achieved, this need not always be true.[2114] An economically strong State might have

2110. *See*, for instance, Rust 2015b m.no. 76; Rust 2015c m.no. 117; Oesterhelt 2015 m.no. 112; Fett 2014, 123; Ribbrock 2004, 145; Bammens 2012, 152–153; Züger 2001, 115; Helde 2000, 95–96.

2111. *See also* Bammens and Vanistendael 2016, secs. 2.1.4.3, 2.3.3.3.3, who argue that the benefits provided for by a tax treaty with a third State are inseparably linked with corresponding concessions granted by that third State and that such benefits, as a result of their reciprocal nature, do not form part of the non-discriminatory treatment under Article 24(1) and (3).

2112. *See also*, critically, Rust 2015b m.no. 76; Rust 2015c m.no. 117; Oesterhelt 2015 m.no. 112; Fett 2014, 121–123.

2113. Horn 1988, 150.

2114. *See also* Avi-Yonah and HJI Panayi 2010, 27; moreover, Fett 2014, 123.

put pressure on a less developed State to accept a particular allocation of taxing rights, and that latter State might have accepted such an allocation in order to conclude an otherwise favourable tax treaty. With respect to such provisions, it is difficult to speak of reciprocity especially if only one Contracting State benefits from them or if these provisions make economic sense for only one Contracting State. In addition, if a Contracting State already unilaterally provided for certain tax benefits under its domestic tax law before concluding a tax treaty, corresponding tax treaty provisions legally obligate both Contracting States to grant such benefits but effectively might not represent reciprocal concessions.[2115]

Of course, it is always possible to regard a tax treaty as a comprehensive package and to find reciprocity in every treaty. To this effect, Working Group No. 23 on Taxation of Dividends observed in its final report of 1971 that 'the provisions [of a tax treaty] – which are usually expressed in a reciprocal form – do not always have the same effects, for a theoretical reciprocity does not necessarily result in equivalence in the respective budgetary sacrifices ... or the economic advantages .... However, reciprocity must be judged on an overall basis, i.e. by considering all the budgetary and economic implications ...'.[2116] But then, the fact remains that a tax treaty may even lose its complete value for a State due to changes in circumstances. For example, consider a tax treaty on estates and inheritances and on gifts. If such a treaty was concluded at a time when both Contracting States maintained taxes on these transfers of property, the Contracting States might have expected to avoid juridical double taxation on a reciprocal basis and to reciprocally retain taxing rights only with respect to particular sources of property. If one Contracting State later abolishes all estate, inheritance, and gifts taxes, the tax treaty ceases to have practical effects on that State's taxing rights. While it can still be argued that the legal rights and obligations under the tax treaty have not changed and remain reciprocal, only one State has to face actual tax consequences. Therefore, it is difficult to argue that, for the State that has maintained its taxes and for which the tax treaty continues to have major effects, the rights and obligations remain linked to those of the other State that abolished its taxes and for which the tax treaty ceased to have practical effects. A perceived imbalance of legal rights and obligations has rather arisen. Guglielmo Maisto actually notes that, in some States, when the treaty regime is the result of the application of the principle of reciprocity, the abolition of estate, inheritance, and gifts taxes by the other Contracting State would necessitate termination as the legal constitutional basis for concluding the tax treaty and restricting the power to tax would no longer exist.[2117]

All of these difficulties in determining the exact meaning and the practical consequences of the principle of reciprocity with respect to a concrete tax treaty put into doubt whether the treaty makers of another tax treaty really intended to limit the scope of the non-discrimination obligations of Article 24 on the basis of this principle. If the application of Article 24 differed depending on whether reciprocal rights and obligations are at stake, an in-depth enquiry into reciprocity would be required. In this

2115. *See also* Avi-Yonah and HJI Panayi 2010, 27.
2116. OECD, CFA/WP1(71)6, p. 18.
2117. Maisto 2011b, 256.

respect, the Contracting States might have even tacitly agreed that they have a reciprocal right to extend tax treaty benefits to persons who are not residents or nationals of either Contracting State. This reciprocal right would allow them to meet their non-discrimination obligations of other tax and non-tax conventions. Put differently, the tax treaty might implicitly and reciprocally permit a unilateral extension of tax treaty benefits. Such an extension, therefore, need not question the reciprocal nature of the rights and obligations but might rather make use of reciprocal rights. If this is true, there appears to be little grounds for a limited scope of the non-discrimination rules. Article 24 should apply to and extend all tax benefits that a Contracting State grants to its nationals or residents regardless of whether they are provided for under domestic tax law or enshrined in another tax treaty.

[c] OECD Commentary on Article 24(2)

The OECD Commentary appears to further support an extension of tax treaty benefits to persons who are not within the scope of a tax treaty but can claim non-discriminatory treatment due to Article 24 of another tax treaty. It interprets the non-discrimination clause on stateless persons of Article 24(2) as extending certain reciprocal benefits that are granted to residents but not to stateless persons under a tax treaty concluded with a third State unless Article 24(2) gets modified. Therefore, it suggests an alternative provision because '[s]ome States may consider that the provisions of paragraph 2 are too liberal insofar as they entitle stateless persons … to claim equality of treatment … in their State of residence and thus benefit in particular … from the provisions of double taxation conventions concluded by it with third States'.[2118] Under this alternative provision, stateless persons cannot claim non-discriminatory treatment in their residence State but only in the source State.[2119]

Apparently, the OECD Commentary acknowledges that Article 24(2) could extend benefits granted under a tax treaty between the residence State and a third State to stateless persons who are residents of the first-mentioned State and who would not be eligible for such tax treaty benefits without the non-discrimination obligations of Article 24(2). This view assumes that the tax treaty between the residence State and the third State at least partly relies on nationality.[2120] As double taxation conventions very seldom presuppose a particular nationality for their application,[2121] the concerns voiced in the OECD Commentary appear of little practical relevance. Nevertheless, if the tax treaty between the residence State and the third State indeed requires

2118. 2014 OECD Commentary on Article 24, para. 31 (similarly 1977: para. 19; 1992–2005: para. 17; 2008–2012: para. 31). This cited explanation was added by Working Group No. 4 upon request of Working Party No. 1 of the Committee on Fiscal Affairs, although reportedly Working Party No. 1 did not mention double taxation conventions concluded with third States. *See* OECD, DAF/CFA/WP1/71.3, p. 1; OECD, DAF/CFA/WP1/71.10, p. 4.

2119. 2008–2017 OECD Commentary on Article 24, para. 31 (1977: para. 19; 1992–2005: para. 17).

2120. *See also* Raad 1986, 87.

2121. *See* already OEEC, FC/WP4(57)1, p. 3, where Working Party No. 4 of the OEEC Fiscal Committee stated that 'since the War Conventions for the avoidance of double taxation have, with a few exceptions, been based not on nationality but on the fact of fiscal domicile'.

nationality for its application or for certain benefits,[2122] stateless persons would not be eligible for tax treaty benefits on a reciprocal basis. Article 24(2) of the tax treaty between the residence State and the source State could then extend such tax treaty benefits to stateless persons who are residents of the first-mentioned State, and this result can only be prevented by deviating from the wording of Article 24(2) of the OECD Model.

What matters is that the OECD Commentary is not concerned with reciprocity. If a tax treaty limits its scope of application or certain benefits to nationals of a Contracting State on a reciprocal basis, an extension of these tax treaty benefits to stateless persons under Article 24(2) of another tax treaty influences that reciprocity. It influences it no less than if a tax treaty limits its application to residents of a Contracting State on a reciprocal basis and Article 24(3) of another tax treaty extends certain tax treaty benefits to persons who are residents of neither Contracting State, that is, to PEs of non-resident enterprises.

[d] Deleted Statements on MFN Clauses

It should be noted, however, that the 1977 OECD Commentary was contradictory in this respect. Despite the statements on Article 24(2) that support non-discriminatory tax treatment regardless of whether benefits are granted under domestic tax law or by a reciprocal tax treaty, the following statements denied an extension of tax treaty benefits to a PE:[2123]

> While an enterprise of a State (A) can normally claim, in respect of the permanent establishment which it possesses in another State (B), the benefit of the provisions of the convention between those States A and B, it nevertheless cannot, should such permanent establishment derive income from a third State (C), invoke the provisions of the convention between States B and C for the benefit of such permanent establishment, since it, the enterprise, is in fact resident of neither of those two States (cf. Article 1). This is the consequence of the well-known principle of the relative effect of treaties, which means that they have effect only as between the Contracting States.
>
> Nor could such an enterprise invoke for this purpose a most-favoured-nation clause, however general its terms, included in a treaty or agreement concluded between States A and B. In fact, it has always been accepted that such a clause did not apply in the case of double taxation conventions because these are essentially based on the principle of reciprocity. It should, however, be noted that some States have made provision in their double taxation conventions enabling the provisions of the latter to be applied, 'in special cases', to permanent establishments of enterprises of a third State.

2122. Kees van Raad mentions that certain tax treaty provisions may be based on nationality; this in particular concerns Article 4(2)(c) and Article 19(1)(b)(i) and (2)(b). *See* Raad 1986, 87. In addition, tax treaty provisions could deviate from the OECD Model by granting particular benefits only to residents who are nationals of one or both of the Contracting State.

2123. 1977 OECD Commentary on Article 24, paras 54–55.

On the one hand, the 1977 OECD Commentary provided a rather obvious statement, namely, that treaties have effect only as between the Contracting States. Article 34 of the VCLT already states that '[a] treaty does not create either obligations or rights for a third State without its consent'. This says nothing about a Contracting State unilaterally extending benefits of a tax treaty to persons who are not, as such, eligible for these benefits.[2124] On the other hand, the 1977 OECD Commentary apparently tried to limit the scope of non-discrimination provisions even if they are not part of a tax treaty: MFN clauses generally cannot address reciprocal double taxation conventions regardless of how broadly they are framed.

Indeed, a historical analysis reveals that those statements in the 1977 OECD Commentary intended to limit the scope of the non-discrimination obligations to national legislation, although initially it was accepted that an MFN clause could, in principle, extend tax treaty benefits. Already in 1966, the Delegate for Luxembourg pointed out that Article 24(3) was concerned only with discrimination due to national legislation and not with discrimination due to the provisions of a bilateral tax treaty.[2125] Later on, in 1971, the Austrian Delegation reiterated that it did not believe that advantages or reliefs (apparently with regard to relief from juridical double taxation) provided for under internal law or in other bilateral conventions should be extended to PEs. In this context, it is reported that the Fiscal Committee had previously expressed agreement with this view, namely, that advantages accorded by one Contracting State to PEs of the other Contracting State need not be extended to PEs of third States.[2126] Subsequently, Working Group No. 4 suggested including in the OECD Commentary that it seems logical to take the view that equality of treatment under Article 24(3) can apply only in the context of the relations between the two Contracting States. Hence, while PEs can, on such grounds, avail themselves of the more favourable provisions in the internal law of the source State, they are not entitled to claim any benefits resulting from a convention to which the residence State is not a party (i.e., a convention between the source State and a third State). According to the Working Group, '[t]his is a consequence of what is known as the relative effect of treaties, whose provisions normally do not operate in regard to other States than the signatory States, subject to the application of the MFN clause which, as is known, is not common in double taxation conventions'.[2127]

While these proposals were adopted by Working Party No. 1, the Rapporteur was also asked to consider whether a State should extend to PEs unilateral reliefs which the provisions of its internal law gave (in absence of a convention) to resident enterprises, such as full set-off for taxes paid abroad.[2128] An extension of a credit for foreign tax under Article 24(3) in the source State was then favoured by Working Group No. 4 if such credit is stipulated by internal law, provided that it is not also claimed in the residence State. For unknown reasons, however, Working Group No. 4 substantially

2124. *See also* Fett 2014, 120–121.
2125. *See* OECD, TFD/FC/211, p. 3.
2126. *See* OECD, DAF/FC/71.6, p. 3; OECD, DAF/CFA/WP1/71.3, p. 3.
2127. *See* OECD, DAF/CFA/WP1/71.10, p. 10; moreover, OECD, DAF/CFA/WP1/71.10(Add.1), pp. 5–6.
2128. *See* OECD, DAF/CFA/WP1/72/3, p. 5.

modified the explanations on tax treaty relief, notably, by stating that an enterprise of the residence State cannot invoke an MFN clause laid down – be it in the most generous terms – in a treaty or agreement concluded between the residence State and the source State in order to claim relief that would be available to resident enterprises of the source State under a tax treaty between the source State and a third State. In addition, Working Party No. 4 successfully suggested including in the OECD Commentary that 'it has always been accepted that such [an MFN] clause could have no application in relation to double taxation conventions, because these are essentially based on the principle of reciprocity'.[2129]

While such a result might have been envisaged from a policy perspective and explains why Article 24 is not about MFN treatment, it appears doubtful that the principle of reciprocity as embodied in a bilateral tax treaty can set limits on MFN clauses of other international agreements such as WTO agreements and bilateral investment agreements. For instance, Article XIV(e) of the GATS contains an explicit exception from the MFN treatment obligations of Article II of the GATS regarding double taxation conventions (*see also* Chapter 2 section §2.05[A]). While the MFN treatment obligations could require an extension of reciprocal tax treaty benefits to other WTO Members, a deviation from MFN treatment is justified only due to this general exception in the GATS. It does not appear convincing to argue that the GATS non-discrimination rules cannot extend tax treaty benefits or are, by implication, limited in their scope just because tax treaties are concluded on a reciprocal basis and have effects only between the Contracting States. In fact, Working Group No. 4 of Working Party No. 1 of the Committee on Fiscal Affairs, when drafting the 1977 OECD Commentary on Article 24, initially admitted that MFN clauses could extend tax treaty benefits, although it tried to alleviate concerns about this 'unintended' result by claiming that such clauses might not extend to matters of taxation and would have to be worded without the least ambiguity.[2130] For good reasons, therefore, the statements of the 1977 OECD Commentary on the principle of reciprocity and the consequent inapplicability of MFN clauses were deleted in 1992.

2129. *See* OECD, CFA/WP1(72)8, pp. 12–13; moreover, OECD, DAF/CFA/2584, pp. 8–9; OECD, CFA/WP1(73)6, pp. 14–15; OECD, DAF/CFA/WP1(73)8, pp. 4–5 (adoption).

2130. OECD, DAF/CFA/WP1/71.10(Add.1), p. 5: 'By way of exception ... an international treaty or agreement can profit Third States if a clause expressed to be for the benefit of Third States is contained in a prior agreement. This, as is known, is principally the case with the "most-favoured-nation clause", which is encountered in a number of treaties, and in particular in treaties known as treaties of friendship, commerce, navigation, establishment, etc. However, for such a clause to avail ... it is further necessary that it be worded without the least ambiguity. Moreover, according to the precedents, the subject-matter of the treaty containing it must be the same as that of the particularly favourable treaty the benefit of which is claimed. These requirements set particularly strict limits on the applicability of the most-favoured-nation clause which to that extent reduce its practical import.' *See also* OECD, DAF/CFA/WP1/72/3, p. 5 (adoption), but then differently in OECD, CFA/WP1(72)8, p. 13; moreover, OECD, DAF/CFA/2584, pp. 8–9; OECD, CFA/WP1(73)6, pp. 14–15; OECD, DAF/CFA/WP1(73)8, pp. 4–5 (adoption).

[e] Benefits Restricted to EU Nationals

Article 24 is based on the principle of reciprocity. It expects that both Contracting States will avoid discrimination against the other Contracting State's nationals and residents. Even though various international conventions, including tax treaties, are also based on the principle of reciprocity, this does not mean that Article 24 is prohibited from extending the benefits of such conventions. In fact, Article 24(1) may even lead to a de facto extension of the EU fundamental freedoms to non-EU nationals when the fundamental freedoms require an EU Member State to grant certain benefits to its own nationals who are active in the EU and when these benefits are not available to non-EU nationals who are in otherwise identical circumstances, that is also active in the EU.[2131] Under Article 24(1), comparison is made to that Member State's own nationals (NT) and not to nationals of other EU Member States (MFN treatment). From this perspective, if Article 24(1) is generally able to extend to non-EU nationals the benefits that are granted under EU law only to EU nationals, it is difficult to see why Article 24(3) should not be able to extend to PEs the benefits that are derived from a tax treaty with a third State and generally limited to residents of a Contracting State.

EU law does not seem to forbid a unilateral extension of tax benefits that an EU Member State is required to grant to other (and its own) EU nationals. It also does not seem to forbid a removal of EU discrimination by turning a tax distinction into a completely neutral tax measure that favours both EU and non-EU nationals or both residents and non-residents.[2132] If, for example, an EU Member State, in meeting its EU law obligations, grants an option to be assessed on a net basis to all non-residents regardless of their nationality (*Gerritse*)[2133] or permits all persons regardless of their residence and nationality to deduct certain special expenditures that relate to taxable income (*Conijn*),[2134] it is not clear why this neutral tax treatment should raise concerns from an EU law perspective just because it also benefits nationals and residents of third States. Additionally, if such neutral treatment does not raise concerns, it is not clear why this should change if these benefits are initially limited to EU nationals but extended to nationals of third States through Article 24(1). When a national of a third

2131. *See* Lüdicke 2017; Freeden, Häck, and Schaumburg 2017 m.no. 4.53; Haslehner 2016c, 23–25; Haslehner 2016a m.no. 9; Schaumburg 2015; Bruns 2013 m.nos. 36, 69; Haslehner 2012, 617–618; Haslehner 2009, 163–167; Haslehner 2007, 444–449; Zalasiński 2007; Gosch 2007, 1560; Schnitger 2006, 83–100; Dommes and Metzler 2006, 133–134; Sedemund 2006, 2785–2786; Lüdicke 2005, 485–486; Sedemund 2005, 1144; Bizek 2003, 74–75; Schnitger 2003, 750; Fekar and Schnitger 2002; Schnitger 2002, 713–716; Sedemund 2002, 395; Lüdicke 1997, 669–674; Kumpf and Roth 1996, 263. Niels Bammens argues, by contrast, that tax advantages granted as a result of specific regional instruments seeking to achieve legal integration (e.g., the EU Treaty) do not form part of the 'national treatment' to which the object of comparison is entitled when it is ascertained under Article 24 whether that object of comparison is treated more favourably than the subject of comparison. *See* Bammens 2016, 121; Bammens 2013b, 181; Bammens 2012, 418–420, 459–460; to this effect, also Rust 2015c m.nos. 53, 166b; Rust 2010, 635–637; Rust 2006, 88–91.

2132. *See also* Fekar and Schnitger 2002, 82–84; moreover, Lüdicke 2017, 296–297; Schnitger 2006, 85–87.

2133. CJEU, 12 June 2003, C-234/01, *Gerritse*. *See also* Dziurdź 2010a, 49–52.

2134. CJEU, 6 July 2006, C-346/04, *Conijn*.

State is a resident of or conducts business in an EU Member State, Article 24(1) obligates that State or any other Member State concerned to extend all benefits that it gives to its own (and other) EU nationals in otherwise identical circumstances. It does not matter whether it grants these benefits under domestic tax law without implementing EU law obligations, under domestic tax law by implementing EU law obligation, or directly under EU law because domestic tax law is violating EU law obligations.

It should be noted, however, that differences in residence may continue to be relevant under Article 24(1).[2135] In addition, as the EU fundamental freedoms (except for the free movement of capital) require not only EU nationality but also a certain cross-border intra-EU element, that is they do not protect purely domestic situations or activities carried on from or in a non-EU Member State, a national of a third State has to fulfil such material requirements as well in order to claim non-discriminatory tax treatment under Article 24(1). When the EU fundamental freedoms, therefore, condemn tax distinctions based on residence as prohibited tax discrimination because of nationality but only so far as intra-EU situations are concerned, it cannot be said that a resident of a third State is comparable to a resident of an EU Member State and that such tax distinctions should be prohibited under Article 24(1) as well;[2136] only Article 24(3), (4) or (5) can be relied on by comparing to resident persons of that EU Member State. An EU Member State may thus limit equal treatment of residents and non-residents to intra-EU situations without violating the non-discrimination obligations of Article 24(1). For this reason (and because there are many more advantages that do not relate to taxation),[2137] Article 24(1) does not automatically confer all advantages that are normally linked to the accession to the EU.[2138] Finally, if EU law should be opposed to a unilateral extension of certain tax benefits because, for instance, this extension would affect rules of EU law that implement a common EU policy,[2139] it could be argued that differences in legal circumstances that are inevitably linked to EU nationality are relevant for the purposes of comparability under Article 24(1). A denial of equal treatment could thereby be justified in order not to conflict with EU law requirements, although such situations are not readily apparent.[2140]

[3] No Apparent Policy Reason Against an Extension

A major argument against extending tax treaty benefits via Article 24(3) lies in the principle of reciprocity. Overall, however, it does not appear to be convincing to rely on the concept of reciprocity as enshrined in one tax treaty in order to restrict the non-discrimination obligations of another tax treaty. Rather, given that both conventions include non-discrimination provisions and aim at avoiding juridical double

2135. *See also* Bruns 2013 m.no. 69.
2136. *See*, to this effect, Haslehner 2007 fn. 82 on p. 448; Schnitger 2006, 100.
2137. *See*, to this effect, Schnitger 2002, 715.
2138. *See*, differently, Rust 2010, 636.
2139. *See* Avery Jones 1998, 102. *See*, moreover, on Article 351(3) of the TFEU (previously Article 307(3) of the EC Treaty), Kofler 2007, 817–819, who distinguishes between primary and secondary EU law; similarly, Rust 2006, 86–87.
2140. *See* again Fekar and Schnitger 2002, 82–84.

taxation in a comprehensive way, it can be argued that the Contracting States agreed to reciprocally extend to PEs all tax treaty benefits that they grant under another tax treaty. Thus, State A and State B have agreed in Article 24(3) of their tax treaty that State A will extend all treaty benefits to PEs that it grants under its tax treaty with State C, and they have agreed that State B will reciprocally extend all treaty benefits to PEs that it grants under its tax treaty with State C. Additionally, State C and State A as well as State C and State B have agreed in their conventions that they will reciprocally grant treaty benefits to PEs in order to avoid discrimination and juridical double taxation. In terms of Article 1, the Contracting States might have not only agreed that they aim at limiting the convention's scope 'to persons who are residents of one or both of the Contracting States' but implicitly also that they do not object to an extension of treaty benefits to other persons not covered by that convention, notably, to persons who are a resident of neither Contracting State but who maintain a PE in a Contracting State, as this furthers the goal of avoiding juridical double taxation in triangular situations. As both Contracting States will thus extend tax treaty benefits to persons who are not covered by Article 1 but who can rely on non-discrimination provisions of another tax treaty, they have reciprocally agreed to extend tax treaty benefits beyond the scope of Article 1.

As a consequence, irrespective of whether the benefits with regard to international juridical double taxation are granted under domestic or tax treaty law, no inevitably linked but relevant differences in circumstances can be established. When considering the aim of preventing juridical double taxation and the objective of Article 24(3) to put PEs on an equal footing with resident enterprises,[2141] Article 24(3) obligates the Contracting States to extend benefits they grant under a tax treaty with a third State to PEs.[2142] A different view could actually allow the Contracting States to

2141. *See also*, to this effect, Rust 2015b m.no. 75; Rust 2015c m.no. 116, who states that the object and purpose of Article 24(3) 'require a wide protection against discrimination', that Article 24(3) 'aims to achieve an equal playing field in the area of taxation between dependent branches and independent corporations', and that '[t]he legal status of a discrimination should not be decisive' because otherwise the source State 'could still grant competitive advantages to its own enterprises by inserting tax benefits not into its domestic law but rather into its tax treaties'; similarly, Rust 2010, 639; Lang, Lüdicke, and Riedweg 2006, 76.

2142. *See also*, to this effect, Haslehner 2016a m.no. 25; Loukota and Jirousek 2016 m.no. 77; Rust 2015b m.nos. 34, 73–76; Rust 2015c m.nos. 114–117; Wassermeyer and Schwenke 2016 m.no. 52; Schänzle 2015 m.no. 19; Eilers 2015 m.no. 10; Fett 2014, 116–124; Balestieri 2015, 425–426; Kubaile 2013 m.nos. 53–56; Pannwitz 2012 m.no. 27; Rust 2010, 639; Haslehner 2009, 263–267, 378; Zhai 2009, 1108; Peeters 2008, 675; Lang, Lüdicke, and Riedweg 2006, 75–78; Tumpel and Stangl 2006, 88–89; Göschl, Kovar, and Wahrlich 2005, 118; Lüdicke 2005, 485; Gomes Behrndt 2004, 64–67; Langoth 2004, 25–26; Ribbrock 2004, 137–158; Toifl 2003, 332; Friedhelm 2002, 616; Züger 2001, 113–115; Helde 2000, 92–99; Staringer 2000, 250; Fischer-Zernin 1997 m.nos. 17, 31; Staringer 1994, 81–84; García Prats 1994, 477–481; Gouthière 1994, 300; differently, Bammens and Vanistendael 2017, sec. 2.3.3.3.3, in which the authors speak of '[t]he current majority opinion' that Article 24(3) does not require extending tax treaty benefits but only refer to the now deleted statements in the 1977 OECD Commentary on Article 24, para. 54; to this effect, Bammens 2016, 102; Vogel 1997 m.nos. 36, 132b; Debatin 1981 III m.no. 329; Piltz 1981, 225–226; moreover, Raad 1986, 152, who relies on the same statements in the 1977 OECD Commentary on the well-known principle of the relative effect of treaties; but *see also* Raad 2012, 166–167; Raad 1988b, 348, where he distinguishes between a reduction in the third State and a credit in the source State and

circumvent the non-discrimination obligations of Article 24 by discriminating through international law. For example, if a State's unilateral measures eliminate international juridical double taxation, a distinction based on nationality or residence can be scrutinized under Article 24 (*see* section §4.04[D][2][a]). It is difficult to see why this State should be able to avoid discrimination under Article 24 by concluding a tax treaty that eliminates international juridical double taxation and, thus, continue to discriminate through international law.[2143] Article 24 must rather cover tax distinctions based on nationality and residence even if they have their origin in international law.[2144]

It should be noted that Article 24(3) may not fully eliminate international juridical double taxation in triangular situations even though it contributes to this objective. For instance, a third State may levy a higher tax under its domestic tax law than it would be allowed to levy under the tax treaty it has concluded with the source State. Even when the source State extends the tax treaty benefits to a PE under Article 24(3) of the tax treaty between the residence State and the source State, this does not change the fact that the tax treaty between the source State and the third State is not applicable. Thus, the third State is under no obligation to limit its taxing rights (unless a tax treaty between the residence State and the third State is in force and provides otherwise); only the source State is obligated to provide for non-discriminatory tax treatment. At the same time, the source State is not obligated to credit a higher tax than it would be required to credit under the tax treaty with the third State or a higher tax than has actually been paid in the third State.[2145] This credit obligation in the source State under

confirms an obligation of the source State to grant the same foreign tax credit to PEs as it grants under the tax treaty between the source State and the third State to its own residents; moreover, Raad 1993, 299, where he further regards the Commentary's prior statements on the well-known principle of the relative effect of treaties as erroneous as far as the obligations of the source State under Article 24(3) are concerned.

2143. *See also*, to this effect, Lang, Lüdicke, and Riedweg 2006, 76; moreover, Rust 2015b m.no. 75; Rust 2015c m.no. 116; Kubaile 2013 m.no. 55; Züger 2001, 114; Helde 2000, 96–97; Staringer 1994, 83.

2144. *See also* Haslehner 2012, 616.

2145. *See*, for instance, Balestieri 2015, 419; Oesterhelt 2015 m.nos. 116, 118–119; Lang, Lüdicke, and Riedweg 2006, 77; Tumpel and Stangl 2006, 88–89; Göschl, Kovar, and Wahrlich 2005, 118–120; Langoth 2004, 27; Ribbrock 2004, 154–156; Züger 2001, 115; Helde 2000, 101–103; Staringer 1994, 86–87; García Prats 1994, 480–481; Raad 1993, 299; differently, Toifl 2003, 334, who argues that the source State should be obliged to credit a higher amount of tax than it would be required to credit under the tax treaty with the third State if such a higher amount tax is actually levied in conformance with the tax treaty between the residence State and the third State. *See*, moreover, Fett 2014, 132–139. As Emily Fett rightly observes, an actual change in residence could also lead to a change in the amount of tax imposed in the third State because the third State would be allowed to levy a lower or higher amount of tax under the tax treaty with the source State than it is allowed to levy under the tax treaty with the residence State. Therefore, it might appear inconsistent that the source State may credit only a lower amount of tax under Article 24(3) if resident enterprises would also receive a lower tax credit but is not required to credit a higher amount of tax even if resident enterprises would receive a higher tax credit as the third State would be allowed to levy a higher amount of tax. *See also* Zhai 2009, 1109, who distinguishes between an overall approach (credit for the tax effectively levied in the third State regardless of the limitation in the tax treaty between the source State and the third State) and a per-country approach (credit for the tax prescribed in the tax treaty between the source State and the third State regardless of the tax effectively levied in the third State), compares these approaches to the solution suggested by the 2008–2017 OECD Commentary on Article 24, para. 70 (credit for the tax effectively levied in the third State but

Article 24(3) is thus limited to the tax that the third State would levy in accordance with the provisions of the tax treaty between the source State and the third State even though, in fact, the provisions of the tax treaty between the source State and the third State do not limit the third State's taxing rights. As a result, the source State may credit, under Article 24(3), the tax paid in the third State in the same amount as if a resident enterprise was at stake, but the tax paid in the third State may be higher than this credit obligation. International juridical double taxation may remain unrelieved.[2146] However, just because the objective of preventing international juridical double taxation cannot be fully achieved in all situations or because not all situations of juridical double taxation are within the scope of Article 24(3) does not speak for any limitation of the scope of Article 24(3). Conversely, the scope of Article 24(3) cannot be extended to provide full relief from juridical double taxation in all situations involving a PE. The main purpose of Article 24(3) remains to prevent tax discrimination and not to prevent juridical double taxation in triangular situations by granting better treatment to PEs than to resident enterprises.[2147]

[4] No Relief but Merely a Shifting of Tax Revenue?

If the source State extends treaty benefits to a PE under Article 24(3) and credits tax paid in a third State in order to provide relief from juridical double taxation, a lower amount of tax is paid in that State. This has no impact on the residence State if it uses the exemption method pursuant to Article 23 A and, therefore, exempts the income or capital that is attributable to the PE. However, if the residence State employs the credit method pursuant to Article 23 B, non-discriminatory tax treatment may merely shift tax revenue from the source State to the residence State without benefiting the taxpayer in question; the tax burden in the source State decreases but the tax burden in the residence State increases. Benefits granted by the source State to the PE are consequently voided by the residence State, arguably establishing relevant differences in circumstances for the purposes of Article 24(3). Whereas non-resident enterprises are subject to tax not only in the source State but also in the residence State, thereby allowing the residence State to offset tax advantages granted under Article 24(3)

limited to the tax prescribed in the tax treaty between the source State and the third State), and concludes that '[n]one of them are both theoretically convincing and practically acceptable'. It is submitted in this study that since a 'but for' test is a hypothetical test which is merely applied in a bilateral context, it appears consequent to consider how resident enterprises would be taxed in the source State, including the source State's lower or higher credit obligation, but without taking account of how the third State would treat such enterprises. Thus, if the source State would be required to credit a potentially higher amount of tax under the tax treaty between the source State and the third State than can be levied in the third State under the applicable tax treaty between the residence State and the third State, this does not influence the fact that the third State actually levies a lower amount of tax and that the source State's in principle higher credit obligation under Article 23 A(2) or 23 B(1), which is extended to a permanent establishment under Article 24(3), remains limited to 'an amount equal to the tax paid in that other State [the third State]'.

2146. *See also*, to this effect, Oesterhelt 2015 m.no. 117; Fett 2014, 137; Ribbrock 2004, 156; Helde 2000, 103; Staringer 1994, 87; García Prats 1994, 480–481.

2147. *See also*, to this effect, Lang, Lüdicke, and Riedweg 2006, 77.

through a lower tax credit, resident enterprises of the source State are subject to tax only in the source State (or at least no credit obligations arise in other States) which allows the source State to effectively provide relief from juridical double taxation.

It can be replied that the credit method pursuant to Article 23 B may, in many cases, lead to an offsetting of tax advantages that are granted in the source State under Article 24.[2148] It cannot be argued that, in all of these cases, the non-discrimination obligations should become inapplicable.[2149] Rather, whether there is tax treatment that is less favourable under Article 24(3) must be judged by looking at the taxation on the PE and thus disregarding whether a lower tax in the source State is offset by a higher tax in the residence State.

Article 24(3) is not about the overall tax burden but about the taxation on the PE. When the taxation on the PE in the source State is less favourably levied, it is prohibited regardless of whether the obligations of Article 24(3) have influence on the overall tax burden of the taxpayer in question.[2150] In this respect, Alexander Rust also comments that, in order to find out whether there is discrimination in the source State, 'the possibility to credit the taxes in the residence State ... is to be disregarded' and that, for the purposes of applying Article 24, 'it makes no difference if the discriminatory tax burden is or could be compensated ... [in the residence State] even if the ultimate tax consequences do not cause the taxpayer to suffer a combined, higher overall tax burden in the two Contracting States'.[2151] A disadvantageous treatment in the source State cannot be compensated by tax advantages granted in the residence State.[2152] A credit obligation in the residence State under Article 23 B has no impact on whether there is discrimination under Article 24(3). Thus, the source State must grant relief from juridical double taxation even if this relief is offset by the residence State and does not lead to a reduction of the overall tax burden.[2153] Inevitably linked differences in legal circumstances with regard to whether a tax benefit may be compensated by another State as well as corresponding differences in credit obligations are irrelevant for the purposes of Article 24(3).

2148. *See* Loukota 1991, according to whom it speaks against a non-reciprocal extension of rules that provide relief from economic double taxation that non-discriminatory tax treatment under Article 24(3) in the source State may only lead to a shift in tax revenue from the source State to the residence State if the latter State applies the credit method; critically Haslehner 2009, 331–332.
2149. *See also* Haslehner 2009 fn. 1191 on p. 287.
2150. *See* already Raad 1986, 141, who states that apparently it is not permitted under Article 24(3) to extend the comparative tax burden of the non-resident taxpayer to include any taxes paid to the residence State of the enterprise in respect of the PE profits (notably, when the residence State may levy taxes on PE profits but is obligated to grant a credit for foreign tax).
2151. Rust 2015b m.no. 5; likewise, Rust 2015c m.no. 4.
2152. *See supra* n. 1888.
2153. *See also*, to this effect, Avery Jones, Depret, et al. 1991b, 336, who emphasize that what happens in the residence State should be irrelevant for establishing taxation that is less favourable in the source State and that no problem of double credit arises because the tax in the source State will be reduced by the credit and this, in turn, reduces the amount of the credit in the residence State for the tax on the profits of the PE; the overall result is the same (unlike if the profits of the PE are exempt in the residence State); similarly, Bammens 2012, 299; Lang, Lüdicke, and Riedweg 2006, 75–76.

[5] *Difference Between Credit and Exemption?*

The OECD Commentary deals only with the extension to PEs of the benefit of the credit provisions of double taxation conventions concluded with third States and, notably, with credit obligations for dividends and interest.[2154] It does not explicitly deal with situations when the source State would be required to exempt income or capital under the tax treaty between the source State and a third State if the PE was a resident enterprise.

Such cases involving tax exemptions may be seldom but are not impossible.[2155] Certain functions that are physically performed in the third State may be attributable to the PE in the source State under the tax treaty between the residence State and the source State. For instance, the personnel of the PE may leave the PE's premises in order to visit clients and customers, to collect information, to negotiate with suppliers in the third State,[2156] or simply to deliver products or provide services in the third State. Such activities in isolation may neither meet the definition of a PE under the treaty between the residence State and the third State nor would they necessarily meet the definition of a PE under the treaty between the residence State and the source State if they were carried on in the source State.[2157] However, they could establish a PE in the third State under the tax treaty between the source State and the third State if, for instance, the definition of a PE in that treaty includes a concept of a services PE.[2158] Thus, if the actual PE was a resident enterprise of the source State, the business profits derived from its functions would be attributable to a PE situated in the third State under Article 7(1) of the treaty between the source State and the third State. As a consequence, the business profits would be exempt in the source State under Article 23 A of that treaty.

2154. 2008–2017 OECD Commentary on Article 24, paras 67–72 (1992–2005: paras 49–54).

2155. *See also* Rust 2015b m.nos. 74, 77; Rust 2015c m.nos. 115, 118; Rust 2004, 391, who mentions cases of an inter-company dividend exemption and of income from immovable property located in a third State. According to the Attribution of Profits Report 2010, the place of use of a tangible asset (including immovable property) is decisive for its economic ownership in the absence of circumstances in a particular case that warrant a different view. *See* OECD, Attribution of Profits Report 2010, paras 75, 174. Therefore, it could be argued that immovable property located in a third State cannot be attributed to a PE in the source State under Article 7(2) as it is not used in the source State (it is actually used in the third State where it is physically located). Accordingly, Article 24(3) cannot require an exemption of income derived from such immovable property since the income is not taxable in the source State anyway. Nevertheless, some authors believe that immovable property situated in a third State might be effectively connected to a PE under Article 7(2) and, therefore, might require relief from juridical double taxation under Article 24(3). *See*, for instance, Raad 1988b, 348. Although this view is not rejected by the Report because circumstances in a particular case may warrant a deviation from the place of use, in the following, a different example concerning a 'sub-PE' will be dealt with.

2156. Dziurdź 2014, 158.

2157. *See*, by contrast, Stieglitz 2004, 103, 111, 125, who apparently deals only with activities that would meet the definition of a PE under the treaty between the residence State and the source State; therefore, he assumes that, under this treaty, the income from such activities carried on in the third State, that is, the income from the hypothetically independent sub-PE in the third State, cannot be allocated to the PE in the source State but remains taxable only in the residence State; to this effect, also Loukota and Jirousek 2016 m.no. 87.

2158. *See*, for instance, 2017 OECD Commentary on Article 5, paras 132 et seq. (2008–2014: paras 42.11 et seq.).

This situation may be called a sub-PE,[2159] but it is no different from a situation involving dividends or interest; certain items of income (business profits, notably, dividends, interest, or other profits) are attributable to the PE in the source State under the tax treaty between the residence State and the source State even though these items of income have a connection to the third State and would be taxable in the third State under the tax treaty between the source State and the third State if the PE in the source State was a resident enterprise and eligible for tax treaty benefits.

In principle, it should not matter under Article 24(3) whether the tax treaty benefits to which resident enterprises of the source State are eligible consist in exemptions or tax credits.[2160] However, ordinary tax credits differ from exemptions as they ensure taxation in the same amount as the crediting State envisages under its domestic tax law. If the source State provides for a particular level of taxation, credit obligations in the source State thus ensure that the whole enterprise does not pay less tax than would be due in the source State without a tax credit. By contrast, if the source State is obliged to exempt income or capital that is related to a third State in order to avoid juridical double taxation at the level of a PE in the source State, the tax actually paid by the whole enterprise might be lower than that which would be due in the source State without the non-discrimination obligations of Article 24(3).

From a policy perspective, this need not be a problem. With regard to resident enterprises of the source State that are eligible for an exemption under Article 23 A, the source State also cannot ensure a particular level of taxation but is obligated to exempt regardless of what the tax burden on the whole enterprise will actually be. Thus, as Emily Fett correctly points out, the income at issue that is attributable to the PE in the source State would also escape taxation if it were derived by a resident enterprise of the source State; the relief in the source State merely places the PE in the same position as a resident enterprise of that State.[2161] However, an exemption in the source State under Article 24(3) may appear to be problematic if a tax treaty exists between the residence

2159. *See*, for instance, Rust 2015b m.no. 77; Rust 2015c m.no. 118; Fett 2014, 36–39, 139–140; Yong 2010, 154–155; Zhai 2009, 1119–1121; Raad 1988b, 349. It should be noted that, according to Alexander Rust and Michael Lang, income attributable to a PE in the third State should not be attributed to a PE in the source State; the concept of a sub-PE is not in line with Article 7. *See* Rust 2015b m.no. 77; in detail, Lang 2005b. In some situations, however, the income might *not* be attributable to a PE in the third State when taking the definition of a PE under the tax treaty between the residence State and the source State as a basis (for instance, no fixed place of business in the third State and no concept of a services PE in the tax treaty between the residence State and the source State); the income might then be attributable to a PE in the source State. This does not prevent the same income from being attributable to a PE in the third State as far as the definition under the tax treaty between the source State and the third State is concerned (for instance, services would lead to a services PE in the third State under the tax treaty between the source State and the third State). It follows that only if the definitions of a PE are identical, a concept of a sub-PE can be rejected.

2160. *See also* Haslehner 2009, 366–367, who welcomes an exemption under Article 24(3) of profits attributable to a foreign (sub-)PE; Raad 1988b, 348–349, who mentions real property as well as sub-PEs and favours double taxation relief without distinguishing between exemption and tax credit; moreover, Loukota and Jirousek 2016 m.no. 86; Toifl 2003, 333, 335; Martín Jiménez, García Prats, and Calderón Carrero 2001, 242; Helde 2000, 90; García Prats 1994, 479; Raad 1993, 299; not least, to this effect, Fett 2014, 114, 139–140.

2161. Fett 2014, 108–109.

State and the third State that prevents the third State from taxing. Since the definitions in the double taxation conventions between the States involved may differ from each other,[2162] it is possible that all States are prevented from taxing:

- Under the tax treaty between the residence State and the source State, certain items of income or capital are taxable in the source State at the level of a PE under Article 7(1) while the residence State provides for an exemption under Article 23 A.
- Under the tax treaty between the source State and the third State, a (sub-)PE would be deemed to exist in the third State and, thus, the source State grants a corresponding tax exemption under Article 24(3) in connection with Articles 7(1) and 23 A.
- Under the tax treaty between the residence State and the third State, no PE is deemed to exist in the third State and, thus, only the residence State is allowed to tax under Article 7(1).

It follows that, if a resident enterprise of the source State carrying on the same activities as the PE in the source State would establish a (sub-)PE in the third State and, therefore, would be exempted in the source State under Article 23 A, an extension of these tax treaty benefits to the PE in the source State might lead to double non-taxation. This double non-taxation would not depend on a State's decision under domestic tax law but would purely derive from tax treaty obligations.[2163] A combination of three conventions together with their allocation rules and non-discrimination obligations could lead to the result that all three States would be required to exempt the income or capital at issue. International juridical double taxation would be avoided but arguably to a greater extent than envisaged by all of the three States that are involved.[2164] If such problems would not arise with resident enterprises of the source State, inevitably

2162. *See also* Zhai 2009, 1120, who emphasizes that there may be different definitions of a PE and, therefore, a mismatch may arise.

2163. *See*, by contrast, Fett 2014, 108–109, who discusses situations of double non-taxation when the third State does not seek to impose tax under its domestic tax law; similarly, with regard to EU law, Jann 1996, 171; critically Martín Jiménez, García Prats, and Calderón Carrero 2001, 246.

2164. *See*, moreover, Fett 2014, 129–130, who is concerned with situations in which certain items of income are attributable to both a PE in the source State and a sub-PE in the third State. If both States would have to provide relief from juridical double taxation by granting an exemption under Article 24(3) of the tax treaty between the residence State and the source State and the tax treaty between the residence State and the third State, respectively, certain items of income could remain untaxed in either State. This result would require, however, that the profits that are attributable to a PE in the source State under the tax treaty between the residence State and the source State would not only be attributable to a (sub-)PE in the third State under the tax treaty between the source State and the third State but that these profits that are also attributable to a PE in the third State under the tax treaty between the residence State and the source State would additionally be attributable to a (sub-)PE in the source State under the tax treaty between the source State and the third State. Such situations seem very unlikely because the same tax treaty – the tax treaty between the source State and the third State – would have to attribute the profits differently depending on whether the source State or the third State extends the benefits of Article 7 in conjunction with Article 23 A in order to meet its non-discrimination obligations.

linked but relevant differences in legal circumstances could prevent comparability under Article 24(3) in a concrete case.

Such a situation of non-taxation is not specific to the non-discrimination obligations but may arise in other circumstances as well, most prominently, when Contracting States interpret or understand tax treaty provisions differently and, therefore, all view themselves as being prevented from taxing. In addition, the OECD Commentary mentioned before 2017 a similar situation that can arise under Article 24(3) that does not only involve tax exemptions but also tax credits:[2165]

> [A] permanent establishment situated in a Contracting State of an enterprise resident of another Contracting State (the State of residence) receives dividends, interest or royalties from a third State .... Another question that arises with triangular cases is that of abuses. If the Contracting State of which the enterprise is a resident exempts from tax the profits of the permanent establishment located in the other Contracting State, there is a danger that the enterprise will transfer assets such as shares, bonds or patents to permanent establishments in States that offer very favourable tax treatment, and in certain circumstances the resulting income may not be taxed in any of the three States. To prevent such practices, which may be regarded as abusive, a provision can be included in the convention between the State of which the enterprise is a resident and the third State ... stating that an enterprise can claim the benefits of the convention only if the income obtained by the permanent establishment situated in the other State is taxed normally in the State of the permanent establishment.

On initial consideration, it is not necessarily clear how this situation relates to Article 24(3). However, imagine that the third State has concluded a tax treaty with the residence State in which it agreed on a substantial reduction of source or withholding tax for dividends or interest. Presumably, the third State agreed on this reduction because it assumed that the income will be taxed in the residence State instead and subject to a credit obligation for any remaining tax paid in the third State. However, under the tax treaty between the residence State and the source State, the first-mentioned State agreed to exempt the income that is attributable to the PE in the source State. Since the income at issue (dividends or interest) is attributable to the PE, it is not taxed in the residence State. This might not constitute a problem to the third State as long as the source State in which the PE is located imposes a sufficiently high tax which continues to justify the tax reduction in the third State. However, if the source State 'offer[s] very favourable tax treatment'[2166] by not taxing dividends or interest, the third State may be displeased with the legally binding tax reduction it has granted vis-à-vis the residence State; it would not have granted this tax reduction vis-à-vis the source State or had it known that the income will remain largely untaxed. Additionally, this 'very favourable tax treatment'[2167] may either be achieved by imposing a very low tax or no tax at all under domestic law or by imposing a tax that is reduced by a tax credit granted under Article 24(3). Thus, the source State might not only impose a very favourable tax treatment under domestic law but, with the same result, lower taxation

2165. 2008–2014 OECD Commentary on Article 24, para. 71 (1992–2005: para. 53).
2166. *Ibid.*, para. 71.
2167. *Ibid.*, para. 71.

by avoiding juridical double taxation in a non-discriminatory manner. From the perspective of the third State, however, it might not necessarily matter why the income is taxed low or not at all – the third State might not intend to grant a substantial reduction of source or withholding tax in such a situation.

All of these considerations do not lead the OECD Commentary to the conclusion that the scope of Article 24(3) should be rethought or limited. Rather, the OECD Commentary suggested before 2017 to modify the tax treaty between the residence State and the third State in order to subject the reduction of source or withholding tax in the third State to additional conditions.[2168] Article 10 of the Multilateral Convention[2169] and Article 29(8) of the 2017 OECD Model now contain such a provision.[2170] Therefore, it can be concluded that, even though at least partly unintended or policy-wise questionable cases of double non-taxation may arise in some cases, this should neither lead to distinctions between tax benefits depending on whether they are granted as tax exemptions or tax credits nor should this lead to a limitation of the scope of Article 24(3). Article 24(3) is rather able to contribute to the avoidance of international juridical double taxation in triangular situations by extending all tax treaty benefits to PEs that are available to resident enterprises. All inevitably linked differences in legal or factual circumstances that may exist in a particular case must be regarded as irrelevant for the purposes of comparability under Article 24(3).

[E] Relief from Economic Double Taxation

[1] Overview of the Issues under Article 24(3) and (5)

States avoid economic double taxation in many different ways and in the hands of different persons. It is particularly possible to distinguish whether a State relieves economic double taxation at the shareholder or corporate level. In the former case, the shareholder receives some form of relief through a full or partial exemption, a reduced rate of tax on dividends, or an imputation credit for tax paid by the company that generated profits. In the latter case, the company benefits from a lower rate of tax for distributed profits or a deduction for distributions.[2171]

Economic double taxation is of little concern to a tax treaty unless it relates to transfer pricing adjustments under Article 9, but the non-discrimination provisions of Article 24 are an exception. If a State avoids economic double taxation by granting tax benefits to resident or domestic-owned enterprises, it may be required to do so with

2168. *Ibid.*, para. 71.
2169. Multilateral Convention to Implement Tax Treaty Related Measures to Prevent BEPS (2016).
2170. As a result, the 2017 OECD Commentary on Article 24, para. 71 has been modified and now refers to Article 29(8) of the OECD Model.
2171. *See* Ault 1992, 578–579, who describes several generic models that have been the basis for specific integration systems that treat corporate and investor taxes in a unified or coordinated manner: on the one hand, relief at the corporate level, notably, a lower rate of tax for distributed profits (split-rate) or a deduction for distributions, and, on the other hand, relief at the shareholder level consisting of either an imputation or shareholder credit or in an exemption or reduced rate of tax on dividends. *See*, moreover, Gammie 2010, 164–165.

non-resident or foreign-owned enterprises as well. In this respect, three situations are relevant under Article 24, the first dealing with measures that avoid economic double taxation at the level of enterprises that receive dividends, and the second and third dealing with measures that avoid economic double taxation at the level of enterprises that distribute their generated profits:

- First, a non-resident enterprise (the shareholder) maintains a PE in a State and receives dividends that are attributable to the PE. It is unclear whether Article 24(3) requires the State to extend to the PE domestic tax benefits that aim at avoiding economic double taxation if these benefits are available only to resident enterprises (section §4.04[E][2]).
- Second, a foreign-owned resident enterprise of a State pays dividends to its non-resident shareholders. It is unclear whether Article 24(5) obligates the State to extend domestic tax benefits to the resident enterprise that aim at avoiding economic double taxation if these benefits are available only to domestic-owned enterprises (section §4.04[E][3]).
- Third, a non-resident enterprise maintains a PE in a State and pays dividends to its shareholders that stem from business profits that are attributable to the PE. It is unclear whether Article 24(3) requires the State to extend domestic tax benefits to the PE that aim at avoiding economic double taxation if these benefits are available only to resident enterprises (section §4.04[E][4]).

In the following, it will be demonstrated that a 'but for' test may establish prima facie discrimination in all three situations. A substantive analysis, however, discloses various arguments against discrimination, which might be reflected in inevitably linked differences in circumstances in a concrete case. Whether such differences are also relevant from a tax treaty perspective and thus prevent comparability and discrimination is nevertheless doubtful. Therefore, it will be submitted that a State is, in principle, obligated to avoid economic double taxation at the level of both resident and non-resident enterprises under Article 24(3) and at the level of both foreign-owned and domestic-owned enterprises under Article 24(5).

[2] Receiving Dividends as a Non-resident

[a] Avoiding Double Taxation

In many countries, special rules exist for the taxation of dividends distributed between companies.[2172] Such rules aim at avoiding economic double taxation, that is taxation of the same income in the hands of different persons. When a company (the subsidiary) earns income and subsequently distributes it as dividends to a corporate shareholder (the parent company), the income is subject to tax twice, once in the hands of the subsidiary and once in the hands of the parent company. If the State of the parent company is not satisfied with economic double taxation and, therefore, provides for

2172. 2008–2017 OECD Commentary on Article 24, para. 48 (1977: para. 31; 1992–2005: para. 29).

special treatment at the level of the parent company (notably, a dividend or participation exemption or a tax credit for underlying tax, that is an imputation or indirect tax credit),[2173] the question arises whether such treatment should, by effect of the provisions of Article 24(3), also be enjoyed by PEs in respect of dividends on holdings forming part of their assets.[2174]

When economic double taxation is avoided only at the level of resident enterprises, a 'but for' test establishes prima facie discrimination. A change in residence leads to a change in tax treatment in regard to the relief from economic double taxation. Thus, initially, residence appears to be the reason for different tax treatment under Article 24(3). Since economic double taxation may arise with both PEs and resident enterprises, no differences in circumstances appear to exist in this respect. This view is also mentioned in the OECD Commentary:[2175]

> Some States consider that such special treatment should be accorded to permanent establishments. They take the view that such treatment was enacted in order to avoid double taxation on profits made by a subsidiary and distributed to a parent company. In principle, profits tax should be levied once, in the hands of the subsidiary performing the profit-generating activities. The parent company should be exempted from tax on such profits when received from the subsidiary or should, under the indirect credit method, be given relief for the taxation borne by the subsidiary. In cases where shares are held as direct investment by a permanent establishment the same principle implies that such a permanent establishment receiving dividends from the subsidiary should likewise be granted the special treatment in view of the fact that a profits tax has already been levied in the hands of the subsidiary.

However, it can be argued that, while resident enterprises receive relief from economic double taxation in only one State, non-resident enterprises could benefit in two States, notably, in their residence State under domestic tax law and in the source State under Article 24(3). Arguably, resident and non-resident enterprises, therefore, are not in similar legal circumstances. Although differences in tax treatment are formally based on residence, it could thus be argued that the actual reason is to ensure that relief from economic double taxation is not granted twice. The second sentence of Article 24(3) 'is designed mainly to ensure that such persons [non-resident individuals] do not obtain greater advantages than residents, through entitlement to personal allowances and reliefs for family responsibilities, both in the State of which they are residents, by the application of its domestic laws, and in the other State by virtue of the principle of equal treatment'.[2176] In a similar way, inevitably linked but relevant differences in circumstances arguably prevent comparability when the non-resident enterprise is already entitled to relief from economic double taxation. This does not necessarily mean that such relief is covered by the second sentence of Article 24(3)

2173. In order to provide relief from economic double taxation in the form of a tax credit, the parent company is entitled to credit against its own tax liability the corporation tax that the subsidiary paid on its profits to the extent that this tax is attributable to the dividends received by the parent company. *See*, for instance, Raad 1986, 147, 150.
2174. 2008–2017 OECD Commentary on Article 24, para. 48 (1977: para. 31; 1992–2005: para. 29).
2175. 2008–2017 OECD Commentary on Article 24, para. 49 (1977: para. 32; 1992–2005: para. 30).
2176. 2008–2017 OECD Commentary on Article 24, para. 36 (1977: para. 24; 1992–2005: para. 22).

and, therefore, excluded from the scope of the non-discrimination clause.[2177] If the residence State provides no relief from economic double taxation under its domestic tax law, there would exist no inevitably linked differences in circumstances with regard to double benefits and, consequently, discrimination under Article 24(3) would not be avoided. In all other cases, by contrast, when the residence State already provides relief from economic double taxation, the source State should not be obligated under Article 24(3) to provide relief as well.

In order to regard such inevitably linked differences in circumstances concerning double benefits as relevant in a concrete case, the reason for different tax treatment from a domestic perspective as reflected in these differences in circumstances must also be relevant from a tax treaty perspective. Only then can the reason for different tax treatment not be equated with the protected characteristic of residence despite a formal overlap in a concrete case. It is doubtful whether this substantive analysis can succeed in justifying different tax treatment and thereby avoid discrimination because of residence under Article 24(3):[2178]

> [I]t is hardly conceivable ... to leave it to the State where the head office of the parent company is situated to give relief from double taxation brought about by a second levying of tax in the State of the permanent establishment. The State of the parent company, in which no activities giving rise to the doubly taxed profits have taken place, will normally exempt the profits in question or will levy a profits tax which is not sufficient to bear a double credit (*i.e.* for the profits tax on the subsidiary as well as for such tax on the permanent establishment).

Even if the residence State already grants relief from economic double taxation under domestic tax law, this relief may be insufficient. Thus, the State of the parent company might not be able to avoid economic double taxation by itself.[2179] While it is true that relief might potentially be granted twice, both in the residence State under domestic tax law and in the source State under Article 24(3), the dividends that bring a burden of economic double taxation are, in principle, also taxed twice, both in the residence State and in the source State. Only if favourable tax treatment is extended under Article 24(3) to the PE in the source State may the objective of avoiding economic double taxation thus be achieved. Against this background, there is no excuse for refusing PEs all of the tax benefits granted to resident enterprises that provide some form of relief from economic double taxation.[2180] If the principal aim of the domestic

---

2177. *See*, differently, Debatin 1970, 135–136 and Sass 1966, 109–110, according to whom a participation exemption is related to the personal (or general) aspects of the non-resident parent company and not to the sphere of activity of the PE; critically Raad 1986, 148; Hintzen 1976, 2227; Vogel 1970, 354–355 (and *see also supra* n. 1124).

2178. 2008–2017 OECD Commentary on Article 24, para. 49 (1977: para. 32; 1992–2005: para. 30).

2179. *See*, for instance, Wandl 2015, 446–447.

2180. *See also*, to this effect, Rust 2015b m.no. 71, who comments that Article 24(3) requires the source State 'to grant an imputation credit to the PE in the same way it accords this benefit to domestic enterprises' and that '[t]he denial of an imputation credit should be regarded as more burdensome taxation at the level of the PE'; similarly with regard to dividend or participation exemptions, Rust 2015b m.no. 78; Rust 2015c m.no. 119; moreover, Haslehner 2016a m.no. 70; Wandl 2015, 460; Oesterhelt 2015 m.nos. 90–92; Pinto Nogueira 2015, 302; Raad 2012, 165; Bammens 2012, 253–255 Garrido 2009, 169; Haslehner 2009, 331–333;

tax measure under scrutiny is to avoid economic double taxation and if this aim can only be achieved by granting relief twice, both in the residence State and in the source State, there is no reason to deny relief from economic double taxation to PEs of non-resident enterprises under Article 24(3) on the basis of 'double benefits'. It follows that inevitably linked differences in circumstances with regard to benefits already granted to non-resident enterprises in their residence State remain irrelevant for the purposes of comparability. A measure that grants relief from economic double taxation only to resident enterprises remains prima facie discriminatory as far as a PE is concerned.

[b] Redistributions and Tax Revenue

Just because the main objective of the domestic tax measure under scrutiny speaks against justification of differences in tax treatment between resident and non-resident enterprises when relief from economic double taxation is already granted in the residence State does not exclude other reasons for different tax treatment that could be based on inevitably linked but relevant differences in circumstances. In particular, concerns about a loss of tax revenue can arise if a tax benefit that is conferred to avoid economic double taxation cannot be compensated for by subsequent taxation:[2181]

> Other States, on the contrary, consider that assimilating permanent establishments to their own enterprises does not entail any obligation to accord such special treatment to the former. They justify their position on various grounds. The purpose of such special treatment is to avoid economic double taxation of dividends and it should be for the recipient company's State of residence and not the permanent establishment's State to bear its cost, because it is more interested in the aim in view. Another reason put forward relates to the sharing of tax revenue between States. The loss of tax revenue incurred by a State in applying such special treatment is partly offset by the taxation of the dividends when they are redistributed by the parent company which has enjoyed such treatment (withholding tax on dividends, shareholder's tax). A State which accorded such treatment to permanent establishments would not have the benefit of such a compensation.

If the source State in which the PE of a non-resident enterprise is situated argues that the residence State of that enterprise is more interested in the aim of avoiding economic double taxation and, therefore, should bear the costs, this does not appear to constitute a legitimate argument against discrimination under Article 24(3).[2182] It can be doubted whether such differences in interest are reflected in, or constitute, differences in legal or factual circumstances that are inevitably linked to residence in a concrete case. However, even if such inevitably linked differences in circumstances

Staringer and Schneeweiss 2007, 240–241; Tumpel and Stangl 2006, 87; Rust 2004, 396; Gouthière 1994, 300; Avery Jones, Depret, et al. 1991b, 334–335, with reference to Raad 1986, 147–148; Lechner 1990, 12–14; Storck 1980, 91–92 (with regard to taxation of capital); Bellstedt 1973, 370–372, 435; Vogel 1970, 353–357; Rädler and Raupach 1966, 392, 393; Heining and Timbart 1961 m.no. 144; differently, Debatin 1970, 135–136; Sass 1966, 109–110.

2181. 2008–2017 OECD Commentary on Article 24, para. 50 (1977: para. 33; 1992–2005: para. 31).

2182. *See also*, critically, Lechner 1990, 13.

exist and genuinely explain why the domestic tax measure under scrutiny distinguishes between resident and non-resident enterprises, they are unlikely to be acceptable from a tax treaty perspective.[2183] On the one hand, it should not be possible for the source State to circumvent the non-discrimination obligations by submitting that it does not want to bear the cost of non-discrimination or that some other State should bear the cost. On the other hand, even if it is acknowledged that the residence State is more interested in the purpose of avoiding economic double taxation than the source State, this eliminates neither the source State's aim of avoiding economic double taxation nor the aim of Article 24(3) to contribute to equal conditions of competition between resident and non-resident enterprises in the source State.

If the residence State is unable to avoid economic double taxation in particular because it exempts the profits that are attributable to the PE under Article 23 A or levies a tax that is not sufficient to bear both a tax credit under Article 23 B and an imputation or indirect tax credit, the source State should be obligated to avoid economic double taxation under Article 24(3) because the perhaps more interested residence State, in fulfilling its tax treaty obligations, is unable to do so. From a different point of view, the residence State has done all within its power to avoid economic double taxation by not taxing the dividends under Article 23 A (or by actually granting relief from economic double taxation), which leaves the perhaps less interested source State with an obligation to avoid economic double taxation in order to succeed in both States' aim. Of course, if the residence State grants no relief through an exemption or tax credit even though it should be more interested in such relief, the source State might question why it should nevertheless grant relief, which might even lead to a shifting of tax revenue from the source State to the residence State without benefiting the taxpayer in question.[2184] This argument, however, could be true for any tax benefit and, therefore, does not suffice for justifying differences in tax treatment (*see* section §4.04[D][4]).

Some States further believe that their avoidance of economic double taxation should be partly compensated for 'by the taxation of the dividends when they are redistributed by the parent company which has enjoyed such treatment (withholding tax on dividends, shareholder's tax)'.[2185] When the source State grants relief from economic double taxation to a resident company, it may tax a subsequent redistribution in the hands of the company's shareholders, usually in the form of a withholding tax on dividends. If the shareholder is a resident, the source State retains full taxing rights under Article 7(1) or 21 unless the shareholder maintains a PE in another State. If the shareholder is a non-resident, the source State may either tax the dividends within the limits imposed by Article 10(2) or, if the shareholder maintains a PE in the source State, tax them fully under Article 10(4) in conjunction with Article 7(1). It follows that the source State is allowed to tax a subsequent redistribution regardless of whether the shareholder of the resident company is a resident or non-resident. This may convince the source State to avoid economic double taxation at the level of the resident company prior to a redistribution.

2183. *See*, to this effect, Pinto Nogueira 2015, 301.
2184. *See also* Loukota 1991; critically Haslehner 2009, 331–332.
2185. 2008–2017 OECD Commentary on Article 24, para. 50 (1977: para. 33; 1992–2005: para. 31).

By contrast, '[a] State which accorded such treatment to permanent establishments would not have the benefit of such a compensation'.[2186] A PE is merely a legal concept that is employed for tax treaty purposes; it cannot, as such, distribute dividends. If a non-resident company maintains a PE in the source State, the company as a whole distributes dividends to its shareholders. As a consequence, the source State is generally prevented from taxing a redistribution in the hands of the company's shareholders. Article 10(2) does not grant the source State any taxing rights when dividends are paid by a non-resident company to a non-resident shareholder. Article 10(5) further states that '[w]here a company which is a resident of a Contracting State derives profits or income from the other Contracting State [that is the source State in which the company maintains a permanent establishment], that other State may not impose any tax on the dividends paid by the company'.

It appears that the source State receives a compensation for its avoidance of economic double taxation only when it grants relief to a resident company, not to a PE. This difference in legal and factual circumstances, that is the fact that PEs, as such, do not distribute dividends and that subsequent taxation depends on whether resident or non-resident enterprises are involved could be regarded as a relevant comparability factor for the purposes of Article 24(3) despite its inevitable link to residence in a concrete case. Arguably, the source State limits tax benefits to resident enterprises not because of residence but because of differences in taxation of redistributions (*see* Figure 4.32).[2187]

2186. *Ibid.*, para. 50.

2187. *See also* OECD, Article 24 Discussion Draft 2007, para. 55, where it is noted that the main argument put forward in the OECD Commentary against extending the benefits for the avoidance of economic double taxation to PEs is the fact that, in the case of dividends received by a resident company, a withholding tax may be levied upon a subsequent redistribution of the dividends by that company whereas, in the case of dividends received by a PE, Article 10(5) would prevent the State where the PE is located from levying such a withholding tax upon a subsequent redistribution.

Figure 4.32 Article 24(3) and Taxation of Redistributions

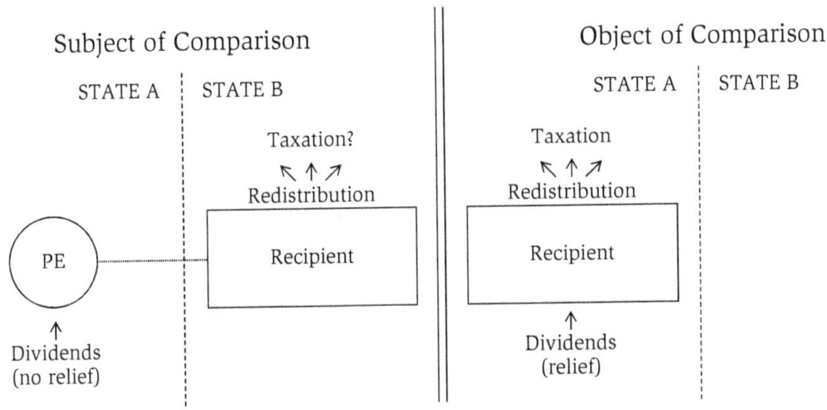

It is questionable whether a tax distinction on the basis of residence can really be seen as pursuing such an independent objective. On the one hand, the source State may be prevented from taxing a subsequent redistribution even if it eliminates economic double taxation in the hands of a resident company. When a resident company of the source State pays dividends to a resident shareholder who maintains a PE abroad to which these dividends are attributable under Article 7, the source State may be required to exempt that shareholder's business profits under Article 23 A. It would not be compensated for its loss of tax revenue.[2188] On the other hand, when a non-resident company that maintains a PE in the source State pays dividends to a resident shareholder or to a non-resident shareholder who also maintains a PE in the source State, that State may receive full compensation for its loss of tax revenue in accordance with Article 10(5).[2189] Lastly, if a company decides not to (re)distribute dividends or any profit,[2190] there might never be compensation for relief from economic double taxation regardless of residence. As differences in residence are often unrelated to differences in subsequent taxation and, thus, as residence constitutes an imperfect substitute for a compensation, this questions a genuine intent to distinguish between resident and non-resident enterprises because of such differences in subsequent taxation.

It must further be considered that certain legal and factual differences in circumstances between PEs and resident enterprises will always persist, including the fact that a PE, as such, does not distribute dividends and that the source State has

2188. To be precise, if the resident shareholder is a company, it may again redistribute the dividends received, potentially leading to a compensation. However, this cannot happen if the resident shareholder is an individual who maintains an exempt PE.

2189. Article 10(5) of the OECD Model does not prohibit the source State to tax 'insofar as such dividends are paid to a resident [the shareholder] of that other State [the source State] or insofar as the holding in respect of which the dividends are paid is effectively connected with a permanent establishment [of the shareholder] situated in that other State [the source State]'.

2190. *See* Pinto Nogueira 2015, 301; Garrido 2009, 168; Lechner 1990, 13.

different taxing rights under the tax treaty with regard to dividend distributions depending on whether a PE or a resident enterprise is at stake. Such differences in circumstances should not be seen as a 'blank cheque' to treat PEs differently from resident enterprises. For instance, the fact that a PE cannot distribute dividends or that dividend distributions of a non-resident company will be taxed differently than those of a resident company can hardly explain why a PE should not 'be accorded the same right as resident enterprises to deduct the trading expenses that are, in general, authorised by the taxation law to be deducted from taxable profits' or 'the same facilities with regard to depreciation and reserves'.[2191]

If the criterion of residence should be regarded as a proxy for subsequent taxation from a domestic perspective,[2192] it must still be decided whether this purpose of ensuring subsequent taxation or otherwise granting no relief from economic double taxation can be distinguished from prohibited tax discrimination by reason of residence from a tax treaty perspective. Article 24(3) aims at putting PEs on an equal footing with resident enterprises in order to contribute to conditions of competition that are not distorted by taxation (*see* Chapter 3 section §3.03[D][1]). This objective cannot be achieved if PEs suffer a higher tax burden than resident enterprises, notably, if only resident enterprises are granted relief from economic double taxation. It is true that the taxation of redistributions partly depends on residence and, therefore, the domestic tax measure under scrutiny might rely on residence in order to roughly approximate differences in subsequent taxation. Article 24(3) also does not appear to forbid the source State to grant relief only when subsequent taxation is ensured, in particular as such taxation might be independent of residence in some situations. A change in residence, however, only potentially leads to a change in subsequent taxation of redistributed dividends, whereas a distinction based on residence disadvantages all non-resident enterprises. It is thus uncertain whether residence will actually influence subsequent taxation. Only a *potential* difference in subsequent taxation is inevitably linked to residence. This does not appear to suffice for justifying a negative impact on the conditions of competition in basically all cases involving PEs of non-resident enterprises to which dividends are attributable.

There is also a parallel discussion in the OECD Commentary regarding the question of whether a dividend exemption that is based on incorporation is made because of nationality under Article 24(1) if, in a bilateral context, incorporation (nationality) and residence are formally indistinguishable from each other (*see* section §4.03[A][2][c]). The OECD Commentary argues that 'residence is a relevant factor in this case (as can be concluded, for example, from paragraph 5 of Article 10, which would prevent the subsequent taxation of dividends paid by a non-resident company but not those paid by a resident company)'.[2193] This implies that the OECD Commentary equates differences in residence with potential differences in the subsequent

2191. 2008–2017 OECD Commentary on Article 24, para. 40 (1977: para. 26; 1992–2005: para. 24).

2192. It has to be acknowledged that a direct reference to subsequent taxation of redistributed dividends might cause timing issues if economic double taxation is avoided before a redistribution of dividends takes place, which arguably requires using residence as a proxy for subsequent taxation.

2193. 2008–2017 OECD Commentary on Article 24, para. 21 (Example 2).

taxation of dividends. Following this view that residence is a relevant factor under Article 24(1) and the reason for different tax treatment despite an inevitable link to nationality, Article 24(3) should prohibit such discrimination because of residence when a PE is involved.

This view is further supported by the OECD Commentary's explanations on branch profits taxes, often distinguished from branch level interest taxes,[2194] which generally violate the non-discrimination provisions of Article 24(3):[2195]

> In some States, the profits of a permanent establishment of an enterprise of another Contracting State are taxed at a higher rate than the profits of enterprises of that State. This additional tax, sometimes referred to as a 'branch tax', may be explained by the fact that if a subsidiary of the foreign enterprise earned the same profits as the permanent establishment and subsequently distributed these profits as a dividend, an additional tax would be levied on these dividends in accordance with paragraph 2 of Article 10. Where such tax is simply expressed as an additional tax payable on the profits of the permanent establishment, it must be considered as a tax levied on the profits of the activities of the permanent establishment itself and not as a tax on the enterprise in its capacity as owner of the permanent establishment. Such a tax would therefore be contrary to paragraph 3.

The main reason for a 'branch tax' is the fact that a PE, by its very nature, does not distribute dividends. No additional tax is levied in the source State when the PE repatriates its profits to the residence State and, in principle, when the non-resident enterprise to which the PE belongs distributes dividends to its shareholders. A subsidiary in the source State, by contrast, would trigger an additional tax which could be levied in accordance with Article 10(2). This background, however, does not constitute a sufficient justification for discrimination. A 'branch tax' must be considered as a tax levied on the profits of the activities of the PE itself and is contrary to the non-discrimination obligations of Article 24(3).[2196]

It is important to keep in mind that a 'branch tax' tries to assimilate taxation to a dividend distribution from a hypothetically separate PE (subsidiary) to a hypothetically

2194. On this distinction, *see* 2008–2017 OECD Commentary on Article 24, para. 61; moreover, Loukota and Jirousek 2016 m.no. 35; Rust 2015b m.no. 69; Bammens 2012, 248–251; L. Hinnekens and Hinnekens 2008, 28–29; Bennett 2006, 447–448; Goldberg and Glicklich 1992, 93–95; Ault and Tillinghast 1992, 266–268.

2195. 2008–2017 OECD Commentary on Article 24, para. 60. *See also* Nikolakakis 2012, 185–186, who comments that the prohibition of imposing the economic and functional equivalent of withholding taxes in the form of branch profits taxes gives rise to somewhat of an incoherent result, though not necessarily to an incoherent analysis, of the application of the provisions of the OECD Model.

2196. *See*, moreover, Rust 2015b m.no. 69; Rust 2015c m.no. 107, who explains that, although branch profits taxes aim to treat an investment through a subsidiary and a PE in the same way, they are nevertheless discriminatory for the purposes of Article 24(3). The branch profits tax is equivalent to the withholding tax on dividends distributed from a resident subsidiary to a non-resident parent company as the profit transfer from a PE to its head office (repatriation) is a non-tax event. However, the withholding tax on dividends constitutes a tax at the level of the parent company. When looking at the tax burden at the level of the PE and comparing it to the tax burden of a resident enterprise, the withholding tax thus cannot be taken into account. As a result, the branch profits tax is an additional tax that is only levied on the PE but not on comparable resident enterprises. *See also* Haslehner 2016a m.no. 23.

separate head office (parent company). A PE of a non-resident enterprise is further treated differently because actual redistributions to shareholders might not be taxable due to that enterprise's foreign residence. After all, if all dividend distributions of a non-resident enterprise would be taxable like dividend distributions of a resident subsidiary, there would be no need for a 'branch tax'. Article 24(3) does not seem to prohibit linking the taxation on the PE to residence-independent characteristics of the enterprise's shareholders as long as the taxation of the shareholders is not simply added up for the purposes of determining the appropriate level of taxation on the PE.[2197] Thus, the fact alone that a 'branch tax' indirectly takes account of how the enterprise's shareholders are taxed would not necessarily be problematic under Article 24(3). Nevertheless,[2198] the taxation of redistributions should have no bearing on the taxation of the PE if the former depends on the enterprise's residence either because the PE is not a resident subsidiary that would be able to distribute dividends or because the PE belongs to a non-resident enterprise that actually distributes dividends. When no relief from economic double taxation is granted at the level of a PE with regard to dividends that are attributable to it as business profits, the profits of the activities of the PE itself are taxed. A tax benefit that provides relief from economic double taxation and that is available only to resident enterprises, therefore, should be extended to PEs under Article 24(3).

All in all, a reasonable and potentially legitimate objective, that is, ensuring subsequent taxation when relief from economic double taxation is granted and thereby

2197. *See* Zorman 2003, 292–293, who argues that the taxation of redistributions should not be taken into account under Article 24(3) because this is a matter of taxing the parent company (the hypothetically independent head office) and not a matter of taxing the subsidiary (the hypothetically independent PE); moreover, Bammens 2012, 204–206, and Kerfs 1994, 115, who report that the Brussels Court of Appeal (Cour d'Appel Bruxelles), in its decisions of 28 May 1993 and 17 June 1993, regarded arguments related to the taxation of redistributions as irrelevant since the tax withheld upon the later redistribution by the receiving company (i.e., the company receiving dividends and claiming relief from economic double taxation) is a tax on the account of the shareholder and not on the account of the receiving company itself; similarly, Bammens 2012, 209–210. It can be critically noted that, of course, the enterprise to which the PE belongs, if it was a resident enterprise, would not be taxed on the later redistribution (although it could be obligated to withhold tax), only its shareholders would be taxed. This taxation, therefore, is not protected under Article 24(3) and does not influence the question of whether the taxation on the PE is less favourably levied: the amount of tax levied on the recipient of the redistributed dividends is no benchmark for the appropriate amount of tax that may be levied on the PE. Yet, if it is assumed, for the sake of argument, that the taxation of the redistribution has no connection to residence but solely depends on other factors such as whether the shareholder is an individual or corporation or how long the shareholder has been participating in the enterprise, Article 24(3) does not prohibit taking account of such factors, either directly or indirectly by referring to the taxation of the redistribution. It is not clear, however, whether this should also hold true if the taxation of the redistributed dividends in the hands of the shareholder depends on the residence of the protected enterprise and, therefore, if a prima facie discriminatory reference to residence is made. Whether the reason for different tax treatment still lies in the taxation of the redistribution (despite an inevitable link to the protected characteristic) or rather in the protected characteristic of residence is a matter for a substantive analysis.

2198. Indeed, the Article 24 Discussion Draft 2007 mentions that it is not clear to what extent the policy concern about taxation of a subsequent redistribution in the context of measures for the avoidance of economic double taxation is different from the problem arising from branch taxation. *See* OECD, Article 24 Discussion Draft 2007, para. 56.

connecting certain benefits to certain sacrifices, does not prevail over the objective of putting PEs on an equal footing with resident enterprises. This result presupposes that the overarching aim of the domestic tax measure is to avoid economic double taxation, that economic double taxation may arise with both PEs and resident enterprises, and that differences in residence have only a remote connection to differences in subsequent taxation and to a compensation for a loss of tax revenue; regardless of residence, redistributions may, or may not, be taxable in a concrete case or no redistributions may take place. In such circumstances, better arguments speak for prohibited tax discrimination under Article 24(3) if PEs are denied relief from economic double taxation. Although differences in subsequent taxation may be inevitably linked to differences in residence in a concrete case, they should be regarded as irrelevant for comparability purposes when a domestic tax measure denies relief from economic double taxation on the basis of residence and without specifically referring to subsequent taxation. If a Contracting State is really concerned with subsequent taxation, it should directly refer to redistributions and their taxation instead of using an arguably inadequate and discriminatory criterion of residence.

[c] *Risk of Transferring Holdings*

Another argument for why economic double taxation should not be avoided with PEs under Article 24(3) relates to concerns about tax planning and receiving otherwise unavailable relief from economic double taxation by using PEs:[2199]

> [T]here is a risk that companies of one State might transfer their holdings in companies of another State to their permanent establishments in that other State for the sole purpose of availing themselves of such treatment.

This argument emphasizes that a company might envisage benefitting from favourable tax treatment in the source State that is granted to PEs under Article 24(3), that is avoidance of economic double taxation. In some situations, the residence State might not provide sufficient relief from economic double taxation. If holdings, therefore, are transferred to a PE in the source State, the residence State might exempt the income of the PE under Article 23 A while the source State might avoid economic double taxation under Article 24(3) to a greater extent than the residence State would do if it retained taxing rights. Lastly, the repatriation of the dividends from the source State to the residence State generally leads to no tax consequences and, in particular, to no withholding tax.

When economic double taxation is better avoided in the source State than in the residence State is a result of the differences between the tax systems of the Contracting States. Apparently, the Contracting States have introduced different relief methods under their domestic tax laws that may be more or less beneficial to a particular taxpayer. It is then always possible to find some situations in which the source State taxes the activities of a PE more favourably than the residence State would tax if the

2199. 2008–2017 OECD Commentary on Article 24, para. 50 (1977: para. 33; 1992–2005: para. 31).

same activities were carried on within its territory. However, this should not justify taxation that is less favourable on the PEs in the source State when compared to that of resident enterprises which carry on the same activities in the source State. For instance, if the source State deducts additional trading expenses or levies a lower tax rate than the residence State but denies such benefits to PEs, there could also be a risk that companies of the residence State might transfer their business to their PEs in the source State for the sole purpose of availing themselves of such treatment. Nevertheless, the fact that the Contracting States have not harmonized their tax systems and taxpayers, therefore, might benefit from being active in the source State by maintaining a PE does not appear to constitute a legitimate consideration under Article 24(3). In fact, it is even doubtful whether this consideration can be reflected in inevitably linked differences in legal or factual circumstances. A change in residence with a 'but for' test leads neither to a change in the place where the activities at issue are carried on nor to a change in the part of the enterprise to which the holding in the company that pays the dividends economically belongs.

Besides that, there are many good reasons for why holdings in companies might be transferred and attributable to a PE in the source State.[2200] All of these reasons make it doubtful whether concerns about potential tax benefits are able to justify differences in tax treatment between PEs and resident enterprises under Article 24(3).

[d] Conditional upon Redistribution

Another argument against avoidance of economic double taxation at the level of PEs concerns measures that are conditional upon redistribution of the dividends:[2201]

> [W]hen such treatment is made conditional upon redistribution of the dividends, its extension to permanent establishments would not be justified, for in such a case the permanent establishment, which is only a part of a company of another State and does not distribute dividends, would be more favourably treated than a resident company.

A tax benefit that aims at avoiding economic double taxation may not simply be limited to residents. It may be conditional upon redistribution of the dividends that are received by the taxpayer in question. A PE as a tax treaty concept cannot redistribute

2200. 2008–2017 OECD Commentary on Article 24, para. 51 (1977: para. 34; 1992–2005: para. 32). *See also* OECD, FC/WP4(71)1, p. 18, where the Rapporteur of Working Party No. 4 of the Fiscal Committee mentioned that the possession of a holding by a PE need not be a matter of the free choice of the enterprise but may be dictated by considerations of necessity, which are, in general, of two kinds: (1) the possession and management of such holdings is incident to the business of the branch; or (2) certain financial institutions are required to deposit a certain amount of assets, mainly shares, as security for the performance of their obligations. *See*, moreover, DAF/CFA/WP1/71.10, p. 5. Perhaps because some Delegates considered it incorrect to rely on legal regulations rather than on whether holdings were effectively connected to a PE, Working Party No. 1 of Committee on Fiscal Affairs asked Working Group No. 4, which succeeded Working Party No. 4 when Working Party No. 1 was established, to reconsider the inclusion of the comments relating to 'considerations of necessity'. *See* OECD, DAF/CFA/WP1/71.3, p. 2; OECD, DAF/CFA/WP1/72/3, p. 4.

2201. 2008–2017 OECD Commentary on Article 24, para. 50 (1977: para. 33; 1992–2005: para. 31).

the dividends; only the non-resident company to which the PE belongs can do so. If a resident enterprise does not redistribute the dividends, it also is not eligible for favourable tax treatment. Thus, not only all non-resident enterprises with a PE in the source State but also certain resident enterprises of the source State are denied special treatment. No relief from economic double taxation is provided to both non-residents and certain residents.

If some residents are treated less favourably as well does not a priori prevent discrimination because of residence in a concrete case. There still remain resident enterprises that may benefit from special treatment while all non-resident enterprises with a PE are denied such benefits. With a 'but for' test, the legal circumstances of the whole non-resident enterprise to which a PE belongs must be taken into account, including its legal structure[2202] and its redistribution of dividends. Whether a non-resident enterprise redistributes dividends is not a characteristic that would be inevitably linked to that enterprise's residence. A non-resident enterprise that redistributes dividends, therefore, must be compared to a resident enterprise that also redistributes dividends. In such a case, there is a difference in tax treatment that is prima facie discriminatory. Conversely, a non-resident enterprise that does not redistribute dividends must be compared to a resident enterprise that also does not redistribute dividends. As both are treated identically and economic double taxation is not avoided in both cases, tax discrimination under Article 24(3) can be denied.

When a 'but for' test leads to prima facie discrimination, the follow-up issue is whether inevitably linked differences in legal or factual circumstances may nevertheless prevent comparability and justify differences in tax treatment. Following the argument mentioned in the OECD Commentary, the fact that a PE, as such, does not redistribute the dividends could be considered an inevitably linked but relevant difference in circumstances. Although the non-resident enterprise at issue redistributes the dividends that are subject to economic double taxation, it arguably matters that the PE does not redistribute the dividends. If Article 24(3) would extend tax benefits to the PE that are conditional upon redistribution, the PE 'would be more favourably treated than a resident company'.[2203]

In order to confirm or deny discrimination under Article 24(3), it is necessary to consider why the domestic tax measure under scrutiny does not bluntly refer to residence but to redistribution. A reason for the condition of redistribution could be that the source State is looking for compensation for the loss of tax revenue that arises due to its special treatment. While the source State intends to avoid economic double taxation at the level of a company, it does not aim at doing so before it can ensure that a redistribution of the dividends takes place and thus not before it can tax the shareholder and recipient of such dividends instead of the distributing company. When applying Article 24(3), the source State takes into account that a PE of a non-resident company is not, in fact, legally separate and independent and, therefore, it cannot redistribute dividends. This fact is important to the source State since it establishes relevant differences in circumstances with regard to the expected compensation. Since

2202. *See also* 2008–2017 OECD Commentary on Article 24, para. 37.
2203. 2008–2017 OECD Commentary on Article 24, para. 50 (1977: para. 33; 1992–2005: para. 31).

PEs do not distribute dividends, they do not lead to a sufficient nexus for the taxation of the recipient of such dividends. Rather, the income of the PE may be repatriated without any tax consequences in the source State and thus without providing the source State with compensation and tax revenue. For these reasons, economic double taxation is not avoided at the level of PEs. In offering solutions for such concerns, the OECD Commentary implicitly confirms this fear about losing compensation and tax revenue.[2204]

The argument about PEs not being able to distribute dividends but being able to repatriate dividends without taxation in the source State is difficult to distinguish from the argument that '[t]he loss of tax revenue incurred by a State in applying such special treatment is partly offset by the taxation of the dividends when they are redistributed by the parent company which has enjoyed such treatment (withholding tax on dividends, shareholder's tax)'[2205] (*see* section §4.04[E][2][b]). Instead of directly pointing to such an envisaged compensation for a loss of tax revenue, the fact that a PE cannot redistribute the dividends is used to defend the domestic tax measure under scrutiny because that measure is, in fact, conditional upon redistribution.

Differences in legal and factual circumstances between PEs and resident enterprises with regard to dividend distributions and repatriation always exist. Simply taking these differences into account and making a tax benefit conditional upon redistribution, therefore, is not sufficient to justify differences in tax treatment. Otherwise, every tax benefit that a State wants to deny to PEs could be made conditional upon redistribution, even tax benefits consisting in a deduction of trading expenses. While some resident enterprises would also suffer from tax treatment that is less favourable, all PEs of non-resident enterprises would suffer. Thus, it is necessary to explain why, in a particular case, these differences are relevant to the domestic tax measure under scrutiny and should prevent discrimination under Article 24(3).

If the source State makes avoidance of economic double taxation conditional upon redistribution of dividends, it presumably makes the purpose of receiving compensation for its tax concession more explicit. Instead of assuming that all income of resident enterprises will, at some point of time, be redistributed, leading to some future compensation, the source State makes relief from economic double taxation conditional upon a redistribution of dividends and, thus, conditional upon immediate compensation. If this is true, however, there is no argument for completely denying relief from economic double taxation; the aim of Article 24(3) to put PEs on an equal footing with resident enterprises should still prevail. A PE is always treated less favourably because it is assumed that a PE is never able to distribute dividends. This is even so if the non-resident enterprise to which the PE belongs redistributes the dividends at issue and when the recipient of the dividends is a resident of the source State or maintains a PE therein and is fully taxable in that State (*see* again section §4.04[E][2][b]). At least in these cases when the source State would receive full compensation for its relief from economic double taxation, it is difficult to argue that

2204. 2008-2017 OECD Commentary on Article 24, para. 53 (1977: para. 36; 1992-2005: para. 34).
2205. 2008-2017 OECD Commentary on Article 24, para. 50 (1977: para. 33; 1992-2005: para. 31). *See also* Wandl 2015, 451; Bammens 2012, 254.

inevitably linked differences in circumstances with regard to the redistribution of dividends should be regarded as relevant for the purposes of comparability. Since Article 24(3) does not disregard the remainder of the non-resident enterprise and other facts and circumstances that may influence the taxation on the PE, it also takes account of the fact that the non-resident enterprise redistributes the dividends at issue and that different tax treatment is not indispensable for reaching the aims of the domestic tax measure under scrutiny, that is avoiding economic double taxation only when there is compensation for such relief.[2206]

In addition, in preparation of the 1977 OECD Model, Working Group No. 4 of Working Party No. 1 stated that, if concerns about an unduly privileged treatment cannot be alleviated through a withholding tax as suggested in the OECD Commentary,[2207] it nevertheless appears justified to extend the treatment of inter-company dividends to PEs as long as its application is limited in such a manner that the difference in the taxation borne by dividends received by PEs and dividends received directly by resident enterprises remains within the limits of the reduced rate specified in Article 10(2).[2208] This approach, which is still reflected in the OECD Commentary,[2209] would meet concerns of Eduard Lechner that, without a dividend exemption at the level of PEs, such dividends would be subject to a high tax rate (for instance, formerly in Austria around 40%), whereas subsequent taxation of redistributed dividends would be usually limited to 5% under Article 10(2).[2210] It may be argued that there is no legal basis for such an approach under Article 24(3) without adaptations.[2211] However, if the objective of linking the relief from economic double taxation to the subsequent taxation of dividends is recognized as a legitimate objective under Article 24(3), it can also be argued that this objective is reflected in inevitably linked but relevant differences in legal circumstances to the extent the relief does not exceed the reduced tax burden pursuant to Article 10(2). If no relief is granted up to the envisaged level of subsequent taxation, there is no discrimination due to differences in legal circumstances between PEs of non-resident enterprises and resident enterprises. If no relief is granted above the envisaged level of subsequent taxation, discrimination by reason of residence under Article 24(3) has to be confirmed.

2206. To be sure, it should again be mentioned (*see supra* n. 2177) that, according to Helmut Debatin and Gert Sass, Article 24(3) does not cover personal (or general) circumstances of both individual and corporate taxpayers and that relief from economic double taxation, therefore, can be refused to PEs. *See* Debatin 1970, 134–136; Sass 1966, 107–110. However, it is doubtful whether Article 24(3) broadly excludes personal circumstances from its scope and whether relief from economic double taxation can be considered a personal aspect of taxation. *See* Raad 1986, 148; Hintzen 1976, 2227; Vogel 1970, 354–355.

2207. 2008–2017 OECD Commentary on Article 24, para. 53 (1977: para. 36; 1992–2005: para. 34).

2208. OECD, CFA/WP1(72)8, pp. 8–9.

2209. 2008–2017 OECD Commentary on Article 24, para. 54 (1977: para. 37; 1992–2005: para. 35).

2210. Lechner 1990, 13.

2211. *See*, to this effect, Lechner 1990, 13; moreover, OECD, CFA/WP1(72)8, p. 9.

[3] *Distributing Dividends to Non-residents*

[a] *Integration of Shareholder's Tax?*

If a State avoids economic double taxation at the level of the company that generated profits, it may distinguish whether the company distributes its profits to resident or non-resident shareholders. It may deny tax benefits if a non-resident shareholder is at stake as this shareholder is not taxable in that State. This raises the question of whether such a limitation of tax benefits directly based on the shareholder's residence may be scrutinized under the ownership non-discrimination clause of Article 24(5).

To be sure, Article 24(5) does not prohibit different taxation of resident and non-resident shareholders. It is only concerned with the taxation of resident enterprises based on whether these enterprises have resident or non-resident shareholders. Therefore, if a Contracting State avoids economic double taxation or integrates taxes only at the level of resident shareholders, this cannot be objected under Article 24(5).[2212] This only constitutes a problem under Article 24(3) if non-resident shareholders maintain a PE (*see* already section §4.04[E][2]).

Issues under Article 24(5) arise if relief from economic double taxation is granted to domestic-owned enterprises but not to foreign-owned enterprises. In this respect, economic double taxation may be avoided by deducting a profit distribution from the tax base of a resident enterprise or by granting a tax rate reduction:[2213]

- In the first case, the profits of the resident enterprise are initially part of the tax base and subject to tax. If the enterprise distributes the profits to its shareholders, the distribution can be deducted from the tax base. In the amount of the distributed profits, no tax is due. The reason for this tax benefit lies in the belief that, instead of taxing the profits in the hands of both the resident enterprise and the shareholders (economic double taxation), they should be taxed only once in the hands of the shareholders. By granting a deduction for the profit distribution, taxation in the hands of the resident enterprise is avoided. However, if the shareholders are not resident in the State concerned, they are not fully subject to tax in that State on the dividends received. Since no economic double taxation arises in that State, no deduction for the profit distribution may be granted.
- In the second case, the profits of the resident enterprise are initially subject to tax at a tax rate that does not consider the fact that these profits will be distributed to its shareholders and subjected to tax a second time in their hands (economic double taxation). If the enterprise distributes the profits, the tax rate is reduced in order to consider the subsequent taxation. Such a system is

2212. *See*, in detail, Bammens 2012, 380–384; moreover, Rust 2015b m.no. 108; Rust 2015c m.no. 164; Rust 2010, 641; Goldberg and Glicklich 1992, 100; Avery Jones, Depret, et al. 1991b, 342; Raad 1986, 186, 190; Green 1994, 149; in general Avery Jones, Baker, et al. 2011b, 195; Avery Jones, Baker, et al. 2011a, 553; critically Salditt 1971, 476–477; Mersmann 1971, 311. *See also* 2008–2017 OECD Commentary on Article 24, para. 76 (1963: para. 18; 1977–2005: para. 57).

2213. Rust 2015b m.no. 108; Rust 2015c m.no. 164.

also called a split-rate company tax system as the State of the resident enterprise 'collect[s] company tax on distributed profits at a lower rate than on retained profits which results in a lower company tax burden on profits distributed by a subsidiary to its parent company'.[2214] Again, such a favourable reduction of the tax rate may be granted only if the profit distribution is made to resident shareholders (*see* Figure 4.33).

Figure 4.33 Article 24(5) and Split-Rate Company Tax System

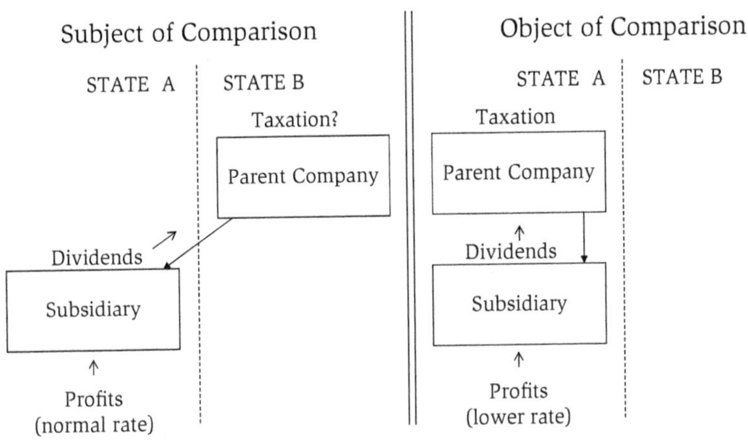

Such distinctions between profit distributions to resident and non-resident shareholders can be scrutinized under Article 24(5). A resident enterprise is taxed other or more burdensome depending on whether it has resident or non-resident shareholders. As a change in the shareholder's residence leads to a change in tax treatment, a 'but for' test establishes prima facie discrimination. Nevertheless, in order to confirm discrimination because of the shareholder's residence, it is necessary to evaluate the reasons for this distinction from a domestic perspective and whether these reasons, if reflected in inevitably linked differences in circumstances in a concrete case, may be brought into balance with the aims of Article 24(5).

A main reason for such a distinction under domestic tax law has already been noted: resident and non-resident shareholders are subject to different taxation in the State concerned. As that State is prepared to avoid economic double taxation in the hands of the resident enterprise only if it can tax the shareholder instead, it draws a corresponding distinction. If the shareholder is a resident, the State is prepared to give up taxation of the resident company by substituting this taxation with the taxation of the resident shareholder. It thereby avoids economic double taxation but ensures single taxation within its territory. If the shareholder is a non-resident, the State is not prepared to give up taxation of the resident company because it might not be able to

2214. 1992–2017 OECD Commentary on Article 10, para. 64 (1977: para. 62).

ensure single taxation within its territory by taxing the shareholder. Although the non-resident shareholder might be subject to tax in another State, and economic double taxation might arise in a cross-border context, this is apparently of no concern to the allegedly discriminating State.

Article 24(5) is likely concerned with the Contracting States turning juridical into economic double taxation (*see* Chapter 3 section §3.03[E][2]). Whether a State is allowed to tax resident or non-resident shareholders should play no role in taxing resident enterprises. If a non-resident shareholder is involved, the State of the resident enterprise has different taxing rights than it would have with a resident shareholder. If the State of the resident enterprise is displeased with such limited taxing rights, it nevertheless cannot disadvantage the resident enterprise by providing for 'any taxation or any requirement connected therewith which is other or more burdensome than the taxation and connected requirements to which other similar [domestic-owned] enterprises ... are or may be subjected'. This background indicates that if a State does not provide relief from economic double taxation to foreign-owned enterprises when such enterprises distribute profits to their non-resident shareholders, this constitutes prohibited tax discrimination under Article 24(5). As the State has generally agreed in the tax treaty not to tax non-resident shareholders or to limit its taxing rights in order to avoid international juridical double taxation, it cannot take foreign residence or missing taxing rights as a reason to contribute to economic double taxation by not granting otherwise available relief, that is by denying a deduction of a profit distribution or a lower tax rate.[2215]

[b] Borderline Case: The UK Act

This conclusion that differences in treatment between domestic-owned and foreign-owned enterprises are prohibited under Article 24(5) so far as relief from economic double taxation is concerned seems not to be shared by the OECD Commentary:[2216]

> A similar example [where the different treatment is not dependent on the fact that the capital of the company is owned or controlled by non-residents but, rather, on the fact that dividends paid to non-residents are taxed differently] would be that of a State that levies a tax on resident companies that make distributions to their shareholders regardless of whether or not they are residents or non-residents, but which, in order to avoid a multiple application of that tax, would not apply it to distributions made to related resident companies that are themselves subject to the tax upon their own distributions. The fact that the latter exemption would not apply to distributions to non-resident companies should not be considered to violate paragraph 5. In that case, it is not because the capital of the resident company is owned or controlled by non-residents that it is treated differently; it is because it makes distributions to companies that, under the provisions of the treaty, cannot be subjected to the same tax when they re-distribute the dividends received from that resident company. In this example, all resident companies are

2215. *See also*, to this effect, Rust 2015b m.no. 108; Rust 2015c m.no. 164; Goldberg and Glicklich 1992, 100.
2216. 2008–2017 OECD Commentary on Article 24, para. 78.

> treated the same way regardless of who owns or controls their capital and the different treatment is restricted to cases where distributions are made in circumstances where the distribution tax could be avoided.

The OECD Commentary appears to take a view that is difficult to reconcile with the objective of the non-discrimination clause. It deals with measures that aim at avoiding economic double taxation, namely, a multiple application of tax, and that concern a tax on resident companies. That tax does not apply 'to distributions made to related resident companies that are themselves subject to the tax upon their own distributions'.[2217] At a first glance, the State is prepared to avoid economic double taxation by not taxing a distribution at the level of a resident company only if it can ensure taxation within its territory, that is taxation of a subsequent redistribution. According to the OECD Commentary, even though the residence of the shareholders is used as the decisive criterion for the different tax treatment, this is not the actual reason. The less favourable treatment is provided because the resident company 'makes distributions to companies that, *under the provisions of the treaty*, cannot be subjected to the same tax when they re-distribute the dividends received from that resident company' (emphasis added).[2218] Thus, the OECD Commentary itself admits that differences in taxing rights under the provisions of the treaty between the State of the company and the State of the shareholder motivated the tax distinction under scrutiny. Such motives, however, are in opposition to Article 24(5) and should, in principle, lead to prohibited tax discrimination because of the shareholder's residence (*see* again Chapter 3 section §3.03[E][2]).

Nevertheless, it should be mentioned that the OECD Commentary does not focus on the taxation of shareholders in general as influenced by their residence, including the taxation of individuals who participate in the resident company, but only on the taxation of corporate shareholders that 'cannot be subjected to the same [corporate or distribution] tax when they *re-distribute the dividends* received from that resident company' (emphasis added).[2219] These statements, therefore, are closely related to the UK case *Boake Allen* (also known as *NEC Semi-Conductors*)[2220] that dealt with the now abolished advanced corporation tax (ACT) that was part of the UK imputation system. Philip Baker describes this system as follows:[2221]

> [W]hen a UK resident company paid a dividend, the company was required to account to the Inland Revenue for an amount of 'advance corporation tax' (ACT), which was calculated as a percentage of the amount of the dividend. This ACT had two functions. First, it was a prepayment of the paying company's own corporation tax liability and could be credited against that 'mainstream corporation tax'. Of course, if the company had no taxable profits for that period but nevertheless

2217. *Ibid.*, para. 78.
2218. *Ibid.*, para. 78.
2219. *Ibid.*, para. 78.
2220. UK House of Lords, *Boake Allen Ltd v. HMRC*, 23 May 2007, [2007] UKHL 25. On this case and its development, *see* Bammens 2012, 165–166, 420–435; Avery Jones, Baker, et al. 2011a, 558–560; Avery Jones, Baker, et al. 2011b, 199–202; Boulogne 2011, 174; Kalungi 2009; Cleave 2008; Cleave 2007; Avery Jones 2007; Oliver 2004; Baker 2004, 207–211.
2221. Baker 2004, 208.

paid a dividend, the ACT was an absolute tax cost. The second function was that the payment of ACT allowed the Inland Revenue to grant a dividend tax credit to the recipient shareholder ....

Where a UK resident subsidiary paid a dividend to its UK resident parent, the system operated so that the parent did not again have to pay ACT when it eventually paid a dividend on to its shareholders. There might be a timing disadvantage, however, if the subsidiary paid a dividend on which it had to account for ACT at the time of payment, and there was then a significant delay before the parent paid a dividend to its shareholders. Largely for that reason, UK domestic legislation ... provided for a 'group income election'. Where a UK resident subsidiary and its UK resident parent entered into such an election, no ACT was payable when the subsidiary paid a dividend to its parent, but the parent then had to pay ACT if it subsequently paid a dividend on to its shareholders.

On the one hand, resident corporations that received dividends from a resident subsidiary were subject to ACT on their own distributions that allowed postponing earlier payment of that tax at the level of the resident subsidiary thereby generally leading to a cash-flow advantage (group income election). On the other hand, all non-resident corporations (but also all resident and non-resident individuals and resident tax-exempt corporations) were not subject to ACT which prohibited postponement of payment and required different tax treatment at the level of the resident subsidiary. It was considered, among other things, that since not only ownership by non-resident persons but also ownership by resident individuals led to treatment that was less favourable (payment of ACT), the shareholder's residence was not the reason for different tax treatment under Article 24(5). This analysis of the scope and design of the domestic tax measure under scrutiny rather implied that the actual grounds for the tax distinction at issue was the shareholder's liability to pay ACT, not the shareholder's residence.[2222] Although liability to pay ACT, in many cases, coincided with full tax liability to corporate tax as far as non-exempt corporations were concerned[2223] (a 'but for' test, therefore, established prima facie discrimination), a distinction between liability to pay ACT and residence was made in substance. Liability to pay ACT, even though inevitably linked to residence in a concrete case, was regarded as a relevant characteristic that rendered situations of foreign-owned and domestic-owned enterprises incomparable.

2222. *See* UK House of Lords, *Boake Allen Ltd v. HMRC*, 23 May 2007, [2007] UKHL 25, paras 16–17 (Lord Hoffmann): 'Does [the domestic tax measure under scrutiny] discriminate on the grounds that the capital of the subsidiary is controlled by a non-resident company? In my opinion it plainly does not. ... [A]n individual US shareholder and the company he controls in the UK could not elect, but the reason is not because the company is subject to US control. An individual UK shareholder and his company could not elect either, for the same reason that a non-resident company cannot elect. It is because an individual is not liable to corporation tax. An election is a joint decision by two entities paying and receiving dividends that one rather than the other will be liable for ACT. This is not a concept which can meaningfully be applied when one of the entities is not liable for ACT at all.' *See also*, however, Schwarz 2015, secs. 24–300 (p. 407), who prefers the view that the ownership by non-residents and not the way in which those non-residents were taxed (liability to pay ACT) gave rise to the difference in treatment; moreover, Kalungi 2009, 139–142.

2223. *See also*, to this effect, Cleave 2008, 95; Cleave 2007, 606.

It should be mentioned that, in the UK case *FCE Bank*,[2224] a case concerning the UK group relief system, resident enterprises were not entitled to group relief if they were both owned by a resident or non-resident individual or by a non-resident corporation. Without a common resident parent company, there could be no group between resident enterprises. This was reminiscent of the previously decided *Boake Allen* case in which a resident enterprise was also not entitled to a group income election if it was owned by a resident or non-resident individual or by a non-resident corporation because payment of ACT – advance *corporation* tax – existed only in a corporate context. From a purely formal perspective, in both cases, tax benefits were denied to a resident enterprise if that enterprise was owned by a resident individual, which should have arguably implied in both cases that the shareholder's residence was not the actual grounds for such a denial.

Despite that, in *FCE Bank*, the shareholder's residence was recognized as the sole reason for different tax treatment. Unlike in *Boake Allen*, prohibited tax discrimination under Article 24(5) was confirmed. While the scope and design of the UK group relief system arguably implied that it mattered whether the shareholder was liable to UK corporation tax, not whether the shareholder was a resident, this did not suffice for rejecting discrimination. Only grouping of profits and losses between resident enterprises was claimed under Article 24(5) which in no way affected the tax position of the shareholder or the UK's right to tax its resident enterprises. In *Boake Allen*, by contrast, the scrutinized tax measure necessarily involved both the resident enterprise and the non-resident shareholder which rendered liability to pay ACT a relevant characteristic.

A comparison of the decisions in *FCE Bank* and *Boake Allen* confirms that, if certain resident shareholders (notably, resident individuals) also trigger tax disadvantages, which means that residence does not matter in such situations, this may point to a particular objective of the domestic tax measure: liability to pay ACT or liability to UK corporation tax. This does not suffice, however, for a denial of discrimination under Article 24(5) or for a definite decision on the grounds for different tax treatment from a domestic and tax treaty perspective in a concrete case: different legal contexts and, in particular differences in the role and involvement of the shareholder, may lead to different assessments and outcomes.[2225]

2224. UK Court of Appeal, *HMRC v. FCE Bank plc*, 17 October 2012, [2012] EWCA Civ 1290. On this case and its development, *see* Cleave 2013b; Cleave 2013a; Last 2013; Baker 2013, 351–354; Bammens 2012, 445–448; Baker 2011.

2225. *See*, however, Bammens 2012, 431–432, who contrasts the *Boake Allen* decision with the German *Delaware* decision on fiscal unity. He argues that, in the first decision, the benefit at issue was denied if the shareholder was not a company *or* if it was a non-resident. Since the benefit was also denied if the shareholder was a resident individual, the distinguishing criterion could not be equated to foreign ownership. He further assumes that, in the second decision, the benefit at issue was denied if the shareholder was a non-resident *and* if it did not have a PE. Since the distinguishing criterion left no cases in which the benefit was denied even though the shareholder was a resident, it could be equated to foreign ownership (foreign ownership was a necessary precondition for the benefit to be denied). Yet, as far as can be seen, a fiscal unity was denied either if the shareholder was a non-resident *and* if it did not have a PE *or*, alternatively, if the shareholder was not a company. In both decisions, therefore, resident individuals or non-resident individuals with a PE precluded tax benefits: they were

It has been further submitted that Article 24(5) does not address the taxation of the shareholder if, for instance, a State imposes withholding tax on dividends paid to a non-resident shareholder but not on dividends paid to a resident shareholder. 'Its object therefore is to ensure equal treatment for taxpayers residing in the same State, and not to subject foreign capital, in the hands of the partners or shareholders, to identical treatment to that applied to domestic capital.'[2226] Given that the payment of ACT is concerned with the payment of the dividend to the shareholders and, thus, with the taxation of domestic or foreign capital in the hands of resident or non-resident shareholders, respectively, not with the taxation of the resident enterprise on its profits, an argument against discrimination can be made. Although ACT is levied or not levied (group income election) on the resident enterprise and does not constitute a withholding tax on the dividend, the payment of ACT still does not relate to the profits of that enterprise, which arguably puts it outside the scope of Article 24(5).[2227] However, if the payment of ACT is really concerned with the payment of the dividend to the shareholders and, therefore, different treatment depends on whether the shareholders are subject to UK corporation tax and ACT, the resident company is, in fact, treated differently because its shareholders are not subject to tax in the UK, a reason which is difficult to reconcile with the objectives of Article 24(5).[2228]

If a resident parent company and a resident subsidiary are allowed to make a group income election that the former rather than the latter will be liable for ACT, differences in liability to pay ACT at the level of the parent company appear relevant not in isolation but for the purposes of determining whether this group income election can fulfil its purpose: mere postponement of liability to pay ACT leading to a liquidity or cash-flow advantage. To this effect, when group consolidation is claimed between a resident subsidiary and a non-resident parent company under Article 24(5) in order to postpone payment of tax through consolidation of profits and losses, it matters whether this postponement could become indefinite and thereby establish differences in circumstances between domestic and cross-border situations.[2229] While discrimination because of the shareholder's residence and tax liability is prohibited, non-discriminatory tax treatment should not lead to a modification of taxing rights by extending group consolidation cross-border; differences in taxing rights and corresponding differences in whether tax is merely postponed or completely abandoned may prevent comparability (*see* section §4.04[C][3]). Similarly, if a group income election would completely eliminate liability to pay ACT in cross-border situations even though its purpose is merely to postpone payment, differences in liability to pay

---

not liable to pay ACT and, therefore, were not eligible for a group income election or not liable to corporate tax and could not participate in a fiscal unity.

2226. 2008–2017 OECD Commentary on Article 24, para. 76 (1963: para. 18; 1977–2005: para. 57). *See*, moreover, 2008–2017 OECD Commentary on Article 24, para. 78. John F. Avery Jones, Philip Baker, et al. state to this effect that 'such withholding obligations are [not] within the scope of the ownership provision because withholding tax is a means of collecting tax on the owner'. *See* Avery Jones, Baker, et al. 2011b, 188–189; Avery Jones, Baker, et al. 2011a, 546; similarly, Haslehner 2016a m.no. 36; Rust 2015c m.no. 164.

2227. Oliver 2004, 82–83; Oliver 1977, 152–153. *See also*, similarly, Baker 2004, 210.

2228. *See also* Kalungi 2009, 141–142.

2229. *See also*, to this effect, Haslehner 2016a m.no. 36.

ACT indicate relevant differences between mere postponement and permanent relief.[2230] This view presupposes that ACT is a tax on resident enterprises (although it has consequences for shareholders as well) and that Article 24(5) does not aim at prohibiting a State from taxing its resident enterprises sooner or later, that is depending on whether a regime allows transferring profits or losses or liability for ACT to another resident enterprise. However, Niels Bammens argues that, since the ACT that is paid functions as a prepayment for 'mainstream corporation tax', the tax position of the shareholder (liability to pay ACT) is irrelevant for the cash-flow advantage and should not be taken into account for comparability purposes. As a consequence, the denial of the cash-flow advantage should be considered to constitute discrimination under Article 24(5).[2231]

All of these arguments demonstrate that discrimination cannot be determined without a substantive analysis that takes account of the purposes of Article 24(5) and how these purposes stand against the former UK imputation system and the concept of ACT. If it is objectively established that, from a UK perspective, the reason for different tax treatment lies not in the shareholder's residence but in liability to pay ACT, it is nevertheless necessary to determine whether this reason should be equated with a prohibited tax distinction under Article 24(5) due to an inevitable link with the shareholder's residence in a concrete case or whether it can succeed as a legitimate tax distinction from a tax treaty perspective. As long as a Contracting State imposes a higher tax on resident enterprises solely because the shareholders are not taxable in that State – they are taxable in the other Contracting State instead – discrimination should be confirmed whereas concerns about (non-)taxation of resident enterprises on their taxable profits appear legitimate. It is difficult to decide on which side the ACT system with its group income election falls. However, as far as liquidity or cash-flow advantages are concerned, there are some grounds to believe that this aspect should be covered by Article 24(5) thereby leading to prohibited tax discrimination if a distinction between foreign-owned and domestic-owned enterprises is made.

[4] Distributing Dividends as a Non-resident

[a] Arguments Against Discrimination

If a non-resident enterprise maintains a PE in a State and pays dividends to its shareholders that stem from business profits that are attributable to the PE, the

2230. *See* UK House of Lords, *Boake Allen Ltd v. HMRC*, 23 May 2007, [2007] UKHL 25, para. 19 (Lord Hoffmann): 'In my respectful opinion, it is not possible to decouple the positions of parent and subsidiary … To allow an election by a group with a US-resident parent would not be to give a relief available to a group with a UK-resident parent. It would be something different in kind. It would not be an election as to who would be liable for ACT but as to whether the group should pay it at all.' This argument was rejected by the CJEU in its decision of 8 March 2001, C-397/98 and C-410/98, *Metallgesellschaft and Hoechst*, but according to the UK House of Lords, the prohibition on discrimination implied by the EU freedom of establishment has an altogether different purpose from the prohibition on discrimination in the double taxation conventions.

2231. Bammens 2012, 433–434, 1026.

question arises whether Article 24(3) requires the State to extend domestic tax benefits that aim at avoiding economic double taxation to the PE if these benefits are available only to resident enterprises (*see* Figure 4.34). The OECD Commentary answers this question in the negative.[2232] It first refers to the fact that Article 24(3) is concerned only with the activities of a PE:[2233]

> [T]he equal treatment principle of paragraph 3 only applies to the taxation of the permanent establishment's own activities. That principle, therefore, is restricted to a comparison between the rules governing the taxation of the permanent establishment's own activities and those applicable to similar business activities carried on by an independent resident enterprise. ... [R]ules related to the distribution of the profits of a resident enterprise cannot be extended to a permanent establishment under paragraph 3 as they do not relate to the business activities of the permanent establishment (see paragraph 59 below).

This idea is further explained as follows:[2234]

> Since a permanent establishment, by its very nature, does not distribute dividends, the tax treatment of distributions made by the enterprise to which the permanent establishment belongs is therefore outside the scope of paragraph 3. Paragraph 3 is restricted to the taxation of the profits from the activities of the permanent establishment itself and does not extend to the taxation of the enterprise as a whole. This is confirmed by the second sentence of the paragraph, which confirms that tax aspects related to the taxpayer that owns the permanent establishment, such as personal allowances and deductions, are outside the scope of the paragraph. [[2235]] Thus, issues related to various systems for the integration of the corporate and shareholder's taxes (*e.g.* advance corporate tax, *précompte mobilier*, computation of franked income and related dividend tax credits) are outside the scope of the paragraph.

2232. *See also* Loukota and Jirousek 2016 m.no. 29.
2233. 2008–2017 OECD Commentary on Article 24, para. 41.
2234. *Ibid.*, para. 59.
2235. *See supra* n. 1124.

Figure 4.34 Article 24(3) and Split-Rate Company Tax System

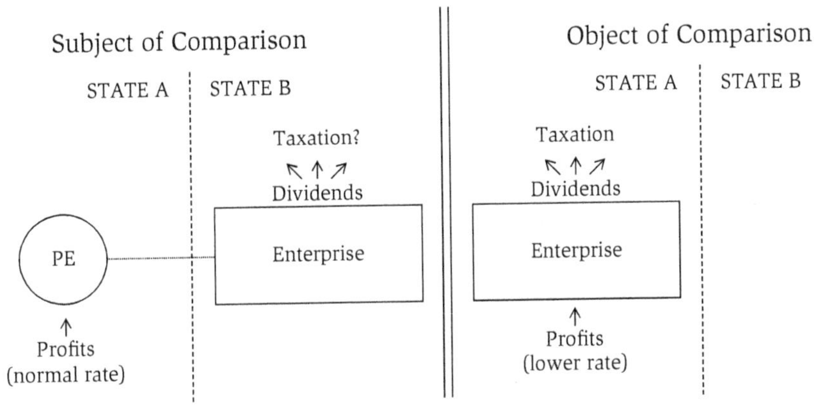

In one aspect, the OECD Commentary can be fully supported: Article 24(3) addresses '[t]he taxation on a permanent establishment'. Consequently, only 'the taxation of the permanent establishment's own activities'[2236] is under scrutiny, not the taxation of the activities carried on by other parts of the non-resident enterprise.[2237] If the income at issue is not attributable to the PE, the PE non-discrimination rule is not applicable. Even more, when other persons and, notably, shareholders are taxed differently based on whether they are invested in a resident or non-resident enterprise, this distinction cannot be scrutinized under Article 24(3). If a measure of a State avoids economic double taxation at the shareholder's level only when dividends are received from resident enterprises, it cannot be extended to dividends from non-resident enterprises even when these non-resident enterprises maintain a PE in that State.[2238]

2236. 2008–2017 OECD Commentary on Article 24, para. 41.

2237. As discussed in section §4.04[B], however, this does not mean that other activities are irrelevant in determining the appropriate level of taxation of the PE's own activities.

2238. *See*, for instance, Rust 2015b m.no. 71; Rust 2015c m.no. 111. This result was not that clear before 2008: 'As regards the imputation system ("*avoir fiscal*" or "tax credit"), it seems doubtful, at least on a literal interpretation of the provisions of paragraph 3, whether it should be extended to non-resident companies in respect of dividends paid out of profits made by their permanent establishments. In fact, it has identical effects to those of the split-rate system but these effects are not immediate as they occur only at the time of the shareholder's personal taxation. From a purely economic and financial standpoint, however, it is conceivable that such profits should be treated as though they were profits of a distinct company in State A where the permanent establishment of a company which is a resident of State B is situated, and, to the extent that they are distributed, carry the *avoir fiscal* or tax credit. But to take the matter further, to avoid all discrimination it is necessary that this advantage should already have been accorded to shareholders who are residents of State B of companies which are residents of State A. From the practical standpoint, the two States concerned should, of course, agree upon the conditions and procedures for allowing the *avoir fiscal* or tax credit to shareholders who are themselves residents of either State, of the companies concerned that are residents of State B.' *See* 1992–2005 OECD Commentary on Article 24, para. 42 (1977: para. 44); moreover, OECD, DAF/CFA/WP1/71.10, pp. 8–9; OECD, DAF/CFA/WP1/72/3, p. 5; OECD, CFA/WP1(72)8, pp. 10–11; OECD, DAF/CFA/2584, p. 7; OECD, CFA/WP1(73)6, pp. 12–13; OECD, DAF/CFA/WP1(73)8, pp. 4–5.

Nevertheless, various options for the avoidance of economic double taxation are at a State's disposal. Some may operate at the level of the shareholder, but some may operate at the level of the distributing company or require the involvement of both. Although all of these different techniques may lead to the same result, that is avoidance of economic double taxation,[2239] it matters under Article 24(3) what method is specifically employed by a Contracting State and whether it applies at the level of the shareholder or at the level of the distributing company.[2240]

Of particular interest are measures that provide for a reduction of the applicable tax rate in order to avoid economic double taxation. Such measures are part of a split-rate company tax system in which company tax on distributed profits is collected at a lower rate than on retained profits.[2241] They operate solely at the level of the distributing company. Yet, the tax rate may not be reduced if a non-resident company is at stake that distributes profits it derived through a PE to its resident or non-resident[2242] shareholders. In this case, the source State in which the PE of the distributing company is located distinguishes based on residence and may thereby contribute to unrelieved economic double taxation. At the same time, Article 24(3) can prevent economic double taxation by requiring the source State to lower its tax rate on the distributed profits provided that these profits stem from activities carried on in the source State through the PE.

When a non-resident company distributes profits, these profits do not necessarily stem from the activities carried on in the source State through a PE. Rather, the whole enterprise distributes profits if it was successful in its overall business. Apparently, the OECD Commentary puts emphasis on this fact by stating that '[s]ince a permanent establishment, by its very nature, does not distribute dividends, the tax treatment of distributions made by the enterprise to which the permanent establishment belongs is therefore outside the scope of paragraph 3'.[2243] While it is without question that a PE, as such, does not distribute dividends, the question remains whether the PE should be granted favourable tax treatment when the non-resident enterprise to which the PE belongs distributes dividends.[2244] Additionally, while a non-resident enterprise may

2239. *See also* Sass 1966, 108–109.

2240. *See*, for instance, Rust 2015b m.no. 72; Rust 2015c m.no. 112, according to whom '[i]t is true that a split-rate system at the level of the distributing corporation and an imputation credit at the level of the shareholder constitute two different methods for the avoidance of economic double taxation that lead to the same result', but '[f]or the application of Article 24(3) … it is important whether or not the benefit is granted at the level of the corporation'.

2241. 1992–2017 OECD Commentary on Article 10, para. 64 (1977: para. 62).

2242. A State's measure may not only distinguish based on whether the distributing company is a resident or a non-resident of that State but also based on whether the ultimate shareholders are residents or non-residents of that State. With regard to the latter distinction, it is up to Article 24(5) to prevent discrimination at the level of the (resident) distributing company based on whether resident or non-resident shareholders are at stake (*see* section §4.04[E][3]). If no such distinction based on the shareholder's residence is permitted under Article 24(5), the only question under Article 24(3) remains whether the State may distinguish based on whether the distributing company is a resident or non-resident of that State.

2243. 2008–2017 OECD Commentary on Article 24, para. 59.

2244. *See also* Rust 2015b m.no. 72; Rust 2015c m.no. 113, who admits that 'a PE is not able to make a dividend distribution' but responds that '[t]he taxpayer protected by Article 24(3) …, however, is the corporation … with regard to the profit attributable to the PE' and that '[t]he

distribute dividends that are not fully derived from the activities carried on in the source State through a PE, the question remains whether economic double taxation should be avoided to the extent the dividends are actually derived from such activities. It is thus unclear whether the dividend distribution can be traced back to business profits that are attributable to a PE in the source State and, therefore, whether the taxation on a PE is less favourably levied if no lower tax rate is granted with regard to distributed profits.

When approaching this question under Article 24(3), it must be ensured that the taxation is on a PE and that the tax measure under scrutiny, therefore, is within the scope of the PE non-discrimination clause. This particularly depends on whether the dividend distributions can be traced back to the activities of a PE in the source State. If the dividend distributions stem from such activities, Article 24(3) is applicable and a 'but for' test establishes prima facie discrimination in all cases when a change in residence leads to a change in tax treatment. It must then be assessed whether inevitably linked differences in circumstances speak against an extension of the domestic tax measure that aims at avoiding economic double taxation.

[b] Linking Distributions to Profits

It is not prohibited under Article 24(3) to consider the activities of the whole enterprise in order to determine whether the taxation on a PE is at stake and what is the relevant benchmark for non-discriminatory taxation. It has been argued above that a State may calculate its progressive tax rate on the basis of the income or capital of the whole enterprise even when it taxes only the activities carried on in the source State through a PE (*see* section §4.04[B]). The tax rate establishes a relevant connection between the taxation on a PE and the activities of the whole enterprise. As far as a split-rate company tax system is concerned, the tax rate similarly establishes a connection between the taxation on a PE and the profit distribution of the whole non-resident enterprise. In both cases, only the taxation on a PE can be scrutinized, but non-discriminatory taxation on a PE depends on factors that are related to the whole non-resident enterprise. The tax rate of a split-rate corporate tax system that is applicable to the PE thus depends on the profit distribution of the whole non-resident enterprise and on the extent the profit distribution relates to the profits of the PE.

In simple cases, the determination of which amount of a profit distribution relates to a PE in the source State might not pose any particular problems. If an enterprise of the residence State maintains a PE in the source State and all activities of that enterprise

corporation can distribute the profits earned in the PE'; similarly, Rust 2010, 638–639. *See*, moreover, Raad 1986, 150, who mentions that, even though a PE cannot make the decision necessary for the split-rate system, viz. how much of the profits to distribute (*see* Rädler and Raupach 1966, 393), it is not the PE but the foreign resident who is the person entitled to non-discriminatory treatment; this foreign resident is certainly able to make the required decision (*see* Vogel 1970, 354). *See*, not least, Haslehner 2009, 311.

are carried on by that PE,[2245] the whole profit distribution relates to the PE under Article 24(3). In particular if the residence State exempts all profits that are attributable to the PE under Article 23 A, only the source State is able to avoid economic double taxation by extending a favourable tax rate to the PE.

In other cases, however, when some parts of the enterprise suffer losses but other parts achieve profits, it might be suitable to link certain amounts of a profit distribution to one part of the enterprise but not to another. Depending on whether such a connection between the profit distribution and the profits of a PE can be established in a particular case, Article 24(3) might require non-discriminatory tax treatment with respect to a split-rate corporate tax system or indeed, as the OECD Commentary argues, the taxation on a PE may not be sufficiently connected to the profit distribution.[2246] However, the OECD Commentary mentioned before 2008 that '[a]s a practical rule, the tax could … be calculated at the reduced rate (applicable to distributed profits) on that proportion of an establishment's profits which corresponds to the ratio between the profit distributed by the company to which it belongs and the latter's total profit; the remaining profit could be taxed at the higher rate. Of course, the two Contracting States would have to consult together and exchange all information necessary for giving practical effect to this solution'.[2247]

In this context, it should be noted that a mismatch between the time when the PE achieves profits and the time when these profits are distributed by the non-resident enterprise to its shareholders does not restrict Article 24(3) in comparing the tax treatment of the PE to the treatment of resident enterprises.[2248] Such a timing mismatch can complicate matters in determining which part of the profit distribution actually stems from profits that were previously attributable to the PE in the source State. It should also be considered, however, that resident enterprises may be exempted on a part of their profits and, therefore, even with resident enterprises, there might be a need for determining which amount of a profit distribution relates to taxable profits. If there is a method available under domestic tax law to connect profits to particular distributions, no other method should be applied in the context of PEs under Article 24(3).

[c] Differences in Circumstances?

Since the profit distribution of the whole non-resident enterprise is not linked to the protected characteristic of residence, a 'but for' test requires comparing to a resident enterprise that makes such a profit distribution. As soon as it is confirmed that this

2245. This may be the case if a company is incorporated in a Contracting State but carries on all substantial business activities in the other Contracting State and if Article 4(3) of the tax treaty, in deviation from the OECD Model, determines residence based on incorporation.

2246. *See also* Raad 1986, 150, who admits that a determination by the source State on the basis of its own law, of the profits of the entire enterprise, and the amount of the profit distributed complicates matters.

2247. 1992–2005 OECD Commentary on Article 24, para. 41 (1977: para. 43); this solution is also mentioned by Hohenwarter and Weninger 2006, 262; Vogel 1970, 354; Rädler and Raupach 1966, 391.

2248. *See*, to this effect, Rust 2015b m.nos. 66, 72; Rust 2015c m.nos. 104, 112.

profit distribution at least partly stems from the profits of a PE, a 'but for' test establishes prima facie discrimination. It follows that, if a State has a split-rate company tax system, it must apply a lower tax rate to the profits of a PE when the income of the whole enterprise is distributed to its shareholders and when identifiable amounts of the distributed income stem from the activities of the PE unless inevitably linked but relevant differences in circumstances can be identified on a substantive basis.

It is noteworthy that, before 2008, the OECD Commentary mentioned that most OECD member countries that have adopted a split-rate system:[2249]

> do not consider themselves bound by the provisions of paragraph 3 to extend it to permanent establishments of non-resident companies. This attitude is based, in particular, on the view that the split-rate is only one element amongst others (in particular a withholding tax on distributed income) in a system of taxing company profits and dividends which must be considered as a whole and is therefore, both for legal and technical reasons, of domestic application only. The State where the permanent establishment is situated could claim the right not to tax such profits at the reduced rate as, generally, it does not tax the dividends distributed by the company to which the permanent establishment belongs.
>
> This view is, however, disputed. The States in favour of extending the split-rate system to permanent establishments urge that as the essential feature of this system is a special technique of taxing profits which enterprises in a corporate form derive from their activities, and is designed to afford immediate relief from the double taxation levied on the profits distributed, it should be applied to permanent establishments in bilateral conventions against double taxation. It is generally recognised that, by the effects of their provisions, such conventions necessarily result in some integration of the taxation systems of the Contracting States. On this account, it is perfectly conceivable that profits made in a State (A) by a permanent establishment of a company resident in another State (B) should be taxed in State A according to the split-rate system. ... Similar considerations apply to systems where distributions of profits made can be deducted from the taxable income of a company.

These statements can be traced back to various discussions in preparation of the 1977 OECD Model which led to no agreement as to whether Article 24(3) requires extending a split-rate system to PEs.[2250] When the OECD Fiscal Committee discussed this issue at length, the Delegates for Austria, Germany, and Norway argued that it did not constitute discrimination to tax a PE at the higher (undistributed) rate, whereas the Delegates for France, Luxembourg, Netherlands, and Switzerland took the contrary view.[2251] As no conclusion was reached and it was impossible to adopt a general

2249. 1992–2005 OECD Commentary on Article 24, paras 40–41 (1977: paras 42–43).

2250. Already in 1966, the Delegate for Japan stated that discrimination that might be permissible includes split-rates of tax according to whether or not profits were distributed, since a State would not know whether or not the profits of a PE of a non-resident company were to be distributed. *See* OECD, TFD/FC/211, p. 3; moreover, OECD, FC(64)1, p. 3. Similarly, Working Party No. 4 of the OECD Fiscal Committee noted that Germany, Belgium, and Austria had a split-rate system, and there would not appear to be any contradiction between this situation and Article 24. *See* OECD, FC/WP4(69)1, pp. 6–7, 14.

2251. OECD, DAF/FC/70.5, p. 3; OECD, DAF/FC/70.5 Corrigendum. It was argued that no discrimination under Article 24(3) arises because (a) the purpose of the lower rate was (i) to

solution, Working Party No. 1 of the Committee on Fiscal Affairs, which succeeded the Fiscal Committee with regard to the work on the OECD Model, asked to prepare comments taking into account these conflicting views.[2252]

Just as the source State may not be prepared to avoid economic double taxation at the level of a PE by granting an exemption or credit for underlying tax when that PE receives dividends, it might not be prepared to avoid economic double taxation by applying a lower tax rate when that PE makes profits that are subsequently distributed by the whole enterprise to the shareholders. As a PE, by its very nature, 'does not distribute dividends',[2253] the source State faces different tax consequences when compared to resident enterprises and may not be rewarded with compensation for its avoidance of economic double taxation.[2254] This issue has already been dealt with in detail above (*see* section §4.04[E][2]). Very similar inevitably linked differences may exist in a concrete case regardless of whether a non-resident enterprise that maintains a PE receives or distributes dividends. In both situations, economic double taxation may be at stake, the PE is not able to distribute dividends, and subsequent taxation may depend on residence. Although concerns about subsequent taxation and compensation for a tax benefit could, in principle, be regarded as legitimate under Article 24(3), they are not able to explain and justify a general tax distinction between resident and non-resident enterprises in regard to measures that aim at avoiding economic double taxation.

Where a non-resident company distributes profits realized by a PE to its shareholders, the situation is not substantially different than when a non-resident company receives dividends that are attributable to a PE. In both cases, the whole enterprise is the taxpayer in question and thus economic double taxation is related to the whole enterprise. Since the PE suffers a tax burden on the distributed profits or the

---

encourage distributions, and PEs could not do this, (ii) to take account of the fact that further taxation was going to be imposed at the shareholder level, which was not the case with PEs; (b) the lower rate should be regarded in the same way as a personal allowance as it was a special rate for distributions; (c) to apply the lower rate to PEs would give them an advantage over national firms. It was argued against this view that (a) while the profits may not be taxed at the shareholder level in the State of the PE, they would be taxed in the other State; (b) the reason for the lower rate of increasing reliance on share capital rather than loans applied to PEs as well; (c) when a State changed from a classical to a split-rate system, the rate on undistributed profits had to be higher than the rate under the classical system to make up for the loss of revenue due to the lower rate on distributed profits so that rates of tax on PEs increased simply as a result of a change of internal tax system; (d) when the total activities of a PE were carried out in the State concerned, the higher rate put them at a disadvantage over subsidiaries.

2252. *See* OECD, DAF/CFA/WP1/71.10, pp. 7–8; OECD, DAF/CFA/WP1/71.10(Add.1), p. 4 (Working Group No. 4 addressed various arguments and was rather in favour of discrimination whenever profits made by the PE are transferred to the head office of the company and included in the profits distributed by the latter); OECD, DAF/CFA/WP1/72/3, pp. 4–5 (Working Party No. 1 recognized that it was impossible to adopt a general solution in the Commentary); OECD, CFA/WP1(72)8, pp. 9–10 (new proposal of Working Group No. 4); OECD, DAF/CFA/2584, p. 6; OECD, CFA/WP1(73)6, pp. 11–12; OECD, DAF/CFA/WP1(73)8, pp. 4–5 (adoption with slight amendments).

2253. 2014 OECD Commentary on Article 24, paras 50, 59 (1992–2005: para. 31; 1977: para. 33).

2254. *See also* Sass 1966, 108–109, who is concerned with a loss of tax revenue because of no subsequent taxation.

dividends that are received, the question arises whether measures that aim at avoiding economic double taxation at the level of resident enterprises should be extended under Article 24(3) to PEs. The aim of putting PEs on an equal footing with resident enterprises generally prevails over unspecified concerns about compensation for a tax benefit. Also, the fact that the tax rate under scrutiny refers to the distributed profits of the whole enterprise does not alter the fact that the taxation is on the PE. Whether a higher or lower tax rate is applied, it is applied to the income that is attributable to the PE. This means that, contrary to the statements of the OECD Commentary, the non-discrimination obligations of Article 24(3) protect non-resident enterprises with regard to measures that avoid economic double taxation through a lower tax rate when the whole enterprise distributes profits to its shareholders.[2255]

2255. *See also*, to this effect, Rust 2015b m.no. 72; Rust 2015c m.nos. 112–113; Rust 2010, 638–639; Haslehner 2009, 310–311; Bammens 2012, 381, 1018–1019; Bellstedt 1973, 370–372; Mersmann 1971, 311; Vogel 1970, 353–357; differently, Debatin 1970, 136, who argues that a split-rate company tax system pursues the capital market policy of allowing higher dividend distributions and consequently refers to the conduct of the companies after the realization of profits; therefore, such a system does not concern the activities carried on through a PE within the meaning of Article 24(3); similarly, Sass 1966, 108–109; moreover, Storck 1980, 95–96.

CHAPTER 5

Conceptual Implications for Non-discrimination Law

In this study, first, the concept of non-discrimination under the GATT and GATS has been examined (Chapter 2). This analysis allowed demonstrating how 'likeness', 'less favourable treatment', and general exceptions determine whether substantive WTO obligations are violated and how these steps of analysis can take account of regulatory purposes. Afterwards, the concept of non-discrimination under Article 24 of the OECD Model has been scrutinized (Chapter 3). Although a mechanical approach to comparability is advocated, it is not always clear how to deal with differences in circumstances that are inevitably linked to a protected characteristic. A two-step approach to comparability has thus been suggested and applied (Chapter 4). This two-step approach deals with most differences in circumstances in a mechanical manner by applying a traditional 'but for' test (first step) but keeps interlinked characteristics to a substantive analysis (second step).

WTO law and double taxation conventions are largely independent of each other because they pursue different goals and have a different legal context. Nevertheless, conceptual implications can be drawn from the non-discrimination provisions of both areas of law. In fact, the analysed non-discrimination clauses bring important insights about conceptual issues that any non-discrimination rule may face. Both areas of law approach cases of discrimination in different ways with different tools and for different reasons, but they often face similar challenges. This chapter aims at addressing common aspects from a conceptual perspective and to reach general conclusions on the concept of non-discrimination.

§5.01 BALANCING DECISIONS ARE INHERENT AND INDISPENSABLE

When interpreting the non-discrimination rules of the WTO Agreement and, in particular, the general MFN and NT rules of the GATT and GATS, it is often indispensable to strike a balance between trade liberalization and other societal values such as environmental sustainability and consumer protection.[2256] On the one hand, the WTO Members have agreed to certain multilateral trade disciplines including non-discrimination. On the other hand, they have preserved their regulatory autonomy. It is a delicate and sensible issue to reconcile these different interests. In a similar way, Article 24 of the OECD Model seeks to establish a balance between unjustified tax distinctions that may have a negative impact on cross-border business and legitimate tax distinctions based on, for example, differences in liability to tax or ability to pay.[2257] On the one hand, the Contracting States have agreed to enter into a bilateral tax treaty in order to avoid international juridical double taxation, cooperate in tax matters, and eliminate discrimination. On the other hand, they intend to retain sovereignty in domestic tax matters. It is disputed where the appropriate balance lies between these competing policy interests.

Neither the general MFN and NT rules of the GATT and GATS nor the non-discrimination provisions of Article 24 of the OECD Model have been handcrafted with perfect precision and accuracy. Rather, they are ambiguous and open to different meanings and interpretations. With regard to comparability, terms such as 'like products',[2258] 'directly competitive or substitutable products',[2259] 'like services and service suppliers',[2260] 'in the same circumstances',[2261] 'the same activities',[2262] and 'similar enterprises'[2263] initially have no clear meaning. It is thus necessary to consider their context and what objectives a particular non-discrimination provision pursues.[2264] Based on such considerations, the same term 'like products' may have a narrower meaning for the purposes of one NT provision[2265] and a broader meaning for the purposes of another[2266] even when both condemn protectionism or the term 'similar enterprises'[2267] is understood as being very close if not identical to 'in the same circumstances'.[2268] With regard to a condemned disadvantage, very different terms are used as well such as 'in excess of',[2269] 'not similarly taxed',[2270] 'less favourable

2256. *See* Chapter 2 section §2.02[E].
2257. *See* Chapter 4 section §4.01[A].
2258. Articles I:1, III:2, first sentence and III:4 of the GATT.
2259. Article III:2, second sentence of the GATT (Interpretative Note *Ad* Article III:2).
2260. Articles II:1 and XVII of the GATS.
2261. Article 24(1) and (2) of the OECD Model.
2262. Article 24(3) of the OECD Model.
2263. Article 24(5) of the OECD Model.
2264. *See also*, to this effect, H. Horn and Mavroidis 2004, 42.
2265. Article III:2, first sentence of the GATT.
2266. Article III:4 of the GATT.
2267. Article 24(5) of the OECD Model.
2268. Article 24(1) and (2) of the OECD Model.
2269. Article III:2, first sentence of the GATT.
2270. Article III:2, second sentence of the GATT (Interpretative Note *Ad* Article III:2).

treatment',[2271] 'other or more burdensome taxation',[2272] and 'less favourable taxation'.[2273] Under both the GATT and GATS and the OECD Model, there is a tendency to give these different terms different meanings not only because different terms are used but also because, in a broader context, these terms express an intention to reach a certain balance.

Non-discrimination provisions normally rely on different tools for identifying a violation of substantive obligations, the most important of which are comparability, less favourable treatment, and exceptions or justifications. Under WTO law and Article 24 of the OECD Model, comparability and certain differences in impact or treatment are a prerequisite whereas exceptions or justifications may or may not be available. In other areas of non-discrimination law, by contrast, a comparison of persons need not be an indispensable requirement for what is considered to be discrimination.[2274] A comparability requirement may even be highly problematic. For instance, before courts and legislatures moved away from the need for a comparator at all, discrimination in pregnancy cases was denied as there could be no pregnant men or comparison was made to ill men thereby stigmatizing pregnancy as unhealthy.[2275] What steps of analysis are available, how they are construed, and which requirements must be fulfilled depends on each individual non-discrimination rule as well as its context and object and purpose.

Since comparability, less favourable treatment, and exceptions or justifications interact with each other[2276] and together contribute to a broader objective, the interpretation of each step of analysis requires consideration of what other steps are available and what scope they are intended to have. A broad concept of comparability may speak for a less intrusive concept of less favourable treatment (*de minimis* threshold, group-based approach, disparate impact) and for a more liberal or evolutionary interpretation of exceptions or justifications. Otherwise, potentially every domestic measure could be branded as illegitimate discrimination which is a result that is often not intended. Comparability may thus become a threshold that needs to be passed in order to turn to a more concrete and fine-tuned analysis. Conversely, an

2271. Article III:4 of the GATT; Articles II:1 and XVII of the GATS.
2272. Article 24(1), (2) and (5) of the OECD Model.
2273. Article 24(3) of the OECD Model.
2274. On problems with comparators, *see*, for instance, Goldberg 2011; Fredman 2011, 168–175; McColgan 2006. *See*, moreover, Directive 2006/54/EC of 5 July 2006 on the implementation of the principle of equal opportunities and equal treatment of men and women in matters of employment and occupation (recast), OJ L 204, 26 July 2006, pp. 23–36, in which Article 2(1)(c) and (d) defines 'harassment' and 'sexual harassment' based on the purpose or effect of certain conduct without requiring comparison. Article 2(2) states that, for the purposes of this Directive, discrimination includes harassment and sexual harassment. *See also*, similarly, Article 3(c) and (d) and Article 4(2) of the Directive 2010/41/EU of 7 July 2010 on the application of the principle of equal treatment between men and women engaged in an activity in a self-employed capacity and repealing Council Directive 86/613/EEC, OJ L 180, 15 July 2010, pp. 1–6. Of course, if discrimination is defined as requiring comparison; there is no discrimination without comparison. However, these examples demonstrate that what can morally and legally be understood as unjustified treatment and discrimination need not require an analysis of comparability in order to be prohibited.
2275. Fredman 2011, 169–171, with further references.
2276. *See also* Mitchell, Heaton, and Henckels 2016, 37.

intended coverage of only de jure or similar forms of discrimination may indicate a narrow concept of comparability. Since only differences in a protected characteristic, as such, cannot be employed as grounds for different treatment, there is less need for exceptions or justifications. In addition, a narrow concept of comparability already avoids discrimination in many situations, which gives room for a test of less favourable treatment in which any difference in treatment or a single better-treated person, product, or service and service supplier suffices for discrimination. If comprehensive exceptions or justifications are available, it seems less important to consider legitimate interests as an issue of comparability or less favourable treatment. Conversely, a lack of exceptions or justifications may lead to a narrower concept of comparability that avoids too many situations of incidental discrimination or to a more sophisticated concept of less favourable treatment that even incorporates a justification analysis.[2277]

This interdependence of different steps of analysis has been utilized by the Appellate Body. In principle, common standards of likeness and less favourable treatment are applied. Under the WTO Agreement, comparability is generally about a competitive relationship[2278] and prohibited treatment is about a measure's detrimental impact on this competitive relationship.[2279] Despite that, the precise conditions for discrimination differ and are highly context dependent since different meanings are given to the same or different terms in order to achieve a similar overall balance. For instance, the general principle of Article III:1 of the GATT informs different NT provisions in different ways,[2280] the concept of 'like products' may be narrower or broader depending on which NT provision is at stake,[2281] and the same term 'like products' in Article I:1 of the GATT may have different meanings depending on whether tariffs or other measures are under scrutiny.[2282] As the Appellate Body has observed in *Japan – Alcoholic Beverages II* (1996), '[t]he accordion of "likeness" stretches and squeezes in different places as different provisions of the *WTO Agreement* are applied'.[2283]

Although only Article XVII of the GATS indicates a concept of de facto discrimination by stating that formally identical or formally different treatment may be considered to be less favourable, all MFN and NT rules of the GATT and GATS have

2277. *See also* Ortino 2012, 52 ('while a narrow justification exception usually tends to correspond to a narrow discrimination requirement, an open-ended justification usually corresponds to a broad discrimination test'). *See*, moreover, Mitchell, Heaton, and Henckels 2016, 37, who rightly warn about circular arguments if *consequences* of a particular interpretation (a greater or lesser overall restriction on a party's freedom of action) are themselves treated as a *reason for* a particular interpretation being chosen. However, no such circular arguments arise if it can be established what overall balance a particular instrument aims to achieve. If an instrument indicates in its preamble that environmental protection is a legitimate interest, if an undisputedly broad concept of comparability touches upon regulatory measures that genuinely pursue such interests, and if no general exceptions or justifications are available may influence how 'less favourable treatment' should be interpreted.

2278. *See* Chapter 2 section §2.03[E][1].

2279. *See* Chapter 2 section §2.04[B][1].

2280. *See* Chapter 2 section §2.03[D][4].

2281. *See* Chapter 2 section §2.03[E][2][a].

2282. *See* Chapter 2 section §2.03[E][2][b].

2283. AB Report, *Japan – Alcoholic Beverages II*, 1996, p. 21.

such a broad scope in order to achieve their common objective of avoiding discrimination without allowing for circumventions.[2284] However, this potentially broad scope is limited by a rather sophisticated group-based 'less favourable treatment' test under which some better-treated 'like' products or services and service suppliers do not suffice for discrimination.[2285] Since the TBT Agreement that furthers the objectives of the GATT contains no general exceptions clause, the combined MFN and NT rule in Article 2.1 of the TBT Agreement incorporates a justification defence into 'less favourable treatment'[2286] thereby taking account of legitimate regulatory distinctions and reaching a similar overall balance as the GATT. Therefore, differences in wording do not prevent the application of similar concepts while identical terms may have very different meanings if they are embedded in different contexts. What matters is the object and purpose of the WTO Agreement and the overall balance it aims to achieve.

Turning to Article 24 of the OECD Model, the non-discrimination provisions contain different comparability requirements, but the approach to comparability is similar.[2287] On the one hand, comparability is construed narrowly in order to eliminate discrimination only in certain precise circumstances. It is further believed that despite many differences in wording, a 'same circumstances' requirement is inherent in all non-discrimination provisions. All relevant circumstances except for the protected characteristic must be the same, and virtually all circumstances are relevant.[2288] This approach limits the scope of the non-discrimination clauses to de jure discrimination[2289] and largely eliminates a need for separate justifications that are arguably not available under Article 24.[2290] On the other hand, it is recognized that certain differences in circumstances should not prevent comparability in all situations because, otherwise, no scope of application would remain. Under Article 24(3), the fact that a PE, as such, does not distribute dividends generally does not prevent comparability. However, it is suggested that it might prevent comparability in some cases that concern the elimination of economic double taxation.[2291]

Article 24(1), (2), and (5) uses the expression 'other or more burdensome taxation' and prohibits all differences in treatment unless they favour protected persons.[2292] Under Article 24(3), by contrast, residents and non-residents may be treated differently as long as such treatment does not result in 'less favourable taxation', that is in a higher tax burden.[2293] A distinction between 'other or more burdensome taxation' and 'less favourable taxation' is made in order to grant the Contracting States greater autonomy in treating residents and non-residents differently for arguably legitimate reasons. Overall, the scope of Article 24 is rather narrow and leaves the Contracting States' sovereignty in domestic tax matters largely untouched.

2284. *See* Chapter 2 section §2.04[A][1].
2285. *See* Chapter 2 section §2.04[B][3].
2286. *See* Chapter 2 section §2.04[C][3].
2287. *See* Chapter 3 section §3.04[A].
2288. *See* Chapter 3 section §3.05[A].
2289. *See* Chapter 3 section §3.05[B].
2290. *See* Chapter 3 section §3.05[C].
2291. *See* Chapter 4 sections §4.04[E][2][d] and §4.04[E][4][a].
2292. *See* Chapter 3 section §3.02[A][1].
2293. *See* Chapter 3 section §3.02[B][1].

This intended balance is not necessarily clear from the wording of the non-discrimination provisions, a wording that is imprecise and uses different terms for not always apparent reasons, but it can be derived from various other means of interpretation and particularly from the context.

It is thus noteworthy how the WTO non-discrimination provisions and those of Article 24 employ various available tools to reach their intended balance. Both address comparability and differences in treatment but in a very different way. Article 24 pursues a narrow concept of comparability by requiring identity of almost all circumstances; WTO law pursues a broader concept because products or services and service suppliers need not be identical. Article 24 enshrines a rather simple comparison of treatments because treatments may be formally different, different in amount, or formally identical; WTO law enshrines a more sophisticated concept that covers de facto discrimination and requires establishing an adverse impact based on a group comparison. Article 24, starting with a narrow concept of comparability, regards most tax distinctions as legitimate; WTO law has a much more intrusive impact on domestic regulation, but various exceptions from a violation of substantive WTO obligations are available. Last, but not least, when such exceptions are missing, this has repercussions on less favourable treatment (TBT Agreement).[2294] All of these steps of analysis work together and influence each other in order to achieve an appropriate balance between various policy interests. Additionally, all of these steps leave at least some room for discretion and different judgments such as in determining and weighing the relevant factors of 'likeness' or the relevant differences in legal or factual circumstances. Therefore, it is crucial to understand what objectives a particular non-discrimination provision pursues and how these objectives connect to other provisions and goals. While the wording of the analysed non-discrimination provisions is rather ambiguous, their context allows to better understand where the equilibrium between illegitimate and justified distinctions lies.

§5.02 STEPS OF ANALYSIS MAY BE INTERCHANGEABLE

Perhaps the most important lesson learned from WTO law is that regulatory purposes and policy objectives may be considered not only as exceptions (i.e., justifications) but also for determining 'likeness' and 'less favourable treatment'. It thus seems wrong to categorically disregard arguments against discrimination under Article 24 of the OECD Model solely because they are considered to be justifications or because they actually are justifications in other areas of law. Such an approach rather risks concealing value judgments as to why a particular argument is irrelevant instead of making these judgments transparent.

Since the general exceptions clauses under the GATT and GATS are exhaustive, tension arises between the limited number of legitimate regulatory purposes and the emergence of new societal values that might not have been anticipated when the GATT and GATS were drafted. This may be resolved by liberally interpreting the general

2294. *See* Chapter 2 section §2.04[C][3].

exceptions clauses – 'exhaustible natural resources' may cover clean air and sea turtles,[2295] 'necessary' involves a flexible weighing and balancing test[2296] – or by considering regulatory purposes as an issue of 'likeness'. Under the aim and effects test, whether a domestic measure pursues a legitimate regulatory purpose is relevant in determining whether competing products are 'like'.[2297] If a measure genuinely aims at encouraging the consumption of low alcohol beer over beer with a high alcohol content specifically for the purposes of protecting human life and health and upholding public morals, this may render high alcohol beer unlike low alcohol beer even when these products are in a competitive relationship.

Although the Appellate Body rejected the aim and effects test, it did not do so for conceptual reasons. It predominantly relied on textual differences between the non-discrimination provisions.[2298] An objective aim and effects test further remains a separate step of analysis in determining whether a measure is applied so as to afford protection to domestic production under the second sentence of Article III:2 of the GATT.[2299] Objectives of a regulatory measure such as the prevention of health risks arguably continue to influence 'likeness' in disguise, hidden behind supposedly objective factors such as physical characteristics and consumers' tastes and habits.[2300] Finally, for the purposes of other international agreements such as NAFTA Chapter 11 on investment protection, the aim and effects test continues to be applied in practice as part of a 'like circumstances' test.[2301]

Both the GATT and GATS as well as the TBT Agreement envisage a similar balance between trade and non-trade objectives. Being part of a single undertaking, they respect the regulatory autonomy of the WTO Members and recognize various regulatory purposes such as the aim of protecting and preserving the environment.[2302] Under the GATT and GATS, the general exceptions clauses[2303] are mainly responsible for taking account of such regulatory purposes.[2304] Under the TBT Agreement, by contrast, no general exceptions clause is available. Yet, it is clear from the context that trade liberalization should not always trump other societal values and that the Members' regulatory autonomy should be respected. To solve this tension under the combined MFN and NT rule of Article 2.1 of the TBT Agreement, it was suggested to consider regulatory purposes as an issue of 'likeness'. However, the Appellate Body decided to consider regulatory purposes as an issue of 'less favourable treatment'. It has to be determined whether a detrimental impact 'stems exclusively from legitimate

2295. *See* Chapter 2 section §2.05[A].
2296. *See* Chapter 2 section §2.05[B].
2297. *See* Chapter 2 section §2.03[D].
2298. *See* Chapter 2 section §2.03[D][4].
2299. *See* Chapter 2 section §2.03[D][5].
2300. *See* Chapter 2 section §2.03[E][3].
2301. *See*, for instance, Ortino 2012, 27, 52; Delimatsis et al. 2011, 266; Diebold 2011a, 125; Diebold 2011b, 840, 848–849, 851; DiMascio and Pauwelyn 2008, 72–74, 82–83; in detail and critically, Mitchell, Heaton, and Henckels 2016, 78–88.
2302. *See* Chapter 2 section §2.02[E].
2303. Article XX of the GATT; Article XIV of the GATS.
2304. *See* Chapter 2 section §2.05[A].

regulatory distinctions'.[2305] This criterion incorporates a justification and proportionality analysis into 'less favourable treatment'. A technical regulation is not legitimate if it is not even-handed, that is disproportionate, not calibrated, or applied in an arbitrary or discriminatory manner.

In practice, therefore, it need not matter whether regulatory purposes and policy objectives are considered as separate exceptions or justifications, as an issue of 'less favourable treatment' or as an issue of 'likeness', that is comparability.[2306] It is possible to draft non-discrimination rules in a way that policy objectives are addressed by the condition of comparability (Article 24, aim and effects test), by the requirement of less favourable treatment (Article 2.1 of the TBT Agreement), or by explicit exceptions or justifications (general MFN and NT rules of the GATT and GATS). While comparability, less favourable treatment, and exceptions or justifications are, in principle, interchangeable, this does not mean that policy objectives must always be of the same legal and practical relevance. Whereas one non-discrimination rule can be subject to an extensive list of justifications or, to this effect, provide for an open list of legitimate interests that deny 'likeness' or 'less favourable treatment', another non-discrimination rule may only know a very limited number of exceptions or, such as Article 24 of the OECD Model, permit a balancing of different interests only in rather limited situations, that is, when inevitably linked differences in circumstances exist in a concrete case. What role certain policy objectives play – this also includes the questions of whether they are regarded as legitimate, need to meet requirements of proportionality, and succeed in prevailing over other interests – depends on each individual non-discrimination clause and not on how many steps of analysis are available.

It could be argued that comparability, less favourable treatment, and exceptions or justifications should be kept separate because this contributes to a clear structure of analysis.[2307] Otherwise, if policy objectives influence comparability or less favourable treatment, this makes an analysis unsystematic and hampers transparency. It is true that structured approaches to non-discrimination are usually preferred in order to address all arguments in a clear and systematic way. However, it is also possible to rely on several steps of analysis including steps for considering legitimate policy interests and their proportionate implementation in order to determine comparability or less favourable treatment. Accordingly, non-discrimination provisions that are not subject to any exceptions or justifications may balance various policy interests against each other without raising concerns about transparency. Article 2.1 of the TBT Agreement is an example. The question of whether a detrimental impact on imports 'stems exclusively from legitimate regulatory distinctions' constitutes a separate step of analysis

2305. *See* Chapter 2 section §2.04[C][3].

2306. *See*, by contrast, Mitchell, Heaton, and Henckels 2016, 139, who argue that, if a legitimate objective is considered as a matter of 'less favourable treatment', a relatively unimportant legitimate objective does not shield a measure that has severe protectionist effects whereas, under a justificatory approach, a less significant purpose might nonetheless justify a measure. However, it remains open why, conceptually, a relatively unimportant legitimate objective should not suffice for no 'less favourable treatment' or why under a justificatory approach a measure should not be justified only by a relatively important purpose.

2307. *See*, for instance, Diebold 2011b, 849.

that determines, together with a preceding analysis of that detrimental impact, whether there is 'less favourable treatment'.[2308] Although only one criterion – 'less favourable treatment' – is expressly mentioned in Article 2.1 of the TBT Agreement, a two-step analysis is required as if separate exceptions and proportionality requirements were available.

Nevertheless, it is not only a matter of legal technique whether arguments are considered as issues of comparability, less favourable treatment, or exceptions or justifications. When a distinction between discrimination and justifications for discrimination is made, there may be different legal consequences attached to these steps of analysis. A 'rule–exception' relationship, for instance, may indicate a shift of the burden of proof thereby making a separation of different steps of analysis important in practice.[2309] Therefore, the precise meaning of a 'justification' may become crucial not because there is an overarching conceptual difference between certain steps of analysis but because the law by itself stipulates differences on some basis and attaches different legal consequences to them.

At the same time, WTO law demonstrates how difficult it is to precisely define what is an exception or justification. For the purposes of the burden of proof, there is a distinction made between exceptions from substantive WTO obligations and exclusions that merely limit or define an obligation's scope. This distinction is often far from clear-cut. Even if a provision uses the term 'except', this does not mean that an exception is at stake.[2310] Even if the non-discrimination analysis allows for no separate justifications (Article 2.1 of the TBT Agreement), this does not mean that the respondent may wait until the claimant has proven all conditions for discrimination.[2311] If the claimant establishes a prima facie case of inconsistency, the burden may 'shift' to the respondent, which may then require the respondent to bring forward legitimate policy interests that justify its measure at the level of 'less favourable treatment'.

From a normative perspective, it is also not irrelevant at which stage of analysis policy interests are addressed.[2312] It might matter whether there is no discrimination or if discrimination is justified. It is, for many people, unacceptable to regard toxic and non-toxic products as comparable when they are in a competitive relationship and to require justification for a discriminatory ban of life-threatening products. Such an approach arguably values trade liberalization as a more important goal than protection of human life or health or is simply ignorant of essential differences that exist between toxic and non-toxic products. If a WTO Member genuinely pursues legitimate regulatory purposes of apparently highest importance, such purposes may consequently influence 'likeness' and 'less favourable treatment' and thereby prevent discrimination even when justifications are available. In *EC – Asbestos* (2001), special weight was given to certain physical characteristics and consumers' tastes and habits were asserted

2308. *See* Chapter 2 section §2.04[C][3].
2309. *See* Chapter 2 section §2.06.
2310. *See* Chapter 2 section §2.06[D].
2311. *See* Chapter 2 section §2.06[E].
2312. *See* Chapter 2 section §2.03[D][3].

without conclusive evidence arguably because there were no protectionist aims, but there were life-threatening products at stake.[2313] This difference between no discrimination and justified discrimination[2314] 'is not in what we do – the end result is the same – but in who we are in doing what we do'.[2315]

Because comparability is construed so narrowly under Article 24 of the OECD Model, there generally is no need to separately consider a measure's purposes in order to justify differences in tax treatment. All differences in circumstances automatically prevent comparability and thereby avoid a threat of discrimination.[2316] Only if there are no relevant differences in circumstances but a difference in treatment remains does this effect lead to prohibited tax discrimination. Yet, problems arise when there is an overlap between protected and unprotected characteristics in a concrete case.[2317] A domestic tax measure may distinguish because of a protected characteristic (nationality or residence) or pursue an arguably legitimate objective that is reflected in a linked but unprotected characteristic (e.g., avoidance of hybrid mismatch arrangements). A formal approach to comparability is not able to distinguish between such situations in every case. Therefore, it may lead to results that are difficult to reconcile with the envisaged balance and the objectives of the non-discrimination provisions.

It is consequently no surprise that various arguments that could be seen as a matter of justification are openly or covertly evaluated in determining comparability; they render differences in legal or factual circumstances relevant or not.[2318] For example, the fact that a measure genuinely aims at countering hybrid mismatch arrangements in order to prevent non-taxation in both Contracting States is able to justify differences in tax treatment (differences in the existence of a hybrid mismatch are relevant for comparability purposes) even if a change in the protected characteristic leads to a change in tax treatment in a concrete case.[2319] While mechanical tests are the preferred option for determining discrimination under Article 24, in practice, these tests are supplemented with additional arguments as soon as they lead to inconsistent or incomprehensible results. Such additional arguments consider a measure's aims by analysing its scope and design in order to determine the actual reason for different tax treatment. They and all underlying value judgments should be openly addressed and discussed in order to avoid a lack of clarity in the application of supposedly value-free tests.

In this study, a two-step approach for analysing comparability under Article 24 of the OECD Model has been suggested. First, a traditional 'but for' test almost automatically accepts all justifications for different treatment that are reflected in differences in

2313. *See* Chapter 2 section §2.03[E][3].
2314. It might also matter whether general exceptions for legitimate policy interests are de facto unavailable due to a strict interpretation of their nexus requirements or whether discriminatory measures can more easily be justified but subsequently, under the chapeau, an inappropriate application of provisionally justified measures leads to a violation of substantive WTO obligations.
2315. Weiler 2009, 769.
2316. *See* Chapter 4 section §4.01[C].
2317. *See* Chapter 3 section §3.06.
2318. *See* Chapter 4 section §4.02[A].
2319. *See* Chapter 3 section §3.06[D].

circumstances in a concrete case except for differences in a protected characteristic and in inevitably linked attributes.[2320] Second, a substantive analysis deals with justifications that are reflected in differences in a protected characteristic or in inevitably linked attributes as if a separate analysis of justifications was conducted.[2321] This approach thus considers, as a separate step of analysis, what aims a domestic tax measure pursues and whether these objectively identified aims are legitimate from a tax treaty perspective. It arguably improves transparency and clarity of decision-making by addressing all arguments openly, not rejecting them automatically, and avoiding undisclosed value judgments.

This approach also goes well with the conceptual implications that can be derived from WTO law. As far as the outcome is concerned, it may not matter at which stage of analysis aims and regulatory purposes are considered: as an issue of comparability under Article 24, as an issue of 'likeness' under the aim and effects test, as an issue of 'less favourable treatment' under Article 2.1 of the TBT Agreement, or as an issue of exceptions or justifications when applying the general MFN and NT rules of the GATT and GATS. All of the mentioned steps of analysis are, in principle, suitable for appropriately dealing with arguments for and against a violation of substantive obligations. It is more important to consider what balance a particular non-discrimination provision aims to achieve, in which cases it attempts to limit a State's autonomy and sovereignty for a greater goal, and how this intended balance can be reached in a structured way with all of the available tools. Since the non-discrimination clauses of Article 24 of the OECD Model aim at preventing discrimination in certain precise circumstances,[2322] there are good arguments for construing comparability in a narrow manner (first step)[2323] and for addressing all remaining arguments for and against a violation of substantive obligations as an issue of comparability (second step).[2324] Similarly as with the aim and effects test, whether differences in circumstances are relevant in a concrete case and, therefore, save a scrutinized measure from being discriminatory despite its otherwise condemned effects depends on what aims that measure pursues and whether these objectively identified aims are legitimate from a tax treaty perspective.

§5.03 AIMS OF MEASURES ARE NOT ABOUT SUBJECTIVE INTENT

Integrating an aim test or a justification defence into 'likeness' or 'less favourable treatment' has been met with criticism and concerns about subjectivity. However, when taking a closer look, it becomes clear that the aims of domestic legislation need not be about subjective intentions inhabiting the minds of individual legislators or regulators or about alleged purposes that succeed in justifying measures without conclusive evidence. Aims can be identified objectively.

2320. *See* Chapter 4 section §4.02[C].
2321. *See* Chapter 4 section §4.02[D].
2322. *See* Chapter 3 section §3.03.
2323. *See* Chapter 4 section §4.02[C].
2324. *See* Chapter 4 section §4.02[D].

As far as exceptions or justifications are concerned, it appears undisputed that aims matter. It is necessary to determine what aims a domestic measure pursues, whether these aims are recognized as legitimate by an exceptions clause and whether they are pursued in a proportionate manner and, therefore, prevail over other aims that are pursued by the WTO Agreement. While an MFN or NT rule might focus only on disproportionate effects and condemn every measure that has a disparate impact on foreign origin, exceptions or justifications focus on aims in order to find an appropriate balance between trade and non-trade objectives. While a Member may submit different and seemingly innocent reasons for discriminatory measures, not every reason can automatically be accepted as a legitimate explanation of discrimination. It is necessary to verify whether a Member indeed pursues such aims before continuing with a flexible assessment of legitimacy under an exceptions clause.

All supposedly legitimate aims alleged by a WTO Member need to be objectively verified by considering texts of statutes, legislative history, pronouncements of government agencies, or officials as well as the structure and operation of the measure in question and any other evidence.[2325] If the measure does not make and cannot be expected to make a meaningful contribution to an aim, it will unlikely justify discrimination. This lack of suitability also indicates that the aim might only be a pretext. If the measure has protectionist effects and if such effects were foreseeable before its introduction, if the measure provides for an exceptionally high burden that does not find any meaningful explanation, or if the measure fails to rely on considerably less trade restrictive but equally available and effective means to achieve its desired goal and level of protection, this constitutes evidence for protectionist intentions. Conversely, if the measure has protectionist effects only due to unforeseen changes in the marketplace or if the measure's requirements and legal consequences contribute to a legitimate policy interest in an effective and proportionate manner, this speaks against protectionist aims. It is not necessary to rely, for instance, on legislative materials in order to determine the measure's objective. It is also not necessary to fail with this assessment when open declarations or statements are missing. How the measure is designed, how it operates, how it fits into a system of other measures that may pursue similar aims, what treatment it provides for, what actual, expected and potential effects it has all contribute to an objective determination of aims.

Objectively identified aims also matter under Article 24 of the OECD Model. Pursuant to the OECD Commentary, comparability must be determined 'from the point of view of the application of the ordinary taxation laws and regulations'.[2326] It is further argued that only relevant differences in circumstances prevent comparability. Whether differences are relevant must be established from the perspective of the domestic tax measure at issue.[2327] Perhaps the most visible evaluation of a measure's aims takes place when an analysis of comparability reaches beyond a traditional 'but for' test. With this test, only the facts and circumstances of a concrete case matter; the protected characteristic is deemed to be different, and all other circumstances are left unchanged.

2325. *See* Chapter 2 sections §2.03[D][3] and §2.03[D][6].
2326. 2008–2017 OECD Commentary on Article 24, para. 7 (1963: para. 2; 1977–2005: para. 3).
2327. *See* Chapter 3 section §3.05[A].

Nevertheless, there is a tendency to argue for or against discrimination by pointing to other cases with somewhat different facts and circumstances and by analysing how these other cases are treated.[2328] A measure's scope and design as well as its architecture and application are referred to in order to identify the actual reason for different tax treatment for the purposes of the non-discrimination clauses of Article 24 of the OECD Model.

At this point, it is worth considering why aims matter under the WTO Agreement. In principle, non-discrimination provisions may be designed in many different ways:[2329] they may merely look at language,[2330] include or exclude close substitutes,[2331] rely on effects only, on aims only,[2332] on both aims and effects, or use other combinations. If both aims and effects are relevant, different relationships between these factors are possible such as discriminatory effects suffice for discrimination unless legitimate aims can be established, both discriminatory effects and illegitimate aims are needed, either illegitimate aims or discriminatory effects suffice, or an overall assessment is made by balancing these and potentially other factors against each other. All of these approaches leave open how to precisely define relevant aims and effects, that is when the same or different treatment has discriminatory effects and what aims are legitimate or illegitimate. As long as non-discrimination provisions succeed in their goal with their individual approach, there is no reason to be worried.[2333] Just as both aims and effects may require objective evidence and evaluation, both may leave room for some discretion and value judgments. Yet, the wording of non-discrimination provisions is often ambiguous and does not precisely lay down which approach to follow, although one solution may be more suitable than another depending on what objectives a particular non-discrimination rule pursues.

Under WTO law, aims are included as an express or implicit requirement for discrimination[2334] or justification[2335] because, in combination with effects, they are perceived to achieve a more appropriate balance between trade and non-trade objectives. Since market forces are unpredictable and market circumstances change constantly, every facially neutral measure could coincidentally have a disparate impact on foreign origin without any bad faith. By merely looking at effects, almost every

2328. *See*, in particular, Chapter 3 section §3.06[D].
2329. *See also* Ortino 2012, 16–19; Ortino 2009, 139–140, who distinguishes between language, effect, inherence, and intent.
2330. *See*, for instance, Ortino 2004, 219, who states that 'the search for [de jure] discrimination does not go beyond an analysis of the mere text of the measure at issue'.
2331. For example, entitlement to a passport could be equated with nationality as far as individuals are concerned even though not all nationals need to be entitled to a passport.
2332. In such a case, even a failed attempt to achieve discriminatory effects could be branded as discrimination which could have some value for political or societal reasons, whereas discriminatory effects would be irrelevant as long as there is no proof of illegitimate aims (but, arguably, discriminatory effects could constitute evidence for such aims).
2333. Of course, a non-discrimination provision's precise goal may not always be easy to discern. However, the point is that there is no conceptually better or worse approach in the abstract.
2334. Article III:2, second sentence of the GATT ('so as to afford protection to domestic production'); Article 2.1 of the TBT Agreement ('stems exclusively from legitimate regulatory distinctions'); aim and effects test under the GATT 1947.
2335. Article XX of the GATT; Article XIV of the GATS.

measure could potentially conflict with non-discrimination obligations. This result would severely limit the WTO Members' regulatory autonomy which is a result that the WTO Agreement does not intend. By considering a measure's aims when evaluating exceptions or establishing discrimination (for instance, by denying discrimination when legitimate aims exist but not when no or only illegitimate aims can be established), more policy space is granted to WTO Members. The question is not whether regulatory purposes should be considered for the purposes of establishing a violation of substantive WTO obligations. The question is how those objectively identified aims of a domestic measure should be considered: as a matter of 'likeness' or 'less favourable treatment' or also or only when dealing with exceptions, that is justifications.

What is true under the WTO Agreement is arguably also true under Article 24 of the OECD Model. It would be possible to apply a traditional 'but for' test and to rely on effects only, that is whether this test indicates the same or different treatment in a concrete case. However, this analysis would lead to results that are difficult to reconcile with the balance that Article 24 aims to achieve.[2336] Article 24 does not intend to prohibit the Contracting States from employing nationality as a criterion for full tax liability or from countering hybrid mismatch arrangements in cross-border situations. In some situations, measures that pursue such aims would violate non-discrimination obligations if, in a concrete case, a change in the protected characteristic leads to a change in tax treatment and if only this effect mattered. By taking aims into account, it is possible to distinguish between two kinds of measures: measures that genuinely pursue interests that are not illegitimate from a tax treaty perspective even if a 'but for' test leads to prima facie discrimination in a concrete case and measures that use their allegedly legitimate aims as a pretext for distinctions that run against the object and purpose of Article 24 and its non-discrimination clauses. Whether objectively identified aims are legitimate and, therefore, lead to inevitably linked but relevant differences in legal or factual circumstances must be evaluated from a tax treaty perspective; not every difference in circumstances that is relevant from a domestic perspective can automatically be accepted and thereby justify differences in treatment.

WTO law demonstrates that even objective characteristics have no value without a benchmark and such a benchmark does not necessarily lead to clear results.[2337] Supposedly objective factors such as physical characteristics require judgment as to which characteristics matter in a concrete case and how they should be weighed and balanced against other supposedly objective factors such as end-uses and consumers' preferences. Thus, differences in physical characteristics have a very different weight and value if they reflect differences between toxicity and non-toxicity of fibres than if they reflect differences in taste between vodka and shōchū.

2336. *See* Chapter 4 section §4.02[A].
2337. *See* Chapter 2 section §2.03[B][1].

§5.04 FORMAL APPROACHES ARE OFTEN INCONCLUSIVE

Under both WTO law and Article 24 of the OECD Model, formal approaches to non-discrimination are inconclusive and, therefore, problematic. It has already been mentioned that by applying a 'but for' test and looking only at effects, unintended results may be reached if there is an overlap of protected and unprotected characteristics in a concrete case. It does not appear convincing to automatically confirm or deny discrimination simply because different treatment is also or not only based on a protected characteristic in this or other cases. By confirming discrimination, Article 24 would appear to be overinclusive. It would condemn too many measures even if they are not in opposition to any objective of a non-discrimination provision but rather rely on legitimate interests that merely happen to overlap with a protected characteristic. By denying discrimination, Article 24 would appear to be under-inclusive. It would accept too many measures as being legitimate even if they run against an objective of a non-discrimination provision by using a supposedly unprotected characteristic as a pretext for discriminatory treatment.

This does not mean that it would be impossible to live with such deficiencies of Article 24 and to accept them as the lesser of two evils: a mechanical approach that is potentially over- or under-inclusive but also easier to apply and a substantive approach that is more accurate in addressing Article 24's objectives but also more sophisticated. However, it is submitted in this study that, even though many people try to adhere to a supposedly simple mechanical approach to non-discrimination, in practice, arguments that cannot be brought together with such an approach are, nevertheless, considered. A formal analysis of discrimination is supplemented with substantive considerations. If a measure de jure refers to nationality, the actual reason for different treatment under Article 24(1) may be residence.[2338] If a measure does not discriminate de jure based on nationality, the actual reason for different treatment may be nationality provided that a sufficiently close substitute such as a passport requirement is employed.[2339] Since a non-discrimination test should not fail to prohibit some distinctions that should be prohibited and prohibit some distinctions that should not be prohibited,[2340] preference is given to a more accurate and appropriate balance between domestic and tax treaty objectives.

Similar problems also arise with de jure discrimination under WTO law.[2341] It could be argued that, as soon as a regulatory measure expressly relies on origin of products or services and service suppliers, it must automatically violate an MFN or NT obligation under the GATT or GATS. Indeed, as the Appellate Body confirmed in *Argentina – Financial Services* (2016), there is a presumption of 'likeness' in such cases. If products or services and service suppliers differ only with respect to their origin, there arguably is no apparent reason for denying comparability and treating them differently. However, this presumption of 'likeness' can be rebutted if it is

2338. *See* Chapter 3 section §3.06[C].
2339. *See* Chapter 3 section §3.06[B].
2340. *See* Hudec 1998, 626.
2341. *See* Chapter 3 section §3.06[D].

established that a regulatory distinction is not based *exclusively* on origin. This leads to a regular and in-depth analysis of 'likeness'. In *Argentina – Financial Services* (2016), regulatory measures relied on a list of jurisdictions and thereby de jure referred to certain origin. Nevertheless, as origin was allegedly used as a proxy for cooperation in tax matters and tax transparency, it remained unclear whether origin was the only reason for different treatment and, thus, whether 'likeness' could be presumed. If products or services and service suppliers are indeed identical in every respect except for their origin, this generally is a compelling reason to presume their 'likeness'.[2342] If a domestic regulatory measure distinguishes de jure by reason of origin, however, this does not necessarily mean that it distinguishes between such identical products or services and service suppliers; they may still differ in important characteristics that are directly connected to their origin and could render them 'unlike'. Just as facially neutral measures can de facto refer to foreign origin, origin-based measures can de facto refer to a potentially legitimate factor. In fact, when explicit exceptions or justifications for de jure discrimination are available, it is hard to imagine how a measure that formally refers to origin should succeed in being justified if such a reference to origin would automatically lead to a distinction that is based *exclusively* on origin.

Explicit references to origin also do not necessarily imply 'less favourable treatment' under WTO law.[2343] On the one hand, formal distinctions based on origin do not lead to 'less favourable treatment' if they do not modify the conditions of competition between 'like' products or services and service suppliers. A reference to origin may not only grant a favour instead of a disadvantage but may also have no or insufficient effects on the conditions of competition. On the other hand, measures that treat all 'like' products or services and service suppliers identically may lead to 'less favourable treatment' if they modify the conditions of competition through such formally equal treatment. For the purposes of establishing 'less favourable treatment', it is initially irrelevant whether a measure provides for formally identical or formally different treatment.

Although a reference to a protected characteristic may appear suspicious, raise a presumption of 'likeness', indicate 'less favourable treatment', require stricter scrutiny, or lead to prima facie discrimination with a 'but for' test, this does not mean that discrimination can be established in all cases. Certain distinction formally by reason of origin, nationality, or residence may be legitimate if the objectives of the measure under scrutiny and the objectives of the non-discrimination provision at issue are taken into account. Although formal approaches for analysing discrimination are appealing because of their straightforward application, they raise tension when they are unable to distinguish between overlapping characteristics or to find an appropriate balance between conflicting interests. Both under WTO law and Article 24 of the OECD Model, there is a tendency to rely on formal approaches and assumptions as far as they are helpful and suitable but to supplement or replace them with substantive approaches as soon as they have reached their conceptual limitations.

2342. *See* Chapter 2 section §2.03[B][1].
2343. *See* Chapter 3 section §3.06[D].

It is further difficult to find a clear dividing line between de jure (direct) and de facto (indirect) discrimination even in supposedly straightforward cases such as in a situation when a passport requirement is employed as a substitute for nationality. This requirement arguably introduces a third category of 'disguised' de jure discrimination.[2344] It may also be difficult to define when two characteristics are 'inextricably linked' to each other because perfect substitutes are seldom or presuppose decisions on a particular perspective.[2345] Whether a measure de jure refers to a protected characteristic, therefore, should conceptually play no decisive role. Under Article 24 of the OECD Model, direct discrimination can be established regardless of whether a domestic tax measure directly refers to a protected characteristic.[2346] Under the GATT and GATS, the general exceptions are available regardless of whether a regulatory measure discriminates de jure or de facto. Consequently, it does not appear convincing to argue that the 'stems exclusively from a legitimate regulatory distinction' analysis under Article 2.1 of the TBT Agreement should only be available when a technical regulation does not de jure discriminate against imports, although the Appellate Body seems to take a different view.[2347] Similarly, 'less favourable treatment' under Article III of the GATT is determined by comparing the group of 'like' imported products to the group of 'like' domestic products.[2348] It can be questioned why 'less favourable treatment' should be determined on a completely different basis if a regulatory measures de jure refers to origin.[2349] By too strictly distinguishing between de jure and de facto discrimination, even subtle changes in legal technique could trigger substantial differences in outcome. If all wine is considered to be 'like', it should not matter whether the US state of Mississippi favours Mississippi wine thereby de jure referring to origin or wine from a variety of the Muscadine grape that basically grows only in Mississippi, is used mostly by Mississippi vintners, and amounts for the major part of the Mississippi wine production. As further demonstrated by the well-known example of the 1904 German tariff concession to Switzerland that lowered the tariff on female cattle older than one and a half year that were reared at a spot at least 300 metres above sea level and having at least one month's grazing each year at a spot at least 800 metres above sea level[2350] measures that discriminate de jure can be transformed into measures that require taking into account the factual circumstances at issue.

All of this does not suggest that it is irrelevant whether a measure de jure refers to a protected characteristic or that such reference can have no impact on whether discrimination exists. On the contrary, a measure that is overtly discriminatory can be expected to have very different effects than a facially neutral measure and may thereby provide objective evidence for illegitimate aims. When effects or aims matter for the

2344. *See* Chapter 3 section §3.06[B].
2345. *See* Chapter 3 section §3.06[C][5].
2346. *See* Chapter 4 section §4.02[B].
2347. *See* Chapter 2 section §2.04[C][3].
2348. *See* Chapter 2 section §2.04[B][3].
2349. *See*, however, Ehring 2014, 53–54.
2350. *See Zusatzvertrag zum Handels- und Zollvertrage zwischen dem Deutschen Reiche und der Schweiz vom 10. Dezember 1891*, Fassung vom 12. November 1904, Deutsches Reichsgesetzblatt vom 24. Mai 1905, Nummer 21, Seiten 330–355, Anlage A.

purposes of establishing discrimination, it also matters whether a measure directly refers to a protected characteristic, employs a facially neutral but close substitute, or uses a criterion that bears no or only a distant relationship to a protected characteristic. Article 24 of the OECD Model pursues a very narrow concept of comparability as it compares only two persons to each other.[2351] Whether a measure de jure refers to a protected characteristic or to some facially neutral characteristic might not lead to different results in a concrete case if those characteristics overlap. However, different results in other cases in which there is no inevitable link help to establish the actual reason for different tax treatment and thereby to distinguish between overlapping characteristics on a substantive basis.[2352]

In addition, the question of how close a facially neutral criterion is connected to origin could also have some impact on 'less favourable treatment' under WTO law. A minimal asymmetry and imbalance in treatment between the group of 'like' imported products and the group of 'like' domestic products could suffice for 'less favourable treatment' if a facially neutral characteristic advantages or disadvantages only a small number of 'like' products or services and service suppliers but is an almost perfect substitute for certain origin. Conversely, a greater disparate impact could be required for characteristics that are more distant. This approach would require a judgment as to how close certain characteristics are related to each other and how this influences a particular standard of 'less favourable treatment'. Similar considerations are arguably involved when the intensity of the competitive relationship or the extent of differential treatment is taken into account.[2353] A single but flexible standard of 'less favourable treatment' could thus avoid a 'cliff effect' that can arise when different standards are applied based on a sometimes artificial distinction between de jure and de facto discrimination.[2354]

Article 24 of the OECD Model and the MFN and NT rules of the GATT and GATS are different in substance but face similar conceptual challenges: how to find an appropriate balance between competing interests, how to apply available tools for assessing discrimination despite an ambiguous wording, how to determine and deal with aims of domestic measures, and how to employ formal approaches to non-discrimination that may provide easy solutions but not always lead to conclusive or convincing results. It is submitted in this study that all non-discrimination provisions inevitably balance between different interests. Therefore, it is crucial to take into account the objectives of the non-discrimination provisions and how they relate to other objectives of a particular instrument. Also, many arguments that can be seen as

2351. *See* Chapter 4 section §4.02[C][1].
2352. *See* Chapter 4 section §4.02[D][3].
2353. Confer Ehring 2002, 966; concurring Vranes 2009, 235.
2354. *See also* Vranes 2009, 225–240, 248–249, who acknowledges that 'almost any *de jure* discriminatory measure can be transformed into *de facto* discriminatory measures' (p. 233), basically accepts that two different standards exist for a finding of de jure and de facto discrimination (pp. 225–240), but also suggests that a 'disguised' measure that intends to indirectly discriminate because of origin can be regarded as essentially amounting to de jure discrimination (pp. 229, 248–249). However, this approach merely shifts the discussion to a different level, that is, to the distinction between 'disguised' de jure discrimination and de facto discrimination.

a matter of exceptions or justifications may just as well turn into a matter of comparability or less favourable treatment particularly if no exceptions or justifications are available. Whether the aims of a domestic measure should be considered in an analysis of discrimination depends on each individual non-discrimination provision and on what objectives it pursues. Such considerations are not about subjective or indiscernible intentions. Rather, they promote a more precise balance between competing policy interests. Last, but not least, the MFN and NT rules of the GATT and GATS and Article 24 of the OECD Model demonstrate that formal approaches should be used with caution as they may be inconclusive or lead to results that are difficult to reconcile with the objectives that are pursued by the non-discrimination provisions.

CHAPTER 6
Summary and Conclusions

§6.01 GENERAL NON-DISCRIMINATION RULES OF THE GATT AND GATS

Non-discrimination is a central WTO obligation.[2355] All major agreements, in particular, the GATT,[2356] the GATS,[2357] and the TRIPS Agreement[2358] include non-discrimination provisions that require MFN and NT. Despite many differences in wording, the non-discrimination rules concerning trade in goods and services generally condemn 'less favourable treatment' of 'like products' or 'like services and service suppliers'. They thereby intend to contribute to trade liberalization and to avoid protectionism. At the same time, the WTO Members have a recognized right to regulate and pursue specific policy interests. WTO law, therefore, seeks to establish a balance between trade and non-trade objectives.[2359] Where this balance lies depends on the meanings of 'likeness' and 'less favourable treatment' and on the availability of exceptions that may justify discriminatory measures.

For the purposes of establishing 'likeness', it is necessary to specify the relevant characteristics, the degree of similarity, and the relevant perspective.[2360] GATT 1947 jurisprudence initially relied on an objective standard of 'likeness' and was mainly concerned with physical characteristics. However, physical characteristics are only a more or less suitable proxy for other factors that really matter, such as substitutability and competitive relationships.[2361] With the Border Tax Adjustments report of 1970,

2355. Chapter 2 section §2.02[A].
2356. Chapter 2 section §2.02[B].
2357. Chapter 2 section §2.02[C].
2358. Chapter 2 section §2.02[D].
2359. Chapter 2 section §2.02[E].
2360. Chapter 2 section §2.03[A].
2361. Chapter 2 section §2.03[B].

economic considerations started to become an open part of the 'likeness' analysis, recognizing that the GATT is an economic agreement essentially concerned with competitiveness. Four general criteria have been employed ever since: the products' properties, the products' end-uses, the consumers' tastes and habits, and tariff classifications – but always on a case-by-case basis and, therefore, without discussion of their relative relevance and weight.[2362] A few years before the creation of the WTO, a purpose-oriented standard of 'likeness' was introduced: the aim and effects test. Although this standard was not fully developed, it allowed denying 'likeness' when a measure had no protectionist aims and effects, that is when a measure pursued legitimate policy interests.[2363] Soon, the Appellate Body rejected the aim and effects test under both the GATT and GATS especially for textual reasons and adhered to a competitive standard of 'likeness'. A determination of 'likeness' is, fundamentally, a determination about the nature and extent of a competitive relationship between and among products.[2364]

The aim and effects test relied on the general principle enshrined in Article III:1 of the GATT that internal measures should not be applied so as to afford protection to domestic production. Conversely, measures without protective aims and effects should not lead to discrimination. Besides being better aligned with the object and purpose of the non-discrimination rules, the aim and effects test responded to concerns that bona fide regulation could incidentally result in treatment that was less favourable and end up in an unjustified violation of substantive WTO obligations which would have severely limited the Members' regulatory autonomy. While such concerns have been lessened by rejecting the notion that different treatment of some 'like products' suffices for de facto discrimination and by applying the general exceptions in a flexible manner, they have not been dispelled. Various arguments against the aim and effects test have been brought forward: the general exceptions could be rendered meaningless; it might be too difficult to determine a measure's aims; there is no guidance on which aims are legitimate; other approaches to 'likeness' are more objective – and all of these arguments appear largely unfounded.[2365] Despite that, textual differences between the non-discrimination rules ultimately led to a rejection of the aim and effects test.[2366]

It seems that the Appellate Body had concerns about the aim and effects test because aims could imply an enquiry into the minds of legislators or regulators.[2367] It can be argued, however, that the aim and effects test was never intended to do so. A measure's aims can be determined on an objective basis just as under a justification analysis.[2368] The second sentence of Article III:2 of the GATT that refers specifically to Article III:1 even requires a separate analysis of a 'protective application' in order to establish discrimination. This is an aim and effects test but for subjective and

2362. Chapter 2 section §2.03[C].
2363. Chapter 2 section §2.03[D].
2364. Chapter 2 section §2.03[E].
2365. Chapter 2 section §2.03[D][3].
2366. Chapter 2 section §2.03[D][4].
2367. Chapter 2 section §2.03[D][5].
2368. Chapter 2 section §2.03[D][6].

indiscernible intentions.[2369] Moreover, it is notable that, in *EC – Asbestos* (2001), the Appellate Body denied 'likeness' of life-threatening asbestos and substitute products despite their competitive relationship. At first sight, the physical properties and consumers' tastes and habits played a decisive role, but the Appellate Body's decision is difficult to understand without the health risks at stake for which a justification defence was available.[2370] Although the end result is the same, it actually matters whether the health risks are considered at the 'likeness' or justification stage: either human life and health or trade liberalization can be perceived as the more important value under the WTO framework.[2371]

Only the NT rule of the GATS expressly states that formally identical or formally different treatment may be considered to be less favourable. Nevertheless, it is undisputed that the general MFN and NT rules of the GATT and GATS all cover both de jure and de facto discrimination.[2372] Origin-based measures are regarded as being discriminatory by definition. However, even when a measure directly refers to origin, neither 'likeness' nor 'less favourable treatment' can automatically be established. It must be ascertained that this distinction is based *exclusively* on origin or that it modifies the conditions of competition, respectively.[2373]

Since the MFN and NT rules of the GATT and GATS employ a competitive standard of 'less favourable treatment',[2374] a formal difference in treatment between 'like' products or services and service suppliers is neither necessary nor sufficient to show a violation of a non-discrimination obligation. What matters is whether a measure modifies the conditions of competition in the relevant market.[2375] It can be argued that, for the purposes of establishing whether identical or different treatment is 'less favourable', any imported product can be compared to any 'like' domestic (NT) or other foreign (MFN) product; the whole group of 'like' imported products must be compared to a corresponding group; or differences in characteristics between 'like' products may establish relevant subgroups; and comparison is possible only within each of these subgroups.[2376] Under the first approach, basically every distinction between 'like' products or services and service suppliers would amount to 'less favourable treatment' thereby severely limiting the regulatory autonomy of WTO Members. Under the third approach, basically every origin-neutral distinction between 'like' products or services and service suppliers would be acceptable. Thus, the Appellate Body decided in *EC – Asbestos* (2001) that, for a violation of the NT obligation, the group of 'like' imported products must be compared to and treated less favourably than the group of 'like' domestic products. It does not suffice to find some 'like' domestic products that enjoy better treatment than some 'like' imported products. It further does not matter that some 'like' domestic products may be burdened as

2369. Chapter 2 section §2.03[D][5].
2370. Chapter 2 section §2.03[E][3].
2371. Chapter 2 section §2.03[D][3].
2372. Chapter 2 section §2.04[A][1].
2373. Chapter 2 section §2.04[A][2].
2374. Chapter 2 section §2.04[B].
2375. Chapter 2 section §2.04[B][1].
2376. Chapter 2 section §2.04[B][2].

well or that some 'like' imported products may also be favoured or that burdened products may predominantly consist of 'like' domestic products – as long as the proportion between burdened and favoured 'like' imported products is higher than the proportion of burdened and favoured 'like' domestic products.[2377]

It has been suggested to consider regulatory purposes as an issue of 'less favourable treatment'. If a measure pursues legitimate policy interests and only incidentally has a disparate impact on imported products, this should not lead to 'less favourable treatment'.[2378] *Dominican Republic – Import and Sale of Cigarettes* (2005) seemed to support such a purpose-oriented standard of 'less favourable treatment'. However, the Appellate Body clarified that there must be a genuine relationship between the measure at issue and its disparate impact. While, arguably, some distant and minor effects of a measure do not suffice for 'less favourable treatment' if these effects are influenced by other factors, it remains unclear on what basis priority can be given to such other explanations for a measure's disparate impact.[2379]

In *US – Clove Cigarettes* (2012), the Appellate Body accepted a purpose-oriented standard of 'less favourable treatment' under Article 2.1 of the TBT Agreement. Although there is no justification defence for this combined MFN and NT obligation, the TBT Agreement does not intend to disregard the regulatory autonomy of WTO Members.[2380] Conversely, the Appellate Body denied a similar standard of 'less favourable treatment' under the MFN and NT rules of both the GATT and GATS in particular because WTO Members can resort to general exceptions.[2381] Article 2.1 of the TBT Agreement thus incorporates a justification defence, including a proportionality analysis, into 'less favourable treatment'. This means that discrimination can be denied under Article 2.1 of the TBT Agreement if a disparate impact stems exclusively from legitimate regulatory distinctions. With or without express justifications, a similar overall balance between trade and non-trade objectives is thereby achieved.

Article XX of the GATT and Article XIV of the GATS contain a closed list of general exceptions that may justify violations of substantive WTO obligations. This list is exhaustive and does not necessarily cover all supposedly legitimate policy interests. While a liberal and evolutionary interpretation of the general exceptions may provide rescue for almost all environmental-friendly measures, progressive taxes on luxury goods and targeted rules against harmful tax competition may serve as examples for which no appropriate exceptions might be available. In such cases, WTO Members try to defend their regulatory measures by arguing against 'likeness' or 'less favourable treatment' based on purpose-oriented standards.[2382]

As the general exception clauses of the GATT and GATS use different terms for the required nexus that measures must establish to a legitimate policy objective in order to be provisionally justified, this might suggest that protection of human life or health ('necessary') is subject to stricter scrutiny than other aims ('relating to'). A

2377. Chapter 2 section §2.04[B][3].
2378. Chapter 2 section §2.04[C][1].
2379. Chapter 2 section §2.04[C][2].
2380. Chapter 2 section §2.04[C][3].
2381. Chapter 2 section §2.04[C][4].
2382. Chapter 2 section §2.05[A].

flexible and holistic approach to 'necessary' has lessened such concerns. In order to determine whether a measure is necessary, a series of factors must be weighed and balanced against each other including the relative importance of the common interests or values that the measure intends to protect, the extent to which the measure contributes to the realization of the end pursued, and the extent to which the measure produces trade-restrictive effects. In this light, it must further be considered whether WTO-consistent or less inconsistent alternative measures are reasonably available and all of this without questioning a WTO Member's right to determine the appropriate level of protection.[2383]

A broad interpretation and flexible application of the general exceptions implies that the WTO framework is not ignorant of many important societal values that are unrelated to trade. At the same time, the chapeau is able to ensure that WTO Members do not abuse or misuse the general exceptions. It subjects the application of provisionally justified measures to additional scrutiny by prohibiting arbitrary or unjustifiable discrimination between WTO Members or a disguised restriction on trade. This allows maintaining a balance of rights and obligations: the right of a Member to invoke a general exception, on the one hand, and the rights of the other Members to trade without discrimination and other restrictions, on the other hand. Where the line of equilibrium is located must be determined on a case-by-case basis.[2384]

It is not precisely clear what 'burden of proof' means under the WTO dispute settlement system, what the standards of proof for establishing a prima facie case are, and why the burden of proof 'shifts' or 'moves' after establishing such a prima facie case.[2385] Thus, the precise meaning and consequences of burden-shifting and a prima facie case remain controversial.[2386] While the complainant has to establish a prima facie case of discrimination, the respondent has to establish a prima facie case of an exception. As the burden may 'shift', however, the burden to provide evidence that alternative measures are reasonably available may be on the complainant.[2387] Whether the initial burden of proof is on the complainant or respondent also depends on whether an exception is at stake. In this context, a distinction between 'exceptions' and 'exclusions' is made, although those concepts are difficult to distinguish.[2388] An argument against the aim and effects test relates to the burden of proof. Yet, the concept of a prima facie case puts into doubt whether the burden of proof would differ substantially if regulatory purposes were a matter of 'likeness' instead of a justification defence. Under the aim and effects test, protectionist purposes could be presumed if the respondent provides no evidence for legitimate purposes thereby procedurally requiring the respondent to justify its measures at the level of 'likeness'.[2389]

2383. Chapter 2 section §2.05[B].
2384. Chapter 2 section §2.05[C].
2385. Chapter 2 section §2.06[A].
2386. Chapter 2 section §2.06[B].
2387. Chapter 2 section §2.06[C].
2388. Chapter 2 section §2.06[D].
2389. Chapter 2 section §2.06[E].

§6.02 ARTICLE 24 OF THE OECD MODEL: TENSIONS AND UNRESOLVED ISSUES

Article 24 of the OECD Model contains provisions dealing with the elimination of tax discrimination. It provides certain specific grounds that a State may not use to discriminate for the purposes of taxation. In relation to nationals of the treaty partner State, Article 24 prohibits discrimination by reason of nationality (paragraph 1)[2390] and contains similar protection for stateless persons (paragraph 2).[2391] In relation to residents of the treaty partner State, Article 24 prohibits discrimination in cases of PEs belonging to treaty partner residents (paragraph 3),[2392] deductions of certain payments and debts to treaty partner residents (paragraph 4),[2393] and enterprises owned or controlled by treaty partner residents (paragraph 5).[2394] All of the non-discrimination provisions apply to taxes of every kind and description, although the meaning of 'residence' may pose special problems with taxes on transactions such as with VAT.[2395]

Article 24 is not a general prohibition of tax discrimination and may be criticized for its too limited scope, though it is related to the overall goal of double taxation conventions to avoid impediments to international trade.[2396] As most States distinguish between residents (full tax liability) and non-residents (limited tax liability) under their domestic laws, the OECD Model is influenced by this distinction.[2397] Unlike residence, nationality plays a minor role in taxation. Distinctions based on nationality, therefore, seem arbitrary and are prohibited under Article 24(1)[2398] unless nationality is used as grounds for full tax liability.[2399] Article 24(3) protects PEs of non-resident enterprises in order to contribute to equal conditions of competition in economically similar situations in the source State.[2400] It excludes personal allowances, reliefs, and reductions based on the assumption that they will already be granted in the residence State.[2401] The deductibility non-discrimination clause of Article 24(4) is concerned with the Contracting States turning prevented juridical double taxation into unrelieved economic double taxation and thereby impeding the agreed allocation of taxing rights. Differences in the deductibility of payments and debts based on differences in residence or taxing rights, therefore, are prohibited.[2402] Similar considerations may apply to the ownership non-discrimination clause of Article 24(5).[2403] Based on the objectives of Article 24(3), (4), and (5), it can further be concluded that the tiebreaker

2390. Chapter 3 section §3.02[A][1].
2391. Chapter 3 section §3.02[A][2].
2392. Chapter 3 section §3.02[B][1].
2393. Chapter 3 section §3.02[B][2].
2394. Chapter 3 section §3.02[B][3].
2395. Chapter 3 section §3.02[C].
2396. Chapter 3 section §3.03[A].
2397. Chapter 3 section §3.03[B].
2398. Chapter 3 section §3.03[C][1].
2399. Chapter 3 section §3.03[C][2].
2400. Chapter 3 section §3.03[D][1].
2401. Chapter 3 section §3.03[D][2].
2402. Chapter 3 section §3.03[E][1].
2403. Chapter 3 section §3.03[E][2].

rules for cases of dual residence do not limit the scope of the non-discrimination provisions related to residence.[2404]

Despite many differences in wording, the non-discrimination provisions of Article 24 pursue a common concept of comparability: all relevant aspects except for the specific grounds that are protected by a non-discrimination clause must be the same.[2405] Yet, the express comparability requirements raise issues that are specific to each non-discrimination provision.[2406] It can be argued that similar circumstances suffice for 'the same circumstances' under Article 24(1) if all differences in circumstances are irrelevant,[2407] comparability under Article 24(3) is not literally limited to 'the same activities' (the activities of the whole non-resident enterprise may be important),[2408] the requirement of deductibility 'under the same conditions' leaves open how comparability under Article 24(4) should be established,[2409] and 'other similar enterprises' under Article 24(5) need not be purely domestic-owned but may have foreign shareholders as well.[2410] In addition, even under a common concept of comparability, the decisive issue is how the relevant and irrelevant differences in circumstances can be determined in a concrete case and thus which aspects must be the same in order to establish comparability.[2411]

Based on the current approach to non-discrimination, all or almost all differences in circumstances except for the protected attribute are relevant and suffice for rejecting discrimination.[2412] Only if basically everything except for the protected attribute is the same, comparability can be established. Only situations of direct (de jure) discrimination are covered by Article 24[2413] while no justification for discriminatory treatment is available.[2414] This strict and mechanical concept of comparability arguably ensures a limited scope of application without a need for balancing decisions. It seems to avoid policy considerations and value judgments.

However, this approach to non-discrimination under Article 24 raises serious conceptual issues when protected and unprotected attributes overlap.[2415] A category of 'disguised' discrimination is introduced which is arguably different from indirect (de facto) discrimination. At the same time, even a passport requirement is not inextricably linked to nationality in all cases and, therefore, could not be covered by Article 24(1).[2416] While, in most cases, differences in nationality are linked to differences in passport entitlement, not all nationals need to be entitled to a passport, and some foreigners may be entitled as well. Conversely, residence of corporations might appear

2404. Chapter 3 section §3.03[F].
2405. Chapter 3 section §3.04[A].
2406. Chapter 3 section §3.04[B].
2407. Chapter 3 section §3.04[B][1].
2408. Chapter 3 section §3.04[B][2].
2409. Chapter 3 section §3.04[B][3].
2410. Chapter 3 section §3.04[B][4].
2411. Chapter 3 section §3.04[C].
2412. Chapter 3 section §3.05[A].
2413. Chapter 3 section §3.05[B].
2414. Chapter 3 section §3.05[C].
2415. Chapter 3 section §3.06[A].
2416. Chapter 3 section §3.06[B].

to be a better proxy for nationality than a passport of individuals if incorporation leads to full tax liability and tax treaty residence.[2417] When a protected characteristic (nationality) overlaps with an unprotected characteristic (residence),[2418] it can be argued that a distinction based on either characteristic automatically[2419] or never[2420] leads to discrimination, the tiebreaker rules of Article 4(2) and (3) must be considered in order to determine tax treaty residence,[2421] residence may only be ignored if it is irrelevant or inextricably linked to nationality,[2422] or residence plays a special role and, unlike other interchangeable characteristics, is always relevant for comparability purposes.[2423] It seems impossible to apply a strict comparability standard in a mechanical manner to distinguish between relevant and irrelevant differences in circumstances.[2424]

Non-deductibility rules that target hybrid mismatch arrangements raise concerns about discrimination because of the recipient's residence under Article 24(4).[2425] It can be argued that situations with and without a hybrid mismatch are not comparable to each other because all circumstances must be identical.[2426] Yet, a change in the recipient's residence may, in a concrete case, lead to a change in tax treatment. This test confirms an inevitable link between a hybrid mismatch criterion and residence and consequently speaks in favour of discrimination under Article 24(4).[2427] Ignoring factual circumstances in order to make payments to non-resident recipients (without a PE) comparable to equally treated payments to resident recipients (with a PE) does not solve this issue because better-treated payments to resident recipients (without a PE) then become comparable as well.[2428] Two at first sight forceful arguments are nevertheless submitted against discrimination: payments to resident recipients are disadvantaged as well,[2429] and not all payments to non-residents are disadvantaged.[2430] This arguably demonstrates that the recipient's residence is not the reason for different tax treatment. A closer analysis reveals that these arguments not only may fail to avoid discrimination in some situations but also are based on undisclosed judgments about how closely a facially neutral criterion must be linked to a protected characteristic in order to constitute 'disguised' discrimination under Article 24(4).[2431]

2417. Chapter 3 section §3.06[C].
2418. Chapter 3 section §3.06[C][1].
2419. Chapter 3 section §3.06[C][2].
2420. Chapter 3 section §3.06[C][3].
2421. Chapter 3 section §3.06[C][4].
2422. Chapter 3 section §3.06[C][5].
2423. Chapter 3 section §3.06[C][6].
2424. Chapter 3 section §3.06[C][7].
2425. Chapter 3 section §3.06[D][1].
2426. Chapter 3 section §3.06[D][2].
2427. Chapter 3 section §3.06[D][3].
2428. Chapter 3 section §3.06[D][4].
2429. Chapter 3 section §3.06[D][5].
2430. Chapter 3 section §3.06[D][6].
2431. Chapter 3 section §3.06[D][7].

§6.03 ARTICLE 24 OF THE OECD MODEL: SUGGESTED COMPARABILITY TEST

Article 24 eliminates tax discrimination for specific policy reasons and not without impact on domestic policy interests. It thereby establishes a balance between domestic and tax treaty objectives, that is between legitimate distinctions and unjustified discrimination. While this balance is largely predetermined through various requirements for Article 24's application, it cannot always be identified with a simple comparability test and without policy considerations.[2432] Although several arguments can be brought forward against a separate analysis of justification – Article 24 explicitly lists all protected characteristics, should have a narrow scope, should not allow for value judgments, should be interpreted in an identical manner by different courts – a complete denial of justification is not necessarily convincing and does not solve most of these issues.[2433] However, the scope of Article 24 is indeed narrowly defined which means that potential justification can generally be considered as an issue of comparability. Thus, there is little need for a separate analysis. Since this conceptual interchangeability of comparability and justification is not always recognized, there is an observable risk that relevant arguments are dismissed without providing a reasonable explanation other than that justification has no place under Article 24.[2434] Article 24 also contains certain exceptions from non-discrimination obligations which basically justify discrimination for specific policy reasons.[2435] Finally, various statements of the OECD Commentary about justified differences in tax treatment evidence that Article 24 is concerned with policy objectives when assessing comparability.[2436]

A traditional 'but for' test for identifying discrimination under Article 24 – but for the protected characteristic, would the tax treatment be different? – has conceptual limitations. It is only able to prove that nationality or residence is *not* the reason for different tax treatment and not that nationality or residence *is* the reason.[2437] It further should not matter under Article 24 whether a domestic tax measure expressly refers to a protected characteristic or rather employs a closely related substitute.[2438] Since a 'but for' test is not able to identify discrimination with certainty and since facially neutral tax measures might also be discriminatory, a two-step approach is suggested in this study for systematically approaching cases of discrimination under Article 24. First, an adapted 'but for' test establishes whether a measure is prima facie discriminatory in a concrete case.[2439] Second, a substantive analysis determines whether nationality or residence is indeed the reason for different tax treatment or whether inevitably linked

2432. Chapter 4 section §4.01[A].
2433. Chapter 4 section §4.01[B].
2434. Chapter 4 section §4.01[C].
2435. Chapter 4 section §4.01[D].
2436. Chapter 4 section §4.01[E].
2437. Chapter 4 section §4.02[A].
2438. Chapter 4 section §4.02[B].
2439. Chapter 4 section §4.02[C].

but relevant attributes prevent comparability.[2440] All arguments and policy considerations can succeed in justifying different tax treatment under Article 24 if they are reflected in inevitably linked differences in legal or factual circumstances in a concrete case and if these differences are relevant from a domestic and tax treaty perspective.

It is not clear from the wording of Article 24 whether comparison should be made between a group of protected persons and a group of comparable persons or between the taxpayer at issue and one single hypothetical taxpayer. Systematic considerations speak for the latter approach which avoids questions about a disparate impact and about discrimination through formally equal treatment.[2441] Therefore, it makes sense to begin the non-discrimination analysis with a 'but for' test that requires everything except for the protected characteristic of nationality or residence to be the same. Yet, differences in circumstances that are inevitably linked to differences in nationality or residence in a concrete case should not prevent comparability. With a 'but for' test, they must be deemed to be different as well.[2442] If a measure refers to a protected characteristic or to an inevitably linked attribute in a concrete case, it is prima facie discriminatory regardless of how other cases are treated and whether an inevitable link exists in other cases.[2443]

Inevitably linked but unprotected characteristics are neither always relevant nor can they always be disregarded for comparability purposes. A substantive analysis must determine their relevance. This substantive analysis not only focuses on the taxpayer in question. It also considers the tax treatment of other cases in order to determine *why* a certain distinction is made from a domestic perspective and whether this reason is compatible with or contravenes the objectives of the non-discrimination provisions.[2444] While comparability cannot be assessed without taking the aims of a domestic tax measure into account, not every allegedly legitimate reason for different tax treatment can automatically be accepted under Article 24.[2445] An assessment of a measure's aims must rely on that measure's wording, scope, design, architecture, and structure. If a domestic tax measure employs a facially neutral attribute instead of a protected characteristic, this may lead to different effects, not necessarily in a concrete case but in other cases, and thereby provide evidence for certain policy aims. Such aims may further be reflected in inevitably linked differences in legal or factual circumstances in a concrete case and, if viewed as legitimate and relevant from a tax treaty perspective, prevent comparability. Questions of whether nationals or residents are disadvantaged as well and whether not all foreigners or non-residents are disadvantaged are part of this substantive analysis.[2446] The suggested two-step approach for identifying discrimination under Article 24,[2447] therefore, can deal with interconnected characteristics without a risk of undisclosed judgments in particular when differences

2440. Chapter 4 section §4.02[D].
2441. Chapter 4 section §4.02[C][1].
2442. Chapter 4 section §4.02[C][2].
2443. Chapter 4 section §4.02[C][3].
2444. Chapter 4 section §4.02[D][1].
2445. Chapter 4 section §4.02[D][2].
2446. Chapter 4 section §4.02[D][3].
2447. Chapter 4 section §4.02[E].

in nationality indicate differences in residence[2448] and differences in residence lead to differences in a hybrid mismatch or low or no taxation.[2449]

As long as nationality and residence do not overlap, a 'but for' test rejects discrimination under Article 24(1) with regard to all facially neutral measures that refer to residence. If there is an overlap in some cases, however, a 'but for' test establishes prima facie discrimination when a change in nationality inevitably leads to a change in residence and thus in tax treatment or when nationality is directly employed as grounds for a distinction.[2450] Whether nationality or residence or perhaps some other inevitably linked characteristic is the reason for different tax treatment can only be determined by a substantive analysis. This is confirmed by several examples of the OECD Commentary. Depending on the objective of the domestic tax measure under scrutiny and how this objective relates to Article 24(1) and the tax treaty as a whole, inevitably linked differences in tax treaty residence but not in domestic residence might avoid comparability, inevitably linked differences in domestic residence might be seen as a suitable proxy for legitimate concerns about tax information, or inevitably linked differences in both tax treaty residence and domestic residence might be irrelevant.[2451]

It is possible to distinguish between non-deductibility rules that specifically target hybrid mismatch arrangements, rules that target all cases of low or no taxation, and rules that target situations when payments are not subject to tax in a State because of a tax exemption, no full or limited tax liability, or a loss of taxing rights. All of these rules may be prima facie discriminatory with a 'but for' test as a change in the recipient's residence may lead to a change in tax treatment and thereby avoid a tax disadvantage in a concrete case.[2452] A substantive analysis, however, is able to distinguish between these kinds of rules. Since Article 24(4) is only concerned with the Contracting States compensating for a loss of taxing rights by turning prevented juridical double taxation into unrelieved economic double taxation, inevitably linked differences in the existence of a hybrid mismatch and low or no taxation are relevant and prevent comparability. This is true even if a non-deductibility rule disadvantages only payments to non-resident recipients. Conversely, inevitably linked differences in tax liability and taxing rights are irrelevant for the purposes of Article 24(4). A rule of a State that denies a deduction when payments to non-resident recipients are not taxed in that State, therefore, may lead to prohibited tax discrimination under Article 24(4) even if it also disadvantages payments to tax-exempt resident recipients.[2453]

An in-depth analysis of various other selected cases of potential discrimination – different methods of income attribution and treatment of non-arm's-length payments, in particular by thin capitalization rules;[2454] calculation of progressive tax rates and deduction of foreign losses;[2455] application of group taxation and consolidation regimes

2448. Chapter 4 section §4.03[A].
2449. Chapter 4 section §4.03[B].
2450. Chapter 4 section §4.03[A][1].
2451. Chapter 4 section §4.03[A][2].
2452. Chapter 4 section §4.03[B][1].
2453. Chapter 4 section §4.03[B][2].
2454. Chapter 4 section §4.04[A].
2455. Chapter 4 section §4.04[B].

to non-resident enterprises;[2456] and relief of juridical[2457] and economic[2458] double taxation – reveals that non-discrimination under Article 24 is a complex undertaking. When a 'but for' test establishes prima facie discrimination, often arguments for or against discrimination can be traced back to inevitably linked differences in legal or factual circumstances. Whether these differences are relevant and prevent comparability or whether the Contracting States intended to avoid discrimination under Article 24 despite such inevitably linked differences in circumstances in a concrete case is the decisive question. This question can only be answered by examining the objectives of the domestic tax measure under scrutiny and the objectives of the applicable non-discrimination provisions together with the provisions' context. It is necessary to determine where the intended and agreed balance lies between the need to prevent unjustified discrimination and the need to take account of legitimate distinctions, that is whether differences in tax treatment are justified or must be equated with a prohibited tax distinction.

§6.04 CONCEPTUAL IMPLICATIONS FOR NON-DISCRIMINATION LAW

All non-discrimination provisions including those of the GATT and GATS and Article 24 of the OECD Model necessarily establish a balance between different and often competing policy interests. For this purpose, they use different tools and impose different requirements for their application. In order to establish discrimination, even comparability is not indispensable but commonly relied on together with less favourable treatment and exceptions or justifications. All of these steps of analysis interact with each other which means that any express requirements cannot be interpreted in isolation without regard to their context and what balance a particular instrument aims to achieve. Identical terms may have very different meanings if they are embedded in different contexts, and different terms may have similar meanings. Although the non-discrimination provisions of the GATT and GATS and Article 24 of the OECD Model contain ambiguous terms that are open to different meanings and interpretations, their context allows better understanding of where the equilibrium between illegitimate and justified distinctions lies.[2459]

If a non-discrimination provision does not allow for justification, arguments against a violation of substantive obligations should not be disregarded because of their supposed justificatory nature. All arguments that could be justification grounds might also be an issue of comparability or less favourable treatment. Thus, what aims a domestic measure pursues, whether these aims are legitimate, and whether they are pursued in a proportionate manner is not a matter reserved to exceptions or justification. With regard to transparency and predictability, there is also no preference for a separate analysis of justification. An analysis of comparability or less favourable treatment may be structured into several parts of which one might be concerned with

2456. Chapter 4 section §4.04[C].
2457. Chapter 4 section §4.04[D].
2458. Chapter 4 section §4.04[E].
2459. Chapter 5 section §5.01.

aims and their legitimacy. Yet, if non-discrimination law draws a distinction on whatever basis between an analysis of discrimination and an analysis of exceptions or justification, this might have implications for the burden of proof. In addition, despite reaching the same end result, a denial of discrimination may have different normative implications when compared to a successful justification of discrimination. The difference between no discrimination and justified discrimination, therefore, is not only a matter of legal technique.[2460]

Aims of domestic legislation need not be about subjective intentions inhabiting the minds of individual legislators or regulators or about alleged purposes that succeed in justifying measures without conclusive evidence. Aims can be identified objectively, in particular, by considering a measure's scope and design as well as its actual, expected, and potential effects. This is true regardless of whether aims are relevant for the purposes of justifying discriminatory measures or for establishing comparability or treatment that is less favourable. Although a non-discrimination provision can be based on effects only, aims are often taken into account in order to distinguish more precisely between illegitimate and justified distinctions.[2461]

Formal approaches to non-discrimination are often inconclusive and, therefore, problematic. Since a non-discrimination test should not fail to prohibit some distinctions that should be prohibited and prohibit some distinctions that should not be prohibited, preference is given to a more accurate and appropriate balance between different and often competing objectives by supplementing a formal analysis with substantive considerations. A measure that de jure refers to a protected characteristic is neither automatically discriminatory under Article 24 of the OECD Model nor can 'likeness' and 'less favourable treatment' automatically be established under WTO law. Just as facially neutral measures can de facto refer to foreign origin, origin-based measures can de facto refer to a potentially legitimate factor. It is further difficult to find a clear dividing line between de jure and de facto discrimination even in supposedly straightforward cases. Nevertheless, a measure that de jure refers to a protected characteristic or employs a close substitute might have very different effects than a measure that uses a facially neutral criterion. It might, therefore, pursue very different aims. Although a formal reference to a protected characteristic may appear suspicious, raise a presumption of 'likeness', indicate 'less favourable treatment', require stricter scrutiny, or lead to prima facie discrimination with a 'but for' test, this is not the end of a non-discrimination analysis; substantive considerations may still indicate that there is no discrimination.[2462]

2460. Chapter 5 section §5.02.
2461. Chapter 5 section §5.03.
2462. Chapter 5 section §5.04.

Bibliography

Abbott, Frederick M., Thomas Cottier, and Francis Gurry. 2015. *International Intellectual Property in an Integrated World Economy*. 3rd ed. Aspen Casebook Series. New York: Wolters Kluwer.

Adda, Marco. 2008. 'Can a Permanent Establishment Be a "Legitimate Heir" in a Domestic Consolidated Tax Regime?'. *European Taxation* 48 (5): 238–244.

Adonnino, Pietro. 1993. 'General Report'. In *Non-discrimination Rules in International Taxation*, edited by International Fiscal Association, 19–71. Cahiers de Droit Fiscal International – Studies on International Fiscal Law, LXXVIIIb. Deventer: Kluwer Law; Taxation Publishers.

Aigner, Hans-Jörgen. 2004. *Hinzurechnungsbesteuerung und DBA-Recht*. Schriftenreihe zum Internationalen Steuerrecht 32. Vienna: Linde.

Alcover, Maria, and Ana María Garcés. 2016. 'The Interpretation of "Treatment No Less Favourable" Under Article III:4 of the GATT 1994 and Article 2.1 of the TBT Agreement: A Comparative Analysis'. *Global Trade and Customs Journal* 11 (9): 360–368.

Allevato Neto, Murillo Estevam. 2015. 'Cross-Border Tax Consolidation under Article 24(5) of the OECD Model'. In *Non-discrimination in European and Tax Treaty Law: Open Issues and Recent Challenges*, edited by Kasper Dziurdź, and Christoph Marchgraber, 553–574. Series on International Tax Law 94. Vienna: Linde.

Andenas, Mads, and Stefan Zleptnig. 2008. 'Proportionality and Balancing in WTO Law: A Comparative Perspective'. In *The World Trade Organization and Trade in Services*, edited by Kern Alexander and Mads Andenas, 147–171. Leiden; Boston: Martinus Nijhoff Publishers.

Ankersmit, Laurens J., and Jessica C. Lawrence. 2012. 'The Future of Environmental Labelling: *US – Tuna II* and the Scope of the TBT'. *Legal Issues of Economic Integration* 39 (1): 127–147.

Antoniolli, Walter. 1956. 'Gleichheit vor dem Gesetz: Wiener Juristische Gesellschaft – Sitzung vom 7. November 1956'. *Österreichische Juristen-Zeitung* 24 (23/24): 646–648.

Appleton, Arthur E. 1997. 'GATT Article XX's Chapeau: A Disguised "Necessary" Test?: The WTO Appellate Body's Ruling in *United States – Standards for Reformulated and Conventional Gasoline*'. *Review of European Community and International Environmental Law (Review of European, Comparative and International Environmental Law)* 6 (2): 131–138.

Appleton, Arthur E. 2014. 'National Treatment under the TBT Agreement'. In *The Principle of National Treatment in International Economic Law: Trade, Investment and Intellectual Property*, edited by Anselm Kamperman Sanders, 92–124. European Intellectual Property Institutes Network Series. Cheltenham; Northampton: Edward Elgar Publishing.

Arnold, Brian J. 1991. *Tax Discrimination Against Aliens, Non-residents, and Foreign Activities: Canada, Australia, New Zealand, the United Kingdom and the United States*. Canadian Tax Papers 90. Toronto: Canadian Tax Foundation.

Arnold, Brian J. 2009a. 'Tax Treaty News'. *Bulletin for International Taxation* 63 (7): 266–271.

Arnold, Brian J. 2009b. 'The 2008 Update of the OECD Model: An Introduction'. *Bulletin for International Taxation* 63 (5): 178–182.

Arnold, Brian J. 2011. 'Tax Treaty News'. *Bulletin for International Taxation* 65 (7): 367–374.

Ault, Hugh J. 1992. 'Corporate Integration, Tax Treaties and the Division of the International Tax Base: Principles and Practices'. *Tax Law Review* 47 (3): 565–608.

Ault, Hugh J. 1993. 'The Role of the OECD Commentaries in the Interpretation of Tax Treaties'. In *Essays on International Taxation: To Sidney I. Roberts – With Esteem and Affection from the Participating Authors and the Partners of Roberts & Holland*, edited by Herbert H. Alpert and Kees van Raad, 61–68. Series on International Taxation 15. Deventer: Kluwer Law; Taxation Publishers.

Ault, Hugh J., and Brian J. Arnold. 2010. *Comparative Income Taxation: A Structural Analysis*. 3rd ed. New York; Alphen on the Rhine: Aspen Publishers; Kluwer Law International.

Ault, Hugh J., and Philip T. Kaplan. 1980. 'International Developments - Another View'. *Journal of Corporate Taxation* 7: 78–87.

Ault, Hugh J., and Jacques Sasseville. 2010. 'Taxation and Non-discrimination: A Reconsideration'. *World Tax Journal* 2 (2): 101–125.

Ault, Hugh J., and David R. Tillinghast. 1992. *Federal Income Tax Project: International Aspects of United States Income Taxation II: Proposals of the American Law Institute on United States Income Tax Treaties*. Philadelphia: American Law Institute.

Avery Jones, John F. 1996. 'Carry on Discriminating'. *European Taxation* 36 (2): 46–49.

Avery Jones, John F. 1998. 'Flows of Capital Between the EU and Third Countries and the Consequences of Disharmony in European International Tax Law'. *EC Tax Review* 7 (2): 95–106.

Avery Jones, John F. 2006. 'The Interaction Between Tax Treaty Provisions and Domestic Law'. In *Tax Treaties and Domestic Law*, edited by Guglielmo Maisto, 123–158. EC and International Tax Law Series 2. Amsterdam: IBFD.

Avery Jones, John F. 2007. 'The Non-discrimination Article Is about Discrimination--Official'. *British Tax Review* 52 (4): 349–350.

Avery Jones, John F. 2009. 'Understanding the OECD Model Tax Convention: The Lesson of History'. *Florida Tax Review* 10 (1): 1–49.

Avery Jones, John F., Philip Baker, Luc De Broe, Maarten J. Ellis, Kees van Raad, Jean-Pierre Le Gall, Sanford H. Goldberg, et al. 2011a. 'Article 24(5) of the OECD Model in Relation to Intra-group Transfers of Assets and Profits and Losses'. *British Tax Review* 56 (5): 535–586.

Avery Jones, John F., et al. 2011b. 'Art. 24(5) of the OECD Model in Relation to Intra-group Transfers of Assets and Profits and Losses'. *World Tax Journal* 3 (2): 179–225.

Avery Jones, John F., and Catherine Bobbett. 1999. 'Triangular Treaty Problems: A Summary of the Discussion in Seminar E at the IFA Congress in London'. *Bulletin for International Fiscal Documentation (Bulletin for International Taxation)* 53 (1): 16–20.

Avery Jones, John F., and Catherine Bobbett. 2008. 'Interpretation of the Non-discrimination Article of the OECD Model'. *Bulletin for International Taxation* 62 (2): 50–55.

Avery Jones, John F., Henri-Robert Depret, Micheline van de Wiele, Maarten J. Ellis, Kees van Raad, Pierre Fontaneau, Pierre-Marie Fontaneau, et al. 1991a. 'The Non-discrimination Article in Tax Treaties–II'. *British Tax Review* 36 (11/12): 421–452.

Avery Jones, John F., et al. 1991b. 'The Non-discrimination Article in Tax Treaties'. *European Taxation* 31 (10): 310–347.

Avi-Yonah, Reuven S., and Christiana HJI Panayi. 2010. 'Rethinking Treaty Shopping: Lessons from the European Union'. In *Tax Treaties: Building Bridges Between Law and Economics*, edited by Michael Lang, Pasquale Pistone, Josef Schuch, Claus Staringer, Alfred Storck, and Martin Zagler, 21–50. Amsterdam: IBFD.

Bagci, Recep. 2019. 'Comparing Similar Enterprises under Article 24(5) of the OECD Model: Non-discrimination and MFN Treatment in the Context of the Netherlands Group Taxation Regime'. *European Taxation* 59 (1): 23–32.

Baker, Philip. 2004. 'Review of Recent Treaty Cases – *NatWest II*, *NEC* and *SA Andritz*'. *Bulletin for International Fiscal Documentation (Bulletin for International Taxation)* 58 (5): 205–212.

Baker, Philip. 2006. *Double Taxation Conventions: A Manual on the OECD Model Tax Convention on Income and on Capital*. 10/11. London: Sweet & Maxwell.

Baker, Philip. 2011. 'Great Britain: FCE Bank PLC v Her Majesty's Revenue and Customs'. In *Tax Treaty Case Law around the Globe – 2011*, edited by Michael Lang, Pasquale Pistone, Josef Schuch, Claus Staringer, Alfred Storck, Luc De Broe, Peter Essers, Eric C.C.M. Kemmeren, and Frans Vanistendael, 455–461. Series on International Tax Law 70. Vienna: Linde.

Baker, Philip. 2013. 'United Kingdom: Group Relief'. In *Tax Treaty Case Law Around the Globe 2012*, edited by Eric C.C.M. Kemmeren, Daniël S. Smit, Peter Essers, Luc De Broe, Michael Lang, Pasquale Pistone, Josef Schuch, Claus Staringer, and Alfred Storck, 351–356. Series on International Tax Law 78. Amsterdam; Vienna: IBFD; Linde.

Baker, Philip, and Richard S. Collier. 2006. 'General Report'. In *The Attribution of Profits to Permanent Establishments*, edited by International Fiscal Association, 21–67. Cahiers de Droit Fiscal International – Studies on International Fiscal Law 91b. Amersfoort: Sdu Fiscale & Financiële Uitgevers.

Balestieri, Stefano. 2015. 'Juridical Double Taxation Relief under Article 24(3) of the OECD Model: The PE Country's Obligations'. In *Non-discrimination in European and Tax Treaty Law: Open Issues and Recent Challenges*, edited by Kasper Dziurdź, and Christoph Marchgraber, 403–426. Series on International Tax Law 94. Vienna: Linde.

Bammens, Niels. 2012. *The Principle of Non-discrimination in International and European Tax Law*. IBFD Doctoral Series 24. Amsterdam: IBFD.

Bammens, Niels. 2013a. 'Articles 24(4) and 24(5) of the OECD Model Applied to Domestic Thin Capitalization Rules'. *World Tax Journal* 5 (2): 148–171.

Bammens, Niels. 2013b. 'The Interaction Between the Interpretation of Article 24 OECD MC and the Non-discrimination Standard Developed by the CJEU'. *EC Tax Review* 22 (4): 172–186.

Bammens, Niels. 2016. 'The Non-discrimination Analysis under the OECD Model as Compared to the EU Fundamental Freedoms'. In *International Tax Law: New Challenges to and from Constitutional and Legal Pluralism*, edited by Joachim Englisch, 97–135. Amsterdam: IBFD.

Bammens, Niels, and Frans Vanistendael. 2016. 'Article 24: Non-discrimination. Global Tax Treaty Commentaries'. IBFD. 30 April 2016. http://online.ibfd.org/document/gttc_article24.

Bammens, Niels, and Frans Vanistendael. 2017. 'Article 24: Non-discrimination. Global Tax Treaty Commentaries'. IBFD. 1 March 2017. http://online.ibfd.org/document/gttc_article24.

Baranger, Séverine. 2004. 'Supreme Court Rules on Thin Capitalization Provisions: Decisions of the Supreme Administrative Court of 30 December 2003'. *European Taxation* 44 (6): 287–290.

Barceló III, John J. 2009. 'Burden of Proof, Prima Facie Case and Presumption in WTO Dispute Settlement'. *Cornell International Law Journal* 42 (1, Winter): 23–43.

Bartels, Lorand. 2015. 'The Chapeau of the General Exceptions in the WTO GATT and GATS Agreements: A Reconstruction'. *American Journal of International Law* 109 (1): 95–125.

Behrens, Stefan. 2011. 'Organschaft über die Grenze aufgrund des DBA-Diskriminierungsverbots?'. *Die Unternehmensbesteuerung* 4 (9): 665–752.

Behrens, Stefan. 2012. 'Keine sog. Organschaft über die Grenze aufgrund des DBA-Diskriminierungsverbots: Anmerkungen zum Nichtanwendungserlass vom 27.12.2011'. *Betriebs-Berater* 67 (8): 485–490.

Beiser, Reinhold. 1991. 'Der Verlustvortrag beschränkt Steuerpflichtiger im Licht des zwischenstaatlichen Steuerrechts'. *Steuer und Wirtschaft International* 1 (1): 15–18.

Bellstedt, Christoph. 1973. *Die Besteuerung international verflochtener Gesellschaften*. 3rd ed. Cologne: Dr. Otto Schmidt.

Bendlinger, Stefan. 2011. 'Neuer OECD-Bericht zur Betriebsstättendefinition'. *Steuer und Wirtschaft International* 21 (12): 531–538.

Bennett, Mary C. 2006. 'The David R. Tillinghast Lecture – Nondiscrimination in International Tax Law: A Concept in Search of a Principle'. *Tax Law Review* 59 (4, Summer): 439–485.

Berrisch, Georg M. 2003. 'Das Allgemeine Zoll- und Handelsabkommen (GATT 1994)'. In *WTO-Handbuch*, edited by Hans-Joachim Prieß, and Georg M. Berrisch, 71–167. Munich: C.H. Beck.

Betten, Rijkele. 1989. 'Netherlands: Denial of Certificate of Residence to Dual Resident Company'. *European Taxation* 29 (11): 371–373.

Beyer, Vincent. 2018. 'Direct Taxes and the GATS: Substantive and Procedural Defences for Non-compliant Income Tax Measures'. *Journal of World Trade* 52 (3): 351–373.

Bhuta, Harshal. 2015. 'Progressive Tax Rates in a Profit or Loss Situation under Article 24(3) of the OECD Model'. In *Non-discrimination in European and Tax Treaty Law: Open Issues and Recent Challenges*, edited by Kasper Dziurdź, and Christoph Marchgraber, 377–402. Series on International Tax Law 94. Vienna: Linde.

Bizek, Barbara. 2003. 'Anwendung der Grundfreiheiten auf Doppelbesteuerungsabkommen'. In *Die Auswirkungen der Diskriminierungsverbote in der Praxis*, edited by Gerd Konezny, and Ulf Zehetner, 59–83. Schriftenreihe zum Internationalen Steuerrecht 28. Vienna: Linde.

Boekhorst, Paul J. te. 1991. 'Austria: Loss Carryforward for Permanent Establishments: Decree of the Austrian Federal Ministry of Finance'. *European Taxation* 31 (12): 412–414.

Boulogne, Gerard Frederik. 2011. 'Group Taxation Within the European Union: Did *Papillon* and Art. 24(5) of the OECD Model Tax Convention Create a Butterfly Effect?'. *European Taxation* 51 (5): 171–178.

Bourgeois, Marc, and Adeline Römer. 2009. 'Effects of Existing Tax Treaties on VAT (Relevance of Arts. 24–27 OECD Model for VAT/GST)'. In *Value Added Tax and Direct Taxation: Similarities and Differences*, edited by Michael Lang, Peter Melz, and Eleonor Kristoffersson, 1231–1268. Amsterdam: IBFD.

Bown, Chad P., and Joel P. Trachtman. 2009. '*Brazil – Measures Affecting Imports of Retreaded Tyres*: A Balancing Act'. *World Trade Review* 8 (1): 85–135.

Böckli, Peter. 1979. 'Die Verweigerung der Steuergutschrift gegenüber Steuerausländern nach der deutschen Körperschaftsteuerreform 1977 aus der Sicht eines Vertragsstaates'. *Steuer und Wirtschaft* 56 (1): 1–15.

Böhmer, Julian. 2014. 'Zur Anwendung des DBA-Diskriminierungsverbots in Fällen schädlicher Gesellschafter-Fremdfinanzierung'. *Internationale Steuer-Rundschau* 3 (5): 163–165.

Brandstetter, Patricia. 2011. *'Taxes Covered': A Study of Article 2 of the OECD Model Tax Conventions*. Amsterdam: IBFD.

Brauner, Yariv. 2014. 'USA: The United Airlines Flight Attendants' Saga Continues'. In *Tax Treaty Case Law Around the Globe 2013*, edited by Michael Lang, Jeffrey Owens, Pasquale Pistone, Josef Schuch, Claus Staringer, Alfred Storck, Peter Essers, Eric C.C.M. Kemmeren, and Daniël S. Smit, 339–347. Series on International Tax Law 81. Amsterdam; Vienna: IBFD; Linde.

Bravo, Nathalie. 2016. 'The Multilateral Tax Instrument and Its Relationship with Tax Treaties'. *World Tax Journal* 8 (3): 279–304.

Bree, Axel. 1998. 'Article XX GATT – Quo Vadis? The Environmental Exception after the Shrimp/Turtle Appellate Body Report'. *Dickinson Journal of International Law* 17 (1): 99–134.

Breining-Kaufmann, Christine. 2001. 'Ein Sieg für die Umwelt? – Der Entscheid der WTO im Asbest-Streit zwischen Kanada und der Europäischen Union'. *Aktuelle Juristische Praxis / Pratique Juridique Actuelle*, no. 10: 1169–1180.

Brendt, Jörg. 2003. 'Verstößt § 8a KStG auch gegen das Diskriminierungsverbot des Art. 24 Abs. 5 OECD-MA?'. *Internationale Wirtschaftsbriefe*, no. 19 (October): 897–904.

Bronckers, Marco, and Natalie McNelis. 1999. 'Rethinking the "Like Product" Definition in WTO Antidumping Law'. *Journal of World Trade* 33 (3): 73–91.

Bronckers, Marco, and Natalie McNelis. 2000. 'Rethinking the "Like Product" Definition in GATT 1994: Anti-dumping and Environmental Protection'. In *Regulatory Barriers and the Principle of Non-discrimination in World Trade Law*, edited by Thomas Cottier, and Petros C. Mavroidis, 345–385. World Trade Forum 2. Michigan: University of Michigan Press.

Bronselaer, Kim, and Werner Heyvaert. 2009. 'Non-discrimination'. In *The New US-Belgium Double Tax Treaty: A Belgian and EU Perspective*, edited by Anne Van de Vijver, 493–522. Ghent: Larcier.

Broude, Tomer. 2007. 'Genetically Modified Rules: The Awkward Rule-Exception–Right Distinction in *EC–Biotech*'. *World Trade Review* 6 (2): 215–231.

Broude, Tomer, and Philip I. Levy. 2014. 'Do You Mind If I Don't Smoke? Products, Purpose and Indeterminacy in *US – Measures Affecting the Production and Sale of Clove Cigarettes*'. *World Trade Review* 13 (2): 357–392.

Brown, Catherine, and Jack Mintz. 2010. 'On the Relationship Between International Tax Neutrality and Non-discrimination Clauses under Tax Treaties for Source-Based Taxes'. In *Tax Treaties: Building Bridges Between Law and Economics*, edited by Michael Lang, Pasquale Pistone, Josef Schuch, Claus Staringer, Alfred Storck, and Martin Zagler, 581–606. Amsterdam: IBFD.

Brugger, Florian. 2008. 'Austria'. In *International and EC Tax Aspects of Groups of Companies*, edited by Guglielmo Maisto, 175–207. EC and International Tax Law Series 4. Amsterdam: IBFD.

Bruns, Silke. 2007. 'Seminar E: Fragen im Bereich der Diskriminierungsverbote (IFA/OECD)'. *Internationales Steuerrecht* 16 (16): 579–582.

Bruns, Silke. 2008. 'Taxation and Non-discrimination: Clarification and Reconsideration by the OECD'. *European Taxation* 48 (9): 484–492.

Bruns, Silke. 2013. 'Art. 24'. In *Doppelbesteuerungsabkommen: Kommentar*, edited by Jens Schönfeld, and Xaver Ditz. Cologne: Dr. Otto Schmidt.

Bunkley, Nick. 2011. 'Lacking Parts, G.M. Will Close Plant'. *The New York Times*, March.

Burgstaller, Eva. 2004. 'Conseil d'Etat zur französischen Unterkapitalisierungsregel: Widerspruch zu DBA- und EU-Recht'. *Steuer und Wirtschaft International* 14 (6): 285–292.

Burgstaller, Eva. 2005. 'Die Kriterien für die Festlegung des Quellenstaates nach den Doppelbesteuerungsabkommen bei Dividenden'. In *Die Verteilung der Besteuerungsrechte zwischen Ansässigkeits- und Quellenstaat im Recht der Doppelbesteuerungsabkommen*, edited by Wolfgang Gassner, Michael Lang, Josef Schuch, and Claus Staringer, 217–246. Vienna: Linde.

Burgstaller, Eva, and Christine Obermair. 2006. 'Das Gesellschafterdiskriminierungsverbot'. In *Die Diskriminierungsverbote im Recht der Doppelbesteuerungsabkommen*, edited by Michael Lang, Josef Schuch, and Claus Staringer, 167–203. Vienna: Linde.

Burton, Steven J. 1982. 'Comment on "Empty Ideas": Logical Positivist Analyses of Equality and Rules'. *Yale Law Journal* 91 (6): 1136–1152.

Búrca, Gráinne de. 2002. 'Unpacking the Concept of Discrimination in EC and International Trade Law'. In *The Law of the Single European Market: Unpacking the Premises*, edited by Catherine Barnard, and Joanne Scott, 181–195. Oxford; Portland, Oregon: Hart Publishing.

Carlson, Geoffrey. 2016. 'Argentina – Measures Relating to Trade in Goods and Services (Argentina–Financial Services), DS453'. *World Trade Review* 15 (4): 706–708.

Chang, Howard F. 2000. 'Toward a Greener GATT: Environmental Trade Measures and the Shrimp-Turtle Case'. *Southern California Law Review* 74 (1): 31–47.

Charnovitz, Steve. 1991. 'Exploring the Environmental Exceptions in GATT Article XX'. *Journal of World Trade* 25 (5): 37–55.

Charnovitz, Steve. 1994. 'Green Roots, Bad Pruning: GATT Rules and Their Application to Environmental Trade Measures'. *Tulane Environmental Law Journal* 7 (2, Summer): 299–352.

Charnovitz, Steve. 1997. 'WTO's *Alcoholic Beverages* Decision'. *Review of European Community and International Environmental Law (Review of European, Comparative and International Environmental Law)* 6 (2): 198–203.

Charnovitz, Steve. 1998. 'The Moral Exception in Trade Policy'. *Virginia Journal of International Law* 38 (4, Summer): 689–745.

Charnovitz, Steve. 2002. 'The Law of Environmental "PPMs" in the WTO: Debunking the Myth of Illegality'. *Yale Journal of International Law* 27 (1, Winter): 59–110.

Charnovitz, Steve. 2007. 'The WTO's Environmental Progress'. *Journal of International Economic Law* 10 (3): 685–706.

Charnovitz, Steve, Lorand Bartels, Robert Howse, Jane Bradley, Joost Pauwelyn, and Donald H. Regan. 2004. 'The Appellate Body's GSP decision'. *World Trade Review* 3 (2): 239–265.

Chemerinsky, Erwin. 1983. 'In Defense of Equality: A Reply to Professor Westen'. *Michigan Law Review* 81 (3): 575–599.

Choi, Won-Mog. 2002. 'Overcoming the "Aim and Effect" Theory: Interpretation of the "Like Product" in GATT Article III'. *U.C. Davis Journal of International Law and Policy* 8 (1, Winter): 107–131.

Cleave, Brian. 2007. '*Boake Allen Limited and Others v HMRC*–Group Income Elections and Non-discrimination'. *British Tax Review* 52 (5): 604–608.

Cleave, Brian. 2008. '*Boake Allen* (or *NEC Semi-Conductors*): Non-discrimination, Advance Corporation Tax, Tax Treaties and the Free Movement of Capital'. *European Taxation* 48 (2): 91–95.

Cleave, Brian. 2013a. '*FCE Bank plc v HMRC*: Applying *Boake Allen* to Group Relief'. *British Tax Review* 58 (2): 126–131.

Cleave, Brian. 2013b. 'The *FCE* Case: Former United Kingdom Group Relief and Treaty Discrimination'. *Bulletin for International Taxation* 67 (8): 414–420.

Colares, Juscelino F., and William P. Canterberry. 2017. '*US–COOL*: How the Appellate Body Misconstrued the National Treatment Principle, Severely Restricting Agency Discretion to Promulgate Mandatory, Pro-consumer Labeling Rules'. *Journal of World Trade* 51 (1): 105–130.

Conconi, Paola, and Tania Voon. 2016. '*EC–Seal Products*: The Tension Between Public Morals and International Trade Agreements'. *World Trade Review* 15 (2): 211–234.

Condon, Bradly J. 2014. 'Treaty Structure and Public Interest Regulation in International Economic Law'. *Journal of International Economic Law* 17 (2): 333–353.

Connolly, Katherine. 2015. 'Finding Space for Regulatory Autonomy in GATS Article XVII after *EC – Seals*: Public Services and the "Likeness" of Public and Private Service Providers'. *Legal Issues of Economic Integration* 42 (1): 57–84.

Conrad, Christiane R. 2011. *Processes and Production Methods (PPMs) in WTO Law: Interfacing Trade and Social Goals*. Cambridge: Cambridge University Press.

Cordewener, Axel. 2002. *Europäische Grundfreiheiten und nationales Steuerrecht: Konvergenz des Gemeinschaftsrechts und Kohärenz der direkten Steuern in der Rechtsprechung des EuGH*. Rechtsordnung und Steuerwesen 29. Cologne: Dr. Otto Schmidt.

Cosbey, Aaron, and Petros C. Mavroidis. 2014. 'Heavy Fuel: Trade and Environment in the GATT/WTO Case Law'. *Review of European Community & International Environmental Law* 23 (3): 288–301.

Cossy, Mireille. 2008. 'Some Thoughts on the Concept of "Likeness" in the GATS'. In *GATS and the Regulation of International Trade in Services*, edited by Marion Panizzon, Nicole Pohl, and Pierre Sauvé, 327–357. Cambridge: Cambridge University Press.

Cottier, Thomas, Panagiotis Delimatsis, and Nicolas F. Diebold. 2008. 'Article XIV GATS'. In *WTO – Trade in Services*, edited by Rüdiger Wolfrum, Peter-Tobias Stoll, and Clemens Feinäugle, 287–328. Max Planck Commentaries on World Trade Law 6. Leiden; Boston: Martinus Nijhoff Publishers.

Cottier, Thomas, and Matthias Oesch. 2012. 'Direct and Indirect Discrimination in WTO and EU Law'. In *Liberalising Trade in the EU and the WTO: A Legal*

Comparison, edited by Sanford E. Gaines, Birgitte Egelund Olsen, and Karsten Engsig Sørensen, 141–175. Cambridge: Cambridge University Press.

Cottier, Thomas, and Lena Schneller. 2014. 'The Philosophy of Non-discrimination in International Trade Regulation'. In *The Principle of National Treatment in International Economic Law: Trade, Investment and Intellectual Property*, edited by Anselm Kamperman Sanders, 3–33. European Intellectual Property Institutes Network Series. Cheltenham; Northampton: Edward Elgar Publishing.

Crowley, Meredith A., and Robert Howse. 2014. '*Tuna–Doplhin II*: A Legal and Economic Analysis of the Appellate Body Report'. *World Trade Review* 13 (2): 321–355.

Curzon, Gerard. 1965. *Multilateral Commercial Diplomacy: The General Agreement on Tariffs and Trade and Its Impact on National Commercial Policies and Techniques*. London: Michael Joseph.

D'Amato, Anthony. 1983. 'Is Equality a Totally Empty Idea?'. *Michigan Law Review* 81 (3): 600–603.

Damen, Stephan. 2001. 'Netherlands Supreme Court Rules on the Residence of Dual Resident Companies under Tax Treaties with Third Countries'. *Bulletin for International Fiscal Documentation (Bulletin for International Taxation)* 55 (7): 290–292.

Danon, Robert J. 2004. 'Cross-Border Transfers of Participations Within a Group: A Note on a Recent Judgment Rendered by the Swiss Supreme Court'. *Intertax* 32 (6/7): 336–339.

Davey, William J., and Keith E. Maskus. 2013. '*Thailand–Cigarettes (Philippines)*: A More Serious Role for the "Less Favourable Treatment" Standard of Article III:4'. *World Trade Review* 12 (2): 163–193.

Davey, William J., and Joost Pauwelyn. 2000. 'MFN Unconditionality: A Legal Analysis of the Concept in View of its Evolution in the GATT/WTO Jurisprudence with Particular Reference to the Issue of "Like Product"'. In *Regulatory Barriers and the Principle of Non-discrimination in World Trade Law*, edited by Thomas Cottier, and Petros C. Mavroidis, 13–50. World Trade Forum 2. Michigan: University of Michigan Press.

Davies, Arwel. 2009. 'Interpreting the Chapeau of GATT Article XX in Light of the "New" Approach in *Brazil-Tyres*'. *Journal of World Trade* 43 (3): 507–539.

Davis, Alex. 2017. 'The *Shochu* Conundrum: Economics and the General Agreement on Tariffs and Trade Article III'. *Global Trade and Customs Journal* 12 (1): 32–38.

Debatin, Helmut. 1963a. 'Das OECD-Musterabkommen zur Vermeidung der internationalen Doppelbesteuerung'. *Außenwirtschaftsdienst des Betriebs-Beraters (Recht der Internationalen Wirtschaft)* 9 (10): 289–295.

Debatin, Helmut. 1963b. *Grundzüge der Abkommen zur Vermeidung der internationalen Doppelbesteuerung*. Sonderdruck der Steuer- und Wirtschafts-Kurzpost 118. Freiburg im Breisgau: Rudolf Haufe Verlag.

Debatin, Helmut. 1965. 'Steuerbefreiung mit Progressionsvorbehalt als Methode zur Vermeidung der Doppelbesteuerung'. *Außenwirtschaftsdienst des Betriebs-Beraters (Recht der Internationalen Wirtschaft)* 11 (2): 41–50.

Debatin, Helmut. 1970. 'Das Verbot steuerlicher Diskriminierung'. *Deutsche Steuer-Zeitung* 57 (9): 129–136.

Debatin, Helmut. 1972. 'Der deutsch-schweizerische Steuervertrag (I)'. *Der Betrieb* 25 (41): 1939–1945.

Debatin, Helmut. 1980. 'Entwicklungsaspekte des internationalen Steuerrechts'. *Recht der Internationalen Wirtschaft* 26 (1): 3–10.

Debatin, Helmut. 1981. 'Vorbemerkungen: Systematik des internationalen Steuerrechts und Grundzüge des deutschen Außensteuerrechts'. In *Doppelbesteuerung*, edited by Rudolf Korn, Georg Dietz, and Helmut Debatin, 43rd ed. Munich: C.H. Bech.

De Broe, Luc. 2008. *International Tax Planning and Prevention of Abuse: A Study under Domestic Tax Law, Tax Treaties and EC Law in Relation to Conduit and Base Companies*. Doctoral Series 14. Amsterdam: IBFD.

De Broe, Luc, and Niels Bammens. 2009. 'Truck Center – Belgian Withholding Tax on Interest Payments to Non-resident Companies Does Not Violate EC Law: A Critical Look at the ECJ's Judgment in Truck Center'. *EC Tax Review* 18 (3): 131–137.

Delimatsis, Panagiotis, Nicolas F. Diebold, Martín Molinuevo, Marion Panizzon, and Pierre Sauvé. 2011. 'Developing Trade Rules for Services: A Case of Fragmented Coherence?'. In *The Prospects of International Trade Regulation: From Fragmentation to Coherence*, edited by Thomas Cottier, and Panagiotis Delimatsis, 245–283. Cambridge: Cambridge University Press.

Demschner, Daniela, and Markus Stefaner. 2009. 'Gruppenbesteuerung: Sandwichgruppen möglich?'. *Steuer und Wirtschaft International* 19 (1): 9–23.

Desai, Mihir A., and James R. Hines Jr. 2003. 'Evaluating International Tax Reform'. *National Tax Journal* 56 (3): 487–502.

Desmedt, Axel. 2001. 'Proportionality in WTO Law'. *Journal of International Economic Law* 4 (3): 441–480.

Diebold, Nicolas F. 2010. *Non-discrimination in International Trade in Services: 'Likeness' in WTO/GATS*. Cambridge: Cambridge University Press.

Diebold, Nicolas F. 2011a. 'Assessing Competition in International Economic Law: A Comparison of "Market Definition" and "Comparability"'. *Legal Issues of Economic Integration* 38 (2): 115–141.

Diebold, Nicolas F. 2011b. 'Standards of Non-discrimination in International Economic Law'. *International and Comparative Law Quarterly* 60 (4): 831–865.

DiMascio, Nicholas, and Joost Pauwelyn. 2008. 'Non-discrimination in Trade and Investment Treaties: Worlds Apart or Two Sides of the Same Coin?'. *American Journal of International Law* 102 (1): 48–89.

Díaz Prado, Fabiola Angélica. 2015. 'Influence of Article 24 on Taxes Not Covered by Article 2 of the OECD Model'. In *Non-discrimination in European and Tax Treaty Law: Open Issues and Recent Challenges*, edited by Kasper Dziurdź, and Christoph Marchgraber, 575–594. Series on International Tax Law 94. Vienna: Linde.

Djanani, Christiana, and Thomas Hartmann. 2000. 'Der Progressionsvorbehalt im Nichtansässigkeitsstaat und bei subjektiven Qualifikationskonflikten'. *Internationales Steuerrecht* 9 (11): 321–325.

Doernberg, Richard L. 1995. 'Overriding Tax Treaties: The U.S. Perspective'. *Emory International Law Review* 9 (1, Spring): 71–132.

Doernberg, Richard L., and Kees van Raad. 1990. 'The Legality of the Earnings-Stripping Provision under U.S Income Tax Treaties'. *Tax Notes International* 2 (2): 199–206.

Dommes, Sabine, and Judith Herdin. 2004. 'The Consequences of the Tie-Breaker Rule for Dual Resident Companies'. *Steuer und Wirtschaft International* 14 (9): 450–455.

Dommes, Sabine, and Vanessa E. Metzler. 2006. 'Das Staatsangehörigendiskriminierungsverbot bei natürlichen Personen'. In *Die Diskriminierungsverbote im Recht der Doppelbesteuerungsabkommen*, edited by Michael Lang, Josef Schuch, and Claus Staringer, 93–135. Vienna: Linde.

Dommes, Sabine, and Josef Schuch. 2007. 'Gruppenbesteuerung und Doppelbesteuerungsabkommen'. In *Grundfragen der Gruppenbesteuerung*, edited by Michael Lang, Josef Schuch, Claus Staringer, and Markus Stefaner, 347–384. Vienna: Linde.

Dorn, Herbert. 1926. 'Der deutsch-italienische Doppelbesteuerungsvertrag: Eine Übersicht'. *Steuer und Wirtschaft* 5 (1): 97–118.

Dörr, Oliver. 2012. 'Article 32'. In *Vienna Convention on the Law of Treaties: A Commentary*, edited by Oliver Dörr, and Kirsten Schmalenbach, 571–586. Berlin; Heidelberg: Springer.

Dötsch, Ewald. 2011. 'Künftig Nullbesteuerung auslandsbeherrschter inländischer Kapitalgesellschaften? Zugleich Anmerkung zu BFH, Urt. v. 9. 2. 2011 – I R 54, 55/10, Der Konzern 2011, 236'. *Der Konzern* 9 (6–7): 267–268.

Du, Ming. 2010. 'Autonomy in Setting Appropriate Level of Protection under the WTO Law: Rhetoric or Reality?'. *Journal of International Economic Law* 13 (4): 1077–1102.

Du, Ming. 2011. 'The Rise of National Regulatory Autonomy in the GATT/WTO Regime'. *Journal of International Economic Law* 14 (3): 639–675.

Du, Ming. 2015. 'Taking Stock: What Do We Know, and Do Not Know, about the National Treatment Obligation in the GATT/WTO Legal System?'. *Chinese Journal of Global Governance* 1 (1): 67–95.

Du, Ming. 2016. '"Treatment No Less Favorable" and the Future of National Treatment Obligation in GATT Article III:4 after *EC–Seal Products*'. *World Trade Review* 15 (1): 139–163.

Dürrschmidt, Daniel. 2015. 'Artikel 3'. In *Doppelbesteuerungsabkommen der Bundesrepublik Deutschland auf dem Gebiet der Steuern vom Einkommen und Vermögen: Kommentar auf der Grundlage der Musterabkommen*, edited by Moris Lehner, 6th ed. Munich: C.H. Beck.

Dziurdź, Kasper. 2010a. 'Bemessungsgrundlage und Steuersatz von Quellensteuern aus gemeinschaftsrechtlicher Sicht'. In *Quellensteuern: Der Steuerabzug bei Zahlungen an ausländische Empfänger*, edited by Michael Lang, Josef Schuch, and Claus Staringer, 47–65. Vienna: Linde.

Dziurdź, Kasper. 2010b. 'Non-discrimination (Article 24 OECD Model'. In *Europe–China Tax Treaties*, edited by Michael Lang, Jianwen Liu, and Gongliang

Tang, 237–259. EUCOTAX Series on European Taxation 26. Alphen on the Rhine: Kluwer Law International.

Dziurdź, Kasper. 2010c. 'Umsatzsteuerbefreiung für Kleinunternehmer und Diskriminierungsverbote in Doppelbesteuerungsabkommen'. *Steuer und Wirtschaft International* 20 (6): 266–271.

Dziurdź, Kasper. 2013a. 'Article 15 of the OECD Model: The 183-Day Rule and the Meaning of "Borne by a Permanent Establishment"'. *Bulletin for International Taxation* 67 (3): 122–127.

Dziurdź, Kasper. 2013b. '"Circularly Linked" Rules Countering Deduction and Non-inclusion Schemes: Some Thoughts on a Tie-Breaker Test'. *Bulletin for International Taxation* 67 (6): 306–310.

Dziurdź, Kasper. 2013c. *Kurzfristige Arbeitnehmerüberlassung Im internationalen Steuerrecht*. Schriftenreihe zum Internationalen Steuerrecht 75. Vienna: Linde.

Dziurdź, Kasper. 2014. 'Attribution of Functions and Profits to a Dependent Agent PE: Different Arm's Length Principles under Articles 7(2) and 9?'. *World Tax Journal* 6 (2): 135–167.

Dziurdź, Kasper. 2016. 'Non-discrimination and Harmful Tax Competition under WTO Law and Article 24 of the OECD Model'. In *Non-discrimination in Tax Treaties: Selected Issues from a Global Perspective*, edited by Dennis Weber and Pasquale Pistone, 167–223. EC and International Tax Law Series 14. Amsterdam: IBFD.

Dziurdź, Kasper, and Christoph Marchgraber. 2015. 'Non-discrimination in European and Tax Treaty Law: An Overview.' In *Non-discrimination in European and Tax Treaty Law: Open Issues and Recent Challenges*, edited by Kasper Dziurdź and Christoph Marchgraber, 1–16. Series on International Tax Law 94. Vienna: Linde.

Dziurdź, Kasper, and Frank Pötgens. 2014. 'Cross-Border Short-Term Employment'. *Bulletin for International Taxation* 68 (8): 404–414.

Ehring, Lothar. 2002. '*De Facto* Discrimination in World Trade Law: National and Most-Favoured-Nation Treatment–or Equal Treatment?'. *Journal of World Trade* 36 (5): 921–977.

Dziurdź, Kasper. 2014. 'National Treatment under the GATT 1994: Jurisprudential Developments on *De Facto* Discrimination'. In *The Principle of National Treatment in International Economic Law: Trade, Investment and Intellectual Property*, edited by Anselm Kamperman Sanders, 34–54. European Intellectual Property Institutes Network Series. Cheltenham; Northampton: Edward Elgar Publishing.

Eigelshoven, Axel. 2015. 'Artikel 9'. In *Doppelbesteuerungsabkommen der Bundesrepublik Deutschland auf dem Gebiet der Steuern vom Einkommen und Vermögen: Kommentar auf der Grundlage der Musterabkommen*, edited by Moris Lehner, 6th ed. Munich: C.H. Beck.

Eilers, Stephan. 2015. 'Triangular Cases'. In *Doppelbesteuerung – Festgabe: Zum 75. Geburtstag von Prof. Dr. Dr. h.c. Franz Wassermeyer – 75 Beiträge zum Recht der DBA*, edited by Franz Wassermeyer, 107–113. Munich: C.H. Beck.

Elliffe, Craig. 2013a. 'Trans-tasman Thin Capitalisation Rules and Treaties: Implications for New Zealand and Australia on Tighter Thin Capitalisation Ratios'. *Australian Tax Forum* 28 (3): 605–640.

Elliffe, Craig. 2013b. 'Unfinished Business: Domestic Thin Capitalization Rules and the Non-discrimination Article in the OECD Model'. *Bulletin for International Taxation* 67 (1): 26–38.

Engel, Benjamin, and Lukas Hilbert. 2012. 'Keine Betriebsstätte nach Art. 5 OECD-MA bei Land- und Forstwirtschaft: BFH-Urteil (I R 26/11) zum DBA Spanien 1966'. *Internationale Wirtschaftsbriefe*, no. 9: 316–321.

Engelschalk, Michael. 1988. *Die Besteuerung von Steuerausländern auf Bruttobasis: Bestandsaufnahme, Rechtliche Grenzen, Alternativen*. Steuerwissenschaft 28. Heidelberg: C.F. Müller.

Englisch, Joachim. 2008. *Wettbewerbsgleichheit im grenzüberschreitenden Handel mit Schlussfolgerungen für indirekte Steuern*. Tübingen: Mohr Siebeck.

Faller, Christine. 2003. 'Die Auswirkungen des Betriebstättendiskriminierungsverbots im österreichischen Steuerrecht'. In *Die Auswirkungen der Diskriminierungsverbote in der Praxis*, edited by Gerd Konezny, and Ulf Zehetner, 35–58. Schriftenreihe zum Internationalen Steuerrecht 28. Vienna: Linde.

Farber, Daniel A., and Robert E. Hudec. 1996. 'GATT Legal Restraints on Domestic Environmental Regulations'. In *Fair Trade and Harmonization: Prerequisites for Free Trade? – Legal Analysis*, edited by Jagdish Bhagwati, and Robert E. Hudec, 2:59–94. Cambridge, Massachusetts; London, England: The MIT Press.

Farrell, Jennifer E. 2013. *The Interface of International Trade Law and Taxation: Defining the Role of the WTO*. IBFD Doctoral Series 26. Amsterdam: IBFD.

Fauchald, Ole Kristian. 2003. 'Flexibility and Predictability under the World Trade Organization's Non-discrimination Clauses'. *Journal of World Trade* 37 (3): 443–482.

Fekar, Pavel, and Arne Schnitger. 2002. 'Art. 24 Abs. 1 OECD-MA als Eintrittsklausel zur mittelbaren und unmittelbaren Anwendung der Grundfreiheiten des EG-Vertrages für Drittstaatler'. *Steuer und Wirtschaft International* 12 (2): 76–85.

Fett, Emily. 2014. *Triangular Cases: The Application of Bilateral Income Tax Treaties in Multilateral Situations*. IBFD Doctoral Series 29. Amsterdam: IBFD.

Firlinger, Robert. 1995. 'Die abkommensrechtliche Ansässigkeit und die Methoden zur Vermeidung der Doppelbesteuerung'. In *Die Methoden zur Vermeidung der Doppelbesteuerung: Anrechnungs- und Befreiungsmethode*, edited by Wolfgang Gassner, Michael Lang, and Eduard Lechner, 307–329. Vienna: Linde.

Fischer-Zernin, Justus. 1997. 'Art. 24 OECD-MA'. In *DBA-Kommentar*, edited by Helmut Becker, Horst-Dieter Höppner, Siegfried Grotherr, and Heinz-Klaus Kroppen, Grundwerk. Herne: Neue Wirtschafts-Briefe.

Flett, James. 2013. 'WTO Space for National Regulation: Requiem for a Diagonal Vector Test'. *Journal of International Economic Law* 16 (1): 37–90.

Flett, James. 2014. 'National Treatment under the General Agreement on Trade in Services'. In *The Principle of National Treatment in International Economic Law: Trade, Investment and Intellectual Property*, edited by Anselm Kamperman Sanders, 55–91. European Intellectual Property Institutes Network Series. Cheltenham; Northampton: Edward Elgar Publishing.

Flick, Hans, and Franz Wassermeyer. 1974. 'Der Einführungserlaß zum Außensteuergesetz (II)'. *Finanz-Rundschau* 29 (23): 574–581.

Flores Elizondo, Cecilia J. 2014. 'European Communities – Measures Prohibiting the Importation and Marketing of Seal Products'. *Manchester Journal of International Economic Law* 11 (2): 312–321.

Footer, Mary, and Saman Zia-Zarifi. 2002. 'European Communities – Measures Affecting Asbestos and Asbestos-Containing Products: The World Trade Organization on Trial for Its Handling of Occupational Health and Safety Issues'. *Melbourne Journal of International Law* 3 (1): 120–142.

Foster, Caroline E. 2010. 'Burden of Proof in International Courts and Tribunals'. *Australian Year Book of International Law* 29: 27–86.

Fredman, Sandra. 2011. *Discrimination Law.* 2nd ed. Clarendon Law Series. Oxford: Oxford University Press.

Freeden, Arne von, Nils Häck, and Harald Schaumburg. 2017. *Internationales Steuerrecht.* 4th ed. Cologne: Dr. Otto Schmidt.

Friedhelm, Jacob. 2002. 'Discriminatory Tax Treatment of German Permanent Establishments – The Rebirth of an Old Problem'. *Tax Management International Journal* 31 (13): 613–617.

Friedlander, Lara. 2002. 'The Role of Non-discrimination Clauses in Bilateral Income Tax Treaties after GATT 1994'. *British Tax Review* 47 (2): 71–118.

Frotscher, Gerrit. 2011. 'Grenzüberschreitende Organschaft – wo stehen wir?'. *Internationales Steuerrecht* 20 (18): 697–703.

Gaines, Sanford E. 2001. 'The WTO's Reading of the GATT Article XX Chapeau: A Disguised Restriction on Environmental Measures'. *University of Pennsylvania Journal of International Law* 22 (4, Winter): 739–862.

Gaines, Sanford E., and Birgitte Egelund Olsen. 2012. 'Trade and Social Objectives'. In *Liberalising Trade in the EU and the WTO: A Legal Comparison*, edited by Sanford E. Gaines, Birgitte Egelund Olsen, and Karsten Engsig Sørensen, 203–233. Cambridge: Cambridge University Press.

Gammie, Malcolm. 2010. 'Non-discrimination and the Taxation of Cross-Border Dividends'. *World Tax Journal* 2 (2): 162–174.

García Prats, Francisco Alfredo. 1994. 'Triangular Cases and Residence as a Basis for Alleviating International Double Taxation: Rethinking the Subjective Scope of Double Tax Treaties'. *Intertax* 22 (11): 473–491.

Gardiner, Richard K. 2015. *Treaty Interpretation.* 2nd ed. Oxford: Oxford University Press.

Garrido, Bruno. 2009. 'Interaction Between the Interpretation of the Non-discrimination Provisions in Tax Treaties and in the EC Treaty: An Apparent Rather than Real Conflict'. *EC Tax Review* 18 (14): 157–178.

Gassner, Wolfgang. 1970. *Gleichheitssatz und Steuerrecht: Eine Aufgabe für Juristen und Wirtschaftswissenschaftler.* Gelbe Briefe 64. Vienna: Instituts für Finanzwissenschaft und Steuerrecht.

Gassner, Wolfgang, and Michael Lang. 2000a. *Das Leistungsfähigkeitsprinzip im Einkommen-und Körperschaftsteuerrecht: Dogmatische Grundfragen – Rechtspolitischer Stellenwert. Verhandlungen des Vierzehnten Österreichischen Juristentages Wien 2000.* Vol. III/1. Vienna: Manz.

Gassner, Wolfgang, and Michael Lang. 2000b. 'Die mangelnde Leistungsfähigkeit des Leistungsfähigkeitsprinzips'. *Österreichische Steuerzeitung* 53 (22): 643–644.

Gennep, Christo J.A.M. van. 1991. 'International: Dual-Resident Companies: The Second Sentence of Article 4(1) of the OECD Model Convention of 1977'. *European Taxation* 31 (5): 141–146.

Gerdes, Imke. 2004. 'Dual Resident Employers and Employees from Third States'. In *Triangular Tax Cases*, edited by Franz Philipp Sutter, and Ulf Zehetner, 195–215. Schriftenreihe zum Internationalen Steuerrecht 34. Vienna: Linde.

Gifford, William C. 1978. 'Permanent Establishments under the Nondiscrimination Clause in Income Tax Treaties'. *Cornell International Law Journal* 11 (1, Winter): 51–70.

Glicklich, Peter A., and Sanford H. Goldberg. 1993. 'United States'. In *Non-discrimination Rules in International Taxation*, edited by International Fiscal Association, 715–741. Cahiers de Droit Fiscal International – Studies on International Fiscal Law, LXXVIIIb. Deventer: Kluwer Law; Taxation Publishers.

Goldberg, Sanford H., and Peter A. Glicklich. 1992. 'Treaty-Based Nondiscrimination: Now You See It Now You Don't'. *Florida Tax Review* 1 (2): 51–113.

Goldberg, Suzanne B. 2011. 'Discrimination by Comparison'. *Yale Law Journal* 120 (4): 728–812.

Gomes Behrndt, Marco Antônio. 2004. 'Passive Income (Dividends, Interests or Royalties) Received by a Permanent Establishment from a Third State'. In *Triangular Tax Cases*, edited by Franz Philipp Sutter, and Ulf Zehetner, 49–76. Schriftenreihe zum Internationalen Steuerrecht 34. Vienna: Linde.

Gosch, Dietmar. 2007. 'Vielerlei Gleichheiten – Das Steuerrecht im Spannungsfeld von bilateralen, supranationalen und verfassungsrechtlichen Anforderungen'. *Deutsches Steuerrecht* 45 (36): 1553–1561.

Gosch, Dietmar. 2012a. 'Rechtsprechungs-Highlights zum Unternehmenssteuerrecht der Kapitalgesellschaften'. In *Steuerberater-Jahrbuch 2011/2012: zugleich Bericht über den 63. Fachkongress der Steuerberater Köln, 11. und 12. Oktober 2011*, edited by Thomas Rödder, Manfred Günkel, and Ursula Niemann, 9–29. Cologne: Dr. Otto Schmidt.

Gosch, Dietmar. 2012b. 'Über Cross Border-Organschaften: Abkehr des BFH vom strikten Inlandsbezug'. *Internationale Wirtschaftsbriefe*, no. 19: 694–707.

Gouthière, Bruno. 1994. 'Removal of Discrimination – A Never-Ending Story'. *European Taxation* 34 (9): 296–302.

Gouthière, Bruno. 2002. 'Thin Capitalization Rules and the Non-discrimination Principle'. *European Taxation* 42 (4): 159–163.

Göschl, Alexius, Herbert Kovar, and Ronald Wahrlich. 2005. 'Dreiecksverhältnisse im Recht der Doppelbesteuerungsabkommen'. In *Praxis des Internationalen Steuerrechts: Festschrift für Helmut Loukota zum 65. Geburtstag*, edited by Michael Lang, and Heinz Jirousek, 111–130. Vienna: Linde.

Graetz, Michael J. 2001. 'The David R. Tillinghast Lecture – Taxing International Income: Inadequate Principles, Outdated Concepts, and Unsatisfactory Policies'. *Tax Law Review* 54 (3, Spring): 261–336.

Graetz, Michael J. 2003. *Foundations of International Income Taxation*. New York: Foundation Press.

Graf zu Ortenburg, Joachim. 1975. 'Abgrenzungsfragen bei der erweiterten beschränkten Einkommensteuerpflicht'. *Deutsches Steuerrecht* 13 (17): 483–488.

Grando, Michelle T. 2006. 'Allocating the Burden of Proof in WTO Disputes: A Critical Analysis'. *Journal of International Economic Law* 9 (3): 615–656.

Grando, Michelle T. 2009. *Evidence, Proof, and Fact-Finding in WTO Dispute Settlement*. 1st ed. Oxford: Oxford University Press.

Green, Robert A. 1994. 'The Troubled Rule of Nondiscrimination in Taxing Foreign Direct Investment'. *Law and Policy in International Business* 26 (1): 113–164.

Green, Robert A. 1998. 'Antilegalistic Approaches to Resolving Disputes Between Governments: A Comparison of the International Tax and Trade Regumes'. *Yale Journal of International Law* 23 (1, Winter): 79–139.

Greenawalt, Kent. 1983. 'How Empty Is the Idea of Equality'. *Columbia Law Review* 83 (5): 1167–1185.

Greenawalt, Kent. 1997. '"Prescriptive Equality": Two Steps Forward'. *Harvard Law Review* 110 (6): 1265–1290.

Gross, Jakob B. 2003. 'OECD Defensive Measures Against Harmful Tax Competition Legality under WTO'. *Intertax* 31 (11): 390–400.

Grotherr, Siegfried. 2016. 'Art. 23 A/Art. 23 B OECD-MA'. In *DBA-Kommentar*, edited by Dietmar Gosch, Heinz-Klaus Kroppen, and Siegfried Grotherr, 29th ed. Herne: Neue Wirtschafts-Briefe.

Großmann, Klaus. 1995. *Doppelt ansässige Kapitalgesellschaften im internationalen Steuerrecht: Insbesondere im Verhältnis Deutschland–USA*. Münchener Schriften zum Internationalen Steuerrecht 20. Munich: C.H. Beck.

Grynberg, Roman, and Bridget Chilala. 2001. 'WTO Compatibility of the OECD Defensive Measures Against Harmful Tax Competition'. *Journal of World Investment* 2 (3): 507–527.

Grynberg, Roman, and Bridget Chilala. 2002. 'WTO Compatibility of the OECD Defensive Measures Against Harmful Tax Competition'. In *International Tax Competition: Globalisation and Fiscal Sovereignty*, edited by Rajiv Biswas, 151–176. London: Commonwealth Secretariat.

Gupta, Ramón R. 1997. 'Appellate Body Interpretation of the WTO Agreement: A Critique in Light of *Japan–Taxes on Alcoholic Beverages*'. *Pacific Rim Law and Policy Journal* 6 (3): 683–716.

Gusmeroli, Michele. 2005. 'Triangular Cases and the Interest and Royalties Directive: Untying the Gordian Knot? – Part 1'. *European Taxation* 45 (1): 2–13.

Haag, Charles T. 1995. 'Legitimizing "Environmental" Legislation under the GATT in Light of the CAFE Panel Report: *More Fuel for Protectionists?*'. *University of Pittsburgh Law Review* 57 (1, Fall): 79–105.

Hageböke, Jens. 2004. 'Art. 24 OECD-MA'. In *Außensteuergesetz – Doppelbesteuerungsabkommen: Kommentar*, edited by Günther Strunk, Bert Kaminski, and Stefan Köhler, Grundwerk. Bonn: Stotax Stollfuß Medien.

Hageböke, Jens. 2005. 'Art. 24 OECD-MA'. In *Außensteuergesetz – Doppelbesteuerungsabkommen: Kommentar*, edited by Günther Strunk, Bert Kaminski, and Stefan Köhler, 3rd ed. Bonn: Stotax Stollfuß Medien.

Hageböke, Jens, and Volker Käbisch. 2006. 'Zur Ausdehnung des Anwendungsbereichs des UmwStG i.d.F. SEStEG-E auf Grund der Diskriminierungsverbote in Art. 24 OECD-MA'. *Internationales Steuerrecht* 15 (24): 849–855.

Hahn, Hartmut. 2005. 'DBA- und EG-rechtliche Diskriminierungsverbote - zwei Paar Schuhe: Anmerkungen und Überlegungen zum BMF-Schreiben vom 8. 12. 2004 und zum sog. Delaware-Urteil des BFH'. *Betriebs-Berater* 60 (10): 521–529.

Hahn, Michael, Nathalie Diaz, Rachel Liechti-McKee, Tetyana Payosova, and Andrea Schläpfer. 2016. 'The Jurisprudence of the World Trade Organization in 2015'. *Swiss Review of International and European Law* 26 (2): 327–357.

Hariharan, Srikanth. 2012. 'Standard of Review and Burden of Proof in WTO Jurisprudence'. *Journal of World Investment and Trade* 13 (5): 795–811.

Haslehner, Werner. 2007. 'Die Ausdehnung des Anwendungsbereichs der europäischen Grundfreiheiten durch Verfassungs- und DBA-Recht'. *taxlex* 3 (9a): 440–449.

Haslehner, Werner. 2009. *Das Betriebsstättendiskriminierungsverbot im Internationalen Steuerrecht*. Schriftenreihe zum Internationalen Steuerrecht 58. Vienna: Linde.

Haslehner, Werner. 2012. 'Tackling Complex Discrimination in International Taxation'. *British Tax Review* 57 (5): 596–622.

Haslehner, Werner. 2016a. 'Art 24 Gleichbehandlung'. In *DBA: Doppelbesteuerungsabkommen – Kommentar*, edited by Dietmar Aigner, Georg Kofler, and Michael Tumpel, 1st ed. Vienna: Linde.

Haslehner, Werner. 2016b. 'Luxembourg: The Effect of a Tax Treaty Tie-Breaker for Dual Residents'. In *Tax Treaty Case Law Around the Globe 2015*, edited by Michael Lang, Alexander Rust, Jeffrey Owens, Pasquale Pistone, Josef Schuch, Claus Staringer, Alfred Storck, Peter Essers, Eric C.C.M. Kemmeren, and Daniël S. Smit, 43–50. Series on International Tax Law 97. Amsterdam; Vienna: IBFD; Linde.

Haslehner, Werner. 2016c. 'Nationality Non-discrimination and Article 24 OECD Model: Perennial Issues, Recent Trends and New Approaches'. In *Non-discrimination in Tax Treaties: Selected Issues from a Global Perspective*, edited by Dennis Weber, and Pasquale Pistone, 1–26. EC and International Tax Law Series 14. Amsterdam: IBFD.

Haslinger, Katharina, and Michael Petritz. 2006. 'DBA- und WTO-Diskriminierungsverbote: Gemeinsamkeiten und Unterschiede'. In *Die Diskriminierungsverbote im Recht der Doppelbesteuerungsabkommen*, edited by Michael Lang, Josef Schuch, and Claus Staringer, 349–383. Vienna: Linde.

Heining, Arnold, and Alban Timbart. 1961. *Kommentar zum deutsch-französischen Doppelbesteuerungsabkommen*. Edited by Bundesverband der Deutschen Industrie and Conseil National du Patronat Français. Cologne; Paris.

Helde, Stefanie. 2000. *Dreiecksverhältnisse im Internationalen Steuerrecht unter Beteiligung einer Betriebstätte*. Steuerfragen der Wirtschaft 13. Cologne: Dr. Otto Schmidt.

Hellwig, Peter. 1973. 'Das Außensteuergesetz, eine Problembereicherung für die Steuerfachwelt: Kleine Auslese'. *Deutsche Steuer-Zeitung* 61 (1/2): 13–19.

Helminen, Marjaana. 2007. 'Non-discrimination and the Nordic Multilateral Double Taxation Convention'. *Bulletin for International Taxation* 61 (3): 103–108.

Hestermeyer, Holger P. 2011. 'Article III GATT.' In *WTO – Trade in Goods*, edited by Rüdiger Wolfrum, Peter-Tobias Stoll, and Holger P. Hestermeyer, 78–165. Max Planck Commentaries on World Trade Law 5. Leiden; Boston: Martinus Nijhoff Publishers.

Hey, Johanna. 2015. 'Steuersystem und Steuerverfassungsrecht'. In *Steuerrecht*, edited by Klaus Tipke, 22nd ed. Cologne: Dr. Otto Schmidt.

Hinnekens, Luc. 1995. 'Compatibility of Bilateral Tax Treaties with European Community Law – Application of the Rules'. *EC Tax Review* 4 (4): 202–237.

Hinnekens, Luc, and Philippe Hinnekens. 2008. 'General Report'. In *Non-discrimination at the Cross-Roads of International Taxation*, edited by International Fiscal Association, 15–54. Cahiers de Droit Fiscal International – Studies on International Fiscal Law 93a. Amersfoort: Sdu Fiscale & Financiële Uitgevers.

Hinnekens, Philippe. 2008. 'Non-discrimination Article in OECD Model Convention Needs Fundamental Review'. *EC Tax Review* 17 (6): 248–249.

Hintsanen, Lari, and Päivi Viitanen. 2004. 'Finland: Supreme Administrative Court Ruling on the Finland–US Tax Treaty Non-discrimination Clause: Decision of the Supreme Administrative Court of 22 June 2004'. *European Taxation* 44 (10): 460–462.

Hintzen, Lothar. 1976. 'Die Diskriminierungsvorschrift der Doppelbesteuerungsabkommen und ihre Verbesserung'. *Der Betrieb* 29 (47): 2226–2229.

Hofbauer, Ines. 2004a. 'Das Meistbegünstigungsprinzip in den deutschen und österreichischen Doppelbesteuerungsabkommen'. *Internationales Steuerrecht* 13 (19): 667–672.

Hofbauer, Ines. 2004b. 'To What Extent Does the OECD Harmful Tax Competition Project Violate the Most-Favoured-Nation Obligations under WTO Law'. *European Taxation* 44 (9): 400–403.

Hofbauer, Ines. 2005a. *Das Prinzip der Meistbegünstigung im grenzüberschreitenden Ertragsteuerrecht: Eine Betrachtung anhand des Internationalen Wirtschaftsrechts und des Rechts der Doppelbesteuerungsabkommen*. Schriftenreihe zum Internationalen Steuerrecht 40. Vienna: Linde.

Hofbauer, Ines. 2005b. 'Most-Favoured-Nation Clauses in Double Taxation Conventions – A Worldwide Overview'. *Intertax* 33 (10): 445–453.

Hofbauer, Ines. 2006. 'DBA-Diskriminierungsverbote und gemeinschaftsrechtliche Grundfreiheiten – Meistbegünstigung'. In *Die Diskriminierungsverbote im Recht der Doppelbesteuerungsabkommen*, edited by Michael Lang, Josef Schuch, and Claus Staringer, 289–318. Vienna: Linde.

Hofstätter, Matthias, and Gernot Ressler. 2006. 'Das Schuldnerdiskriminierungsverbot in Art 24 Abs 4 OECD-MA'. In *Die Diskriminierungsverbote im Recht der*

Doppelbesteuerungsabkommen, edited by Michael Lang, Josef Schuch, and Claus Staringer, 205–230. Vienna: Linde.

Hohenwarter, Daniela. 2004. 'Losses in Triangular Situations'. In *Triangular Tax Cases*, edited by Franz Philipp Sutter, and Ulf Zehetner, 219–262. Schriftenreihe zum Internationalen Steuerrecht 34. Vienna: Linde.

Hohenwarter, Daniela. 2010. *Verlustverwertung im Konzern*. Schriften und aktuelle Beiträge zum österreichischen Abgabenrecht 59. Vienna: LexisNexis.

Hohenwarter, Daniela, and Patrick Weninger. 2006. 'DBA-Diskriminierungsverbote: Auswahl der Vergleichsobjekte, Rechtfertigungsgründe und Verhältnismäßigkeitsgrundsatz'. In *Die Diskriminierungsverbote im Recht der Doppelbesteuerungsabkommen*, edited by Michael Lang, Josef Schuch, and Claus Staringer, 231–264. Vienna: Linde.

Holmes, Kevin, and Sebastian Löser. 2004. '58th IFA Congress, 2004 – Summary of Discussion on Subjects I and II'. *Bulletin for International Fiscal Documentation (Bulletin for International Taxation)* 58 (11): 534–537.

Hoor, Oliver R. 2012. 'Comments on the OECD Discussion Draft on the Meaning of "Permanent Establishment"'. *Tax Notes International* 65 (3): 207–214.

Horn, Frank. 1988. *Reservations and Interpretative Declarations to Multilateral Treaties*. The Hague: T.M.C. Asser Instituut.

Horn, Henrik, and Petros C. Mavroidis. 2004. 'Still Hazy after All These Years: The Interpretation of National Treatment in the GATT/WTO Case-Law on Tax Discrimination'. *European Journal of International Law* 15 (1): 39–69.

Horn, Henrik, and Petros C. Mavroidis. 2008. 'The Permissible Reach of National Environmental Policies'. *Journal of World Trade* 42 (6): 1107–1178.

Horn, Henrik, and Petros C. Mavroidis. 2009a. 'Burden of Proof in Environmental Disputes in the WTO: Legal Aspects'. *European Energy and Environmental Law Review* 18 (2): 112–140.

Horn, Henrik, and Petros C. Mavroidis. 2009b. 'Burden of Proof in Environmental Disputes in the WTO: Legal Aspects'. *European Energy and Environmental Law Review* 18 (2): 112–140.

Horn, Henrik, and Joseph H.H. Weiler. 2003. 'EC – Asbestos: European Communities – Measures Affecting Asbestos and Asbestos-Containing Products'. In *The WTO Case Law of 2001*, edited by Henrik Horn, and Petros C. Mavroidis, 14–40. The American Law Institute Reporters' Studies. Cambridge: Cambridge University Press.

Horn, Henrik, and Joseph H.H. Weiler. 2003. 2004. '*EC – Asbestos*: European Communities – Measures Affecting Asbestos and Asbestos-Containing Products'. *World Trade Review* 3 (1): 129–151.

Hosson, Fred C. de, and Geerten M.M. Michielse. 1989. 'Treaty Aspects of the "Thin Capitalisation" Issue – A Review of the OECD Report'. *Intertax* 17 (11): 476–484.

Houston-McMillan. 2016. 'The Legitimate Regulatory Distinction Test: Incomplete and Inadequate for the Particular Purposes of the TBT Agreement'. *World Trade Review* 15 (4): 543–562.

Howse, Robert. 2002. 'The Appellate Body Rulings in the *Shrimp/Turtle* Case: A New Legal Baseline for the Trade and Environment Debate'. *Columbia Journal of Environmental Law* 27 (2): 491–521.

Howse, Robert. 2012. 'Regulatory Measures'. In *The Oxford Handbook on the World Trade Organization*, edited by Amrita Narlikar, Martin Daunton, and Robert M. Stern, 441–460. Oxford: Oxford University Press.

Howse, Robert. 2016. 'The World Trade Organization 20 Years On: Global Governance by Judiciary'. *European Journal of International Law* 27 (1): 9–77.

Howse, Robert, Joanna Langille, and Katie Sykes. 2015. 'Pluralism in Practice: Moral Legislation and the Law of the WTO after *Seal Products*'. *George Washington International Law Review* 48 (1): 81–150.

Howse, Robert, and Philip I. Levy. 2013. 'The TBT Panels: *US–Cloves, US–Tuna, US–COOL*'. *World Trade Review* 12 (2): 327–375.

Howse, Robert, and Damien J. Neven. 2003. 'US – Shrimp: United States – Import Prohibition of Certain Shrimp and Shrimp Products: Recourse to Article 21.5 of the DSU by Malaysia'. In *The WTO Case Law of 2001*, edited by Henrik Horn, and Petros C. Mavroidis, 41–71. The American Law Institute Reporters' Studies. Cambridge: Cambridge University Press.

Howse, Robert, and Donald H. Regan. 2000. 'The Product/Process Distinction – An Illusory Basis for Disciplining "Unilateralism" in Trade Policy'. *European Journal of International Law* 11 (2): 249–289.

Howse, Robert, and Elisabeth Türk. 2001. 'The WTO Impact on Internal Regulations – A Case Study of the Canada–EC Asbestos Dispute'. In *The EU and the WTO: Legal and Constitutional Issues*, edited by Gráinne de Búrca, and Joanne Scott, 283–328. Oxford; Portland, Oregon: Hart Publishing.

Howse, Robert, and Elisabeth Türk. 2006. 'The WTO Impact on Internal Regulations: A Case Study of the *Canada–EC Asbestos* Dispute'. In *Trade and Human Health and Safety*, edited by George A. Bermann, and Petros C. Mavroidis, 77–117. Cambridge: Cambridge University Press.

Hoyos Jiménez, Catalina. 2016. 'Non-discrimination on the Basis of Nationality in IIAs: A Latin American Tax Perspective'. In *Non-discrimination in Tax Treaties: Selected Issues from a Global Perspective*, edited by Dennis Weber, and Pasquale Pistone, 27–38. EC and International Tax Law Series 14. Amsterdam: IBFD.

Hruschka, Franz, and Stefan Bendlinger. 2003. 'Der Verlustvortrag für österreichische Betriebsstätten deutscher Unternehmer'. *Steuer und Wirtschaft International* 13 (6): 271–278.

Hudec, Robert E. 1990. *The GATT Legal System and World Trade Diplomacy*. 2nd ed. Salem (New Hampshire): Butterworth Legal Publishers.

Hudec, Robert E. 1993. *Enforcing International Trade Law: The Evolution of the Modern GATT Legal System*. Salem (New Hampshire): Butterworth Legal Publishers.

Hudec, Robert E. 1996. 'GATT Legal Restraints on the Use of Trade Measures Against Foreign Environmental Practices'. In *Fair Trade and Harmonization: Prerequisites for Free Trade? – Legal Analysis*, edited by Jagdish Bhagwati, and Robert E. Hudec, 2:95–174. Cambridge, Massachusetts; London, England: The MIT Press.

Hudec, Robert E. 1998. 'GATT/WTO Constraints on National Regulation: Requiem for an "Aim and Effects" Test'. *The International Lawyer* 32 (3, Fall): 619–649.

Hudec, Robert E. 2000a. '"Like Product": The Differences in Meaning in GATT Articles I and III'. In *Regulatory Barriers and the Principle of Non-discrimination in World Trade Law*, edited by Thomas Cottier, and Petros C. Mavroidis, 101–123. World Trade Forum 2. Michigan: University of Michigan Press.

Hudec, Robert E. 2000b. 'The Product-Process Doctrine in GATT/WTO Jurisprudence'. In *New Directions in International Economic Law: Essays in Honour of John H. Jackson*, edited by Marco Bronckers, and Reinhard Quick, 187–217. The Hague: Kluwer Law International.

Huemer, Edgar. 1996. *Die unbeschränkte Steuerpflicht natürlicher Personen: Innerstaatliches Recht und Doppelbesteuerungsabkommen*. Schriftenreihe zum Internationalen Steuerrecht 2. Vienna: Linde.

Hughes, David. 1996. 'Non-discrimination: A Consideration of Article 24(5) OECD Model Convention'. *Bulletin for International Fiscal Documentation (Bulletin for International Taxation)* 50 (9): 390–393.

Iacovides, Marios C. 2014. 'Marginal Consumers, Marginalized Economics: Whose Tastes and Habits Should the WTO Panels and Appellate Body Consider when Assessing "Likeness"?'. *Journal of World Trade* 48 (2): 323–350.

Isakova, Irina Viktorovna. 2015. 'Thin Capitalization Rules under Article 24(4) and 24(5) of the OECD Model'. In *Non-discrimination in European and Tax Treaty Law: Open Issues and Recent Challenges*, edited by Kasper Dziurdź, and Christoph Marchgraber, 511–531. Series on International Tax Law 94. Vienna: Linde.

Ismer, Roland. 2012. 'Gruppenbesteuerung statt Organschaft im Ertragsteuerrecht?'. *Deutsches Steuerrecht* 50 (17): 821–829.

Ismer, Roland. 2015. 'Artikel 23.' In *Doppelbesteuerungsabkommen der Bundesrepublik Deutschland auf dem Gebiet der Steuern vom Einkommen und Vermögen: Kommentar auf der Grundlage der Musterabkommen*, edited by Moris Lehner, 6th ed. Munich: C.H. Beck.

Ismer, Roland, and Katharina Riemer. 2015. 'Article 4'. In *Klaus Vogel on Double Taxation Conventions*, edited by Ekkehart Reimer, and Alexander Rust, 4th ed. Alphen on the Rhine: Kluwer Law International.

Jackson, John H. 1989. 'National Treatment Obligations and Non-tariff Barriers'. *Michigan Journal of International Law* 10 (1, Winter): 207–224.

Jackson, John H. 2000a. 'Comments on *Shrimp/Turtle* and the Product/Process Distinction'. *European Journal of International Law* 11 (2): 303–307.

Jackson, John H. 2000b. *The Jurisprudence of GATT and the WTO: Insights on Treaty Law and Economic Relations*. Cambridge: Cambridge University Press.

Jann, Martin. 1996. 'How Does Community Law Affect Benefits Available to Non-resident Taxpayers under Tax Treaties?'. *EC Tax Review* 5 (4): 168–171.

Jeffery, Ramon J. 1999. *The Impact of State Sovereignty on Global Trade and International Taxation*. Series on International Taxation 23. London: Kluwer Law International.

Kalungi, Ronald. 2009. 'Confusion Worse Confounded: What *Boake Allen* Teaches Us about the (Non-) Incorporation and Interpretation of Double Taxation Treaties in the United Kingdom'. *British Tax Review* 54 (1): 129–154.

Kamperman Sanders, Anselm. 2014. 'National Treatment under the TRIPS Agreement'. In *The Principle of National Treatment in International Economic Law: Trade, Investment and Intellectual Property*, edited by Anselm Kamperman Sanders, 286–299. European Intellectual Property Institutes Network Series. Cheltenham; Northampton: Edward Elgar Publishing.

Kane, Mitchell A. 2006. 'Ownership Neutrality, Ownership Distortions, and International Tax Welfare Benchmarks'. *Virginia Tax Review* 26 (1, Summer): 53–79.

Kaplan, Philip T. 1992. 'Reuters Ltd. v. Tax Appeals Tribunal: Tax Planning Opportunity for Banks and Other Companies with Branches in the United States of America'. *British Tax Review* 37: 285–287.

Kapterian, Gisele. 2010. 'A Critique of WTO Jurisprudence on "Necessity"'. *International and Comparative Law Quarterly* 59 (1): 89–127.

Karst, Kenneth L. 1983. 'Why Equality Matters'. *Georgia Law Review* 17 (2, Winter): 245–289.

Kempinger, Corinna. 2007. 'Sonderausgaben und beschränkte Betriebsstättenverluste'. *Steuer und Wirtschaft International* 17 (6): 258–266.

Kennedy, Matthew. 2015. 'Blurred Lines: Reading TRIPS with GATT Glasses'. *Journal of World Trade* 49 (5): 735–755.

Kerfs, Philip. 1994. 'Taxation of Permanent Establishments in Conflict with Non-discrimination Provisions in Tax Treaties: Decisions of the Brussels Court of Appeal of 28 May 1993 and 17 June 1993'. *European Taxation* 34 (4): 114–116.

Kim, Ho Cheol. 2007. 'Burden of Proof and the *Prima Facie* Case: The Evolving History and Its Applications in the WTO Jurisprudence'. *Richmond Journal of Global Law and Business* 6 (3): 245–263.

Klabbers, Jan. 2009. *Treaty Conflict and the European Union*. Cambridge: Cambridge University Press.

Knobbe-Keuk, Brigitte. 1992. 'Germany: Developments in Thin Capitalization and Some Legal Obstacles to Legislation'. *European Taxation* 32 (12): 405–408.

Knobbe-Keuk, Brigitte. 1993. 'Wieder einmal ein Entwurf zu § 8a KStG – Wiederauflage einer Regelung zur Gesellschafterfremdfinanzierung im Standortsicherungsgesetz'. *Der Betrieb* 46 (2): 60–66.

Kofler, Georg. 2007. *Doppelbesteuerungsabkommen und Europäisches Gemeinschaftsrecht*. Schriftenreihe zum Internationalen Steuerrecht 47. Vienna: Linde.

Kofler, Georg. 2009. 'Der Verlustvortrag für beschränkt Steuerpflichtige nach § 102 Abs 2 Z 2 EStG'. *Steuer und Wirtschaft International* 19 (10): 477–485.

Kofler, Georg. 2015. 'Article 9'. In *Klaus Vogel on Double Taxation Conventions*, edited by Ekkehart Reimer, and Alexander Rust, 4th ed. Alphen on the Rhine: Kluwer Law International.

Kolb, Andreas, Michael Lang, Helmut Loukota, Robert Waldburger, Mike Waters, and Ulrich Wolff. 2002. 'Server as a Permanent Establishment and Dual Resident Companies – Case Studies'. *Steuer und Wirtschaft International* 12 (10): 477–480.

Korinek, Karl, and Michael Holoubek. 1991. 'Gleichheitsgrundsatz und Abgabenrecht'. In *Steuerbilanzreform und Verfassungsrecht*, edited by Wolfgang Gassner and Eduard Lechner, 73–100. Aktuelle Beiträge zum österreichischen Abgabenrecht 17. Vienna: Orac.

Korinek, Karl, and Michael Holoubek. 1999. 'Austria'. In *The Principle of Equality in European Taxation*, edited by Gerard T.K. Meussen, 35–49. EUCOTAX Series on European Taxation 2. London: Kluwer Law International.

Kort, Jan W.J. de. 2001. 'HR 28 February 2001, nr 35.557: The Supreme Court of the Netherlands Reaches a Questionable Decision in a Triangular Dividend Withholding Tax Case'. *Intertax* 29 (12): 402–406.

Kostohryz, Jiří. 2015. 'Ownership Non-discrimination under Article 24(5) of the OECD Model in the Case of Low-Taxed Payments'. In *Non-discrimination in European and Tax Treaty Law: Open Issues and Recent Challenges*, edited by Kasper Dziurdź, and Christoph Marchgraber, 533–552. Series on International Tax Law 94. Vienna: Linde.

Krabbe, Helmut. 1984. 'Maßnahmen gegen unangemessene Gesellschafterfremdfinanzierung und das Recht der Doppelbesteuerungsabkommen'. *Recht der Internationalen Wirtschaft* 30 (2): 127–130.

Krabbe, Helmut. 1985. 'Verlustberücksichtigung bei Auslandseinkünften'. In *Grundfragen des Internationalen Steuerrechts*, edited by Klaus Vogel, 79–89. Cologne: Dr. Otto Schmidt.

Krajewski, Markus, and Maika Engelke. 2008. 'Article XVII GATS'. In *WTO – Trade in Services*, edited by Rüdiger Wolfrum, Peter-Tobias Stoll, and Clemens Feinäugle, 329–420. Max Planck Commentaries on World Trade Law 6. Leiden; Boston: Martinus Nijhoff Publishers.

Kruse, Rudi. 2013. 'Process and Production Methods and Burden of Proof: A Procedural Limitation on the "Like" Products Debate'. *International Trade and Business Law Review* 16: 377–393.

Kubaile, Heiko. 2013. 'Art. 25: Diskriminierungsverbot'. In *Doppelbesteuerungsabkommen Deutschland–Schweiz: Steuern vom Einkommen und Vermögen, Nachlass- und Erbschaftsteuern – Kommentar*, edited by Franz Wassermeyer, Michael Kempermann, Johannes Baßler, and Nils Häck, 38th ed. Cologne: Dr. Otto Schmidt.

Kuleshova, Yulia. 2005. 'Trends in the Interpretation of Non Discrimination Clauses'. In *Tax Treaty Policy and Development*, edited by Markus Stefaner, and Mario Züger, 451–475. Schriftenreihe zum Internationalen Steuerrecht 39. Vienna: Linde.

Kumpf, Wolfgang. 1982. *Besteuerung inländischer Betriebstätten von Steuerausländern*. Praxis des Internationalen Steuerrechts 2. Cologne: Dr. Otto Schmidt.

Kumpf, Wolfgang, and Andreas Roth. 1996. 'Wahlbesteuerung für beschränkt Einkommensteuerpflichtige? Zur Besteuerung von nicht im Inland ansässigen natürlichen Personen im System der Einkommensteuer'. *Steuer und Wirtschaft* 73 (3): 259–266.

Kusch, Karsten, and Thomas Schöneborn. 2012. 'Grenzüberschreitende Organschaft – Finanzverwaltung lehnt neuere BFH-Rechtsprechung ab'. *NWB Steuer- und Wirtschaftsrecht*, no. 15: 1231–1236.

Lang, Michael. 1990. 'Betriebsstättendiskriminierungsverbot und Verlustvortrag für beschränkt Steuerpflichtige'. *Steuer und Wirtschaft International* 0 (2): 34–38.

Lang, Michael. 1991. *Hybride Finanzierungen im Internationalen Steuerrecht: Rechtsgrundlagen der Doppelbesteuerungsabkommen zur Beurteilung von Mischformen zwischen Eigen- und Fremdkapital*. Schriften zum österreichischen Abgabenrecht 30. Vienna: Orac.

Lang, Michael. 1992. *Doppelbesteuerungsabkommen und innerstaatliches Recht: Die Einordnung von Doppelbesteuerungsabkommen in die österreichische Rechtsordnung*. Schriften zum österreichischen Abgabenrecht 31. Vienna: Orac.

Lang, Michael. 1994a. 'Die Bedeutung des Musterabkommens und des Kommentars des OECD-Steuerausschusses für die Auslegung von Doppelbesteuerungsabkommen'. In *Aktuelle Entwicklungen im Internationalen Steuerrecht: Das neue Musterabkommen der OECD*, edited by Wolfgang Gassner, Michael Lang, and Eduard Lechner, 11–41. Vienna: Linde.

Lang, Michael. 1994b. 'Unterkapitalisierung'. In *Aktuelle Entwicklungen im Internationalen Steuerrecht: Das neue Musterabkommen der OECD*, edited by Wolfgang Gassner, Michael Lang, and Eduard Lechner, 127–156. Vienna: Linde.

Lang, Michael. 1996. 'Die Bindung der Doppelbesteuerungsabkommen an die Grundfreiheiten des EU-Rechts'. In *Doppelbesteuerungsabkommen und EU-Recht: Auswirkungen auf die Abkommenspraxis*, edited by Wolfgang Gassner, Michael Lang, and Eduard Lechner, 25–42. Vienna: Linde.

Lang, Michael. 1999. 'Steuerliche Behandlung von Betriebsstättenverlusten aus deutsch-österreichischen Wirtschaftsbeziehungen in Österreich'. In *Aufwand und Verluste bei internationalen Steuersachverhalten*, edited by Detlev J. Piltz, and Harald Schaumburg, 137–162. Forum der Internationalen Besteuerung 16. Cologne: Dr. Otto Schmidt.

Lang, Michael. 2000a. 'Die Besteuerung von Einkünften bei unterschiedlichen Personen aus dem Blickwinkel des DBA-Rechts'. *Steuer und Wirtschaft International* 10 (11): 527–535.

Lang, Michael. 2000b. 'Personengesellschaften im DBA-Recht'. *Steuer und Wirtschaft International* 10 (2): 60–66.

Lang, Michael. 2000c. 'Qualifikationskonflikte bei Personengesellschaften'. *Internationales Steuerrecht* 9 (5): 129–134.

Lang, Michael. 2000d. *The Application of the OECD Model Tax Convention to Partnerships: A Critical Analysis of the Report Prepared by the OECD Committee on Fiscal Affairs*. Schriftenreihe zum Internationalen Steuerrecht 11. Vienna: Linde.

Lang, Michael. 2001. 'Taxation of Income in the Hands of Different Taxpayers from the Viewpoint of Tax Treaty Law'. *Bulletin for International Fiscal Documentation (Bulletin for International Taxation)* 55 (12): 596–600.

Lang, Michael. 2003a. 'Abkommens- und gemeinschaftsrechtliche Anforderungen an die Organschaft'. *Österreichische Steuerzeitung* 56 (11): 254–261.

Lang, Michael. 2003b. 'Der doppelt ansässige Organträger aus abkommensrechtlicher Sicht'. *Steuer und Wirtschaft International* 13 (5): 215–222.

Lang, Michael. 2005a. 'Das EuGH-Urteil in der Rechtssache D. – Gerät der Motor der Steuerharmonisierung ins Stottern?'. *Steuer und Wirtschaft International* 15 (8): 365–375.

Lang, Michael. 2005b. 'Die Unterbetriebsstätte im Abkommensrecht'. In *Körperschaftsteuer – Internationales Steuerrecht – Doppelbesteuerung: Festschrift für Franz Wassermeyer zum 65. Geburtstag*, edited by Rudolf Gocke, Dietmar Gosch, and Michael Lang, 709–721. Munich: C.H. Beck.

Lang, Michael. 2005c. 'Ist die Schumacker-Rechtsprechung am Ende? Die Verpflichtung zur Berücksichtigung der persönlichen Verhältnisse und des Familienstandes in einem der Mitgliedstaaten'. *Recht der Internationalen Wirtschaft* 51 (5): 336–344.

Lang, Michael. 2006. 'Die Arbeiten der OEEC und der OECD zur Schaffung der Diskriminierungsverbote'. In *Die Diskriminierungsverbote im Recht der Doppelbesteuerungsabkommen*, edited by Michael Lang, Josef Schuch, and Claus Staringer, 31–48. Vienna: Linde.

Lang, Michael. 2007a. 'Die Maßgeblichkeit des innerstaatlichen Rechts für die DBA-Auslegung in der jüngsten Rechtsprechung des VwGH'. *Steuer und Wirtschaft International* 17 (5): 199–206.

Lang, Michael. 2007b. 'Non-discrimination – What Does History Teach Us?'. In *Mélanges en l'honneur de Jean-Pierre Le Gall: Fiscalité et entreprise: politiques et pratiques*, 103–108. Paris: Dalloz.

Lang, Michael. 2008. 'Die Ansässigkeit als das Kriterium für die Besteuerung im Quellenstaat nach den Verteilungsnormen des OECD-Musterabkommens'. In *Die Ansässigkeit im Recht der Doppelbesteuerungsabkommen*, edited by Michael Lang, Josef Schuch, and Claus Staringer, 225–237. Vienna: Linde.

Lang, Michael. 2011a. 'Art. 24 OECD Model Convention, Residence and VAT'. In *VAT in an EU and International Perspective: Essays in Honour of Han Kogels*, edited by Henk van Arendonk, Sjaak Jansen, and René van der Paardt, 331–337. Amsterdam: IBFD.

Lang, Michael. 2011b. 'Art. 3 Abs. 2 OECD-MA und die Auslegung von Doppelbesteuerungsabkommen'. *Internationale Wirtschaftsbriefe*, no. 8: 281–294.

Lang, Michael. 2011c. 'Austria: Exemption Method and Progression'. In *Tax Treaty Case Law Around the Globe – 2011*, edited by Michael Lang, Pasquale Pistone, Josef Schuch, Claus Staringer, Alfred Storck, Luc De Broe, Peter Essers, Eric C.C.M. Kemmeren, and Frans Vanistendael, 383–390. Series on International Tax Law 70. Vienna: Linde.

Lang, Michael. 2011d. 'Der Begriff *Unternehmen* und Art. 24 OECD-Musterabkommen'. *Steuer und Wirtschaft International* 21 (1): 9–20.

Lang, Michael. 2014. 'Doppelbesteuerungsabkommen und Gleichheitsgrundsatz'. *Steuer und Wirtschaft International* 24 (2): 58–74.

Lang, Michael, and Florian Brugger. 2008. 'The Role of the OECD Commentary in Tax Treaty Interpretation'. *Austrialian Tax Forum* 23: 95–108.

Lang, Michael, and Walter Loukota. 2003. 'Das Erfordernis der Beibringung eines inländischen Besteuerungsnachweises nach § 102 Abs. 1 Z 3 Satz 2 EStG'. *Steuer und Wirtschaft International* 13 (2): 67–78.

Lang, Michael, Jürgen Lüdicke, and Peter Riedweg. 2006. 'Steueranrechnung und Betriebsstättendiskriminierungsverbot der DBA bei Dreieckssachverhalten'. *Internationales Steuerrecht* 15 (3): 73–78.

Lang, Michael, Pasquale Pistone, Josef Schuch, Claus Staringer, and Alfred Storck, eds. 2013. *Beneficial Ownership: Recent Trends*. Amsterdam: IBFD.

Langoth, Bernd. 2004. 'Treaty Entitlement of Permanent Establishments'. In *Triangular Tax Cases*, edited by Franz Philipp Sutter, and Ulf Zehetner, 19–47. Schriftenreihe zum Internationalen Steuerrecht 34. Vienna: Linde.

Last, Alison. 2013. 'FCE Bank PLC'. *Highlights & Insights on European Taxation* 6 (2): 35–38.

Lazarski, Henry. 1989. 'France: 3% Tax on Real Property: The Supreme Civil Court Overrules the Tax Administration's First Decision Concerning the Interpretation of Non-discrimination Clauses'. *European Taxation* 29 (8): 285–288.

Lazarski, Henry. 2005. 'Surprising French Supreme Administrative Court Decision on the Interpretation of a Non-discrimination Clause'. *European Taxation* 45 (8): 352–353.

Lechner, Eduard. 1982. 'Das Befreiungssystem mit Progressionsvorbehalt als bilaterale Maßnahme zur Vermeidung der internationalen Doppelbesteuerung'. *Finanz Journal* 21: 91–95.

Lechner, Eduard. 1990. 'Schachtelprivileg und Diskriminierungsverbot'. *Steuer und Wirtschaft International* 0 (1): 9–14.

Lechner, Eduard. 1995. 'Befreiungsmethode und Einkommensermittlung'. In *Die Methoden zur Vermeidung der Doppelbesteuerung: Anrechnungs- und Befreiungsmethode*, edited by Wolfgang Gassner, Michael Lang, and Eduard Lechner, 137–152. Vienna: Linde.

Lechner, Eduard. 1996. 'Die Auswirkungen des EU-Rechts auf die "Befreiung" von Verlusten nach den Doppelbesteuerungsabkommen'. In *Doppelbesteuerungsabkommen und EU-Recht: Auswirkungen auf die Abkommenspraxis*, edited by Wolfgang Gassner, Michael Lang, and Eduard Lechner, 85–98. Vienna: Linde.

Lehner, Moris. 1995. 'Auswirkungen der Steuerharmonisierung auf das Recht der Doppelbesteuerungsabkommen'. In *Rechtsfragen des europäischen Steuer-, Außenwirtschafts- und Zollrechts: Münsteraner Symposion 1994*, edited by Dieter Birk, and Dirk Ehlers, 18–32. Cologne: Dr. Otto Schmidt.

Lehner, Moris. 2000. 'The Influence of EU Law on Tax Treaties from a German Perspective'. *Bulletin for International Fiscal Documentation (Bulletin for International Taxation)* 54 (8): 461–470.

Lehner, Moris. 2001. 'Der Einfluss des Europarechts auf die Doppelbesteuerungsabkommen'. *Internationales Steuerrecht* 10 (11, Summer): 329–337.

Lehner, Moris. 2008. 'Artikel 4'. In *Doppelbesteuerungsabkommen der Bundesrepublik Deutschland auf dem Gebiet der Steuern vom Einkommen und Vermögen: Kommentar auf der Grundlage der Musterabkommen*, edited by Moris Lehner, 5th ed. Munich: C.H. Beck.

Lehner, Moris. 2015. 'Artikel 4'. In *Doppelbesteuerungsabkommen der Bundesrepublik Deutschland auf dem Gebiet der Steuern vom Einkommen und Vermögen: Kommentar auf der Grundlage der Musterabkommen*, edited by Moris Lehner, 6th ed. Munich: C.H. Beck.

Levy, Philip I., and Donald H. Regan. 2015. '*EC–Seal Products*: Seals and Sensibilities (TBT Aspects of the Panel and Appellate Body Reports)'. *World Trade Review* 14 (2): 337–379.

Li, Guojun. 2010. 'National Treatment under the General Agreement on Trade in Services'. *Cambridge Student Law Review* 6 (1): 74–93.

Link, Simon Patrick. 2008. 'Application of Tax Treaties to Companies Subject to National Group Taxation Regimes'. In *International and EC Tax Aspects of Groups of Companies*, edited by Guglielmo Maisto, 137–146. EC and International Tax Law Series 4. Amsterdam: IBFD.

Loukota, Helmut. 1989a. *Internationale Steuerfälle: Handbuch für die Praxis*. Vienna: Orac.

Loukota, Helmut. 1989b. 'Steuerreform und internationales Steuerrecht'. *Österreichische Steuerzeitung* 42 (3): 25–30.

Loukota, Helmut. 1990a. 'Internationale Verlustverwertung: Kritik am falschen Ende'. *Österreichische Steuerzeitung* 43 (14): 162–164.

Loukota, Helmut. 1990b. 'Verlustvortrag für Steuerausländer: Mit Maß und Ziel'. *Österreichische Steuerzeitung* 43 (6): 62–64.

Loukota, Helmut. 1991. 'Beteiligungsertragsbefreiung für ausländische Unternehmen?'. *Steuer und Wirtschaft International* 1 (1): 5–7.

Loukota, Helmut. 2005. 'Das DBA-Diskriminierungsverbot – Eine Bestandsaufnahme der Verwaltungspraxis'. *Steuer und Wirtschaft International* 15 (2): 56–66.

Loukota, Helmut, and Heinz Jirousek. 2016. *Internationales Steuerrecht: Innerstaatliche Vorschriften und zwischenstaatliche Vereinbarungen – mit Erläuterungen unter Berücksichtigung der Rechtsprechung*. 39th ed. Vienna: Manz.

Loukota, Walter. 2005. 'Verbot der Betriebsstättendiskriminierung – DBA-Recht versus EG-Recht.' In *Praxis des Internationalen Steuerrechts: Festschrift für Helmut Loukota zum 65. Geburtstag*, edited by Michael Lang and Heinz Jirousek, 329–347. Vienna: Linde.

Loukota, Walter. 2006. 'DBA-Diskriminierungsverbote und gemeinschaftsrechtliche Grundfreiheiten – Gemeinsamkeiten und Unterschiede'. In *Die Diskriminierungsverbote im Recht der Doppelbesteuerungsabkommen*, edited by Michael Lang, Josef Schuch, and Claus Staringer, 265–288. Vienna: Linde.

Loukota, Walter, and Markus Stefaner. 2005. 'Bestimmung der Quelle bei Zinsen und Lizenzgebühren nach Art 11 und 12 OECD-MA'. In *Die Verteilung der Besteuerungsrechte zwischen Ansässigkeits- und Quellenstaat im Recht der Doppelbesteuerungsabkommen*, edited by Wolfgang Gassner, Michael Lang, Josef Schuch, and Claus Staringer, 247–272. Vienna: Linde.

Lüdicke, Jürgen. 1997. 'Die Besteuerung Nichtansässiger im Spannungsverhältnis zwischen Gemeinschaftsrecht und Doppelbesteuerungsabkommen'. In *Gedächtnisschrift für Brigitte Knobbe-Keuk*, edited by Wolfgang Schön, 647–674. Cologne: Dr. Otto Schmidt.

Lüdicke, Jürgen. 1999. 'Doppelansässigkeit, Ansässigkeitswechsel und Progressionsvorbehalt'. In *Unternehmenspolitik und Internationale Besteuerung: Festschrift für Lutz Fischer zum 60. Geburtstag*, edited by Hans-Jochen Kleineidam, 731–750. Berlin: Erich Schmidt Verlag.

Lüdicke, Jürgen. 2005. 'Darf im internationalen Steuerrecht noch differenziert werden?'. In *Körperschaftsteuer – Internationales Steuerrecht – Doppelbesteuerung: Festschrift für Franz Wassermeyer zum 65. Geburtstag*, edited by Rudolf Gocke, Dietmar Gosch, and Michael Lang, 473–488. Munich: C.H. Beck.

Lüdicke, Jürgen. 2011a. 'Das DBA-Gespenst bei der Organschaft'. *Internationales Steuerrecht* 20 (19): 740–747.

Lüdicke, Jürgen. 2011b. 'Re Shareholder Discrimination by German Thin Capitalisation Rules'. *International Tax Law Reports* 13 (5): 646–649.

Lüdicke, Jürgen. 2011c. 'Re Treaty Discrimination and Fiscal Unity'. *International Tax Law Reports* 13 (6): 839–849.

Lüdicke, Jürgen. 2015. 'Ansässigkeit'. In *Doppelbesteuerung – Festgabe: Zum 75. Geburtstag von Prof. Dr. Dr. h.c. Franz Wassermeyer – 75 Beiträge zum Recht der DBA*, edited by Franz Wassermeyer, 87–96. Munich: C.H. Beck.

Lüdicke, Jürgen. 2017. 'EU-Grundfreiheiten, DBA-Diskriminierungsverbot nach der Staatsangehörigkeit und Treaty Override: An American in Paris'. *Internationales Steuerrecht* 26 (8): 289–299.

Lüdicke, Jürgen, Jürg B. Altorfer, Gauthier Blanluet, Daniela Hohenwarter-Mayr, Koichi Inoue, Steve Suarez, and Carolin Lange-Hückstädt. 2014. 'Cross-Border Loss Utilization'. *Bulletin for International Taxation* 68 (6/7): 376–383.

Lüdicke, Jürgen, and Sabine Rödel. 2004. 'Generalthema II: Gruppenbesteuerung'. *Internationales Steuerrecht* 13 (16): 549–554.

Lüers, Jan-Carl. 2013. 'Artikel 1'. In *TRIPs: Internationales und europäisches Recht des geistigen Eigentums – Kommentar*, edited by Jan Busche, Peter-Tobias Stoll, and Andreas Wiebe, 2nd ed., 89–102. Cologne: Carl Heymanns.

Lüthi, Daniel. 1991. 'Thin Capitalisation of Companies in International Tax Law'. *Intertax* 19 (10): 446–453.

Lyal, Richard. 2003. 'Non-discrimination and Direct Tax in Community Law'. *EC Tax Review* 12 (2): 68–74.

Lydgate, Emily. 2011. 'Consumer Preferences and the National Treatment Principle: Emerging Environmental Regulations Prompt a New Look at an Old Problem'. *World Trade Review* 10 (2): 165–188.

Lydgate, Emily. 2016. 'Sorting out Mixed Messages under the WTO National Treatment Principle: A Proposed Approach'. *World Trade Review* 15 (3): 423–450.

Maisto, Guglielmo. 2011a. 'European VAT and Tax Treaties'. In *VAT in an EU and International Perspective: Essays in Honour of Han Kogels*, edited by Henk van Arendonk, Sjaak Jansen, and René van der Paardt. Amsterdam: IBFD.

Maisto, Guglielmo. 2011b. 'The Pursuit of Harmonization Regarding Taxes on Death and the International Implications'. *Bulletin for International Taxation* 65 (4/5): 253–259.

Marceau, Gabrielle. 2013. 'The New TBT Jurisprudence in *US – Clove Cigarettes*, WTO *US – Tuna II*, and *US – COOL*'. *Asian Journal of WTO and International Health Law and Policy* 8 (1): 1–39.

Marceau, Gabrielle. 2014. 'A Comment on the Appellate Body Report in *EC-Seal Products* in the Context of the Trade and Environment Debate'. *Review of European Community & International Environmental Law* 23 (3): 318–328.

Marceau, Gabrielle, and Joel P. Trachtman. 2014. 'A Map of the World Trade Organization Law of Domestic Regulation of Goods: The Technical Barriers to Trade Agreement, the Sanitary and Phytosanitary Measures Agreement, and the General Agreement on Tariffs and Trade'. *Journal of World Trade* 48 (2): 351–432.

Marres, Otto. 2016a. 'Interest Deduction Limitations: When to Apply Articles 9 and 24(4) of the OECD Model?'. In *Non-discrimination in Tax Treaties: Selected Issues from a Global Perspective*, edited by Dennis Weber, and Pasquale Pistone, 39–69. EC and International Tax Law Series 14. Amsterdam: IBFD.

Marres, Otto. 2016b. 'Interest Deduction Limitations: When to Apply Articles 9 and 24(4) of the OECD Model'. *European Taxation* 56 (1): 2–14.

Martín Jiménez, Adolfo J. 2005. 'Defining the Objective Scope of Income Tax Treaties: The Impact of Other Treaties and EC Law on the Concept of Tax in the OECD Model'. *Bulletin for International Fiscal Documentation (Bulletin for International Taxation)* 59 (10): 432–444.

Martín Jiménez, Adolfo J., Francisco Alfredo García Prats, and José Manuel Calderón Carrero. 2001. 'Triangular Cases, Tax Treaties and EC Law: The *Saint-Gobain* Decision of the ECJ'. *Bulletin for International Fiscal Documentation (Bulletin for International Taxation)* 55 (6): 241–253.

Mason, Ruth. 2010. 'Tax Discrimination and Capital Neutrality'. *World Tax Journal* 2 (2): 126–138.

Mason, Ruth, and Michael S. Knoll. 2012. 'What Is Tax Discrimination?', *The Yale Law Journal* 121 (5): 1014–1116.

Masui, Yoshihiro. 2004. 'General Report'. In *Group Taxation*, edited by International Fiscal Association, 21–67. Cahiers de Droit Fiscal International – Studies on International Fiscal Law 89b. Amersfoort: Sdu Fiscale & Financiële Uitgevers.

Mattern, Oliver. 2014. 'BFH I R 30/12: Auswirkungen der DBA-Diskriminierungsverbote in Art. 24 Abs. 3 und 4 OECD-MA auf Zins- bzw. Lizenzabzugsbeschränkungen'. *Internationales Steuerrecht* 23 (15): 558–560.

Matthews, Kathleen. 1993. 'Nondiscrimination: Should Article 24 of the OECD Model Treaty Be Completely Rewritten?'. *Tax Notes International* 7 (18): 1083–1087.

Mattoo, Aaditya. 1997. 'National Treatment in the GATS: Corner-Stone or Pandora's Box?'. *Journal of World Trade* 31 (1): 107–135.

Mattoo, Aaditya, and Arvind Subramanian. 1998. 'Regulatory Autonomy and Multilateral Disciplines: The Dilemma and a Possible Resolution'. *Journal of International Economic Law* 1 (2): 303–322.

Mavroidis, Petros C. 2000a. '"Like Products": Some Thoughts at the Positive and Normative Level'. In *Regulatory Barriers and the Principle of Non-discrimination in World Trade Law*, edited by Thomas Cottier, and Petros C. Mavroidis, 125–135. World Trade Forum 2. Michigan: University of Michigan Press.

Mavroidis, Petros C. 2000b. 'Trade and Environment after the *Shrimps–Turtles* Litigation'. *Journal of World Trade* 34 (1): 73–88.

Mavroidis, Petros C. 2004. 'Development of WTO Dispute Settlement Procedures Through Case-Law (We Will Fix It)'. In *The WTO Dispute Settlement System 1995–2003*, edited by Federico Ortino, and Ernst-Ulrich Petersmann, 153–176. Studies in Transnational Economic Law 18. The Hague: Kluwer Law International.

Mavroidis, Petros C. 2013. 'Driftin' Too Far from Shore – Why the Test for Compliance with the TBT Agreement Developed by the WTO Appellate Body Is Wrong, and What Should the AB Have Done Instead'. *Journaltitle* 12 (3): 509–531.

Mavroidis, Petros C. 2015. 'Sealed with a Doubt: EU, Seals, and the WTO'. *European Journal of Risk Regulation* 6 (3): 388–395.

Mavroidis, Petros C., and Kamal Saggi. 2014. 'What Is Not so Cool about *US–COOL* Regulations? A Critical Analysis of the Appellate Body's Ruling on *US–COOL*'. *World Trade Review* 13 (2): 299–320.

McColgan, Aileen. 2006. 'Cracking the Comparator Problem: Discrimination, "Equal" Treatment and the Role of Comparisons'. *European Human Rights Law Review* 6: 650–677.

McConnell, Irene. 2002. 'The Asbestos Case at the World Trade Organization: The Treatment of Public Health Regulations under the General Agreement of Tariffs and Trade 1994 and the Agreement on Technical Barriers to Trade'. *Tulsa Journal of Comparative and International Law* 10 (1, Fall): 153–182.

McDonald, Janet. 1993. 'Greening the GATT: Harmonizing Free Trade and Environmental Protection in the New World Order'. *Environmental Law* 23 (2): 397–474.

McDorman, Ted L. 1991. 'The GATT Consistency of U.S Fish Import Embargoes to Stop Driftnet Fishing and Save Whales, Dolphins and Turtles'. *George Washington Journal of International Law and Economics* 24 (3): 477–525.

McGrady, Benn. 2012. 'Appellate Body Report, *United States – Clove Cigarettes*'. *European Journal of Risk Regulation* 3 (2): 251–256.

McRae, Donald M. 2000. 'GATT Article XX and the WTO Appellate Body'. In *New Directions in International Economic Law: Essays in Honour of John H. Jackson*, edited by Marco Bronckers, and Reinhard Quick, 219–236. The Hague: Kluwer Law International.

McRae, Donald M. 2012. 'MFN in the GATT and the WTO'. *Asian Journal of WTO and International Health Law and Policy* 7 (1): 1–23.

Meilicke, Wienand. 1980. 'Ausländer-Diskriminierung bei der stillen Gesellschaft'. *Finanz-Rundschau* 35 (5): 105–109.

Meilicke, Wienand. 1981. 'Germany: Recent German Legislative Proposals Result in Tax Discrimination Against Foreign-Owned Enterprises'. *Tax Management International Journal* 10 (9): 26–29.

Melloni, Mattia. 2005. *The Principle of National Treatment in the GATT: A Survey of the Jurisprudence, Practice and Policy*. Bruxelles: Emile Bruylant.

Meltzer, Joshua, and Amelia Porges. 2013. 'Beyond Discrimination? The WTO Parses the *TBT Agreement* in *US – Clove Cigarettes, US – Tuna II (Mexico)* and *US – COOL*'. *Melbourne Journal of International Law* 14 (2): 699–726.

Mersmann, Wolfgang. 1971. 'Diskriminierung ausländischer Beteiligungen bei der Körperschaftsteuerreform?'. *Deutsche Steuer-Zeitung* 59 (19): 310–313.

Michielse, Geerten M.M. 1997. 'Treaty Aspects of Thin Capitalization'. *Bulletin for International Fiscal Documentation (Bulletin for International Taxation)* 51 (12): 565–573.

Mitchell, Andrew D., David Heaton, and Caroline Henckels. 2016. *Non-discrimination and the Role of Regulatory Purpose in International Trade and Investment Law*. Elgar International Investment Law. Cheltenham; Northampton: Edward Elgar Publishing.

Mitchell, Andrew D., and Caroline Henckels. 2013. 'Variations on a Theme: Comparing the Concept of "Necessity" in International Investment Law and WTO Law'. *Chicago Journal of International Law* 14 (1, Summer): 93–164.

Mitchell, Andrew D., and Tania Voon. 2011. 'Regulating Tobacco Flavors: Implications of WTO Law'. *Boston University International Law Journal* 29 (2, Summer): 383–425.

Mitra, Rahul Krishna. 2007. 'OECD's Public Discussion Draft on Non-discrimination: A Critical Analysis'. *Tax Planning International Review* 34 (6): 3–7.

Mitschke, Wolfgang. 2011. 'Keine Diskriminierung nach Art. XX Abs. 4 DBA-Großbritannien in Fällen ausländerbeherrschter Inlandskapitalgesellschaften'. *Internationales Steuerrecht* 20 (14): 537–542.

Moldenhauer, David T. 1995a. 'Application of the Nationality Non-discrimination Clause of Tax Treaties to Nonresident Companies: An Evaluation of the French Judicial Position (I)'. *International Business Law Journal* 1: 73–106.

Moldenhauer, David T. 1995b. 'Application of the Nationality Non-discrimination Clause of Tax Treaties to Nonresident Companies: An Evaluation of the French Judicial Position (II)'. *International Business Law Journal* 2: 215–239.

Montini, Massimiliano. 1997. 'The Nature and Function of the Necessity and Proportionality Principles in the Trade and Environment Context'. *Review of European Community and International Environmental Law (Review of European, Comparative and International Environmental Law)* 6 (2): 121–130.

Moritz, Martin. 2003. *Das Diskriminierungsverbot im Spannungsverhältnis zu Gleichbehandlung und Gerechtigkeit: Seine Möglichkeiten und Grenzen am besonderen Beispiel der direkten Besteuerung*. Vienna: Verlag Österreich.

Mössner, Jörg Manfred. 1985. 'Die Methoden zur Vermeidung der Doppelbesteuerung: Vorzüge, Nachteile, aktuelle Probleme'. In *Grundfragen des Internationalen Steuerrechts*, edited by Klaus Vogel, 135–169. Cologne: Dr. Otto Schmidt.

Mössner, Jörg Manfred. 2011. 'Gewerbesteuerliche Organschaft zwischen einem in Großbritannien ansässigen Organträger und einer inländischen Organgesellschaft über eine inländische Zwischenholding'. *Internationales Steuerrecht* 20 (9): 345–350.

Muller, Gilles. 2016. 'National Treatment and the GATS: Lessons from Jurisprudence'. *Journal of World Trade* 50 (5): 819–844.

Muller, Gilles. 2017. 'De Facto Discrimination under GATS National Treatment: Has the Genie of Trade Liberalization Been Let out of the Bottle?'. *Legal Issues of Economic Integration* 44 (2): 151–172.

Munhoz Ribeiro, Fernando. 2015. 'Comparability Assessment under the Non-discrimination Clause of Article 24 of the OECD Model'. In *Non-discrimination in European and Tax Treaty Law: Open Issues and Recent Challenges*, edited by Kasper Dziurdź, and Christoph Marchgraber, 335–352. Series on International Tax Law 94. Vienna: Linde.

Musgrave, Peggy B. 2005a. 'Capital Export Neutrality'. In *The Encyclopedia of Taxation & Tax Policy*, edited by Joseph J. Cordes, Robert D. Ebel, and Jane G. Gravelle, 2nd ed., 45–46. Washington, D.C.: The Urban Institute Press.

Musgrave, Peggy B. 2005b. 'Capital Import Neutrality'. In *The Encyclopedia of Taxation & Tax Policy*, edited by Joseph J. Cordes, Robert D. Ebel, and Jane G. Gravelle, 2nd ed., 50–51. Washington, D.C.: The Urban Institute Press.

Müller, Klaus-Dieter. 2015. 'Der Progressionsvorbehalt im Abkommen und im nationalen Recht'. In *Doppelbesteuerung – Festgabe: Zum 75. Geburtstag von Prof. Dr. Dr. h.c. Franz Wassermeyer – 75 Beiträge zum Recht der DBA*, edited by Franz Wassermeyer, 447–454. Munich: C.H. Beck.

Neumann, Jan, and Elisabeth Türk. 2003a. 'Necessity Revisited: Proportionality in World Trade Organization Law after *Korea – Beef, EC – Asbestos* and *EC – Sardines*'. *Journal of World Trade* 37 (1): 199–233.

Neumann, Jan, and Elisabeth Türk. 2003b. 'Necessity Revisited – Proportionality in WTO Law after *EC – Asbestos*'. In *WTO-Recht und Globalisierung*, edited by Martin Nettesheim, and Gerald G. Sander, 103–144. Tübinger Schriften zum internationalen und europäischen Recht 68. Berlin: Duncker & Humblot.

Neven, Damien J., and Joel P. Trachtman. 2013. '*Philippines – Taxes on Distilled Spirits*: Like Products and Market Definition'. *World Trade Review* 12 (2): 297–326.

Nielsen, Laura, and Maria-Alejandra Calle. 2013. 'Systemic Implications of the EU – Seal Products Case'. *Asian Journal of WTO and International Health Law and Policy* 8 (1): 41–75.

Nieminen, Martti. 2015a. 'Dual Role of the OECD Commentaries – Part 1'. *Intertax* 43 (11): 636–659.

Nieminen, Martti. 2015b. 'Dual Role of the OECD Commentaries: Part 2'. *Intertax* 43 (12): 773–795.

Nikolakakis, Angelo. 2012. 'Intercompany Dividends and Non-discrimination under the OECD MC: Economic Double Taxation, Branch Taxes and Customary Discrimination'. In *Taxation of Intercompany Dividends under Tax Treaties and EU Law*, edited by Guglielmo Maisto, 169–188. EC and International Tax Law Series 8. Amsterdam: IBFD.

Nitikman, Joel A. 2000. 'The Interaction of Canada's Thin Capitalization Rule and the Canada–United States Tax Treaty'. *International Tax Journal* 26 (1, Winter): 20–64.

Norpoth, Johannes. 2013. 'Mysteries of the TBT Agreement Resolved? Lessons to Learn for Climate Policies and Developing Country Exporters from Recent TBT Disputes'. *Journal of World Trade* 47 (3): 575–600.

Nottage, Hunter, and Alejandro Sánchez. 2012. 'Navigating Uncharted Waters: A Review of *US-Tuna II*'. *Global Trade and Customs Journal* 7 (2): 59–65.

Oberascher, Friederike. 2006. 'Das Staatsangehörigendiskriminierungsverbot des Art 24 OECD-MA in einer historischen Längsschnittanalyse'. In *Die Diskriminierungsverbote im Recht der Doppelbesteuerungsabkommen*, edited by Michael Lang, Josef Schuch, and Claus Staringer, 49–68. Vienna: Linde.

Oberascher, Friederike, and Claus Staringer. 2007. 'Gruppenträger und Gruppenmitglied'. In *Grundfragen der Gruppenbesteuerung*, edited by Michael Lang, Josef Schuch, Claus Staringer, and Markus Stefaner, 29–50. Vienna: Linde.

O'Brien, James G. 1978. 'The Nondiscrimination Article in Tax Treaties'. *Law and Policy in International Business* 10 (2): 545–612.

Oesterhelt, Stefan. 2015. 'Art. 24'. In *Internationales Steuerrecht: Kommentar zum Schweizerischen Steuerrecht*, edited by Martin Zweifel, Michael Beusch, and René Matteotti. Basel: Helbing Lichtenhahn.

Oliver, David. 1977. 'Discrimination'. *British Tax Review* 22: 148–153.

Oliver, David. 1989. 'Other Similar Enterprises'. *British Tax Review* 34 (5): 141–146.

Oliver, David. 1993. 'Differential Treatment or Discrimination?'. *British Tax Review* 38 (6): 435–441.

Oliver, David. 2004. 'Other Similar Enterprises – *NEC Semi-Conductors Ltd and others v Inland Revenue*'. *British Tax Review* 49 (2): 80–84.

Orava, Stephen J. 2002. 'Potential WTO Claims in Response to Countermeasures under the OECD's Recommendations Applicable to Alleged Tax Havens'. In *International Tax Competition: Globalisation and Fiscal Sovereignty*, edited by Rajiv Biswas, 177–197. London: Commonwealth Secretariat.

Ortino, Federico. 2004. 'WTO Jurisprudence on *De Jure* and *De Facto* Discrimination'. In *The WTO Dispute Settlement System 1995–2003*, edited by Federico Ortino, and Ernst-Ulrich Petersmann, 217–262. Studies in Transnational Economic Law 18. The Hague: Kluwer Law International.

Ortino, Federico. 2008. 'The Principle of Non-discrimination and Its Exceptions in GATS: Selected Legal Issues'. In *The World Trade Organization and Trade in Services*, edited by Kern Alexander, and Mads Andenas, 173–204. Leiden; Boston: Martinus Nijhoff Publishers.

Ortino, Federico. 2009. 'GATT'. In *The Oxford Handbook of International Trade Law*, edited by Daniel Bethlehem, Donald M. McRae, Rodney Neufeld, and Isabelle Van Damme, 129–156. Oxford: Oxford University Press.

Ortino, Federico. 2012. 'From "Non-discrimination" to "Reasonableness": A Paradigm Shift in International Economic Law?'. In *Globalization, Technologies and Legal Revolution: The Impact of Global Changes on Territorial and Cultural Diversities, on Supranational Integration and Constitutional Theory – Liber Amicorum in Memory of Sergio Ortino*, edited by Francesco Palermo, Giovanni Poggeschi, Günther Rautz, and Jens Woelk, 13–60. Schriftenreihe der Europäischen Akademie Bozen, Bereich 'Minderheiten und Autonomien' 21. Baden-Baden: Nomos.

Pannwitz, Kurt von. 2012. 'Artikel 24 MA'. In *Außensteuergesetz / Doppelbesteuerungsabkommen*, edited by Florian Haase, 2nd ed. Heidelberg: C.F. Müller.

Papotti, Raul-Angelo. 2003. 'Treaty Non-discrimination Clauses in Group Consolidation Situations'. *Intertax* 31 (10): 320–328.

Partiti, Enrico. 2013. 'The Appellate Body Report in *US – Tuna II* and Its Impact on Eco-Labelling and Standardization'. *Legal Issues of Economic Integration* 40 (1): 73–94.

Patrick, Robert J., Jr. 1978. 'A Comparison of the United States and OECD Model Income Tax Conventions'. *Law and Policy in International Business* 10 (2): 613–718.

Pauwelyn, Joost. 1998. 'Evidence, Proof and Persuasion in WTO Dispute Settlement: Who Bears the Burden?'. *Journal of International Economic Law* 1 (2): 227–258.

Pauwelyn, Joost. 2008. 'Comment: The Unbearable Lightness of Likeness'. In *GATS and the Regulation of International Trade in Services*, edited by Marion Panizzon, Nicole Pohl, and Pierre Sauvé, 358–369. Cambridge: Cambridge University Press.

Pauwelyn, Joost. 2010. 'The Dog That Barked But Didn't Bite: 15 Years of Intellectual Property Disputes at the WTO'. *Journal of International Dispute Settlement* 1 (2): 389–429.

Peeters, Bernard. 2008. 'On Anti-Discrimination Provisions and Permanent Establishments in "Bilateral Triangular Situations"'. In *A Vision of Taxes Within and Outside European Borders: Festschrift in Honor of Prof. Dr. Frans Vanistendael*, edited by Luc Hinnekens, and Philippe Hinnekens, 669–678. Alphen on the Rhine: Kluwer Law International.

Penttilä, Seppo. 2008. 'Finland'. In *Non-discrimination at the Cross-Roads of International Taxation*, edited by International Fiscal Association, 257–266. Cahiers de Droit Fiscal International – Studies on International Fiscal Law 93a. Amersfoort: Sdu Fiscale & Financiële Uitgevers.

Peters, Cees, and Margreet Snellaars. 2001. 'Non-discrimination and Tax Law: Structure and Comparison of the Various Non-discrimination Clauses'. *EC Tax Review* 10 (1): 13–18.

Peters, Christopher J. 1997. 'Equality Revisited'. *Harvard Law Review* 110 (6): 1210–1264.

Peters, Christopher J. 1999. 'Slouching Towards Equality'. *Iowa Law Review* 84 (4): 801–818.

Peters, Christopher J. 2000. 'Outcomes, Reasons, and Equality'. *Boston University Law Review* 80 (4): 1095–1126.

Pfitzer, James Headen, and Sheila Sabune. 2008. 'Burden-Shifting in WTO Dispute Settlement: The Prima Facie Doctrine'. *Bridges* 12 (2): 18.

Pfitzer, James Headen, and Sheila Sabune. 2009. *Burden of Proof in WTO Dispute Settlement: Contemplating Preponderance of the Evidence*. ICTSD Dispute Settlement and Legal Aspects of International Trade 9. Geneva: International Centre for Trade; Sustainable Development (ICTSD).

Philipp, Alfred. 1971. *Befreiungssystem mit Progressionsvorbehalt und Anrechnungsverfahren: Probleme des zwischenstaatlichen Steuerrechtes*. Vienna: Orac.

Piérola, Fernando. 2012. 'The Treatment of "Likeness" and a New Rejection of the "Aim and Effects" Test in *US – Clove Cigarettes*'. *Global Trade and Customs Journal* 7 (7/8): 347–348.

Pillai, Rajesh. 2002. 'National Treatment and WTO Dispute Settlement'. *World Trade Review* 1 (3): 321–343.

Piltz, Detlev J. 1981. *Die Personengesellschaften im internationalen Steuerrecht der Bundesrepublik Deutschland*. Heidelberg: Verlagsgesellschaft Recht und Wirtschaft.

Piltz, Detlev J. 1996. 'General Report'. In *International Aspects of Thin Capitalization*, edited by International Fiscal Association, 83–139. Cahiers de Droit Fiscal International – Studies on International Fiscal Law 81b. The Hague: Kluwer Law International.

Pinetz, Erik, and Karoline Spies. 2014a. 'Ergebniskonsolidierung inländischer Schwestergesellschaften im Rahmen des § 9 KStG (Teil I)'. *Zeitschrift für Gesellschaftsrecht und angrenzendes Steuerrecht* 13 (9): 470–475.

Pinetz, Erik, and Karoline Spies. 2014b. 'Ergebniskonsolidierung inländischer Schwestergesellschaften im Rahmen des § 9 KStG (Teil II)'. *Zeitschrift für Gesellschaftsrecht und angrenzendes Steuerrecht* 13 (10): 510–519.

Pinto Nogueira, João Félix. 2015. 'Portugal: PE and Non-discrimination Regarding Domestic Relief for Double Economic Taxation'. In *Tax Treaty Case Law Around the Globe 2014*, edited by Eric C.C.M. Kemmeren, Daniël S. Smit, Peter Essers, Michael Lang, Jeffrey Owens, Pasquale Pistone, Alexander Rust, Josef Schuch, Claus Staringer, and Alfred Storck, 293–303. Series on International Tax Law 89. Amsterdam; Vienna: IBFD; Linde.

Pinto Nogueira, João Félix. 2017. 'Portugal: Non-discrimination and Access to Domestic Law Incentives for Individuals in the Residence State'. In *Tax Treaty Case Law Around the Globe 2016*, edited by Eric Kemmeren, Daniël S. Smit, Peter Essers, Michael Lang, Pasquale Pistone, Josef Schuch, Claus Staringer, Alfred Storck, Jeffrey Owens, and Alexander Rust, 385–396. Amsterdam; Vienna: IBFD; Linde.

Pitkänen, Sami. 2015. 'Consolidating Group Members with a PE of a Foreign Enterprise under Article 24(3) of the OECD Model'. In *Non-discrimination in European and Tax Treaty Law: Open Issues and Recent Challenges*, edited by Kasper Dziurdź, and Christoph Marchgraber, 461–486. Series on International Tax Law 94. Vienna: Linde.

Porges, Amelia, and Joel P. Trachtman. 2003. 'Robert Hudec and Domestic Regulation: The Resurrection of Aim and Effects'. *Journal of World Trade* 37 (4): 783–799.

Pott, Hans-Michael. 1982. 'Die Vereinbarkeit des Entwurfs eines § 8a KStG (KStÄndGE 1982) mit dem Völkerrecht'. *Steuer und Wirtschaft* 59 (3): 223–230.

Pöllath, Reinhard, and Albert J. Rädler. 1980. 'Die vorgeschlagene Erweiterung des § 8 Abs.3 KStG – Voraussetzungen und Wirkungen nach innerstaatlichem und Abkommensrecht'. *Betriebs-Berater* 35 (21).

Pöllath, Reinhard, and Albert J. Rädler. 1982a. 'Gewinnberichtigungen zwischen verbundenen Unternehmen ohne Rücksicht auf Abkommensrecht?'. *Der Betrieb* 35 (11): 561–565.

Pöllath, Reinhard, and Albert J. Rädler. 1982b. 'Gewinnberichtigungen zwischen verbundenen Unternehmen ohne Rücksicht auf Abkommensrecht? (II)'. *Der Betrieb* 35 (12): 617–620.

Pöschl, Magdalena. 2008. *Gleichheit vor dem Gesetz*. Forschungen aus Staat und Recht 147. Vienna: Springer.

Princen, Savina, and Marcel Gérard. 2008. 'International Tax Consolidation in the European Union: Evidence of Heterogeneity'. *European Taxation* 48 (4): 174–184.

Qin, Julia Ya. 2005. 'Defining Nondiscrimination under the Law of the World Trade Organization'. *Boston University International Law Journal* 23 (2): 215–297.

Raad, Kees van. 1982. 'Netherlands Withholding Tax on Dividends Paid to Foreign Parent Companies and Nondiscrimination Clauses?'. *Intertax* 10 (5): 183–187.

Raad, Kees van. 1986. *Nondiscrimination in International Tax Law*. Series on International Taxation 6. Deventer: Kluwer Law; Taxation Publishers.

Raad, Kees van. 1988a. 'Dual Residence'. *European Taxation* 28 (8): 241–246.

Raad, Kees van. 1988b. 'Issues in the Application of Tax Treaty Non-discrimination Clauses'. *Bulletin for International Fiscal Documentation (Bulletin for International Taxation)* 42 (8/9): 347–351.

Raad, Kees van. 1988c. 'Steuergestaltung durch Doppelsitz von Kapitalgesellschaften in der internationalen Praxis'. In *Steuergestaltung durch doppelt ansässige Gesellschaften?*, edited by Rainer Hausmann, Kees van Raad, Arndt Raupach, and Winfried Veelken, 1–11. Munich: C.H. Beck.

Raad, Kees van. 1988d. 'The Netherlands Model Income Tax Treaty'. *Intertax* 16 (8–9): 241–250.

Raad, Kees van. 1990. 'Netherlands: Dual Residence and 1977 OECD Model Treaty Article 4(1), Second Sentence'. *European Taxation* 30 (1): 27–29.

Raad, Kees van. 1992. '1992 Additions to Articles 3(2) (Interpretation) and 24 (Non-discrimination) of the 1992 OECD Model and Commentary'. *Intertax* 20 (12): 671–676.

Raad, Kees van. 1993. 'The 1992 OECD Model Treaty: Triangular Cases'. *European Taxation* 33 (9): 298–301.

Raad, Kees van. 1995. 'The Impact of the EC Treaty's Fundamental Freedoms Provisions on EU Member States' Taxation in Border-Crossing Situations – Current State of Affairs'. *EC Tax Review* 4 (4): 190–201.

Raad, Kees van. 2001. 'Fractional Taxation Taxation of Multi-State Income of EU Resident Individuals – A Proposal'. In *Liber Amicorum Sven-Olof Lodin*, edited by Krister Andersson, Peter Melz, and Christer Silfverberg, 211–221. Series on International Taxation 27. Stockholm: Kluwer Law International.

Raad, Kees van. 2005. 'Nondiscrimination in Taxation of Cross-Border Income under the OECD Model and EC Treaty Rules – A Concise Comparison and Assessment'. In *A Tax Globalist: The Search for the Borders of International Taxation – Essays in Honour of Maarten J. Ellis*, 129–143. Amsterdam: IBFD.

Raad, Kees van. 2008. 'Non-discrimination under Tax Treaties Regarding Groups of Companies'. In *International and EC Tax Aspects of Groups of Companies*, edited by Guglielmo Maisto, 157–171. EC and International Tax Law Series 4. Amsterdam: IBFD.

Raad, Kees van. 2009. '2008 OECD Model: Operation and Effect of Article 4(1) in Dual Residence Issues under the Updated Commentary'. *Bulletin for International Taxation* 63 (5): 187–190.

Raad, Kees van. 2010. 'Non-residents – Personal Allowances, Deduction of Personal Expenses and Tax Rates'. *World Tax Journal* 2 (2): 154–161.

Raad, Kees van. 2012. 'Intercompany Dividends and Non-discrimination under the OECD Model'. In *Taxation of Intercompany Dividends under Tax Treaties and EU Law*, edited by Guglielmo Maisto, 161–168. EC and International Tax Law Series 8. Amsterdam: IBFD.

Raad, Kees van, and Alexander Bosman. 2016. 'Nondiscrimination from the Perspective of the OECD Model and the Treaty on the Functioning of the European Union: Structural and Conceptual Issues'. In *Comparative Fiscal Federalism*, edited by Reuven S. Avi-Yonah, and Michael Lang, 2nd ed., 67–81. EUCOTAX Series on European Taxation 14. Alphen on the Rhine: Kluwer Law International.

Raupach, Arndt. 1966. 'Diskriminierungsverbote und Gleichbehandlungsklauseln in Doppelbesteuerungsabkommen: Systematik, Geltungsbereich und Bedeutung für die deutsche Gesellschaftsteuer'. *Außenwirtschaftsdienst des Betriebs-Beraters (Recht der Internationalen Wirtschaft)* 12 (5): 85–92.

Rädler, Albert J., and Arndt Raupach. 1966. *Deutsche Steuern bei Auslandsbeziehungen*. Munich: C.H. Beck.

Regan, Donald H. 2001. 'Judicial Review of Member-State Regulation of Trade Within a Federal or Quasi-Federal System: Protectionism and Balancing, Da Capo'. *Michigan Law Review* 99 (8): 1853–1902.

Regan, Donald H. 2002. 'Regulatory Purpose and "Like Products" in Article III:4 of the GATT (With Additional Remarks on Article III:2)'. *Journal of World Trade* 36 (3): 443–478.

Regan, Donald H. 2003. 'Further Thoughts on the Role of Regulatory Purpose under Article III of the General Agreement on Tariffs and Trade: A Tribute to Bob Hudec'. *Journal of World Trade* 37 (4): 737–760.

Regan, Donald H. 2006a. 'Regulatory Purpose and "Like Products" in Article III:4 of the GATT (with Additional Remarks on Article III:2)'. In *Trade and Human Health and Safety*, edited by George A. Bermann, and Petros C. Mavroidis, 190–223. Cambridge: Cambridge University Press.

Regan, Donald H. 2006b. 'What Are Trade Agreements For? – Two Conflicting Stories Told by Economists, with a Lesson for Lawyers'. *Journal of International Economic Law* 9 (4): 951–988.

Regan, Donald H. 2007. 'The Meaning of "Necessary" in GATT Article XX and GATS Article XIV: The Myth of Cost–Benefit Balancing'. *World Trade Review* 6 (3): 347–369.

Reid, Emily. 2010. 'Regulatory Autonomy in the EU and WTO: Defining and Defending Its Limits'. *Journal of World Trade* 44 (4): 877–901.

Reimer, Ekkehart. 2014. 'Permanent Establishment in the OECD Model Tax Convention'. In *Permanent Establishments: A Domestic Taxation, Bilateral Tax Treaty and OECD Perspective*, edited by Ekkehart Reimer, Stefan Schmid, and Marianne Orell, 3rd ed. Alphen on the Rhine: Kluwer Law International.

Reimer, Ekkehart. 2015. 'Artikel 6'. In *Doppelbesteuerungsabkommen der Bundesrepublik Deutschland auf dem Gebiet der Steuern vom Einkommen und Vermögen: Kommentar auf der Grundlage der Musterabkommen*, edited by Moris Lehner, 6th ed. Munich: C.H. Beck.

Reyes, Arantxa. 2011. 'Non-discrimination of Permanent Establishments'. In *Permanent Establishments in International and EU Tax Law*, edited by Florian Brugger, and Patrick Plansky, 287–303. Series on International Tax Law 68. Vienna: Linde.

Ribbrock, Martin. 2004. *Dreieckssachverhalte im Internationalen Steuerrecht: Probleme bei der Besteuerung von Betriebstätten mit Zinseinkünften aus Drittstaaten*. Schriftenreihe Steuerrecht in Forschung und Praxis 5. Hamburg: Verlag Dr. Kovač.

Ribbrock, Martin. 2005. 'Auslegung von DBA-Diskriminierungsverboten: Bedeutung der Grundfreiheiten – Besprechung des BMF-Schreibens vom 8. 12. 2004'. *Europäisches Wirtschafts- und Steuerrecht* 15 (9): 401–405.

Riemenschneider, Sven. 1995. *Abkommensberechtigung von Personengesellschaften und abkommensrechtliche Behandlung der Einkünfte aus Beteiligungen inländischer Gesellschafter an ausländischen Personengesellschaften*. Frankfurt am Main: Peter Lang.

Rienstra, John G. 2017. 'United States – Individual Taxation. Country Analyses'. IBFD. 1 January 2017. https://online.ibfd.org/document/ita_us_chaphead.

Rodríguez Nepote, Isabel. 2011. 'Article 24 Non-discrimination'. In *History of Tax Treaties: The Relevance of the OECD Documents for the Interpretation of Tax Treaties*, edited by Thomas Ecker, and Gernot Ressler, 663–684. Series on International Tax Law 69. Vienna: Linde.

Roessler, Frieder. 1996. 'Diverging Domestic Policies and Multilateral Trade Integration'. In *Fair Trade and Harmonization: Prerequisites for Free Trade? – Legal Analysis*, edited by Jagdish Bhagwati, and Robert E. Hudec, 2:21–56. Cambridge, Massachusetts; London, England: The MIT Press.

Roessler, Frieder. 2000. *The Legal Structure, Functions & Limits of the World Trade Order: A Collection of Essays*. London: Cameron May.

Roessler, Frieder. 2003. 'Beyond the Ostensible: A Tribute to Professor Robert Hudec's Insights on the Determination of the Likeness of Products under the National Treatment Provisions of the General Agreement on Tariffs and Trade'. *Journal of World Trade* 37 (4): 771–781.

Rosenbloom, H. David. 1991. 'Toward a New Tax Treaty Policy for a New Decade'. *American Journal of Tax Policy* 9 (1, Spring): 77–94.

Rosenfeld, Michel. 1988. 'Substantive Equality and Equal Opportunity: A Jurisprudential Appraisal'. *California Law Review* 74 (5): 1687–1712.

Rödder, Thomas, and Jens Schönfeld. 2011. 'Dokument Abschied (auslandsbeherrschter) inländischer Kapitalgesellschaften von der deutschen Ertragsteuerpflicht? Erste Anmerkungen zum überraschenden Urteil des BFH v. 9. 2. 2011 (I R 54, 55/10, DStR 2011, 762)'. *Deutsches Steuerrecht* 49 (19): 886–890.

Ruiz Fabri, Hélène. 2014. 'Is There a Case – Legally and Politically – for Direct Effect of WTO Obligations?'. *European Journal of International Law* 25 (1): 151–173.

Russo, Raffaele. 2004. 'Tax Treatment of "Dealings" Between Different Parts of the Same Enterprise under Article 7 of the OECD Model: Almost a Century of Uncertainty'. *Bulletin for International Fiscal Documentation (Bulletin for International Taxation)* 58 (10): 472–485.

Russo, Raffaele. 2008. 'The 2008 OECD Model: An Overview'. *European Taxation* 48 (9): 459–466.

Rust, Alexander. 2003a. 'Artikel 24'. In *Doppelbesteuerungsabkommen der Bundesrepublik Deutschland auf dem Gebiet der Steuern vom Einkommen und Vermögen: Kommentar auf der Grundlage der Musterabkommen*, edited by Moris Lehner, 4th ed. Munich: C.H. Beck.

Rust, Alexander. 2003b. 'Ermöglichen Diskriminierungsverbote eine Organschaft über die Grenze? Anmerkung zum Urteil des BFH vom 29. 1. 2003, IStR 2003, 422'. *Internationales Steuerrecht* 12 (19): 658–661.

Rust, Alexander. 2004. 'Diskriminierungsverbote verbieten Diskriminierungen! Anmerkung zum Urteil des FG Hamburg vom 2. 9. 2003 (IStR 2004, 385)'. *Internationales Steuerrecht* 13 (11): 391–396.

Rust, Alexander. 2005. 'Diskriminierungsverbote der DBA: BFH-Urt. v. 29. 1. 2003, I R 6/99, zu Art. 24 Abs. 24 DBA-USA'. *Internationales Steuerrecht* 14 (1): 26–28.

Rust, Alexander. 2006. 'Meistbegünstigungsklauseln in den Doppelbesteuerungsabkommen'. In *Meistbegünstigung im Steuerrecht der EU-Staaten: Beiträge von Siegbert Alber, Christoph Herrmann, Ekkehart Reimer, Alexander Rust, Stefan Enchelmaier, Axel Cordewener, Josef Schuch, Joachim Englisch, Pasquale Pistone, Clemens Philipp Schindler und Albert J. Rädler mit Diskussionsbeiträgen eines Münchener Symposions*, edited by Axel Cordewener, Stefan Enchelmaier, and Clemens Philipp Schindler, 77–92. Münchener Schriften zum Internationalen Steuerrecht 26. Munich: C.H. Beck.

Rust, Alexander. 2010. 'International Tax Neutrality and Non-discrimination – A Legal Perspective'. In *Tax Treaties: Building Bridges Between Law and Economics*, edited by Michael Lang, Pasquale Pistone, Josef Schuch, Claus Staringer, Alfred Storck, and Martin Zagler, 629–649. Amsterdam: IBFD.

Rust, Alexander. 2013a. 'Germany: Cross-Border Group Consolidation'. In *Tax Treaty Case Law Around the Globe 2012*, edited by Eric C.C.M. Kemmeren, Daniël S. Smit, Peter Essers, Luc De Broe, Michael Lang, Pasquale Pistone, Josef Schuch, Claus Staringer, and Alfred Storck, 357–363. Series on International Tax Law 78. Amsterdam; Vienna: IBFD; Linde.

Rust, Alexander. 2013b. 'Gleichbehandlungsgebote und Diskriminierungsverbote im Internationalen Steuerrecht'. In *Internationales Steuerrecht: 37. Jahrestagung der Deutschen Steuerjuristischen Gesellschaft e.V. Linz, 10. und 11. September 2012*, edited by Markus Achatz, 71–85. Veröffentlichungen der Deutschen Steuerjuristischen Gesellschaft e.V. 36. Cologne: Dr. Otto Schmidt.

Rust, Alexander. 2015a. 'Article 23'. In *Klaus Vogel on Double Taxation Conventions*, edited by Ekkehart Reimer and Alexander Rust, 4th ed. Alphen on the Rhine: Kluwer Law International.

Rust, Alexander. 2015b. 'Article 24'. In *Klaus Vogel on Double Taxation Conventions*, edited by Ekkehart Reimer and Alexander Rust, 4th ed. Alphen on the Rhine: Kluwer Law International.

Rust, Alexander. 2015c. 'Artikel 24'. In *Doppelbesteuerungsabkommen der Bundesrepublik Deutschland auf dem Gebiet der Steuern vom Einkommen und Vermögen: Kommentar auf der Grundlage der Musterabkommen*, edited by Moris Lehner, 6th ed. Munich: C.H. Beck.

Rust, Alexander. 2015d. 'BEPS Action 2: 2014 Deliverable–Neutralising the Effects of Hybrid Mismatch Arrangements and Its Compatibility with the Non-discrimination Provisions in Tax Treaties and the Treaty on the Functioning of the European Union'. *British Tax Review* 60 (3): 308–324.

Rust, Alexander. 2015e. 'Der BEPS Aktionspunkt 2 zur Neutralisierung der Effekte hybrider Gestaltungen und seine Vereinbarkeit mit den Diskriminierungsverboten der Doppelbesteuerungsabkommen und des AEUV'. In *Grundfragen des Europäischen Steuerrechts*, edited by Wolfgang Schön and Caroline Heber, 89–108. MPI Studies in Tax Law and Public Finance 5. Berlin; Heidelberg: Springer.

Rybnik, Daniel. 2014. 'Tax Havens: Paradigm Shift'. *International Transfer Pricing Journal* 21 (4): 275–277.

Saccardo, Nicola. 2003. 'Art. 24(3) of the OECD Model Convention: The Significance of the Expression "*Taxation on a Permanent Establishment*" in Cross-Border Reorganizations'. *Intertax* 31 (8/9): 271–279.

Salditt, Franz. 1971. 'Das körperschaftsteuerliche Anrechnungsverfahren: Die Behandlung des gebietsfremden Anteilseigners'. *Außenwirtschaftsdienst des Betriebs-Beraters (Recht der Internationalen Wirtschaft)* 16 (10): 474–480.

Santiago, Bruno. 2009. 'Non-discrimination Provisions at the Intersection of EC and International Tax Law'. *European Taxation* 49 (5): 249–262.

Sarnoff, Joshua D. 1999a. 'Equality as Uncertainty'. *Iowa Law Review* 84 (3): 377–411.

Sarnoff, Joshua D. 1999b. 'I Come to Praise Morality, Not to Bury It'. *Iowa Law Review* 84 (4): 819–826.

Sass, Gert. 1966. 'Zur Auslegung der in Doppelbesteuerungsabkommen übernommenen OECD-Klausel über die Nichtdiskriminierung von Betriebsstätten'. *Außenwirtschaftsdienst des Betriebs-Beraters (Recht der Internationalen Wirtschaft)* 11 (4): 106–110.

Sasseville, Jacques. 2006. 'A Tax Treaty Perspective: Special Issues'. In *Tax Treaties and Domestic Law*, edited by Guglielmo Maisto, 37–61. EC and International Tax Law Series 2. Amsterdam: IBFD.

Sasseville, Jacques. 2008. 'Treaty Recognition of Groups of Companies'. In *International and EC Tax Aspects of Groups of Companies*, edited by Guglielmo Maisto, 129–136. EC and International Tax Law Series 4. Amsterdam: IBFD.

Sasseville, Jacques. 2013. 'Canada: Transfer of Losses.' In *Tax Treaty Case Law Around the Globe 2012*, edited by Eric C.C.M. Kemmeren, Daniël S. Smit, Peter Essers, Luc De Broe, Michael Lang, Pasquale Pistone, Josef Schuch, Claus Staringer, and Alfred Storck, 339–349. Series on International Tax Law 78. Amsterdam; Vienna: IBFD; Linde.

Scapa Passalacqua, Anna B., and Lars A. Henie. 2005. 'The Norwegian Group Contribution System in Cross-Border Situations'. *Intertax* 33 (3): 37–44.

Schaumburg, Harald. 2015. 'Diskriminierungsverbote von Staatsangehörigen'. In *Doppelbesteuerung – Festgabe: Zum 75. Geburtstag von Prof. Dr. Dr. h.c. Franz Wassermeyer – 75 Beiträge zum Recht der DBA*, edited by Franz Wassermeyer, 121–127. Munich: C.H. Beck.

Schänzle, Thomas. 2015. 'Abkommensrechtliches Diskriminierungsverbot'. In *Doppelbesteuerung – Festgabe: Zum 75. Geburtstag von Prof. Dr. Dr. h.c. Franz Wassermeyer – 75 Beiträge zum Recht der DBA*, edited by Franz Wassermeyer, 495–503. Munich: C.H. Beck.

Schilcher, Michael, and Markus Stefaner. 2006. 'Die Anwendung des Staatsangehörigendiskriminierungsverbots (Art 24 Abs 1 OECD-MA) auf juristische Personen und Personengesellschaften'. In *Die Diskriminierungsverbote im Recht der Doppelbesteuerungsabkommen*, edited by Michael Lang, Josef Schuch, and Claus Staringer, 137–165. Vienna: Linde.

Schlager, Christoph. 2008. 'Die Einschränkung der Ansässigkeit bei bloß inländischen Einkunftsquellen nach Art 4 Abs 1 Satz 2 OECD-MA'. In *Die Ansässigkeit im Recht der Doppelbesteuerungsabkommen*, edited by Michael Lang, Josef Schuch, and Claus Staringer, 87–108. Vienna: Linde.

Schneeweiss, Hermann. 2006. 'Betriebsstättendiskriminierungsverbot: Kein Verlustvortrag für beschränkt Steuerpflichtige bei doppelter Verlustverwertung'. *Steuer und Wirtschaft International* 16 (7): 312–317.

Schnitger, Arne. 2002. 'Geltung der Grundfreiheiten des EGV für Drittstaatsangehörige im Steuerrecht'. *Internationales Steuerrecht* 11 (20): 711–716.

Schnitger, Arne. 2003. 'Das Ende der Bruttobesteuerung beschränkt Steuerpflichtiger: Die Lehren der Rs. Gerritse'. *Finanz-Rundschau* 85 (15): 745–756.

Schnitger, Arne. 2006. *Die Grenzen der Einwirkung der Grundfreiheiten des EG-Vertrages auf das Ertragsteuerrecht*. Düsseldorf: IDW Verlag.

Schnitger, Arne. 2014. 'Urteil des EuGH in der Rs. SCA als Katalysator für eine deutsche Organschaftsreform – jetzt geht's los (?)'. *Internationales Steuerrecht* 23 (16): 587–591.

Schnitger, Arne, and Christina Berliner. 2011. 'Die Anwendung der deutschen Organschaft bei grenzüberschreitenden Sachverhalten'. *Internationales Steuerrecht* 20 (19): 753–762.

Schnitger, Arne, and Michael Oskamp. 2014. 'Empfehlungen der OECD zur Neutralisierung von Hybrid Mismatches auf Abkommensebene'. *Internationales Steuerrecht* 23 (11): 385–393.

Schoenbaum, Thomas J. 1997. 'International Trade and Protection of the Environment: The Continuing Search for Reconciliation'. *American Journal of International Law* 91 (2): 268–313.

Schön, Wolfgang. 2004. 'World Trade Organization Law and Tax Law'. *Bulletin for International Fiscal Documentation (Bulletin for International Taxation)* 58 (7): 283–296.

Schön, Wolfgang. 2006. 'Diskriminierung im Steuerrecht'. In *Die Diskriminierungsverbote im Recht der Doppelbesteuerungsabkommen*, edited by Michael Lang, Josef Schuch, and Claus Staringer, 13–30. Vienna: Linde.

Schön, Wolfgang. 2016. 'Destination-Based Income Taxation and WTO Law: A Note'. In *Practical Problems in European and International Tax Law: Essays in Honour of Manfred Mössner*, edited by Heike Jochum, Peter Essers, Michael Lang, Norbert Winkeljohann, and Bertil Wiman, 429–451. Amsterdam: IBFD.

Schön, Wolfgang, Andreas Bakrozis, Johannes Becker, Tobias Beuchert, Martin Boer, Nadja Dwenger, Andreas Gerten, et al. 2014. 'Debt and Equity in Domestic and International Tax Law – A Comparative Policy Analysis'. *British Tax Review* 59 (2): 146–217.

Schuch, Josef. 1998a. 'Organschaft und Gruppenbesteuerung im Abkommensrecht'. In *Besteuerung von Unternehmensgruppen: Bestandsaufnahme und Vorschläge zur Reform der Organschaft im Körperschaftsteuerrecht*, edited by Wolfgang Gassner, Michael Lang, and Werner Wiesner, 173–198. Vienna: Linde.

Schuch, Josef. 1998b. *Verluste im Recht der Doppelbesteuerungsabkommen*. Schriftenreihe zum Internationalen Steuerrecht 8. Vienna: Linde.

Schuch, Josef, and Katharina Fürnsinn. 2015. 'Art. 24 Österreich'. In *Doppelbesteuerung: OECD-Musterabkommen – DBA Österreich–Deutschland*, edited by Franz Wassermeyer, Christian Kaeser, Michael Lang, and Josef Schuch, 3rd ed., 2835–2848. Munich; Vienna: C.H. Beck; Linde.

Schuch, Josef, and Alexander Stieglitz. 2006. 'DBA- und EU-Diskriminierungsverbote und Verfahrensrecht'. In *Die Diskriminierungsverbote im Recht der Doppelbesteuerungsabkommen*, edited by Michael Lang, Josef Schuch, and Claus Staringer, 407–433. Vienna: Linde.

Schwarz, Jonathan. 2015. *Schwarz on Tax Treaties*. 4th ed. Kingston upon Thames: Wolters Kluwer.

Schwenke, Michael. 2013. 'Grenzüberschreitende Organschaft – Anmerkungen zu den Neuregelungen im Gesetz zur Änderung und Vereinfachung der Unternehmensbesteuerung und des steuerlichen Reisekostenrechts'. *Internationale Steuer-Rundschau* 2 (2): 41–46.

Scott, Cordia. 2001. 'OECD "Harmful" Tax Competition Move May Violate WTO Obligations, Expert Says'. *Tax Notes International* 22 (18): 2146–2147.

Sedemund, Jan. 2002. 'Direkte und mittelbare Reichweite der Grundfreiheiten des EG-Vertrags am Beispiel des § 8a KStG'. *Internationales Steuerrecht* 11 (11): 390–396.

Sedemund, Jan. 2005. 'DBA- und EG-rechtliche Diskriminierungsverbote – zwei Paar Schuhe? – Eine Replik auf den Beitrag von *Hahn* im Betriebs-Berater 2005, 521'. *Betriebs-Berater* 60 (21): 1144–1145.

Sedemund, Jan. 2006. 'Die mittelbare Wirkung der Grundfreiheiten für in Drittstaaten ansässige Unternehmen nach den EuGH-Urteilen Fidium Finanz AG und Cadbury Schweppes'. *Betriebs-Berater* 61 (51/52): 2781–2786.

Serpin, Pelin. 2016. 'The Public Morals Exception after the WTO Seal Products Dispute: Has the Exception Swallowed the Rules?'. *Columbia Business Law Review* 2016 (1): 217–251.

Shalav, Sarig, and Cees Faber. 2005. 'Non-discrimination under Tax Treaties'. In *The Attribution of Profits to Permanent Establishments: The Taxation of Intra-Company Dealings*, edited by Raffaele Russo, 447–458. Amsterdam: IBFD.

Silva, Bruno da. 2013. 'Felixstowe Dock and Railway Company and Others'. *Highlights & Insights on European Taxation* 6 (1): 107–117.

Silva, Bruno da. 2016a. 'Reconsidering the Application and Interpretation of Anti-treaty Shopping Rules in the Context of Developing Countries'. *Intertax* 44 (3): 227–246.

Silva, Bruno da. 2016b. 'Revisiting the Application of the Capital Ownership Non-discrimination Provision in Tax Treaties'. In *Non-discrimination in Tax Treaties: Selected Issues from a Global Perspective*, edited by Dennis Weber, and Pasquale Pistone, 71–132. EC and International Tax Law Series 14. Amsterdam: IBFD.

Simons, Kenneth W. 1985. 'Equality as a Comparative Right'. *Boston University Law Review* 65 (3): 387–482.

Simons, Kenneth W. 2000. 'The Logic of Egalitarian Norms'. *Boston University Law Review* 80 (3): 693–771.

Simpson, Claire. 2005. 'Re A Oy and B Oy: KHO:2004:65'. *International Tax Law Reports* 7 (3): 288–323.

Sinclair, Ian. 1984. *The Vienna Convention on the Law of Treaties*. 2nd ed. Manchester; Dover: Manchester University Press.

Smit, Daniël S. 2016. 'Netherlands: Dutch Supreme Court 31 January 2014, BNB 2014/77: Worldwide Taxation of Non-resident Taxpayers for Purposes of Calculating the Average Tax Rate: Tax Treaty Override?'. In *Tax Treaty Case Law Around the Globe 2015*, edited by Michael Lang, Alexander Rust, Jeffrey Owens, Pasquale Pistone, Josef Schuch, Claus Staringer, Alfred Storck, Peter Essers, Eric C.C.M. Kemmeren, and Daniël S. Smit, 301–311. Series on International Tax Law 97. Amsterdam; Vienna: IBFD; Linde.

Smit, Pim M. 2002. 'Treaty Residence of a Company in a Triangular Situation: Decision of the Supreme Court of 28 February 2001'. *European Taxation* 42 (4): 155–158.

Snelson, James H. 1996. 'Can GATT Article III Recover from Its Head-On Collision with *United States – Taxes on Automobiles*?'. *Minnesota Journal of Global Trade* 5 (2, Summer): 467–502.

Sommerhalder, Ruud A. 1996. 'Approaches to Thin Capitalization'. *European Taxation* 36 (3): 82–95.

Sparagna, Giovanna Terese. 2004. 'United States'. In *Group Taxation*, edited by International Fiscal Association, 711–732. Cahiers de Droit Fiscal International – Studies on International Fiscal Law 89b. Amersfoort: Sdu Fiscale & Financiële Uitgevers.

Staringer, Claus. 1994. 'Triangular Cases'. In *Aktuelle Entwicklungen im Internationalen Steuerrecht: Das neue Musterabkommen der OECD*, edited by Wolfgang Gassner, Michael Lang, and Eduard Lechner, 67–90. Vienna: Linde.

Staringer, Claus. 1999. *Besteuerung doppelt ansässiger Kapitalgesellschaften*. Vienna: Linde.

Staringer, Claus. 2000. 'Die Besteuerung von Dividenden nach der Revision des DBA Österreich-Schweiz'. *Steuer und Wirtschaft International* 10 (6): 245–253.

Staringer, Claus. 2005. 'Der Einfluss der Gruppenbesteuerung auf die Unternehmensorganisation'. *Österreichische Steuerzeitung* 58 (22): 495–502.

Staringer, Claus. 2008. 'Die Ansässigkeit aufgrund des Wohnsitzes, des ständigen Aufenthalts, des Ortes der Geschäftsleitung oder eines anderen ähnlichen Merkmals nach Art 4 Abs 1 OECD-MA'. In *Die Ansässigkeit im Recht der Doppelbesteuerungsabkommen*, edited by Michael Lang, Josef Schuch, and Claus Staringer, 67–86. Vienna: Linde.

Staringer, Claus, and Angelika Jettmar. 2006. 'Gleichheitsgrundsatz und DBA-Diskriminierungsverbote'. In *Die Diskriminierungsverbote im Recht der Doppelbesteuerungsabkommen*, edited by Michael Lang, Josef Schuch, and Claus Staringer, 385–406. Vienna: Linde.

Staringer, Claus, and Hermann Schneeweiss. 2007. 'Tax Treaty Non-discrimination and EC Freedoms'. In *Tax Treaty Law and EC Law*, edited by Michael Lang, Josef Schuch, and Claus Staringer, 227–246. Schriftenreihe zum Internationalen Steuerrecht 46. Vienna: Linde.

Ståhl, Kristina. 2000. 'The Application of the Treaty Non-discrimination Principle in Sweden'. *Intertax* 28 (5): 195–199.

Stieglitz, Alexander. 2004. 'The Sub-permanent Establishment in a Third State'. In *Triangular Tax Cases*, edited by Franz Philipp Sutter, and Ulf Zehetner, 99–126. Schriftenreihe zum Internationalen Steuerrecht 34. Vienna: Linde.

Storck, Alfred. 1980. *Ausländische Betriebstätten im Ertrag- und Vermögensteuerrecht: Taxation of Foreign Permanent Establishments*. Frankfurt am Main; Deventer: Alfred Metzner Verlag; Kluwer.

Sykes, Alan O. 2003. 'The Least Restrictive Means'. *University of Chicago Law Review* 70 (1, Winter): 403–419.

Taniguchi, Yasuhei. 2008. 'Understanding the Concept of Prima Facie Proof in WTO Dispute Settlement'. In *The WTO: Governance, Dispute Settlement, and Developing Countries*, edited by Merit E. Janow, Victoria Donaldson, and Alan Yanovich, 553–572. New York: Juris Publishing.

Thiel, Servaas van. 2005. 'General Report'. In *WTO and Direct Taxation*, edited by Michael Lang, Judith Herdin, and Ines Hofbauer, 13–47. Schriftenreihe zum Internationalen Steuerrecht 35. Vienna: Linde.

Thömmes, Otmar. 1997. 'Tatbestandsmäßigkeit und Rechtfertigung steuerlicher Diskriminierungsverbote nach EG-Recht'. In *Gedächtnisschrift für Brigitte Knobbe-Keuk*, edited by Wolfgang Schön, 795–834. Cologne: Dr. Otto Schmidt.

Ting, Antony. 2013. *The Taxation of Corporate Groups under Consolidation: An International Comparison*. Cambridge: Cambridge University Press.

Tobler, Christa. 2005. *Indirect Discrimination: A Case Study into the Development of the Legal Concept of Indirect Discrimination under EC Law*. Social Europe Series 10. Antwerpen; Oxford: Intersentia.

Toifl, Gerald. 1996. 'Die EU-Grundfreiheiten und die Diskriminierungsverbote der Doppelbesteuerungsabkommen'. In *Doppelbesteuerungsabkommen und EU-Recht: Auswirkungen auf die Abkommenspraxis*, edited by Wolfgang Gassner, Michael Lang, and Eduard Lechner, 139–180. Vienna: Linde.

Toifl, Gerald. 2003. *Personengesellschaften im Recht der Doppelbesteuerungsabkommen unter besonderer Berücksichtigung der gemeinschafts- und abkommensrechtlichen Diskriminierungsverbote*. Schriftenreihe zum Internationalen Steuerrecht 22. Vienna: Linde.

Toifl, Gerald. 2004. 'Gemeinschaftsrechtskonforme Interpretation der DBA-rechtlichen Diskriminierungsverbote'. *Steuer und Wirtschaft International* 14 (7): 325–332.

Tomazela, Ramon. 2015. 'BEPS Action 2: Missing Proposals on Hybrid Financial Instruments – Part 1'. 14 August 2015. http://www.kluwertaxlawblog.com/blog/2015/08/14/.

Torres Bernárdez, Santiago. 1998. 'Interpretation of Treaties by the International Court of Justice Following the Adoption of the 1969 Vienna Convention on the Law of Treaties'. In *Liber Amicorum Professor Ignaz Seidl-Hohenveldern in Honour of His 80th Birthday*, edited by Gerhard Hafner, Gerhard Loibl, Alfred Rest, Lilly Sucharipa-Behrmann, and Karl Zemanek, 721–748. The Hague: Kluwer Law International.

Trebilcock, Michael J., and Robert Howse. 2005. *The Regulation of International Trade*. 3rd ed. Abingdon: Routledge.

Trenkwalder, Verena. 2005. 'Grenzüberschreitende Gruppe und Abkommensrecht'. In *Gruppenbesteuerung: Kommentar und systematische Darstellungen*, edited by Peter Quantschnigg, Markus Achatz, Ernst Haidenthaler, Verena Trenkwalder, and Michael Tumpel, 411–433. Vienna: Linde.

Tsai, Edward S. 1999. '"Like" Is a Four-Letter Word – GATT Article III's "Like Product" Conundrum'. *Berkeley Journal of International Law* 17 (1): 26–60.

Tumpel, Michael. 1992. 'EWR-Diskriminierungsverbote und Direkte Steuern'. *ecolex*, 655–659.

Tumpel, Michael. 1994. *Harmonisierung der direkten Unternehmensbesteuerung in der EU*. Schriftenreihe Europa des Bundeskanzleramts 4. Vienna: Österreichische Staatsdruckerei.

Tumpel, Michael, and Christian Stangl. 2006. 'Das Betriebstättendiskriminierungsverbot'. In *Die Diskriminierungsverbote im Recht der Doppelbesteuerungsabkommen*, edited by Michael Lang, Josef Schuch, and Claus Staringer, 69–91. Vienna: Linde.

Tussman, Jospeh, and Jacobus tenBroek. 1949. 'The Equal Protection of the Laws'. *California Law Review* 37 (3): 341–381.

Unterhalter, David. 2008. 'The Burden of Proof in WTO Dispute Settlement'. In *The WTO: Governance, Dispute Settlement, and Developing Countries*, edited by Merit E. Janow, Victoria Donaldson, and Alan Yanovich, 543–552. New York: Juris Publishing.

Unterhalter, David. 2009. 'Allocating the Burden of Proof in WTO Dispute Settlement Proceedings'. *Cornell International Law Journal* 42 (2): 209–221.

Valinaki, Fay. 2016. '"Repairing the Defects" of Article 2.1 of the WTO Technical Barriers to Trade Agreement: An Amendment Proposal'. *Legal Issues of Economic Integration* 43 (1): 65–96.

Valkenburg, Koos W. 1995. 'Netherlands: Holding Structures and Exemptions from Capital Duty: An Overview of Recent Developments Concerning Non-discrimination Provisions in Tax Treaties'. *European Taxation* 35 (6): 170–178.

Van Brussel, Yves. 2015. 'The Relevance of Residence as a Safeguard in Article 24(1) of the OECD Model'. In *Non-discrimination in European and Tax Treaty Law: Open Issues and Recent Challenges*, edited by Kasper Dziurdź, and Christoph Marchgraber, 353–376. Series on International Tax Law 94. Vienna: Linde.

Van Calster, Geert. 2001. 'Getting There Slowly: International Trade Law and Public Health in the WTO Asbestos Panel'. *European Environmental Law Review (European Energy and Environmental Law Review)* 10 (4): 113–119.

Van den Bossche, Peter. 2008. 'Looking for Proportionality in WTO Law'. *Legal Issues of Economic Integration* 35 (3): 283–294.

Van den Bossche, Peter, and Werner Zdouc. 2013. *The Law and Policy of the World Trade Organization: Text, Cases and Materials*. 3rd ed. Cambridge: Cambridge University Press.

Vanistendael, Frans. 2008. 'Group Taxation under Domestic Law: Common Law Versus Civil Law Countries'. In *International and EC Tax Aspects of Groups of Companies*, edited by Guglielmo Maisto, 45–91. EC and International Tax Law Series 4. Amsterdam: IBFD.

Vanistendael, Frans. 2010. 'Taxation and Non-discrimination, a Reconsideration of Withholding Taxes in the OECD'. *World Tax Journal* 2 (2): 175–191.

Vanistendael, Frans. 2016. 'Non-discrimination: Can the EU Learn from the OECD Model Convention and Vice Versa?'. In *Non-discrimination in Tax Treaties: Selected Issues from a Global Perspective*, edited by Dennis Weber, and Pasquale Pistone, 225–254. EC and International Tax Law Series 14. Amsterdam: IBFD.

Vann, Richard. 2009. '"Liable to Tax" and Company Residence under Tax Treaties'. In *Residence of Companies under Tax Treaties and EC Law*, edited by Guglielmo Maisto, 197–271. EC and International Tax Law Series 5. Amsterdam: IBFD.

Verhoosel, Gaëtan. 2002. *National Treatment and WTO Dispute Settlement: Adjudicating the Boundaries of Regulatory Autonomy*. Oxford; Portland, Oregon: Hart Publishing.

Villiger, Mark E. 2009. *Commentary on the 1969 Vienna Convention on the Law of Treaties*. Leiden; Boston: Martinus Nijhoff Publishers.

Vinnitskiy, Danil V. 2016. 'Non-discrimination in Tax Treaties – Art. 24(4) and (5) OECD MC: A Russian Approach to Tax Treaty Interpretation'. In *Non-discrimination in Tax Treaties: Selected Issues from a Global Perspective*, edited by Dennis Weber, and Pasquale Pistone, 133–166. EC and International Tax Law Series 14. Amsterdam: IBFD.

Vogel, Klaus. 1970. 'Das Verbot der Betriebstättendiskriminierung im Körperschaftsteuerrecht: Dargestellt am Beispiel des deutsch-französischen Doppelbesteuerungsabkommens von 1959'. *Außenwirtschaftsdienst des Betriebs-Beraters (Recht der Internationalen Wirtschaft)* 16 (8): 349–357.

Vogel, Klaus. 1982. 'Ausländische Gerichtsentscheidungen als Anregung für den deutschen Steuerrechtler'. *Steuer und Wirtschaft* 59 (1): 66–70.

Vogel, Klaus. 1996. 'Wesen und Wirkungen der Freistellung: Besonders bei negativen Einkünften und Vermögenswerten'. In *Freistellung im internationalen Steuerrecht: Beiträge von Klaus Vogel, Franz Wassermeyer, Albrecht E. H. Schäfer, Helmut Krabbe, Hansgeorg Hauser mit Diskussionsbeiträgen eines Münchener Symposions*, edited by Klaus Vogel, Franz Wassermeyer, Albrecht E. H. Schäfer, Helmut Krabbe, and Hansgeorg Hauser, 1–19. Münchener Schriften zum Internationalen Steuerrecht 21. Munich: C.H. Beck.

Vogel, Klaus. 1997. *Klaus Vogel on Double Taxation Conventions: A Commentary to the OECD-, UN- and US Model Conventions for the Avoidance of Double Taxation on Income and Capital – With Particular Reference to German Treaty Practice*. 3rd ed. London: Kluwer Law International.

Vogel, Klaus. 2002a. 'Tax Treaty News'. *Bulletin for International Fiscal Documentation (Bulletin for International Taxation)* 56 (1): 2–3.

Vogel, Klaus. 2002b. 'Tax Treaty News'. *Bulletin for International Fiscal Documentation (Bulletin for International Taxation)* 56 (7): 286–287.

Vogel, Klaus. 2003. 'Tax Treaty News'. *Bulletin for International Fiscal Documentation (Bulletin for International Taxation)* 57 (2): 39–40.

Vogel, Klaus. 2005. '"State of Residence" May as Well Be 'State of Source' – There Is No Contradiction'. *Bulletin for International Fiscal Documentation (Bulletin for International Taxation)* 59 (10): 420–423.

Vogel, Klaus. 2008. 'Artikel 23'. In *Doppelbesteuerungsabkommen der Bundesrepublik Deutschland auf dem Gebiet der Steuern vom Einkommen und Vermögen: Kommentar auf der Grundlage der Musterabkommen*, edited by Moris Lehner, 5th ed. Munich: C.H. Beck.

Voon, Tania. 2012. 'United States–Measures Affecting the Production and Sale of Clove Cigarettes'. *American Journal of International Law* 106 (4): 824–830.

Vranes, Erich. 2009. *Trade and the Environment: Fundamental Issues in International Law, WTO Law, and Legal Theory*. Oxford: Oxford University Press.

Waldron, Jeremy. 1991. 'The Substance of Equality'. *Michigan Law Review* 89 (6): 1350–1370.

Wandl, Klemens S. 2015. 'Prevention of Economic Double Taxation under Article 24(3) of the OECD Model'. In *Non-discrimination in European and Tax Treaty Law: Open Issues and Recent Challenges*, edited by Kasper Dziurdź, and Christoph Marchgraber, 427–460. Series on International Tax Law 94. Vienna: Linde.

Warren, Alvin C., Jr. 2001. 'Income Tax Discrimination Against International Commerce'. *Tax Law Review* 54 (2, Winter): 131–170.

Wassermeyer, Franz, and Christian Kaeser. 2013. 'Art. 4 MA'. In *Doppelbesteuerung: Kommentar zu allen deutschen Doppelbesteuerungsabkommen*, edited by Franz Wassermeyer, 122nd ed. Munich: C.H. Beck.

Wassermeyer, Franz, and Michael Schwenke. 2016. 'Art. 24 MA'. In *Doppelbesteuerung: Kommentar zu allen deutschen Doppelbesteuerungsabkommen*, edited by Franz Wassermeyer, Christian Kaeser, Michael Schwenke, and Klaus-Dieter Drüen, 134th ed. Munich: C.H. Beck.

Wattel, Peter. 2000. 'Progressive Taxation of Non-residents and Intra-EC Allocation of Personal Tax Allowances: Why *Schumacker*, *Asscher*, *Gilly* and *Gschwind* Do Not Suffice'. *European Taxation* 40 (6): 210–223.

Wattel, Peter. 2015. 'Non-discrimination *à la Cour*: The ECJ's (Lack of) Comparability Analysis in Direct Tax Cases'. *European Taxation* 55 (12): 542–553.

Wattel, Peter. 2016. 'Non-discrimination à la Cour: The ECJ's (Lack of) Comparability Analysis in Direct Tax Cases'. In *Non-discrimination in Tax Treaties: Selected Issues from a Global Perspective*, edited by Dennis Weber, and Pasquale Pistone, 255–282. EC and International Tax Law Series 14. Amsterdam: IBFD.

Weiler, Joseph H. H. 2009. 'Law, Culture, and Values in the WTO – Gazing into the Crystal Ball'. In *The Oxford Handbook of International Trade Law*, edited by Daniel Bethlehem, Donald M. McRae, Rodney Neufeld, and Isabelle Van Damme, 749–772. Oxford: Oxford University Press.

Westen, Peter. 1982a. 'On "Confusing Ideas": Reply'. *Yale Law Journal* 91 (6): 1153–1165.

Westen, Peter. 1982b. 'The Empty Idea of Equality'. *Harvard Law Review* 95 (3): 537–596.

Westen, Peter. 1983a. 'The Meaning of Equality in Law, Science, Math, and Morals: A Reply'. *Michigan Law Review* 81 (3): 604–663.

Westen, Peter. 1983b. 'To Lure the Tarantula from Its Hole: A Response'. *Columbia Law Review* 83 (5): 1186–1208.

Westen, Peter. 1990. *Speaking of Equality: An Analysis of the Rhetorical Force of 'Equality' in Moral and Legal Discourse*. Studies in Moral, Political and Legal Philosophy. Princeton: Princeton University Press.

Westin, Richard A. 1997. *Environmental Tax Initiatives and Multilateral Trade Agreements: Dangerous Collisions*. Cambridge: Kluwer Law international.

Widhalm, Christian. 1995. 'Rechtsgrundlagen und Anwendungsbereich des Progressionsvorbehalts'. In *Die Methoden zur Vermeidung der Doppelbesteuerung: Anrechnungs- und Befreiungsmethode*, edited by Wolfgang Gassner, Michael Lang, and Eduard Lechner, 153–171. Vienna: Linde.

Widmer, Max. 1993a. 'Zuteilung und Besteuerung der Unternehmensgewinne bei Betriebstätten'. In *Handbuch des Internationalen Steuerrechts der Schweiz*, edited by Ernst Höhn, 2nd ed., 226–288. Schriftenreihe Finanzwissenschaft und Finanzrecht 38. Berne: Haupt.

Widmer, Max. 1993b. 'Zuteilung und Besteuerung der Unternehmensgewinne bei Betriebstätten'. In *Handbuch des Internationalen Steuerrechts der Schweiz*, edited by Ernst Höhn, 2nd ed., 204–253. Schriftenreihe Finanzwissenschaft und Finanzrecht 38. Berne: Haupt.

Wiers, Jochem, and James Mathis. 2001. 'The Report of the Appellate Body in the *Asbestos* Dispute: *WTO Appellate Body Report 12 March 2001, WT/DS135/AB/R, European Communities – Measures Affecting Asbestos and Asbestos-Containing Products*'. *Legal Issues of Economic Integration* 28 (2): 211–225.

Wiesner, Werner, and Gunter Mayr. 2005. 'Aktuelle Zweifelsfragen zur Gruppenbesteuerung'. *Recht der Wirtschaft* 23 (9): 566–572.

Wiman, Bertil. 2000. 'Equalizing the Income Tax Burden in a Group of Companies'. *Intertax* 28 (10): 352–359.

Wiman, Bertil. 2013. 'Sweden: Non-deductibility of Interest Payments'. In *Tax Treaty Case Law Around the Globe 2012*, edited by Eric C.C.M. Kemmeren, Daniël S. Smit, Peter Essers, Luc De Broe, Michael Lang, Pasquale Pistone, Josef Schuch, Claus Staringer, and Alfred Storck, 329–337. Series on International Tax Law 78. Amsterdam; Vienna: IBFD; Linde.

Wittendorff, Jens. 2010. *Transfer Pricing and the Arm's Length Principle in International Tax Law*. Series on International Taxation 35. Alphen on the Rhine: Kluwer Law International.

World Trade Organization. 1995. *GATT Analytical Index: Guide to GATT Law and Practice*. 6th ed. Vol. 1. Geneva: World Trade Organization; Bernan Press.

World Trade Organization. 2008. *10 Benefits of the WTO Trading System*. 1st ed. Geneva: World Trade Organization.

World Trade Organization. 2012. *WTO Analytical Index: Guide to WTO Law and Practice*. 3rd ed. Vol. 1. Geneva: World Trade Organization.

World Trade Organization. 2015. *Understanding the WTO*. 5th ed. Geneva: World Trade Organization.

Wunderlich, Caroline. 2009. 'Artikel 24'. In *DBA Deutschland/USA Doppelbesteuerungsabkommen*, edited by Dieter Endres, Friedhelm Jacob, Marion Gohr, and Martin Klein. Munich: C.H. Beck.

Wundsam, Walter, and Hans Zöchling. 1990. 'Nochmals: Verlustverrechnung für Steuerausländer: Zweierlei Maß und Ziel'. *Österreichische Steuerzeitung* 43 (9): 100–102.

Yong, Singyuan. 2010. 'Triangular Treaty Cases: Putting Permanent Establishments in Their Proper Place'. *Bulletin for International Taxation* 64 (3): 152–164.

Young, Margaret A. 2014. 'Trade Measures to Address Environmental Concerns in Faraway Places: Jurisdictional Issues'. *Review of European Community & International Environmental Law* 23 (3): 302–317.

Zalasiński, Adam. 2007. 'Article 24(1) of the OECD Model Convention and the Exclusion of MFN Treatment–A Comment on the OECD Public Discussion Draft'. *Intertax* 35 (8/9): 460–472.

Zanutto Velasques, Rodolfo. 2015. 'Creditor Non-discrimination under Article 24(4) of the OECD Model in the Case of Deduction and Non-inclusion Schemes'. In *Non-discrimination in European and Tax Treaty Law: Open Issues and Recent Challenges*, edited by Kasper Dziurdź, and Christoph Marchgraber, 487–509. Series on International Tax Law 94. Vienna: Linde.

Zedalis, Rex J. 1994. 'A Theory of the GATT "Like" Product Common Language Cases'. *Vanderbilt Journal of Transnational Law* 27 (1): 33–134.

Zedalis, Rex J. 1997. 'Product v. Non-product Based Distinctions in GATT Article III Trade and Environment Jurisprudence: Recent Developments'. *European Environmental Law Review (European Energy and Environmental Law Review)* 6 (4): 108–112.

Zell, Joshua A. 2016. 'Just Between You and Me: Mutual Recognition Agreements and the Most-Favoured Nation Principle'. *World Trade Review* 15 (1): 3–23.

Zhai, Gang. 2009. 'Triangular Cases Involving Income Attributable to PEs'. *Tax Notes International* 53 (12): 1105–1123.

Zhou, Weihuan. 2012a. 'The Role of Regulatory Purpose under Articles III:2 and 4 – Toward Consistency Between Negotiating History and WTO Jurisprudence'. *World Trade Review* 11 (1): 81–118.

Zhou, Weihuan. 2012b. '*US – Clove Cigarettes* and *US – Tuna II (Mexico)*: Implications for the Role of Regulatory Purpose under Article III:4 of the GATT'. *Journal of International Economic Law* 15 (4): 1075–1122.

Zorman, Gregor. 2003. 'The Non-discrimination of Permanent Establishment under Tax Treaty Law'. In *Permanent Establishments in International Tax Law*, edited by Hans-Jörgen Aigner, and Mario Züger, 275–296. Schriftenreihe zum Internationalen Steuerrecht 29. Vienna: Linde.

Zöchling, Hans. 1990. 'Die Verlustverrechnung für beschränkt Steuerpflichtige: Österreich auf dem Weg zur Unitary Taxation?'. *Österreichische Steuerzeitung* 43 (5): 50–51.

Zöchling, Hans. 1993. 'Austria'. In *Non-discrimination Rules in International Taxation*, edited by International Fiscal Association, 297–320. Cahiers de Droit Fiscal International – Studies on International Fiscal Law, LXXVIIIb. Deventer: Kluwer Law; Taxation Publishers.

Zöchling, Hans. 1994. 'Diskriminierungsverbote im österreichischen Steuerrecht'. *Steuer und Wirtschaft International* 4 (1): 16–21.

Züger, Mario. 2001. 'Die Bedeutung von Diskriminierungsverboten für die Lösung von Zurechnungskonflikten bei Personengesellschaften'. *Steuer und Wirtschaft International* 11 (3): 111–120.

Table of Cases

GATT 1947

Working Party Reports

Brazil – Internal Taxes (1949)

Australia – Ammonium Sulphate (1950)

Border Tax Adjustments (1970)

Panel Reports

Germany – Sardines (1952)

EEC – Animal Feed Proteins (1978)

Spain – Unroasted Coffee (1981)

WTO

Panel Reports

Appellate Body Reports

Article 24

Austria

Belgium

Finland

France

Germany

Netherlands

Spain

Sweden

United Kingdom

United States of America

European Union

OEEC/OECD Materials

Steering Group

General

DAF/CFA/2584

Working Party No. 1 on Double Taxation of the Committee on Fiscal Affairs, Steering Group, *Non-discrimination*, DAF/CFA/2584, 1 March 1973., 299, 403, 481, 517, 522

Minutes

DAFFE/CFA/WP1/MR/M(97)1

Working Party No. 1 on Double Taxation of the Committee on Fiscal Affairs, Steering Group on the Revision of the Model Tax Convention, *Summary Record of the Eleventh Meeting of the Steering Group on the Revision of the Model Tax Convention (Held on 17 February 1997)*, DAFFE/CFA/WP1/MR/M(97)1, 15 July 1997 (distribution)., 215

Working Party No. 1

General

CFA/WP1(73)10

Working Party No. 1 on Double Taxation of the Committee on Fiscal Affairs, *Revised Articles and Commentaries of the 1963 OECD Draft Convention*, CFA/WP1(73)10, 12 November 1973., 143, 144, 194

DAF/CFA/WP1/71.3

Working Party No. 1 on Double Taxation of the Committee on Fiscal Affairs, *Summary of Discussions at the First Meeting of the Working Party N° 1 on Double Taxation (held from 22nd to 25th June, 1971)*, DAF/CFA/WP1/71.3, 26 July 1971., 150, 299, 402, 478, 480

DAF/CFA/WP1/72/3

Working Party No. 1 on Double Taxation of the Committee on Fiscal Affairs, *Summary of Discussions at the Third Meeting of Working Party No. 1 on Double Taxation (held from 11th to 14th January, 1972)*, DAF/CFA/WP1/72/3, 14 February 1972., 144, 150, 299, 403, 480, 481, 504, 517, 522

DAF/CFA/WP1/73.1

Working Party No. 1 on Double Taxation of the Committee on Fiscal Affairs, *Meeting of the Steering Group of Working Party N°1 on Double Taxation*, DAF/CFA/WP1/73.1, 4 January 1973., 403

DAF/CFA/WP1/73.2

Working Party No. 1 on Double Taxation of the Committee on Fiscal Affairs, *Conclusions of the First Meeting of the Steering Group (held on 18/19th January, 1973) (Note by the Secretariat)*, DAF/CFA/WP1/73.2, 26 January 1973., 147, 299, 403

DAF/CFA/WP1/73.5

Working Party No. 1 on Double Taxation of the Committee on Fiscal Affairs, *Summary of Discussions at the Seventh Meeting of Working Party N° 1 on Double Taxation (13th - 15th February, 1973)*, DAF/CFA/WP1/73.5, 11 April 1973., 147, 409

DAF/CFA/WP1(73)8

Working Party No. 1 on Double Taxation of the Committee on Fiscal Affairs, *Summary of Discussions at the Eight Meeting of Working Party N° 1 on Double Taxation (8th - 11th May, 1973)*, DAF/CFA/WP1(73)8, 5 July 1973., 299, 404, 481, 517, 522

DAF/CFA/WP1/73.11

Working Party No. 1 on Double Taxation of the Committee on Fiscal Affairs, *Non-discrimination - Revision of Article 24 of the OECD Draft Convention*, DAF/CFA/WP1/73.11, 23 August 1973., 299, 404

DAF/CFA/WP1/73.12

Working Party No. 1 on Double Taxation of the Committee on Fiscal Affairs, *Note on the Ninth Meeting (Tuesday 18th - Thursday 20th September 1973)*, DAF/CFA/WP1/73.12, 5 October 1973., 299, 404

DAF/CFA/WP1(73)13

Working Party No. 1 on Double Taxation of the Committee on Fiscal Affairs, *Summary of Discussions at the Ninth Meeting of Working Party N° 1 on Double Taxation (18th-21st September, 1973)*, DAF/CFA/WP1(73)13, 5 November 1973., 143, 299, 404

DAF/CFA/WP1/75.8

Working Party No. 1 on Double Taxation of the Committee on Fiscal Affairs, *Summary of Discussions at the Fifteenth Meeting of Working Party No. 1 on Double Taxation (held from 4th to 7th March, 1975)*, DAF/CFA/WP1/75.8, 26 March 1975., 410

DAF/CFA/WP1/75.14

Working Party No. 1 on Double Taxation of the Committee on Fiscal Affairs, *Summary of Discussion Concerning the Seventeenth Meeting of Working Party No. 1 on Double Taxation (held from 7th to 10th October, 1975)*, DAF/CFA/WP1/75.14, 30 October 1975., 410, 411

DAF/CFA/WP1/76.19

Working Party No. 1 on Double Taxation of the Committee on Fiscal Affairs, *Revised Commentary of the 1963 Draft Convention (Note by the Secretariat)*, DAF/CFA/WP1/76.19, 5 November 1976., 144, 411

DAFFE/CFA/WP1(91)1

Working Party No. 1 on Double Taxation of the Committee on Fiscal Affairs, *Scope of the Article on Non-discrimination (Note by the Delegate for France)*, DAFFE/CFA/WP1(91)1, 22 March 1991., 175, 253

DAFFE/CFA/WP1(91)5

Working Party No. 1 on Double Taxation of the Committee on Fiscal Affairs, *Scope of the Article on Non-discrimination (Note by the Delegate for France)*, DAFFE/CFA/WP1(91)5, 24 August 1991., 176

DAFFE/CFA/WP1(92)4

Working Party No. 1 on Double Taxation of the Committee on Fiscal Affairs, *Scope of the Non-discrimination Article: Questionnaire and Summary of Country Replies (Note by the Secretariat)*, DAFFE/CFA/WP1(92)4, 10 February 1992., 176

DAFFE/CFA/WP1(92)17

Working Party No. 1 on Double Taxation of the Committee on Fiscal Affairs, *Summary of Replies to the Questionnaire on the Article on Non-discrimination (Note by the Secretariat)*, DAFFE/CFA/WP1(92)17, 5 August 1992., 176

DAFFE/CFA/WP1(94)9

Working Party No. 1 on Double Taxation of the Committee on Fiscal Affairs, *The 1995 Update to the Model Tax Convention (Note by the Secretariat)*, DAFFE/CFA/WP1(94)9, 8 November 1994., 148

DAFFE/CFA/WP1/MR(95)2

Working Party No. 1 on Double Taxation of the Committee on Fiscal Affairs, Steering Group on the Revision of the Model Convention, *Preparing for the 1996 Update*, DAFFE/CFA/WP1/MR(95)2, 7 February 1995., 148, 215, 471

DAFFE/CFA/WP1(95)5

Working Party No. 1 on Double Taxation of the Committee on Fiscal Affairs, *Steering Group Recommendations for Update 'A' to the Model Tax Convention (Note by the Secretariat)*, DAFFE/CFA/WP1(95)5, 15 February 1995., 148, 471

DAFFE/CFA/WP1(95)5/REV1

Working Party No. 1 on Double Taxation of the Committee on Fiscal Affairs, *Working Party Proposals for the 1995+ Update to the Model Tax Convention (Note by the Secretariat)*, DAFFE/CFA/WP1(95)5REV1, 30 June 1995., 148, 471

DAFFE/CFA/WP1(95)5/REV2

Working Party No. 1 on Double Taxation of the Committee on Fiscal Affairs, *Working Party Proposals for the 1995+ Update to the Model Tax Convention (Note by the Secretariat)*, DAFFE/CFA/WP1(95)5REV2, 17 August 1995., 148, 471

DAFFE/CFA/WP1(95)5/REV3

Working Party No. 1 on Double Taxation of the Committee on Fiscal Affairs, *Working Party Proposals for the 1995+ Update*, DAFFE/CFA/WP1(95)5REV3, 22 December 1995 (distribution)., 148, 471

DAFFE/CFA/WP1(96)17

Working Party No. 1 on Double Taxation of the Committee on Fiscal Affairs, *Proposals for the Next Update to the Model Tax Convention*, DAFFE/CFA/WP1(96)17, 27 August 1996 (distribution)., 471

Minutes

DAFFE/CFA/WP1/M(91)1

Working Party No. 1 on Double Taxation of the Committee on Fiscal Affairs, *Summary Record of the Fifty-First Meeting of Working Party No. 1 (held on 22, 23 and 25 April 1991)*, DAFFE/CFA/WP1/M(91)1, 26 April 1991., 175

DAFFE/CFA/WP1/M(91)2

Working Party No. 1 on Double Taxation of the Committee on Fiscal Affairs, *Summary Record of the Fifty-Second Meeting of Working Party No. 1 (held on 10, 11 and 12 September 1991)*, DAFFE/CFA/WP1/M(91)2, 11 October 1991., 176

DAFFE/CFA/WP1/M(92)1

Working Party No. 1 on Double Taxation of the Committee on Fiscal Affairs, *Summary Record of the Fifty-Third Meeting of Working Party No. 1 (held on 18, 19 and 20 February 1992)*, DAFFE/CFA/WP1/M(92)1, 9 March 1991., 176

DAFFE/CFA/WP1/M(97)1

Working Party No. 1 on Double Taxation of the Committee on Fiscal Affairs, *Summary Record of the 63rd Meeting of Working Party No. 1 (Held on 18, 19 and 20 February 1997)*, DAFFE/CFA/WP1/M(97)1, 11 July 1997 (distribution)., 471

Working Group No. 4

CFA/WP1(71)1

Working Party No. 1 on Double Taxation of the Committee on Fiscal Affairs, Working Group No. 4, *Fourth Report on Amendments to be made to Article 24 of the Draft Convention relating to Non-discrimination*, received on 27 May 1971, CFA/WP1(71)1, 8 June 1971., 143, 144, 145, 150, 185, 186, 194, 299

CFA/WP1(76)1

Working Party No. 1 on Double Taxation of the Committee on Fiscal Affairs, Working Group No. 15, *Third Report of Working Group No. 15 (Switzerland – Ireland – Japan – Netherlands): Questions Connected with the Methods for Elimination of Double Taxation*, CFA/WP1(76)1, 16 January 1976., 410, 411

CFA/WP1(76)4

Working Party No. 1 on Double Taxation of the Committee on Fiscal Affairs, Working Group No. 15, *Questions Connected with the Methods for Elimination of Double Taxation (Note by the Secretariat)*, CFA/WP1(76)4, 8 March 1976., 410, 411

Working Group No. 23

CFA/WP1(71)6

Working Party No. 1 on Double Taxation of the Committee on Fiscal Affairs, Working Group No. 23, *Final Report – Part I: Double Taxation of Dividends received by an Individual (Note by the Secretary of the Committee)*, CFA/WP1(71)6, 30 December 1971., 477

Fiscal Committee

General

FC(58)2

Fiscal Committee, *Draft Report by the Fiscal Committee on its Activities (Note by the Secretariat)*, FC(58)2, 13 February 1958., 160, 165, 172, 183

FC(58)2(Rev. 1) Part I and II

Fiscal Committee, *Draft Report by the Fiscal Committee on its Activities (Note by the Secretariat)*, FC(58)2(Rev. 1) Part I and II, 19 April 1958., 161, 165, 172, 183

FC(64)1

Fiscal Committee, *Note by the Japanese Delegation on the Position of Japan in relation to the Draft Double Taxation Convention on Income and Capital (Note by the Secretariat of the Committee)*, FC(64)1, 5 August 1964., 521

DAF/FC/69.17

Fiscal Committee, *Notes on Discussion of Reports of Working Parties N° 4, 28, 29 and 30 during the 33rd Session of the Fiscal Committee held from 9th to 12th December, 1969*, DAF/FC/69.17, 29 December 1969., 143

DAF/FC/70.5

Fiscal Committee, *Notes on Discussion of Reports of Working Parties N° 4, 26 and 28 during the 34th Session of the Fiscal Committee held from 3rd to 6th March, 1970*, DAF/FC/70.5, 23 March 1970., 143, 144, 145, 149, 161, 194, 209, 521

DAF/FC/70.5 Corrigendum

Fiscal Committee, *Notes on Discussion of Reports of Working Parties N° 4, 26 and 28 during the 34th Session of the Fiscal Committee held from 3rd to 6th March, 1970*, DAF/FC/70.5 Corrigendum, 5 May 1970., 521

DAF/FC/71.6

Fiscal Committee, *Note on the Discussions at the 39th Session of the Fiscal Committee, held from 20th to 23rd April, 1971 on Non-discrimination (Working Party No. 4) and the Taxation of Shipping and Air Transport Profits (Working Party No. 29)*, DAF/FC/71.6, 24 May 1971., 143, 144, 145, 150, 162, 185, 186, 194, 299, 480

Minutes

FC/M(56)1

Fiscal Committee, *Minutes of the 1st Session held at the Château de la Muette, Paris, on Wednesday 23rd and Thursday 24th May, 1956*, FC/M(56)1, 6 June 1956., 142, 173

FC/M(57)2

Fiscal Committee, *Minutes of the 4th Session held at the Château de la Muette, Paris, on Tuesday 4th, Wednesday 5th, Thursday 6th and Friday 7th June, 1957*, FC/M(57)2, 3 July 1957., 146, 153, 155, 160, 206, 209

FC/M(57)3

Fiscal Committee, *Minutes of the 5th Session held at the Château de la Muette, Paris, on Tuesday 1st, Wednesday 2nd and Thursday 3rd October, 1957*, FC/M(57)3, 5 November 1957., 174, 184, 206

FC/M(58)1

Fiscal Committee, *Minutes of the 6th Session held at the Château de la Muette, Paris, on Monday 25th, Tuesday 26th and Wednesday 27th November, 1957*, FC/M(58)1, 6 January 1958., 184

FC/M(58)2

Fiscal Committee, *Minutes of the 7th Session held at the Château de la Muette, Paris, on Tuesday 25th, Wednesday 26th and Thursday 27th February, 1958*, FC/M(58)2, 29 March 1958., 217

Official Publications

Discussion Drafts

Index

G

H

I

N

O

P

R

V

W

SERIES ON INTERNATIONAL TAXATION

1. Alberto Xavier, *The Taxation of Foreign Investment in Brazil,* 1980 (ISBN 90-200-0582-0).
2. Hugh J. Ault & Albert J. Rädler, *The German Corporation Tax Law with 1980 Amendments,* 1981 (ISBN 90-200-0642-8).
3. Paul R. McDaniel & Hugh J. Ault, *Introduction to United States International Taxation,* 1981 (ISBN 90-6544-004-6).
4. Albert J. Rädler, *German Transfer Pricing/Prix de Transfer en Allemagne,* 1984 (ISBN 90-6544-143-3).
5. Paul R. McDaniel & Stanley S. Surrey, *International Aspects of Tax Expenditures: A Comparative Study,* 1985 (ISBN 90-654-4163-8).
6. Kees van Raad, *Nondiscrimination in International Tax Law,* 1986 (ISBN 90-6544-266-9).
7. Sijbren Cnossen (ed.), *Tax Coordination in the European Community,* 1987 (ISBN 90-6544-272-3).
8. Ben Terra, *Sales Taxation. The Case of Value Added Tax in the European Community,* 1989 (ISBN 90-6544-381-9).
9. Rutsel S.J. Martha, *The Jurisdiction to Tax in International Law: Theory and Practice of Legislative Fiscal Jurisdiction,* 1989 (ISBN 90-654-4416-5).
10. Paul R. McDaniel & Hugh J. Ault, *Introduction to United States International Taxation* (3rd revised edition), 1989 (ISBN 90-6544-423-8).
11. Manuel Pires, *International Juridicial Double Taxation of Income,* 1989 (ISBN 90-6544-426-2).
12. A.H.M. Daniels, *Issues in International Partnership Taxation,* 1991 (ISBN 90-654-4577-3).
13. Arvid A. Skaar, *Permanent Establishment: Erosion of a Tax Treaty Principle,* 1992 (ISBN 90-6544-594-3).
14. Cyrille David & Geerten M.M. Michielse (eds), *Tax Treatment of Financial Instruments,* 1996 (ISBN 90-654-4666-4).
15. Herbert H. Alpert & Kees van Raad (eds), *Essays on International Taxation,* 1993 (ISBN 90-654-4781-4).
16. Wolfgang Gassner, Michael Lang & Eduard Lechner (eds), *Tax Treaties and EC Law,* 1997 (ISBN 90-411-0680-4).
17. Glória Teixeira, *Taxing Corporate Profits in the EU,* 1997 (ISBN 90-411-0703-7).
18. Michael Lang et al. (eds), *Multilateral Tax Treaties,* 1998 (ISBN 90-411-0704-5).
19. Stef van Weeghel, *The Improper Use of Tax Treaties,* 1998 (ISBN 90-411-0737-1).
20. Klaus Vogel (ed.), *Interpretation of Tax Law and Treaties and Transfer Pricing in Japan and Germany,* 1998 (ISBN 90-411-9655-2).
21. Bertil Wiman (ed.), *International Studies in Taxation: Law and Economics; Liber Amicorum Leif Mutén,* 1999 (ISBN 90-411-9692-7).
22. Alfonso J. Martín Jiménez, *Towards Corporate Tax Harmonization in the European Community,* 1999 (ISBN 90-411-9690-0).

23. Ramon J. Jeffery, *The Impact of State Sovereignty on Global Trade and International Taxation*, 1999 (ISBN 90-411-9703-6).
24. A.J. Easson, *Taxation of Foreign Direct Investment*, 1999 (ISBN 90-411-9741-9).
25. Marjaana Helminen, *The Dividend Concept in International Tax Law: Dividend Payments Between Corporate Entities*, 1999 (ISBN 90-411-9765-6).
26. Paul Kirchhof, Moris Lehner, Kees van Raad, Arndt Raupach & Michael-Rodi (eds), *International and Comparative Taxation: Essays in Honour of Klaus Vogel*, 2002 (ISBN 90-411-9841-5).
27. Krister Andersson, Peter Melz & Christer Silfverberg (eds), *Liber Amicorum Sven-Olof Lodin*, 2001 (ISBN 90-411-9850-4).
28. Juan Martín Jovanovich, *Customs Valuation and Transfer Pricing: Is It Possible to Harmonize Customs and Tax Rules?*, Second Edition, 2018 (ISBN 978-90-411-6134-5).
29. Stefano Simontacchi, *Taxation of Capital Gains under the OECD Model Convention: With Special Regard to Immovable Property*, 2007 (ISBN 978-90-411-2549-1).
30. Michael Lang, Josef Schuch, & Claus Staringer (eds), *Tax Treaty Law and EC Law*, 2007 (ISBN 978-90-411-2629-0).
31. Duncan Bentley, *Taxpayers' Rights: Theory Origin and Implementation*, 2007 (ISBN 978-90-411-2650-4).
32. Sergio André Rocha, *Interpretation of Double Taxation Conventions: General Theory and Brazilian Perspective*, 2008 (ISBN 978-90-411-2822-5).
33. Robert F. van Brederode, *Systems of General Sales Taxation: Theory, Policy and Practice*, 2009 (ISBN 978-90-411-2832-4).
34. John G. Head & Richard Krever (eds), *Tax Reform in the 21st Century: A Volume in Memory of Richard Musgrave*, 2009 (ISBN 978-90-411-2829-4).
35. Jens Wittendorff, *Transfer Pricing and the Arm's Length Principle in International Tax Law*, 2010 (ISBN 978-90-411-3270-3).
36. Marjaana Helminen, *The International Tax Law Concept of Dividend*, Second Edition, 2017 (ISBN 978-90-411-8394-1).
37. Robert F. van Brederode (ed.), *Immovable Property under VAT: A Comparative Global Analysis*, 2011 (ISBN 978-90-411-3126-3).
38. Dennis Weber & Stef van Weeghel, *The 2010 OECD Updates: Model Tax Convention & Transfer Pricing Guidelines - A Critical Review*, 2011 (ISBN 978-90-411-3812-5).
39. Yariv Brauner & Martin James McMahon, Jr. (eds), *The Proper Tax Base: Structural Fairness from an International and Comparative Perspective—Essays in Honour of Paul McDaniel*, 2012 (ISBN 978-90-411-3286-4).
40. Robert F. van Brederode (ed.), *Science, Technology and Taxation*, 2012 (ISBN 978-90-411-3125-6).
41. Oskar Henkow, *The VAT/GST Treatment of Public Bodies*, 2013 (ISBN 978-90-411-4663-2).
42. Jean Schaffner, *How Fixed Is a Permanent Establishment?*, 2013 (ISBN 978-90-411-4662-5).

43. Miguel Correia, *Taxation of Corporate Groups*, 2013 (ISBN 978-90-411-4841-4).
44. Veronika Daurer, *Tax Treaties and Developing Countries*, 2014 (ISBN 978-90-411-4982-4).
45. Claire Micheau, *State Aid, Subsidy and Tax Incentives under EU and WTO Law*, 2014 (ISBN 978-90-411-4555-0).
46. Robert F. van Brederode & Richard Krever (eds), *Legal Interpretation of Tax Law*, 2014 (ISBN 978-90-411-4945-9).
47. Radhakishan Rawal, *Taxation of Cross-border Services*, 2014 (ISBN 978-90-411-4947-3).
48. João Dácio Rolim, *Proportionality and Fair Taxation*, 2014 (ISBN 978-90-411-5838-3).
49. Paulo Rosenblatt, *General Anti-avoidance Rules for Major Developing Countries*, 2015 (ISBN 978-90-411-5839-0).
50. Gaspar Lopes Dias V.S., *Tax Arbitrage through Cross-Border Financial Engineering*, 2015 (ISBN 978-90-411-5875-8).
51. Geerten M.M. Michielse & Victor Thuronyi (eds), *Tax Design Issues Worldwide*, 2015 (ISBN 978-90-411-5610-5).
52. Oktavia Weidmann, *Taxation of Derivatives*, 2015 (ISBN 978-90-411-5977-9).
53. Chris Evans, Richard Krever & Peter Mellor (eds), *Tax Simplification*, 2015 (ISBN 978-90-411-5976-2).
54. Reuven Avi-Yonah & Joel Slemrod (eds), *Taxation and Migration*, 2015 (ISBN 978-90-411-6136-9).
55. Alexander Bosman, *Other Income under Tax Treaties: An Analysis of Article 21 of the OECD Model Convention*, 2015 (ISBN 978-90-411-6610-4).
56. John Abrahamson, *International Taxation of Manufacturing and Distribution*, 2016 (ISBN 978-90-411-6664-7).
57. Frederik Boulogne, *Shortcomings in the EU Merger Directive*, 2016 (ISBN 978-90-411-6713-2).
58. Angelika Meindl-Ringler, *Beneficial Ownership in International Tax Law*, 2016 (ISBN 978-90-411-6833-7).
59. Andreas Waltrich, *Cross-Border Taxation of Permanent Establishments: An International Comparison*, 2016 (ISBN 978-90-411-6832-0).
60. Sergio André Rocha & Allison Christians (eds), *Tax Sovereignty in the BEPS Era*, 2017 (ISBN 978-90-411-6707-1).
61. Peter Antony Wilson, *BRICS and International Tax Law*, 2018 (ISBN 978-90-411-9435-0).
62. Louise Otis, Brigitte Alepin & Blanca Moreno-Dodson (eds), *Winning the Tax Wars: Tax Competition and Cooperation*, 2018 (ISBN 978-90-411-9460-2).
63. Marta Castelon, *International Taxation of Income from Services under Double Taxation Conventions: Development, Practice and Policy*, 2018 (ISBN 978-90-411-9594-4).
64. D.M. Broekhuijsen, *A Multilateral Tax Treaty: Designing an Instrument to Modernise International Tax Law*, 2018 (ISBN 978-90-411-9872-3).

65. John Abrahamson, *International Taxation of Energy Production and Distribution*, 2018 (ISBN 978-90-411-9101-4).
66. Leopoldo Parada, *Double Non-taxation and the Use of Hybrid Entities: An Alternative Approach in the New Era of BEPS*, 2018 (ISBN 978-90-411-9991-1).
67. Richard Snoeij, *International Tax Aspects of Sovereign Wealth Investors: A Source State Perspective*, 2018 (ISBN 978-90-411-9431-2).
68. Aleksandra Bal, *Taxation, Virtual Currency and Blockchain*, 2019 (ISBN 978-94-035-0103-1).
69. Werner Haslehner, Georg Kofler, Katerina Pantazatou & Alexander Rust (eds), *Tax and the Digital Economy: Challenges and Proposals for Reform*, 2019 (ISBN 978-94-035-0361-5).
70. Eva Escribano, *Jurisdiction to Tax Corporate Income Pursuant to the Presumptive Benefit Principle: A Critical Analysis of Structural Paradigms Underlying Corporate Income Taxation and Proposals for Reform*, 2019 (ISBN 978-94-035-0640-1).
71. Jérôme Monsenego & Jan Bjuvberg (eds), *International Taxation in a Changing Landscape: Liber Amicorum in Honour of Bertil Wiman*, 2019 (ISBN 978-90-411-9234-9).
72. Kasper Dziurdź, *Non-discrimination in Tax Treaty Law and World Trade Law: The Impact of Formal, Substantive, and Subjective Approaches*, 2019 (ISBN 978-94-035-0904-4).

www.ingramcontent.com/pod-product-compliance
Lightning Source LLC
LaVergne TN
LVHW020003031026
849161LV00023B/867